WEBSTER'S
Spanish-English Dictionary
for Students

SECOND EDITION

Created in Cooperation with the Editors of
MERRIAM-WEBSTER

FEDERAL
STREET
PRESS

A Division of Merriam-Webster, Incorporated
Springfield, Massachusetts

This edition published by
Federal Street Press,
A Division of Merriam-Webster, Incorporated
P.O. Box 281
Springfield, MA 01102

Federal Street Press books are available for bulk purchase for sales promotion
and premium use. For details write the manager of special sales,
Federal Street Press, P.O. Box 281, Springfield, MA 01102

ISBN   978-1-59695-165-5

4th printing   Webcom, Toronto, ON   8/2016   Jouve

Printed in Canada

Contents

Preface

This Spanish-English Dictionary is a concise reference to the core vocabulary of Spanish and English. Its 40,000 entries and over 50,000 translations provide up-to-date coverage of the basic vocabulary and idioms in both languages. In addition, the book includes many specifically Latin-American words and phrases.

This book shares many details of presentation with larger Spanish-English dictionaries, but for reasons of conciseness it also has a number of features uniquely its own. Users need to be familiar with the following major features of this dictionary.

Main entries follow one another in strict alphabetical order, without regard to intervening spaces or hyphens. The Spanish letter combinations *ch* and *ll* are alphabetized within the letters *C* and *L;* however, the Spanish letter *ñ* is alphabetized separately between *N* and *O.*

Homographs (words spelled the same but having different meanings or parts of speech) are run on at a single main entry if they are closely related. Run-on homograph entries are replaced in the text by a boldfaced swung dash (as **haber** . . . *v aux* . . . — ∼ *nm* . . .). Homographs of distinctly different origin (as **date**[1] and **date**[2]) are given separate entries.

Run-on entries for related words that are not homographs may also follow the main entry. Thus we have the main entry **calcular** *vt* followed by run-on entries for — **calculador, -dora** *adj* . . . — **calculadora** *nf* . . . and — **cálculo** *nm*. However, if a related word falls later in the alphabet than a following unrelated main entry, it will be entered at its own place; **ear** and its run-on — **eardrum** precede the main entry **earl** which is followed by the main entry **earlobe.**

Variant spellings appear at the main entry separated by *or* (as **judgment** *or* **judgement, paralyze** *or Brit* **paralyse,** or **cacahuate** *or* **cacahuete**).

Inflected forms of English verbs, adjectives, adverbs, and nouns are shown when they are irregular (as **wage** . . . **waged, waging; ride** . . . **rode, ridden; good** . . . **better, best;** or **fly** . . . *n, pl* **flies**) or when there might be doubt about their spelling (as **ego** . . . *n, pl* **egos**). Inflected forms of Spanish irregular verbs are shown in the section Conjugation of Spanish Verbs on page v; numerical references to this table are included at the main entry (as **poseer** {20} *vt*). Irregular plurals of Spanish nouns or adjectives are shown at the main entry (as **ladrón, -drona** *n, mpl* **-drones**).

Cross-references are provided to lead the user to the appropriate main entry (as **mice** → **mouse** or **sobrestimar** → **sobreestimar**).

The grammatical function of entry words is indicated by an italic **functional label** (as *vt, adj, or nm*). Italic **usage labels** may be added at the entry or sense as well (as **timbre** *nm* . . . **4** *Lat* : postage stamp, **center** *or Brit* **centre** . . . *n* . . ., or **garra** *nf* . . . **2** *fam* : hand, paw). These labels are also included in the translations (**bag** *n* . . . **2** HANDBAG : bolso *m*, cartera *f Lat*).

Usage notes are occasionally placed before a translation to clarify meaning or use (as **que** *conj* . . . **2** (*in comparisons*) : than).

Synonyms may appear before the translation word(s) in order to provide context for the meaning of an entry word or sense (as **sitio** *nm* . . . **2** ESPACIO : room, space; or **meet** . . . *vt* . . . **2** SATISFY : satisfacer).

Bold notes are sometimes used before a translation to introduce a plural sense or a common phrase using the main entry word (as **mueble** *nm* . . . **2** ∼s *nmpl* : furniture, furnishings, or **call** . . . *vt* . . . **2** ∼ **off** : cancelar). Note that when an entry word is repeated in a bold note, it is replaced by a swung dash.

Conjugation of Spanish Verbs

Simple Tenses

-AR Verbs (hablar)		-ER Verbs (comer)		-IR Verbs (vivir)	
PRESENT INDICATIVE TENSE					
hablo	hablamos	como	comemos	vivo	vivimos
hablas	habláis	comes	coméis	vives	vivís
habla	hablan	come	comen	vive	viven
PRESENT SUBJUNCTIVE TENSE					
hable	hablemos	coma	comamos	viva	vivamos
hables	habléis	comas	comáis	vivas	viváis
hable	hablen	coma	coman	viva	vivan
PRETERIT INDICATIVE TENSE					
hablé	hablamos	comí	comimos	viví	vivimos
hablaste	hablasteis	comiste	comisteis	viviste	vivisteis
habló	hablaron	comió	comieron	vivió	vivieron
IMPERFECT INDICATIVE TENSE					
hablaba	hablábamos	comía	comíamos	vivía	vivíamos
hablabas	hablabais	comías	comíais	vivías	vivíais
hablaba	hablaban	comía	comían	vivía	vivían
IMPERFECT SUBJUNCTIVE TENSE					
hablara	habláramos	comiera	comiéramos	viviera	viviéramos
hablaras	hablarais	comieras	comierais	vivieras	vivierais
hablara	hablaran	comiera	comieran	viviera	vivieran
or		*or*		*or*	
hablase	hablásemos	comiese	comiésemos	viviese	viviésemos
hablases	hablaseis	comieses	comieseis	vivieses	vivieseis
hablase	hablasen	comiese	comiesen	viviese	viviesen
FUTURE INDICATIVE TENSE					
hablaré	hablaremos	comeré	comeremos	viviré	viviremos
hablarás	hablaréis	comerás	comeréis	vivirás	viviréis
hablará	hablarán	comerá	comerán	vivirá	vivirán
FUTURE SUBJUNCTIVE TENSE					
hablare	habláremos	comiere	comiéremos	viviere	viviéremos
hablares	hablareis	comieres	comiereis	vivieres	viviereis
hablare	hablaren	comiere	comieren	viviere	vivieren
CONDITIONAL TENSE					
hablaría	hablaríamos	comería	comeríamos	viviría	viviríamos
hablarías	hablaríais	comerías	comeríais	vivirías	viviríais
hablaría	hablarían	comería	comerían	viviría	vivirían
IMPERATIVE TENSE					
	hablemos		comamos		vivamos
habla	hablad	come	comed	vive	vivid
hable	hablen	coma	coman	viva	vivan
PRESENT PARTICIPLE (GERUND) TENSE					
hablando		comiendo		viviendo	
PAST PARTICIPLE TENSE					
hablado		comido		vivido	

Compound Tenses

1. Perfect Tenses

The perfect tenses are formed with *haber* and the past participle:

PRESENT PERFECT
> he hablado, etc. (*indicative*);
> haya hablado, etc. (*subjunctive*)

PAST PERFECT
> había hablado, etc. (*indicative*);
> hubiera hablado, etc. (*subjunctive*)
> *or*
> hubiese hablado, etc. (*subjunctive*)

PRETERIT PERFECT
> hube hablado, etc. (*indicative*)

FUTURE PERFECT
> habré hablado, etc. (*indicative*)

CONDITIONAL PERFECT
> habría hablado, etc. (*indicative*)

2. Progressive Tenses

The progressive tenses are formed with *estar* and the present participle:

PRESENT PROGRESSIVE
> estoy llamando, etc. (*indicative*);
> esté llamando, etc. (*subjunctive*)

IMPERFECT PROGRESSIVE
> estaba llamando, etc. (*indicative*);
> estuviera llamando, etc. (*subjunctive*)
> *or*
> estuviese llamando, etc. (*subjunctive*)

PRETERIT PROGRESSIVE
> estuve llamando, etc. (*indicative*)

FUTURE PROGRESSIVE
> estaré llamando, etc. (*indicative*)

CONDITIONAL PROGRESSIVE
> estaría llamando, etc. (*indicative*)

PRESENT PERFECT PROGRESSIVE
> he estado llamando, etc. (*indicative*);
> haya estado llamando, etc. (*subjunctive*)

PAST PERFECT PROGRESSIVE
> había estado llamando, etc. (*indicative*);
> hubiera estado llamando, etc. (*subjunctive*)
> *or*
> hubiese estado llamando, etc. (*subjunctive*)

Irregular Verbs

The *imperfect subjunctive*, the *future subjunctive*, the *conditional*, and most forms of the *imperative* are not included in the model conjugations, but can be derived as follows:

The *imperfect subjunctive* and the *future subjunctive* are formed from the third person plural form of the preterit tense by removing the last syllable (-*ron*) and adding the appropriate suffix:

PRETERIT INDICATIVE, THIRD PERSON PLURAL (querer)	quisieron
IMPERFECT SUBJUNCTIVE (querer)	quisiera, quisieras, etc. *or* quisiese, quisieses, etc.
FUTURE SUBJUNCTIVE (querer)	quisiere, quisieres, etc.

The conditional uses the same stem as the future indicative:

FUTURE INDICATIVE (poner)	pondré, pondrás, etc.
CONDITIONAL (poner)	pondría, pondrías, etc.

The third person singular, first person plural, and third person plural forms of the *imperative* are the same as the corresponding forms of the present subjunctive.

The second person singular form of the *imperative* is generally the same as the third person singular of the present indicative. Exceptions are noted in the model conjugations list.

The second person plural *(vosotros)* form of the *imperative* is formed by removing the final -*r* of the infinitive form and adding a -*d* (ex.: *oír* → *oíd*).

Model Conjugations of Irregular Verbs

The model conjugations below include the following simple tenses: the *present indicative* (*IND*), the *present subjunctive* (*SUBJ*), the *preterit indicative* (*PRET*), the *imperfect indicative* (*IMPF*), the *future indicative* (*FUT*), the second person singular form of the *imperative* (*IMPER*) when it differs from the third person singular of the present indicative, the *gerund* or *present participle* (*PRP*), and the *past participle* (*PP*). Each set of conjugations is preceded by the corresponding infinitive form of the verb, shown in bold type. Only tenses containing irregularities are listed, and the irregular verb forms within each tense are displayed in bold type.

Each irregular verb entry in the Spanish-English section of this dictionary is cross-referenced by number to one of the following model conjugations. These cross-reference numbers are shown in curly braces { } immediately following the entry's functional label.

1 **abolir** *(defective verb)* : *IND* abolimos, abolís *(other forms not used)*; *SUBJ (not used)*; *IMPER (only second person plural is used)*

2 **abrir** : *PP* abierto

3 **actuar** : *IND* **actúo, actúas, actúa**, actuamos, actuáis, **actúan**; *SUBJ* **actúe, actúes, actúe**, actuemos, actuéis, **actúen**; *IMPER* **actúa**

4 **adquirir** : *IND* **adquiero, adquieres, adquiere**, adquirimos, adquirís, **adquieren**; *SUBJ* **adquiera, adquieras, adquiera**, adquiramos, adquiráis, **adquieran**; *IMPER* **adquiere**

5 **airar** : *IND* **aíro, aíras, aíra**, airamos, airáis, **aíran**; *SUBJ* **aíre, aíres, aíre**, airemos, airéis, **aíren**; *IMPER* **aíra**

6 **andar** : *PRET* **anduve, anduviste, anduvo, anduvimos, anduvisteis, anduvieron**

7 **asir** : *IND* **asgo**, ases, ase, asimos, asís, asen; *SUBJ* **asga, asgas, asga, asgamos, asgáis, asgan**

8 **aunar** : *IND* **aúno, aúnas, aúna**, aunamos, aunáis, **aúnan**; *SUBJ* **aúne, aúnes, aúne**, aunemos, aunéis, **aúnen**; *IMPER* **aúna**

9 **avergonzar** : *IND* **avergüenzo, avergüenzas, avergüenza**, avergonzamos, avergonzáis, **avergüenzan**; *SUBJ* **avergüence, avergüences, avergüence**, avergoncemos, avergoncéis, **avergüencen**; *PRET* **avergoncé**; *IMPER* **avergüenza**

10 **averiguar** : *SUBJ* **averigüe, averigües, averigüe, averigüemos, averigüéis, averigüen;** *PRET* **averigüé,** averiguaste, averiguó, averiguamos, averiguasteis, averiguaron

11 **bendecir** : *IND* **bendigo, bendices, bendice,** bendecimos, bendecís, **bendicen;** *SUBJ* **bendiga, bendigas, bendiga, bendigamos, bendigáis, bendigan;** *PRET* **bendije, bendijiste, bendijo, bendijimos, bendijisteis, bendijeron;** *IMPER* **bendice**

12 **caber** : *IND* **quepo,** cabes, cabe, cabemos, cabéis, caben; *SUBJ* **quepa, quepas, quepa, quepamos, quepáis, quepan;** *PRET* **cupe, cupiste, cupo, cupimos, cupisteis, cupieron;** *FUT* **cabré, cabrás, cabrá, cabremos, cabréis, cabrán**

13 **caer** : *IND* **caigo,** caes, cae, caemos, caéis, caen; *SUBJ* **caiga, caigas, caiga, caigamos, caigáis, caigan;** *PRET* **caí, caíste, cayó, caímos, caísteis, cayeron;** *PRP* **cayendo;** *PP* **caído**

14 **cocer** : *IND* **cuezo, cueces, cuece,** cocemos, cocéis, **cuecen;** *SUBJ* **cueza, cuezas, cueza, cozamos, cozáis, cuezan;** *IMPER* **cuece**

15 **coger** : *IND* **cojo,** coges, coge, cogemos, cogéis, cogen; *SUBJ* **coja, cojas, coja, cojamos, cojáis, cojan**

16 **colgar** : *IND* **cuelgo, cuelgas, cuelga,** colgamos, colgáis, **cuelgan;** *SUBJ* **cuelgue, cuelgues, cuelgue, colguemos, colguéis, cuelguen;** *PRET* **colgué,** colgaste, colgó, colgamos, colgasteis, colgaron; *IMPER* **cuelga**

17 **concernir** (*defective verb; used only in the third person singular and plural of the present indicative, present subjunctive, and imperfect subjunctive*) see 25 **discernir**

18 **conocer** : *IND* **conozco,** conoces, conoce, conocemos, conocéis, conocen; *SUBJ* **conozca, conozcas, conozca, conozcamos, conozcáis, conozcan**

19 **contar** : *IND* **cuento, cuentas, cuenta,** contamos, contáis, **cuentan;** *SUBJ* **cuente, cuentes, cuente,** contemos, contéis, **cuenten;** *IMPER* **cuenta**

20 **creer** : *PRET* **creí, creíste, creyó, creímos, creísteis, creyeron;** *PRP* **creyendo;** *PP* **creído**

21 **cruzar** : *SUBJ* **cruce, cruces, cruce, crucemos, crucéis, crucen;** *PRET* **crucé,** cruzaste, cruzó, cruzamos, cruzasteis, cruzaron

22 **dar** : *IND* **doy,** das, da, damos, **dais,** dan; *SUBJ* **dé,** des, **dé,** demos, **deis,** den; *PRET* **di,** diste, dio, dimos, disteis, dieron

23 **decir** : *IND* **digo, dices, dice,** decimos, decís, **dicen;** *SUBJ* **diga, digas, diga, digamos, digáis, digan;** *PRET* **dije, dijiste, dijo, dijimos, dijisteis, dijeron;** *FUT* **diré, dirás, dirá, diremos, diréis, dirán;** *IMPER* **di;** *PRP* **diciendo;** *PP* **dicho**

24 **delinquir** : *IND* **delinco,** delinques, delinque, delinquimos, delinquís, delinquen; *SUBJ* **delinca, delincas, delinca, delincamos, delincáis, delincan**

25 **discernir** : *IND* **discierno, disciernes, discierne,** discernimos, discernís, **disciernen;** *SUBJ* **discierna, disciernas, discierna,** discernamos, discernáis, **disciernan;** *IMPER* **discierne**

26 **distinguir** : *IND* **distingo,** distingues, distingue, distinguimos, distinguís, distinguen; *SUBJ* **distinga, distingas, distinga, distingamos, distingáis, distingan**

27 **dormir** : *IND* **duermo, duermes, duerme,** dormimos, dormís, **duermen;** *SUBJ* **duerma, duermas, duerma, durmamos, durmáis, duerman;** *PRET* dormí, dormiste, **durmió,** dormimos, dormisteis, **durmieron;** *IMPER* **duerme;** *PRP* **durmiendo**

28 **elegir** : *IND* **elijo, eliges, elige,** elegimos, elegís, **eligen;** *SUBJ* **elija, elijas, elija, elijamos, elijáis, elijan;** *PRET* elegí, elegiste, **eligió,** elegimos, elegisteis, **eligieron;** *IMPER* **elige;** *PRP* **eligiendo**

29 **empezar** : *IND* **empiezo, empiezas, empieza,** empezamos, empezáis, **empiezan;** *SUBJ* **empiece, empieces, empiece,** empecemos, empecéis, **empiecen;** *PRET* **empecé,** empezaste, empezó, empezamos, empezasteis, empezaron; *IMPER* **empieza**

30 **enraizar** : *IND* **enraízo, enraízas, enraíza,** enraizamos, enraizáis, **enraízan;** *SUBJ* **enraíce, enraíces, enraíce,** enraicemos, enraicéis, **enraícen;** *PRET* **enraicé,** enraizaste, enraizó, enraizamos, enraizasteis, enraizaron; *IMPER* **enraíza**

31 **erguir** : *IND* **irgo** *or* **yergo**, **irgues** *or* **yergues**, **irgue** *or* **yergue**, erguimos, erguís, **irguen** *or* **yerguen**; *SUBJ* **irga** *or* **yerga**, **irgas** *or* **yergas**, **irga** *or* **yerga**, **irgamos**, **irgáis**, **irgan** *or* **yergan**; *PRET* erguí, erguiste, **irguió**, erguimos, erguisteis, **irguieron**; *IMPER* **irgue** *or* **yergue**; *PRP* **irguiendo**

32 **errar** : *IND* **yerro**, **yerras**, **yerra**, erramos, erráis, **yerran**; *SUBJ* **yerre**, **yerres**, **yerre**, erremos, erréis, **yerren**; *IMPER* **yerra**

33 **escribir** : *PP* **escrito**

34 **estar** : *IND* **estoy**, **estás**, **está**, estamos, estáis, **están**; *SUBJ* **esté**, **estés**, **esté**, estemos, estéis, **estén**; *PRET* **estuve**, **estuviste**, **estuvo**, **estuvimos**, **estuvisteis**, **estuvieron**; *IMPER* **está**

35 **exigir** : *IND* **exijo**, exiges, exige, exigimos, exigís, exigen; *SUBJ* **exija**, **exijas**, **exija**, **exijamos**, **exijáis**, **exijan**

36 **forzar** : *IND* **fuerzo**, **fuerzas**, **fuerza**, forzamos, forzáis, **fuerzan**; *SUBJ* **fuerce**, **fuerces**, **fuerce**, **forcemos**, **forcéis**, **fuercen**; *PRET* **forcé**, forzaste, forzó, forzamos, forzasteis, forzaron; *IMPER* **fuerza**

37 **freír** : *IND* **frío**, **fríes**, **fríe**, **freímos**, freís, **fríen**; *SUBJ* **fría**, **frías**, **fría**, **friamos**, **friáis**, **frían**; *PRET* freí, **freíste**, **frió**, **freímos**, **freísteis**, **frieron**; *IMPER* **fríe**; *PRP* **friendo**; *PP* **frito**

38 **gruñir** : *PRET* gruñí, gruñiste, **gruñó**, gruñimos, gruñisteis, **gruñeron**; *PRP* **gruñendo**

39 **haber** : *IND* **he**, **has**, **ha**, **hemos**, habéis, **han**; *SUBJ* **haya**, **hayas**, **haya**, **hayamos**, **hayáis**, **hayan**; *PRET* **hube**, **hubiste**, **hubo**, **hubimos**, **hubisteis**, **hubieron**; *FUT* **habré**, **habrás**, **habrá**, **habremos**, **habréis**, **habrán**; *IMPER* **he**

40 **hacer** : *IND* **hago**, haces, hace, hacemos, hacéis, hacen; *SUBJ* **haga**, **hagas**, **haga**, **hagamos**, **hagáis**, **hagan**; *PRET* **hice**, **hiciste**, **hizo**, **hicimos**, **hicisteis**, **hicieron**; *FUT* **haré**, **harás**, **hará**, **haremos**, **haréis**, **harán**; *IMPER* **haz**; *PP* **hecho**

41 **huir** : *IND* **huyo**, **huyes**, **huye**, huimos, huís, **huyen**; *SUBJ* **huya**, **huyas**, **huya**, **huyamos**, **huyáis**, **huyan**; *PRET* huí, huiste, **huyó**, huimos, huisteis, **huyeron**; *IMPER* **huye**; *PRP* **huyendo**

42 **imprimir** : *PP* **impreso**

43 **ir** : *IND* **voy**, **vas**, **va**, **vamos**, **vais**, **van**; *SUBJ* **vaya**, **vayas**, **vaya**, **vayamos**, **vayáis**, **vayan**; *PRET* **fui**, **fuiste**, **fue**, **fuimos**, **fuisteis**, **fueron**; *IMPF* **iba**, **ibas**, **iba**, **íbamos**, **ibais**, **iban**; *IMPER* **ve**; *PRP* **yendo**; *PP* **ido**

44 **jugar** : *IND* **juego**, **juegas**, **juega**, jugamos, jugáis, **juegan**; *SUBJ* **juegue**, **juegues**, **juegue**, **juguemos**, **juguéis**, **jueguen**; *PRET* **jugué**, jugaste, jugó, jugamos, jugasteis, jugaron; *IMPER* **juega**

45 **lucir** : *IND* **luzco**, luces, luce, lucimos, lucís, lucen; *SUBJ* **luzca**, **luzcas**, **luzca**, **luzcamos**, **luzcáis**, **luzcan**

46 **morir** : *IND* **muero**, **mueres**, **muere**, morimos, morís, **mueren**; *SUBJ* **muera**, **mueras**, **muera**, **muramos**, **muráis**, **mueran**; *PRET* morí, moriste, **murió**, morimos, moristeis, **murieron**; *IMPER* **muere**; *PRP* **muriendo**; *PP* **muerto**

47 **mover** : *IND* **muevo**, **mueves**, **mueve**, movemos, movéis, **mueven**; *SUBJ* **mueva**, **muevas**, **mueva**, movamos, mováis, **muevan**; *IMPER* **mueve**

48 **nacer** : *IND* **nazco**, naces, nace, nacemos, nacéis, nacen; *SUBJ* **nazca**, **nazcas**, **nazca**, **nazcamos**, **nazcáis**, **nazcan**

49 **negar** : *IND* **niego**, **niegas**, **niega**, negamos, negáis, **niegan**; *SUBJ* **niegue**, **niegues**, **niegue**, **neguemos**, **neguéis**, **nieguen**; *PRET* **negué**, negaste, negó, negamos, negasteis, negaron; *IMPER* **niega**

50 **oír** : *IND* **oigo**, **oyes**, **oye**, **oímos**, oís, **oyen**; *SUBJ* **oiga**, **oigas**, **oiga**, **oigamos**, **oigáis**, **oigan**; *PRET* oí, **oíste**, **oyó**, **oímos**, **oísteis**, **oyeron**; *IMPER* **oye**; *PRP* **oyendo**; *PP* **oído**

51 **oler** : *IND* **huelo**, **hueles**, **huele**, olemos, oléis, **huelen**; *SUBJ* **huela**, **huelas**, **huela**, olamos, oláis, **huelan**; *IMPER* **huele**

Conjugation of Spanish Verbs

52 **pagar** : *SUBJ* **pague, pagues, pague, paguemos, paguéis, paguen;** *PRET* **pagué,** pagaste, pagó, pagamos, pagasteis, pagaron

53 **parecer** : *IND* **parezco,** pareces, parece, parecemos, parecéis, parecen; *SUBJ* **parezca, parezcas, parezca, parezcamos, parezcáis, parezcan**

54 **pedir** : *IND* **pido, pides, pide,** pedimos, pedís, **piden;** *SUBJ* **pida, pidas, pida, pidamos, pidáis, pidan;** *PRET* pedí, pediste, **pidió,** pedimos, pedisteis, **pidieron;** *IMPER* **pide;** *PRP* **pidiendo**

55 **pensar** : *IND* **pienso, piensas, piensa,** pensamos, pensáis, **piensan;** *SUBJ* **piense, pienses, piense,** pensemos, penséis, **piensen;** *IMPER* **piensa**

56 **perder** : *IND* **pierdo, pierdes, pierde,** perdemos, perdéis, **pierden;** *SUBJ* **pierda, pierdas, pierda,** perdamos, perdáis, **pierdan;** *IMPER* **pierde**

57 **placer** : *IND* **plazco,** places, place, placemos, placéis, placen; *SUBJ* **plazca, plazcas, plazca, plazcamos, plazcáis, plazcan;** *PRET* plací, placiste, plació *or* **plugo,** placimos, placisteis, placieron *or* **pluguieron**

58 **poder** : *IND* **puedo, puedes, puede,** podemos, podéis, **pueden;** *SUBJ* **pueda, puedas, pueda,** podamos, podáis, **puedan;** *PRET* **pude, pudiste, pudo, pudimos, pudisteis, pudieron;** *FUT* **podré, podrás, podrá, podremos, podréis, podrán;** *IMPER* **puede;** *PRP* **pudiendo**

59 **podrir** *or* **pudrir** : *PP* **podrido** *(all other forms based on* pudrir*)*

60 **poner** : *IND* **pongo,** pones, pone, ponemos, ponéis, ponen; *SUBJ* **ponga, pongas, ponga, pongamos, pongáis, pongan;** *PRET* **puse, pusiste, puso, pusimos, pusisteis, pusieron;** *FUT* **pondré, pondrás, pondrá, pondremos, pondréis, pondrán;** *IMPER* **pon;** *PP* **puesto**

61 **producir** : *IND* **produzco,** produces, produce, producimos, producís, producen; *SUBJ* **produzca, produzcas, produzca, produzcamos, produzcáis, produzcan;** *PRET* **produje, produjiste, produjo, produjimos, produjisteis, produjeron**

62 **prohibir** : *IND* **prohíbo, prohíbes, prohíbe,** prohibimos, prohibís, **prohíben;** *SUBJ* **prohíba, prohíbas, prohíba,** prohibamos, prohibáis, **prohíban;** *IMPER* **prohíbe**

63 **proveer** : *PRET* proveí, **proveíste, proveyó, proveímos, proveísteis, proveyeron;** *PRP* **proveyendo;** *PP* **provisto**

64 **querer** : *IND* **quiero, quieres, quiere,** queremos, queréis, **quieren;** *SUBJ* **quiera, quieras, quiera,** queramos, queráis, **quieran;** *PRET* **quise, quisiste, quiso, quisimos, quisisteis, quisieron;** *FUT* **querré, querrás, querrá, querremos, querréis, querrán;** *IMPER* **quiere**

65 **raer** : *IND* rao *or* **raigo** *or* **rayo,** raes, rae, raemos, raéis, raen; *SUBJ* **raiga** *or* **raya, raigas** *or* **rayas, raiga** *or* **raya, raigamos** *or* **rayamos, raigáis** *or* **rayáis, raigan** *or* **rayan;** *PRET* **raí, raíste, rayó, raímos, raísteis, rayeron;** *PRP* **rayendo;** *PP* **raído**

66 **reír** : *IND* **río, ríes, ríe, reímos,** reís, **ríen;** *SUBJ* **ría, rías, ría, riamos, riáis, rían;** *PRET* reí, **reíste, rió, reímos, reísteis, rieron;** *IMPER* **ríe;** *PRP* **riendo;** *PP* **reído**

67 **reñir** : *IND* **riño, riñes, riñe,** reñimos, reñís, **riñen;** *SUBJ* **riña, riñas, riña, riñamos, riñáis, riñan;** *PRET* reñí, reñiste, **riñó,** reñimos, reñisteis, **riñeron;** *PRP* **riñendo**

68 **reunir** : *IND* **reúno, reúnes, reúne,** reunimos, reunís, **reúnen;** *SUBJ* **reúna, reúnas, reúna,** reunamos, reunáis, **reúnan;** *IMPER* **reúne**

69 **roer** : *IND* roo *or* **roigo** *or* **royo,** roes, roe, roemos, roéis, roen; *SUBJ* roa *or* **roiga** *or* **roya,** roas *or* **roigas** *or* **royas,** roa *or* **roiga** *or* **roya,** roamos *or* **roigamos** *or* **royamos,** roáis *or* **roigáis** *or* **royáis,** roan *or* **roigan** *or* **royan;** *PRET* roí, **roíste, royó, roímos, roísteis, royeron;** *PRP* **royendo;** *PP* **roído**

70 **romper** : *PP* **roto**

71 **saber** : *IND* **sé,** sabes, sabe, sabemos, sabéis, saben; *SUBJ* **sepa, sepas, sepa, sepamos, sepáis, sepan;** *PRET* **supe, supiste, supo, supimos, supisteis, supieron;** *FUT* **sabré, sabrás, sabrá, sabremos, sabréis, sabrán**

72 **sacar** : *SUBJ* **saque, saques, saque, saquemos, saquéis, saquen;** *PRET* **saqué,** sacaste, sacó, sacamos, sacasteis, sacaron

73 **salir** : *IND* **salgo,** sales, sale, salimos, salís, salen; *SUBJ* **salga, salgas, salga, salgamos, salgáis, salgan;** *FUT* **saldré, saldrás, saldrá, saldremos, saldréis, saldrán;** *IMPER* **sal**

74 **satisfacer** : *IND* **satisfago,** satisfaces, satisface, satisfacemos, satisfacéis, satisfacen; *SUBJ* **satisfaga, satisfagas, satisfaga, satisfagamos, satisfagáis, satisfagan;** *PRET* **satisfice, satisficiste, satisfizo, satisficimos, satificisteis, satisficieron;** *FUT* satisfaré, satisfarás, satisfará, satisfaremos, satisfaréis, satisfarán;** *IMPER* **satisfaz** *or* **satisface;** *PP* **satisfecho**

75 **seguir** : *IND* **sigo, sigues, sigue,** seguimos, seguís, **siguen;** *SUBJ* **siga, sigas, siga, sigamos, sigáis, sigan;** *PRET* seguí, seguiste, **siguió,** seguimos, seguisteis, **siguieron;** *IMPER* **sigue;** *PRP* **siguiendo**

76 **sentir** : *IND* **siento, sientes, siente,** sentimos, sentís, **sienten;** *SUBJ* **sienta, sientas, sienta, sintamos, sintáis, sientan;** *PRET* sentí, sentiste, **sintió,** sentimos, sentisteis, **sintieron;** *IMPER* **siente;** *PRP* **sintiendo**

77 **ser** : *IND* **soy, eres, es, somos, sois, son;** *SUBJ* **sea, seas, sea, seamos, seáis, sean;** *PRET* **fui, fuiste, fue, fuimos, fuisteis, fueron;** *IMPF* **era, eras, era, éramos, erais, eran;** *IMPER* **sé;** *PRP* **siendo;** *PP* **sido**

78 **soler** *(defective verb; used only in the present, preterit, and imperfect indicative, and the present and imperfect subjunctive) see 47* **mover**

79 **tañer** : *PRET* tañí, tañiste, **tañó,** tañimos, tañisteis, **tañeron;** *PRP* **tañendo**

80 **tener** : *IND* **tengo, tienes, tiene,** tenemos, tenéis, **tienen;** *SUBJ* **tenga, tengas, tenga, tengamos, tengáis, tengan;** *PRET* **tuve, tuviste, tuvo, tuvimos, tuvisteis, tuvieron;** *FUT* **tendré, tendrás, tendrá, tendremos, tendréis, tendrán;** *IMPER* **ten**

81 **traer** : *IND* **traigo,** traes, trae, traemos, traéis, traen; *SUBJ* **traiga, traigas, traiga, traigamos, traigáis, traigan;** *PRET* **traje, trajiste, trajo, trajimos, trajisteis, trajeron;** *PRP* **trayendo;** *PP* **traído**

82 **trocar** : *IND* **trueco, truecas, trueca,** trocamos, trocáis, **truecan;** *SUBJ* **trueque, trueques, trueque, troquemos, troquéis, truequen;** *PRET* **troqué,** trocaste, trocó, trocamos, trocasteis, trocaron; *IMPER* **trueca**

83 **uncir** : *IND* **unzo,** unces, unce, uncimos, uncís, uncen; *SUBJ* **unza, unzas, unza, unzamos, unzáis, unzan**

84 **valer** : *IND* **valgo,** vales, vale, valemos, valéis, valen; *SUBJ* **valga, valgas, valga, valgamos, valgáis, valgan;** *FUT* **valdré, valdrás, valdrá, valdremos, valdréis, valdrán**

85 **variar** : *IND* **varío, varías, varía,** variamos, variáis, **varían;** *SUBJ* **varíe, varíes, varíe,** variemos, variéis, **varíen;** *IMPER* **varía**

86 **vencer** : *IND* **venzo,** vences, vence, vencemos, vencéis, vencen; *SUBJ* **venza, venzas, venza, venzamos, venzáis, venzan**

87 **venir** : *IND* **vengo, vienes, viene,** venimos, venís, **vienen;** *SUBJ* **venga, vengas, venga, vengamos, vengáis, vengan;** *PRET* **vine, viniste, vino, vinimos, vinisteis, vinieron;** *FUT* **vendré, vendrás, vendrá, vendremos, vendréis, vendrán;** *IMPER* **ven;** *PRP* **viniendo**

88 **ver** : *IND* **veo, ves, ve, vemos, veis, ven;** *PRET* **vi, viste, vio, vimos, visteis, vieron;** *IMPER* **ve;** *PRP* **viendo;** *PP* **visto**

89 **volver** : *IND* **vuelvo, vuelves, vuelve,** volvemos, volvéis, **vuelven;** *SUBJ* **vuelva, vuelvas, vuelva,** volvamos, volváis, **vuelvan;** *IMPER* **vuelve;** *PP* **vuelto**

90 **yacer** : *IND* **yazco** *or* **yazgo** *or* **yago,** yaces, yace, yacemos, yacéis, yacen; *SUBJ* **yazca** *or* **yazga** *or* **yaga, yazcas** *or* **yazgas** *or* **yagas, yazca** *or* **yazga** *or* **yaga, yazcamos** *or* **yazgamos** *or* **yagamos, yazcáis** *or* **yazgáis** *or* **yagáis, yazcan** *or* **yazgan** *or* **yagan;** *IMPER* **yace** *or* **yaz**

Irregular English Verbs

INFINITIVE	PAST	PAST PARTICIPLE
arise	arose	arisen
awake	awoke	awoken *or* awaked
be	was, were	been
bear	bore	borne
beat	beat	beaten *or* beat
become	became	become
befall	befell	befallen
begin	began	begun
behold	beheld	beheld
bend	bent	bent
beseech	beseeched *or* besought	beseeched *or* besought
beset	beset	beset
bet	bet	bet
bid	bade *or* bid	bidden *or* bid
bind	bound	bound
bite	bit	bitten
bleed	bled	bled
blow	blew	blown
break	broke	broken
breed	bred	bred
bring	brought	brought
build	built	built
burn	burned *or* burnt	burned *or* burnt
burst	burst	burst
buy	bought	bought
can	could	—
cast	cast	cast
catch	caught	caught
choose	chose	chosen
cling	clung	clung
come	came	come
cost	cost	cost
creep	crept	crept
cut	cut	cut
deal	dealt	dealt
dig	dug	dug
do	did	done
draw	drew	drawn
dream	dreamed *or* dreamt	dreamed *or* dreamt
drink	drank	drunk *or* drank
drive	drove	driven
dwell	dwelled *or* dwelt	dwelled *or* dwelt
eat	ate	eaten
fall	fell	fallen
feed	fed	fed
feel	felt	felt
fight	fought	fought
find	found	found
flee	fled	fled
fling	flung	flung
fly	flew	flown

INFINITIVE	PAST	PAST PARTICIPLE
forbid	forbade	forbidden
forecast	forecast	forecast
forego	forewent	foregone
foresee	foresaw	foreseen
foretell	foretold	foretold
forget	forgot	forgotten *or* forgot
forgive	forgave	forgiven
forsake	forsook	forsaken
freeze	froze	frozen
get	got	got *or* gotten
give	gave	given
go	went	gone
grind	ground	ground
grow	grew	grown
hang	hung	hung
have	had	had
hear	heard	heard
hide	hid	hidden *or* hid
hit	hit	hit
hold	held	held
hurt	hurt	hurt
keep	kept	kept
kneel	knelt *or* kneeled	knelt *or* kneeled
know	knew	known
lay	laid	laid
lead	led	led
lean	leaned	leaned
leap	leaped *or* leapt	leaped *or* leapt
learn	learned	learned
leave	left	left
lend	lent	lent
let	let	let
lie	lay	lain
light	lit *or* lighted	lit *or* lighted
lose	lost	lost
make	made	made
may	might	—
mean	meant	meant
meet	met	met
mow	mowed	mowed *or* mown
pay	paid	paid
put	put	put
quit	quit	quit
read	read	read
rend	rent	rent
rid	rid	rid
ride	rode	ridden
ring	rang	rung
rise	rose	risen
run	ran	run
saw	sawed	sawed *or* sawn
say	said	said
see	saw	seen
seek	sought	sought
sell	sold	sold

INFINITIVE	PAST	PAST PARTICIPLE
send	sent	sent
set	set	set
shake	shook	shaken
shall	should	—
shear	sheared	sheared *or* shorn
shed	shed	shed
shine	shone *or* shined	shone *or* shined
shoot	shot	shot
show	showed	shown *or* showed
shrink	shrank *or* shrunk	shrunk *or* shrunken
shut	shut	shut
sing	sang *or* sung	sung
sink	sank *or* sunk	sunk
sit	sat	sat
slay	slew	slain
sleep	slept	slept
slide	slid	slid
sling	slung	slung
smell	smelled *or* smelt	smelled *or* smelt
sow	sowed	sown *or* sowed
speak	spoke	spoken
speed	sped *or* speeded	sped *or* speeded
spell	spelled	spelled
spend	spent	spent
spill	spilled	spilled
spin	spun	spun
spit	spit *or* spat	spit *or* spat
split	split	split
spoil	spoiled	spoiled
spread	spread	spread
spring	sprang *or* sprung	sprung
stand	stood	stood
steal	stole	stolen
stick	stuck	stuck
sting	stung	stung
stink	stank *or* stunk	stunk
stride	strode	stridden
strike	struck	struck
swear	swore	sworn
sweep	swept	swept
swell	swelled	swelled *or* swollen
swim	swam	swum
swing	swung	swung
take	took	taken
teach	taught	taught
tear	tore	torn
tell	told	told
think	thought	thought
throw	threw	thrown
thrust	thrust	thrust
tread	trod	trodden *or* trod
wake	woke	woken *or* waked
waylay	waylaid	waylaid
wear	wore	worn
weave	wove *or* weaved	woven *or* weaved

INFINITIVE	PAST	PAST PARTICIPLE
wed	wedded	wedded
weep	wept	wept
will	would	—
win	won	won
wind	wound	wound
withdraw	withdrew	withdrawn
withhold	withheld	withheld
withstand	withstood	withstood
wring	wrung	wrung
write	wrote	written

Abbreviations in this Work

adj	adjective	*nmf*	masculine or feminine noun
adv	adverb		
adv	adverbial phrase	*nmfpl*	plural noun invariable for gender
algn	alguien (someone)		
art	article	*nmfs & pl*	noun invariable for both gender and number
Brit	Great Britain	*nmpl*	masculine plural noun
conj	conjunction		
conj phr	conjunctive phrase	*nms & pl*	invariable singular or plural masculine noun
esp	especially		
etc	et cetera	*npl*	plural noun
f	feminine	*ns & pl*	noun invariable for plural
fam	familiar or colloquial	*pl*	plural
fpl	feminine plural	*pp*	past participle
interj	interjection	*prep*	preposition
Lat	Latin America	*prep phr*	prepositional phrase
m	masculine	*pron*	pronoun
mf	masculine or feminine	*s.o.*	someone
mpl	masculine plural	*sth*	something
n	noun	*usu*	usually
nf	feminine noun	*v*	verb
nfpl	feminine plural noun	*v aux*	auxiliary verb
nfs & pl	invariable singular or plural feminine noun	*vi*	intransitive verb
		v impers	impersonal verb
nm	masculine noun	*vr*	reflexive verb
		vt	transitive verb

Spanish-English
Dictionary

A

a¹ *nf* : a, first letter of the Spanish alphabet
a² *prep* **1** : to **2 ~ las dos** : at two o'clock
3 al día siguiente : (on) the following day
4 ~ pie : on foot **5 de lunes ~ viernes**
: from Monday until Friday **6 tres veces**
~ la semana : three times per week **7 ~**
la : in the manner of, like
abadía *nf* : abbey
abajo *adv* **1** : down, below, downstairs **2**
~ de *Lat* : under, beneath **3 de ~** : (at
the) bottom **4 hacia ~** : downwards
abalanzarse {21} *vr* : hurl oneself, rush
abandonar *vt* **1** : abandon, leave **2** RENUN-
CIAR A : give up — **abandonarse** *vr* **1**
: neglect oneself **2 ~ a** : give oneself over
to — **abandonado, -da** *adj* **1** : abandoned,
deserted **2** DESCUIDADO : neglected **3** DES-
ALIÑADO : slovenly — **abandono** *nm* **1**
: abandonment, neglect **2 por ~** : by default
abanico *nm* : fan — **abanicar** {72} *vt* : fan
abaratar *vt* : lower the price of — **abara-**
tarse *vr* : become cheaper
abarcar {72} *vt* **1** : cover, embrace **2** *Lat*
: monopolize
abarrotar *vt* : pack, cram — **abarrotes**
nmpl Lat **1** : groceries **2 tienda de ~**
: grocery store
abastecer {53} *vt* : supply, stock — **abas-**
tecimiento *nm* : supply, provisions —
abasto *nm* **1** : supply **2 no dar ~ a** : be
unable to cope with
abatir *vt* **1** : knock down, shoot down **2**
DEPRIMIR : depress — **abatirse** *vr* **1** : get
depressed **2 ~ sobre** : swoop down on
— **abatido, -da** *adj* : dejected, depressed
— **abatimiento** *nm* : depression, dejection
abdicar {72} *v* : abdicate — **abdicación** *nf*,
pl **-ciones** : abdication
abdomen *nm, pl* **-dómenes** : abdomen —
abdominal *adj* : abdominal
abecé *nm* : ABC — **abecedario** *nm* : alphabet
abedul *nm* : birch
abeja *nf* : bee — **abejorro** *nm* : bumblebee
aberración *nf, pl* **-ciones** : aberration
abertura *nf* : opening
abeto *nm* : fir (tree)
abierto, -ta *adj* : open
abigarrado, -da *adj* : multicolored
abismo *nm* : abyss, chasm — **abismal** *adj*
: vast, enormous
abjurar *vi* **~ de** : abjure
ablandar *vt* : soften (up) — **ablandarse** *vr*
: soften

abnegarse {49} *vr* : deny oneself — **abne-**
gado, -da *adj* : self-sacrificing — **abnega-**
ción *nf, pl* **-ciones** : self-denial
abochornar *vt* : embarrass — **abochor-**
narse *vr* : get embarrassed
abofetear *vt* : slap
abogado, -da *n* : lawyer — **abogacía** *nf*
: legal profession — **abogar** {52} *vi* **~**
por : plead for, defend
abolengo *nm* : lineage
abolir {1} *vt* : abolish — **abolición** *nf, pl*
-ciones : abolition
abollar *vt* : dent — **abolladura** *nf* : dent
abominar *vt* : abominate — **abominable**
adj : abominable — **abominación** *nf, pl*
-ciones : abomination
abonar *vt* **1** : pay (a bill, etc.) **2** : fertilize
(the soil) — **abonarse** *vr* : subscribe —
abonado, -da *n* : subscriber — **abono** *nm*
1 : payment, installment **2** FERTILIZANTE
: fertilizer **3** : season ticket (to the theater,
etc.)
abordar *vt* **1** : tackle (a problem) **2** : accost,
approach (a person) **3** *Lat* : board — **abor-**
daje *nm* : boarding
aborigen *nmf, pl* **-rígenes** : aborigine — **~**
adj : aboriginal, native
aborrecer {53} *vt* : abhor, detest — **aborre-**
cible *adj* : hateful — **aborrecimiento** *nm*
: loathing
abortar *vi* : have a miscarriage — *vt* : abort
— **aborto** *nm* : abortion, miscarriage
abotonar *vt* : button — **abotonarse** *vr*
: button up
abovedado, -da *adj* : vaulted
abrasar *vt* : burn, scorch — **abrasarse** *vr*
: burn up — **abrasador, -dora** *adj* : burning
abrasivo, -va *adj* : abrasive — **abrasivo** *nm*
: abrasive
abrazar {21} *vt* : hug, embrace — **abra-**
zarse *vr* : embrace — **abrazadera** *nf*
: clamp — **abrazo** *nm* : hug, embrace
abrebotellas *nms & pl* : bottle opener —
abrelatas *nms & pl* : can opener
abrevadero *nm* : watering trough
abreviar *vt* **1** : shorten, abridge **2** : abbreviate (a word) — **abreviación** *nf, pl* **-cio-**
nes : shortening — **abreviatura** *nf* : abbreviation
abridor *nm* : bottle opener, can opener
abrigar {52} *vt* **1** : wrap up (in clothing) **2**
ALBERGAR : cherish, harbor — **abrigarse**
vr : dress warmly — **abrigado, -da** *adj* **1**
: sheltered **2** : warm, wrapped up (of per-

sons) — **abrigo** *nm* **1** : coat, overcoat **2**
REFUGIO : shelter, refuge
abril *nm* : April
abrillantar *vt* : polish, shine
abrir {2} *vt* **1** : open **2** : unlock, undo — *vi*
: open up — **abrirse** *vr* **1** : open up **2** : clear
up (of weather)
abrochar *vt* : button, fasten — **abrocharse**
vr : fasten, do up
abrogar {52} *vt* : annul, repeal
abrumar *vt* : overwhelm — **abrumador,**
-dora *adj* : overwhelming, oppressive
abrupto, -ta *adj* **1** ESCARPADO : steep **2** ÁS-
PERO : rugged, harsh **3** REPENTINO : abrupt
absceso *nm* : abscess
absolución *nf, pl* **-ciones 1** : absolution **2**
: acquittal (in law)
absoluto, -ta *adj* **1** : absolute, unconditional
2 en absoluto : not at all — **absoluta-**
mente *adv* : absolutely
absolver {89} *vt* **1** : absolve **2** : acquit (in
law)
absorber *vt* **1** : absorb **2** : take up (time,
energy, etc.) — **absorbente** *adj* **1** : absorbent **2** INTERESANTE : absorbing — **absor-**
ción *nf, pl* **-ciones** : absorption — **absorto,**
-ta *adj* : absorbed, engrossed
abstemio, -mia *adj* : abstemious — ~ *n*
: teetotaler
abstenerse {80} *vr* : abstain, refrain —
abstención *nf, pl* **-ciones** : abstention —
abstinencia *nf* : abstinence
abstracción *nf, pl* **-ciones** : abstraction —
abstracto, -ta *adj* : abstract — **abstraer**
{81} *vt* : abstract — **abstraerse** *vr* : lose
oneself in thought — **abstraído, -da** *adj*
: preoccupied
absurdo, -da *adj* : absurd, ridiculous — **ab-**
surdo *nm* : absurdity
abuchear *vt* : boo, jeer — **abucheo** *nm*
: booing
abuelo, -la *n* **1** : grandfather, grandmother **2**
abuelos *nmpl* : grandparents
abulia *nf* : apathy, lethargy
abultar *vi* : bulge, be bulky — *vt* : enlarge,
expand — **abultado, -da** *adj* : bulky
abundar *vi* : abound, be plentiful — **abun-**
dancia *nf* : abundance — **abundante** *adj*
: abundant
aburrir *vt* : bore — **aburrirse** *vr* : get bored
— **aburrido, -da** *adj* **1** : bored **2** TEDIOSO
: boring — **aburrimiento** *nm* : boredom
abusar *vi* **1** : go too far **2** ~ **de** : abuse —
abusivo, -va *adj* : outrageous, excessive —
abuso *nm* : abuse
abyecto, -ta *adj* : abject, wretched
acá *adv* : here, over here
acabar *vi* **1** : finish, end **2** ~ **de** : have just
(done something) **3** ~ **con** : put an end to
4 ~ **por** : end up (doing sth) — *vt* : finish

— **acabarse** *vr* : come to an end — **aca-**
bado, -da *adj* **1** : finished, perfect **2** AGO-
TADO : old, worn-out — **acabado** *nm* : finish
academia *nf* : academy — **académico, -ca**
adj : academic
acaecer {53} *vi* : happen, occur
acallar *vt* : quiet, silence
acalorar *vt* : stir up, excite — **acalorarse** *vr*
: get worked up — **acalorado, -da** *adj*
: emotional, heated
acampar *vi* : camp — **acampada** *nf* **ir de** ~
: go camping
acanalado, -da *adj* **1** : grooved **2** : corrugated (of iron, etc.)
acantilado *nm* : cliff
acaparar *vt* **1** : hoard **2** MONOPOLIZAR
: monopolize
acápite *nm Lat* : paragraph
acariciar *vt* **1** : caress **2** : cherish (hopes,
ideas, etc.)
ácaro *nm* : mite
acarrear *vt* **1** : haul, carry **2** OCASIONAR
: give rise to — **acarreo** *nm* : transport
acaso *adv* **1** : perhaps, maybe **2 por si** ~
: just in case
acatar *vt* : comply with, respect — **acata-**
miento *nm* : compliance, respect
acatarrarse *vr* : catch a cold
acaudalado, -da *adj* : wealthy, rich
acaudillar *vt* : lead
acceder *vi* **1** : agree **2** ~ **a** : gain access to,
enter
acceso *nm* **1** : access **2** ENTRADA : entrance
3 : attack, bout (of an illness) — **accesible**
adj : accessible
accesorio *nm* : accessory — **accesorio, -ria**
adj : incidental
accidentado, -da *adj* **1** : eventful, turbulent
2 : rough, uneven (of land, etc.) **3** HERIDO
: injured — ~ *n* : accident victim
accidental *adj* : accidental — **accidentarse**
vr : have an accident — **accidente** *nm* **1**
: accident **2** : unevenness (of land)
acción *nf, pl* **-ciones 1** : action **2** ACTO
: act, deed **3** : share, stock (in finance) —
accionar *vt* : activate — *vi* : gesticulate —
accionista *nmf* : stockholder
acebo *nm* : holly
acechar *vt* : watch, stalk — **acecho** *nm*
estar al ~ **por** : be on the lookout for
aceite *nm* : oil — **aceitar** *vt* : oil — **aceitera**
nf **1** : oilcan **2** : cruet (in cookery) **3** *Lat*
: oil refinery — **aceitoso, -sa** *adj* : oily
aceituna *nf* : olive
acelerar *v* : accelerate — **acelerarse** *vr*
: hurry up — **aceleración** *nf, pl* **-ciones**
: acceleration — **acelerador** *nm* : accelera-
tor
acelga *nf* : (Swiss) chard

acentuar {3} *vt* **1** : accent **2** ENFATIZAR : emphasize, stress — **acentuarse** *vr* : stand out — **acento** *nm* **1** : accent **2** ÉNFASIS : stress, emphasis

acepción *nf, pl* **-ciones** : sense, meaning

aceptar *vt* : accept — **aceptable** *adj* : acceptable — **aceptación** *nf, pl* **-ciones** **1** : acceptance **2** ÉXITO : success

acequia *nf* : irrigation ditch

acera *nf* : sidewalk

acerbo, -ba *adj* : harsh, caustic

acerca *prep* ~ **de** : about, concerning

acercar {72} *vt* : bring near or closer — **acercarse** *vr* : approach, draw near

acero *nm* **1** : steel **2** ~ **inoxidable** : stainless steel

acérrimo, -ma *adj* **1** : staunch, steadfast **2** : bitter (of an enemy)

acertar {55} *vt* : guess correctly — *vi* **1** ATINAR : be accurate **2** ~ **a** : manage to — **acertado, -da** *adj* : correct, accurate

acertijo *nm* : riddle

acervo *nm* : heritage

acetona *nf* : acetone, nail-polish remover

achacar {72} *vt* : attribute, impute

achacoso, -sa *adj* : sickly

achaparrado, -da *adj* : squat, stocky

achaque *nm* : aches and pains

achatar *vt* : flatten

achicar {72} *vt* **1** : make smaller **2** ACOBARDAR : intimidate **3** : bail out (water) — **achicarse** *vr* : become intimidated

achicharrar *vt* : scorch, burn to a crisp

achicoria *nf* : chicory

aciago, -ga *adj* : fateful, unlucky

acicalar *vt* : dress up, adorn — **acicalarse** *vr* : get dressed up

acicate *nm* **1** : spur **2** INCENTIVO : incentive

ácido, -da *adj* : acid, sour — **acidez** *nf, pl* **-deces** : acidity — **ácido** *nm* : acid

acierto *nm* **1** : correct answer **2** HABILIDAD : skill, sound judgment

aclamar *vt* : acclaim — **aclamación** *nf, pl* **-ciones** : acclaim, applause

aclarar *vt* **1** CLARIFICAR : clarify, explain **2** : rinse (clothing) **3** ~ **la voz** : clear one's throat — *vi* : clear up — **aclararse** *vr* : become clear — **aclaración** *nf, pl* **-ciones** : explanation — **aclaratorio, -ria** *adj* : explanatory

aclimatar *vt* : acclimatize — **aclimatarse** *vr* ~ **a** : get used to — **aclimatación** *nf, pl* **-ciones** : acclimatization

acné *nm* : acne

acobardar *vt* : intimidate — **acobardarse** *vr* : become frightened

acodarse *vr* ~ **en** : lean (one's elbows) on

acoger {15} *vt* **1** REFUGIAR : shelter **2** RECIBIR : receive, welcome — **acogerse** *vr* **1** : take refuge **2** ~ **a** : resort to — **acoge-**

dor, -dora *adj* : cozy, welcoming — **acogida** *nf* **1** : welcome **2** REFUGIO : refuge

acolchar *vt* : pad

acólito *nm* MONAGUILLO : altar boy

acometer *vt* **1** : attack **2** EMPRENDER : undertake — *vi* ~ **contra** : rush against — **acometida** *nf* : attack, assault

acomodar *vt* **1** ADAPTAR : adjust **2** COLOCAR : put, make a place for — **acomodarse** *vr* **1** : settle in **2** ~ **a** : adapt to — **acomodado, -da** *adj* : well-to-do — **acomodaticio, -cia** *adj* : accommodating, obliging — **acomodo** *nm* : job, position

acompañar *vt* **1** : accompany **2** ADJUNTAR : enclose — **acompañamiento** *nm* : accompaniment — **acompañante** *nmf* **1** COMPAÑERO : companion **2** : accompanist (in music)

acompasado, -da *adj* : rhythmic, measured

acomplejar *vt* : give a complex, make neurotic

acondicionar *vt* : fit out, equip — **acondicionado, -da** *adj* : equipped

acongojar *vt* : distress, upset — **acongojarse** *vr* : get upset

aconsejar *vt* : advise — **aconsejable** *adj* : advisable

acontecer {53} *vi* : occur, happen — **acontecimiento** *nm* : event

acopiar *vt* : gather, collect — **acopio** *nm* : collection, stock

acoplar *vt* : couple, connect — **acoplarse** *vr* : fit together — **acoplamiento** *nm* : connection, coupling

acorazado, -da *adj* : armored — **acorazado** *nm* : battleship

acordar {19} *vt* **1** : agree (on) **2** *Lat* : award — **acordarse** *vr* : remember

acorde *adj* **1** : in agreement **2** ~ **con** : in keeping with — ~ *nm* : chord (in music)

acordeón *nm, pl* **-deones** : accordion

acordonar *vt* **1** : cordon off **2** : lace up (shoes)

acorralar *vt* : corner, corral

acortar *vt* : shorten, cut short — **acortarse** *vr* : get shorter

acosar *vt* : hound, harass — **acoso** *nm* : harassment

acostar {19} *vt* : put to bed — **acostarse** *vr* **1** : go to bed **2** TUMBARSE : lie down

acostumbrar *vt* : accustom — *vi* ~ **a** : be in the habit of — **acostumbrarse** *vr* ~ **a** : get used to — **acostumbrado, -da** *adj* **1** HABITUADO : accustomed **2** HABITUAL : usual

acotar *vt* **1** ANOTAR : annotate **2** DELIMITAR : mark off (land) — **acotación** *nf, pl* **-ciones** : marginal note — **acotado, -da** *adj* : enclosed

acre *adj* **1** : pungent **2** MORDAZ : harsh, biting

acrecentar {55} *vt* : increase — **acrecenta-miento** *nm* : growth, increase

acreditar *vt* **1** : accredit, authorize **2** PRO-BAR : prove — **acreditarse** *vr* : prove one-self — **acreditado, -da** *adj* **1** : reputable **2** : accredited (in politics, etc.)

acreedor, -dora *adj* : worthy — ~ *n* : credi-tor

acribillar *vt* **1** : riddle, pepper **2** ~ **a** : ha-rass with

acrílico *nm* : acrylic

acrimonia *nf or* **acritud** *nf* **1** : pungency **2** RESENTIMIENTO : bitterness, acrimony

acrobacia *nf* : acrobatics — **acróbata** *nmf* : acrobat — **acrobático, -ca** *adj* : acrobatic

acta *nf* **1** : certificate **2** : minutes *pl* (of a meeting)

actitud *nf* **1** : attitude **2** POSTURA : posture, position

activar *vt* **1** : activate **2** ESTIMULAR : stimu-late, speed up — **actividad** *nf* : activity — **activo, -va** *adj* : active — **activo** *nm* : assets *pl*

acto *nm* **1** ACCIÓN : act, deed **2** : act (in theater) **3 en el** ~ : right away

actor *nm* : actor — **actriz** *nf, pl* **-trices** : ac-tress

actual *adj* : present, current — **actualidad** *nf* **1** : present time **2** ~**es** *nfpl* : current affairs — **actualizar** {21} *vt* : modernize — **actualización** *nf, pl* **-ciones** : moderniza-tion — **actualmente** *adv* : at present, nowa-days

actuar {3} *vi* **1** : act, perform **2** ~ **de** : act as

acuarela *nf* : watercolor

acuario *nm* : aquarium

acuartelar *vt* : quarter (troops)

acuático, -ca *adj* : aquatic, water

acuchillar *vt* : knife, stab

acudir *vi* **1** : go, come **2** ~ **a** : be present at, attend **3** ~ **a** : turn to

acueducto *nm* : aqueduct

acuerdo *nm* **1** : agreement **2 de** ~ : OK, all right **3 de** ~ **con** : in accordance with **4 estar de** ~ : agree

acumular *vt* : accumulate — **acumularse** *vr* : pile up — **acumulación** *nf, pl* **-ciones** : accumulation — **acumulador** *nm* : sto-rage battery — **acumulativo, -va** *adj* : cu-mulative

acunar *vt* : rock

acuñar *vt* **1** : mint (money) **2** : coin (a word)

acuoso, -sa *adj* : watery

acupuntura *nf* : acupuncture

acurrucarse {72} *vr* : curl up, nestle

acusar *vt* **1** : accuse **2** MOSTRAR : reveal, show — **acusación** *nf, pl* **-ciones** : accusa-tion, charge — **acusado, -da** *adj* : promi-nent, marked — ~ *n* : defendant

acuse *nm* ~ **de recibo** : acknowledgment of receipt

acústica *nf* : acoustics — **acústico, -ca** *adj* : acoustic

adagio *nm* **1** REFRÁN : adage, proverb **2** : adagio (in music)

adaptar *vt* **1** : adapt **2** AJUSTAR : adjust, fit — **adaptarse** *vr* ~ **a** : adapt to — **adapta-ble** *adj* : adaptable — **adaptación** *nf, pl* **-ciones** : adaptation — **adaptador** *nm* : adapter (in electricity)

adecuar {8} *vt* : adapt, make suitable — **adecuarse** *vr* ~ **a** : be appropriate for — **adecuado, -da** *adj* : suitable, appropriate

adelantar *vt* **1** : advance, move forward **2** PASAR : overtake **3** : pay in advance — **ade-lantarse** *vr* **1** : move forward, get ahead **2** : be fast (of a clock) — **adelantado, -da** *adj* **1** : advanced, ahead **2** : fast (of a clock) **3 por** ~ : in advance — **adelante** *adv* **1** : ahead, forward **2** ¡~! : come in! **3 más** ~ : later on, further on — **adelanto** *nm* **1** : advance **2** *or* ~ **de dinero** : advance pay-ment

adelgazar {21} *vt* : make thin — *vi* : lose weight

ademán *nm, pl* **-manes 1** GESTO : gesture **2** ~**es** *nmpl* : manners **3 en** ~ **de** : as if to

además *adv* **1** : besides, furthermore **2** ~ **de** : in addition to, as well as

adentro *adv* : inside, within — **adentrarse** *vr* ~ **en** : go into, get inside of

adepto, -ta *n* : follower, supporter

aderezar {21} *vt* : season, dress — **aderezo** *nm* : dressing, seasoning

adeudar *vt* **1** : debit **2** DEBER : owe — **adeudo** *nm* **1** DÉBITO : debit **2** *Lat* : debt

adherirse {76} *vr* : adhere, stick — **adhe-rencia** *nf* : adherence — **adhesión** *nf, pl* **-siones 1** : adhesion **2** APOYO : support — **adhesivo, -va** *adj* : adhesive — **adhe-sivo** *nm* : adhesive

adición *nf, pl* **-ciones** : addition — **adicio-nal** *adj* : additional

adicto, -ta *adj* : addicted — ~ *n* : addict

adiestrar *vt* : train

adinerado, -da *adj* : wealthy

adiós *nm, pl* **adioses 1** : farewell **2** ¡~! : good-bye!

aditamento *nm* : attachment, accessory

aditivo *nm* : additive

adivinar *vt* **1** : guess **2** PREDECIR : foretell — **adivinación** *nf, pl* **-ciones** : guessing, prediction — **adivinanza** *nf* : riddle — **adi-vino, -na** *n* : fortune-teller

adjetivo *nm* : adjective

adjudicar {72} *vt* : award — **adjudicarse** *vr* : appropriate — **adjudicación** *nf, pl* **-cio-nes** : awarding

adjuntar *vt* : enclose (with a letter, etc.) —

adjunto, -ta *adj* : enclosed, attached — ~ *n* : assistant
administración *nf, pl* **-ciones 1** : administration **2** : administering (of a drug, etc.) **3** DIRECCIÓN : management — **administrador, -dora** *n* : administrator, manager — **administrar** *vt* **1** : manage, run **2** : administer (a drug, etc.) — **administrativo, -va** *adj* : administrative
admirar *vt* : admire — **admirarse** *vr* : be amazed — **admirable** *adj* : admirable — **admiración** *nf, pl* **-ciones 1** : admiration **2** ASOMBRO : amazement — **admirador, -dora** *n* : admirer
admitir *vt* **1** : admit **2** ACEPTAR : accept — **admisible** *adj* : admissible, acceptable — **admisión** *nf, pl* **-siones 1** : admission **2** ACEPTACIÓN : acceptance
ADN *nm* : DNA
adobe *nm* : adobe
adobo *nm* : marinade
adoctrinar *vt* : indoctrinate — **adoctrinamiento** *nm* : indoctrination
adolecer {53} *vi* ~ **de** : suffer from
adolescente *adj & nmf* : adolescent — **adolescencia** *nf* : adolescence
adonde *conj* : where
adónde *adv* : where
adoptar *vt* : adopt (a child), take (a decision) — **adopción** *nf, pl* **-ciones** : adoption — **adoptivo, -va** *adj* : adopted, adoptive
adoquín *nm, pl* **-quines** : cobblestone
adorar *vt* : adore, worship — **adorable** *adj* : adorable — **adoración** *nf, pl* **-ciones** : adoration, worship
adormecer {53} *vt* **1** : make sleepy **2** ENTUMECER : numb — **adormecerse** *vr* : doze off — **adormecimiento** *nm* : drowsiness — **adormilarse** *vr* : doze
adornar *vt* : decorate, adorn — **adorno** *nm* : ornament, decoration
adquirir {4} *vt* **1** : acquire **2** COMPRAR : purchase — **adquisición** *nf, pl* **-ciones 1** : acquisition **2** COMPRA : purchase
adrede *adv* : intentionally, on purpose
adscribir {33} *vt* : assign, appoint
aduana *nf* : customs (office) — **aduanero, -ra** *adj* : customs — ~ *n* : customs officer
aducir {61} *vt* : cite, put forward
adueñarse *vr* ~ **de** : take possession of
adular *vt* : flatter — **adulación** *nf, pl* **-ciones** : adulation, flattery — **adulador, -dora** *adj* : flattering — ~ *n* : flatterer
adulterar *vt* : adulterate
adulterio *nm* : adultery — **adúltero, -ra** *n* : adulterer
adulto, -ta *adj & n* : adult
adusto, -ta *adj* : stern, severe
advenedizo, -za *n* : upstart
advenimiento *nm* : advent, arrival

adverbio *nm* : adverb — **adverbial** *adj* : adverbial
adversario, -ria *n* : adversary, opponent — **adverso, -sa** *adj* : adverse — **adversidad** *nf* : adversity
advertir {76} *vt* **1** AVISAR : warn **2** NOTAR : notice — **advertencia** *nf* : warning
adviento *nm* : Advent
adyacente *adj* : adjacent
aéreo, -rea *adj* : aerial, air
aerobic *nm* : aerobics *pl*
aerodeslizador *nm* : hovercraft
aerodinámico, -ca *adj* : aerodynamic
aeródromo *nm* : airfield
aerogenerador *nm* : wind-powered generator
aerolínea *nf* : airline
aeromozo, -za *n* : flight attendant, steward *m*, stewardess *f*
aeronave *nf* : aircraft
aeropuerto *nm* : airport
aerosol *nm* : aerosol, spray
afable *adj* : affable — **afabilidad** *nf* : affability
afán *nm, pl* **afanes 1** ANHELO : eagerness **2** EMPEÑO : effort, hard work — **afanarse** *vr* : toil — **afanosamente** *adv* : industriously, busily — **afanoso, -sa** *adj* **1** : eager **2** TRABAJOSO : arduous
afear *vt* : make ugly, disfigure
afección *nf, pl* **-ciones** : ailment, complaint
afectar *vt* : affect — **afectación** *nf, pl* **-ciones** : affectation — **afectado, -da** *adj* : affected
afectivo, -va *adj* : emotional
afecto *nm* : affection — **afecto, -ta** *adj* ~ **a** : fond of — **afectuoso, -sa** *adj* : affectionate, caring
afeitar *vt* : shave — **afeitarse** *vr* : shave — **afeitada** *nf* : shave
afeminado, -da *adj* : effeminate
aferrarse {55} *vr* : cling, hold on
afianzar {21} *vt* : secure, strengthen — **afianzarse** *vr* : become established
afiche *nm* Lat : poster
afición *nf, pl* **-ciones 1** : penchant, fondness **2** PASATIEMPO : hobby — **aficionado, -da** *n* **1** ENTUSIASTA : enthusiast, fan **2** AMATEUR : amateur — **aficionarse** *vr* ~ **a** : become interested in
afilar *vt* : sharpen — **afilado, -da** *adj* : sharp — **afilador** *nm* : sharpener
afiliarse *vr* ~ **a** : join, become a member of — **afiliación** *nf, pl* **-ciones** : affiliation — **afiliado, -da** *adj* : affiliated
afín *adj, pl* **afines** : related, similar — **afinidad** *nf* : affinity, similarity
afinar *vt* **1** : tune **2** PULIR : perfect, refine
afirmar *vt* **1** : state, affirm **2** REFORZAR : strengthen — **afirmación** *nf, pl* **-ciones**

: statement, affirmation — **afirmativo, -va** *adj* : affirmative

afligir {35} *vt* **1** : afflict **2** APENAR : distress — **afligirse** *vr* : grieve — **aflicción** *nf, pl* **-ciones** : grief, sorrow — **afligido -da** *adj* : sorrowful, distressed

aflojar *vt* **1** : loosen, slacken — *vi* : ease up — **aflojarse** *vr* : become loose, slacken

aflorar *vi* : come to the surface, emerge — **afloramiento** *nm* : outcrop

afluencia *nf* : influx — **afluente** *nm* : tributary

afortunado, -da *adj* : fortunate, lucky — **afortunadamente** *adv* : fortunately

afrentar *vt* : insult — **afrenta** *nf* : affront, insult

africano, -na *adj* : African

afrontar *vt* : confront, face

afuera *adv* **1** : out **2** : outside, outdoors — **afueras** *nfpl* : outskirts

agachar *vt* : lower — **agacharse** *vr* : crouch, stoop

agalla *nf* **1** BRANQUIA : gill **2 tener ~s** *fam* : have guts

agarrar *vt* **1** ASIR : grasp **2** *Lat* : catch — **agarrarse** *vr* : hold on, cling — **agarradera** *nf Lat* : handle — **agarrado, -da** *adj fam* : stingy — **agarre** *nm* : grip, grasp — **agarrón** *nm, pl* **-rones** : tug, pull

agasajar *vt* : fête, wine and dine — **agasajo** *nm* : lavish attention

agave *nm* : agave

agazaparse *vr* : crouch down

agencia *nf* : agency, office — **agente** *nmf* : agent, officer

agenda *nf* **1** : agenda **2** LIBRETA : notebook

ágil *adj* : agile — **agilidad** *nf* : agility

agitar *vt* **1** : agitate, shake **2** : wave, flap (wings, etc.) **3** PERTURBAR : stir up — **agitarse** *vr* **1** : toss about **2** INQUIETARSE : get upset — **agitación** *nf, pl* **-ciones 1** : agitation, shaking **2** INTRANQUILIDAD : restlessness — **agitado, -da** *adj* **1** : agitated, excited **2** : choppy, rough (of the sea)

aglomerar *vt* : amass — **aglomerarse** *vr* : crowd together

agnóstico, -ca *adj & n* : agnostic

agobiar *vt* **1** : oppress **2** ABRUMAR : overwhelm — **agobiado, -da** *adj* : weary, weighed down — **agobiante** *adj* : oppressing, oppressive

agonizar {21} *vi* : be dying — **agonía** *nf* **1** : death throes **2** PENA : agony — **agonizante** *adj* : dying

agorero, -ra *adj* : ominous

agostar *vt* : wither

agosto *nm* : August

agotar *vt* **1** : deplete, use up **2** CANSAR : exhaust, weary — **agotarse** *vr* **1** : run out, give out **2** CANSARSE : get tired — **agotado,**

-da *adj* **1** CANSADO : exhausted **2** : sold out — **agotador, -dora** *adj* : exhausting — **agotamiento** *nm* : exhaustion

agraciado, -da *adj* **1** : attractive **2** AFORTUNADO : fortunate

agradar *vi* : be pleasing — **agradable** *adj* : pleasant, agreeable — **agrado** *nm* **1** : taste, liking **2 con ~** : with pleasure

agradecer {53} *vt* : be grateful for, thank — **agradecido, -da** *adj* : grateful — **agradecimiento** *nm* : gratitude

agrandar *vt* : enlarge — **agrandarse** *vr* : grow larger

agrario, -ria *adj* : agrarian, agricultural

agravar *vt* **1** : make heavier **2** EMPEORAR : aggravate, worsen — **agravarse** *vr* : get worse

agraviar *vt* : insult — **agravio** *nm* : insult

agredir {1} *vt* : attack

agregar {52} *vt* : add, attach — **agregado, -da** *n* : attaché — **agregado** *nm* : aggregate

agresión *nf, pl* **-siones** : aggression, attack — **agresividad** *nf* : aggressiveness — **agresivo, -va** *adj* : aggressive — **agresor, -sora** *n* : aggressor, attacker

agreste *adj* : rugged, wild

agriar *vt* : sour — **agriarse** *vr* **1** : turn sour (of milk, etc.) **2** : become embittered

agrícola *adj* : agricultural — **agricultura** *nf* : agriculture, farming — **agricultor, -tora** *n* : farmer

agridulce *adj* **1** : bittersweet **2** : sweet-and-sour (in cooking)

agrietar *vt* : crack — **agrietarse** *vr* **1** : crack **2** : chap

agrimensor, -sora *n* : surveyor

agrio, agria *adj* : sour

agrupar *vt* : group together — **agruparse** *vr* : form a group — **agrupación** *nf, pl* **-ciones** : group, association — **agrupamiento** *nm* : grouping

agua *nf* **1** : water **2 ~ oxigenada** : hydrogen peroxide **3 ~s negras** *or* **~s residuales** : sewage

aguacate *nm* : avocado

aguacero *nm* : downpour

aguado, -da *adj* **1** : watery **2** *Lat fam* : soft, flabby — **aguar** {10} *vt* **1** : water down, dilute **2 ~ la fiesta** *fam* : spoil the party

aguafuerte *nm* : etching

aguanieve *nf* : sleet

aguantar *vt* **1** SOPORTAR : bear, withstand **2** SOSTENER : hold — *vi* : hold out, last — **aguantarse** *vr* **1** : resign oneself **2** CONTENERSE : restrain oneself — **aguante** *nm* **1** : patience **2** RESISTENCIA : endurance

aguardar *vt* : await

aguardiente *nm* : clear brandy

aguarrás *nm* : turpentine

agudo, -da *adj* **1** : acute, sharp **2** : shrill,

high-pitched (in music) — **agudeza** *nf* **1** : sharpness **2** : witticism

agüero *nm* : augury, omen

aguijón *nm, pl* **-jones 1** : stinger (of an insect) **2** ESTÍMULO : goad, stimulus — **aguijonear** *vt* : goad

águila *nf* : eagle

aguja *nf* **1** : needle **2** : hand (of a clock) **3** : spire (of a church)

agujero *nm* : hole

agujeta *nf* **1** *Lat* : shoelace **2** ~s *nfpl* : (muscular) stiffness

aguzar {21} *vt* **1** : sharpen **2** ~ **el oído** : prick up one's ears

ahí *adv* **1** : there **2 por** ~ : somewhere, thereabouts

ahijado, -da *n* : godchild, godson *m,* goddaughter *f*

ahínco *nm* : eagerness, zeal

ahogar {52} *vt* **1** : drown **2** ASFIXIAR : smother — **ahogarse** *vr* : drown — **ahogo** *nm* : breathlessness

ahondar *vt* : deepen — *vi* : elaborate, go into detail

ahora *adv* **1** : now **2** ~ **mismo** : right now

ahorcar {72} *vt* : hang, kill by hanging — **ahorcarse** *vr* : hang oneself

ahorita *adv Lat fam* : right now

ahorrar *vt* : save, spare — *vi* : save up — **ahorrarse** *vr* : spare oneself — **ahorro** *nm* : saving

ahuecar {72} *vt* **1** : hollow out **2** : cup (one's hands)

ahumar {8} *vt* : smoke, cure — **ahumado, -da** *adj* : smoked

ahuyentar *vt* : scare away, chase away

airado, -da *adj* : irate, angry

aire *nm* **1** : air **2** ~ **acondicionado** : air-conditioning **3 al** ~ **libre** : in the open air, outdoors — **airear** *vt* : air, air out

aislar {5} *vt* **1** : isolate **2** : insulate (in electricity) — **aislamiento** *nm* **1** : isolation **2** : (electrical) insulation

ajar *vt* **1** : crumple, wrinkle **2** ESTROPEAR : spoil

ajedrez *nm* : chess

ajeno, -na *adj* **1** : someone else's **2** EXTRAÑO : alien **3** ~ **a** : foreign to

ajetreado, -da *adj* : hectic, busy — **ajetrearse** *vr* : bustle about — **ajetreo** *nm* : hustle and bustle

ají *nm, pl* **ajíes** *Lat* : chili pepper

ajo *nm* : garlic

ajustar *vt* **1** : adjust, adapt **2** ACORDAR : agree on **3** SALDAR : settle — **ajustarse** *vr* : fit, conform — **ajustable** *adj* : adjustable — **ajustado, -da** *adj* **1** : close, tight **2** CEÑIDO : tight-fitting — **ajuste** *nm* : adjustment

ajusticiar *vt* : execute, put to death

al (*contraction of* **a** *and* **el**) → **a**²

ala *nf* **1** : wing **2** : brim (of a hat)

alabanza *nf* : praise — **alabar** *vt* : praise

alacena *nf* : cupboard, larder

alacrán *nm, pl* **-cranes** : scorpion

alado, -da *adj* : winged

alambre *nm* : wire

alameda *nf* **1** : poplar grove **2** : tree-lined avenue — **álamo** *nm* : poplar

alarde *nm* : show, display — **alardear** *vi* : boast

alargar {52} *vt* **1** : extend, lengthen **2** PROLONGAR : prolong — **alargarse** *vr* : become longer — **alargador** *nm* : extension cord

alarido *nm* : howl, shriek

alarmar *vt* : alarm — **alarma** *nf* : alarm — **alarmante** *adj* : alarming

alba *nf* : dawn

albahaca *nf* : basil

albañil *nm* : bricklayer, mason

albaricoque *nm* : apricot

albedrío *nm* **libre** ~ : free will

alberca *nf* **1** : reservoir, tank **2** *Lat* : swimming pool

albergar {52} *vt* : house, lodge — **albergue** *nm* **1** : lodging **2** REFUGIO : shelter **3** ~ **juvenil** : youth hostel

albóndiga *nf* : meatball

alborear *v impers* : dawn — **albor** *nm* : dawning — **alborada** *nf* : dawn

alborotar *vt* : excite, stir up — *vi* : make a racket — **alborotarse** *vr* : get excited — **alborotado, -da** *adj* : excited, agitated — **alborotador, -dora** *n* : agitator, rioter — **alboroto** *nm* : ruckus

alborozar {21} *vt* : gladden — **alborozo** *nm* : joy

álbum *nm* : album

alcachofa *nf* : artichoke

alcalde, -desa *n* : mayor

alcance *nm* **1** : reach **2** ÁMBITO : range, scope

alcancía *nf* : money box

alcantarilla *nf* : sewer, drain

alcanzar {21} *vt* **1** : reach **2** LLEGAR A : catch up with **3** LOGRAR : achieve, attain — *vi* **1** : suffice, be enough **2** ~ **a** : manage to

alcaparra *nf* : caper

alcázar *nm* : fortress, castle

alce *nm* : moose, European elk

alcoba *nf* : bedroom

alcohol *nm* : alcohol — **alcohólico, -ca** *adj & n* : alcoholic — **alcoholismo** *nm* : alcoholism

aldaba *nf* : door knocker

aldea *nf* : village — **aldeano, -na** *n* : villager

aleación *nf, pl* **-ciones** : alloy

aleatorio, -ria *adj* : random

aleccionar *vt* : instruct, teach

aledaño, -ña *adj* : bordering — **aledaños** *nmpl* : outskirts

alegar {52} *vt* : assert, allege — *vi Lat* : argue — **alegato** *nm* **1** : allegation (in law) **2** *Lat* : argument

alegoría *nf* : allegory — **alegórico, -ca** *adj* : allegorical

alegrar *vt* : make happy, cheer up — **alegrarse** *vr* : be glad — **alegre** *adj* **1** CONTENTO : glad, happy **2** : colorful, bright — **alegremente** *adv* : happily — **alegría** *nf* : joy, cheer

alejar *vt* **1** : remove, move away **2** ENAJENAR : estrange — **alejarse** *vr* : move away, drift apart — **alejado, -da** *adj* : remote — **alejamiento** *nm* **1** : removal **2** : estrangement (of persons)

alemán, -mana *adj, mpl* **-manes** : German — **alemán** *nm* : German (language)

alentar {55} *vt* : encourage — **alentador, -dora** *adj* : encouraging

alergia *nf* : allergy — **alérgico, -ca** *adj* : allergic

alero *nm* : eaves *pl*

alertar *vt* : alert — **alerta** *adv* : on the alert — **alerta** *adj & nf* : alert

aleta *nf* **1** : fin, flipper **2** : small wing

alevosía *nf* : treachery — **alevoso, -sa** *adj* : treacherous

alfabeto *nm* : alphabet — **alfabético, -ca** *adj* : alphabetical — **alfabetismo** *nm* : literacy — **alfabetizar** {21} *vt* **1** : teach literacy **2** : alphabetize

alfalfa *nf* : alfalfa

alfarería *nf* : pottery

alféizar *nm* : sill, windowsill

alfil *nm* : bishop (in chess)

alfiler *nm* **1** : pin **2** BROCHE : brooch — **alfiletero** *nm* : pincushion

alfombra *nf* : carpet, rug — **alfombrilla** *nf* : small rug, mat

alga *nf* : seaweed

álgebra *nf* : algebra

algo *pron* **1** : something **2** ~ **de** : some, a little — ~ *adv* : somewhat, rather

algodón *nm, pl* **-dones** : cotton

alguacil *nm* : constable, bailiff

alguien *pron* : somebody, someone

alguno, -na *adj* (**algún** *before masculine singular nouns*) **1** : some, any **2** (*in negative constructions*) : not any, not at all **3 algunas veces** : sometimes — ~ *pron* **1** : one, someone, somebody **2 algunos, -nas** *pron pl* : some, a few

alhaja *nf* : jewel

alharaca *nf* : fuss

aliado, -da *n* : ally — ~ *adj* : allied — **alianza** *nf* : alliance — **aliarse** {85} *vr* : form an alliance

alias *adv & nm* : alias

alicaído, -da *adj* : depressed

alicates *nmpl* : pliers

aliciente *nm* **1** : incentive **2** : attraction (to a place)

alienar *vt* : alienate — **alienación** *nf, pl* **-ciones** : alienation

aliento *nm* **1** : breath **2** ÁNIMO : encouragement, strength

aligerar *vt* **1** : lighten **2** APRESURAR : hasten, quicken

alimaña *nf* : pest, vermin

alimentar *vt* : feed, nourish — **alimentarse** *vr* ~ **con** : live on — **alimentación** *nf, pl* **-ciones 1** : feeding **2** NUTRICIÓN : nourishment — **alimenticio, -cia** *adj* : nourishing — **alimento** *nm* : food, nourishment

alinear *vt* : align, line up — **alinearse** *vr* ~ **con** : align oneself with — **alineación** *nf, pl* **-ciones 1** : alignment **2** : lineup (in sports)

aliño *nm* : dressing, seasoning — **aliñar** *vt* : season, dress

alisar *vt* : smooth

alistarse *vr* : join up, enlist — **alistamiento** *nm* : enlistment

aliviar *vt* : relieve, soothe — **aliviarse** *vr* : recover, get better — **alivio** *nm* : relief

aljibe *nm* : cistern, tank

allá *adv* **1** : there, over there **2 más** ~ : farther away **3 más** ~ **de** : beyond

allanar *vt* **1** : smooth, level out **2** *Spain* : break into (a house) **3** *Lat* : raid — **allanamiento** *nm* **1** *Spain* : breaking and entering **2** *Lat* : raid

allegado, -da *n* : close friend, relation

allí *adv* : there, over there

alma *nf* : soul

almacén *nm, pl* **-cenes 1** : warehouse **2** *Lat* : shop, store **3 grandes almacenes** : department store — **almacenamiento** *or* **almacenaje** *nm* : storage — **almacenar** *vt* : store

almádena *nf* : sledgehammer

almanaque *nm* : almanac

almeja *nf* : clam

almendra *nf* **1** : almond **2** : kernel (of nuts, fruit, etc.)

almiar *nm* : haystack

almíbar *nm* : syrup

almidón *nm, pl* **-dones** : starch — **almidonar** *vt* : starch

almirante *nm* : admiral

almohada *nf* : pillow — **almohadilla** *nf* : small pillow, pad — **almohadón** *nm, pl* **-dones** : bolster, large cushion

almorranas *nfpl* : hemorrhoids, piles

almorzar {36} *vi* : have lunch — *vt* : have for lunch — **almuerzo** *nm* : lunch

alocado, -da *adj* : crazy, wild

áloe *or* **aloe** *nm* : aloe

alojar *vt* : house, lodge — **alojarse** *vr*

: lodge, room — **alojamiento** *nm* : lodging, accommodations *pl*

alondra *nf* : lark

alpaca *nf* : alpaca

alpinismo *nm* : mountain climbing — **alpinista** *nmf* : mountain climber

alpiste *nm* : birdseed

alquilar *vt* : rent, lease — **alquilarse** *vr* : be for rent — **alquiler** *nm* : rent, rental

alquitrán *nm, pl* **-tranes** : tar

alrededor *adv* **1** : around, about **2** ~ **de** : approximately — **alrededor de** *prep phr* : around — **alrededores** *nmpl* : outskirts

alta *nf* : discharge (of a patient)

altanería *nf* : haughtiness — **altanero, -ra** *adj* : haughty

altar *nm* : altar

altavoz *nm, pl* **-voces** : loudspeaker

alterar *vt* **1** : alter, modify **2** PERTURBAR : disturb — **alterarse** *vr* : get upset — **alteración** *nf, pl* **-ciones 1** : alteration **2** ALBOROTO : disturbance — **altera- do, -da** *adj* : upset

altercado *nm* : altercation, argument

alternar *vi* **1** : alternate **2** ~ **con** : socialize with — *vt* : alternate — **alternarse** *vr* : take turns — **alternativa** *nf* : alternative — **alternativo, -va** *adj* : alternating, alternative — **alterno, -na** *adj* : alternate

Alteza *nf* : Highness

altiplano *nm* : high plateau

altitud *nf* : altitude

altivez *nf, pl* **-veces** : haughtiness — **altivo, -va** *adj* : haughty

alto, -ta *adj* **1** : tall, high **2** RUIDOSO : loud — **alto** *adv* **1** ARRIBA : high **2** : loud, loudly — ~ *nm* **1** ALTURA : height, elevation **2** : stop, halt — ~ *interj* : halt!, stop! — **altoparlante** *nm Lat* : loudspeaker

altruista *adj* : altruistic — **altruismo** *nm* : altruism

altura *nf* **1** : height **2** ALTITUD : altitude **3 a la** ~ **de** : near, up by

alubia *nf* : kidney bean

alucinar *vi* : hallucinate — **alucinación** *nf, pl* **-ciones** : hallucination

alud *nm* : avalanche

aludir *vi* : allude, refer — **aludido, -da** *adj* **darse por** ~ : take it personally

alumbrar *vt* **1** : light, illuminate **2** PARIR : give birth to — **alumbrado** *nm* : (electric) lighting — **alumbramiento** *nm* : childbirth

aluminio *nm* : aluminum

alumno, -na *n* : pupil, student

alusión *nf, pl* **-siones** : allusion

aluvión *nm, pl* **-viones** : flood, barrage

alzar {21} *vt* : lift, raise — **alzarse** *vr* : rise (up) — **alza** *nf* : rise — **alzamiento** *nm* : uprising

ama → **amo**

amabilidad *nf* : kindness — **amable** *adj* : kind, nice

amaestrar *vt* : train

amagar {52} *vt* **1** : show signs of **2** AMENAZAR : threaten — *vi* : be imminent — **amago** *nm* **1** INDICIO : sign **2** AMENAZA : threat

amainar *vi* : abate

amamantar *v* : breast-feed, nurse

amanecer {53} *v impers* : dawn — *vi* : wake up — ~ *nm* : dawn, daybreak

amanerado *adj* : affected, mannered

amansar *vt* **1** : tame **2** APACIGUAR : soothe — **amansarse** *vr* : calm down

amante *adj* ~ **de** : fond of — ~ *nmf* : lover

amañar *vt* : rig, tamper with

amapola *nf* : poppy

amar *vt* : love

amargar {52} *vt* : make bitter — **amargado, -da** *adj* : embittered — **amargo, -ga** *adj* : bitter — **amargo** *nm* : bitterness — **amargura** *nf* : bitterness, grief

amarillo, -lla *adj* : yellow — **amarillo** *nm* : yellow

amarrar *vt* **1** : moor **2** ATAR : tie up

amasar *vt* **1** : knead **2** : amass (a fortune, etc.)

amateur *adj & nmf* : amateur

amatista *nf* : amethyst

ambages *nmpl* **sin** ~ : without hesitation, straight to the point

ámbar *nm* : amber

ambición *nf, pl* **-ciones** : ambition — **ambicionar** *vt* : aspire to — **ambicioso, -sa** *adj* : ambitious

ambiente *nm* **1** AIRE : atmosphere **2** MEDIO : environment, surroundings *pl* — **ambiental** *adj* : environmental

ambigüedad *nf* : ambiguity — **ambiguo, -gua** *adj* : ambiguous

ámbito *nm* : domain, sphere

ambos, -bas *adj & pron* : both

ambulancia *nf* : ambulance

ambulante *adj* : traveling, itinerant

ameba *nf* : amoeba

amedrentar *vt* : intimidate

amén *nm* **1** : amen **2** ~ **de** : in addition to

amenaza *nf* : threat (**amenazas de muerte/ bomba** death/bomb threats)

amenazar {21} *vt* : threaten

amenizar {21} *vt* : make pleasant, enliven — **ameno, -na** *adj* : pleasant

americano, -na *adj* : American

ameritar *vt Lat* : deserve

ametralladora *nf* : machine gun

amianto *nm* : asbestos

amiba → **ameba**

amígdala *nf* : tonsil — **amigdalitis** *nf* : tonsilitis

amigo, -ga *adj* : friendly, close — ~ *n* : friend — **amigable** *adj* : friendly

amilanar *vt* : daunt — **amilanarse** *vr* : lose heart

aminorar *vt* : diminish

amistad *nf* : friendship — **amistoso, -sa** *adj* : friendly

amnesia *nf* : amnesia

amnistía *nf* : amnesty

amo, ama *n* **1** : master *m*, mistress *f* **2 ama de casa** : homemaker, housewife **3 ama de llaves** : housekeeper

amodorrado, -da *adj* : drowsy

amolar {19} *vt* **1** : grind, sharpen **2** MOLESTAR : annoy

amoldar *vt* : adapt, adjust — **amoldarse** *vr* ~ **a** : adapt to

amonestar *vt* : admonish, warn — **amonestación** *nf, pl* **-ciones** : admonition, warning

amoníaco *or* **amoniaco** *nm* : ammonia

amontonar *vt* : pile up — **amontonarse** *vr* : pile up (of things), form a crowd (of persons)

amor *nm* : love

amordazar {21} *vt* : gag

amorío *nm* : love affair — **amoroso, -sa** *adj* **1** : loving **2** *Lat* : sweet, lovable

amortado, -da *adj* : black-and-blue

amortiguar {10} *vt* : muffle, soften, tone down — **amortiguador** *nm* : shock absorber

amortizar {21} *vt* : pay off — **amortización** *nf* : repayment

amotinar *vt* : incite (to riot) — **amotinarse** *vr* : riot, rebel

amparar *vt* : shelter, protect — **ampararse** *vr* **1** ~ **de** : take shelter from **2** ~ **en** : have recourse to — **amparo** *nm* : refuge, protection

ampliar {85} *vt* **1** : expand **2** : enlarge (a photograph) — **ampliación** *nf, pl* **-ciones 1** : expansion, enlargement **2** : extension (of a building)

amplificar {72} *vt* : amplify — **amplificador** *nm* : amplifier

amplio, -plia *adj* : broad, wide, ample — **amplitud** *nf* **1** : breadth, extent **2** ESPACIOSIDAD : spaciousness

ampolla *nf* **1** : blister **2** : vial, ampoule — **ampollarse** *vr* : blister

ampuloso, -sa *adj* : pompous

amputar *vt* : amputate — **amputación** *nf, pl* **-ciones** : amputation

amueblar *vt* : furnish (a house, etc.)

amurallar *vt* : wall in

anacardo *nm* : cashew nut

anaconda *nf* : anaconda

anacrónico, -ca *adj* : anachronistic — **anacronismo** *nm* : anachronism

ánade *nmf* : duck

anagrama *nm* : anagram

anales *nmpl* : annals

analfabeto, -ta *adj & n* : illiterate — **analfabetismo** *nm* : illiteracy

analgésico *nm* : painkiller, analgesic

analizar {21} *vt* : analyze — **análisis** *nm* : analysis — **analítico, -ca** *adj* : analytical, analytic

analogía *nf* : analogy — **análogo, -ga** *adj* : analogous

ananá *or* **ananás** *nm, pl* **-nás** : pineapple

anaquel *nm* : shelf

anaranjado, -da *adj* : orange-colored

anarquía *nf* : anarchy — **anarquista** *adj & nmf* : anarchist

anatomía *nf* : anatomy — **anatómico, -ca** *adj* : anatomic, anatomical

anca *nf* **1** : haunch **2** ~**s de rana** : frogs' legs

ancestral *adj* : ancestral

ancho, -cha *adj* : wide, broad, ample — **ancho** *nm* : width

anchoa *nf* : anchovy

anchura *nf* : width, breadth

anciano, -na *adj* : aged, elderly — ~ *n* : elderly person

ancla *nf* : anchor — **anclar** *v* : anchor

andadas *nfpl* **1** : tracks **2 volver a las** ~ : go back to one's old ways

andadura *nf* : walking, journey

andaluz, -luza *adj & n, mpl* **-luces** : Andalusian

andamio *nm* : scaffold

andanada *nf* **1** : volley **2 soltar una** ~ : reprimand

andanzas *nfpl* : adventures

andar {6} *vi* **1** CAMINAR : walk **2** IR : go, travel **3** FUNCIONAR : run, work **4** ~ **en** : rummage around in **5** ~ **por** : be approximately — *vt* : cover, travel — ~ *nm* : gait, walk

andén *nm, pl* **-denes 1** : (train) platform **2** *Lat* : sidewalk

andino, -na *adj* : Andean

andorrano, -na *adj* : Andorran

andrajos *nmpl* : tatters — **andrajoso, -sa** *adj* : ragged

anécdota *nf* : anecdote

anegar {52} *vt* : flood — **anegarse** *vr* **1** : be flooded **2** AHOGARSE : drown

anemia *nf* : anemia — **anémico, -ca** *adj* : anemic

anestesia *nf* : anesthesia — **anestésico, -ca** *adj* : anesthetic — **anestésico** *nm* : anesthetic

anexar *vt* : annex, attach — **anexo, -xa** *adj* : attached — **anexo** *nm* : annex

anfibio, -bia *adj* : amphibious — **anfibio** *nm* : amphibian

anfiteatro *nm* : amphitheater

anfitrión, -triona *n, mpl* **-triones** : host, hostess *f*

ángel *nm* : angel — **angelical** *adj* : angelic, angelical

angloparlante *adj* : English-speaking

anglosajón, -jona *adj, mpl* **-jones** : Anglo-Saxon

angosto, -ta *adj* : narrow

anguila *nf* : eel

ángulo *nm* **1** : angle **2** ESQUINA : corner — **angular** *adj* : angular — **anguloso, -sa** *adj* : angular

angustiar *vt* **1** : anguish, distress **2** INQUIETAR : worry — **angustiarse** *vr* : get upset — **angustia** *nf* **1** : anguish **2** INQUIETUD : worry — **angustioso, -sa** *adj* **1** : anguished **2** INQUIETANTE : distressing

anhelar *vt* : yearn for, crave — **anhelante** *adj* : yearning, longing — **anhelo** *nm* : longing

anidar *vi* : nest

anillo *nm* : ring

ánima *n* : soul

animación *nf, pl* **-ciones 1** VIVEZA : liveliness **2** BULLICIO : hustle and bustle — **animado, -da** *adj* : cheerful, animated — **animador, -dora** *n* **1** : (television) host **2** : cheerleader

animadversión *nf, pl* **-siones** : animosity

animal *nm* : animal — ~ *nmf* : brute, beast — ~ *adj* : brutish

animar *vt* **1** ALENTAR : encourage **2** ALEGAR : cheer up — **animarse** *vr* **1** : liven up **2** ~ **a** : get up the nerve to

ánimo *nm* **1** : spirit, soul **2** HUMOR : mood, spirits *pl* **3** ALIENTO : encouragement

animosidad *nf* : animosity, ill will

animoso, -sa *adj* : spirited, brave

aniquilar *vt* : annihilate — **aniquilación** *n, pl* **-ciones** : annihilation

anís *nm* : anise

aniversario *nm* : anniversary

ano *nm* : anus

anoche *adv* : last night

anochecer {53} *vi* : get dark — ~ *nm* : dusk, nightfall

anodino, -na *adj* : insipid, dull

anomalía *nf* : anomaly

anonadado, -da *adj* : dumbfounded

anónimo, -ma *adj* : anonymous — **anonimato** *nm* : anonymity

anorexia *nf* : anorexia

anormal *adj* : abnormal — **anormalidad** *nf* : abnormality

anotar *vt* **1** : annotate **2** APUNTAR : jot down — **anotación** *nf, pl* **-ciones** : annotation, note

anquilosarse *vr* **1** : become paralyzed **2** ESTANCARSE : stagnate — **anquilosami-**

ento *nm* **1** : paralysis **2** ESTANCAMIENTO : stagnation

ansiar {85} *vt* : long for — **ansia** *nf* **1** INQUIETUD : uneasiness **2** ANGUSTIA : anguish **3** ANHELO : longing — **ansiedad** *nf* : anxiety — **ansioso, -sa** *adj* **1** : anxious **2** DESEOSO : eager

antagónico, -ca *adj* : antagonistic — **antagonismo** *nm* : antagonism — **antagonista** *nmf* : antagonist

antaño *adv* : yesteryear, long ago

antártico, -ca *adj* : antarctic

ante¹ *nm* **1** : elk, moose **2** GAMUZA : suede

ante² *prep* **1** : before, in front of **2** : in view of **3** ~ **todo** : above all

anteanoche *adv* : the night before last

anteayer *adv* : the day before yesterday

antebrazo *nm* : forearm

anteceder *vt* : precede — **antecedente** *adj* : previous, prior — ~ *nm* : precedent — **antecesor, -sora** *n* **1** : ancestor **2** PREDECESOR : predecessor

antedicho, -cha *adj* : aforesaid

antelación *nf, pl* **-ciones 1** : advance notice **2 con** ~ : in advance

antemano *adv* **de** ~ : beforehand

antena *nf* : antenna

antenoche → **anteanoche**

anteojos *nmpl* **1** : glasses, eyeglasses **2** ~ **bifocales** : bifocals

antepasado, -da *n* : ancestor

antepecho *nm* : ledge

antepenúltimo, -ma *adj* : third from last

anteponer {60} *vt* **1** : place before **2** PREFERIR : prefer

anterior *adj* **1** : previous, earlier **2** DELANTERO : front — **anterioridad** *nf* **con** ~ : beforehand, in advance — **anteriormente** *adv* : previously

antes *adv* **1** : before, earlier **2** ANTERIORMENTE : previously **3** PRIMERO : first **4** MEJOR : rather **5** ~ **de** : before, previous to **6** ~ **que** : before

antesala *nf* : waiting room

antiaéreo, -rea *adj* : antiaircraft

antibiótico *nm* : antibiotic

anticipar *vt* **1** : move up (a date, etc.) **2** : pay in advance — **anticiparse** *vr* **1** : be early **2** ADELANTARSE : get ahead — **anticipación** *nf, pl* **-ciones 1** : anticipation **2 con** ~ : in advance — **anticipado, -da** *adj* **1** : advance, early **2 por** ~ : in advance — **anticipo** *nm* **1** : advance (payment) **2** : foretaste

anticoncepción *nf, pl* **-ciones** : contraception — **anticonceptivo, -va** *adj* : contraceptive — **anticonceptivo** *nm* : contraceptive

anticongelante *nm* : antifreeze

anticuado, -da *adj* : antiquated, outdated

anticuario, -ria *n* : antique dealer — **anticuario** *nm* : antique shop
anticuerpo *nm* : antibody
antídoto *nm* : antidote
antier → **anteayer**
antiestético, -ca *adj* : unsightly
antifaz *nm, pl* **-faces** : mask
antífona *nf* : anthem
antigualla *nf* : relic, old thing
antiguo, -gua *adj* **1** : ancient, old **2** ANTERIOR : former **3** ANTICUADO : old-fashioned **4 muebles antiguos** : antique furniture — **antiguamente** *adv* **1** : long ago **2** ANTES : formerly — **antigüedad** *nf* **1** : antiquity **2** : seniority (in the workplace) **3** ~**es** *nfpl* : antiques
antihigiénico, -ca *adj* : unsanitary
antihistamínico *nm* : antihistamine
antiinflamatorio, -ria *adj* : anti-inflammatory
antílope *nm* : antelope
antinatural *adj* : unnatural
antipatía *nf* : aversion, dislike — **antipático, -ca** *adj* : unpleasant
antirreglamentario, -ria *adj* : unlawful
antirrobo, -ba *adj* : antitheft
antisemita *adj* : anti-Semitic — **antisemitismo** *nm* : anti-Semitism
antiséptico, -ca *adj* : antiseptic — **antiséptico** *nm* : antiseptic
antisocial *adj* : antisocial
antítesis *nf* : antithesis
antiviral *adj* : antiviral
antivirus *nm, pl* **antivirus** : antivirus software
antojarse *vr* **1** APETECER : crave **2** PARECER : seem, appear — **antojadizo, -za** *adj* : capricious — **antojo** *nm* : whim, craving
antología *nf* : anthology
antorcha *nf* : torch
antro *nm* : dive, den
antropófago, -ga *nmf* : cannibal
antropología *nf* : anthropology
anual *adj* : annual, yearly — **anualidad** *nf* : annuity — **anuario** *nm* : yearbook, annual
anudar *vt* : knot — **anudarse** *vr* : tie, knot
anular *vt* : annul, cancel — **anulación** *nf, pl* **-ciones** : annulment, cancellation
anunciar *vt* **1** : announce **2** : advertise (products) — **anunciante** *nmf* : advertiser — **anuncio** *nm* **1** : announcement **2** *or* ~ **publicitario** : advertisement
anzuelo *nm* **1** : fishhook **2 morder el** ~ : take the bait
añadir *vt* : add — **añadidura** *nf* **1** : additive, addition **2 por** ~ : in addition, furthermore
añejo, -ja *adj* : aged, vintage
añicos *nmpl* **hacer(se)** ~ : smash to pieces
añil *adj & nm* : indigo (color)
año *nm* **1** : year **2 Año Nuevo** : New Year

añorar *vt* : long for, miss — **añoranza** *nf* : nostalgia
añoso, -sa *adj* : aged, old
aorta *nf* : aorta
apabullar *vt* : overwhelm
apacentar {55} *vt* : pasture, graze
apachurrar *vt Lat* : crush
apacible *adj* : gentle, mild
apaciguar {10} *vt* : appease, pacify — **apaciguarse** *vr* : calm down
apadrinar *vt* **1** : be a godparent to **2** : sponsor (an artist, etc.)
apagar {52} *vt* **1** : turn or switch off **2** EXTINGUIR : extinguish, put out — **apagarse** *vr* **1** EXTINGUIRSE : go out **2** : die down — **apagado, -da** *adj* **1** : off, out **2** : dull, subdued (of colors, sounds, etc.) — **apagador** *nm Lat* : (light) switch — **apagón** *nm, pl* **-gones** : blackout
apalancar {72} *vt* **1** LEVANTAR : jack up **2** ABRIR : pry open — **apalancamiento** *nm* : leverage
apalear *vt* : beat up, thrash
aparador *nm* **1** : sideboard **2** *Lat* : shop window
aparato *nm* **1** : machine, appliance, apparatus **2** : system (in anatomy) **3** OSTENTACIÓN : ostentation — **aparatoso, -sa** *adj* **1** : ostentatious **2** ESPECTACULAR : spectacular
aparcar {72} *v Spain* : park — **aparcamiento** *nm Spain* **1** : parking **2** : parking lot
aparcero, -ra *n* : sharecropper
aparear *vt* : mate, pair up — **aparearse** *vr* : mate
aparecer {53} *vi* **1** : appear **2** PRESENTARSE : show up — **aparecerse** *vr* : appear
aparejar *vt* **1** : rig (a ship) **2** : harness (an animal) — **aparejado, -da** *adj* **llevar** ~ : entail — **aparejo** *nm* **1** : equipment, gear **2** : harness (for an animal) **3** : rigging (for a ship)
aparentar *vt* **1** : seem **2** FINGIR : feign — **aparente** *adj* : apparent, seeming
aparición *nf, pl* **-ciones** **1** : appearance **2** FANTASMA : apparition — **apariencia** *nf* **1** : appearance, look **2 en** ~ : apparently
apartado *nm* **1** : section, paragraph **2** ~ **postal** : post office box
apartamento *nm* : apartment
apartar *vt* **1** ALEJAR : move away **2** SEPARAR : set aside, separate — **apartarse** *vr* **1** : move away **2** DESVIARSE : stray — **aparte** *adv* **1** : apart, separately **2** ADEMÁS : besides
apasionar *vt* : excite, fascinate — **apasionarse** *vr* : get excited — **apasionado, -da** *adj* : passionate, excited — **apasionante** *adj* : exciting

apatía *nf* : apathy — **apático, -ca** *adj* : apathetic

apearse *vr* **1** : dismount **2** : get out of or off (a vehicle)

apedrear *vt* : stone

apegarse {52} *vr* ～ **a** : become attached to, grow fond of — **apegado, -da** *adj* : devoted — **apego** *nm* : fondness

apelar *vi* **1** : appeal **2** ～ **a** : resort to — **apelación** *nf, pl* **-ciones** : appeal

apellido *nm* : last name, surname — **apellidarse** *vr* : have for a last name

apenar *vt* : sadden — **apenarse** *vr* **1** : grieve **2** *Lat* : become embarrassed

apenas *adv* : hardly, scarcely — ～ *conj* : as soon as

apéndice *nm* : appendix — **apendicitis** *nf* : appendicitis

apercibir *vt* **1** : warn **2** *Lat* : notice — **apercibirse** *vr* ～ **de** : notice — **apercibimiento** *nm* : warning

aperitivo *nm* **1** : appetizer **2** : aperitif

apero *nm* : tool, implement

apertura *nf* : opening

apesadumbrar *vt* : sadden — **apesadumbrarse** *vr* : be weighed down

apestar *vi* : stink — **apestoso, -sa** *adj* : stinking, foul

apetecer {53} *vt* : crave, long for — **apetecible** *adj* : appealing

apetito *nm* : appetite — **apetitoso, -sa** *adj* : appetizing

ápice *nm* **1** : apex, summit **2** PIZCA : bit, smidgen

apilar *vt* : pile up — **apilarse** *vr* : pile up

apiñar *vt* : pack, cram — **apiñarse** *vr* : crowd together

apio *nm* : celery

apisonadora *nf* : steamroller

aplacar {72} *vt* : appease, placate — **aplacarse** *vr* : calm down

aplanar *vt* : flatten, level

aplastar *vt* : crush — **aplastante** *adj* : overwhelming

aplaudir *v* : applaud — **aplauso** *nm* **1** : applause **2** : acclaim

aplazar {21} *vt* : postpone, defer — **aplazamiento** *nm* : postponement

aplicar {72} *vt* : apply — **aplicarse** *vr* : apply oneself — **aplicable** *adj* : applicable — **aplicación** *nf, pl* **-ciones** : application — **aplicado, -da** *adj* : diligent

aplomo *nm* : aplomb

apocarse {72} *vr* : belittle oneself — **apocado, -da** *adj* : timid — **apocamiento** *nm* : timidity

apodar *vt* : nickname

apoderar *vt* : empower — **apoderarse** *vr* ～ **de** : seize — **apoderado, -da** *n* : agent, proxy

apodo *nm* : nickname

apogeo *nm* : peak, height

apología *nf* : defense, apology

apoplegía *nf* : stroke, apoplexy

aporrear *vt* : bang on, beat

aportar *vt* : contribute — **aportación** *nf, pl* **-ciones** : contribution

apostar[1] {19} *v* : bet, wager

apostar[2] *vt* : station, post

apostillar *vt* : annotate — **apostilla** *nf* : note

apóstol *nm* : apostle

apóstrofo *nm* : apostrophe

apostura *nf* : elegance, grace

apoyar *vt* **1** : support **2** INCLINAR : lean, rest — **apoyarse** *vr* ～ **en** : lean on, rest on — **apoyo** *nm* : support

apreciar *vt* **1** ESTIMAR : appreciate **2** EVALUAR : appraise — **apreciable** *adj* : considerable — **apreciación** *nf, pl* **-ciones** **1** : appreciation **2** VALORACIÓN : appraisal — **aprecio** *nm* **1** : appraisal **2** ESTIMA : esteem

aprehender *vt* : apprehend — **aprehensión** *nf, pl* **-siones** : apprehension, capture

apremiar *vt* : urge — *vi* : be urgent — **apremiante** *adj* : pressing, urgent — **apremio** *nm* : urgency

aprender *v* : learn — **aprenderse** *vr* : memorize

aprendiz, -diza *n, mpl* **-dices** : apprentice, trainee — **aprendizaje** *nm* : apprenticeship

aprensión *nf, pl* **-siones** : apprehension, dread — **aprensivo, -va** *adj* : apprehensive

apresar *vt* : capture, seize — **apresamiento** *nm* : seizure, capture

aprestar *vt* : make ready — **aprestarse** *vr* : get ready

apresurar *vt* : speed up — **apresurarse** *vr* : hurry — **apresuradamente** *adv* : hurriedly, hastily — **apresurado, -da** *adj* : in a rush

apretar {55} *vt* **1** : press, push (a button) **2** : tighten (a knot, etc.) **3** ESTRECHAR : squeeze — *vi* **1** : press (down) **2** : fit too tightly — **apretón** *nm, pl* **-tones** **1** : squeeze **2** ～ **de manos** : handshake — **apretado, -da** *adj* **1** : tight **2** *fam* : tightfisted

aprieto *nm* : predicament, jam

aprisa *adv* : quickly

aprisionar *vt* : imprison

aprobar {19} *vt* **1** : approve of **2** : pass (an exam, etc.) — *vi* : pass — **aprobación** *nf, pl* **-ciones** : approval

aprontar *vt* : prepare, ready **ó aprontarse** *vr* : get ready

apropiarse *vr* ～ **de** : take possession of, appropriate — **apropiación** *nf, pl* **-ciones**

: appropriation — **apropiado, -da** *adj*
: appropriate

aprovechar *vt* : take advantage of, make good use of — *vi* : be of use — **aprovecharse** *vr* ~ **de** : take advantage of — **aprovechado, -da** *adj* **1** : diligent **2** OPORTUNISTA : opportunistic

aproximar *vt* : bring closer — **aproximarse** *vr* : approach — **aproximación** *nf, pl* **-ciones** : approximation — **aproximadamente** *adv* : approximately — **aproximado, -da** *adj* : approximate

apto, -ta *adj* **1** : suitable **2** CAPAZ : capable — **aptitud** *nf* : aptitude, capability

apuesta *nf* : bet, wager

apuesto, -ta *adj* : elegant, good-looking

apuntalar *vt* : prop up, shore up

apuntar *vt* **1** : aim, point **2** ANOTAR : jot down **3** SEÑALAR : point at **4** : prompt (in theater) — **apuntarse** *vr* **1** : sign up **2** : score, chalk up (a victory, etc.) — **apunte** *nm* : note

apuñalar *vt* : stab

apurar *vt* **1** : hurry, rush **2** AGOTAR : use up **3** PREOCUPAR : trouble — **apurarse** *vr* **1** : worry **2** *Lat* : hurry up — **apuradamente** *adv* : with difficulty — **apurado, -da** *adj* **1** : needy **2** DIFÍCIL : difficult **3** *Lat* : rushed — **apuro** *nm* **1** : predicament, jam **2** *Lat* : hurry

aquejar *vt* : afflict

aquel, aquella *adj, mpl* **aquellos** : that, those

aquél, aquélla *pron, mpl* **aquéllos 1** : that (one), those (ones) **2** : the former

aquello *pron* : that, that matter

aquí *adv* **1** : here **2** AHORA : now **3 por** ~ : hereabouts

aquietar *vt* : calm — **aquietarse** *vr* : calm down

ara *nf* **1** : altar **2 en** ~**s de** : for the sake of

árabe *adj* : Arab, Arabic — ~ *nm* : Arabic (language)

arado *nm* : plow

arancel *nm* : tariff

arándano *nm* : blueberry

araña *nf* **1** : spider **2** LÁMPARA : chandelier

arañar *v* : scratch, claw — **arañazo** *nm* : scratch

arar *v* : plow

arbitrar *v* **1** : arbitrate **2** : referee, umpire (in sports) — **arbitraje** *nm* : arbitration — **arbitrario, -ria** *adj* : arbitrary — **arbitrio** *nm* **1** : (free) will **2** JUICIO : judgment — **árbitro, -tra** *n* **1** : arbitrator **2** : referee, umpire (in sports)

árbol *nm* : tree — **arboleda** *nf* : grove

arbusto *nm* : shrub, bush

arca *nf* **1** : ark **2** COFRE : chest

arcada *nf* **1** : arcade **2** ~**s** *nfpl* : retching

arcaico, -ca *adj* : archaic

arcano, -na *adj* : arcane, secret

arce *nm* : maple tree

archipiélago *nm* : archipelago

archivar *vt* : file — **archivador** *nm* : filing cabinet — **archivo** *nm* **1** : file **2** : archives *pl*

arcilla *nf* : clay

arco *nm* **1** : arch **2** : bow (in sports, music, etc.) **3** : arc (in geometry) **4** ~ **iris** : rainbow

arder *vi* : burn

ardid *nm* : scheme, ruse

ardiente *adj* **1** : burning **2** FOGOSO : ardent

ardilla *nf* **1** : squirrel **2** ~ **listada** : chipmunk

ardor *nm* **1** : burning **2** ENTUSIASMO : passion, ardor

arduo, -dua *adj* : arduous

área *nf* : area

arena *nf* **1** : sand **2** PALESTRA : arena — **arenoso, -sa** *adj* : sandy, gritty

arenque *nm* : herring

arete *nm* *Lat* : earring

argamasa *nf* : mortar

argentino, -na *adj* : Argentinian, Argentine

argolla *nf* : hoop, ring

argot *nm* : slang

argüir {41} *vt* **1** : argue **2** DEMOSTRAR : prove, show — *vi* : argue

argumentar *vt* : argue, contend — **argumentación** *nf, pl* **-ciones** : (line of) argument — **argumento** *nm* **1** : argument, reasoning **2** TRAMA : plot, story line

árido, -da *adj* : dry, arid — **aridez** *nf, pl* **-deces** : aridity

arisco, -ca *adj* : surly

aristocracia *nf* : aristocracy — **aristócrata** *nmf* : aristocrat — **aristocrático, -ca** *adj* : aristocratic

aritmética *nf* : arithmetic — **aritmético, -ca** *adj* : arithmetic, arithmetical

arma *nf* **1** : weapon (**arma nuclear** nuclear weapon) (**arma química/biológica** chemical/biological weapon) (**arma de destrucción masiva** weapon of mass destruction) **2 armas** *nfpl* : armed forces **3 arma blanca**: sharp weapon **4 arma de fuego** : firearm

armar *vt* **1** : arm **2** MONTAR : assemble — **armada** *nf* : navy — **armado, -da** *adj* : armed — **armadura** *nf* **1** : armor **2** ARMAZÓN : framework — **armamento** *nm* : armament, arms *pl*

armario *nm* **1** : (clothes) closet **2** : cupboard, cabinet

armazón *nmf, pl* **-zones** : frame, framework

armisticio *nm* : armistice

armonizar {21} *vt* **1** : harmonize **2** : reconcile (differences, etc.) — *vi* : harmonize, go together — **armonía** *nf* : harmony — **armónica** *nf* : harmonica — **armónico, -ca** *adj* : harmonic — **armonioso, -sa** *adj* : harmonious

arnés *nm, pl* **-neses** : harness

aro *nm* **1** : hoop, ring **2** *Lat* : earring

aroma *nm* : aroma, scent — **aromático, -ca** *adj* : aromatic

arpa *nf* : harp

arpón *nm, pl* **-pones** : harpoon

arquear *vt* : arch, bend — **arquearse** *vr* : bend, bow

arqueología *nf* : archaeology — **arqueológico, -ca** *adj* : archaeological — **arqueólogo, -ga** *n* : archaeologist

arquero, -ra *n* **1** : archer **2** PORTERO : goalkeeper, goalie

arquetipo *nm* : archetype

arquitectura *nf* : architecture — **arquitecto, -ta** *n* : architect — **arquitectónico, -ca** *adj* : architectural

arrabal *nm* **1** : slum **2** ~es *nmpl* : outskirts

arracimarse *vr* : cluster together

arraigar {52} *vi* : take root, become established — **arraigarse** *vr* : settle down — **arraigado, -da** *adj* : deeply rooted, well established — **arraigo** *nm* : roots *pl*

arrancar {72} *vt* **1** : pull out, tear off **2** : start (an engine), boot (a computer) — *vi* **1** : start an engine **2** : get going — **arranque** *nm* **1** : starter (of a car) **2** ARREBATO : outburst **3 punto de** ~ : starting point

arrasar *vt* **1** : destroy, devastate **2** LLENAR : fill to the brim

arrastrar *vt* **1** : drag **2** ATRAER : draw, attract — *vi* : hang down, trail — **arrastrarse** *vr* **1** : crawl, creep **2** HUMILLARSE : grovel — **arrastre** *nm* **1** : dragging **2** : trawling (for fish)

arrear *vt* : urge on

arrebatar *vt* **1** : snatch, seize **2** CAUTIVAR : captivate — **arrebatarse** *vr* : get carried away — **arrebatado, -da** *adj* : hotheaded, rash — **arrebato** *nm* : outburst

arreciar *vi* : intensify, worsen

arrecife *nm* : reef

arreglar *vt* **1** COMPONER : fix **2** ORDENAR : tidy up **3** SOLUCIONAR : solve, work out — **arreglarse** *vr* **1** : get dressed (up) **2** **arreglárselas** *fam* : get by, manage — **arreglado, -da** *adj* **1** : fixed, repaired **2** ORDENADO : tidy **3** SOLUCIONADO : settled, sorted out **4** ATAVIADO : smart, dressed-up — **arreglo** *nm* **1** : arrangement **2** REPARACIÓN : repair **3** ACUERDO : agreement

arremangarse {52} *vr* : roll up one's sleeves

arremeter *vi* : attack, charge — **arremetida** *nf* : attack, onslaught

arremolinarse *vr* **1** : crowd around, mill about **2** : swirl (about)

arrendar {55} *vt* : rent, lease — **arrendador, -dora** *n* : landlord, landlady *f* — **arrendamiento** *nm* : rent, rental — **arrendatario, -ria** *n* : tenant, renter

arrepentirse {76} *vr* **1** : regret, be sorry **2** : repent (for one's sins) — **arrepentido, -da** *adj* : repentant — **arrepentimiento** *nm* : regret, repentance

arrestar *vt* : arrest, detain — **arresto** *nm* : arrest

arriar *vt* : lower

arriba *adv* **1** (*indicating position*) : above, overhead **2** (*indicating direction*) : up, upwards **3** : upstairs (of a house) **4** ~ **de** : more than **5 de** ~ **abajo** : from top to bottom

arribar *vi* **1** : arrive **2** : dock, put into port — **arribista** *nmf* : parvenu, upstart — **arribo** *nm* : arrival

arriendo → **arrendimiento**

arriesgar {52} *vt* : risk, venture — **arriesgarse** *vr* : take a chance — **arriesgado, -da** *adj* : risky

arrimar *vt* : bring closer, draw near — **arrimarse** *vr* : approach

arrinconar *vt* **1** : corner, box in **2** ABANDONAR : push aside

arroba *nf* **1** : at sign (**arroba merriam-webster punto com** @ merriam-webster dot com) **2** : former unit of measurement

arrobar *vt* : entrance — **arrobarse** *vr* : be enraptured — **arrobamiento** *nm* : rapture, ecstasy

arrodillarse *vr* : kneel (down)

arrogancia *nf* : arrogance — **arrogante** *adj* : arrogant

arrojar *vt* **1** : hurl, cast **2** EMITIR : give off, spew out **3** PRODUCIR : yield — **arrojarse** *vr* : throw oneself — **arrojado, -da** *adj* : daring — **arrojo** *nm* : boldness, courage

arrollar *vt* **1** : sweep away **2** DERROTAR : crush, overwhelm **3** : run over (with a vehicle) — **arrollador, -dora** *adj* : overwhelming

arropar *vt* : clothe, cover (up) — **arroparse** *vr* : wrap oneself up

arroyo *nm* **1** RIACHUELO : stream **2** : gutter (in a street)

arroz *nm, pl* **arroces** : rice

arrugar {52} *vt* : wrinkle, crease — **arrugarse** *vr* : get wrinkled — **arruga** *nf* : wrinkle, crease

arruinar *vt* : ruin, wreck — **arruinarse** *vr* **1** : be ruined **2** EMPOBRECERSE : go bankrupt

arrullar *vt* : lull to sleep — *vi* : coo — **arrullo** *nm* **1** : lullaby **2** : cooing (of doves)

arrumbar *vt* : lay aside

arsenal *nm* : arsenal

arsénico *nm* : arsenic
arte *nmf (usually m in singular, f in plural)* **1** : art **2** HABILIDAD : skill **3** ASTUCIA : cunning, cleverness **4** → **bello**
artefacto *nm* : artifact, device
arteria *nf* : artery
artesanía *nm* **1** : craftsmanship **2** : handicrafts *pl* — **artesanal** *adj* : handmade — **artesano, -na** *n* : artisan, craftsman
ártico, -ca *adj* : arctic
articular *vt* : articulate — **articulación** *nf, pl* -ciones **1** : articulation, pronunciation **2** COYUNTURA : joint
artículo *nm* **1** : article **2** ~s de primera necesidad : essentials **3** ~s de tocador : toiletries
artífice *nmf* : artisan, craftsman
artificial *adj* : artificial
artificio *nm* **1** HABILIDAD : skill **2** APARATO : device **3** ARDID : artifice, ruse — **artificioso, -sa** *adj* : cunning, deceptive
artillería *nf* : artillery
artilugio *nm* : gadget
artimaña *nf* : ruse, trick
artista *nmf* **1** : artist **2** ACTOR : actor, actress *f* — **artístico, -ca** *adj* : artistic
artritis *nms & pl* : arthritis — **artrítico, -ca** *adj* : arthritic
arveja *nf Lat* : pea
arzobispo *nm* : archbishop
as *nm* : ace
asa *nf* : handle
asado, -da *adj* : roasted, grilled — **asado** *nm* : roast — **asador** *nm* : spit — **asaduras** *nfpl* : offal, entrails
asalariado, -da *n* : wage earner — ~ *adj* : salaried
asaltar *vt* **1** : assault **2** ROBAR : mug, rob — **asaltante** *nmf* **1** : assailant **2** ATRACADOR : mugger, robber — **asalto** *nm* **1** : assault **2** ROBO : mugging, robbery
asamblea *nf* : assembly, meeting
asar *vt* : roast, grill — **asarse** *vr fam* : roast, feel the heat
asbesto *nm* : asbestos
ascender {56} *vi* **1** : ascend, rise up **2** : be promoted (in a job) **3** ~ a : amount to — *vt* : promote — **ascendencia** *nf* : ancestry, descent — **ascendiente** *nmf* : ancestor — ~ *nm* : influence — **ascensión** *nf, pl* -siones : ascent — **ascenso** *nm* **1** : ascent, rise **2** : promotion (in a job) — **ascensor** *nm* : elevator
asco *nm* **1** : disgust **2 hacer** ~s de : turn up one's nose at **3 me da** ~ : it makes me sick
ascua *nf* **1** : ember **2 estar en** ~s *fam* : be on edge
asear *vt* : clean, tidy up — **asearse** *vr* : get cleaned up — **aseado, -da** *adj* : clean, tidy

asediar *vt* **1** : besiege **2** ACOSAR : harass — **asedio** *nm* **1** : siege **2** ACOSO : harassment
asegurar *vt* **1** : assure **2** FIJAR : secure **3** : insure (a car, house, etc.) — **asegurarse** *vr* : make sure
asemejarse *vr* **1** : be similar **2** ~ a : look like, resemble
asentar {55} *vt* **1** : set down **2** INSTALAR : set up, establish **3** *Lat* : state — **asentarse** *vr* **1** : settle **2** ESTABLECERSE : settle down — **asentado, -da** *adj* : settled, established
asentir {76} *vi* : assent, agree — **asentimiento** *nm* : assent
aseo *nm* : cleanliness
asequible *adj* : accessible, attainable
aserrar {55} *vt* : saw — **aserradero** *nm* : sawmill — **aserrín** *nm, pl* -rrines : sawdust
asesinar *vt* **1** : murder **2** : assassinate — **asesinato** *nm* **1** : murder **2** : assassination — **asesino, -na** *n* **1** : murderer, killer **2** : assassin
asesorar *vt* : advise, counsel — **asesorarse** *vr* ~ de : consult — **asesor, -sora** *n* : advisor, consultant — **asesoramiento** *nm* : advice, counsel
asestar {55} *vt* **1** : aim (a weapon) **2** : deal (a blow)
aseverar *vt* : assert — **aseveración** *nf, pl* -ciones : assertion
asfalto *nm* : asphalt
asfixiar *vt* : asphyxiate, suffocate — **asfixiarse** *vr* : suffocate — **asfixia** *nf* : asphyxiation, suffocation
así *adv* **1** : like this, like that, thus **2** ~ de : so, that (much) **3** ~ que : so, therefore **4** ~ que : as soon as **5** ~ como : as well as — ~ *adj* : such, like that — ~ *conj* AUNQUE : even though
asiático, -ca *adj* : Asian, Asiatic
asidero *nm* : handle
asiduo, -dua *adj* : frequent, regular
asiento *nm* : seat
asignar *vt* **1** : assign, allocate **2** DESTINAR : appoint — **asignación** *nf, pl* -ciones **1** : assignment **2** SUELDO : salary, pay — **asignatura** *nf* : subject, course
asilo *nm* **1** : asylum, home **2** REFUGIO : refuge, shelter — **asilado, -da** *n* : inmate
asimilar *vt* : assimilate — **asimilarse** *vr* ~ a : resemble
asimismo *adv* **1** : similarly, likewise **2** TAMBIÉN : as well, also
asir {7} *vt* : seize, grasp — **asirse** *vr* ~ a : cling to
asistir *vi* ~ a : attend, be present at — *vt* : assist — **asistencia** *nf* **1** : attendance **2** AYUDA : assistance — **asistente** *nmf* **1** : assistant **2 los** ~s : those present

asma *nf* : asthma — **asmático, -ca** *adj* : asthmatic

asno *nm* : ass, donkey

asociar *vt* : associate — **asociarse** *vr* **1** : form a partnership **2** ~ **a** : join, become a member of — **asociación** *nf*, *pl* **-ciones** : association — **asociado, -da** *adj* : associate, associated — ~ *n* : associate, partner

asolar {19} *vt* : devastate

asomar *vt* : show, stick out — *vi* : appear, show — **asomarse** *vr* **1** : appear **2** : stick one's head out (of a window)

asombrar *vt* : amaze, astonish — **asombrarse** *vr* : be amazed — **asombro** *nm* : amazement, astonishment — **asombroso, -sa** *adj* : amazing, astonishing

asomo *nm* **1** : hint, trace **2 ni por** ~ : by no means

aspaviento *nm* : exaggerated gestures, fuss

aspecto *nm* **1** : aspect **2** APARIENCIA : appearance, look

áspero, -ra *adj* : rough, harsh — **aspereza** *nf* : roughness, harshness

aspersión *nf*, *pl* **-siones** : sprinkling — **aspersor** *nm* : sprinkler

aspiración *nf*, *pl* **-ciones 1** : breathing in **2** ANHELO : aspiration

aspiradora *nf* : vacuum cleaner

aspirar *vi* ~ **a** : aspire to — *vt* : inhale, breathe in — **aspirante** *nmf* : applicant, candidate

aspirina *nf* : aspirin

asquear *vt* : sicken, disgust

asquerosidad *nf* : filth, foulness — **asqueroso, -sa** *adj* : disgusting, sickening

asta *nf* **1** : flagpole **2** CUERNO : antler, horn **3** : shaft (of a spear) — **astado, -da** *adj* : horned

asterisco *nm* : asterisk

asteroide *nm* : asteroid

astigmatismo *nm* : astigmatism

astillar *vt* : splinter — **astilla** *nf* : splinter, chip

astillero *nm* : shipyard

astral *adj* : astral

astringente *adj* & *nm* : astringent

astro *nm* **1** : heavenly body **2** : star (of movies, etc.)

astrología *nf* : astrology

astronauta *nmf* : astronaut — **astronáutica** *nf* : astronautics

astronave *nf* : spaceship

astronomía *nf* : astronomy — **astronómico, -ca** *adj* : astronomical — **astrónomo, -ma** *n* : astronomer

astucia *nf* **1** : astuteness **2** ARDID : cunning, guile — **astuto, -ta** *adj* **1** : astute **2** TAIMADO : crafty

asueto *nm* : time off, break

asumir *vt* : assume — **asunción** *nf*, *pl* **-ciones** : assumption

asunto *nm* **1** : matter, affair **2** NEGOCIO : business

asustar *vt* : scare, frighten — **asustarse** *vr* ~ **de** : be frightened of — **asustadizo, -za** *adj* : jumpy, skittish — **asustado, -da** *adj* : frightened, afraid

atacar {72} *v* : attack — **atacante** *nmf* : attacker

atado *nm* : bundle

atadura *nf* : tie, bond

atajada *nf* : save (in sports)

atajar *vt* : block, cut off — *vi* ~ **por** : take a shortcut through — **atajo** *nm* : shortcut

atañer {79} *vi* ~ **a** : concern, have to do with

ataque *nm* **1** : attack, assault **2** ACCESO : fit **3** ~ **de nervios** : nervous breakdown

atar *vt* : tie up, tie down — **atarse** *vr* : tie (up)

atardecer {53} *v impers* : get dark — ~ *nm* : late afternoon, dusk

atareado, -da *adj* : busy

atascar {72} *vt* **1** : block, clog **2** ESTORBAR : hinder — **atascarse** *vr* **1** OBSTRUIRSE : become obstructed **2** : get bogged down — **atasco** *nm* **1** : blockage **2** EMBOTELLAMIENTO : traffic jam

ataúd *nm* : coffin

ataviar {85} *vt* : dress (up) — **ataviarse** *vr* : dress up — **atavío** *nm* : attire

atemorizar {21} *vt* : frighten — **atemorizarse** *vr* : get scared

atención *nf*, *pl* **-ciones 1** : attention **2 prestar** ~ : pay attention **3 llamar la** ~ : attract attention — ~ *interj* : attention!, watch out!

atender {56} *vt* **1** : attend to **2** CUIDAR : look after **3** : heed (advice, etc.) — *vi* : pay attention

atenerse {80} *vr* ~ **a** : abide by

atentamente *adv* **1** : attentively **2 le saluda** ~ : sincerely yours

atentar {55} *vi* ~ **contra** : make an attempt on — **atentado** *nm* : attack

atento, -ta *adj* **1** : attentive, mindful **2** CORTÉS : courteous

atenuar {3} *vt* **1** : dim (lights), tone down (colors, etc.) **2** DISMINUIR : lessen — **atenuante** *nmf* : extenuating circumstances

ateo, atea *adj* : atheistic — ~ *n* : atheist

aterciopelado, -da *adj* : velvety, downy

aterido, -da *adj* : frozen stiff

aterrar {55} *vt* : terrify — **aterrador, -dora** *adj* : terrifying

aterrizar {21} *vi* : land — **aterrizaje** *nm* : landing

aterrorizar {21} *vt* : terrify

atesorar *vt* : hoard, amass

atestar {55} *vt* **1** : crowd, pack **2** : testify to (in law) — **atestado, -da** *adj* : stuffed, packed

atestiguar {10} *vt* : testify to

atiborrar *vt* : stuff, cram — **atiborrarse** *vr* : stuff oneself

ático *nm* **1** : penthouse **2** DESVÁN : attic

atildado, -da *adj* : smart, neat

atinar *vi* : be on target

atípico, -ca *adj* : atypical

atirantar *vt* : tighten

atisbar *vt* **1** : spy on **2** VISLUMBRAR : catch a glimpse of — **atisbo** *nm* : sign, hint

atizar {21} *vt* **1** : poke (a fire) **2** : rouse, stir up (passions, etc.) — **atizador** *nm* : poker

atlántico, -ca *adj* : Atlantic

atlas *nm* : atlas

atleta *nmf* : athlete — **atlético, -ca** *adj* : athletic — **atletismo** *nm* : athletics

atmósfera *nf* : atmosphere — **atmosférico, -ca** *adj* : atmospheric

atolondrado, -da *adj* **1** : scatterbrained **2** ATURDIDO : bewildered, dazed

átomo *nm* : atom — **atómico, -ca** *adj* : atomic — **atomizador** *nm* : atomizer

atónito, -ta *adj* : astonished, amazed

atontar *vt* : stun, daze

atorar *vt* : block — **atorarse** *vr* : get stuck

atormentar *vt* : torment, torture — **atormentarse** *vr* : torment oneself, agonize — **atormentador, -dora** *n* : tormenter

atornillar *vt* : screw

atorrante *nmf Lat* : bum, loafer

atosigar {52} *vt* : harass, annoy

atracar {72} *vi* : dock, land — *vt* : hold up, mug — **atracarse** *vr fam* ~ **de** : gorge oneself with — **atracadero** *nm* : dock, pier — **atracador, -dora** *n* : robber, mugger

atracción *nf, pl* **-ciones** : attraction

atraco *nm* : holdup, robbery

atractivo, -va *adj* : attractive — **atractivo** *nm* : attraction, appeal

atraer {81} *vt* : attract

atragantarse *vr* : choke

atrancar {72} *vt* : block, bar — **atrancarse** *vr* : get blocked, get stuck

atrapar *vt* : trap, capture

atrás *adv* **1** DETRÁS : back, behind **2** ANTES : before, earlier **3 para** ~ *or* **hacia** ~ : backwards

atrasar *vt* **1** : put back (a clock) **2** DEMORAR : delay — *vi* : lose time — **atrasarse** *vr* : fall behind — **atrasado, -da** *adj* **1** : late, overdue **2** : backward (of countries, etc.) **3** : slow (of a clock) — **atraso** *nm* **1** RETRASO : delay **2** : backwardness **3** ~**s** *nmpl* : arrears

atravesar {55} *vt* **1** CRUZAR : cross **2** TRASPASAR : pierce **3** : lay across (a road, etc.) **4** : go through (a situation) — **atravesarse** *vr* : be in the way

atrayente *adj* : attractive

atreverse *vr* : dare — **atrevido, -da** *adj* **1** : bold **2** INSOLENTE : insolent — **atrevimiento** *nm* **1** : boldness **2** DESCARO : insolence

atribuir {41} *vt* **1** : attribute **2** : confer (powers, etc.) — **atribuirse** *vr* : take credit for

atribular *vt* : afflict, trouble

atributo *nm* : attribute

atrincherar *vt* : entrench — **atrincherarse** *vr* : dig oneself in

atrocidad *nf* : atrocity

atronador, -dora *adj* : thunderous

atropellar *vt* **1** : run over **2** : violate, abuse (a person) — **atropellarse** *vr* : rush — **atropellado, -da** *adj* : hasty — **atropello** *nm* : abuse, outrage

atroz *adj, pl* **atroces** : atrocious

atuendo *nm* : attire

atufar *vt* : vex — **atufarse** *vr* : get angry

atún *nm, pl* **atunes** : tuna

aturdir *vt* **1** : stun, shock **2** CONFUNDIR : bewilder — **aturdido, -da** *adj* : dazed, bewildered

audaz *adj, pl* **-daces** : bold, daring — **audacia** *nf* : boldness, audacity

audible *adj* : audible

audición *nf, pl* **-ciones** **1** : hearing **2** : audition (in theater, etc.)

audiencia *nf* : audience

audífono *nm* **1** : hearing aid **2** ~**s** *nmpl Lat* : headphones, earphones

audiovisual *adj* : audiovisual

auditar *vt* : audit — **auditor, -tora** *n* : auditor

auditorio *nm* **1** : auditorium **2** PÚBLICO : audience

auge *nm* **1** : peak **2** : (economic) boom

augurar *vt* : predict, foretell — **augurio** *nm* : omen

augusto, -ta *adj* : august

aula *nf* : classroom

aullar {8} *vi* : howl — **aullido** *nm* : howl

aumentar *vt* : increase, raise — *vi* : increase, grow — **aumento** *nm* : increase, rise

aun *adv* **1** : even **2** ~ **así** : even so

aún *adv* **1** : still, yet **2 más** ~ : furthermore

aunar {8} *vt* : join, combine — **aunarse** *vr* : unite

aunque *conj* **1** : though, although, even if **2** ~ **sea** : at least

aureola *nf* **1** : halo **2** FAMA : aura

auricular *nm* **1** : telephone receiver **2** ~**es** *nmpl* : headphones

aurora *nf* : dawn

ausentarse *vr* : leave, go away — **ausencia** *nf* : absence — **ausente** *adj* : absent — ~

nmf **1** : absentee **2** : missing person (in law)
auspicios *nmpl* : sponsorship, auspices
austero, -ra *adj* : austere — **austeridad** *nf* : austerity
austral *adj* : southern
australiano, -na *adj* : Australian
austriaco *or* **austríaco, -ca** *adj* : Austrian
auténtico, -ca *adj* : authentic, genuine — **autenticidad** *nf* : authenticity
auto *nm* : auto, car
autoayuda *nf* : self-help
autobiografía *nf* : autobiography — **autobiográfico, -ca** *adj* : autobiographical
autobús *nm*, *pl* **-buses** : bus
autocompasión *nf* : self-pity
autocontrol *nm* : self-control
autocracia *nf* : autocracy
autóctono, -na *adj* : indigenous, native
autodefensa *nf* : self-defense
autodidacta *adj* : self-taught
autodisciplina *nf* : self-discipline
autoestop → **autostop**
autografiar *vt* : autograph — **autógrafo** *nm* : autograph
autómata *nm* : automaton
automático, -ca *adj* : automatic — **automatización** *nf*, *pl* **-ciones** : automation — **automatizar** {21} *vt* : automate
automotor, -triz *adj*, *fpl* **-trices** : self-propelled
automóvil *nm* : automobile — **automovilista** *nmf* : motorist — **automovilístico, -ca** *adj* : automobile, car
autonomía *nf* : autonomy — **autónomo, -ma** *adj* : autonomous
autopista *nf* : expressway, highway
autopropulsado, -da *adj* : self-propelled
autopsia *nf* : autopsy
autor, -tora *n* **1** : author **2** : perpetrator (of a crime)
autoridad *nf* : authority — **autoritario, -ria** *adj* : authoritarian
autorizar {21} *vt* : authorize, approve — **autorización** *nf*, *pl* **-ciones** : authorization — **autorizado, -da** *adj* **1** PERMITIDO : authorized **2** : authoritative
autorretrato *nm* : self-portrait
autoservicio *nm* **1** : self-service restaurant **2** SUPERMERCADO : supermarket
autostop *nm* **1** : hitchhiking **2 hacer ～** : hitchhike — **autostopista** *nmf* : hitchhiker
autosuficiente *adj* : self-sufficient
auxiliar *vt* : aid, assist — ～ *adj* : auxiliary — ～ *nmf* **1** : assistant, helper **2 ～ de vuelo** : flight attendant — **auxilio** *nm* **1** : aid, assistance **2 primeros ～s** : first aid
avalancha *nf* : avalanche

avalar *vt* : guarantee, endorse — **aval** *nm* : guarantee, endorsement
avanzar {21} *v* : advance, move forward — **avance** *nm* : advance — **avanzado, -da** *adj* : advanced
avaricia *nf* : greed, avarice — **avaricioso, -sa** *adj* : avaricious, greedy — **avaro, -ra** *adj* : miserly — ～ *n* : miser
avasallar *vt* : overpower, subjugate — **avasallador, -dora** *adj* : overwhelming
avatar *nm* **1** : avatar **2 avatares** *nmpl* : vagaries, vicissitudes
ave *nf* : bird
avecinarse *vr* : approach
avecindarse *vr* : settle, take up residence
avellana *nf* : hazelnut
avena *nf* **1** : oats *pl* **2** *or* **harina de ～** : oatmeal
avenida *nf* : avenue
avenir {87} *vt* : reconcile, harmonize — **avenirse** *vr* : agree, come to terms
aventajar *vt* : be ahead of, surpass
aventar {55} *vt* **1** : fan **2** : winnow (grain) **3** *Lat* : throw, toss
aventurar *vt* : venture, risk — **aventurarse** *vr* : take a risk — **aventura** *nf* **1** : adventure **2** RIESGO : risk **3** AMORÍO : love affair — **aventurado, -da** *adj* : risky — **aventurero, -ra** *adj* : adventurous — ～ *n* : adventurer
avergonzar {9} *vt* : shame, embarrass — **avergonzarse** *vr* : be ashamed, be embarrassed
averiar {85} *vt* : damage — **averiarse** *vr* : break down — **avería** *nf* **1** : damage **2** : breakdown (of an automobile) — **averiado, -da** *adj* **1** : damaged, faulty **2** : broken down (of an automobile)
averiguar {10} *vt* **1** : find out **2** INVESTIGAR : investigate — **averiguación** *nf*, *pl* **-ciones** : investigation, inquiry
aversión *nf*, *pl* **-siones** : aversion, dislike
avestruz *nm*, *pl* **-truces** : ostrich
aviación *nf*, *pl* **-ciones** : aviation — **aviador, -dora** *n* : aviator
aviar {85} *vt* : prepare, make ready
ávido, -da *adj* : eager, avid — **avidez** *nf*, *pl* **-deces** : eagerness
avío *nm* **1** : preparation, provision **2 ～s** *nmpl* : gear, equipment
avión *nm*, *pl* **aviones** : airplane — **avioneta** *nf* : light airplane
avisar *vt* **1** : notify **2** ADVERTIR : warn — **aviso** *nm* **1** : notice **2** ADVERTENCIA : warning **3** *Lat* : advertisement, ad **4 estar sobre ～** : be on the alert
avispa *nf* : wasp — **avispón** *nm*, *pl* **-pones** : hornet
avispado, -da *adj fam* : clever, sharp
avistar *vt* : catch sight of

avivar *vt* **1** : enliven, brighten **2** : arouse (desire, etc.) **3** : intensify (pain)

axila *nf* : underarm, armpit

axioma *nm* : axiom

ay *interj* **1** : oh! **2** : ouch!, ow!

ayer *adv* : yesterday — ~ *nm* : yesteryear, days gone by

ayote *nm Lat* : pumpkin

ayudar *vt* : help, assist — **ayudarse** *vr* ~ **de** : make use of — **ayuda** *nf* : help, assistance — **ayudante** *nmf* : helper, assistant

ayunar *vi* : fast — **ayunas** *nfpl* **en** ~ : fasting — **ayuno** *nm* : fast

ayuntamiento *nm* **1** : town hall, city hall (building) **2** : town or city council

azabache *nm* : jet

azada *nf* : hoe — **azadonar** *vt* : hoe

azafata *nf* : stewardess *f*

azafrán *nm, pl* **-franes** : saffron

azalea *nf* : azalea

azar *nm* **1** : chance **2 al** ~ : at random — **azaroso, -sa** *adj* : hazardous (of a journey, etc.), eventful (of a life)

azorar *vt* **1** : alarm **2** DESCONCERTAR : embarrass — **azorarse** *vr* : get embarrassed

azotar *vt* : beat, whip — **azote** *nm* **1** LÁTIGO : whip, lash **2** CALAMIDAD : scourge

azotea *nf* : flat or terraced roof

azteca *adj* : Aztec

azúcar *nmf* : sugar — **azucarado, -da** *adj* : sugary — **azucarera** *nf* : sugar bowl — **azucarero, -ra** *adj* : sugar

azufre *nm* : sulphur

azul *adj & nm* : blue — **azulado, -da** *adj* : bluish

azulejo *nm* **1** : ceramic tile **2** *Lat* : bluebird

azur *n* : azure, sky blue

azuzar {21} *vt* : incite, urge on

B

b *nf* : b, second letter of the Spanish alphabet

babear *vi* : drool, slobber — **baba** *nf* : saliva, drool

babel *nmf* : bedlam

babero *nm* : bib

babor *nm* : port (side)

babosa *nf* : slug — **baboso, -sa** *adj* **1** : slimy **2** *Lat fam* : silly

babucha *nf* : slipper

babuino *nm* : baboon

bacalao *nm* : cod

bache *nm* **1** : pothole, rut **2** DIFICULTADES : bad time

bachiller *nmf* : high school graduate — **bachillerato** *nm* : high school diploma

bacon *nm Spain* : bacon

bacteria *nf* : bacterium

bagaje *nm* : baggage, luggage

bagatela *nf* : trinket

bagre *nm* : catfish

bahía *nf* : bay

bailar *v* : dance — **bailarín, -rina** *n, mpl* **-rines** : dancer — **baile** *nm* **1** : dance **2** FIESTA : dance party, ball

bajar *vt* **1** : bring down, lower **2** DESCENDER : go down, come down — *vi* : descend, drop — **bajarse** *vr* ~ **de** : get out of, get off — **baja** *nf* **1** : fall, drop **2** CESE : dismissal **3** PERMISO : sick leave **4** : (military) casualty — **bajada** *nf* **1** : descent, drop **2** PENDIENTE : slope

bajeza *nf* : lowness, meanness

bajío *nm* : sandbank, shoal

bajo, -ja *adj* **1** : low, lower **2** : short (in stature) **3** : soft, faint (of sounds) **4** VIL : base, vile — **bajo** *adv* **1** : low **2 habla más** ~ : speak more softly — ~ *nm* **1** : ground floor **2** DOBLADILLO : hem **3** : bass (in music) — ~ *prep* : under, below — **bajón** *nm, pl* **-jones** : sharp drop, slump

bala *nf* **1** : bullet **2** : bale (of cotton, etc.)

balada *nf* : ballad

balancear *vt* **1** : balance **2** : swing (one's arms, etc.), rock (a boat) — **balancearse** *vr* : swing, sway — **balance** *nm* **1** : balance **2** : balance sheet — **balanceo** *nm* : swaying, rocking

balancín *nm, pl* **-cines** **1** : seesaw **2** MECEDORA : rocking chair

balanza *nf* : scales *pl*, balance

balar *vi* : bleat

balaustrada *nf* : balustrade, banister

balazo *nm* **1** DISPARO : shot **2** : bullet wound

balbucear *vi* **1** : stammer, stutter **2** : babble (of a baby) — **balbuceo** *nm* : stammering, muttering, babbling

balcón *nm, pl* **-cones** : balcony

balde *nm* **1** : bucket, pail **2 en** ~ : in vain

baldío, -día *adj* **1** : uncultivated **2** INÚTIL : useless — **baldío** *nm* : wasteland

baldosa *nf* : floor tile

balear *vt Lat* : shoot (at) — **baleo** *nm Lat* : shot, shooting

balido *nm* : bleat

balín *nm, pl* **-lines** : pellet

balística *nf* : ballistics — **balístico, -ca** *adj* : ballistic

baliza *nf* **1** : buoy **2** : beacon (for aircraft)

ballena *nf* : whale

ballesta *nf* **1** : crossbow **2** : spring (of an automobile)

ballet *nm* : ballet

balneario *nm* : spa

balompié *nm* : soccer

balón *nm, pl* **-lones** : ball — **baloncesto** *nm* : basketball — **balonvolea** *nm* : volleyball

balsa *nf* **1** : raft **2** ESTANQUE : pond, pool

bálsamo *nm* : balsam, balm — **balsámico, -ca** *adj* : soothing

balsero -ra *n* : boat person, refugee

baluarte *nm* : bulwark, bastion

bambolear *vi* : sway, swing — **bambolearse** *vr* : sway, rock

bambú *nm, pl* **-búes** *or* **-bús** : bamboo

banal *adj* : banal

banana *nf Lat* : banana — **banano** *nm Lat* : banana

banca *nf* **1** : banking **2** BANCO : bench — **bancario, -ria** *adj* : bank, banking — **bancarrota** *nf* : bankruptcy — **banco** *nm* **1** : bank **2** BANCA : stool, bench, pew **3** : school (of fish)

banda *nf* **1** : band, strip **2** : band (in music) **3** PANDILLA : gang **4** : flock (of birds) **5** ~ **sonora** : sound track — **bandada** *nf* : flock (of birds), school (of fish)

bandazo *nm* : lurch

bandeja *nf* : tray, platter

bandera *nf* : flag, banner

banderilla *nf* : banderilla

banderín *nm, pl* **-rines** : pennant, small flag

bandido, -da *n* : bandit

bando *nm* **1** : proclamation, edict **2** PARTIDO : faction, side

bandolero, -ra *n* : bandit

banjo *nm* : banjo

banquero, -ra *n* : banker

banqueta *nf* **1** : stool, footstool **2** *Lat* : sidewalk

banquete *nm* : banquet

bañar *vt* **1** : bathe, wash **2** SUMERGIR : immerse **3** CUBRIR : coat, cover — **bañarse** *vr* **1** : take a bath **2** : go swimming — **bañera** *nf* : bathtub — **bañista** *nmf* : bather — **baño** *nm* **1** : bath, swim **2** BAÑERA : bathtub **3** ¿donde está el ~? : where is the bathroom? **4** ~ **María** : double boiler

baqueta *nf* **1** : ramrod **2** ~**s** *nfpl* : drumsticks

bar *nm* : bar, tavern

barajar *vt* **1** : shuffle (cards) **2** CONSIDERAR : consider — **baraja** *nf* : deck of cards

baranda *nf* : rail, railing — **barandal** *nm* : handrail, banister

barato, -ta *adj* : cheap — **barato** *adv* : cheap, cheaply — **barata** *nf Lat* : sale, bargain — **baratija** *nf* : trinket — **baratillo** *nm* : secondhand store, flea market

barba *nf* **1** : beard, stubble **2** BARBILLA : chin

barbacoa *nf* : barbecue

barbaridad *nf* **1** : barbarity, cruelty **2** ¡qué ~! : that's outrageous! — **barbarie** *nf* : barbarism, savagery — **bárbaro, -ra** *adj* : barbaric

barbecho *nm* : fallow land

barbero, -ra *n* : barber — **barbería** *nf* : barbershop

barbilla *nf* : chin

barbudo, -da *adj* : bearded

barca *nf* **1** : boat **2** ~ **de pasaje** : ferryboat — **barcaza** *nf* : barge — **barco** *nm* : boat, ship

barítono *nm* : baritone

barman *nm* : bartender

barnizar {21} *vt* **1** : varnish **2** : glaze (ceramics) — **barniz** *nm, pl* **-nices** **1** : varnish **2** : glaze (on ceramics)

barómetro *nm* : barometer

barón *nm, pl* **-rones** : baron — **baronesa** *nf* : baroness

barquero *nm* : boatman

barquillo *nm* : wafer, cone

barra *nf* **1** : bar, rod, stick **2** : counter (of a bar, etc.)

barraca *nf* **1** : hut, cabin **2** CASETA : booth, stall

barranco *nm or* **barranca** *nf* : ravine, gorge, gully

barredera *nf* : street-sweeping machine

barrenar *vt* : drill — **barrena** *nf* : drill, auger

barrer *v* : sweep

barrera *nf* : barrier

barreta *nf* : crowbar

barriada *nf* : district, quarter

barrica *nf* : cask, keg

barricada *nf* : barricade

barrida *nf* **1** : sweep **2** : slide (in sports)

barrido *nm* : sweep, sweeping

barriga *nf* : belly

barril *nm* **1** : barrel, keg **2 de** ~ : draft

barrio *nm* **1** : neighborhood **2** ~ **bajo** : slums *pl*

barro *nm* **1** : mud **2** ARCILLA : clay **3** GRANO : pimple, blackhead — **barroso, -sa** *adj* : muddy

barrote *nm* : bar (on a window)

barrunto *nm* **1** : suspicion **2** INDICIO : sign, indication

bártulos *nmpl* : things, belongings

barullo *nm* : racket, ruckus

basa *nf* : base, pedestal — **basar** *vt* : base — **basarse** *vr* ~ **en** : be based on

báscula *nf* : scales *pl*

base *nf* **1** : base **2** FUNDAMENTO : basis, foundation **3** ~ **de datos** : database — **básico, -ca** *adj* : basic

basquetbol *or* **básquetbol** *nm Lat* : basketball

bastar *vi* : be enough, suffice — **bastante** *adv* **1** : fairly, rather **2** SUFICIENTE : enough — ~ *adj* : enough, sufficient — ~ *pron* : enough

bastardo, -da *adj & n* : bastard

bastidor *nm* **1** : frame **2** : wing (in theater) **3 entre** ~**es** : behind the scenes, backstage

bastilla *nf* : hem

bastión *nf, pl* **-tiones** : bastion, stronghold

basto, -ta *adj* : coarse, rough

bastón *nm, pl* **-tones** **1** : cane, walking stick **2** : baton (in parades)

basura *nf* : garbage, rubbish — **basurero, -ra** *n* : garbage collector

bata *nf* **1** : bathrobe, housecoat **2** : smock (of a doctor, laboratory worker, etc.)

batallar *vi* : battle, fight — **batalla** *nf* **1** : battle, fight, struggle **2 de** ~ : ordinary, everyday — **batallón** *nm, pl* **-llones** : battalion

batata *nf* : yam, sweet potato

batear *v* : bat, hit — **bate** *nm* : baseball bat — **bateador, -dora** *n* : batter, hitter

batería *nf* **1** : battery **2** : drums *pl* **3** ~ **de cocina** : kitchen utensils *pl*

batir *vt* **1** : beat, whip **2** DERRIBAR : knock down — **batirse** *vr* : fight — **batido** *nm* : milk shake — **batidor** *nm* : eggbeater, whisk — **batidora** *nf* : electric mixer

batuta *nf* : baton

baúl *nm* : trunk, chest

bautismo *nm* : baptism — **bautismal** *adj* : baptismal — **bautizar** {21} *vt* : baptize — **bautizo** *nm* : baptism, christening

baya *nf* : berry

bayeta *nf* : cleaning cloth

bayoneta *nf* : bayonet

bazar *nm* : bazaar

bazo *nm* : spleen

bazofia *nf fam* : rubbish, hogwash

beato, -ta *adj* : blessed

bebé *nm* : baby

beber *v* : drink — **bebedero** *nm* : watering trough — **bebedor, -dora** *n* : (heavy) drinker — **bebida** *nf* : drink, beverage — **bebido, -da** *adj* : drunk

beca *nf* : grant, scholarship

becerro, -rra *n* : calf

befa *nf* : jeer, taunt

beige *adj & nm* : beige

beisbol *or* **béisbol** *nm* : baseball — **beisbolista** *nmf* : baseball player

beldad *nf* : beauty

belén *nf, pl* **-lenes** : Nativity scene

belga *adj* : Belgian

beliceño, -ña *adj* : Belizean

bélico, -ca *adj* : military, war — **belicoso, -sa** *adj* : warlike

beligerancia *nf* : belligerence — **beligerante** *adj & nmf* : belligerent

belleza *nf* : beauty — **bello, -lla** *adj* **1** : beautiful **2 bellas artes** : fine arts

bellota *nf* : acorn

bemol *adj & nm* : flat (in music)

bendecir {11} *vt* **1** : bless **2** ~ **la mesa** : say grace — **bendición** *nf, pl* **-ciones** : benediction, blessing — **bendito, -ta** *adj* **1** : blessed, holy **2** DICHOSO : fortunate **3 ¡bendito sea Dios!** : thank goodness!

benefactor, -tora *n* : benefactor

beneficiar *vt* : benefit, assist — **beneficiarse** *vr* : benefit, profit — **beneficiario, -ria** *n* : beneficiary — **beneficio** *nm* **1** : gain, profit **2** BIEN : benefit — **beneficioso, -sa** *adj* : beneficial — **benéfico, -ca** *adj* : charitable

benemérito, -ta *adj* : worthy

beneplácito *nm* : approval, consent

benévolo, -la *adj* : benevolent, kind — **benevolencia** *nf* : benevolence, kindness

bengala *nf or* **luz de** ~ : flare

benigno, -na *adj* **1** : mild **2** : benign (in medicine) — **benignidad** *nf* : mildness, kindness

benjamín, -mina *n, mpl* **-mines** : youngest child

beodo, -da *adj & n* : drunk

berenjena *nf* : eggplant

berma *nf* : shoulder (of a road)

berrear *vi* **1** : bellow, low **2** : bawl, howl (of a person) — **berrido** *nm* **1** : bellowing **2** : howl, scream (of a person)

berro *nm* : watercress

berza *nf* : cabbage

besar *vt* : kiss — **besarse** *vr* : kiss (each other) — **beso** *nm* : kiss

bestia *nf* : beast, animal — **bestial** *adj* : bestial, brutal — **bestialidad** *nf* : brutality

betabel *nm Lat* : beet

betún *nm, pl* **-tunes** : shoe polish

bianual *adj* : biannual

biberón *nm, pl* **-rones** : baby's bottle

Biblia *nf* : Bible — **bíblico, -ca** *adj* : biblical

bibliografía *nf* : bibliography — **bibliográfico, -ca** *adj* : bibliographic, bibliographical

biblioteca *nf* : library — **bibliotecario, -ria** *n* : librarian

bicarbonato *nm* ~ **de soda** : baking soda

bicentenario *nm* : bicentennial

bíceps *nms & pl* : biceps

bicho *nm* : small animal, bug

bicicleta *nf* : bicycle — **bici** *nf fam* : bike

bicolor *adj* : two-tone

bidón *nm, pl* **-dones** : large can, drum

bien *adv* **1** : well, good **2** CORRECTAMENTE : correctly, right **3** MUY : very, quite **4** DE BUENA GANA : willingly **5** ~ **que** : although **6** **más** ~ : rather — **bien** *adj* **1** : all right, well **2** AGRADABLE : pleasant, nice **3** SATISFACTORIO : satisfactory **4** CORRECTO : correct, right — **bien** *nm* **1** : good **2** ~**es** *nmpl* : property, goods

bienal *adj* & *nf* : biennial

bienaventurado, -da *adj* : blessed, fortunate

bienestar *nm* : welfare, well-being

bienhechor, -chora *n* : benefactor

bienintencionado, -da *adj* : well-meaning

bienvenido, -da *adj* : welcome — **bienvenida** *nf* **1** : welcome **2 dar la** ~ **a** : welcome (s.o.)

bife *nm Lat* : steak

bifocales *nmpl* : bifocals

bifurcarse {72} *vr* : fork — **bifurcación** *nf, pl* **-ciones** : fork, branch

bigamia *nf* : bigamy

bigote *nm* **1** : mustache **2** ~**s** *nmpl* : whiskers (of an animal)

bikini *nm* : bikini

bilingüe *adj* : bilingual

bilis *nf* : bile

billar *nm* : pool, billiards

billete *nm* **1** : bill, banknote **2** BOLETO : ticket — **billetera** *nf* : billfold, wallet

billón *nm, pl* **-llones** : trillion

bimensual, -suale *adj* : twice a month — **bimestral** *adj* : bimonthly

binario, -ria *adj* : binary

bingo *nm* : bingo

binoculares *nmpl* : binoculars

biodegradable *adj* : biodegradable

biofísica *nf* : biophysics

biografía *nf* : biography — **biográfico, -ca** *adj* : biographical — **biógrafo, -fa** *n* : biographer

biología *nf* : biology — **biológico, -ca** *adj* : biological, biologic — **biólogo, -ga** *n* : biologist

biombo *nm* : folding screen

biomecánica *nf* : biomechanics

biopsia *nf* : biopsy

bioquímica *nf* : biochemistry — **bioquímico, -ca** *adj* : biochemical

biotecnología *nf* : biotechnology

bipartidista *adj* : bipartisan

bípedo *nm* : biped

biquini → **bikini**

birlar *vt fam* : swipe, pinch

bis *adv* **1** : twice (in music) **2** : A (in an address) — ~ *nm* : encore

bisabuelo, -la *n* : great-grandfather *m*, great-grandmother *f*

bisagra *nf* : hinge

bisecar {72} *vt* : bisect

biselar *vt* : bevel

bisexual *adj* : bisexual

bisiesto *adj* **año** ~ : leap year

bisnieto, -ta *n* : great-grandson *m*, great-granddaughter *f*

bisonte *nm* : bison, buffalo

bisoño, -ña *n* : novice

bistec *nm* : steak

bisturí *nm* : scalpel

bisutería *nf* : costume jewelry

bit *nm* : bit (unit of information)

bitácora *nf* **1** : ship's log **2** BLOG : blog

bizco, -ca *adj* : cross-eyed

bizcocho *nm* : sponge cake

bizquear *vi* : squint — **bizquera** *nf* : squint

blanco, -ca *adj* : white — **blanco, -ca** *n* : white person — **blanco** *nm* **1** : white **2** DIANA : target, bull's-eye **3** : blank (space) — **blancura** *nf* : whiteness

blandir {1} *vt* : wave, brandish

blando, -da *adj* **1** : soft, tender **2** DÉBIL : weak-willed **3** INDULGENTE : lenient — **blandura** *nf* **1** : softness, tenderness **2** DEBILIDAD : weakness **3** INDULGENCIA : leniency

blanquear *vt* **1** : whiten, bleach **2** : launder (money) — *vi* : turn white — **blanqueador** *nm Lat* : bleach

blasfemar *vi* : blaspheme — **blasfemia** *nf* : blasphemy — **blasfemo, -ma** *adj* : blasphemous

bledo *nm* **no me importa un** ~ *fam* : I couldn't care less

blindaje *nm* : armor, armor plating — **blindado, -da** *adj* : armored

bloc *nm, pl* **blocs** : (writing) pad

blog *nm, pl* **blogs** BITÁCORA : blog

bloquear *vt* **1** OBSTRUIR : block, obstruct **2** : blockade — **bloque** *nm* **1** : block **2** : bloc (in politics) — **bloqueo** *nm* **1** OBSTRUCCIÓN : blockage **2** : blockade

blusa *nf* : blouse — **blusón** *nm, pl* **-sones** : smock

boato *nm* : showiness

bobina *nf* : bobbin, reel

bobo, -ba *adj* : silly, stupid — ~ *n* : fool, simpleton

boca *nf* **1** : mouth **2** ENTRADA : entrance **3** ~ **arriba** : faceup **4** ~ **abajo** : facedown, prone **5** ~ **de riego** : hydrant

bocacalle *nf* : entrance (to a street)

bocado *nm* **1** : bite, mouthful **2** : bit (of a bridle) — **bocadillo** *nm Spain* : sandwich

bocajarro *nm* **a** ~ : point-blank

bocallave *nf* : keyhole

bocanada *nf* **1** : swallow, swig **2** : puff, gust (of smoke, wind, etc.)

boceto *nm* : sketch, outline

bochorno *nm* **1** VERGÜENZA : embarrassment **2** : muggy weather — **bochornoso, -sa** *adj* **1** VERGONZOSO : embarrassing **2** : muggy, sultry

bocina *nf* **1** : horn **2** : mouthpiece (of a telephone) — **bocinazo** *nm* : honk, toot

boda *nf* : wedding

bodega *nf* **1** : wine cellar **2** : warehouse **3** : hold (of a ship or airplane) **4** *Lat* : grocery store

bofetear *vt* : slap — **bofetada** *nf or* **bofetón** *nm* : slap (in the face)

boga *nf* : fashion, vogue

bohemio, -mia *adj & n* : bohemian

boicotear *vt* : boycott — **boicot** *nm, pl* **-cots** : boycott

boina *nf* : beret

bola *nf* **1** : ball **2** *fam* : fib

bolera *nf* : bowling alley

boleta *nf Lat* : ticket — **boletería** *nf Lat* : ticket office

boletín *nm, pl* **-tines** **1** : bulletin **2** ~ **de noticias** : news release

boleto *nm* : ticket

boliche *nm* **1** : bowling **2** BOLERA : bowling alley

bolígrafo *nm* : ballpoint pen

bolillo *nm* : bobbin

boliviano, -na *adj* : Bolivian

bollo *nm* : bun, sweet roll

bolo *nm* **1** : bowling pin **2** ~**s** *nmpl* : bowling

bolsa *nf* **1** : bag **2** *Lat* : pocketbook, purse **3 la Bolsa** : the stock market — **bolsillo** *nm* : pocket — **bolso** *nm Spain* : pocketbook, handbag

bomba *nf* **1** : bomb **2** ~ **de gasolina** : gas pump

bombachos *nmpl* : baggy trousers

bombardear *vt* : bomb, bombard — **bombardeo** *nm* : bombing, bombardment — **bombardero** *nm* : bomber (airplane)

bombear *vt* : pump — **bombero, -ra** *n* : firefighter

bombilla *nf* : lightbulb — **bombillo** *nm Lat* : lightbulb

bombo *nm* **1** : bass drum **2 a** ~**s y platillos** : with a great fanfare

bombón *nm, pl* **-bones** : candy, chocolate

bonachón, -chona *adj, mpl* **-chones** *fam* : good-natured

bonanza *nf* **1** : fair weather (at sea) **2** PROSPERIDAD : prosperity

bondad *nf* : goodness, kindness — **bondadoso, -sa** *adj* : kind, good

boniato *nm* : sweet potato

bonificación *nf, pl* **-ciones** **1** : bonus, extra **2** DESCUENTO : discount

bonito, -ta *adj* : pretty, lovely

bono *nm* **1** : bond **2** VALE : voucher

boquear *vi* : gasp — **boqueada** *nf* : gasp

boquerón *nm, pl* **-rones** : anchovy

boquete *nm* : gap, opening

boquiabierto, -ta *adj* : open-mouthed, speechless

boquilla *nf* : mouthpiece (of a musical instrument)

borbollar *vi* : bubble

borbotar *or* **borbotear** *vi* : boil, bubble, gurgle — **borbotón** *nm, pl* **-tones** **1** : spurt **2 salir a borbotones** : gush out

bordar *v* : embroider — **bordado** *nm* : embroidery, needlework

borde *nm* **1** : border, edge **2 al** ~ **de** : on the verge of — **bordear** *vt* : border — **bordillo** *nm* : curb

bordo *nm* **a** ~ : aboard, on board

borla *nf* **1** : pom-pom, tassel **2** : powder puff

borracho, -cha *adj & n* : drunk — **borrachera** *nf* : drunkenness

borrar *vt* : erase, blot out — **borrador** *nm* **1** : rough draft **2** : eraser (for a blackboard)

borrascoso, -sa *adj* : stormy

borrego, -ga *n* : lamb, sheep — **borrego** *nm Lat* : false rumor, hoax

borrón *nm, pl* **-rrones** **1** : smudge, blot **2** ~ **y cuenta nueva** : let's forget about it — **borroso, -sa** *adj* **1** : blurry, smudgy **2** INDISTINTO : vague, hazy

bosque *nm* : woods, forest — **boscoso, -sa** *adj* : wooded

bosquejar *vt* : sketch (out) — **bosquejo** *nm* : outline, sketch

bostezar {21} *vi* : yawn — **bostezo** *nm* : yawn

bota *nf* : boot

botánica *nf* : botany — **botánico, -ca** *adj* : botanical

botar *vt* **1** : throw, hurl **2** *Lat* : throw away **3** : launch (a ship) — *vi* : bounce

bote *nm* **1** : small boat **2** *Spain* : can **3** TARRO : jar **4** SALTO : bounce, jump

botella *nf* : bottle

botín *nm, pl* **-tines** **1** : ankle boot **2** DESPOJOS : booty, plunder

botiquín *nm, pl* **-quines** **1** : medicine cabinet **2** : first-aid kit

botón *nm, pl* **-tones** **1** : button **2** YEMA : bud — **botones** *nmfs & pl* : bellhop

botulismo *nm* : botulism

boutique *nf* : boutique

bóveda *nf* : vault

boxear *vi* : box — **boxeador, -dora** *n* : boxer — **boxeo** *nm* : boxing

boya *nf* : buoy — **boyante** *adj* **1** : buoyant **2** PRÓSPERO : prosperous, thriving

bozal *nm* **1** : muzzle **2** : halter (for a horse)

bracear *vi* **1** : wave one's arms **2** NADAR : swim, crawl

bracero, -ra *n* : day laborer

bragas *nf Spain* : panties

bragueta *nf* : fly, pants zipper
braille *adj & nm* : braille
bramante *nm* : twine, string
bramar *vi* **1** : bellow, roar **2** : howl (of the wind) — **bramido** *nm* : bellow, roar
brandy *nm* : brandy
branquia *nf* : gill
brasa *nf* : ember
brasier *nm Lat* : brassiere
brasileño, -ña *adj* : Brazilian
bravata *nf* **1** : boast, bravado **2** AMENAZO : threat
bravo, -va *adj* **1** : fierce, savage **2** : rough (of the sea) **3** *Lat* : angry — ~ *interj* : bravo!, well done! — **bravura** *nf* **1** FERO-CIDAD : fierceness **2** VALENTÍA : bravery
braza *nf* **1** : breaststroke **2** : fathom (measurement) — **brazada** *nf* : stroke (in swimming)
brazalete *nm* **1** : bracelet **2** : (cloth) armband
brazo *nm* **1** : arm **2** : branch (of a river, etc.) **3** ~ **derecho** : right-hand man **4** ~**s** *nmpl* : hands, laborers
brea *nf* : tar
brebaje *nm* : concoction
brecha *nf* : breach, gap
brécol *nm* : broccoli
bregar {52} *vi* **1** LUCHAR : struggle **2** TRA-BAJAR : work hard — **brega** *nf* **andar a la** ~ : struggle
breña *nf or* **breñal** *nm* : scrubland, brush
breve *adj* **1** : brief, short **2** **en** ~ : shortly, in short — **brevedad** *nf* : brevity, shortness — **brevemente** *adv* : briefly
brezal *nm* : moor, heath — **brezo** *nm* : heather
bricolaje *or* **bricolage** *nm* : do-it-yourself
brida *nf* : bridle
brigada *nf* **1** : brigade **2** EQUIPO : gang, team, squad
brillar *vi* : shine, sparkle — **brillante** *adj* : brilliant, shiny — ~ *nm* : diamond — **bri-llantez** *nf* : brilliance — **brillo** *nm* **1** : luster, shine **2** ESPLENDOR : splendor — **brilloso, -sa** *adj* : shiny
brincar {72} *vi* : jump about, frolic — **brinco** *nm* : jump, skip
brindar *vi* : drink a toast — *vt* : offer, provide — **brindarse** *vr* : offer one's assistance — **brindis** *nm* : drink, toast
brío *nm* **1** : force, determination **2** ÁNIMO : spirit, verve — **brioso, -sa** *adj* : spirited, lively
brisa *nf* : breeze
británico, -ca *adj* : British
brizna *nf* **1** : strand, thread **2** : blade (of grass)
brocado *nm* : brocade
brocha *nf* : paintbrush

broche *nm* **1** : fastener, clasp **2** ALFILER : brooch
brocheta *nf* : skewer
brócoli *nm* : broccoli
bromear *vi* : joke, fool around — **broma** *nf* : joke, prank — **bromista** *adj* : fun-loving, joking — ~ *nmf* : joker, prankster
bronca *nf fam* : fight, row
bronce *nm* : bronze — **bronceado, -da** *adj* : suntanned — **bronceado** *nm* : tan — **broncearse** *vr* : get a suntan
bronco, -ca *adj* **1** : harsh, rough **2** : untamed, wild (of a horse)
bronquitis *nf* : bronchitis
broqueta *nf* : skewer
brotar *vi* **1** : bud, sprout **2** : stream, gush (of a river, tears, etc.) **3** : arise (of feelings, etc.) **4** : break out (in medicine) — **brote** *nm* **1** : outbreak **2** : sprout, bud, shoot (of plants)
brujería *nf* : witchcraft — **bruja** *nf* **1** : witch **2** *fam* : old hag — **brujo** *nm* : warlock, sorcerer — **brujo, -ja** *adj* : bewitching
brújula *nf* : compass
bruma *nf* : haze, mist — **brumoso, -sa** *adj* : hazy, misty
bruñir {38} *vt* : burnish, polish
brusco, -ca *adj* **1** SÚBITO : sudden, abrupt **2** TOSCO : brusque, rough — **brusquedad** *nf* : abruptness, brusqueness
brutal *adj* : brutal — **brutalidad** *nf* : brutality
bruto, -ta *adj* **1** : brutish, stupid **2** : crude (of petroleum, etc.), uncut (of diamonds) **3** **peso** ~ : gross weight — ~ *n* : brute
bucal *adj* : oral
bucear *vi* **1** : dive, swim underwater **2** ~ **en** : delve into — **buceo** *nm* : (underwater) diving
bucle *nm* : curl
budín *nm, pl* **-dines** : pudding
budismo *nm* : Buddhism — **budista** *adj & nmf* : Buddhist
buenamente *adv* **1** : easily **2** VOLUNTARIA-MENTE : willingly
buenaventura *nf* **1** : good luck **2** **decir la** ~ **a uno** : tell s.o.'s fortune
bueno, -na *adj* (**buen** *before masculine singular nouns*) **1** : good **2** AMABLE : kind **3** APROPIADO : appropriate **4** SALUDABLE : well, healthy **5** : nice, fine (of weather) **6** **buenos días** : hello, good day **7** **buenas noches** : good night **8** **buenas tardes** : good afternoon, good evening — **bueno** *interj* : OK!, all right!
buey *nm* : ox, steer
búfalo *nm* : buffalo
bufanda *nf* : scarf
bufar *vi* : snort — **bufido** *nm* : snort
bufet *or* **bufé** *nm* : buffet-style meal

bufete *nm* **1** : law practice **2** MESA : writing desk

bufo, -fa *adj* : comic — **bufón, -fona** *n, mpl* **-fones** : buffoon, jester — **bufonada** *nf* : wisecrack

buhardilla *nf* : attic, garret

búho *nm* : owl

buitre *nm* : vulture

bujía *nf* : spark plug

bulbo *nm* : bulb (of a plant)

bulevar *nm* : boulevard

búlgaro, -ra *adj* : Bulgarian

bulla *nf* : uproar, racket

bulldozer *nm* : bulldozer

bullicio *nm* **1** : uproar **2** AJETREO : hustle and bustle — **bullicioso, -sa** *adj* : noisy, boisterous

bullir {38} *vi* **1** : boil **2** AJETREARSE : bustle, stir

bulto *nm* **1** : package, bundle **2** VOLUMEN : bulk, size **3** FORMA : form, shape **4** PROTUBERANCIA : lump, swelling

bumerán *nm, pl* **-ranes** : boomerang

buñuelo *nm* : fried pastry

buque *nm* : ship

burbujear *vi* : bubble — **burbuja** *nf* : bubble

burdel *nm* : brothel

burdo, -da *adj* : coarse, rough

burgués, -guesa *adj & n, mpl* **-gueses** : bourgeois — **burguesía** *nf* : bourgeoisie

burlar *vt* : trick, deceive — **burlarse** *vr* ~ **de** : make fun of — **burla** *nf* **1** MOFA : mockery, ridicule **2** BROMA : joke, trick

burlesco, -ca *adj* : comic, funny

burlón, -lona *adj, mpl* **-lones** : mocking

burocracia *nf* : bureaucracy — **burócrata** *nmf* : bureaucrat — **burocrático, -ca** *adj* : bureaucratic

burrito *nm* : burrito

burro, -rra *n* **1** : donkey **2** *fam* : dunce — ~ *adj* : stupid — **burro** *nm* **1** : sawhorse **2** *Lat* : stepladder

bus *nm* : bus

buscador¹ *nm* : search engine

buscador² -dora *n* : hunter (for treasure, etc.), prospector

buscar {72} *vt* **1** : look for, seek **2 ir a** ~ **a uno** : fetch s.o. — *vi* : search — **busca** *nf* : search — **búsqueda** *nf* : search

busto *nm* : bust (in sculpture)

butaca *nf* **1** : armchair **2** : seat (in a theatre)

butano *nm* : butane

buzo *nm* : diver

buzón *nm, pl* **-zones** : mailbox

byte *nm* : byte

C

c *nf* : c, third letter of the Spanish alphabet

cabal *adj* **1** : exact **2** COMPLETO : complete — **cabales** *nmpl* **no estar en sus** ~ : not be in one's right mind

cabalgar {52} *vi* : ride — **cabalgata** *nf* : cavalcade

caballa *nf* : mackerel

caballería *nf* **1** : cavalry **2** CABALLO : horse, mount — **caballeriza** *nf* : stable

caballero *nm* **1** : gentleman **2** : knight (rank) — **caballerosidad** *nf* : chivalry — **caballeroso, -sa** *adj* : chivalrous

caballete *nm* **1** : ridge (of a roof) **2** : easel (for a canvas) **3** : bridge (of the nose)

caballito *nm* **1** : rocking horse **2** ~**s** *nmpl* : merry-go-round

caballo *nm* **1** : horse **2** : knight (in chess) **3** ~ **de fuerza** : horsepower

cabaña *nf* : cabin, hut

cabaret *nm, pl* **-rets** : nightclub, cabaret

cabecear *vi* **1** : shake one's head, nod **2** : pitch, lurch (of a boat)

cabecera *nf* **1** : head (of a bed, etc.) **2** : heading (in a text) **3 médico de** ~ : family doctor

cabecilla *nmf* : ringleader

cabello *nm* : hair — **cabelludo, -da** *adj* : hairy

caber {12} *vi* **1** : fit, go (into) **2 no cabe duda** : there's no doubt

cabestro *nm* : halter

cabeza *nf* **1** : head **2 de** ~ : head first — **cabezada** *nf* **1** : butt (of the head) **2 dar** ~**s** : nod off

cabezal *nm* : bolster, headrest

cabida *nf* **1** : room, capacity **2 dar** ~ **a** : accomodate, find room for

cabina *nf* **1** : booth **2** : cab (of a truck, etc.) **3** : cabin, cockpit (of an airplane)

cabizbajo, -ja *adj* : downcast

cable *nm* : cable

cabo *nm* **1** : end, stub **2** TROZO : bit **3** : corporal (in the military) **4** : cape (in geography) **5 al fin y al** ~ : after all **6 llevar a** ~ : carry out, do

cabra *nf* : goat

cabriola *nf* **1** : leap, skip **2 hacer ∼s** : prance around

cabrito *nm* : kid (goat)

cacahuate *or* **cacahuete** *nm* : peanut

cacao *nm* **1** : cacao (tree) **2** : cocoa (drink)

cacarear *vi* : crow, cackle — *vt fam* : boast about

cacería *nf* : hunt

cacerola *nf* : pan, saucepan

cacharro *nm* **1** *fam* : thing, piece of junk **2** *fam* : jalopy **3 ∼s** *nmpl* : pots and pans

cachear *vt* : search, frisk

cachemir *nm or* **cachemira** *nf* : cashmere

cachete *nm Lat* : cheek — **cachetada** *nf Lat* : slap

cacho *nm* **1** *fam* : piece, bit **2** *Lat* : horn

cachorro, -rra *n* **1** : cub **2** PERRITO : puppy

cactus *or* **cacto** *nm* : cactus

cada *adj* : each, every

cadalso *nm* : scaffold

cadáver *nm* : corpse

cadena *nf* **1** : chain **2** : (television) channel **3 ∼ de montaje** : assembly line

cadencia *nf* : cadence

cadera *nf* : hip

cadete *nmf* : cadet

caducar {72} *vi* : expire — **caducidad** *nf* : expiration

caer {13} *vi* **1** : fall, drop **2 ∼ bien a uno** : be to one's liking **3 dejar ∼** : drop **4 me cae bien** : I like him, I like him — **caerse** *vr* : drop, fall (down)

café *nm* **1** : coffee **2** : café — **∼** *adj Lat* : brown — **cafetera** *nf* : coffeepot — **cafetería** *nf* : coffee shop, cafeteria — **cafeína** *nf* : caffeine

caficultor -tora *n* : coffee grower

caficultura *nf* : coffee industry

caída *nf* **1** : fall, drop **2** PENDIENTE : slope

caimán *nm, pl* **-manes** : alligator

caja *nf* **1** : box, case **2** : checkout counter, cashier's desk (in a store) **3 ∼ fuerte** : safe **4 ∼ registradora** : cash register — **cajero, -ra** *n* **1** : cashier **2** : (bank) teller — **cajetilla** *nf* : pack (of cigarettes) — **cajón** *nm, pl* **-jones 1** : drawer (in furniture) **2** : large box, crate

cajuela *nf Lat* : trunk (of a car)

cal *nf* : lime

cala *nf* : cove

calabaza *nf* **1** : pumpkin, squash, gourd **2 dar ∼s a** *fam* : give the brush-off to — **calabacín** *nm, pl* **-cines** *or* **calabacita** *nf Lat* : zucchini

calabozo *nm* **1** : prison **2** CELDA : cell

calamar *nm* : squid

calambre *nm* **1** ESPASMO : cramp **2** : (electric) shock

calamidad *nf* : calamity

calar *vt* **1** : soak (through) **2** PERFORAR : pierce — **calarse** *vr* : get drenched

calavera *nf* : skull

calcar {72} *vt* **1** : trace **2** IMITAR : copy, imitate

calcetín *nm, pl* **-tines** : sock

calcinar *vt* : char

calcio *nm* : calcium

calcomanía *nf* : decal

calcular *vt* : calculate, estimate — **calculador, -dora** *adj* : calculating — **calculadora** *nf* : calculator — **cálculo** *nm* **1** : calculation **2** : calculus (in mathematics and medicine) **3 ∼ biliar** : gallstone

caldera *nf* **1** : cauldron **2** : boiler (for heating, etc.) — **caldo** *nm* : broth, stock

calefacción *nf, pl* **-ciones** : heating, heat

calendario *nm* : calendar

calentamiento *nm* **1** : heating, warming: calentamiento global **global warming 2** : warm-up (in sports)

calentar {55} *vt* : heat (up), warm (up) — **calentarse** *vr* : get warm, heat up — **calentador** *nm* : heater — **calentura** *nf* : temperature, fever

calibre *nm* **1** : caliber **2** DIÁMETRO : bore, diameter — **calibrar** *vt* : calibrate

calidad *nf* **1** : quality **2 en ∼ de** : as, in the capacity of

cálido, -da *adj* : hot, warm

calidoscopio *nm* : kaleidoscope

caliente *adj* **1** : hot **2** ACALORADO : heated, fiery

calificar {72} *vt* **1** : qualify **2** EVALUAR : rate **3** : grade (an exam, etc.) — **calificación** *nf, pl* **-ciones 1** : qualification **2** EVALUACIÓN : rating **3** NOTA : grade — **calificativo, -va** *adj* : qualifying — **calificativo** *nm* : qualifier, epithet

caligrafía *nf* : penmanship

calistenia *nf* : calisthenics

cáliz *nm, pl* **-lices** : chalice

caliza *nf* : limestone

callar *vi* : keep quiet, be silent — *vt* **1** : silence, hush **2** OCULTAR : keep secret — **callarse** *vr* : remain silent — **callado, -da** *adj* : quiet, silent

calle *nf* : street, road — **callejear** *vi* : wander about the streets — **callejero, -ra** *adj* **1** : street **2 perro callejero** : stray dog — **callejón** *nm, pl* **-jones 1** : alley **2 ∼ sin salida** : dead-end street

callo *nm* : callus, corn

calma *nf* : calm, quiet — **calmante** *adj* : soothing — **∼** *nm* : tranquilizer — **calmar** *vt* : calm, soothe — **calmarse** *vr* : calm down — **calmo, -ma** *adj Lat* : calm — **calmoso, -sa** *adj* **1** : calm **2** LENTO : slow

calor *nm* **1** : heat, warmth **2 tener ~** : be hot — **caloría** *nf* : calorie

calumnia *nf* : slander, libel — **calumniar** *vt* : slander, libel

caluroso, -sa *adj* **1** : hot **2** : warm, enthusiastic (of applause, etc.)

calvo, -va *adj* : bald — **calvicie** *nf* : baldness

calza *nf* : wedge

calzada *nf* : roadway

calzado *nm* : footwear — **calzar** {21} *vt* **1** : wear (shoes) **2** : put shoes on (s.o.)

calzones *nmpl Lat* : panties — **calzoncillos** *nmpl* : underpants, briefs

cama *nf* : bed

camada *nf* : litter, brood

camafeo *nm* : cameo

cámara *nf* **1** : chamber **2** *or* **~ fotográfica** : camera **3** : house (in government)

camarada *nmf* : comrade — **camaradería** *nf* : camaraderie

camarero, -ra *n* **1** : waiter, waitress *f* **2** : steward *m*, stewardess *f* (on a ship, etc.) — **camarera** *nf* : chambermaid *f*

camarín *nm, pl* **-rines** : dressing room

camarón *nm, pl* **-rones** : shrimp

camarote *nm* : cabin, stateroom

cambiar *vt* **1** : change **2** CANJEAR : exchange — *vi* **1** : change **2** : shift gears (of an automobile) — **cambiarse** *vr* **1** : change (clothing) **2** : move (to a new address) — **cambiable** *adj* : changeable

cambio *nm* **1** : change, alteration (**cambio climático** climate change) (**cambio de domicilio** change of address) **2** : exchange (of goods, etc.) **3** : change (money) **4 a cambio (de)** : in exchange (for) **5 en ~** : however, on the other hand

camello *nm* : camel

camilla *nf* : stretcher — **camillero** *nm* : orderly (in a hospital)

caminar *vi* : walk — *vt* : cover (a distance) — **caminata** *nf* : hike

camino *nm* **1** : road, path **2** RUTA : way **3 a medio ~** : halfway (there) **4 ponerse en ~** : set out

camión *nm, pl* **-miones 1** : truck **2** *Lat* : bus — **camionero, -ra** *n* **1** : truck driver **2** *Lat* : bus driver — **camioneta** *nm* : light truck, van

camisa *nf* **1** : shirt **2 ~ de fuerza** : straitjacket — **camiseta** *nf* : T-shirt, undershirt — **camisón** *nm, pl* **-sones** : nightshirt, nightgown

camorra *nf fam* : fight, trouble

camote *nm Lat* : sweet potato

campamento *nm* : camp

campana *nf* : bell — **campanada** *nf* : stroke (of a bell), peal — **campanario** *nm* : bell tower — **campanilla** *nf* : (small) bell

campaña *nf* **1** : countryside **2** : (military or political) campaign

campeón, -peona *n, mpl* **-peones** : champion — **campeonato** *nm* : championship

campesino, -na *n* : peasant, farm laborer — **campestre** *adj* : rural, rustic

camping *nm* **1** : campsite **2 hacer ~** : go camping

campiña *nf* : countryside

campo *nm* **1** : field **2** CAMPIÑA : countryside, country **3** CAMPAMENTO : camp

camuflaje *nm* : camouflage — **camuflar** *vt* : camouflage

cana *nf* : gray hair

canadiense *adj* : Canadian

canal *nm* **1** : canal **2** MEDIO : channel **3** : (radio or television) channel — **canalizar** {21} *vt* : channel

canalete *nm* : paddle (of a canoe)

canalla *nf* : rabble — **~** *nmf fam* : swine, bastard

canapé *nm* **1** : canapé **2** SOFÁ : sofa, couch

canario *nm* : canary

canasta *nf* : basket — **canasto** *nm* : large basket

cancelar *vt* **1** : cancel **2** : pay off, settle (a debt) — **cancelación** *nf, pl* **-ciones 1** : cancellation **2** : payment in full (of a debt)

cáncer *nm* : cancer — **canceroso, -sa** *adj* : cancerous

cancha *nf* : court, field (for sports)

canciller *nm* : chancellor

canción *nf, pl* **-ciones 1** : song **2 ~ de cuna** : lullaby — **cancionero** *nm* : songbook

candado *nm* : padlock

candela *nf* : candle — **candelabro** *nm* : candelabra — **candelero** *nm* **1** : candlestick **2 estar en el ~** : be in the limelight

candente *adj* : red-hot

candidato, -ta *n* : candidate — **candidatura** *nf* : candidacy

cándido, -da *adj* : naïve — **candidez** *nf* **1** : simplicity **2** INGENUIDAD : naïveté

candil *nm* : oil lamp — **candilejas** *nfpl* : footlights

candor *nm* : naïveté, innocence

canela *nf* : cinnamon

cangrejo *nm* : crab

canguro *nm* : kangaroo

caníbal *nmf* : cannibal — **canibalismo** *nm* : cannibalism

canicas *nfpl* : (game of) marbles

canino, -na *adj* : canine — **canino** *nm* : canine (tooth)

canjear *vt* : exchange — **canje** *nm* : exchange, trade

cano, -na *adj* : gray, gray-haired

canoa *nf* : canoe

canon *nm, pl* **cánones** : canon

canonizar {21} *vt* : canonize

canoso, -sa *adj* : gray, gray-haired

cansar *vt* : tire (out) — *vi* : be tiring — **cansarse** *vr* : get tired — **cansado, -da** *adj* 1 : tired 2 PESADO : tiresome — **cansancio** *nm* : fatigue, weariness

cantalupo *nm* : cantaloupe

cantar *v* : sing — ~ *nm* : song — **cantante** *nmf* : singer

cántaro *nm* 1 : pitcher, jug 2 **llover a** ~**s** *fam* : rain cats and dogs

cantautor -tora *n* : singer-songwriter

cantera *nf* : quarry (excavation)

cantidad *nf* 1 : quantity, amount 2 **una** ~ **de** : lots of

cantimplora *nf* : canteen, water bottle

cantina *nf* 1 : canteen, cafeteria 2 *Lat* : tavern, bar

canto *nm* 1 : singing, song 2 BORDE, LADO : edge 3 **de** ~ : on end, sideways 4 ~ **rodado** : boulder — **cantor, -tora** *adj* 1 : singing 2 **pájaro** ~ : songbird — ~ *n* : singer

caña *nf* 1 : cane, reed 2 ~ **de pescar** : fishing pole

cáñamo *nm* : hemp

cañería *nf* : pipes, piping — **caño** *nm* 1 : pipe 2 : spout (of a fountain) — **cañón** *nm, pl* **-ñones** 1 : cannon 2 : barrel (of a gun) 3 : canyon (in geography)

caoba *nf* : mahogany

caos *nm* : chaos — **caótico, -ca** *adj* : chaotic

capa *nf* 1 : cape, cloak 2 : coat (of paint, etc.), coating (in cooking) 3 ESTRATO : layer, stratum 4 : (social) class

capacidad *nf* 1 : capacity 2 APTITUD : ability

capacitar *vt* : train, qualify — **capacitación** *nf, pl* **-ciones** : training

caparazón *nm, pl* **-zones** : shell

capataz *nmf, pl* **-taces** : foreman

capaz *adj, pl* **-paces** 1 : capable, able 2 ESPACIOSO : spacious

capellán *nm, pl* **-llanes** : chaplain

capilla *nf* : chapel

capital *adj* 1 : capital 2 PRINCIPAL : chief, principal — ~ *nm* : capital (assets) — ~ *nf* : capital (city) — **capitalismo** *nm* : capitalism — **capitalista** *adj & nmf* : capitalist, capitalistic — **capitalizar** {21} *vt* : capitalize

capitán, -tana *n, mpl* **-tanes** : captain

capitolio *nm* : capitol

capitular *vi* : capitulate, surrender — **capitulación** *nf, pl* **-ciones** : surrender

capítulo *nm* : chapter

capó *nm* : hood (of a car)

capote *nm* : cloak, cape

capricho *nm* : whim, caprice — **caprichoso, -sa** *adj* : whimsical, capricious

cápsula *nf* : capsule

captar *vt* 1 : grasp 2 ATRAER : gain, attract (interest, etc.) 3 : harness (waters)

capturar *vt* : capture, seize — **captura** *nf* : capture, seizure

capucha *nf* : hood (of clothing)

capullo *nm* 1 : cocoon 2 : (flower) bud

caqui *adj & nm* : khaki

cara *nf* 1 : face 2 ASPECTO : appearance 3 *fam* : nerve, gall 4 ~ **a** *or* **de** ~ **a** : facing

carabina *nf* : carbine

caracol *nm* 1 : snail 2 *Lat* : conch 3 RIZO : curl

carácter *nm, pl* **-racteres** 1 : character 2 ÍNDOLE : nature — **característica** *nf* : characteristic — **característico, -ca** *adj* : characteristic — **caracterizar** {21} *vt* : characterize

caramba *interj* : oh my!, good grief!

carámbano *nm* : icicle

caramelo *nm* 1 : caramel 2 DULCE : candy

carátula *nf* 1 CARETA : mask 2 : jacket (of a record, etc.) 3 *Lat* : face (of a watch)

caravana *nf* 1 : caravan 2 REMOLQUE : trailer

caray → **caramba**

carbohidrato *nm* : carbohydrate

carbón *nm, pl* **-bones** 1 : coal 2 : charcoal (for drawing) — **carboncillo** *nm* : charcoal — **carbonero, -ra** *adj* : coal — **carbonizar** {21} *vt* : char — **carbono** *nm* : carbon — **carburador** *nm* : carburetor — **carburante** *nm* : fuel

carcajada *nf* : loud laugh, guffaw

cárcel *nf* : jail, prison — **carcelero, -ra** *n* : jailer

carcinógeno *nm* : carcinogen

carcomer *vt* : eat away at — **carcomido, -da** *adj* : worm-eaten

cardenal *nm* 1 : cardinal 2 CONTUSIÓN : bruise

cardíaco *or* **cardiaco, -ca** *adj* : cardiac, heart

cárdigan *nm, pl* **-gans** : cardigan

cardinal *adj* : cardinal

cardiólogo, -ga *n* : cardiologist

cardo *nm* : thistle

carear *vt* : bring face-to-face

carecer {53} *vi* ~ **de** : lack — **carencia** *nf* : lack, want — **carente** *adj* ~ **de** : lacking (in)

carestía *nf* 1 : high cost 2 ESCASEZ : dearth, scarcity

careta *nf* : mask

cargada *nf* : joke

cargar {52} *vt* 1 : load 2 : charge (a battery,

a purchase, etc.) **3** LLEVAR : carry **4** ~ **de** : burden with — *vi* **1** : load **2** ~ **con** : pick up, carry away — **carga** *nf* **1** : load **2** CARGAMENTO : freight, cargo **3** RESPONSABILIDAD : burden **4** : charge (in electricity, etc.) — **cargado, -da** *adj* **1** : loaded, burdened **2** PESADO : heavy, stuffy **3** : charged (of a battery) **4** FUERTE : strong, concentrated — **cargamento** *nm* : cargo, load — **cargo** *nm* **1** : charge **2** PUESTO : position, office

cariarse *vr* : decay (of teeth)

caribe *adj* : Caribbean

caricatura *nf* **1** : caricature **2** : (political) cartoon — **caricaturizar** *vt* : caricature

caricia *nf* : caress

caridad *nf* **1** : charity **2** LIMOSNA : alms *pl*

caries *nfs & pl* : cavity (in a tooth)

cariño *nm* : affection, love — **cariñoso, -sa** *adj* : affectionate, loving

carisma *nf* : charisma — **carismático, -ca** *adj* : charismatic

caritativo, -va *adj* : charitable

cariz *nm, pl* **-rices** : appearance, aspect

carmesí *adj & nm* : crimson

carmín *nm, pl* **-mines** *or* ~ **de labios** : lipstick

carnada *nf* : bait

carnal *adj* **1** : carnal **2** primo ~ : first cousin

carnaval *nm* : carnival

carne *nf* **1** : meat **2** : flesh (of persons or fruits) **3** ~ **de cerdo** : pork **4** ~ **de gallina** : goose bumps **5** ~ **de ternera** : veal

carné *nm* → **carnet**

carnero *nm* **1** : ram, sheep **2** : mutton (in cooking)

carnet *nm* **1** ~ **de conducir** : driver's license **2** ~ **de identidad** : identification card, ID

carnicería *nf* **1** : butcher shop **2** MATANZA : slaughter — **carnicero, -ra** *n* : butcher

carnívoro, -ra *adj* : carnivorous — **carnívoro** *nm* : carnivore

carnoso, -sa *adj* : fleshy

caro, -ra *adj* **1** : expensive **2** QUERIDO : dear — **caro** *adv* : dearly

carpa *nf* **1** : carp **2** TIENDA : tent

carpeta *nf* : folder

carpintería *nf* : carpentry — **carpintero, -ra** *n* : carpenter

carraspear *vi* : clear one's throat — **carraspera** *nf* **1** : hoarseness **2** tener ~ : have a frog in one's throat

carrera *nf* **1** : running, run **2** COMPETICIÓN : race **3** : course (of studies) **4** PROFESIÓN : career, profession

carreta *nf* : cart, wagon

carrete *nm* : reel, spool

carretera *nf* : highway, road

carretilla *nf* : wheelbarrow

carril *nm* **1** : lane (of a road) **2** : rail (for a railroad)

carrillo *nm* : cheek

carrito *nm* : cart, trolley

carrizo *nm* : reed

carro *nm* **1** : wagon, cart **2** *Lat* : automobile, car — **carrocería** *nf* : body (of an automobile)

carroña *nf* : carrion

carroza *nf* **1** : carriage **2** : float (in a parade)

carruaje *nm* : carriage

carrusel *nm* : merry-go-round, carousel

carta *nf* **1** : letter **2** NAIPE : playing card **3** : charter (of an organization, etc.) **4** MENÚ : menu **5** MAPA : map, chart

cartel *nm* : poster, bill — **cartelera** *nf* : billboard

cartera *nf* **1** : briefcase **2** BILLETERA : wallet **3** *Lat* : pocketbook, handbag — **carterista** *nmf* : pickpocket

cartero, -ra *nm* : mail carrier, mailman *m*

cartílago *nm* : cartilage

cartilla *nf* **1** : primer, reader **2** : booklet, record (of a savings account, etc.)

cartón *nm, pl* **-tones** **1** : cardboard **2** : carton (of cigarettes, etc.)

cartucho *nm* : cartridge

casa *nf* **1** : house **2** HOGAR : home **3** EMPRESA : company, firm **4** ~ **flotante** : houseboat

casar *vt* : marry — *vi* : go together, match up — **casarse** *vr* **1** : get married **2** ~ **con** : marry — **casado, -da** *adj* : married — **casamiento** *nm* **1** : marriage **2** BODA : wedding

cascabel *nm* : small bell

cascada *nf* : waterfall

cascanueces *nms & pl* : nutcracker

cascar {72} *vt* : crack (a shell, etc.) — **cascarse** *vr* : crack, chip — **cáscara** *nf* : skin, peel, shell — **cascarón** *nm, pl* **-rones** : eggshell

casco *nm* **1** : helmet **2** : hull (of a boat) **3** : hoof (of a horse) **4** : fragment (of ceramics, etc.) **5** : center (of a town) **6** ENVASE : empty bottle

caserío *nm* **1** *Spain* : country house **2** POBLADO : hamlet

casero, -ra *adj* **1** : homemade **2** DOMÉSTICO : domestic, household — ~ *n* : landlord, landlady *f*

caseta *nf* : booth, stall

casete → **cassette**

casi *adv* **1** : almost, nearly **2** (*in negative phrases*) : hardly

casilla *nf* **1** : compartment, pigeonhole **2** CASETA : booth **3** : box (on a form)

casino *nm* **1** : casino **2** : (social) club

caso *nm* **1** : case **2** en ~ **de** : in the event

of **3 hacer** ~ : pay attention **4 no venir al** ~ : be beside the point

caspa *nf* : dandruff

casquete *nm* **1** : skullcap **2 casquete glaciar** : ice cap **3 casquete polar** : polar ice cap **4 casquete corto** : crew cut

cassette *nmf* : cassette

casta *nf* **1** : lineage, descent **2** : breed (of animals) **3** : caste (in India)

castaña *nf* : chestnut

castañetear *vi* : chatter (of teeth)

castaño, -ña *adj* : chestnut (color)

castañuela *nf* : castanet

castellano *nm* : Spanish, Castilian (language)

castidad *nf* : chastity

castigar {52} *vt* **1** : punish **2** : penalize (in sports) — **castigo** *nm* **1** : punishment **2** : penalty (in sports)

castillo *nm* : castle

casto, -ta *adj* : chaste, pure — **castizo, -za** *adj* : pure, traditional (in style)

castor *nm* : beaver

castrar *vt* : castrate

castrense *adj* : military

casual *adj* : chance, accidental — **casualidad** *nf* **1** : coincidence **2 por** ~ *or* **de** ~ : by chance — **casualmente** *adv* : by chance

cataclismo *nm* : cataclysm

catalán, -lana *adj, mpl* **-lanes** : Catalan — **catalán** *nm* : Catalan (language)

catalizador *nm* : catalyst

catalogar {52} *vt* : catalog, classify — **catálogo** *nm* : catalog

catapulta *nf* : catapult

catar *vt* : taste, sample

catarata *nf* **1** : waterfall **2** : cataract (in medicine)

catarro *nm* RESFRIADO : cold

catástrofe *nf* : catastrophe, disaster — **catastrófico, -ca** *adj* : catastrophic, disastrous

catecismo *nm* : catechism

cátedra *nf* : chair (at a university)

catedral *nf* : cathedral

catedrático, -ca *n* : professor

categoría *nf* **1** : category **2** RANGO : rank **3 de** ~ : first-rate — **categórico, -ca** *adj* : categorical

católico, -ca *adj & n* : Catholic — **catolicismo** *nm* : Catholicism

catorce *adj & nm* : fourteen — **catorceavo** *nm* : fourteenth

catre *nm* : cot

cauce *nm* **1** : riverbed **2** VÍA : channel, means *pl*

caucho *nm* : rubber

caución *nf, pl* **-ciones** : security, guarantee

caudal *nm* **1** : volume of water, flow **2** RIQUEZA : wealth

caudillo *nm* : leader, commander

causar *vt* : cause, provoke — **causa** *nf* **1** : cause **2** RAZÓN : reason **3** : case (in law) **4 a** ~ **de** : because of

cáustico, -ca *adj* : caustic

cautela *nf* : caution — **cauteloso, -sa** *adj* : cautious — **cautelosamente** *adv* : cautiously, warily

cautivar *vt* **1** : capture **2** ENCANTAR : captivate — **cautiverio** *nm* : captivity — **cautivo, -va** *adj & n* : captive

cauto, -ta *adj* : cautious

cavar *v* : dig

caverna *nf* : cavern, cave

cavidad *nf* : cavity

cavilar *vi* : ponder

cayado *nm* : crook, staff

cazar {21} *vt* **1** : hunt **2** ATRAPAR : catch, bag — *vi* : go hunting — **caza** *nf* **1** : hunt, hunting **2** : game (animals) — **cazador, -dora** *n* : hunter

cazo *nm* **1** : saucepan **2** CUCHARÓN : ladle — **cazuela** *nf* : casserole

CD *nm* : CD, compact disc

cebada *nf* : barley

cebar *vt* **1** : bait **2** : feed, fatten (animals) **3** : prime (a firearm, etc.) — **cebo** *nm* **1** CARNADA : bait **2** : charge (of a firearm)

cebolla *nf* : onion — **cebolleta** *nf* : scallion, green onion — **cebollino** *nm* : chive

cebra *nf* : zebra

cecear *vi* : lisp — **ceceo** *nm* : lisp

cedazo *nm* : sieve

ceder *vi* **1** : yield, give way **2** DISMINUIR : diminish, abate — *vt* : cede, hand over

cedro *nm* : cedar

cédula *nf* : document, certificate

cegar {49} *vt* **1** : blind **2** TAPAR : block, stop up — *vi* : be blinded, go blind — **ceguera** *nf* : blindness

ceja *nf* : eyebrow

cejar *vi* : give in, back down

celada *nf* : trap, ambush

celador, -dora *n* : guard, warden

celda *nf* : cell (of a jail)

celebrar *vt* **1** : celebrate **2** : hold (a meeting), say (Mass) **3** ALEGRARSE DE : be happy about — **celebrarse** *vr* : take place — **celebración** *nf, pl* **-ciones** : celebration — **célebre** *adj* : famous, celebrated — **celebridad** *nf* : celebrity

celeridad *nf* : swiftness, speed

celeste *adj* **1** : celestial, heavenly **2** *or* **azul** ~ : sky blue — **celestial** *adj* : celestial, heavenly

celibato *nm* : celibacy — **célibe** *adj* : celibate

celo *nm* **1** : zeal **2 en** ~ : in heat **3** ~**s** *nmpl* : jealousy **4 tener** ~**s** : be jealous

celofán *nm, pl* **-fanes** : cellophane
celoso, -sa *adj* **1** : jealous **2** DILIGENTE : zealous
célula *nf* : cell
celular¹ *adj* : cellular
celular² *nm* : cell phone
celulitis *nf* : cellulite
celulosa *nf* : cellulose
cementerio *nm* : cemetery
cemento *nm* **1** : cement **2** ~ **armado** : reinforced concrete
cena *nf* : supper, dinner
cenagal *nm* : bog, quagmire — **cenagoso** *adj* : swampy
cenar *vi* : have dinner, have supper — *vt* : have for dinner or supper
cenicero *nm* : ashtray
cenit *nm* : zenith
ceniza *nf* : ash
censo *nm* : census
censurar *vt* **1** : censor **2** REPROBAR : censure, criticize — **censura** *nf* **1** : censorship **2** REPROBACIÓN : censure, criticism
centavo *nm* **1** : cent **2** : centavo (unit of currency)
centellear *vi* : sparkle, twinkle — **centella** *nf* **1** : flash **2** CHISPA : spark — **centelleo** *nm* : twinkling, sparkle
centenar *nm* : hundred — **centenario** *nm* : centennial
centeno *nm* : rye
centésimo, -ma *adj* : hundredth
centígrado *adj* : centigrade, Celsius
centigramo *nm* : centigram
centímetro *nm* : centimeter
centinela *nmf* : sentinel, sentry
central *adj* : central — ~ *nf* : main office, headquarters — **centralita** *nf* : switchboard — **centralizar** {21} *vt* : centralize
centrar *vt* : center — **centrarse** *vr* ~ **en** : focus on — **céntrico, -ca** *adj* : central — **centro** *nm* **1** : center **2** : downtown (of a city) **3** ~ **de mesa** : centerpiece
centroamericano, -na *adj* : Central American
ceñir {67} *vt* **1** : encircle **2** : fit (s.o.) tightly — **ceñirse** *vr* ~ **a** : limit oneself to — **ceñido, -da** *adj* : tight
ceño *nm* **1** : frown **2 fruncir el** ~ : knit one's brow, frown
cepillo *nm* **1** : brush **2** : (carpenter's) plane **3** ~ **de dientes** : toothbrush — **cepillar** *vt* **1** : brush **2** : plane (wood)
cera *nf* **1** : wax, beeswax **2** : floor wax, furniture wax
cerámica *nf* **1** : ceramics *pl* **2** : (piece of) pottery
cerca¹ *nf* : fence — **cercado** *nm* : enclosure
cerca² *adv* **1** : close, near **2** ~ **de** : near,

close to **3** ~ **de** : nearly, almost — **cercano, -na** *adj* : near, close — **cercanía** *nf* **1** : proximity **2** ~**s** *nfpl* : outskirts
cercar {72} *vt* **1** : fence in **2** RODEAR : surround
cerciorarse *vr* ~ **de** : make sure of
cerco *nm* **1** : circle, ring **2** ASEDIO : siege **3** *Lat* : fence
cerda *nf* : bristle
cerdo *nm* **1** : pig, hog **2** ~ **macho** : boar
cereal *adj & nm* : cereal
cerebro *nm* : brain — **cerebral** *adj* : cerebral
ceremonia *nf* : ceremony — **ceremonial** *adj* : ceremonial — **ceremonioso, -sa** *adj* : ceremonious
cereza *nf* : cherry
cerilla *nf* : match — **cerillo** *nm Lat* : match
cerner {56} *or* **cernir** *vt* : sift — **cernerse** *vr* **1** : hover **2** ~ **sobre** : loom over — **cernidor** *nm* : sieve
cero *nm* : zero
cerrar {55} *vt* **1** : close, shut **2** : turn off (a faucet, etc.) **3** : bring to an end — *vi* **1** : close up, lock up **2** : close down (a business, etc.) — **cerrarse** *vr* **1** : close, shut **2** TERMINAR : come to a close, end — **cerrado, -da** *adj* **1** : closed, shut, locked **2** : overcast (of weather) **3** : sharp (of a curve) **4** : thick, broad (of an accent) — **cerradura** *nf* : lock — **cerrajero, -ra** *n* : locksmith
cerro *nm* : hill
cerrojo *nm* : bolt, latch
certamen *nm, pl* **-támenes** : competition, contest
certero, -ra *adj* : accurate, precise
certeza *nf* : certainty — **certidumbre** *nf* : certainty
certificar {72} *vt* **1** : certify **2** : register (mail) — **certificado, -da** *adj* : certified, registered — **certificado** *nm* : certificate
cervato *nm* : fawn
cerveza *nf* **1** : beer **2** ~ **de barril** : draft beer — **cervecería** *nf* **1** : brewery **2** BAR : beer hall, bar
cesar *vi* : cease, stop — *vt* : dismiss, lay off — **cesación** *nf, pl* **-ciones** : cessation, suspension — **cesante** *adj* **1** : laid off **2** *Lat* : unemployed — **cesantía** *nf Lat* : unemployment
cesárea *nf* : cesarean (section)
cese *nm* **1** : cessation, stop **2** DESTITUCIÓN : dismissal
césped *nm* : lawn, grass
cesta *nf* : basket — **cesto** *nm* **1** : (large) basket **2** ~ **de basura** : wastebasket
cetro *nm* : scepter
chabacano *nm Lat* : apricot
chabola *nf Spain* : shack, shanty
chacal *nm* : jackal

cháchara *nf fam* : gabbing, chatter
chacra *nf Lat* : (small) farm
chafar *vt fam* : flatten, crush
chal *nm* : shawl
chaleco *nm* : vest
chalet *nm Spain* : house
chalupa *nf* **1** : small boat **2** *Lat* : small stuffed tortilla
chamarra *nf* : jacket
chamba *nf Lat fam* : job
champaña *or* **champán** *nm* : champagne
champiñón *nm, pl* **-ñones** : mushroom
champú *nm, pl* **-pús** *or* **-púes** : shampoo
chamuscar {72} *vt* : scorch
chance *nm Lat* : chance, opportunity
chancho *nm Lat* : pig
chanclos *nmpl* : galoshes
chantaje *nm* : blackmail — **chantajear** *vt* : blackmail
chanza *nf* : joke, jest
chapa *nf* **1** : sheet, plate **2** INSIGNIA : badge — **chapado, -da** *adj* **1** : plated **2 chapado a la antigua** : old-fashioned
chaparrón *nm, pl* **-rrones** : downpour
chapotear *vi* : splash
chapucero, -ra *adj* : shoddy, sloppy — **chapuza** *nf* : botched job
chapuzón *nm, pl* **-zones** : dip, short swim
chaqueta *nf* : jacket
charca *nf* : pond — **charco** *nm* : puddle
charlar *vi* : chat — **charla** *nf* : chat, talk — **charlatán, -tana** *adj, mpl* **-tanes** : talkative — ∼ *n* **1** : chatterbox **2** FARSANTE : charlatan
charol *nm* **1** : patent leather **2** BARNIZ : varnish
chasco *nm* **1** : trick, joke **2** DECEPCIÓN : disappointment
chasis *nms & pl* : chassis
chasquear *vt* **1** : click (the tongue), snap (one's fingers) **2** : crack (a whip) — **chasquido** *nm* **1** : click, snap **2** : crack (of a whip)
chat *nm, pl* **chats** : chat room
chatarra *nf* : scrap (metal)
chato, -ta *adj* **1** : pug-nosed **2** APLANADO : flat
chauvinismo *nm* : chauvinism — **chauvinista** *adj* : chauvinist, chauvinistic
chaval, -vala *n fam* : kid, boy *m*, girl *f*
checo, -ca *adj* : Czech — **checo** *nm* : Czech (language)
chef *nm* : chef
cheque *nm* : check — **chequera** *nf* : checkbook
chequear *vt Lat* **1** : check, inspect, verify **2** : check in (baggage) — **chequeo** *nm* **1** : (medical) checkup **2** *Lat* : check, inspection
chica → **chico**

chicano, -na *adj* : Chicano, Mexican-American
chícharo *nm Lat* : pea
chicharrón *nm, pl* **-rrones** : pork rind
chichón *nm, pl* **-chones** : bump
chicle *nm* : chewing gum
chico, -ca *adj* : little, small — ∼ *n* : child, boy *m*, girl *f*
chiflar *vt* : whistle at, boo — *vi Lat* : whistle — **chiflado, -da** *adj fam* : crazy, nuts — **chiflido** *nm* : whistling
chile *nm* : chili pepper
chileno, -na *adj* : Chilean
chillar *vi* **1** : shriek, scream **2** CHIRRIAR : screech, squeal — **chillido** *nm* **1** : scream **2** CHIRRIDO : screech, squeal — **chillón, -llona** *adj, mpl* **-llones** : shrill, loud
chimenea *nf* **1** : chimney **2** HOGAR : fireplace
chimpancé *nm* : chimpanzee
chinche *nf* : bedbug
chino, -na *adj* : Chinese — **chino** *nm* : Chinese (language)
chiquillo, -lla *n* : kid, child
chiquito, -ta *adj* : tiny — ∼ *n* : little child, tot
chiribita *nf* : spark
chiripa *nf* **1** : fluke **2 de** ∼ : by sheer luck
chirivía *nf* : parsnip
chirriar {85} *vi* **1** : squeak, creak **2** : screech (of brakes, etc.) — **chirrido** *nm* **1** : squeak, creak **2** : screech (of brakes)
chisme *nm* : (piece of) gossip — **chismear** *vi* : gossip — **chismoso, -sa** *adj* : gossipy — ∼ *n* : gossip
chispear *vi* : spark — **chispa** *nf* : spark
chisporrotear *vi* : crackle, sizzle — **chisporroteo** *nm* : crackle
chiste *nm* : joke, funny story — **chistoso, -sa** *adj* : funny, witty
chivo, -va *n* : kid, young goat
chocar {72} *vi* **1** : crash, collide **2** ENFRENTARSE : clash — **chocante** *adj* **1** : striking, shocking **2** *Lat* : unpleasant, rude
choclo *nm Lat* : ear of corn, corncob
chocolate *nm* : chocolate
chofer *or* **chófer** *nm* **1** : chauffeur **2** CONDUCTOR : driver
choque *nm* **1** : shock **2** : crash, collision (of vehicles) **3** CONFLICTO : clash
chorizo *nm* : chorizo, sausage
chorrear *vi* **1** : drip **2** BROTAR : pour out, gush — **chorro** *nm* **1** : stream, jet **2** HILO : trickle
chovinismo → **chauvinismo**
choza *nf* : hut, shack
chubasco *nm* : downpour, squall
chuchería *nf* **1** : knickknack, trinket **2** DULCE : sweet

chueco, -ca adj Lat : crooked
chuleta nf : cutlet, chop
chulo, -la adj fam : cute, pretty
chupar vt 1 : suck 2 ABSORBER : absorb 3 fam : guzzle — vi : suckle — chupada nf : suck, sucking — chupete nm 1 : pacifier 2 Lat : lollipop
churro nm 1 : fried dough 2 fam : botch, mess
chusco, -ca adj : funny
chusma nf : riffraff, rabble
chutar vi : shoot (in soccer)
cianuro nm : cyanide
ciber- pref : cyber-
cicatriz nf, pl -trices : scar — cicatrizar {21} vi : form a scar, heal
cíclico, -ca adj : cyclical
ciclismo nm : cycling — ciclista nmf : cyclist
ciclo nm : cycle
ciclón nm, pl -clones : cyclone
ciego, -ga adj : blind — ciegamente adv : blindly
cielo nm 1 : sky 2 : heaven (in religion)
ciempiés nms & pl : centipede
cien adj : a hundred, hundred — ~ nm : one hundred
ciénaga nf : swamp, bog
ciencia nf 1 : science 2 a ~ cierta : for a fact
cieno nm : mire, mud, silt
científico, -ca adj : scientific — ~ n : scientist
ciento adj (used in compound numbers) : one hundred — ~ nm 1 : hundred, group of a hundred 2 por ~ : percent
cierre nm 1 : closing, closure 2 BROCHE : fastener, clasp
cierto, -ta adj 1 : true 2 SEGURO : certain 3 por ~ : as a matter of fact
ciervo, -va n : deer, stag m, hind f
cifra nf 1 : number, figure 2 : sum (of money, etc.) 3 CLAVE : code, cipher — cifrar vt 1 : write in code 2 ~ la esperanza en : pin all one's hopes on
cigarrillo nm : cigarrette — cigarro nm 1 : cigarette 2 PURO : cigar
cigüeña nf : stork
cilantro nm : cilantro, coriander
cilindro nm : cylinder — cilíndrico, -ca adj : cylindrical
cima nf : peak, summit
címbalo nm : cymbal
cimbrar or cimbrear vt : shake, rock — cimbrarse or cimbrearse vr : sway
cimentar {55} vt 1 : lay the foundation of 2 : cement, strengthen (relations, etc.) — cimientos nmpl : base, foundation(s)
cinc nm : zinc

cincel nm : chisel — cincelar vt : chisel
cinco adj & nm : five
cincuenta adj & nm : fifty — cincuentavo, -va adj : fiftieth — cincuentavo nm : fiftieth
cine nm : cinema, movies pl — cinematográfico, -ca adj : movie, film
cínico, -ca adj : cynical — ~ n : cynic — cinismo nm : cynicism
cinta nf 1 : ribbon, band 2 ~ adhesiva : adhesive tape 3 ~ métrica : tape measure 4 ~ magnetofónica : magnetic tape
cinto nm : belt, girdle — cintura nf : waist — cinturón nm, pl -rones 1 : belt 2 ~ de seguridad : seat belt
ciprés nm, pl -preses : cypress
circo nm : circus
circuito nm : circuit
circulación nf, pl -ciones 1 : circulation 2 TRÁFICO : traffic — circular vi 1 : circulate 2 : drive (a vehicle) — ~ adj : circular
círculo nm : circle
circuncidar vt : circumcise — circuncisión nf, pl -siones : circumcision
circundar vt : surround
circunferencia nf : circumference
circunscribir {33} vt : confine, limit — circunscribirse vr ~ a : limit oneself to — circunscripción nf, pl -ciones : district, constituency
circunspecto, -ta adj : circumspect, cautious
circunstancia nf : circumstance — circunstancial adj : chance — circunstante nmf 1 : bystander 2 los ~s : those present
circunvalación nf, pl -ciones 1 : encircling 2 carretera de ~ : bypass
cirio nm : candle
ciruela nf 1 : plum 2 ~ pasa : prune
cirugía nf : surgery — cirujano, -na n : surgeon
cisma nf : schism
cisne nm : swan
cisterna nf : cistern
cita nf 1 : appointment, date 2 REFERENCIA : quote, quotation — citación nf, pl -ciones : summons — citar vt 1 : quote, cite 2 CONVOCAR : make an appointment with 3 : summon (in law) — citarse vr ~ con : arrange to meet
cítrico nm : citrus (fruit)
ciudad nf : city, town — ciudadano, -na n 1 : citizen 2 HABITANTE : resident — ciudadanía nf : citizenship
cívico, -ca adj : civic
civil adj : civil — ~ nmf : civilian — civilidad nf : civility — civilización nf, pl -cio-

nes : civilization — **civilizar** {21} *vt* : civilize

cizaña *nf* : discord, rift

clamar *vi* : clamor, cry out — **clamor** *nm* : clamor, outcry — **clamoroso, -sa** *adj* : clamorous, loud

clan *nm* : clan

clandestino, -na *adj* : clandestine, secret

clara *nf* : egg white

claraboya *nf* : skylight

claramente *adv* : clearly

clarear *v impers* **1** : dawn **2** ACLARAR : clear up — *vi* : be transparent

claridad *nf* **1** : clarity, clearness **2** LUZ : light

clarificar {72} *vt* : clarify — **clarificación** *nf, pl* **-ciones** : clarification

clarín *nm, pl* **-rines** : bugle

clarinete *nm* : clarinet

clarividente *adj* **1** : clairvoyant **2** PERSPICAZ : perspicacious — **clarividencia** *nf* **1** : clairvoyance **2** PERSPICACIA : farsightedness

claro *adv* **1** : clearly **2** POR SUPUESTO : of course, surely — ~ *nm* **1** : clearing, glade **2** ~ **de luna** : moonlight — **claro, -ra** *adj* **1** : clear, bright **2** : light (of colors) **3** EVIDENTE : clear, evident

clase *nf* **1** : class **2** TIPO : sort, kind

clásico, -ca *adj* : classic, classical — **clásico** *nm* : classic

clasificar {72} *vt* **1** : classify, sort out **2** : rate, rank (a hotel, a team, etc.) — **clasificarse** *vr* : qualify (in competitions) — **clasificación** *nf, pl* **-ciones** **1** : classification **2** : league (in sports)

claudicar {72} *vi* : back down

claustro *nm* : cloister

claustrofobia *nf* : claustrophobia — **claustrofóbico, -ca** *adj* : claustrophobic

cláusula *nf* : clause

clausurar *vt* : close (down) — **clausura** *nf* : closure, closing

clavada *nf* : slam dunk (in basketball)

clavado *nm Lat* : dive

clavar *vt* **1** : nail, hammer **2** HINCAR : drive in, plunge

clave *nf* **1** CIFRA : code **2** SOLUCIÓN : key **3** : clef (in music) — ~ *adj* : key

clavel *nm* : carnation

clavicémbalo *nm* : harpsichord

clavícula *nf* : collarbone

clavija *nf* **1** : peg, pin **2** : (electric) plug

clavo *nm* **1** : nail **2** : clove (spice)

claxon *nm, pl* **cláxones** : horn (of an automobile)

clemencia *nf* : clemency, mercy — **clemente** *adj* : merciful

clerical *adj* : clerical — **clérigo, -ga** *n* : clergyman, cleric — **clero** *nm* : clergy

clic *nm, pl* **clics** : click (**haz clic aquí** click here) (**doble clic** double click)

cliché *nm* **1** : cliché **2** : negative (of a photograph)

cliente, -ta *n* : customer, client — **clientela** *nf* : clientele, customers *pl*

clima *nm* **1** : climate **2** AMBIENTE : atmosphere — **climático, -ca** *adj* : climatic

climatizar {21} *vt* : air-condition — **climatizado, -da** *adj* : air-conditioned

clímax *nm* : climax

clinch *nm* : clinch (in boxing)

clínica *nf* : clinic — **clínico, -ca** *adj* : clinical

clip *nm, pl* **clips** : (paper) clip

cloaca *nf* : sewer

clon *nm* : clone

clonar *vt* : clone

cloquear *vi* : cluck — **cloqueo** *nm* : cluck, clucking

cloro *nm* : chlorine

clóset *nm Lat, pl* **clósets** : (built-in) closet, cupboard

club *nm* : club

coacción *nf, pl* **-ciones** : coercion — **coaccionar** *vt* : coerce

coagular *v* : clot, coagulate — **coagularse** *vr* : coagulate — **coágulo** *nm* : clot

coalición *nf, pl* **-ciones** : coalition

coartada *nf* : alibi

coartar *vt* : restrict, limit

cobarde *nmf* : coward — ~ *adj* : cowardly — **cobardía** *nf* : cowardice

cobaya *nf* : guinea pig

cobertizo *nm* : shelter, shed

cobertor *nm* : bedspread

cobertura *nf* **1** : cover **2** : coverage (of news, etc.)

cobijar *vt* : shelter — **cobijarse** *vr* : take shelter — **cobija** *nf Lat* : blanket — **cobijo** *nm* : shelter

cobra *nf* : cobra

cobrar *vt* **1** : charge, collect **2** : earn (a salary, etc.) **3** ADQUERIR : acquire, gain **4** : cash (a check) — *vi* : be paid — **cobrador, -dora** *n* **1** : collector **2** : conductor (of a bus, etc.)

cobre *nm* : copper

cobro *nm* : collection (of money), cashing (of a check)

cocaína *nf* : cocaine

cocción *nf, pl* **-ciones** : cooking

cocear *vi* : kick

cocer {14} *vt* **1** : cook **2** HERVIR : boil

coche *nm* **1** : car, automobile **2** : coach (of a train) **3** *or* ~ **de caballos** : carriage **4** ~ **fúnebre** : hearse — **cochecito** *nm* : baby carriage, stroller — **cochera** *nf* : garage, carport

cochino, -na *n* : pig, hog — ~ *adj fam* : dirty, filthy — **cochinada** *nf fam* : dirty thing — **cochinillo** *nm* : piglet

cocido, -da *adj* **1** : boiled, cooked **2 bien** ~ : well-done — **cocido** *nm* : stew

cociente *nm* : quotient

cocina *nf* **1** : kitchen **2** : (kitchen) stove **3** : (art of) cooking, cuisine — **cocinar** *v* : cook — **cocinero, -ra** *n* : cook, chef

coco *nm* : coconut

cocodrilo *nm* : crocodile

coctel *or* **cóctel** *nm* **1** : cocktail **2** FIESTA : cocktail party

codazo *nm* **1** : nudge **2 dar un** ~ **a** : elbow, nudge

codicia *nf* : greed — **codiciar** *vt* : covet — **codicioso, -sa** *adj* : covetous, greedy

código *nm* **1** : code **2** ~ **postal** : zip code **3** ~ **morse** : Morse code

codo *nm* : elbow

codorniz *nf, pl* **-nices** : quail

coexistir *vi* : coexist

cofre *nm* : chest, coffer

coger {15} *vt* **1** : take (hold of) **2** ATRAPAR : catch **3** : pick up (from the ground) **4** : pick (fruit, etc.) — **cogerse** *vr* : hold on

cohechar *vt* : bribe — **cohecho** *nm* : bribe, bribery

coherencia *nf* : coherence — **coherente** *adj* : coherent — **cohesión** *nf, pl* **-siones** : cohesion

cohete *nm* : rocket

cohibir {62} *vt* **1** : restrict **2** : inhibit (a person) — **cohibirse** *vr* : feel inhibited — **cohibido, -da** *adj* : inhibited, shy

coincidir *vi* **1** : coincide **2** ~ **con** : agree with — **coincidencia** *nf* : coincidence

cojear *vi* **1** : limp **2** : wobble (of furniture, etc.) — **cojera** *nf* : limp

cojín *nm, pl* **-jines** : cushion — **cojinete** *nm* **1** : pad, cushion **2** : bearing (of a machine)

cojo, -ja *adj* **1** : lame **2** : wobbly (of furniture) — ~ *n* : lame person

col *nf* **1** : cabbage **2** ~ **de Bruselas** : Brussels sprout

cola *nf* **1** : tail **2** FILA : line (of people) **3** : end (of a line) **4** PEGAMENTO : glue **5** ~ **de caballo** : ponytail

colaborar *vi* : collaborate — **colaboración** *nf, pl* **-ciones** : collaboration — **colaborador, -dora** *n* **1** : collaborator **2** : contributor (to a periodical)

colada *nf Spain* **1** : laundry **2 hacer la** ~ : do the washing

colador *nm* : colander, strainer

colapso *nm* : collapse

colar {19} *vt* : strain, filter — **colarse** *vr* : sneak in, gate-crash

colcha *nf* : bedspread, quilt — **colchón** *nm, pl* **-chones** : mattress — **colchoneta** *nf* : mat

colear *vi* : wag its tail

colección *nf, pl* **-ciones** : collection — **coleccionar** *vt* : collect — **coleccionista** *nmf* : collector — **colecta** *nf* : collection (of donations)

colectividad *nf* : community — **colectivo, -va** *adj* : collective — **colectivo** *nm* **1** : collective **2** *Lat* : city bus

colector *nm* : sewer

colega *nmf* : colleague

colegio *nm* **1** : school **2** : (professional) college — **colegial, -giala** *n* : schoolboy *m*, schoolgirl *f*

colegir {28} *vt* : gather

cólera *nm* : cholera — ~ *nf* : anger, rage — **colérico, -ca** *adj* **1** : bad-tempered **2** FURIOSO : angry

colesterol *nm* : cholesterol

coleta *nf* : pigtail

colgar {16} *vt* **1** : hang **2** : hang up (a telephone) **3** : hang out (laundry) — *vi* : hang up — **colgante** *adj* : hanging — ~ *nm* : pendant

colibrí *nm* : hummingbird

cólico *nm* : colic

coliflor *nf* : cauliflower

colilla *nf* : (cigarette) butt

colina *nf* : hill

colindar *vi* ~ **con** : be adjacent to — **colindante** *adj* : adjacent

coliseo *nm* : coliseum

colisión *nf, pl* **-siones** : collision — **colisionar** *vi* ~ **contra** : collide with

collar *nm* **1** : necklace **2** : collar (for pets)

colmar *vt* **1** : fill to the brim **2** : fulfill (a wish, etc.) **3** ~ **de** : shower with — **colmado, -da** *adj* : heaping

colmena *nf* : beehive

colmillo *nm* **1** : canine (tooth) **2** : fang (of a dog, etc.), tusk (of an elephant)

colmo *nm* **1** : height, limit **2 ¡eso es el** ~ ! : that's the last straw!

colocar {72} *vt* **1** PONER : place, put **2** : find a job for — **colocarse** *vr* **1** SITUARSE : position oneself **2** : get a job — **colocación** *nf, pl* **-ciones** **1** : placement, placing **2** EMPLEO : position, job

colombiano, -na *adj* : Colombian

colon *nm* : (intestinal) colon

colonia *nf* **1** : colony **2** PERFUME : cologne **3** *Lat* : residential area — **colonial** *adj* : colonial — **colonizar** {21} *vt* : colonize — **colonización** *nf, pl* **-ciones** : colonization — **colono, -na** *n* : settler, colonist

coloquial *adj* : colloquial — **coloquio** *nm* **1** : talk, discussion **2** CONGRESO : conference

color *nm* : color — **colorado, -da** *adj* : red
— **colorear** *vt* : color — **colorete** *nm*
: rouge — **colorido** *nm* : colors *pl*, coloring
colosal *adj* : colossal
columna *nf* **1** : column **2** ～ **vertebral**
: spine, backbone — **columnista** *nmf* : columnist
columpiar *vt* : push (on a swing) — **columpiarse** *vr* : swing — **columpio** *nm* : swing
coma[1] *nm* : coma
coma[2] *nf* : comma
comadre *nf* **1** : godmother of one's child, mother of one's godchild **2** *fam* : (female) friend — **comadrear** *vi fam* : gossip
comadreja *nf* : weasel
comadrona *nf* : midwife
comandancia *nf* : command headquarters, command — **comandante** *nmf* **1** : commander **2** : major (in the military) — **comando** *nm* **1** : commando **2** *Lat* : command
comarca *nf* : region, area
combar *vt* : bend, curve
combatir *vt* : combat, fight against — *vi*
: fight — **combate** *nm* **1** : combat **2** : fight (in boxing) — **combatiente** *nmf* : combatant, fighter
combinar *vt* **1** : combine **2** : put together, match (colors, etc.) — **combinarse** *vr* : get together — **combinación** *nf, pl* **-ciones 1** : combination **2** : connection (in travel)
combustible *nm* : fuel — ～ *adj* : combustible — **combustión** *nf, pl* **-tiones** : combustion
comedia *nf* : comedy
comedido, -da *adj* : moderate
comedor *nm* : dining room
comensal *nmf* : diner, dinner guest
comentar *vt* **1** : comment on, discuss **2** MENCIONAR : mention — **comentario** *nm* **1** : comment, remark **2** ANÁLISIS : commentary — **comentarista** *nmf* : commentator
comenzar {29} *v* : begin, start
comer *vt* **1** : eat **2** *fam* : eat up, eat into — *vi*
1 : eat **2** CENAR : have a meal **3 dar de** ～
: feed — **comerse** *vr* : eat up
comercio *nm* **1** : commerce, trade **2** NEGOCIO : business — **comercial** *adj* : commercial — **comercializar** {21} *vt* : market — **comerciante** *nmf* : merchant, dealer — **comerciar** *vi* : do business, trade
comestible *adj* : edible — **comestibles** *nmpl* : groceries, food
cometa *nm* : comet — ～ *nf* : kite
cometer *vt* **1** : commit **2** ～ **un error** : make a mistake — **cometido** *nm* : assignment, task
comezón *nf, pl* **-zones** : itchiness, itching

comicios *nmpl* : elections
cómico, -ca *adj* : comic, comical — ～ *n* : comic, comedian
comida *nf* **1** ALIMENTO : food **2** *Spain* : lunch **3** *Lat* : dinner **4 tres** ～**s al día** : three meals a day
comienzo *nm* : beginning
comillas *nfpl* : quotation marks
comino *nm* : cumin
comisario, -ria *n* : commissioner — **comisaría** *nf* : police station
comisión *nf, pl* **-siones 1** : commission **2** COMITÉ : committee
comité *nm* : committee
como *conj* **1** : as, since **2 sí** : if — ～ *prep* **1** : like, as **2 así** ～ : as well as — ～ *adv* **1** : as **2** APROXIMADAMENTE : around, about
cómo *adv* **1** : how **2** ～ **no** : by all means **3** ¿～ **te llamas?** : what's your name?
cómoda *nf* : chest of drawers
comodidad *nf* : comfort, convenience
comodín *nm, pl* **-dines** : joker (in playing cards)
cómodo, -da *adj* **1** : comfortable **2** ÚTIL : handy, convenient
comoquiera *adv* **1** : in any way **2** ～ **que** : however
compacto, -ta *adj* : compact
compadecer {53} *vt* : feel sorry for — **compadecerse** *vr* ～ **de** : take pity on
compadre *nm* **1** : godfather of one's child, father of one's godchild **2** *fam* : buddy
compañero, -ra *n* : companion, partner — **compañerismo** *nm* : companionship
compañía *nf* : company
comparar *vt* : compare — **comparable** *adj* : comparable — **comparación** *nf, pl* **-ciones** : comparison — **comparativo, -va** *adj* : comparative
comparecencia *nf* **1** : appearance (in court) **2 orden de comparecencia** : subpoena, summons
comparecer *vt* : appear (before a court, etc.)
compartimiento *or* **compartimento** *nm* : compartment
compartir *vt* : share
compás *nm, pl* **-pases 1** : compass **2** : rhythm, time (in music)
compasión *nf, pl* **-siones** : compassion, pity — **compasivo, -va** *adj* : compassionate
compatible *adj* : compatible — **compatibilidad** *nf* : compatibility
compatriota *nmf* : compatriot, fellow countryman
compeler *vt* : compel
compendiar *vt* : summarize — **compendio** *nm* : summary
compensar *vt* : compensate for — **compensación** *nf, pl* **-ciones** : compensation

competir

competir {54} *vi* : compete — **competencia** *nf* **1** : competition, rivalry **2** CAPACIDAD : competence — **competente** *adj* : competent — **competición** *nf, pl* **-ciones** : competition — **competidor, -dora** *n* : competitor

compilar *vt* : compile

compinche *nmf fam* : friend, chum

complacer {57} *vt* : please — **complacerse** *vr* ~ **en** : take pleasure in — **complaciente** *adj* : obliging, helpful

complejidad *nf* : complexity — **complejo, -ja** *adj* : complex — **complejo** *nm* : complex

complementar *vt* : complement — **complementario, -ria** *adj* : complementary — **complemento** *nm* **1** : complement **2** : object (in grammar)

completar *vt* : complete — **completo, -ta** *adj* **1** : complete **2** PERFECTO : perfect **3** LLENO : full — **completamente** *adv* : completely

complexión *nf, pl* **-xiones** : constitution, build

complicar {72} *vt* **1** : complicate **2** IMPLICAR : involve — **complicación** *nf, pl* **-ciones** : complication — **complicado, -da** *adj* : complicated, complex

cómplice *nmf* : accomplice — ~ *adj* : conspiratorial, knowing

complot *nm, pl* **-plots** : conspiracy, plot

componer {60} *vt* **1** : make up, compose **2** : compose, write (a song) **3** ARREGLAR : fix, repair — **componerse** *vr* ~ **de** : consist of — **componente** *adj & nm* : component, constituent

comportarse *vr* : behave — **comportamiento** *nm* : behavior

composición *nf, pl* **-ciones** : composition — **compositor, -tora** *n* : composer, songwriter

compostura *nf* **1** : composure **2** REPARACIÓN : repair

comprar *vt* : buy, purchase — **compra** *nf* **1** : purchase **2 ir de** ~**s** : go shopping — **comprador, -dora** *n* : buyer, shopper

comprender *vt* **1** : comprehend, understand **2** ABARCAR : cover, include — **comprensible** *adj* : understandable — **comprensión** *nf, pl* **-siones** : understanding — **comprensivo, -va** *adj* : understanding

compresa *nf* **1** : compress **2** *or* ~ **higiénica** : sanitary napkin

compresión *nf, pl* **-siones** : compression — **comprimido** *nm* : pill, tablet — **comprimir** *vt* : compress

comprobar {19} *vt* **1** VERIFICAR : check **2** DEMOSTRAR : prove — **comprobación** *nf, pl* **-ciones** : verification, check — **compro-**

bante *nm* **1** : proof **2** RECIBO : receipt, voucher

comprometer *vt* **1** : compromise **2** ARRIESGAR : jeopardize **3** OBLIGAR : commit, put under obligation — **comprometerse** *vr* **1** : commit oneself **2** ~ **con** : get engaged to — **comprometedor, -dora** *adj* : compromising — **comprometido, -da** *adj* **1** : compromising, awkward **2** : engaged (to be married) — **compromiso** *nm* **1** : obligation, commitment **2** : (marriage) engagement **3** ACUERDO : agreement **4** APURO : awkward situation

compuesto, -ta *adj* **1** : compound **2** ~ **de** : made up of, consisting of — **compuesto** *nm* : compound

compulsivo, -va *adj* : compelling, urgent

computar *vt* : compute, calculate — **computadora** *nf or* **computador** *nm* **1** : computer **2** ~ **portátil** : laptop computer — **cómputo** *nm* : calculation

comulgar {52} *vi* : receive Communion

común *adj, pl* **-munes 1** : common **2** ~ **y corriente** : ordinary **3 por lo** ~ : generally

comuna *nf* : commune — **comunal** *adj* : communal

comunicar {72} *vt* : communicate — **comunicarse** *vr* **1** : communicate **2** ~ **con** : get in touch with — **comunicación** *nf, pl* **-ciones** : communication — **comunicado** *nm* : communiqué — **comunicativo, -va** *adj* : communicative

comunidad *nf* : community

comunión *nf, pl* **-niones** : communion, Communion

comunismo *nm* : Communism — **comunista** *adj & nmf* : Communist

con *prep* **1** : with **2** A PESAR DE : in spite of **3** (*before an infinitive*) : by **4** ~ **(tal) que** : so long as

cóncavo, -va *adj* : concave

concebir {54} *v* : conceive — **concebible** *adj* : conceivable

conceder *vt* **1** : grant, bestow **2** ADMITIR : concede

concejal, -jala *n* : councilman, alderman

concentrar *vt* : concentrate — **concentrarse** *vr* : concentrate — **concentración** *nf, pl* **-ciones** : concentration

concepción *nf, pl* **-ciones** : conception — **concepto** *nm* **1** : concept **2** OPINIÓN : opinion

concernir {17} *vi* ~ **a** : concern — **concerniente** *adj* ~ **a** : concerning

concertar {55} *vt* **1** : arrange, coordinate **2** (*used before an infinitive*) : agree **3** : harmonize (in music) — *vi* : be in harmony

concesión *nf, pl* **-siones 1** : concession **2** : awarding (of prizes, etc.)

concha *nf* : shell

conciencia *nf* **1** : conscience **2** CONO-CIMIENTO : consciousness, awareness — **concientizar** {21} *vt Lat* : make aware — **concientizarse** *vr Lat* ~ **de** : realize

concienzudo, -da *adj* : conscientious

concierto *nm* **1** : concert **2** : concerto (musical composition)

conciliar *vt* : reconcile — **conciliación** *nf, pl* **-ciones** : reconciliation

concilio *nm* : council

conciso, -sa *adj* : concise

conciudadano, -na *n* : fellow citizen

concluir {41} *vt* : conclude — *vi* : come to an end — **conclusión** *nf, pl* **-siones** : conclusion — **concluyente** *adj* : conclusive

concordar {19} *vi* : agree — *vt* : reconcile — **concordancia** *nf* : agreement — **concordia** *nf* : harmony, concord

concretar *vt* : make concrete, specify — **concretarse** *vr* : become definite, take shape — **concreto, -ta** *adj* **1** : concrete **2** DETERMINADO : specific **3 en** ~ : specifically — **concreto** *nm Lat* : concrete

concurrir *vi* **1** : come together, meet **2** ~ **a** : take part in — **concurrencia** *nf* : audience, turnout — **concurrido, -da** *adj* : busy, crowded

concursar *vi* : compete, participate — **concursante** *nmf* : competitor — **concurso** *nm* **1** : competition **2** CONCURRENCIA : gathering **3** AYUDA : help, cooperation

condado *nm* : county

conde, -desa *n* : count *m*, countess *f*

condenar *vt* **1** : condemn, damn **2** : sentence (a criminal) — **condena** *nf* **1** : condemnation **2** SENTENCIA : sentence — **condenación** *nf, pl* **-ciones** : condemnation, damnation

condensar *vt* : condense — **condensación** *nf, pl* **-ciones** : condensation

condesa *nf* → **conde**

condescender {56} *vi* **1** : acquiesce, agree **2** ~ **a** : condescend to — **condescendiente** *adj* : condescending

condición *nf, pl* **-ciones** **1** : condition, state **2** CALIDAD : capacity, position — **condicional** *adj* : conditional

condimento *nm* : condiment, seasoning

condolerse {47} *vr* : sympathize — **condolencia** *nf* : condolence

condominio *nm* **1** : joint ownership **2** *Lat* : condominium

condón *nm, pl* **-dones** : condom

conducir {61} *vt* **1** DIRIGIR : direct, lead **2** MANEJAR : drive — *vi* **1** : drive **2** ~ **a** : lead to — **conducirse** *vr* : behave

conducta *nf* : behavior, conduct

conducto *nm* : conduit, duct

conductor, -tora *n* : driver

conectar *vt* **1** : connect **2** ENCHUFAR : plug in — *vi* : connect

conejo, -ja *n* : rabbit — **conejera** *nf* : (rabbit) hutch

conexión *nf, pl* **-xiones** : connection — **conexo, -xa** *adj* : connected

confabularse *vr* : conspire, plot

confeccionar *vt* : make (up), prepare — **confección** *nf, pl* **-ciones** **1** : making, preparation **2** : tailoring, dressmaking

confederación *nf, pl* **-ciones** : confederation

conferencia *nf* **1** : lecture **2** REUNIÓN : conference

conferir {76} *vt* : confer, bestow

confesar {55} *v* : confess — **confesarse** *vr* : go to confession — **confesión** *nf, pl* **-siones** **1** : confession **2** CREDO : religion, creed

confeti *nm* : confetti

confianza *nf* **1** : trust (**de poca confianza** untrustworthy) **2** : confidence, self-confidence

confiar {85} *vi* : trust — *vt* : entrust — **confiable** *adj* : trustworthy, reliable — **confiado, -da** *adj* **1** : confident **2** CRÉDULO : trusting

confidencia *nf* : confidence, secret — **confidencial** *adj* : confidential — **confidencialidad** *nf* : confidentiality — **confidente** *nmf* **1** : confidant, confidante *f* **2** : (police) informer

configuración *nf, pl* **-ciones** : configuration, shape

confín *nm, pl* **-fines** : boundary, limit — **confinar** *vt* **1** : confine **2** DESTERRER : exile

confirmar *vt* : confirm — **confirmación** *nf, pl* **-ciones** : confirmation

confiscar {72} *vt* : confiscate

confitería *nm* : candy store

confitura *nf* : jam

conflagración *nf, pl* **-ciones** **1** : war, conflict **2** INCENDIO : fire

conflicto *nm* : conflict

confluencia *nf* : junction, confluence

conformar *vt* : shape, make up — **conformarse** *vr* **1** RESIGNARSE : resign oneself **2** ~ **con** : content oneself with — **conforme** *adj* **1** : content, satisfied **2** ~ **a** : in accordance with — ~ *conj* : as — **conformidad** *nf* **1** : agreement **2** RESIGNACIÓN : resignation

confortar *vt* : comfort — **confortable** *adj* : comfortable

confrontar *vt* **1** : confront **2** COMPARAR : compare — *vi* : border — **confrontarse** *vr* ~ **con** : face up to — **confrontación** *nf, pl* **-ciones** : confrontation

confundir *vt* : confuse, mix up — **confun-**

dirse *vr* : make a mistake, be confused —
confusión *nf*, *pl* **-siones** : confusion —
confuso, -sa *adj* **1** : confused **2** INDISTINTO
: hazy, indistinct — **congelar** *vt* : freeze —
congelarse *vr* : freeze — **congelación** *nf*,
pl **-ciones** : freezing — **congelado, -da** *adj*
: frozen — **congelador** *nm* : freezer
congeniar *vi* : get along
congestión *nf*, *pl* **-tiones** : congestion —
congestionado, -da *adj* : congested
congoja *nf* : anguish, grief
congraciarse *vr* : ingratiate oneself
congratular *vt* : congratulate
congregar {52} *vt* : bring together — **congregarse** *vr* : congregate — **congregación**
nf, *pl* **-ciones** : congregation, gathering
congreso *nm* : congress — **congresista**
nmf : member of congress
conjeturar *vt* : guess, conjecture — **conjetura** *nf* : guess, conjecture
conjugar {52} *vt* : conjugate — **conjugación** *nf*, *pl* **-ciones** : conjugation
conjunción *nf*, *pl* **-ciones** : conjunction
conjunto, -ta *adj* : joint — **conjunto** *nm* **1**
: collection **2** : outfit (of clothing) **3** GRUPO
: band **4 en ~** : as a whole
conjurar *vt* : ward off — *vi* : conspire, plot
conllevar *vt* : entail
conmemorar *vt* : commemorate — **conmemoración** *nf*, *pl* **-ciones** : commemoration — **conmemorativo, -va** *adj* : com-
memorative
conmigo *pron* : with me
conminar *vt* : threaten
conmiseración *nf*, *pl* **-ciones** : pity, commi-
seration
conmocionar *vt* : shock — **conmoción** *nf*,
pl **-ciones** **1** : shock, upheaval **2** *or* **~
cerebral** : concussion
conmover {47} *vt* **1** : move, touch **2** SACU-
DIR : shake (up) — **conmoverse** *vr* : be
moved — **conmovedor, -dora** *adj* : moving, touching
conmutador *nm* **1** : (electric) switch **2** *Lat*
: switchboard
cono *nm* : cone
conocer {18} *vt* **1** : know **2** : meet (a person), get to know (a city, etc.) **3** RECONO-
CER : recognize — **conocerse** *vr* **1** : meet,
get to know each other **2** : know oneself —
conocedor, -dora *adj* & *n* : expert — **conocido, -da** *adj* : well-known — **~** *n* : acquaintance — **conocimiento** *nm* **1**
: knowledge **2** SENTIDO : consciousness
conque *conj* : so
conquistar *vt* : conquer — **conquista** *nf*
: conquest — **conquistador, -dora** *adj*
: conquering — **conquistador** *nm* : conqueror

consabido, -da *adj* **1** : well-known **2** HABI-
TUEL : usual
consagrar *vt* **1** : consecrate **2** DEDICAR : devote — **consagración** *nf*, *pl* **-ciones** : consecration
consciencia *nf* → **conciencia** — **consciente** *adj* : conscious, aware
consecución *nf*, *pl* **-ciones** : attainment
consecuencia *nf* **1** : consequence **2 en ~**
: accordingly — **consecuente** *adj* : consistent
consecutivo, -va *adj* : consecutive
conseguir {75} *vt* **1** : get, obtain **2 ~
hacer algo** : manage to do sth
consejo *nm* **1** : advice, counsel **2** : council
(assembly) — **consejero, -ra** *n* : adviser,
counselor
consenso *nm* : consensus
consentir {76} *vt* **1** : allow, permit **2** MIMAR
: pamper, spoil — *vi* : consent — **consenti-
miento** *nm* : consent, permission
conserje *nmf* : caretaker, janitor
conservar *vt* **1** : preserve **2** GUARDAR
: keep, conserve — **conservarse** *vr* : keep
— **conserva** *nf* **1** : preserve(s) **2 ~s** *nfpl*
: canned goods — **conservación** *nf*, *pl*
-ciones : conservation, preservation —
conservador, -dora *adj* & *n* : conservative
— **conservatorio** *nm* : conservatory
considerar *vt* **1** : consider **2** RESPETAR : respect — **considerable** *adj* : considerable
— **consideración** *nf*, *pl* **-ciones** **1** : consideración **2** RESPETO : respect — **considerado, -da** *adj* **1** : considerate **2** RESPETADO
: respected
consigna *nf* **1** ESLOGAN : slogan **2** ORDEN
: orders **3** : checkroom (for baggage)
consigo *pron* : with her, with him, with you,
with oneself
consiguiente *adj* **1** : consequent **2 por ~**
: consequently
consistir *vi* **~ en** **1** : consist of **2** : lie in,
consist in — **consistencia** *nf* : consistency
— **consistente** *adj* **1** : firm, solid **2 ~ en**
: consisting of
consolar {19} *vt* : console, comfort — **consolarse** *vr* : console oneself — **consolación** *nf*, *pl* **-ciones** : consolation
consolidar *vt* : consolidate — **consolidación** *nf*, *pl* **-ciones** : consolidation
consomé *nm* : consommé
consonante *adj* : consonant, harmonious —
~ *nf* : consonant
consorcio *nm* : consortium
conspirar *vi* : conspire, plot — **conspiración** *nf*, *pl* **-ciones** : conspiracy — **conspi-
rador, -dora** *n* : conspirator
constancia *nf* **1** : record, evidence **2** PERSE-
VERANCIA : perseverance — **constante** *adj*

: constant — **constantemente** *adv* : constantly, continually

constar *vi* **1** : be evident, be clear **2** ~ **de** : consist of

constatar *vt* **1** : verify **2** AFIRMAR : state, affirm

constelación *nf, pl* **-ciones** : constellation

consternación *nf, pl* **-ciones** : consternation

constipado, -da *adj* estar ~ : have a cold — **constipado** *nm* : cold — **constiparse** *vr* : catch a cold

constituir {41} *vt* **1** FORMAR : constitute, form **2** FUNDAR : establish, set up — **constituirse** *vr* ~ **en** : set oneself up as — **constitución** *nf, pl* **-ciones** : constitution — **constitucional** *adj* : constitutional — **constitutivo, -va** *adj* : constituent — **constituyente** *adj & nm* : constituent

constreñir {67} *vt* **1** : force, compel **2** RESTRINGIR : restrict, limit

construir {41} *vt* : build, construct — **construcción** *nf, pl* **-ciones** : construction, building — **constructivo, -va** *adj* : constructive — **constructor, -tora** *n* : builder

consuelo *nm* : consolation, comfort

consuetudinario, -ria *adj* : customary

cónsul *nmf* : consul — **consulado** *nm* : consulate

consultar *vt* : consult — **consulta** *nf* : consultation — **consultor, -tora** *n* : consultant — **consultorio** *nm* : office (of a doctor or dentist)

consumar *vt* **1** : consummate, complete **2** : commit (a crime)

consumir *vt* : consume — **consumirse** *vr* : waste away — **consumición** *nf, pl* **-ciones 1** : consumption **2** : drink (in a restaurant) — **consumido, -da** *adj* : thin, emaciated — **consumidor, -dora** *n* : consumer — **consumo** *nm* : consumption

consumismo *nm* : consumerism

contabilidad *nf* **1** : accounting, bookkeeping **2** : accountancy (profession) — **contable** *nmf Spain* : accountant, bookkeeper

contactar *vi* ~ **con** : get in touch with, contact — **contacto** *nm* : contact

contado, -da *adj* : numbered, few — **contado** *nm* **al** ~ : (in) cash

contador, -dora *n Lat* : accountant — **contador** *nm* : meter

contagiar *vt* **1** : infect **2** : transmit (a disease) — **contagiarse** *vr* **1** : be contagious **2** : become infected (with a disease) — **contagio** *nm* : contagion, infection — **contagioso, -sa** *adj* : contagious, infectious

contaminar *vt* : contaminate, pollute — **contaminación** *nf, pl* **-ciones** : contamination, pollution

contar {19} *vt* **1** : count **2** NARRAR : tell — *vi* **1** : count **2** ~ **con** : rely on, count on

contemplar *vt* **1** MIRAR : look at, behold **2** CONSIDERAR : contemplate — **contemplación** *nf, pl* **-ciones** : contemplation

contemporáneo, -nea *adj & n* : contemporary

contender {56} *vi* : contend, compete — **contendiente** *nmf* : competitor

contener {80} *vt* **1** : contain **2** RESTRINGIR : restrain, hold back — **contenerse** *vr* : restrain oneself — **contenedor** *nm* : container — **contenido, -da** *adj* : restrained — **contenido** *nm* : contents *pl*

contentar *vt* : please, make happy — **contentarse** *vr* ~ **con** : be satisfied with — **contento, -ta** *adj* : glad, happy, contented

contestar *vt* : answer — *vi* : reply, answer back — **contestación** *nf, pl* **-ciones** : answer, reply

contexto *nm* : context

contienda *nf* **1** COMBATE : dispute, fight **2** COMPETICIÓN : contest

contigo *pron* : with you

contiguo, -gua *adj* : adjacent

continente *nm* : continent — **continental** *adj* : continental

contingencia *nf* : contingency — **contingente** *adj & nm* : contingent

continuar {3} *v* : continue — **continuación** *nf, pl* **-ciones 1** : continuation **2** **a** ~ : next, then — **continuidad** *nf* : continuity — **continuo, -nua** *adj* **1** : continuous, steady **2** FRECUENTE : continual

contorno *nm* **1** : outline **2** ~**s** *nmpl* : surrounding area

contorsión *nf, pl* **-siones** : contortion

contra *prep* **1** : against **2 en** ~ : against — ~ *nm* **los pros y los** ~**s** : the pros and cons

contraatacar {72} *v* : counterattack — **contraataque** *nm* : counterattack

contrabajo *nm* : double bass

contrabalancear *vt* : counterbalance

contrabandista *nmf* : smuggler — **contrabando** *nm* **1** : smuggling **2** : contraband (goods)

contracción *nf, pl* **-ciones** : contraction

contrachapado *nm* : plywood

contradecir {11} *vt* : contradict — **contradicción** *nf, pl* **-ciones** : contradiction — **contradictorio, -ria** *adj* : contradictory

contraer {81} *vt* **1** : contract **2** ~ **matrimonio** : get married — **contraerse** *vr* : contract, tighten up

contrafuerte *nm* : buttress

contragolpe *nm* : backlash

contralto *nmf* : contralto

contrapartida *nf* : compensation

contrapelo: **a** ~ *adv phr* : the wrong way

contrapeso *nm* : counterbalance
contraponer {60} *vt* **1** : counter, oppose **2**
COMPARAR : compare
contraproducente *adj* : counterproductive
contrariar {85} *vt* **1** : oppose **2** MOLESTAR
: vex, annoy — **contrariedad** *nf* **1** : obstacle **2** DISGUSTO : annoyance — **contrario,**
-ria *adj* **1** OPUESTO : opposite **2 al contra-**
rio : on the contrary **3 ser ~ a** : be opposed
to
contrarrestar *vt* : counteract
contrasentido *nm* : contradiction (in terms)
contraseña *nf* : password
contrastar *vt* **1** : check, verify **2** RESISTIR
: resist — *vi* : contrast — **contraste** *nm*
: contrast
contratar *vt* **1** : contract for **2** : hire, engage
(workers)
contratiempo *nm* **1** : mishap **2** DIFICULTAD
: setback
contrato *nm* : contract — **contratista** *nmf*
: contractor
contraventana *nf* : shutter
contribuir {41} *vi* **1** : contribute **2** : pay
taxes — **contribución** *nf, pl* **-ciones 1**
: contribution **2** IMPUESTO : tax — **contri-**
buyente *nmf* **1** : contributor **2** : taxpayer
contrincante *nmf* : opponent
contrito, -ta *adj* : contrite
controlar *vt* **1** : control **2** COMPROBAR : monitor, check — **control** *nm* **1** : control **2**
VERIFICACIÓN : inspection, check — **con-**
trolador, -dora *n* : controller
controversia *nf* : controversy
contundente *adj* **1** : blunt **2** : forceful, convincing (of arguments, etc.)
contusión *nf, pl* **-siones** : bruise
convalecencia *nf* : convalescence — **con-**
valeciente *adj* & *nmf* : convalescent
convencer {86} *vt* : convince, persuade —
convencerse *vr* : be convinced — **conven-**
cimiento *nm* : conviction, belief
convención *nf, pl* **-ciones** : convention —
convencional *adj* : conventional
convenir {87} *vi* **1** : be suitable, be advisable **2 ~ en** : agree on — **conveniencia** *nf*
1 : convenience **2** : suitability (of an action,
etc.) — **conveniente** *adj* **1** : convenient **2**
ACONSEJABLE : suitable, advisable **3** PRO-
VECHOSO : useful — **convenio** *nm* : agreement, pact
convento *nm* : convent, monastery
converger {15} *or* **convergir** *vi* : converge
conversar *vi* : converse, talk — **conversa-**
ción *nf, pl* **-ciones** : conversation
conversatorio *nm* : talk, discussion
conversión *nf, pl* **-siones** : conversion —
converso, -sa *n* : convert
convertir {76} *vt* : convert — **convertirse**

vr ~ **en** : turn into — **convertible** *adj* &
nm : convertible
convexo, -xa *adj* : convex
convicción *nf, pl* **-ciones** : conviction —
convicto, -ta *adj* : convicted
convidar *vt* : invite — **convidado, -da** *n*
: guest
convincente *adj* : convincing
convite *nm* **1** : invitation **2** : banquet
convivir *vi* : live together — **convivencia** *nf*
: coexistence, living together
convocar {72} *vt* : convoke, call together
convulsión *nf, pl* **-siones 1** : convulsion **2**
TRASTORNO : upheaval — **convulsivo, -va**
adj : convulsive
conyugal *adj* : conjugal — **cónyuge** *nmf*
: spouse, partner
coñac *nm* : cognac, brandy
cooperar *vi* : cooperate — **cooperación** *nf,*
pl **-ciones** : cooperation — **cooperativa** *nf*
: cooperative, co-op — **cooperativo, -va**
adj : cooperative
coordenada *nf* : coordinate
coordinar *vt* : coordinate — **coordinación**
nf, pl **-ciones** : coordination — **coordina-**
dor, -dora *n* : coordinator
copa *nf* **1** : glass, goblet **2** : cup (in sports)
3 tomar una ~ : have a drink
copia *nf* : copy — **copiar** *vt* : copy
copioso, -sa *adj* : copious, abundant
copla *nf* **1** : (popular) song **2** ESTROFA
: verse, stanza
copo *nm* **1** : flake **2** *or* **~ de nieve** : snowflake
coquetear *vi* : flirt — **coqueteo** *nm* : flirt-
ing, flirtation — **coqueto, -ta** *adj* : flirtatious — **~** *n* : flirt
coraje *nm* **1** : valor, courage **2** IRA : anger
coral[1] *nm* : coral
coral[2] *adj* : choral — **~** *nf* : choir, chorale
Corán *nm* **el ~** : the Koran
coraza *nf* **1** : armor plating **2** : shell
corazón *nm, pl* **-zones 1** : heart **2** : core (of
fruit) **3 mi ~** : my darling — **corazonada**
nf **1** : hunch **2** IMPULSO : impulse
corbata *nf* : tie, necktie
corchete *nm* **1** : hook and eye, clasp **2**
: square bracket (punctuation mark)
corcho *nm* : cork
cordel *nm* : cord, string
cordero *nm* : lamb
cordial *adj* : cordial — **cordialidad** *nf* : cor-
diality
cordillera *nf* : mountain range
córdoba *nf* : córdoba (Nicaraguan unit of
currency)
cordón *nm, pl* **-dones 1** : cord **2 ~ poli-**
cial : (police) cordon **3 cordones** *nmpl*
: shoelaces
cordura *nf* : sanity

corear *vt* : chant
coreografía *nf* : choreography
cornamenta *nf* : antlers *pl*
corneta *nf* : bugle
coro *nm* **1** : chorus **2** : (church) choir
corona *nf* **1** : crown **2** : wreath, garland (of flowers) — **coronación** *nf, pl* **-ciones** : coronation — **coronar** *vt* : crown
coronel *nm* : colonel
coronilla *nf* **1** : crown (of the head) **2 estar hasta la ~** : be fed up
corporación *nf, pl* **-ciones** : corporation
corporal *adj* : corporal, bodily
corporativo, -va *adj* : corporate
corpulento, -ta *adj* : stout
corral *nm* **1** : farmyard **2** : pen, corral (for animals) **3** *or* **corralito** : playpen
correa *nf* **1** : strap, belt **2** : leash (for a dog, etc.)
corrección *nf, pl* **-ciones** **1** : correction **2** : correctness, propriety (of manners) — **correccional** *nm* : reformatory — **correctivo, -va** *adj* : corrective — **correcto, -ta** *adj* **1** : correct, right **2** CORTÉS : polite
corredizo, -za *adj* : sliding
corredor, -dora *n* **1** : runner, racer **2** AGENTE : agent, broker — **corredor** *nm* : corridor, hallway
corregir {28} *vt* : correct — **corregirse** *vr* : mend one's ways
correlación *nf, pl* **-ciones** : correlation
correo *nm* **1** : mail **2 ~ aéreo** : airmail
correr *vi* **1** : run, race **2** : flow (of a river, etc.) **3** : pass (of time) — *vt* **1** : run **2** RECORRER : travel over, cover **3** : draw (curtains) — **correrse** *vr* **1** : move along **2** : run (of colors)
corresponder *vi* **1** : correspond **2** PERTENECER : belong **3** ENCAJAR : fit **4 ~ a** : reciprocate, repay — **corresponderse** *vr* : write to each other — **correspondencia** *nf* **1** : correspondence **2** : connection (of a train, etc.) — **correspondiente** *adj* : corresponding, respective — **corresponsal** *nmf* : correspondent
corretear *vi* : run about, scamper
corrida *nf* **1** : run **2** *or* **~ de toros** : bullfight — **corrido, -da** *adj* **1** : straight, continuous **2** *fam* : worldly
corriente *adj* **1** : current **2** NORMAL : common, ordinary **3** : running (of water, etc.) — **~** *nf* **1** : current (of water, electricity, etc.), draft (of air) **2** TENDENCIA : tendency, trend — **~** *nm* **al ~ 1** : up-to-date **2** ENTERADO : aware, informed
corrillo *nm* : clique, circle — **corro** *nm* : ring, circle (of people)
corroborar *vt* : corroborate
corroer {69} *vt* **1** : corrode (of metals) **2**

: erode, wear away — **corroerse** *vr* : corrode
corromper *vt* **1** : corrupt **2** PUDRIR : rot — **corrompido, -da** *adj* : corrupt
corrosión *nf, pl* **-siones** : corrosion — **corrosivo, -va** *adj* : corrosive
corrupción *nf, pl* **-ciones** **1** : corruption **2** DESCOMPOSICIÓN : decay, rot — **corrupto, -ta** *adj* : corrupt
corsé *nm* : corset
cortar *vt* **1** : cut **2** RECORTAR : cut out **3** QUITAR : cut off — *vi* : cut — **cortarse** *vr* **1** : cut oneself **2** : be cut off (on the telephone) **3** : curdle (of milk) **4 ~ el pelo** : have one's hair cut — **cortada** *nf Lat* : cut — **cortante** *adj* : cutting, sharp
cortauñas *nms & pl* : nail clippers
corte[1] *nm* **1** : cutting **2** ESTILO : cut, style **3 ~ de pelo** : haircut
corte[2] *nf* **1** : court **2 hacer la ~ a** : court, woo — **cortejar** *vt* : court, woo
cortejo *nm* **1** : entourage **2** NOVIAZGO : courtship **3 ~ fúnebre** : funeral procession
cortés *adj* : courteous, polite — **cortesía** *nf* : courtesy, politeness
corteza *nf* **1** : bark **2** : crust (of bread) **3** : rind, peel (of fruit)
cortina *nm* : curtain
corto, -ta *adj* **1** : short **2** ESCASO : scarce **3** *fam* : timid, shy **4 ~ de vista** : nearsighted — **cortocircuito** *nm* : short circuit
corvo, -va *adj* : curved, bent
cosa *nf* **1** : thing **2** ASUNTO : matter, affair **3 ~ de** : about **4 poca ~** : nothing much
cosechar *v* : harvest, reap — **cosecha** *nf* **1** : harvest, crop **2** : vintage (of wine)
coser *v* : sew
cosmético, -ca *adj* : cosmetic — **cosmético** *nm* : cosmetic
cósmico, -ca *adj* : cosmic
cosmopolita *adj* : cosmopolitan
cosmos *nm* : cosmos
cosquillas *nfpl* **1** : tickling **2 hacer ~** : tickle — **cosquilleo** *nm* : tickling sensation, tingle
costa *nf* **1** : coast, shore **2 a toda ~** : at any cost
costado *nm* **1** : side **2 al ~** : alongside
costar {19} *v* : cost
costarricense *or* **costarriqueño, -ña** *adj* : Costa Rican
coste *nm* → **costo** — **costear** *vt* : pay for
costero, -ra *adj* : coastal
costilla *nf* **1** : rib **2** CHULETA : chop, cutlet
costo *nm* : cost, price — **costoso, -sa** *adj* : costly
costra *nf* : scab
costumbre *nf* **1** : custom, habit **2 de ~** : usual

costura *nf* **1** : sewing, dressmaking **2** PUNTADAS : seam — **costurera** *nf* : dressmaker
cotejar *vt* : compare
cotidiano, -na *adj* : daily
cotizar {21} *vt* : quote, set a price on — **cotización** *nf, pl* **-ciones** : quotation, price — **cotizado, -da** *adj* : in demand
coto *nm* : enclosure, reserve
cotorra *nf* **1** : small parrot **2** *fam* : chatterbox — **cotorrear** *vi fam* : chatter, gab
coyote *nm* : coyote
coyuntura *nf* **1** : joint **2** SITUACIÓN : situation, moment
coz *nm, pl* **coces** : kick (of an animal)
cráneo *nf* : cranium, skull
cráter *nm* : crater
crear *vt* : create — **creación** *nf, pl* **-ciones** : creation — **creativo, -va** *adj* : creative — **creador, -dora** *n* : creator
crecer {53} *vi* **1** : grow **2** AUMENTAR : increase — **crecido, -da** *adj* **1** : full-grown **2** : large (of numbers) — **creciente** *adj* **1** : growing, increasing **2** : crescent (of the moon) — **crecimiento** *nm* **1** : growth **2** AUMENTO : increase
credenciales *nfpl* : credentials
credibilidad *nf* : credibility
crédito *nm* : credit
credo *nm* : creed
crédulo, -la *adj* : credulous, gullible
creer {20} *v* **1** : believe **2** SUPONER : suppose, think — **creerse** *vr* : regard oneself as — **creencia** *nf* : belief — **creíble** *adj* : believable, credible — **creído, -da** *adj fam* : conceited
crema *nf* : cream
cremación *nf, pl* **-ciones** : cremation
cremallera *nf* : zipper
cremoso, -sa *adj* : creamy
crepe *nmf* : crepe, pancake
crepitar *vi* : crackle
crepúsculo *nm* : twilight, dusk
crespo, -pa *adj* : curly, frizzy
crespón *nm, pl* **-pones** : crepe (fabric)
cresta *nf* **1** : crest **2** : comb (of a rooster)
cretino, -na *n* : cretin
creyente *nmf* : believer
criar {85} *vt* **1** : nurse (a baby) **2** EDUCAR : bring up, rear **3** : raise, breed (animals) — **cría** *nf* **1** : breeding, rearing **2** : young animal — **criadero** *nm* : farm, hatchery — **criado, -da** *n* : servant, maid *f* — **criador, -dora** *n* : breeder — **crianza** *nf* : upbringing, rearing
criatura *nf* **1** : creature **2** NIÑO : baby, child
crimen *nm, pl* **crímenes** : crime — **criminal** *adj & nmf* : criminal
críquet *nm* : cricket (game)
crin *nf* : mane
criollo, -lla *adj & n* : Creole

cripta *nf* : crypt
crisantemo *nm* : chrysanthemum
crisis *nf* **1** : crisis **2** ~ **nerviosa** : nervous breakdown
crispar *vt* **1** : tense (muscles), clench (one's fist) **2** IRRITAR : irritate, set on edge — **crisparse** *vr* : tense up
cristal *nm* **1** : crystal **2** VIDRIO : glass, piece of glass — **cristalería** *nf* : glassware — **cristalino, -na** *adj* : crystalline — **cristalino** *nm* : lens (of the eye) — **cristalizar** {21} *vi* : crystallize
cristiano, -na *adj & n* : Christian — **cristianismo** *nm* : Christianity — **Cristo** *nm* : Christ
criterio *nm* **1** : criterion **2** JUICIO : judgment, opinion
criticar {72} *vt* : criticize — **crítica** *nf* **1** : criticism **2** RESEÑA : review, critique — **crítico, -ca** *adj* : critical — ~ *n* : critic, reviewer
croar *vi* : croak
cromo *nm* : chromium, chrome
cromosoma *nm* : chromosome
crónica *nf* **1** : chronicle **2** : (news) report
crónico, -ca *adj* : chronic
cronista *nmf* : reporter, newscaster
cronología *nf* : chronology — **cronológico, -ca** *adj* : chronological
cronometrar *vt* : time, clock — **cronómetro** *nm* : chronometer, stopwatch
croqueta *nf* : croquette
croquis *nms & pl* : (rough) sketch
cruce *nm* **1** : crossing **2** : crossroads, intersection **3** ~ **peatonal** : crosswalk
crucero *nm* **1** : cruise **2** : cruiser (ship)
crucial *adj* : crucial
crucificar {72} *vt* : crucify — **crucifijo** *nm* : crucifix — **crucifixión** *nf, pl* **-fixiones** : crucifixion
crucigrama *nm* : crossword puzzle
crudo, -da *adj* **1** : harsh, crude **2** : raw (of food) — **crudo** *nm* : crude oil
cruel *adj* : cruel — **crueldad** *nf* : cruelty
crujir *vi* : rustle, creak, crackle, crunch — **crujido** *nm* : rustle, creak, crackle, crunch — **crujiente** *adj* : crunchy, crisp
cruzar {21} *vt* **1** : cross **2** : exchange (words) — **cruzarse** *vr* **1** : intersect **2** : pass each other — **cruz** *nf, pl* **cruces** : cross — **cruzada** *nf* : crusade — **cruzado, -da** *adj* : crossed — **cruzado** *nm* : crusader
cuaderno *nm* : notebook
cuadra *nf* **1** : stable **2** *Lat* : (city) block
cuadrado, -da *adj* : square — **cuadrado** *nm* : square
cuadragésimo, -ma *adj* : fortieth, forty- — ~ *n* : fortieth, forty- (in a series)
cuadrar *vi* **1** : conform, agree **2** : add up,

tally (numbers) — *vt* : square — **cuadrarse** *vr* : stand at attention

cuadrilátero *nm* **1** : quadrilateral **2** : ring (in sports)

cuadrilla *nf* : gang, group

cuadro *nm* **1** : square **2** PINTURA : painting **3** DESCRIPCIÓN : picture, description **4** : staff, management (of an organization) **5** CUADRADO : check, square **6** : (baseball) diamond

cuadrúpedo *nm* : quadruped

cuadruple *adj* : quadruple — **cuadruplicar** {72} *vt* : quadruple

cuajar *vi* **1** : curdle **2** COAGULAR : clot, coagulate **3** : set (of pudding, etc.) **4** AFIANZARSE : catch on — *vt* **1** : curdle **2** ~ **de** : fill with

cual *pron* **1** el ~, la ~, los ~es, las ~es : who, whom, which **2** lo ~ : which **3** cada ~ : everyone, everybody — ~ *prep* : like, as

cuál *pron* : which (one), what (one) — ~ *adj* : which, what

cualidad *nf* : quality, trait

cualquiera (**cualquier** *before nouns*) *adj, pl* **cualesquiera** : any, whatever — ~ *pron, pl* **cualesquiera** : anyone, whatever

cuán *adv* : how

cuando *conj* **1** : when **2** SI : since, if **3** ~ **más** : at the most **4 de vez en** ~ : from time to time — ~ *prep* : during, at the time of

cuándo *adv* **1** : when **2** ¿desde ~? : since when?

cuantía *nf* **1** : quantity, extent **2** IMPORTANCIA : importance — **cuantioso, -sa** *adj* : abundant, considerable

cuantificar {72} *vt* : quantify

cuanto *adv* **1** : as much as **2** ~ **antes** : as soon as possible **3 en** ~ : as soon as **4 en** ~ **a** : as for, as regards — **cuanto, -ta** *adj* : as many, whatever — ~ *pron* **1** : as much as, all that, everything **2 unos cuantos, unas cuantas** : a few

cuánto *adv* : how much, how many — **cuánto, -ta** *adj* : how much, how many — ~ *pron* : how much, how many

cuarenta *adj & nm* : forty — **cuarentavo, -va** *adj* : fortieth — **cuarentavo** *nm* : fortieth

cuarentena *nf* : quarantine

Cuaresma *nf* : Lent

cuartear *vt* : quarter, divide up — **cuartearse** *vr* : crack, split

cuartel *nm* **1** : barracks *pl* **2** ~ **general** : headquarters **3 no dar** ~ : show no mercy

cuarteto *nm* : quartet

cuarto, -ta *adj* : fourth — ~ *n* : fourth (in a series) — **cuarto** *nm* **1** : quarter, fourth **2** HABITACIÓN : room

cuarto oscuro *nm* : darkroom

cuarzo *nm* : quartz

cuatro *adj & nm* : four — **cuatrocientos, -tas** *adj* : four hundred — **cuatrocientos** *nms & pl* : four hundred

cuba *nf* : cask, barrel

cubano, -na *adj* : Cuban

cubeta *nf* **1** : keg, cask **2** *Lat* : pail, bucket

cúbico, -ca *adj* : cubic, cubed — **cubículo** *nm* : cubicle

cubierta *nf* **1** : cover, covering **2** : (automobile) tire **3** : deck (of a ship) — **cubierto** *nm* **1** : cutlery, place setting **2 a** ~ : under cover

cubo *nm* **1** : cube **2** *Spain* : pail, bucket **3** : hub (of a wheel)

cubrecama *nm* : bedspread

cubrir {2} *vt* : cover — **cubrirse** *vr* **1** : cover oneself **2** : cloud over

cucaracha *nf* : cockroach

cuchara *nf* : spoon — **cucharada** *nf* : spoonful — **cucharilla** *or* **cucharita** *nf* : teaspoon — **cucharón** *nm, pl* -rones : ladle

cuchichear *vi* : whisper — **cuchicheo** *nm* : whisper

cuchilla *nf* **1** : (kitchen) knife **2** ~ **de afeitar** : razor blade — **cuchillada** *nf* : stab, knife wound — **cuchillo** *nm* : knife

cuclillas *nfpl* **en** ~ : squatting, crouching

cuco *nm* : cuckoo — **cuco, -ca** *adj fam* : pretty, cute

cucurucho *nm* : ice-cream cone

cuello *nm* **1** : neck **2** : collar (of clothing)

cuenca *nf* **1** : river basin **2** : (eye) socket — **cuenco** *nm* **1** : bowl **2** CONCAVIDAD : hollow

cuenta *nf* **1** : calculation, count **2** : (bank) account **3** FACTURA : check, bill **4** : bead (for a necklace, etc.) **5 darse** ~ : realize **6 tener en** ~ : bear in mind

cuento *nm* **1** : story, tale **2** ~ **de hadas** : fairy tale

cuerda *nf* **1** : cord, rope, string **2** ~**s vocales** : vocal cords **3 dar** ~ **a** : wind up

cuerdo, -da *adj* : sane, sensible

cuerno *nm* **1** : horn **2** : antlers *pl* (of a deer)

cuero *nm* **1** : leather, hide **2** ~ **cabelludo** : scalp

cuerpo *nm* **1** : body **2** : corps (in the military, etc.)

cuervo *nm* : crow

cuesta *nf* **1** : slope **2 a** ~**s** : on one's back **3** ~ **abajo** : downhill **4** ~ **arriba** : uphill

cuestión *nf, pl* -tiones : matter, affair — **cuestionar** *vt* : question — **cuestionario** *nm* **1** : questionnaire **2** : quiz (in school)

cueva *nf* : cave

cuidar *vt* **1** : take care of, look after **2** : pay attention to (details, etc.) — *vi* **1** ~ **de** : look after **2** ~ **de que** : make sure that — **cuidarse** *vr* : take care of oneself — **cuidado** *nm* **1** : care **2** PREOCUPACIÓN : worry, concern **3 tener** ~ : be careful **4 ¡cuidado!** : watch out!, careful! — **cuidadoso, -sa** *adj* : careful — **cuidadosamente** *adv* : carefully

culata *nf* : butt (of a gun) — **culatazo** *nf* : kick, recoil

culebra *nf* : snake

culinario, -ria *adj* : culinary

culminar *vi* : culminate — **culminación** *nf, pl* **-ciones** : culmination

culo *nm fam* : backside, bottom

culpa *nf* **1** : fault, blame **2** PECADO : sin **3 echar la** ~ **a** : blame **4 tener la** ~ : be at fault — **culpabilidad** *nf* : guilt — **culpable** *adj* : guilty — ~ *nmf* : culprit, guilty party — **culpar** *vt* : blame

cultivar *vt* : cultivate — **cultivo** *nm* **1** : farming, cultivation **2** ~s : crops

culto, -ta *adj* : cultured, educated — **culto** *nm* **1** : worship **2** : (religious) cult — **cultura** *nf* : culture — **cultural** *adj* : cultural

culturismo *nm* : bodybuilding

cumbre *nf* : summit, top

cumpleaños *nms & pl* : birthday

cumplido, -da *adj* **1** : complete, full **2** CORTÉS : courteous — **cumplido** *nm* : compliment, courtesy

cumplimentar *vt* **1** : congratulate **2** CUMPLIR : carry out — **cumplimiento** *nm* : carrying out, performance

cumplir *vt* **1** : accomplish, carry out **2** : keep (a promise), observe (a law, etc.) **3** : reach (a given age) — *vi* **1** : expire, fall due **2** ~ **con el deber** : do one's duty — **cumplirse** *vr* **1** : expire **2** REALIZARSE : come true

cúmulo *nm* **1** : heap, pile **2** : cumulus (cloud)

cuna *nf* **1** : cradle **2** ORIGEN : birthplace

cundir *vi* **1** PROPAGARSE : spread, propagate **2** : go a long way

cuneta *nf* : ditch (in a road), gutter (in a street)

cuña *nf* : wedge

cuñado, -da *n* : brother-in-law *m*, sister-in-law *f*

cuota *nf* **1** : fee, dues **2** CUPO : quota **3** *Lat* : installment, payment

cupo *nm* **1** : quota, share **2** *Lat* : capacity, room

cupón *nm, pl* **-pones** : coupon

cúpula *nf* : dome, cupola

cura *nf* : cure, treatment — ~ *nm* : priest — **curación** *nf, pl* **-ciones** : healing — **curar** *vt* **1** : cure **2** : dress (a wound) **3** CURTIR : tan (hides) — **curarse** *vr* : get well

curiosear *vi* **1** : snoop, pry **2** : browse (in a store) — *vt* : look over — **curiosidad** *nf* : curiosity — **curioso, -sa** *adj* **1** : curious, inquisitive **2** RARO : unusual, strange

currículum *nm, pl* **-lums** *or* **currículo** *nm* : résumé, curriculum vitae

cursar *vt* **1** : take (a course), study **2** ENVIAR : send, pass on

cursi *adj fam* : affected, pretentious

cursiva *nf* : italics *pl*

curso *nm* **1** : course **2** : (school) year **3 en** ~ : under way **4 en** ~ : current

curtir *vt* **1** : tan **2** : harden (skin, features, etc.) — **curtiduría** *nf* : tannery

curva *nf* **1** : curve, bend **2** ~ **de nivel** : contour — **curvo, -va** *adj* : curved, bent

cúspide *nf* : apex, peak

custodia *nf* : custody — **custodiar** *vt* : guard, look after — **custodio, -dia** *n* : guardian

cutáneo, -nea *adj* : skin

cutícula *nf* : cuticle

cutis *nms & pl* : skin, complexion

cuyo, -ya *adj* **1** : whose, of whom, of which **2 en cuyo caso** : in which case

D

d *nf* : d, fourth letter of the Spanish alphabet

dádiva *nf* : gift, handout — **dadivoso, -sa** *adj* : generous

dado, -da *adj* **1** : given **2 dado que** : provided that, since — **dados** *nmpl* : dice

daga *nf* : dagger

daltónico, -ca *adj* : color-blind

dama *nf* **1** : lady **2** ~s *nfpl* : checkers

damnificar {72} *vt* : damage, injure

danés, -nesa *adj* : Danish — **danés** *nm* : Danish (language)

danzar {21} *v* : dance — **danza** *nf* : dance, dancing

dañar *vt* : damage, harm — **dañarse** *vr* **1** : be damaged **2** : hurt oneself — **dañino, -na** *adj* : harmful — **daño** *nm* **1** : damage, harm **2** ~s **y perjuicios** : damages

dar {22} *vt* **1** : give **2** PRODUCIR : yield, produce **3** : strike (the hour) **4** MOSTRAR : show — *vi* **1** ~ **como** : consider, regard as **2** ~ **con** : run into, meet **3** ~ **contra** : knock against **4** ~ **para** : be enough for — **darse** *vr* **1** : happen **2** ~ **contra** : bump into **3** ~ **por** : consider oneself **4 dárselas de** : pose as

dardo *nm* : dart

dársena *nf* : dock

datar *vt* : date — *vi* ~ **de** : date from

dátil *nm* : date (fruit)

dato *nm* **1** : fact **2** ~s *nmpl* : data

de *prep* **1** : of **2** ~ **Managua** : from Managua **3** ~ **niño** : as a child **4** ~ **noche** : at night **5 las tres** ~ **la mañana** : three o'clock in the morning **6 más** ~ **10** : more than 10

deambular *vi* : wander about, stroll

debajo *adv* **1** : underneath **2** ~ **de** : under, underneath **3 por** ~ : below, beneath

debatir *vt* : debate — **debatirse** *vr* : struggle — **debate** *nm* : debate

deber *vt* : owe — *v aux* **1** : have to, should **2** (*expressing probability*) : must — **deberse** *vr* ~ **a** : be due to — ~ *nm* **1** : duty **2** ~**es** *nmpl* : homework — **debido, -da** *adj* ~ **a** : due to, owing to

débil *adj* : weak, feeble — **debilidad** *nf* : weakness — **debilitar** *vt* : weaken — **debilitarse** *vr* : get weak — **débilmente** *adv* : weakly, faintly

débito *nm* **1** : debit **2** DEUDA : debt

debutar *vi* : debut — **debut** *nm, pl* ~**s** : debut — **debutante** *nf* : debutante *f*

década *nf* : decade

decadencia *nf* : decadence — **decadente** *adj* : decadent

decaer {13} *vi* : decline, weaken

decano, -na *n* : dean

decapitar *vt* : behead

decena *nf* : ten, about ten

decencia *nf* : decency

decenio *nm* : decade

decente *adj* : decent

decepcionar *vt* : disappoint — **decepción** *nf, pl* -**ciones** : disappointment

decibelio *or* **decibel** *nm* : decibel

decidir *vt* : decide, determine — *vi* : decide — **decidirse** *vr* : make up one's mind — **decididamente** *adv* : definitely, decidedly — **decidido, -da** *adj* : determined, resolute

decimal *adj* : decimal

décimo, -ma *adj & n* : tenth

decimoctavo, -va *adj* : eighteenth — ~ *n* : eighteenth (in a series)

decimocuarto, -ta *adj* : fourteenth — ~ *n* : fourteenth (in a series)

decimonoveno, -na *or* **decimonono, -na**

adj : nineteenth — ~ *n* : nineteenth (in a series)

decimoquinto, -ta *adj* : fifteenth — ~ *n* : fifteenth (in a series)

decimoséptimo, -ma *adj* : seventeenth — ~ *n* : seventeenth (in a series)

decimosexto, -ta *adj* : sixteenth — ~ *n* : sixteenth (in a series)

decimotercero, -ra *adj* : thirteenth — ~ *n* : thirteenth (in a series)

decir {23} *vt* **1** : say **2** CONTAR : tell **3 es** ~ : that is to say **4 querer** ~ : mean — **decirse** *vr* **1** : tell oneself **2 ¿cómo se dice...en español?** : how do you say...in Spanish? — ~ *nm* : saying, expression

decisión *nf, pl* -**siones** : decision — **decisivo, -va** *adj* : decisive

declarar *vt* : declare — *vi* : testify — **declararse** *vr* **1** : declare oneself **2** : break out (of a fire, an epidemic, etc.) — **declaración** *nf, pl* -**ciones** : statement

declinar *v* : decline

declive *nm* **1** : decline **2** PENDIENTE : slope

decolorar *vt* : bleach — **decolorarse** *vr* : fade

decoración *nf, pl* -**ciones** : decoration — **decorado** *nm* : stage set — **decorar** *vt* : decorate — **decorativo, -va** *adj* : decorative

decoro *nm* : decency, decorum — **decoroso, -sa** *adj* : decent, proper

decrecer {53} *vi* : decrease

decrépito, -ta *adj* : decrepit

decretar *vt* : decree — **decreto** *nm* : decree

dedal *nm* : thimble

dedicar {72} *vt* : dedicate — **dedicarse** *vr* ~ **a** : devote oneself to — **dedicación** *nf, pl* -**ciones** : dedication — **dedicatoria** *nf* : dedication, inscription

dedo *nm* **1** : finger **2** ~ **del pie** : toe

deducir {61} *vt* **1** INFERIR : deduce **2** DESCONTAR : deduct — **deducción** *nf, pl* -**ciones** : deduction

defecar {72} *vi* : defecate

defecto *nm* : defect — **defectuoso, -sa** *adj* : defective, faulty

defender {56} *vt* : defend — **defenderse** *vr* : defend oneself — **defensa** *nf* : defense — **defensiva** *nf* : defensive — **defensivo, -va** *adj* : defensive — **defensor, -sora** *n* **1** : defender **2** *or* **abogado defensor** : defense counsel

deferencia *nf* : deference — **deferente** *adj* : deferential

deficiencia *nf* : deficiency — **deficiente** *adj* : deficient

déficit *nm, pl* -**cits** : deficit

definir *vt* : define — **definición** *nf, pl* -**ciones** : definition — **definitivo, -va** *adj* **1** : definitive **2 en definitiva** : in short

deformar *vt* **1** : deform **2** : distort (the truth, etc.) — **deformación** *nf, pl* **-ciones** : distortion — **deforme** *adj* : deformed — **deformidad** *nf* : deformity

defraudar *vt* **1** : defraud **2** DECEPCIONAR : disappoint

degenerar *vi* : degenerate — **degenerado, -da** *adj* : degenerate

degradar *vt* **1** : degrade **2** : demote (in the military)

degustar *vt* : taste

dehesa *nf* : pasture

deidad *nf* : deity

dejar *vt* **1** : leave **2** ABANDONAR : abandon **3** PERMITIR : allow — *vi* ~ **de** : quit — **dejado, -da** *adj* : slovenly, careless

dejo *nm* **1** : aftertaste **2** : (regional) accent

delantal *nm* : apron

delante *adv* **1** : ahead **2** ~ **de** : in front of

delantera *nf* **1** : front **2 tomar la** ~ : take the lead — **delantero, -ra** *adj* : front, forward — ~ *n* : forward (in sports)

delatar *vt* : denounce, inform against

delegar {52} *vt* : delegate — **delegación** *nf, pl* **-ciones** : delegation — **delegado, -da** *n* : delegate, representative

deleitar *vt* : delight, please — **deleite** *nm* : delight

deletrear *vi* : spell (out)

delfín *nm, pl* **-fines** : dolphin

delgado, -da *adj* : thin

deliberar *vi* : deliberate — **deliberación** *nf, pl* **-ciones** : deliberation — **deliberado, -da** *adj* : deliberate, intentional

delicadeza *nf* **1** : delicacy, daintiness **2** SUAVIDAD : gentleness **3** TACTO : tact — **delicado, -da** *adj* **1** : delicate **2** SENSIBLE : sensible **3** DISCRETO : tactful

delicia *nf* : delight — **delicioso, -sa** *adj* **1** : delightful **2** RICO : delicious

delictivo, -va *adj* : criminal

delimitar *vt* : define, set the boundaries of

delincuencia *nf* : delinquency, crime — **delincuente** *adj & nmf* : delinquent, criminal — **delinquir** {24} *vi* : break the law

delirante *adj* : delirious — **delirar** *vi* **1** : be delirious **2** ~ **por** *fam* : rave about — **delirio** *nm* **1** : delirium **2** ~ **de grandeza** : delusions of grandeur

delito *nm* : crime

delta *nm* : delta

demacrado, -da *adj* : emaciated

demandar *vt* **1** : sue **2** PEDIR : demand **3** *Lat* : require — **demanda** *nf* **1** : lawsuit **2** PETICIÓN : request **3 la oferta y la** ~ : supply and demand — **demandante** *nmf* : plaintiff

demás *adj* : rest of the, other — ~ *pron* **1**

lo (la, los, las) ~ : the rest, others **2 por** ~ : extremely **3 por lo** ~ : otherwise **4 y** ~ : and so on

demasiado *adv* **1** : too **2** : too much — ~ *adj* : too much, too many

demencia *nf* : madness — **demente** *adj* : insane, mad

democracia *nf* : democracy — **demócrata** *nmf* : democrat — **democrático, -ca** *adj* : democratic

demoler {47} *vt* : demolish — **demolición** *nf, pl* **-ciones** : demolition

demonio *nm* : devil, demon

demorar *v* : delay — **demorarse** *vr* : take a long time — **demora** *nf* : delay

demostrar {19} *vt* **1** : demonstrate **2** MOSTRAR : show — **demostración** *nf, pl* **-ciones** : demonstration

demudar *vt* : change, alter

denegar {49} *vt* **1** : deny, refuse — **denegación** *nf, pl* **-ciones** : denial, refusal

denigrar *vt* **1** : denigrate **2** INJURIAR : insult

denominador *nm* : denominator

denotar *vt* : denote, show

densidad *nf* : density — **denso, -sa** *adj* : dense

dental *adj* : dental — **dentado, -da** *adj* : toothed, notched — **dentadura** *nf* ~ **postiza** : dentures *pl* — **dentífrico** *nm* : toothpaste — **dentista** *nmf* : dentist

dentro *adv* **1** : in, inside **2** ~ **de poco** : soon, shortly **3 por** ~ : inside

denuedo *nm* : courage

denunciar *vt* **1** : denounce **2** : report (a crime) — **denuncia** *nf* **1** : accusation **2** : (police) report

departamento *nm* **1** : department **2** *Lat* : apartment

depender *vi* **1** : depend **2** ~ **de** : depend on — **dependencia** *nf* **1** : dependence, dependency **2** SUCURSAL : branch office — **dependiente** *adj* : dependent — **dependiente, -ta** *n* : clerk, salesperson

deplorar *vt* : deplore, regret

deponer {60} *vt* : remove from office, depose

deportar *vt* : deport — **deportación** *nf, pl* **-ciones** : deportation

deporte *nm* : sport, sports *pl* — **deportista** *nmf* : sportsman *m*, sportswoman *f* — **deportivo, -va** *adj* **1** : sporty **2 artículos deportivos** : sporting goods

depositar *vt* **1** : put, place **2** : deposit (in a bank, etc.) — **depósito** *nm* **1** : deposit **2** ALMACÉN : warehouse

depravado, -da *adj* : depraved

depreciarse *vr* : depreciate — **depreciación** *nf* : depreciation

depredador *nm* : predator

deprimir *vt* : depress — **deprimirse** *vr* : get depressed — **depresión** *nf, pl* **-siones** : depression

derecha *nf* **1** : right side **2** : right wing (in politics) — **derechista** *adj* : right-wing

derecho[1] *adv* **1** : straight **2** : upright **3** : directly

derecho[2], **-cha** *adj* **1** : right **2** : right-hand (**el margen derecho** the right-hand margin) **3** RECTO : straight, upright, erect (**siéntate derecho** sit up straight)

derecho[3] *nm* **1** : right (**derechos humanos** human rights) **2** : law (**derecho civil** civil law) **3** : right side (of cloth or clothing)

deriva *nf* **1** : drift **2 a la ∼** : adrift — **derivación** *nf, pl* **-ciones** : derivation — **derivar** *vi* **1** : drift **2 ∼ de** : derive from

derramamiento *nm* **∼ de sangre** : bloodshed

derramar *vt* **1** : spill **2** : shed (tears, blood) — **derramarse** *vr* : overflow — **derrame** *nm* **1** : spilling **2** : discharge, hemorrhage

derrapar *vi* : skid — **derrape** *nm* : skid

derretir {54} *vt* : melt, thaw — **derretirse** *vr* **1** : melt, thaw **2 ∼ por** *fam* : be crazy about

derribar *vt* **1** : demolish **2** : bring down (a plane, a tree, etc.) **3** : overthrow (a government, etc.)

derrocar {72} *vt* : overthrow

derrochar *vt* : waste, squander — **derrochador, -dora** *n* : spendthrift — **derroche** *nm* : extravagance, waste

derrotar *vt* : defeat — **derrota** *nf* : defeat

derruir {41} *vt* : demolish, tear down

derrumbar *vt* : demolish, knock down — **derrumbarse** *vr* : collapse, break down — **derrumbamiento** *nm* : collapse — **derrumbe** *nm* : collapse

desabotonar *vt* : unbutton, undo

desabrido, -da *adj* : bland

desabrochar *vt* : unbutton, undo — **desabrocharse** *vr* : come undone

desacato *nm* **1** : disrespect **2** : contempt (of court) — **desacatar** *vt* : defy, disobey

desacertado, -da *adj* : mistaken, wrong — **desacertar** {55} *vi* : be mistaken — **desacierto** *nm* : mistake, error

desaconsejar *vt* : advise against — **desaconsejable** *adj* : inadvisable

desacreditar *vt* : discredit

desactivar *vt* : deactivate

desacuerdo *nm* : disagreement

desafiar {85} *vt* : defy, challenge — **desafiante** *adj* : defiant

desafilado, -da *adj* : blunt

desafinado, -da *adj* : out-of-tune, off-key

desafío *nm* : challenge, defiance

desafortunado, -da *adj* : unfortunate — **desafortunadamente** *adv* : unfortunately

desagradar *vt* : displease — **desagradable** *adj* : disagreeable, unpleasant

desagradecido, -da *adj* : ungrateful

desagrado *nm* **1** : displeasure **2 con ∼** : reluctantly

desagravio *nm* : amends, reparation

desagregarse {52} *vr* : disintegrate

desaguar {10} *vi* : drain, empty — **desagüe** *nm* **1** : drainage **2** : drain (of a sink, etc.)

desahogar {52} *vt* **1** : relieve **2** : give vent to (anger, etc.) — **desahogarse** *vr* : let off steam, unburden oneself — **desahogado, -da** *adj* **1** : roomy **2** ADINERADO : comfortable, well-off — **desahogo** *nm* **1** : relief **2 con ∼** : comfortably

desahuciar *vt* **1** : deprive of hope **2** DESALOJAR : evict — **desahucio** *nm* : eviction

desaire *nm* : snub, rebuff — **desairar** *vt* : snub, slight

desalentar {55} *vt* : discourage — **desaliento** *nm* : discouragement

desaliñado, -da *adj* : slovenly

desalmado, -da *adj* : heartless, cruel

desalojar *vt* **1** : evacuate **2** DESAHUCIAR : evict

desamparar *vt* : abandon — **desamparo** *nm* : abandonment, desertion

desamueblado, -da *adj* : unfurnished

desangrarse *vr* : lose blood, bleed to death

desanimar *vt* : discourage — **desanimarse** *vr* : get discouraged — **desanimado, -da** *adj* : downhearted, despondent — **desánimo** *nm* : discouragement

desanudar *vt* : untie

desaparecer {53} *vi* : disappear — **desaparecido, -da** *n* : missing person — **desaparición** *nf, pl* **-ciones** : disappearance

desapasionado, -da *adj* : dispassionate

desapego *nm* : indifference

desapercibido, -da *adj* : unnoticed

desaprobar {19} *vt* : disapprove of — **desaprobación** *nf, pl* **-ciones** : disapproval

desaprovechar *vt* : waste

desarmar *vt* **1** : disarm **2** DESMONTAR : dismantle, take apart — **desarme** *nm* : disarmament

desarraigar {52} *vt* : uproot, root out

desarreglar *vt* **1** : mess up **2** : disrupt (plans, etc.) — **desarreglado, -da** *adj* : disorganized — **desarreglo** *nm* : untidiness, disorder

desarrollar *vt* : develop — **desarrollarse** *vr* : take place — **desarrollo** *nm* : development

desarticular *vt* **1** : break up, dismantle **2** : dislocate (a bone)

desaseado, -da *adj* **1** : dirty **2** DESORDENADO : messy

desastre *nm* : disaster — **desastroso, -sa** *adj* : disastrous

desatar *vt* **1** : undo, untie **2** : unleash (passions) — **desatarse** *vr* **1** : come undone **2** DESENCADENARSE : break out, erupt

desatascar {72} *vt* : unclog

desatender {56} *vt* **1** : disregard **2** : neglect (an obligation, etc.) — **desatento, -ta** *adj* : inattentive

desatinado, -da *adj* : foolish, silly

desautorizado, -da *adj* : unauthorized

desavenencia *nf* : disagreement

desayunar *vi* : have breakfast — *vt* : have for breakfast — **desayuno** *nm* : breakfast

desbancar {72} *vt* : oust

desbarajuste *nm* : disorder, confusion

desbaratar *vt* : ruin, destroy — **desbaratarse** *vr* : fall apart

desbocarse {72} *vr* : run away, bolt

desbordar *vt* **1** : overflow **2** : exceed (limits) — **desbordarse** *vr* : overflow — **desbordamiento** *nm* : overflow

descabellado, -da *adj* : crazy

descafeinado, -da *adj* : decaffeinated

descalabrar *vt* : hit on the head — **descalabro** *nm* : misfortune, setback

descalificar {72} *vt* : disqualify — **descalificación** *nf, pl* **-ciones** : disqualification

descalzarse {21} *vr* : take off one's shoes — **descalzo, -za** *adj* : barefoot

descaminar *vt* : mislead, lead astray

descansar *v* : rest — **descanso** *nm* **1** : rest **2** : landing (of a staircase) **3** : intermission (in theater), halftime (in sports)

descapotable *adj & nm* : convertible

descarado, -da *adj* : insolent, shameless

descargable *adj* : downloadable

descargar {52} *vt* **1** : unload **2** : discharge (a firearm, etc.) — **descarga** *nf* **1** : unloading **2** : discharge (of a firearm, of electricity, etc.) — **descargo** *nm* **1** : unloading **2** : discharge (of a duty, etc.) **3** : defense (in law)

descarnado, -da *adj* : scrawny, gaunt

descaro *nm* : insolence, nerve

descarrilar *vi* : derail — **descarrilarse** *vr* : be derailed

descartar *vt* : reject — **descartarse** *vr* : discard

descascarar *vt* : peel, shell, husk

descender {56} *vt* **1** : go down **2** BAJAR : lower — *vi* **1** : descend **2** ~ **de** : be descended from — **descendiencia** *nf* **1** : descendants *pl* **2** LINAJE : lineage, descent — **descendiente** *nmf* : descendant — **descenso** *nm* **1** : descent **2** : drop, fall (in level, in temperature, etc.)

descifrar *vt* : decipher, decode

descolgar {16} *vt* **1** : take down **2** : pick up, answer (the telephone)

descolorarse *vr* : fade — **descolorido, -da** *adj* : faded, discolored

descomponer {60} *vt* : break down — **descomponerse** *vr* **1** : rot, decompose **2** *Lat* : break down — **descompuesto, -ta** *adj* *Lat* : out of order

descomunal *adj* : enormous

desconcertar {55} *vt* : disconcert, confuse — **desconcertante** *adj* : confusing — **desconcierto** *nm* : confusion, bewilderment

desconectar *vt* : disconnect

desconfiar {85} *vi* ~ **de** : distrust — **desconfiado, -da** *adj* : distrustful — **desconfianza** *nf* : distrust

descongelar *vt* **1** : thaw, defrost **2** : unfreeze (assets)

descongestionante *nm* : decongestant

desconocer {18} *vt* : not know, fail to recognize — **desconocido, -da** *adj* : unknown — ~ *n* : stranger

desconsiderado, -da *adj* : inconsiderate

desconsolar *vt* : distress — **desconsolado, -da** *adj* : heartbroken — **desconsuelo** *nm* : grief, sorrow

descontar {19} *vt* : discount

descontento, -ta *adj* : dissatisfied — **descontento** *nm* : discontent

descontinuar *vt* : discontinue

descorazonado, -da *adj* : discouraged

descorrer *vt* : draw back

descortés *adj, pl* **-teses** : rude — **descortesía** *nf* : discourtesy, rudeness

descoyuntar *vt* : dislocate

descrédito *nm* : discredit

descremado, -da *adj* : nonfat, skim

describir {33} *vt* : describe — **descripción** *nf, pl* **-ciones** : description — **descriptivo, -va** *adj* : descriptive

descubierto, -ta *adj* **1** : exposed, uncovered **2 al descubierto** : in the open — **descubierto** *nm* : deficit, overdraft

descubrir {2} *vt* **1** : discover **2** REVELAR : reveal — **descubrimiento** *nm* : discovery

descuento *nm* : discount

descuidar *vt* : neglect — **descuidarse** *vr* **1** : be careless **2** ABANDONARSE : let oneself go — **descuidado, -da** *adj* **1** : careless, sloppy **2** DESATENDIDO : neglected — **descuido** *nm* : neglect, carelessness

desde *prep* **1** : from (a place), since (a time) **2** ~ **luego** : of course

desdén *nm* : scorn, disdain — **desdeñar** *vt* : scorn — **desdeñoso, -sa** *adj* : disdainful

desdicha *nf* **1** : misery **2** DESGRACIA : misfortune — **desdichado, -da** *adj* : unfortunate, unhappy

desear *vt* : wish, want — **deseable** *adj* : desirable

desecar *vt* : dry up

desechar *vt* **1** : throw away **2** RECHAZAR : reject — **desechable** *adj* : disposable — **desechos** *nmpl* : rubbish

desembarazarse {21} *vr* ~ **de** : get rid of

desembarcar {72} *vi* : disembark — *vt* : unload — **desembarcadero** *nm* : jetty, landing pier — **desembarco** *nm* : landing

desembocar {72} *vi* ~ **en 1** : flow into **2** : lead to (a result) — **desembocadura** *nf* **1** : mouth (of a river) **2** : opening, end (of a street)

desembolsar *vt* : pay out — **desembolso** *nm* : payment, outlay

desembragar *vi* : disengage the clutch

desempacar {72} *v Lat* : unpack

desempate *nm* : tiebreaker

desempeñar *vt* **1** : play (a role) **2** : redeem (from a pawnshop) — **desempeñarse** *vr* : get out of debt

desempleo *nm* : unemployment — **desempleado, -da** *adj* : unemployed

desempolvar *vt* : dust

desencadenar *vt* **1** : unchain **2** : trigger, unleash (protests, crises, etc.) — **desencadenarse** *vr* : break loose

desencajar *vt* **1** : dislocate **2** DESCONECTAR : disconnect

desencanto *nm* : disillusionment

desenchufar *vt* : disconnect, unplug

desenfadado, -da *adj* : carefree, confident — **desenfado** *nm* : confidence, ease

desenfrenado, -da *adj* : unrestrained — **desenfreno** *nm* : abandon, lack of restraint

desenganchar *vt* : unhook

desengañar *vt* : disillusion — **desengaño** *nm* : disappointment

desenlace *nm* : ending, outcome

desenmarañar *vt* : disentangle

desenmascarar *vt* : unmask

desenredar *vt* : untangle — **desenredarse** *vr* ~ **de** : extricate oneself from

desenrollar *vt* : unroll, unwind

desentenderse {56} *vr* ~ **de** : want nothing to do with

desenterrar {55} *vt* : dig up, disinter

desentonar *vi* **1** : be out of tune **2** : clash (of colors, etc.)

desenvoltura *nf* : confidence, ease

desenvolver {89} *vt* : unfold, unwrap — **desenvolverse** *vr* : unfold, develop

desenvuelto, -ta *adj* : confident, self-assured

deseo *nm* : desire — **deseoso, -sa** *adj* : eager, anxious

desequilibrar *vt* : throw off balance — **desequilibrado, -da** *adj* : unbalanced — **desequilibrio** *nm* : imbalance

desertar *vt* : desert — **deserción** *nf, pl -cio-*nes : desertion — **desertor, -tora** *n* : deserter

desesperar *vt* : exasperate — *vi* : despair — **desesperarse** *vr* : become exasperated — **desesperación** *nf, pl* -ciones : desperation, despair — **desesperado, -da** *adj* : desperate, hopeless

desestimar *vt* : reject

desfalcar {72} *vt* : embezzle — **desfalco** *nm* : embezzlement

desfallecer {53} *vi* **1** : weaken **2** DESMAYARSE : faint

desfavorable *adj* : unfavorable

desfigurar *vt* **1** : disfigure, mar **2** : distort (the truth)

desfiladero *nm* : mountain pass, gorge

desfilar *vi* : march, parade — **desfile** *nm* : parade, procession

desfogar {52} *vt* : vent — **desfogarse** *vr* : let off steam

desgajar *vt* : tear off, break apart — **desgajarse** *vr* : come off

desgana *nf* **1** : lack of appetite **2** : lack of enthusiasm, reluctance

desgarbado, -da *adj* : gawky, ungainly

desgarrar *vt* : tear, rip — **desgarrador, -dora** *adj* : heartbreaking — **desgarro** *nm* : tear

desgastar *vt* : wear away, wear down — **desgaste** *nm* : deterioration, wear and tear

desgracia *nf* **1** : misfortune **2 caer en ~** : fall into disgrace **3 por ~** : unfortunately — **desgraciadamente** *adv* : unfortunately — **desgraciado, -da** *adj* : unfortunate

deshabitado, -da *adj* : uninhabited

deshacer {40} *vt* **1** : undo **2** DESTRUIR : destroy, ruin **3** DISOLVER : dissolve **4** : break (an agreement), cancel (plans, etc.) — **deshacerse** *vr* **1** : come undone **2** ~ **de** : get rid of **3** ~ **en** : lavish, heap (praise, etc.) — **deshecho, -cha** *adj* **1** : undone **2** DESTROZADO : destroyed, ruined

desheredar *vt* : disinherit

deshidratar *vt* : dehydrate

deshielo *nm* : thaw

deshilachar *vt* : unravel — **deshilacharse** *vr* : fray

deshonesto, -ta *adj* : dishonest

deshonrar *vt* : dishonor, disgrace — **deshonra** *nf* : dishonor — **deshonroso, -sa** *adj* : dishonorable

deshuesar *vt* **1** : pit (a fruit) **2** : bone, debone (meat)

desidia *nf* **1** : indolence **2** DESASEO : sloppiness

desierto, -ta *adj* : deserted, uninhabited — **desierto** *nm* : desert

designar *vt* : designate — **designación** *nf, pl* -ciones : appointment (to an office, etc.)

designio *nm* : plan

desigual *adj* **1** : unequal **2** DISPAREJO : uneven — **desigualdad** *nf* : inequality
desilusionar *vt* : disappoint, disillusion — **desilusión** *nf, pl* **-siones** : disappointment, disillusionment
desinfectar *vt* : disinfect — **desinfectante** *adj & nm* : disinfectant
desinflar *vt* : deflate — **desinflarse** *vr* : deflate, go flat
desinhibido, -da *adj* : uninhibited
desintegrar *vt* : disintegrate — **desintegrarse** *vr* : disintegrate — **desintegración** *nf, pl* **-ciones** : disintegration
desinteresado, -da *adj* : unselfish, generous — **desinterés** *nm* : unselfishness
desistir *vi* ~ **de** : give up
desleal *adj* : disloyal — **deslealtad** *nf* : disloyalty
desleír {66} *vt* : dilute, dissolve
desligar {52} *vt* **1** : untie **2** SEPARAR : separate — **desligarse** *vr* : extricate oneself
desliz *nm, pl* **-lices** : slip, mistake — **deslizar** {21} *vt* : slide, slip — **deslizarse** *vr* : slide, glide
deslucido, -da *adj* : dingy, tarnished
deslumbrar *vt* : dazzle — **deslumbrante** *adj* : dazzling, blinding
deslustrar *vt* : tarnish, dull
desmán *nm, pl* **-manes** : outrage, excess
desmandarse *vr* : get out of hand
desmantelar *vt* : dismantle
desmañado, -da *adj* : clumsy
desmayar *vi* : lose heart — **desmayarse** *vr* : faint — **desmayo** *nm* : faint
desmedido, -da *adj* : excessive
desmejorar *vt* : impair — *vi* : deteriorate
desmemoriado, -da *adj* : forgetful
desmentir {76} *vt* : deny — **desmentido** *nm* : denial
desmenuzar {21} *vt* **1** : crumble **2** EXAMINAR : scrutinize — **desmenuzarse** *vr* : crumble
desmerecer {53} *vt* : be unworthy of — *vi* : decline in value
desmesurado, -da *adj* : excessive
desmigajar *vt* : crumble
desmontar *vt* **1** : dismantle, take apart **2** ALLANAR : level — *vi* : dismount
desmoralizar {21} *vt* : demoralize
desmoronarse *vr* : crumble
desnivel *nm* : unevenness
desnudar *vt* : undress, strip — **desnudarse** *vr* : get undressed — **desnudez** *nf, pl* **-deces** : nudity, nakedness — **desnudo, -da** *adj* : nude, naked — **desnudo** *nm* : nude
desnutrición *nf, pl* **-ciones** : malnutrition
desobedecer {53} *v* : disobey — **desobediencia** *nf* : disobedience — **desobediente** *adj* : disobedient

desocupar *vt* : empty, vacate — **desocupado, -da** *adj* **1** : vacant **2** DESEMPLEADO : unemployed
desodorante *adj & nm* : deodorant
desolado, -da *adj* **1** : desolate **2** DESCONSOLADO : devastated, distressed — **desolación** *nf, pl* **-ciones** : desolation
desorden *nm, pl* **desórdenes** : disorder, mess — **desordenado, -da** *adj* : untidy — **desordenadamente** *adv* : in a disorderly way
desorganizar {21} *vt* : disorganize — **desorganización** *nf, pl* **-ciones** : disorganization
desorientar *vt* : disorient, confuse — **desorientarse** *vr* : lose one's way
desovar *vi* : spawn
despachar *vt* **1** : deal with (a task, etc.) **2** ENVIAR : dispatch, send **3** : wait on, serve (customers) — **despacho** *nm* **1** : dispatch, shipment **2** OFICINA : office
despacio *adv* : slowly
desparramar *vt* : spill, scatter, spread
despavorido, -da *adj* : terrified
despecho *nm* **1** : spite **2 a** ~ **de** : despite, in spite of
despectivo, -va *adj* **1** : pejorative **2** DESPRECIATIVO : contemptuous
despedazar {21} *vt* : tear apart
despedir {54} *vt* **1** : see off **2** DESTITUIR : dismiss, fire **3** DESPRENDER : emit — **despedirse** *vr* : say good-bye — **despedida** *nf* : farewell, good-bye
despegar {52} *vt* : detach, unstick — *vi* : take off — **despegado, -da** *adj* : cold, distant — **despegue** *nm* : takeoff
despeinar *vt* : ruffle (hair) — **despeinado, -da** *adj* : disheveled, unkempt
despejar *vt* : clear, free — *vi* : clear up — **despejado, -da** *adj* **1** : clear, fair **2** LÚCIDO : clear-headed
despellejar *vt* : skin (an animal)
despensa *nf* : pantry, larder
despeñadero *nm* : precipice
desperdiciar *vt* : waste — **desperdicio** *nm* **1** : waste **2** ~**s** *nmpl* : scraps
desperfecto *nm* : flaw, defect
despertar {55} *vi* : awaken, wake up — *vt* : wake, rouse — **despertador** *nm* : alarm clock
despiadado, -da *adj* : pitiless, merciless
despido *nm* : dismissal, layoff
despierto, -ta *adj* : awake
despilfarrar *vt* : squander — **despilfarrador, -dora** *n* : spendthrift — **despilfarro** *nm* : extravagance, wastefulness
despistar *vt* : throw off the track, confuse — **despistarse** *vr* : lose one's way — **despistado, -da** *adj* **1** : absentminded **2** DES-

ORIENTADO : confused — **despiste** *nm* **1**
: absentmindedness **2** ERROR : mistake

desplazar {21} *vt* : displace — **desplazarse**
vr : travel

desplegar {49} *vt* : unfold, spread out —
despliegue *nm* : display

desplomarse *vr* : collapse

desplumar *vt* **1** : pluck **2** *fam* : fleece

despoblado, -da *adj* : uninhabited, deserted
— **despoblado** *nm* : deserted area

despojar *vt* : strip, deprive — **despojos**
nmpl **1** : plunder **2** RESTOS : remains, scraps

desportillar *vt* : chip — **desportillarse** *vr*
: chip — **desportilladura** *nf* : chip, nick

despota *nmf* : despot

despotricar *vi* : rant (and rave)

despreciar *vt* : despise, scorn — **despreciable** *adj* **1** : despicable **2 una cantidad** ~
: a negligible amount — **desprecio** *nm*
: disdain, scorn

desprender *vt* **1** : detach, remove **2** EMITIR
: give off — **desprenderse** *vr* **1** : come off
2 DEDUCIRSE : be inferred, follow — **desprendimiento** *nm* ~ **de tierras** : landslide

despreocupado, -da *adj* : carefree, unconcerned

desprestigiar *vt* : discredit — **desprestigiarse** *vr* : lose face

desprevenido, -da *adj* : unprepared

desproporcionado, -da : out of proportion

despropósito *nm* : (piece of) nonsense, absurdity

desprovisto, -ta *adj* ~ **de** : lacking in

después *adv* **1** : afterward **2** ENTONCES
: then, next **3** ~ **de** : after **4 después (de)
que** : after **5** ~ **de todo** : after all

despuntado, -da *adj* : blunt, dull

desquiciar *vt* : drive crazy

desquitarse *vr* **1** : retaliate **2** ~ **con** : take
it out on, get back at — **desquite** *nm* : revenge

destacar {72} *vt* : emphasize — *vi* : stand
out — **destacado, -da** *adj* : outstanding

destapar *vt* : open, uncover — **destapador**
nm Lat : bottle opener

destartalado, -da *adj* : dilapidated

destellar *vi* : flash, sparkle — **destello** *nm*
: sparkle, twinkle, flash

destemplado, -da *adj* **1** : out of tune **2** MAL
: out of sorts **3** : unpleasant (of weather)

desteñir {67} *vt* : fade, bleach — *vi* : run,
fade — **desteñirse** *vr* : fade

desterrar {55} *vt* : banish, exile — **deste-
rrado, -da** *n* : exile

destetar *vt* : wean

destiempo *adv* **a** ~ : at the wrong time

destierro *nm* : exile

destilar *vt* : distill — **destilería** *nf* : distillery

destinar *vt* **1** : assign, allocate **2** NOMBRAR
: appoint — **destinado, -da** *adj* : destined

— **destinatario, -ria** *n* : addressee — **destino** *nm* **1** : destiny **2** RUMBO : destination

destituir {41} *vt* : dismiss — **destitución** *nf,
pl* **-ciones** : dismissal

destornillar *vt* : unscrew — **destornillador**
nm : screwdriver

destreza *nf* : skill, dexterity

destrozar {21} *vt* : destroy, wreck — **des-
trozos** *nmpl* : damage, destruction

destrucción *nf, pl* **-ciones** : destruction —
destructivo, -va *adj* : destructive — **destruir** {41} *vt* : destroy

desunir *vt* : split, divide

desusado, -da *adj* **1** : obsolete **2** INSÓLITO
: unusual — **desuso** *nm* **caer en** ~ : fall
into disuse

desvaído, -da *adj* **1** : pale, washed-out **2**
BORROSO : vague, blurred

desvalido, -da *adj* : destitute, needy

desvalijar *vt* : rob

desván *nm, pl* **-vanes** : attic

desvanecer {53} *vt* : make disappear —
desvanecerse *vr* **1** : vanish **2** DESMAYARSE
: faint

desvariar {85} *vi* : be delirious — **desvarío**
nm : delirium

desvelar *vt* : keep awake — **desvelarse** *vr*
: stay awake — **desvelo** *nm* **1** : sleepless-
ness **2** ~**s** *nmpl* : efforts

desvencijado, -da *adj* : dilapidated, rickety

desventaja *nf* : disadvantage

desventura *nf* : misfortune

desvergonzado, -da *adj* : shameless —
desvergüenza *nf* : shamelessness

desvestir {54} *vt* : undress — **desvestirse**
vr : get undressed

desviación *nf, pl* **-ciones 1** : deviation **2**
: detour (in a road) — **desviar** {85} *vt* : divert, deflect — **desviarse** *vr* **1** : branch off
2 APARTARSE : stray — **desvío** *nm* : diversion, detour

detallar *vt* : detail — **detallado, -da** *adj* : detailed, thorough — **detalle** *nm* **1** : detail **2**
al ~ : retail — **detallista** *adj* : retail — ~
nmf : retailer

detectar *vt* : detect — **detective** *nmf* : detective

detener {80} *vt* **1** : arrest, detain **2** PARAR
: stop **3** RETRASAR : delay — **detenerse** *vr*
1 : stop **2** DEMORARSE : linger — **detención**
nf, pl **-ciones** : arrest, detention

detergente *nm* : detergent

deteriorar *vt* : damage — **deteriorarse** *vr*
: wear out, deteriorate — **deteriorado, -da**
adj : damaged, worn — **deterioro** *nm* : deterioration, damage

determinar *vt* **1** : determine **2** MOTIVAR
: bring about **3** DECIDIR : decide — **deter-
minarse** *vr* : decide — **determinación** *nf,
pl* **-ciones 1** : determination **2 tomar una**

~ : make a decision — **determinado, -da**
adj **1** : determined **2** ESPECÍFICO : specific
detestar *vt* : detest
detonar *vi* : explode, detonate — **detonación** *nf, pl* **-ciones** : detonation
detrás *adv* **1** : behind **2 ~ de** : in back of
3 por ~ : from behind
detrimento *nm* **en ~ de** : to the detriment of
deuda *nf* : debt — **deudor, -dora** *n* : debtor
devaluar {3} *vt* : devalue — **devaluarse** *vr* : depreciate
devastar *vt* : devastate — **devastador, -dora** *adj* : devastating
devenir {87} *vi* **1** : come about **2 ~ en** : become, turn into
devoción *nf, pl* **-ciones** : devotion
devolución *nf, pl* **-ciones** : return
devolver {89} *vt* **1** RESTITUIR : give back **2** : refund, pay back — *vi* : vomit — **devolverse** *vr Lat* : return, come back
devorar *vt* : devour
devoto, -ta *adj* : devout — **~** *n* : devotee
día *nm* **1** : day **2** : daytime **3 al ~** : up-to-date **4 en pleno ~** : in broad daylight
diabetes *nf* : diabetes — **diabético, -ca** *adj* & *n* : diabetic
diablo *nm* : devil — **diablillo** *nm* : imp, rascal — **diablura** *nf* : prank — **diabólico, -ca** *adj* : diabolic, diabolical
diafragma *nm* : diaphragm
diagnosticar {72} *vt* : diagnose — **diagnóstico, -ca** *adj* : diagnostic — **diagnóstico** *nm* : diagnosis
diagonal *adj* & *nf* : diagonal
diagrama *nm* : diagram
dial *nm* : dial (of a radio, etc.)
dialecto *nm* : dialect
dialogar {52} *vi* : have a talk — **diálogo** *nm* : dialogue
diamante *nm* : diamond
diámetro *nm* : diameter
diana *nf* **1** : reveille **2** BLANCO : target, bull's-eye
diario, -ria *adj* : daily — **diario** *nm* **1** : diary **2** PERIÓDICO : newspaper — **diariamente** *adv* : daily
diarrea *nf* : diarrhea
dibujar *vt* **1** : draw **2** DESCRIBIR : portray — **dibujante** *nmf* : draftsman *m*, draftswoman *f* — **dibujo** *nm* **1** : drawing **2 ~s animados** : (animated) cartoons
diccionario *nm* : dictionary
dicha *nf* **1** ALEGRÍA : happiness **2** SUERTE : good luck — **dicho** *nm* : saying, proverb — **dichoso, -sa** *adj* **1** : happy **2** AFORTUNADO : lucky
diciembre *nm* : December
dictar *vt* **1** : dictate **2** : pronounce (a sen-

tence), deliver (a speech) — **dictado** *nm* : dictation — **dictador, -dora** *n* : dictator — **dictadura** *nf* : dictatorship
diecinueve *adj* & *nm* : nineteen — **diecinueveavo, -va** *adj* : nineteenth
dieciocho *adj* & *nm* : eighteen — **dieciochoavo, -va** *or* **dieciochavo, -va** *adj* : eighteenth
dieciséis *adj* & *nm* : sixteen — **dieciseisavo, -va** *adj* : sixteenth
diecisiete *adj* & *nm* : seventeen — **diecisieteavo, -va** *adj* : seventeenth
diente *nm* **1** : tooth **2** : prong, tine (of a fork, etc.) **3 ~ de ajo** : clove of garlic **4 ~ de león** : dandelion
diesel *adj* & *nm* : diesel
diestra *nf* : right hand — **diestro, -tra** *adj* **1** : right **2** HÁBIL : skillful
dieta *nf* : diet — **dietético, -ca** *adj* : dietetic, dietary
diez *adj* & *nm, pl* **dieces** : ten
difamar *vt* : slander, libel — **difamación** *nf, pl* **-ciones** : slander, libel
diferencia *nf* : difference — **diferenciar** *vt* : distinguish between — **diferenciarse** *vr* : differ — **diferente** *adj* : different
diferir {76} *vt* : postpone — *vi* : differ
difícil *adj* : difficult — **dificultad** *nf* : difficulty — **dificultar** *vt* : hinder, obstruct
difteria *nf* : diphtheria
difundir *vt* **1** : spread (out) **2** : broadcast (television, etc.)
difunto, -ta *adj* & *n* : deceased
difusión *nf, pl* **-siones** : spreading
digerir {76} *vt* : digest — **digerible** *adj* : digestible — **digestión** *nf, pl* **-tiones** : digestion — **digestivo, -va** *adj* : digestive
digitalizar {21} *vt* : digitalize
dígito *nm* : digit — **digital** *adj* : digital
dignarse *vr* **~ a** : deign to
dignatario, -ria *n* : dignitary — **dignidad** *nf* : dignity — **digno, -na** *adj* : worthy
digresión *nf, pl* **-ciones** : digression
dilapidar *vt* : waste, squander
dilatar *vt* **1** : expand, dilate **2** PROLONGAR : prolong **3** POSPONER : postpone
dilema *nm* : dilemma
diligencia *nf* **1** : diligence **2** TRÁMITE : procedure, task — **diligente** *adj* : diligent
diluir {41} *vt* : dilute
diluvio *nm* **1** : flood **2** LLUVIA : downpour
dimensión *nf, pl* **-siones** : dimension
diminuto, -ta *adj* : minute, tiny
dimitir *vi* : resign — **dimisión** *nf, pl* **-siones** : resignation
dinámico, -ca *adj* : dynamic
dinamita *nf* : dynamite
dínamo *or* **dinamo** *nmf* : dynamo
dinastía *nf* : dynasty

dineral *nm* : large sum, fortune
dinero *nm* : money
dinosaurio *nm* : dinosaur
diócesis *nfs & pl* : diocese
dios, diosa *n* : god, goddess *f*
Dios *nm* : (**si Dios quiere** God willing) (**¡Dios me libre** God/heaven forbid!) (**que Dios te bendiga** God bless you)
dióxido de carbono *nm* : carbon dioxide
diploma *nm* : diploma — **diplomado, -da** *adj* : qualified, trained
diplomacia *nf* : diplomacy — **diplomático, -ca** *adj* : diplomatic — ∼ *n* : diplomat
diputación *nf, pl* **-ciones** : delegation — **diputado, -da** *n* : delegate
dique *nm* : dike
dirección *nf, pl* **-ciones 1** : address **2** SENTIDO : direction **3** GESTIÓN : management **4** : steering (of an automobile) — **direccional** *nf Lat* : turn signal, blinker — **directa** *nf* : high gear — **directiva** *nf* : board of directors — **directivo, -va** *adj* : managerial — ∼ *n* : manager, director — **directo, -ta** *adj* **1** : direct **2** DERECHO : straight — **directamente** *adv* : directly — **director, -tora** *n* **1** : director, manager **2** : conductor (of an orchestra) — **directorio** *nm* : directory — **directriz** *nf, pl* **-trices** : guideline
dirigencia *nf* : leaders *pl*, leadership — **dirigente** *nmf* : director, leader
dirigible *nm* : dirigible, blimp
dirigir {35} *vt* **1** : direct, lead **2** : address (a letter, etc.) **3** ENCAMINAR : aim **4** : conduct (music) — **dirigirse** *vr* **1** ∼ **a** : go towards **2** ∼ **a algn** : speak to s.o., write to s.o.
discernir {25} *vt* : discern, distinguish — **discernimiento** *nm* : discernment
disciplinar *vt* : discipline — **disciplina** *nf* : discipline
discípulo, -la *n* : disciple, follower
disco *nm* **1** : disc, disk **2** : discus (in sports) **3** ∼ **compacto** : compact disc
discordante *adj* : discordant — **discordia** *nf* : discord
discoteca *nf* : disco, discotheque
discreción *nf, pl* **-ciones** : discretion
discrepancia *nf* **1** : discrepancy **2** DESACUERDO : disagreement — **discrepar** *vi* : differ, disagree
discreto, -ta *adj* : discreet
discriminar *vt* **1** : discriminate against **2** DISTINGUIR : distinguish — **discriminación** *nf, pl* **-ciones** : discrimination
disculpar *vt* : excuse, pardon — **disculparse** *vr* : apologize — **disculpa** *nf* **1** : apology **2** EXCUSA : excuse
discurrir *vi* **1** : pass, go by **2** REFLEXIONAR : ponder, reflect
discurso *nm* : speech, discourse

discutir *vt* **1** : discuss **2** CUESTIONAR : dispute — *vi* : argue — **discusión** *nf, pl* **-siones 1** : discussion **2** DISPUTA : argument — **discutible** *adj* : debatable
disecar {72} *vt* : dissect — **disección** *nf, pl* **-ciones** : dissection
diseminar *vt* : disseminate, spread
disentería *nf* : dysentery
disentir {76} *vi* ∼ **de** : disagree with — **disentimiento** *nm* : disagreement, dissent
diseñar *vt* : design — **diseñador, -dora** *n* : designer — **diseño** *nm* : design
disertación *nf, pl* **-ciones 1** : lecture **2** : (written) dissertation
disfrazar {21} *vt* : disguise — **disfrazarse** *vr* ∼ **de** : disguise oneself as — **disfraz** *nm, pl* **-fraces 1** : disguise **2** : costume (for a party, etc.)
disfrutar *vt* : enjoy — *vi* : enjoy oneself
disgustar *vt* : upset, annoy — **disgustarse** *vr* **1** : get annoyed **2** ENEMISTARSE : fall out (with s.o.) — **disgusto** *nm* **1** : annoyance, displeasure **2** RIÑA : quarrel
disidente *adj & nmf* : dissident
disimular *vt* : conceal, hide — *vi* : pretend — **disimulo** *nm* : pretense
disipar *vt* **1** : dispel **2** DERROCHAR : squander
diskette *nm* : floppy disk, diskette
dislexia *nf* : dyslexia — **disléxico, -ca** *adj* : dyslexic
dislocar {72} *vt* : dislocate — **dislocarse** *vr* : become dislocated
disminuir {41} *vt* : reduce — *vi* : decrease, drop — **disminución** *nf, pl* **-ciones** : decrease
disociar *vt* : dissociate
disolver {89} *vt* : dissolve — **disolverse** *vr* : dissolve
disparar *vi* : shoot, fire — *vt* : shoot — **dispararse** *vr* : shoot up, skyrocket
disparatado, -da *adj* : absurd — **disparate** *nm* : nonsense, silly thing
disparejo, -ja *adj* : uneven — **disparidad** *nf* : difference, disparity
disparo *nm* : shot
dispensar *vt* **1** : dispense, distribute **2** DISCULPAR : excuse
dispersar *vt* : disperse, scatter — **dispersarse** *vr* : disperse — **dispersión** *nf, pl* **-siones** : scattering
disponer {60} *vt* **1** : arrange, lay out **2** ORDENAR : decide, stipulate — *vi* ∼ **de** : have at one's disposal — **disponerse** *vr* ∼ **a** : be ready to — **disponibilidad** *nf* : availability — **disponible** *adj* : available
disposición *nf, pl* **-ciones 1** : arrangement **2** APTITUD : aptitude **3** : order, provision (in law) **4 a** ∼ **de** : at the disposal of

dispositivo *nm* : device, mechanism
dispuesto, -ta *adj* : prepared, ready
disputar *vi* **1** : argue **2** COMPETIR : compete — *vt* : dispute — **disputa** *nf* : dispute, argument
disquete → **diskette**
distanciar *vt* : space out — **distanciarse** *vr* : grow apart — **distancia** *nf* : distance — **distante** *adj* : distant
distinguir {26} *vt* : distinguish — **distinguirse** *vr* : distinguish oneself, stand out — **distinción** *nf, pl* -ciones : distinction — **distintivo, -va** *adj* : distinctive — **distinto, -ta** *adj* **1** : different **2** CLARO : distinct, clear
distorsión *nf, pl* -siones : distortion
distraer {81} *vt* **1** : distract **2** DIVERTIR : entertain — **distraerse** *vr* **1** : get distracted **2** ENTRETENERSE : amuse oneself — **distracción** *nf, pl* -ciones **1** : amusement **2** DESPISTE : absentmindedness — **distraído, -da** *adj* : distracted, absentminded
distribuir {41} *vt* : distribute — **distribución** *nf, pl* -ciones : distribution — **distribuidor, -dora** *n* : distributor
distrito *nm* : district
disturbio *nm* : disturbance
disuadir *vt* : dissuade, discourage — **disuasivo, -va** *adj* : deterrent
diurno, -na *adj* : day, daytime
divagar {52} *vi* : digress
diván *nm, pl* -vanes : divan, couch
divergir {35} *vi* **1** : diverge **2** ∼ **en** : differ on
diversidad *nf* : diversity
diversificar {72} *vt* : diversify
diversión *nf, pl* -siones : fun, entertainment
diverso, -sa *adj* : diverse
divertir {76} *vt* : entertain — **divertirse** *vr* : enjoy oneself, have fun — **divertido, -da** *adj* : entertaining
dividendo *nm* : dividend
dividir *vt* **1** : divide **2** REPARTIR : distribute
divinidad *nf* : divinity — **divino, -na** *adj* : divine
divisa *nf* **1** : currency **2** EMBLEMA : emblem
divisar *vt* : discern, make out
división *nf, pl* -siones : division — **divisor** *nm* : denominator
divorciar *vt* : divorce — **divorciarse** *vr* : get a divorce — **divorciado, -da** *n* : divorcé *m*, divorcée *f* — **divorcio** *nm* : divorce
divulgar {52} *vt* **1** : divulge, reveal **2** PROPAGAR : spread, circulate
dizque *adv Lat* : supposedly, apparently
doblar *vt* **1** : double **2** PLEGAR : fold **3** : turn (a corner) **4** : dub (a film) — *vi* : turn — **doblarse** *vr* **1** : double over **2** ∼ **a** : give in to — **dobladillo** *nm* : hem — **doble** *adj & nm* : double — ∼ *nmf* : stand-in, double — **doblemente** *adv* : doubly — **doblegar**

{52} *vt* : force to yield — **doblegarse** *vr* : give in — **doblez** *nm, pl* -bleces : fold, crease
doce *adj & nm* : twelve — **doceavo, -va** *adj* : twelfth — **docena** *nf* : dozen
docente *adj* : teaching
dócil *adj* : docile
doctor, -tora *n* : doctor — **doctorado** *nm* : doctorate
doctrina *nf* : doctrine
documentar *vt* : document — **documentación** *nf, pl* -ciones : documentation — **documental** *adj & nm* : documentary — **documento** *nm* : document
dogma *nm* : dogma — **dogmático, -ca** *adj* : dogmatic
dólar *nm* : dollar
doler {47} *vi* **1** : hurt **2 me duelen los pies** : my feet hurt — **dolerse** *vr* ∼ **de** : complain about — **dolor** *nm* **1** : pain **2** PENA : grief **3** ∼ **de cabeza** : headache **4** ∼ **de estómago** : stomachache — **dolorido, -da** *adj* **1** : sore **2** AFLIGIDO : hurt — **doloroso, -sa** *adj* : painful
domar *vt* : tame, break in
domesticar {72} *vt* : domesticate, tame — **doméstico, -ca** *adj* : domestic
domicilio *nm* : home, residence
dominar *vt* **1** : dominate, control **2** : master (a subject, a language, etc.) — **dominarse** *vr* : control oneself — **dominación** *nf, pl* -ciones : domination — **dominante** *adj* : dominant
domingo *nm* : Sunday — **dominical** *adj* **periódico** ∼ : Sunday newspaper
dominio *nm* **1** : authority **2** : mastery (of a subject) **3** TERRITORIO : domain
dominó *nm, pl* -nós : dominoes *pl* (game)
don¹ *nm* : courtesy title preceding a man's first name
don² *nm* **1** : gift **2** TALENTO : talent — **donación** *nf, pl* -ciones : donation — **donador, -dora** *n* : donor
donaire *nm* : grace, charm
donar *vt* : donate — **donante** *nmf* : donor — **donativo** *nm* : donation
donde *conj* : where — ∼ *prep Lat* : over by
dónde *adv* **1** : where **2 ¿de** ∼ **eres?** : where are you from? **3 ¿por** ∼**?** : whereabouts?
dondequiera *adv* **1** : anywhere **2** ∼ **que** : wherever, everywhere
doña *nf* : courtesy title preceding a woman's first name
doquier *adv* **por** ∼ : everywhere
dorar *vt* **1** : gild **2** : brown (food) — **dorado, -da** *adj* : gold, golden
dormir {27} *vt* : put to sleep — *vi* : sleep — **dormirse** *vr* : fall asleep — **dormido, -da** *adj* **1** : asleep **2** ENTUMECIDO : numb —

dormilón, -lona *n* : sleepyhead, late riser — **dormitar** *vi* : doze — **dormitorio** *nm* **1** : bedroom **2** : dormitory (in a college)
dorso *nm* : back
dos *adj & nm* : two — **doscientos, -tas** *adj* : two hundred — **doscientos** *nms & pl* : two hundred
dosel *nm* : canopy
dosis *nfs & pl* : dose, dosage
dotar *vt* **1** : provide, equip **2** ~ **de** : endow with — **dotación** *nf, pl* **-ciones 1** : endowment, funding **2** PERSONAL : personnel — **dote** *nf* **1** : dowry **2** ~**s** *nfpl* : gift, talent
dragar {52} *vt* : dredge — **draga** *nf* : dredge
dragón *nm, pl* **-gones** : dragon
drama *nm* : drama — **dramático, -ca** *adj* : dramatic — **dramatizar** {21} *vt* : dramatize — **dramaturgo, -ga** *n* : dramatist, playwright
drástico, -ca *adj* : drastic
drenar *vt* : drain — **drenaje** *nm* : drainage
droga *nf* : drug — **drogadicto, -ta** *n* : drug addict — **drogar** {52} *vt* : drug — **drogarse** *vr* : take drugs — **droguería** *nf* : drugstore
dromedario *nm* : dromedary
dual *adj* : dual
ducha *nf* : shower — **ducharse** *vr* : take a shower
ducho, -cha *adj* : experienced, skilled

duda *nf* : doubt — **dudar** *vt* : doubt — *vi* ~ **en** : hesitate to — **dudoso, -sa** *adj* **1** : doubtful **2** SOSPECHOSO : questionable
duelo *nm* **1** : duel **2** LUTO : mourning
duende *nm* : elf, imp
dueño, -na *n* **1** : owner **2** : landlord, landlady *f*
dulce *adj* **1** : sweet **2** : fresh (of water) **3** SUAVE : mild, gentle — ~ *nm* : candy, sweet — **dulzura** *nf* : sweetness
duna *nf* : dune
dúo *nm* : duo, duet
duodécimo, -ma *adj* : twelfth — ~ *n* : twelfth (in a series)
dúplex *nms & pl* : duplex (apartment)
duplicar {72} *vt* **1** : double **2** : duplicate, copy (a document, etc.) — **duplicado, -da** *adj* : duplicate — **duplicado** *nm* : copy
duque *nm* : duke — **duquesa** *nf* : duchess
durabilidad *nf* : durability
duración *nf, pl* **-ciones** : duration, length
duradero, -ra *adj* : durable, lasting
durante *prep* **1** : during **2** ~ **una hora** : for an hour
durar *vi* : endure, last
durazno *nm Lat* : peach
duro *adv* : hard — **duro, -ra** *adj* **1** : hard **2** SEVERO : harsh — **dureza** *nf* **1** : hardness **2** SEVERIDAD : harshness

E

e[1] *nf* : e, fifth letter of the Spanish alphabet
e[2] *conj* (*used instead of* **y** *before words beginning with i or hi*) : and
ebanista *nmf* : cabinetmaker
ébano *nm* : ebony
e–book *nm, pl* **e–books** : e-book, electronic book
ebrio, -bria *adj* : drunk
ebullición *nf, pl* **-ciones** : boiling
echar *vt* **1** : throw, cast **2** EXPULSAR : expel, dismiss **3** : give off, emit (smoke, sparks, etc.) **4** BROTAR : sprout **5** PONER : put (on) **6** ~ **a perder** : spoil, ruin **7** ~ **de menos** : miss — **echarse** *vr* **1** : throw oneself **2** ACOSTARSE : lie down **3** ~ **a** : start (to)
eclesiástico, -ca *adj* : ecclesiastic — ~ *nm* : clergyman
eclipse *nm* : eclipse — **eclipsar** *vi* : eclipse
eco *nm* : echo
ecología *nf* : ecology — **ecológico, -ca** *adj* : ecological — **ecologista** *nmf* : ecologist

economía *nf* **1** : economy **2** : economics (science) — **economico, -ca** *adj* **1** : economic, economical **2** BARATO : inexpensive — **economista** *nmf* : economist — **economizar** {21} *v* : save
ecosistema *nm* : ecosystem
ecuación *nf, pl* **-ciones** : equation
ecuador *nm* : equator
ecuánime *adj* **1** : even-tempered **2** : impartial (in law)
ecuatoriano, -na *adj* : Ecuadorian, Ecuadorean, Ecuadoran
ecuestre *adj* : equestrian
edad *nf* **1** : age **2 Edad Media** : Middle Ages *pl* **3 ¿qué** ~ **tienes?** : how old are you?
edición *nf, pl* **-ciones 1** : publishing, publication **2** : edition (of a book, etc.)
edicto *nm* : edict
edificar {72} *vt* : build — **edificio** *nm* : building

editar *vt* **1** : publish **2** : edit (a film, a text, etc.) — **editor, -tora** *n* **1** : publisher **2** : editor — **editorial** *adj* : publishing — ~ *nm* : editorial — ~ *nf* : publishing house

edredón *nm, pl* **-dones** : (down) comforter, duvet

educar {72} *vt* **1** : educate **2** CRIAR : bring up, raise **3** : train (the body, the voice, etc.) — **educación** *nf, pl* **-ciones** **1** : education **2** MODALES : (good) manners *pl* — **educado, -da** *adj* : polite — **educador, -dora** *n* : educator — **educativo, -va** *adj* : educational

efectivo, -va *adj* **1** : effective **2** REAL : real — **efectivo** *nm* : cash — **efectivamente** *adv* **1** : really **2** POR SUPUESTO : yes, indeed — **efectuar** {3} *vt* : bring about, carry out

efecto *nm* **1** : effect **2 en ~** : actually, in fact **3 efecto secundario** : side effect **4 efectos** *nmpl* : effects (**efectos especiales** special effects)

efervescente *adj* : effervescent — **efervescencia** *nf* : effervescence

eficaz *adj, pl* **-caces** **1** : effective **2** EFICIENTE : efficient — **eficacia** *nf* **1** : effectiveness **2** EFICIENCIA : efficiency

eficiente *adj* : efficient — **eficiencia** *nf* : efficiency

efímero, -ra *adj* : ephemeral

efusivo, -va *adj* : effusive

egipcio, -cia *adj* : Egyptian

ego *nm* : ego — **egocéntrico, -ca** *adj* : egocentric — **egoísmo** *nm* : egoism — **egoísta** *adj* : egoistic — ~ *nmf* : egoist

egresar *vi* : graduate — **egresado, -da** *n* : graduate — **egreso** *nm* : graduation, commencement

eje *nm* **1** : axis **2** : axle (of a wheel, etc.)

ejecutar *vt* **1** : execute, put to death **2** REALIZAR : carry out — **ejecución** *nf, pl* **-ciones** : execution

ejecutivo, -va *adj & n* : executive

ejemplar *adj* : exemplary — ~ *nm* **1** : copy, issue **2** EJEMPLO : example — **ejemplificar** {72} *vt* : exemplify — **ejemplo** *nm* **1** : example **2 por ~** : for example

ejercer {86} *vt* **1** : practice (a profession) **2** : exercise (a right, etc.) — *vi* **~ de** : practice as, work as — **ejercicio** *nm* **1** : exercise **2** : practice (of a profession, etc.)

ejército *nm* : army

el, la *art, pl* **los, las** : the — **el** *pron* (*referring to masculine nouns*) **1** : the one **2 ~ que** : he who, whoever, the one that

él *pron* : he, him

elaborar *vt* **1** : manufacture, produce **2** : draw up (a plan, etc.)

elástico, -ca *adj* : elastic — **elástico** *nm* : elastic — **elasticidad** *nf* : elasticity

elección *nf, pl* **-ciones** **1** : election **2** SELECCIÓN : choice — **elector, -tora** *n* : voter — **electorado** *nm* : electorate — **electoral** *adj* : electoral

electricidad *nf* : electricity — **eléctrico, -ca** *adj* : electric, electrical — **electricista** *nmf* : electrician — **electrificar** {72} *vt* : electrify — **electrizar** {21} *vt* : electrify, thrill — **electrocutar** *vt* : electrocute

electrodo *nm* : electrode

electrodoméstico *nm* : electric appliance

electromagnético, -ca *adj* : electromagnetic

electrón *nm, pl* **-trones** : electron — **electrónico, -ca** *adj* : electronic — **electrónica** *nf* : electronics

elefante, -ta *n* : elephant

elegante *adj* : elegant — **elegancia** *nf* : elegance

elegía *nf* : elegy

elegir {28} *vt* **1** : elect **2** ESCOGER : choose, select — **elegible** *adj* : eligible

elemento *nm* : element — **elemental** *adj* **1** : elementary, basic **2** ESENCIAL : fundamental

elenco *nm* : cast (of actors)

elevar *vt* **1** : raise, lift **2** ASCENDER : elevate (in a hierarchy), promote — **elevarse** *vr* : rise — **elevación** *nf, pl* **-ciones** : elevation — **elevador** *nm* **1** : hoist **2** *Lat* : elevator

eliminar *vt* : eliminate — **eliminación** *nf, pl* **-ciones** : elimination

elipse *nf* : ellipse — **elíptico, -ca** *adj* : elliptical, elliptic

elite *or* **élite** *nf* : elite

elixir *or* **elíxir** *nm* : elixir

ella *pron* : she, her — **ello** *pron* : it — **ellos, ellas** *pron pl* **1** : they, them **2 de ellos, de ellas** : theirs

elocuente *adj* : eloquent — **elocuencia** *nf* : eloquence

elogiar *vt* : praise — **elogio** *nm* : praise

eludir *vt* : avoid, elude

email *nm, pl* **emails:** e-mail

emanar *vi* **~ de** : emanate from

emancipar *vt* : emancipate — **emanciparse** *vr* : free oneself — **emancipación** *nf, pl* **-ciones** : emancipation

embadurnar *vt* : smear, daub

embajada *nf* : embassy — **embajador, -dora** *n* : ambassador

embalar *vt* : wrap up, pack — **embalaje** *nm* : packing

embaldosar *vt* : pave with tiles

embalsamar *vt* : embalm

embalse *nm* : dam, reservoir

embarazar {21} *vt* **1** : make pregnant **2** IMPEDIR : restrict, hamper — **embarazada** *adj* : pregnant — **embarazo** *nm* **1** : preg-

nancy **2** IMPEDIMENTO : hindrance, obstacle — **embarazoso, -sa** *adj* : embarrassing
embarcar {72} *vt* : load — **embarcarse** *vr* : embark, board — **embarcación** *nf, pl* **-ciones** : boat, craft — **embarcadero** *nm* : pier, jetty — **embarco** *nm* : embarkation
embargar {52} *vt* **1** : seize, impound **2** : overwhelm (with emotion, etc.) — **embargo** *nm* **1** : embargo **2** : seizure (in law) **3 sin ~** : nevertheless
embarque *nm* : loading (of goods), boarding (of passengers)
embarrancar {72} *vi* : run aground
embarullarse *vr fam* : get mixed up
embaucar {72} *vt* : trick, swindle — **embaucador, -dora** *n* : swindler
embeber *vt* : absorb — *vi* : shrink — **embeberse** *vr* : become absorbed
embelesar *vt* : enchant, delight — **embelesado, -da** *adj* : spellbound
embellecer {53} *vt* : embellish, beautify
embestir {54} *vt* : attack, charge at — *vi* : charge, attack — **embestida** *nf* **1** : attack **2** : charge (of a bull)
emblema *nm* : emblem
embobar *vt* : amaze, fascinate
embocadura *nf* **1** : mouth (of a river, etc.) **2** : mouthpiece (of an instrument)
émbolo *nm* : piston
embolsarse *vr* : put in one's pocket
emborracharse *vr* : get drunk
emborronar *vt* **1** : smudge, blot **2** GARABATEAR : scribble
emboscar {72} *vt* : ambush — **emboscada** *nf* : ambush
embotar *vt* : dull, blunt
embotellar *vt* : bottle (up) — **embotellamiento** *nm* : traffic jam
embrague *nm* : clutch — **embragar** {52} *vi* : engage the clutch
embriagarse {52} *vr* : get drunk — **embriagado, -da** *adj* : intoxicated, drunk — **embriagador, -dora** *adj* : intoxicating — **embriaguez** *nf* : drunkenness
embrión *nm, pl* **-briones** : embryo
embrollo *nm* : tangle, confusion
embrujar *vt* : bewitch — **embrujo** *nm* : spell, curse
embrutecer *vt* : brutalize
embudo *nm* : funnel
embuste *nm* : lie — **embustero, -ra** *adj* : lying — **~** *n* : liar, cheat
embutir *vt* : stuff — **embutido** *nm* : sausage, cold meat
emergencia *nf* : emergency
emerger {15} *vi* : emerge, appear
emigrar *vi* **1** : emigrate **2** : migrate (of animals) — **emigración** *nf, pl* **-ciones** **1** : emigration **2** : migration (of animals) — **emigrante** *adj & nmf* : emigrant

eminente *adj* : eminent — **eminencia** *nf* : eminence
emitir *vt* **1** : emit **2** EXPRESAR : express (an opinion, etc.) **3** : broadcast (on radio or television) **4** : issue (money, stamps, etc.) — **emisión** *nf, pl* **-siones** **1** : emission **2** : broadcast (on radio or television) **3** : issue (of money, etc.) — **emisora** *nf* : radio station
emoción *nf, pl* **-ciones** : emotion — **emocional** *adj* : emotional — **emocionante** *adj* **1** : moving, touching **2** APASIONANTE : exciting, thrilling — **emocionar** *vt* **1** : move, touch **2** APASIONAR : excite, thrill — **emocionarse** *vr* **1** : be moved **2** APASIONARSE : get excited — **emotivo, -va** *adj* **1** : emotional **2** CONMOVEDOR : moving
emoticón *nm, pl* **-cones** : emoticon
emoticono : emoticón
empacar {72} *vt Lat* : pack
empachar *vt* : give indigestion to — **empacharse** *vr* : get indigestion — **empacho** *nm* : indigestion
empadronarse *vr* : register to vote
empalagoso, -sa *adj* : excessively sweet, cloying
empalizada *nf* : palisade (fence)
empalmar *vt* : connect, link — *vi* : meet, converge — **empalme** *nm* **1** : connection, link **2** : junction (of a railroad, etc.)
empanada *nf* : pie, turnover — **empanadilla** *nf* : meat or seafood pie
empanar *vt* : bread (in cooking)
empantanar *vt* : flood — **empantanarse** *vr* **1** : become flooded **2** : get bogged down
empañar *vt* **1** : steam (up) **2** : tarnish (one's reputation, etc.) — **empañarse** *vr* : fog up
empapar *vt* : soak — **empaparse** *vr* : get soaking wet
empapelar *vt* : wallpaper
empaquetar *vt* : pack, package
emparedado, -da *adj* : walled in, confined — **emparedado** *nm* : sandwich
emparejar *vt* : match up, pair — **emparejarse** *vr* : pair off
emparentado, -da *adj* : related, kindred
empastar *vt* : fill (a tooth) — **empaste** *nm* : filling
empatar *vi* : result in a draw, be tied — **empate** *nm* : draw, tie
empedernido, -da *adj* : inveterate, hardened
empedrar {55} *vt* : pave (with stones) — **empedrado** *nm* : paving, pavement
empeine *nm* : instep
empeñar *vt* : pawn — **empeñarse** *vr* **1** : insist, persist **2** ENDEUDARSE : go into debt **3** **~ en** : make an effort to — **empeñado, -da** *adj* **1** : determined, committed **2** EN-

DEUDADO : in debt — **empeño** *nm* **1** : determination, effort **2 casa de ~s** : pawnshop

empeorar *vi* : get worse — *vt* : make worse

empequeñecer {53} *vt* : diminish, make smaller

emperador *nm* : emperor — **emperatriz** *nf*, *pl* -**trices** : empress

empezar {29} *v* : start, begin

empinar *vt* : raise — **empinarse** *vr* : stand on tiptoe — **empinado, -da** *adj* : steep

empírico, -ca *adj* : empirical

emplasto *nm* : poultice

emplazar {21} *vt* **1** : summon, subpoena **2** SITUAR : place, locate — **emplazamiento** *nm* **1** : location, site **2** CITACIÓN : summons, subpoena

emplear *vt* **1** : employ **2** USAR : use — **emplearse** *vr* **1** : get a job **2** USARSE : be used — **empleado, -da** *n* : employee — **empleador, -dora** *n* : employer — **empleo** *nm* **1** : occupation, job **2** USO : use

empobrecer {53} *vt* : impoverish — **empobrecerse** *vr* : become poor

empollar *vi* : brood (eggs) — *vt* : incubate

empolvarse *vr* : powder one's face

empotrar *vt* : fit, build into — **empotrado, -da** *adj* : built-in

emprender *vt* : undertake, begin — **emprendedor, -dora** *adj* : enterprising

empresa *nf* **1** COMPAÑIA : company, firm **2** TAREA : undertaking — **empresarial** *adj* : business, managerial — **empresario, -ria** *n* **1** : businessman *m*, businesswoman *f* **2** : impresario (in theater), promoter (in sports)

empujar *v* : push — **empuje** *nm* : impetus, drive — **empujón** *nm*, *pl* -**jones** : push, shove

empuñar *vt* : grasp, take hold of

emular *vt* : emulate

en *prep* **1** : in **2** DENTRO DE : into, inside (of) **3** SOBRE : on **4 ~ avión** : by plane **5 ~ casa** : at home

enajenar *vt* : alienate — **enajenación** *nf*, *pl* -**ciones** : alienation

enagua *nf* : slip, petticoat

enaltecer {53} *vt* : praise, extol

enamorar *vt* : win the love of — **enamorarse** *vr* : fall in love — **enamorado, -da** *adj* : in love — **~** *n* : lover, sweetheart

enano, -na *adj & n* : dwarf

enarbolar *vt* **1** : hoist, raise **2** : brandish (arms, etc.)

enardecer {53} *vt* : stir up, excite

encabezar {21} *vt* **1** : head, lead **2** : put a heading on (an article, a list, etc.) — **encabezamiento** *nm* **1** : heading **2** : headline (in a newspaper)

encabritarse *vr* : rear up

encadenar *vt* **1** : chain, tie (up) **2** ENLAZAR : connect, link

encajar *vt* : fit (together) — *vi* **1** : fit **2** CUADRAR : conform, tally — **encaje** *nm* : lace

encalar *vt* : whitewash

encallar *vi* : run aground

encaminar *vt* : direct, aim — **encaminarse** *vr* **~ a** : head for — **encaminado, -da** *adj* **~ a** : aimed at, designed to

encandilar *vt* : dazzle

encanecer {53} *vi* : turn gray

encantar *vt* : enchant, bewitch — *vi* **me encanta esta canción** : I love this song — **encantado, -da** *adj* **1** : delighted **2** HECHIZADO : bewitched — **encantador, -dora** *adj* : charming, delightful — **encantamiento** *nm* : enchantment, spell — **encanto** *nm* **1** : charm, fascination **2** HECHIZO : spell

encapotarse *vr* : cloud over — **encapotado, -da** *adj* : overcast

encapricharse *vr* **~ con** : be infatuated with

encapuchado, -da *adj* : hooded

encaramar *vt* : lift up — **encaramarse** *vr* **~ a** : climb up on

encarar *vt* : face, confront

encarcelar *vt* : imprison — **encarcelamiento** *nm* : imprisonment

encarecer {53} *vt* : increase, raise (price, value, etc.) — **encarecerse** *vr* : become more expensive

encargar {52} *vt* **1** : put in charge of **2** PEDIR : order — **encargarse** *vr* **~ de** : take charge of — **encargado, -da** *adj* : in charge — **~** *n* : manager, person in charge — **encargo** *nm* **1** : errand **2** TAREA : assignment, task **3** PEDIDO : order

encariñarse *vr* **~ con** : become fond of

encarnar *vt* : embody — **encarnación** *nf*, *pl* -**ciones** : embodiment — **encarnado, -da** *adj* **1** : incarnate **2** ROJO : red

encarnizarse {21} *vr* **~ con** : attack viciously — **encarnizado, -da** *adj* : bitter, bloody

encarrilar *vt* : put on the right track

encasillar *vt* : pigeonhole

encauzar {21} *vt* : channel

encender {56} *vt* **1** : light, set fire to **2** PRENDER : switch on, start **3** AVIVAR : arouse (passions, etc.) — **encenderse** *vr* **1** : get excited **2** RUBORIZARSE : blush — **encendedor** *nm* : lighter — **encendido, -da** *adj* : lit, on — **encendido** *nm* : ignition (switch)

encerar *vt* : wax, polish — **encerado, -da** *adj* : waxed — **encerado** *nm* : blackboard

encerrar {55} *vt* **1** : lock up, shut away **2** CONTENER : contain

encestar *vi* : score (in basketball)

enchilada *nf* : enchilada

enchufar *vt* : plug in, connect — **enchufe** *nm* : plug, socket

encía *nf* : gum (tissue)

encíclica *nf* : encyclical

enciclopedia *nf* : encyclopedia — **enciclopédico, -ca** *adj* : encyclopedic

encierro *nm* **1** : confinement **2** : sit-in (at a university, etc.)

encima *adv* **1** : on top **2** ADEMÁS : as well, besides **3** ~ **de** : on, over, on top of **4 por** ~ **de** : above, beyond

encinta *adj* : pregnant

enclenque *adj* : weak, sickly

encoger {15} *v* : shrink — **encogerse** *vr* **1** : shrink **2** : cower, cringe **3** ~ **de hombros** : shrug (one's shoulders) — **encogido, -da** *adj* **1** : shrunken **2** TÍMIDO : shy

encolar *vt* : glue, stick

encolerizar {21} *vt* : enrage, infuriate — **encolerizarse** *vr* : get angry

encomendar {55} *vt* : entrust

encomienda *nf* **1** : charge, mission **2** *Lat* : parcel

encono *nm* : rancor, animosity

encontrar {19} *vt* **1** : find **2** : meet, encounter (difficulties, etc.) — **encontrarse** *vr* **1** : meet **2** HALLARSE : find oneself, be — **encontrado, -da** *adj* : contrary, opposing

encorvar *vt* : bend, curve — **encorvarse** *vr* : bend over, stoop

encrespar *vt* **1** : curl **2** IRRITAR : irritate — **encresparse** *vr* **1** : curl one's hair **2** IRRITARSE : get annoyed **3** : become choppy (of the sea)

encrucijada *nf* : crossroads

encuadernar *vt* : bind (a book) — **encuadernación** *nf, pl* **-ciones** : bookbinding

encuadrar *vt* **1** : frame **2** ENCAJAR : fit **3** COMPRENDER : contain, include

encubrir {2} *vt* : conceal, cover (up) — **encubierto, -ta** *adj* : covert — **encubrimiento** *nm* : cover-up

encuentro *nm* : meeting, encounter

encuestar *vt* : poll, take a survey of — **encuesta** *nf* **1** : investigation, inquiry **2** SONDEO : survey — **encuestador, -dora** *n* : pollster

encumbrado, -da *adj* : eminent, distinguished

encurtir *vt* : pickle

endeble *adj* : weak, feeble — **endeblez** *nf* : weakness, frailty

endemoniado, -da *adj* : wicked

enderezar {21} *vt* **1** : straighten (out) **2** : put upright, stand on end

endeudarse *vr* : go into debt — **endeudado, -da** *adj* : indebted, in debt — **endeudamiento** *nm* : debt

endiablado, -da *adj* **1** : wicked, diabolical **2** : complicated, difficult

endibia *or* **endivia** *nf* : endive

endosar *vt* : endorse — **endoso** *nm* : endorsement

endulzar {21} *vt* **1** : sweeten **2** : soften, mellow (a tone, a response, etc.) — **endulzante** *nm* : sweetener

endurecer {53} *vt* : harden — **endurecerse** *vr* : become hardened

enema *nm* : enema

enemigo, -ga *adj* : hostile — ~ *n* : enemy — **enemistad** *nf* : enmity — **enemistar** *vt* : make enemies of — **enemistarse** *vr* ~ **con** : fall out with

energía *nf* : energy — **enérgico, -ca** *adj* : energetic, vigorous, forceful

enero *nm* : January

enervar *vt* **1** : enervate, weaken **2** *fam* : get on one's nerves

enésimo, -ma *adj* **por enésima vez** : for the umpteenth time

enfadar *vt* : annoy, make angry — **enfadarse** *vr* : get annoyed — **enfado** *nm* : anger, annoyance — **enfadoso, -sa** *adj* : annoying

enfatizar {21} *vt* : emphasize — **énfasis** *nms & pl* : emphasis — **enfático, -ca** *adj* : emphatic

enfermar *vt* : make sick — *vi* : get sick — **enfermedad** *nf* : sickness, disease — **enfermería** *nf* : infirmary — **enfermero, -ra** *n* : nurse — **enfermizo, -za** *adj* : sickly — **enfermo, -ma** *adj* : sick — ~ *n* : sick person, patient

enflaquecer {53} *vi* : lose weight

enfocar {72} *vt* **1** : focus (on) **2** : consider (a problem, etc.) — **enfoque** *nm* : focus

enfrascarse {72} *vr* ~ **en** : immerse oneself in, get caught up in

enfrentar *vt* **1** : confront, face **2** : bring face to face — **enfrentarse** *vr* ~ **con** : confront, clash with — **enfrente** *adv* **1** : opposite **2** ~ **de** : in front of

enfriar {85} *vt* : chill, cool — **enfriarse** *vr* **1** : get cold **2** RESFRIARSE : catch a cold — **enfriamiento** *nm* **1** : cooling off **2** CATARRO : cold

enfurecer {53} *vt* : infuriate — **enfurecerse** *vr* : fly into a rage

enfurruñarse *vr fam* : sulk

engalanar *vt* : decorate — **engalanarse** *vr* : dress up

enganchar *vt* : hook, snag, catch — **engancharse** *vr* **1** : get caught **2** ALISTARSE : enlist

engañar *vt* **1** EMBAUCAR : trick, deceive **2** : cheat on, be unfaithful to — **engañarse** *vr*

1 : deceive oneself **2** EQUIVOCARSE : be mistaken — **engaño** *nm* : deception, deceit — **engañoso, -sa** *adj* : deceptive, deceitful

engatusar *vt* : coax, cajole

engendrar *vt* **1** : beget **2** : engender, give rise to (suspicions, etc.)

englobar *vt* : include, embrace

engomar *vt* : glue

engordar *vt* : fatten — *vi* : gain weight

engorroso, -sa *adj* : bothersome

engranar *v* : mesh, engage — **engranaje** *nm* : gears *pl*

engrandecer {53} *vt* **1** : enlarge **2** ENALTE- CER : exalt

engrapar *vt Lat* : staple — **engrapadora** *nf Lat* : stapler

engrasar *v* : lubricate, grease — **engrase** *nm* : lubrication

engreído, -da *adj* : conceited

engrosar {19} *vt* : swell — *vi* : gain weight

engrudo *nm* : paste

engullir {38} *vt* : gulp down, gobble up

enhebrar *vt* : thread

enhorabuena *nf* : congratulations *pl*

enigma *nm* : enigma — **enigmático, -ca** *adj* : enigmatic

enjabonar *vt* : soap (up), lather

enjaezar {21} *vt* : harness

enjalbegar {52} *vt* : whitewash

enjambrar *vi* : swarm — **enjambre** *nm* : swarm

enjaular *vt* **1** : cage **2** *fam* : jail

enjuagar {52} *vt* : rinse — **enju- ague** *nm* **1** : rinse **2** ~ **bucal** : mouthwash

enjugar {52} *vt* **1** : wipe away (tears) **2** : wipe out (debt)

enjuiciar *vt* **1** : prosecute **2** JUZGAR : try

enjuto, -ta *adj* : gaunt, lean

enlace *nm* **1** : bond, link **2** : junction (of a highway, etc.)

enlatar *vt* : can

enlazar {21} *vt* : join, link — *vi* ~ **con** : link up with

enlistarse *vr Lat* : enlist

enlodar *vt* : cover with mud

enloquecer {53} *vt* : drive crazy — **enloquecerse** *vr* : go crazy

enlosar *vt* : pave, tile

enlutarse *vr* : go into mourning

enmarañar *vt* **1** : tangle **2** COMPLICAR : complicate **3** CONFUNDIR : confuse — **enmarañarse** *vr* **1** : get tangled up **2** CON- FUNDIRSE : become confused

enmarcar {72} *vt* : frame

enmascarar *vt* : mask

enmendar {55} *vt* **1** : amend **2** CORREGIR : emend, correct — **enmendarse** *vr* : mend one's ways — **enmienda** *nf* **1** : amendment **2** CORRECCIÓN : correction

enmohecerse {53} *vr* **1** : become moldy **2** OXIDARSE : rust

enmudecer {53} *vt* : silence — *vi* : fall silent

ennegrecer {53} *vt* : blacken

ennoblecer {53} *vt* : ennoble, dignify

enojar *vt* **1** : anger **2** MOLESTAR : annoy — **enojarse** *vr* ~ **con** : get upset with — **enojo** *nm* **1** : anger **2** MOLESTIA : annoyance — **enojoso, -sa** *adj* : annoying

enorgullecer {53} *vt* : make proud — **enorgullecerse** *vr* ~ **de** : pride oneself on

enorme *adj* : enormous — **enormemente** *adv* : enormously, extremely — **enormidad** *nf* : enormity

enraizar {30} *vi* : take root

enredadera *nf* : climbing plant, vine

enredar *vt* **1** : tangle up, entangle **2** CON- FUNDIR : confuse **3** IMPLICAR : involve — **enredarse** *vr* **1** : become entangled **2** ~ **en** : get mixed up in — **enredo** *nm* **1** : tangle **2** EMBROLLO : confusion, mess — **enredoso, -sa** *adj* : tangled up, complicated

enrejado *nm* **1** : railing **2** REJILLA : grating, grille **3** : trellis (for plants)

enrevesado, -da *adj* : complicated

enriquecer {53} *vt* : enrich — **enriquecerse** *vr* : get rich

enrojecer {53} *vt* : redden — **enrojecerse** *vr* : blush

enrolar *vt* : enlist — **enrolarse** *vr* ~ **en** : enlist in

enrollar *vt* : roll up, coil

enroscar {72} *vt* **1** : roll up **2** ATORNILLAR : screw in

ensalada *nf* : salad

ensalzar {21} *vt* : praise

ensamblar *vt* : assemble, fit together

ensanchar *vt* **1** : widen **2** AMPLIAR : expand — **ensanche** *nm* **1** : widening **2** : (urban) expansion, development

ensangrentado, -da *adj* : bloody, bloodstained

ensañarse *vr* : act cruelly

ensartar *vt* : string, thread

ensayar *vi* : rehearse — *vt* : try out, test — **ensayo** *nm* **1** : essay **2** PRUEBA : trial, test **3** : rehearsal (in theater, etc.)

enseguida *adv* : right away, immediately

ensenada *nf* : inlet, cove

enseñar *vt* **1** : teach **2** MOSTRAR : show — **enseñanza** *nf* **1** EDUCACIÓN : education **2** INSTRUCCIÓN : teaching

enseres *nmpl* **1** : equipment **2** ~ **domésticos** : household goods

ensillar *vt* : saddle (up)

ensimismarse *vr* : lose oneself in thought

ensombrecer {53} *vt* : cast a shadow over, darken

ensoñación *nf, pl* **-ciones** : fantasy, daydream

ensordecer {53} *vt* : deafen — *vi* : go deaf — **ensordecedor, -dora** *adj* : deafening

ensortijar *vt* : curl

ensuciar *vt* : soil — **ensuciarse** *vr* : get dirty

ensueño *nm* : daydream, fantasy

entablar *vt* : initiate, start

entallar *vt* : tailor, fit (clothing) — *vi* : fit

entarimado *nm* : floorboards, flooring

ente *nm* **1** : being **2** ORGANISMO : body, organization

entender {56} *vt* **1** : understand **2** OPINAR : think, believe — *vi* **1** : understand **2** ～ **de** : know about, be good at — **entenderse** *vr* **1** : understand each other **2** LLEVARSE BIEN : get along well — ～ *nm* **a mi** ～ : in my opinion — **entendido, -da** *adj* **1** : understood **2 eso se da por** ～ : that goes without saying **3 tener** ～ : be under the impression — **entendimiento** *nm* **1** : understanding **2** INTELIGENCIA : intellect

enterar *vt* : inform — **enterarse** *vr* : find out, learn — **enterado, -da** *adj* : well-informed

entereza *nf* **1** HONRADEZ : integrity **2** FORTALEZA : fortitude **3** FIRMEZA : resolve

enternecer {53} *vt* : move, touch

entero, -ra *adj* **1** : whole **2** TOTAL : absolute, total **3** INTACTO : intact — **entero** *nm* : integer, whole number

enterrar {55} *vt* : bury

entibiar *vt* : cool (down) — **entibiarse** *vr* : become lukewarm

entidad *nf* **1** : entity **2** ORGANIZACIÓN : body, organization

entierro *nm* **1** : burial **2** : funeral (ceremony)

entomología *nf* : entomology — **entomólogo, -ga** *n* : entomologist

entonar *vt* : sing, intone — *vi* : be in tune

entonces *adv* **1** : then **2 desde** ～ : since then

entornado, -da *adj* : half-closed, ajar

entorno *nm* : surroundings *pl*, environment

entorpecer {53} *vt* **1** : hinder, obstruct **2** : numb, dull (wits, reactions, etc.)

entrada *nf* **1** : entrance, entry **2** BILLETE : ticket **3** COMIENZO : beginning **4** : inning (in baseball) **5** ～**s** *nfpl* : income **6 tener** ～**s** : have a receding hairline

entraña *nf* **1** : core, heart **2** ～**s** *nfpl* VÍSCERAS : entrails, innards — **entrañable** *adj* : close, intimate — **entrañar** *vt* : involve

entrar *vi* **1** : enter **2** EMPEZAR : begin — *vt* : introduce, bring in

entre *prep* **1** : between **2** : among

entreabrir {2} *vt* : leave ajar — **entreabierto, -ta** *adj* : half-open, ajar

entreacto *nm* : intermission

entrecejo *nm* **fruncir el** ～ : knit one's brows, frown

entrecortado, -da *adj* : faltering (of the voice), labored (of breathing)

entrecruzar {21} *vi* : intertwine

entredicho *nm* : doubt, question

entregar {52} *vt* : deliver, hand over — **entregarse** *vr* : surrender — **entrega** *nf* **1** : delivery **2** DEDICACIÓN : dedication, devotion **3** ～ **inicial** : down payment

entrelazar {21} *vt* : intertwine — **entrelazarse** *vr* : become intertwined

entremés *nm, pl* **-meses 1** : hors d'oeuvre **2** : short play (in theater)

entremeterse → **entrometerse**

entremezclar *vt* : mix (up)

entrenar *vt* : train, drill — **entrenarse** *vr* : train — **entrenador, -dora** *n* : trainer, coach — **entranamiento** *nm* : training

entrepierna *nf* : crotch

entresacar {72} *vt* : pick out, select

entresuelo *nm* : mezzanine

entretanto *adv* : meanwhile — ～ *nm* **en el** ～ : in the meantime

entretener {80} *vt* **1** : entertain **2** DESPISTAR : distract **3** RETRASAR : delay, hold up — **entretenerse** *vr* **1** : amuse oneself **2** DEMORARSE : dawdle — **entretenido, -da** *adj* : entertaining — **entretenimiento** *nm* **1** : entertainment, amusement **2** PASATIEMPO : pastime

entrever {88} *vt* : catch a glimpse of, make out

entrevistar *vt* : interview — **entrevista** *nf* : interview — **entrevistador, -dora** *n* : interviewer

entristecer {53} *vt* : sadden

entrometerse *vr* : interfere — **entrometido, -da** *adj* : meddling, nosy — *n* : meddler

entroncar {72} *vi* : be related, be connected

entumecer {53} *vt* : make numb — **entumecerse** *vr* : go numb — **entumecido, -da** *adj* **1** : numb **2** : stiff (of muscles, etc.)

enturbiar *vt* : cloud — **enturbiarse** *vr* : become cloudy

entusiasmar *vt* : fill with enthusiasm — **entusiasmarse** *vr* : get excited — **entusiasmo** *nm* : enthusiasm — **entusiasta** *adj* : enthusiastic — ～ *nmf* : enthusiast

enumerar *vt* : enumerate, list — **enumeración** *nf, pl* **-ciones** : enumeration, count

enunciar *vt* : enunciate — **enunciación** *nf, pl* **-ciones** : enunciation

envalentonar *vt* : make bold, encourage — **envalentonarse** *vr* : be brave

envanecerse {53} *vr* : become vain

envasar *vt* **1** : package **2** : bottle, can — **envase** *nm* **1** : packaging **2** RECIPIENTE : container **3** : jar, bottle, can

envejecer {53} *v* : age — **envejecido, -da** *adj* : aged, old — **envejecimiento** *nm* : aging

envenenar *vt* : poison — **envenenamiento** *nm* : poisoning

envergadura *nf* **1** ALCANCE : scope **2** : span (of wings, etc.)

envés *nm, pl* **-veses** : reverse side

enviar {85} *vt* : send — **enviado, -da** *n* : envoy, correspondent

envidiar *vt* : envy — **envidia** *nf* : envy, jealousy — **envidioso, -sa** *adj* : jealous, envious

envilecer {53} *vt* : degrade, debase — **envilecimiento** *nm* : degradation

envío *nm* **1** : sending, shipment **2** : remittance (of funds)

enviudar *vi* : be widowed

envolver {89} *vt* **1** : wrap **2** RODEAR : surround **3** IMPLICAR : involve — **envoltorio** *nm or* **envoltura** *nf* : wrapping, wrapper

enyesar *vt* **1** : plaster **2** ESCAYOLAR : put in a plaster cast

enzima *nf* : enzyme

épico, -ca *adj* : epic — **épica** *nf* : epic

epidemia *nf* : epidemic — **epidémico, -ca** *adj* : epidemic

epilepsia *nf* : epilepsy — **epiléptico, -ca** *adj & n* : epileptic

epílogo *nm* : epilogue

episodio *nm* : episode

epitafio *nm* : epitaph

epíteto *nm* : epithet

época *nf* **1** : epoch, period **2** ESTACIÓN : season

epopeya *nf* : epic poem

equidad *nf* : equity, justice

equilátero, -ra *adj* : equilateral

equilibrar *vt* : balance — **equilibrado, -da** *adj* : well-balanced — **equilibrio** *nm* **1** : balance, equilibrium **2** JUICIO : good sense

equinoccio *nm* : equinox

equipaje *nm* : baggage, luggage

equipar *vt* : equip

equiparar *vt* **1** IGUALAR : make equal **2** COMPARAR : compare — **equiparable** *adj* : comparable

equipo *nm* **1** : equipment **2** : team, crew (in sports, etc.)

equitación *nf, pl* **-ciones** : horseback riding

equitativo, -va *adj* : equitable, fair, just

equivaler {84} *vi* : be equivalent — **equivalencia** *nf* : equivalence — **equivalente** *adj & nm* : equivalent

equivocar {72} *vt* : mistake, confuse — **equivocarse** *vr* : make a mistake — **equivocación** *nf, pl* **-ciones** : error, mistake — **equivocado, -da** *adj* : mistaken, wrong

equívoco, -ca *adj* : ambiguous — **equívoco** *nm* : misunderstanding

era *nf* : era

erario *nm* : public treasury, funds *pl*

erección *nf, pl* **-ciones** : erection

erguir {31} *vt* : raise, lift — **erguirse** *vr* : rise (up) — **erguido, -da** *adj* : erect, upright

erigir {35} *vt* : build, erect — **erigirse** *vr* ~ **en** : set oneself up as

erizarse {21} *vr* : bristle, stand on end — **erizado, -da** *adj* : bristly

erizo *nm* **1** : hedgehog **2** ~ **de mar** : sea urchin

ermitaño, -ña *n* : hermit

erosionar *vt* : erode — **erosión** *nf, pl* **-siones** : erosion

erótico, -ca *adj* : erotic

erradicar {72} *vt* : eradicate

errar {32} *vt* : miss — *vi* **1** : be wrong, be mistaken **2** VAGAR : wander — **errado, -da** *adj Lat* : wrong, mistaken

errata *nf* : misprint

errático, -ca *adj* : erratic

error *nm* : error — **erróneo, -nea** *adj* : erroneous, mistaken

eructar *vi* : belch, burp — **eructo** *nm* : belch, burp

erudito, -ta *adj* : erudite, learned

erupción *nf, pl* **-ciones** **1** : eruption **2** SARPULLIDO : rash

esa, ésa → **ese, ése**

esbelto, -ta *adj* : slender, slim

esbozar {21} *vt* : sketch, outline — **esbozo** *nm* : sketch, outline

escabechar *vt* : pickle — **escabeche** *nm* : brine (for pickling)

escabel *nm* : footstool

escabroso, -sa *adj* **1** : rugged, rough **2** ESPINOSO : thorny, difficult **3** ATREVIDO : shocking, risqué

escabullirse {38} *vr* : slip away, escape

escalar *vt* : climb, scale — *vi* : escalate — **escala** *nf* **1** : scale **2** ESCALERA : ladder **3** : stopover (of an airplane, etc.) — **escalada** *nf* : ascent, climb — **escalador, -dora** *n* ALPINISTA : mountain climber

escaldar *vt* : scald

escalera *nf* **1** : stairs *pl*, staircase **2** ESCALA : ladder **3** ~ **mecánica** : escalator

escalfar *vt* : poach

escalinata *nf* : flight of stairs

escalofrío *nm* : shiver, chill — **escalofriante** *adj* : chilling, horrifying

escalonar *vt* **1** : stagger, spread out **2** : terrace (land) — **escalón** *nm, pl* **-lones** : step, rung

escama *nf* **1** : scale (of fish or reptiles) **2** : flake (of skin) — **escamoso, -sa** *adj* : scaly

escamotear *vt* **1** : conceal **2** ~ **algo a algn** : rob s.o. of sth

escandalizar {21} *vt* : scandalize — **escandalizarse** *vr* : be shocked — **escándalo** *nm* **1** : scandal **2** ALBOROTO : scene, commotion — **escandaloso, -sa** *adj* **1** : shocking, scandalous **2** RUIDOSO : noisy

escandinavo, -va *adj* : Scandinavian

escáner *nm* : scanner

escaño *nm* **1** : seat (in a legislative body) **2** BANCO : bench

escapar *vi* : escape, run away — **escaparse** *vr* **1** : escape **2** : leak out (of gas, water, etc.) — **escapada** *nf* : escape

escaparate *nm* : store window

escapatoria *nf* : loophole, way out

escape *nm* **1** : leak (of gas, water, etc.) **2** : exhaust (from a vehicle)

escarabajo *nm* : beetle

escarbar *vt* **1** : dig, scratch, poke **2** ~ **en** : pry into

escarcha *nf* : frost (on a surface)

escarlata *adj & nf* : scarlet — **escarlatina** *nf* : scarlet fever

escarmentar {55} *vi* : learn one's lesson — **escarmiento** *nm* : lesson, punishment

escarnecer {53} *vt* : ridicule, mock — **escarnio** *nm* : ridicule, mockery

escarola *nf* : escarole, endive

escarpa *nf* : steep slope — **escarpado, -da** *adj* : steep

escasear *vi* : be scarce — **escasez** *nf, pl* **-seces** : shortage, scarcity — **escaso, -sa** *adj* **1** : scarce **2** ~ **de** : short of

escatimar *vt* : be sparing with, skimp on

escayolar *vt* : put in a plaster cast — **escayola** *nf* **1** : plaster (for casts) **2** : plaster cast

escena *nf* **1** : scene **2** ESCENARIO : stage — **escenario** *nm* **1** : setting, scene **2** ESCENA : stage — **escénico, -ca** *adj* : scenic

escepticismo *nm* : skepticism — **escéptico, -ca** *adj* : skeptical — ~ *n* : skeptic

esclarecer {53} *vt* : shed light on, clarify

esclavo, -va *n* : slave — **esclavitud** *nf* : slavery — **esclavizar** {21} *vt* : enslave

esclerosis *nf* ~ **múltiple** : multiple sclerosis

esclusa *nf* : floodgate, lock (of a canal)

escoba *nf* : broom

escocer {14} *vi* : sting

escocés, -cesa *adj, mpl* **-ceses 1** : Scottish **2** : tartan, plaid — **escocés** *nm, pl* **-ceses** : Scotch (whiskey)

escoger {15} *vt* : choose — **escogido, -da** *adj* : choice, select

escolar *adj* : school — ~ *nmf* : student, pupil

escolta *nmf* : escort — **escoltar** *vt* : escort, accompany

escombros *nmpl* : ruins, rubble

esconder *vt* : hide, conceal — **esconderse**

vr : hide — **escondidas** *nfpl* **1** *Lat* : hide-and-seek **2 a** ~ : secretly, in secret — **escondite** *nm* **1** : hiding place **2** : hide-and-seek (game) — **escondrijo** *nm* : hiding place

escopeta *nf* : shotgun

escoplo *nm* : chisel

escoria *nf* **1** : slag **2** : dregs *pl* (of society, etc.)

escorpión *nm, pl* **-piones** : scorpion

escote *nm* **1** : (low) neckline **2 pagar a** ~ : go Dutch

escotilla *nf* : hatchway

escribir {33} *v* : write — **escribirse** *vr* **1** : write to one another, correspond **2** : be spelled — **escribiente** *nmf* : clerk — **escrito, -ta** *adj* : written — **escritos** *nmpl* : writings — **escritor, -tora** *n* : writer — **escritorio** *nm* : desk — **escritura** *nf* **1** : handwriting **2** : deed (in law)

escroto *nm* : scrotum

escrúpulo *nm* : scruple — **escrupuloso, -sa** *adj* : scrupulous

escrutar *vt* **1** : scrutinize **2** : count (votes) — **escrutinio** *nm* **1** : scrutiny **2** : count (of votes)

escuadra *nf* **1** : square (instrument) **2** : fleet (of ships), squad (in the military) — **escuadrón** *nm, pl* **-drones** : squadron

escuálido, -da *adj* **1** : skinny **2** SUCIO : squalid

escuchar *vt* **1** : listen to **2** *Lat* : hear — *vi* : listen

escudo *nm* **1** : shield **2** *or* ~ **de armas** : coat of arms

escudriñar *vt* : scrutinize, examine

escuela *nf* : school

escueto, -ta *adj* : plain, simple

esculpir *v* : sculpt — **escultor, -tora** *n* : sculptor — **escultura** *nf* : sculpture

escupir *v* : spit

escurrir *vt* **1** : drain **2** : wring out (clothes) — *vi* **1** : drain **2** : drip-dry (of clothes) — **escurrirse** *vr* **1** : drain **2** *fam* : slip away — **escurridizo, -da** *adj* : slippery, evasive — **escurridor** *nm* **1** : dish drainer **2** COLADOR : colander

ese, esa *adj, mpl* **esos** : that, those

ése, ésa *pron, mpl* **ésos** : that one, those ones *pl*

esencia *nf* : essence — **esencial** *adj* : essential

esfera *nf* **1** : sphere **2** : dial (of a watch) — **esférico, -ca** *adj* : spherical

esfinge *nf* : sphinx

esforzar {36} *vt* : strain — **esforzarse** *vr* : make an effort — **esfuerzo** *nm* : effort

esfumarse *vr* : fade away, vanish

esgrimir *vt* **1** : brandish, wield **2** : make use

of (an argument, etc.) — **esgrima** *nf* **1**
: fencing **2 hacer ~** : fence
esguince *nm* : sprain, strain
eslabonar *vt* : link, connect — **eslabón** *nm*,
pl **-bones** : link
eslavo, -va *adj* : Slavic
eslogan *nm*, *pl* **-lóganes** : slogan
esmaltar *vt* : enamel — **esmalte** *nm* **1** : enamel **2 ~ de uñas** : nail polish
esmerado, -da *adj* : careful
esmeralda *nf* : emerald
esmerarse *vr* : take great care
esmeril *nm* : emery
esmoquin *nm*, *pl* **-móquines** : tuxedo
esnob *nmf*, *pl* **esnobs** : snob — **~** *adj*
: snobbish
eso *pron* (*neuter*) **1** : that **2 ¡~ es!** : that's
it!, that's right! **3 en ~** : at that point, then
esófago *nm* : esophagus
esos, ésos → ese, ése
espabilarse *vr* **1** : wake up **2 DARSE PRISA**
: get moving — **espabilado, -da** *adj* **1**
: awake **2 LISTO** : bright, clever
espaciar *vt* : space out, spread out — **espacial** *adj* : space — **espacio** *nm* **1** : space **2**
~ exterior : outer space — **espacioso, -sa**
adj : spacious
espada *nf* **1** : sword **2 ~s** *nfpl* : spades (in
playing cards)
espagueti *nm or* **espaguetis** *nmpl* : spaghetti
espalda *nf* **1** : back **2 ~ s** *nfpl* : shoulders,
back
espantar *vt* : scare, frighten — **espantarse**
vr : become frightened — **espantajo** *nm or*
espantapájaros *nms & pl* : scarecrow —
espanto *nm* : fright, fear — **espantoso,
-sa** *adj* **1** : frightening, horrific **2 TERRIBLE**
: awful, terrible
español, -ñola *adj* : Spanish — **español** *nm*
: Spanish (language)
esparadrapo *nm* : adhesive bandage
esparcir {83} *vt* : scatter, spread — **espar-
cirse** *vr* **1** : be scattered, spread out **2 DI-
VERTIRSE** : enjoy oneself
espárrago *nm* : asparagus
espasmo *nm* : spasm — **espasmódico, -ca**
adj : spasmodic
espátula *nf* : spatula
especia *nf* : spice
especial *adj & nm* : special — **especialidad**
nf : specialty — **especialista** *nmf* : specialist — **especializarse** {21} *vr* **~ en** : specialize in — **especialmente** *adv* : especially
especie *nf* **1** : species **2 CLASE** : type, kind
especificar {72} *vt* : specify — **especificación** *nf*, *pl* **-ciones** : specification — **específico, -ca** *adj* : specific
espécimen *nm*, *pl* **espécimenes** : specimen

espectáculo *nm* **1** : show, performance **2**
VISIÓN : spectacle, view — **espectacular**
adj : spectacular — **espectador, -dora** *n*
: spectator
espectro *nm* **1** : spectrum **2 FANTASMA**
: ghost
especulación *nf*, *pl* **-ciones** : speculation
espejo *nm* : mirror — **espejismo** *nm* **1** : mirage **2 ILUSIÓN** : illusion
espeluznante *adj* : terrifying, hair- raising
esperar *vt* **1** : wait for **2 CONTAR CON** : expect **3 ~ que** : hope (that) — *vi* : wait —
espera *nf* : wait — **esperanza** *nf* : hope,
expectation — **esperanzado, -da** *adj*
: hopeful — **esperanzar** {21} *vt* : give hope
to
esperma *nmf* **1** : sperm **2 ~ de ballena**
: blubber
esperpento *nm* : (grotesque) sight, fright
espesar *vt* : thicken — **espesarse** *vr*
: thicken — **espeso, -sa** *adj* : thick, heavy
— **espesor** *nm* : thickness, density — **es-
pesura** *nf* **1 ESPESOR** : thickness **2** : thicket
espetar *vt* : blurt (out)
espiar {85} *vt* : spy on — *vi* : spy — **espía**
nmf : spy
espiga *nf* : ear (of wheat, etc.)
espina *nf* **1** : thorn **2** : (fish) bone **3 ~
dorsal** : spine, backbone
espinaca *nf* **1** : spinach (plant) **2 ~s** *nfpl*
: spinach (food)
espinazo *nm* : spine, backbone
espinilla *nf* **1** : shin **2 GRANO** : blackhead,
pimple
espinoso, -sa *adj* **1** : prickly **2** : bony (of
fish) **3** : difficult, thorny (of problems, etc.)
espionaje *nm* : espionage
espiral *adj & nf* : spiral
espirar *v* : breathe out, exhale
espíritu *nm* **1** : spirit **2 Espíritu Santo**
: Holy Spirit — **espiritual** *adj* : spiritual —
espiritualidad *nf* : spirituality
espita *nf* : spigot, faucet
espléndido, -da *adj* **1** : splendid **2 GE-
NEROSO** : lavish — **esplendor** *nm* : splendor
espliego *nm* : lavender
espolear *vt* : spur on
espoleta *nf* : fuse
espolvorear *vt* : sprinkle, dust
esponja *nf* **1** : sponge **2 tirar la ~** : throw
in the towel — **esponjoso, -sa** *adj* : spongy
espontaneidad *nf* : spontaneity — **espontáneo, -nea** *adj* : spontaneous
espora *nf* : spore
esporádico, -ca *adj* : sporadic
esposo, -sa *n* : spouse, wife *f*, husband *m*
— **esposar** *vt* : handcuff — **esposas** *nfpl*
: handcuffs

esprintar *vi* : sprint (in sports) — **esprint** *nm* : sprint
espuela *nf* : spur
espumar *vt* : skim — **espuma** *nf* **1** : foam, froth **2** : (soap) lather **3** : head (on beer) — **espumoso, -sa** *adj* **1** : foamy, frothy **2** : sparkling (of wine)
esqueleto *nm* : skeleton
esquema *nf* : outline, sketch
esquí *nm* **1** : ski **2** : skiing (sport) **3** ~ **acuático** : waterskiing — **esquiador, -dora** *n* : skier — **esquiar** {85} *vi* : ski
esquilar *vt* : shear
esquimal *adj* : Eskimo
esquina *nf* : corner
esquirol *nm* : strikebreaker, scab
esquivar *vt* **1** : evade, dodge (a blow) **2** EVITAR : avoid — **esquivo, -va** *adj* : shy, elusive
esquizofrenia *nf* : schizophrenia — **esquizofrénico, -ca** *adj & n* : schizophrenic
esta, ésta → **este**[1], **éste**
estable *adj* : stable — **estabilidad** *nf* : stability — **estabilizar** {21} *vt* : stabilize
establecer {53} *vt* : establish — **establecerse** *vr* : establish oneself, settle — **establecimiento** *nm* : establishment
establo *nm* : stable
estaca *nf* : stake — **estacada** *nf* **1** : (picket) fence **2 dejar en la** ~ : leave in a lurch
estación *nf, pl* **-ciones 1** : season **2** ~ **de servicio** : gas station — **estacionar** *v* : park — **estacionamiento** *nm* : parking — **estacionario, -ria** *adj* : stationary
estadía *nf Lat* : stay
estadio *nm* **1** : stadium **2** FASE : phase, stage
estadista *nmf* : statesman
estadística *nf* : statistics — **estadístico, -ca** *adj* : statistical
estado *nm* **1** : state **2** ~ **civil** : marital status
estadounidense *adj & nmf* : American (from the United States)
estafar *vt* : swindle, defraud — **estafa** *nf* : swindle, fraud — **estafador, -dora** *n* : cheat, swindler
estallar *vi* **1** : explode **2** : break out (of war, an epidemic, etc.) **3** ~ **en llamas** : burst into flames — **estallido** *nm* **1** : explosion **2** : report (of a gun) **3** : outbreak (of war, etc.)
estampar *vt* : stamp, print — **estampa** *nf* **1** : print, illustration **2** ASPECTO : appearance — **estampado, -da** *adj* : printed
estampida *nf* : stampede
estampilla *nf* : stamp
estancarse {72} *vr* **1** : stagnate **2** : come to a halt — **estancado, -da** *adj* : stagnant

estancia *nf* **1** : stay **2** HABITACIÓN : (large) room **3** *Lat* : (cattle) ranch
estanco, -ca *adj* : watertight
estándar *adj & nm* : standard — **estandarizar** {21} *vt* : standardize
estandarte *nm* : standard, banner
estanque *nm* **1** : pool, pond **2** : reservoir (for irrigation)
estante *nm* : shelf — **estantería** *nf* : shelves *pl*, bookcase
estaño *nm* : tin
estar {34} *v aux* : be — *vi* **1** : be **2** : be at home **3** QUEDARSE : stay, remain **4** ¿**cómo estás?** : how are you? **5** ~ **a** : cost **6** ~ **bien (mal)** : be well (sick) **7** ~ **para** : be in the mood for **8** ~ **por** : be in favor of **9** ~ **por** : be about to — **estarse** *vr* : stay, remain
estarcir {83} *vt* : stencil
estárter *nm* : choke (of an automobile)
estatal *adj* : state, national
estático, -ca *adj* **1** : static **2** INMÓVIL : unmoving, still — **estática** *nf* : static
estatua *nf* : statue
estatura *nf* : height
estatus *nm* : status, prestige
estatuto *nm* : statute — **estatutario, -ria** *adj* : statutory
este[1], **esta** *adj, mpl* **estos** : this, these
este[2] *adj* : eastern, east — **este** *nm* **1** : east **2** : east wind **3 el Este** : the Orient
éste, ésta *pron, mpl* **éstos 1** : this one, these ones *pl* **2** : the latter
estela *nf* **1** : wake (of a ship) **2** : trail (of smoke, etc.)
estera *nf* : mat
estéreo *adj & nm* : stereo — **estereofónico, -ca** *adj* : stereophonic
estereotipo *nm* : stereotype
estéril *adj* **1** : sterile **2** : infertile — **esterilidad** *nf* **1** : sterility **2** : infertility — **esterilizar** {21} *vt* : sterilize
estética *nf* : aesthetics — **estético, -ca** *adj* : aesthetic
estiércol *nm* : dung, manure
estigma *nm* : stigma — **estigmatizar** {21} *vt* : stigmatize
estilarse {21} *vr* : be in fashion
estilo *nm* **1** : style **2** MANERA : fashion, manner — **estilista** *nmf* : stylist
estima *nf* : esteem, regard — **estimación** *nf, pl* **-ciones 1** : esteem **2** VALORACIÓN : estimate — **estimado, -da** *adj* **Estimado señor** : Dear Sir — **estimar** *vt* **1** : esteem, respect **2** VALORAR : value, estimate **3** CONSIDERAR : consider
estimular *vt* **1** : stimulate **2** ALENTAR : encourage — **estimulante** *adj* : stimulating — ~ *nm* : stimulant — **estímulo** *nm* : stimulus

estío *nm* : summertime
estipular *vt* : stipulate
estirar *vt* : stretch (out), extend — **estirado, -da** *adj* **1** : stretched, extended **2** ALTA-NERO : stuck-up, haughty — **estiramiento** *nm* ~ **facial** : face-lift — **estirón** *nm, pl* **-rones** : pull, tug
estirpe *nf* : lineage, stock
estival *adj* : summer
esto *pron (neuter)* **1** : this **2 en** ~ : at this point **3 por** ~ : for this reason
estofa *nf* **1** : class, quality **2 de baja** ~ : low-class
estofar *vt* : stew — **estofado** *nm* : stew
estoicismo *nm* : stoicism — **estoico, -ca** *adj* : stoic, stoical — ~ *n* : stoic
estómago *nm* : stomach — **estomacal** *adj* : stomach
estorbar *vt* : obstruct — *vi* : get in the way — **estorbo** *nm* **1** : obstacle **2** MOLESTIA : nuisance
estornino *nm* : starling
estornudar *vi* : sneeze — **estornudo** *nm* : sneeze
estos, éstos → **este, éste**
estrabismo *nm* : squint
estrado *nm* : platform, stage
estrafalario, -ria *adj* : eccentric, bizarre
estragar {52} *vt* : devastate — **estragos** *nmpl* **1** : ravages **2 hacer** ~ **en** *or* **causar** ~ **entre** : wreak havoc with
estragón *nm* : tarragon
estrangular *vt* : strangle — **estrangulación** *nf* : strangulation
estratagema *nf* : stratagem
estrategia *nf* : strategy — **estratégico, -ca** *adj* : strategic
estrato *nm* : stratum
estratosfera *nf* : stratosphere
estrechar *vt* **1** : narrow **2** : strengthen (a bond) **3** ABRAZAR : embrace **4** ~ **la mano a uno** : shake s.o.'s hand — **estrecharse** *vr* : narrow — **estrechez** *nf, pl* **-checes 1** : narrowness **2 estrecheces** *nfpl* : financial problems — **estrecho, -cha** *adj* **1** : tight, narrow **2** ÍNTIMO : close — **estrecho** *nm* : strait
estrella *nf* **1** : star **2** DESTINO : destiny **3** ~ **de mar** : starfish — **estrellado, -da** *adj* **1** : starry **2** : star-shaped
estrellar *v* : crash — **estrellarse** *vr* ~ **contre** : smash into
estremecer {53} *vt* : cause to shudder — *vi* : tremble, shake — **estremecerse** *vr* : shudder, shiver (with emotion) — **estremecimiento** *nm* : shaking, shivering
estrenar *vt* **1** : use for the first time **2** : premiere, open (a film, etc.) — **estrenarse** *vr* : make one's debut — **estreno** *nm* : debut, premiere

estreñirse {67} *vr* : be constipated — **estreñimiento** *nm* : constipation
estrépito *nm* : clamor, din — **estrepitoso, -sa** *adj* : noisy, clamorous
estrés *nm, pl* **estreses** : stress — **estresante** *adj* : stressful — **estresar** *vt* : stress (out)
estría *nf* : groove
estribaciones *nfpl* : foothills
estribar *vi* ~ **en** : stem from, lie in
estribillo *nm* : refrain, chorus
estribo *nm* **1** : stirrup **2** : running board (of a vehicle) **3** CONTRAFUERTE : buttress **4 perder los** ~**s** : lose one's temper
estribor *nm* : starboard
estricto, -ta *adj* : strict
estridente *adj* : strident, shrill
estrofa *nf* : stanza, verse
estropajo *nm* : scouring pad
estropear *vt* **1** : ruin, spoil **2** DAÑAR : damage — **estropearse** *vr* **1** : go bad **2** AVE-RIARSE : break down — **estropicio** *nm* : damage, havoc
estructura *nf* : structure — **estructural** *adj* : structural
estruendo *nm* : din, roar — **estruendoso, -sa** *adj* : thunderous
estrujar *vt* : squeeze
estuario *nm* : estuary
estuche *nm* : kit, case
estuco *nm* : stucco
estudiar *v* : study — **estudiante** *nmf* : student — **estudiantil** *adj* : student — **estudio** *nm* **1** : study **2** OFICINA : studio, office **3** ~**s** *nmpl* : studies, education **4** : studio (for filming, etc.) **5** : studio (apartment) — **estudioso, -sa** *adj* : studious
estufa *nf* : stove, heater
estupefaciente *adj & nm* : narcotic — **estupefacto, -ta** *adj* : astonished
estupendo, -da *adj* : stupendous, marvelous
estúpido, -da *adj* : stupid — **estupidez** *nf, pl* **-deces** : stupidity
estupor *nm* **1** : stupor **2** ASOMBRO : amazement
etapa *nf* : stage, phase
etcétera : et cetera, and so on
éter *nm* : ether
etéreo, -rea *adj* : ethereal
eterno, -na *adj* : eternal — **eternidad** *nf* : eternity — **eternizarse** {21} *vr* : take forever
ética *nf* : ethics — **ético, -ca** *adj* : ethical
etimología *nf* : etymology
etíope *adj* : Ethiopian
etiqueta *nf* **1** : tag, label **2** PROTOCOLO : etiquette **3 de** ~ : formal, dressy — **etiquetar** *vt* : label
étnico, -ca *adj* : ethnic

eucalipto *nm* : eucalyptus

Eucaristía *nf* : Eucharist, communion

eufemismo *nm* : euphemism — **eufemístico, -ca** *adj* : euphemistic

euforia *nf* : euphoria — **eufórico, -ca** *adj* : euphoric

euro *nm* : euro

europeo, -pea *adj* : European

eutanasia *nf* : euthanasia

evacuar *vt* : evacuate, vacate — *vi* : have a bowel movement — **evacuación** *nf, pl* **-ciones** : evacuation

evadir *vt* : evade, avoid — **evadirse** *vr* : escape

evaluar {3} *vt* : evaluate — **evaluación** *nf, pl* **-ciones** : evaluation

evangelio *nm* : gospel — **evangélico, -ca** *adj* : evangelical — **evangelismo** *nm* : evangelism

evaporar *vt* : evaporate — **evaporarse** *vr* : evaporate, disappear — **evaporación** *nf, pl* **-ciones** : evaporation

evasión *nf, pl* **-siones** 1 : evasion 2 FUGA : escape — **evasiva** *nf* : excuse, pretext — **evasivo, -va** *adj* : evasive

evento *nm* : event

eventual *adj* 1 : temporary 2 POSIBLE : possible — **eventualidad** *nf* : possibility, eventuality

evidencia *nf* 1 : evidence, proof 2 **poner en ~** : demonstrate — **evidenciar** *vt* : demonstrate, show — **evidente** *adj* : evident — **evidentemente** *adj* : evidently, apparently

evitar *vt* 1 : avoid 2 IMPEDIR : prevent — **evitable** *adj* : avoidable

evocar {72} *vt* : evoke

evolución *nf, pl* **-ciones** : evolution — **evolucionar** *vi* : evolve

exacerbar *vt* 1 : exacerbate 2 IRRITAR : irritate

exacto, -ta *adj* : precise, exact — **exactamente** *adv* : exactly — **exactitud** *nf* : precision, accuracy

exagerar *v* : exaggerate — **exageración** *nf, pl* **-ciones** : exaggeration — **exagerado, -da** *adj* : exaggerated

exaltar *vt* 1 : exalt, extol 2 EXCITAR : excite, arouse — **exaltarse** *vr* : get worked-up — **exaltado, -da** *adj* : worked up, hotheaded

examen *nm, pl* **exámenes** 1 : examination, test 2 ANÁLISIS : investigation — **examinar** *vt* 1 : examine 2 ESTUDIAR : study, inspect — **examinarse** *vr* : take an exam

exánime *adj* : lifeless

exasperar *vt* : exasperate, irritate — **exasperación** *nf, pl* **-ciones** : exasperation

excavar *v* : excavate — **excavación** *nf, pl* **-ciones** : excavation

exceder *vt* : exceed, surpass — **excederse** *vr* : go too far — **excedente** *adj & nm* : surplus, excess

excelente *adj* : excellent — **excelencia** *nf* 1 : excellence 2 **Su Excelencia** : His/Her Excellency

excéntrico, -ca *adj & n* : eccentric — **excentricidad** *nf* : eccentricity

excepción *nf, pl* **-ciones** : exception — **excepcional** *adj* : exceptional

excepto *prep* : except (for) — **exceptuar** {3} *vt* : exclude, except

exceso *nm* 1 : excess 2 **~ de velocidad** : speeding — **excesivo, -va** *adj* : excessive

excitar *vt* : excite, arouse — **excitarse** *vr* : get excited — **excitable** *adj* : excitable — **excitación** *nf, pl* **-ciones** : excitement, agitation, arousal — **excitante** *adj* : exciting

exclamar *v* : exclaim — **exclamación** *nf, pl* **-ciones** : exclamation

excluir {41} *vt* : exclude — **exclusión** *nf, pl* **-siones** : exclusion — **exclusivo, -va** *adj* : exclusive

excomulgar {52} *vt* : excommunicate — **excomunión** *nf, pl* **-niones** : excommunication

excremento *nm* : excrement

exculpar *vt* : exonerate

excursión *nf, pl* **-siones** : excursion — **excursionista** *nmf* 1 : tourist, sightseer 2 : hiker

excusar *vt* 1 : excuse 2 EXIMIR : exempt — **excusarse** *vr* : apologize — **excusa** *nf* 1 : excuse 2 DISCULPA : apology

exento, -ta *adj* : exempt

exequias *nfpl* : funeral rites

exhalar *vt* 1 : exhale 2 : give off (an odor, etc.)

exhaustivo, -va *adj* : exhaustive — **exhausto, -ta** *adj* : exhausted, worn-out

exhibir *vt* : exhibit, show — **exhibición** *nf, pl* **-ciones** : exhibition

exhortar *vt* : exhort, admonish

exigir {35} *vt* : demand, require — **exigencia** *nf* : demand, requirement — **exigente** *adj* : demanding

exiguo, -gua *adj* : meager

exiliar *vt* : exile — **exiliarse** *vr* : go into exile — **exiliado, -da** *adj* : exiled, in exile — **~** *n* : exile — **exilio** *nm* : exile

eximir *vt* : exempt

existir *vi* : exist — **existencia** *nf* 1 : existence 2 **~s** *nfpl* MERCANCÍA : goods, stock — **existente** *adj* : existing

éxito *nm* 1 : success, hit 2 **tener ~** : be successful — **exitoso, -sa** *adj Lat* : successful

éxodo *nm* : exodus

exorbitante *adj* : exorbitant

exorcizar {21} *vt* : exorcize — **exorcismo** *nm* : exorcism

exótico, -ca *adj* : exotic

expandir *vt* : expand — **expandirse** *vr* : spread — **expansión** *nf, pl* **-siones** : expansion — **expansivo, -va** *adj* : expansive

expatriarse {85} *vr* **1** : emigrate **2** EXILIARSE : go into exile — **expatriado, -da** *adj & n* : expatriate

expectativa *nf* **1** : expectation, hope **2** ~s *nfpl* : prospects

expedición *nf, pl* **-ciones** : expedition

expediente *nm* **1** : expedient **2** DOCUMENTOS : file, record **3** INVESTIGACIÓN : inquiry, proceedings

expedir {54} *vt* **1** : issue **2** ENVIAR : dispatch — **expedito, -ta** *adj* : free, clear

expeler *vt* : expel, eject

expendedor, -dora *n* : dealer, seller

expensas *nfpl* **1** : expenses **2 a** ~ **de** : at the expense of

experiencia *nf* : experience

experimentar *vi* **1** : experiment — *vt* **1** : experiment with, test out **2** SENTIR : experience, feel — **experimentado, -da** *adj* : experienced — **experimental** *adj* : experimental — **experimento** *nm* : experiment

experto, -ta *adj & n* : expert

expiar {85} *vt* : atone for

expirar *vi* **1** : expire **2** MORIR : die

explayar *vt* : extend — **explayarse** *vr* **1** : spread out **2** HABLAR : speak at length

explicar {72} *vt* : explain — **explicarse** *vr* : understand — **explicación** *nf, pl* **-ciones** : explanation — **explicativo, -va** *adj* : explanatory

explícito, -ta *adj* : explicit

explorar *vt* : explore — **exploración** *nf, pl* **-ciones** : exploration — **explorador, -dora** *n* : explorer, scout — **exploratorio, -ria** *adj* : exploratory

explosión *nf, pl* **-siones** **1** : explosion **2** : outburst (of anger, laughter, etc.) — **explosivo, -va** *adj* : explosive — **explosivo** *nm* : explosive

explotar *vt* **1** : exploit **2** : operate, run (a factory, etc.), work (a mine) — *vi* : explode — **explotación** *nf, pl* **-ciones** **1** : exploitation **2** : running (of a business), working (of a mine)

exponer {60} *vt* **1** : expose **2** : explain, set out (ideas, theories, etc.) **3** EXHIBIR : exhibit, display — *vi* : exhibit — **exponerse** *vr* ~ **a** : expose oneself to

exportar *vt* : export — **exportaciones** *nfpl* : exports — **exportador, -dora** *n* : exporter

exposición *nf, pl* **-ciones** **1** : exposure **2** : exhibition (of objects, art, etc.) **3** : exposition, setting out (of ideas, etc.) — **expositor, -tora** *n* **1** : exhibitor **2** : exponent (of a theory, etc.)

exprés *nms & pl* **1** : express (train) **2** *or* **café** ~ : espresso

expresamente *adv* : expressly, on purpose

expresar *vt* : express — **expresarse** *vr* : express oneself — **expresión** *nf, pl* **-siones** : expression — **expresivo, -va** *adj* **1** : expressive **2** CARIÑOSO : affectionate

expreso, -sa *adj* : express — **expreso** *nm* : express train, express

exprimir *vt* **1** : squeeze **2** EXPLOTAR : exploit — **exprimidor** *nm* : squeezer, juicer

expuesto, -ta *adj* **1** : exposed **2** PELIGROSO : risky, dangerous

expulsar *vt* : expel, eject — **expulsión** *nf, pl* **-siones** : expulsion

exquisito, -ta *adj* **1** : exquisite **2** RICO : delicious — **exquisitez** *nf* **1** : exquisiteness **2** : delicacy, special dish

éxtasis *nms & pl* : ecstasy — **extático, -ta** *adj* : ecstatic

extender {56} *vt* **1** : spread out **2** : draw up (a document), write out (a check) — **extenderse** *vr* **1** : extend, spread **2** DURAR : last — **extendido, -da** *adj* **1** : widespread **2** : outstretched (of arms, wings, etc.)

extensamente *adv* : extensively

extensión *nf, pl* **-siones** **1** : extension **2** AMPLITUD : expanse **3** ALCANCE : range, extent — **extenso, -sa** *adj* : extensive

extenuar {3} *vt* : exhaust, tire out

exterior *adj* **1** : exterior, external **2** EXTRANJERO : foreign — ~ *nm* **1** : outside **2 en el** ~ : abroad — **exteriorizar** {21} *vt* : show, reveal — **exteriormente** *adv* : outwardly, externally

exterminar *vt* : exterminate — **exterminación** *nf, pl* **-ciones** : extermination — **exterminio** *nm* : extermination

externo, -na *adj* : external

extinguir {26} *vt* **1** : extinguish (a fire) **2** : put an end to, wipe out — **extinguirse** *vr* **1** : go out (of fire, light, etc.) **2** : become extinct — **extinción** *nf, pl* **-ciones** : extinction — **extinguidor** *nm Lat* : fire extinguisher — **extinto, -ta** *adj* : extinct — **extintor** *nm* : fire extinguisher

extirpar *vt* : remove, eradicate

extorsión *nf, pl* **-siones** **1** : extortion **2** MOLESTIA : trouble

extra *adv* : extra — ~ *adj* **1** ADICIONAL : additional **2** : top-quality — ~ *nmf* : extra (in movies) — ~ *nm* : extra (expense)

extraditar *vt* : extradite
extraer {81} *vt* : extract — **extracción** *nf, pl*
-ciones : extraction — **extracto** *nm* **1** : extract **2** RESUMEN : abstract, summary
extranjero, -ra *adj* : foreign — ~ *n* : foreigner — **extranjero** *nm* : foreign countries *pl*
extrañar *vt* : miss (someone) — **extrañarse** *vr* : be surprised — **extrañeza** *nf* : surprise — **extraño, -ña** *adj* **1** : foreign **2** RARO : strange, odd — ~ *n* : stranger
extraoficial *adj* : unofficial
extraordinario, -ria *adj* : extraordinary
extrasensorial *adj* : extrasensory
extraterrestre *adj & nmf* : extraterrestrial
extravagante *adj* : extravagant, outrageous — **extravagancia** *nf* : extravagance, outlandishness

extraviar {85} *vt* : lose, misplace — **extraviarse** *vr* : get lost — **extravío** *nm* : loss
extremar *vt* : carry to extremes — **extremarse** *vr* : do one's utmost — **extremadamente** *adv* : extremely — **extremado, -da** *adj* : extreme — **extremidad** *nf* **1** : tip, end **2** ~**es** *nfpl* : extremities — **extremista** *adj & nmf* : extremist — **extremo, -ma** *adj* **1** : extreme **2 en caso** ~ : as a last resort — **extremo** *nm* **1** : end **2 en** ~ : in the extreme, extremely **3 en ultimo** ~ : as a last resort
extrovertido -da *adj* : extroverted — ~ *n* : extrovert
exuberante *adj* : exuberant — **exuberancia** *nf* : exuberance
exudar *vt* : exude
eyacular *vi* : ejaculate — **eyaculación** *nf, pl* **-ciones** : ejaculation

F

f *nf* : f, sixth letter of the Spanish alphabet
fabricar {72} *vt* **1** : manufacture **2** CONSTRUIR : build, construct **3** INVENTAR : fabricate — **fábrica** *nf* : factory — **fabricación** *nf, pl* **-ciones** : manufacture — **fabricante** *nmf* : manufacturer
fábula *nf* **1** : fable **2** MENTIRA : story, lie
fabuloso, -sa *adj* : fabulous
facción *nf, pl* **-ciones** **1** : faction **2** ~**es** *nfpl* RASGOS : features
faceta *nf* : facet
facha *nf* : appearance, look
fachada *nf* : façade
facial *adj* : facial
fácil *adj* **1** : easy **2** PROBABLE : likely — **fácilmente** *adv* : easily, readily — **facilidad** *nf* **1** : facility, ease **2** ~**es** *nfpl* : facilities, services — **facilitar** *vt* **1** : facilitate **2** PROPORCIONAR : provide, supply
facsímil *or* **facsímile** *nm* **1** COPIA : facsimile, copy **2** : fax
factible *adj* : feasible
factor *nm* : factor
factoría *nf* : factory
factura *nf* **1** : bill, invoice **2** HECHURA : making, manufacture — **facturar** *vt* **1** : bill for **2** : check in (baggage, etc.)
facultad *nf* **1** : faculty, ability **2** AUTORIDAD : authority **3** : school (of a university) — **facultativo, -va** *adj* : optional
faena *nf* **1** : task, job **2** ~**s domésticas** : housework

fagot *nm* : bassoon
faisán *nm, pl* **-sanes** : pheasant
faja *nf* **1** : sash **2** : girdle, corset **3** : strip (of land)
fajo *nm* : bundle, sheaf
falda *nf* **1** : skirt **2** : side, slope (of a mountain)
falible *adj* : fallible
fálico, -ca *adj* : phallic
fallar *vi* : fail, go wrong — *vt* **1** : pronounce judgment on **2** ERRAR : miss — **falla** *nf* **1** : flaw, defect **2** : (geological) fault
fallecer {53} *vi* : pass away, die — **fallecimiento** *nm* : demise, death
fallido, -da *adj* : failed, unsuccessful
fallo *nm* **1** : error **2** SENTENCIA : sentence, verdict
falo *nm* : phallus, penis
falsear *vt* : falsify, distort — **falsedad** *nf* **1** : falseness **2** MENTIRA : falsehood, lie — **falsificación** *nf, pl* **-ciones** : forgery, fake — **falsificador, -dora** *n* : forger — **falsificar** {72} *vt* **1** : counterfeit, forge **2** ALTERAR : falsify — **falso, -sa** *adj* **1** : false, untrue **2** FALSIFICADO : counterfeit, forged
falta *nf* **1** CARENCIA : lack **2** DEFECTO : defect, fault, error **3** AUSENCIA : absence **4** : offense, misdemeanor (in law) **5** : foul (in sports) **6 hacer** ~ : be lacking, be needed **7 sin** ~ : without fail — **faltar** *vi* **1** : be lacking, be needed **2** : be missing **3** QUEDAR : remain, be left **4 ¡no faltaba más!**

: don't mention it! — **falto, -ta** *adj* ~ **de** : lacking (in)

fama *nf* **1** : fame **2** REPUTACIÓN : reputation

famélico, -ca *adj* : starving

familia *nf* : family — **familiar** *adj* **1** : familial, family **2** CONOCIDO : familiar **3** : informal (of language, etc.) — ~ *nmf* : relation, relative — **familiaridad** *nf* : familiarity — **familiarizarse** {21} *vr* ~ **con** : familiarize oneself with

famoso, -sa *adj* : famous

fanático, -ca *adj* : fanatic, fanatical — ~ *n* : fanatic — **fanatismo** *nm* : fanaticism

fanfarria *nf* : fanfare

fanfarrón, -rrona *adj, mpl* **-rrones** *fam* : boastful — ~ *n fam* : braggart — **fanfarronear** *vi* : boast, brag

fango *nm* : mud, mire — **fangoso, -sa** *adj* : muddy

fantasear *vi* : fantasize, daydream — **fantasía** *nf* **1** : fantasy **2** IMAGINACIÓN : imagination

fantasma *nm* : ghost, phantom — **fantasmal** *adj* : ghostly

fantástico, -ca *adj* : fantastic

FAQ *nm, pl* **FAQs** : FAQ

fardo *nm* : bundle

farfullar *v* : jabber, gabble

farmacéutico, -ca *adj* : pharmaceutical — ~ *n* : pharmacist — **farmacia** *nf* : drugstore, pharmacy

faro *nm* **1** : lighthouse **2** : headlight (of an automobile) — **farol** *nm* **1** LINTERNA : lantern **2** FAROLA : streetlight — **farola** *nf* **1** : lamppost **2** FAROL : streetlight

farsa *nf* : farce — **farsante** *nmf* : charlatan, fraud

fascículo *nm* : installment, part (of a publication)

fascinar *vt* : fascinate — **fascinación** *nf, pl* **-ciones** : fascination — **fascinante** *adj* : fascinating

fascismo *nm* : fascism — **fascista** *adj* & *nmf* : fascist

fase *nf* : phase

fastidiar *vt* : annoy, bother — *vi* : be annoying or bothersome — **fastidio** *nm* : annoyance — **fastidioso, -sa** *adj* : annoying, bothersome

fatal *adj* **1** : fateful **2** MORTAL : fatal **3** *fam* : awful, terrible — **fatalidad** *nf* **1** : fate, destiny **2** DESGRACIA : misfortune

fatídico, -ca *adj* : fateful, momentous

fatiga *nf* : fatigue — **fatigado, -da** *adj* : weary, tired — **fatigar** {52} *vt* : tire — **fatigarse** *vr* : get tired — **fatigoso, -sa** *adj* : fatiguing, tiring

fatuo, -tua *adj* **1** : fatuous **2** PRESUMIDO : conceited

fauna *nf* : fauna

favor *nm* **1** : favor **2 a** ~ **de** : in favor of **3 por** ~ : please — **favorable** *adj* **1** : favorable **2 ser** ~ **a** : be in favor of — **favorecedor, -dora** *adj* : flattering — **favorecer** {53} *vt* **1** AYUDAR : favor **2** : look well on, suit — **favoritismo** *nm* : favoritism — **favorito, -ta** *adj* & *n* : favorite

fax *nm* : fax — **faxear** *vt* : fax

faz *nf, pl* **faces** : face, countenance

fe *nf* **1** : faith **2 dar** ~ **de** : bear witness to **3 de buena** ~ : in good faith

fealdad *nf* : ugliness

febrero *nm* : February

febril *adj* : feverish

fecha *nf* **1** : date **2** ~ **de caducidad** *or* ~ **de vencimiento** : expiration date **3** ~ **límite** : deadline — **fechar** *vt* : date, put a date on

fechoría *nf* : misdeed

fécula *nf* : starch (in food)

fecundar *vt* **1** : fertilize (an egg) **2** : make fertile — **fecundo, -da** *adj* : fertile

federación *nf, pl* **-ciones** : federation — **federal** *adj* : federal

felicidad *nf* **1** : happiness **2 ¡~es!** : best wishes!, congratulations!, happy birthday! — **felicitación** *nf, pl* **-ciones** : congratulation — **felicitar** *vt* : congratulate — **felicitarse** *vr* ~ **de** : be glad about

feligrés, -gresa *n, mpl* **-greses** : parishioner

felino, -na *adj* & *n* : feline

feliz *adj, pl* **-lices** **1** : happy **2** AFORTUNADO : fortunate **3 Feliz Navidad** : Merry Christmas

felpa *nf* **1** : plush **2** : terry cloth (for towels, etc.)

felpudo *nm* : doormat

femenino, -na *adj* **1** : feminine **2** : female (in biology) — **femenino** *nm* : feminine (in grammar) — **femineidad** *nf* : femininity — **feminismo** *nm* : feminism — **feminista** *adj* & *nmf* : feminist

fenómeno *nm* : phenomenon — **fenomenal** *adj* **1** : phenomenal **2** *fam* : fantastic, terrific

feo, fea *adj* **1** : ugly **2** DESAGRADABLE : unpleasant, nasty

féretro *nm* : coffin

feria *nf* **1** : fair, market **2** FIESTA : festival, holiday **3** *Lat fam* : small change — **feriado, -da** *adj* **día feriado** : public holiday

fermentar *v* : ferment — **fermentación** *nf, pl* **-ciones** : fermentation — **fermento** *nm* : ferment

feroz *adj, pl* **-roces** : ferocious, fierce — **ferocidad** *nf* : ferocity, fierceness
férreo, -rrea *adj* 1 : iron 2 **vía férrea** : railroad track
ferretería *nf* : hardware store
ferrocarril *nm* : railroad, railway — **ferroviario, -ria** *adj* : rail, railroad
ferry *nm, pl* **ferrys** : ferry
fértil *adj* : fertile, fruitful — **fertilidad** *nf* : fertility — **fertilizante** *nm* : fertilizer — **fertilizar** *vt* : fertilize
fervor *nm* : fervor, zeal — **ferviente** *adj* : fervent
festejar *vt* 1 : celebrate 2 AGASAJAR : entertain, wine and dine — **festejo** *nm* : celebration, festivity
festín *nm, pl* **-tines** : banquet, feast
festival *nm* : festival — **festividad** *nf* : festivity — **festivo, -va** *adj* 1 : festive 2 **día festivo** : holiday
fetiche *nm* : fetish
fétido, -da *adj* : foul-smelling, fetid
feto *nm* : fetus — **fetal** *adj* : fetal
feudal *adj* : feudal
fiable *adj* : reliable — **fiabilidad** *nf* : reliability
fiado, -da *adj* : on credit — **fiador, -dora** *n* : bondsman, guarantor
fiambres *nfpl* : cold cuts
fianza *nf* 1 : bail, bond 2 **dar** ~ : pay a deposit
fiar {85} *vt* 1 : guarantee 2 : sell on credit — *vi* **ser de** ~ : be trustworthy — **fiarse** *vr* ~ **de** : place trust in
fiasco *nm* : fiasco
fibra *nf* 1 : fiber 2 ~ **de vidrio** : fiberglass
ficción *nf, pl* **-ciones** : fiction
ficha *nf* 1 : token 2 TARJETA : index card 3 : counter, chip (in games) — **fichar** *vt* : file, index — **fichero** *nm* 1 : card file 2 : filing cabinet
ficticio, -cia *adj* : fictitious
fidedigno, -na *adj* : reliable, trustworthy
fidelidad *nf* : fidelity, faithfulness
fideo *nm* : noodle
fiebre *nf* 1 : fever 2 ~ **del heno** : hay fever 3 ~ **palúdica** : malaria
fiel *adj* 1 : faithful, loyal 2 PRECISO : accurate, reliable — ~ *nm* 1 : pointer (of a scale) 2 **los** ~**es** : the faithful — **fielmente** *adv* : faithfully
fieltro *nm* : felt
fiero, -ra *adj* : fierce, ferocious — **fiera** *nf* : wild animal, beast
fierro *nm Lat* : iron (bar)
fiesta *nf* 1 : party 2 DÍA FESTIVO : holiday, feast day

figura *nf* 1 : figure 2 FORMA : shape, form — **figurar** *vi* 1 : figure (in), be included (among) 2 DESTACAR : stand out — *vt* : represent — **figurarse** *vr* : imagine
fijar *vt* 1 : fasten, affix 2 CONCRETAR : set, fix — **fijarse** *vr* 1 : settle 2 ~ **en** : notice, pay attention to — **fijo, -ja** *adj* 1 : fixed, firm 2 PERMANENTE : permanent
fila *nf* 1 : line, file, row 2 **ponerse en** ~ : line up
filantropía *nf* : philanthropy — **filantrópico, -ca** *adj* : philanthropic — **filántropo, -pa** *n* : philanthropist
filatelia *nf* : philately, stamp collecting
filete *nm* : fillet
filial *adj* : filial — ~ *nf* : affiliate, subsidiary
filigrana *nf* 1 : filigree 2 : watermark (on paper)
filipino, -na *adj* : Filipino
filmar *vt* : film, shoot — **filme** *or* **film** *nm* : film, movie
filo *nm* 1 : edge 2 **dar** ~ **a** : sharpen
filón *nm, pl* **-lones** 1 : vein (of minerals) 2 *fam* : gold mine
filoso, -sa *adj Lat* : sharp
filosofía *nf* : philosophy — **filosófico, -ca** *adj* : philosophical — **filósofo, -fa** *n* : philosopher
filtrar *v* : filter — **filtrarse** *vr* : leak out, seep through — **filtro** *nm* : filter
fin *nm* 1 : end 2 OBJETIVO : purpose, aim 3 **en** ~ : well, in short 4 ~ **de semana** : weekend 5 **por** ~ : finally, at last
final *adj* : final — ~ *nm* : end, conclusion — ~ *nf* : final (in sports) — **finalidad** *nf* : purpose, aim — **finalista** *nmf* : finalist — **finalizar** {21} *v* : finish, end — **finalmente** *adv* : finally
financiar *vt* : finance, fund — **financiero, -ra** *adj* : financial — ~ *n* : financier — **finanzas** *nfpl* : finance
finca *nf* 1 : farm, ranch 2 *Lat* : country house
fingir {35} *v* : feign, pretend — **fingido, -da** *adj* : false, feigned
finito, -ta *adj* : finite
finlandés, -desa *adj* : Finnish
fino, -na *adj* 1 : fine 2 DELGADO : slender 3 REFINADO : refined 4 AGUDO : sharp, keen — **finura** *nf* 1 : fineness 2 REFINAMIENTO : refinement
firma *nf* 1 : signature 2 : (act of) signing 3 EMPRESA : firm, company
firmamento *nm* : firmament, sky
firmar *v* : sign
firme *adj* 1 : firm, resolute 2 ESTABLE : steady, stable — **firmeza** *nf* 1 : strength, resolve 2 ESTABILIDAD : firmness, stability

fiscal *adj* : fiscal — ~ *nmf* : district attorney — **fisco** *nm* : (national) treasury
fisgar {52} *vt* : pry into — *vi* : pry — **fisgón, -gona** *n, mpl* **-gones** : snoop, busybody
física *nf* : physics — **físico, -ca** *adj* : physical — ~ *n* : physicist — **físico** *nm* : physique
fisiología *nf* : physiology — **fisiológico, -ca** *adj* : physiological — **fisiólogo, -ga** *n* : physiologist
fisioterapia *nf* : physical therapy — **fisioterapeuta** *nmf* : physical therapist
fisonomía *nf* : features *pl*, appearance
fisura *nf* : fissure
fláccido, -da *or* **flácido, -da** *adj* : flaccid, flabby
flaco, -ca *adj* **1** : thin, skinny **2** DÉBIL : weak
flagrante *adj* : flagrant
flamante *adj* **1** : bright, brilliant **2** NUEVO : brand-new
flamenco, -ca *adj* **1** : flamenco (of music or dance) **2** : Flemish — **flamenco** *nm* **1** : flamingo **2** : flamenco (music or dance)
flaquear *vi* : weaken, flag — **flaqueza** *nf* **1** : thinness **2** DEBILIDAD : weakness
flash *nm* : flash
flatulencia *nf* : flatulence
flauta *nf* **1** : flute **2** ~ **dulce** : recorder — **flautín** *nm, pl* **-tines** : piccolo — **flautista** *nmf* : flutist
flecha *nf* : arrow
fleco *nm* **1** : fringe **2** *Lat* : bangs *pl*
flema *nf* : phlegm — **flemático, -ca** *adj* : phlegmatic
flequillo *nm* : bangs *pl*
fletar *vt* **1** : charter, rent **2** *Lat* : transport — **flete** *nm* **1** : charter **2** : shipping (charges) **3** *Lat* : transport, freight
flexible *adj* : flexible — **flexibilidad** *nf* : flexibility
flirtear *vi* : flirt
flojo, -ja *adj* **1** SUELTO : loose, slack **2** DÉBIL : weak **3** PEREZOSO : lazy — **flojera** *nf fam* : lethargy
flor *nf* : flower — **flora** *nf* : flora — **floral** *adj* : floral — **floreado, -da** *adj* : flowered — **florear** *vi Lat* : flower, bloom — **florecer** {53} *vi* **1** : bloom, blossom **2** PROSPERAR : flourish — **floreciente** *adj* : flourishing — **florero** *nm* : vase — **florido, -da** *adj* : flowery — **florista** *nmf* : florist — **floritura** *nf* : frill, flourish
flota *nf* : fleet
flotar *vi* : float — **flotador** *nm* **1** : float **2** : life preserver (for a swimmer) — **flotante** *adj* : floating, buoyant — **flote: a** ~ *adv phr* : afloat

flotilla *nf* : flotilla, fleet
fluctuar {3} *vi* : fluctuate — **fluctuación** *nf, pl* **-ciones** : fluctuation
fluir {41} *vi* : flow — **fluidez** *nf* **1** : fluidity **2** : fluency (of language, etc.) — **fluido, -da** *adj* **1** : fluid **2** : fluent (of language) — **fluido** *nm* : fluid — **flujo** *nm* : flow
fluorescente *adj* : fluorescent
fluoruro *nm* : fluoride
fluvial *adj* : river
fobia *nf* : phobia
foca *nf* : seal (animal)
foco *nm* **1** : focus **2** : spotlight, floodlight (in theater, etc.) **3** *Lat* : lightbulb
fofo, -fa *adj* : flabby
fogata *nf* : bonfire
fogón *nm, pl* **-gones** : burner
fogoso, -sa *adj* : ardent
folklore *nm* : folklore — **folklórico, -ca** *adj* : folk, traditional
follaje *nm* : foliage
folleto *nm* : pamphlet, leaflet
fomentar *vt* : promote, encourage — **fomento** *nm* : promotion, encouragement
fonda *nf* : boarding house
fondear *vt* : sound out, examine — *vi* : anchor
fondillos *nmpl* : seat (of pants, etc.)
fondo *nm* **1** : bottom **2** : rear, back, end **3** PROFUNDIDAD : depth **4** : background (of a painting, etc.) **5** *Lat* : slip, petticoat **6** ~ **s** *nmpl* : funds, resources **7 a** ~ : thoroughly, in depth **8 en el** ~ : deep down
fonético, -ca *adj* : phonetic — **fonética** *nf* : phonetics
fontanería *nf Spain* : plumbing — **fontanero, -ra** *n Spain* : plumber
footing *nm* **1** : jogging **2 hacer** ~ : jog
forajido, -da *n* : bandit, outlaw
foráneo, -nea *adj* : foreign, strange
forastero, -ra *n* : stranger, outsider
forcejear *vi* : struggle — **forcejeo** *nm* : struggle
forense *adj* : forensic
forja *nf* : forge — **forjar** *vt* **1** : forge **2** CREAR, FORMAR : build up, create
forma *nf* **1** : form, shape **2** MANERA : manner, way **3 en** ~ : fit, healthy **4** ~ **s** *nfpl* : appearances, conventions — **formación** *nf, pl* **-ciones** **1** : formation **2** EDUCACIÓN : training
formal *adj* **1** : formal **2** SERIO : serious **3** FIABLE : dependable, reliable — **formalidad** *nf* **1** : formality **2** SERIEDAD : seriousness **3** FIABILIDAD : reliability
formar *vt* **1** : form, shape **2** CONSTITUIR : constitute **3** EDUCAR : train, educate — **formarse** *vr* **1** DESARROLLARSE : develop, take shape **2** EDUCARSE : be educated

formato *nm* : format
formidable *adj* **1** : tremendous **2** *fam* : fantastic, terrific
fórmula *nf* : formula
formular *vt* **1** : formulate, draw up **2** : make, lodge (a complaint, etc.)
formulario *nm* : form
fornido, -da *adj* : well-built, burly
foro *nm* : forum
forraje *nm* : forage, fodder — **forrajear** *vi* : forage
forrar *vt* **1** : line (a garment) **2** : cover (a book) — **forro** *nm* **1** : lining **2** CUBIERTA : book cover
fortalecer {53} *vt* : strengthen — **fortaleza** *nf* **1** : fortress **2** FUERZA : strength **3** : (moral) fortitude
fortificar {72} *vt* : fortify — **fortificación** *nf*, *pl* **-ciones** : fortification
fortuito, -ta *adj* : fortuitous, chance
fortuna *nf* **1** SUERTE : fortune, luck **2** RIQUEZA : wealth, fortune **3** por ~ : fortunately
forzar {36} *vt* **1** : force **2** : strain (one's eyes) — **forzosamente** *adv* : necessarily — **forzoso, -sa** *adj* : necessary, inevitable
fosa *nf* **1** : pit, ditch **2** TUMBA : grave **3** ~s nasales : nostrils
fósforo *nm* **1** : phosphorus **2** CERILLA : match — **fosforescente** *adj* : phosphorescent
fósil *nm* : fossil
foso *nm* **1** : ditch **2** : pit (of a theater) **3** : moat (of a castle)
foto *nf* : photo
fotocopia *nf* : photocopy — **fotocopiadora** *nf* : photocopier — **fotocopiar** *vt* : photocopy
fotogénico, -ca *adj* : photogenic
fotografía *nf* **1** : photography **2** : photograph, picture — **fotografiar** {85} *vt* : photograph — **fotográfico, -ca** *adj* : photographic — **fotógrafo, -fa** *n* : photographer
fotosíntesis *nf* : photosynthesis
fracasar *vi* : fail — **fracaso** *nm* : failure
fracción *nf*, *pl* **-ciones 1** : fraction **2** : faction (in politics) — **fraccionamiento** *nm* *Lat* : housing development
fractura *nf* : fracture — **fracturarse** *vr* : fracture, break (a bone)
fragancia *nf* : fragrance, scent — **fragante** *adj* : fragrant
fragata *nf* : frigate
frágil *adj* **1** : fragile **2** DÉBIL : frail, delicate — **fragilidad** *nf* **1** : fragility **2** DEBILIDAD : frailty
fragmento *nm* : fragment
fragor *nm* : clamor, din

fragoso, -sa *adj* : rough, rugged
fragua *nf* : forge — **fraguar** {10} *vt* **1** : forge **2** IDEAR : concoct — *vi* : harden, solidify
fraile *nm* : friar, monk
frambuesa *nf* : raspberry
francés, -cesa *adj*, *mpl* **-ceses** : French — **francés** *nm* : French (language)
franco, -ca *adj* **1** : frank, candid **2** : free (in commerce) — **franco** *nm* : franc
francotirador, -dora *n* : sniper
franela *nf* : flannel
franja *nf* **1** : stripe, band **2** FLECO : fringe
franquear *vt* **1** : clear (a path, etc.) **2** : cross over (a doorstep, etc.) **3** : pay postage on (mail) — **franqueo** *nm* : postage
franqueza *nf* : frankness
frasco *nm* : small bottle, vial, flask
frase *nf* **1** : phrase **2** ORACIÓN : sentence
fraternal *adj* : brotherly, fraternal — **fraternidad** *nf* : brotherhood, fraternity — **fraternizar** {21} *vi* : fraternize — **fraterno, -na** *adj* : brotherly, fraternal
fraude *nm* : fraud — **fraudulento, -ta** *adj* : fraudulent
fray *nm* (*used in titles*) : brother, friar
frazada *nf* *Lat* : blanket
frecuencia *nf* **1** : frequency **2** con ~ : often, frequently — **frecuentar** *vt* : frequent, haunt — **frecuente** *adj* : frequent
fregadero *nm* : kitchen sink
fregar {49} *vt* **1** : scrub, wash **2** *Lat fam* : annoy — *vi Lat fam* : be a pest
freír {37} *vt* : fry
fregona *nf Spain* : mop
frenar *vt* **1** : brake **2** RESTRINGIR : curb, check
frenesí *nm* : frenzy — **frenético, -ca** *adj* : frantic, frenzied
freno *nm* **1** : brake **2** : bit (of a bridle) **3** CONTROL : check, restraint
frente *nm* **1** : front **2** : facade (of a building) **3** al ~ de : at the head of **4** ~ a : opposite **5** de ~ : (facing) forward **6** hacer ~ a : face up to, brave — ~ *nf* : forehead
fresa *nf* : strawberry
fresco, -ca *adj* **1** : fresh **2** FRÍO : cool **3** *fam* : insolent, nervy — **fresco** *nm* **1** : fresh air **2** FRESCOR : coolness **3** : fresco (art or painting) — **frescor** *nm* : coolness, cool air — **frescura** *nf* **1** : freshness **2** FRÍO : coolness **3** *fam* : nerve, insolence
fresno *nm* : ash (tree)
frialdad *nf* **1** : coldness **2** INDIFERENCIA : indifference
fricción *nf*, *pl* **-ciones 1** : friction **2** MASAJE : rubbing, massage — **friccionar** *vt* : rub
frigidez *nf* : frigidity
frigorífico *nm Spain* : refrigerator
frijol *nm Lat* : bean

frío, fría *adj* **1** : cold **2** INDIFERENTE : cool, indifferent — **frío** *nm* **1** : cold **2** INDIFERENCIA : coldness, indifference **3 hacer ~** : be cold (outside) **4 tener ~** : be cold, feel cold

frito, -ta *adj* **1** : fried **2** *fam* : fed up

frívolo, -la *adj* : frivolous — **frivolidad** *nf* : frivolity

fronda *nf* **1** : frond **2** *or* **~s** *nfpl* : foliage — **frondoso, -sa** *adj* : leafy

frontera *nf* : border, frontier — **fronterizo, -za** *adj* : border, on the border — **frontero, -ra** *adj* : facing, opposite

frotar *vt* : rub — **frotarse** *vr* **~ las manos** : rub one's hands

fructífero, -ra *adj* : fruitful

frugal *adj* : frugal, thrifty — **frugalidad** *adj* : frugality

fruncir {83} *vt* **1** : gather (in pleats) **2 ~ el ceño** : frown **3 ~ la boca** : purse one's lips

frustrar *vt* : frustrate — **frustrarse** *vr* : fail — **frustración** *nf, pl* **-ciones** : frustration — **frustrado, -da** *adj* **1** : frustrated **2** FRACASADO : failed, unsuccessful — **frustrante** *adj* : frustrating

fruta *nf* : fruit — **frutilla** *nf Lat* : strawberry — **fruto** *nm* **1** : fruit **2** RESULTADO : result, consequence

fucsia *adj & nm* : fuchsia

fuego *nm* **1** : fire **2** : flame, burner (on a stove) **3 ~s artificiales** *nmpl* : fireworks **4 ¿tienes fuego?** : have you got a light?

fuelle *nm* : bellows

fuente *nf* **1** : fountain **2** MANANTIAL : spring **3** ORIGEN : source **4** PLATO : platter, serving dish

fuera *adv* **1** : outside, out **2** : abroad, away **3 ~ de** : outside of, beyond **4 ~ de** : aside from, in addition to

fuerte *adj* **1** : strong **2** : bright (of colors), loud (of sounds) **3** EXTREMO : intense **4** DURO : hard — **~** *adv* **1** : strongly, hard **2** : loudly **3** MUCHO : abundantly, a lot — **~** *nm* **1** : fort **2** ESPECIALIDAD : strong point

fuerza *nf* **1** : strength **2** VIOLENCIA : force **3** PODER : power, might **4 ~s armadas** *nfpl* : armed forces **5 a ~ de** : by dint of **6 a la ~** : necessarily

fuga *nf* **1** : flight, escape **2** : fugue (in music) **3** ESCAPE : leak — **fugarse** {52} *vr* : flee, run away — **fugaz** *adj, pl* **-gaces** : fleeting — **fugitivo, -va** *adj & n* : fugitive

fulano, -na *n* : so-and-so, what's-his-name, what's-her-name

fulgor *nm* : brilliance, splendor

fulminar *vt* **1** : strike with lightning **2** : strike down (with an illness, etc.) — **fulminante** *adj* : devastating

fumar *v* : smoke — **fumarse** *vr* **1** : smoke **2** *fam* : squander — **fumador, -dora** *n* : smoker

funámbulo, -la *n* : tightrope walker

función *nf, pl* **-ciones** **1** : function **2** TRABAJOS : duties *pl* **3** : performance, show (in theater) — **funcional** *adj* : functional — **funcionamiento** *nm* **1** : functioning **2 en ~** : in operation — **funcionar** *vi* **1** : function, run, work **2 no funciona** : out of order — **funcionario, -ria** *n* : civil servant, official

funda *nf* **1** : cover, sheath **2** *or* **~ de almohada** : pillowcase

fundar *vt* **1** ESTABLECER : found, establish **2** BASAR : base — **fundarse** *vr* **~ en** : be based on — **fundación** *nf, pl* **-ciones** : foundation — **fundador, -dora** *n* : founder — **fundamental** *adj* : fundamental, basic — **fundamentalmente** *adv* : basically — **fundamentar** *vt* **1** : lay the foundations for **2** BASAR : base — **fundamento** *nm* **1** : foundation **2 ~s** *nmpl* : fundamentals

fundir *vt* **1** : melt down, smelt **2** FUSIONAR : fuse, merge — **fundirse** *vr* **1** : blend, merge **2** DERRETIRSE : melt **3** : burn out (of a lightbulb) — **fundición** *nf, pl* **-ciones** **1** : smelting **2** : foundry

fúnebre *adj* **1** : funeral **2** LÚGUBRE : gloomy

funeral *adj* : funeral, funerary — **~** *nm* **1** : funeral **2 ~es** *nmpl* EXEQUIAS : funeral (rites) — **funeraria** *nf* : funeral home

funesto, ta *adj* : terrible, disastrous

fungir {35} *vi Lat* : act, function

furgón *nm, pl* **-gones** **1** : van, truck **2** : freight car (of a train) **3 ~ de cola** : caboose — **furgoneta** *nf* : van

furia *nf* **1** CÓLERA : fury, rage **2** VIOLENCIA : violence — **furibundo, -da** *adj* : furious — **furioso, -sa** *adj* **1** : furious, irate **2** INTENSO : intense, violent — **furor** *nm* : fury

furtivo, -va *adj* : furtive

furúnculo *nm* : boil

fuselaje *nm* : fuselage

fusible *nm* : fuse

fusil *nm* : rifle — **fusilar** *vt* : shoot (by firing squad)

fusión *nf, pl* **-siones** **1** : fusion **2** UNIÓN : union, merger — **fusionar** *vt* **1** : fuse **2** UNIR : merge — **fusionarse** *vr* : merge

futbol *or* **fútbol** *nm* **1** : soccer **2 ~ americano** : football — **futbolista** *nmf* : soccer player, football player

fútil *adj* : trifling, trivial

futuro, -ra *adj* : future — **futuro** *nm* : future

G

g *nf* : g, seventh letter of the Spanish alphabet

gabán *nm*, *pl* **-banes** : topcoat, overcoat

gabardina *nf* **1** : trench coat, raincoat **2** : gabardine (fabric)

gabinete *nm* **1** : cabinet (in government) **2** : (professional) office

gacela *nf* : gazelle

gaceta *nf* : gazette

gachas *nfpl* : porridge

gacho, -cha *adj* : drooping

gaélico, -ca *adj* : Gaelic

gafas *nfpl* **1** : eyeglasses **2 ∼ de sol** : sunglasses

gaita *nf* : bagpipes *pl*

gajo *nm* : segment (of fruit)

gala *nf* **1** : gala **2 de ∼** : formal **3 hacer ∼ de** : display, show off **4 ∼s** *nfpl* : finery

galáctico, -ca *adj* : galactic

galán *nm*, *pl* **-lanes** **1** : leading man (in theater) **2** *fam* : boyfriend

galante *adj* : gallant — **galantear** *vt* : court, woo — **galantería** *nf* **1** : gallantry **2** CUMPLIDO : compliment

galápago *nm* : (aquatic) turtle

galardón *nm*, *pl* **-dones** : reward

galaxia *nf* : galaxy

galera *nf* : galley

galería *nf* **1** : corridor **2** : gallery, balcony (in a theater)

galés, -lesa *adj*, *mpl* **-leses** : Welsh

galgo *nm* : greyhound

galimatías *nms & pl* : gibberish

gallardía *nf* **1** : bravery **2** ELEGANCIA : elegance — **gallardo, -da** *adj* **1** : brave **2** APUESTO : elegant, good-looking

gallego, -ga *adj* : Galician

galleta *nf* **1** : (sweet) cookie **2** : (salted) cracker

gallina *nf* **1** : hen **2 ∼ de Guinea** : guinea fowl — **gallinero** *nm* : henhouse, (chicken) coop — **gallo** *nm* : rooster, cock

galón *nm*, *pl* **-lones** **1** : gallon **2** : stripe (military insignia)

galopar *vi* : gallop — **galope** *nm* : gallop

galvanizar {21} *vt* : galvanize

gama *nf* **1** : range, spectrum **2** : scale (in music)

gamba *nf* : large shrimp, prawn

gamuza *nf* **1** : chamois (animal) **2** : chamois (leather), suede

gana *nf* **1** : desire, wish **2** APETITO : appetite **3 de buena ∼** : willingly, heartily **4 de mala ∼** : unwillingly **5 no me da la ∼** : I don't feel like it **6 tener ∼s de** : feel like, be in the mood for

ganado *nm* **1** : cattle *pl*, livestock **2 ∼ ovino** : sheep *pl* **3 ∼ porcino** : swine *pl* — **ganadería** *nf* **1** : cattle raising **2** GANADO : livestock

ganador, -dora *adj* : winning — **∼** *n* : winner

ganancia *nf* : profit

ganar *vt* **1** : earn **2** : win (in games, etc.) **3** CONSEGUIR : gain **4** ADQUERIR : get, obtain **5 ∼ a algn** : win over s.o., beat s.o. — *vi* : win — **ganarse** *vr* **1** : win, gain **2 ∼ la vida** : make a living

gancho *nm* **1** : hook **2** HORQUILLA : hairpin **3** *Lat* : (clothes) hanger

gandul, -dula *adj & n fam* : good-for-nothing — **gandul** *nm Lat* : pigeon pea

ganga *nf* : bargain

gangrena *nf* : gangrene

gángster *nmf* : gangster

ganso, -sa *n* : goose, gander *m* — **gansada** *nf* : silly thing, nonsense

gañir {38} *vi* : yelp — **gañido** *nm* : yelp

garabatear *v* : scribble — **garabato** *nm* : scribble

garaje *nm* : garage

garantizar {21} *vt* : guarantee — **garante** *nmf* : guarantor — **garantía** *nf* **1** : guarantee, warranty **2** FIANZA : surety

garapiñar *vt* : candy (fruits, etc.)

garbanzo *nm* : chickpea, garbanzo

garbo *nm* : grace, elegance — **garboso, -sa** *adj* : graceful, elegant

gardenia *nf* : gardenia

garfio *nm* : hook, gaff

garganta *nf* **1** : throat **2** CUELLO : neck **3** DESFILADERO : ravine, gorge — **gargantilla** *nf* : necklace

gárgara *nf* **1** : gargling, gargle **2 hacer ∼s** : gargle

gárgola *nf* : gargoyle

garita *nf* **1** : sentry box **2** CABAÑA : cabin, hut

garito *nm* : gambling den

garra *nf* **1** : claw, talon **2** *fam* : hand, paw

garrafa *nf* : decanter, carafe — **garrafón** *nm*, *pl* **-fones** : large decanter or bottle

garrapata *nf* : tick

garrocha *nf* **1** : lance, pike **2** *Lat* : pole (in sports)

garrote *nm* : club, cudgel

garúa *nf Lat* : drizzle

garza *nf* : heron

garzón, -zona *nm, pl* **-zones** : waiter *m*, waitress *f*

gas *nm* 1 : gas 2 ~ **lacrimógeno** : tear gas

gasa *nf* : gauze

gaseosa *nf* : soda, soft drink

gasolina *nf* : gasoline, gas — **gasoil** *or* **gasóleo** *nm* : diesel fuel — **gasolinera** *nf* : gas station, service station

gastar *vt* 1 : spend 2 CONSUMIR : consume, use up 3 DESPERDICIAR : squander, waste — **gastarse** *vr* 1 : spend 2 DETERIORARSE : wear out — **gastado, -da** *adj* 1 : spent 2 : worn-out (of clothing, etc.) — **gastador, -dora** *n* : spendthrift — **gasto** *nm* 1 : expense, expenditure 2 ~s **generales** : overhead

gástrico, -ca *adj* : gastric

gastronomía *nf* : gastronomy — **gastrónomo, -ma** *n* : gourmet

gatas: a ~ *adv phr* : on all fours

gatear *vi* : crawl, creep

gatillo *nm* : trigger — **gatillero** *nm Mex* : gunman

gato, -ta *n* : cat — **gatito, -ta** *n* : kitten — **gato** *nm* : jack (for an automobile)

gaucho *nm* : gaucho

gaveta *nf* : drawer

gavilla *nf* 1 : sheaf 2 PANDILLA : gang

gaviota *nf* : gull, seagull

gay *adj* : gay (homosexual)

gaza *nf* : loop

gazpacho *nm* : gazpacho

géiser *nm* : geyser

gelatina *nf* : gelatin

gema *nf* : gem

gemelo, -la *adj & n* : twin — **gemelo** *nm* 1 : cuff link 2 ~s *nmpl* : binoculars

gemir {54} *vi* : moan, groan, whine — **gemido** *nm* : moan, groan, whine

gen *or* **gene** *nm* : gene

genealogía *nf* : genealogy — **genealógico, -ca** *adj* : genealogical

generación *nf, pl* **-ciones** : generation

generador *nm* : generator

general *adj* 1 : general 2 **en** ~ *or* **por lo** ~ : in general, generally — ~ *nmf* : general — **generalidad** *nf* 1 : generalization 2 MAYORÍA : majority — **generalizar** {21} *vi* : generalize — *vt* : spread (out) — **generalizarse** *vr* : become widespread — **generalmente** *adv* : usually, generally

generar *vt* : generate

género *nm* 1 : kind, sort 2 : gender (in grammar) 3 ~ **humano** : human race — **genérico, -ca** *adj* : generic

generoso, -sa *adj* 1 : generous, unselfish 2 : ample (in quantity) — **generosidad** *nf* : generosity

génesis *nfs & pl* : genesis

genética *nf* : genetics — **genético, -ca** *adj* : genetic

genial *adj* 1 : brilliant 2 ESTUPENDO : great, terrific

genio *nm* 1 : genius 2 CARÁCTER : temper, disposition 3 : genie (in mythology)

genital *adj* : genital — **genitales** *nmpl* : genitals

genocidio *nm* : genocide

gente *nf* 1 : people 2 *fam* : relatives *pl*, folks *pl* 3 **ser buena** ~ : be nice, be kind

gentil *adj* 1 AMABLE : kind 2 : gentile (in religion) — **gentileza** *nf* : kindness, courtesy

gentío *nm* : crowd, mob

gentuza *nf* : riffraff, rabble

genuflexión *nf, pl* **-xiones** : genuflection

genuino, -na *adj* : genuine

geografía *nf* : geography — **geográfico, -ca** *adj* : geographic, geographical

geología *nf* : geology — **geológico, -ca** *adj* : geologic, geological

geometría *nf* : geometry — **geométrico, -ca** *adj* : geometric, geometrical

geranio *nm* : geranium

gerencia *nf* : management — **gerente** *nmf* : manager

geriatría *nf* : geriatrics — **geriátrico, -ca** *adj* : geriatric

germen *nm, pl* **gérmenes** : germ

germinar *vi* : germinate, sprout

gestación *nf, pl* **-ciones** : gestation

gesticular *vi* : gesticulate, gesture — **gesticulación** *nf, pl* **-ciones** : gesticulation

gestión *nf, pl* **-tiones** 1 : procedure, step 2 ADMINISTRACIÓN : management — **gestionar** *vt* 1 : negotiate, work towards 2 ADMINISTRAR : manage, handle

gesto *nm* 1 : gesture 2 : (facial) expression 3 MUECA : grimace

gigante *adj & nm* : giant — **gigantesco, -ca** *adj* : gigantic

gimnasia *nf* : gymnastics — **gimnasio** *nm* : gymnasium, gym — **gimnasta** *nmf* : gymnast

gimotear *vi* : whine, whimper

ginebra *nf* : gin

ginecología *nf* : gynecology — **ginecólogo, -ga** *n* : gynecologist

gira *nf* : tour

girar *vi* : turn (around), revolve — *vt* 1 : turn, twist, rotate 2 : draft (checks) 3 : transfer (funds)

girasol *nm* : sunflower

giratorio, -ria *adj* : revolving

giro *nm* 1 : turn, rotation 2 LOCUCIÓN : expression 3 ~ **bancario** : bank draft 4 ~ **postal** : money order

giroscopio *nm* : gyroscope

gis *nm Lat* : chalk

gitano, -na *adj & n* : Gypsy

glaciar *nm* : glacier — **glacial** *adj* : glacial, icy

gladiador *nm* : gladiator

glándula *nf* : gland

glasear *vt* : glaze, ice (cake, etc.) — **glaseado** *nm* : icing

glicerina *nf* : glycerin

globo *nm* **1** : globe **2** : balloon **3** ~ **ocular** : eyeball — **global** *adj* **1** : global **2** TOTAL : total, overall

glóbulo *nm* : blood cell, corpuscle

gloria *nf* : glory

glorieta *nf* **1** : bower, arbor **2** *Spain* : rotary, traffic circle

glorificar {72} *vt* : glorify

glorioso, -sa *adj* : glorious

glosario *nm* : glossary

glotón, -tona *adj, mpl* **-tones** : gluttonous — ~ *n* : glutton — **glotonería** *nf* : gluttony

glucosa *nf* : glucose

gnomo *nm* : gnome

gobernar {55} *v* **1** : govern, rule **2** DIRIGIR : direct, manage **3** : steer (a boat, etc.) — **gobernación** *nf, pl* **-ciones** : governing, government — **gobernador, -dora** *n* : governor — **gobernante** *adj* : ruling, governing — ~ *n* : ruler, leader — **gobierno** *nm* : government

goce *nm* : enjoyment

gol *nm* : goal (in sports)

golf *nm* : golf — **golfista** *nmf* : golfer

golfo *nm* : gulf

golondrina *nf* **1** : swallow **2** ~ **de mar** : tern

golosina *nf* : sweet, candy — **goloso, -sa** *adj* : fond of sweets

golpe *nm* **1** : blow **2** PUÑETAZO : punch **3** : knock (on a door, etc.) **4 de** ~ : suddenly **5 de un** ~ : all at once **6** ~ **de estado** : coup d'etat — **golpear** *vt* **1** : hit, punch **2** : slam, bang (a door, etc.) — *vi* : knock (at a door)

goma *nf* **1** CAUCHO : rubber **2** PEGAMENTO : glue **3** *or* ~ **elástica** : rubber band **4** ~ **de mascar** : chewing gum **5** ~ **de borrar** : eraser

gong *nm* : gong

gordo, -da *adj* **1** : fat, plump **2** GRUESO : thick **3** : fatty (of meat) **4** *fam* : big, serious — ~ *n* : fat person — **gorda** *nf Lat* : thick corn tortilla — **gordo** *nm* **1** GRASA : fat **2** : jackpot (in a lottery) — **gordura** *nf* : fatness, flab

gorgotear *vi* : gurgle, bubble

gorila *nm* : gorilla

gorjear *vi* **1** : chirp, tweet **2** : gurgle (of a baby) — **gorjeo** *nm* : chirping

gorra *nf* **1** : cap, bonnet **2 de** ~ *fam* : for free

gorrear *vt fam* : bum, scrounge

gorrión *nm, pl* **-rriones** : sparrow

gorro *nm* **1** : cap, bonnet **2 de** ~ *fam* : for free

gota *nf* **1** : drop **2** : gout (in medicine) — **gotear** *vi* : drip, leak — **goteo** *nm* : drip, dripping — **gotera** *nf* : leak

gótico, -ca *adj* : Gothic

gozar {21} *vi* **1** : enjoy oneself **2** ~ **de algo** : enjoy sth

gozne *nm* : hinge

gozo *nm* **1** : joy **2** PLACER : enjoyment, pleasure — **gozoso, -sa** *adj* : joyful, glad

grabar *vt* **1** : engrave **2** : record, tape — **grabación** *nf, pl* **-ciones** : recording — **grabado** *nm* : engraving — **grabadora** *nf* : tape recorder

gracia *nf* **1** : grace **2** FAVOR : favor, kindness **3** HUMOR : humor, wit **4** ~**s** *nfpl* : thanks **5** ¡(muchas) ~**s!** : thank you (very much)! — **gracioso, -sa** *adj* : funny, amusing

grada *nf* **1** : step, stair **2** : row (in a theater, etc.) **3** ~**s** *nfpl* : bleachers, grandstand — **gradación** *nf, pl* **-ciones** : gradation, scale — **gradería** *nf* : rows *pl*, stands *pl* — **grado** *nm* **1** : degree **2** : grade (in school) **3 de buen** ~ : willingly

graduar {3} *vt* **1** : regulate, adjust **2** MARCAR : calibrate **3** : confer a degree on (in education) — **graduarse** *vr* : graduate (from a school) — **graduación** *nf, pl* **-ciones 1** : graduation **2** : alcohol content, proof — **graduado, -da** *n* : graduate — **gradual** *adj* : gradual — **gradualmente** *adv* : little by little, gradually

gráfico, -ca *adj* : graphic — **gráfica** *nf* : graph — **gráfico** *nm* **1** : graph **2** : graphic (in computers)

gragea *nf* : pill, tablet

grajo *nm* : rook (bird)

gramática *nf* : grammar — **gramatical** *adj* : grammatical

gramo *nm* : gram

gran → **grande**

grana *nf* : scarlet

granada *nf* **1** : pomegranate **2** : grenade (in the military)

granate *nm* : garnet

grande *adj* (**gran** *before singular nouns*) **1** : large, big **2** ALTO : tall **3** : great (in quality, intensity, etc.) **4** *Lat* : grown-up — **grandeza** *nf* **1** : greatness **2** NOBLEZA : nobility — **grandiosidad** *nf* : grandeur — **grandioso, -sa** *adj* : grand, magnificent

granel: a ~ *adv phr* **1** : in bulk **2** : in abundance

granero *nm* : barn, granary

granito *nm* : granite
granizar {21} *v impers* : hail — **granizada** *nf* : hailstorm — **granizado** *nm* : iced drink — **granizo** *nm* : hail
granja *nf* : farm — **granjero, -ra** *n* : farmer
grano *nm* 1 : grain 2 SEMILLA : seed 3 : (coffee) bean 4 BARRO : pimple
granuja *nmf* : rascal
grapa *nf* : staple — **grapadora** *nf* : stapler — **grapar** *vt* : staple
grasa *nf* 1 : grease 2 : fat (in cooking, etc.) — **grasiento, -ta** *adj* : greasy, oily — **graso, -sa** *adj* : fatty, greasy, oily — **grasoso, -sa** *adj Lat* : greasy, oily
gratificar {72} *vt* 1 : give a tip or bonus to 2 SATISFACER : gratify, satisfy — **gratificación** *nf, pl* **-ciones** 1 : bonus, tip, reward 2 SATISFACCIÓN : gratification
gratis *adv & adj* : free
gratitud *nf* : gratitude
grato, -ta *adj* : pleasant, agreeable
gratuito, -ta *adj* 1 : gratuitous, unwarranted 2 GRATIS : free
grava *nf* : gravel
gravar *vt* 1 : tax 2 CARGAR : burden — **gravamen** *nm, pl* **-vámenes** 1 : burden, obligation 2 IMPUESTO : tax
grave *adj* 1 : grave, serious 2 : deep, low (of a voice, etc.) — **gravedad** *nf* : gravity
gravilla *nf* : gravel
gravitar *vi* 1 : gravitate 2 ~ **sobre** : weigh on — **gravitación** *nf, pl* **-ciones** : gravitation
gravoso, -sa *adj* : costly, burdensome
graznar *vi* : caw, quack, honk — **graznido** *nm* : caw, quack, honk
gregario, -ria *adj* : gregarious
gremio *nm* : guild, (trade) union
greñas *nfpl* : shaggy hair, mop
griego, -ga *adj* : Greek — **griego** *nm* : Greek (language)
grieta *nf* : crack, crevice
grifo *nm Spain* : faucet, tap
grillete *nm* : shackle
grillo *nm* 1 : cricket 2 ~**s** *nmpl* : fetters, shackles
grima *nf* **dar** ~ : annoy, irritate
gringo, -ga *adj & n Lat fam* : Yankee, gringo
gripe *nf or* **gripa** *nf Lat* : flu, influenza
gris *adj & nm* : gray
gritar *v* : shout, scream, cry — **grito** *nm* 1 : shout, scream, cry 2 **dar** ~**s** : shout
grosella *nf* : currant
grosería *nf* 1 : vulgar remark 2 DESCORTESÍA : rudeness — **grosero, -ra** *adj* 1 : coarse, vulgar 2 DESCORTÉS : rude
grosor *nm* : thickness
grotesco, -ca *adj* : grotesque, hideous
grúa *nf* : crane, derrick

grueso, -sa *adj* 1 : thick 2 CORPULENTO : stout, heavy — **gruesa** *nf* : gross — **grueso** *nm* 1 GROSOR : thickness 2 : main body, mass 3 **en** ~ : wholesale
grulla *nf* : crane (bird)
grumo *nm* : lump, clot — **grumoso, -sa** *adj* : lumpy
gruñir {38} *vi* 1 : growl, grunt 2 *fam* : grumble — **gruñido** *nm* 1 : growl, grunt 2 *fam* : grumble — **gruñón, -ñona** *adj, mpl* **-ñones** *fam* : grumpy, grouchy — ~ *n fam* : grouch
grupa *nf* : rump, hindquarters *pl*
grupo *nm* : group
gruta *nf* : grotto
guacamayo *nm or* **guacamaya** *nf Lat* : macaw
guacamole *nm* : guacamole
guadaña *nf* : scythe
guagua *nf Lat* 1 : baby 2 AUTOBÚS : bus
guajalote, -ta *or* **guajolote, -ta** *n Lat* : turkey
guante *nm* : glove
guapo, -pa *adj* : handsome, good-looking
guaraní *nm* : Guarani (language of Paraguay)
guarda *nmf* 1 : keeper, custodian 2 GUARDIÁN : security guard — **guardabarros** *nms & pl* : fender — **guardabosque** *nmf* : forest ranger — **guardacostas** *nmfs & pl* : coast guard vessel — **guardaespaldas** *nmfs & pl* : bodyguard — **guardameta** *nmf* : goalkeeper — **guardapolvo** *nm* : overalls *pl* — **guardar** *vt* 1 : keep 2 PROTEGER : guard, protect 3 RESERVAR : save — **guardarse** *vr* ~ **de** 1 : refrain from 2 : guard against — **guardarropa** *nm* 1 : cloakroom, checkroom 2 ARMARIO : wardrobe
guardería *nf* : nursery, day-care center
guardia *nf* 1 : guard, vigilence 2 TURNO : duty, watch — ~ *nmf* 1 : guard 2 *or* ~ **municipal** : police officer — **guardián, -diana** *n, mpl* **-dianes** **1** : guardian, keeper 2 GUARDA : security guard
guarecer {53} *vt* : shelter, protect — **guarecerse** *vr* : take shelter
guarida *nf* 1 : den, lair (of animals) 2 : hideout (of persons)
guarnecer {53} *vt* 1 : adorn, garnish 2 : garrison (an area) — **guarnición** *nf, pl* **-ciones** 1 : garnish, trimming 2 : (military) garrison
guasa *nf fam* 1 : joke 2 **de** ~ : in jest — **guasón, -sona** *adj, mpl* **-sones** *fam* : joking, witty — ~ *n fam* : joker
guatemalteco, -ca *adj* : Guatemalan
guay *adj* : cool, neat, great
guayaba *nf* : guava
gubernamental *or* **gubernativo, -va** *adj* : governmental

guepardo *nm* : cheetah
güero, -ra *adj Lat* : blond, fair
guerra *nf* **1** : war, warfare **2** LUCHA : conflict, struggle — **guerrear** *vi* : wage war — **guerrero, -ra** *adj* **1** : war, fighting **2** BELICOSO : warlike — **~** *n* : warrior — **guerrilla** *nf* : guerrilla warfare — **guerrillero, -ra** *adj & n* : guerrilla
gueto *nm* : ghetto
guiar {85} *vt* **1** : guide, lead **2** ACONSEJAR : advise — **guiarse** *vr* : be guided by, go by — **guía** *nf* **1** : guidebook **2** ORIENTACIÓN : guidance — **~** *nmf* : guide, leader
guijarro *nm* : pebble
guillotina *nf* : guillotine
guinda *nf* : morello (cherry)
guiñar *vi* : wink — **guiño** *nm* : wink
guión *nm, pl* **guiones** **1** : script, screenplay **2** : hyphen, dash (in punctuation) — **guionista** *nmf* : scriptwriter, screenwriter

guirnalda *nf* : garland
guisa *nf* **1** : manner, fashion **2 a ~ de** : by way of **3 de tal ~** : in such a way
guisado *nm* : stew
guisante *nm* : pea
guisar *vt* : cook — **guiso** *nm* : stew, casserole
guitarra *nf* : guitar — **guitarrista** *nmf* : guitarist
gula *nf* : gluttony
gusano *nm* **I** : worm **2** : maggot (larva)
gustar *vt* **1** : taste **2** *Lat* : like — *vi* **1** : be pleasing **2 como guste** : as you like **3 me gustan los dulces** : I like sweets — **gusto** *nm* **1** : taste **2** PLACER : pleasure, liking **3 a ~** : comfortable, at ease **4 al ~** : to taste **5 mucho ~** : pleased to meet you — **gustoso, -sa** *adj* **1** : tasty **2** AGRADABLE : pleasant **3 hacer algo ~** : do sth willingly
gutural *adj* : guttural

H

h *nf* : h, eighth letter of the Spanish alphabet
haba *nf* : broad bean
habanero, -ra *adj* : Havanan — **habano** *nm* : Havana cigar
haber {39} *v aux* **1** : have, has **2 ~ de** : must — *v impers* **1** : there is, there are **2 hay que** : it is necessary (to) **3 ¿qué hay?** *or* **¿qué hubo?** : how's it going? — **~** *nm* **1** : assets *pl* **2** : credit side (in accounting) **3 ~es** *nmpl* : income, earnings
habichuela *nf* **1** : bean **2 ~ verde** : string bean
hábil *adj* **1** : able, skillful **2** LISTO : clever **3 horas ~es** : business hours — **habilidad** *nf* : ability, skill
habilitar *vt* **1** : equip, furnish **2** AUTORIZAR : authorize
habiloso -sa *adj* : bright, smart, clever
habitar *vt* : inhabit — *vi* : reside, dwell — **habitable** *adj* : habitable, inhabitable — **habitación** *nf, pl* **-ciones** **1** : room, bedroom **2** MORADA : dwelling, abode **3** : habitat (in biology) — **habitante** *nmf* : inhabitant, resident — **hábitat** *nm* : habitat
hábito *nm* : habit — **habitual** *adj* : habitual, usual — **habituar** {3} *vt* : accustom, habituate — **habituarse** *vr* **~ a** : get used to
hablar *vi* **1** : speak, talk **2 ~ de** : mention, talk about **3 ~ con** : talk to, speak with — *vt* **1** : speak (a language) **2** DISCUTIR : discuss — **hablarse** *vr* **1** : speak to each

other **2 se habla inglés** : English spoken — **habla** *nf* **1** : speech **2** IDIOMA : language, dialect **3 de ~ inglesa** : English-speaking — **hablador, -dora** *adj* : talkative — **~** *n* : chatterbox — **habladuría** *nf* **1** : rumor **2 ~s** *nfpl* : gossip — **hablante** *nmf* : speaker
hacedor, -dora *n* : creator, maker
hacendado, -da *n* : landowner, rancher
hacer {40} *vt* **1** : do, perform **2** CONSTRUIR, CREAR : make **3** OBLIGAR : force, oblige — *vi* : act — *v impers* **1 ~ calor/viento** : be hot/be windy **2 ~ falta** : be necessary **3 hace mucho tiempo** : a long time ago **4 no lo hace** : it doesn't matter — **hacerse** *vr* **1** VOLVERSE : become **2** : pretend (to be) **3 ~ a** : get used to **4 se hace tarde** : it's getting late
hacha *nf* **1** : hatchet, ax **2** ANTORCHA : torch
hachís *nm* : hashish
hacia *prep* **1** : toward, towards **2** CERCA DE : near, around, about **3 ~ abajo** : downward **4 ~ adelante** : forward
hacienda *nf* **1** : estate, ranch **2** BIENES : property **3** *Lat* : livestock **4 Hacienda** : department of revenue
hacinar *vt* : stack
hada *nf* : fairy
hado *nm* : fate
halagar {52} *vt* : flatter — **halagador, -dora** *adj* : flattering — **halago** *nm* : flattery —

halagüeño, -ña *adj* **1** : flattering **2** PROME-TEDOR : promising
halcón *nm, pl* **-cones** : hawk, falcon
halibut *nm, pl* **-buts** : halibut
hálito *nm* : breath
hallar *vt* **1** : find **2** DESCUBRIR : discover, find out — **hallarse** *vr* : be, find oneself — **hallazgo** *nm* : discovery, find
halo *nm* : halo
hamaca *nf* : hammock
hambre *nf* **1** : hunger **2** INANICIÓN : starvation, famine **3 tener** ~ : be hungry — **hambriento, -ta** *adj* : hungry, starving — **hambruna** *nf* : famine
hamburguesa *nf* : hamburger
hampa *nf* : underworld — **hampón, -pona** *n, mpl* **-pones** : criminal, thug
hámster *nm* : hamster
hándicap *nm* : handicap (in sports)
hangar *nm* : hangar
haragán, -gana *adj, mpl* **-ganes** : lazy, idle — ~ *n* : slacker, idler — **haraganear** : be lazy, loaf
harapiento, -ta *adj* : ragged, in rags — **harapos** *nmpl* : rags, tatters
harina *nf* : flour
hartar *vt* **1** : glut, satiate **2** FASTIDIAR : annoy — **hartarse** *vr* **1** : gorge oneself **2** CANSARSE : get fed up — **harto, -ta** *adj* **1** : full, satiated **2** CANSADO : tired, fed up — **harto** *adv* : extremely, very — **hartura** *nf* **1** : surfeit **2** ABUNDANCIA : abundance, plenty
hasta *prep* **1** : until, up until (in time) **2** : as far as, up to (in space) **3** ¡~ **luego!** : see you later! **4** ~ **que** : until — ~ *adv* : even
hastiar {85} *vt* **1** : make weary, bore **2** ASQUEAR : sicken — **hastiarse** *vr* ~ **de** : get tired of — **hastío** *nm* **1** : weariness, tedium **2** REPUGNANCIA : disgust
hato *nm* **1** : flock, herd **2** : bundle (of possessions)
haya *nf* : beech
haz *nm, pl* **haces** **1** : bundle, sheaf **2** : beam (of light)
hazaña *nf* : feat, exploit
hazmerreír *nm fam* : laughingstock
he {39} *v impers* ~ **aquí** : here is, here are, behold
hebilla *nf* : buckle
hebra *nf* : strand, thread
hebreo, -brea *adj* : Hebrew — **hebreo** *nm* : Hebrew (language)
hecatombe *nm* : disaster
hechizo *nm* **1** : spell **2** ENCANTO : charm, fascination — **hechicería** *nf* : sorcery, witchcraft — **hechicero, -ra** *n* : sorcerer, sorceress *f* — **hechizar** {21} *vt* **1** : bewitch **2** CAUTIVAR : charm

hecho, -cha *adj* **1** : made, done **2** : ready-to-wear (of clothing) **3** ~ **y derecho** : full-fledged, mature — **hecho** *nm* **1** : fact **2** SUCESO : event **3** ACTO : act, deed **4 de** ~ : in fact — **hechura** *nf* **1** : making, creation **2** FORMA : shape, form **3** : build (of the body) **4** ARTESANÍA : workmanship
heder {56} *vi* : stink, reek — **hediondez** *nf, pl* **-deces** : stench — **hediondo, -da** *adj* : stinking — **hedor** *nm* : stench
helar {55} *v* : freeze — **helarse** *vr* : freeze up, freeze over — **helado, -da** *adj* **1** : freezing cold **2** CONGELADO : frozen — **helada** *nf* : frost — **heladería** *nf* : ice-cream parlor — **helado** *nm* : ice cream — **heladora** *nf* : freezer
helecho *nm* : fern
hélice *nf* **1** : propeller **2** ESPIRAL : spiral, helix
helicóptero *nm* : helicopter
helio *nm* : helium
hembra *nf* **1** : female **2** MUJER : woman
hemisferio *nm* : hemisphere
hemorragia *nf* **1** : hemorrhage **2** ~ **nasal** : nosebleed
hemorroides *nfpl* : hemorrhoids, piles
henchir {54} *vt* : stuff, fill
hender {56} *vt* : cleave, split — **hendidura** *nf* : crevice, fissure
henequén *nm, pl* **-quenes** : sisal
heno *nm* : hay
hepatitis *nf* : hepatitis
heraldo *nm* : herald
herbolario, -ria *n* : herbalist
heredar *vt* : inherit — **heredad** *nm* : rural property, estate — **heredero, -ra** *n* : heir, heiress *f* — **hereditario, -ria** *adj* : hereditary
hereje *nmf* : heretic — **herejía** *nf* : heresy
herencia *nf* **1** : inheritance **2** : heredity (in biology)
herir {76} *vt* **1** : injure, wound **2** : hurt (feelings, pride, etc.) — **herida** *nf* : injury, wound — **herido, -da** *adj* **1** : injured, wounded **2** : hurt (of feelings, pride, etc.) — ~ *n* : injured person, casualty
hermano, -na *n* : brother *m*, sister *f* — **hermanastro, -tra** *n* : half brother *m*, half sister *f* — **hermandad** *nf* : brotherhood
hermético, -ca *adj* : hermetic, watertight
hermoso, -sa *adj* : beautiful, lovely — **hermosura** *nf* : beauty
hernia *nf* : hernia
héroe *nm* : hero — **heroico, -ca** *adj* : heroic — **heroína** *nf* **1** : heroine **2** : heroin (narcotic) — **heroísmo** *nm* : heroism
herradura *nf* : horseshoe
herramienta *nf* : tool
herrero, -ra *n* : blacksmith

herrumbre *nf* : rust

hervir {76} *v* : boil — **hervidero** *nm* **1** : mass, swarm **2** : hotbed (of intrigue, etc.) — **hervidor** *nm* : kettle — **hervor** *nm* **1** : boiling **2** ENTUSIASMO : fervor, ardor

heterogéneo, -nea *adj* : heterogeneous

heterosexual *adj & nmf* : heterosexual

hexágono *nm* : hexagon — **hexagonal** *adj* : hexagonal

hez *nf, pl* **heces** : dregs *pl,* scum

hiato *nm* : hiatus

hibernar *vi* : hibernate — **hibernación** *nf, pl* **-ciones** : hibernation

híbrido, -da *adj* : hybrid — **híbrido** *nm* : hybrid

hidalgo, -ga *n* : nobleman *m,* noblewoman *f*

hidratante *adj* : moisturizing

hidrato *nm* ~ **de carbono** : carbohydrate

hidráulico, -ca *adj* : hydraulic

hidroavión *nm, pl* **-aviones** : seaplane

hidroeléctrico, -ca *adj* : hydroelectric

hidrofobia *nf* : rabies

hidrógeno *nm* : hydrogen

hidroplano *nm* : hydroplane

hiedra *nf* **1** : ivy **2** ~ **venenosa** : poison ivy

hiel *nm* **1** : bile **2** AMARGURA : bitterness

hielo *nm* **1** : ice **2** FRIALDAD : coldness **3 romper el** ~ : break the ice

hiena *nf* : hyena

hierba *nf* **1** : herb **2** CÉSPED : grass **3 mala** ~ : weed — **hierbabuena** *nf* : mint

hierro *nm* **1** : iron **2** ~ **fundido** : cast iron

hígado *nm* : liver

higiene *nf* : hygiene — **higiénico, -ca** *adj* : hygienic

higo *nm* : fig

hijo, -ja *n* **1** : son *m,* daughter *f* **2 hijos** *nmpl* : children, offspring — **hijastro, -tra** *n* : stepson *m,* stepdaughter *f*

hilar *v* **1** : spin **2** ~ **delgado** : split hairs — **hilado** *nm* : yarn, thread

hilaridad *nf* : hilarity

hilera *nf* : file, row

hilo *nm* **1** : thread **2** LINO : linen **3** ALAMBRE : wire **4** : trickle (of water, etc.) **5** ~ **dental** : dental floss

hilvanar *vt* **1** : baste, tack **2** : put together (ideas, etc.)

himno *nm* **1** : hymn **2** ~ **nacional** : national anthem

hincapié *nm* **hacer** ~ **en** : emphasize, stress

hincar {72} *vt* : drive in, plunge — **hincarse** *vr* ~ **de rodillas** : kneel (down)

hinchar *vt Spain* : inflate, blow up — **hincharse** *vr* **1** : swell (up) **2** *Spain fam* : stuff

oneself — **hinchado, -da** *adj* **1** : swollen **2** POMPOSO : pompous — **hinchazón** *nf, pl* **-zones** : swelling

hindú *adj & nmf* : Hindu — **hinduismo** *nm* : Hinduism

hinojo *nm* : fennel

hiperactivo, -va *adj* : hyperactive

hiperenlace *nm* : hyperlink

hipermercado *nm* : large supermarket, hypermarket

hipersensible *adj* : oversensitive

hipertensión *nf, pl* **-siones** : hypertension, high blood pressure

hípico, -ca *adj* : equestrian, horse

hipil → **huipil**

hipnosis *nfs & pl* : hypnosis — **hipnótico, -ca** *adj* : hypnotic — **hipnotismo** *nm* : hypnotism — **hipnotizador, -dora** *n* : hypnotist — **hipnotizar** {21} *vt* : hypnotize

hipo *nm* **1** : hiccup, hiccups *pl* **2 tener** ~ : have hiccups

hipocondríaco, -ca *adj* : hypochondriacal — ~ *n* : hypochondriac

hipocresía *nf* : hypocrisy — **hipócrita** *adj* : hypocritical — ~ *nmf* : hypocrite

hipodérmico, -ca *adj* : hypodermic

hipódromo *nm* : racetrack

hipopótamo *nm* : hippopotamus

hipoteca *nf* : mortgage — **hipotecar** {72} *vt* : mortgage

hipótesis *nfs & pl* : hypothesis — **hipotético, -ca** *adj* : hypothetical

hiriente *adj* : hurtful, offensive

hirsuto, -ta *adj* **1** : hairy **2** : bristly, wiry (of hair)

hirviente *adj* : boiling

hispano, -na *or* **hispánico, -ca** *adj & n* : Hispanic — **hispanoamericano, -na** *adj* : Latin-American — ~ *n* : Latin American — **hispanohablante** *or* **hispanoparlante** *adj* : Spanish-speaking

histeria *nf* : hysteria — **histérico, -ca** *adj* : hysterical — **histerismo** *nm* : hysteria

historia *nf* **1** : history **2** CUENTO : story — **historiador, -dora** *n* : historian — **historial** *nm* : record, background — **histórico, -ca** *adj* **1** : historical **2** IMPORTANTE : historic, important — **historieta** *nf* : comic strip

hito *nm* : milestone, landmark

hocico *nm* : snout, muzzle

hockey *nm* : hockey

hogar *nm* **1** : home **2** CHIMENEA : hearth, fireplace — **hogareño, -ña** *adj* **1** : home-loving **2** DOMÉSTICO : home, domestic

hoguera *nf* : bonfire

hoja *nf* **1** : leaf **2** : sheet (of paper) **3** ~ **de afeitar** : razor blade — **hojalata** *nf* : tinplate — **hojaldre** *nm* : puff pastry — **hojear** *vt* : leaf through — **hojuela** *nf Lat* : flake

hola *interj* : hello!, hi!

holandés, -desa *adj, mpl* **-deses** : Dutch

holgado, -da *adj* **1** : loose, baggy **2** : comfortable (of an economic situation, a victory, etc.) — **holgazán, -zana** *adj, mpl* **-zanes** : lazy — ~ *n* : slacker, idler — **holgazanear** *vi* : laze about, loaf — **holgura** *nf* **1** : looseness **2** BIENESTAR : comfort, ease

hollín *nm, pl* **-llines** : soot

holocausto *nm* : holocaust

hombre *nm* **1** : man **2 el** ~ : mankind **3** ~ **de estado** : statesman **4** ~ **de negocios** : businessman

hombrera *nf* **1** : shoulder pad **2** : epaulet (of a uniform)

hombría *nf* : manliness

hombro *nm* : shoulder

hombruno, -na *adj* : mannish

homenaje *nm* **1** : homage **2 rendir** ~ **a** : pay tribute to

homeopatía *nf* : homeopathy

homicidio *nm* : homicide, murder — **homicida** *adj* : homicidal, murderous — ~ *nmf* : murderer

homogéneo, -nea *adj* : homogeneous

homólogo, -ga *adj* : equivalent — ~ *n* : counterpart

homosexual *adj & nmf* : homosexual — **homosexualidad** *nf* : homosexuality

hondo, -da *adj* : deep — **hondo** *adv* : deeply — **hondonada** *nf* : hollow — **hondura** *nf* : depth

hondureño, -ña *adj* : Honduran

honesto, -ta *adj* : decent, honorable — **honestidad** *nf* : honesty, integrity

hongo *nm* **1** : mushroom **2** : fungus (in botany and medicine)

honor *nm* : honor — **honorable** *adj* : honorable — **honorario, -ria** *adj* : honorary — **honorarios** *nmpl* : payment, fee — **honra** *nf* : honor — **honradez** *nf, pl* **-deces** : honesty, integrity — **honrado, -da** *adj* : honest, upright — **honrar** *vt* : honor — **honrarse** *vr* : be honored — **honroso, -sa** *adj* : honorable

hora *nf* **1** : hour **2** : (specific) time **3** CITA : appointment **4 a la última** ~ : at the last minute **5** ~ **punta** : rush hour **6 media** ~ : half an hour **7 ¿qué** ~ **es?** : what time is it? **8** ~**s de oficina** : office hours **9** ~**s extraordinarias** : overtime

horario *nm* : schedule, timetable

horca *nf* **1** : gallows *pl* **2** : pitchfork (in agriculture)

horcajadas: a ~ *adv phr* : astride

horda *nf* : horde

horizonte *nm* : horizon — **horizontal** *adj* : horizontal

horma *nf* **1** : form, mold, last **2** : shoe tree

hormiga *nf* : ant

hormigón *nm, pl* **-gones** : concrete

hormigueo *nm* : tingling, pins and needles

hormiguero *nm* **1** : anthill **2** : swarm (of people)

hormona *nf* : hormone

horno *nm* **1** : oven (for cooking) **2** : small furnace, kiln — **hornada** *nf* : batch — **hornear** *vt* : bake — **hornillo** *nf* : portable stove

horóscopo *nm* : horoscope

horquilla *nf* **1** : hairpin, bobby pin **2** HORCA : pitchfork

horrendo, -da *adj* : horrendous, awful — **horrible** *adj* : horrible — **horripilante** *adj* : horrifying — **horror** *nm* **1** : horror, dread **2** ATROCIDAD : atrocity — **horrorizar** {21} *vt* : horrify, terrify — **horrorizarse** *vr* : be horrified — **horroroso, -sa** *adj* : horrifying, dreadful

hortaliza *nf* : (garden) vegetable — **hortelano, -na** *n* : truck farmer — **horticultura** *nf* : horticulture

hosco, -ca *adj* : sullen, gloomy

hospedar *vt* : put up, lodge — **hospedarse** *vr* : stay, lodge — **hospedaje** *nm* : lodging

hospital *nm* : hospital — **hospitalario, -ria** *adj* : hospitable — **hospitalidad** *nf* : hospitality — **hospitalizar** {21} *vt* : hospitalize

hostería *nf* : small hotel, inn

hostia *nf* : host (in religion)

hostigar {52} *vt* **1** : whip **2** ACOSAR : harass, pester

hostil *adj* : hostile — **hostilidad** *nf* : hostility

hotel *nm* : hotel — **hotelero, -ra** *adj* : hotel — ~ *n* : hotel manager, hotelier

hoy *adv* **1** : today **2 de** ~ **en adelante** : from now on **3** ~ **(en) día** : nowadays **4** ~ **mismo** : this very day

hoyo *nm* : hole — **hoyuelo** *nm* : dimple

hoz *nf, pl* **hoces** : sickle

huarache *nm* : huarache (sandal)

hueco, -ca *adj* **1** : hollow, empty **2** ESPONJOSO : soft, spongy **3** RESONANTE : resonant — **hueco** *nm* **1** : hollow, cavity **2** : recess (in a wall, etc.) **3** ~ **de escalera** : stairwell

huelga *nf* **1** : strike **2 declararse en** ~ : go on strike — **huelguista** *nmf* : striker

huella *nf* **1** : footprint **2** VESTIGIO : track, mark **3** ~ **digital** *or* ~ **dactilar** : fingerprint

huérfano, -na *n* : orphan — ~ *adj* : orphaned

huerta *nf* : truck farm — **huerto** *nm* **1** : vegetable garden **2** : (fruit) orchard

hueso *nm* **1** : bone **2** : pit, stone (of a fruit)
huésped, -peda *n* : guest — **huésped** *nm* : host (organism)
huesudo, -da *adj* : bony
huevo *nm* **1** : egg **2** ∼**s estrellados** : fried eggs **3** ∼**s revueltos** : scrambled eggs — **hueva** *nf* : roe
huida *nf* : flight, escape — **huidizo, -za** *adj* **1** : shy **2** FUGAZ : fleeting
huipil *nm Lat* : traditional embroidered blouse or dress
huir {41} *vi* **1** : escape, flee **2** ∼ **de** : shun, avoid
hule *nm* **1** : oilcloth **2** *Lat* : rubber
humano, -na *adj* **1** : human **2** COMPASIVO : humane — **humano** *nm* : human (being) — **humanidad** *nf* **1** : humanity, mankind **2** BENEVOLENCIA : humaneness **3** ∼**es** *nfpl* : humanities — **humanismo** *nm* : humanism — **humanista** *nmf* : humanist — **humanitario, -ria** *adj & n* : humanitarian
humear *vi* : smoke, steam — **humareda** *nf* : cloud of smoke
humedad *nf* **1** : dampness **2** : humidity (in meteorology) — **humedecer** {53} *vt* : moisten, dampen — **humedecerse** *vr* : become moist — **húmedo, -da** *adj* **1** : moist, damp **2** : humid (in meteorology)
humildad *nf* : humility — **humilde** *adj* : humble — **humillación** *nf, pl* **-ciones**

: humiliation — **humillante** *adj* : humiliating — **humillar** *vt* : humiliate — **humillarse** *vr* : humble oneself
humo *nm* **1** : smoke, steam, fumes **2** ∼**s** *nmpl* : airs, conceit
humor *nm* **1** : mood, temper **2** GRACIA : humor **3 de buen** ∼ : in a good mood — **humorismo** *nm* : humor, wit — **humorista** *nmf* : humorist, comedian — **humorístico, -ca** *adj* : humorous
hundir *vt* **1** : sink **2** : destroy, ruin (a building, plans, etc.) — **hundirse** *vr* **1** : sink **2** DERRUMBARSE : collapse — **hundido, -da** *adj* : sunken — **hundimiento** *nm* **1** : sinking **2** DERRUMBE : collapse
húngaro, -ra *adj* : Hungarian
huracán *nm, pl* **-canes** : hurricane
huraño, -ña *adj* : unsociable
hurgar {52} *vi* ∼ **en** : rummage around in
hurón *nm, pl* **-rones** : ferret
hurra *interj* : hurrah!, hooray!
hurtadillas: a ∼ *adv phr* : stealthily, on the sly
hurtar *vt* : steal — **hurto** *nm* **1** ROBO : theft **2** : stolen property
husmear *vt* : sniff out, pry into — *vi* : nose around
huy *interj* : ow!, ouch!

I

i *nf* : i, ninth letter of the Spanish alphabet
ibérico, -ca *adj* : Iberian — **ibero, -ra** *or* **íbero, -ra** *adj* : Iberian
iceberg *nm, pl* **-bergs** : iceberg
icono *nm* : icon
ictericia *nf* : jaundice
ida *nf* **1** : outward journey **2** ∼ **y vuelta** : round-trip **3** ∼**s y venidas** : comings and goings
idea *nf* **1** : idea **2** OPINIÓN : opinion
ideal *adj & nm* : ideal — **idealismo** *nm* : idealism — **idealista** *adj* : idealistic — ∼ *nmf* : idealist — **idealizar** {21} *vt* : idealize
idear *vt* : devise, think up
ídem *nm* : the same, ditto
identidad *nf* : identity — **idéntico, -ca** *adj* : identical — **identificar** {72} *vt* : identify — **identificarse** *vr* **1** : identify oneself **2**

∼ **con** : identify with — **identificación** *nf, pl* **-ciones** : identification
ideología *nf* : ideology — **ideológico, -ca** *adj* : ideological
idílico, -ca *adj* : idyllic
idioma *nm* : language — **idiomático, -ca** *adj* : idiomatic
idiosincrasia *nf* : idiosyncrasy — **idiosincrásico, -ca** *adj* : idiosyncratic
idiota *adj* : idiotic — ∼ *nmf* : idiot — **idiotez** *nf* : idiocy
ídolo *nm* : idol — **idolatrar** *vt* : idolize — **idolatría** *nf* : idolatry
idóneo, -nea *adj* : suitable, fitting — **idoneidad** *nf* : fitness, suitability
iglesia *nf* : church
iglú *nm* : igloo
ignición *nf, pl* **-ciones** : ignition
ignífugo, -ga *adj* : fire-resistant, fireproof

ignorar *vt* **1** : ignore **2** DESCONOCER : be unaware of — **ignorancia** *nf* : ignorance — **ignorante** *adj* : ignorant — ～ *nmf* : ignorant person

igual *adv* **1** : in the same way **2 por** ～ : equally — ～ *adj* **1** : equal **2** IDÉNTICO : the same **3** LISO : smooth, even **4** SEMEJANTE : similar — ～ *nmf* : equal, peer — **igualar** *vt* **1** : make equal **2** : be equal to **3** NIVELAR : level (off) — **igualdad** *nf* **1** : equality **2** UNIFORMIDAD : uniformity — **igualmente** *adv* : likewise

iguana *nf* : iguana

ijada *nf* : flank

ilegal *adj* : illegal

ilegible *adj* : illegible

ilegítimo, -ma *adj* : illegitimate — **ilegitimidad** *nf* : illegitimacy

ileso, -sa *adj* : unharmed

ilícito, -ta *adj* : illicit

ilimitado, -da *adj* : unlimited

ilógico, -ca *adj* : illogical

iluminar *vt* : illuminate — **iluminarse** *vr* : light up — **iluminación** *nf, pl* **-ciones 1** : illumination **2** ALUMBRADO : lighting

ilusionar *vt* : excite — **ilusionarse** *vr* : get one's hopes up — **ilusión** *nf, pl* **-siones 1** : illusion **2** ESPERANZA : hope — **ilusionado, -da** *adj* : excited

iluso -sa *adj* : naïve, gullible — ～ *n* : dreamer, visionary — **ilusorio, -ria** *adj* : illusory

ilustrar *vt* **1** : illustrate **2** ACLARAR : explain — **ilustración** *nf, pl* **-ciones 1** : illustration **2** SABER : learning **3 la Ilustración** : the Enlightenment — **ilustrado, -da** *adj* **1** : illustrated **2** ERUDITO : learned — **ilustrador, -dora** *n* : illustrator

ilustre *adj* : illustrious

imagen *nf, pl* **imágenes** : image, picture

imaginar *vt* : imagine — **imaginarse** *vr* : imagine — **imaginación** *nf, pl* **-ciones** : imagination — **imaginario, -ria** *adj* : imaginary — **imaginativo, -va** *adj* : imaginative

imán *nm, pl* **imanes** : magnet — **imantar** *vt* : magnetize

imbécil *adj* : stupid, idiotic — ～ *nmf* : idiot

imborrable *adj* : indelible

imbuir {41} *vt* ～ **de** : imbue with

imitar *vt* **1** COPIAR : imitate, copy **2** : impersonate — **imitación** *nf, pl* **-ciones 1** COPIA : imitation, copy **2** : impersonation — **imitador, -dora** *n* : impersonator

impaciencia *nf* : impatience — **impacientar** *vt* : make impatient, exasperate — **impacientarse** *vr* : grow impatient — **impaciente** *adj* : impatient

impacto *nm* : impact

impar *adj* : odd — ～ *nm* : odd number

imparcial *adj* : impartial — **imparcialidad** *nf* : impartiality

impartir *vt* : impart, give

impasible *adj* : impassive

impasse *nm* : impasse

impávido, -da *adj* : fearless

impecable *adj* : impeccable, spotless

impedir {54} *vt* **1** : prevent **2** DIFICULTAR : impede, hinder — **impedido, -da** *adj* : disabled — **impedimento** *nm* : obstacle, impediment

impeler *vt* : drive, propel

impenetrable *adj* : impenetrable

impenitente *adj* : unrepentant

impensable *adj* : unthinkable — **impensado, -da** *adj* : unexpected

imperar *vi* **1** : reign, rule **2** PREDOMINAR : prevail — **imperante** *adj* : prevailing

imperativo, -va *adj* : imperative — **imperativo** *nm* : imperative

imperceptible *adj* : imperceptible

imperdible *nm* : safety pin

imperdonable *adj* : unforgivable

imperfección *nf, pl* **-ciones** : imperfection — **imperfecto, -ta** *adj* : imperfect — **imperfecto** *nm* : imperfect (tense)

imperial *adj* : imperial — **imperialismo** *nm* : imperialism — **imperialista** *adj* & *nmf* : imperialist

impericia *nf* : lack of skill

imperio *nm* **1** : empire **2** DOMINIO : rule — **imperioso, -sa** *adj* **1** : imperious **2** URGENTE : pressing, urgent

impermeable *adj* **1** : waterproof **2** ～ **a** : impervious to — ～ *nm* : raincoat

impersonal *adj* : impersonal

impertinente *adj* : impertinent — **impertinencia** *nf* : impertinence

ímpetu *nm* **1** : impetus **2** ENERGÍA : energy, vigor **3** VIOLENCIA : force — **impetuoso, -sa** *adj* : impetuous — **impetuosidad** *nf* : impetuosity

impío, -pía *adj* : impious, ungodly

implacable *adj* : implacable

implantar *vt* **1** : implant **2** ESTABLECER : establish, introduce

implemento *nm* *Lat* : implement, tool

implicar {72} *vt* **1** : involve, implicate **2** SIGNIFICAR : imply — **implicación** *nf, pl* **-ciones** : implication

implícito, -ta *adj* : implicit

implorar *vt* : implore

imponer {60} *vt* **1** : impose **2** : command (respect, etc.) — *vi* : be imposing — **imponerse** *vr* **1** : assert oneself, command respect **2** PREVALECER : prevail — **imponente** *adj* : imposing, impressive — **imponible** *adj* : taxable

impopular *adj* : unpopular — **impopularidad** *nf* : unpopularity

importación *nf, pl* **-ciones 1** : importation **2 importaciones** *nfpl* : imports — **importado, -da** *adj* : imported — **importador, -dora** *adj* : importing — ~ *n* : importer

importancia *nf* : importance — **importante** *adj* : important

importar *vi* **1** : matter, be important (**no importa** it doesn't matter, it's not important) (**no me importa** I don't care) **2** : bother (**si no te importa** if you don't mind) — *vt* **1** : import **2** ASCENDER A : amount to, cost

importe *nm* **1** : price **2** CANTIDAD : sum, amount

importunar *vt* : bother — **importuno, -na** *adj* **1** : inopportune **2** MOLESTO : bothersome

imposible *adj* : impossible — **imposibilidad** *nf* : impossibility

imposición *nf, pl* **-ciones 1** : imposition **2** IMPUESTO : tax

impostor, -tora *n* : impostor

impotente *adj* : powerless, impotent — **impotencia** *nf* : impotence

impracticable *adj* **1** : impracticable **2** INTRANSITABLE : impassable

impreciso, -sa *adj* : vague, imprecise — **imprecisión** *nf, pl* **-siones 1** : vagueness **2** ERROR : inaccuracy

impredecible *adj* : unpredictable

impregnar *vt* : impregnate

imprenta *nf* **1** : printing **2** : printing shop, press

imprescindible *adj* : essential, indispensable

impresión *nf, pl* **-siones 1** : impression **2** IMPRENTA : printing — **impresionable** *adj* : impressionable — **impresionante** *adj* : impressive — **impresionar** *vt* **1** : impress **2** CONMOVER : affect, move — *vi* : make an impression — **impresionarse** *vr* **1** : be impressed **2** CONMOVERSE : be affected

impreso, -sa *adj* : printed — **impreso** *nm* **1** FORMULARIO : form **2** ~**s** *nmpl* : printed matter — **impresor, -sora** *n* : printer — **impresora** *nf* : (computer) printer

imprevisible *adj* : unforeseeable — **imprevisto, -ta** *adj* : unexpected, unforeseen

imprimir {42} *vt* **1** : print **2** DAR : impart, give

improbable *adj* : improbable — **improbabilidad** *nf* : improbability

improcedente *adj* : inappropriate

improductivo, -va *adj* : unproductive

improperio *nm* : insult

impropio, -pia *adj* **1** : inappropriate **2** INCORRECTO : incorrect

improvisar *v* : improvise — **improvisado,**

-da *adj* : improvised, impromptu — **improvisación** *nf, pl* **-ciones** : improvisation — **improviso**: **de** ~ *adv phr* : suddenly

imprudente *adj* : imprudent, rash — **imprudencia** *nf* : imprudence, carelessness

impúdico, -ca *adj* : shameless, indecent

impuesto *nm* **1** : tax **2** ~ **sobre la renta** : income tax

impugnar *vt* : challenge, contest

impulsar *vt* : propel, drive — **impulsividad** *nf* : impulsiveness — **impulsivo, -va** *adj* : impulsive — **impulso** *nm* **1** : drive, thrust **2** MOTIVACIÓN : impulse

impune *adj* : unpunished — **impunidad** *nf* : impunity

impuro, -ra *adj* : impure — **impureza** *nf* : impurity

imputar *vt* : impute, attribute

inacabable *adj* : interminable, endless

inaccesible *adj* : inaccessible

inaceptable *adj* : unacceptable

inactivo, -va *adj* : inactive — **inactividad** *nf* : inactivity

inadaptado, -da *adj* : maladjusted — ~ *n* : misfit

inadecuado, -da *adj* **1** : inadequate **2** INAPROPIADO : inappropriate

inadmisible *adj* : inadmissible

inadvertido, -da *adj* **1** : unnoticed **2** DISTRAÍDO : distracted — **inadvertencia** *nf* : oversight

inagotable *adj* : inexhaustible

inaguantable *adj* : unbearable

inalámbrico, -ca *adj* : wireless, cordless

inalcanzable *adj* : unreachable, unattainable

inalterable *adj* **1** : unchangeable **2** : impassive (of character) **3** : fast (of colors)

inanición *nf, pl* **-ciones** : starvation, famine

inanimado, -da *adj* : inanimate

inaplicable *adj* : inapplicable

inapreciable *adj* : imperceptible

inapropiado, -da *adj* : inappropriate

inarticulado, -da *adj* : inarticulate

inasequible *adj* : unattainable

inaudito, -ta *adj* : unheard-of, unprecedented

inaugurar *vt* : inaugurate — **inauguración** *nf, pl* **-ciones** : inauguration — **inaugural** *adj* : inaugural

inca *adj* : Inca, Incan

incalculable *adj* : incalculable

incandescencia *nf* : incandescence — **incandescente** *adj* : incandescent

incansable *adj* : tireless

incapacitar *vt* : incapacitate, disable — **incapacidad** *nf* : incapacity, inability — **incapaz** *adj, pl* **-paces** : incapable

incautar *vt* : confiscate, seize

incendiar *vt* : set fire to, burn (down) — **incendiarse** *vr* : catch fire — **incendiario, -ria** *adj* : incendiary — **~** *n* : arsonist — **incendio** *nm* **1** : fire **2 ~ premeditado** : arson
incentivo *nm* : incentive
incertidumbre *nf* : uncertainty
incesante *adj* : incessant
incesto *nm* : incest — **incestuoso, -sa** *adj* : incestuous
incidencia *nf* **1** : impact **2** SUCESO : incident — **incidental** *adj* : incidental — **incidente** *nm* : incident
incidir *vi* **~ en 1** : fall into (a habit, mistake, etc.) **2** INFLUIR EN : affect, influence
incienso *nm* : incense
incierto, -ta *adj* : uncertain
incinerar *vt* **1** : incinerate **2** : cremate (a corpse) — **incineración** *nf, pl* **-ciones 1** : incineration **2** : cremation (of a corpse) — **incinerador** *nm* : incinerator
incipiente *adj* : incipient
incisión *nf, pl* **-siones** : incision
incisivo, -va *adj* : incisive — **incisivo** *nm* : incisor
incitar *vt* : incite, rouse
incivilizado, -da *adj* : uncivilized
inclinar *vt* : tilt, lean — **inclinarse** *vr* **1** : lean (over) **2 ~ a** : be inclined to — **inclinación** *nf, pl* **-ciones 1** : inclination **2** LADEAR : incline, tilt
incluir {41} *vt* **1** : include **2** ADJUNTAR : enclose — **inclusión** *nf, pl* **-siones** : inclusion — **inclusive** *adv* : up to and including — **inclusivo, -va** *adj* : inclusive — **incluso** *adv* : even, in fact — **incluso, -sa** *adj* : enclosed
incógnito, -ta *adj* **1** : unknown **2 de ~** : incognito
incoherente *adj* : incoherent — **incoherencia** *nf* : incoherence
incoloro, -ra *adj* : colorless
incombustible *adj* : fireproof
incomible *adj* : inedible
incomodar *vt* **1** : inconvenience **2** ENFADAR : bother, annoy — **incomodarse** *vr* **1** : take the trouble **2** ENFADARSE : get annoyed — **incomodidad** *nf* : discomfort — **incómodo, -da** *adj* **1** : uncomfortable **2** INCONVENIENTE : inconvenient, awkward
incomparable *adj* : incomparable
incompatible *adj* : incompatible — **incompatibilidad** *nf* : incompatibility
incompetente *adj* : incompetent — **incompetencia** *nf* : incompetence
incompleto, -ta *adj* : incomplete
incomprendido, -da *adj* : misunderstood — **incomprensible** *adj* : incomprehensible — **incomprensión** *nf, pl* **-siones** : lack of understanding

incomunicado, -da *adj* **1** : isolated **2** : in solitary confinement
inconcebible *adj* : inconceivable
inconcluso, -sa *adj* : unfinished
incondicional *adj* : unconditional
inconformista *adj & nmf* : nonconformist
inconfundible *adj* : unmistakable
incongruente *adj* : incongruous
inconmensurable *adj* : vast, immeasurable
inconsciente *adj* **1** : unconscious, unaware **2** IRREFLEXIVO : reckless — **~** *nm* **el ~** : the unconscious — **inconsciencia** *nf* **1** : unconsciousness **2** INSENSATEZ : thoughtlessness
inconsecuente *adj* : inconsistent — **inconsecuencia** *nf* : inconsistency
inconsiderado, -da *adj* : inconsiderate
inconsistente *adj* **1** : flimsy **2** : watery (of a sauce, etc.) **3** : inconsistent (of an argument) — **inconsistencia** *nf* : inconsistency
inconsolable *adj* : inconsolable
inconstante *adj* : changeable, unreliable — **inconstancia** *nf* : inconstancy
inconstitucional *adj* : unconstitutional
incontable *adj* : countless
incontenible *adj* : irrepressible
incontestable *adj* : indisputable
incontinente *adj* : incontinent — **incontinencia** *nf* : incontinence
inconveniente *adj* **1** : inconvenient **2** INAPROPIADO : inappropriate — **~** *nm* : obstacle, problem — **inconveniencia** *nf* **1** : inconvenience **2** : tactless remark
incorporar *vt* **1** AGREGAR : incorporate, add **2** : mix (in cooking) — **incorporarse** *vr* **1** : sit up **2 ~ a** : join — **incorporación** *nf, pl* **-ciones** : incorporation
incorrecto, -ta *adj* **1** : incorrect **2** DESCORTÉS : impolite
incorregible *adj* : incorrigible
incrédulo, -la *adj* : incredulous — **incredulidad** *nf* : incredulity, disbelief
increíble *adj* : incredible, unbelievable
incrementar *vt* : increase — **incremento** *nm* : increase
incriminar *vt* **1** : incriminate **2** ACUSAR : accuse
incrustar *vt* : set, inlay — **incrustarse** *vr* : become embedded
incubar *vt* : incubate — **incubadora** *nf* : incubator
incuestionable *adj* : unquestionable
inculcar {72} *vt* : instill
inculpar *vt* : accuse, charge
inculto, -ta *adj* **1** : uneducated **2** : uncultivated (of land)
incumplimiento *nm* **1** : noncompliance **2 ~ de contrato** : breach of contract

incurable *adj* : incurable

incurrir *vi* ~ **en 1** : incur (expenses, etc.) **2** : fall into, commit (crimes)

incursión *nf, pl* **-siones** : raid

indagar {52} *vt* : investigate — **indagación** *nf, pl* **-ciones** : investigation

indebido, -da *adj* : undue

indecente *adj* : indecent, obscene — **indecencia** *nf* : indecency, obscenity

indecible *adj* : inexpressible

indecisión *nf, pl* **-siones** : indecision — **indeciso, -sa** *adj* **1** : undecided **2** IRRESOLUTO : indecisive

indefenso, -sa *adj* : defenseless, helpless

indefinido, -da *adj* : indefinite — **indefinidamente** *adv* : indefinitely

indeleble *adj* : indelible

indemnizar {21} *vt* : indemnify, compensate — **indemnización** *nf, pl* **-ciones** : compensation

independiente *adj* : independent — **independencia** *nf* : independence — **independizarse** {21} *vr* : become independent

indescifrable *adj* : indecipherable

indescriptible *adj* : indescribable

indeseable *adj* : undesirable

indestructible *adj* : indestructible

indeterminado, -da *adj* : indeterminate

indicar {72} *vt* **1** : indicate **2** MOSTRAR : show — **indicación** *nf, pl* **-ciones 1** : sign, indication **2 indicaciones** *nfpl* : directions — **indicador** *nm* **1** : sign, signal **2** : gauge, dial, meter — **indicativo, -va** *adj* : indicative — **indicativo** *nm* : indicative (mood)

índice *nm* **1** : indication **2** : index (of a book, etc.) **3** : index finger **4** ~ **de natalidad** : birth rate

indicio *nm* : indication, sign

indiferente *adj* **1** : indifferent **2 me es** ~ : it doesn't matter to me — **indiferencia** *nf* : indifference

indígena *adj* : indigenous, native — ~ *nmf* : native

indigente *adj & nmf* : indigent — **indigencia** *nf* : poverty

indigestión *nf, pl* **-tiones** : indigestion — **indigesto, -ta** *adj* : indigestible

indignar *vt* : outrage, infuriate — **indignarse** *vr* : become indignant — **indignación** *nf, pl* **-ciones** : indignation — **indignado, -da** *adj* : indignant — **indignidad** *nf* : indignity — **indigno, -na** *adj* : unworthy

indio, -dia *adj* **1** : American Indian **2** : Indian (from India)

indirecta *nf* **1** : hint **2 lanzar una** ~ : drop a hint — **indirecto, -ta** *adj* : indirect

indisciplina *nf* : lack of discipline — **indisciplinado, -da** *adj* : undisciplined

indiscreto, -ta *adj* : indiscreet — **indiscreción** *nf, pl* **-ciones 1** : indiscretion **2** : tactless remark

indiscriminado, -da *adj* : indiscriminate

indiscutible *adj* : indisputable

indispensable *adj* : indispensable

indisponer {60} *vt* **1** : upset, make ill **2** ENEMISTAR : set against, set at odds — **indisponerse** *vr* **1** : become ill **2** ~ **con** : fall out with — **indisposición** *nf, pl* **-ciones** : indisposition, illness — **indispuesto, -ta** *adj* : unwell, indisposed

indistinto, -ta *adj* : indistinct

individual *adj* : individual — **individualidad** *nf* : individuality — **individualizar** {21} *vt* : individualize — **individuo** *nm* : individual

indivisible *adj* : indivisible

índole *nf* **1** : nature, character **2** TIPO : type, kind

indolente *adj* : indolent, lazy — **indolencia** *nf* : indolence, laziness

indoloro, -ra *adj* : painless

indómito, -ta *adj* : indomitable

indonesio, -sia *adj* : Indonesian

inducir {61} *vt* **1** : induce **2** DEDUCIR : infer

indudable *adj* : beyond doubt — **indudablemente** *adv* : undoubtedly

indulgente *adj* : indulgent — **indulgencia** *nf* : indulgence

indultar *vt* : pardon, reprieve — **indulto** *nm* : pardon, reprieve

industria *nf* : industry — **industrial** *adj* : industrial — ~ *nmf* : industrialist, manufacturer — **industrialización** *nf, pl* **-ciones** : industrialization — **industrializar** {21} *vt* : industrialize — **industrioso, -sa** *adj* : industrious

inédito, -ta *adj* : unpublished

inefable *adj* : inexpressible

ineficaz *adj, pl* **-caces 1** : ineffective **2** INEFICIENTE : inefficient

ineficiente *adj* : inefficient — **ineficiencia** *nf* : inefficiency

inelegible *adj* : ineligible

ineludible *adj* : unavoidable, inescapable

inepto, -ta *adj* : inept — **ineptitud** *nf* : ineptitude

inequívoco, -ca *adj* : unequivocal

inercia *nf* : inertia

inerme *adj* : unarmed, defenseless

inerte *adj* : inert

inesperado, -da *adj* : unexpected

inestable *adj* : unstable — **inestabilidad** *nf* : instability

inevitable *adj* : inevitable

inexacto, -ta *adj* **1** : inexact **2** INCORRECTO : incorrect, wrong

inexistente *adj* : nonexistent

inexorable *adj* : inexorable
inexperiencia *nf* : inexperience — **inexperto, -ta** *adj* : inexperienced, unskilled
inexplicable *adj* : inexplicable
infalible *adj* : infallible
infame *adj* **1** : infamous, vile **2** *fam* : horrible — **infamia** *nf* : infamy, disgrace
infancia *nf* : infancy — **infanta** *nf* : infanta, princess — **infante** *nm* **1** : infante, prince **2** : infantryman (in the military) — **infantería** *nf* : infantry — **infantil** *adj* **1** : child's, children's **2** INMADURO : childish
infarto *nm* : heart attack
infatigable *adj* : tireless
infectar *vt* : infect — **infectarse** *vr* : become infected — **infección** *nf, pl* **-ciones** : infection — **infeccioso, -sa** *adj* : infectious — **infecto, -ta** *adj* **1** : infected **2** : foul, sickening
infecundo, -da *adj* : infertile
infeliz *adj, pl* **-lices** : unhappy — **infelicidad** *nf* : unhappiness
inferior *adj & nmf* : inferior — **inferioridad** *nf* : inferiority
inferir {76} *vt* **1** DEDUCIR : infer **2** : cause (harm or injury)
infernal *adj* : infernal, hellish
infestar *vt* : infest
infiel *adj* : unfaithful — **infidelidad** *nf* : infidelity
infierno *nm* **1** : hell **2 el quinto ~** *fam* : the middle of nowhere
infiltrar *vt* : infiltrate — **infiltrarse** *vr* : infiltrate
infinidad *nf* **1** : infinity **2 una ~ de** : countless — **infinitivo** *nm* : infinitive — **infinito, -ta** *adj* : infinite — **infinito** *nm* : infinity
inflación *nf, pl* **-ciones** : inflation — **inflacionario, -ria** *or* **inflacionista** *adj* : inflationary
inflamar *vt* : inflame — **inflamable** *adj* : flammable, inflammable — **inflamación** *nf, pl* **-ciones** : inflammation — **inflamatorio, -ria** *adj* : inflammatory
inflar *vt* **1** : inflate **2** EXAGERAR : exaggerate — **inflarse** *vr* ~ **de** : swell (up) with
inflexible *adj* : inflexible — **inflexión** *nf, pl* **-xiones** : inflection
infligir {35} *vt* : inflict
influencia *nf* : influence — **influenciar** → **influir**
influenza *nf* : influenza
influir {41} *vt* : influence — *vi* ~ **en** *or* ~ **sobre** : have an influence on — **influjo** *nm* : influence — **influyente** *adj* : influential
infografía *nf* : computer graphics *pl*
información *nf, pl* **-ciones** **1** : information **2** NOTICIAS : news **3** : directory assistance (on the telephone)

informal *adj* **1** : informal **2** IRRESPONSABLE : unreliable
informar *v* : inform — **informarse** *vr* : get information, find out — **informante** *nmf* : informant — **informática** *nf* : information technology — **informativo, -va** *adj* : informative — **informatizar** {21} *vt* : computerize
informe *adj* : shapeless — ~ *nm* **1** : report **2 ~s** *nmpl* : information, data **3 ~s** *nmpl* : references (for employment)
infortunado, -da *adj* : unfortunate — **infortunio** *nm* : misfortune
infracción *nf, pl* **-ciones** : violation, infraction
infraestructura *nf* : infrastructure
infrahumano, -na *adj* : subhuman
infranqueable *adj* **1** : impassable **2** INSUPERABLE : insurmountable
infrarrojo, -ja *adj* : infrared
infrecuente *adj* : infrequent
infringir {35} *vt* : infringe
infructuoso, -sa *adj* : fruitless
infundado, -da *adj* : unfounded, baseless
infundir *vt* : instill, infuse — **infusión** *nf, pl* **-siones** : infusion
ingeniar *vt* : invent, think up
ingeniería *nf* : engineering — **ingeniero, -ra** *n* : engineer
ingenio *nm* **1** : ingenuity **2** AGUDEZA : wit **3** MÁQUINA : device, apparatus **4 ~ azucarero** *Lat* : sugar refinery — **ingenioso, -sa** *adj* **1** : ingenious **2** AGUDO : clever, witty — **ingeniosamente** *adv* : cleverly
ingenuidad *nf* : naïveté, ingenuousness — **ingenuo, -nua** *adj* : naïve
ingerir {76} *vt* : ingest, consume
ingle *nf* : groin
inglés, -glesa *adj, mpl* **-gleses** : English — **inglés** *nm* : English (language)
ingrato, -ta *adj* **1** : ungrateful **2 un trabajo ingrato** : a thankless task — **ingratitud** *nf* : ingratitude
ingrediente *nm* : ingredient
ingresar *vt* : deposit — *vi* ~ **en** : enter, be admitted into, join — **ingreso** *nm* **1** : entrance, entry **2** : admission (into a hospital, etc.) **3 ~s** *nmpl* : income, earnings
inhábil *adj* **1** : unskillful, clumsy **2 ~ para** : unsuited for — **inhabilidad** *nf* : unskillfulness
inhabitable *adj* : uninhabitable — **inhabitado, -da** *adj* : uninhabited
inhalar *vt* : inhale — **inhalación** *nf* : inhalation
inherente *adj* : inherent
inhibir *vt* : inhibit — **inhibición** *nf, pl* **-ciones** : inhibition

inhóspito, -ta *adj* : inhospitable
inhumano, -na *adj* : inhuman, inhumane —
 inhumanidad *nf* : inhumanity
iniciar *vt* : initiate, begin — **iniciación** *nf, pl*
 -ciones 1 : initiation **2** COMIENZO : beginning — **inicial** *adj* & *nf* : initial — **iniciativa**
 nf : initiative — **inicio** *nm* : start, beginning
inigualado, -da *adj* : unequaled
ininterrumpido, -da *adj* : uninterrupted
injerirse {76} *vr* : interfere — **injerencia** *nf*
 : interference
injertar *vt* : graft — **injerto** *nm* : graft
injuriar *vt* : insult — **injuria** *nf* : insult — **in-**
 jurioso, -sa *adj* : insulting, abusive
injusticia *nf* : injustice, unfairness — **in-**
 justo, -ta *adj* : unfair, unjust
inmaculado, -da *adj* : immaculate
inmaduro, -ra *adj* **1** : immature **2** : unripe
 (of fruit) — **inmadurez** *nf* : immaturity
inmediaciones *nfpl* : surrounding area
inmediato, -ta *adj* **1** : immediate **2** CONTI-
 GUO : adjoining **3 de ～** : immediately,
 right away **4 ～ a** : next to, close to — **in-**
 mediatamente *adv* : immediately
inmejorable *adj* : excellent
inmenso, -sa *adj* : immense, vast — **inmen-**
 sidad *nf* : immensity
inmerecido, -da *adj* : undeserved
inmersión *nf, pl* **-siones** : immersion
inmigrar *vi* : immigrate — **inmigración** *nf,*
 pl **-ciones** : immigration — **inmigrante** *adj*
 & *nmf* : immigrant
inminente *adj* : imminent, impending — **in-**
 minencia *nf* : imminence
inmiscuirse {41} *vr* : interfere
inmobiliario, -ria *adj* : real estate, property
inmodesto, -ta *adj* : immodest
inmoral *adj* : immoral — **inmoralidad** *nf*
 : immorality
inmortal *adj* & *nmf* : immortal — **inmortali-**
 dad *nf* : immortality
inmóvil *adj* : motionless, still — **inmovilizar**
 {21} *vt* : immobilize
inmueble *nm* : building, property
inmundicia *nf* : filth, trash — **inmundo, -da**
 adj : dirty, filthy
inmunizar {21} *vt* : immunize — **inmune**
 adj : immune — **inmunidad** *nf* : immunity
 — **inmunización** *nf, pl* **-ciones** : immunization
inmutable *adj* : unchangeable
innato, -ta *adj* : innate
innecesario, -ria *adj* : unnecessary, needless
innegable *adj* : undeniable
innoble *adj* : ignoble
innovar *vt* : introduce — *vi* : innovate — **in-**
 novación *nf, pl* **-ciones** : innovation — **in-**
 novador, -dora *adj* : innovative — **～** *n*
 : innovator

innumerable *adj* : innumerable
inocencia *nf* : innocence — **inocente** *adj* &
 nmf : innocent — **inocentón, -tona** *adj, mpl*
 -tones : naive — **～** *n* : simpleton, dupe
inocular *vt* : inoculate — **inoculación** *nf, pl*
 -ciones : inoculation
inocuo, -cua *adj* : innocuous
inodoro, -ra *adj* : odorless — **inodoro** *nm*
 : toilet
inofensivo, -va *adj* : inoffensive, harmless
inolvidable *adj* : unforgettable
inoperable *adj* : inoperable
inoperante *adj* : ineffective
inopinado, -da *adj* : unexpected
inoportuno, -na *adj* : untimely, inopportune
inorgánico, -ca *adj* : inorganic
inoxidable *adj* **1** : rustproof **2 acero ～**
 : stainless steel
inquebrantable *adj* : unwavering
inquietar *vt* : disturb, worry — **inquietarse**
 vr : worry — **inquietante** *adj* : disturb-
 ing, worrisome — **inquieto, -ta** *adj*
 : anxious, worried — **inquietud** *nf* : anxiety,
 worry
inquilino, -na *n* : tenant
inquirir {4} *vi* : make inquiries — *vt* : investigate
insaciable *adj* : insatiable
insalubre *adj* : unhealthy
insatisfecho, -cha *adj* **1** : unsatisfied **2**
 DESCONTENTO : dissatisfied
inscribir {33} *vt* **1** : enroll, register **2** GRA-
 BAR : inscribe, engrave — **inscribirse** *vr*
 : register — **inscripción** *nf, pl* **-ciones 1**
 : inscription **2** REGISTRO : registration
insecto *nm* : insect — **insecticida** *nm* : insecticide
inseguro, -ra *adj* **1** : insecure **2** PELIGROSO
 : unsafe **3** DUDOSO : uncertain — **inseguri-**
 dad *nf* **1** : insecurity **2** PELIGRO : lack of
 safety **3** DUDA : uncertainty
inseminar *vt* : inseminate — **inseminación**
 nf, pl **-ciones** : insemination
insensato, -ta *adj* : senseless, foolish —
 insensatez *nf* : foolishness, thoughtlessness
insensible *adj* **1** : insensitive, unfeeling **2**
 : numb (in medicine) **3** IMPERCEPTIBLE
 : imperceptible — **insensibilidad** *nf* : insensitivity
inseparable *adj* : inseparable
insertar *vt* : insert
insidia *nf* : snare, trap — **insidioso, -sa** *adj*
 : insidious
insigne *adj* : noted, famous
insignia *nf* **1** : insignia, badge **2** BANDERA
 : flag
insignificante *adj* : insignificant, negligible
insincero, -ra *adj* : insincere

insinuar {3} *vt* : insinuate — **insinuarse** *vr*
~ **en** : worm one's way into — **insinua-**
ción *nf, pl* -**ciones** : insinuation — **insi-**
nuante *adj* : insinuating, suggestive
insípido, -da *adj* : insipid
insistir *v* : insist — **insistencia** *nf* : insis-
tence — **insistente** *adj* : insistent
insociable *adj* : unsociable
insolación *nf, pl* -**ciones** : sunstroke
insolencia *nf* : insolence — **insolente** *adj*
: insolent
insólito, -ta *adj* : rare, unusual
insoluble *adj* : insoluble
insolvencia *nf* : insolvency, bankruptcy —
insolvente *adj* : insolvent, bankrupt
insomnio *nm* : insomnia — **insomne** *nmf*
: insomniac
insondable *adj* : unfathomable
insonorizado, -da *adj* : soundproof
insoportable *adj* : unbearable
insospechado, -da *adj* : unexpected
insostenible *adj* : untenable
inspeccionar *vt* : inspect — **inspección** *nf,*
pl -**ciones** : inspection — **inspector, -tora**
n : inspector
inspirar *vt* : inspire — *vi* : inhale — **inspi-**
rarse *vr* : be inspired — **inspiración** *nf, pl*
-**ciones 1** : inspiration **2** RESPIRACIÓN : inhalation — **inspirador, -dora** *adj* : inspirational
instalar *vt* : install — **instalarse** *vr* : settle
— **instalación** *nf, pl* -**ciones** : installation
instancia *nf* **1** : request **2 en última** ~
: ultimately, as a last resort
instantáneo, -nea *adj* : instantaneous, instant — **instantánea** *nf* : snapshot — **ins-**
tante *nm* **1** : instant **2 a cada** ~ : frequently, all the time **3 al** ~ : immediately
instar *vt* : urge, press
instaurar *vt* : establish — **instauración** *nf,*
pl -**ciones** : establishment
instigar {52} *vt* : incite, instigate — **instiga-**
dor, -dora *n* : instigator
instinto *nm* : instinct — **instintivo, -va** *adj*
: instinctive
institución *nf, pl* -**ciones** : institution —
institucional *adj* : institutional — **institu-**
cionalizar {21} *vt* : institutionalize — **ins-**
tituir {41} *vt* : institute, establish
— **instituto** *nm* : institute — **institutriz** *nf,*
pl -**trices** : governess
instruir {41} *vt* : instruct — **instrucción** *nf,*
pl -**ciones 1** : instruction **2 instrucciones**
nfpl : instructions, directions — **instruc-**
tivo, -va *adj* : instructive — **instructor,**
-tora *n* : instructor
instrumento *nm* : instrument — **instrumen-**
tal *adj* : instrumental
insubordinarse *vr* : rebel — **insubordi-**

nado, -da *adj* : insubordinate — **insubordi-**
nación *nf, pl* -**ciones** : insubordination
insuficiente *adj* : insufficient, inadequate —
insuficiencia *nf* **1** : insufficiency, inade-
quacy **2** ~ **cardíaca** : heart failure
insufrible *adj* : insufferable
insular *adj* : insular, island
insulina *nf* : insulin
insulso, -sa *adj* **1** : insipid, bland **2** soso
: dull
insultar *vt* : insult — **insultante** *adj* : insulting — **insulto** *nm* : insult
insuperable *adj* : insurmountable
insurgente *adj & nmf* : insurgent
insurrección *nf, pl* -**ciones** : insurrection,
uprising
intachable *adj* : irreproachable
intacto, -ta *adj* : intact
intangible *adj* : intangible
integrar *vt* : integrate — **integrarse** *vr* : become integrated — **integración** *nf, pl* -**cio-**
nes : integration — **integral** *adj* **1** : integral
2 pan ~ : whole grain bread — **íntegro,**
-gra *adj* **1** : honest, upright **2** ENTERO
: whole, complete — **integridad** *nf* **1** REC-
TITUD : integrity **2** TOTALIDAD : wholeness
intelecto *nm* : intellect — **intelectual** *adj &*
nmf : intellectual
inteligencia *nf* : intelligence — **inteligente**
adj : intelligent — **inteligible** *adj* : intelligible
intemperie *nf* **a la** ~ : in the open air, outside
intempestivo, -va *adj* : untimely, inopportune
intención *nf, pl* -**ciones** : intention, intent
— **intencionado, -da** *adj* **1** : intended **2**
bien ~ : well-meaning **3 mal** ~ : malicious — **intencional** *adj* : intentional
intensidad *nf* : intensity — **intensificar**
{72} *vt* : intensify — **intensificarse** *vr* : intensify — **intensivo, -va** *adj* : intensive —
intenso, -sa *adj* : intense
intentar *vt* : attempt, try — **intento** *nm* **1**
: intention **2** TENTATIVA : attempt
interactuar {3} *vi* : interact — **interacción**
nf, pl -**ciones** : interaction — **interactivo,**
-va *adj* : interactive
intercalar *vt* : insert, intersperse
intercambio *nm* : exchange — **intercambia-**
ble *adj* : interchangeable — **intercambiar**
vt : exchange, trade
interceder *vi* : intercede
interceptar *vt* : intercept — **intercepción** *nf,*
pl -**ciones** : interception
intercesión *nf, pl* -**siones** : intercession
interés *nm, pl* -**reses** : interest — **intere-**
sado, -da *adj* **1** : interested **2** EGOISTA
: selfish — **interesante** *adj* : interesting —

interesar *vt* : interest — *vi* : be of interest — **interesarse** *vr* : take an interest

interfaz *nf, pl* **-faces** : interface

interferir {76} *vi* : interfere — *vt* : interfere with — **interferencia** *nf* : interference

interfón *nm, pl* **-fones** : intercom

interfono *nm* : intercom

interino, -na *adj* : temporary, interim — **interiormente** *adv* : inwardly

interior *adj* : interior, inner — ~ *nm* : interior, inside — **interiormente** *adv* : inwardly

interjección *nf, pl* **-ciones** : interjection

interlocutor, -tora *n* : speaker

intermediario, -ria *adj & n* : intermediary

intermedio, -dia *adj* : intermediate — **intermedio** *nm* : intermission

interminable *adj* : interminable, endless

intermisión *nf, pl* **-siones** : intermission, pause

intermitente *adj* : intermittent — ~ *nm* : blinker, turn signal

internacional *adj* : international

internar *vt* : commit, confine — **internarse** *vr* : penetrate — **internado** *nm* : boarding school — **interno, -na** *adj* : internal — ~ *n* **1** : boarder **2** : inmate (in a jail, etc.)

internauta *nmf* : Internet user

Internet *or* **internet** *nmf* : Internet

interponer {60} *vt* : interpose — **interponerse** *vr* : intervene

interpretar *vt* **1** : interpret **2** : play, perform (in theater, etc.) — **interpretación** *nf, pl* **-ciones** : interpretation — **intérprete** *nmf* **1** TRADUCTOR : interpreter **2** : performer (of music)

interrogar {52} *vt* : interrogate, question — **interrogación** *nf, pl* **-ciones 1** : interrogation **2 signo de** ~ : question mark — **interrogativo, -va** *adj* : interrogative — **interrogatorio** *nm* : interrogation, questioning

interrumpir *v* : interrupt — **interrupción** *nf, pl* **-ciones** : interruption — **interruptor** *nm* : (electrical) switch

intersección *nf, pl* **-ciones** : intersection

intervalo *nm* : interval

intervenir {87} *vi* **1** : take part **2** MEDIAR : intervene — *vt* **1** : tap (a telephone) **2** INSPECCIONAR : audit **3** OPERAR : operate on — **intervención** *nf, pl* **-ciones 1** : intervention **2** : audit (in business) **3** *or* ~ **quirúrgica** : operation — **interventor, -tora** *n* : inspector, auditor

intestino *nm* : intestine — **intestinal** *adj* : intestinal

intimar *vi* ~ **con** : become friendly with — **intimidad** *nf* **1** : private life **2** AMISTAD : intimacy

intimidar *vt* : intimidate

íntimo, -ma *adj* **1** : intimate, close **2** PRIVADO : private

intolerable *adj* : intolerable — **intolerancia** *nf* : intolerance — **intolerante** *adj* : intolerant

intoxicar {72} *vt* : poison — **intoxicación** *nf, pl* **-ciones** : poisoning

intranquilizar {21} *vt* : make uneasy — **intranquilizarse** *vr* : be anxious — **intranquilidad** *nf* : uneasiness, anxiety — **intranquilo, -la** *adj* : uneasy, worried

intransigente *adj* : unyielding, intransigent

intransitable *adj* : impassable

intransitivo, -va *adj* : intransitive

intrascendente *adj* : unimportant, insignificant

intravenoso, -sa *adj* : intravenous

intrépido, -da *adj* : intrepid, fearless

intrigar {52} *v* : intrigue — **intriga** *nf* : intrigue — **intrigante** *adj* : intriguing

intrincado, -da *adj* : intricate, involved

intrínseco, -ca *adj* : intrinsic — **intrínsecamente** *adv* : intrinsically, inherently

introducción *nf, pl* **-ciones** : introduction — **introducir** {61} *vt* **1** : introduce **2** METER : insert — **introducirse** *vr* ~ **en** : penetrate, get into — **introductorio, -ria** *adj* : introductory

intromisión *nf, pl* **-siones** : interference

introvertido, -da *adj* : introverted — ~ *n* : introvert

intrusión *nf, pl* **-siones** : intrusion — **intruso, -sa** *adj* : intrusive — ~ *n* : intruder

intuir {41} *vt* : sense — **intuición** *nf, pl* **-ciones** : intuition — **intuitivo, -va** *adj* : intuitive

inundar *vt* : flood — **inundarse** *vr* ~ **de** : be inundated with — **inundación** *nf, pl* **-ciones** : flood

inusitado, -da *adj* : unusual, uncommon

inútil *adj* **1** : useless **2** INVÁLIDO : disabled — **inutilidad** *nf* : uselessness — **inutilizar** {21} *vt* **1** : make useless **2** INCAPACITAR : disable

invadir *vt* : invade

invalidez *nf, pl* **-deces 1** : invalidity **2** : disability (in medicine) — **inválido, -da** *adj & n* : invalid

invalorable *adj Lat* : invaluable

invariable *adj* : invariable

invasión *nf, pl* **-siones** : invasion — **invasor, -sora** *adj* : invading — ~ *n* : invader

invencible *adj* : invincible

inventar *vt* **1** : invent **2** : fabricate, make up (a word, an excuse, etc.) — **invención** *nf, pl* **-ciones 1** : invention **2** MENTIRA : lie, fabrication

inventario *nm* : inventory

inventiva *nf* : inventiveness — **inventivo,**

-va *adj* : inventive — **inventor, -tora** *n* : inventor
invernadero *nm* : greenhouse
invernal *adj* : winter
inverosímil *adj* : unlikely
inversión *nf, pl* **-siones 1** : inversion, reversal **2** : investment (of money, time, etc.)
inverso, -sa *adj* **1** : inverse **2** CONTRARIO : opposite **3 a la inversa** : the other way around, inversely
inversor, -sora *n* : investor
invertebrado, -da *adj* : invertebrate — **invertebrado** *nm* : invertebrate
invertir {76} *vt* **1** : invert, reverse **2** : invest (money, time, etc.) — *vi* : make an investment
investidura *nf* : investiture
investigar {52} *vt* **1** : investigate **2** ESTUDIAR : research — *vi* ~ **sobre** : do research into — **investigación** *nf, pl* **-ciones 1** : investigation **2** ESTUDIO : research — **investigador, -dora** *n* : investigator, researcher
investir {54} *vt* : invest
inveterado, -da *adj* : deep-seated, inveterate
invicto, -ta *adj* : undefeated
invierno *nm* : winter
invisible *adj* : invisible — **invisibilidad** *nf* : invisibility
invitar *vt* : invite — **invitación** *nf, pl* **-ciones** : invitation — **invitado, -da** *n* : guest
invocar {72} *vt* : invoke — **invocación** *nf, pl* **-ciones** : invocation
involuntario, -ria *adj* : involuntary
invulnerable *adj* : invulnerable
inyectar *vt* : inject — **inyección** *nf, pl* **-ciones** : injection, shot — **inyectado, -da** *adj* **ojos inyectados** : bloodshot eyes
ion *nm* : ion — **ionizar** {21} *vt* : ionize
ir {43} *vi* **1** : go **2** FUNCIONAR : work, function **3** CONVENIR : suit **4 ¿cómo te va?** : how are you? **5** ~ **con prisa** : be in a hurry **6** ~ **por** : follow, go along **7 vamos** : let's go — *v aux* **1** ~ **a** : be going to, be about to **2** ~ **caminando** : take a walk **3 vamos a ver** : we shall see — **irse** *vr* : go away, be gone
ira *nf* : rage, anger — **iracundo, -da** *adj* : irate, angry
iraní *adj* : Iranian
iraquí *adj* : Iraqi

iris *nms & pl* **1** : iris (of the eye) **2 arco** ~ : rainbow
irlandés, -desa *adj, mpl* **-deses** : Irish
ironía *nf* : irony — **irónico, -ca** *adj* : ironic, ironical
irracional *adj* : irrational
irradiar *vt* : radiate, irradiate
irrazonable *adj* : unreasonable
irreal *adj* : unreal
irreconciliable *adj* : irreconcilable
irreconocible *adj* : unrecognizable
irrecuperable *adj* : irretrievable
irreductible *adj* : unyielding
irreemplazable *adj* : irreplaceable
irreflexivo, -va *adj* : rash, unthinking
irrefutable *adj* : irrefutable
irregular *adj* : irregular — **irregularidad** *nf* : irregularity
irrelevante *adj* : irrelevant
irreparable *adj* : irreparable
irreprimible *adj* : irrepressible
irreprochable *adj* : irreproachable
irresistible *adj* : irresistible
irresoluto, -ta *adj* : indecisive, irresolute
irrespetuoso, -sa *adj* : disrespectful
irresponsable *adj* : irresponsible — **irresponsabilidad** *nf* : irresponsibility
irreverente *adj* : irreverent
irreversible *adj* : irreversible
irrevocable *adj* : irrevocable
irrigar {52} *vt* : irrigate — **irrigación** *nf, pl* **-ciones** : irrigation
irrisorio, -ria *adj* : laughable, ridiculous
irritar *vt* : irritate — **irritarse** *vr* : get annoyed — **irritable** *adj* : irritable — **irritación** *nf, pl* **-ciones** : irritation — **irritante** *adj* : irritating
irrompible *adj* : unbreakable
irrumpir *vi* ~ **en** : burst into
isla *nf* : island
islámico, -ca *adj* : Islamic, Muslim
islandés, -desa *adj, mpl* **-deses** : Icelandic
isleño, -ña *n* : islander
israelí *adj* : Israeli
istmo *nm* : isthmus
italiano, -na *adj* : Italian — **italiano** *nm* : Italian (language)
itinerario *nm* : itinerary
izar {21} *vt* : hoist, raise
izquierda *nf* : left — **izquierdista** *adj & nmf* : leftist — **izquierdo, -da** *adj* : left

J

j *nf* : j, tenth letter of the Spanish alphabet

jabalí *nm, pl* **-líes** : wild boar

jabalina *nf* : javelin

jabón *nm, pl* **-bones** : soap — **jabonar** *vt* : soap (up) — **jabonera** *nf* : soap dish — **jabonoso, -sa** *adj* : soapy

jaca *nf* : pony

jacinto *nm* : hyacinth

jactarse *vr* : boast, brag — **jactancia** *nf* : boastfulness, bragging — **jactancioso, -sa** *adj* : boastful

jadear *vi* : pant, gasp — **jadeante** *adj* : panting, breathless — **jadeo** *nm* : gasp, panting

jaez *nm, pl* **jaeces** **1** : harness **2 jaeces** *nmpl* : trappings

jaguar *nm* : jaguar

jaiba *nf Lat* : crab

jalapeño *nm Lat* : jalapeño pepper

jalar *v Lat* : pull, tug

jalea *nf* : jelly

jaleo *nm fam* **1** : uproar, racket **2 armar un ~** : raise a ruckus

jalón *nm, pl* **-lones** *Lat* : pull, tug

jamaicano, -na *or* **jamaiquino, -na** *adj* : Jamaican

jamás *adv* **1** : never **2 para siempre ~** : for ever and ever

jamelgo *nm* : nag (horse)

jamón *nm, pl* **-mones** **1** : ham **2 ~ serrano** : cured ham

Januká *nmf* : Hanukkah

japonés, -nesa *adj, mpl* **-neses** : Japanese — **japonés** *nm* : Japanese (language)

jaque *nm* **1** : check (in chess) **2 ~ mate** : checkmate

jaqueca *nf* : headache, migraine

jarabe *nm* : syrup

jardín *nm, pl* **-dines** **1** : garden **2 ~ infantil** *or* **~ de niños** *Lat* : kindergarten — **jardinería** *nf* : gardening — **jardinero, -ra** *n* : gardener

jarra *nf* : pitcher, jug — **jarro** *nm* : pitcher — **jarrón** *nm, pl* **-rrones** : vase

jaula *nf* : cage

jauría *nf* : pack of hounds

jazmín *nm, pl* **-mines** : jasmine

jazz *nm* : jazz

jeans *nmpl* : jeans

jefe, -fa *n* **1** : chief, leader **2** PATRÓN : boss **3 ~ de cocina** : chef — **jefatura** *nf* **1** : leadership **2** SEDE : headquarters

jengibre *nm* : ginger

jeque *nm* : sheikh, sheik

jerarquía *nf* **1** : hierarchy **2** RANGO : rank — **jerárquico, -ca** *adj* : hierarchical

jerez *nm, pl* **-reces** : sherry

jerga *nf* **1** : coarse cloth **2** ARGOT : jargon, slang

jerigonza *nf* **1** : jargon **2** GALIMATÍAS : gibberish

jeringa *or* **jeringuilla** *nf* : syringe — **jeringar** {52} *vt fam* : annoy, pester

jeroglífico *nm* : hieroglyphic

jersey *nm, pl* **-seys** : jersey

jesuita *adj & nm* : Jesuit

Jesús *nm* : Jesus

jilguero *nm* : goldfinch

jinete *nmf* : horseman, horsewoman *f*, rider

jirafa *nf* : giraffe

jirón *nm, pl* **-rones** : shred, tatter

jitomate *nm Lat* : tomato

jockey *nmf, pl* **-keys** : jockey

jocoso, -sa *adj* : humorous, jocular

jofaina *nf* : washbowl

jolgorio *nm* : merrymaking

jornada *nf* **1** : day's journey **2** : working day — **jornal** *nm* : day's pay — **jornalero, -ra** *n* : day laborer

joroba *nf* : hump — **jorobado, -da** *adj* : hunchbacked, humpbacked — **~** *n* : hunchback — **jorobar** *vt fam* : annoy

jota *nf* **1** : iota, jot **2 no veo ni ~** : I can't see a thing

joven *adj, pl* **jóvenes** : young — **~** *nmf* : young man *m*, young woman *f*, youth

jovial *adj* : jovial, cheerful

joya *nf* : jewel — **joyería** *nf* : jewelry store — **joyero, -ra** *n* : jeweler — **joyero** *nm* : jewelry box

juanete *nm* : bunion

jubilación *nf, pl* **-ciones** : retirement — **jubilado, -da** *adj* : retired — **~** *nmf* : retiree — **jubilar** *vt* : retire, pension off — **jubilarse** *vr* : retire — **jubileo** *nm* : jubilee

júbilo *nm* : joy, jubilation — **jubiloso, -sa** *adj* : joyous, jubilant

judaísmo *nm* : Judaism

judía *nf* **1** : bean **2** *or* **~ verde** : green bean, string bean

judicial *adj* : judicial

judío, -día *adj* : Jewish — **~** *n* : Jew

judo *nm* : judo

juego *nm* **1** : game **2** : playing (of children, etc.) **3** *or* **~s de azar** : gambling **4** CONJUNTO : set **5 estar en ~** : be at stake **6 fuera de ~** : offside (in sports) **7 hacer ~** : go together, match **8 ~ de manos** : conjuring trick **9 poner en ~** : bring into play

juerga *nf fam* : spree, binge

jueves *nms & pl* : Thursday
juez *nmf, pl* **jueces 1** : judge **2** ÁRBITRO : umpire, referee
jugar {44} *vi* **1** : play **2** : gamble (in a casino, etc.) **3** APOSTAR : bet **4** ~ **(al) tenis** : play tennis — *vt* : play — **jugarse** *vr* : risk, gamble (away) — **jugada** *nf* **1** : play, move **2** TRETA : (dirty) trick — **jugador, -dora** *n* **1** : player **2** : gambler
juglar *nm* : minstrel
jugo *nm* **1** : juice **2** SUSTANCIA : substance, essence — **jugoso, -sa** *adj* **1** : juicy **2** SUSTANCIAL : substantial, important
juguete *nm* : toy — **juguetear** *vi* : play — **juguetería** *nf* : toy store — **juguetón, -tona** *adj, mpl* **-tones** : playful
juicio *nm* **1** : judgment **2** RAZÓN : reason, sense **3 a mi** ~ : in my opinion — **juicioso, -sa** *adj* : wise, sensible
julio *nm* : July
junco *nm* : reed, rush
jungla *nf* : jungle
junio *nm* : June
juntar *vt* **1** UNIR : join, unite **2** REUNIR : collect — **juntarse** *vr* **1** : join (together) **2** REUNIRSE : meet, get together — **junta** *nf* **1** : board, committee **2** REUNIÓN : meeting **3** : (political) junta **4** : joint, gasket — **junto, -ta** *adj* **1** : joined **2** PRÓXIMO : close, adjacent **3** (*used adverbially*) : together **4** ~ **a** : next to **5** ~ **con** : together with — **juntura** *nf* : joint
Júpiter *nm* : Jupiter
jurar *v* **1** : swear **2** ~ **en falso** : commit perjury — **jurado** *nm* **1** : jury **2** : juror, member of a jury — **juramento** *nm* : oath
jurídico, -ca *adj* : legal
jurisdicción *nf, pl* **-ciones** : jurisdiction
jurisprudencia *nf* : jurisprudence
justamente *adv* **1** : fairly, justly **2** PRECISAMENTE : precisely, exactly
justicia *nf* : justice, fairness
justificar {72} *vt* **1** : justify **2** DISCULPAR : excuse, vindicate — **justificación** *nf, pl* **-ciones** : justification
justo, -ta *adj* **1** : just, fair **2** EXACTO : exact **3** APRETADO : tight — **justo** *adv* **1** : just, exactly **2** ~ **a tiempo** : just in time
juvenil *adj* : youthful — **juventud** *nf* **1** : youth **2** JÓVENES : young people
juzgar {52} *vt* **1** : try (a case in court) **2** ESTIMAR : judge, consider **3 a** ~ **por** : judging by — **juzgado** *nm* : court, tribunal

K

k *nf* : k, eleventh letter of the Spanish alphabet
kaki → **caqui**
karate *or* **kárate** *nm* : karate
kilo *nm* : kilo — **kilogramo** *nm* : kilogram
kilómetro *nm* : kilometer — **kilometraje** *nm* : distance in kilometers, mileage — **kilométrico, -ca** *adj fam* : end-less
kilovatio *nm* : kilowatt
kiosco *nm* → **quiosco**

L

l *nf* : l, twelfth letter of the Spanish alphabet
la *pron* **1** : her, it **2** (*formal*) : you **3** ~ **que** : the one who — ~ *art* → **el**
laberinto *nm* : labyrinth, maze
labia *nf fam* : gift of gab
labio *nm* : lip
labor *nf* **1** : work, labor **2** TAREA : task **3** ~**es domésticas** : housework — **laborable** *adj* **día** ~ : business day — **laborar** *vi* : work — **laboratorio** *nm* : laboratory, lab — **laborioso, -sa** *adj* : laborious
labrar *vt* **1** : cultivate, till **2** : work (metals), carve (stone, wood) **3** CAUSAR : cause, bring about — **labrado, -da** *adj* **1** : cultivated, tilled **2** : carved, wrought — **labrador, -dora** *n* : farmer — **labranza** *nf* : farming
laca *nf* **1** : lacquer **2** : hair spray
lacayo *nm* : lackey
lacerar *vt* : lacerate

lacio, -cia *adj* 1 : limp 2 : straight (of hair)
lacónico, -ca *adj* : laconic
lacra *nf* : scar
lacrar *vt* : seal — lacre *nm* : sealing wax
lacrimógeno, -na *adj* gas lacrimógeno
: tear gas — lacrimoso, -sa *adj* : tearful
lácteo, -tea *adj* 1 : dairy 2 Vía Láctea
: Milky Way
ladear *vt* : tilt — ladearse *vr* : lean
ladera *nf* : slope, hillside
ladino, -na *adj* : crafty
lado *nm* 1 : side 2 al ∼ : next door, nearby
3 al ∼ de : beside, next to 4 de ∼ : sideways 5 por otro ∼ : on the other hand 6
por todos ∼s : everywhere, all around
ladrar *vi* : bark — ladrido *nm* : bark
ladrillo *nm* : brick
ladrón, -drona *n, mpl* -drones : thief
lagarto *nm* : lizard — lagartija *nf* : (small)
lizard
lago *nm* : lake
lágrima *nf* : tear
laguna *nf* 1 : lagoon 2 VACÍO : gap
laico, -ca *adj* : lay, secular — ∼ *n* : layman
m, layperson
lamentar *vt* 1 : regret, be sorry about 2 lo
lamento : I'm sorry — lamentarse *vr* : lament — lamentable *adj* 1 : deplorable 2
TRISTE : sad, pitiful — lamento *nm* : lament, moan
lamer *vt* 1 : lick 2 : lap (against) — lamida
nf : lick
lámina *nf* 1 PLANCHA : sheet 2 DIBUJO
: plate, illustration — laminar *vt* : laminate
lámpara *nf* : lamp
lampiño, -ña *adj* : beardless, hairless
lana *nf* 1 : wool 2 de ∼ : woolen
lance *nm* 1 : event, incident 2 : throw (of
dice, etc.) 3 RIÑA : quarrel
lanceta *nf* : lancet
lancha *nf* 1 : boat, launch 2 ∼ motora
: motorboat
langosta *nf* 1 : lobster 2 : locust (insect)
— langostino *nm* : prawn, crayfish
languidecer {53} *vi* : languish — languidez
nf, pl -deces : languor — lánguido, -da *adj*
: languid, listless
lanilla *nf* : nap (of fabric)
lanudo, -da *adj* : woolly
lanza *nf* : spear, lance
lanzar {21} *vt* 1 : throw 2 : shoot (a glance),
give (a sigh, etc.) 3 : launch (a missile, a
project) — lanzarse *vr* : throw oneself —
lanzamiento *nm* : throwing, launching
lapicero *nm* : (mechanical) pencil
lápida *nf* : tombstone
lapidar *vt* : stone
lápiz *nm, pl* -pices 1 : pencil 2 ∼ de labios : lipstick

lapso *nm* : lapse (of time) — lapsus *nms &*
pl : lapse, slip (of the tongue)
largar {52} *vt* 1 AFLOJAR : loosen, slacken 2
fam : give — largarse *vr fam* : go away,
beat it — largo, -ga *adj* 1 : long 2 a la
larga : in the long run 3 a lo largo : lengthwise 4 a lo largo de : along — largo *nm*
: length — largometraje *nm* : feature film
— largueza *nf* : generosity
laringe *nf* : larynx — laringitis *nfs & pl*
: laryngitis
larva *nf* : larva
las → el
lascivo, -va *adj* : lascivious, lewd
láser *nm* : laser
lastimar *vt* : hurt — lastimarse *vr* : hurt
oneself — lástima *nf* 1 : pity 2 dar ∼ : be
pitiful 3 me dan ∼ : I feel sorry for them
4 ¡qué ∼! : what a shame! — lastimero,
-ra *adj* : pitiful, wretched — lastimoso, -sa
adj : pitiful, terrible
lastre *nm* : ballast
lata *nf* 1 : tinplate 2 : (tin) can 3 *fam* : nuisance, bore 4 dar (la) lata a *fam* : bother,
annoy
latente *adj* : latent
lateral *adj* : side, lateral
latido *nm* 1 : beat, throb 2 ∼ del corazón
: heartbeat
latifundio *nm* : large estate
látigo *nm* : whip — latigazo *nm* : lash
latín *nm* : Latin (language)
latino, -na *adj* 1 : Latin 2 : Latin-American
— ∼ *n* : Latin American — latinoamericano, -na *adj* : Latin-American — ∼ *n*
: Latin American
latir *vi* : beat, throb
latitud *nf* : latitude
latón *nm, pl* -tones : brass
latoso, -sa *adj fam* : annoying
laúd *nm* : lute
laudable *adj* : laudable
laureado, -da *adj* : prize-winning
laurel *nm* 1 : laurel 2 : bay leaf (in cooking)
lava *nf* : lava
lavar *vt* : wash — lavarse *vr* 1 : wash oneself 2 ∼ las manos : wash one's hands —
lavable *adj* : washable — lavabo *nm* 1
: sink 2 RETRETE : lavatory, toilet — lava-
dero *nm* : laundry room — lavado *nm*
: wash, washing — lavadora *nf* : washing
machine — lavamanos *nms & pl* : washbowl — lavandería *nf* : laundry (service)
— lavaplatos *nms & pl* 1 : dishwasher 2
Lat : kitchen sink — lavativa *nf* : enema —
lavatorio *nm* : lavatory, washroom — lavavajillas *nms & pl* : dishwasher
laxante *adj & nm* : laxative — laxo, -xa *adj*
: loose
lazo *nm* 1 VÍNCULO : link, bond 2 LAZADA

: bow **3** : lasso, lariat — **lazada** *nf* : bow, loop

le *pron* **1** : (to) her, (to) him, (to) it **2** (*formal*) : (to) you **3** (*as direct object*) : him, you

leal *adj* : loyal, faithful — **lealtad** *nf* : loyalty, allegiance

lebrel *nm* : hound

lección *nf, pl* **-ciones 1** : lesson **2** : lecture (in a classroom)

leche *nf* **1** : milk **2** ~ **descremada** *or* ~ **desnatada** : skim milk **3** ~ **en polvo** : powdered milk — **lechera** *nf* : milk jug — **lechería** *nf* : dairy store — **lechero, -ra** *adj* : dairy — ~ *n* : milkman *m*, milk dealer

lecho *nm* : bed

lechón, -chona *n, mpl* **-chones** : suckling pig

lechoso, -sa *adj* : milky

lechuga *nf* : lettuce

lechuza *nf* : owl

lector, -tora *n* : reader — **lectura** *nf* **1** : reading **2** ESCRITOS : reading matter

leer {20} *v* : read

legación *nf, pl* **-ciones** : legation

legado *nm* **1** : legacy **2** ENVIADO : legate, emissary

legajo *nm* : dossier, file

legal *adj* : legal — **legalidad** *nf* : legality — **legalizar** {21} *vt* : legalize — **legalización** *nf, pl* **-ciones** : legalization

legar {52} *vt* : bequeath

legendario, -ria *adj* : legendary

legible *adj* : legible

legión *nf, pl* **-giones** : legion — **legionario, -ria** *n* : legionnaire

legislar *vi* : legislate — **legislación** *nf, pl* **-ciones** : legislation — **legislador, -dora** *n* : legislator — **legislatura** *nf* : legislature

legítimo, -ma *adj* **1** : legitimate **2** GENUINO : authentic — **legitimidad** *nf* : legitimacy

lego, -ga *adj* **1** : secular, lay **2** IGNORANTE : ignorant — ~ *n* : layman *m*, layperson

legua *nf* : league

legumbre *nf* : vegetable

leído, -da *adj* : well-read

lejano, -na *adj* : distant, far away — **lejanía** *nf* : distance

lejía *nf* : bleach

lejos *adv* **1** : far (away) **2** a lo ~ : in the distance **3** de ~ *or* desde ~ : from afar **4** ~ **de** : far from

lelo, -la *adj* : silly, stupid

lema *nm* : motto

lencería *nf* **1** : linen **2** : (women's) lingerie

lengua *nf* **1** : tongue **2** IDIOMA : language **3** morderse la ~ : hold one's tongue

lenguado *nm* : sole, flounder

lenguaje *nm* : language

lengüeta *nf* **1** : tongue (of a shoe) **2** : reed (of a musical instrument)

lengüetada *nf* **beber a** ~**s** : lap (up)

lente *nmf* **1** : lens **2** ~**s** *nmpl* : eyeglasses **3** ~**s de contacto** : contact lenses

lenteja *nf* : lentil — **lentejuela** *nf* : sequin

lento, -ta *adj* : slow — **lento** *adv* : slowly — **lentitud** *nf* : slowness

leña *nf* : firewood — **leñador, -dora** *n* : lumberjack, woodcutter — **leño** *nm* : log

león, -ona *n, mpl* **leones** : lion, lioness *f*

leopardo *nm* : leopard

leotardo *nm* : leotard, tights *pl*

lepra *nf* : leprosy — **leproso, -sa** *n* : leper

lerdo, -da *adj* **1** TORPE : clumsy **2** TONTO : slow-witted

les *pron* **1** : (to) them, (to) you **2** (*as direct object*) : them, you

lesbiano, -na *adj* : lesbian — **lesbiana** *nf* : lesbian — **lesbianismo** *nm* : lesbianism

lesión *nf, pl* **-siones** : lesion, wound — **lesionado, -da** *adj* : injured, wounded — **lesionar** *vt* **1** : injure, wound **2** DAÑAR : damage

letal *adj* : lethal

letanía *nf* : litany

letárgico, -ca *adj* : lethargic — **letargo** *nm* : lethargy

letra *nf* **1** : letter **2** ESCRITURA : handwriting **3** : lyrics *pl* (of a song) **4** ~ **de cambio** : bill of exchange **5** ~**s** *nfpl* : arts — **letrado, -da** *adj* : learned — **letrero** *nm* : sign, notice

letrina *nf* : latrine

leucemia *nf* : leukemia

levadizo, -za *adj* **puente levadizo** : drawbridge

levadura *nf* **1** : yeast **2** ~ **en polvo** : baking powder

levantar *vt* **1** : lift, raise **2** RECOGER : pick up **3** CONSTRUIR : erect, put up **4** ENCENDER : rouse, stir up **5** ~ **la mesa** *Lat* : clear the table — **levantarse** *vr* **1** : rise, stand up **2** : get out of bed **3** SUBLEVARSE : rise up — **levantamiento** *nm* **1** : raising, lifting **2** SUBLEVACIÓN : uprising

levante *nm* **1** : east **2** : east wind

levar *vt* ~ **anclas** : weigh anchor

leve *adj* **1** : light, slight **2** : minor, trivial (of wounds, sins, etc.) — **levedad** *nf* : lightness — **levemente** *adv* : lightly, slightly

léxico *nm* : vocabulary, lexicon

ley *nf* **1** : law **2** **de (buena)** ~ : genuine, pure (of metals)

leyenda *nf* **1** : legend **2** : caption (of an illustration, etc.)

liar {85} *vt* **1** : bind, tie (up) **2** : roll (a cigarette) **3** CONFUNDIR : confuse, muddle — **liarse** *vr* : get mixed up

libanés, -nesa *adj, mpl* **-neses** : Lebanese

libelo *nm* **1** : libel **2** : petition (in court)
libélula *nf* : dragonfly
liberación *nf, pl* **-ciones** : liberation, deliverance
liberal *adj & nmf* : liberal — **liberalidad** *nf* : generosity, liberality
liberar *vt* : liberate, free — **libertad** *nf* **1** : freedom, liberty **2** ~ **bajo fianza** : bail **3** ~ **condicional** : parole **4 en** ~ : free — **libertar** *vt* : set free
libertinaje *nm* : licentiousness — **libertino, -na** *n* : libertine
libido *nf* : libido
libio, -bia *adj* : Libyan
libra *nf* **1** : pound **2** ~ **esterlina** : pound sterling
librar *vt* **1** : free, save **2** : wage, fight (a battle) **3** : draw, issue (a check, etc.) — **librarse** *vr* ~ **de** : free oneself from, get rid of
libre *adj* **1** : free **2** : unoccupied (of space), spare (of time) **3 al aire** ~ : in the open air **4** ~ **de impuestos** : tax-free
librea *nf* : livery
libro *nm* **1** : book **2** ~ **de bolsillo** : paperback — **librería** *nf* : bookstore — **librero, -ra** *n* : bookseller — **librero** *nm Lat* : bookcase — **libreta** *nf* : notebook
licencia *nf* **1** : license, permit **2** PERMISO : permission **3** : (military) leave — **licenciado, -da** *n* **1** : graduate **2** *Lat* : lawyer — **licenciar** *vt* : dismiss, discharge — **licenciarse** *vr* : graduate — **licenciatura** *nf* : degree
licencioso, -sa *adj* : licentious
liceo *nm* : high school
licitar *vt* : bid for
lícito, -ta *adj* **1** : lawful, legal **2** JUSTO : just, fair
licor *nm* **1** : liquor **2** : liqueur — **licorera** *nf* : decanter
licuadora *nf* : blender — **licuado** *nm* : milk shake — **licuar** {3} *vt* : liquefy
lid *nf* **1** : fight **2 en buena** ~ : fair and square
líder *adj* : leading — ~ *nmf* : leader — **liderato** *or* **liderazgo** *nm* : leadership
lidia *nf* : bullfight — **lidiar** *v* : fight
liebre *nf* : hare
lienzo *nm* **1** : cotton or linen cloth **2** : canvas (for a painting) **3** PARED : wall
liga *nf* **1** : league **2** *Lat* : rubber band **3** : garter (for stockings) — **ligadura** *nf* **1** ATADURA : tie, bond **2** : ligature (in medicine or music) — **ligamento** *nm* : ligament — **ligar** {52} *vt* : bind, tie (up)
ligero, -ra *adj* **1** : light, lightweight **2** LEVE : slight **3** ÁGIL : agile **4** FRÍVOLO : lighthearted, superficial — **ligeramente** *adv* : lightly, slightly — **ligereza** *nf* **1** : light-

ness **2** : flippancy (of character), thoughtlessness (of actions) **3** AGILIDAD : agility
light *adj* : light, low-calorie
lija *nf* : sandpaper — **lijar** *vt* : sand
lila *nf* : lilac
lima *nf* **1** : file **2** : lime (fruit) **3** ~ **para uñas** : nail file — **limar** *vt* : file
limbo *nm* : limbo
limitar *vt* : limit — *vi* ~ **con** : border on — **limitación** *nf, pl* **-ciones** : limitation, limit — **límite** *nm* **1** : limit **2** CONFÍN : boundary, border **3** ~ **de velocidad** : speed limit **4 fecha** ~ : deadline — **limítrofe** *adj* : bordering
limo *nm* : slime, mud
limón *nm, pl* **-mones** **1** : lemon **2** ~ **verde** *Lat* : lime — **limonada** *nf* : lemonade
limosna *nf* **1** : alms **2 pedir** ~ : beg — **limosnero, -ra** *n* : beggar
limpiabotas *nmfs & pl* : bootblack
limpiaparabrisas *nms & pl* : windshield wiper
limpiar *vt* **1** : clean, wipe (away) **2** ~ **en seco** : dry-clean — **limpieza** *nf* **1** : cleanliness **2** : (act of) cleaning — **limpio** *adv* : cleanly, fairly — **limpio, -pia** *adj* **1** : clean, neat **2** HONRADO : honest **3** NETO : net, clear
limusina *nf* : limousine
linaje *nm* : lineage, ancestry
linaza *nf* : linseed
lince *nm* : lynx
linchar *vt* : lynch
lindar *vi* ~ **con** : border on — **lindante** *adj* : bordering — **linde** *nmf or* **lindero** *nm* : boundary
lindo, -da *adj* **1** : pretty, lovely **2 de lo lindo** *fam* : a lot
línea *nf* **1** : line **2** ~ **de conducta** : course of action **3 en** ~ : on-line **4 guardar la** ~ : watch one's figure — **lineal** *adj* : linear
lingote *nm* : ingot
lingüista *nmf* : linguist — **lingüística** *nf* : linguistics — **lingüístico, -ca** *adj* : linguistic
linimento *nm* : liniment
lino *nm* **1** : flax (plant) **2** : linen (fabric)
linóleo *nm* : linoleum
linterna *nf* **1** FAROL : lantern **2** : flashlight
lío *nm* **1** : bundle **2** *fam* : mess, trouble **3** *fam* : (love) affair
liofilizar {21} *vt* : freeze-dry
liquen *nm* : lichen
liquidar *vt* **1** : liquefy **2** : liquidate (merchandise, etc.) **3** : settle, pay off (a debt, etc.) — **liquidación** *nf, pl* **-ciones** **1** : liquidation **2** REBAJA : clearance sale — **líquido, -da** *adj* **1** : liquid **2** NETO : net — **líquido** *nm* : liquid
lira *nf* : lyre

lírico, -ca adj : lyric, lyrical — **lírica** nf : lyric poetry

lirio nm : iris

lisiado, -da adj : disabled — ∼ n : disabled person — **lisiar** vt : disable, cripple

liso, -sa adj 1 : smooth 2 PLANO : flat 3 SENCILLO : plain 4 **pelo** ∼ : straight hair

lisonjear vt : flatter — **lisonja** nf : flattery

lista nf 1 : stripe 2 ENUMERACIÓN : list 3 : menu (in a restaurant) — **listado, -da** adj : striped

listo, -ta adj 1 : clever, smart 2 PREPARADO : ready

listón nm, pl **-tones** 1 : ribbon 2 : strip (of wood)

lisura nf : smoothness

litera nf : bunk bed, berth

literal adj : literal

literatura nf : literature — **literario, -ria** adj : literary

litigar {52} vi : litigate — **litigio** nm 1 : litigation 2 **en** ∼ : in dispute

litografía nf 1 : lithography 2 : lithograph (picture)

litoral adj : coastal — ∼ nm : shore, seaboard

litro nm : liter

liturgia nf : liturgy — **litúrgico, -ca** adj : liturgical

liviano, -na adj 1 LIGERO : light 2 INCONSTANTE : fickle

lívido, -da adj : livid

llaga nf : sore, wound

llama nf 1 : flame 2 : llama (animal)

llamar vt 1 : call 2 : call up (on the telephone) — vi : phone, call 2 : knock, ring (at the door) — **llamarse** vr 1 : be called 2 **¿cómo te llamas?** : what's your name? — **llamada** nf : call — **llamado, -da** adj : named, called — **llamamiento** nm : call, appeal

llamarada nf 1 : blaze 2 : flushing (of the face)

llamativo, -va adj : flashy, showy

llamear vi : flame, blaze

llano, -na adj 1 : flat 2 : straightforward (of a person, a message, etc.) 3 SENCILLO : plain, simple — **llano** nm : plain — **llaneza** nf : simplicity

llanta nf 1 : rim (of a wheel) 2 Lat : tire

llanto nm : crying, weeping

llanura nf : plain

llave nf 1 : key 2 Lat : faucet 3 INTERRUPTOR : switch 4 **cerrar con** ∼ : lock 5 ∼ **inglesa** : monkey wrench — **llavero** nm : key chain

llegar {52} vi 1 : arrive, come 2 ALCANZAR : reach 3 BASTAR : be enough 4 ∼ **a** : manage to 5 ∼ **a ser** : become — **llegada** nf : arrival

llenar vt : fill (up), fill in — **lleno, -na** adj 1 : full 2 **de lleno** : completely — **lleno** nm : full house

llevar vt 1 : take, carry 2 CONDUCIR : lead 3 : wear (clothing, etc.) 4 TENER : have 5 **llevo una hora aquí** : I've been here for an hour — **llevarse** vr 1 : take (away) 2 ∼ **bien** : get along well — **llevadero, -ra** adj : bearable

llorar vi : cry, weep — **lloriquear** vi : whimper, whine — **lloro** nm : crying — **llorón, -rona** n, mpl **-rones** : crybaby, whiner — **lloroso, -sa** adj : tearful

llover {47} v impers : rain — **llovizna** nf : drizzle — **lloviznar** v impers : drizzle

lluvia nf : rain — **lluvioso, -sa** adj : rainy

lo pron 1 : him, it 2 (formal, masculine) : you 3 ∼ **que** : what, that which — ∼ art 1 : the 2 ∼ **mejor** : the best (part) 3 **sé** ∼ **bueno que eres** : I know how good you are

loa nf : praise — **loable** adj : praiseworthy — **loar** vt : praise

lobo, -ba n : wolf

lóbrego, -ga adj : gloomy

lóbulo nm : lobe

local adj : local — ∼ nm : premises pl — **localidad** nf : town, locality — **localizar** {21} vt : localize 2 ENCONTRAR : locate — **localizarse** vr : be located

loción nf, pl **-ciones** : lotion

loco, -ca adj 1 : crazy, insane 2 **a lo loco** : wildly, recklessly 3 **volverse** ∼ : go mad — ∼ n 1 : crazy person, lunatic 2 **hacerse el loco** : act the fool

locomoción nf, pl **-ciones** : locomotion — **locomotora** nf : engine, locomotive

locuaz adj, pl **-cuaces** : talkative, loquacious

locución nf, pl **-ciones** : expression, phrase

locura nf 1 : insanity, madness 2 INSENSATEZ : crazy act, folly

locutor, -tora n : announcer

locutorio nm : phone booth

lodo nm : mud — **lodazal** nm : quagmire

logaritmo nm : logarithm

lógica nf : logic — **lógico, -ca** adj : logical — **logística** nf : logistics pl

logotipo nm : logo

lograr vt 1 : achieve, attain 2 CONSEGUIR : get, obtain 3 ∼ **hacer** : manage to do — **logro** nm : achievement, success

loma nf : hill, hillock

lombriz nf, pl **-brices** : worm

lomo nm 1 : back (of an animal) 2 : spine (of a book) 3 ∼ **de cerdo** : pork loin

lona nf : canvas

loncha nf : slice (of bacon, etc.)

lonche nm Lat : lunch — **lonchería** nf Lat : luncheonette

longaniza *nf* : sausage
longevidad *nf* : longevity — **longevo, -va** *adj* : long-lived
longitud *nf* **1** : longitude **2** LARGO : length
lonja → **loncha**
loro *nm* : parrot
los, las *pron* **1** : them **2** : you **3 los que, las que** : those who, the ones who — **los** *art* → **el**
losa *nf* **1** : flagstone **2** *or* ~ **sepulcral** : tombstone
lote *nm* **1** : batch, lot **2** *Lat* : plot of land
lotería *nf* : lottery
loto *nm* : lotus
loza *nf* : crockery, earthenware
lozano, -na *adj* **1** : healthy-looking, vigorous **2** : luxuriant (of plants) — **lozanía** *nf* **1** : (youthful) vigor **2** : luxuriance (of plants)
lubricar {72} *vt* : lubricate — **lubricante** *adj* : lubricating — ~ *nm* : lubricant
lucero *nm* : bright star
luchar *vi* **1** : fight, struggle **2** : wrestle (in sports) — **lucha** *nf* **1** : struggle, fight **2** : wrestling (sport) — **luchador, -dora** *n* : fighter, wrestler
lucidez *nf, pl* **-deces** : lucidity — **lúcido, -da** *adj* : lucid
lucido, -da *adj* : magnificent, splendid
luciérnaga *nf* : firefly, glowworm
lucir {45} *vi* **1** : shine **2** *Lat* : appear, seem — *vt* **1** : wear, sport **2** OSTENTAR : show off — **lucirse** *vr* **1** : shine, excel **2** PRESUMIR : show off — **lucimiento** *nm* **1** : brilliance **2** ÉXITO : brilliant performance, success

lucrativo, -va *adj* : lucrative — **lucro** *nm* : profit
luego *adv* **1** : then **2** : later (on) **3 desde** ~ : of course **4 ¡hasta** ~**!** : see you later! **5** ~ **que** : as soon as — ~ *conj* : therefore
lugar *nm* **1** : place **2** ESPACIO : space, room **3 dar** ~ **a** : give rise to **4 en** ~ **de** : instead of **5 tener** ~ : take place
lugarteniente *nmf* : deputy
lúgubre *adj* : gloomy
lujo *nm* **1** : luxury **2 de** ~ : deluxe — **lujoso, -sa** *adj* : luxurious
lujuria *nf* : lust
lumbre *nf* **1** : fire **2 poner en la** ~ : put on the stove
luminoso, -sa *adj* : shining, luminous
luna *nf* **1** : moon **2** : (window) glass **3** ESPEJO : mirror **4** ~ **de miel** : honeymoon — **lunar** *adj* : lunar — ~ *nm* : mole, beauty spot
lunes *nms & pl* : Monday
lupa *nf* : magnifying glass
lúpulo *nm* : hops
lustrar *vt* : shine, polish — **lustre** *nm* **1** BRILLO : luster, shine **2** ESPLENDOR : glory — **lustroso, -sa** *adj* : lustrous, shiny
luto *nm* **1** : mourning **2 estar de** ~ : be in mourning
luxación *nf, pl* **-ciones** : dislocation
luz *nf, pl* **luces 1** : light **2** : lighting (in a room, etc.) **3** *fam* : electricity **4 a la** ~ **de** : in light of **5 dar a** ~ : give birth **6 sacar a la** ~ : bring to light

M

m *nf* : m, 13th letter of the Spanish alphabet
macabro, -bra *adj* : macabre
macarrón *nm, pl* **-rrones 1** : macaroon **2 macarrones** *nmpl* : macaroni
maceta *nf* : flowerpot
machacar {72} *vt* : crush, grind — *vi* ~ **sobre** : go on about — **machacón, -cona** *adj, mpl* **-cones** : tiresome, boring
machete *nm* : machete — **machetear** *vt* : hack with a machete
macho *adj* **1** : male **2** *fam* : macho — ~ *nm* **1** : male **2** *fam* : he-man — **machista** *nm* : male chauvinist
machucar {72} *vt* **1** : beat, crush **2** : bruise (fruit)
macizo, -za *adj* : solid — **macizo** *nm* ~ **de flores** : flower bed

mácula *nf* : stain
madeja *nf* : skein, hank
madera *nf* **1** : wood **2** : lumber (for construction) **3** ~ **dura** : hardwood — **madero** *nm* : piece of lumber, plank
madre *nf* **1** : mother **2** ~ **política** : mother-in-law — **madrastra** *nf* : stepmother
madreselva *nf* : honeysuckle
madriguera *nf* : burrow, den
madrileño, -ña *adj* : of or from Madrid
madrina *nf* **1** : godmother **2** : bridesmaid (at a wedding)
madrugada *nf* : dawn, daybreak — **madrugador, -dora** *n* : early riser
madurar *v* **1** : mature **2** : ripen (of fruit) — **madurez** *nf, pl* **-reces 1** : maturity **2** : ripe-

ness (of fruit) — **maduro, -ra** *adj* **1** : mature **2** : ripe (of fruit)
maestría *nf* : mastery, skill — **maestro, -tra** *adj* : masterly, skilled — **~** *n* **1** : teacher (in grammar school) **2** EXPERTO : expert, master
Mafia *nf* : Mafia
magia *nf* : magic — **mágico, -ca** *adj* : magic, magical
magisterio *nm* : teachers *pl*, teaching profession
magistrado, -da *n* : magistrate, judge
magistral *adj* **1** : masterful **2** : magisterial (of an attitude, etc.)
magnánimo, -ma *adj* : magnanimous — **magnanimidad** *nf* : magnanimity
magnate *nmf* : magnate, tycoon
magnesia *nf* : magnesia — **magnesio** *nm* : magnesium
magnético, -ca *adj* : magnetic — **magnetismo** *nm* : magnetism — **magnetizar** {21} *vt* : magnetize
magnetófono *nm* : tape recorder
magnificencia *nf* : magnificence — **magnífico, -ca** *adj* : magnificent
magnitud *nf* : magnitude
magnolia *nf* : magnolia
mago, -ga *n* **1** : magician **2 los Reyes Magos** : the Magi
magro, -gra *adj* **1** : lean **2** MEZQUINO : poor, meager
magullar *vt* : bruise — **magulladura** *nf* : bruise
mahometano, -na *adj* : Islamic, Muslim — **~** *n* : Muslim
maicena *nf* : cornstarch
maíz *nm* : corn
maja *nf* : pestle
majadero, -ra *adj* : foolish, silly — **~** *n* : fool
majar *vt* : crush
majestad *nf* **1** : majesty **2 Su Majestad** : His/Her Majesty — **majestuoso, -sa** *adj* : majestic
majo, -ja *adj* **1** : nice **2** GUAPO : good-looking
mal *adv* **1** : badly, poorly **2** INCORRECTAMENTE : incorrectly **3** DIFÍCILMENTE : with difficulty, hardly **4 de ~ en peor** : from bad to worse **5 menos ~** : it's just as well — **~** *nm* **1** : evil **2** DAÑO : harm, damage **3** ENFERMEDAD : illness — **~** *adj* → **malo**
malabarismo *nm* : juggling — **malabarista** *nmf* : juggler
malacostumbrar *vt* : spoil, pamper — **malacostumbrado, -da** *adj* : spoiled
malaria *nf* : malaria
malasio, -sia *adj* : Malaysian
malaventura *nf* : misfortune — **malaventurado, -da** *adj* : unfortunate

malayo, -ya *adj* : Malay, Malayan
malcriado, -da *adj* : bad-mannered, spoiled
maldad *nf* **1** : evil **2** : evil deed
maldecir {11} *vt* : curse, damn — *vi* **1** : curse, swear **2 ~ de** : speak ill of — **maldición** *nf, pl* **-ciones** : curse — **maldito, -ta** *adj fam* : damned
maleable *adj* : malleable
maleante *nmf* : crook
malecón *nm, pl* **-cones** : jetty
maleducado, -da *adj* : rude
maleficio *nm* : curse — **maléfico, -ca** *adj* : evil, harmful
malentendido *nm* : misunderstanding
malestar *nm* **1** : discomfort **2** INQUIETUD : uneasiness
maleta *nf* **1** : suitcase **2 hacer la ~** : pack one's bags — **maletero, -ra** *n* : porter — **maletero** *nm* : trunk (of an automobile) — **maletín** *nm, pl* **-tines 1** PORTAFOLIO : briefcase **2** : overnight bag
malévolo, -la *adj* : malevolent — **malevolencia** *nf* : malevolence
maleza *nf* **1** : underbrush **2** MALAS HIERBAS : weeds *pl*
malgastar *vt* : waste, squander
malhablado, -da *adj* : foul-mouthed
malhechor, -chora *n* : criminal, delinquent
malhumorado, -da *adj* : bad-tempered, cross
malicia *nf* : malice — **malicioso, -sa** *adj* : malicious
maligno, -na *adj* **1** : malignant **2** PERNICIOSO : harmful, evil
malla *nf* **1** : mesh **2 ~s** *nfpl* : tights
malo, -la *adj* (**mal** *before masculine singular nouns*) **1** : bad **2** : poor (in quality) **3** ENFERMO : unwell **4 estar de malas** : be in a bad mood — **~** *n* : villain, bad guy (in movies, etc.)
malograr *vt* : waste — **malograrse** *vr* **1** FRACASAR : fail **2** : die young — **malogro** *nm* : failure
maloliente *adj* : smelly
malpensado, -da *adj* : malicious, nasty
malsano, -na *adj* : unhealthy
malsonante *adj* : rude
malta *nf* : malt
maltratar *vt* : mistreat
maltrecho, -cha *adj* : battered
malvado, -da *adj* : evil, wicked
malvavisco *nm* : marshmallow
malversar *vt* : embezzle — **malversación** *nf, pl* **-ciones** : embezzlement
mama *nf* : teat (of an animal), breast (of a woman)
mamá *nf fam* : mom, mama
mamar *vi* **1** : suckle **2 dar de ~ a** : breast-feed — *vt* **1** : suckle, nurse **2** : learn from

childhood, grow up with — **mamario, -ria** *adj* : mammary

mamarracho *nm fam* : mess, sight

mambo *nm* : mambo

mamífero, -ra *adj* : mammalian — **mamífero** *nm* : mammal

mamografía *nf* : mammogram

mampara *nf* : screen, room divider

mampostería *nf* : masonry

manada *nf* **1** : flock, herd, pack **2 en ~** : in droves

manar *vi* **1** : flow **2 ~ en** : be rich in — **manantial** *nm* **1** : spring **2** ORIGEN : source

manchar *vt* **1** : stain, spot, mark **2** : tarnish (a reputation, etc.) — **mancharse** *vr* : get dirty — **mancha** *nf* : stain

mancillar *vt* : sully, stain

manco, -ca *adj* : one-armed, one- handed

mancomunar *vt* : combine, join — **mancomunarse** *vr* : unite — **mancomunidad** *nf* : union

mandar *vt* **1** : command, order **2** ENVIAR : send **3** *Lat* : hurl, throw — *vi* **1** : be in charge **2 ¿mande?** *Lat* : yes?, pardon? — **mandadero, -ra** *nm* : messenger — **mandado** *nm* : errand — **mandamiento** *nm* **1** : order, warrant **2** : commandment (in religion)

mandarina *nf* : mandarin orange, tangerine

mandato *nm* **1** : term of office **2** ORDEN : mandate — **mandatario, -ria** *n* **1** : leader (in politics) **2** : agent (in law)

mandíbula *nf* : jaw, jawbone

mandil *nm* : apron

mando *nm* **1** : command, leadership **2 al ~ de** : in charge of **3 ~ a distancia** : remote control

mandolina *nf* : mandolin

mandón, -dona *adj, mpl* **-dones** : bossy

manecilla *nf* : hand (of a clock), pointer

manejar *vt* **1** : handle, operate **2** : manage (a business, etc.) **3** : manipulate (a person) **4** *Lat* : drive (a car) — **manejarse** *vr* **1** : manage, get by **2** *Lat* : behave — **manejo** *nm* **1** : handling, use **2** : management (of a business, etc.)

manera *nf* **1** : way, manner **2 de ~ que** : so that **3 de ninguna ~** : by no means **4 de todas ~s** : anyway

manga *nf* **1** : sleeve **2** MANGUERA : hose

mango *nm* **1** : hilt, handle **2** : mango (fruit)

mangonear *vt fam* : boss around — *vi* **1** : be bossy **2** HOLGAZANEAR : loaf, fool around

manguera *nf* : hose

maní *nm, pl* **-níes** *Lat* : peanut

manía *nf* **1** : mania, obsession **2** MODA PASAJERA : craze, fad **3** ANTIPATÍA : dislike — **maníaco, -ca** *adj* : maniacal — **~** *n* : maniac

maniatar *vt* : tie the hands of

maniático, -ca *adj* : obsessive, fussy — **~** *n* : fussy person, fanatic

manicomio *nm* : insane asylum

manicura *nf* : manicure — **manicuro, -ra** *n* : manicurist

manido, -da *adj* : stale, hackneyed

manifestar {55} *vt* **1** : demonstrate, show **2** DECLARAR : express, declare — **manifestarse** *vr* **1** : become evident **2** : demonstrate (in politics) — **manifestación** *nf, pl* **-ciones 1** : manifestation, sign **2** : demonstration (in politics) — **manifestante** *nmf* : protester, demonstrator — **manifiesto, -ta** *adj* : manifest, evident — **manifiesto** *nm* : manifesto

manija *nf* : handle

manillar *nm* : handlebars *pl*

maniobra *nf* : maneuver — **maniobrar** *v* : maneuver

manipular *vt* **1** : manipulate **2** MANEJAR : handle — **manipulación** *nf, pl* **-ciones** : manipulation

maniquí *nmf, pl* **-quíes** : mannequin, model — **~** *nm* : mannequin, dummy

manirroto, -ta *adj* : extravagant — **~** *n* : spendthrift

manito -ta ²**mano**

manivela *nf* : crank

manjar *nm* : delicacy, special dish

mano *nf* **1** : hand **2** : coat (of paint, etc.) **3 a ~** *or* **a la ~** : at hand, nearby **4 dar la ~** : shake hands **5 de segunda ~** : secondhand **6 ~ de obra** : labor, manpower

manojo *nm* : bunch

manopla *nf* : mitten

manosear *vt* **1** : handle excessively **2** : fondle (a person)

manotazo *nm* : slap

mansalva : a ~ *adv phr* : at close range, without risk

mansarda *nf* : attic

mansedumbre *nf* **1** : gentleness **2** : tameness (of an animal)

mansión *nf, pl* **-siones** : mansion

manso, -sa *adj* **1** : gentle **2** : tame (of an animal)

manta *nf* **1** : blanket **2** *Lat* : poncho

manteca *nf* : lard, fat — **mantecoso, -sa** *adj* : greasy

mantel *nm* : tablecloth — **mantelería** *nf* : table linen

mantener {80} *vt* **1** : support **2** CONSERVAR : preserve **3** : keep up, maintain (relations, correspondence, etc.) **4** AFIRMAR : affirm — **mantenerse** *vr* **1** : support oneself **2 ~ firme** : hold one's ground — **manteni-**

miento *nm* **1** : maintenance **2** SUSTENTO : sustenance

mantequilla *nf* : butter — **mantequera** *nf* : churn — **mantequería** *nf* : dairy

mantilla *nf* : mantilla

manto *nm* : cloak

mantón *nm, pl* **-tones** : shawl

manual *adj* : manual — ~ *nm* : manual, handbook

manubrio *nm* **1** : handle, crank **2** *Lat* : handlebars *pl*

manufactura *nf* **1** : manufacture **2** FÁBRICA : factory

manuscrito *nm* : manuscript — **manuscrito, -ta** *adj* : handwritten

manutención *nf, pl* **-ciones** : maintenance

manzana *nf* **1** : apple **2** : (city) block — **manzanar** *nm* : apple orchard — **manzano** *nm* : apple tree

maña *nf* **1** : skill **2** ASTUCIA : cunning, guile

mañana *adv* : tomorrow — ~ *nm* **el ~** : the future — ~ *nf* : morning

mañoso, -sa *adj* **1** : skillful **2** *Lat* : finicky

mapa *nm* : map — **mapamundi** *nm* : map of the world

mapache *nm* : raccoon

maqueta *nf* : model, mock-up

maquillaje *nm* : makeup — **maquillarse** *vr* : put on makeup

máquina *nf* **1** : machine **2** LOCOMOTORA : locomotive **3 a toda ~** : at full speed **4** ~ **de escribir** : typewriter — **maquinación** *nf, pl* **-ciones** : machination — **maquinal** *adj* : mechanical — **maquinaria** *nf* **1** : machinery **2** : mechanism, works *pl* (of a watch, etc.) — **maquinilla** *nf* : small machine — **maquinista** *nmf* **1** : machinist **2** : (railroad) engineer

mar *nmf* **1** : sea **2 alta ~** : high seas *pl*

maraca *nf* : maraca

maraña *nf* **1** : thicket **2** ENREDO : tangle, mess

maratón *nm, pl* **-tones** : marathon

maravilla *nf* **1** : wonder, marvel **2** : marigold (flower) — **maravillar** *vt* : astonish — **maravillarse** *vr* : be amazed — **maravilloso, -sa** *adj* : marvelous

marca *nf* **1** : mark **2** : brand (on livestock) **3** *or* ~ **de fábrica** : trademark **4** : record (in sports) — **marcado, -da** *adj* : marked — **marcador** *nm* **1** : scoreboard **2** *Lat* : marker, felt-tipped pen

marcapasos *nms & pl* : pacemaker

marcar {72} *vt* **1** : mark **2** : brand (livestock) **3** INDICAR : indicate, show **4** : dial (a telephone, etc.) **5** : score (in sports) — *vi* **1** : score **2** : dial (on the telephone, etc.)

marcha *nf* **1** : march **2** : hike, walk **3** : pace, speed (**a toda marcha** at top speed) **4** : gear (of an automobile) **5** : departure **6** : march (en música) **7** : course (**la marcha de los acontecimientos** the course of events) **8 en ~** : in motion, in gear, under way (**ponerse en marcha** to set off)

marchar *vi* **1** : go **2** CAMINAR : walk **3** FUNCIONAR : work, run — **marcharse** *vr* : leave, go

marchitarse *vr* : wither, wilt — **marchito, -ta** *adj* : withered

marcial *adj* : martial, military

marco *nm* **1** : frame **2** : goalposts *pl* (in sports) **3** ENTORNO : setting, framework

marea *nf* : tide — **marear** *vt* **1** : make nauseous or dizzy **2** CONFUNDIR : confuse — **marearse** *vr* **1** : become nauseated or dizzy **2** CONFUNDIRSE : get confused — **mareado, -da** *adj* **1** : sick, nauseous **2** ATURDIDO : dazed, dizzy

maremoto *nm* : tidal wave

mareo *nm* **1** : nausea, seasickness **2** VÉRTIGO : dizziness

marfil *nm* : ivory

margarina *nf* : margarine

margarita *nf* : daisy

margen *nm, pl* **márgenes 1** : edge, border **2** : margin (of a page, etc.) — **marginado, -da** *adj* **1** : alienated **2 clases marginadas** : underclass — ~ *n* : outcast — **marginal** *adj* : marginal — **marginar** *vt* : ostracize, exclude

mariachi *nm* : mariachi musician or band

maridaje *nm* : marriage, union — **marido** *nm* : husband

marihuana *or* **mariguana** *or* **marijuana** *nf* : marijuana

marimba *nf* : marimba

marina *nf* **1** : coast **2** *or* ~ **de guerra** : navy, fleet

marinada *nf* : marinade — **marinar** *vt* : marinate

marinero, -ra *adj* **1** : sea, marine **2** : seaworthy (of a ship) — **marinero** *nm* : sailor — **marino, -na** *adj* : marine — **marino** *nm* : seaman, sailor

marioneta *nf* : puppet, marionette

mariposa *nf* **1** : butterfly **2** ~ **nocturna** : moth

mariquita *nf* : ladybug

marisco *nm* **1** : shellfish **2** ~**s** *nmpl* : seafood

marisma *nf* : salt marsh

marítimo, -ma *adj* : maritime, shipping

mármol *nm* : marble

marmota *nf* ~ **de América** : groundhog

marquesina *nf* : marquee, (glass) canopy

marrano, -na *n* **1** : pig, hog **2** *fam* : slob

marrar *vt* : miss (a target) — *vi* : fail

marrón *adj & nm, pl* **-rrones** : brown
marroquí *adj* : Moroccan
marsopa *nf* : porpoise
marsupial *nm* : marsupial
Marte *nm* : Mars
martes *nms & pl* : Tuesday
martillo *nm* **1** : hammer **2 ~ neumático**
: jackhammer — **martillar** *or* **martillear** *v*
: hammer
mártir *nmf* : martyr — **martirio** *nm* : martyr-
dom — **martirizar** {21} *vt* **1** : martyr **2**
ATORMENTAR : torment
marxismo *nm* : Marxism — **marxista** *adj &*
nmf : Marxist
marzo *nm* : March
mas *conj* : but
más *adv* **1** : more **2 el/la/lo ~** : (the) most
3 (*in negative constructions*) : (any) longer
4 ¡qué día ~ bonito! : what a beautiful
day! — **~** *adj* **1** : more **2** : most **3 ¿quién**
~? : who else? — **~** *prep* : plus — **~**
pron **1 a lo ~** : at most **2 de ~** : extra,
spare **3 ~ o menos** : more or less **4 ¿tie-**
nes ~? : do you have more?
masa *nf* **1** : mass, volume **2** : dough (in
cooking) **3 ~s** *nfpl* : people, masses
masacre *nf* : massacre
masaje *nm* : massage — **masajear** *vt* : massage
mascar {72} *v* : chew
máscara *nf* : mask — **mascarada** *nf* : masquerade — **mascarilla** *nf* : mask (in mede-
cine, etc.)
mascota *nf* : mascot
masculino, -na *adj* **1** : masculine, male **2**
VARONIL : manly **3** : masculine (in grammar) — **masculinidad** *nf* : masculinity
mascullar *v* : mumble
masilla *nf* : putty
masivo, -va *adj* : mass, large-scale
masón *nm, pl* **-sones** : Mason, Freemason
— **masónico, -ca** *adj* : Masonic
masoquismo *nm* : masochism — **maso-**
quista *adj* : masochistic — **~** *nmf* : masochist
masticar {72} *v* : chew
mástil *nm* **1** : mast **2** ASTA : flagpole **3**
: neck (of a stringed instrument)
mastín *nm, pl* **-tines** : mastiff
masturbarse *vr* : masturbate — **masturba-**
ción *nf, pl* **-ciones** : masturbation
mata *nf* : bush, shrub
matadero *nm* : slaughterhouse
matador *nm* : matador, bullfighter
matamoscas *nms & pl* : flyswatter
matar *vt* **1** : kill **2** : slaughter (animals) —
matarse *vr* **1** : be killed **2** SUICIDARSE
: commit suicide — **matanza** *nf* : slaughter,
killing
matasanos *nms & pl fam* : quack

matasellos *nms & pl* : postmark
mate *adj* : matte, dull — **~** *nm* **1** : maté **2**
jaque ~ : checkmate
matemáticas *nfpl* : mathematics — **mate-**
mático, -ca *adj* : mathematical — **~** *n*
: mathematician
materia *nf* **1** ASUNTO : matter **2** MATERIAL
: material — **material** *adj* **1** : material **2**
daños ~es : property damage — **~** *nm* **1**
: material **2** EQUIPO : equipment, gear —
materialismo *nm* : materialism — **materia-**
lista *adj* : materialistic — **materializar**
{21} *vt* : bring to fruition — **materializarse**
vr : materialize — **materialmente** *adv* : absolutely
maternal *adj* : maternal — **maternidad** *nf* **1**
: motherhood **2** : maternity hospital — **ma-**
terno, -na *adj* **1** : maternal **2 lengua ma-**
terna : mother tongue
matinal *adj* : morning
matinée *or* **matiné** *nf* : matinee
matiz *nm, pl* **-tices 1** : nuance **2** : hue, shade
(of colors) — **matizar** {21} *vt* **1** : blend
(colors) **2** : qualify (a statement, etc.) **3 ~**
de : tinge with
matón *nm, pl* **-tones 1** : bully **2** CRIMINAL
: gangster, hoodlum
matorral *nm* : thicket
matraca *nf* **1** : rattle, noisemaker **2 dar la**
~ a : pester
matriarcado *nm* : matriarchy
matrícula *nf* **1** : list, roll, register **2** INSCRIP-
CIÓN : registration **3** : license plate (of an
automobile) — **matricular** *vt* : register —
matricularse *vr* : register, matriculate
matrimonio *nm* **1** : marriage **2** PAREJA
: (married) couple — **matrimonial** *adj*
: marital
matriz *nf, pl* **-trices 1** : matrix **2** : uterus,
womb (in anatomy)
matrona *nf* : matron
matutino, -na *adj* : morning
maullar {8} *vi* : meow — **maullido** *nm*
: meow
maxilar *nm* : jaw, jawbone
máxima *nf* : maxim
máxime *adv* : especially
máximo, -ma *adj* : maximum, highest —
máximo *nm* **1** : maximum **2 al ~** : to the
full
maya *adj* : Mayan
mayo *nm* : May
mayonesa *nf* : mayonnaise
mayor *adj* **1** (*comparative of* **grande**) : bigger, larger, greater, older **2** (*superlative of*
grande) : biggest, largest, greatest, oldest **3**
al por ~ : wholesale **4 ~ de edad** : of
(legal) age — **~** *nmf* **1** : major (in the
military) **2** ADULTO : adult **3 ~es** *nmfpl*
: grown-ups — **mayoral** *nm* : foreman

mayordomo *nm* : butler

mayoreo *nm Lat* : wholesale

mayoría *nf* : majority

mayorista *adj* : wholesale — ~ *nmf* : wholesaler

mayormente *adv* : primarily

mayúscula *nf* : capital letter — **mayúsculo, -la** *adj* 1 : capital, uppercase 2 **un fallo mayúsculo** : a terrible mistake

maza *nf* : mace (weapon)

mazapán *nm, pl* **-panes** : marzipan

mazmorra *nf* : dungeon

mazo *nm* 1 : mallet 2 MAJA : pestle

mazorca *nf* ~ **de maíz** : corncob

me *pron* 1 (*direct object*) : me 2 (*indirect object*) : to me, for me, from me 3 (*reflexive*) : myself, to myself, for myself, from myself

mecánica *nf* : mechanics — **mecánico, -ca** *adj* : mechanical — ~ *n* : mechanic

mecanismo *nm* : mechanism — **mecanización** *nf, pl* **-ciones** : mechanization — **mecanizar** {21} *vt* : mechanize

mecanografiar {85} *vt* : type — **mecanografía** *nf* : typing — **mecanógrafo, -fa** *n* : typist

mecate *nm Lat* : rope

mecedora *nf* : rocking chair

mecenas *nmfs & pl* : patron, sponsor — **mecenazgo** *nm* : patronage, sponsorship

mecer {86} *vt* 1 : rock 2 : push (on a swing) — **mecerse** *vr* : rock, swing

mecha *nf* 1 : fuse (of a bomb, etc.) 2 : wick (of a candle)

mechero *nm* 1 : burner 2 *Spain* : cigarette lighter

mechón *nm, pl* **-chones** : lock (of hair)

medalla *nf* : medal — **medallón** *nm, pl* **-llones** 1 : medallion 2 : locket (jewelry)

media *nf* 1 : average 2 ~**s** *nfpl* : stockings 3 **a** ~**s** : by halves, halfway

mediación *nf, pl* **-ciones** : mediation

mediado, -da *adj* 1 : half full, half empty, half over 2 : halfway through — **mediados** *nmpl* **a** ~ **de** : halfway through, in the middle of

mediador, -dora *n* : mediator

medialuna *nf* 1 : crescent 2 : croissant (pastry)

medianamente *adv* : fairly

medianero, -ra *adj* **pared medianera** : dividing wall

mediano, -na *adj* 1 : medium, average 2 MEDIOCRE : mediocre

medianoche *nf* : midnight

mediante *prep* : through, by means of

mediar *vi* 1 : be in the middle 2 INTERVENIR : mediate 3 ~ **entre** : be between

medicación *nf, pl* **-ciones** : medication — **medicamento** *nm* : medicine — **medicar** {72} *vt* : medicate — **medicarse** *vr* : take medicine — **medicina** *nf* : medicine — **medicinal** *adj* : medicinal

medición *nf, pl* **-ciones** : measurement

médico, -ca *adj* : medical — ~ *n* : doctor, physician

medida *nf* 1 : measurement, measure 2 MODERACIÓN : moderation 3 GRADO : extent, degree 4 **tomar** ~**s** : take steps — **medidor** *nm Lat* : meter, gauge

medieval *adj* : medieval

medio, -dia *adj* 1 : half 2 MEDIANO : average 3 **una media hora** : half an hour 4 **la clase media** : the middle class — **medio** *adv* : half — ~ *nm* 1 : half 2 MANERA : means *pl*, way 3 **en** ~ **de** : in the middle of 4 ~ **ambiente** : environment 5 ~**s** *nmpl* : means, resources

mediocre *adj* : mediocre, average — **mediocridad** *nf* : mediocrity

mediodía *nm* : noon, midday

medioevo *nm* : Middle Ages

medir {54} *vt* 1 : measure 2 CONSIDERAR : weigh, consider — **medirse** *vr* : be moderate

meditar *vi* : meditate, contemplate — *vt* 1 : think over, consider 2 PLANEAR : plan, work out — **meditación** *nf, pl* **-ciones** : meditation

mediterráneo, -nea *adj* : Mediterranean

medrar *vt* : flourish, thrive

medroso, -sa *adj* : fearful

médula *nf* 1 : marrow 2 ~ **espinal** : spinal cord

medusa *nf* : jellyfish

megabyte *nm* : megabyte

megáfono *nm* : megaphone

mejicano → **mexicano**

mejilla *nf* : cheek

mejillón *nm, pl* **-llones** : mussel

mejor *adv* 1 (*comparative*) : better 2 (*superlative*) : best 3 **a lo** ~ : maybe, perhaps — ~ *adj* 1 (*comparative of* **bueno** *or* **bien**) : better 2 (*superlative of* **bueno** *or* **bien**) : best 3 **lo** ~ : the best thing 4 **tanto** ~ : so much the better — **mejora** *nf* : improvement

mejorana *nf* : marjoram

mejorar *vt* : improve — *vi* : improve, get better

mejunje *nm* : concoction, brew

melancolía *nf* : melancholy — **melancólico, -ca** *adj* : melancholic, melancholy

melaza *nf* : molasses

melena *nf* 1 : long hair 2 : mane (of a lion)

melindroso, -sa *adj* 1 : affected 2 *Lat* : finicky

mella *nf* : chip, nick — **mellado, -da** *adj* : chipped, jagged

mellizo, -za *adj & n* : twin

melocotón *nm, pl* **-tones** : peach
melodía *nf* : melody — **melódico, -ca** *adj* : melodic
melodrama *nm* : melodrama — **melodramático, -ca** *adj* : melodramatic
melón *nm, pl* **-lones** : melon
meloso, -sa *adj* **1** : sweet, honeyed **2** EMPALAGOSO : cloying
membrana *nf* : membrane
membrete *nm* : letterhead, heading
membrillo *nm* : quince
membrudo, -da *adj* : muscular, burly
memorable *adj* : memorable
memorándum *or* **memorando** *nm, pl* **-dums** *or* **-dos 1** : memorandum **2** AGENDA : notebook
memoria *nf* **1** : memory **2** RECUERDO : remembrance **3** INFORME : report **4 de ~** : by heart **5 ~s** *nfpl* : memoirs — **memorizar** {21} *vt* : memorize
mena *nf* : ore
menaje *nm* : household goods *pl*, furnishings *pl*
mencionar *vt* : mention, refer to — **mención** *nf, pl* **-ciones** : mention
mendaz *adj, pl* **-daces** : lying
mendigar {52} *vi* : beg — *vt* : beg for — **mendicidad** *nf* : begging — **mendigo, -ga** *n* : beggar
mendrugo *nm* : crust (of bread)
menear *vt* **1** : move, shake **2** : sway (one's hips) **3** : wag (a tail) — **menearse** *vr* **1** : sway, shake, move **2** *fam* : hurry up
menester *nm* **ser ~** : be necessary — **menestroso, -sa** *adj* : needy
menguar *vt* : diminish, lessen — *vi* **1** : decline, decrease **2** : wane (of the moon) — **mengua** *nf* : decrease, decline
menopausia *nf* : menopause
menor *adj* (*comparative of* **pequeño**) : smaller, lesser, younger **2** (*superlative of* **pequeño**) : smallest, least, youngest **3** : minor (in music) **4 al por ~** : retail — ~ *nmf* : minor, juvenile
menos *adv* **1** (*comparative*) : less **2** (*superlative*) : least **3 ~ de** : fewer than — ~ *adj* **1** (*comparative*) : less, fewer **2** (*superlative*) : least, fewest — ~ *prep* **1** : minus **2** EXCEPTO : except — ~ *pron* **1** : less, fewer **2 al ~** *or* **por lo ~** : at least **3 a ~ que** : unless — **menoscabar** *vt* **1** : lessen **2** ESTROPEAR : harm, damage — **menospreciar** *vt* **1** DESPRECIAR : scorn **2** SUBESTIMAR : undervalue — **menosprecio** *nm* : contempt
mensaje *nm* : message — **mensajero, -ra** *n* : messenger
menso, -sa *adj Lat fam* : foolish, stupid
menstruar {3} *vi* : menstruate — **menstruación** *nf* : menstruation

mensual *adj* : monthly — **mensualidad** *nf* **1** : monthly payment **2** : monthly salary
mensurable *adj* : measurable
menta *nf* **1** : mint, peppermint **2 ~ verde** : spearmint
mental *adj* : mental — **mentalidad** *nf* : mentality
mentar {55} *vt* : mention, name
mente *nf* : mind
mentir {76} *vi* : lie — **mentira** *nf* : lie — **mentirilla** *nf* : fib — **mentiroso, -sa** *adj* : lying — ~ *n* : liar
mentís *nms & pl* : denial
mentol *nm* : menthol
mentón *nm, pl* **-tones** : chin
menú *nm, pl* **-nús** : menu
menudear *vi* : occur frequently — **menudeo** *nm Lat* : retail, retailing
menudillos *nmpl* : giblets
menudo, -da *adj* **1** : small, insignificant **2 a ~** : often
meñique *nm or* **dedo ~** : little finger, pinkie
meollo *nm* **1** : marrow **2** ESENCIA : essence, core
mercado *nm* **1** : market **2 ~ de valores** : stock market — **mercadería** *nf* : merchandise, goods *pl*
mercancía *nf* : merchandise, goods *pl* — **mercante** *nmf* : merchant, dealer — **mercantil** *adj* : commercial
mercenario, -ria *adj & n* : mercenary
mercería *nf* : notions store
mercurio *nm* : mercury
Mercurio *nm* : Mercury (planet)
merecer {53} *vt* : deserve — *vi* : be worthy — **merecedor, -dora** *adj* : deserving, worthy — **merecido** *nm* **recibir su ~** : get one's just deserts
merendar {55} *vi* : have an afternoon snack — *vt* : have as an afternoon snack — **merendero** *nm* **1** : snack bar **2** : picnic area
merengue *nm* **1** : meringue **2** : merengue (dance)
meridiano, -na *adj* **1** : midday **2** CLARO : crystal-clear — **meridiano** *nm* : meridian — **meridional** *adj* : southern
merienda *nf* : afternoon snack, tea
mérito *nm* : merit, worth — **meritorio, -ria** *adj* : deserving — ~ *n* : intern, trainee
mermar *vi* : decrease — *vt* : reduce, cut down — **merma** *nf* : decrease
mermelada *nf* : marmalade, jam
mero, -ra *adj* **1** : mere, simple **2** *Lat fam* (*used as an intensifier*) : very, real — **mero** *adv Lat fam* **1** : nearly, almost **2 aquí ~** : right here
merodear *vi* **1** : maraud **2 ~ por** : prowl about (a place)
mes *nm* : month

mesa *nf* **1** : table **2** COMITÉ : committee, board

mesarse *vr* ~ **los cabellos** : tear one's hair

meseta *nf* : plateau

Mesías *nm* : Messiah

mesilla *nf* : small table

mesón *nm, pl* **-sones** : inn — **mesonero, -ra** *nm* : innkeeper

mestizo, -za *adj* **1** : of mixed ancestry **2** HÍBRIDO : hybrid — ~ *n* : person of mixed ancestry

mesura *nf* : moderation — **mesurado, -da** *adj* : moderate, restrained

meta *nf* : goal, objective

metabolismo *nm* : metabolism

metafísica *nf* : metaphysics — **metafísico, -ca** *adj* : metaphysical

metáfora *nf* : metaphor — **metafórico, -ca** *adj* : metaphoric, metaphorical

metal *nm* **1** : metal **2** : brass section (in an orchestra) — **metálico, -ca** *adj* : metallic, metal — **metalurgia** *nf* : metallurgy

metamorfosis *nfs & pl* : metamorphosis

metano *nm* : methane

metedura *nf* ~ **de pata** *fam* : blunder

meteoro *nm* : meteor — **meteórico, -ca** *adj* : meteoric — **meteorito** *nm* : meteorite — **meteorología** *nf* : meteorology — **meteorólogo, -ga** *adj* : meteorological, meteorologic — ~ *n* : meteorologist

meter *vt* **1** : put (in) **2** : place (in a job, etc.) **3** ENREDAR : involve **4** CAUSAR : make, cause **5** : spread (a rumor) **6** *Lat* : strike (a blow) — **meterse** *vr* **1** : get in, enter **2** ~ **en** : get involved in, meddle in **3** ~ **con** *fam* : pick a fight with

meticuloso, -sa *adj* : meticulous

método *nm* : method — **metódico, -ca** *adj* : methodical — **metodología** *nf* : methodology

metomentodo *nmf fam* : busybody

metralla *nf* : shrapnel — **metralleta** *nf* : submachine gun

métrico, -ca *adj* : metric, metrical

metro *nm* **1** : meter **2** : subway (train)

metrópoli *nf or* **metrópolis** *nfs & pl* : metropolis — **metropolitano, -na** *adj* : metropolitan

mexicano, -na *adj* : Mexican — **mexicoamericano, -na** *adj* : Mexican-American

mezcla *nf* **1** : mixture **2** ARGAMASA : mortar — **mezclar** *vt* **1** : mix, blend **2** CONFUNDIR : mix up, muddle **3** INVOLUCRAR : involve — **mezclarse** *vr* **1** : get mixed up **2** : mingle (socially) — **mezcolanza** *nf* : mixture

mezclilla *nf Lat* : denim

mezquino, -na *adj* **1** : mean, petty **2** ESCASO : meager — **mezquindad** *nf* : meanness, stinginess

mezquita *nf* : mosque

mezquite *nm* : mesquite

mi *adj* : my

mí *pron* **1** : me **2** *or* ~ **mismo,** ~ **misma** : myself **3 a** ~ **no me importa** : it doesn't matter to me

miajas → **migajas**

miau *nm* : meow

mica *nf* : mica

mico *nm* : (long-tailed) monkey

microbio *nm* : microbe, germ — **microbiología** *nf* : microbiology

microbús *nm, pl* **-buses** : minibus

microchip *nm, pl* **microchips** : microchip

microcosmos *nms & pl* : microcosm

microfilm *nm, pl* **-films** : microfilm

micrófono *nm* : microphone

microondas *nms & pl* : microwave (oven)

microorganismo *nm* : microorganism

microscopio *nm* : microscope — **microscópico, -ca** *adj* : microscopic

miedo *nm* **1** : fear **2 dar** ~ : be frightening — **miedoso, -sa** *adj* : fearful

miel *nf* : honey

miembro *nm* **1** : member **2** EXTREMIDAD : limb, extremity

mientras *adv or* ~ **tanto** : meanwhile, in the meantime — ~ *conj* **1** : while, as **2** ~ **que** : while, whereas **3** ~ **viva** : as long as I live

miércoles *nms & pl* : Wednesday

mies *nf* : (ripe) corn, grain

miga *nf* : crumb — **migajas** *nfpl* **1** : breadcrumbs **2** SOBRAS : leftovers

migración *nf, pl* **-ciones** : migration

migraña *nf* : migraine

migrar *vi* : migrate

mijo *nm* : millet

mil *adj & nm* : thousand

milagro *nm* : miracle — **milagroso, -sa** *adj* : miraculous

milenio *nm* : millennium

milésimo, -ma *adj* : thousandth

milicia *nf* **1** : militia **2** : military (service)

miligramo *nm* : milligram

mililitro *nm* : milliliter

milímetro *nm* : millimeter

militante *adj & nmf* : militant

militar *adj* : military — ~ *nmf* : soldier — **militarizar** {21} *vt* : militarize

milla *nf* : mile

millar *nm* : thousand

millón *nm, pl* **-llones** **1** : million **2 mil millones** : billion — **millonario, -ria** *n* : millionaire — **millonésimo, -ma** *adj* : millionth

mimar *vt* : pamper, spoil

mimbre *nm* : wicker

mímica *nf* **1** : mime, sign language **2** IMITACIÓN : mimicry

mimo *nm* : pampering — ~ *nmf* : mime

mina *nf* **1** : mine **2** : lead (for pencils) — **minar** *vt* **1** : mine **2** DEBILITAR : undermine

mineral *adj* : mineral — ~ *nm* **1** : mineral **2** : ore (of a metal)

minería *nf* : mining — **minero, -ra** *adj* : mining — ~ *n* : miner

miniatura *nf* : miniature

minifalda *nf* : miniskirt

minifundio *nm* : small farm

minimizar {21} *vt* : minimize

mínimo, -ma *adj* **1** : minimum **2** MINÚSCULO : minute **3 en lo más** ~ : in the slightest — **mínimo** *nm* : minimum

minino, -na *n fam* : pussycat

ministerio *nm* : ministry — **ministro, -tra** *n* **1** : minister, secretary **2 primer ministro** : prime minister

minoría *nf* : minority

minorista *adj* : retail — ~ *nmf* : retailer

minoritario, -ria *adj* : minority

minucia *nf* : trifle, small detail — **minucioso, -sa** *adj* **1** : detailed **2** METICULOSO : thorough

minué *nm* : minuet

minúsculo, -la *adj* : minuscule, tiny

minusvalía *nf* : handicap, disability — **minusválido, -da** *adj* : disabled

minuta *nf* **1** : bill, fee **2** BORRADOR : rough draft

minuto *nm* : minute — **minutero** *nm* : minute hand

mío, mía *adj* **1** : mine **2 una amiga mía** : a friend of mine — ~ *pron* **el mío, la mía** : mine, my own

miope *adj* : nearsighted

mirar *vt* **1** : look at **2** OBSERVAR : watch **3** CONSIDERAR : consider — *vi* **1** : look **2** ~ **a** : face, overlook **3** ~ **por** : look after — **mirarse** *vr* **1** : look at oneself **2** : look at each other — **mira** *nf* **1** : sight (of a firearm or instrument) **2** INTENCIÓN : aim, objective — **mirada** *nf* : look — **mirado, -da** *adj* **1** : careful **2** CONSIDERADO : considerate **3 bien** ~ : well thought of — **mirador** *nm* **1** BALCÓN : balcony **2** : lookout, vantage point — **miramiento** *nm* : consideration

mirlo *nm* : blackbird

misa *nf* : Mass

miscelánea *nf* : miscellany

miserable *adj* **1** : poor **2** LASTIMOSO : miserable, wretched — **miseria** *nf* **1** : poverty **2** DESGRACIA : misfortune, misery

misericordia *nf* : mercy — **misericordioso, -sa** *adj* : merciful

mísero, -ra *adj* : wretched, miserable

misil *nm* : missile

misión *nf, pl* **-siones** : mission — **misionero, -ra** *adj & n* : missionary

mismo *adv* (*used for emphasis*) : right, exactly — **mismo, -ma** *adj* **1** : same **2** (*used for emphasis*) : very **3** : -self **4 por lo** ~ : for that reason

misoginia *nf* : misogyny — **misógino** *nm* : misogynist

misterio *nm* : mystery — **misterioso, -sa** *adj* : mysterious

mística *nf* : mysticism — **místico, -ca** *adj* : mystic, mystical — ~ *n* : mystic

mitad *nf* **1** : half **2** MEDIO : middle

mítico, -ca *adj* : mythical, mythic

mitigar {52} *vt* : mitigate

mitin *nm, pl* **mítines** : (political) meeting

mito *nm* : myth — **mitología** *nm* : mythology — **mitológico, -ca** *adj* : mythological

mixto, -ta *adj* **1** : mixed, joint **2** : coeducational (of a school)

mnemónico, -ca *adj* : mnemonic

mobiliario *nm* : furniture

mocasín *nm, pl* **-sines** : moccasin

mochila *nf* : backpack, knapsack

moción *nf, pl* **-ciones** : motion

moco *nm* **1** : mucus **2 limpiarse los** ~**s** : wipe one's nose — **mocoso, -sa** *n fam* : kid, brat

moda *nf* **1** : fashion, style **2 a la** ~ *or* **de** ~ : in style, fashionable **3** ~ **pasajera** : fad — **modal** *adj* : modal — **modales** *nmpl* : manners — **modalidad** *nf* : type, kind

modelar *vt* : model, mold — **modelo** *adj* : model — ~ *nm* : model, pattern — ~ *nmf* : model, mannequin

módem *or* **modem** [ˈmoDEm] *nm* : modem

moderar *vt* **1** : moderate **2** : reduce (speed, etc.) **3** PRESIDIR : chair (a meeting) — **moderarse** *vr* : restrain oneself — **moderación** *nf, pl* **-ciones** : moderation — **moderado, -da** *adj & n* : moderate — **moderador, -dora** *n* : moderator, chairperson

moderno, -na *adj* : modern — **modernismo** *nm* : modernism — **modernizar** {21} *vt* : modernize

modesto, -ta *adj* : modest — **modestia** *nf* : modesty

modificar {72} *vt* : modify, alter — **modificación** *nf, pl* **-ciones** : alteration

modismo *nm* : idiom

modista *nmf* **1** : dressmaker **2** : (fashion) designer

modo *nm* **1** : way, manner **2** : mood (in grammar) **3** : mode (in music) **4 a** ~ **de** : by way of **5 de** ~ **que** : so (that) **6 de todos** ~**s** : in any case, anyway

modorra *nf* : drowsiness

modular *vt* : modulate — **modulación** *nf, pl* **-ciones** : modulation

módulo *nm* : module, unit

mofa *nf* : ridicule, mockery — **mofarse** *vr* ~ **de** : make fun of

mofeta *nf* : skunk

moflete *nm fam* : fat cheek — **mofletudo, -da** *adj fam* : fat-cheeked, chubby

mohín *nm, pl* **-hines** : grimace — **mohino, -na** *adj* : sulky

moho *nm* **1** : mold, mildew **2** ÓXIDO : rust — **mohoso, -sa** *adj* **1** : moldy **2** OXIDADO : rusty

moisés *nm, pl* **-seses** : bassinet, cradle

mojar *vt* **1** : wet, moisten **2** : dunk (food) — **mojarse** *vr* : get wet — **mojado, -da** *adj* : wet, damp

mojigato, -ta *adj* : prudish — **~** *n* : prude

mojón *nm, pl* **-jones** : boundary stone, marker

molar *nm* : molar

moldear *vt* : mold, shape — **molde** *nm* : mold, form — **moldura** *nf* : molding

mole[1] *nf* : mass, bulk

mole[2] *nm* **1** : Mexican chili sauce **2** : meat served with mole

molécula *nf* : molecule — **molecular** *adj* : molecular

moler {47} *vt* : grind, crush

molestar *vt* **1** : annoy, bother **2 no ~** : do not disturb — *vi* : be a nuisance — **molestarse** *vr* **1** : bother **2** OFENDERSE : take offense — **molestia** *nf* **1** : annoyance, nuisance **2** MALESTAR : discomfort — **molesto, -ta** *adj* **1** : annoyed **2** FASTIDIOSO : annoying **3** INCÓMODO : in discomfort — **molestoso, -sa** *adj* : bothersome, annoying

molido, -da *adj* **1** : ground (of meat, etc.) **2** *fam* : worn out, exhausted

molino *nm* **1** : mill **2 ~ de viento** : windmill — **molinero, -ra** *n* : miller — **molinillo** *nm* : grinder, mill

mollera *nf* **1** : crown (of the head) **2** *fam* : brains *pl*

molusco *nm* : mollusk

momento *nm* **1** : moment, instant **2** : (period of) time **3** : momentum (in physics) **4 de ~** : for the moment **5 de un ~ a otro** : any time now — **momentáneamente** *adv* : momentarily — **momentáneo, -nea** *adj* **1** : momentary **2** PASAJERO : temporary

momia *nf* : mummy

monada *nf* **1** : attractive person **2** : cute or pretty thing

monaguillo *nm* : altar boy

monarca *nmf* : monarch — **monarquía** *nf* : monarchy

monasterio *nm* : monastery — **monástico, -ca** *adj* : monastic

mondadientes *nms & pl* : toothpick

mondar *vt* : peel

mondongo *nm* : innards *pl*, guts *pl*

moneda *nf* **1** : coin **2** : currency (of a country) — **monedero** *nm* : change purse

monetario, -ria *adj* : monetary

monitor *nm* : monitor

monja *nf* : nun — **monje** *nm* : monk

mono, -na *n* : monkey — **~** *adj fam* : lovely, cute

monogamia *nf* : monogamy — **monógamo -ma** *adj* : monogamous

monografía *nf* : monograph

monograma *nm* : monogram

monolingüe *adj* : monolingual

monólogo *nm* : monologue

monopatín *nm, pl* **-tines** : scooter, skateboard

monopolio *nm* : monopoly — **monopolizar** {21} *vt* : monopolize

monosílabo *nm* : monosyllable — **monosilábico, -ca** *adj* : monosyllabic

monoteísmo *nm* : monotheism — **monoteísta** *adj* : monotheistic

monotonía *nf* : monotony — **monótono, -na** *adj* : monotonous

monovolumen *nm, pl* **-lúmenes** : minivan

monóxido *nm* **~ de carbono** : carbon monoxide

monstruo *nm* : monster — **monstruosidad** *nf* : monstrosity — **monstruoso, -sa** *adj* : monstrous

monta *nf* : importance, value

montaje *nm* **1** : assembly **2** : staging (in theater), editing (of films)

montaña *nf* **1** : mountain **2 ~ rusa** : roller coaster — **montañero, -ra** *n* : mountain climber — **montañoso, -sa** *adj* : mountainous

montar *vt* **1** : mount **2** ESTABLECER : establish **3** ENSAMBLAR : assemble, put together **4** : stage (a performance) **5** : cock (a gun) — *vi* **1 ~ a caballo** : ride horseback **2 ~ en bicicleta** : get on a bicycle

monte *nm* **1** : mountain **2** BOSQUE : woodland **3** *or* **~ bajo** : scrubland **4 ~ de piedad** : pawnshop

montés *adj, pl* **-teses** : wild (of animals or plants)

montículo *nm* : mound, hillock

montón *nm, pl* **-tones** **1** : heap, pile **2 un ~ de** *fam* : lots of

montura *nf* **1** : mount (horse) **2** SILLA : saddle **3** : frame (of glasses)

monumento *nm* : monument — **monumental** *adj fam* : monumental, huge

monzón *nm, pl* **-zones** : monsoon

moño *nm* **1** : bun (of hair) **2** *Lat* : bow (knot)

mora *nf* **1** : mulberry **2** ZARZAMORA : blackberry

morada *nf* : residence, dwelling

morado, -da *adj* : purple — **morado** *nm* : purple

moral *adj* : moral — **~** *nf* **1** : ethics, morals *pl* **2** ÁNIMO : morale — **moraleja** *nf* : moral (of a story) — **moralidad** *nf* : morality — **moralista** *adj* : moralistic — ~ *nmf* : moralist

morar *vi* : live, reside

morboso, -sa *adj* : morbid

mordaz *adj* : caustic, scathing — **mordacidad** *nf* : bite, sharpness

mordaza *nf* : gag

morder {47} *v* : bite — **mordedura** *nf* : bite (of an animal)

mordisquear *vt* : nibble (on) — **mordisco** *nm* : nibble, bite

moreno, -na *adj* **1** : dark-haired, brunette **2** : dark-skinned — ~ *n* **1** : brunette **2** : dark-skinned person

moretón *nm, pl* **-tones** : bruise

morfina *nf* : morphine

morir {46} *vi* **1** : die **2** APAGARSE : die out, go out — **morirse** *vr* **1** ~ **de** : die of **2** ~ **por** : be dying for — **moribundo, -da** *adj* : dying

moro, -ra *adj* : Moorish — ~ *n* : Moor

moroso, -sa *adj* : delinquent, in arrears — **morosidad** *nf* : delinquency (in payment)

morral *nm* : backpack

morriña *nf* : homesickness

morro *nm* : snout

morsa *nf* : walrus

morse *nm* : Morse code

mortaja *nf* : shroud

mortal *adj* **1** : mortal **2** : deadly (of a wound, an enemy, etc.) — ~ *nmf* : mortal — **mortalidad** *nf* : mortality — **mortandad** *nf* : death toll

mortero *nm* : mortar

mortífero, -ra *adj* : deadly, lethal

mortificar {72} *vt* **1** : mortify **2** ATORMENTAR : torment — **mortificarse** *vr* : be distressed

mosaico *nm* : mosaic

mosca *nf* : fly

moscada *adj* → **nuez**

mosquearse *vr fam* **1** : become suspicious **2** ENFADARSE : get annoyed

mosquito *nm* : mosquito — **mosquitero** *nm* **1** : (window) screen **2** : mosquito net

mostachón *nm, pl* **-chones** : macaroon

mostaza *nf* : mustard

mostrador *nm* : counter (in a store)

mostrar {19} *vt* : show — **mostrarse** *vr* : show oneself, appear

mota *nf* : spot, speck — **moteado, -da** *adj* : speckled, spotted

mote *nm* : nickname

motel *nm* : motel

motín *nm, pl* **-tines 1** : riot, uprising **2** : mutiny (of troops)

motivo *nm* **1** : motive, cause **2** : motif (in art, music, etc.) — **motivación** *nf, pl* **-ciones** : motivation — **motivar** *vt* **1** : cause **2** IMPULSAR : motivate

moto *nf* : motorcycle, motorbike — **motocicleta** *nf* : motorcycle — **motociclista** *nmf* : motorcyclist

motoneta *nf* : scooter

motor, -triz *or* **-tora** *adj* : motor — **motor** *nm* : motor, engine — **motorista** *nmf* **1** : motorcyclist **2** *Lat* : motorist

mover {47} *vt* **1** : move, shift **2** : shake (the head) **3** PROVOCAR : provoke — **moverse** *vr* **1** : move (over) **2** APRESURARSE : get a move on — **movedizo, -za** *adj* : movable, shifting — **movible** *adj* : movable

móvil *adj* : mobile — ~ *nm* **I** MOTIVO : motive **2** : mobile — **movilidad** *nf* : mobility — **movilizar** {21} *vt* : mobilize

movimiento *nm* **1** : movement, motion **2** ~ **sindicalista** : labor movement

mozo, -za *adj* : young — ~ *n* **1** : young man *m,* young woman *f* **2** *Lat* : waiter *m,* waitress *f*

MP3 *nm, pl* **MP3** : MP3

muchacho, -cha *n* : kid, boy *m,* girl *f*

muchedumbre *nf* : crowd

mucho *adv* **1** : very much, a lot **2** : long, a long time — **mucho, -cha** *adj* **1** : a lot of, many, much **2 muchas veces** : often — ~ *pron* : a lot, many, much

mucosidad *nf* : mucus

muda *nf* **1** : molting (of animals) **2** : change (of clothing) — **mudanza** *nf* **1** : change **2** TRASLADO : move, change of residence — **mudar** *v* **1** : molt, shed **2** CAMBIAR : change — **mudarse** *vr* **1** : change (one's clothes) **2** TRASLADARSE : move (one's residence)

mudo, -da *adj* **1** : mute **2** SILENCIOSO : silent

mueble *nm* **1** : piece of furniture **2** ~**s** *nmpl* : furniture, furnishings

mueca *nf* **1** : grimace, face **2 hacer** ~**s** : makes faces

muela *nf* **1** : tooth, molar **2** ~ **de juicio** : wisdom tooth

muelle *adj* : soft — ~ *nm* **1** : wharf, jetty **2** RESORTE : spring

muérdago *nm* : mistletoe

muerte *nf* : death — **muerto, -ta** *adj* **1** : dead **2** : dull (of colors, etc.) — ~ *nm* : dead person, deceased

muesca *nf* : nick, notch

muestra *nf* **1** : sample **2** SEÑAL : sign, show

mugir {35} *vi* : moo, bellow — **mugido** *nm* : mooing, bellowing

mugre *nf* : grime, filth — **mugriento, -ta** *adj* : filthy, grimy

muguete *nm* : lily of the valley

mujer *nf* **1** : woman **2** ESPOSA : wife **3** ~ **de negocios** : businesswoman

mulato, -ta *adj & n* : mulatto

muleta *nf* **1** : crutch **2** APOYO : prop, support
mullido, -da *adj* : soft, spongy
mulo, -la *n* : mule
multa *nf* : fine — **multar** *vt* : fine
multicolor *adj* : multicolored
multicultural *adj* : multicultural
multimedia *adj* : multimedia
multinacional *adj* : multinational
multiplicar {72} *v* : multiply — **multiplicarse** *vr* : multiply, reproduce — **múltiple** *adj* : multiple — **multiplicación** *nf, pl* **-ciones** : multiplication — **múltiplo** *nm* : multiple
multitud *nf* : crowd, multitude
mundo *nm* **1** : world **2 todo el ~** : everyone, everybody — **mundanal** *adj* : worldly — **mundano, -na** *adj* **1** : worldly, earthly **2 la vida mundana** : high society — **mundial** *adj* : world, worldwide
municiones *nfpl* : ammunition
municipal *adj* : municipal — **municipio** *nm* **1** : municipality **2** AYUNTAMIENTO : town council
muñeca *nf* **1** : doll **2** : wrist (in anatomy) — **muñeco** *nm* **1** : boy doll **2** MANIQUÍ : dummy, puppet
muñon *nm, pl* **-ñones** : stump (of an arm or leg)
mural *adj & nm* : mural — **muralla** *nf* : wall, rampart

murciélago *nm* : bat (animal)
murmullo *nm* **1** : murmur, murmuring **2** : rustling (of leaves, etc.)
murmurar *vi* **1** : murmur, whisper **2** CRITICAR : gossip
muro *nm* : wall
musa *nf* : muse
musaraña *nf* : shrew
músculo *nm* : muscle — **muscular** *adj* : muscular — **musculatura** *nf* : muscles *pl* — **musculoso, -sa** *adj* : muscular
muselina *nf* : muslin
museo *nm* : museum
musgo *nm* : moss — **musgoso, -sa** *adj* : mossy
música *nf* : music — **musical** *adj* : musical — **músico, -ca** *adj* : musical — **~** *n* : musician
musitar *vt* : mumble
muslo *nm* : thigh
musulmán, -mana *adj & n, mpl* **-manes** : Muslim
mutar *v* : mutate — **mutación** *nf, pl* **-ciones** : mutation — **mutante** *adj & nmf* : mutant
mutilar *vt* : mutilate — **mutilación** *nf, pl* **-ciones** : mutilation
mutuo, -tua *adj* : mutual
muy *adv* **1** : very, quite **2** DEMASIADO : too

N

n *nf* : n, 14th letter of the Spanish alphabet
nabo *nm* : turnip
nácar *nm* : mother-of-pearl
nacer {48} *vi* **1** : be born **2** : hatch (of an egg), sprout (of a plant) **3** SURGIR : arise, spring up — **nacido, -da** *adj & n* **recién ~** : newborn — **naciente** *adj* **1** : new, growing **2** : rising (of the sun) — **nacimiento** *nm* **1** : birth **2** : source (of a river) **3** ORIGEN : beginning **4** BELÉN : Nativity scene
nación *nf, pl* **-ciones** : nation, country — **nacional** *adj* : national — **~** *nmf* : national, citizen — **nacionalidad** *nf* : nationality — **nacionalismo** *nm* : nationalism — **nacionalista** *adj & nmf* : nationalist — **nacionalizar** {21} *vt* **1** : nationalize **2** : naturalize (as a citizen) — **nacionalizarse** *vr* : become naturalized
nada *pron* **1** : nothing **2 de ~** : you're welcome **3 ~ más** : nothing else, nothing more — **~** *adv* : not at all — **~** *nf* **la ~** : nothingness

nadar *v* : swim — **nadador, -dora** *n* : swimmer
nadería *nf* : small thing, trifle
nadie *pron* : nobody, no one
nado: a ~ *adv phr* : swimming
nafta *nf Lat* : gasoline
naipe *nm* : playing card
nalgas *nfpl* : buttocks, bottom
nana *nf* : lullaby
naranja *adj & nm* : orange (color) — **~** *nf* : orange (fruit) — **naranjal** *nm* : orange grove — **naranjo** *nm* : orange tree
narciso *nm* : narcissus, daffodil
narcótico, -ca *adj* : narcotic — **narcótico** *nm* : narcotic — **narcotizar** {21} *vt* : drug — **narcotraficante** *nmf* : drug trafficker — **narcotráfico** *nm* : drug trafficking
nariz *nf, pl* **-rices 1** : nose **2** OLFATO : sense of smell **3 narices** *nfpl* : nostrils
narrar *vt* : narrate, tell — **narración** *nf, pl* **-ciones** : narration — **narrador, -dora** *n*

: narrator — **narrativa** *nf* : narrative, storytelling

nasal *adj* : nasal

nata *nf Spain* : cream

natación *nf, pl* **-ciones** : swimming

natal *adj* 1 : native, birth — **natalicio** *nm* : birthday — **natalidad** *nf* : birthrate

natillas *nfpl* : custard

natividad *nf* : birth, nativity

nativo, -va *adj & n* : native

natural *adj* 1 : natural 2 NORMAL : normal 3 ~ **de** : native of, from — ~ *nm* 1 : temperament 2 NATIVO : native — **naturaleza** *nf* : nature — **naturalidad** *nf* : naturalness — **naturalista** *adj* : naturalistic — **naturalización** *nf, pl* -ciones : naturalization — **naturalizar** {21} *vt* : naturalize — **naturalizarse** *vr* : become naturalized — **naturalmente** *adv* 1 : naturally 2 POR SUPUESTO : of course

naufragar {52} *vi* 1 : be shipwrecked 2 FRACASAR : fail — **naufragio** *nm* : shipwreck — **náufrago, -ga** *adj* : shipwrecked — ~ *n* : castaway

náusea *nf* 1 : nausea 2 **dar** ~**s** : nauseate 3 ~**s matutinas** : morning sickness — **nauseabundo, -da** *adj* : nauseating

náutico, -ca *adj* : nautical

navaja *nf* : pocketknife, penknife

naval *adj* : naval

nave *nf* 1 : ship 2 : nave (of a church) 3 ~ **espacial** : spaceship

navegar {52} *v* : navigate, sail — **navegable** *adj* : navigable — **navegación** *nf, pl* -ciones : navigation — **navegante** *adj* : sailing, seafaring — ~ *nmf* : navigator

Navidad *nf* 1 : Christmas 2 **feliz** ~ : Merry Christmas — **navideño, -ña** *adj* : Christmas

naviero, -ra *adj* : shipping

nazi *adj & nmf* : Nazi — **nazismo** *nm* : Nazism

neblina *nf* : mist

nebuloso, -sa *adj* 1 : hazy, misty, foggy 2 VAGO : vague, nebulous

necedad *nf* 1 : stupidity 2 **decir** ~**es** : talk nonsense

necesario, -ria *adj* : necessary — **necesariamente** *adv* : necessarily — **necesidad** *nf* 1 : need, necessity 2 POBREZA : poverty 3 ~**es** *nfpl* : hardships — **necesitado, -da** *adj* : needy — **necesitar** *vt* : need — *vi* ~ **de** : have need of

necio, -cia *adj* : silly, dumb

necrología *nf* : obituary

néctar *nm* : nectar

nectarina *nf* : nectarine

neerlandés, -desa *adj, mpl* **-deses** : Dutch — **neerlandés** *nm* : Dutch (language)

nefasto, -ta *adj* 1 : ill-fated 2 *fam* : terrible, awful

negar {49} *vt* 1 : deny 2 REHUSAR : refuse 3 : disown (a person) — **negarse** *vr* : refuse — **negación** *nf, pl* -ciones 1 : denial 2 : negative (in grammar) — **negativa** *nf* 1 : denial 2 RECHAZO : refusal — **negativo, -va** *adj* : negative — **negativo** *nm* : negative (of a photograph)

negligente *adj* : negligent — **negligencia** *nf* : negligence

negociar *vt* : negotiate — *vi* : deal, do business — **negociable** *adj* : negotiable — **negociación** *nf, pl* -ciones : negotiation — **negociante** *nmf* : businessman *m*, businesswoman *f* — **negocio** *nm* 1 : business 2 TRANSACCIÓN : deal 3 ~**s** : business, commerce

negro, -gra *adj* : black, dark — ~ *n* : dark-skinned person — **negro** *nm* : black (color) — **negrura** *nf* : blackness — **negruzco, -ca** *adj* : blackish

nene, -na *n fam* : baby, small child

nenúfar *nm* : water lily

neón *nm* : neon

neoyorquino, -na *adj* : of or from New York

nepotismo *nm* : nepotism

Neptuno *nm* : Neptune

nervio *nm* 1 : nerve 2 : sinew (in meat) 3 VIGOR : vigor, energy 4 **tener** ~**s** : be nervous — **nerviosismo** *nf* : nervousness — **nervioso, -sa** *adj* 1 : nervous, anxious 2 **sistema nervioso** : nervous system

nervudo, -da *adj* : sinewy

neto, -ta *adj* 1 : clear, distinct 2 : net (of weight, salaries, etc.)

neumático *nm* : tire

neumonía *nf* : pneumonia

neurología *nf* : neurology — **neurológico, -ca** *adj* : neurological, neurologic — **neurólogo, -ga** *n* : neurologist

neurosis *nfs & pl* : neurosis — **neurótico, -ca** *adj & n* : neurotic

neutral *adj* : neutral — **neutralidad** *nf* : neutrality — **neutralizar** {21} *vt* : neutralize — **neutro, -tra** *adj* 1 : neutral 2 : neuter (in biology and grammar)

neutrón *nm, pl* **-trones** : neutron

nevar {55} *v impers* : snow — **nevada** *nf* : snowfall — **nevado, -da** *adj* 1 : snow-covered, snowy 2 : snow-white — **nevasca** *nf* : snowstorm

nevera *nf* : refrigerator

nevisca *nf* : light snowfall, flurry

nexo *nm* : link, connection

ni *conj* **1** : neither, nor **2** ~ **que** : as if **3** ~ **siquiera** : not even

nicaragüense *adj* : Nicaraguan

nicho *nm* : niche

nicotina *nf* : nicotine

nidada *nf* : brood (of chicks, etc.)

nido *nm* **1** : nest **2** GUARIDA : hiding place, den

niebla *nf* : fog, mist

nieto, -ta *n* **1** : grandson *m,* granddaughter *f* **2 nietos** *nmpl* : grandchildren

nieve *nf* : snow

nigeriano, -na *adj* : Nigerian

nilón *or* **nilon** *nm, pl* **-lones** : nylon

nimio, -mia *adj* : insignificant, trivial — **nimiedad** *nf* **1** : trifle **2** INSIGNIFICANCIA : triviality

ninfa *nf* : nymph

ninguno, -na (**ningún** *before masculine singular nouns*) *adj* : no, not any — ~ *pron* **1** : neither, none **2** : no one, nobody

niña *nf* **1** : pupil (of the eye) **2 la** ~ **de los ojos** : the apple of one's eye

niño, -ña *n* : child, boy *m,* girl *f* — ~ *adj* **1** : young **2** INFANTIL : immature, childish — **niñero, -ra** *n* : baby-sitter, nanny — **niñez** *nf, pl* **-ñeces** : childhood

nipón, -pona *adj* : Japanese

níquel *nm* : nickel

nítido, -da *adj* : clear, sharp — **nitidez** *nf, pl* **-deces** : clarity, sharpness

nitrato *nm* : nitrate

nitrógeno *nm* : nitrogen

nivel *nm* **1** : level, height **2** ~ **de vida** : standard of living — **nivelar** *vt* : level (out)

no *adv* **1** : not **2** (*in answer to a question*) : no **3 ¡como** ~**!** : of course! **4** ~ **bien** : as soon as **5** ~ **fumador** : non-smoker — ~ *nm* : no

noble *adj & nmf* : noble — **nobleza** *nf* : nobility

noche *nf* **1** : night, evening **2 buenas** ~**s** : good evening, good night **3 de** ~ *or* **por la** ~ : at night **4 hacerse de** ~ : get dark — **Nochebuena** *nf* : Christmas Eve — **nochecita** *nf* : dusk — **Nochevieja** *nf* : New Year's Eve

noción *nf, pl* **-ciones 1** : notion, concept **2 nociones** *nfpl* : rudiments

nocivo, -va *adj* : harmful, noxious

nocturno, -na *adj* **1** : night **2** : nocturnal (of animals, etc.) — **nocturno** *nm* : nocturne

nogal *nm* **1** : walnut tree **2** ~ **americano** : hickory

nómada *nmf* : nomad — ~ *adj* : nomadic

nomás *adv Lat* : only, just

nombrar *vt* **1** : appoint **2** CITAR : mention — **nombrado, -da** *adj* : famous, well-known — **nombramiento** *nm* : appointment, nomination — **nombre** *nm* **1** : name **2** SUSTANTIVO : noun **3** FAMA : fame, renown **4** ~ **de pila** : first name

nómina *nf* : payroll

nominal *adj* : nominal

nominar *vt* : nominate — **nominación** *nf, pl* **-ciones** : nomination

nomo *nm* : gnome

non *adj* : odd, not even — ~ *nm* : odd number

nonagésimo, -ma *adj & n* : ninetieth

nopal *nm* : nopal, prickly pear

nordeste *or* **noreste** *adj* **1** : northeastern **2** : northeasterly (of wind, etc.) — ~ *nm* : northeast

nórdico, -ca *adj* : Scandinavian

noreste → **nordeste**

noria *nf* **1** : waterwheel **2** : Ferris wheel (at a fair, etc.)

norma *nf* : rule, norm, standard — **normal** *adj* **1** : normal **2 escuela** ~ : teacher-training college — **normalidad** *nf* : normality — **normalizar** {21} *vt* **1** : normalize **2** ESTANDARIZAR : standardize — **normalizarse** *vr* : return to normal — **normalmente** *adv* : ordinarily, generally

noroeste *adj* **1** : northwestern **2** : northwesterly (of wind, etc.) — ~ *nm* : northwest

norte *adj* : north, northern — ~ *nm* **1** : north **2** : north wind

norteamericano, -na *adj* : North American

norteño, -ña *adj* : northern

noruego, -ga *adj* : Norwegian — **noruego** *nm* : Norwegian (language)

nos *pron* **1** (*direct object*) : us **2** (*indirect object*) : to us, for us, from us **3** (*reflexive*) : ourselves **4** : each other, one another

nosotros, -tras *pron* **1** (*subject*) : we **2** (*object*) : us **3** *or* ~ **mismos** : ourselves

nostalgia *nf* **1** : nostalgia **2 sentir** ~ **por** : be homesick for — **nostálgico, -ca** *adj* : nostalgic

nota *nf* **1** : note **2** : grade, mark (in school) **3** CUENTA : bill, check — **notable** *adj* : noteworthy, notable — **notar** *vt* : notice — **notarse** *vr* : be evident, seem

notario, -ria *n* : notary (public)

noticia *nf* **1** : news item, piece of news **2** ~**s** *nfpl* : news — **noticiario** *nm* : newscast — **noticiero** *nm Lat* : newscast

notificar {72} *vt* : notify — **notificación** *nf, pl* **-ciones** : notification

notorio, -ria *adj* **1** : obvious **2** CONOCIDO

: well-known — **notoriedad** *nf* : fame, notoriety

novato, -ta *adj* : inexperienced — ~ *n* : beginner, novice

novecientos, -tas *adj* : nine hundred — **novecientos** *nms & pl* : nine hundred

novedad *nf* **1** : newness, innovation **2** NOTICIAS : news **3** ~**es** : novelties, latest news — **novedoso, -sa** *adj* : original, novel

novela *nf* **1** : novel **2** : soap opera (on television) — **novelesco, -ca** *adj* **1** : fictional **2** FANTÁSTICO : fabulous — **novelista** *nmf* : novelist

noveno, -na *adj* : ninth — **noveno** *nm* : ninth

noventa *adj & nm* : ninety — **noventavo, -va** *adj* : ninetieth — **noventavo** *nm* : ninetieth

novia → **novio**

noviazgo *nm* : engagement

novicio, -cia *n* : novice

noviembre *nm* : November

novillo, -lla *n* : young bull *m*, heifer *f*

novio, -via *n* **1** : boyfriend *m*, girlfriend *f* **2** PROMETIDO : fiancé *m*, fiancée *f* **3** : bridegroom *m*, bride *f* (at a wedding)

novocaína *nf* : novocaine

nube *nf* : cloud — **nubarrón** *nm, pl* **-rrones** : storm cloud — **nublado, -da** *adj* **1** : cloudy **2** ENTURBIADO : clouded, dim — **nublado** *nm* : storm cloud — **nublar** *vt* **1** : cloud **2** OSCURECER : obscure — **nublarse** *vr* : get cloudy — **nuboso, -sa** *adj* : cloudy

nuca *nf* : nape, back of the neck

núcleo *nm* **1** : nucleus **2** CENTRO : center, core — **nuclear** *adj* : nuclear

nudillo *nm* : knuckle

nudismo *nm* : nudism — **nudista** *adj & nmf* : nudist

nudo *nm* **1** : knot **2** : crux, heart (of a problem, etc.) — **nudoso, -sa** *adj* : knotty, gnarled

nuera *nf* : daughter-in-law

nuestro, -tra *adj* : our — ~ *pron* (*with definite article*) : ours, our own

nuevamente *adv* : again, anew

nueve *adj & nm* : nine

nuevo, -va *adj* **1** : new **2 de nuevo** : again, once more

nuez *nf, pl* **nueces 1** : nut **2** *or* ~ **de nogal** : walnut **3** ~ **de Adán** : Adam's apple **4** ~ **moscada** : nutmeg

nulo, -la *adj* **1** *or* ~ **y sin efecto** : null and void **2** INCAPAZ : useless, inept — **nulidad** *nf* **1** : nullity **2 es una** ~ *fam* : he's a total loss

numerar *vt* : number — **numeración** *nf, pl* **-ciones 1** : numbering **2** NÚMEROS : numbers *pl*, numerals *pl* — **numeral** *adj* : numeral — **número** *nm* **1** : number, numeral **2** : issue (of a publication) **3 sin** ~ : countless — **numérico, -ca** *adj* : numerical — **numeroso, -sa** *adj* : numerous

nunca *adv* **1** : never, ever **2** ~ **más** : never again **3** ~ **jamás** : never ever

nupcial *adj* : nuptial, wedding — **nupcias** *nfpl* : nuptials, wedding

nutria *nf* : otter

nutrir *vt* **1** ALIMENTAR : feed, nourish **2** FOMENTAR : fuel, foster — **nutrición** *nf, pl* **-ciones** : nutrition — **nutrido, -da** *adj* **1** : nourished **2** ABUNDANTE : considerable, abundant — **nutriente** *nm* : nutrient — **nutritivo, -va** *adj* : nourishing, nutritious

O

o¹ *nf* : o, 16th letter of the Spanish alphabet

o² *conj* (**u** *before words beginning with o- or ho-*) **1** : or, either **2** ~ **sea** : in other words

oasis *nms & pl* : oasis

obcecar {72} *vt* : blind (by emotions) — **obcecarse** *vr* : become stubborn

obedecer {53} *vt* : obey — *vi* **1** : obey **2** ~ **a** : respond to **3** ~ **a** : be due to — **obediencia** *nf* : obedience — **obediente** *adj* : obedient

obertura *nf* : overture

obeso, -sa *adj* : obese — **obesidad** *nf* : obesity

obispo *nm* : bishop

objetar *v* : object — **objeción** *nf, pl* **-ciones** : objection

objeto *nm* : object — **objetivo, -va** *adj* : objective — **objetivo** *nm* **1** : objective, goal **2** : lens (in photography, etc.)

objetor, -tora *n* ~ **de conciencia** : conscientious objector

oblicuo, -cua *adj* : oblique
obligar {52} *vt* : require, oblige — **obligarse** *vr* : commit oneself (to do something) — **obligación** *nf, pl* **-ciones** : obligation — **obligado, -da** *adj* **1** : obliged **2** FORZOSO : obligatory — **obligatorio, -ria** *adj* : mandatory
oblongo, -ga *adj* : oblong
oboe *nm* : oboe — ~ *nmf* : oboist
obra *nf* **1** : work, deed **2** : work (of art, literature, etc.) **3** CONSTRUCCIÓN : construction work **4** ~ **maestra** : masterpiece **5** ~**s públicas** : public works — **obrar** *vt* : work, produce — *vi* : act, behave — **obrero, -ra** *adj* **la clase obrera** : the working class — ~ *n* : worker, laborer
obsceno, -na *adj* : obscene — **obscenidad** *nf* : obscenity
obsequiar *vt* **1** : give, present — **obsequio** *nm* : gift, present
observar *vt* **1** : observe, watch **2** ADVERTIR : notice **3** ACATAR : observe, obey **4** COMENTAR : remark — **observación** *nf, pl* **-ciones** : observation — **observador, -dora** *adj* : observant — ~ *n* : observer — **observancia** *nf* : observance — **observatorio** *nm* : observatory
obsesionar *vt* : obsess — **obsesionarse** *vr* : be obsessed — **obsesión** *nf, pl* **-siones** : obsession — **obsesivo, -va** *adj* : obsessive — **obseso, -sa** *adj* : obsessed
obsoleto, -ta *adj* : obsolete
obstaculizar {21} *vt* : hinder — **obstáculo** *nm* : obstacle
obstante: no ~ *conj phr* : nevertheless, however — ~ *prep phr* : in spite of, despite
obstar {21} *vi* ~ **a** *or* ~ **para** : stop, prevent
obstetricia *nf* : obstetrics — **obstetra** *nmf* : obstetrician
obstinarse *vr* : be stubborn — **obstinado, -da** *adj* **1** : obstinate, stubborn **2** TENAZ : persistent
obstruir {41} *vt* : obstruct — **obstrucción** *nf, pl* **-ciones** : obstruction
obtener {80} *vt* : obtain, get
obtuso, -sa *adj* : obtuse
obviar *vt* : get around, avoid
obvio, -via *adj* : obvious — **obviamente** *adv* : obviously, clearly
oca *nf* : goose
ocasión *nf, pl* **-siones** **1** : occasion **2** OPORTUNIDAD : opportunity **3** GANGA : bargain — **ocasional** *adj* **1** : occasional **2** ACCIDENTAL : accidental, chance — **ocasionar** *vt* : cause
ocaso *nm* **1** : sunset **2** DECADENCIA : decline
occidente *nm* **1** : west **2 el Occidente** : the West — **occidental** *adj* : western, Western
océano *nm* : ocean — **oceanografía** *nf* : oceanography
ochenta *adj & nm* : eighty
ocho *adj & nm* : eight — **ochocientos, -tas** *adj* : eight hundred — **ochocientos** *nms & pl* : eight hundred
ocio *nm* **1** : free time, leisure **2** INACTIVIDAD : idleness — **ociosidad** *nf* : idleness, inactivity — **ocioso, -sa** *adj* **1** : idle, inactive **2** INÚTIL : useless
ocre *adj & nm* : ocher
octágono *nm* : octagon — **octagonal** *adj* : octagonal
octava *nf* : octave
octavo, -va *adj & n* : eighth
octeto *nm* : byte
octogésimo, -ma *adj & n* : eightieth
octubre *nm* : October
ocular *adj* : ocular, eye — **oculista** *nmf* : ophthalmologist
ocultar *vt* : conceal, hide — **ocultarse** *vr* : hide — **oculto, -ta** *adj* : hidden, occult
ocupar *vt* **1** : occupy **2** : hold (a position, etc.) **3** : provide work for — **ocuparse** *vr* **1** ~ **de** : concern oneself with **2** ~ **de** : take care of (children, etc.) — **ocupación** *nf, pl* **-ciones** **1** : occupation **2** EMPLEO : job — **ocupado, -da** *adj* **1** : busy **2** : occupied (of a place) **3 señal de ocupado** : busy signal — **ocupante** *nmf* : occupant
ocurrir *vi* : occur, happen — **ocurrirse** *vr* ~ **a** : occur to — **ocurrencia** *nf* **1** : occurrence, event **2** SALIDA : witty remark, quip
oda *nf* : ode
odiar *vt* : hate — **odio** *nm* : hatred — **odioso, -sa** *adj* : hateful
odisea *nf* : odyssey
odontología *nf* : dentistry, dental surgery — **odontólogo, -ga** *n* : dentist, dental surgeon
oeste *adj* : west, western — ~ *nm* **1** : west **2 el Oeste** : the West
ofender *v* : offend — **ofenderse** *vr* : take offense — **ofensa** *nf* : offense, insult — **ofensiva** *nf* : offensive — **ofensivo, -va** *adj* : offensive
oferta *nf* **1** : offer **2 de** ~ : on sale **3** ~ **y demanda** : supply and demand
oficial *adj* : official — ~ *nmf* **1** : skilled worker **2** : officer (in the military)
oficina *nf* : office — **oficinista** *nmf* : office worker
oficio *nm* : trade, profession — **oficioso, -sa** *adj* : unofficial
ofrecer {53} *vt* **1** : offer **2** : provide, present

(an opportunity, etc.) — **ofrecerse** *vr* : volunteer — **ofrecimiento** *nm* : offer
ofrenda *nf* : offering
oftalmología *nf* : ophthalmology — **oftalmólogo, -ga** *n* : ophthalmologist
ofuscar {72} *vt* **1** : blind, dazzle **2** CONFUNDIR : confuse — **ofuscarse** *vr* ~ **con** : be blinded by — **ofuscación** *nf, pl* **-ciones 1** : blindness **2** CONFUSIÓN : confusion
ogro *nm* : ogre
oír {50} *vi* : hear — *vt* **1** : hear **2** ESCUCHAR : listen to **3** ¡oiga! *or* ¡oye! : excuse me!, listen! — **oídas: de** ~ *adv phr* : by hearsay — **oído** *nm* **1** : ear **2** : (sense of) hearing **3 duro de** ~ : hard of hearing
ojal *nm* : buttonhole
ojalá *interj* : I hope so!, if only!
ojear *vt* : eye, look at — **ojeada** *nf* : glimpse, glance
ojeriza *nf* **1** : ill will **2 tener** ~ **a** : have a grudge against
ojo *nm* **1** : eye **2** PERSPICACIA : shrewdness **3** : span (of a bridge) **4** ¡~! : look out!, pay attention!
ola *nf* : wave — **oleada** *nf* : wave, surge — **oleaje** *nm* : swell (of the sea)
olé *interj* : bravo!
oleada *nf* : wave, swell — **oleaje** *nm* : waves *pl*, surf
óleo *nm* **1** : oil **2** CUADRO : oil painting — **oleoducto** *nm* : oil pipeline
oler {51} *vt* : smell — *vi* **1** : smell **2** ~ **a** : smell of — **olerse** *vr fam* : have a hunch about
olfatear *vt* **1** : sniff **2** OLER : sense, sniff out — **olfato** *nm* **1** : sense of smell **2** PERSPICACIA : nose, instinct
Olimpiada *or* **Olimpíada** *nf* : Olympics *pl*, Olympic Games *pl* — **olímpico, -ca** *adj* : Olympic
oliva *nf* : olive — **olivo** *nm* : olive tree
olla *nf* **1** : pot **2** ~ **podrida** : (Spanish) stew
olmo *nm* : elm
olor *nm* : smell — **oloroso, -sa** *adj* : fragrant
olvidar *vt* **I** : forget **2** DEJAR : leave (behind) — **olvidarse** *vr* : forget — **olvidadizo, -za** *adj* : forgetful — **olvido** *nm* **1** : forgetfulness **2** DESCUIDO : oversight
ombligo *nm* : navel
omelette *nmf Lat* : omelet
ominoso, -sa *adj* : ominous
omitir *vt* : omit — **omisión** *nf, pl* **-siones** : omission
ómnibus *nm, pl* **-bus** *or* **-buses** : bus
omnipotente *adj* : omnipotent
omóplato *nm* *or* **omoplato** *nm* : shoulder blade
once *adj & nm* : eleven — **onceavo, -va** *adj & n* : eleventh
onda *nf* : wave — **ondear** *vi* : ripple — **ondulación** *nf, pl* **-ciones** : undulation — **on-**

dulado, -da *adj* : wavy — **ondular** *vt* : wave (hair) — *vi* : undulate, ripple
ónice *nmf or* **ónix** *nm* : onyx
onza *nf* : ounce
opaco, -ca *adj* **1** : opaque **2** DESLUSTRADO : dull
ópalo *nm* : opal
opción *nf, pl* **-ciones** : option — **opcional** *adj* : optional
ópera *nf* : opera
operar *vt* **1** : operate on **2** *Lat* : operate, run (a machine) — *vi* **1** : operate **2** NEGOCIAR : deal, do business — **operarse** *vr* **1** : have an operation **2** OCURRIR : take place — **operación** *nf, pl* **-ciones** **1** : operation **2** TRANSACCIÓN : transaction, deal — **operacional** *adj* : operational — **operador, -dora** *n* **1** : operator **2** : cameraman (for television, etc.)
opereta *nf* : operetta
opinar *vt* : think — *vi* : express an opinion — **opinión** *nf, pl* **-niones** : opinion
opio *nm* : opium
oponer {60} *vt* **1** : raise, put forward (arguments, etc.) **2** ~ **resistencia** : put up a fight — **oponerse** *vr* ~ **a** : oppose, be against — **oponente** *nmf* : opponent
oporto *nm* : port (wine)
oportunidad *nf* : opportunity — **oportunista** *nmf* : opportunist — **oportuno, -na** *adj* **1** : opportune, timely **2** APROPIADO : suitable
opositor, -tora *n* **1** : opponent **2** : candidate (for a position) — **oposición** *nf, pl* **-ciones** : opposition
oprimir *vt* **1** : press, squeeze **2** TIRANIZAR : oppress — **opresión** *nf, pl* **-siones** **1** : oppression **2** ~ **de pecho** : tightness in the chest — **opresivo, -va** *adj* : oppressive — **opresor, -sora** *n* : oppressor
optar *vi* **1** ~ **a** : apply for **2** ~ **por** : choose, opt for
óptica *nf* **1** : optics **2** : optician's (shop) — **óptico, -ca** *adj* : optical — ~ *n* : optician
optimismo *nm* : optimism — **optimista** *adj* : optimistic — ~ *nmf* : optimist
optometría *nf* : optometry — **optometrista** *nmf* : optometrist
opuesto *adj* **1** : opposite **2** CONTRADICTORIO : opposed, conflicting
opulencia *nf* : opulence — **opulento, -ta** *adj* : opulent
oración *nf, pl* **-ciones** **1** : prayer **2** FRASE : sentence, clause
oráculo *nm* : oracle
orador, -dora *n* : speaker
oral *adj* : oral
orar *vi* : pray
órbita *nf* **1** : orbit (in astronomy) **2** : eye socket — **orbitar** *vi* : orbit

orden *nm, pl* **órdenes 1** : order **2 ~ del día** : agenda (at a meeting) **3 ~ público** : law and order — **~** *nf, pl* **órdenes 1** : order (of food) **2 ~ religiosa** : religious order **3 ~ de compra** : purchase order

ordenador *nm Spain* : computer

ordenar *vt* **1** : order, command **2** ARREGLAR : put in order **3** : ordain (a priest) — **ordenanza** *nm* : orderly (in the armed forces) — **~** *nf* : ordinance, regulation

ordeñar *vt* : milk

ordinal *adj & nm* : ordinal

ordinario, -ria *adj* **1** : ordinary **2** GROSERO : common, vulgar

orear *vt* : air

orégano *nm* : oregano

oreja *nf* : ear

orfanato *or* **orfelinato** *nm* : orphanage

orfebre *nmf* : goldsmith, silversmith

orgánico, -ca *adj* : organic

organigrama *nm* : flowchart

organismo *nm* **1** : organism **2** ORGANIZACIÓN : agency, organization

organista *nmf* : organist

organizar {21} *vt* : organize — **organizarse** *vr* : get organized — **organización** *nf, pl* **-ciones** : organization — **organizador, -dora** *n* : organizer

órgano *nm* : organ

orgasmo *nm* : orgasm

orgía *nf* : orgy

orgullo *nm* : pride — **orgulloso, -sa** *adj* : proud

orientación *nf, pl* **-ciones 1** : orientation **2** DIRECCIÓN : direction **3** CONSEJO : guidance

oriental *adj* **1** : eastern **2** : oriental — **~** *nmf* : Oriental

orientar *vt* **1** : orient, position **2** GUIAR : guide, direct — **orientarse** *vr* **1** : orient oneself **2 ~ hacia** : turn towards

oriente *nm* **1** : east, East **2 el Oriente** : the Orient

orificio *nm* : orifice, opening

origen *nm, pl* **orígenes** : origin — **original** *adj & nm* : original — **originalidad** *nf* : originality — **originar** *vt* : give rise to — **originarse** *vr* : originate, arise — **originario, -ria** *adj* **~ de** : native of

orilla *nf* **1** : border, edge **2** : bank (of a river), shore (of the sea)

orinar *vi* : urinate — **orina** *nf* : urine

oriol *nm* : oriole

oriundo, -da *adj* **~ de** : native of

orla *nf* : border

ornamental *adj* : ornamental — **ornamento** *nm* : ornament

ornar *vt* : adorn

ornitología *nf* : ornithology

oro *nm* : gold

orquesta *nf* : orchestra — **orquestar** *vt* : orchestrate

orquídea *nf* : orchid

ortiga *nf* : nettle

ortodoxia *nf* : orthodoxy — **ortodoxo, -xa** *adj* : orthodox

ortografía *nf* : spelling

ortopedia *nf* : orthopedics — **ortopédico, -ca** *adj* : orthopedic

oruga *nf* : caterpillar

orzuelo *nm* : sty (in the eye)

os *pron pl Spain* **1** (*direct or indirect object*) : you, to you **2** (*reflexive*) : yourselves, to yourselves **3** : each other, to each other

osado, -da *adj* : bold, daring — **osadía** *nf* **1** : boldness, daring **2** DESCARO : audacity, nerve

osamenta *nf* : skeleton

osar *vi* : dare

oscilar *vi* **1** : swing, sway **2** FLUCTUAR : fluctuate — **oscilación** *nf, pl* **-ciones 1** : swinging **2** FLUCTUACIÓN : fluctuation

oscuro, -ra *adj* **1** : dark **2** : obscure (of ideas, persons, etc.) **3 a oscuras** : in the dark — **oscurecer** {53} *vt* **1** : darken **2** : confuse, cloud (the mind) **3 al ~** : at nightfall — *v impers* : get dark — **oscurecerse** *vr* : grow dark — **oscuridad** *nf* **1** : darkness **2** : obscurity (of ideas, persons, etc.)

óseo, ósea *adj* : skeletal, bony

oso, osa *n* **1** : bear **2 ~ de peluche** *or* **~ de felpa** : teddy bear

ostensible *adj* : evident, obvious

ostentar *vt* **1** : flaunt, display **2** POSEER : have, hold — **ostentación** *nf, pl* **-ciones** : ostentation — **ostentoso, -sa** *adj* : ostentatious, showy

osteopatía *n* : osteopathy — **osteópata** *nmf* : osteopath

osteoporosis *nf* : osteoporosis

ostra *nf* : oyster

ostracismo *nm* : ostracism

otear *vt* : scan, survey

otoño *nm* : autumn, fall — **otoñal** *adj* : autumn, fall

otorgar {52} *vt* **1** : grant, award **2** : draw up (a legal document)

otro, otra *adj* **1** : another, other **2 otra vez** : again — **~** *pron* **1** : another (one), other (one) **2 los otros, las otras** : the others, the rest

ovación *nf, pl* **-ciones** : ovation

óvalo *nm* : oval — **oval** *or* **ovalado, -da** *adj* : oval

ovario *nm* : ovary

oveja *nf* **1** : sheep, ewe **2 ~ negra** : black sheep

overol *nm Lat* : overalls *pl*

ovillo *nm* **1** : ball (of yarn) **2 hacerse un ~** : curl up (into a ball)

ovni *or* **OVNI** *nm* (*objeto volador no identificado*) : UFO
ovular *vi* : ovulate — **ovulación** *nf, pl* **-ciones** : ovulation
oxidar *vi* : rust — **oxidarse** *vr* : get rusty —

oxidación *nf, pl* **-ciones** : rusting — **oxidado, -da** *adj* : rusty — **óxido** *nm* : rust
oxígeno *nm* : oxygen
oye → **oír**
oyente *nmf* **1** : listener **2** : auditor (student)
ozono *nm* : ozone

P

p *nf* : p, 17th letter of the Spanish alphabet
pabellón *nm, pl* **-llones 1** : pavilion **2** : block, building (in a hospital complex, etc.) **3** : summerhouse (in a garden, etc.) **4** BANDERA : flag
pabilo *nm* : wick
pacer {48} *v* : graze
paces → **paz**
paciencia *nf* : patience — **paciente** *adj & nmf* : patient
pacificar {72} *vt* : pacify, calm — **pacificarse** *vr* : calm down — **pacífico, -ca** *adj* : peaceful, pacific — **pacifismo** *nm* : pacifism — **pacifista** *adj & nmf* : pacifist
pacotilla *nf* **de ～** : second-rate, trashy
pacto *nm* : pact, agreement — **pactar** *vt* : agree on — *vi* : come to an agreement
padecer {53} *vt* : suffer, endure — *vi* **～ de** : suffer from — **padecimiento** *nm* : suffering
padre *nm* **1** : father **2 ～s** *nmpl* : parents — **～** *adj Lat fam* : great, fantastic — **padrastro** *nm* : stepfather — **padrino** *nm* **1** : godfather **2** : best man (at a wedding)
padrón *nm, pl* **-drones** : register, roll
paella *nf* : paella
paga *nf* : pay, wages *pl* — **pagadero, -ra** *adj* : payable
pagano, -na *adj & n* : pagan, heathen
pagar {52} *vt* : pay, pay for — *vi* : pay — **pagaré** *nm* : IOU
página *nf* : page
pago *nm* : payment
país *nm* **1** : country, nation **2** REGIÓN : region, land — **paisaje** *nm* : scenery, landscape — **paisano, -na** *n* : compatriot
paja *nf* **1** : straw **2** *fam* : nonsense
pájaro *nm* **1** : bird **2 ～ carpintero** : woodpecker — **pajarera** *nf* : aviary
pajita *nf* : (drinking) straw
pala *nf* **1** : shovel, spade **2** : blade (of an oar or a rotor) **3** : paddle, racket (in sports)
palabra *nf* **1** : word **2** HABLA : speech **3 tener la ～** : have the floor — **palabrota** *nf* : swearword

palacio *nm* **1** : palace, mansion **2 ～ de justicia** : courthouse
paladar *nm* : palate — **paladear** *vt* : savor
palanca *nf* **1** : lever, crowbar **2** *fam* : leverage, influence **3 ～ de cambio** *or* **～ de velocidades** : gearshift
palangana *nf* : washbowl
palco *nm* : box (in a theater)
palestino, -na *adj* : Palestinian
paleta *nf* **1** : small shovel, trowel **2** : palette (in art) **3** : paddle (in sports, etc.)
paletilla *nf* : shoulder blade
paliar *vt* : alleviate, ease — **paliativo, -va** *adj* : palliative
pálido, -da *adj* : pale — **palidecer** {53} *vi* : turn pale — **palidez** *nf, pl* **-deces** : paleness, pallor
palillo *nm* **1** : small stick **2** *or* **～ de dientes** : toothpick
paliza *nf* : beating
palma *nf* **1** : palm (of the hand) **2** : palm (tree or leaf) **3 batir ～s** : clap, applaud — **palmada** *nf* **1** : pat, slap **2 ～s** *nfpl* : clapping
palmera *nf* : palm tree
palmo *nm* **1** : span, small amount **2 ～ a ～** : bit by bit
palmotear *vi* : applaud — **palmoteo** *nm* : clapping, applause
palo *nm* **1** : stick **2** MANGO : shaft, handle **3** MÁSTIL : mast **4** POSTE : pole **5** GOLPE : blow **6** : suit (of cards)
paloma *nf* : pigeon, dove — **palomilla** *nf* : moth — **palomitas** *nfpl* : popcorn
palpar *vt* : feel, touch — **palpable** *adj* : palpable
palpitar *vi* : palpitate, throb — **palpitación** *nf, pl* **-ciones** : palpitation
palta *nf Lat* : avocado
paludismo *nm* : malaria
pampa *nf* : pampa
pan *nm* **1** : bread **2** : loaf (of bread, etc.) **3 ～ tostado** : toast
pana *nf* : corduroy

panacea *nf* : panacea
panadería *nf* : bakery, bread shop — **panadero, -ra** *n* : baker
panal *nm* : honeycomb
panameño, -ña *adj* : Panamanian
pancarta *nf* : placard, banner
pancito *nm Lat* : (bread) roll
páncreas *nms & pl* : pancreas
panda *nmf* : panda
pandemonio *nm* : pandemonium
pandero *nm* : tambourine — **pandereta** *nf* : (small) tambourine
pandilla *nf* : gang
panecillo *nm Spain* : (bread) roll
panel *nm* : panel
panela *nf* : unrefined sugar
panfleto *nm* : pamphlet
pánico *nm* : panic
panorama *nm* : panorama — **panorámico, -ca** *adj* : panoramic
panqueque *nm Lat* : pancake
pantaletas *nfpl Lat* : panties
pantalla *nf* 1 : screen 2 : lampshade
pantalón *nm, pl* **-lones** 1 *or* **pantalones** *nmpl* : pants *pl*, trousers *pl* 2 **pantalones vaqueros** : jeans
pantano *nm* 1 : swamp, marsh 2 EMBALSE : reservoir — **pantanoso, -sa** *adj* : marshy, swampy
pantera *nf* : panther
pantimedias *nfpl Lat* : panty hose
pantomima *nf* : pantomime
pantorrilla *nf* : calf (of the leg)
pantufla *nf* : slipper
panza *nf* : belly, paunch — **panzón, -zona** *adj, mpl* **-zones** : potbellied
pañal *nm* : diaper
paño *nm* 1 : cloth 2 TRAPO : rag, dust cloth 3 **~ de cocina** : dishcloth 4 **~ higiénico** : sanitary napkin 5 **~s menores** : underwear
pañuelo *nm* 1 : handkerchief 2 : scarf, kerchief
papa[1] *nm* : pope
papa[2] *nf Lat* 1 : potato 2 **~s fritas** : potato chips, french fries
papá *nm fam* 1 : dad, pop 2 **~s** *nmpl* : parents, folks
papada *nf* : double chin
papagayo *nm* : parrot
papal *adj* : papal
papalote *nm Lat* : kite
papanatas *nmfs & pl fam* : simpleton
papaya *nf* : papaya
papel *nm* 1 : paper, sheet of paper 2 : role, part (in theater, etc.) 3 **~ de aluminio** : aluminum foil 4 **~ higiénico** *or* **~ de baño** : toilet paper 5 **~ de lija** : sandpaper 6 **~ pintado** : wallpaper — **papeleo** *nm* : paperwork, red tape — **papelera** *nf*

: wastebasket — **papelería** *nf* : stationery store — **papeleta** *nf* 1 : ticket, slip 2 : ballot (paper)
paperas *nfpl* : mumps
papilla *nf* 1 : baby food, pap 2 **hacer ~** : smash to bits
paquete *nm* 1 : package, parcel 2 : pack (of cigarettes, etc.)
paquistaní *adj* : Pakistani
par *nm* 1 : pair, couple 2 : par (in golf) 3 NOBLE : peer 4 **abierto de ~ en ~** : wide open 5 **sin ~** : without equal — **~** *adj* : even (in number) — **~** *nf* 1 : par 2 **a la ~ que** : at the same time as
para *prep* 1 : for 2 HACIA : towards 3 : (in order) to 4 : around, by (a time) 5 **~ adelante** : forwards 6 **~ atrás** : backwards 7 **~ que** : so (that), in order that
parabienes *nmpl* : congratulations
parábola *nf* : parable
parabrisas *nms & pl* : windshield
paracaídas *nms & pl* : parachute — **paracaidista** *nmf* 1 : parachutist 2 : paratrooper (in the military)
parachoques *nms & pl* : bumper
parada *nf* 1 : stop 2 : (act of) stopping 3 DESFILE : parade — **paradero** *nm* 1 : whereabouts 2 *Lat* : bus stop — **parado, -da** *adj* 1 : idle, stopped 2 *Lat* : standing (up) 3 **bien (mal) parado** : in good (bad) shape
paradoja *nf* : paradox
parafernalia *nf* : paraphernalia
parafina *nf* : paraffin
parafrasear *vt* : paraphrase — **paráfrasis** *nfs & pl* : paraphrase
paraguas *nms & pl* : umbrella
paraguayo, -ya *adj* : Paraguayan
paraíso *nm* : paradise
paralelo, -la *adj* : parallel — **paralelo** *nm* : parallel — **paralelismo** *nm* : similarity
parálisis *nfs & pl* : paralysis — **paralítico, -ca** *adj* : paralytic — **paralizar** {21} *vt* : paralyze
parámetro *nm* : parameter
páramo *nm* : barren plateau
parangón *nm, pl* **-gones** 1 : comparison 2 **sin ~** : matchless
paraninfo *nm* : auditorium, hall
paranoia *nf* : paranoia — **paranoico, -ca** *adj & n* : paranoid
parapeto *nm* : parapet, rampart
parapléjico, -ca *adj & n* : paraplegic
parar *vt* 1 : stop 2 *Lat* : stand, prop — *vi* 1 : stop 2 **ir a ~** : end up, wind up — **pararse** *vr* 1 : stop 2 *Lat* : stand up
pararrayos *nms & pl* : lightning rod
parásito, -ta *adj* : parasitic — **parásito** *nm* : parasite
parasol *nm* : parasol

parcela *nf* : parcel, tract (of land) — **parcelar** *vt* : parcel (up)

parche *nm* : patch

parcial *adj* **1** : partial **2 a tiempo ~** : part-time — **parcialidad** *nf* : partiality, bias

parco, -ca *adj* : sparing, frugal

pardo, -da *adj* : brownish grey

parear *vt* : pair (up)

parecer {53} *vi* **1** : seem, look **2** ASEMEJARSE A : look like, seem like **3 me parece que** : I think that, in my opinion **4 ¿qué te parece?** : what do you think? **5 según parece** : apparently — **parecerse** *vr* **~ a** : resemble — **~** *nm* **1** : opinion **2** ASPECTO : appearance **3 al ~** : apparently — **parecido, -da** *adj* **1** : similar **2 bien parecido** : good-looking — **parecido** *nm* : resemblance, similarity

pared *nf* : wall

parejo, -ja *adj* **1** : even, smooth **2** SEMEJANTE : similar — **pareja** *nf* **1** : couple, pair **2** : partner (person)

parentela *nf* : relatives *pl*, kin — **parentesco** *nm* : relationship, kinship

paréntesis *nms & pl* **1** : parenthesis **2** DIGRESIÓN : digression **3 entre ~** : by the way

paria *nmf* : outcast

paridad *nf* : equality

pariente *nmf* : relative, relation

parir *vi* : give birth, have a baby — *vt* : give birth to

parking *nm* : parking lot

parlamentar *vi* : discuss — **parlamentario, -ria** *adj* : parliamentary — **~** *n* : member of parliament — **parlamento** *nm* : parliament

parlanchín, -china *adj, mpl* **-chines** : talkative, chatty — **~** *n* : chatterbox

parlotear *vi fam* : chatter — **parloteo** *nm fam* : chatter

paro *nm* **1** : stoppage, shutdown **2** DESEMPLEO : unemployment **3** *Lat* : strike **4 ~ cardíaco** : cardiac arrest

parodia *nf* : parody — **parodiar** *vt* : parody

párpado *nm* : eyelid — **parpadear** *vi* **1** : blink **2** : flicker (of light), twinkle (of stars) — **parpadeo** *nm* **1** : blink **2** : flicker (of light), twinkling (of stars)

parque *nm* **1** : park **2 ~ de atracciones** : amusement park

parqué *nm* : parquet

parquear *vt Lat* : park

parquedad *nf* : frugality, moderation

parquímetro *nm* : parking meter

parra *nf* : grapevine

párrafo *nm* : paragraph

parranda *nf fam* : party, spree

parrilla *nf* **1** : broiler, grill **2** : grate (of a chimney, etc.) — **parrillada** *nf* : barbecue

párroco *nm* : parish priest — **parroquia** *nf* **1** : parish **2** : parish church — **parroquial** *adj* : parochial — **parroquiano, -na** *nm* **1** : parishioner **2** CLIENTE : customer

parsimonia *nf* **1** : calm **2** FRUGALIDAD : thrift — **parsimonioso, -sa** *adj* **1** : calm, unhurried **2** FRUGAL : thrifty

parte *nf* **1** : part **2** PORCIÓN : share **3** LADO : side **4** : party (in negotiations, etc.) **5 de ~ de** : on behalf of **6 ¿de ~ de quién?** : who is speaking? **7 en alguna ~** : somewhere **8 en todas ~s** : everywhere **9 tomar ~** : take part — **~** *nm* **1** : report **2 ~ meteorológico** : weather forecast

partero, -ra *n* : midwife

partición *nf, pl* **-ciones** : division, sharing

participar *vi* **1** : participate, take part **2 ~ en** : have a share in — *vt* : notify — **participación** *nf, pl* **-ciones** **1** : participation **2** : share, interest (in a fund, etc.) **3** NOTICIA : notice — **participante** *adj* : participating — **~** *nmf* : participant — **partícipe** *nmf* : participant

participio *nm* : participle

partícula *nf* : particle

particular *adj* **1** : particular **2** PRIVADO : private — **~** *nm* **1** : matter **2** PERSONA : individual — **particularidad** *nf* : peculiarity — **particularizar** {21} *vt* : distinguish, characterize — *vi* : go into details

partir *vt* **1** : split, divide **2** ROMPER : break, crack **3** REPARTIR : share (out) — *vi* **1** : depart **2 ~ de** : start from **3 a ~ de** : as of, from — **partirse** *vr* **1** : split (open) **2** RAJARSE : crack — **partida** *nf* **1** : departure **2** : entry, item (in a register, etc.) **3** JUEGO : game **4** : group (of persons) **5 mala ~** : dirty trick **6 ~ de nacimiento** : birth certificate — **partidario, -ria** *n* : follower, supporter — **partido** *nm* **1** : (political) party **2** : game, match (in sports) **3** PARTIDARIOS : following **4 sacar ~ de** : make the most of

partitura *nf* : (musical) score

parto *nm* **1** : childbirth **2 estar de ~** : be in labor

parvulario *nm* : nursery school

pasa *nf* **1** : raisin **2 ~ de Corinto** : currant

pasable *adj* : passable

pasada *nf* **1** : pass, wipe, coat (of paint, etc.) **2 de ~** : in passing **3 mala ~** : dirty trick — **pasadizo** *nm* : corridor — **pasado, -da** *adj* **1** : past **2** PODRIDO : bad, spoiled **3** ANTICUADO : out-of-date **4 el año pasado** : last year — **pasado** *nm* : past

pasador *nm* **1** CERROJO : bolt **2** : barrette (for the hair)

pasaje *nm* **1** : passage **2** BILLETE : ticket, fare **3** PASILLO : passageway **4** PASAJEROS : passengers *pl* — **pasajero, -ra** *adj* : passing — **~** *n* : passenger

pasamanos *nms & pl* : handrail, banister
pasaporte *nm* : passport
pasar *vi* **1** : pass, go (by) **2** ENTRAR : come in **3** SUCEDER : happen **4** TERMINARSE : be over, end **5** ~ **de** : exceed **6** ¿**qué pasa?** : what's the matter? — *vt* **1** : pass **2** : spend (time) **3** CRUZAR : cross **4** TOLERAR : tolerate **5** SUFRIR : go through, suffer **6** : show (a movie, etc.) **7** **pasarlo bien** : have a good time **8** ~ **por alto** : overlook, omit — **pasarse** *vr* **1** : pass, go away **2** ESTROPEARSE : spoil, go bad **3** OLVIDARSE : slip one's mind **4** EXCEDERSE : go too far
pasarela *nf* **1** : footbridge **2** : gangway (on a ship)
pasatiempo *nm* : pastime, hobby
Pascua *nf* **1** : Easter (Christian feast) **2** : Passover (Jewish feast) **3** NAVIDAD : Christmas
pase *nm* : pass
pasear *vi* : take a walk, go for a ride — *vt* **1** : take for a walk **2** EXHIBIR : parade, show off — **pasearse** *vr* : go for a walk, go for a ride — **paseo** *nm* **1** : walk, ride **2** *Lat* : outing
pasillo *nm* : passage, corridor
pasión *nf, pl* **-siones** : passion
pasivo, -va *adj* : passive — **pasivo** *nm* : liabilities *pl*
pasmar *vt* : astonish, amaze — **pasmarse** *vr* : be astonished — **pasmado, -da** *adj* : stunned, flabbergasted — **pasmo** *nm* : astonishment — **pasmoso, -sa** *adj* : astonishing
paso¹, -sa *adj* : dried (of fruit)
paso² *nm* **1** : step **2** HUELLA : footprint **3** RITMO : pace **4** CRUCE : crossing **5** PASAJE : passage, way through **6** : (mountain) pass **7** **de** ~ : in passing
pasta *nf* **1** : paste **2** MASA : dough **3** *or* ~**s** : pasta **4** ~ **de dientes** *or* ~ **dentífrica** : toothpaste
pastar *v* : graze
pastel *nm* **1** : cake **2** EMPANADA : pie **3** : pastel (crayon) — **pastelería** *nf* : pastry shop
pasteurizar {21} *vt* : pasteurize
pastilla *nf* **1** : pill, tablet **2** : bar (of chocolate, soap, etc.) **3** ~ **para la tos** : lozenge, cough drop
pasto *nm* **1** : pasture **2** *Lat* : grass, lawn — **pastor, -tora** *n* **1** : shepherd **2** : pastor (in religion) — **pastoral** *adj* : pastoral
pata *nf* **1** : paw, leg (of an animal) **2** : foot, leg (of furniture) **3** **meter la** ~ *fam* : put one's foot in it — **patada** *nf* **1** : kick **2** : stamp (of the foot) — **patalear** *vi* **1** : kick **2** : stamp (one's feet)
patata *nf Spain* : potato
patear *vt* : kick — *vi* **1** : kick **2** : stamp (one's feet)

patentar *vt* : patent — **patente** *adj* : obvious, patent — ~ *nf* : patent
paternal *adj* : fatherly, paternal — **paternidad** *nf* **1** : fatherhood **2** : paternity (in law) — **paterno, -na** *adj* : paternal
patético, -ca *adj* : pathetic, moving
patillas *nfpl* : sideburns
patinar *vi* **1** : skate **2** RESBALAR : slip, slide — **patín** *nm, pl* **-tines** : skate — **patinador, -dora** *n* : skater — **patinaje** *nm* : skating — **patinazo** *nm* **1** : skid **2** *fam* : blunder — **patinete** *nm* : scooter
patio *nm* **1** : courtyard, patio **2** *or* ~ **de recreo** : playground
pato, -ta *n* **1** : duck **2** **pagar el pato** *fam* : take the blame — **patito, -ta** *n* : duckling
patología *nf* : pathology — **patológico, -ca** *adj* : pathological
patraña *nf* : hoax
patria *nf* : native land
patriarca *nm* : patriarch
patrimonio *nm* **1** : inheritance **2** : (historical or cultural) heritage
patriota *adj* : patriotic — ~ *nmf* : patriot — **patriótico, -ca** *adj* : patriotic — **patriotismo** *nm* : patriotism
patrocinador, -dora *n* : sponsor — **patrocinar** *vt* : sponsor — **patrocinio** *nm* : sponsorship
patrón, -trona *n, mpl* **-trones** **1** : patron **2** JEFE : boss **3** : landlord, landlady *f* (of a boarding house, etc.) — **patrón** *nm, pl* **-trones** : pattern (in sewing) — **patronato** *nm* **1** : patronage **2** FUNDACIÓN : foundation, trust
patrulla *nf* **1** : patrol **2** : (police) cruiser — **patrullar** *v* : patrol
paulatino, -na *adj* : gradual
pausa *nf* : pause, break — **pausado, -da** *adj* : slow, deliberate
pauta *nf* : guideline
pavimento *nm* : pavement — **pavimentar** *vt* : pave
pavo, -va *n* **1** : turkey **2** **pavo real** : peacock
pavonearse *vr* : strut, swagger
pavor *nm* : dread, terror — **pavoroso, -sa** *adj* : terrifying
payaso, -sa *n* : clown — **payasada** *nf* : antic, buffoonery — **payasear** *vi Lat fam* : clown (around)
paz *nf, pl* **paces** **1** : peace **2** **dejar en** ~ : leave alone **3** **hacer las paces** : make up, reconcile
peaje *nm* : toll
peatón *nm, pl* **-tones** : pedestrian
peca *nf* : freckle
pecado *nm* : sin — **pecador, -dora** *adj* : sinful — ~ *n* : sinner — **pecaminoso, -sa** *adj* : sinful — **pecar** {72} *vi* : sin
pecera *nf* : fishbowl, fish tank

pecho *nm* **1** : chest **2** MAMA : breast **3** CORAZÓN : heart, courage **4 dar el ~** : breastfeed **5 tomar a ~** : take to heart — **pechuga** *nf* : breast (of fowl)
pecoso, -sa *adj* : freckled
pectoral *adj* : pectoral
peculiar *adj* **I** : particular **2** RARO : peculiar, odd — **peculiaridad** *nf* : peculiarity
pedagogía *nf* : education, pedagogy — **pedagogo, -ga** *n* : educator, teacher
pedal *nm* : pedal — **pedalear** *vi* : pedal
pedante *adj* : pedantic, pompous
pedazo *nm* **1** : piece, bit **2 hacerse ~s** : fall to pieces
pedernal *nm* : flint
pedestal *nm* : pedestal
pediatra *nmf* : pediatrician
pedigrí *nm* : pedigree
pedir {54} *vt* **1** : ask for, request **2** : order (food, merchandise, etc.) — *vi* **1** : ask **2 ~ prestado** : borrow — **pedido** *nm* **1** : order **2 hacer un ~** : place an order
pedregoso, -sa *adj* : rocky, stony
pedrería *nf* : precious stones *pl*
pegar {52} *vt* **1** : stick, glue, paste **2** : sew on (a button, etc.) **3** JUNTAR : bring together **4** GOLPEAR : hit, strike **5** PROPINAR : deal (a blow, etc.) **6** : transmit (an illness) **7 ~ un grito** : let out a scream — *vi* **1** : adhere, stick **2** GOLPEAR : hit — **pegarse** *vr* **1** : hit oneself, hit each other **2** ADHERIRSE : stick, adhere **3** CONTAGIARSE : be transmitted — **pegadizo, -za** *adj* : catchy **2** CONTAGIOSO : contagious — **pegajoso, -sa** *adj* **1** : sticky **2** *Lat* : catchy — **pegamento** *nm* : glue
peinar *vt* : comb — **peinarse** *vr* : comb one's hair — **peinado** *nm* : hairstyle, hairdo — **peine** *nm* : comb — **peineta** *nf* : ornamental comb
pelado, -da *adj* **1** : shorn, hairless **2** : peeled (of fruit, etc.) **3** *fam* : bare **4** *fam* : broke, penniless
pelaje *nm* : coat (of an animal), fur
pelar *vt* **1** : cut the hair of (a person) **2** MONDAR : peel (fruit) **3** : pluck (a chicken, etc.), skin (an animal) — **pelarse** *vr* **1** : peel **2** *fam* : get a haircut
peldaño *nm* **1** : step (of stairs) **2** : rung (of a ladder)
pelear *vi* **1** : fight **2** DISCUTIR : quarrel — **pelearse** *vr* : have a fight — **pelea** *nf* **1** : fight **2** DISCUSIÓN : quarrel
peletería *nf* : fur shop
peliagudo, -da *adj* : tricky, difficult
pelícano *nm* : pelican
película *nf* : movie, film
peligro *nm* **1** : danger **2** RIESGO : risk — **peligroso, -sa** *adj* : dangerous

pelirrojo, -ja *adj* : red-haired — **~** *n* : redhead
pellejo *nm* : skin, hide
pellizcar {72} *vt* : pinch — **pellizco** *nm* : pinch
pelo *nm* **1** : hair **2** : coat, fur (of an animal) **3** : pile, nap (of fabric) **4 con ~s y señales** : in great detail **5 no tener ~ en la lengua** *fam* : not to mince words **6 tomar el ~ a algn** *fam* : pull someone's leg — **pelón, -lona** *adj fam, mpl* **-lones** : bald
pelota *nf* : ball
pelotón *nm, pl* **-tones** : squad, detachment
peltre *nm* : pewter
peluca *nf* : wig
peluche *nm* **1** : plush **2 oso de ~** : teddy bear
peludo, -da *adj* : hairy, furry
peluquería *nf* : hairdresser's, barber shop — **peluquero, -ra** *n* : barber, hairdresser
pelusa *nf* : fuzz, lint
pelvis *nfs & pl* : pelvis
pena *nf* **1** : penalty **2** TRISTEZA : sorrow **3** DOLOR : suffering, pain **4** *Lat* : embarrassment **5 a duras ~s** : with great difficulty **6 ¡qué ~!** : what a shame! **7 valer la ~** : be worthwhile
penacho *nm* **1** : crest, tuft **2** : plume (ornament)
penal *adj* : penal — **~** *nm* : prison, penitentiary — **penalidad** *nf* **1** : hardship **2** : penalty (in law) — **penalizar** {21} *vt* : penalize
penalty *nm* : penalty (in sports)
penar *vt* : punish — *vi* : suffer
pendenciero, -ra *adj* : quarrelsome
pender *vi* : hang — **pendiente** *adj* **1** : pending **2 estar ~ de** : be watching out for — **~** *nf* : slope — **~** *nm Spain* : earring
pendón *nm, pl* **-dones** : banner
péndulo *nm* : pendulum
pene *nm* : penis
penetrar *vi* **1** : penetrate **2 ~ en** : go into — *vt* **1** : penetrate **2** : pierce (one's heart, etc.) **3** ENTENDER : fathom, grasp — **penetración** *nf, pl* **-ciones** **1** : penetration **2** PERSPICACIA : insight — **penetrante** *adj* **1** : penetrating **2** : sharp (of odors, etc.), piercing (of sounds) **3** : deep (of a wound, etc.)
penicilina *nf* : penicillin
península *nf* : peninsula — **peninsular** *adj* : peninsular
penitencia *nf* **1** : penitence **2** CASTIGO : penance — **penitenciaría** *nf* : penitentiary — **penitente** *adj & nmf* : penitent
penoso, -sa *adj* **1** : painful, distressing **2** TRABAJOSO : difficult **3** *Lat* : shy
pensar {55} *vi* **1** : think **2 ~ en** : think about — *vt* **1** : think **2** CONSIDERAR : think about **3 ~ hacer algo** : intend to do sth

— **pensador, -dora** *n* : thinker — **pensamiento** *nm* **1** : thought **2** : pansy (flower) — **pensativo, -va** *adj* : pensive, thoughtful

pensión *nf, pl* **-siones 1** : boarding house **2** : (retirement) pension **3** ~ **alimenticia** : alimony — **pensionista** *nmf* **1** : lodger **2** JUBILADO : retiree

pentágono *nm* : pentagon

pentagrama *nm* : staff (in music)

penúltimo, -ma *adj* : next to last, penultimate

penumbra *nf* : half-light

penuria *nf* : dearth, shortage

peña *nf* : rock, crag — **peñasco** *nm* : crag, large rock — **peñón** *nm, pl* **-ñones** : craggy rock

peón *nm, pl* **peones 1** : laborer, peon **2** : pawn (in chess)

peonía *nf* : peony

peor *adv* **1** (*comparative of* **mal**) : worse **2** (*superlative of* **mal**) : worst — ~ *adj* **1** (*comparative of* **malo**) : worse **2** (*superlative of* **malo**) : worst

pepino *nm* : cucumber — **pepinillo** *nm* : pickle, gherkin

pepita *nf* **1** : seed, pip **2** : nugget (of gold, etc.)

pequeño, -ña *adj* : small, little — **pequeñez** *nf, pl* **-ñeces 1** : smallness **2** NIMIEDAD : trifle

pera *nf* : pear — **peral** *nm* : pear tree

percance *nm* : mishap, setback

percatarse *vr* ~ **de** : notice

percepción *nf, pl* **-ciones** : perception — **perceptible** *adj* : perceptible

percha *nf* **1** : perch (for birds) **2** : (coat) hanger **3** : coatrack (on a wall)

percibir *vt* **1** : perceive **2** : receive (a salary, etc.)

percusión *nf, pl* **-siones** : percussion

perder {56} *vt* **1** : lose **2** : miss (an opportunity, etc.) **3** DESPERDICIAR : waste (time) — *vi* : lose — **perderse** *vr* **1** : get lost **2** DESAPARECER : disappear **3** DESPERDICIARSE : be wasted — **perdedor, -dora** *n* : loser — **pérdida** *nf* **1** : loss **2** ESCAPE : leak **3** ~ **de tiempo** : waste of time — **perdido, -da** *adj* **1** : lost **2 un caso perdido** *fam* : a hopeless case

perdigón *nm, pl* **-gones** : shot, pellet

perdiz *nf, pl* **-dices** : partridge

perdón *nm, pl* **-dones** : forgiveness, pardon — **perdón** *interj* : sorry! — **perdonar** *vt* **1** DISCULPAR : forgive **2** : pardon (in law)

perdurar *vi* : last, endure — **perdurable** *adj* : lasting

perecer {53} *vi* : perish, die — **perecedero, -ra** *adj* : perishable

peregrinación *nf, pl* **-ciones** *or* **peregrinaje** *nm* : pilgrimage — **peregrino, -na** *adj*

1 : migratory **2** RARO : unusual, odd — ~ *n* : pilgrim

perejil *nm* : parsley

perenne *adj* & *nm* : perennial

pereza *nf* : laziness — **perezoso, -sa** *adj* : lazy

perfección *nf, pl* **-ciones** : perfection — **perfeccionar** *vt* **1** : perfect **2** MEJORAR : improve — **perfeccionista** *nmf* : perfectionist — **perfecto, -ta** *adj* : perfect

perfidia *nf* : treachery — **pérfido, -da** *adj* : treacherous

perfil *nm* **1** : profile **2** CONTORNO : outline **3** ~**es** *nmpl* RASGOS : features — **perfilar** *vt* : outline — **perfilarse** *vr* **1** : be outlined **2** CONCRETARSE : take shape

perforar *vt* **1** : perforate **2** : drill, bore (a hole) — **perforación** *nf, pl* **-ciones** : perforation — **perforadora** *nf* : (paper) punch

perfume *nm* : perfume, scent — **perfumar** *vt* : perfume — **perfumarse** *vr* : put perfume on

pergamino *nm* : parchment

pericia *nf* : skill

periferia *nf* : periphery, outskirts (of a city, etc.) — **periférico, -ca** *adj* : peripheral

perilla *nf* **1** : goatee **2** *Lat* : knob **3 venir de** ~**s** *fam* : come in handy

perímetro *nm* : perimeter

periódico, -ca *adj* : periodic — **periódico** *nm* : newspaper — **periodismo** *nm* : journalism — **periodista** *nmf* : journalist

período *or* **periodo** *nm* : period

periquito *nm* : parakeet

periscopio *nm* : periscope

perito, -ta *adj* & *n* : expert

perjudicar {72} *vt* : harm, damage — **perjudicial** *adj* : harmful — **perjuicio** *nm* **1** : harm, damage **2 en** ~ **de** : to the detriment of

perjurar *vi* : perjure oneself — **perjurio** *nm* : perjury

perla *nf* **1** : pearl **2 de** ~**s** *fam* : great, just fine

permanecer {53} *vi* : remain — **permanencia** *nf* **1** : permanence **2** : stay, staying (in a place) — **permanente** *adj* : permanent — ~ *nf* : permanent (wave)

permeable *adj* : permeable

permitir *vt* **1** : permit, allow **2 ¿me permite?** : may I? — **permitirse** *vr* : allow oneself — **permisible** *adj* : permissible, allowable — **permisivo, -va** *adj* : permissive — **permiso** *nm* **1** : permission **2** : permit, license (document) **3** : leave (in the military) **4 con** ~ : excuse me

permuta *nf* : exchange

pernicioso, -sa *adj* : pernicious, destructive

pero *conj* : but — ~ *nm* **1** : fault **2** REPARO : objection

perorar *vi* : make a speech — **perorata** *nf* : (long-winded) speech
perpendicular *adj & nf* : perpendicular
perpetrar *vt* : perpetrate
perpetuar {3} *vt* : perpetuate — **perpetuo, -tua** *adj* : perpetual
perplejo, -ja *adj* : perplexed — **perplejidad** *nf* : perplexity
perro, -rra *n* 1 : dog, bitch *f* 2 **perro caliente** : hot dog — **perrera** *nf* : kennel
perseguir {75} *vt* 1 : pursue, chase 2 ACOSAR : persecute — **persecución** *nf, pl* -ciones 1 : pursuit, chase 2 ACOSO : persecution
perseverar *vi* : persevere — **perseverancia** *nf* : perseverance
persiana *nf* : (venetian) blind
persistir *vi* : persist — **persistencia** *nf* : persistence — **persistente** *adj* : persistent
persona *nf* : person — **personaje** *nm* 1 : character (in literature, etc.) 2 : important person, celebrity — **personal** *adj* : personal — ~ *nm* : personnel, staff — **personalidad** *nf* : personality — **personificar** {72} *vi* : personify
perspectiva *nf* 1 : perspective 2 VISTA : view 3 POSIBILIDAD : prospect, outlook
perspicacia *nf* : shrewdness, insight — **perspicaz** *adj, pl* -caces : shrewd, discerning
persuadir *vt* : persuade — **persuadirse** *vr* : become convinced — **persuasión** *nf, pl* -siones : persuasion — **persuasivo, -va** *adj* : persuasive
pertenecer {53} *vi* ~ a : belong to — **perteneciente** *adj* ~ a : belonging to — **pertenencia** *nf* 1 : ownership 2 ~s *nfpl* : belongings
pertinaz *adj, pl* -naces 1 OBSTINADO : obstinate 2 PERSISTENTE : persistent
pertinente *adj* : pertinent, relevant — **pertinencia** *nf* : relevance
perturbar *vt* : disturb — **perturbación** *nf, pl* -ciones : disturbance
peruano, -na *adj* : Peruvian
pervertir {76} *vt* : pervert — **perversión** *nf, pl* -siones : perversion — **perverso, -sa** *adj* : perverse — **pervertido, -da** *adj* : perverted, depraved — ~ *n* : pervert
pesa *nf* 1 : weight 2 ~s : weights (in sports) — **pesadez** *nf, pl* -deces 1 : heaviness 2 *fam* : tediousness, drag
pesadilla *nf* : nightmare
pesado, -da *adj* 1 : heavy 2 LENTO : sluggish 3 MOLESTO : annoying 4 ABURRIDO : tedious 5 DURO : tough, difficult — ~ *n fam* : bore, pest — **pesadumbre** *nf* : grief, sorrow
pésame *nm* : condolences *pl*
pesar *vt* : weigh — *vi* 1 : weigh, be heavy 2 INFLUIR : carry weight 3 **pese a** : despite — ~ *nm* 1 : sorrow, grief 2 REMORDIMIENTO : remorse 3 **a ~ de** : in spite of
pescado *nm* : fish — **pesca** *nf* 1 : fishing 2 PECES : fish *pl*, catch 3 **ir de ~** : go fishing — **pescadería** *nf* : fish market — **pescador, -dora** *n, mpl* -dores : fisherman — **pescar** {72} *vt* 1 : fish for 2 *fam* : catch (a cold, etc.) 3 *fam* : catch hold of, nab — *vi* : fish
pescuezo *nm* : neck (of an animal)
pese a → pesar
pesebre *nm* : manger
pesero *nm Lat* : minibus
peseta *nf* : peseta
pesimismo *nm* : pessimism — **pesimista** *adj* : pessimistic — ~ *nmf* : pessimist
pésimo, -ma *adj* : awful
peso *nm* 1 : weight 2 CARGA : burden 3 : peso (currency) 4 ~ **pesado** : heavyweight
pesquero, -ra *adj* : fishing
pesquisa *nf* : inquiry
pestaña *nf* : eyelash — **pestañear** *vi* : blink — **pestañeo** *nm* : blink
peste *nm* 1 : plague 2 *fam* : stench, stink 3 *Lat fam* : cold, bug — **pesticida** *nm* : pesticide — **pestilencia** *nf* 1 : stench 2 PLAGA : pestilence
pestillo *nm* : bolt, latch
petaca *nf Lat* : suitcase
pétalo *nm* : petal
petardo *nm* : firecracker
petición *nf, pl* -ciones : petition, request
petirrojo *nm* : robin
petrificar {72} *vt* : petrify
petróleo *nm* : oil, petroleum — **petrolero, -ra** *adj* : oil — **petrolero** *nm* : oil tanker
petulante *adj* : insolent, arrogant
peyorativo, -va *adj* : pejorative
pez *nm, pl* **peces** 1 : fish 2 ~ **de colores** : goldfish 3 ~ **espada** : swordfish 4 ~ **gordo** *fam* : big shot
pezón *nm, pl* -zones : nipple
pezuña *nf* : hoof
piadoso, -sa *adj* 1 : compassionate 2 DEVOTO : pious, devout
piano *nm* : piano — **pianista** *nmf* : pianist, piano player
piar {85} *vi* : chirp, tweet
pibe, -ba *n Lat fam* : kid, child
pica *nf* 1 : pike, lance 2 : spade (in playing cards)
picado, -da *adj* 1 : perforated 2 : minced, chopped (of meat, etc.) 3 : decayed (of teeth) 4 : choppy (of the sea) 5 *fam* : annoyed — **picada** *nf* 1 : bite, sting 2 *Lat* : sharp descent — **picadillo** *nm* : minced meat — **picadura** *nf* 1 : sting, bite 2 : (moth) hole

picante *adj* : hot, spicy

picaporte *nm* **1** : door handle **2** ALDABA : door knocker **3** PESTILLO : latch

picar {72} *vt* **1** : sting, bite **2** : peck at, nibble on (food) **3** PERFORAR : prick, puncture **4** TRITURAR : chop, mince — *vi* **1** : bite, take the bait **2** ESCOCER : sting, itch **3** COMER : nibble **4** : be spicy (of food) — **picarse** *vr* **1** : get a cavity **2** ENFADARSE : take offense

picardía *nf* **1** : craftiness **2** TRAVESURA : prank — **picaresco, -ca** *adj* **1** : picaresque **2** TRAVIESO : roguish — **pícaro, -ra** *adj* **1** : mischievous **2** MALICIOSO : villainous — ~ *n* : rascal, scoundrel

picazón *nf, pl* **-zones** : itch

pichón, -chona *n, mpl* **-chones** : (young) pigeon

picnic *nm, pl* **-nics** : picnic

pico *nm* **1** : beak **2** CIMA : peak **3** PUNTA : (sharp) point **4** : pick, pickax (tool) **5 las siete y** ~ : a little after seven — **picotazo** *nm* : peck — **picotear** *vt* : peck — *vi fam* : nibble, pick — **picudo, -da** *adj* : pointy

pie *nm* **1** : foot (in anatomy) **2** : base, bottom, stem **3 al** ~ **de la letra** : word for word **4 dar** ~ **a** : give rise to **5 de** ~ : standing (up) **6 de** ~**s a cabeza** : from top to bottom

piedad *nf* **1** : pity, mercy **2** DEVOCIÓN : piety

piedra *nf* **1** : stone **2** : flint (of a lighter) **3** GRANIZO : hailstone **4** ~ **angular** : cornerstone **5** → **pómez**

piel *nf* **1** : skin **2** CUERO : leather **3** PELO : fur, pelt

pienso *nm* : feed, fodder

pierna *nf* : leg

pieza *nf* **1** : piece, part **2** *or* ~ **de teatro** : play **3** HABITACIÓN : room

pigmento *nm* : pigment — **pigmentación** *nf, pl* **-ciones** : pigmentation

pigmeo, -mea *adj* : pygmy

pijama *nm* : pajamas *pl*

pila *nf* **1** : battery **2** MONTÓN : pile **3** FREGADERO : sink **4** : basin (of a fountain, etc.)

pilar *nm* : pillar

píldora *nf* : pill

pillar *vt* **1** : catch **2** : get (a joke, etc.) — **pillaje** *nm* : pillage — **pillo, -lla** *adj* : crafty — ~ *n* : rascal, scoundrel

piloto *nmf* : pilot — **pilotar** *vt* : pilot

pimienta *nf* : pepper (condiment) — **pimiento** *nm* : pepper (fruit) — **pimentero** *nm* : pepper shaker — **pimentón** *nm, pl* **-tones** **1** : paprika **2** : cayenne pepper

pináculo *nm* : pinnacle

pincel *nm* : paintbrush

pinchar *vt* **1** : pierce, prick **2** : puncture (a tire, etc.) **3** INCITAR : goad — **pinchazo** *nm* **1** : prick **2** : puncture (of a tire, etc.)

pingüino *nm* : penguin

pino *nm* : pine (tree)

pintar *v* : paint — **pintarse** *vr* : put on makeup — **pinta** *nf* **1** : spot **2** : pint (measure) **3** *fam* : appearance — **pintada** *nf* : graffiti — **pinto, -ta** *adj* : speckled, spotted — **pintor, -tora** *n, mpl* **-tores** : painter — **pintoresco, -ca** *adj* : picturesque, quaint — **pintura** *nf* **1** : paint **2** CUADRO : painting

pinza *nf* **1** : clothespin **2** : claw, pincer (of a crab, etc.) **3** ~**s** *nfpl* : tweezers

pinzón *nm, pl* **-zones** : finch

piña *nf* **1** : pine cone **2** ANANÁS : pineapple

piñata *nf* : piñata

piñón *nm, pl* **-ñones** : pine nut

pío¹, pía *adj* **1** : pious **2** : piebald (of a horse)

pío² *nm* : peep, chirp

piojo *nm* : louse

pionero, -ra *n* : pioneer

pipa *nf* **1** : pipe (for smoking) **2** *Spain* : seed, pip

pipí *nm* : pee *fam* (**hacer pipí** to take a pee)

pique *nm* **1** : grudge **2** RIVALIDAD : rivalry **3 irse a** ~ : sink, founder

piqueta *nf* : pickax

piquete *nm* : picket (line) — **piquetear** *v* : picket

piragua *nf* : canoe

pirámide *nf* : pyramid

piraña *nf* : piranha

pirata *adj* : bootleg, pirated — ~ *nmf* : pirate — **piratear** *vt* **1** : bootleg, pirate **2** : hack into (a computer)

piropo *nm* : (flirtatious) compliment

pirueta *nf* : pirouette

pirulí *nm* : (cone-shaped) lollipop

pisada *nf* **1** : footstep **2** HUELLA : footprint

pisapapeles *nms & pl* : paperweight

pisar *vt* **1** : step on **2** HUMILLAR : walk all over, abuse — *vi* : step, tread

piscina *nf* **1** : swimming pool **2** : (fish) pond

piso *nm* **1** : floor, story **2** *Lat* : floor (of a room) **3** *Spain* : apartment

pisotear *vt* : trample (on)

pista *nf* **1** : trail, track **2** INDICIO : clue **3** ~ **de aterrizaje** : runway, airstrip **4** ~ **de baile** : dance floor **5** ~ **de hielo** : ice-skating rink

pistacho *nm* : pistachio

pistola *nf* **1** : pistol, gun **2** PULVERIZADOR : spray gun — **pistolera** *nf* : holster — **pistolero** *nm* : gunman

pistón *nm, pl* **-tones** : piston

pito *nm* **1** SILBATO : whistle **2** CLAXON

: horn — **pitar** *vi* **1** : blow a whistle **2** : beep, honk (of a horn) — *vt* : whistle at — **pitido** *nm* **1** : whistle, whistling **2** : beep (of a horn) — **pitillo** *nm fam* : cigarette

pitón *nm, pl* -**tones** *nm* : python

pitorro *nm* : spout

pivote *nm* : pivot

piyama *nmf Lat* : pajamas *pl*

pizarra *nf* **1** : slate **2** ENCERADO : blackboard — **pizarrón** *nm, pl* -**rrones** *Lat* : blackboard

pizca *nf* **1** : pinch (of salt) **2** ÁPICE : speck, tiny bit **3** *Lat* : harvest

pizza *nf* : pizza — **pizzería** *nf* : pizzeria

placa *nf* **1** : sheet, plate **2** INSCRIPCIÓN : plaque **3** : (police) badge

placenta *nf* : placenta

placer {57} *vt* : please — ~ *nm* : pleasure — **placentero, -ra** *adj* : pleasant, agreeable

plácido, -da *adj* : placid, calm

plaga *nf* **1** : plague **2** CALAMIDAD : disaster — **plagar** {52} *vt* : plague, infest

plagiar *vt* : plagiarize — **plagio** *nm* : plagiarism

plan *nm* **1** : plan **2 en ~ de** : as **3 no te pongas en ese ~** *fam* : don't be that way

plana *nf* **1** : page **2 en primera ~** : on the front page

plancha *nf* **1** : iron (for ironing) **2** : grill (for cooking) **3** LÁMINA : sheet, plate — **planchar** *v* : iron — **planchado** *nm* : ironing

planear *vt* : plan — *vi* : glide — **planeador** *nm* : glider

planeta *nm* : planet

planicie *nf* : plain

planificar {72} *vt* : plan — **planificación** *nf, pl* -**ciones** : planning

planilla *nf Lat* : list, roster

plano, -na *adj* : flat — **plano** *nm* **1** : map, plan **2** : plane (surface) **3** NIVEL : level **4 de ~** : flatly, outright **5 primer ~** : foreground, close-up (in photography)

planta *nf* **1** : plant **2** PISO : floor, story **3** : sole (of the foot) — **plantación** *nf, pl* -**ciones 1** : plantation **2** : (action of) planting — **plantar** *vt* **1** : plant **2** *fam* : deal, land — **plantarse** *vr* : stand firm

plantear *vt* **1** : expound, set forth **2** : raise (a question) **3** CAUSAR : create, pose (a problem) — **plantearse** *vr* : think about, consider

plantel *nm* **1** : staff, team **2** *Lat* : educational institution

plantilla *nf* **1** : insole **2** PATRÓN : pattern, template **3** : staff (of a business, etc.)

plasma *nm* : plasma

plástico, -ca *adj* : plastic — **plástico** *nm* : plastic

plata *nf* **1** : silver **2** *Lat fam* : money **3 ~ de ley** : sterling silver

plataforma *nf* **1** : platform **2 ~ petrolífera** : oil rig **3 ~ de lanzamiento** : launching pad

plátano *nm* **1** : banana **2** : plantain

platea *nf* : orchestra, pit (in a theater)

plateado, -da *adj* **1** : silver, silvery (color) **2** : silver-plated

platicar {72} *vi* : talk, chat — **plática** *nf* : chat, conversation

platija *nf* : flatfish, flounder

platillo *nm* **1** : saucer **2** CÍMBALO : cymbal **3** *Lat* : dish, course

platino *nm* : platinum

plato *nm* **1** : plate, dish **2** : course (of a meal) **3 ~ principal** : entrée

platónico, -ca *adj* : platonic

playa *nf* **1** : beach, seashore **2 ~ de estacionamiento** *Lat* : parking lot

plaza *nf* **1** : square, plaza **2** : seat (in transportation) **3** PUESTO : post, position **4** MERCADO : market, marketplace **5 ~ de toros** : bullring

plazo *nm* **1** : period, term **2** PAGO : installment **3 a largo ~** : long-term

plazoleta *or* **plazuela** *nf* : small square

pleamar *nf* : high tide

plebe *nf* : common people — **plebeyo, -ya** *adj & nm* : plebeian

plegar {49} *vt* : fold, bend — **plegarse** *vr* **1** : give in, yield **2** : jackknife (of a truck) — **plegable** *or* **plegadizo, -za** *adj* : folding, collapsible

plegaria *nf* : prayer

pleito *nm* **1** : lawsuit **2** *Lat* : dispute, fight

plenilunio *nm* : full moon

pleno, -na *adj* **1** : full, complete **2 en plena forma** : in top form **3 en pleno día** : in broad daylight — **plenitud** *nf* : fullness, abundance

pleuresía *nf* : pleurisy

pliego *nm* : sheet (of paper) — **pliegue** *nm* **1** : crease, fold **2** : pleat (in fabric)

plisar *vt* : pleat

plomería *nf Lat* : plumbing — **plomero, -ra** *n Lat* : plumber

plomo *nm* **1** : lead **2** FUSIBLE : fuse

pluma *nf* **1** : feather **2** : (fountain) pen — **plumaje** *nm* : plumage — **plumero** *nm* : feather duster — **plumilla** *nf* : nib — **plumón** *nm, pl* -**mones** : down

plural *adj & nm* : plural — **pluralidad** *nf* : plurality

pluriempleo *nm* **hacer ~** : have more than one job

plus *nm* : bonus

plusvalía *nf* : appreciation, capital gain

plutocracia *nf* : plutocracy

Plutón *nm* : Pluto

plutonio *nm* : plutonium

pluvial *adj* : rain

poblar {19} *vt* **1** : settle, colonize **2** HABI-
TAR : inhabit — **poblarse** *vr* : become
crowded — **población** *nf, pl* **-ciones 1**
: city, town, village **2** HABITANTES : population — **poblado, -da** *adj* **1** : populated **2**
: thick, bushy (of a beard, eyebrows, etc.)
— **poblado** *nm* : village
pobre *adj* **1** : poor **2** ¡~ de mí! : poor me!
— ~ *nmf* **1** : poor person **2** los ~s : the
poor **3** ¡pobre! : poor thing! — **pobreza** *nf*
: poverty
pocilga *nf* : pigsty
poción *nf, pl* **-ciones** *or* **pócima** *nf* : potion
poco, -ca *adj* **1** : little, not much, (a) few **2**
pocas veces : rarely — ~ *pron* **1** : little,
few **2 hace poco** : not long ago **3 poco a**
poco : bit by bit, gradually **4 por poco**
: nearly, just about **5 un poco** : a little, a bit
— **poco** *adv* : little, not much
podar *vt* : prune
podcast *nm, pl* **podcasts** : podcast
poder {58} *v aux* **1** : be able to, can **2** (*expressing possibility*) : might, may **3** (*expressing permission*) : can, may **4 ¿cómo**
puede ser? : how can it be? **5 ¿puedo**
pasar? : may I come in? — *vi* **1** : be possible **2** ~ **con** : cope with, manage **3 no**
puedo más : I've had enough — ~ *nm* **1**
: power **2** POSESIÓN : possession — **pode-**
río *nm* : power — **poderoso, -sa** *adj*
: powerful
podólogo, -ga *n* : chiropodist
podrido, -da *adj* : rotten
poema *nm* : poem — **poesía** *nf* **1** : poetry **2**
POEMA : poem — **poeta** *nmf* : poet — **poé-**
tico, -ca *adj* : poetic
póker *nm* → **póquer**
polaco, -ca *adj* : Polish
polar *adj* : polar — **polarizar** {21} *vt* : polarize
polea *nf* : pulley
polémica *nf* : controversy — **polémico, -ca**
adj : controversial — **polemizar** *vt* : argue
polen *nm, pl* **pólenes** : pollen
policía *nf* : police — ~ *nmf* : police officer,
policeman *m*, policewoman *f* — **policíaco,**
-ca *adj* **1** : police **2 novela policíaca** : detective story
poliéster *nm* : polyester
poligamia *nf* : polygamy — **polígamo, -ma**
n : polygamist
polígono *nm* : polygon
polilla *nf* : moth
polio *or* **poliomielitis** *nf* : polio, poliomyelitis
politécnico, -ca *adj* : polytechnic
política *nf* **1** : politics **2** POSTURA : policy
— **político, -ca** *adj* **1** : political **2 her-**
mano político : brother-in-law — ~ *n*
: politician

póliza *nf or* ~ **de seguros** : insurance policy
polizón *nm, pl* **-zones** : stowaway
pollo, -lla *n* **1** : chicken, chick **2** : chicken
(for cooking) — **pollera** *nf Lat* : skirt — **po-**
llería *nf* : poultry shop — **pollito, -ta** *n*
: chick
polo *nm* **1** : pole **2** : polo (sport) **3** ~ **norte**
: North Pole
poltrona *nf* : easy chair
polución *nf, pl* **-ciones** : pollution
polvo *nm* **1** : powder **2** SUCIEDAD : dust **3**
~s *nmpl* : face powder **4 hacer** ~ *fam*
: crush, shatter — **polvareda** *nf* : cloud of
dust — **polvera** *nf* : compact (for powder)
— **pólvora** *nf* : gunpowder — **polvoriento,**
-ta *adj* : dusty
pomada *nf* : ointment
pomelo *nm* : grapefruit
pómez *nm or* **piedra** ~ *nf* : pumice
pomo *nm* : knob, doorknob
pompa *nf* **1** : (soap) bubble **2** ESPLENDOR
: pomp **3** ~s **fúnebres** : funeral — **pom-**
poso, -sa *adj* **1** : pompous **2** ESPLÉNDIDO
: splendid
pómulo *nm* : cheekbone
ponchar *vt Lat* : puncture — **ponchadura** *nf*
Lat : puncture
ponche *nm* : punch (drink)
poncho *nm* : poncho
ponderar *vt* **1** : consider **2** ALABAR : speak
highly of
poner {60} *vt* **1** : put **2** AGREGAR : add **3**
CONTRIBUIR : contribute **4** SUPONER : suppose **5** DISPONER : arrange, set out **6** : give
(a name), call **7** ENCENDER : turn on **8** ES-
TABLECER : set up, establish **9** : lay (eggs)
— *vi* : lay eggs — **ponerse** *vr* **1** : move
(into a position) **2** : put on (clothing, etc.) **3**
: set (of the sun) **4** ~ **furioso** : become
angry
poniente *nm* **1** OCCIDENTE : west **2** : west
wind
pontífice *nm* : pontiff
pontón *nm, pl* **-tones** : pontoon
ponzoña *nf* : poison, venom
popa *nf* **1** : stern **2 a** ~ : astern
popelín *nm, pl* **-lines** : poplin
popote *nm Lat* : (drinking) straw
populacho *nm* : rabble, masses *pl*
popular *adj* **1** : popular **2** : colloquial (of
language) — **popularidad** *nf* : popularity
— **popularizar** {21} *vt* : popularize — **po-**
puloso, -sa *adj* : populous
póquer *nm* : poker (card game)
por *prep* **1** : for **2** (*indicating an approximate time*) : around, during **3** (*indicating
an approximate place*) : around, about **4** A
TRAVÉS DE : through, along **5** A CAUSA DE
: because of **6** (*indicating rate or ratio*)

: per **7** *or* **~ medio de** : by means of **8**
: times (in mathematics) **9** SEGÚN : as for,
according to **10 estar ~** : be about to **11**
~ ciento : percent **12 ~ favor** : please
13 ~ lo tanto : therefore **14 ¿por qué?**
: why?

porcelana *nf* : porcelain, china
porcentaje *nm* : percentage
porción *nf, pl* **-ciones** : portion, piece
pordiosero, -ra *n* : beggar
porfiar {85} *vi* : insist — **porfiado, -da** *adj*
: obstinate, persistent
pormenor *nm* : detail
pornografía *nf* : pornography — **pornográfico, -ca** *adj* : pornographic
poro *nm* : pore — **poroso, -sa** *adj* : porous
poroto *nm Lat* : bean
porque *conj* **1** : because **2** *or* **por que** : in
order that — **porqué** *nm* : reason
porquería *nf* **1** SUCIEDAD : filth **2** : shoddy
thing, junk
porra *nf* : nightstick, club — **porrazo** *nm*
: blow, whack
portaaviones *nms & pl* : aircraft carrier
portada *nf* **1** : facade **2** : title page (of a
book), cover (of a magazine)
portador, -dora *n* : bearer
portaequipajes *nms & pl* : luggage rack
portafolio *or* **portafolios** *nm, pl* **-lios** **1**
: portfolio **2** MALETÍN : briefcase
portal *nm* **1** : doorway **2** VESTÍBULO : hall,
vestibule
portamonedas *nms & pl* : purse
portar *vt* : carry, bear — **portarse** *vr* : behave
portátil *adj* : portable
portaviones *nm* → **portaaviones**
portavoz *nmf, pl* **-voces** : spokesperson,
spokesman *m*, spokeswoman *f*
portazo *nm* **dar un ~** : slam the door
porte *nm* **1** : transport, freight **2** ASPECTO
: bearing, appearance **3 ~ pagado** : postage paid
portento *nm* : marvel, wonder — **porten-
toso, -sa** *adj* : marvelous
porteño, -ña *adj* : of or from Buenos Aires
portería *nf* **1** : superintendent's office **2**
: goal, goalposts *pl* (in sports) — **portero,
-ra** *n* **1** : goalkeeper, goalie **2** CONSERJE
: janitor, superintendent
portezuela *nf* : door (of an automobile)
pórtico *nm* : portico
portilla *nf* : porthole
portugués, -guesa *adj, mpl* **-gueses** : Portuguese — **portugués** *nm* : Portuguese
(language)
porvenir *nm* : future
pos: en ~ de *adv phr* : in pursuit of
posada *nf* : inn
posaderas *nfpl fam* : backside, bottom

posar *vi* : pose — *vt* : place, lay — **posarse**
vr : settle, rest
posavasos *nms & pl* : coaster
posdata *nf* : postscript
pose *nf* : pose
poseer {20} *vt* : possess, own — **poseedor,
-dora** *n* : possessor, owner — **poseído, -da**
adj : possessed — **posesión** *nf, pl* **-siones**
: possession — **posesionarse** *vr* **~ de**
: take possession of, take over — **posesivo,
-va** *adj* : possessive
posguerra *nf* : postwar period
posibilidad *nf* : possibility — **posibilitar** *vt*
: make possible — **posible** *adj* **1** : possible
2 de ser ~ : if possible
posición *nf, pl* **-ciones** : position — **posi-
cionar** *vt* : position — **posicionarse** *vr*
: take a stand
positivo, -va *adj* : positive
poso *nm* : sediment, (coffee) grounds
posponer {60} *vt* **1** : postpone **2** RELEGAR
: put behind, subordinate
postal *adj* : postal — **~** *nf* : postcard
postdata → **posdata**
poste *nm* : post, pole
póster *nm, pl* **-ters** : poster
postergar {52} *vt* **1** : pass over **2** APLAZAR
: postpone
posteridad *nf* : posterity — **posterior** *adj* **1**
: later, subsequent **2** TRASERO : back, rear
— **posteriormente** *adv* : subsequently,
later
postigo *nm* **1** : small door **2** CONTRAVEN-
TANA : shutter
postizo, -za *adj* : artificial, false
postrarse *vr* : prostrate oneself — **postrado, -da** *adj* : prostrate
postre *nm* : dessert
postular *vt* **1** : advance, propose **2** *Lat*
: nominate — **postulado** *nm* : postulate
póstumo, -ma *adj* : posthumous
postura *nf* : position, stance
potable *adj* : drinkable, potable
potaje *nm* : thick vegetable soup
potasio *nm* : potassium
pote *nm* : jar
potencia *nf* : power — **potencial** *adj & nm*
: potential — **potente** *adj* : powerful
potro, -tra *n* : colt *m*, filly *f* — **potro** *nm*
: horse (in gymnastics)
pozo *nm* **1** : well **2** : shaft (in a mine)
práctica *nf* **1** : practice **2 en la ~** : in practice — **practicable** *adj* : practicable, feasible — **practicante** *adj* : practicing — **~**
nmf : practitioner — **practicar** {72} *vt* **1**
: practice **2** REALIZAR : perform, carry out
— *vi* : practice — **práctico, -ca** *adj* : practical
pradera *nf* : grassland, prairie — **prado** *nm*
: meadow

pragmático, -ca *adj* : pragmatic
preámbulo *nm* : preamble
precario, -ria *adj* : precarious
precaución *nf, pl* **-ciones 1** : precaution **2**
PRUDENCIA : caution, care **3 con ~** : cautiously
precaver *vt* : guard against — **precavido, -da** *adj* : prudent, cautious
preceder *v* : precede — **precedencia** *nf*
: precedence, priority — **precedente** *adj*
: preceding, previous — **~** *nm* : precedent
precepto *nm* : precept
preciado, -da *adj* : prized, valuable — **preciarse** *vr* **~ de** : pride oneself on, boast about
precinto *nm* : seal
precio *nm* : price, cost — **preciosidad** *nf* **1**
VALOR : value **2** : beautiful thing — **precioso, -sa** *adj* **1** HERMOSO : beautiful **2**
VALIOSO : precious
precipicio *nm* : precipice
precipitar *vt* **1** : hasten, speed up **2** ARROJAR
: hurl — **precipitarse** *vr* **1** APRESURARSE
: rush **2** : act rashly **3** ARROJARSE : throw
oneself — **precipitación** *nf, pl* **-ciones 1**
: precipitation **2** PRISA : haste — **precipitadamente** *adv* : in a rush, hastily — **precipitado, -da** *adj* : hasty
preciso, -sa *adj* **1** : precise **2** NECESARIO
: necessary — **precisamente** *adv* : precisely, exactly — **precisar** *vt* **1** : specify,
determine **2** NECESITAR : require — **precisión** *nf, pl* **-siones 1** : precision **2** NECESIDAD : necessity
preconcebido *adj* : preconceived
precoz *adj, pl* **-coces 1** : early **2** : precocious (of children)
precursor, -sora *n* : forerunner
predecesor, -sora *n* : predecessor
predecir {11} *vt* : foretell, predict
predestinado, -da *adj* : predestined
predeterminar *vt* : predetermine
prédica *nf* : sermon
predicado *nm* : predicate
predicar {72} *v* : preach — **predicador, -dora** *n* : preacher
predicción *nf, pl* **-ciones 1** : prediction **2**
PRONÓSTICO : forecast
predilección *nf, pl* **-ciones** : preference —
predilecto, -ta *adj* : favorite
predisponer {60} *vt* : predispose — **predisposición** *nf, pl* **-ciones** : predisposition
predominar *vi* : predominate — **predominante** *adj* : predominant, prevailing — **predominio** *nm* : predominance
preeminente *adj* : preeminent
prefabricado, -da *adj* : prefabricated
prefacio *nm* : preface
preferir {76} *vt* : prefer — **preferencia** *nf* **1**
: preference **2 de ~** : preferably — **prefe-**

rente *adj* : preferential — **preferible** *adj*
: preferable — **preferido, -da** *adj* : favorite
prefijo *nm* **1** : prefix **2** *Spain* : area code
pregonar *vt* : proclaim, announce
pregunta *nf* **1** : question **2 hacer ~s** : ask
questions — **preguntar** *v* : ask — **preguntarse** *vr* : wonder
prehistórico, -ca *adj* : prehistoric
prejuicio *nm* : prejudice
preliminar *adj & nm* : preliminary
preludio *nm* : prelude
prematrimonial *adj* : premarital
prematuro, -ra *adj* : premature
premeditar *vt* : premeditate — **premeditación** *nf, pl* **-ciones** : premeditation
premenstrual *adj* : premenstrual
premio *nm* **1** : prize **2** RECOMPENSA : reward
3 ~ gordo : jackpot — **premiado, -da** *adj*
: prizewinning — **premiar** *vt* **1** : award a
prize to **2** RECOMPENSAR : reward
premisa *nf* : premise
premonición *nf, pl* **-ciones** : premonition
premura *nf* : haste, urgency
prenatal *adj* : prenatal
prenda *nf* **1** : piece of clothing **2** GARANTÍA
: pledge **3** : forfeit (in a game) — **prendar**
vt : captivate — **prendarse** *vr* **~ de** : fall in
love with
prender *vt* **1** SUJETAR : pin, fasten **2** APRESAR : capture **3** : light (a match, etc.) **4** *Lat*
: turn on (a light, etc.) — *vi* **1** : take root **2**
ARDER : catch, burn (of fire) — **prenderse**
vr : catch fire — **prendedor** *nm* *Lat*
: brooch, pin
prensa *nf* : press — **prensar** *vt* : press
preñado, -da *adj* **1** : pregnant **2 ~ de**
: filled with
preocupar *vt* : worry — **preocuparse** *vr* **1**
: worry **2 ~ de** : take care of — **preocupación** *nf, pl* **-ciones** : worry
preparar *vt* : prepare — **prepararse** *vr* : get
ready — **preparación** *nf, pl* **-ciones** : preparation — **preparado, -da** *adj* : prepared,
ready — **preparado** *nm* : preparation —
preparativo, -va *adj* : preparatory, preliminary — **preparativos** *nmpl* : preparations
—**preparatorio, -ria** *adj* : preparatory
preposición *nf, pl* **-ciones** : preposition
prepotente *adj* : arrogant, domineering
prerrogativa *nf* : prerogative
presa *nf* **1** : catch, prey **2** DIQUE : dam **3**
hacer ~ en : seize
presagiar *vt* : presage, forebode — **presagio** *nm* **1** : omen **2** PREMONICIÓN : premonition
presbítero *nm* : presbyter, priest
prescindir *vi* **~ de 1** : do without **2** OMITIR
: dispense with
prescribir {33} *vt* : prescribe — **prescripción** *nf, pl* **-ciones** : prescription

presencia *nf* **1** : presence **2** ASPECTO : appearance — **presenciar** *vt* : be present at, witness

presentar *vt* **1** : present **2** OFRECER : offer, give **3** MOSTRAR : show **4** : introduce (persons) — **presentarse** *vr* **1** : show up **2** : arise, come up (of a problem, etc.) **3** : introduce oneself — **presentación** *nf, pl* -**ciones 1** : presentation **2** : introduction (of persons) **3** ASPECTO : appearance — **presentador, -dora** *n* : presenter, host (of a television program, etc.)

presente *adj* **1** : present **2 tener ~** : keep in mind — **~** *nm* **1** : present **2 entre los ~s** : among those present

presentir {76} *vt* : have a presentiment of — **presentimiento** *nm* : premonition

preservar *vt* : preserve, protect — **preservación** *nf, pl* -**ciones** : preservation — **preservativo** *nm* : condom

presidente, -ta *n* **1** : president **2** : chair, chairperson (of a meeting) — **presidencia** *nf* **1** : presidency **2** : chairmanship (of a meeting) — **presidencial** *adj* : presidential

presidio *nm* : prison — **presidiario, -ria** *n* : convict

presidir *vt* **1** : preside over, chair **2** PREDOMINAR : dominate

presión *nf, pl* -**siones 1** : pressure **2 ~ arterial** : blood pressure **3 hacer ~** : press — **presionar** *vt* **1** : press **2** COACCIONAR : put pressure on

preso, -sa *adj* : imprisoned — **~** *n* : prisoner

prestar *vt* **1** : lend, loan **2** : give (aid) **3 ~ atención** : pay attention — **prestado, -da** *adj* **1** : borrowed, on loan **2 pedir ~** : borrow — **prestamista** *nmf* : moneylender — **préstamo** *nm* : loan

prestidigitación *nf, pl* -**ciones** : sleight of hand — **prestidigitador, -dora** *n* : magician

prestigio *nm* : prestige — **prestigioso, -sa** *adj* : prestigious

presto, -ta *adj* : prompt, ready — **presto** *adv* : promptly, right away

presumir *vt* : presume — *vi* : boast, show off — **presumido, -da** *adj* : conceited, vain — **presunción** *nf, pl* -**ciones 1** : presumption **2** VANIDAD : vanity — **presunto, -ta** *adj* : presumed, alleged — **presuntuoso, -sa** *adj* : conceited

presuponer {60} *vt* : presuppose — **presupuesto** *nm* **1** : budget, estimate **2** SUPUESTO : assumption

presuroso, -sa *adj* : hasty, quick

pretender *vt* **1** : try to **2** AFIRMAR : claim **3** CORTEJAR : court, woo **4 ~ que** : expect — **pretencioso, -sa** *adj* : pretentious — **pretendido** *adj* : supposed — **pretendiente** *nmf* **1** : candidate **2** : pretender (to a throne)

— **~** *nm* : suitor — **pretensión** *nf, pl* -**siones 1** INTENCIÓN : intention, aspiration **2** : claim (to a throne, etc.) **3 pretensiones** *nfpl* : pretensions

pretérito *nm* : past (in grammar)

pretexto *nm* : pretext, excuse

prevalecer {53} *vi* : prevail — **prevaleciente** *adj* : prevailing, prevalent

prevenir {87} *vt* **1** : prevent **2** AVISAR : warn — **prevenirse** {87} *vr* **~ contra** *or* **~ de** : take precautions against — **prevención** *nf, pl* -**ciones 1** : prevention **2** PRECAUCIÓN : precaution **3** PREJUICIO : prejudice — **prevenido, -da** *adj* **1** : prepared, ready **2** PRECAVIDO : cautious — **preventivo, -va** *adj* : preventive

prever {88} *vt* **1** : foresee **2** PLANEAR : plan — **previo, -via** *adj* : previous, prior — **previsible** *adj* : foreseeable — **previsión** *nf, pl* -**siones 1** : foresight **2** PREDICCIÓN : prediction, forecast — **previsor, -sora** *adj* : farsighted, prudent

prieto, -ta *adj* **1** CEÑIDO : tight **2** *Lat fam* : dark-skinned

prima *nf* **1** : bonus **2** : (insurance) premium **3** → **primo**

primario, -ria *adj* **1** : primary **2 escuela primaria** : elementary school

primate *nm* : primate

primavera *nf* **1** : spring (season) **2** : primrose (flower) — **primaveral** *adj* : spring

primero, -ra *adj* (**primer** *before masculine singular nouns*) **1** : first **2** MEJOR : top, leading **3** PRINCIPAL : main, basic **4 de primera** : first-rate — **~** *n* : first (person or thing) — **primero** *adv* **1** : first **2** MÁS BIEN : rather, sooner

primitivo, -va *adj* : primitive

primo, -ma *n* : cousin

primogénito, -ta *adj & n* : firstborn

primor *nm* : beautiful thing

primordial *adj* : basic, fundamental

primoroso, -sa *adj* **1** : exquisite, fine **2** HÁBIL : skillful

princesa *nf* : princess

principado *nm* : principality

principal *adj* : main, principal

príncipe *nm* : prince

principio *nm* **1** : principle **2** COMIENZO : beginning, start **3** ORIGEN : origin **4 al ~** : at first **5 a ~s de** : at the beginning of — **principiante** *nmf* : beginner

pringar {52} *vt* : spatter (with grease) — **pringoso, -sa** *adj* : greasy

prioridad *nf* : priority

prisa *nf* **1** : hurry, rush **2 a ~** *or* **de ~** : quickly **3 a toda ~** : as fast as possible **4 darse ~** : hurry **5 tener ~** : be in a hurry

prisión *nf, pl* -**siones 1** : prison **2** ENCAR-

CELAMIENTO : imprisonment — **prisionero, -ra** *n* : prisoner
prisma *nm* : prism — **prismáticos** *nmpl* : binoculars
privar *vt* **1** : deprive **2** PROHIBIR : forbid **3** *Lat* : knock out — **privarse** *vr* : deprive oneself — **privación** *nf, pl* **-ciones** : deprivation — **privado, -da** *adj* : private — **privativo, -va** *adj* : exclusive
privilegio *nm* : privilege — **privilegiado, -da** *adj* : privileged
pro *prep* : for, in favor of — ∼ *nm* **1** : pro, advantage **2 en ∼ de** : for, in support of **3 los pros y los contras** : the pros and cons
proa *nf* : bow, prow
probabilidad *nf* : probability — **probable** *adj* : probable, likely — **probablemente** *adv* : probably
probar {19} *vt* **1** : try, test **2** : try on (clothing) **3** DEMOSTRAR : prove **4** DEGUSTAR : taste — *vi* : try — **probarse** *vr* : try on (clothing) — **probeta** *nf* : test tube
problema *nm* : problem — **problemático, -ca** *adj* : problematic
proceder *vi* **1** : proceed, act **2** : be appropriate **3** ∼ **de** : come from — **procedencia** *nf* : origin — **procedente** *adj* ∼ **de** : coming from, originating in — **procedimiento** *nm* **1** : procedure, method **2** : proceedings *pl* (in law)
procesar *vt* **1** : prosecute **2** : process (data) — **procesador** *nm* ∼ **de textos** : word processor — **procesamiento** *nm* : processing — **procesión** *nf, pl* **-siones** : procession — **proceso** *nm* **1** : process **2** : trial, proceedings *pl* (in law)
proclamar *vt* : proclaim — **proclama** *nf* : proclamation — **proclamación** *nf, pl* **-ciones** : proclamation
procrear *vi* : procreate — **procreación** *nf, pl* **-ciones** : procreation
procurar *vt* **1** : try, endeavor **2** CONSEGUIR : obtain, procure — **procurador, -dora** *n* : attorney
prodigar {52} *vt* : lavish — **prodigio** *nm* : wonder, prodigy — **prodigioso, -sa** *adj* : prodigious
pródigo, -ga *adj* : extravagant, prodigal
producir {61} *vt* **1** : produce **2** CAUSAR : cause **3** : yield, bear (interest, fruit, etc.) — **producirse** *vr* : take place — **producción** *nf, pl* **-ciones** : production — **productividad** *nf* : productivity — **productivo, -va** *adj* : productive — **producto** *nm* : product — **productor, -tora** *n* : producer
proeza *nf* : exploit
profanar *vt* : profane, desecrate — **profanación** *nf, pl* **-ciones** : desecration — **profano, -na** *adj* : profane
profecía *nf* : prophecy

proferir {76} *vt* **1** : utter **2** : hurl (insults)
profesar *vt* **1** : profess **2** : practice (a profession, etc.) — **profesión** *nf, pl* **-siones** : profession — **profesional** *adj & nmf* : professional — **profesor, -sora** *n* **1** : teacher **2** : professor (at a university, etc.) — **profesorado** *nm* **1** : teaching profession **2** PROFESORES : faculty
profeta *nm* : prophet — **profético, -ca** *adj* : prophetic — **profetista** *nf* : (female) prophet — **profetizar** {21} *vt* : prophesy
prófugo, -ga *adj & n* : fugitive
profundo, -da *adj* **1** HONDO : deep **2** : profound (of thoughts, etc.) — **profundamente** *adv* : deeply, profoundly — **profundidad** *nf* : depth — **profundizar** {21} *vt* : study in depth
profuso, -sa *adj* : profuse — **profusión** *nf, pl* **-siones** : profusion
progenie *nf* : progeny, offspring
programa *nm* **1** : program **2** : curriculum (in education) — **programación** *nf, pl* **-ciones** : programming — **programador, -dora** *n* : programmer — **programar** *vt* **1** : schedule **2** : program (a computer, etc.)
progreso *nm* : progress — **progresar** *vi* : (make) progress — **progresión** *nf, pl* **-ciones** : progression — **progresista** *adj & nmf* : progressive — **progresivo, -va** *adj* : progressive, gradual
prohibir {62} *vt* : prohibit, forbid — **prohibición** *nf, pl* **-ciones** : ban, prohibition — **prohibido, -da** *adj* : forbidden — **prohibitivo, -va** *adj* : prohibitive
prójimo *nm* : neighbor, fellow man
prole *nf* : offspring
proletariado *nm* : proletariat — **proletario, -ria** *adj & n* : proletarian
proliferar *vi* : proliferate — **proliferación** *nf, pl* **-ciones** : proliferation — **prolífico, -ca** *adj* : prolific
prolijo, -ja *adj* : wordy, long-winded
prólogo *nm* : prologue, foreword
prolongar {52} *vt* **1** : prolong **2** ALARGAR : lengthen — **prolongarse** *vr* : last, continue — **prolongación** *nf, pl* **-ciones** : extension
promedio *nm* : average
promesa *nf* : promise — **prometedor, -dora** *adj* : promising, hopeful — **prometer** *vt* : promise — *vi* : show promise — **prometerse** *vr* : get engaged — **prometido, -da** *adj* : engaged — ∼ *n* : fiancé *m*, fiancée *f*
prominente *adj* : prominent — **prominencia** *nf* : prominence
promiscuo, -cua *adj* : promiscuous — **promiscuidad** *nf* : promiscuity
promocionar *vt* : promote — **promoción** *nf, pl* **-ciones** : promotion

promontorio *nm* : promontory

promover {47} *vt* **1** : promote **2** CAUSAR : cause — **promotor, -tora** *n* : promoter

promulgar {52} *vt* **1** : proclaim **2** : enact (a law)

pronombre *nm* : pronoun

pronosticar {72} *vt* : predict, forecast — **pronóstico** *nm* **1** : prediction, forecast **2** : (medical) prognosis

pronto, -ta *adj* **1** : quick, prompt **2** PREPARADO : ready — **pronto** *adv* **1** : soon **2** RAPIDAMENTE : quickly, promptly **3 de ~** : suddenly **4 por lo ~** : for the time being **5 tan ~ como** : as soon as

pronunciar *vt* **1** : pronounce **2** : give, deliver (a speech) — **pronunciarse** *vr* **1** : declare oneself **2** SUBLEVARSE : revolt — **pronunciación** *nf, pl* **-ciones** : pronunciation

propagación *nf, pl* **-ciones** : propagation

propaganda *nf* **1** : propaganda **2** PUBLICIDAD : advertising

propagar {52} *vt* : propagate, spread — **propagarse** *vr* : propagate

propano *nm* : propane

propasarse *vr* : go too far

propensión *nf, pl* **-siones** : inclination, propensity — **propenso, -sa** *adj* : prone, inclined

propiamente *adv* : exactly

propicio, -cia *adj* : favorable, propitious

propiedad *nf* **1** : property **2** PERTINENCIA : ownership, possession — **propietario, -ria** *n* : owner, proprietor

propina *nf* : tip

propinar *vt* : give, deal (a blow, etc.)

propio, -pia *adj* **1** : own **2** APROPIADO : proper, appropriate **3** CARACTERÍSTICO : characteristic, typical **4** MISMO : himself, herself, oneself

proponer {60} *vt* **1** : propose **2** : nominate (a person) — **proponerse** *vr* : propose, intend

proporción *nf, pl* **-ciones** : proportion — **proporcionado, -da** *adj* : proportionate — **proporcional** *adj* : proportional — **proporcionar** *vt* **1** : provide **2** AJUSTAR : adapt, proportion

proposición *nf, pl* **-ciones** : proposal, proposition

propósito *nm* **1** : purpose, intention **2 a ~** : incidentally, by the way **3 a ~** : on purpose, intentionally

propuesta *nf* **1** : proposal **2** : offer (of employment, etc.)

propulsar *vt* **1** : propel, drive **2** PROMOVER : promote — **propulsión** *nf, pl* **-siones** : propulsion

prorrogar {52} *vt* **1** : extend **2** APLAZAR : postpone — **prórroga** *nf* **1** : extension, deferment **2** : overtime (in sports)

prorrumpir *vi* : burst forth, break out

prosa *nf* : prose

proscribir {33} *vt* **1** : prohibit, ban **2** DESTERRAR : exile — **proscripción** *nf, pl* **-ciones 1** : ban **2** DESTIERRO : banishment — **proscrito, -ta** *adj* : banned — **~** *n* : exile, outlaw

proseguir {75} *v* : continue — **prosecución** *nf, pl* **-ciones** : continuation

prospección *nf, pl* **-ciones** : prospecting, exploration

prospecto *nm* : prospectus

prosperar *vi* : prosper, thrive — **prosperidad** *nf* : prosperity — **próspero, -ra** *adj* : prosperous, flourishing

prostituir {41} *vt* : prostitute — **prostitución** *nf, pl* **-ciones** : prostitution — **prostituta** *nf* : prostitute

protagonista *nmf* : protagonist — **protagonizar** *vt* : star in

proteger {15} *vt* : protect — **protegerse** *vr* : protect oneself — **protección** *nf, pl* **-ciones** : protection — **protector, -tora** *adj* : protective — **~** *n* : protector — **protegido, -da** *n* : protégé

proteína *nf* : protein

protestar *v* : protest — **protesta** *nf* : protest — **protestante** *adj & nmf* : Protestant

protocolo *nm* : protocol

prototipo *nm* : prototype

protuberancia *nf* : protuberance — **protuberante** *adj* : protuberant

provecho *nm* **1** : benefit, advantage **2 ¡buen ~!** : enjoy your meal! — **provechoso, -sa** *adj* : profitable, beneficial

proveer {63} *vt* : provide, supply — **proveedor, -dora** *n* : supplier

provenir {87} *vi* **~ de** : come from

proverbio *nm* : proverb — **proverbial** *adj* : proverbial

providencia *nf* **1** : providence **2** PRECAUCIÓN : precaution — **providencial** *adj* : providential

provincia *nf* : province — **provincial** *adj* : provincial — **provinciano, -na** *adj* : provincial, parochial

provisión *nf, pl* **-siones** : provision — **provisional** *adj* : provisional

provocar {72} *vt* **1** : provoke, cause **2** IRRITAR : irritate — **provocación** *nf, pl* **-ciones** : provocation — **provocativo, -va** *adj* : provocative

próximo, -ma *adj* **1** CERCANO : near **2** SIGUIENTE : next — **próximamente** *adv* : shortly, soon — **proximidad** *nf* **1** : proximity **2 ~es** *nfpl* : vicinity

proyectar *vt* **1** : plan **2** LANZAR : throw, hurl **3** : cast (light) **4** : show (a film) — **proyección** *nf, pl* **-ciones** : projection — **proyectil**

nm : missile — **proyecto** *nm* : plan, project — **proyector** *nm* : projector
prudencia *nf* : prudence, care — **prudente** *adj* : prudent, sensible
prueba *nf* **1** : proof, evidence **2** : test (in education, medicine, etc.) **3** : event (in sports) **4 a ~ de agua** : waterproof
psicoanálisis *nm* : psychoanalysis — **psicoanalista** *nmf* : psychoanalyst — **psicoanalizar** {21} *vt* : psychoanalyze
psicología *nf* : psychology — **psicológico, -ca** *adj* : psychological — **psicólogo, -ga** *n* : psychologist
psicópata *nmf* : psychopath
psicosis *nfs & pl* : psychosis
psicoterapia *nf* : psychotherapy — **psicoterapeuta** *nmf* : psychotherapist
psicótico, -ca *adj & n* : psychotic
psiquiatría *nf* : psychiatry — **psiquiatra** *nmf* : psychiatrist — **psiquiátrico, -ca** *adj* : psychiatric
psíquico, -ca *adj* : psychic
púa *nf* **1** : sharp point **2** : tooth (of a comb) **3** : thorn (of a plant), quill (of a porcupine, etc.) **4** : (guitar) pick
pubertad *nf* : puberty
publicar {72} *vt* **1** : publish **2** DIVULGAR : divulge, disclose — **publicación** *nf, pl* **-ciones** : publication
publicidad *nf* **1** : publicity **2** : advertising (in marketing) — **publicista** *nmf* : publicist — **publicitar** *vt* **1** : publicize **2** : advertise (a product, etc.) — **publicitario, -ria** *adj* : advertising
público, -ca *adj* : public — **público** *nm* **1** : public **2** : audience (of theater, etc.), spectators *pl* (of sports)
puchero *nm* **1** : (cooking) pot **2** GUISADO : stew **3 hacer ~s** : pout
púdico, -ca *adj* : modest
pudiente *adj* : wealthy
pudín *nm, pl* **-dines** : pudding
pudor *nm* : modesty — **pudoroso, -sa** *adj* : modest
pudrir {59} *vt* **1** : rot **2** *fam* : annoy — **pudrirse** *vr* : rot
pueblo *nm* **1** : town, village **2** NACIÓN : people, nation
puente *nm* **1** : bridge **2 hacer ~** : have a long weekend **3 ~ levadizo** : drawbridge
puerco, -ca *n* **1** : pig **2 puerco espín** : porcupine — **~** *adj* : dirty, filthy
pueril *adj* : childish
puerro *nm* : leek
puerta *nf* **1** : door, gate **2 a ~ cerrada** : behind closed doors
puerto *nm* **1** : port **2** : (mountain) pass **3** REFUGIO : haven
puertorriqueño, -ña *adj* : Puerto Rican
pues *conj* **1** : since, because **2** POR LO TANTO : so, therefore **3** (*used interjectionally*) : well, then

puesta *nf* **1 ~ a punto** : tune-up **2 ~ de sol** : sunset **3 ~ en marcha** : starting up — **puesto, -ta** *adj* **1** : put, set **2** VESTIDO : dressed — **puesto** *nm* **1** : place **2** EMPLEO : position, job **3** : stand, stall (in a market) **4 ~ avanzado** : outpost — **~ que** *conj* : since, given that
púgil *nm* : boxer
pugnar *vi* : fight — **pugna** *nf* : fight, battle
pulcro, -cra *adj* : tidy, neat
pulga *nf* **1** : flea **2 tener malas ~s** : have a bad temper
pulgada *nf* : inch — **pulgar** *nm* **1** : thumb **2** : big toe
pulir *vt* **1** : polish **2** REFINAR : touch up, perfect
pulla *nf* : cutting remark, gibe
pulmón *nm, pl* **-mones** : lung — **pulmonar** *adj* : pulmonary — **pulmonía** *nf* : pneumonia
pulpa *nf* : pulp
pulpería *nf Lat* : grocery store
púlpito *nm* : pulpit
pulpo *nm* : octopus
pulsar *vt* **1** : press (a button), strike (a key) **2** : play (music) — **pulsación** *nf, pl* **-ciones** **1** : beat, throb **2** : keystroke (on a typewriter, etc.)
pulsera *nf* : bracelet
pulso *nm* **1** : pulse **2** : steadiness (of hand)
pulular *vi* : swarm
pulverizar {21} *vt* **1** : pulverize, crush **2** : spray (a liquid) — **pulverizador** *nm* : atomizer, spray
puma *nf* : puma
punitivo, -va *adj* : punitive
punta *nf* **1** : tip, end **2** : point (of a needle, etc.) **3 ~ del dedo** : fingertip **4 sacar ~ a** : sharpen
puntada *nf* **1** : stitch **2 ~s** *nfpl* : seam
puntal *nm* : prop, support
puntapié *nm* : kick
puntear *vt* : pluck (a guitar)
puntería *nf* : aim, marksmanship
puntiagudo, -da *adj* : sharp, pointed
puntilla *nf* **1** : lace edging **2 de ~s** : on tiptoe
punto *nm* **1** : dot, point **2** : period (in punctuation) **3** ASUNTO : item, question **4** LUGAR : spot, place **5** MOMENTO : moment **6** : point (in a score) **7** PUNTADA : stitch **8 a las dos en ~** : at two o'clock sharp **9 dos ~s** : colon **10 hasta cierto ~** : up to a point **11 ~ de partida** : starting point **12 ~ muerto** : deadlock **13 ~ y coma** : semicolon
puntocom *nm pl* **puntocom**: dot-com

puntuación *nf, pl* **-ciones 1** : punctuation **2** : scoring, score (in sports)

puntual *adj* **1** : prompt, punctual **2** EXACTO : accurate, detailed — **puntualidad** *nf* **1** : punctuality **2** EXACTITUD : accuracy

puntuar {3} *vt* : punctuate — *vi* : score (in sports)

punzar {21} *vt* : prick, puncture — **punzada** *nf* **1** PINCHAZO : prick **2** : sharp pain — **punzante** *adj* **1** : sharp **2** MORDAZ : biting, caustic

puñado *nm* **1** : handful **2 a ~s** : by the handful

puñal *nm* : dagger — **puñalada** *nf* : stab

puño *nm* **1** : fist **2** : cuff (of a shirt) **3** : handle, hilt (of a sword, etc.) — **puñetazo** *nm* : punch (with the fist)

pupila *nf* : pupil (of the eye)

pupitre *nm* : desk

puré *nm* **1** : purée **2 ~ de papas** *or* **~ de patatas** *Spain* : mashed potatoes

pureza *nf* : purity

purga *nf* : purge — **purgar** {52} *vt* : purge — **purgatorio** *nm* : purgatory

purificar {72} *vt* : purify — **purificación** *nf, pl* **-ciones** : purification

puritano, -na *adj* : puritanical — **~** *n* : puritan

puro, -ra *adj* **1** : pure **2** SIMPLE : plain, simple **3** *Lat fam* : only, just — **puro** *nm* : cigar

púrpura *nf* : purple — **purpúreo, -rea** *adj* : purple

pus *nm* : pus

pusilánime *adj* : cowardly

puta *nf* : whore

putrefacción *nf, pl* **-ciones** : putrefaction, rot — **pútrido, -da** *adj* : putrid, rotten

Q

q *nf* : q, 18th letter of the Spanish alphabet

que *conj* **1** : that **2** (*in comparisons*) : than **3** (*introducing a reason or cause*) : so that, or else **4 es ~** : the thing is that **5 yo ~ tú** : if I were you — **~** *pron* **1** (*referring to persons*) : who, whom **2** (*referring to things*) : that, which **3 el (la, lo, las, los) ~** : he (she, it, they) who, whoever, the one(s) that

qué *adv* **1** : how, what **2 ¡~ lindo!** : how lovely! — **~** *adj* : what, which — **~** *pron* **1** : what **2 ¿~ crees?** : what do you think?

quebrar {55} *vt* : break — *vi* : go bankrupt — **quebrarse** *vr* : break — **quebrada** *nf* : ravine, gorge — **quebradizo, -za** *adj* : breakable, fragile — **quebrado, -da** *adj* **1** : bankrupt **2** : rough, uneven (of land, etc.) **3** ROTO : broken — **quebrado** *nm* : fraction — **quebradura** *nf* : crack, fissure — **quebrantar** *vt* **1** : break **2** DEBILITAR : weaken — **quebranto** *nm* **1** : harm, damage **2** AFLICCIÓN : grief, pain

queda *nf* → **toque**

quedar *vi* **1** PERMANECER : remain, stay **2** ESTAR : be **3** FALTAR : be left **4** : fit, look (of clothing, etc.) **5 no queda lejos** : it's not far **6 ~ en** : agree to, agree on — **quedarse** *vr* **1** : stay **2 ~ con** : keep

quedo, -da *adj* : quiet, still — **quedo** *adv* : softly, quietly

quehacer *nm* **1** : task **2 ~es** *nmpl* : chores

queja *nf* : complaint — **quejarse** *vr* **1** : complain **2** GEMIR : moan, groan — **quejido** *nm* : moan, whimper — **quejoso, -sa** *adj* : complaining, whining

quemar *vt* **1** : burn **2** MALGASTAR : squander — *vi* : burn — **quemarse** *vr* **1** : burn oneself **2** : burn (up) **3** : get sunburned — **quemado, -da** *adj* **1** : burned **2** AGOTADO : burned-out **3 estar ~** : be fed up — **quemador** *nm* : burner — **quemadura** *nf* : burn — **quemarropa: a ~** *adj & adv phr* : point-blank

querella *nf* **1** : dispute, quarrel **2** : charge (in law)

querer {64} *vt* **1** : want **2** AMAR : love **3 ~ decir** : mean **4 ¿quieres pasarme la leche?** : please pass the milk **5 sin ~** : unintentionally — **~** *nm* : love — **querido, -da** *adj* : dear, beloved — **~** *n* **1** : darling **2** AMANTE : lover

queroseno *nm* : kerosene

querubín *nm, pl* **-bines** : cherub

queso *nm* : cheese — **quesadilla** *nf Lat* : quesadilla

quicio *nm* **1 estar fuera de ~** : be beside oneself **2 sacar de ~** : drive crazy

quiebra *nf* **1** : break **2** BANCARROTA : bankruptcy

quien *pron, pl* **quienes 1** (*subject*) : who **2** (*object*) : whom **3** (*indefinite*) : whoever, anyone, some people

quién *pron, pl* **quiénes 1** (*subject*) : who **2**

(*object*) : whom **3 ¿de ~ es este lápiz?** : whose pencil is this?

quienquiera *pron, pl* **quienesquiera** : whoever, whomever

quieto, -ta *adj* **1** : calm, quiet **2** INMÓVIL : still — **quietud** *nf* : stillness

quijada *nf* : jaw, jawbone (of an animal)

quilate *nm* : carat, karat

quilla *nf* : keel

quimera *nf* : illusion — **quimérico, -ca** *adj* : fanciful

química *nf* : chemistry — **químico, -ca** *adj* : chemical — **~** *n* : chemist

quince *adj & nm* : fifteen — **quinceañero, -ra** *n* : fifteen-year-old, teenager — **quincena** *nf* : two-week period, fortnight — **quincenal** *adj* : semimonthly, twice a month

quincuagésimo, -ma *adj & n* : fiftieth

quinientos, -tas *adj* : five hundred — **quinientos** *nms & pl* : five hundred

quinina *nf* : quinine

quinqué *nm* : oil lamp

quinta *nf* : country house, villa

quintaesencia *nf* : quintessence

quinteto *nm* : quintet

quinto, -ta *adj & n* : fifth — **quinto** *nm* : fifth

quiosco *nm* : kiosk, newsstand

quiropráctico, -ca *n* : chiropractor

quirúrgico, -ca *adj* : surgical

quisquilloso, -sa *adj* : fastidious, fussy

quiste *nm* : cyst

quitar *vt* **1** : remove, take away **2** : take off (clothes) **3** : get rid of, relieve (pain, etc.) — **quitarse** *vr* **1** : withdraw, leave **2** : take off (one's clothes) **3 ~ de** : give up (a habit) **4 ~ de encima** : get rid of — **quitaesmalte** *nm* : nail-polish remover — **quitamanchas** *nms & pl* : stain remover — **quitanieves** *nm* : snowplow — **quitasol** *nm* : parasol

quizá *or* **quizás** *adv* : maybe, perhaps

R

r *nf* : r, 19th letter of the Spanish alphabet

rábano *nm* **1** : radish **2 ~ picante** : horseradish

rabí *nmf, pl* **-bíes** : rabbi

rabia *nf* **1** : rage, anger **2** : rabies (disease) — **rabiar** *vi* **1** : be furious **2** : be in great pain **3 ~ por** : be dying for — **rabioso, -sa** *adj* **1** : enraged, furious **2** : rabid, having rabies

rabino, -na *n* : rabbi

rabo *nm* **1** : tail **2 el ~ del ojo** : the corner of one's eye

racha *nf* **1** : gust of wind **2** SERIE : series, string — **racheado, -da** *adj* : gusty

racial *adj* : racial

racimo *nm* : bunch, cluster

raciocinio *nm* : reason, reasoning

ración *nf, pl* **-ciones 1** : share, ration **2** : helping (of food)

racional *adj* : rational — **racionalizar** {21} *vt* : rationalize

racionar *vt* : ration — **racionamiento** *nm* : rationing

racismo *nm* : racism — **racista** *adj & nmf* : racist

radar *nm* : radar

radiación *nf, pl* **-ciones** : radiation

radiactivo, -va *adj* : radioactive — **radiactividad** *nf* : radioactivity

radiador *nm* : radiator

radiante *adj* : radiant

radical *adj & nmf* : radical

radicar {72} *vi* **~ en** : lie in, be rooted in

radio *nm* **1** : radius **2** : spoke (of a wheel) **3** : radium (element) — **~** *nmf* : radio

radioactivo, -va *adj* : radioactive — **radioactividad** *nf* : radioactivity

radiodifusión *nf, pl* **-siones** : broadcasting — **radioemisora** *nf* : radio station — **radioescucha** *nmf* : listener — **radiofónico, -ca** *adj* : radio

radiografía *nf* : X ray — **radiografiar** {85} *vt* : x-ray

radiología *nf* : radiology — **radiólogo, -ga** *n* : radiologist

raer {65} *vt* : scrape off

ráfaga *nf* **1** : gust (of wind) **2** : flash (of light)

raído, -da *adj* : worn, shabby

raíz *nf, pl* **raíces 1** : root **2** ORIGEN : origin, source **3 echar raíces** : take root

raja *nf* **1** : crack, slit **2** RODAJA : slice — **rajar** *vt* : crack, split — **rajarse** *vr* **1** : crack, split open **2** *fam* : back out

rajatabla: a ~ *adv phr* : strictly, to the letter

ralea *nf* : sort, kind

ralentí *nm* : neutral (gear)

rallar *vt* : grate — **rallador** *nm* : grater

rama *nf* : branch — **ramaje** *nm* : branches *pl* — **ramal** *nm* : branch (of a railroad, etc.) — **ramificarse** {72} *vr* : branch (off) — **ramillete** *nm* **1** : bouquet **2** GRUPO : cluster, bunch — **ramo** *nm* **1** : branch **2** RAMILLETE : bouquet

rampa *nf* : ramp, incline

rana *nf* **1** : frog **2** ~ **toro** : bullfrog

rancho *nm* : ranch, farm — **ranchero, -ra** *n* : rancher, farmer

rancio, -cia *adj* **1** : rancid **2** : aged (of wine)

rango *nm* **1** : rank **2** : (social) standing

ranúnculo *nm* : buttercup

ranura *nf* : groove, slot

rapar *vt* **1** : shave **2** : crop (hair)

rapaz *adj, pl* **-paces** : rapacious, predatory

rápido, -da *adj* : rapid, quick — **rápidamente** *adv* : rapidly, fast — **rapidez** *nf* : speed — **rápido** *adv* : quickly, fast — ~ *nm* **1** : express train **2** ~s *nmpl* : rapids

rapiña *nf* **1** : plunder **2 ave de** ~ : bird of prey

rapsodia *nf* : rhapsody

raptar *vt* : kidnap — **rapto** *nm* : kidnapping — **raptor, -tora** *n* : kidnapper

raqueta *nf* : racket (in sports)

raro, -ra *adj* **1** : rare **2** EXTRAÑO : odd, strange — **raramente** *adv* : rarely, infrequently — **rareza** *nf* : rarity

ras *nm* **a** ~ **de** : level with

rascacielos *nms & pl* : skyscraper

rascar {72} *vt* **1** : scratch **2** RASPAR : scrape — **rascarse** *vr* : scratch oneself

rasgar {52} *vt* : rip, tear — **rasgarse** *vr* : rip

rasgo *nm* **1** : stroke (of a pen) **2** CARACTERÍSTICA : trait, characteristic **3** ~s *nmpl* FACCIONES : features

rasguear *vt* : strum

rasguñar *vt* : scratch — **rasguño** *nm* : scratch

raso, -sa *adj* **1** : level, flat **2** : low (of a flight) **3 soldado raso** : private (in the army) — **raso** *nm* : satin

raspar *vt* **1** : scrape **2** LIMAR : file down, smooth — *vi* : be rough — **raspadura** *nf* **1** : scratch **2** ~s *nfpl* : scrapings

rastra *nf* **1** : rake **2 a** ~s : unwillingly — **rastrear** *vt* : track, trace — **rastrero, -ra** *adj* **1** : creeping **2** DESPRECIABLE : despicable — **rastrillar** *vt* : rake — **rastrillo** *nm* : rake — **rastro** *nm* **1** : trail, track **2** SEÑAL : sign

rasurar *vt Lat* : shave — **rasurarse** *vr Lat* : shave

rata *nf* : rat

ratear *vt* : steal — **ratero, -ra** *n* : thief

ratificar {72} *vt* : ratify — **ratificación** *nf, pl* **-ciones** : ratification

rato *nm* **1** : while **2 al poco** ~ : shortly after **3 pasar el** ~ : pass the time

ratón *nm, pl* **-tones** : mouse — **ratonera** *nf* : mousetrap

raudal *nm* **1** : torrent **2 a** ~es : in abundance — **raudo, -da** *adj* : swift

raya *nf* **1** : line **2** LISTA : stripe **3** : part (in the hair) — **rayar** *vt* : scratch — *vi* **1 al** ~ **el día** : at daybreak **2** ~ **en** : border on — **rayarse** *vr* : get scratched

rayo *nm* **1** : ray, beam **2** : bolt of lightning **3** ~s X : X rays

rayón *nm* : rayon

raza *nf* **1** : (human) race **2** : breed (of animals) **3 de** ~ : thoroughbred, pedigreed

razón *nf, pl* **-zones 1** : reason **2 dar** ~ : inform **3 en** ~ **de** : because of **4 tener** ~ : be right — **razonable** *adj* : reasonable — **razonamiento** *nm* : reasoning — **razonar** *v* : reason, think

reacción *nf, pl* **-ciones** : reaction — **reaccionar** *vi* : react — **reaccionario, -ria** *adj & n* : reactionary

reacio, -cia *adj* : resistant, stubborn

reactivar *vt* : reactivate, revive

reactor *nm* **1** : jet (airplane) **2** ~ **nuclear** : nuclear reactor

reajustar *vt* : readjust — **reajuste** *nm* : readjustment

real *adj* **1** : royal **2** VERDADERO : real, true

realce *nm* **1** : relief **2 dar** ~ : highlight

realeza *nf* : royalty

realidad *nf* **1** : reality **2 en** ~ : actually, in fact

realismo *nm* : realism — **realista** *adj* : realistic — ~ *nmf* : realist

realizar {21} *vt* **1** : carry out **2** : achieve (a goal) **3** : produce (a film or play) **4** : realize (a profit) — **realizarse** *vr* **1** : fulfill oneself **2** : come true (of a dream, etc.) — **realización** *nf, pl* **-ciones** : execution, realization

realmente *adv* : really, actually

realzar {21} *vt* : highlight, enhance

reanimar *vt* : revive

reanudar *vt* : resume, renew — **reanudarse** *vr* : resume

reaparecer {53} *vi* : reappear — **reaparición** *nf, pl* **-ciones** : reappearance

reavivar *vt* : revive

rebajar *vt* **1** : lower, reduce **2** HUMILLAR : humiliate — **rebajarse** *vr* **1** : humble oneself **2** ~ **a** : stoop to — **rebaja** *nf* **1** : reduction **2** DESCUENTO : discount **3** ~s *nfpl* : sales

rebanada *nf* : slice

rebaño *nm* **1** : herd **2** : flock (of sheep)

rebasar *vt* : surpass, exceed

rebatir *vt* : refute

rebelarse *vr* : rebel — **rebelde** *adj* : rebellious — ~ *nmf* : rebel — **rebeldía** *nf* : rebelliousness — **rebelión** *nf, pl* **-liones** : rebellion

reblandecer *vt* : soften

rebobinar *vt* : rewind

rebosar *vi* **1** : overflow **2** ~ **de** : be bursting with — *vt* : overflow with

rebotar *vi* : bounce, rebound — **rebote** *nm* **1** : bounce **2 de** ~ : on the rebound

rebozar {21} *vt* : coat in batter

rebuscado, -da *adj* : pretentious

rebuznar *vi* : bray

recabar *vt* **1** : obtain, collect **2** ~ **fondos** : raise money

recado *nm* **1** MENSAJE : message **2** *Spain* : errand

recaer {13} *vi* **1** : relapse **2** ~ **sobre** : fall on — **recaída** *nf* : relapse

recalcar {72} *vt* : emphasize, stress

recalcitrante *adj* : recalcitrant

recalentar {55} *vt* **1** : overheat **2** : reheat, warm up (food) — **recalentarse** *vr* : overheat

recámara *nf* **1** : chamber (of a firearm) **2** *Lat* : bedroom

recambio *nm* **1** : spare part **2** : refill (for a pen, etc.)

recapitular *vt* : recapitulate, sum up — **recapitulación** *nf, pl* **-ciones** : recapitulation

recargar {52} *vt* **1** : overload **2** : recharge (a battery), reload (a firearm, etc.) — **recargado, -da** *adj* : overly elaborate — **recargo** *nm* : surcharge

recato *nm* : modesty — **recatado, -da** *adj* : modest, demure

recaudar *vt* : collect — **recaudación** *nf, pl* **-ciones** : collection — **recaudador, -dora** *n* ~ **de impuestos** : tax collector

recelar *vt* : distrust, fear — **recelo** *nm* : distrust, suspicion — **receloso, -sa** *adj* : distrustful, suspicious

recepción *nf, pl* **-ciones** : reception — **recepcionista** *nmf* : receptionist

receptáculo *nm* : receptacle

receptivo, -va *adj* : receptive — **receptor, -tora** *n* : recipient — **receptor** *nm* : receiver (of a radio, etc.)

recesión *nf, pl* **-siones** : recession

receso *nm Lat* : recess, adjournment

receta *nf* **1** : recipe **2** : prescription (in medicine)

rechazar {21} *vt* **1** : reject, refuse **2** REPELER : repel **3** : reflect (light) — **rechazo** *nm* : rejection

rechinar *vi* **1** : squeak, creak **2** : grind, gnash (one's teeth)

rechoncho, -cha *adj fam* : chubby

recibir *vt* **1** : receive **2** ACOGER : welcome — *vi* : receive visitors — **recibidor** *nm* : vestibule, entrance hall — **recibimiento** *nm* : reception, welcome — **recibo** *nm* : receipt

reciclar *vt* **1** : recycle **2** : retrain (workers) — **reciclaje** *nm* : recycling

recién *adv* **1** : newly, recently **2** ~ **casados** : newlyweds — **reciente** *adj* : recent — **recientemente** *adv* : recently

recinto *nm* **1** ÁREA : area, site

recio, -cia *adj* : tough, strong

recipiente *nm* : container, receptacle — ~ *nmf* : recipient

recíproco, -ca *adj* : reciprocal, mutual

recitar *vt* : recite — **recital** *nm* : recital

reclamar *vt* : demand, ask for — *vi* : complain — **reclamación** *nf, pl* **-ciones** **1** : claim, demand **2** QUEJA : complaint — **reclamo** *nm* **1** : lure (in hunting) **2** *Lat* : inducement, attraction

reclinar *vt* : rest, lean — **reclinarse** *vr* : recline, lean back

recluir {41} *vt* : confine, lock up — **recluirse** *vr* : shut oneself away — **reclusión** *nf, pl* **-siones** : imprisonment — **recluso, -sa** *n* : prisoner

recluta *nmf* : recruit — **reclutamiento** *nm* : recruitment — **reclutar** *vt* : recruit, enlist

recobrar *vt* : recover, regain — **recobrarse** *vr* ~ **de** : recover from

recodo *nm* : bend

recoger {15} *vt* **1** : collect, gather **2** COGER : pick up **3** LIMPIAR, ORDENAR : clean up, tidy (up) — **recogerse** *vr* : retire, withdraw — **recogedor** *nm* : dustpan — **recogido, -da** *adj* : quiet, secluded

recolección *nf, pl* **-ciones** **1** : collection **2** COSECHA : harvest

recomendar {55} *vt* : recommend — **recomendación** *nf, pl* **-ciones** : recommendation

recompensar *vt* : reward — **recompensa** *nf* : reward

reconciliar *vt* : reconcile — **reconciliarse** *vr* : be reconciled — **reconciliación** *nf, pl* **-ciones** : reconciliation

recóndito, -ta *adj* : hidden

reconfortar *vt* : comfort

reconocer {18} *vt* **1** : recognize **2** ADMITIR : admit **3** EXAMINAR : examine — **reconocible** *adj* : recognizable — **reconocido, -da** *adj* **1** : recognized, accepted **2** AGRADECIDO : grateful — **reconocimiento** *nm* **1** : recognition **2** AGRADECIMIENTO : gratitude **3** : (medical) examination

reconsiderar *vt* : reconsider

reconstruir {41} *vt* : reconstruct — **reconstrucción** *nf, pl* **-ciones** : reconstruction

recopilar *vt* **1** RECOGER : collect, gather **2** : compile — **recopilación** *nf, pl* **-ciones** : collection, compilation

récord *nm, pl* **-cords** : record

recordar {19} *vt* 1 ACORDARSE DE : remember 2 : remind — *vi* : remember — **recordatorio** *nm* : reminder

recorrer *vt* 1 : travel through 2 : cover (a distance) — **recorrido** *nm* 1 : journey, trip 2 TRAYECTO : route, course

recortar *vt* 1 : reduce 2 CORTAR : cut (out) 3 : trim (hair) — **recortarse** *vr* : stand out — **recorte** *nm* 1 : cut, cutting 2 ~s de **periódicos** : newspaper clippings

recostar {19} *vt* : lean, rest — **recostarse** *vr* : lie down

recoveco *nm* 1 : bend 2 RINCÓN : nook, corner

recrear *vt* 1 : recreate 2 ENTRETENER : entertain — **recrearse** *vr* : to enjoy oneself — **recreativo, -va** *adj* : recreational — **recreo** *nm* 1 : recreation, amusement 2 : recess, break (at school)

recriminar *vt* : reproach

recrudecer {53} *vi* : worsen — **recrudecerse** *vr* : intensify, get worse

rectángulo *nm* : rectangle — **rectangular** *adj* : rectangular

rectificar {72} *vt* 1 : rectify, correct 2 AJUSTAR : straighten (out) — **rectitud** *nf* 1 : straightness 2 : (moral) rectitude — **recto, -ta** *adj* 1 : straight 2 ÍNTEGRO : upright, honorable — **recto** *nm* : rectum

rector, -tora *adj* : governing, managing — ~ *n* : rector — **rectoría** *nf* : rectory

recubrir {2} *vt* : cover, coat

recuento *nm* : count, recount

recuerdo *nm* 1 : memory 2 : souvenir, remembrance (of a journey, etc.) 3 ~s *nmpl* SALUDOS : regards

recuperar *vt* 1 : recover, retrieve 2 ~ el **tiempo perdido** : make up for lost time — **recuperarse** *vr* ~ **de** : recover from — **recuperación** *nf, pl* **-ciones** 1 : recovery 2 ~ **de datos** : data retrieval

recurrir *vi* ~ **a** : turn to (a person), resort to (force, etc.) — **recurso** *nm* 1 : recourse, resort 2 : appeal (in law) 3 ~s *nmpl* : resources

red *nf* 1 : net 2 SISTEMA : network, system 3 **la Red** : the Internet

redactar *vt* : write (up), draft — **redacción** *nf, pl* **-ciones** 1 : writing, drafting 2 : editing (of a newspaper, etc.) — **redactor, -tora** *n* : editor

redada *nf* 1 : (police) raid 2 : catch (in fishing)

redescubrir {2} *vt* : rediscover

redención *nf, pl* **-ciones** : redemption — **redentor, -tora** *adj* : redeeming

redil *nm* : fold, pen

rédito *nm* : interest, yield

redoblar *vt* : redouble

redomado, -da *adj* : out-and-out

redondear *vt* 1 : make round 2 : round off (a number, etc.) — **redonda** *nf* 1 : whole note (in music) 2 **a la** ~ : in the surrounding area — **redondel** *nm* 1 : ring, circle 2 : bullring — **redondo, -da** *adj* 1 : round 2 PERFECTO : excellent

reducir {61} *vt* : reduce — **reducirse** *vr* ~ **a** : come down to, amount to — **reducción** *nf, pl* **-ciones** : reduction — **reducido, -da** *adj* 1 : reduced, limited 2 PEQUEÑO : small

redundante *adj* : redundant — **redundancia** *nf* : redundancy

reedición *nf, pl* **-ciones** : reprint

reembolsar *vt* : refund, reimburse, repay — **reembolso** *nm* : refund, reimbursement

reemplazar {21} *vt* : replace — **reemplazo** *nm* : replacement

reencarnación *nf, pl* **-ciones** : reincarnation

reencuentro *nm* : reunion

reestructurar *vt* : restructure

refaccionar *vt Lat* : repair, renovate — **refacciones** *nfpl Lat* : repairs, renovations

referir {76} *vt* 1 : tell 2 REMITIR : refer — **referirse** *vr* ~ **a** : refer to — **referencia** *nf* 1 : reference 2 **hacer** ~ **a** : refer to — **referéndum** *nm, pl* **-dums** : referendum — **referente** *adj* ~ **a** : concerning

refinar *vt* : refine — **refinado, -da** *adj* : refined — **refinamiento** *nm* : refinement — **refinería** *nf* : refinery

reflector *nm* 1 : reflector 2 : spotlight, searchlight, floodlight

reflejar *vt* : reflect — **reflejarse** *vr* : be reflected — **reflejo** *nm* 1 : reflection 2 : (physical) reflex 3 ~s *nmpl* : highlights (in hair)

reflexionar *vi* : reflect, think — **reflexión** *nf, pl* **-xiones** : reflection, thought — **reflexivo, -va** *adj* 1 : reflective, thoughtful 2 : reflexive (in grammar)

reflujo *nm* : ebb (tide)

reforma *nf* 1 : reform 2 ~s *nfpl* : renovations — **reformador, -dora** *n* : reformer — **reformar** *vt* 1 : reform 2 : renovate, repair (a house, etc.) — **reformarse** *vr* : mend one's ways — **reformatorio** *nm* : reformatory

reforzar {36} *vt* : reinforce

refrán *nm, pl* **-franes** : proverb, saying

refregar {49} *vt* : scrub

refrenar *vt* 1 : rein in (a horse) 2 CONTENER : restrain — **refrenarse** *vr* : restrain oneself

refrendar *vt* : approve, endorse

refrescar {72} *vt* 1 : refresh, cool 2 : brush up on (knowledge) — *vi* : turn cooler — **refrescante** *adj* : refreshing — **refresco** *nm* : soft drink

refriega *nf* : scuffle, skirmish

refrigerar *vt* **1** : refrigerate **2** CLIMATIZAR : air-condition — **refrigeración** *nf, pl* **-ciones 1** : refrigeration **2** AIRE ACONDICIONADO : air-conditioning — **refrigerador** *nmf Lat* : refrigerator — **refrigerio** *nm* : refreshments *pl*

refrito, -ta *adj* : refried — **refrito** *nm* : rehash

refuerzo *nm* : reinforcement

refugiar *vt* : shelter — **refugiarse** *vr* : take refuge — **refugiado, -da** *n* : refugee — **refugio** *nm* : refuge, shelter

refulgir {35} *vi* : shine brightly

refunfuñar *vi* : grumble, groan

refutar *vt* : refute

regadera *nf* **1** : watering can **2** *Lat* : shower head, shower

regalar *vt* **1** : give (as a gift) — **regalarse** *vr* ~ **con** : treat oneself to

regaliz *nm, pl* **-lices** : licorice

regalo *nm* **1** : gift, present **2** PLACER : pleasure, delight

regalón, -lona *adj* : spoiled (of a person)

regañadientes: a ~ *adv phr* : reluctantly, unwillingly

regañar *vt* : scold — *vi* **1** QUEJARSE : grumble **2** *Spain* : quarrel — **regañon, -ñona** *adj, mpl* **-ñones** *fam* : grumpy, irritable

regar {49} *vt* **1** : irrigate, water **2** ESPARCIR : scatter

regatear *vt* **1** : haggle over **2** ESCATIMAR : skimp on — *vi* : bargain, haggle

regazo *nm* : lap (of a person)

regenerar *vt* : regenerate

regentar *vt* : run, manage

reggae *nm* : reggae

régimen *nm, pl* **regímenes 1** : regime **2** DIETA : diet **3** ~ **de vida** : lifestyle

regimiento *nm* : regiment

regio, -gia *adj* : royal, regal

región *nf, pl* **-giones** : region, area — **regional** *adj* : regional

regir {28} *vt* **1** : rule **2** ADMINISTRAR : manage, run **3** DETERMINAR : govern, determine — *vi* : apply, be in force — **regirse** *vr* ~ **por** : be guided by

registrar *vt* **1** : register **2** GRABAR : record, tape **3** : search (a house, etc.), frisk (a person) — **registrarse** *vr* **1** : register **2** : be recorded (of temperatures, etc.) — **registrador, -dora** *adj* **caja registradora** : cash register — ~ *n* : registrar — **registro** *nm* **1** : registration **2** : register (book) **3** : registry (office) **4** : range (of a voice, etc.) **5** INSPECCIÓN : search

regla *nf* **1** : rule, regulation **2** : ruler (for measuring) **3** MENSTRUACIÓN : period — **reglamentación** *nf, pl* **-ciones 1** : regulation **2** REGLAS : rules *pl* — **reglamentar** *vt* : regulate — **reglamentario, -ria** *adj* : regulation, official — **reglamento** *nm* : regulations *pl*, rules *pl*

regocijar *vt* : gladden, delight — **regocijarse** *vr* : rejoice — **regocijo** *nm* : delight, rejoicing

regodearse *vr* : be delighted — **regodeo** *nm* : delight

regordete *adj fam* : chubby

regresar *vi* : return, come back, go back — *vt Lat* : give back — **regresión** *nf, pl* **-siones** : regression — **regresivo, -va** *adj* : regressive — **regreso** *nm* **1** : return **2 estar de** ~ : be back, be home again

reguero *nm* **1** : irrigation ditch **2** SEÑAL : trail, trace **3 correr como un** ~ **de pólvora** : spread like wildfire

regular *adj* **1** : regular **2** MEDIANO : medium, average **3 por lo** ~ : in general — ~ *vt* : regulate, control — **regulación** *nf, pl* **-ciones** : regulation, control — **regularidad** *nf* : regularity — **regularizar** {21} *vt* : normalize, make regular

rehabilitar *vt* **1** : rehabilitate **2** : reinstate (s.o. in a position) **3** : renovate (a building, etc.) — **rehabilitación** *nf* **1** : rehabilitation **2** : reinstatement (in a position) **3** : renovation (of a building, etc.)

rehacer {40} *vt* **1** : redo **2** REPARAR : repair — **rehacerse** *vr* **1** : recover **2** ~ **de** : get over

rehén *nm, pl* **-henes** : hostage

rehuir {41} *vt* : avoid, shun

rehusar {8} *v* : refuse

reimprimir *vt* : reprint — **reimpresión** *nf, pl* **-siones** : reprinting, reprint

reina *nf* : queen — **reinado** *nm* : reign — **reinante** *adj* : reigning — **reinar** *vi* **1** : reign **2** PREVALECER : prevail

reincidir *vi* : backslide, relapse

reino *nm* : kingdom, realm

reintegrar *vt* **1** : reinstate **2** : refund (money), reimburse (expenses, etc.) — **reintegrarse** *vr* ~ **a** : return to — **reintegro** *nm* : reimbursement

reír {66} *vi* : laugh — *vt* : laugh at — **reírse** *vr* : laugh

reiterar *vt* : repeat, reiterate

reivindicar {72} *vt* **1** : claim **2** RESTAURAR : restore

reja *nf* : grille, grating — **rejilla** *nf* : grille, grate, screen

rejuvenecer {53} *vt* : rejuvenate — **rejuvenecerse** *vr* : be rejuvenated

relación *nf, pl* **-ciones 1** : relation, connection **2** COMUNICACIÓN : relationship, relations *pl* **3** RELATO : account **4** LISTA : list **5 con** ~ **a** *or* **en** ~ **a** : in relation to — **relacionar** *vt* : relate, connect — **relacionarse** *vr* ~ **con** : be connected to, interact with

relajar *vt* : relax — **relajarse** *vr* : relax —

relajación *nf, pl* **-ciones** : relaxation — **relajado, -da** *adj* **1** : relaxed **2** : dissolute, lax (in behavior)

relamerse *vr* : smack one's lips, lick its chops

relámpago *nm* : flash of lightning — **relampaguear** *vi* : flash

relatar *vt* : relate, tell

relativo, -va *adj* **1** : relative **2 en lo relativo a** : with regard to — **relatividad** *nf* : relativity

relato *nm* **1** : account, report **2** CUENTO : story, tale

releer {20} *vt* : reread

relegar {52} *vt* : relegate

relevante *adj* : outstanding, important

relevar *vt* **1** : relieve, take over from **2 ∼ de** : exempt from — **relevo** *nm* **1** : relief, replacement **2 carrera de ∼s** : relay race

relieve *nm* **1** : relief (in art, etc.) **2** IMPORTANCIA : prominence, importance **3 poner en ∼** : emphasize

religión *nf, pl* **-giones** : religion — **religioso, -sa** *adj* : religious — **∼** *n* : monk *m*, nun *f*

relinchar *vi* : neigh, whinny — **relincho** *nm* : neigh, whinny

reliquia *nf* **1** : relic **2 ∼ de familia** : family heirloom

rellenar *vt* **1** : refill **2** : stuff, fill (in cooking) — **relleno, -na** *adj* : stuffed, filled — **relleno** *nm* : stuffing, filling

reloj *nm* **1** : clock **2** *or* **∼ de pulsera** : wristwatch **3 ∼ de arena** : hourglass **4 como un ∼** : like clockwork

relucir {45} *vi* **1** : glitter, shine **2 sacar a ∼** : bring up, mention — **reluciente** *adj* : brilliant, shining

relumbrar *vi* : shine brightly

remachar *vt* **1** : rivet **2** RECALAR : stress, drive home — **remache** *nm* : rivet

remanente *nm* : remainder, surplus

remanso *nm* : pool

remar *vi* : row

rematar *vt* **1** : conclude, finish up **2** MATAR : finish off **3** LIQUIDAR : sell off cheaply **4** *Lat* : auction — *vi* **1** : shoot (in sports) **2** TERMINAR : end — **rematado, -da** *adj* : utter, complete — **remate** *nm* **1** : shot (in sports) **2** FIN : end

remedar *vt* : imitate, mimic

remediar *vt* **1** : remedy, repair **2** : solve (a problem) **3** EVITAR : avoid — **remedio** *nm* **1** : remedy, cure **2** SOLUCIÓN : solution **3 sin ∼** : hopeless

rememorar *vi* : recall

remendar {55} *vt* : mend

remesa *nf* **1** : remittance **2** : shipment (of merchandise)

remezón *nm, pl* **-zones** *Lat* : mild earthquake, tremor

remiendo *nm* : mend, patch

remilgado, -da *adj* **1** : prudish **2** AFECTADO : affected — **remilgo** *nm* : primness, affectation

reminiscencia *nf* : reminiscence

remisión *nf, pl* **-siones** : remission

remiso, -sa *adj* **1** : reluctant **2** NEGLIGENTE : remiss

remitir *vt* **1** : send, remit **2 ∼ a** : refer to, direct to — *vi* : subside, let up — **remite** *nm* : return address — **remitente** *nmf* : sender (of a letter, etc.)

remo *nm* : paddle, oar

remodelar *vt* **1** : remodel **2** : restructure (an organization)

remojar *vt* : soak, steep — **remojo** *nm* **poner en ∼** : soak

remolacha *nf* : beet

remolcar {72} *vt* : tow, tug — **remolcador** *nm* : tugboat

remolino *nm* **1** : whirlwind, whirlpool **2** : crowd (of people) **3** : cowlick (of hair)

remolque *nm* **1** : towing, tow **2** : trailer (vehicle)

remontar *vt* **1** : overcome **2** SUBIR : go up — **remontarse** *vr* **1** : soar **2 ∼ a** : date from, go back to

rémora *nf* : hindrance

remorder {47} *vt* : trouble, worry — **remordimiento** *nm* : remorse

remoto, -ta *adj* : remote — **remotamente** *adv* : remotely, slightly

remover {47} *vt* **1** : stir **2** : move around, turn over (earth, embers, etc.) **3** REAVIVIR : bring up again **4** DESPEDIR : fire, dismiss

remunerar *vt* : remunerate

renacer {48} *vi* : be reborn, revive — **renacimiento** *nm* **1** : rebirth, revival **2 el Renacimiento** : the Renaissance

renacuajo *nm* : tadpole, pollywog

rencilla *nf* : quarrel

renco, -ca *adj* *Lat* : lame

rencor *nm* **1** : rancor, hostility **2 guardar ∼** : hold a grudge — **rencoroso, -sa** *adj* : resentful

rendición *nf, pl* **-ciones** : surrender — **rendido, -da** *adj* **1** : submissive **2** AGOTADO : exhausted

rendija *nf* : crack, split

rendir {54} *vt* **1** : render, give **2** PRODUCIR : yield, produce **3** CANSAR : exhaust — *vi* : make progress, go a long way — **rendirse** *vr* : surrender, give up — **rendimiento** *nm* **1** : performance **2** : yield, return (in finance, etc.)

renegar {49} *vt* : deny — *vi* **1** QUEJARSE : grumble **2 ∼ de** ABJURAR : renounce, disown — **renegado, -da** *n* : renegade

renglón *nm, pl* **-glones 1** : line (of writing) **2** *Lat* : line (of products)

reno *nm* : reindeer

renombre *nm* : renown — **renombrado, -da** *adj* : famous, renowned

renovar {19} *vt* **1** : renew, restore **2** : renovate (a building, etc.) — **renovación** *nf, pl* **-ciones 1** : renewal **2** : renovation (of a building, etc.)

renquear *vi* : limp, hobble

rentar *vt* **1** : produce, yield **2** *Lat* : rent — **renta** *nf* **1** : income **2** ALQUILER : rent **3 impuesto sobre la** ~ : income tax — **rentable** *adj* : profitable

renunciar *vi* **1** : resign **2** ~ **a** : renounce, relinquish — **renuncia** *nf* **1** : renunciation **2** DIMISIÓN : resignation

reñir {67} *vi* ~ **con** : argue with, fall out with — *vt* **1** : scold **2** DISPUTAR : fight — **reñido, -da** *adj* **1** : hard-fought **2** ~ **con** : on bad terms with

reo, rea *n* **1** : accused, defendant **2** CULPABLE : culprit

reojo *nm* **de** ~ : out of the corner of one's eye

reorganizar {21} *vt* : reorganize

repantigarse {52} *vr* : sprawl out

reparar *vt* **1** : repair, fix **2** : make amends for (an offense, etc.) — *vi* **1** ~ **en** ADVERTIR : take notice of **2** ~ **en** CONSIDERAR : consider — **reparación** *nf, pl* **-ciones 1** : reparation, amends **2** ARREGLO : repair — **reparo** *nm* **1** : reservation, objection **2 poner** ~**s a** : object to

repartir *vt* **1** : allocate **2** DISTRIBUIR : distribute **3** ESPARCIR : spread — **repartición** *nf, pl* **-ciones** : distribution — **repartidor, -dora** *n* : delivery person, distributor — **reparto** *nm* **1** : allocation **2** DISTRIBUCIÓN : delivery **3** : cast (of characters)

repasar *vt* **1** : review, go over **2** ZURCIR : mend — **repaso** *nm* **1** : review **2** : mending (of clothes)

repeler *vt* **1** : repel **2** REPUGNAR : disgust — **repelente** *adj* : repellent, repulsive

repente *nm* **1** : fit, outburst **2 de** ~ : suddenly — **repentino, -na** *adj* : sudden

repercutir *vi* **1** : reverberate **2** ~ **en** : have repercussions on — **repercusión** *nf, pl* **-siones** : repercussion

repertorio *nm* : repertoire

repetir {54} *vt* **1** : repeat **2** : have a second helping of (food) — **repetirse** *vr* **1** : repeat oneself **2** : recur (of an event, etc.) — **repetición** *nf, pl* **-ciones 1** : repetition **2** : rerun, repeat (of a program, etc.) — **repetido, -da** *adj* **1** : repeated **2 repetidas veces** : repeatedly, time and again — **repetitivo, -va** *adj* : repetitive, repetitious

repicar {72} *vt* : ring — *vi* : ring out, peal — **repique** *nm* : ringing, pealing

repisa *nf* **1** : shelf, ledge **2** ~ **de ventana** : windowsill

replegar {49} *vt* : fold — **replegarse** *vr* : retreat, withdraw

repleto, -ta *adj* **1** : replete, full **2** ~ **de** : packed with

replicar {72} *vt* : reply, retort — *vi* : answer back — **réplica** *nf* **1** RESPUESTA : reply **2** COPIA : replica, reproduction

repliegue *nm* **1** : fold **2** : (military) withdrawal

repollo *nm* : cabbage

reponer {60} *vt* **1** : replace **2** REPLICAR : reply — **reponerse** *vr* : recover

reportar *vt* **1** : yield, bring **2** *Lat* : report — **reportaje** *nm* : article, (news) report — **reporte** *nm Lat* : report — **reportero, -ra** *n* : reporter

reposar *vi* **1** DESCANSAR : rest **2** : stand, settle (of liquids, dough, etc.) — **reposado, -da** *adj* : calm, relaxed — **reposición** *nf, pl* **-ciones** **1** : replacement **2** : rerun, repeat (of a program, etc.) — **reposo** *nm* : rest

repostar *vi* **1** : stock up on **2** : refuel (an airplane, etc.) — *vi* : fill up, refuel

reprender *vt* : reprimand, scold — **reprensible** *adj* : reprehensible

represalia *nf* **1** : reprisal **2 tomar** ~**s** : retaliate

represar *vt* : dam

representar *vt* **1** : represent **2** : perform (a play, etc.) **3** APARENTAR : look, appear as — **representación** *nf, pl* **-ciones 1** : representation **2** : performance (of a play, etc.) **3 en** ~ **de** : on behalf of — **representante** *nmf* **1** : representative **2** ACTOR : performer — **representativo, -va** *adj* : representative

represión *nf, pl* **-siones** : repression

reprimenda *nf* : reprimand

reprimir *vt* **1** : repress **2** : suppress (a rebellion, etc.)

reprobar {19} *vt* **1** : reprove, condemn **2** *Lat* : fail (an exam, etc.)

reprochar *vt* : reproach — **reprocharse** *vr* : reproach oneself — **reproche** *nm* : reproach

reproducir {61} *vt* : reproduce — **reproducirse** *vr* **1** : breed, reproduce **2** : recur (of an event, etc.) — **reproducción** *nf, pl* **-ciones** : reproduction — **reproductor, -tora** *adj* : reproductive

reptil *nm* : reptile

república *nf* : republic — **republicano, -na** *adj & n* : republican

repudiar *vt* : repudiate

repuesto *nm* : spare (auto) part

repugnar *vt* : disgust — **repugnancia** *nf* : disgust — **repugnante** *adj* : disgusting

repujar *vt* : emboss

repulsivo, -va *adj* : repulsive

reputar *vt* : consider, deem — **reputación** *nf, pl* **-ciones** : reputation

requerir {76} *vt* **1** : require **2** : summon, send for (a person)

requesón *nm, pl* **-sones** : cottage cheese

réquiem *nm* : requiem

requisito *nm* **1** : requirement **2** ~ **previo** : prerequisite

res *nf* **1** : beast, animal **2** *Lat or* **carne de** ~ : beef

resabio *nm* **1** VICIO : bad habit, vice **2** DEJO : aftertaste

resaca *nf* **1** : undertow **2 tener** ~ : have a hangover

resaltar *vi* **1** : stand out **2 hacer** ~ : bring out, highlight — *vt* : emphasize

resarcir {83} *vt* : compensate, repay — **resarcirse** *vr* ~ **de** : make up for

resbalar *vi* **1** : slip, slide **2** : skid (of an automobile) — **resbalarse** *vr* : slip, skid — **resbaladizo, -za** *adj* : slippery — **resbalón** *nm, pl* **-lones** : slip — **resbaloso, -sa** *adj Lat* : slippery

rescatar *vt* **1** : rescue, ransom **2** RECUPERAR : recover, get back — **rescate** *nm* **1** : rescue **2** : ransom (money) **3** RECUPERACIÓN : recovery

rescindir *vt* : cancel — **rescisión** *nf, pl* **-siones** : cancellation

rescoldo *nm* : embers *pl*

resecar {72} *vt* : dry (out) — **resecarse** *vr* : dry up — **reseco, -ca** *adj* : dry, dried-up

resentirse {76} *vr* **1** : suffer, be weakened **2** OFENDERSE : be offended **3** ~ **de** : feel the effects of — **resentido, -da** *adj* : resentful — **resentimiento** *nm* : resentment

reseñar *vt* **1** : review **2** DESCRIBIR : describe — **reseña** *nf* **1** : review, report **2** DESCRIPCIÓN : description

reservar *vt* **1** : reserve **2** GUARDAR : keep, save — **reservarse** *vr* **1** : save oneself **2** : keep for oneself — **reserva** *nf* **1** : reservation **2** PROVISIÓN : reserve **3 de** ~ : spare, in reserve — **reservación** *nf, pl* **-ciones** : reservation — **reservado, -da** *adj* **1** : reserved **2** : confidential (of a document, etc.)

resfriar {85} *vt* : cool — **resfriarse** *vr* **1** : cool off **2** CONSTIPARSE : catch a cold — **resfriado** *nm* CATARRO : cold — **resfrío** *nm Lat* : cold

resguardar *vt* : protect — **resguardarse** *vr* : protect oneself — **resguardo** *nm* **1** : protection **2** RECIBO : receipt

residir *vi* **1** : reside, live **2** ~ **en** : lie in — **residencia** *nf* **1** : residence **2** *or* ~ **universitaria** : dormitory — **residencial** *adj* : residential — **residente** *adj & nmf* : resident

residuo *nm* **1** : residue **2** ~**s** *nmpl* : waste — **residual** *adj* : residual

resignar *vt* : resign — **resignarse** *vr* ~ **a** : resign oneself to — **resignación** *nf, pl* **-ciones** : resignation

resina *nf* **1** : resin **2** ~ **epoxídica** : epoxy

resistir *vt* **1** AGUANTAR : stand, bear **2** : withstand (temptation, etc.) — *vi* : resist — **resistirse** *vr* ~ **a** : be resistant to — **resistencia** *nf* **1** : resistance **2** AGUANTE : endurance, stamina — **resistente** *adj* : resistant, strong, tough

resma *nf* : ream

resollar {19} *vi* : breathe heavily, pant

resolver {89} *vt* **1** : resolve **2** DECIDIR : decide — **resolverse** *vr* : make up one's mind — **resolución** *nf, pl* **-ciones** **1** : resolution **2** DECISIÓN : decision **3** FIRMEZA : determination, resolve

resonar {19} *vi* : resound — **resonancia** *nf* **1** : resonance **2** CONSECUENCIAS : impact, repercussions *pl* — **resonante** *adj* : resonant, resounding

resoplar *vi* **1** : puff, pant **2** : snort (with annoyance)

resorte *nm* **1** MUELLE : spring **2 tocar** ~**s** : pull strings

respaldar *vt* : back, endorse — **respaldarse** *vr* : lean back — **respaldo** *nm* **1** : back (of a chair, etc.) **2** APOYO : support, backing

respectar *vt* : concern, relate to — **respectivo, -va** *adj* : respective — **respecto** *nm* **1** **al** ~ : in this respect **2** ~ **a** : in regard to, concerning

respetar *vt* : respect — **respetable** *adj* : respectable — **respeto** *nm* **1** : respect **2 presentar sus** ~**s** : pay one's respects — **respetuoso, -sa** *adj* : respectful

respingo *nm* : start, jump

respirar *v* : breathe — **respiración** *nf, pl* **-ciones** : respiration, breathing — **respiratorio, -ria** *adj* : respiratory — **respiro** *nm* **1** : breath **2** DESCANSO : respite, break

resplandecer {53} *vi* : shine — **resplandeciente** *adj* : shining, gleaming — **resplandor** *nm* **1** : brilliance, gleam **2** : flash (of lightning, etc.)

responder *vt* : answer, reply — *vi* **1** : answer **2** REPLICAR : answer back **3** ~ **a** : respond to **4** ~ **de** : answer for (something)

responsable *adj* : responsible — **responsabilidad** *nf* : responsibility

respuesta *nf* **1** : answer, reply **2** REACCIÓN : response

resquebrajar *vt* : split, crack — **resquebrajarse** *vr* : crack

resquicio *nm* **1** : crack, crevice **2** VESTIGIO : trace, glimmer

resta *nf* : subtraction

restablecer {53} *vt* : reestablish, restore —

restablecerse *vr* : recover — **restableci-miento** *nm* : restoration, recovery
restallar *vi* : crack, crackle
restar *vt* **1** : deduct, subtract **2** DISMINUIR : minimize — *vi* : be left — **restante** *adj* **1** : remaining **2 lo** ~ : the rest
restauración *nf, pl* **-ciones** : restoration
restaurante *nm* : restaurant
restaurar *vt* : restore
restituir {41} *vt* : return, restore — **resti-tución** *nf, pl* **-ciones** : restitution
resto *nm* **1** : rest, remainder **2** ~**s** *nmpl* : leftovers **3** *or* ~**s mortales** : mortal remains
restregar {49} *vt* : rub, scrub — **restre-garse** *vr* : rub
restringir {35} *vt* : restrict, limit — **restric-ción** *nf, pl* **-ciones** : restriction, limitation — **restrictivo, -va** *adj* : restrictive
resucitar *vt* : resuscitate, revive — *vi* : come back to life
resuelto, -ta *adj* : determined, resolved
resuello *nm* : heavy breathing, panting
resultar *vi* **1** : succeed, work out **2** SALIR : turn out (to be) **3** ~ **de** : be the result of **4** ~ **en** : result in — **resultado** *nm* : result, outcome
resumir *v* : summarize, sum up — **resumen** *nm, pl* **-súmenes 1** : summary **2 en** ~ : in short
resurgir {35} *vi* : reappear, revive — **resur-gimiento** *nm* : resurgence — **resurrección** *nf, pl* **-ciones** : resurrection
retahíla *nf* : string, series
retal *nm* : remnant
retardar *vt* **1** RETRASAR : delay **2** POSPONER : postpone
retazo *nm* **1** : remnant, scrap **2** : fragment (of a text, etc.)
retener {80} *vt* **1** : retain, keep **2** : withhold (funds, etc.) **3** DETENER : detain — **reten-ción** *nf, pl* **-ciones 1** : retention **2** : deduc-tion, withholding (of funds)
reticente *adj* : reluctant — **reticencia** *nf* : reluctance
retina *nf* : retina
retintín *nm, pl* **-tines 1** : tinkling, jingle **2 con** ~ : sarcastically
retirar *vt* **1** : remove, take away **2** : with-draw (funds, statements, etc.) — **retirarse** *vr* **1** : retreat, withdraw **2** JUBILARSE : retire — **retirada** *nf* **1** : withdrawal **2 batirse en** ~ : beat a retreat — **retirado, -da** *adj* **1** : remote, secluded **2** JUBILADO : retired — **retiro** *nm* **1** : retreat **2** JUBILACIÓN : retire-ment **3** *Lat* : withdrawal
reto *nm* : challenge, dare
retocar {72} *vt* : touch up
retoño *nm* : sprout, shoot

retoque *nm* **1** : retouching **2 el último** ~ : the finishing touch
retorcer {14} *vt* **1** : twist, contort **2** : wring out (clothes, etc.) — **retorcerse** *vr* **1** : get twisted up **2** : squirm, writhe (in pain) — **retorcijón** *nm, pl* **-jones** : cramp, spasm — **retorcimiento** *nm* : twisting, wringing out
retórica *nf* : rhetoric — **retórico, -ca** *adj* : rhetorical
retornar *v* : return — **retorno** *nm* : return
retozar {21} *vi* : frolic, romp — **retozón, -zona** *adj* : playful, frisky
retractarse *vr* **1** : withdraw, back down **2** ~ **de** : take back, retract
retraer {81} *vt* : retract — **retraerse** *vr* : withdraw — **retraído, -da** *adj* : with-drawn, shy
retrasar *vt* **1** : delay, hold up **2** APLAZAR : postpone **3** : set back (a clock) — **retra-sarse** *vr* **1** : be late **2** : fall behind (in work, etc.) — **retrasado, -da** *adj* **1** : retarded **2** : in arrears (of payments) **3** : backward (of a country) **4** : slow (of a clock) — **retraso** *nm* **1** : delay **2** SUBDESARROLLO : back-wardness **3** ~ **mental** : mental retardation
retratar *vt* **1** : portray **2** FOTOGRAFIAR : pho-tograph **3** DIBUJAR : paint a portrait of — **retrato** *nm* **1** : portrayal **2** DIBUJO : portrait **3** FOTOGRAFÍA : photograph
retrete *nm* : restroom, toilet
retribuir {41} *vt* **1** : pay **2** RECOMPENSAR : reward — **retribución** *nf, pl* **-ciones 1** : payment **2** RECOMPENSA : reward
retroactivo, -va *adj* : retroactive
retroceder *vi* **1** : go back, turn back **2** CEDER : back down — **retroceso** *nm* **1** : backward movement **2** : backing down
retrógrado, -da *adj & nmf* : reactionary
retrospectiva *nf* : hindsight — **retrospec-tivo, -va** *adj* : retrospective
retrovisor *nm* : rearview mirror
retumbar *vi* : resound, reverberate, rumble
reumatismo *nm* : rheumatism
reunir {68} *vt* **1** : unite, join **2** TENER : have, possess **3** RECOGER : gather, collect — **reu-nirse** *vr* : meet, gather — **reunión** *nf, pl* **-niones 1** : meeting **2** : (social) gathering, reunion
revalidar *vt* : confirm, ratify
revancha *nf* **1** : revenge **2** : rematch (in sports)
revelar *vt* **1** : reveal, disclose **2** : develop (film) — **revelación** *nf, pl* **-ciones** : revela-tion — **revelado** *nm* : developing (of film) — **revelador, -dora** *adj* : revealing
reventar {55} *v* : burst, blow up — **reven-tarse** *vr* : burst — **reventón** *nm, pl* **-tones** : blowout, flat tire

reverberar *vi* : reverberate — **reverberación** *nf, pl* **-ciones** : reverberation
reverenciar *vt* : revere — **reverencia** *nf* **1** : bow, curtsy **2** VENERACIÓN : reverence — **reverendo, -da** *adj & nmf* : reverend — **reverente** *adj* : reverent
reversa *nf Lat* : reverse (gear)
reverso *nm* **1** : back, reverse **2 el ~ de la medalla** : the complete opposite — **reversible** *adj* : reversible
revertir {76} *vi* **1** : revert **2 ~ en** : result in
revés *nm, pl* **-veses 1** : back, wrong side **2** CONTRATIEMPO : setback **3** BOFETADA : slap **4** : backhand (in sports) **5 al ~** : the other way around, upside down, inside out
revestir {54} *vt* **1** : coat, cover **2** ASUMIR : take on, assume — **revestimiento** *nm* : covering, coating
revisar *vt* **1** : examine, inspect **2** : check over, overhaul (machinery, etc.) **3** MODIFICAR : revise — **revisión** *nf, pl* **-siones 1** : revision **2** INSPECCIÓN : inspection, check — **revisor, -sora** *n* : inspector
revistar *vt* : review, inspect (troops, etc.) — **revista** *nf* **1** : magazine, journal **2** : revue (in theater) **3 pasar ~** : review, inspect
revivir *vi* : revive, come alive again — *vt* : relive
revocar {72} *vt* : revoke
revolcar {82} *vt* : knock over, knock down — **revolcarse** *vr* : roll around
revolotear *vi* : flutter, flit — **revoloteo** *nm* : fluttering, flitting
revoltijo *nm* : mess, jumble
revoltoso, -sa *adj* : rebellious
revolución *nf, pl* **-ciones** : revolution — **revolucionar** *vt* : revolutionize — **revolucionario, -ria** *adj & n* : revolutionary
revolver {89} *vt* I : mix, stir **2** : upset (one's stomach) **3** DESORGANIZAR : mess up — **revolverse** *vr* **1** : toss and turn **2** VOLVERSE : turn around
revólver *nm* : revolver
revuelo *nm* : commotion
revuelta *nf* : uprising, revolt — **revuelto, -ta** *adj* **1** : choppy, rough **2** DESORDENADO : messed up **3 huevos revueltos** : scrambled eggs
rey *nm* : king
reyerta *nf* : brawl, fight
rezagarse {52} *vr* : fall behind, lag
rezar {21} *vi* **1** : pray **2** DECIR : say — *vt* : say, recite — **rezo** *nm* : prayer
rezongar {52} *vi* : gripe, grumble
rezumar *v* : ooze
ría *nf* : estuary
riachuelo *nm* : brook, stream
riada *nf* : flood
ribera *nf* : bank, shore

ribetear *vt* : border, trim — **ribete** *nm* **1** : border, trim **2** : embellishment
rico, -ca *adj* **1** : rich, wealthy **2** ABUNDANTE : abundant **3** SABROSO : rich, tasty — **~** *n* : rich person
ridiculizar {21} *vt* : ridicule — **ridículo, -la** *adj* : ridiculous — **ridículo** *nm* **1 hacer el ~** : make a fool of oneself **2 poner en ~** : ridicule
riego *nm* : irrigation
riel *nm* : rail
rienda *nf* **1** : rein **2 dar ~ suelta a** : give free rein to
riesgo *nm* : risk
rifa *nf* : raffle — **rifar** *vt* : raffle (off) — **rifarse** *vr fam* : fight over
rifle *nm* : rifle
rígido, -da *adj* **1** : rigid, stiff **2** SEVERO : harsh, strict — **rigidez** *nf, pl* **-deces 1** : rigidity, stiffness **2** SEVERIDAD : harshness, strictness
rigor *nm* **1** : rigor, harshness **2** EXACTITUD : precision **3 de ~** : essential, obligatory — **riguroso, -sa** *adj* : rigorous
rima *nf* **1** : rhyme **2 ~s** *nfpl* : verse, poetry — **rimar** *vi* : rhyme
rimbombante *adj* : showy, pompous
rímel *nm* : mascara
rincón *nm, pl* **-cones** : corner, nook
rinoceronte *nm* : rhinoceros
riña *nf* **1** : fight, brawl **2** DISPUTA : dispute, quarrel
riñón *nm, pl* **-ñones** : kidney
río *nm* **1** : river **2** TORRENTE : torrent, stream
riqueza *nf* **1** : wealth **2** ABUNDANCIA : richness **3 ~s naturales** : natural resources
risa *nf* **1** : laughter, laugh **2 dar ~ a algn** : make s.o. laugh **3 morirse de la ~** *fam* : die laughing
risco *nm* : crag, cliff
risible *adj* : laughable
ristra *nf* : string, series
risueño, -ña *adj* : cheerful, smiling
ritmo *nm* **1** : rhythm **2** VELOCIDAD : pace, speed — **rítmico, -ca** *adj* : rhythmical
rito *nm* : rite, ritual — **ritual** *adj & nm* : ritual
rival *adj & nmf* : rival — **rivalidad** *nf* : rivalry, competition — **rivalizar** {21} *vi* **~ con** : rival, compete with
rizar {21} *vt* **1** : curl **2** : ripple (a surface) — **rizarse** *vr* : curl — **rizado, -da** *adj* **1** : curly **2** : choppy (of water) — **rizo** *nm* **1** : curl **2** : ripple (in water) **3** : loop (in aviation)
róbalo *nm* : bass (fish)
robar *vt* **1** : steal **2** : burglarize (a house, etc.) **3** SECUESTRAR : kidnap — **robo** *nm* : robbery, theft
roble *nm* : oak

robot *nm, pl* **-bots** : robot — **robótica** *nf*
: robotics

robustecer {53} *vt* : make stronger,
strengthen — **robusto, -ta** *adj* : robust,
sturdy

roca *nf* : rock, boulder

roce *nm* **1** : rubbing, chafing **2** RASGUÑO
: graze, scratch **3 tener un ~ con** : have a
brush with

rociar {85} *vt* : spray, sprinkle — **rocío** *nm*
: dew

rocoso, -sa *adj* : rocky

rodaja *nf* : slice

rodar {19} *vi* **1** : roll, roll down, roll along
2 GIRAR : turn, go around **3** : travel (of a
vehicle) **4** : film (of movies, etc.) — *vt* **1**
: film, shoot **2** : break in (a vehicle) — **ro-
daje** *nm* **1** : filming, shooting **2** : breaking
in (of a vehicle)

rodear *vt* **1** : surround, encircle **2** *Lat*
: round up (cattle) — **rodearse** *vr* ~ **de**
: surround oneself with — **rodeo** *nm* **1**
: rodeo, roundup **2** DESVÍO : detour **3 andar
con ~s** : beat around the bush

rodilla *nf* : knee

rodillo *nm* **1** : roller **2** : rolling pin (for pastry)

roer {69} *vt* **1** : gnaw **2** ATORMENTAR : eat
away at, torment — **roedor** *nm* : rodent

rogar {16} *vt* : beg, request — *vi* : pray

rojo, -ja *adj* **1** : red **2 ponerse ~** : blush
— **rojo** *nm* : red — **rojez** *nf* : redness — **rojizo, -za** *adj* : reddish

rollizo, -za *adj* : plump, chubby

rollo *nm* **1** : roll, coil **2** *fam* : boring speech,
lecture

romance *nm* **1** : romance **2** : Romance (language)

romano, -na *adj & n* : Roman

romántico, -ca *adj* : romantic — **romanti-
cismo** *nm* : romanticism

romería *nf* : pilgrimage, procession

romero *nm* : rosemary

romo, -ma *adj* : blunt, dull

rompecabezas *nms & pl* : puzzle

romper {70} *vt* **1** : break **2** RASGAR : rip,
tear **3** : break off (relations), break (a contract) — *vi* **1** : break (of the day, waves,
etc.) **2 ~ a** : begin to, burst out with **3 ~
con** : break off with — **romperse** *vr* : break

ron *nm* : rum

roncar {72} *vi* : snore — **ronco, -ca** *adj*
: hoarse

ronda *nf* **1** : rounds *pl*, patrol **2** : round (of
drinks, etc.) — **rondar** *vt* **1** : patrol **2** : hang
around (a place) **3** : be approximately (an
age, a number, etc.) — *vi* **1** : be on patrol **2**
MERODEAR : prowl about

ronquera *nf* : hoarseness

ronquido *nm* : snore

ronronear *vi* : purr — **ronroneo** *nm* : purr,
purring

ronzar {21} *vt* : munch, crunch

roña *nf* **1** : mange **2** SUCIEDAD : dirt, filth
— **roñoso, -sa** *adj* **1** : mangy **2** SUCIO
: dirty **3** *fam* : stingy

ropa *nf* **1** : clothes *pl*, clothing **2 ~ interior**
: underwear — **ropaje** *nm* : robes *pl*, regalia
— **ropero** *nm* : wardrobe, closet

rosa *nf* : rose (flower) — ~ *adj* : rose-
colored — ~ *nm* : rose (color) — **rosado,
-da** *adj* **1** : pink **2 vino rosado** : rosé —
rosado *nm* : pink (color) — **rosal** *nm*
: rosebush

rosario *nm* : rosary

rosbif *nm* : roast beef

rosca *nf* **1** : thread (of a screw) **2** ESPIRAL
: ring, coil

roseta *nf* : rosette

rosquilla *nf* : doughnut

rostro *nm* : face

rotación *nf, pl* **-ciones** : rotation — **rotativo,
-va** *adj* : rotary, revolving

roto, -ta *adj* : broken, torn

rotonda *nf* : traffic circle, rotary

rótula *nf* : kneecap

rótulo *nm* **1** : heading, title **2** ETIQUETA
: label, sign

rotundo, -da *adj* : categorical, absolute

rotura *nf* : break, tear, fracture

rozar {21} *vt* **1** : graze, touch lightly **2**
APROXIMARSE DE : touch on, border on — *vi*
: scrape, rub — **rozarse** *vr* **1** : rub, chafe **2**
~ **con** *fam* : rub elbows with — **rozadura**
nf : scratch

rubí *nm, pl* **rubíes** : ruby

rubicundo, -da *adj* : ruddy

rubio, -bia *adj & n* : blond

rubor *nm* : flush, blush — **ruborizarse** {21}
vr : blush

rúbrica *nf* **1** : flourish (in writing) **2** TÍTULO
: title, heading

rudeza *nf* : roughness, coarseness

rudimentos *nmpl* : rudiments, basics — **rudimentario, -ria** *adj* : rudimentary

rudo, -da *adj* **1** : rough, harsh **2** GROSERO
: coarse, unpolished

rueda *nf* **1** : wheel **2** CORRO : circle, ring **3**
RODAJA : (round) slice **4 ir sobre ~s** : go
smoothly — **ruedo** *nm* : bullring

ruego *nm* : request

rugir {35} *vi* : roar — **rugido** *nm* : roar

rugoso, -sa *adj* **1** : rough **2** ARRUGADO
: wrinkled

ruibarbo *nm* : rhubarb

ruido *nm* : noise — **ruidoso, -sa** *adj* : loud,
noisy

ruina *nf* **1** : ruin, destruction **2** COLAPSO
: collapse **3 ~s** *nfpl* : ruins, remains —
ruinoso, -sa *adj* : run-down, dilapidated

ruiseñor *nm* : nightingale
ruleta *nf* : roulette
rulo *nm* : curler, roller
rumano, -na *adj* : Romanian, Rumanian
rumba *nf* : rumba
rumbo *nm* **1** : direction, course **2** ESPLENDI-DEZ : lavishness **3 con ~ a** : bound for, heading for **4 perder el ~** : go off course
rumiar *vt* : mull over — *vi* : chew the cud — **rumiante** *adj* & *nm* : ruminant
rumor *nm* **1** : rumor **2** MURMULLO : murmur — **rumorearse** *or* **rumorarse** *vr* : be ru-

mored — **rumoroso, -sa** *adj* : murmuring, babbling
ruptura *nf* **1** : break, rupture **2** : breach (of a contract) **3** : breaking off (of relations)
rural *adj* : rural
ruso, -sa *adj* : Russian — **ruso** *nm* : Russian (language)
rústico, -ca *adj* **1** : rural, rustic **2 en rús-tica** : in paperback
ruta *nf* : route
rutina *nf* : routine — **rutinario, -ria** *adj* : routine

S

s *nf* : s, 20th letter of the Spanish alphabet
sábado *nm* : Saturday
sábana *nf* : sheet
sabandija *nf* : bug
saber {71} *vt* **1** : know **2** SER CAPAZ DE : know how to, be able to **3** ENTERARSE : learn, find out **4 a ~** : namely — *vi* **1** : taste **2 ~ de** : know about — **~** *nm* : knowledge — **sabelotodo** *nmf fam* : know-it-all — **sabido, -da** *adj* : well-known — **sabiduría** *nf* **1** : wisdom **2** CO-NOCIMIENTO : learning, knowledge — **sa-biendas: a ~** *adv phr* : knowingly — **sabio, -bia** *adj* **1** : learned **2** PRUDENTE : wise, sensible
sabor *nm* : flavor, taste — **saborear** *vt* : savor
sabotaje *nm* : sabotage — **saboteador, -dora** *n* : saboteur — **sabotear** *vt* : sabotage
sabroso, -sa *adj* : delicious, tasty
sabueso *nm* **1** : bloodhound **2** *fam* : sleuth
sacacorchos *nms & pl* : corkscrew
sacapuntas *nms & pl* : pencil sharpener
sacar {72} *vt* **1** : take out **2** OBTENER : get, obtain **3** EXTRAER : extract, withdraw **4** : bring out (a book, a product, etc.) **5** : take (photos), make (copies) **6** QUITAR : remove **7 ~ adelante** : bring up (children), carry out (a project, etc.) **8 ~ la lengua** : stick out one's tongue — *vi* : serve (in sports)
sacarina *nf* : saccharin
sacerdote, -tisa *n* : priest *m*, priestess *f* — **sacerdocio** *nm* : priesthood — **sacerdotal** *adj* : priestly
saciar *vt* : satisfy
saco *nm* **1** : bag, sack **2** : sac (in anatomy) **3** *Lat* : jacket
sacramento *nm* : sacrament — **sacramen-tal** *adj* : sacramental

sacrificar {72} *vt* : sacrifice — **sacrificarse** *vr* : sacrifice oneself — **sacrificio** *nm* : sac-rifice
sacrilegio *nm* : sacrilege — **sacrílego, -ga** *adj* : sacrilegious
sacro, -cra *adj* : sacred — **sacrosanto, -ta** *adj* : sacrosanct
sacudir *vt* **1** : shake **2** GOLPEAR : beat **3** CONMOVER : shake up, shock — **sacudirse** *vr* : shake off — **sacudida** *nf* **1** : shaking **2** : jolt (of a train, etc.), tremor (of an earth-quake) **3** : (emotional) shock
sádico, -ca *adj* : sadistic — **~** *n* : sadist — **sadismo** *nm* : sadism
saeta *nf* : arrow
safari *nm* : safari
sagaz *adj, pl* **-gaces** : shrewd, sagacious — **sagacidad** *nf* : shrewdness
sagrado, -da *adj* : sacred, holy
sal *nf* : salt
sala *nf* **1** : room, hall **2** : living room (of a house) **3 ~ de espera** : waiting room
salar *vt* : salt — **salado, -da** *adj* **1** : salty **2** GRACIOSO : witty **3 agua salada** : salt water
salario *nm* : salary, wage
salchicha *nf* : sausage — **salchichón** *nf, pl* **-chones** : salami-like cold cut
saldar *vt* **1** : settle, pay off **2** VENDER : sell off — **saldo** *nm* **1** : balance (of an account) **2 ~s** *nmpl* : remainders, sale items
salero *nm* : saltshaker
salir {73} *vi* **1** : go out, come out **2** PARTIR : leave **3** APARECER : appear **4** RESULTAR : turn out **5** : rise (of the sun) **6 ~ ade-lante** : get by **7 ~ con** : go out with, date **8 ~ de** : come from — **salirse** *vr* **1** : leave **2** ESCAPARSE : leak out, escape **3** SOLTARSE : come off **4 ~ con la suya** : get one's

own way — **salida** *nf* **1** : exit **2** : (action of) leaving, departure **3** SOLUCIÓN : way out **4** : leak (of gas, liquid, etc.) **5** OCURRENCIA : witty remark **6** ~ **de emergencia** : emergency exit **7** ~ **del sol** : sunrise —
saliente *adj* **1** : departing, outgoing **2** DESTACADO : outstanding
saliva *nf* : saliva
salmo *nm* : psalm
salmón *nm, pl* **-mones** : salmon
salmuera *nf* : brine
salón *nm, pl* **-lones** **1** : lounge, sitting room **2** ~ **de belleza** : beauty salon **3** ~ **de clase** : classroom
salpicar {72} *vt* **1** : splash, spatter **2** ~ **de** : pepper with — **salpicadera** *nf Lat* : fender — **salpicadura** *nf* : splash
salsa *nf* **1** : sauce **2** : (meat) gravy **3** : salsa (music)
saltamontes *nms & pl* : grasshopper
saltar *vi* **1** : jump, leap **2** REBOTAR : bounce **3** : come off (of a button, etc.) **4** ROMPERSE : shatter **5** ESTALLAR : explode, blow up — *vt* **1** : jump (over) **2** OMITIR : skip, miss — **saltarse** *vr* **1** : come off **2** OMITIR : skip, miss
saltear *vt* : sauté
saltimbanqui *nmf* : acrobat
salto *nm* **1** : jump, leap **2** : dive (into water) **3** ~ **de agua** : waterfall — **saltón, -tona** *adj, mpl* **-tones** : bulging, protruding
salud *nf* **1** : health **2** ¡**salud!** : here's to your health! **3** ¡**salud!** *Lat* : bless you! (when someone sneezes) — **saludable** *adj* : healthy
saludar *vt* **1** : greet, say hello to **2** : salute (in the military) — **saludo** *nm* **1** : greeting **2** : (military) salute **3** ~**s** : best wishes, regards
salva *nf* ~ **de aplausos** : round of applause
salvación *nf, pl* **-ciones** : salvation
salvado *nm* : bran
salvador, -dora *n* : savior, rescuer
salvadoreño, -ña *adj* : (El) Salvadoran
salvaguardar *vt* : safeguard
salvaje *adj* **1** : wild **2** PRIMITIVO : savage, primitive — ~ *nmf* : savage
salvar *vt* **1** : save, rescue **2** RECORRER : cover, travel **3** SUPERAR : overcome — **salvarse** *vr* : save oneself — **salvavidas** *nms & pl* **1** : life preserver **2 bote** ~ : lifeboat
salvia *nf* : sage (plant)
salvo, -va *adj* : safe — **salvo** *prep* **1** : except (for), save **2** ~ **que** : unless
samba *nf* : samba
San → santo

sanar *vt* : heal, cure — *vi* : recover — **sanatorio** *nm* **1** : sanatorium **2** HOSPITAL : clinic, hospital
sanción *nf, pl* **-ciones** : sanction — **sancionar** *vt* : sanction
sandalia *nf* : sandal
sándalo *nm* : sandalwood
sandía *nf* : watermelon
sandwich ["sandwitS, "saNgwitS] *nm, pl* **-wiches** [-dwitSes, -gwi-] : sandwich
saneamiento *nm* : sanitation
sangrar *vt* **1** : bleed **2** : indent (a paragraph) — *vi* : bleed — **sangrante** *adj* : bleeding — **sangre** *nf* **1** : blood **2 a** ~ **fría** : in cold blood — **sangriento, -ta** *adj* : bloody
sanguijuela *nf* : leech
sanguinario, -ria *adj* : bloodthirsty — **sanguíneo, -nea** *adj* : blood
sano, -na *adj* **1** : healthy **2** : (morally) wholesome **3** ENTERO : intact **4 sano y salvo** : safe and sound — **sanidad** *nf* **1** : health **2** : public health, sanitation — **sanitario, -ria** *adj* : sanitary, health — **sanitario** *nm Lat* : toilet
santiamén *nm* **en un** ~ : in no time at all
santo, -ta *adj* **1** : holy **2 Santo, Santa (San** *before masculine names except those beginning with D or T)* : Saint — ~ *n* : saint — **santo** *nm* **1** : saint's day **2** *Lat* : birthday — **santidad** *nf* : holiness, sanctity — **santiguarse** {10} *vr* : cross oneself — **santuario** *nm* : sanctuary
saña *nf* **1** : fury **2** BRUTALIDAD : viciousness
sapo *nm* : toad
saque *nm* : serve (in tennis, etc.), throw-in (in soccer)
saquear *vt* : sack, loot — **saqueador, -dora** *n* : looter — **saqueo** *nm* : sacking, looting
sarampión *nm* : measles *pl*
sarape *nm Lat* : serape
sarcasmo *nm* : sarcasm — **sarcástico, -ca** *adj* : sarcastic
sardina *nf* : sardine
sardónico, -ca *adj* : sardonic
sargento *nmf* : sergeant
sarpullido *nm* : rash
sartén *nmf, pl* **-tenes** : frying pan
sastre, -tra *n* : tailor — **sastrería** *nf* **1** : tailoring **2** : tailor's shop
Satanás *nm* : Satan — **satánico, -ca** *adj* : satanic
satélite *nm* : satellite
sátira *nf* : satire — **satírico, -ca** *adj* : satirical
satisfacer {74} *vt* **1** : satisfy **2** CUMPLIR : fulfill, meet **3** PAGAR : pay — **satisfacerse** *vr* **1** : be satisfied **2** VENGARSE

: take revenge — **satisfacción** *nf, pl* **-ciones** : satisfaction — **satisfactorio, -ria** *adj* : satisfactory — **satisfecho, -cha** *adj* : satisfied

saturar *vt* : saturate — **saturación** *nf, pl* **-ciones** : saturation

Saturno *nm* : Saturn

sauce *nm* : willow

sauna *nmf* : sauna

savia *nf* : sap

saxofón *nm, pl* **-fones** : saxophone

sazón *nf, pl* **-zones** **1** : seasoning **2** MADUREZ : ripeness **3 a la ~** : at that time, then **4 en ~** : ripe, in season — **sazonar** *vt* : season

se *pron* **1** (*reflexive*) : himself, herself, itself, oneself, yourself, yourselves, themselves **2** (*indirect object*) : (to) him, (to) her, (to) you, (to) them **3** : each other, one another **4 ~ dice que** : it is said that **5 ~ habla inglés** : English spoken

sebo *nm* **1** : fat **2** : tallow (for candles, etc.) **3** : suet (for cooking)

secar {72} *v* : dry — **secarse** *vr* : dry (up) — **secador** *nm* : hair dryer — **secadora** *nf* : (clothes) dryer

sección *nf, pl* **-ciones** : section

seco, -ca *adj* **1** : dry **2** : dried (of fruits, etc.) **3** TAJANTE : sharp, brusque **4** *fam* : thin, skinny **5 a secas** : simply, just **6 en seco** : suddenly

secretar *vt* : secrete — **secreción** *nf, pl* **-ciones** : secretion

secretario, -ria *n* : secretary — **secretaría** *nf* : secretariat

secreto, -ta *adj* : secret — **secreto** *nm* **1** : secret **2 en ~** : in confidence

secta *nf* : sect

sector *nm* : sector

secuaz *nmf, pl* **-cuaces** : follower, henchman

secuela *nf* : consequence

secuencia *nf* : sequence

secuestrar *vt* **1** : kidnap **2** : hijack (an airplane, etc.) **3** EMBARGAR : confiscate, seize — **secuestrador, -dora** *n* **1** : kidnapper **2** : hijacker (of an airplane, etc.) — **secuestro** *nm* **1** : kidnapping **2** : hijacking (of an airplane, etc.) **3** : seizure (of goods)

secular *adj* : secular

secundar *vt* : support, second — **secundario, -ria** *adj* : secondary

sed *nf* **1** : thirst **2 tener ~** : be thirsty

seda *nf* : silk

sedal *nm* : fishing line

sedar *vt* : sedate — **sedante** *adj & nm* : sedative

sede *nf* **1** : seat, headquarters **2 Santa Sede** : Holy See

sedentario, -ria *adj* : sedentary

sedición *nf, pl* **-ciones** : sedition — **sedicioso, -sa** *adj* : seditious

sediento, -ta *adj* : thirsty

sedimento *nm* : sediment

sedoso, -sa *adj* : silky, silken

seducir {61} *vt* **1** : seduce **2** ATRAER : captivate, charm — **seducción** *nf, pl* **-ciones** : seduction — **seductor, -tora** *adj* **1** : seductive **2** ENCANTADOR : charming — **~** *n* : seducer

segar {49} *vt* : reap — **segador, -dora** *n* : reaper, harvester

seglar *adj* : lay, secular — **~** *nm* : layperson, layman *m*, laywoman *f*

segmento *nm* : segment

segregar {52} *vt* : segregate — **segregación** *nf, pl* **-ciones** : segregation

seguir {75} *vt* : follow — *vi* : go on, continue — **seguida: en ~** *adv phr* : right away — **seguido** *adv* **1** : straight (ahead) **2** *Lat* : often — **seguido, -da** *adj* **1** : continuous **2** CONSECUTIVO : consecutive — **seguidor, -dora** *n* : follower

según *prep* : according to — **~** *adv* : it depends — **~** *conj* : as, just as

segundo, -da *adj* : second — **~** *n* : second (one) — **segundo** *nm* : second (unit of time)

seguridad *nf* **1** : safety, security **2** : (financial) security (**seguridad social** Social Security) **3** CERTEZA : certainty, assurance **4** : confidence, self-confidence

seguro, -ra *adj* **1** : safe **2** FIRME : secure **3** CIERTO : sure, certain **4** FIABLE : reliable — **seguramente** *adv* : for sure, surely — **seguro** *adv* : certainly — **~** *nm* **1** : insurance **2** : safety (device)

seis *adj & nm* : six — **seiscientos, -tas** *adj* : six hundred — **seiscientos** *nms & pl* : six hundred

seísmo *nm* : earthquake

selección *nf, pl* **-ciones** : selection — **seleccionar** *vt* : select, choose — **selectivo, -va** *adj* : selective — **selecto, -ta** *adj* : choice, select

sellar *vt* **1** : seal **2** TIMBRAR : stamp — **sello** *nm* **1** : seal **2** TIMBRE : stamp **3** *or* **~ distintivo** : hallmark

selva *nf* **1** : jungle **2** BOSQUE : forest

semáforo *nm* : traffic light

semana *nf* : week — **semanal** *adj* : weekly — **semanario** *nm* : weekly

semántica *nf* : semantics — **semántico, -ca** *adj* : semantic

semblante *nm* **1** : countenance, face **2** APARIENCIA : look

sembrar {55} *vt* **1** : sow **2 ~ de** : strew with

semejar *vi* : resemble — **semejarse** *vr* : look alike — **semejante** *adj* 1 : similar 2 TAL : such — **~** *nm* : fellowman — **semejanza** *nf* : similarity

semen *nm* : semen — **semental** *nm* 1 : stud 2 **caballo ~** : stallion

semestre *nm* : semester

semiconductor *nm* : semiconductor

semifinal *nf* : semifinal

semilla *nf* : seed — **semillero** *nm* 1 : nursery (for plants) 2 HERVIDERO : hotbed, breeding ground

seminario *nm* 1 : seminary 2 CURSO : seminar, course

sémola *nf* : semolina

senado *nm* : senate — **senador, -dora** *n* : senator

sencillo, -lla *adj* 1 : simple 2 ÚNICO : single — **sencillez** *nf* : simplicity

senda *nf* *or* **sendero** *nm* : path, way

sendos, -das *adj pl* : each, both

senil *adj* : senile

seno *nm* 1 : breast, bosom 2 : sinus (in anatomy) 3 **~ materno** : womb

sensación *nf, pl* **-ciones** : feeling, sensation — **sensacional** *adj* : sensational — **sensacionalista** *adj* : sensationalistic, lurid

sensato, -ta *adj* : sensible — **sensatez** *nf* : good sense

sensibilidad *nf* 1 : sensitivity, sensibility 2 SENSACIÓN : feeling

sensible *adj* 1 : sensitive 2 APRECIABLE : considerable, significant — **sensitivo, -va** *or* **sensorial** *adj* : sense, sensory

sensual *adj* : sensual, sensuous — **sensualidad** *nf* : sensuality

sentar {55} *vt* 1 : seat, sit 2 ESTABLECER : establish, set — *vi* 1 : suit 2 **~ bien a** : agree with (of food or drink) — **sentarse** *vr* : sit (down) — **sentado, -da** *adj* 1 : sitting, seated 2 **dar por sentado** : take for granted

sentencia *nf* 1 FALLO : sentence, judgment 2 MÁXIMA : saying — **sentenciar** *vt* : sentence

sentido, -da *adj* 1 : heartfelt, sincere 2 SENSIBLE : touchy, sensitive — **sentido** *nm* 1 : sense 2 CONOCIMIENTO : consciousness 3 DIRECCIÓN : direction 4 **doble ~** : double entendre 5 **~ común** : common sense 6 **~ del humor** : sense of humor 7 **~ único** : one-way

sentimiento *nm* 1 : feeling, emotion 2 PESAR : regret — **sentimental** *adj* : sentimental — **sentimentalismo** *nm* : sentimentality

sentir {76} *vt* 1 : feel 2 OÍR : hear 3 LAMENTAR : be sorry for 4 **lo siento** : I'm sorry — *vi* : feel — **sentirse** *vr* : feel

seña *nf* 1 : sign 2 **~s** *nfpl* DIRECCIÓN : address 3 **~s particulares** : distinguishing marks

señal *nf* 1 : signal 2 AVISO, INDICIO : sign 3 DEPÓSITO : deposit 4 **dar ~es de** : show signs of 5 **en ~ de** : as a token of — **señalado, -da** *adj* : notable — **señalar** *vt* 1 INDICAR : indicate, point out 2 MARCAR : mark 3 FIJAR : fix, set — **señalarse** *vr* : distinguish oneself

señor, -ñora *n* 1 : gentleman *m*, man *m*, lady *f*, woman *f* 2 : Sir *m*, Madam *f* 3 : Mr. *m*, Mrs. *f* 4 **señora** : wife *f* 5 **el Señor** : the Lord — **señorial** *adj* : stately — **señorita** *nf* 1 : young lady, young woman 2 : Miss

señuelo *nm* 1 : decoy 2 TRAMPA : bait, lure

separar *vt* 1 : separate 2 QUITAR : detach, remove 3 APARTAR : move away 4 DESTITUIR : dismiss — **separarse** *vr* 1 APARTARSE : separate 2 : part company — **separación** *nf, pl* **-ciones** : separation — **separado, -da** *adj* 1 : separate 2 : separated (of persons) 3 **por separado** : separately

septentrional *adj* : northern

séptico, -ca *adj* : septic

septiembre *nm* : September

séptimo, -ma *adj* : seventh — **~** *n* : seventh

sepulcro *nm* : tomb, sepulchre — **sepultar** *vt* : bury — **sepultura** *nf* 1 : burial 2 TUMBA : grave

sequedad *nf* : dryness — **sequía** *nf* : drought

séquito *nm* : retinue, entourage

ser {77} *vi* 1 : be 2 **a no ~ que** : unless 3 **¿cuánto es?** : how much is it? 4 **es más** : what's more 5 **~ de** : belong to 6 **~ de** : come from 7 **son las diez** : it's ten o'clock — **~** *nm* 1 ENTE : being 2 **~ humano** : human being

serbio, -bia *adj* : Serb, Serbian

serenar *vt* : calm — **serenarse** *vr* : calm down — **serenata** *nf* : serenade — **serenidad** *nf* : serenity — **sereno, -na** *adj* 1 : serene, calm 2 : fair, clear (of weather) — **sereno** *nm* : night watchman

serie *nf* 1 : series 2 **fabricación en ~** : mass production 3 **fuera de ~** : extraordinary — **serial** *nm* : serial

serio, -ria *adj* 1 : serious 2 RESPONSABLE : reliable 3 **en serio** : seriously — **seriedad** *nf* : seriousness

sermón *nm, pl* **-mones** : sermon — **sermonear** *vt* : lecture, reprimand

serpentear *vi* : twist, wind — **serpiente** *nf* 1 : serpent, snake 2 **~ de cascabel** : rattlesnake

serrado, -da *adj* : serrated

serrano, -na *adj* **1** : mountain **2 jamón serrano** : cured ham

serrar {55} *vt* : saw — **serrín** *nm, pl* **-rrines** : sawdust — **serrucho** *nm* : saw, handsaw

servicio *nm* **1** : service **2** ~**s** *nmpl* : restroom — **servicial** *adj* : obliging, helpful —

servidor, -dora *n* **1** : servant **2 su seguro servidor** : yours truly — **servidumbre** *nf* **1** : servitude **2** CRIADOS : help, servants *pl* — **servil** *adj* : servile

servilleta *nf* : napkin

servir {54} *vt* : serve — *vi* **1** : work, function **2** VALER : be of use — **servirse** *vr* **1** : help oneself **2 sírvase sentarse** : please have a seat

sesenta *adj & nm* : sixty

sesgo *nm* : bias, slant

sesión *nf, pl* **-siones 1** : session **2** : showing (of a film), performance (of a play)

seso *nm* : brain — **sesudo, -da** *adj* **1** : sensible **2** *fam* : brainy

seta *nf* : mushroom

setecientos, -tas *adj* : seven hundred — **setecientos** *nms & pl* : seven hundred

setenta *adj & nm* : seventy

setiembre *nm* → **septiembre**

seto *nm* **1** : fence **2** ~ **vivo** : hedge

seudónimo *nm* : pseudonym

severo, -ra *adj* **1** : harsh, severe **2** : strict (of a teacher, etc.) — **severidad** *nf* : severity

sexagésimo, -ma *adj & n* : sixtieth

sexo *nm* : sex — **sexismo** *nm* : sexism — **sexista** *adj & nmf* : sexist

sexteto *nm* : sextet

sexto, -ta *adj & n* : sixth

sexual *adj* : sexual — **sexualidad** *nf* : sexuality

sexy *adj, pl* **sexy** *or* **sexys** : sexy

si *conj* **1** : if **2** (*in indirect questions*) : whether **3** ~ **bien** : although **4** ~ **no** : otherwise, or else

sí[1] *adv* **1** : yes **2 creo que** ~ : I think so **3 porque** ~ *fam* : (just) because — ~ *nm* : consent

sí[2] *pron* **1 de por** ~ *or* **en** ~ : by itself, in itself, per se **2 fuera de** ~ : beside oneself **3 para** ~ **(mismo)** : to himself, to herself, for himself, for herself **4 entre** ~ : among themselves

sico- → **psico-**

SIDA *or* **sida** *nm* : AIDS

siderurgia *nf* : iron and steel industry

sidra *nf* : (hard) cider

siega *nf* **1** : harvesting **2** : harvest (time)

siembra *nf* **1** : sowing **2** : sowing season

siempre *adv* **1** : always **2** *Lat* : still **3 para** ~ : forever, for good **4** ~ **que** : whenever, every time **5** ~ **que** *or* ~ **y cuando** : provided that

sien *nf* : temple

sierra *nf* **1** : saw **2** CORDILLERA : mountain range **3 la** ~ : the mountains *pl*

siervo, -va *n* : slave

siesta *nf* : nap, siesta

siete *adj & nm* : seven

sífilis *nf* : syphilis

sifón *nm, pl* **-fones** : siphon

sigilo *nm* : secrecy

sigla *nf* : acronym, abbreviation

siglo *nm* **1** : century **2 hace** ~**s** : for ages

significar {72} *vt* **1** : mean, signify **2** EXPRESAR : express — **significación** *nf, pl* **-ciones 1** : significance, importance **2** : meaning (of a word, etc.) — **significado, -da** *adj* : well-known — **significado** *nm* : meaning — **significativo, -va** *adj* : significant

signo *nm* **1** : sign **2** ~ **de admiración** : exclamation point **3** ~ **de interrogación** : question mark

siguiente *adj* : next, following

sílaba *nf* : syllable

silbar *v* **1** : whistle **2** ABUCHEAR : hiss, boo — **silbato** *nm* : whistle — **silbido** *nm* **1** : whistle, whistling **2** ABUCHEO : hiss, booing

silenciar *vt* : silence — **silenciador** *nm* : muffler — **silencio** *nm* : silence — **silencioso, -sa** *adj* : silent, quiet

silicio *nm* : silicon

silla *nf* **1** : chair **2** *or* ~ **de montar** : saddle **3** ~ **de ruedas** : wheelchair — **sillón** *nm, pl* **-llones** : armchair, easy chair

silo *nm* : silo

silueta *nf* **1** : silhouette **2** CONTORNO : outline, shape

silvestre *adj* : wild

silvicultura *nf* : forestry

símbolo *nm* : symbol — **simbólico, -ca** *adj* : symbolic — **simbolismo** *nm* : symbolism — **simbolizar** {21} *vt* : symbolize

simetría *nf* : symmetry — **simétrico, -ca** *adj* : symmetrical, symmetric

simiente *nf* : seed

símil *nm* **1** : simile **2** COMPARACIÓN : comparison — **similar** *adj* : similar, alike

simio *nm* : ape

simpatía *nf* **1** : liking, affection **2** AMABILIDAD : friendliness — **simpático, -ca** *adj* **1** : nice, likeable **2** AMABLE : pleasant, kind — **simpatizante** *nmf* : sympathizer — **simpatizar** {21} *vi* **1** : get along, hit it off **2** ~ **con** : sympathize with

simple *adj* **1** SENCILLO : simple **2** MERO : pure, sheer **3** TONTO : simpleminded —

~ *n* : fool, simpleton — **simpleza** *nf* **1** : simpleness **2** TONTERÍA : silly thing —
simplicidad *nf* : simplicity — **simplificar** {72} *vt* : simplify
simposio *or* **simposium** *nm* : symposium
simular *vt* **1** : simulate **2** FINGIR : feign — **simulacro** *nm* : simulation, drill
simultáneo, -nea *adj* : simultaneous
sin *prep* **1** : without **2** ~ **que** : without
sinagoga *nf* : synagogue
sincero, -ra *adj* : sincere — **sinceramente** *adv* : sincerely — **sinceridad** *nf* : sincerity
síncopa *nf* : syncopation
sincronizar {21} *vt* : synchronize
sindicato *nm* : (labor) union — **sindical** *adj* : union, labor
síndrome *nm* : syndrome
sinfín *nm* **1** : endless number **2 un ~ de** : no end of
sinfonía *nf* : symphony — **sinfónico, -ca** *adj* : symphonic
singular *adj* **1** : exceptional, outstanding **2** PECULIAR : peculiar **3** : singular (in grammar) — ~ *nm* : singular — **singularizar** {21} *vt* : single out — **singularizarse** *vr* : stand out
siniestro, -tra *adj* **1** : sinister **2** IZQUIERDO : left — **siniestro** *nm* : disaster
sinnúmero *nm* → **sinfín**
sino *conj* **1** : but, rather **2** EXCEPTO : except, save
sinónimo, -ma *adj* : synonymous — **sinónimo** *nm* : synonym
sinopsis *nfs & pl* : synopsis
sinrazón *nf, pl* -**zones** : wrong
síntaxis *nfs & pl* : syntax
síntesis *nfs & pl* : synthesis — **sintético, -ca** *adj* : synthetic — **sintetizar** {21} *vt* **1** : synthesize **2** RESUMIR : summarize
síntoma *nm* : symptom — **sintomático, -ca** *adj* : symptomatic
sintonía *nf* **1** : tuning in (of a radio) **2 en ~ con** : in tune with — **sintonizar** {21} *vt* : tune (in) to
sinuoso, -sa *adj* : winding
sinvergüenza *nmf* : scoundrel
sionismo *nm* : Zionism
siquiera *adv* **1** : at least **2 ni ~** : not even — ~ *conj* : even if
sirena *nf* **1** : mermaid **2** : siren (of an ambulance, etc.)
sirio, -ria *adj* : Syrian
sirviente, -ta *n* : servant, maid *f*
sisear *vi* : hiss — **siseo** *nm* : hiss
sismo *nm* : earthquake — **sísmico, -ca** *adj* : seismic
sistema *nm* **1** : system **2 por ~** : systematically — **sistemático, -ca** *adj* : systematic
sitiar *vt* : besiege
sitio *nm* **1** : place, site **2** ESPACIO : room,

space **3** CERCO : siege **4 en cualquier ~** : anywhere
situar {3} *vt* : situate, place — **situarse** *vr* **1** : be located **2** ESTABLECERSE : get oneself established — **situación** *nf, pl* -**ciones** : situation, position — **situado, -da** *adj* : situated, placed
slip *nm* : briefs *pl*, underpants *pl*
smoking *nm* : tuxedo
SMS *nm, pl* **SMS** : text message
so *prep* : under
sobaco *nm* : armpit
sobar *vt* **1** : finger, handle **2** : knead (dough) — **sobado, -da** *adj* : worn, shabby
soberanía *nf* : sovereignty — **soberano, -na** *adj & n* : sovereign
soberbia *nf* : pride, arrogance — **soberbio, -bia** *adj* : proud, arrogant
sobornar *vt* : bribe — **soborno** *nm* **1** : bribe **2** : (action of) bribery
sobrar *vi* **1** : be more than enough **2** RESTAR : be left over — **sobra** *nf* **1** : surplus **2 de ~** : to spare **3 ~s** *nfpl* : leftovers — **sobrado, -da** *adj* : more than enough — **sobrante** *adj* : remaining
sobre[1] *nm* : envelope
sobre[2] *prep* **1** : on, on top of **2** POR ENCIMA DE : over, above **3** ACERCA DE : about **4 ~ todo** : especially, above all
sobrecama *nmf Lat* : bedspread
sobrecargar {52} *vt* : overload, overburden
sobrecoger {15} *vt* : startle — **sobrecogerse** *vr* : be startled
sobrecubierta *nf* : dust jacket
sobredosis *nfs & pl* : overdose
sobreentender {56} *vt* : infer, understand — **sobreentenderse** *vr* : be understood
sobreestimar *vt* : overestimate
sobregiro *nm* : overdraft
sobrellevar *vt* : endure, bear
sobremesa *nf* **de ~** : after-dinner
sobrenatural *adj* : supernatural
sobrenombre *nm* : nickname
sobrentender → **sobreentender**
sobrepasar *vt* : exceed
sobreponer {60} *vt* **1** : superimpose **2** ANTEPONER : put before — **sobreponerse** *vr* **~ a** : overcome
sobresalir {73} *vi* **1** : protrude **2** DESTACARSE : stand out — **sobresaliente** *adj* : outstanding
sobresaltar *vt* : startle — **sobresaltarse** *vr* : start, jump up — **sobresalto** *nm* : fright
sobrestimar → **sobreestimar**
sobretodo *nm* : overcoat
sobrevenir {87} *vi* : happen, ensue
sobrevivencia *nf* → **supervivencia**
sobreviviente *adj & nmf* → **superviviente**
sobrevivir *vi* : survive — *vt* : outlive
sobrevolar {19} *vt* : fly over

sobriedad *nf* **1** : sobriety **2** MODERACIÓN : restraint

sobrino, -na *n* : nephew *m*, niece *f*

sobrio, -bria *adj* : sober

socarrón, -rrona *adj*, *mpl* **-rrones** : sarcastic

socavar *vt* : undermine

sociable *adj* : sociable — **social** *adj* : social — **socialismo** *nm* : socialism — **socialista** *adj* & *nmf* : socialist — **sociedad** *nf* **1** : society **2** EMPRESA : company **3** ~ **anónima** : incorporated company — **socio, -cia** *n* **1** : partner **2** MIEMBRO : member — **sociología** *nf* : sociology — **sociólogo, -ga** *n* : sociologist

socorrer *vt* : help — **socorrista** *nmf* : lifeguard — **socorro** *nm* : help

soda *nf* : soda (water)

sodio *nf* : sodium

sofá *nm* : couch, sofa

sofisticación *nf*, *pl* **-ciones** : sophistication — **sofisticado, -da** *adj* : sophisticated

sofocar {72} *vt* **1** : suffocate, smother **2** : put out (a fire), stifle (a rebellion, etc.) — **sofocarse** *vr* **1** : suffocate **2** *fam* : get upset — **sofocante** *adj* : suffocating, stifling

sofreír {66} *vt* : sauté

soga *nf* : rope

soja *nf* → **soya**

sojuzgar *vt* : subdue, subjugate

sol *nm* **1** : sun **2 hacer** ~ : be sunny

solamente *adv* : only, just

solapa *nf* **1** : lapel (of a jacket) **2** : flap (of an envelope) — **solapado, -da** *adj* : secret, underhanded

solar[1] *adj* : solar, sun

solar[2] *nm* : lot, site

solariego, -ga *adj* : ancestral

solaz *nm*, *pl* **-laces** **1** : solace **2** DESCANSO : relaxation — **solazarse** {21} *vr* : relax

soldado *nm* **1** : soldier **2** ~ **raso** : private

soldar {19} *vt* : weld, solder — **soldador** *nm* : soldering iron — **soldador, -dora** *n* : welder

soleado, -da *adj* : sunny

soledad *nf* : loneliness, solitude

solemne *adj* : solemn — **solemnidad** *nf* : solemnity

soler {78} *vi* **1** : be in the habit of **2 suele llegar tarde** : he usually arrives late

solicitar *vt* **1** : request, solicit **2** : apply for (a job, etc.) — **solicitante** *nmf* : applicant — **solícito, -ta** *adj* : solicitous, obliging — **solicitud** *nf* **1** : concern **2** PETICIÓN : request **3** : application (for a job, etc.)

solidaridad *nf* : solidarity

sólido, -da *adj* **1** : solid **2** : sound (of an argument, etc.) — **sólido** *nm* : solid — **solidez** *nf* : solidity — **solidificar** {72} *vt* : solidify — **solidificarse** *vr* : solidify, harden

soliloquio *nm* : soliloquy

solista *nmf* : soloist

solitario, -ria *adj* **1** : solitary **2** AISLADO : lonely, deserted — ~ *n* : recluse — **solitaria** *nf* : tapeworm — **solitario** *nm* : solitaire

sollozar {21} *vi* : sob — **sollozo** *nm* : sob

solo, -la *adj* **1** : alone **2** AISLADO : lonely **3 a solas** : alone, by oneself — **solo** *nm* : solo

sólo *adv* : just, only

solomillo *nm* : sirloin

solsticio *nm* : solstice

soltar {19} *vt* **1** : release **2** DEJAR CAER : let go of, drop **3** DESATAR : unfasten, undo — **soltarse** *vr* **1** : break free **2** DESATARSE : come undone

soltero, -ra *adj* : single, unmarried — ~ *n* **1** : bachelor *m*, single woman *f* **2 apellido de soltera** : maiden name

soltura *nf* **1** : looseness **2** : fluency (in language) **3** AGILIDAD : agility, ease

soluble *adj* : soluble

solución *nf*, *pl* **-ciones** : solution — **solucionar** *vt* : solve, resolve

solventar *vt* **1** : settle, pay **2** RESOLVER : resolve — **solvente** *adj* & *nm* : solvent

sombra *nf* **1** : shadow **2** : shade (of a tree, etc.) **3** ~**s** *nfpl* : darkness, shadows — **sombreado, -da** *adj* : shady

sombrero *nm* : hat

sombrilla *nf* : parasol, umbrella

sombrío, -bría *adj* : dark, somber, gloomy

somero, -ra *adj* : superficial

someter *vt* **1** : subjugate **2** SUBORDINAR : subordinate **3** : subject (to treatment, etc.) **4** PRESENTAR : submit, present — **someterse** *vr* **1** : submit, yield **2** ~ **a** : undergo

somnífero, -ra *adj* : soporific — **somnífero** *nm* : sleeping pill — **somnoliento, -ta** *adj* : drowsy, sleepy

somos → **ser**

son[1] → **ser**

son[2] *nm* **1** : sound **2 en** ~ **de** : as, in the manner of

sonajero *nm* : (baby's) rattle

sonámbulo, -la *n* : sleepwalker

sonar {19} *vi* **1** : sound **2** : ring (as a bell) **3** : look or sound familiar **4** ~ **a** : sound like — **sonarse** *vr or* ~ **las narices** : blow one's nose

sonata *nf* : sonata

sondear *vt* **1** : sound, probe **2** : survey, sound out (opinions, etc.) — **sondeo** *nm* **1** : sounding, probing **2** ENCUESTA : survey, poll

soneto *nm* : sonnet

sónico, -ca *adj* : sonic

sonido *nm* : sound

sonoro, -ra *adj* **1** : resonant, sonorous **2**
RUIDOSO : loud
sonreír {66} *vi* : smile — **sonreírse** *vr*
: smile — **sonriente** *adj* : smiling — **son-**
risa *nf* : smile
sonrojar *vt* : cause to blush — **sonrojarse** *vr*
: blush — **sonrojo** *nm* : blush
sonrosado, -da *adj* : rosy, pink
sonsacar {72} *vt* : wheedle (out)
soñar {19} *v* **1** : dream **2** ~ **con** : dream
about **3** ~ **despierto** : daydream — **soña-**
dor, -dora *adj* : dreamy — ~ *n* : dreamer
— **soñoliento, -ta** *adj* : sleepy, drowsy
sopa *nf* : soup
sopesar *vt* : weigh, consider
soplar *vi* : blow — *vt* : blow out, blow off,
blow up — **soplete** *nm* : blowtorch —
soplo *nm* : puff, gust
soplón, -plona *n, pl* **-plones** *fam* : sneak
sopor *nm* : drowsiness — **soporífero, -ra**
adj : soporific
soportar *vt* **1** SOSTENER : support **2** AGUAN-
TAR : bear — **soporte** *nm* : support
soprano *nmf* : soprano
sor *nf* : Sister (in religion)
sorber *vt* **1** : sip **2** ABSORBER : absorb **3**
CHUPAR : suck up — **sorbete** *nm* : sherbet
— **sorbo** *nm* **1** : sip, swallow **2 beber a**
~**s** : sip
sordera *nf* : deafness
sórdido, -da *adj* : sordid, squalid
sordo, -da *adj* **1** : deaf **2** : muted (of a
sound) — **sordomudo, -da** *n* : deaf-mute
sorna *nf* : sarcasm
sorprender *vt* : surprise — **sorprenderse** *vr*
: be surprised — **sorprendente** *adj* : surprising — **sorpresa** *nf* : surprise
sortear *vt* **1** : raffle off, draw lots for **2**
ESQUIVAR : dodge — **sorteo** *nm* : drawing,
raffle
sortija *nf* **1** : ring **2** : ringlet (of hair)
sortilegio *nm* **1** HECHIZO : spell **2** HECHI-
CERÍA : sorcery
sosegar {49} *vt* : calm, pacify — **sose-**
garse *vr* : calm down — **sosegado, -da** *adj*
: calm, tranquil — **sosiego** *nm* : calm
soslayo: de ~ *adv phr* : obliquely, sideways
soso, -sa *adj* **1** : insipid, tasteless **2** ABU-
RRIDO : dull
sospechar *vt* : suspect — **sospecha** *nf*
: suspicion — **sospechoso, -sa** *adj* : suspicious — ~ *n* : suspect
sostener {80} *vt* **1** : support **2** SUJETAR
: hold **3** MANTENER : sustain, maintain —
sostenerse *vr* **1** : stand (up) **2** CONTINUAR
: remain **3** SUSTENTARSE : support oneself
— **sostén** *nm, pl* **-tenes 1** APOYO : support
2 SUSTENTO : sustenance **3** : brassiere, bra

— **sostenido, -da** *adj* **1** : sustained **2**
: sharp (in music) — **sostenido** *nm* : sharp
sótano *nm* : basement
soterrar {55} *vt* **1** : bury **2** ESCONDER : hide
soto *nm* : grove
soviético, -ca *adj* : Soviet
soy → **ser**
soya *nf* : soy
spam *nm, pl* **spams** : spam
Sr. *nm* : Mr. — **Sra.** *nf* : Mrs., Ms. — **Srta.** *or*
Srita. *nf* : Miss, Ms.
su *adj* **1** : his, her, its, their, one's **2** (*formal*)
: your
suave *adj* **1** : soft **2** LISO : smooth **3** APACI-
BLE : gentle, mild — **suavidad** *nf* **1** : softness, smoothness **2** APACIBILIDAD : mildness, gentleness — **suavizar** {21} *vt*
: soften, smooth
subalimentado, -da *adj* : undernourished,
underfed
subalterno, -na *adj* **1** SUBORDINADO : subordinate **2** SECUNDARIO : secondary — ~ *n*
: subordinate
subarrendar {55} *vt* : sublet
subasta *nf* : auction — **subastar** *vt* : auction
(off)
subcampeón, -peona *n, mpl* **-peones**
: runner-up
subcomité *nm* : subcommittee
subconsciente *adj & nm* : subconscious
subdesarrollado, -da *adj* : underdeveloped
subdirector, -tora *n* : assistant manager
súbdito, -ta *n* : subject
subdividir *vt* : subdivide — **subdivisión** *nf,*
pl **-siones** : subdivision
subestimar *vt* : underestimate
subir *vt* **1** : climb, go up **2** LLEVAR : bring
up, take up **3** AUMENTAR : raise — *vi* **1**
: go up, come up **2** ~ **a** : get in (a car), get
on (a bus, etc.) — **subirse** *vr* **1** : climb (up)
2 ~ **a** : get in (a car), get on (a bus, etc.) **3**
~ **a la cabeza** : go to one's head — **su-**
bida *nf* **1** : ascent, climb **2** AUMENTO : rise
3 PENDIENTE : slope — **subido, -da** *adj* **1**
: bright, strong **2** ~ **de tono** : risqué
súbito, -ta *adj* **1** : sudden **2 de súbito** : all
of a sudden, suddenly
subjetivo, -va *adj* : subjective
subjuntivo, -va *adj* : subjunctive — **subjun-**
tivo *nm* : subjunctive (case)
sublevar *vt* : stir up, incite to rebellion —
sublevarse *vr* : rebel — **sublevación** *nf, pl*
-ciones : uprising, rebellion
sublime *adj* : sublime
submarino, -na *adj* : underwater — **subma-**
rino *nm* : submarine — **submarinismo** *nm*
: scuba diving
subordinar *vt* : subordinate — **subordi-**
nado, -da *adj & n* : subordinate
subproducto *nm* : by-product

subrayar *vt* **1** : underline **2** ENFATIZAR : emphasize, stress

subrepticio, -cia *adj* : surreptitious

subsanar *vt* **1** : rectify, correct **2** : make up for (a deficiency), overcome (an obstacle)

subscribir → **suscribir**

subsidio *nm* : subsidy, benefit

subsiguiente *adj* : subsequent

subsistir *vi* **1** : live, subsist **2** SOBREVIVIR : survive — **subsistencia** *nf* : subsistence

substancia *nf* → **sustancia**

subterfugio *nm* : subterfuge

subterráneo, -nea *adj* : underground, subterranean — **subterráneo** *nm* : underground passage

subtítulo *nm* : subtitle

suburbio *nm* **1** : suburb **2** : slum (outside a city) — **suburbano, -na** *adj* : suburban

subvencionar *vt* : subsidize — **subvención** *nf, pl* **-ciones** : subsidy, grant

subvertir {76} *vt* : subvert — **subversión** *nf, pl* **-siones** : subversion — **subversivo, -va** *adj & n* : subversive

subyacente *adj* : underlying

subyugar {52} *vt* : subjugate, subdue

succión *nf, pl* **-ciones** : suction — **succionar** *vt* : suck up, draw in

sucedáneo *nm* : substitute

suceder *vi* **1** : happen, occur **2 ~ a** : follow **3 suceda lo que suceda** : come what may — **sucesión** *nf, pl* **-siones** : succession — **sucesivo, -va** *adj* : successive — **suceso** *nm* **1** : event **2** INCIDENTE : incident — **sucesor, -sora** *n* : successor

suciedad *nf* **1** : dirtiness **2** MUGRE : dirt, filth

sucinto, -ta *adj* : succinct, concise

sucio, -cia *adj* : dirty, filthy

suculento, -ta *adj* : succulent

sucumbir *vi* : succumb

sucursal *nf* : branch (of a business)

sudadera *nf* : sweatshirt — **sudado, -da** *adj* : sweaty

sudafricano, -na *adj* : South African

sudamericano, -na *adj* : South American

sudar *vi* : sweat

sudeste → **sureste**

sudoeste → **suroeste**

sudor *nm* : sweat — **sudoroso, -sa** *adj* : sweaty

sueco, -ca *adj* : Swedish — **sueco** *nm* : Swedish (language)

suegro, -gra *n* **1** : father-in-law *m*, mother-in-law *f* **2 suegros** *nmpl* : in-laws

suela *nf* : sole (of a shoe)

sueldo *nm* : salary, wage

suelo *nm* **1** : ground **2** : floor (in a house) **3** TIERRA : soil, land

suelto, -ta *adj* : loose, free — **suelto** *nm* : loose change

sueño *nm* **1** : dream **2 coger el ~** : get to sleep **3 tener ~** : be sleepy

suero *nm* **1** : whey **2** : serum (in medicine)

suerte *nf* **1** : luck, fortune **2** AZAR : chance **3** DESTINO : fate **4** CLASE : sort, kind **5 por ~** : luckily **6 tener ~** : be lucky

suéter *nm* : sweater

suficiencia *nf* **1** CAPACIDAD : competence, proficiency **2** PRESUNCIÓN : smugness — **suficiente** *adj* **1** : enough, sufficient **2** PRESUNTUOSO : smug — **suficientemente** *adv* : enough

sufijo *nm* : suffix

sufragio *nm* : suffrage, vote

sufrir *vt* **1** : suffer **2** SOPORTAR : bear, stand — *vi* : suffer — **sufrido, -da** *adj* **1** : long-suffering **2** : sturdy, serviceable (of clothing) — **sufrimiento** *nm* : suffering

sugerir {76} *vt* : suggest — **sugerencia** *nf* : suggestion — **sugestión** *nf, pl* **-tiones** : suggestion — **sugestionable** *adj* : impressionable — **sugestionar** *vt* : influence — **sugestivo, -va** *adj* **1** : suggestive **2** ESTIMULANTE : interesting, stimulating

suicidio *nm* : suicide — **suicida** *adj* : suicidal — **~** *nmf* : suicide (victim) — **suicidarse** *vr* : commit suicide

suite *nf* : suite

suizo, -za *adj* : Swiss

sujetar *vt* **1** : hold (on to) **2** FIJAR : fasten **3** DOMINAR : subdue — **sujetarse** *vr* **1 ~ a** : hold on to, cling to **2 ~ a** : abide by — **sujeción** *nf, pl* **-ciones** **1** : fastening **2** DOMINACIÓN : subjection — **sujetador** *nm* Spain : brassiere, bra — **sujetapapeles** *nms & pl* : paper clip — **sujeto, -ta** *adj* **1** : fastened **2 ~ a** : subject to — **sujeto** *nm* **1** : individual **2** : subject (in grammar)

sulfuro *nm* : sulfur — **sulfúrico, -ca** *adj* : sulfuric

sultán *nm, pl* **-tanes** : sultan

suma *nf* **1** : sum, total **2** : addition (in mathematics) **3 en ~** : in short — **sumamente** *adv* : extremely — **sumar** *vt* **1** : add (up) **2** TOTALIZAR : add up to, total — *vi* : add up — **sumarse** *vr* **~ a** : join

sumario, -ria *adj* : concise — **sumario** *nm* **1** : summary **2** : indictment (in law)

sumergir {35} *vt* : submerge, plunge — **sumergirse** *vr* : be submerged — **sumergible** *adj* : waterproof (of a watch, etc.)

sumidero *nm* : drain

suministrar *vt* : supply, provide — **suministro** *nm* : supply, provision

sumir *vt* : plunge, immerse — **sumirse** *vr* **~ en** : sink into

sumisión *nf, pl* **-siones** : submission — **sumiso, -sa** *adj* : submissive

sumo, -ma *adj* **1** : highest, supreme **2 de suma importancia** : of great importance

suntuoso, -sa *adj* : sumptuous, lavish
super *or* **súper** *nm fam* : supermarket
superabundancia *nf* : overabundance
superar *vt* **1** : surpass, outdo **2** VENCER
: overcome — **superarse** *vr* : improve oneself
superávit *nm* : surplus
superestructura *nf* : superstructure
superficie *nf* **1** : surface **2** ÁREA : area —
superficial *adj* : superficial
superfluo, -flua *adj* : superfluous
superintendente *nmf* : supervisor, superintendent
superior *adj* **1** : superior **2** : upper (of a
floor, etc.) **3 ~ a** : above, higher than —
~ *nm* : superior — **superioridad** *nf* : superiority
superlativo, -va *adj* : superlative — **superlativo** *nm* : superlative
supermercado *nm* : supermarket
superpoblado, -da *adj* : overpopulated
supersónico, -ca *adj* : supersonic
superstición *nf, pl* **-ciones** : superstition —
supersticioso, -sa *adj* : superstitious
supervisar *vt* : supervise, oversee — **supervisión** *nf, pl* **-siones** : supervision — **supervisor, -sora** *n* : supervisor
supervivencia *nf* : survival — **superviviente** *adj* : surviving — **~** *nmf* : survivor
suplantar *vt* : supplant, replace
suplemento *nm* : supplement — **suplementario, -ria** *adj* : supplementary
suplente *adj & nmf* : substitute
suplicar {72} *vt* : beg, entreat — **súplica** *nf*
: plea, entreaty
suplicio *nm* : ordeal, torture
suplir *vt* **1** : make up for **2** REEMPLAZAR
: replace
supo, etc. → **saber**
suponer {60} *vt* **1** : suppose, assume **2**
SIGNIFICAR : mean **3** IMPLICAR : involve,
entail — **suposición** *nf, pl* **-ciones** : sup-
position
supositorio *nm* : suppository
supremo, -ma *adj* : supreme — **supremacía** *nf* : supremacy
suprimir *vt* **1** : suppress, eliminate **2** : delete (text) — **supresión** *nf, pl* **-siones** **1**
: suppression, elimination **2** : deletion (of
text)
supuesto, -ta *adj* **1** : supposed, alleged **2
por supuesto** : of course — **supuesto** *nm*
: assumption — **supuestamente** *adv* : allegedly
sur *nm* **1** : south, South **2** : south wind **3 del
~** : south, southerly
surafricano, -na → **sudafricano**
suramericano, -na → **sudamericano**
surcar {72} *vt* **1** : plow (earth) **2** : cut

through (air, water, etc.) — **surco** *nm*
: groove, furrow, rut
sureño, -ña *adj* : southern, Southern — **~** *n*
: Southerner
sureste *adj* **1** : southeast, southeastern **2**
: southeasterly (of wind, etc.) — **~** *nm*
: southeast, Southeast
surf *or* **surfing** *nm* : surfing
surfista *nmf* : surfer
surgir {35} *vi* **1** : arise **2** APARECER : appear
— **surgimiento** *nm* : rise, emergence
suroeste *adj* **1** : southwest, southwestern **2**
: southwesterly (of wind, etc.) — **~** *nm*
: southwest, Southwest
surtir *vt* **1** : supply, provide **2 ~ efecto**
: have an effect — **surtirse** *vr* **~ de** : stock
up on — **surtido, -da** *adj* **1** : assorted, varied **2** : stocked (with merchandise) — **surtido** *nm* : assortment, selection — **surtidor**
nm : gas pump
susceptible *adj* **1** : susceptible, sensitive **2
~ de** : capable of — **susceptibilidad** *nf*
: sensitivity
suscitar *vt* : provoke, arouse
suscribir {33} *vt* **1** : sign (a formal document) **2** RATIFICAR : endorse — **suscribirse** *vr* **~ a** : subscribe to — **suscripción**
nf, pl **-ciones** : subscription — **suscriptor,
-tora** *n* : subscriber
susodicho, -cha *adj* : aforementioned
suspender *vt* **1** : suspend **2** COLGAR : hang
3 *Spain* : fail (an exam, etc.) — **suspensión** *nf, pl* **-siones** : suspension — **suspenso** *nm* **1** *Spain* : failure (in an exam,
etc.) **2** *Lat* : suspense
suspicaz *adj, pl* **-caces** : suspicious
suspirar *vi* : sigh — **suspiro** *nm* : sigh
sustancia *nf* **1** : substance **2 sin ~** : shallow, lacking substance — **sustancial** *adj*
: substantial, significant — **sustancioso,
-sa** *adj* : substantial, solid
sustantivo *nm* : noun
sustentar *vt* **1** : support **2** ALIMENTAR : sustain, nourish **3** MANTENER : maintain —
sustentarse *vr* : support oneself — **sus-
tentación** *nf, pl* **-ciones** : support
— **sustento** *nm* **1** : means of support, livelihood **2** ALIMENTO : sustenance
sustituir {41} *vt* : replace, substitute — **sustitución** *nf, pl* **-ciones** : replacement, substitution — **sustituto, -ta** *n* : substitute
susto *nm* : fright, scare
sustraer {81} *vt* **1** : remove, take away **2**
: subtract (in mathematics) — **sustraerse**
vr **~ a** : avoid, evade — **sustracción** *nf, pl*
-ciones : subtraction
susurrar *vi* **1** : whisper **2** : murmur (of
water) **3** : rustle (of leaves, etc.) — *vt*

: whisper — **susurro** *nm* **1** : whisper **2** : murmur (of water) **3** : rustle, rustling (of leaves, etc.)

sutil *adj* **1** : delicate, fine **2** : subtle (of fragrances, differences, etc.) — **sutileza** *nf* : subtlety

sutura *nf* : suture

suyo, -ya *adj* **1** : his, her, its, one's, theirs **2** (*formal*) : yours **3 un primo suyo** : a cousin of his/hers — ~ *pron* **1** : his, hers, its (own), one's own, theirs **2** (*formal*) : yours

switch *nm Lat* : switch

T

t *nf* : t, 21st letter of the Spanish alphabet

taba *nf* : anklebone

tabaco *nm* : tobacco — **tabacalero, -ra** *adj* : tobacco

tábano *nm* : horsefly

taberna *nf* : tavern

tabicar {72} *vt* : wall up — **tabique** *nm* : thin wall, partition

tabla *nf* **1** : board, plank **2** LISTA : table, list **3** ~ **de planchar** : ironing board **4** ~**s** *nfpl* : stage, boards *pl* — **tablado** *nm* **1** : flooring **2** PLATAFORMA : platform **3** : (theater) stage — **tablero** *nm* **1** : bulletin board **2** : board (in games) **3** PIZARRA : blackboard **4** ~ **de instrumentos** : dashboard, instrument panel

tableta *nf* **1** : tablet, pill **2** : bar (of chocolate)

tablilla *nf* : slat — **tablón** *nm, pl* **-lones 1** : plank, beam **2** ~ **de anuncios** : bulletin board

tabú *adj* : taboo — **tabú** *nm, pl* **-búes** or **-bús** : taboo

tabular *vt* : tabulate

taburete *nm* : stool

tacaño, -na *adj* : stingy, miserly

tacha *nf* **1** : flaw, defect **2 sin** ~ : flawless

tachar *vt* **1** : cross out, delete **2** ~ **de** : accuse of, label as

tachón *nm, pl* **-chones** : stud, hobnail — **tachuela** *nf* : tack, hobnail

tácito, -ta *adj* : tacit

taciturno, -na *adj* : taciturn

taco *nm* **1** : stopper, plug **2** *Lat* : heel (of a shoe) **3** : cue (in billiards) **4** : taco (in cooking)

tacón *nm, pl* **-cones 1** : heel (of a shoe) **2 de** ~ **alto** : high-heeled

táctica *nf* : tactic, tactics *pl* — **táctico, -ca** *adj* : tactical

tacto *nm* **1** : (sense of) touch, feel **2** DELICADEZA : tact

tafetán *nm, pl* **-tanes** : taffeta

tailandés, -desa *adj* : Thai

taimado, -da *adj* : crafty, sly

tajar *vt* : cut, slice — **tajada** *nf* **1** : slice **2 sacar** ~ *fam* : get one's share — **tajante** *adj* : categorical — **tajo** *nm* **1** : cut, gash **2** ESCARPA : steep cliff

tal *adv* **1** : so, in such a way **2 con** ~ **que** : provided that, as long as **3 ¿qué** ~**?** : how are you?, how's it going? — ~ *adj* **1** : such, such a **2** ~ **vez** : maybe, perhaps — ~ *pron* **1** : such a one, such a thing **2** ~ **para cual** : two of a kind

taladrar *vt* : drill — **taladro** *nm* : drill

talante *nm* **1** HUMOR : mood **2** VOLUNTAD : willingness

talar *vt* : cut down, fell

talco *nm* : talcum powder

talego *nm* : sack

talento *nm* : talent — **talentoso, -sa** *adj* : talented

talismán *nm, pl* **-manes** : talisman, charm

talla *nf* **1** : sculpture, carving **2** ESTATURA : height **3** : size (in clothing) — **tallar** *vt* **1** : sculpt, carve **2** : measure (someone's height)

tallarín *nf, pl* **-rines** : noodle

talle *nm* **1** : waist, waistline **2** FIGURA : figure **3** : measurements *pl* (of clothing)

taller *nm* **1** : workshop **2** : studio (of an artist)

tallo *nm* : stalk, stem

talón *nm, pl* **-lones 1** : heel (of the foot) **2** : stub (of a check) — **talonario** *nm* : checkbook

taltuza *nf* : gopher

tamal *nm* : tamale

tamaño, -ña *adj* : such a, such a big — **tamaño** *nm* **1** : size **2 de** ~ **natural** : lifesize

tambalearse *vr* **1** : teeter, wobble **2** : stagger, totter (of persons)

también *adv* : too, as well, also

tambor *nm* : drum — **tamborilear** *vi* : drum

tamiz *nm* : sieve — **tamizar** {21} *vt* : sift

tampoco *adv* : neither, not either

tampón *nm, pl* **-pones 1** : tampon **2** : ink pad (for stamping)

tan *adv* **1** : so, so very **2** ~ **pronto como** : as soon as **3** ~ **sólo** : only, merely

tanda *nf* **1** TURNO : turn, shift **2** GRUPO : batch, lot, series

tangente *nf* : tangent

tangible *adj* : tangible

tango *nm* : tango

tanque *nm* : tank

tantear *vt* **1** : feel, grope **2** SOPESAR : size up, weigh — *vi* : feel one's way — **tanteador** *nm* : scoreboard — **tanteo** *nm* **1** : weighing, sizing up **2** PUNTUACIÓN : scoring (in sports)

tanto *adv* **1** : so much **2** (*in expressions of time*) : so long — ~ *nm* **1** : certain amount **2** : goal, point (in sports) **3** un ~ : somewhat, rather — **tanto, -ta** *adj* **1** : so much, so many **2** (*in comparisons*) : as much, as many **3** *fam* : however many — ~ *pron* **1** : so much, so many **2 entre** ~ : meanwhile **3 por lo** ~ : therefore

tañer {79} *vt* **1** : ring (a bell) **2** : play (a musical instrument)

tapa *nf* **1** : cover, top, lid **2** *Spain* : snack

tapacubos *nms & pl* : hubcap

tapar *vt* **1** : cover, put a lid on **2** OCULTAR : block out **3** ENCUBRIR : cover up — **tapadera** *nf* **1** : cover, lid **2** : front (to hide a deception)

tapete *nm* **1** : small rug, mat **2** : cover (for a table)

tapia *nf* : (adobe) wall, garden wall — **tapiar** *vt* **1** : wall in **2** : block off (a door, etc.)

tapicería *nf* **1** : upholstery **2** TAPIZ : tapestry — **tapicero, -ra** *n* : upholsterer

tapioca *nf* : tapioca

tapiz *nm, pl* **-pices** : tapestry — **tapizar** {21} *vt* : upholster

tapón *nm, pl* **-pones 1** : cork **2** : cap (for a bottle, etc.) **3** : plug, stopper (for a sink)

tapujo *nm* **sin** ~**s** : openly, outright

taquigrafía *nf* : stenography, shorthand — **taquígrafo, -fa** *n* : stenographer

taquilla *nf* **1** : box office **2** RECAUDACIÓN : earnings *pl,* take — **taquillero, -ra** *adj* **un éxito taquillero** : a box-office hit

tarántula *nf* : tarantula

tararear *vt* : hum

tardar *vi* **1** : take a long time, be late **2 a más** ~ : at the latest — *vt* : take (time) — **tardanza** *nf* : lateness, delay — **tarde** *adv* **1** : late **2** ~ **o temprano** : sooner or later — ~ *nf* **1** : afternoon, evening **2 ¡buenas** ~**s!** : good afternoon!, good evening! **3 en la** ~ *or* **por la** ~ : in the afternoon, in the evening — **tardío, -día** *adj* : late, tardy — **tardo, -da** *adj* : slow

tarea *nf* **1** : task, job **2** : homework (in education)

tarifa *nf* **1** : fare, rate **2** LISTA : price list **3** ARANCEL : duty, tariff

tarima *nf* : platform, stage

tarjeta *nf* **1** : card **2** ~ **de crédito** : credit card **3** ~ **postal** : postcard

tarro *nm* : jar, pot

tarta *nf* **1** : cake **2** TORTA : tart

tartamudear *vi* : stammer, stutter — **tartamudeo** *nm* : stutter, stammer

tartán *nm, pl* **-tanes** : tartan, plaid

tártaro *nm* : tartar

tarugo *nm* **1** : block (of wood) **2** *fam* : blockhead, dunce

tasa *nf* **1** : rate **2** IMPUESTO : tax **3** VALORACIÓN : appraisal — **tasación** *nf, pl* **-ciones** : appraisal — **tasar** *vt* **1** : set the price of **2** VALORAR : appraise, value

tasca *nf* : cheap bar, dive

tatuar {3} *vt* : tattoo — **tatuaje** *nm* : tattoo, tattooing

taurino, -na *adj* : bull, bullfighting — **tauromaquia** *nf* : (art of) bullfighting

taxi *nm, pl* **taxis** : taxi, taxicab — **taxista** *nmf* : taxi driver

taza *nf* **1** : cup **2** : (toilet) bowl — **tazón** *nm, pl* **-zones** : bowl

te *pron* **1** (*direct object*) : you **2** (*indirect object*) : for you, to you, from you **3** (*reflexive*) : yourself, for yourself, to yourself, from yourself

té *nm* : tea

teatro *nm* : theater — **teatral** *adj* : theatrical

techo *nm* **1** : roof **2** : ceiling (of a room) **3** LÍMITE : upper limit, ceiling — **techumbre** *nf* : roofing

tecla *nf* : key (of a musical instrument or a machine) — **teclado** *nm* : keyboard — **teclear** *vt* : type in, enter

técnica *nf* **1** : technique, skill **2** TECNOLOGÍA : technology — **técnico, -ca** *adj* : technical — ~ *n* : technician

tecnología *nf* : technology — **tecnológico, -ca** *adj* : technological

tecolote *nm Lat* : owl

tedio *nm* : boredom — **tedioso, -sa** *adj* : tedious, boring

teja *nf* : tile — **tejado** *nm* : roof

tejer *v* **1** : knit, crochet **2** : weave (on a loom)

tejido *nm* **1** : fabric, cloth **2** : tissue (of the body)

tejón *nm, pl* **-jones** : badger

tela *nf* **1** : fabric, material **2** ~ **de araña** : spiderweb — **telar** *nm* : loom — **telaraña** *nf* : spiderweb, cobweb

tele *nf fam* : TV, television

telecomunicación *nf, pl* **-ciones** : telecommunication

teledifusión *nf, pl* **-siones** : television broadcasting

teledirigido, -da *adj* : remote-controlled
telefonear *v* : telephone, call — **telefónico, -ca** *adj* : telephone — **telefonista** *nmf* : telephone operator — **teléfono** *nm* **1** : telephone **2 llamar por ~** : make a phone call
telegrafiar {85} *v* : telegraph — **telegráfico, -ca** *adj* : telegraphic — **telégrafo** *nm* : telegaph
telegrama *nm* : telegram
telenovela *nf* : soap opera
telepatía *nf* : telepathy — **telepático, -ca** *adj* : telepathic
telescopio *nm* : telescope — **telescópico, -ca** *adj* : telescopic
telespectador, -dora *n* : (television) viewer
telesquí *nm, pl* **-squís** : ski lift
televidente *nmf* : (television) viewer
televisión *nf, pl* **-siones** : television, TV — **televisar** *vt* : televise — **televisor** *nm* : television set
telón *nm, pl* **-lones 1** : curtain (in theater) **2 ~ de fondo** : backdrop, background
tema *nm* : theme
temblar {55} *vi* **1** : tremble, shiver **2** : shake (of a building, the ground, etc.) — **temblor** *nm* **1** : shaking, trembling **2 ~ de tierra** : tremor, earthquake — **tembloroso, -sa** *adj* : trembling, shaky
temer *vt* : fear, dread — *vi* : be afraid — **temerario, -ria** *adj* : reckless — **temeridad** *nf* **1** : recklessness **2** : rash act — **temeroso, -sa** *adj* : fearful — **temor** *nm* : fear, dread
temperamento *nm* : temperament — **temperamental** *adj* : temperamental
temperatura *nf* : temperature
tempestad *nf* : storm — **tempestuoso, -sa** *adj* : stormy
templar *vt* **1** : temper (steel) **2** : moderate (temperature) **3** : tune (a musical instrument) — **templarse** *vr* : warm up, cool down — **templado, -da** *adj* **1** : temperate, mild **2** TIBIO : lukewarm **3** VALIENTE : courageous — **templanza** *nf* **1** : moderation **2** : mildness (of weather)
templo *nm* : temple, synagogue
tempo *nm* : tempo
temporada *nf* **1** : season, time **2** PERÍODO : period, spell — **temporal** *adj* **1** : temporal **2** PROVISIONAL : temporary — **~** *nm* : storm — **temporero, -ra** *n* : temporary or seasonal worker
temporizador *nm* : timer
temprano, -na *adj* : early — **temprano** *adv* : early
tenaz *adj, pl* **-naces** : tenacious — **tenaza** *nf* or **tenazas** *nfpl* **1** : pliers **2** : tongs (for the fireplace, etc.) **3** : claw (of a crustacean)
tendedero *nm* : clothesline
tendencia *nf* : tendency, trend

tender {56} *vt* **1** : spread out, stretch out **2** : hang out (clothes) **3** : lay (cables, etc.) **4** : set (a trap) — *vi* **~ a** : have a tendency towards — **tenderse** *vr* : stretch out, lie down
tendero, -ra *n* : shopkeeper
tendido *nm* **1** : laying (of cables, etc.) **2** : seats *pl*, stand (at a bullfight)
tendón *nm, pl* **-dones** : tendon
tenebroso, -sa *adj* **1** : gloomy, dark **2** SINIESTRO : sinister
tenedor, -dora *n* **1** : holder **2 ~ de libros** : bookkeeper — **tenedor** *nm* : table fork — **teneduría** *nf* **~ de libros** : bookkeeping
tener {80} *vt* **1** : have, possess **2** SUJETAR : hold **3** TOMAR : take **4 ~ frío (hambre,** *etc.)* : be cold (hungry, etc.) **5 ~ ... años** : be ... years old **6 ~ por** : think, consider — *v aux* **1 ~ que** : have to, ought to **2 tenía pensado escribirte** : I've been thinking of writing to you — **tenerse** *vr* **1** : stand up **2 ~ por** : consider oneself
tenería *nf* : tannery
tengo → tener
tenia *nf* : tapeworm
teniente *nmf* : lieutenant
tenis *nms & pl* **1** : tennis **2 ~** *nmpl* : sneakers — **tenista** *nmf* : tennis player
tenor *nm* **1** : tenor **2** : tone, sense (in style)
tensar *vt* **1** : tense, make taut **2** : draw (a bow) — **tensarse** *vr* : become tense — **tensión** *nf, pl* **-siones 1** : tension **2 ~ arterial** : blood pressure — **tenso, -sa** *adj* : tense
tentación *nf, pl* **-ciones** : temptation
tentáculo *nm* : tentacle
tentar {55} *vt* **1** : feel, touch **2** ATRAER : tempt — **tentador, -dora** *adj* : tempting
tentativa *nf* : attempt
tentempié *nm fam* : snack
tenue *adj* **1** : tenuous **2** : faint, weak (of sounds) **3** : light, fine (of thread, rain, etc.)
teñir {67} *vt* **1** : dye **2 ~ de** : tinge with
teología *nf* : theology — **teólogo, -ga** *n* : theologian
teorema *nm* : theorem
teoría *nf* : theory — **teórico, -ca** *adj* : theoretical
tequila *nm* : tequila
terapia *nf* **1** : therapy **2 ~ ocupacional** : occupational therapy — **terapeuta** *nmf* : therapist — **terapéutico, -ca** *adj* : therapeutic
tercermundista *adj* : third-world
tercero, -ra *adj* (**tercer** *before masculine singular nouns*) **1** : third **2 el Tercer Mundo** : the Third World — **~** *n* : third (in a series)
terciar *vt* : sling (sth over one's shoulders),

tilt (a hat) — *vi* **1** : intervene **2** ~ **en** : take part in
tercio *nm* : third
terciopelo *nm* : velvet
terco, -ca *adj* : obstinate, stubborn
tergiversar *vt* : distort, twist
termal *adj* : thermal, hot — **termas** *nfpl* : hot springs
terminar *vt* : conclude, finish — *vi* **1** : finish **2** ACABARSE : come to an end — **terminarse** *vr* **1** : run out **2** ACABARSE : come to an end — **terminación** *nf, pl* **-ciones** : termination, conclusion — **terminal** *adj* : terminal, final — ~ *nm* (*in some regions f*) : (electric or electronic) terminal — ~ *nf* (*in some regions m*) : terminal, station
término *nm* **1** CONCLUSIÓN : end, conclusion **2** : term, expression **3** : period, term of office **4** : place, position **5 por término medio** : on average **6 términos** *nmpl* : terms (of an agreement), specifications — **terminología** *nf* : terminology
termita *nf* : termite
termo *nm* : thermos
termómetro *nm* : thermometer
termóstato *nm* : thermostat
ternero, -ra *n* : calf — **ternera** *nf* : veal
ternura *nf* : tenderness
terquedad *nf* : obstinacy, stubbornness
terracota *nf* : terra-cotta
terraplén *nm, pl* **-plenes** : embankment
terráqueo, -quea *adj* : earth, terrestrial
terrateniente *nmf* : landowner
terraza *nf* **1** : terrace **2** BALCÓN : balcony
terremoto *nm* : earthquake
terreno *nm* **1** : terrain **2** SUELO : earth, ground **3** SOLAR : plot, tract of land — **terreno, -na** *adj* : earthly — **terrestre** *adj* : terrestrial
terrible *adj* : terrible
terrier *nmf* : terrier
territorio *nm* : territory — **territorial** *adj* : territorial
terrón *nm, pl* **-rones** **1** : clod (of earth) **2** ~ **de azúcar** : lump of sugar
terror *nm* : terror — **terrorífico, -ca** *adj* : terrifying — **terrorismo** *nm* : terrorism — **terrorista** *adj & nmf* : terrorist
terroso, -sa *adj* : earthy
terso, -sa *adj* **1** : smooth **2** : polished, flowing (of a style) — **tersura** *nf* : smoothness
tertulia *nf* : gathering, group
tesis *nfs & pl* : thesis
tesón *nm* : persistence, tenacity
tesoro *nm* **1** : treasure **2** : thesaurus (book) **3 el Tesoro** : the Treasury — **tesorero, -ra** *n* : treasurer
testaferro *nm* : figurehead

testamento *nm* : testament, will — **testamentario, -ria** *n* : executor, executrix *f* — **testar** *vi* : draw up a will
testarudo, -da *adj* : stubborn
testículo *nm* : testicle
testificar {72} *v* : testify — **testigo** *nmf* **1** : witness **2** ~ **ocular** : eyewitness — **testimoniar** *vi* : testify — **testimonio** *nm* : testimony
tétano *or* **tétanos** *nm* : tetanus
tetera *nf* : teapot
tetilla *nf* **1** : teat, nipple (of a man) **2** : nipple (of a baby bottle) — **tetina** *nf* : nipple (of a baby bottle)
tétrico, -ca *adj* : somber, gloomy
textil *adj & nm* : textile
texto *nm* : text — **textual** *adj* **1** : textual **2** EXACTO : literal, exact
textura *nf* : texture
tez *nf, pl* **teces** : complexion
ti *pron* **1** : you **2** ~ **mismo,** ~ **misma** : yourself
tía → **tío**
tianguis *nms & pl Lat* : open-air market
tibio, -bia *adj* : lukewarm
tiburón *nm, pl* **-rones** : shark
tic *nm* : tic
tiempo *nm* **1** : time **2** ÉPOCA : age, period **3** : weather (in meteorology) **4** : halftime (in sports) **5** : tempo (in music) **6** : tense (in grammar)
tienda *nf* **1** : store, shop **2** *or* ~ **de campaña** : tent
tiene → **tener**
tienta *nf* **andar a** ~**s** : feel one's way, grope around
tierno, -na *adj* **1** : tender, fresh, young **2** CARIÑOSO : affectionate
tierra *nf* **1** : land **2** SUELO : ground, earth **3** *or* ~ **natal** : native land **4 la Tierra** : the Earth **5 por** ~ : overland **6** ~ **adentro** : inland
tieso, -sa *adj* **1** : stiff, rigid **2** ERGUIDO : erect **3** ENGREÍDO : haughty
tiesto *nm* : flowerpot
tifoideo, -dea *adj* **fiebre tifoidea** : typhoid fever
tifón *nm, pl* **-fones** : typhoon
tifus *nm* : typhus
tigre, -gresa *n* **1** : tiger, tigress *f* **2** *Lat* : jaguar
tijera *nf or* **tijeras** *nfpl* : scissors — **tijeretada** *nf* : cut, snip
tildar *vt* ~ **de** : brand as, call
tilde *nf* **1** : tilde **2** ACENTO : accent mark
tilo *nm* : linden (tree)
timar *vt* : swindle, cheat
timbre *nm* **1** : bell **2** : tone, timbre (of a voice, etc.) **3** SELLO : seal, stamp **4** *Lat* : postage stamp — **timbrar** *vt* : stamp

tímido, -da *adj* : timid, shy — **timidez** *nf* : timidity, shyness

timo *nm fam* : swindle, hoax

timón *nm, pl* **-mones 1** : rudder **2 coger el ~** : take the helm, take charge

tímpano *nm* **1** : eardrum **2 ~s** *nmpl* : timpani, kettledrums

tina *nf* **1** : vat **2** BAÑERA : bathtub

tinieblas *nfpl* **1** : darkness **2 estar en ~ sobre** : be in the dark about

tino *nm* **1** : good judgment, sense **2** TACTO : tact

tinta *nf* **1** : ink **2 saberlo de buena ~** : have it on good authority — **tinte** *nm* **1** : dye, coloring **2** MATIZ : overtone — **tintero** *nm* : inkwell

tintinear *vi* : jingle, tinkle, clink — **tintineo** *nm* : jingle, tinkle, clink

tinto, -ta *adj* **1** : dyed, stained **2** : red (of wine)

tintorería *nf* : dry cleaner (service)

tintura *nf* **1** : dye, tint **2 ~ de yodo** : tincture of iodine

tiña *nf* : ringworm

tío, tía *n* : uncle *m*, aunt *f*

tiovivo *nm* : merry-go-round

típico, -ca *adj* : typical

tiple *nm* : soprano

tipo *nm* **1** : type, kind **2** FIGURA : figure (of a woman), build (of a man) **3** : rate (of interest, etc.) **4** : (printing) type, typeface — **tipo, -pa** *n fam* : guy *m*, gal *f*

tipografía *nf* : typography, printing — **tipográfico, -ca** *adj* : typographical — **tipógrafo, -fa** *n* : printer

tique *or* **tíquet** *nm* : ticket — **tiquete** *nm Lat* : ticket

tira *nf* **1** : strip, strap **2 ~ cómica** : comic strip

tirabuzón *nf, pl* **-zones 1** : corkscrew **2** RIZO : curl, coil

tirada *nf* **1** : throw **2** DISTANCIA : distance **3** IMPRESIÓN : printing, issue — **tirador** *nm* : handle, knob — **tirador, -dora** *n* : marksman *m*, markswoman *f*

tiranía *nf* : tyranny — **tiránico, -ca** *adj* : tyrannical — **tiranizar** {21} *vt* : tyrannize — **tirano, -na** *adj* : tyrannical — **~** *n* : tyrant

tirante *adj* **1** : taut, tight **2** : tense (of a situation, etc.) — **~** *nm* **1** : (shoulder) strap **2 ~s** *nmpl* : suspenders

tirar *vt* **1** : throw **2** DESECHAR : throw away **3** DERRIBAR : knock down **4** DISPARAR : shoot, fire **5** IMPRIMIR : print — *vi* **1** : pull **2** DISPARAR : shoot **3** ATRAER : attract **4** *fam* : get by, manage **5 ~ a** : tend towards — **tirarse** *vr* **1** : throw oneself **2** *fam* : spend (time)

tiritar *vi* : shiver

tiro *nm* **1** : shot, gunshot **2** : shot, kick (in sports) **3** : team (of horses, etc.) **4 a ~** : within range

tiroides *nmf* : thyroid (gland)

tirón *nm, pl* **-rones 1** : pull, yank **2 de un ~** : in one go

tirotear *vt* : shoot at — **tiroteo** *nm* : shooting

tisis *nfs & pl* : tuberculosis

títere *nm* : puppet

titilar *vi* : flicker

titiritero, -ra *n* **1** : puppeteer **2** ACRÓBATA : acrobat

titubear *vi* **1** : hesitate **2** BALBUCEAR : stutter, stammer — **titubeante** *adj* : hesitant, faltering — **titubeo** *nm* : hesitation

titular *vt* : title, call — **titularse** *vr* **1** : be called, be titled **2** LICENCIARSE : receive a degree — **~** *adj* : titular, official — **~** *nm* : headline — **~** *nmf* : holder, incumbent — **título** *nm* **1** : title **2** : degree, qualification (in education)

tiza *nf* : chalk

tiznar *vt* : blacken (with soot, etc.) — **tizne** *nm* : soot

toalla *nf* : towel — **toallero** *nm* : towel rack

tobillo *nm* : ankle

tobogán *nm, pl* **-ganes 1** : toboggan, sled **2** : slide (in a playground, etc.)

tocadiscos *nms & pl* : record player

tocado, -da *adj fam* : touched, not all there — **tocado** *nm* : headgear, headdress

tocador *nm* : dressing table

tocar {72} *vt* **1** : touch, feel **2** MENCIONAR : touch on, refer to **3** : play (a musical instrument) — *vi* **1** : knock, ring **2 ~ en** : touch on, border on

tocayo, -ya *n* : namesake

tocino *nm* **1** : bacon **2** : salt pork (for cooking) — **tocineta** *nf Lat* : bacon

tocólogo, -ga *n* : obstetrician

tocón *nm, pl* **-cones** : stump (of a tree)

todavía *adv* **1** AÚN : still **2** (*in comparisons*) : even **3 ~ no** : not yet

todo, -da *adj* **1** : all **2** CADA, CUALQUIER : every, each **3 a toda velocidad** : at top speed **4 todo el mundo** : everyone, everybody — **~** *pron* **1** : everything, all **2 todos, -das** *pl* : everybody, everyone, all — **todo** *nm* : whole — **todopoderoso, -sa** *adj* : almighty, all-powerful

todoterreno *nm* : all-terrain vehicle

toga *nf* **1** : toga **2** : gown, robe (of a judge, etc.)

toldo *nm* : awning, canopy

tolerar *vt* : tolerate — **tolerancia** *nf* : tolerance — **tolerante** *adj* : tolerant

toma *nf* **1** : capture **2** DOSIS : dose **3** : take (in film) **4** ~ **de corriente** : wall socket, outlet **5** ~ **y daca** : give-and-take —
tomar *vt* **1** : take **2** : have (food or drink) **3** CAPTURAR : capture, seize **4** ~ **el sol** : sunbathe **5** ~ **tierra** : land — *vi* : drink (alcohol) — **tomarse** *vr* **1** : take (time, etc.) **2** : drink, eat, have (food, drink)

tomate *nm* : tomato

tomillo *nm* : thyme

tomo *nm* : volume

ton *nm* **sin** ~ **ni son** : without rhyme or reason

tonada *nf* : tune

tonel *nm* : barrel, cask

tonelada *nf* : ton — **tonelaje** *nm* : tonnage

tónica *nf* **1** : tonic (water) **2** TENDENCIA : trend, tone — **tónico, -ca** *adj* : tonic — **tónico** *nm* : tonic (in medicine)

tono *nm* **1** : tone **2** : shade (of colors) **3** : key (in music)

tontería *nf* **1** : silly thing or remark **2** ESTU-PIDEZ : foolishness **3 decir** ~s : talk nonsense — **tonto, -ta** *adj* **1** : stupid, silly **2 a tontas y a locas** : haphazardly — ~ *n* : fool, idiot

topacio *nm* : topaz

toparse *vr* ~ **con** : run into, come across

tope *nm* **1** : limit, end **2** *or* ~ **de puerta** : doorstop **3** *Lat* : bump — ~ *adj* : maximum

tópico, -ca *adj* **1** : topical, external **2** MA-NIDO : trite — **tópico** *nm* : cliché

topo *nm* : mole (animal)

toque *nm* **1** : (light) touch **2** : ringing, peal (of a bell) **3** ~ **de queda** : curfew **4** ~ **de diana** : reveille — **toquetear** *vt* : finger, handle

tórax *nms & pl* : thorax

torbellino *nm* : whirlwind

torcer {14} *vt* **1** : twist, bend **2** : turn (a corner) **3** : wring (out) — *vi* : turn — **torcerse** *vr* **1** : twist, sprain **2** FRUSTRARSE : go wrong **3** DESVIARSE : go astray — **torcedura** *nf* **1** : twisting **2** ESGUINCE : sprain — **torcido, -da** *adj* : twisted, crooked

tordo, -da *adj* : dappled — **tordo** *nm* : thrush (bird)

torear *vt* **1** : fight (bulls) **2** ELUDIR : dodge, sidestep — *vi* : fight bulls — **toreo** *nm* : bullfighting — **torero, -ra** *n* : bullfighter

tormenta *nf* : storm — **tormento** *nm* **1** : torture **2** ANGUSTIA : torment, anguish — **tormentoso, -sa** *adj* : stormy

tornado *nm* : tornado

tornar *vt* CONVERTIR : render, turn — *vi* : go back, return — **tornarse** *vr* : become, turn into

torneo *nm* : tournament

tornillo *nm* : screw

torniquete *nm* **1** : turnstile **2** : tourniquet (in medicine)

torno *nm* **1** : winch **2** : (carpenter's) lathe **3** ~ **de alfarero** : (potter's) wheel **4** ~ **de banco** : vise **5 en** ~ **a** : around, about

toro *nm* **1** : bull **2** ~s *nmpl* : bullfight

toronja *nf* : grapefruit

torpe *adj* **1** : clumsy, awkward **2** ESTÚPIDO : stupid, dull

torpedear *vt* : torpedo — **torpedo** *nm* : torpedo

torpeza *nf* **1** : clumsiness, awkwardness **2** ESTUPIDEZ : slowness, stupidity

torre *nf* **1** : tower **2** : turret (on a ship, etc.) **3** : rook, castle (in chess)

torrente *nm* **1** : torrent **2** ~ **sanguíneo** : bloodstream — **torrencial** *adj* : torrential

tórrido, -da *adj* : torrid

torsión *nf, pl* **-siones** : twisting

torta *nf* **1** : torte, cake **2** *Lat* : sandwich

tortazo *nm fam* : blow, wallop

tortícolis *nfs & pl* : stiff neck

tortilla *nf* **1** : tortilla **2** *or* ~ **de huevo** : omelet

tórtola *nf* : turtledove

tortuga *nf* **1** : turtle, tortoise **2** ~ **de agua dulce** : terrapin

tortuoso, -sa *adj* : tortuous, winding

tortura *nf* : torture — **torturar** *vt* : torture

tos *nf* **1** : cough **2** ~ **ferina** : whooping cough

tosco, -ca *adj* : rough, coarse

toser *vi* : cough

tosquedad *nf* : coarseness

tostar {19} *vt* **1** : toast **2** BRONCEAR : tan — **tostarse** *vr* : get a tan — **tostada** *nf* **1** : piece of toast **2** *Lat* : tostada — **tostador** *nm* : toaster

tostón *nm, pl* **-tones** *Lat* : fried plantain chip

total *adj & nm* : total — ~ *adv* : so, after all — **totalidad** *nf* : whole — **totalitario, -ria** *adj & n* : totalitarian — **totalitarismo** *nm* : totalitarianism — **totalizar** {21} *vt* : total, add up to

tóxico, -ca *adj* : toxic, poisonous — **tóxico** *nm* : poison — **toxicomanía** *nf* : drug addiction — **toxicómano, -na** *n* : drug addict — **toxina** *nf* : toxin

tozudo, -da *adj* : stubborn

traba *nf* : obstacle, hindrance

trabajar *vi* **1** : work **2** : act, perform (in theater, etc.) — *vt* **1** : work (metal) **2** : knead (dough) **3** MEJORAR : work on, work at — **trabajador, -dora** *adj* : hardworking — ~ *n* : worker — **trabajo** *nm* **1** : work **2** EMPLEO : job **3** TAREA : task **4**

ESFUERZO : effort **5 costar ~** : be difficult
6 ~ en equipo : teamwork **7 ~s** *nmpl*
: hardships, difficulties — **trabajoso, -sa**
adj : hard, laborious

trabalenguas *nms & pl* : tongue twister

trabar *vt* **1** : join, connect **2** OBSTACULIZAR
: impede **3** : strike up (a conversation, etc.)
4 : thicken (sauces) — **trabarse** *vr* **1** : jam
2 ENREDARSE : become entangled **3 se le
traba la lengua** : he gets tongue-tied

trabucar {72} *vt* : mix up

tracción *nf* : traction

tractor *nm* : tractor

tradición *nf, pl* **-ciones** : tradition — **tradicional** *adj* : traditional

traducir {61} *vt* : translate — **traducción** *nf,
pl* **-ciones** : translation — **traductor, -tora**
n : translator

traer {81} *vt* **1** : bring **2** CAUSAR : cause,
bring about **3** CONTENER : carry, have **4**
LLEVAR : wear — **traerse** *vr* **1** : bring along
2 traérselas : be difficult

traficar {72} *vi* **~ en** : traffic in — **trafi-
cante** *nmf* : dealer, trafficker — **tráfico** *nm*
1 : trade (of merchandise) **2** : traffic (of
vehicles)

tragaluz *nf, pl* **-luces** : skylight

tragar {52} *vt* **1** : swallow **2** *fam* : put up
with — *vi* : swallow — **tragarse** *vr* **1**
: swallow **2** ABSORBER : absorb, swallow
up

tragedia *nf* : tragedy — **trágico, -ca** *adj*
: tragic

trago *nm* **1** : swallow, swig **2** *fam* : drink,
liquor — **tragón, -gona** *adj fam* : greedy
— **~** *nmf fam* : glutton

traicionar *vt* : betray — **traición** *nf, pl* **-cio-
nes 1** : betrayal **2** : treason (in law) — **traidor, -dora** *adj* : traitorous, treacherous —
~ *n* : traitor

trailer *nm* : trailer

traje *nm* **1** : dress, costume **2** : (man's) suit
3 ~ de baño : bathing suit

trajinar *vi fam* : rush around — **trajín** *nm, pl*
-jines *fam* : hustle and bustle

trama *nf* **1** : plot **2** : weave, weft (of fabric)
— **tramar** *vt* **1** : plot, plan **2** : weave (fabric)

tramitar *vt* : negotiate — **trámite** *nm* : procedure, step

tramo *nm* **1** : stretch, section **2** : flight (of
stairs)

trampa *nf* **1** : trap **2 hacer ~s** : cheat —
trampear *vt* : cheat

trampilla *nf* : trapdoor

trampolín *nm, pl* **-lines 1** : diving board **2**
: trampoline (in a gymnasium, etc.)

tramposo, -sa *adj* : crooked, cheating — **~**
n : cheat, swindler

tranca *nf* **1** : cudgel, club **2** : bar (for a door
or window)

trance *nm* **1** : critical juncture **2** : (hypnotic) trance **3 en ~ de** : in the process of

tranquilo, -la *adj* : calm, tranquil — **tranquilidad** *nf* : tranquility, peace — **tranquilizante** *nm* : tranquilizer — **tranquilizar**
{21} *vt* : calm, soothe — **tranquilizarse** *vr*
: calm down

trans- *see also* **tras-**

transacción *nf, pl* **-ciones** : transaction

transatlántico, -ca *adj* : transatlantic —
transatlántico *nm* : ocean liner

transbordador *nm* **1** : ferry **2 ~ espacial**
: space shuttle — **transbordar** *vt* : transfer
— *vi* : change (of trains, etc.) — **transbordo** *nm* **hacer ~** : change (trains, etc.)

transcribir {33} *vt* : transcribe — **transcripción** *nf, pl* **-ciones** : transcription

transcurrir *vi* : elapse, pass — **transcurso**
nm : course, progression

transeúnte *nmf* : passerby

transferir {76} *vt* : transfer — **transferencia** *nf* : transfer, transference

transformar *vt* **1** : transform, change **2**
CONVERTIR : convert — **transformarse** *vr*
: be transformed — **transformación** *nf, pl*
-ciones : transformation — **transformador**
nm : transformer

transfusión *nf, pl* **-siones** : transfusion

transgénico[1] **-ca** *adj* : genetically modified

transgénico[2] **-ca** *n* : genetically modified
plant or animal

transgredir {1} *vt* : transgress — **transgresión** *nf* : transgression

transición *nf, pl* **-ciones** : transition

transido, -da *adj* : overcome, stricken

transigir {35} *vi* : give in, compromise

transistor *nm* : transistor

transitar *vi* : go, travel — **transitable** *adj*
: passable

transitivo, -va *adj* : transitive

tránsito *nm* **1** : transit **2** TRÁFICO : traffic **3
hora de máximo ~** : rush hour — **transi-
torio, -ria** *adj* : transitory

transmitir *vt* **1** : transmit **2** : broadcast
(radio, TV, etc.) **3** CEDER : pass on — **transmisión** *nf, pl* **-siones 1** : broadcast **2**
TRANSFERENCIA : transfer **3** : transmission
(of an automobile) — **transmisor** *nm*
: transmitter

transparentarse *vr* : be transparent —
transparente *adj* : transparent

transpirar *vi* : perspire, sweat — **transpiración** *nf, pl* **-ciones** : perspiration, sweat

transponer {60} *vt* : transpose, move —
transponerse *vr* **1** : set (of the sun, etc.) **2**
DORMITAR : doze off

transportar *vt* : transport, carry — **transportarse** *vr* : get carried away — **transporte** *nm* : transport, transportation
transversal *adj* **corte** ~ : cross section
tranvía *nm* : streetcar, trolley
trapear *vt Lat* : mop
trapecio *nm* : trapeze
trapisonda *nf* : scheme, plot
trapo *nm* **1** : cloth, rag **2** ~**s** *nmpl fam* : clothes
tráquea *nf* : trachea, windpipe
traquetear *vi* : rattle around, shake — **traqueteo** *nm* : rattling
tras *prep* **I** DESPUÉS DE : after **2** DÉTRAS DE : behind
tras- *see also* **trans-**
trascender {56} *vi* **1** : leak out, become known **2** EXTENDERSE : spread **3** ~ **de** : transcend — **trascendencia** *nf* : importance — **trascendental** *adj* **1** : transcendental **2** IMPORTANTE : important
trasegar *vt* : move around
trasero, -ra *adj* : rear, back — **trasero** *nm* : buttocks *pl*
trasfondo *nm* **1** : background **2** : undercurrent (of suspicion, etc.)
trasladar *vt* **1** : transfer, move **2** POSPONER : postpone — **trasladarse** *vr* : move, relocate — **traslado** *nm* **1** : transfer, move **2** COPIA : copy
traslapar *vt* : overlap — **traslaparse** *vr* : overlap
traslucirse {45} *vr* **1** : be translucent **2** REVELARSE : be revealed — **traslúcido, -da** : translucent
trasnochar *vi* : stay up all night
traspasar *vt* **1** : pierce, go through **2** EXCEDER : go beyond **3** ATRAVESAR : cross, go across **4** : transfer (a business, etc.) — **traspaso** *nm* : transfer, sale
traspié *nm* **1** : stumble, trip **2** ERROR : blunder
trasplantar *vt* : transplant — **trasplante** *nm* : transplant
trasquilar *vt* : shear
traste *nm* **1** : fret (on a guitar, etc.) **2** *Lat* : (kitchen) utensil **3 dar al** ~ **con** : ruin **4 irse al** ~ : fall through
trastos *nmpl fam* : pieces of junk, stuff
trastornar *vt* **1** : disturb, disrupt **2** VOLVER LOCO : drive crazy — **trastornarse** *vr* : go crazy — **trastornado, -da** *adj* : disturbed, deranged — **trastorno** *nm* **1** : disturbance, disruption **2** : (medical or psychological) disorder
trastrocar *vt* : change, switch around
tratable *adj* : friendly, sociable
tratar *vi* **1** ~ **con** : deal with **2** ~ **de** : try to **3** ~ **de** *or* ~ **sobre** : be about, concern

4 ~ **en** : deal in — *vt* **1** : treat **2** MANEJAR : deal with, handle — **tratarse** *vr* ~ **de** : be about, concern — **tratado** *nm* **1** : treatise **2** CONVENIO : treaty — **tratamiento** *nm* : treatment — **trato** *nm* **1** : treatment **2** ACUERDO : deal, agreement **3** ~**s** *nmpl* : dealings
trauma *nm* : trauma — **traumático, -ca** *adj* : traumatic
través *nm* **1 a** ~ **de** : across, through **2 de** ~ : sideways
travesaño *nm* : crosspiece
travesía *nf* : voyage, crossing (of the sea)
travesura *nf* **1** : prank **2** ~**s** *nfpl* : mischief — **travieso, -sa** *adj* : mischievous, naughty
trayecto *nm* **I** : trajectory, path **2** VIAJE : journey **3** RUTA : route — **trayectoria** *nf* : path, trajectory
traza *nf* **1** : design, plan **2** ASPECTO : appearance — **trazado** *nm* **1** : outline, sketch **2** DISEÑO : plan, layout — **trazar** {21} *vt* **1** : trace, outline **2** : draw up (a plan, etc.) — **trazo** *nm* : stroke, line
trébol *nm* **1** : clover, shamrock **2** ~**es** *nmpl* : clubs (in playing cards)
trece *adj & nm* : thirteen — **treceavo, -va** *adj* : thirteenth — **treceavo** *nm* : thirteenth (fraction)
trecho *nm* **I** : stretch, period **2** DISTANCIA : distance **3 de** ~ **a** ~ : at intervals
tregua *nf* **1** : truce **2 sin** ~ : without respite
treinta *adj & nm* : thirty — **treintavo, -va** *adj* : thirtieth — **treintavo** *nm* : thirtieth (fraction)
tremendo, -da *adj* : tremendous, enormous
trementina *nf* : turpentine
trémulo, -la *adj* : trembling, flickering
tren *nm* **1** : train **2** ~ **de aterrizaje** : landing gear
trenza *nf* : braid, pigtail — **trenzar** {21} *vt* : braid — **trenzarse** *vr Lat* : get involved
trepar *vi* **1** : climb **2** : creep, spread (of a plant) — **treparse** *vr* : climb (up) — **trepador, -dora** *adj* : climbing — **trepadora** *nf* **1** : climbing plant **2** *fam* : social climber
trepidar *vi* : shake, vibrate
tres *adj & nm* : three — **trescientos, -tas** *adj* : three hundred — **trescientos** *nms & pl* : three hundred
treta *nf* : trick
triángulo *nm* : triangle — **triangular** *adj* : triangular
tribu *nf* : tribe — **tribal** *adj* : tribal
tribulación *nf, pl* **-ciones** : tribulation
tribuna *nf* **1** : dais, platform **2** : grandstand, bleachers *pl* (in a stadium)

tribunal *nm* : court, tribunal
tributar *vt* : pay, render — *vi* : pay taxes —
  tributo *nm* **1** : tribute **IMPUESTO** : tax
triciclo *nm* : tricycle
tricolor *adj* : tricolored
tridimensional *adj* : three-dimensional
trigésimo, -ma *adj & n* : thirtieth
trigo *nm* : wheat
trigonometría *nf* : trigonometry
trillado, -da *adj* : trite
trillar *vt* : thresh — **trilladora** *nf* : threshing
  machine
trillizo, -za *n* : triplet
trilogía *nf* : trilogy
trimestral *adj* : quarterly
trinar *vi* : warble
trinchar *vt* : carve
trinchera *nf* **1** : trench, ditch **2** **IMPERMEA-**
  BLE : trench coat
trineo *nm* : sled, sleigh
trinidad *nf* : trinity
trino *nm* : trill, warble
trío *nm* : trio
tripa *nf* **1** : gut, intestine **2** ~s *nfpl fam*
  : belly, tummy
triple *adj & nm* : triple — **triplicar** {72} *vt*
  : triple
trípode *nm* : tripod
tripular *vt* : man — **tripulación** *nf, pl* **-cio-**
  nes : crew — **tripulante** *nmf* : crew member
tris *nm* **estar en un** ~ **de** : be within an
  inch of
triste *adj* **1** : sad **2** **SOMBRÍO** : dismal,
  gloomy **3** **MISERABLE** : sorry, miserable —
  tristeza *nf* : sadness, grief
tritón *nm, pl* **-tones** : newt
triturar *vt* : crush, grind
triunfar *vi* : triumph, win — **triunfal** *adj* : triumphal — **triunfante** *adj* : triumphant —
  triunfo *nm* : triumph, victory
trivial *adj* : trivial
triza *nf* **1** : shred, bit **2 hacer** ~s : smash
  to pieces
trocar {82} *vt* **1** **CONVERTIR** : change **2**
  INTERCAMBIAR : exchange
trocha *nf* : path, trail
trofeo *nm* : trophy
trombón *nm, pl* **-bones 1** : trombone **2**
  : trombonist (musician)
trombosis *nf* : thrombosis
trompa *nf* **1** : trunk (of an elephant), snout **2**
  : horn (musical instrument) **3** : tube (in
  anatomy)
trompeta *nf* : trumpet — **trompetista** *nmf*
  : trumpet player
trompo *nm* : top (toy)
tronada *nf* : thunderstorm — **tronar** {19} *vi*

: thunder, rage — *vt Lat fam* : shoot — *v
  impers* : thunder
tronchar *vt* **1** : snap **2** **TRUNCAR** : cut short
tronco *nm* **1** : trunk (of a tree) **2** : torso (of
  a person) **3 dormir como un** ~ : sleep
  like a log
trono *nm* : throne
tropa *nf* : troops *pl*, soldiers *pl*
tropel *nm* : mob
tropezar {29} *vi* **1** : trip, stumble **2** ~ **con**
  : come up against, run into — **tropezón** *nm,
  pl* **-zones 1** : stumble **2** **EQUIVOCACIÓN**
  : mistake, slip
trópico *nm* : tropic — **tropical** *adj* : tropical
tropiezo *nm* **1** **CONTRATIEMPO** : snag, setback **2** **EQUIVOCACIÓN** : mistake, slip
trotar *vi* **1** : trot **2** *fam* : rush about — **trote**
  nm **1** : trot **2** *fam* : rush, bustle **3 al** ~ : at
  a trot, quickly
trozo *nm* : piece, bit, chunk
trucha *nf* : trout
truco *nm* **1** : knack **2** **ARDID** : trick
trueno *nm* : thunder
trueque *nm* : barter, exchange
trufa *nf* : truffle
truncar {72} *vt* **1** : cut short **2** : thwart, spoil
  (plans, etc.)
tu *adj* : your
tú *pron* : you
tuba *nf* : tuba
tuberculosis *nf* : tuberculosis
tubo *nm* **1** : tube, pipe **2** ~ **de escape**
  : exhaust pipe (of a vehicle) **3** ~ **de des-**
  agüe : drainpipe — **tubería** *nf* : pipes *pl*,
  tubing
tuerca *nf* : nut (for a screw)
tuerto, -ta *adj* : one-eyed, blind in one eye
tuétano *nm* : marrow
tufo *nm* **1** : vapor **2** *fam* : stench, stink
tugurio *nm* : hovel
tulipán *nm, pl* **-panes** : tulip
tullido, -da *adj* : crippled, paralyzed
tumba *nf* : tomb, grave
tumbar *vt* : knock down, knock over — **tum-**
  barse *vr* : lie down — **tumbo** *nm* **dar** ~s
  : jolt, bump around
tumor *nm* : tumor
tumulto *nm* **1** : commotion, tumult **2** **MOTÍN**
  : riot — **tumultuoso, -sa** *adj* : tumultuous
tuna *nf* : prickly pear
túnel *nm* : tunnel
túnica *nf* : tunic
tupé *nm* : toupee
tupido, -da *adj* : dense, thick
turba *nf* **1** : peat **2** **MUCHEDUMBRE** : mob,
  throng
turbación *nf, pl* **-ciones 1** : disturbance **2**
  CONFUSIÓN : confusion
turbante *nm* : turban

turbar *vt* **1** : disturb, upset **2** CONFUNDIR : confuse, bewilder

turbina *nf* : turbine

turbio, -bia *adj* **1** : cloudy, murky **2** : blurred (of vision, etc.) — **turbión** *nm, pl* -**biones** : squall

turbulencia *nf* : turbulence — **turbulento, -ta** *adj* : turbulent

turco, -ca *adj* : Turkish — **turco** *nm* : Turkish (language)

turista *nmf* : tourist — **turismo** *nm* : tourism, tourist industry — **turístico, -ca** *adj* : tourist, travel

turnarse *vr* : take turns, alternate — **turno** *nm* **1** : turn **2** ~ **de noche** : night shift

turquesa *nf* : turquoise

turrón *nm, pl* -**rrones** : nougat

tutear *vt* : address as *tú*

tutela *nf* **1** : guardianship (in law) **2 bajo la** ~ **de** : under the protection of

tuteo *nm* : addressing as *tú*

tutor, -tora *n* **1** : guardian **2** : tutor (in education)

tuyo, -ya *adj* : yours, of yours — ~ *pron* **1 el tuyo, la tuya, lo tuyo, los tuyos, las tuyas** : yours **2 los tuyos** : your family, your friends

U

u¹ *nf* : u, 22d letter of the Spanish alphabet

u² *conj* (*used before words beginning with o- or ho-*) : or

uapití *nm* : American elk, wapiti

ubicar {72} *vt Lat* **1** COLOCAR : place, position **2** LOCALIZAR : find — **ubicarse** *vr* : be located

ubre *nf* : udder

Ud., Uds. → **usted**

uf *interj* : phew!

ufanarse *vr* ~ **de** : boast about — **ufano, -na** *adj* **1** : proud **2** ENGREÍDO : self-satisfied

ujier *nm* : usher

úlcera *nf* : ulcer

ulterior *adj* : later, subsequent — **ulteriormente** *adv* : subsequently

últimamente *adv* : lately, recently

ultimar *vt* **1** : complete, finish **2** *Lat* : kill — **ultimátum** *nm, pl* -**tums** : ultimatum

último, -ma *adj* **1** : last **2** : latest, most recent (in time) **3** : farthest (in space) **4 por último** : finally

ultrajar *vt* : outrage, insult — **ultraje** *nm* : outrage, insult

ultramar *nm* **de** ~ *or* **en** ~ : overseas — **ultramarino, -na** *adj* : overseas — **ultramarinos** *nmpl* **tienda de** ~ : grocery store

ultranza: a ~ *adv phr* : to the extreme — **a** ~ *adj phr* : out-and-out, complete

ultrasónico -ca *adj* : ultrasonic

ultrasonido *nm* : ultrasound

ultravioleta *adj* : ultraviolet

ulular *vi* **1** : hoot (of an owl) **2** : howl (of a wolf, the wind, etc.) — **ululato** *nm* : hoot (of an owl)

umbilical *adj* : umbilical

umbral *nm* : threshold

un, una *art, mpl* **unos 1** : a, an **2 unos** *or* **unas** *pl* : some, a few **3 unos** *or* **unas** *pl* : about, approximately — **un** *adj* → **uno**

unánime *adj* : unanimous — **unanimidad** *nf* : unanimity

uncir {83} *vt* : yoke

undécimo, -ma *adj & n* : eleventh

ungir {35} *vt* : anoint — **ungüento** *nm* : ointment

único, -ca *adj* **1** : only, sole **2** EXCEPCIONAL : unique — ~ *n* : only one — **únicamente** *adv* : only

unicornio *nm* : unicorn

unidad *nf* **1** : unit **2** ARMONÍA : unity — **unido, -da** *adj* **1** : united **2** : close (of friends, etc.)

unificar {72} *vt* : unify — **unificación** *nf, pl* -**ciones** : unification

uniformar *vt* **1** : standardize **2** : put into uniform — **uniformado, -da** *adj* : uniformed — **uniforme** *adj & nm* : uniform — **uniformidad** *nf* : uniformity

unilateral *adj* : unilateral

unir *vt* **1** : unite, join **2** COMBINAR : combine, mix together — **unirse** *vr* **1** : join together **2** ~ **a** : join — **unión** *nf, pl* **uniones 1** : union **2** JUNTURA : joint, coupling

unísono *nm* **al** ~ : in unison

unitario, -ria *adj* : unitary

universal *adj* : universal

universidad *nf* : university, college — **universitario, -ria** *adj* : university, college
universo *nm* : universe
uno, una (**un** *before masculine singular nouns*) *adj* : one — **~** *pron* **1** : one **2 unos, unas** *pl* : some **3 uno(s) a otro(s)** : one another, each other **4 uno y otro** : both — **uno** *nm* : one (number)
untar *vt* **1** : smear, grease **2** *fam* : bribe — **untuoso, -sa** *adj* : greasy, sticky
uña *nf* **1** : nail, fingernail **2** : claw (of a cat, etc.), hoof (of a horse, etc.)
uranio *nm* : uranium
Urano *nm* : Uranus
urbano, -na *adj* : urban, city — **urbanidad** *nf* : politeness, courtesy — **urbanización** *nf, pl* **-ciones** : housing development — **urbanizar** *vt* : develop, urbanize — **urbe** *nf* : large city
urdir *vt* **1** : warp **2** PLANEAR : plot — **urdimbre** *nf* : warp (of a fabric)
urgir {35} *v impers* : be urgent, be pressing — **urgencia** *nf* **1** : urgency **2** EMERGENCIA : emergency — **urgente** *adj* : urgent
urinario, -ria *adj* : urinary — **urinario** *nm* : urinal (place)

urna *nf* **1** : urn **2** : ballot box (for voting)
urraca *nf* : magpie
uruguayo, -ya *adj* : Uruguayan
usar *vt* **1** : use **2** LLEVAR : wear — **usarse 1** EMPLEARSE : be used **2** : be worn, be in fashion — **usado, -da** *adj* **1** : used **2** GASTADO : worn, worn-out — **usanza** *nf* : custom, usage — **uso** *nm* **1** : use **2** DESGASTE : wear and tear **3** USANZA : custom, usage
usted *pron* **1** (*used in formal address; often written as* **Ud.** *or* **Vd.**) : you **2 ~es** *pl* (*often written as* **Uds.** *or* **Vds.**) : you (all)
usual *adj* : usual
usuario, -ria *n* : user
usura *nf* : usury — **usurero, -ra** *n* : usurer
usurpar *vt* : usurp
utensilio *nm* : utensil, tool
útero *nm* : uterus, womb
utilizar {21} *vt* : use, utilize — **útil** *adj* : useful — **útiles** *nmpl* : implements, tools — **utilidad** *nf* : utility, usefulness — **utilitario, -ria** *adj* : utilitarian — **utilización** *nf, pl* **-ciones** : utilization, use
uva *nf* : grape
uy *interj* **1** : oh! **2** : ow!

V

v *nf* : v, 23d letter of the Spanish alphabet
va → ir
vaca *nf* : cow
vacaciones *nfpl* **1** : vacation **2 estar de ~** : be on vacation **3 irse de ~** : go on vacation
vacante *adj* : vacant — **~** *nf* : vacancy
vaciar {85} *vt* **1** : empty (out) **2** AHUECAR : hollow out **3** : cast, mold (a statue, etc.)
vacilar *vi* **1** : hesitate, waver **2** : flicker (of light) **3** TAMBALEARSE : be unsteady, wobble **4** *fam* : joke, fool around — **vacilación** *nf, pl* **-ciones** : hesitation — **vacilante** *adj* **1** : hesitant **2** OSCILANTE : unsteady
vacío, -cía *adj* : empty — **vacío** *nm* **1** : void **2** : vacuum (in physics) **3** HUECO : space, gap
vacuna *nf* : vaccine — **vacunación** *nf, pl* **-ciones** : vaccination — **vacunar** *vt* : vaccinate
vacuno, -na *adj* : bovine
vadear *vt* : ford — **vado** *nm* : ford
vagabundear *vi* : wander — **vagabundo, -da** *adj* **1** : vagrant **2** : stray (of a dog, etc.) — **~** *n* : hobo, bum — **vagancia** *nf* **1** : va-

grancy **2** PEREZA : laziness, idleness — **vagar** {52} *vi* : roam, wander
vagina *nf* : vagina
vago, -ga *adj* **1** : vague **2** PEREZOSO : lazy, idle — **~** *n* : idler, loafer
vagón *nm, pl* **-gones** : car (of a train)
vahído *nm* : dizzy spell
vaho *nm* **1** : breath **2** VAPOR : vapor, steam
vaina *nf* **1** : sheath, scabbard **2** : pod (in botany) **3** *Lat fam* : bother, pain
vainilla *nf* : vanilla
vaivén *nm, pl* **-venes 1** : swinging, swaying **2** : coming and going (of people, etc.) **3 vaivenes** *nmpl* : ups and downs
vajilla *nf* : dishes *pl*
vale *nm* **1** : voucher **2** PAGARÉ : IOU — **valedero, -ra** *adj* : valid
valentía *nf* : courage, bravery
valer {84} *vt* **1** : be worth **2** COSTAR : cost **3** GANAR : gain, earn **4** EQUIVALER A : be equal to — *vi* **1** : have value, cost **2** SER VÁLIDO : be valid, count **3** SERVIR : be of use **4 hacerse ~** : assert oneself **5 más vale** : it's better — **valerse** *vr* **1 ~ de**

: take advantage of **2 ~ solo** *or* **~ por sí mismo** : look after oneself

valeroso, -sa *adj* : courageous

valga, etc. → valer

valía *nf* : worth

validar *vt* : validate — **validez** *nf* : validity — **válido, -da** *adj* : valid

valiente *adj* **1** : brave **2** (*used ironically*) : fine, great

valija *nf* : case, valise

valioso, -sa *adj* : valuable

valla *nf* **1** : fence **2** : hurdle (in sports) — **vallar** *vt* : put a fence around

valle *nm* : valley

valor *nm* **1** : value, worth **2** VALENTÍA : courage, valor **3 objetos de ~** : valuables **4 sin ~** : worthless **5 ~es** *nmpl* : values, principles **6 ~es** *nmpl* : securities, bonds — **valoración** *nf, pl* **-ciones** : valuation — **valorar** *vt* : evaluate, assess

vals *nm* : waltz

válvula *nf* : valve

vamos → ir

vampiro *nm* : vampire

van → ir

vanagloriarse *vr* : boast, brag

vándalo *nm* : vandal — **vandalismo** : vandalism

vanguardia *nf* **1** : vanguard **2** : avant-garde (in art, music, etc.) **3 a la ~** : at/in the forefront

vanidad *nf* : vanity — **vanidoso, -sa** *adj* : vain, conceited

vano, -na *adj* **1** INÚTIL : vain, useless **2** SUPERFICIAL : empty, hollow **3 en vano** : in vain

vapor *nm* **1** : steam, vapor **2 al ~** : steamed — **vaporizador** *nm* : vaporizer — **vaporizar** {21} *vt* : vaporize

vaquero, -ra *n* : cowboy *m,* cowgirl *f* — **vaqueros** *nmpl* : jeans

vara *nf* **1** : stick, rod **2** : staff (of office)

varado, -da *adj* : stranded

variar {85} *vt* **1** : vary **2** CAMBIAR : change, alter — *vi* : vary, change — **variable** *adj & nf* : variable — **variación** *nf, pl* **-ciones** : variation — **variado, -da** *adj* : varied — **variante** *nf* : variant

varicela *nf* : chicken pox

varicoso, -sa *adj* : varicose

variedad *nf* : variety

varilla *nf* : rod, stick

vario, -ria *adj* **1** : varied **2 ~s** *pl* : several

varita *nf* : wand

variz *nf, pl* **-rices** *or* **várices** : varicose vein

varón *nm, pl* **-rones** **1** : man, male **2** NIÑO : boy — **varonil** *adj* : manly

vas → ir

vasco, -ca *adj* : Basque — **vasco** *nm* : Basque (language)

vasija *nf* : container, vessel

vaso *nm* **1** : glass **2** : vessel (in anatomy)

vástago *nm* **1** : offspring, descendent **2** BROTE : shoot **3** VARILLA : rod

vasto, -ta *adj* : vast

vaticinar *vt* : prophesy, predict — **vaticinio** *nm* : prophecy

vatio *nm* : watt

vaya, etc. → ir

Vd., Vds. → usted

ve, etc. → ir, ver

vecinal *adj* : local

vecino, -na *n* **1** : neighbor **2** HABITANTE : resident, inhabitant — **~** *adj* : neighboring — **vecindad** *nf* : neighborhood, vicinity — **vecindario** *nm* **1** : neighborhood **2** VECINOS : community, residents *pl*

vedar *vt* : prohibit — **veda** *nf* **1** : prohibition, ban **2** : closed season (for hunting and fishing) — **vedado** *nm* : preserve (for game, etc.)

vega *nf* : fertile lowland

vegetal *nm* : vegetable, plant — **~** *adj* : vegetable — **vegetación** *nf, pl* **-ciones** : vegetation — **vegetar** *vi* : vegetate — **vegetariano, -na** *adj & n* : vegetarian

vehemente *adj* : vehement

vehículo *nm* : vehicle

veinte *adj & nm* : twenty — **veinteavo, -va** *adj* : twentieth — **veinteavo** *nm* : twentieth — **veintena** *nf* : group of twenty, score

vejar *vt* : mistreat, humiliate — **vejación** *nf, pl* **-ciones** : humiliation

vejez *nf* : old age

vejiga *nf* **1** : bladder **2** AMPOLLA : blister

vela *nf* **1** : candle **2** : sail (of a ship) **3** VIGILIA : vigil **4 pasar la noche en ~** : have a sleepless night

velada *nf* : evening (party)

velar *vt* **1** : hold a wake over **2** CUIDAR : watch over **3** : blur (a photograph) **4** OCULTAR : veil, mask — *vi* **1** : stay awake **2 ~ por** : watch over — **velado, -da** *adj* **1** : veiled, hidden **2** : blurred (of a photograph)

velero *nm* : sailing ship

veleta *nf* : weather vane

vello *nm* **1** : body hair **2** PELUSA : down, fuzz — **vellón** *nm, pl* **-llones** : fleece — **velloso, -sa** *adj* : downy, fluffy — **velludo, -da** *adj* : hairy

velo *nm* : veil

veloz *adj, pl* **-loces** : fast, quick — **velocidad** *nf* **1** : speed, velocity **2** MARCHA : gear (of an automobile) — **velocímetro** *nm* : speedometer

vena *nf* **1** : vein **2** : grain (of wood) **3** DISPOSICIÓN : mood **4 tener ~ de** : have a talent for

venado *nm* **1** : deer **2** : venison (in cooking)

vencer {86} vt **1** : beat, defeat **2** SUPERAR : overcome — vi **1** : win **2** CADUCAR : expire — **vencerse** vr : collapse, give way — **vencedor, -dora** adj : winning — ~ n : winner — **vencido, -da** adj **1** : beaten, defeated **2** CADUCADO : expired **3** : due, payable (in finance) **4 darse por** ~ : give up — **vencimiento** nm **1** : expiration **2** : maturity (of a loan)

venda nf : bandage — **vendaje** nm : bandage, dressing — **vendar** vt **1** : bandage **2** ~ **los ojos** : blindfold

vendaval nm : gale

vender vt : sell — **venderse** vr **1** : be sold **2 se vende** : for sale — **vendedor, -dora** n **1** : seller **2** : salesman m, saleswoman f (in a store)

vendimia nf : grape harvest

vendrá, etc. → **venir**

veneno nm **1** : poison **2** : venom (of a snake, etc.) — **venenoso, -sa** adj : poisonous

venerar vt : venerate, revere — **venerable** adj : venerable — **veneración** nf, pl **-ciones** : veneration, reverence

venéreo, -rea adj : venereal

venezolano, -na adj : Venezuelan

venga → **venir**

vengar {52} vt : avenge — **vengarse** vr : get even, take revenge — **venganza** nf : vengeance, revenge — **vengativo, -va** adj : vindictive, vengeful

venia nf **1** : permission **2** : pardon (in law)

venial adj : venial, petty

venir {87} vi **1** : come **2** LLEGAR : arrive **3** HALLARSE : be, appear **4** QUEDAR : fit **5 que viene** : coming, next **6** ~ **a ser** : turn out to be **7** ~ **bien** : be suitable — **venirse** vr **1** : come **2** ~ **abajo** : fall apart, collapse — **venida** nf **1** : arrival, coming **2** REGRESO : return — **venidero, -ra** adj : coming

venta nf **1** : sale, selling **2 en** ~ : for sale

ventaja nf : advantage — **ventajoso, -sa** adj : advantageous

ventana nf **1** : window **2** ~ **de la nariz** : nostril — **ventanilla** nf **1** : window (of a vehicle or airplane) **2** : ticket window, box office (of a theater, etc.)

ventilar vt : ventilate, air (out) — **ventilación** nf, pl **-ciones** : ventilation — **ventilador** nm : fan, ventilator

ventisca nf : blizzard — **ventisquero** nm : snowdrift

ventoso, -sa adj : windy — **ventosidad** nf : wind, flatulence

ventrílocuo, -cua n : ventriloquist

ventura nf **1** : fortune, luck **2** SATISFACCIÓN : happiness **3 a la** ~ : at random — **venturoso, -sa** adj : fortunate, happy

ver {88} vt **1** : see **2** : watch (television, etc.) — vi **1** : see **2 a** ~ or **vamos a** ~ : let's see **3 no tener nada que** ~ **con** : have nothing to do with **4 ya veremos** : we'll see — **verse** vr **1** : see oneself **2** HALLARSE : find oneself **3** ENCONTRARSE : see each other, meet

vera nf **1** : side, edge **2** : bank (of a river)

veracidad nf : truthfulness

verano nm : summer — **veraneante** nmf : summer vacationer — **veranear** vi : spend the summer — **veraniego, -ga** adj : summer

veras nfpl **de** ~ : really

veraz adj, pl **-races** : truthful

verbal adj : verbal

verbena nf : festival, fair

verbo nm : verb — **verboso, -sa** adj : verbose

verdad nf **1** : truth **2 de** ~ : really, truly **3 ¿verdad?** : right?, isn't that so? — **verdaderamente** adv : really, truly — **verdadero, -dera** adj : true, real

verde adj **1** : green **2** : dirty, risqué (of a joke, etc.) — ~ nm : green — **verdor** nm : greenness

verdugo nm **1** : executioner, hangman **2** : cruel person, tyrant

verdura nf : vegetable(s), green(s)

vereda nf **1** : path, trail **2** Lat : sidewalk

veredicto nm : verdict

vergüenza nf **1** : shame **2** TIMIDEZ : bashfulness, shyness — **vergonzoso, -sa** adj **1** : shameful **2** TÍMIDO : bashful, shy

verídico, -ca adj : true, truthful

verificar {72} vt **1** : verify, confirm **2** EXAMINAR : test, check out — **verificarse** vr **1** : take place **2** : come true (of a prophecy, etc.) — **verificación** nf, pl **-ciones** : verification

verja nf **1** : (iron) gate **2** : rails pl (of a fence) **3** ENREJADO : grating, grille

vermut nm, pl **-muts** : vermouth

vernáculo, -la adj : vernacular

verosímil adj **1** : probable, likely **2** CREÍBLE : credible

verraco nm : boar

verruga nf : wart

versar vi ~ **sobre** : deal with, be about — **versado, -da** adj ~ **en** : versed in

versátil adj **1** : versatile **2** VOLUBLE : fickle

versión nf, pl **-siones** **1** : version **2** TRADUCCIÓN : translation

verso nm **1** : poem, verse **2** : line (of poetry)

vértebra nf : vertebra

verter {56} vt **1** : pour (out) **2** DERRAMAR : spill **3** TIRAR : dump — vi : flow — **vertedero** nm **1** : dump, landfill **2** DESAGÜE : drain, outlet

vertical adj & nf : vertical

vértice *nm* : vertex, apex

vertiente *nf* : slope

vértigo *nm* : vertigo, dizziness — **vertiginoso, -sa** *adj* : dizzy

vesícula *nf* **1** : blister **2** ~ **biliar** : gallbladder

vestíbulo *nm* : vestibule, hall, foyer

vestido *nm* **1** : dress **2** ROPA : clothing, clothes *pl*

vestigio *nm* : vestige, trace

vestir {54} *vt* **1** : dress, clothe **2** LLEVAR : wear — *vi* : dress — **vestirse** *vr* : get dressed — **vestimenta** *nf* : clothing — **vestuario** *nm* **1** : wardrobe, clothes *pl* **2** : dressing room (in a theater), locker room (in sports)

veta *nf* **1** : vein, seam **2** : grain (of wood)

vetar *vt* : veto

veteado, -da *adj* : streaked, veined

veterano, -na *adj & n* : veteran

veterinaria *nf* : veterinary medicine — **veterinario, -ria** *adj* : veterinary — ~ *n* : veterinarian

veto *nm* : veto

vetusto, -ta *adj* : ancient

vez *nf, pl* **veces 1** : time **2** TURNO : turn **3 a la** ~ : at the same time **4 a veces** : sometimes **5 de una** ~ : all at once **6 de una** ~ **para siempre** : once and for all **7 de** ~ **en cuando** : from time to time **8 dos veces** : twice **9 en** ~ **de** : instead of **10 una** ~ : once

vía *nf* **1** : way, road, route **2** MEDIO : means **3** : track, line (of a railroad) **4** : (anatomical) tract **5 en** ~ **de** : in the process of — ~ *prep* : via

viable *adj* : viable, feasible — **viabilidad** *nf* : viability

viaducto *nm* : viaduct

viajar *vi* : travel — **viajante** *nmf* : traveling salesperson — **viaje** *nm* : trip, journey — **viajero, -ra** *adj* : traveling — ~ *n* **1** : traveler **2** PASAJERO : passenger

vial *adj* : road, traffic

víbora *nf* : viper

vibrar *vi* : vibrate — **vibración** *nf, pl* **-ciones** : vibration — **vibrante** *adj* : vibrant

vicario, -ria *n* : vicar

vicepresidente, -ta *n* : vice president

viceversa *adv* : vice versa

vicio *nm* **1** : vice **2** MALA COSTUMBRE : bad habit **3** DEFECTO : defect — **viciado, -da** *adj* **1** : corrupt **2** : stuffy, stale (of air, etc.) — **viciar** *vt* **1** : corrupt **2** ESTROPEAR : spoil, pollute — **vicioso, -sa** *adj* : depraved, corrupt

vicisitud *nf* : vicissitude

víctima *nf* : victim

victoria *nf* : victory — **victorioso, -sa** *adj* : victorious

vid *nf* : vine, grapevine

vida *nf* **1** : life **2** DURACIÓN : lifetime **3 de por** ~ : for life **4 estar con** ~ : be alive

video *or* **vídeo** *nm* **1** : video **2** : VCR, videocassette recorder

videojuego *nm* : video game

vidrio *nm* : glass — **vidriado** *nm* : glaze — **vidriar** *vt* : glaze — **vidriera** *nf* **1** : stained-glass window **2** : glass door **3** *Lat* : shopwindow — **vidrioso, -sa** *adj* **1** : delicate (of a subject, etc.) **2 ojos vidriosos** : glassy eyes

vieira *nf* : scallop

viejo, -ja *adj* : old — ~ *n* **1** : old man *m*, old woman *f* **2 hacerse** ~ : get old

viene, etc. → **venir**

viento *nm* : wind

vientre *nm* **1** : abdomen, belly **2** MATRIZ : womb **3** INTESTINO : bowels *pl*

viernes *nms & pl* **1** : Friday **2 Viernes Santo** : Good Friday

vietnamita *adj & nm* : Vietnamese

viga *nf* : beam, girder

vigencia *nf* **1** : validity **2 entrar en** ~ : go into effect — **vigente** *adj* : valid, in force

vigésimo, -ma *adj & n* : twentieth

vigía *nmf* : lookout

vigilar *vt* : look after, watch over — *vi* : keep watch — **vigilancia** *nf* **1** : vigilance **2 bajo** ~ : under surveillance — **vigilante** *adj* : vigilant — ~ *nmf* : watchman, guard — **vigilia** *nf* **1** : wakefulness **2** : vigil (in religion)

vigor *nm* **1** : vigor **2 entrar en** ~ : go into effect — **vigorizante** *adj* : invigorating — **vigoroso, -sa** *adj* : vigorous

VIH *nm* : HIV

vil *adj* : vile, despicable — **vileza** *nf* **1** : vileness **2** : despicable act — **vilipendiar** *vt* : revile

villa *nf* **1** : town, village **2** : villa (house)

villancico *nm* : (Christmas) carol

villano, -na *n* : villain

vilo *nm* **en** ~ : suspended, in the air

vinagre *nm* : vinegar — **vinagrera** *nf* : cruet — **vinagreta** *nf* : vinaigrette

vincular *vt* : tie, link — **vínculo** *nm* : link, tie, bond

vindicar *vt* **1** : vindicate **2** VENGAR : avenge

vino¹, etc. → **venir**

vino² *nm* : wine

viña *nf or* **viñedo** *nm* : vineyard

vio, etc. → **ver**

viola *nf* : viola

violar *vt* **1** : violate (a law, etc.) **2** : rape (a person) — **violación** *nf, pl* **-ciones 1** : violation, offense **2** : rape (of a person)

violencia *nf* : violence, force — **violentar** *vt* **1** : force **2** : break into (a house, etc.) — **violentarse** *vr* **1** : force oneself **2** AVERGON-

ZARSE : be embarrassed — **violento, -ta** *adj*
1 : violent 2 INCÓMODO : awkward, embarrassing

violeta *adj & nm* : violet (color) — ~ *nf*
: violet (flower)

violín *nm, pl* **-lines** : violin — **violinista** *nmf*
: violinist — **violoncelista** *or* **violonche-
lista** *nmf* : cellist — **violoncelo** *or* **violon-
chelo** *nm* : cello, violoncello

virar *vi* : turn, change direction — **viraje** *nm*
1 : turn, swerve 2 CAMBIO : change

virgen *adj & nmf, pl* **vírgenes** : virgin —
virginal *adj* : virginal — **virginidad** *nf* : virginity

viril *adj* : virile — **virilidad** *nf* : virility

virtual *adj* : virtual

virtud *nf* 1 : virtue 2 **en** ~ **de** : by virtue of
— **virtuoso, -sa** *adj* : virtuous — ~ *n* : virtuoso

viruela *nf* 1 : smallpox 2 **picado de** ~s
: pockmarked

virulento, -ta *adj* : virulent

virus *nms & pl* : virus

visa *nf Lat* : visa — **visado** *nm Spain* : visa

vísceras *nfpl* : entrails — **visceral** *adj* : visceral

viscoso, -sa *adj* : viscous — **viscosidad** *nf*
: viscosity

visera *nf* : visor

visible *adj* : visible — **visibilidad** *nf* : visibility

visión *nf, pl* **-siones** 1 : eyesight 2 APARI-
CIÓN : vision, illusion 3 PUNTO DE VISTA
: view, perspective — **visionario, -ria** *adj &
n* : visionary

visitar *vt* : visit — **visita** *nf* 1 : visit 2 **tener**
~ : have company — **visitante** *adj* : visit-
ing — ~ *nmf* : visitor

vislumbrar *vt* : make out, discern — **vislumbre** *nf* 1 : glimpse, sign 2 RESPLANDOR
: glimmer, gleam

viso *nm* 1 : sheen 2 **tener** ~s **de** : seem,
show signs of

visón *nm, pl* **-sones** : mink

víspera *nf* : eve, day before

vista *nf* 1 : vision, eyesight 2 MIRADA
: look, gaze 3 PANORAMA : view, vista 4
: hearing (in court) 5 **a primera** ~ *or* **a
simple** ~ : at first sight 6 **hacer la** ~
gorda : turn a blind eye 7 **perder de** ~
: lose sight of — **vistazo** *nm* 1 : glance 2
echar un ~ : have a look

visto, -ta *adj* 1 : clear, obvious 2 COMÚN
: commonly seen 3 **estar bien** ~ : be
approved of 4 **estar mal** ~ : be frowned
upon 5 **nunca** ~ : unheard-of 6 **por lo
visto** : apparently 7 **visto que** : since,
given that — **visto** *nm* ~ **bueno** : approval
— ~ *pp* → **ver**

vistoso, -sa *adj* : colorful, bright

visual *adj* : visual — **visualizar** {21} *vt* : visualize

vital *adj* : vital — **vitalicio, -cia** *adj* : life, for
life — **vitalidad** *nf* : vitality

vitamina *nf* : vitamin

viticultor, -tora *n* : winegrower — **viticul-
tura** *nf* : wine growing

vitorear *vt* : cheer, acclaim

vítreo, -trea *adj* : glassy

vitrina *nf* 1 : showcase, display case 2 *Lat*
: shopwindow

vituperar *vt* : censure — **vituperio** *nm* : censure

viudo, -da *n* : widower *m*, widow *f* — ~ *adj*
: widowed — **viudez** *nf* : widowerhood,
widowhood

viva *nm* **dar** ~s : cheer

vivacidad *nf* : vivacity, liveliness

vivamente *adv* 1 : vividly 2 PROFUNDA-
MENTE : deeply, acutely

vivaz *adj, pl* **-vaces** 1 : lively, vivacious 2
AGUDO : vivid, sharp

víveres *nmpl* : provisions, supplies

vivero *nm* 1 : nursery (for plants) 2 : (fish)
hatchery, (oyster) bed

viveza *nf* 1 : liveliness 2 : vividness (of colors, descriptions, etc.) 3 ASTUCIA : sharpness (of mind) — **vívido, -da** *adj* : vivid

vividor, -dora *n* : freeloader

vivienda *nf* 1 : housing 2 MORADA : dwelling

viviente *adj* : living

vivificar {72} *vt* : enliven

vivir *vi* 1 : live, be alive 2 ~ **de** : live on
— *vt* : experience, live (through) — ~ *nm*
1 : life, lifestyle 2 **de mal** ~ : disreputable
— **vivo, -va** *adj* 1 : alive 2 INTENSO : intense, bright 3 ANIMADO : lively 4 ASTUTO
: sharp, quick 5 **en vivo** : live

vocablo *nm* : word — **vocabulario** *nm* : vocabulary

vocación *nf, pl* **-ciones** : vocation — **voca-
cional** *adj* : vocational

vocal *adj* : vocal — ~ *nmf* : member (of a
committee, etc.) — ~ *nf* : vowel — **vocalista** *nmf* : singer, vocalist

vocear *v* : shout — **vocerío** *nm* : shouting

vociferar *vi* : shout

vodka *nmf* : vodka

volar {19} *vi* 1 : fly 2 : blow away (of pa-
pers, etc.) 3 *fam* : disappear 4 **irse volando**
: rush off — *vt* : blow up — **volador, -dora**
adj : flying — **volandas: en** ~ *adv phr* : in
the air — **volante** *adj* : flying — ~ *nm* 1
: steering wheel 2 : shuttlecock (in badmin-
ton) 3 : flounce (of fabric) 4 *Lat* : flier,
circular

volátil *adj* : volatile

volcán *nm, pl* **-canes** : volcano — **volcánico, -ca** *adj* : volcanic

volcar {82} *vt* **1** : upset, knock over **2** VACIAR : empty out — *vi* : overturn — **volcarse** *vr* **1** : overturn, tip over **2** ⁓ **en** : throw oneself into

voleibol *nm* : volleyball

voltaje *nm* : voltage

voltear *vt* : turn over, turn upside down — **voltearse** *vr Lat* : turn (around) — **voltereta** *nf* : somersault

voltio *nm* : volt

voluble *adj* : fickle

volumen *nm, pl* **-lúmenes** : volume — **voluminoso, -sa** *adj* : voluminous

voluntad *nf* **1** : will **2** DESEO : wish **3** INTENCIÓN : intention **4 a** ⁓ : at will **5 buena** ⁓ : goodwill **6 mala** ⁓ : ill will **7 fuerza de** ⁓ : willpower — **voluntario, -ria** *adj* : voluntary — ⁓ *n* : volunteer — **voluntarioso, -sa** *adj* **1** : willing **2** TERCO : stubborn, willful

voluptuoso, -sa *adj* : voluptuous

volver {89} *vi* **1** : return, come or go back **2** ⁓ **a** : return to, do again **3** ⁓ **en sí** : come to — *vt* **1** : turn, turn over, turn inside out **2** CONVERTIR EN : turn (into) **3** ⁓ **loco** : drive crazy — **volverse** *vr* **1** : turn (around) **2** HACERSE : become

vomitar *vi* : vomit — *vt* **1** : vomit **2** : spew (out) — **vómito** *nm* **1** : (action of) vomiting **2** : vomit

voraz *adj, pl* **-races** : voracious

vos *pron Lat* : you

vosotros, -tras *pron Spain* : you, yourselves

votar *vi* : vote — *vt* : vote for — **votación** *nf, pl* **-ciones** : vote, voting — **votante** *nmf* : voter — **voto** *nm* **1** : vote **2** : vow (in religion)

voy → **ir**

voz *nf, pl* **voces 1** : voice **2** GRITO : shout, yell **3** VOCABLO : word, term **4** RUMOR : rumor **5 dar voces** : shout **6 en** ⁓ **alta** : loudly **7 en** ⁓ **baja** : softly

vuelco *nm* : upset, overturning

vuelo *nm* **1** : flight **2** : (action of) flying **3** : flare (of clothing) **4 al** ⁓ : on the wing

vuelta *nf* **1** : turn **2** REVOLUCIÓN : circle, revolution **3** CURVA : bend, curve **4** REGRESO : return **5** : round, lap (in sports) **6** PASEO : walk, drive, ride **7** REVÉS : back, other side **8** *Spain* : change **9 dar** ⁓**s** : spin **10 estar de** ⁓ : be back — **vuelto** *nm Lat* : change

vuestro, -tra *adj Spain* : your, of yours — ⁓ *pron Spain (with definite article)* : yours

vulgar *adj* **1** : vulgar **2** CORRIENTE : common — **vulgaridad** *nf* **1** : vulgarity **2** BANALIDAD : banality — **vulgo** *nm* **el** ⁓ : the masses, common people

vulnerable *adj* : vulnerable — **vulnerabilidad** *nf* : vulnerability

WXYZ

w *nf* : w, 24th letter of the Spanish alphabet

wáter *nm Spain* : toilet

webcam *nf, pl* **webcams** : webcam

webmaster *nmf, pl* **-ters** : webmaster

whisky *nm, pl* **-skys** *or* **-skies** : whiskey

windsurf *nm* : windsurfing

x *nf* : x, 25th letter of the Spanish alphabet

xenofobia *nf* : xenophobia

xilófono *nm* : xylophone

y¹ *nf* : y, 26th letter of the Spanish alphabet

y² *conj* : and

ya *adv* **1** : already **2** AHORA : (right) now **3** MÁS TARDE : later, soon **4** ⁓ **no** : no longer **5** ⁓ **que** : now that, since, inasmuch as

yacer {90} *vi* : lie (on or in the ground) — **yacimiento** *nm* : bed, deposit

yanqui *adj & nmf* : Yankee

yate *nm* : yacht

yegua *nf* : mare

yelmo *nm* : helmet

yema *nf* **1** : bud, shoot **2** : yolk (of an egg) **3** *or* ⁓ **del dedo** : fingertip

yerba *nf* **1** *or* ⁓ **mate** : maté **2** → **hierba**

yermo, -ma *adj* : barren, deserted — **yermo** *nm* : wasteland

yerno *nm* : son-in-law

yerro *nm* : blunder, mistake

yerto, -ta *adj* : stiff

yesca *nf* : tinder

yeso *nm* **1** : gypsum **2** : plaster (for art, construction)

yo *pron* **1** (*subject*) : I **2** (*object*) : me **3 soy** ⁓ : it is I, it's me — ⁓ *nm* : ego, self

yodo *nm* : iodine

yoga *nm* : yoga

yogurt *or* **yogur** *nm* : yogurt

zutano

yuca *nf* : yucca
yugo *nm* : yoke (of oxen)
yugoslavo, -va *adj* : Yugoslavian
yugular *adj* : jugular
yunque *nm* : anvil
yunta *nf* : yoke
yuxtaponer {60} *vt* : juxtapose — **yuxtaposición** *nf, pl* **-ciones** : juxtaposition
z *nf* : z, 27th letter of the Spanish alphabet
zacate *nm Lat* : grass
zafar *vt Lat* : loosen, untie — **zafarse** *vr* **1** : come undone **2** : get free of (an obligation, etc.)
zafio, -fia *adj* : coarse
zafiro *nm* : sapphire
zaga *nf* **a la ~** *or* **en ~** : behind, in the rear
zaguán *nm, pl* **-guanes** : (entrance) hall
zaherir {76} *vt* : hurt (s.o.'s feelings)
zaino, -na *adj* : chestnut (color)
zalamería *nf* : flattery — **zalamero, -ra** *adj* : flattering — **~** *n* : flatterer
zambullirse {38} *vr* : dive, plunge — **zambullida** *nf* : dive, plunge
zanahoria *nf* : carrot
zancada *nf* : stride, step — **zancadilla** *nf* **1** : trip, stumble **2 hacer una ~ a algn** : trip s.o. up
zancos *nmpl* : stilts
zancudo *nm Lat* : mosquito
zángano, -na *n fam* : lazy person, slacker — **zángano** *nm* : drone (bee)
zanja *nf* : ditch, trench — **zanjar** *vt* : settle, resolve
zapallo *nm Lat* : pumpkin — **zapallito** *nm Lat* : zucchini
zapapico *nm* : pickax
zapato *nm* : shoe — **zapatería** *nf* : shoe store — **zapatero, -ra** *n* : shoemaker, cobbler —

zapatilla *nf* **1** : slipper **2** : sneaker (for sports, etc.)
zapping *nm* : channel surfing
zar *nm* : czar
zarandear *vt* **1** : sift **2** SACUDIR : shake
zarcillo *nm* : earring
zarpa *nf* : paw
zarpar *vi* : set sail, raise anchor
zarza *nf* : bramble — **zarzamora** *nf* : blackberry
zigzag *nm, pl* **-zags** *or* **-zagues** : zigzag — **zigzaguear** *vi* : zigzag
zinc *nm* : zinc
zíper *nm Lat* : zipper
zircón *nm, pl* **-cones** : zircon
zócalo *nm* **1** : base (of a column, etc.) **2** : baseboard (of a wall) **3** *Lat* : main square, plaza
zodíaco *nm* : zodiac
zona *nf* : zone, area
zoo *nm* : zoo — **zoología** *nf* : zoology — **zoológico, -ca** *adj* : zoological — **zoológico** *nm* : zoo — **zoólogo, -ga** *n* : zoologist
zopilote *nm Lat* : buzzard
zoquete *nmf fam* : oaf, blockhead
zorrillo *nm Lat* : skunk
zorro, -rra *n* : fox, vixen *f* — **~** *adj* : foxy, sly
zozobra *nf* : anxiety, worry — **zozobrar** *vi* : capsize
zueco *nm* : clog (shoe)
zumbar *vi* : buzz — *vt fam* : hit, beat — **zumbido** *nm* : buzzing
zumo *nf* : juice
zurcir {83} *vt* : darn, mend
zurdo, -da *adj* : left-handed — **~** *n* : left-handed person — **zurda** *nf* : left hand
zutano, -na → **fulano**

English-Spanish
Dictionary

A

a¹ *n, pl* **a's** *or* **as** : a *f*, primera letra del alfabeto inglés

a² *art* (**an** *before vowel or silent h*) **1** : un *m*, una *f* **2** PER : por, a la, al

aback *adv* **be taken** ~ : quedarse desconcertado

abacus *n, pl* **abaci** *or* **abacuses** : ábaco *m*

abandon *vt* **1** DESERT : abandonar **2** GIVE UP : renunciar a — ~ *n* : desenfreno *m* — **abandonment** *n* : abandono *m*

abashed *adj* : avergonzado

abate *vi* **abated; abating** : amainar, disminuir

abattoir *n* : matadero *m*

abbey *n, pl* **-beys** : abadía *f* — **abbot** *n* : abad *m*

abbreviate *vt* **-ated; -ating** : abreviar — **abbreviation** *n* : abreviatura *f*, abreviación *f*

abdicate *v* **-cated; -cating** : abdicar — **abdication** *n* : abdicación *f*

abdomen *n* : abdomen *m*, vientre *m* — **abdominal** *adj* : abdominal

abduct *vt* : secuestrar — **abduction** *n* : secuestro *m*

aberration *n* : aberración *f*

abet *vt* **abetted; abetting** *or* **aid and** ~ : ser cómplice de

abeyance *n* : desuso *m*

abhor *vt* **-horred; -horring** : aborrecer

abide *v* **abode** *or* **abided; abiding** *vt* : soportar, tolerar — *vi* **1** DWELL : morar **2** ~ **by** : atenerse a

ability *n, pl* **-ties** **1** CAPABILITY : aptitud *f*, capacidad *f* **2** SKILL : habilidad *f*

abject *adj* : miserable, desdichado

ablaze *adj* : en llamas

able *adj* **abler; ablest** **1** CAPABLE : capaz, hábil **2** COMPETENT : competente

abnormal *adj* : anormal — **abnormality** *n, pl* **-ties** : anormalidad *f*

aboard *adv* : a bordo — ~ *prep* : a bordo de

abode *n* : morada *f*, domicilio *m*

abolish *vt* : abolir, suprimir — **abolition** *n* : abolición *f*

abominable *adj* : abominable, aborrecible — **abomination** *n* : abominación *f*

aborigine *n* : aborigen *mf*

abort *vt* : abortar — **abortion** *n* : aborto *m* — **abortive** *adj* UNSUCCESSFUL : malogrado

abound *vi* ~ **in** : abundar en

about *adv* **1** APPROXIMATELY : aproximadamente, más o menos **2** AROUND : alrededor **3** **be** ~ **to** : estar a punto de **4** **be up and** ~ : estar levantado — ~ *prep* **1** AROUND : alrededor de **2** CONCERNING : acerca de, sobre

above *adv* : arriba — ~ *prep* **1** : encima de **2** ~ **all** : sobre todo — **aboveboard** *adj* : honrado

abrasive *adj* **1** : abrasivo **2** BRUSQUE : brusco, mordaz

abreast *adv* **1** : al lado **2** **keep** ~ **of** : mantenerse al corriente de

abridge *vt* **abridged; abridging** : abreviar

abroad *adv* **1** : en el extranjero **2** WIDELY : por todas partes **3** **go** ~ : ir al extranjero

abrupt *adj* **1** SUDDEN : repentino **2** BRUSQUE : brusco

abscess *n* : absceso *m*

absence *n* **1** : ausencia *f* **2** LACK : falta *f*, carencia *f* — **absent** *adj* : ausente — **absentee** *n* : ausente *mf* — **absentminded** *adj* : distraído, despistado

absolute *adj* : absoluto — **absolutely** *adv* : absolutamente

absolve *vt* **-solved; -solving** : absolver

absorb *vt* : absorber — **absorbent** *adj* : absorbente — **absorption** *n* : absorción *f*

abstain *vi* ~ **from** : abstenerse de — **abstinence** *n* : abstinencia *f*

abstract *adj* : abstracto — ~ *vt* : extraer — ~ *n* : resumen *m* — **abstraction** *n* : abstracción *f*

absurd *adj* : absurdo — **absurdity** *n, pl* **-ties** : absurdo *m*

abundant *adj* : abundante — **abundance** *n* : abundancia *f*

abuse *vt* **abused; abusing** **1** MISUSE : abusar de **2** MISTREAT : maltratar **3** REVILE : insultar — ~ *n* **1** : abuso *m* **2** INSULTS : insultos *mpl* — **abusive** *adj* : injurioso

abut *vi* **abutted; abutting** ~ **on** : colindar con

abyss *n* : abismo *m* — **abysmal** *adj* : atroz, pésimo

academy *n, pl* **-mies** : academia *f* — **academic** *adj* **1** : académico **2** THEORETICAL : teórico

accelerate *v* **-ated; -ating** : acelerar — **acceleration** *n* : aceleración *f*

accent *vt* : acentuar — ~ *n* : acento *m* — **accentuate** *vt* **-ated; -ating** : acentuar, subrayar

accept *vt* : aceptar — **acceptable** *adj*

: aceptable — **acceptance** *n* **1** : aceptación *f* **2** APPROVAL : aprobación *f*

access *n* : acceso *m* — **accessible** *adj* : accesible, asequible

accessory *n, pl* **-ries 1** : accesorio *m* **2** ACCOMPLICE : cómplice *mf*

accident *n* **1** MISHAP : accidente *m* **2** CHANCE : casualidad *f* — **accidental** *adj* : accidental — **accidentally** *adv* **1** BY CHANCE : por casualidad **2** UNINTENTIONALLY : sin querer

acclaim *vt* : aclamar — ~ *n* : aclamación *f*

acclimatize *vt* **-tized; -tizing** : aclimatar

accommodate *vt* **-dated; -dating 1** ADAPT : acomodar, adaptar **2** SATISFY : complacer, satisfacer **3** HOLD : tener cabida para — **accomodation** *n* **1** : adaptación *f* **2** ~s *npl* LODGING : alojamiento *m*

accompany *vt* **-nied; -nying** : acompañar

accomplice *n* : cómplice *mf*

accomplish *vt* : realizar, llevar a cabo — **accomplishment** *n* **1** COMPLETION : realización *f* **2** ACHIEVEMENT : logro *m*, éxito *m*

accord *n* **1** AGREEMENT : acuerdo *m* **2** of one's own ~ : voluntariamente — **accordance** *n* in ~ with : conforme a, de acuerdo con — **accordingly** *adv* : en consecuencia — **according to** *prep* : según

accordion *n* : acordeón *m*

accost *vt* : abordar

account *n* **1** : cuenta *f* **2** REPORT : relato *m*, informe *m* **3** WORTH : importancia *f* **4** on ~ of : a causa de, debido a **5** on no ~ : de ninguna manera — ~ *vi* **for** : dar cuenta de, explicar — **accountable** *adj* : responsable — **accountant** *n* : contador *m*, -dora *f Lat*; contable *mf Spain* — **accounting** *n* : contabilidad *f*

accrue *vi* **-crued; -cruing** : acumularse

accumulate *v* **-lated; -lating** *vt* : acumular — *vi* : acumularse — **accumulation** *n* : acumulación *f*

accurate *adj* : exacto, preciso — **accuracy** *n* : exactitud *f*, precisión *f*

accuse *vt* **-cused; -cusing** : acusar — **accusation** *n* : acusación *f*

accustomed *adj* **1** : acostumbrado **2** become ~ to : acostumbrarse a

ace *n* : as *m*

ache *vi* **ached; aching** : doler — ~ *n* : dolor *m*

achieve *vt* **achieved; achieving** : lograr, realizar — **achievement** *n* : logro *m*, éxito *m*

acid *adj* : ácido — ~ *n* : ácido *m*

acid rain *n* : lluvia *f* ácida

acknowledge *vt* **-edged; -edging 1** ADMIT : admitir **2** RECOGNIZE : reconocer **3** ~ **receipt of** : acusar recibo de — **acknowledgment** *n* **1** : reconocimiento *m* **2**

THANKS : agradecimiento *m* **3** ~ **of receipt** : acuse *m* de recibo

acne *n* : acné *m*

acorn *n* : bellota *f*

acoustic *or* **acoustical** *adj* : acústico — **acoustics** *ns & pl* : acústica *f*

acquaint *vt* **1** ~ **s.o. with** : poner a algn al corriente de **2** be ~ed with : conocer a (una persona), saber (un hecho) — **acquaintance** *n* **1** : conocimiento *m* **2** : conocido *m*, -da *f* (persona)

acquire *vt* **-quired; -quiring** : adquirir — **acquisition** *n* : adquisición *f*

acquit *vt* **-quitted; -quitting** : absolver

acre *n* : acre *m* — **acreage** *n* : superficie *f* en acres

acrid *adj* : acre

acrobat *n* : acróbata *mf* — **acrobatic** *adj* : acrobático

acronym *n* : siglas *fpl*

across *adv* **1** : de un lado a otro **2** CROSSWISE : a través **3** go ~ : atravesar — ~ *prep* **1** : a través de **2** ~ **the street** : al otro lado de la calle

acrylic *n* : acrílico *m*

act *vi* **1** : actuar **2** PRETEND : fingir **3** FUNCTION : funcionar **4** ~ **as** : servir de — *vt* : interpretar (un papel) — ~ *n* **1** ACTION : acto *m*, acción *f* **2** DECREE : ley *f* **3** : acto *m* (en una obra de teatro), número *m* (en un espectáculo) — **acting** *adj* : interino

action *n* **1** : acción *f* **2** LAWSUIT : demanda *f* **3** take ~ : tomar medidas

activate *vt* **-vated; -vating** : activar

active *adj* **1** : activo **2** LIVELY : enérgico **3** ~ **volcano** : volcán *m* en actividad — **activity** *n, pl* **-ties** : actividad *f*

actor *n* : actor *m* — **actress** *n* : actriz *f*

actual *adj* : real, verdadero — **actually** *adv* : realmente, en realidad

acupuncture *n* : acupuntura *f*

acute *adj* **acuter; acutest 1** : agudo **2** PERCEPTIVE : perspicaz

ad → **advertisement**

adamant *adj* : inflexible

adapt *vt* : adaptar — *vi* : adaptarse — **adaptable** *adj* : adaptable — **adaptation** *n* : adaptación *f* — **adapter** *n* : adaptador *m*

add *vt* **1** : añadir **2** *or* ~ **up** : sumar — *vi* : sumar

addict *n* **1** : adicto *m*, -ta *f* **2** *or* **drug** ~ : drogadicto *m*, -ta *f*; toxicómano *m*, -na *f* — **addiction** *n* : dependencia *f*

addition *n* **1** : suma *f* (en matemáticas) **2** ADDING : adición *f* **3** in ~ : además — **additional** *adj* : adicional — **additive** *n* : aditivo *m*

address *vt* **1** : dirigirse a (una persona) **2** : ponerle la dirección a (una carta) **3**

: tratar (un asunto) — ~ *n* **1** : dirección *f*, domicilio *m* **2** SPEECH : discurso *m*

adept *adj* : experto, hábil

adequate *adj* : adecuado, suficiente

adhere *vi* **-hered; -hering 1** STICK : adherirse **2** ~ **to** : observar — **adherence** *n* **1** : adhesión *f* **2** : observancia *f* (de una ley, etc.) — **adhesive** *adj* : adhesivo — ~ *n* : adhesivo *m*

adjacent *adj* : adyacente, contiguo

adjective *n* : adjetivo *m*

adjoining *adj* : contiguo, vecino

adjourn *vt* : aplazar, suspender — *vi* : suspenderse

adjust *vt* : ajustar, arreglar — *vi* : adaptarse — **adjustable** *adj* : ajustable — **adjustment** *n* : ajuste *m* (a una máquina, etc.), adaptación *f* (de una persona)

ad–lib *v* **-libbed; -libbing** : improvisar

administer *vt* : administrar — **administration** *n* : administración *f* — **administrative** *adj* : administrativo — **administrator** *n* : administrador *m*, -dora *f*

admirable *adj* : admirable

admiral *n* : almirante *m*

admire *vt* **-mired; -miring** : admirar — **admiration** *n* : admiración *f* — **admirer** *n* : admirador *m*, -dora *f*

admit *vt* **-mitted; -mitting 1** : admitir, dejar entrar **2** ACKNOWLEDGE : reconocer — **admission** *n* **1** ADMITTANCE : entrada *f*, admisión *f* **2** ACKNOWLEDGMENT : reconocimiento *m* — **admittance** *n* : admisión *f*, entrada *f*

admonish *vt* : amonestar, reprender

ado *n* **1** : alboroto *m*, bulla *f* **2** without further ~ : sin más (preámbulos)

adolescent *n* : adolescente *mf* — **adolescence** *n* : adolescencia *f*

adopt *vt* : adoptar — **adoption** *n* : adopción *f*

adore *vt* **adored; adoring 1** : adorar **2** LIKE, LOVE : encantarle (algo a uno) — **adorable** *adj* : adorable — **adoration** *n* : adoración *f*

adorn *vt* : adornar — **adornment** *n* : adorno *m*

adrift *adj & adv* : a la deriva

adroit *adj* : diestro, hábil

adult *adj* : adulto — ~ *n* : adulto *m*, -ta *f*

adultery *n, pl* **-teries** : adulterio *m*

advance *v* **-vanced; -vancing** *vt* : adelantar — *vi* : avanzar, adelantarse — ~ *n* **1** : avance *m* **2** PROGRESS : adelanto *m* **3** in ~ : por adelantado — **advancement** *n* : adelanto *m*, progreso *m*

advantage *n* **1** : ventaja *f* **2** take ~ of : aprovecharse de — **advantageous** *adj* : ventajoso

advent *n* **1** ARRIVAL : llegada *f* **2** Advent : Adviento *m*

adventure *n* : aventura *f* — **adventurous** *adj* **1** : intrépido **2** RISKY : arriesgado

adverb *n* : adverbio *m*

adversary *n, pl* **-saries** : adversario *m*, -ria *f*

adverse *adj* : adverso, desfavorable — **adversity** *n, pl* **-ties** : adversidad *f*

advertise *v* **-tised; -tising** *vt* : anunciar — *vi* : hacer publicidad — **advertisement** *n* : anuncio *m* — **advertiser** *n* : anunciante *mf* — **advertising** *n* : publicidad *f*

advice *n* : consejo *m*

advise *vt* **-vised; -vising 1** COUNSEL : aconsejar, asesorar **2** RECOMMEND : recomendar **3** INFORM : informar — **advisable** *adj* : aconsejable — **adviser** *n* : consejero *m*, -ra *f*; asesor *m*, -sora *f* — **advisory** *adj* : consultivo

advocate *vt* **-cated; -cating** : recomendar — ~ *n* : defensor *m*, -sora *f*

aerial *adj* : aéreo — ~ *n* : antena *f*

aerobics *ns & pl* : aeróbic *m*

aerodynamic *adj* : aerodinámico

aerosol *n* : aerosol *m*

aesthetic *adj* : estético

afar *adv* : lejos

affable *adj* : afable

affair *n* **1** : asunto *m*, cuestión *f* **2** or love ~ : amorío *m*, aventura *f*

affect *vt* **1** : afectar **2** FEIGN : fingir — **affection** *n* : afecto *m*, cariño *m* — **affectionate** *adj* : afectuoso, cariñoso

affinity *n, pl* **-ties** : afinidad *f*

affirm *vt* : afirmar — **affirmative** *adj* : afirmativo

affix *vt* : fijar, pegar

afflict *vt* : afligir — **affliction** *n* : aflicción *f*

affluent *adj* : próspero, adinerado

afford *vt* **1** : tener los recursos para, permitirse (el lujo de) **2** PROVIDE : brindar

affront *n* : afrenta *f*

afloat *adv & adj* : a flote

afoot *adj* : en marcha

afraid *adj* **1** be ~ : tener miedo **2** I'm ~ not : me temo que no

African *adj* : africano

after *adv* **1** AFTERWARD : después **2** BEHIND : detrás, atrás — ~ *conj* : después de (que) — ~ *prep* **1** : después de **2** ~ all : después de todo **3** it's ten ~ five : son las cinco y diez

aftereffect *n* : efecto *m* secundario

aftermath *n* : consecuencias *fpl*

afternoon *n* : tarde *f*

afterward *or* **afterwards** *adv* : después, más tarde

again *adv* **1** : otra vez, de nuevo **2** ~ and ~ : una y otra vez **3** then ~ : por otra parte

against *prep* : contra, en contra de

age *n* **1** : edad *f* **2** ERA : era *f*, época *f* **3** be

of ~ : ser mayor de edad   **4 for ~s** : hace
siglos   **5 old ~** : vejez *f* — ~ *vi* **aged;**
aging : envejecer — **aged** *adj*   **1** OLD : anciano, viejo   **2 children ~ 10 to 17** : niños
de 10 a 17 años
agency *n, pl* **-cies** : agencia *f*
agenda *n* : orden *m* del día
agent *n* : agente *mf*, representante *mf*
aggravate *vt* **-vated; -vating**   **1** WORSEN
: agravar, empeorar   **2** ANNOY : irritar
aggregate *adj* : total, global — ~ *n* : total
m
aggression *n* : agresión *f* — **aggressive** *adj*
: agresivo — **aggressor** *n* : agresor *m*, -sora
f
aghast *adj* : horrorizado
agile *adj* : ágil — **agility** *n, pl* **-ties** : agilidad
f
agitate *v* **-tated; -tating** *vt*   **1** SHAKE : agitar
2 TROUBLE : inquietar — **agitation** *n* : agitación *f*, inquietud *f*
agnostic *n* : agnóstico *m*, -ca *f*
ago *adv*   **1** : hace   **2 long ~** : hace mucho
tiempo
agony *n, pl* **-nies**   **1** PAIN : dolor *m*   **2** AN-
GUISH : angustia *f* — **agonize** *vi* **-nized;**
-nizing : atormentarse — **agonizing** *adj*
: angustioso
agree *v* **agreed; agreeing** *vt* **1** : acordar   **2**
~ that : estar de acuerdo de que — *vi*   **1**
: estar de acuerdo   **2** CORRESPOND : concordar   **3 ~ to** : acceder a   **4 this climate**
~s with me : este clima me sienta bien —
agreeable *adj*   **1** PLEASING : agradable   **2**
WILLING : dispuesto — **agreement** *n* : acuerdo *m*
agriculture *n* : agricultura *f* — **agricultural**
adj : agrícola
aground *adv* **run ~** : encallar
ahead *adv*   **1** IN FRONT : delante, adelante
2 BEFOREHAND : por adelantado   **3** LEAD-
ING : a la delantera   **4 get ~** : adelantar
— **ahead of** *prep*   **1** : delante de, antes de
2 get ~ of : adelantarse a
aid *vt* : ayudar — ~ *n* : ayuda *f*, asistencia *f*
AIDS *n* : SIDA *m*, sida *m*
ail *vi* : estar enfermo — **ailment** *n* : enfermedad *f*
aim *vt* : apuntar (un arma), dirigir (una observación) — *vi*   **1** : apuntar   **2** ASPIRE : aspirar — ~ *n*   **1** : puntería *f*   **2** GOAL
: propósito *m*, objetivo *m* — **aimless** *adj*
: sin objetivo
air *vt or* ~ **out** : airear   **2** EXPRESS : expresar   **3** BROADCAST : emitir — ~ *n*   **1** : aire
m   **2 be on the ~** : estar en el aire — **air-**
conditioning *n* : aire *m* acondicionado —
air conditioned *n* : climatizado — **aircraft**
ns & pl   **1** : avión *m*, aeronave *f*   **2 ~ car-**
rier : portaaviones *m* — **air force** *n* : fuerza

f aérea — **airline** *n* : aerolínea *f*, línea *f* aérea
— **airliner** *n* : avión *m* de pasajeros — **air-**
mail *n* : correo *m* aéreo — **airplane** *n*
: avión *m* — **airport** *n* : aeropuerto *m* — **air-**
strip *n* : pista *f* de aterrizaje — **airtight** *adj*
: hermético — **airy** *adj* **airier; -est** : aireado,
bien ventilado
aisle *n*   **1** : pasillo *m*   **2** : nave *f* lateral (de
una iglesia)
ajar *adj* : entreabierto
akin *adj* **~ to** : semejante a
alarm *n*   **1** : alarma *f*   **2** ANXIETY : inquietud
f — *vt* : alarmar, asustar — **alarm clock** *n*
: despertador *m*
alas *interj* : ¡ay!
album *n* : álbum *m*
alcohol *n* : alcohol *m* — **alcoholic** *adj* : alcohólico — ~ *n* : alcohólico *m*, -ca *f* — **al-**
coholism *n* : alcoholismo *m*
alcove *n* : nicho *m*, hueco *m*
ale *n* : cerveza *f*
alert *adj*   **1** WATCHFUL : alerta, atento   **2**
LIVELY : vivo — ~ *n* : alerta *f* — ~ *vt*
: alertar, poner sobre aviso
alfalfa *n* : alfalfa *f*
alga *n, pl* **-gae** : alga *f*
algebra *n* : álgebra *f*
alias *adv* : alias — ~ *n* : alias *m*
alibi *n* : coartada *f*
alien *adj* : extranjero — ~ *n*   **1** FOREIGNER
: extranjero *m*, -ra *f*   **2** EXTRATERRESTRIAL
: extraterrestre *mf*
alienate *vt* **-ated; -ating** : enajenar — **alien-**
ation *n* : enajenación *f*
alight *vi*   **1** LAND : posarse   **2 ~ from**
: apearse de
align *vt* : alinear — **alignment** *n* : alineación
f
alike *adv* : igual, del mismo modo — ~ *adj*
: parecido
alimony *n, pl* **-nies** : pensión *f* alimenticia
alive *adj*   **1** LIVING : vivo, viviente   **2**
LIVELY : animado, activo
all *adv*   **1** COMPLETELY : todo, completamente   **2 ~ the better** : tanto mejor   **3 ~**
the more : aún más, todavía más — ~ *adj*
: todo — ~ *pron*   **1** : todo, -da   **2 ~ in ~**
: en general   **3 not at ~** : de ninguna
manera — **all–around** *adj* versatile : completo
allay *vt*   **1** ALLEVIATE : aliviar   **2** CALM
: aquietar
allege *vt* **-leged; -leging** : alegar — **allega-**
tion *n* : alegato *m*, acusación *f* — **alleged**
adj : presunto — **allegedly** *adv* : supuestamente
allegiance *n* : lealtad *f*
allegory *n, pl* **-ries** : alegoría *f* — **allegorical**
adj : alegórico

allergy *n, pl* **-gies** : alergia *f* — **allergic** *adj* : alérgico

alleviate *vt* **-ated; -ating** : aliviar

alley *n, pl* **-leys** : callejón *m*

alliance *n* : alianza *f*

alligator *n* : caimán *m*

allocate *vt* **-cated; -cating** : asignar — **allocation** *n* : asignación *f*, reparto *m*

allot *vt* **-lotted; -lotting** : asignar — **allotment** *n* : reparto *m*, asignación *f*

allow *vt* **1** PERMIT : permitir **2** GRANT : dar, conceder **3** ADMIT : admitir **4** CONCEDE : reconocer — *vi* ~ **for** : tener en cuenta — **allowance** *n* **1** : pensión *f*, subsidio *m* **2 make** ~**s for** : tener en cuenta, disculpar

alloy *n* : aleación *f*

all right *adv* **1** YES : sí, de acuerdo **2** WELL : bien **3** DEFINITELY : bien, sin duda — ~ *adj* : bien, bueno

all–terrain vehicle *n* : (vehículo *m*) todoterreno *m*

allude *vi* **-luded; -luding** : aludir

allure *vt* **-lured; -luring** : atraer — **alluring** *adj* : atrayente, seductor

allusion *n* : alusión *f*

ally *vi* **-lied; -lying** ~ **oneself with** : aliarse con — ~ *n* : aliado *m*, -da *f*

almanac *n* : almanaque *m*

almighty *adj* : omnipotente, todopoderoso

almond *n* : almendra *f*

almost *adv* : casi

alms *ns & pl* : limosna *f*

alone *adv* : sólo, solamente, únicamente — ~ *adj* : solo

along *adv* **1** FORWARD : adelante **2** ~ **with** : con, junto con **3 all** ~ : desde el principio — ~ *prep* : por, a lo largo de — **alongside** *adv* : al costado — ~ *or* ~ **of** *prep* : al lado de

aloof *adj* : distante, reservado

aloud *adv* : en voz alta

alphabet *n* : alfabeto *m* — **alphabetical** *or* **alphabetic** *adj* : alfabético

already *adv* : ya

also *adv* : también, además

altar *n* : altar *m*

alter *vt* : alterar, modificar — **alteration** *n* : alteración *f*, modificación *f*

alternate *adj* : alterno — ~ *v* **-nated; -nating** : alternar — **alternating current** *n* : corriente *f* alterna — **alternative** *adj* : alternativo — ~ *n* : alternativa *f*

although *conj* : aunque

altitude *n* : altitud *f*

altogether *adv* **1** COMPLETELY : completamente, del todo **2** ON THE WHOLE : en suma, en general

aluminum *n* : aluminio *m*

always *adv* **1** : siempre **2** FOREVER : para siempre

am → **be**

amass *vt* : amasar, acumular

amateur *adj* : amateur — ~ *n* : amateur *mf;* aficionado *m*, -da *f*

amaze *vt* **amazed; amazing** : asombrar — **amazement** *n* : asombro *m* — **amazing** *adj* : asombroso

ambassador *n* : embajador *m*, -dora *f*

amber *n* : ámbar *m*

ambiguous *adj* : ambiguo — **ambiguity** *n, pl* **-ties** : ambigüedad *f*

ambition *n* : ambición *f* — **ambitious** *adj* : ambicioso

ambivalence *n* : ambivalencia *f* — **ambivalent** *adj* : ambivalente

amble *vi or* ~ **along** : andar sin prisa

ambulance *n* : ambulancia *f*

ambush *vt* : emboscar — ~ *n* : emboscada *f*

amen *interj* : amén

amenable *adj* ~ **to** : receptivo a

amend *vt* : enmendar — **amendment** *n* : enmienda *f* — **amends** *ns & pl* **make** ~ **for** : reparar

amenities *npl* : servicios *mpl*, comodidades *fpl*

American *adj* : americano

amethyst *n* : amatista *f*

amiable *adj* : amable, agradable

amicable *adj* : amigable, amistoso

amid *or* **amidst** *prep* : en medio de, entre

amiss *adv* **1** : mal **2 take sth** ~ : tomar algo a mal — ~ *adj* **1** WRONG : malo **2 something is** ~ : algo anda mal

ammonia *n* : amoníaco *m*

ammunition *n* : municiones *fpl*

amnesia *n* : amnesia *f*

amnesty *n, pl* **-ties** : amnistía *f*

among *prep* : entre

amorous *adj* : amoroso

amount *vi* **1** ~ **to** : equivaler a **2** ~ **to** TOTAL : sumar, ascender a — ~ *n* : cantidad *f*

amphibian *n* : anfibio *m* — **amphibious** *adj* : anfibio

amphitheater *n* : anfiteatro *m*

ample *adj* **-pler; -plest 1** SPACIOUS : amplio, extenso **2** ABUNDANT : abundante

amplify *vt* **-fied; -fying** : amplificar — **amplifier** *n* : amplificador *m*

amputate *vt* **-tated; -tating** : amputar — **amputation** *n* : amputación *f*

amuse *vt* **amused; amusing 1** : hacer reír, divertir **2** ENTERTAIN : entretener — **amusement** *n* : diversión *f* — **amusing** *adj* : divertido

an → **a²**

analogy *n, pl* **-gies** : analogía *f* — **analogous** *adj* : análogo

analysis *n, pl* **-yses** : análisis *m* — **analytic** *or* **analytical** *adj* : analítico — **analyze** *vt* **-lyzed; -lyzing** : analizar

anarchy *n* : anarquía *f*

anatomy *n, pl* **-mies** : anatomía *f* — **anatomic** *or* **anatomical** *adj* : anatómico

ancestor *n* : antepasado *m*, -da *f* — **ancestral** *adj* : ancestral — **ancestry** *n* 1 DESCENT : linaje *m*, abolengo *m* 2 ANCESTORS : antepasados *mpl*, **-das** *fpl*

anchor *n* 1 : ancla *f* 2 : presentador *m*, -dora *f* (en televisión) — ~ *vt* 1 : anclar 2 FASTEN : sujetar — *vi* : anclar

anchovy *n, pl* **-vies** *or* **-vy** : anchoa *f*

ancient *adj* : antiguo, viejo

and *conj* 1 : y (*e before words beginning with i- or hi-*) 2 **come ~ see** : ven a ver 3 **more ~ more** : cada vez más 4 **try ~ finish it soon** : trata de terminarlo pronto

anecdote *n* : anécdota *f*

anemia *n* : anemia *f* — **anemic** *adj* : anémico

anesthesia *n* : anestesia *f* — **anesthetic** *adj* : anestésico — ~ *n* : anestésico *m*

anew *adv* : de nuevo, nuevamente

angel *n* : ángel *m* — **angelic** *or* **angelical** *adj* : angélico

anger *vt* : enojar, enfadar — ~ *n* : ira *f*, enojo *m*, enfado *m*

angle *n* 1 : ángulo *m* 2 POINT OF VIEW : perspectiva *f*, punto *m* de vista — **angler** *n* : pescador *m*, -dora *f*

Anglo–Saxon *adj* : anglosajón

angry *adj* **-grier; -est** : enojado, enfadado

anguish *n* : angustia *f*

angular *adj* 1 : angular 2 ~ **features** : rasgos *mpl* angulosos

animal *n* : animal *m*

animate *adj* : animado — ~ *vt* **-mated; -mating** : animar — **animated** *adj* 1 : animado 2 ~ **cartoon** : dibujos *mpl* animados — **animation** *n* : animación *f*

animosity *n, pl* **-ties** : animosidad *f*

anise *n* : anís *m*

ankle *n* : tobillo *m*

annals *npl* : anales *mpl*

annex *vt* : anexar — ~ *n* : anexo *m*

annihilate *vt* **-lated; -lating** : aniquilar — **annihilation** *n* : aniquilación *f*

anniversary *n, pl* **-ries** : aniversario *m*

annotate *vt* **-tated; -tating** : anotar — **annotation** *n* : anotación *f*

announce *vt* **-nounced; -nouncing** : anunciar — **announcement** *n* : anuncio *m* — **announcer** *n* : locutor *m*, -tora *f*

annoy *vt* : fastidiar, molestar — **annoyance** *n* : fastidio *m*, molestia *f* — **annoying** *adj* : molesto, fastidioso

annual *adj* : anual — ~ *n* : anuario *m*

annuity *n, pl* **-ties** : anualidad *f*

annul *vt* **annulled; annulling** : anular — **annulment** *n* : anulación *f*

anoint *vt* : ungir

anomaly *n, pl* **-lies** : anomalía *f*

anonymous *adj* : anónimo — **anonymity** *n* : anonimato *m*

another *adj* 1 : otro 2 **in ~ minute** : en un minuto más — ~ *pron* : otro, otra

answer *n* 1 REPLY : respuesta *f*, contestación *f* 2 SOLUTION : solución *f* — ~ *vt* 1 : contestar a, responder a 2 ~ **the door** : abrir la puerta — *vi* : contestar, responder

ant *n* : hormiga *f*

antagonize *vt* **-nized; -nizing** : provocar la enemistad de — **antagonism** *n* : antagonismo *m*

antarctic *adj* : antártico

antelope *n, pl* **-lope** *or* **-lopes** : antílope *m*

antenna *n, pl* **-nae** *or* **-nas** : antena *f*

anthem *n* : himno *m*

anthology *n, pl* **-gies** : antología *f*

anthropology *n* : antropología *f*

anti–Semitic *adj* : antisemita

antibiotic *adj* : antibiótico — ~ *n* : antibiótico *m*

antibody *n, pl* **-bodies** : anticuerpo *m*

anticipate *vt* **-pated; -pating** 1 FORESEE : anticipar, prever 2 EXPECT : esperar — **anticipation** *n* : anticipación *f*, expectación *f*

antics *npl* : payasadas *fpl*

antidote *n* : antídoto *m*

antifreeze *n* : anticongelante *m*

antipathy *n, pl* **-thies** : antipatía *f*

antiquated *adj* : anticuado

antique *adj* : antiguo — ~ *n* : antigüedad *f* — **antiquity** *n, pl* **-ties** : antigüedad *f*

antiseptic *adj* : antiséptico — ~ *n* : antiséptico *m*

antisocial *adj* 1 : antisocial 2 UNSOCIABLE : poco sociable

antithesis *n, pl* **-eses** : antítesis *f*

antiviral *adj* : antiviral

antivirus *adj* : antiviral

antivirus software *n* : antivirus *m*

antlers *npl* : cornamenta *f*

antonym *n* : antónimo *m*

anus *n* : ano *m*

anvil *n* : yunque *m*

anxiety *n, pl* **-eties** 1 APPREHENSION : inquietud *f*, ansiedad *f* 2 EAGERNESS : anhelo *m* — **anxious** *adj* 1 WORRIED : inquieto, preocupado 2 EAGER : ansioso — **anxiously** *adv* : con ansiedad

any *adv* 1 SOMEWHAT : algo, un poco 2 **it's not ~ good** : no sirve para nada 3 **we can't wait ~ longer** : no podemos esperar más — ~ *adj* 1 : alguno 2 (*in negative* *constructions*) : ningún **3** WHATEVER : cualquier **4 in** ~ **case** : en todo caso — ~ *pron* **1** : alguno, **-na 2** : ninguno, **-na 3 do you want** ~ **more rice?** : ¿quieres más arroz?

anybody → **anyone**

anyhow *adv* **1** : de todas formas **2** HAPHAZARDLY : de cualquier modo

anymore *adv* **not** ~ : ya no

anyone *pron* **1** SOMEONE : alguien **2** WHOEVER : quienquiera **3 I don't see** ~ : no veo a nadie

anyplace → **anywhere**

anything *pron* **1** SOMETHING : algo, alguna cosa **2** (*in negative constructions*) : nada **3** WHATEVER : cualquier cosa, lo que sea

anytime *adv* : en cualquier momento

anyway → **anyhow**

anywhere *adv* **1** : en cualquier parte, dondequiera **2** (*used in questions*) : en algún sitio **3 I can't find it** ~ : no lo encuentro por ninguna parte

apart *adv* **1** : aparte **2** ~ **from** : excepto, aparte de **3 fall** ~ : deshacerse, hacerse pedazos **4 live** ~ : vivir separados **5 take** ~ : desmontar, desmantelar

apartment *n* : apartamento *m*

apathy *n* : apatía *f* — **apathetic** *adj* : apático, indiferente

ape *n* : simio *m*

aperture *n* : abertura *f*

apex *n, pl* **apexes** *or* **apices** : ápice *m*, cumbre *f*

apiece *adv* : cada uno

aplomb *n* : aplomo *m*

apology *n, pl* **-gies** : disculpa *f* — **apologetic** *adj* : lleno de disculpas — **apologize** *vi* **-gized; -gizing** : disculparse, pedir perdón

apostle *n* : apóstol *m*

apostrophe *n* : apóstrofo *m*

appall *vt* : horrorizar — **appalling** *adj* : horroroso

apparatus *n, pl* **-tuses** *or* **-tus** : aparato *m*

apparel *n* : ropa *f*

apparent *adj* **1** OBVIOUS : claro, evidente **2** SEEMING : aparente — **apparently** *adv* : al parecer, por lo visto

apparition *n* : aparición *f*

appeal *vi* **1** ~ **for** : solicitar **2** ~ **to** : apelar a (la bondad de algn, etc.) **3** ~ **to** ATTRACT : atraer a — ~ *n* **1** : apelación *f* (en derecho) **2** REQUEST : llamamiento *m* **3** ATTRACTION : atractivo *m* — **appealing** *adj* : atractivo

appear *vi* **1** : aparecer **2** : comparecer (ante un tribunal), actuar (en el teatro) **3**

SEEM : parecer — **appearance** *n* **1** : aparición *f* **2** LOOK : apariencia *f*, aspecto *m*

appease *vt* **-peased; -peasing** : apaciguar, aplacar

appendix *n, pl* **-dixes** *or* **-dices** : apéndice *m* — **appendicitis** *n* : apendicitis *f*

appetite *n* : apetito *m* — **appetizer** *n* : aperitivo *m* — **appetizing** *adj* : apetitoso

applaud *v* : aplaudir — **applause** *n* : aplauso *m*

apple *n* : manzana *f*

appliance *n* : aparato *m*

apply *v* **-plied; -plying** *vt* **1** : aplicar **2** ~ **oneself** : aplicarse — *vi* **1** : aplicarse **2** ~ **for** : solicitar, pedir — **applicable** *adj* : aplicable — **applicant** *n* : solicitante *mf;* candidato *m*, **-ta** *f* — **application** *n* **1** : aplicación *f* **2** : solicitud *f* (para un empleo, etc.)

appoint *vt* **1** NAME : nombrar **2** FIX, SET : fijar, señalar — **appointment** *n* **1** APPOINTING : nombramiento *m* **2** ENGAGEMENT : cita *f*

apportion *vt* : distribuir, repartir

appraise *vt* **-praised; -praising** : evaluar, valorar — **appraisal** *n* : evaluación *f*

appreciate *v* **-ated; -ating** *vt* **1** VALUE : apreciar **2** UNDERSTAND : darse cuenta de **3 I** ~ **your help** : te agradezco tu ayuda — *vi* : aumentar en valor — **appreciation** *n* **1** GRATITUDE : agradecimiento *m* **2** VALUING : apreciación *f*, valoración *f* — **appreciative** *adj* **1** : apreciativo **2** GRATEFUL : agradecido

apprehend *vt* **1** ARREST : aprehender, detener **2** DREAD : temer **3** COMPREHEND : comprender — **apprehension** *n* **1** ARREST : detención *f*, aprehensión *f* **2** ANXIETY : aprensión *f*, temor *m* — **apprehensive** *adj* : aprensivo, inquieto

apprentice *n* : aprendiz *m*, **-diza** *f*

approach *vt* **1** NEAR : acercarse a **2** : dirigirse a (algn), abordar (un problema, etc.) — *vi* : acercarse — ~ *n* **1** NEARING : acercamiento *m* **2** POSITION : enfoque *m* **3** ACCESS : acceso *m* — **approachable** *adj* : accesible, asequible

appropriate *vt* **-ated; -ating** : apropiarse de — ~ *adj* : apropiado

approve *vt* **-proved; -proving** : aprobar — **approval** *n* : aprobación *f*

approximate *adj* : aproximado — ~ *vt* **-mated; -mating** : aproximarse a — **approximately** *adv* : aproximadamente

apricot *n* : albaricoque *m*, chabacano *m* *Lat*

April *n* : abril *m*

apron *n* : delantal *m*

apropos *adv* : a propósito
apt *adj* **1** FITTING : apto, apropiado **2** LIA-BLE : propenso — **aptitude** *n* : aptitud *f*
aquarium *n, pl* **-iums** *or* **-ia** : acuario *m*
aquatic *adj* : acuático
aqueduct *n* : acueducto *m*
Arab *adj* : árabe — **Arabic** *adj* : árabe — ∼ *n* : árabe *m* (idioma)
arbitrary *adj* : arbitrario
arbitrate *v* **-trated; -trating** : arbitrar — **arbitration** *n* : arbitraje *m*
arc *n* : arco *m*
arcade *n* **1** : arcada *f* **2 shopping** ∼ : galería *f* comercial
arch *n* : arco *m* — ∼ *vt* : arquear — *vi* : arquearse
archaeology *or* **archeology** *n* : arqueología *f* — **archaeological** *adj* : arqueológico — **archaeologist** *n* : arqueólogo *m*, -ga *f*
archaic *adj* : arcaico
archbishop *n* : arzobispo *m*
archery *n* : tiro *m* al arco
archipelago *n, pl* **-goes** *or* **-gos** : archipiélago *m*
architecture *n* : arquitectura *f* — **architect** *n* : arquitecto *m*, -ta *f* — **architectural** *adj* : arquitectónico
archives *npl* : archivo *m*
archway *n* : arco *m* (de entrada)
arctic *adj* : ártico
ardent *adj* : ardiente, fervoroso — **ardor** *n* : ardor *m*, fervor *m*
arduous *adj* : arduo
are → **be**
area *n* **1** REGION : área *f*, zona *f* **2** FIELD : campo *m* **3** ∼ **code** : código *m* de la zona *Lat*, prefijo *m Spain*
aren't (*contraction of* **are not**) → **be**
arena *n* : arena *f*, ruedo *m*
Argentine *or* **Argentinean** *or* **Argentinian** *adj* : argentino
argue *v* **-gued; -guing** *vi* **1** QUARREL : discutir **2** ∼ **against** : argumentar contra — *vt* : argumentar, sostener — **argument** *n* **1** QUARREL : disputa *f*, discusión *f* **2** REASONING : argumentos *mpl*
arid *adj* : árido — **aridity** *n* : aridez *f*
arise *vi* **arose; arisen; arising 1** : levantarse **2** ∼ **from** : surgir de
aristocracy *n, pl* **-cies** : aristocracia *f* — **aristocrat** *n* : aristócrata *mf* — **aristocratic** *adj* : aristocrático
arithmetic *n* : aritmética *f*
ark *n* : arca *f*
arm *n* **1** : brazo *m* **2** WEAPON : arma *f* — ∼ *vt* : armar — **armament** *n* : armamento *m* — **armchair** *n* : sillón *m* — **armed** *adj* **1** ∼ **forces** : fuerzas *fpl* armadas **2** ∼ **robbery** : robo *m* a mano armada

armistice *n* : armisticio *m*
armor *or Brit* **armour** *n* : armadura *f* — **armored** *or Brit* **armoured** *adj* : blindado, acorazado — **armory** *or Brit* **armoury** : arsenal *m*
armpit *n* : axila *f*, sobaco *m*
army *n, pl* **-mies** : ejército *m*
aroma *n* : aroma *m* — **aromatic** *adj* : aromático
around *adv* **1** : de circunferencia **2** NEARBY : por ahí **3** APPROXIMATELY : más o menos, aproximadamente **4 all** ∼ : por todos lados, todo alrededor **5 turn** ∼ : voltearse — ∼ *prep* **1** SURROUNDING : alrededor de **2** THROUGHOUT : por **3** NEAR : cerca de **4** ∼ **the corner** : a la vuelta de la esquina
arouse *vt* **aroused; arousing 1** AWAKE : despertar **2** EXCITE : excitar
arrange *vt* **-ranged; -ranging** : arreglar, poner en orden — **arrangement** *n* **1** ORDER : arreglo *m* **2** ∼**s** *npl* : preparativos *mpl*
array *n* : selección *f*, surtido *m*
arrears *npl* **1** : atrasos *mpl* **2 be in** ∼ : estar atrasado en pagos
arrest *vt* : detener — ∼ *n* **1** : arresto *m*, detención *f* **2 under** ∼ : detenido
arrive *vi* **-rived; -riving** : llegar — **arrival** *n* : llegada *f*
arrogance *n* : arrogancia *f* — **arrogant** *adj* : arrogante
arrow *n* : flecha *f*
arsenal *n* : arsenal *m*
arsenic *n* : arsénico *m*
arson *n* : incendio *m* premeditado
art *n* **1** : arte *m* **2** ∼**s** *npl* : letras *fpl* (en educación) **3 fine** ∼**s** : bellas artes *fpl*
artefact *Brit* → **artifact**
artery *n, pl* **-teries** : arteria *f*
artful *adj* : astuto, taimado
arthritis *n, pl* **-tides** : artritis *f* — **arthritic** *adj* : artrítico
artichoke *n* : alcachofa *f*
article *n* : artículo *m*
articulate *vt* **-lated; -lating** : articular — ∼ *adj* **be** ∼ : expresarse bien
artifact *or Brit* **artefact** *n* : artefacto *m*
artificial *adj* : artificial
artillery *n, pl* **-leries** : artillería *f*
artisan *n* : artesano *m*, -na *f*
artist *n* : artista *mf* — **artistic** *adj* : artístico
as for *prep* : en cuanto a
as if *conj* : como si
as of *prep* : desde, a partir de
as soon as *conj* : tan pronto como
as though → **as if**
as to *prep* : sobre, acerca de

as well as *conj* : tanto como — ~ *prep* : además de, aparte de

as *adv* **1** : tan, tanto **2** ~ **much** : tanto como **3** ~ **tall** ~ : tan alto como **4** ~ **well** : también — ~ *conj* **1** WHILE : mientras **2** (*referring to manner*) : como **3** SINCE : ya que **4** THOUGH : por más que — ~ *prep* **1** : de **2** LIKE : como — ~ *pron* : que

asbestos *n* : asbesto *m*, amianto *m*

ascend *vi* : ascender, subir — *vt* : subir (a) — **ascent** *n* : ascensión *f*, subida *f*

ascertain *vt* : averiguar, determinar

ascribe *vt* **-cribed; -cribing** : atribuir

ash¹ *n* : ceniza *f*

ash² *n* : fresno *m* (árbol)

ashamed *adj* : avergonzado, apenado *Lat*

ashore *adv* **1** : en tierra **2 go** ~ : desembarcar

ashtray *n* : cenicero *m*

Asian *adj* : asiático

aside *adv* **1** : a un lado **2** APART : aparte **3 set** ~ : guardar — **aside from** *prep* **1** BESIDES : además de **2** EXCEPT : aparte de, menos

ask *vt* **1** : preguntar **2** REQUEST : pedir **3** INVITE : invitar — *vi* : preguntar

askance *adv* **look** ~ : mirar de soslayo

askew *adj* : torcido, ladeado

asleep *adj* **1** : dormido **2 fall** ~ : dormirse, quedarse dormido

asparagus *n* : espárrago *m*

aspect *n* : aspecto *m*

asphalt *n* : asfalto *m*

asphyxiate *v* **-ated; -ating** *vt* : asfixiar — **asphyxiation** *n* : asfixia *f*

aspire *vi* **-pired; -piring** : aspirar — **aspiration** *n* : aspiración *f*

aspirin *n*, *pl* **aspirin** *or* **aspirins** : aspirina *f*

ass *n* **1** : asno *m* **2** IDIOT : imbécil *mf*, idiota *mf*

assail *vt* : atacar, asaltar — **assailant** *n* : asaltante *mf*, atacante *mf*

assassin *n* : asesino *m*, -na *f* — **assassinate** *vt* **-nated; -nating** : asesinar — **assassination** *n* : asesinato *m*

assault *n* **1** : ataque *m*, asalto *m* **2** : agresión *f* (contra algn) — *vt* : atacar, asaltar

assemble *v* **-bled; -bling** *vt* **1** GATHER : reunir, juntar **2** CONSTRUCT : montar — *vi* : reunirse — **assembly** *n*, *pl* **-blies 1** MEETING : reunión *f*, asamblea *f* **2** CONSTRUCTING : montaje *m*

assent *vi* : asentir, consentir — ~ *n* : asentimiento *m*

assert *vt* **1** : afirmar **2** ~ **oneself** : hacerse valer — **assertion** *n* : afirmación *f* — **assertive** *adj* : firme, enérgico

assess *vt* : evaluar, valorar — **assessment** *n* : evaluación *f*, valoración *f*

asset *n* **1** : ventaja *f*, recurso *m* **2** ~**s** *npl* : bienes *mpl*, activo *m*

assiduous *adj* : asiduo

assign *vt* **1** APPOINT : designar, nombrar **2** ALLOT : asignar — **assignment** *n* **1** TASK : misión *f* **2** HOMEWORK : tarea *f* **3** ASSIGNING : asignación *f*

assimilate *vt* **-lated; -lating** : asimilar

assist *vt* : ayudar — **assistance** *n* : ayuda *f* — **assistant** *n* : ayudante *mf*

associate *v* **-ated; -ating** *vt* : asociar — *vi* : asociarse — ~ *n* : asociado *m*, -da *f*; socio *m*, -cia *f* — **association** *n* : asociación *f*

assorted *adj* : surtido — **assortment** *n* : surtido *m*, variedad *f*

assume *vt* **-sumed; -suming 1** SUPPOSE : suponer **2** UNDERTAKE : asumir **3** TAKE ON : adquirir, tomar — **assumption** *n* : suposición *f*

assure *vt* **-sured; -suring** : asegurar — **assurance** *n* **1** CERTAINTY : certeza *f*, garantía *f* **2** CONFIDENCE : confianza *f*, seguridad *f* (de sí mismo)

asterisk *n* : asterisco *m*

asthma *n* : asma *m*

astonish *vt* : asombrar — **astonishing** *adj* : asombroso — **astonishment** *n* : asombro *m*

astound *vt* : asombrar, pasmar — **astounding** *adj* : asombroso, pasmoso

astray *adv* **1 go** ~ : extraviarse **2 lead** ~ : llevar por mal camino

astrology *n* : astrología *f*

astronaut *n* : astronauta *mf*

astronomy *n*, *pl* **-mies** : astronomía *f* — **astronomer** *n* : astrónomo *m*, -ma *f* — **astronomical** *adj* : astronómico

astute *adj* : astuto, sagaz — **astuteness** *n* : astucia *f*

asylum *n* **1** : asilo *m* **2 insane** ~ : manicomio *m*

at *prep* **1** : a **2** ~ **home** : en casa **3** ~ **night** : en la noche, por la noche **4** ~ **two o'clock** : a las dos **5 be angry** ~ : estar enojado con **6 laugh** ~ : reírse de — **at all** *adv* **not** ~ : en absoluto, nada

ate → **eat**

atheist *n* : ateo *m*, atea *f* — **atheism** *n* : ateísmo *m*

athlete *n* : atleta *mf* — **athletic** *adj* : atlético — **athletics** *ns* & *pl* : atletismo *m*

atlas *n* : atlas *m*

atmosphere *n* **1** : atmósfera *f* **2** AMBIENCE : ambiente *m* — **atmospheric** *adj* : atmosférico

atom *n* : átomo *m* — **atomic** *adj* : atómico

atomizer *n* : atomizador *m*

atone *vt* **atoned; atoning** ~ **for** : expiar

atrocity *n*, *pl* **-ties** : atrocidad *f* — **atrocious** *adj* : atroz

atrophy *vi* **-phied; -phying** : atrofiarse
attach *vt* **1** : sujetar, atar **2** : adjuntar (un documento, etc.) **3** ～ **importance to** : atribuir importancia a **4 become** ～**ed to s.o.** : encariñarse con algn — **attachment** *n* **1** ACCESSORY : accesorio *m* **2** FONDNESS : cariño *m*
attack *v* : atacar — ～ *n* : ataque *m* — **attacker** *n* : agresor *m*, -sora *f*
attain *vt* : lograr, alcanzar — **attainment** *n* : logro *m*
attempt *vt* : intentar — ～ *n* : intento *m*
attend *vt* : asistir a — *vi* **1** : asistir **2** ～ **to** : ocuparse de — **attendance** *n* **1** : asistencia *f* **2** TURNOUT : concurrencia *f* — **attendant** *n* : encargado *m*, -da *f*; asistente *mf*
attention *n* **1** : atención *f* **2 pay** ～ : prestar atención, hacer caso — **attentive** *adj* : atento
attest *vt* : atestiguar
attic *n* : desván *m*
attire *n* : atavío *m*
attitude *n* **1** : actitud *f* **2** POSTURE : postura *f*
attorney *n*, *pl* **-neys** : abogado *m*, -da *f*
attract *vt* : atraer — **attraction** *n* **1** : atracción *f* **2** APPEAL : atractivo *m* — **attractive** *adj* : atractivo, atrayente
attribute *n* : atributo *m* — ～ *vt* **-tributed; -tributing** : atribuir, imputar
ATV all-terrain vehicle
auburn *adj* : castaño rojizo
auction *n* : subasta *f* — ～ *vt or* ～ **off** : subastar
audacious *adj* : audaz — **audacity** *n*, *pl* **-ties** : audacia *f*, atrevimiento *m*
audible *adj* : audible
audience *n* **1** INTERVIEW : audiencia *f* **2** PUBLIC : público *m*
audiovisual *adj* : audiovisual
audition *n* : audición *f*
auditor *n* **1** : auditor *m*, -tora *f* (de finanzas) **2** STUDENT : oyente *mf*
auditorium *n*, *pl* **-riums** *or* **-ria** : auditorio *m*
augment *vt* : aumentar
augur *vi* ～ **well** : ser de buen agüero
August *n* : agosto *m*
aunt *n* : tía *f*
aura *n* : aura *f*
auspices *npl* : auspicios *mpl*
auspicious *adj* : propicio, prometedor
austere *adj* : austero — **austerity** *n*, *pl* **-ties** : austeridad *f*
Australian *adj* : australiano
authentic *adj* : auténtico
author *n* : autor *m*, -tora *f*
authority *n*, *pl* **-ties** : autoridad *f* — **authoritarian** *adj* : autoritario — **authoritative** *adj* **1** RELIABLE : autorizado **2** DICTATORIAL : autoritario — **authorization** *n* : autorización *f* — **authorize** *vt* **-rized; -rizing** : autorizar
autobiography *n*, *pl* **-phies** : autobiografía *f* — **autobiographical** *adj* : autobiográfico
autograph *n* : autógrafo *m* — ～ *vt* : autografiar
automatic *adj* : automático — **automate** *vt* **-mated; -mating** : automatizar — **automation** *n* : automatización *f*
automobile *n* : automóvil *m*
autonomy *n*, *pl* **-mies** : autonomía *f* — **autonomous** *adj* : autónomo
autopsy *n*, *pl* **-sies** : autopsia *f*
autumn *n* : otoño *m*
auxiliary *adj* : auxiliar — ～ *n*, *pl* **-ries** : auxiliar *mf*
avail *vt* ～ **oneself of** : aprovecharse de — ～ *n* **to no** ～ : en vano — **available** *adj* : disponible — **availability** *n*, *pl* **-ties** : disponibilidad *f*
avalanche *n* : avalancha *f*
avarice *n* : avaricia *f*
avatar *n* : avatar *m*
avenge *vt* **avenged; avenging** : vengar
avenue *n* **1** : avenida *f* **2** MEANS : vía *f*
average *n* : promedio *m* — ～ *adj* **1** MEAN : medio **2** ORDINARY : regular, ordinario — ～ *vt* **-aged; -aging** **1** : hacer un promedio de **2** *or* ～ **out** : calcular el promedio de
averse *adj* **be** ～ **to** : sentir aversión por — **aversion** *n* : aversión *f*
avert *vt* **1** AVOID : evitar, prevenir **2** ～ **one's eyes** : apartar los ojos
aviation *n* : aviación *f* — **aviator** *n* : aviador *m*, -dora *f*
avid *adj* : ávido — **avidly** *adv* : con avidez
avocado *n*, *pl* **-dos** : aguacate *m*
avoid *vt* : evitar — **avoidable** *adj* : evitable
await *vt* : esperar
awake *v* **awoke; awoken** *or* **awaked; awaking** : despertar — ～ *adj* : despierto — **awaken** *v* → **awake**
award *vt* **1** : otorgar, conceder (un premio, etc.) **2** : adjudicar (daños y perjuicios) — ～ *n* **1** PRIZE : premio *m* **2** : adjudicación *f*
aware *adj* **be** ～ **of** : estar consciente de — **awareness** *n* : conciencia *f*
away *adv* **1** (*referring to distance*) : de aquí, de distancia **2 far** ～ : lejos **3 give** ～ : regalar **4 go** ～ : irse **5 right** ～ : en seguida **6 take** ～ : quitar — ～ *adj* **1** ABSENT : ausente **2** ～ **game** : partido *m* fuera de casa
awe *n* : temor *m* reverencial — **awesome** *adj* : imponente, formidable
awful *adj* **1** : terrible, espantoso **2 an** ～ **lot** : muchísimo — **awfully** *adv* : terriblemente

awhile *adv* : un rato

awkward *adj* **1** CLUMSY : torpe **2** EMBARRASSING : embarazoso, delicado **3** DIFFICULT : difícil — **awkwardly** *adv* **1** : con dificultad **2** CLUMSILY : de manera torpe

awning *n* : toldo *m*

awry *adj* **1** ASKEW : torcido **2 go ~** : salir mal

ax *or* **axe** *n* : hacha *f*

axiom *n* : axioma *m*

axis *n, pl* **axes** : eje *m*

axle *n* : eje *m*

B

b *n, pl* **b's** *or* **bs** : b, segunda letra del alfabeto inglés

babble *vi* **-bled; -bling** **1** : balbucear **2** MURMUR : murmurar — **~** *n* : balbuceo *m* (de bebé), murmullo *m* (de voces, de un arroyo)

baboon *n* : babuino *m*

baby *n, pl* **-bies** : bebé *m;* niño *m*, -ña *f* — **baby** *vt* **-bied; -bying** : mimar, consentir — **babyish** *adj* : infantil — **baby-sit** *vi* **-sat; -sitting** : cuidar a los niños

bachelor *n* **1** : soltero *m* **2** GRADUATE : licenciado *m*, -da *f*

back *n* **1** : espalda *f* **2** REVERSE : reverso *m*, dorso *m*, revés *m* **3** REAR : fondo *m*, parte *f* trasera **4** : defensa *mf* (en deportes) — **~** *adv* **1** : atrás **2 be ~** : estar de vuelta **3 go ~** : volver **4 two years ~** : hace dos años — **~** *adj* **1** REAR : de atrás, trasero **2** OVERDUE : atrasado — **~** *vt* **1** SUPPORT : apoyar **2** *or* **~ up** : darle marcha atrás a (un vehículo) — *vi* **1 ~ down** : volverse atrás **2 ~ up** : retroceder — **backache** *n* : dolor *m* de espalda — **backbone** *n* : columna *f* vertebral — **backfire** *vi* **-fired; -firing** : petardear — **backhand** *adv* : de revés, con el revés — **backhanded** *adj* : indirecto — **backing** *n* : apoyo *m*, respaldo *m* — **backlash** *n* : reacción *f* violenta — **backlog** *n* : atrasos *mpl* — **backpack** *n* : mochila *f* — **backstage** *adv & adj* : entre bastidores — **backtrack** *vi* : dar marcha atrás — **backup** *n* **1** SUPPORT : respaldo *m*, apoyo *m* **2** : copia *f* de seguridad (para computadoras) — **backward** *or* **backwards** *adv* **1** : hacia atrás **2 do it ~** : hacerlo al revés **3 fall ~** : caer de espaldas **4 bend over ~s** : hacer todo lo posible — **backward** *adj* **1** : hacia atrás **2** RETARDED : retrasado **3** SHY : tímido **4** UNDERDEVELOPED : atrasado

background *n* **1** : fondo *m* (de un cuadro, etc.), antecedentes *mpl* (de una situación) (**in the background** : en el fondo) **2** EXPERIENCE, TRAINING : experiencia *f* profesional, formación *f* **3** HISTORY : origen *m* (de una persona), antecedentes *mpl*

bacon *n* : tocino *m*, tocineta *f Lat*, bacon *m Spain*

bacteria : bacterias *fpl*

bad *adj* **worse; worst** **1** : malo **2** ROTTEN : podrido **3** SEVERE : grave **4 from ~ to worse** : de mal en peor **5 too ~!** : ¡qué lástima! — **~** *adv* → **badly**

badge *n* : insignia *f*, chapa *f*

badger *n* : tejón *m* — **~** *vt* : acosar

badly *adv* **1** : mal **2** SEVERELY : gravemente **3 want ~** : desear mucho

baffle *vi* **-fled; -fling** : desconcertar

bag *n* **1** : bolsa *f*, saco *m* **2** HANDBAG : bolso *m*, cartera *f Lat* **3** SUITCASE : maleta *f* — **~** *vt* **bagged; bagging** : ensacar, poner en una bolsa

baggage *n* : equipaje *m*

baggy *adj* **-gier; -est** : holgado

bail *n* : fianza *f* — **~** *vt* **1** : achicar (agua de un bote) **2 ~ out** RELEASE : poner en libertad bajo fianza **3 ~ out** EXTRICATE : sacar de apuros

bailiff *n* : alguacil *mf*

bait *vt* **1** : cebar **2** HARASS : acosar — **~** *n* : cebo *m*, carnada *f*

bake *v* **baked; baking** *vt* : cocer al horno — *vi* : cocerse (al horno) — **baker** *n* : panadero *m*, -ra *f* — **bakery** *n, pl* **-ries** : panadería *f*

balance *n* **1** SCALES : balanza *f* **2** COUNTERBALANCE : contrapeso *m* **3** EQUILIBRIUM : equilibrio *m* **4** REMAINDER : resto *m* **5** *or* **bank ~** : saldo *m* — **~** *v* **-anced; -ancing** *vt* **1** : hacer el balance de (una cuenta) **2** EQUALIZE : equilibrar **3** WEIGH : sopesar — *vi* **1** : sostenerse en equilibro **2** : cuadrar (dícese de una cuenta)

balcony *n, pl* **-nies** **1** : balcón *m* **2** : galería *f* (de un teatro)

bald *adj* **1** : calvo **2** WORN : pelado **3 the ~ truth** : la pura verdad

bale *n* : bala *f*, fardo *m*

baleful *adj* : siniestro
balk *vi* ~ **at** : resistarse a
ball bearing *n* : cojinete *m* de bola
ball *n* **1** : pelota *f*, bola *f*, balón *m* **2** DANCE : baile *m* **3** ~ **of string** : ovillo *m* de cuerda
ballad *n* : balada *f*
ballast *n* : lastre *m*
ballerina *n* : bailarina *f*
ballet *n* : ballet *m*
ballistic *adj* : balístico
balloon *n* : globo *m*
ballot *n* **1** : papeleta *f* (de voto) **2** VOTING : votación *f*
ballpoint pen *n* : bolígrafo *m*
ballroom *n* : sala *f* de baile
balm *n* : bálsamo *m* — **balmy** *adj* **balmier; -est** : templado, agradable
baloney *n* NONSENSE : tonterías *fpl*
bamboo *n* : bambú *m*
bamboozle *vt* **-zled; -zling** : engañar, embaucar
ban *vt* **banned; banning** : prohibir — ~ *n* : prohibición *f*
banal *adj* : banal
banana *n* : plátano *m*, banana *f Lat*, banano *m Lat*
band *n* **1** STRIP : banda *f* **2** GROUP : banda *f*, grupo *m*, conjunto *m* — ~ *vi* ~ **together** : unirse, juntarse
bandage *n* : vendaje *m*, venda *f* — ~ *vt* **-daged; -daging** : vendar
bandit *n* : bandido *m*, -da *f*
bandy *vt* **-died; -dying** ~ **about** : circular, repetir
bang *vt* **1** STRIKE : golpear **2** SLAM : cerrar de un golpe — *vi* **1** SLAM : cerrarse de un golpe **2** ~ **on** : golpear — ~ *n* **1** BLOW : golpe *m* **2** NOISE : estrépito *m* **3** SLAM : portazo *m*
bangle *n* : brazalete *m*, pulsera *f*
bangs *npl* : flequillo *m*
banish *vt* : desterrar
banister *n* : pasamanos *m*, barandal *m*
bank *n* **1** : banco *m* **2** : orilla *f*, ribera *f* (de un río) **3** EMBANKMENT : terraplén *m* — ~ *vt* : depositar — *vi* **1** : ladearse (dícese de un avión) **2** : tener una cuenta (en un banco) **3** ~ **on** : contar con — **banker** *n* : banquero *m*, -ra *f* — **banking** *n* : banca *f*
bankrupt *adj* : en bancarrota, en quiebra — **bankruptcy** *n, pl* **-cies** : quiebra *f*, bancarrota *f*
banner *n* : bandera *f*, pancarta *f*
banquet *n* : banquete *m*
banter *n* : bromas *fpl* — ~ *vi* : hacer bromas
baptize *vt.* **-tized; -tizing** : bautizar — **baptism** *n* : bautismo *m*
bar *n* **1** : barra *f* **2** BARRIER : barrera *f*, obstáculo *m* **3** COUNTER : mostrador *m*, barra

f **4** TAVERN : bar *m* **5 behind** ~**s** : entre rejas **6** ~ **of soap** : pastilla *f* de jabón — ~ *vt* **barred; barring 1** OBSTRUCT : obstruir, bloquear **2** EXCLUDE : excluir **3** PROHIBIT : prohibir — ~ *prep* **1** : excepto **2** ~ **none** : sin excepción
barbarian *n* : bárbaro *m*, -ra *f*
barbecue *vt* **-cued; -cuing** : asar a la parrilla — ~ *n* : barbacoa *f*
barbed wire *n* : alambre *m* de púas
barber *n* : barbero *m*, -ra *f*
bar code *n* : código *m* de barras
bare *adj* **1** : desnudo **2** EMPTY : vacío **3** MINIMUM : mero, esencial — **barefaced** *adj* : descarado — **barefoot** *or* **barefooted** *adv & adj* : descalzo — **barely** *adv* : apenas, por poco
bargain *n* **1** AGREEMENT : acuerdo *m* **2** BUY : ganga *f* — ~ *vi* **1** : regatear, negociar **2** ~ **for** : contar con
barge *n* : barcaza *f* — ~ *vi* **barged; barging** ~ **in** : entrometerse, interrumpir
baritone *n* : barítono *m*
bark¹ *vi* : ladrar — ~ *n* : ladrido *m* (de un perro)
bark² *n* : corteza *f* (de un árbol)
barley *n* : cebada *f*
barn *n* : granero *m* — **barnyard** *n* : corral *m*
barometer *n* : barómetro *m*
baron *n* : barón *m* — **baroness** *n* : baronesa *f*
barracks *ns & pl* : cuartel *m*
barrage *n* **1** : descarga *f* (de artillería) **2** : aluvión *m* (de preguntas, etc.)
barrel *n* **1** : barril *m*, tonel *m* **2** : cañón *m* (de un arma de fuego)
barren *adj* : estéril
barricade *vt* **-caded; -cading** : cerrar con barricadas — ~ *n* : barricada *f*
barrier *n* : barrera *f*
barring *prep* : salvo
barrio *n* : barrio *m*
bartender *n* : camarero *m*, -ra *f*
barter *vt* : cambiar, trocar — ~ *n* : trueque *m*
base *n, pl* **bases** : base *f* — ~ *vt* **based; basing** : basar, fundamentar — ~ *adj* **baser; basest** : vil
baseball *n* : beisbol *m*, béisbol *m*
basement *n* : sótano *m*
bash *vt* : golpear violentamente — ~ *n* **1** BLOW : golpe *m* **2** PARTY : fiesta *f*
bashful *adj* : tímido, vergonzoso
basic *adj* : básico, fundamental — **basically** *adv* : fundamentalmente
basil *n* : albahaca *f*
basin *n* **1** WASHBOWL : palangana *f*, lavabo *m* **2** : cuenca *f* (de un río)
basis *n, pl* **bases** : base *f*
bask *vi* ~ **in the sun** : tostarse al sol

basket *n* : cesta *f*, cesto *m* — **basketball** *n* : baloncesto *m*, basquetbol *m Lat*

bass¹ *n, pl* **bass** *or* **basses** : róbalo *m* (pesca)

bass² *n* : bajo *m* (tono, voz, instrumento)

bassoon *n* : fagot *m*

bastard *n* : bastardo *m*, -da *f*

baste *vt* **basted; basting** **1** STITCH : hilvanar **2** : bañar (carne)

bat¹ *n* : murciélago *m* (animal)

bat² *n* : bate *m* — ∼ *vt* **batted; batting** : batear

batch *n* : hornada *f* (de pasteles, etc.), lote *m* (de mercancías), montón *m* (de trabajo), grupo *m* (de personas)

bath *n, pl* **baths** **1** : baño *m* **2** BATHROOM : baño *m*, cuarto *m* de baño **3 take a** ∼ : bañarse — **bathe** *v* **bathed; bathing** *vt* : bañar, lavar — *vi* : bañarse — **bathrobe** *n* : bata *f* (de baño) — **bathroom** *n* : baño *m*, cuarto *m* de baño — **bathtub** *n* : bañera *f*, tina *f* (de baño)

baton *n* : batuta *f*

battalion *n* : batallón *m*

batter *vt* **1** BEAT : golpear **2** MISTREAT : maltratar — ∼ *n* **1** : masa *f* para rebozar **2** HITTER : bateador *m*, -dora *f*

battery *n, pl* **-teries** : batería *f*, pila *f* (de electricidad)

battle *n* **1** : batalla *f* **2** STRUGGLE : lucha *f* — ∼ *vi* **-tled; -tling** : luchar — **battlefield** *n* : campo *m* de batalla — **battleship** *n* : acorazado *m*

bawl *vi* : llorar a gritos

bay window *n* : ventana *f* en saliente

bay¹ *n* INLET : bahía *f*

bay² *n or* ∼ **leaf** : laurel *m*

bay³ *vi* : aullar — ∼ *n* : aullido *m*

bayonet *n* : bayoneta *f*

bazaar *n* **1** : bazar *m* **2** SALE : venta *f* benéfica

be *v* **was , were; been; being; am , is , are** *vi* **1** : ser **2** (*expressing location*) : estar **3** (*expressing existence*) : ser, existir **4** (*expressing a state of being*) : estar, tener — *v impers* **1** (*indicating time*) : ser **2** (*indicating a condition*) : hacer, estar — *v aux* **1** (*expressing occurrence*) : ser **2** (*expressing possibility*) : poderse **3** (*expressing obligation*) : deber **4** (*expressing progression*) : estar

beach *n* : playa *f*

beacon *n* : faro *m*

bead *n* **1** : cuenta *f* **2** DROP : gota *f* **3** ∼**s** *npl* NECKLACE : collar *m*

beak *n* : pico *m*

beam *n* **1** : viga *f* (de madera, etc.) **2** RAY : rayo *m* — ∼ *vi* SHINE : brillar — *vt* BROADCAST : transmitir, emitir

bean *n* **1** : habichuela *f*, frijol *m* **2 coffee** ∼ : grano *m* **3 string** ∼ : judía *f*

bear¹ *n, pl* **bears** *or* **bear** : oso *m*, osa *f*

bear² *v* **bore; borne; bearing** *vt* **1** CARRY : portar **2** ENDURE : soportar — *vi* ∼ **right/left** : doble a la derecha/a la izquierda — **bearable** *adj* : soportable

beard *n* : barba *f*

bearer *n* : portador *m*, -dora *f*

bearing *n* **1** MANNER : comportamiento *m* **2** SIGNIFICANCE : relacíon *f*, importancia *f* **3 get one's** ∼**s** : orientarse

beast *n* : bestia *f*

beat *v* **beat; beaten** *or* **beat; beating** *vt* **1** HIT : golpear **2** : batir (huevos, etc.) **3** DEFEAT : derrotar — *vi* : latir (dícese del corazón) — ∼ *n* **1** : golpe *m* **2** : latido *m* (del corazón) **3** RHYTHM : ritmo *m*, tiempo *m* — **beating** *n* **1** : paliza *f* **2** DEFEAT : derrota *f*

beauty *n, pl* **-ties** : belleza *f* — **beautiful** *adj* : hermoso, lindo — **beautifully** *adv* WONDERFULLY : maravillosamente — **beautify** *vt* **-fied; -fying** : embellecer

beaver *n* : castor *m*

because *conj* : porque — **because of** *prep* : por, a causa de, debido a

beckon *vt* : llamar, hacer señas a — *vi* : hacer una seña

become *v* **-came; -come; -coming** *vi* : hacerse, ponerse — *vt* SUIT : favorecer — **becoming** *adj* **1** SUITABLE : apropiado **2** FLATTERING : favorecedor

bed *n* **1** : cama *f* **2** : cauce *m* (de un río), fondo *m* (del mar) **3** : macizo *m* (de flores) **4 go to** ∼ : irse a la cama — **bedclothes** *npl* : ropa *f* de cama

bed and breakfast *n* : pensión *f* con desayuno

bedlam *n* : confusión *f*, caos *m*

bedraggled *adj* : desaliñado, sucio

bedridden *adj* : postrado en cama

bedroom *n* : dormitorio *m*, recámara *f Lat*

bedspread *n* : colcha *f*

bedtime *n* : hora *f* de acostarse

bee *n* : abeja *f*

beech *n, pl* **beeches** *or* **beech** : haya *f*

beef *n* : carne *f* de vaca, carne *f* de res *Lat* — **beefsteak** *n* : bistec *m*

beehive *n* : colmena *f*

beeline *n* **make a** ∼ **for** : irse derecho a

beep *n* : pitido *m* — ∼ *v* : pitar

beer *n* : cerveza *f*

beet *n* : remolacha *f*

beetle *n* : escarabajo *m*

before *adv* **1** : antes **2 the month** ∼ : el mes anterior — ∼ *prep* **1** (*in space*) : delante de, ante **2** (*in time*) : antes de — ∼ *conj* : antes de que — **beforehand** *adv* : antes

befriend *vt* : hacerse amigo de

beg *v* **begged; begging** *vt* **1** : pedir, mendigar **2** ENTREAT : suplicar — *vi* : mendigar, pedir limosna — **beggar** *n* : mendigo *m*, -ga *f*

begin *v* **-gan; -gun; -ginning** : empezar, comenzar — **beginner** *n* : principiante *mf* — **beginning** *n* : principio *m*, comienzo *m*

begrudge *vt* **-grudged; -grudging 1** : dar de mala gana **2** ENVY : envidiar

behalf *n* **on ~ of** : de parte de, en nombre de

behave *vi* **-haved; -having** : comportarse, portarse — **behavior** *n* : comportamiento *m*, conducta *f*

behind *adv* **1** : detrás **2 fall ~** : atrasarse — **~** *prep* **1** : atrás de, detrás de **2 be ~ schedule** : ir retrasado **3 her friends are ~ her** : tiene el apoyo de sus amigos

behold *vt* **-held; -holding** : contemplar

beige *adj & nm* : beige

being *n* **1** : ser *m* **2 come into ~** : nacer

belated *adj* : tardío

belch *vi* : eructar — **~** *n* : eructo *m*

Belgian *adj* : belga

belie *vt* **-lied; -lying** : contradecir, desmentir

belief *n* **1** TRUST : confianza *f* **2** CONVICTION : creencia *f*, convicción *f* **3** FAITH : fe *f* — **believable** *adj* : creíble — **believe** *v* **-lieved; -lieving** : creer — **believer** *n* : creyente *mf*

belittle *vt* **-littled; -littling** : menospreciar

Belizean *adj* : beliceño *m*, -ña *f*

bell *n* **1** : campana *f* **2** : timbre *m* (de teléfono, de la puerta, etc.)

belligerent *adj* : beligerante

bellow *vi* : bramar, mugir — *vt or* **~ out** : gritar

bellows *ns & pl* : fuelle *m*

belly *n*, *pl* **-lies** : vientre *m*

belong *vi* **1 ~ to** : pertenecer a, ser propiedad de **2 ~ to** : ser miembro de (un club, etc.) **3 where does it ~** : ¿dónde va? — **belongings** *npl* : pertenencias *fpl*, efectos *mpl* personales

beloved *adj* : querido, amado — **~** *n* : querido *m*, -da *f*

below *adv* : abajo — **~** *prep* **1** : abajo de, debajo de **2 ~ average** : por debajo del promedio **3 ~ zero** : bajo cero

belt *n* **1** : cinturón *m* **2** BAND, STRAP : cinta *f*, correa *f* **3** AREA : frente *m*, zona *f* — **~** *vt* **1** : ceñir con un cinturón **2** THRASH : darle una paliza a

bench *n* **1** : banco *m* **2** WORKBENCH : mesa *f* de trabajo **3** COURT : tribunal *m*

bend *v* **bent; bending** *vt* : doblar, torcer —

vi **1** : torcerse **2 ~ over** : inclinarse — **~** *n* : curva *f*, ángulo *m*

beneath *adv* : abajo, debajo — **~** *prep* : bajo, debajo de

benediction *n* : bendición *f*

benefactor *n* : benefactor *m*, -tora *f*

benefit *n* **1** ADVANTAGE : ventaja *f*, provecho *m* **2** AID : asistencia *f*, beneficio *m* — **~** *vt* : beneficiar — *vi* : beneficiarse — **beneficial** *adj* : beneficioso — **beneficiary** *n*, *pl* **-ries** : beneficiario *m*, -ria *f*

benevolent *adj* : benévolo

benign *adj* **1** KIND : benévolo, amable **2** : benigno (en medicina)

bent *adj* **1** : encorvado **2 be ~ on** : estar empeñado en — **~** *n* : aptitud *f*, inclinación *f*

bequeath *vt* : legar — **bequest** *n* : legado *m*

berate *vt* **-rated; -rating** : reprender, regañar

bereaved *adj* : desconsolado, a luto

beret *n* : boina *f*

berry *n*, *pl* **-ries** : baya *f*

berserk *adj* **1** : enloquecido **2 go ~** : volverse loco

berth *n* **1** MOORING : atracadero *m* **2** BUNK : litera *f*

beseech *vt* **-sought** *or* **-seeched; -seeching** : suplicar, implorar

beset *vt* **-set; -setting 1** HARASS : acosar **2** SURROUND : rodear

beside *prep* **1** : al lado de, junto a **2 be ~ oneself** : estar fuera de sí — **besides** *adv* : además — **~** *prep* **1** : además de **2** EXCEPT : excepto

besiege *vt* **-sieged; -sieging** : asediar

best *adj* (*superlative of* **good**) : mejor — **~** *adv* (*superlative of* **well**) : mejor — **~** *n* **1 at ~** : a lo más **2 do one's ~** : hacer todo lo posible **3 the ~** : lo mejor — **best man** *n* : padrino *m* (de boda)

bestow *vt* : otorgar, conceder

bet *n* : apuesta *f* — **~** *v* **bet; betting** *vt* : apostar — *vi* **~ on sth** : apostarle a algo

betray *vt* : traicionar — **betrayal** *n* : traición *f*

better *adj* (*comparative of* **good**) **1** : mejor **2 get ~** : mejorar — **~** *adv* (*comparative of* **well**) **1** : mejor **2 all the ~** : tanto mejor — **~** *n* **1 the ~** : el mejor, la mejor **2 get the ~ of** : vencer a — **~** *vt* **1** IMPROVE : mejorar **2** SURPASS : superar

between *prep* : entre — **~** *adv or* **in ~** : en medio

beverage *n* : bebida *f*

beware *vi* **~ of** : tener cuidado con

bewilder *vt* : desconcertar — **bewilderment** *n* : desconcierto *m*

bewitch *vt* : hechizar, encantar

beyond *adv* : más allá, más lejos (en el espacio), más adelante (en el tiempo) — **∼** *prep* : más allá de

bias *n* **1** PREJUDICE : prejuicio *m* **2** TENDENCY : inclinación *f*, tendencia *f* — **biased** *adj* : parcial

bib *n* : babero *m* (para niños)

Bible *n* : Biblia *f* — **biblical** *adj* : bíblico

bibliography *n, pl* **-phies** : bibliografía *f*

bicarbonate of soda *n* : bicarbonato *m* de soda

biceps *ns & pl* : bíceps *m*

bicker *vi* : reñir

bicycle *n* : bicicleta *f* — **∼** *vi* **-cled; -cling** : ir en bicicleta

bid *vt* **bade** *or* **bid; bidden** *or* **bid; bidding** **1** OFFER : ofrecer **2** **∼** **farewell** : decir adios — **∼** *n* **1** OFFER : oferta *f* **2** ATTEMPT : intento *m*, tentativa *f*

bide *vt* **bode** *or* **bided; bided; biding** **∼** **one's time** : esperar el momento oportuno

bifocals *npl* : anteojos *mpl* bifocales

big *adj* **bigger; biggest** : grande

bigamy *n* : bigamía *f*

bigot *n* : intolerante *mf* — **bigotry** *n, pl* **-tries** : intolerancia *f*, fanatismo *m*

bike *n* **1** BICYCLE : bici *f fam* **2** MOTORCYCLE : moto *f*

bike lane *or* **bicycle lane** *n* : carril *m* para bicicletas

bikini *n* : bikini *m*

bile *n* : bilis *f*

bilingual *adj* : bilingüe

bill *n* **1** BEAK : pico *m* **2** INVOICE : cuenta *f*, factura *f* **3** BANKNOTE : billete *m* **4** LAW : proyecto *m* de ley, ley *f* — **∼** *vt* : pasarle la cuenta a — **billboard** *n* : cartelera *f* — **billfold** *n* : billetera *f*, cartera *f*

billiards *n* : billar *m*

billion *n, pl* **billions** *or* **billion** : mil millones *mpl*

billow *vi* : ondular, hincharse

billy goat *n* : macho *m* cabrío

bin *n* : cubo *m*, cajón *m*

binary *adj* : binario *m*

bind *vt* **bound; binding** **1** TIE : atar **2** OBLIGATE : obligar **3** UNITE : unir **4** BANDAGE : vendar **5** : encuadernar (un libro) — **binder** *n* FOLDER : carpeta *f* — **binding** *n* : encuadernación *f* (de libros)

binge *n* : juerga *f fam*

bingo *n, pl* **-gos** : bingo *m*

binoculars *npl* : binoculares *mpl*, gemelos *mpl*

biochemistry *n* : bioquímica *f*

biography *n, pl* **-phies** : biografía *f* — **biographer** *n* : biógrafo *m*, **-fa** *f* — **biographical** *adj* : biográfico

biological weapon *n* : arma *f* biológica

biology *n* : biología *f* — **biological** *adj* : biológico — **biologist** *n* : biólogo *m*, **-ga** *f*

biotechnology *n* : biotecnología *f* — **biotechnological** *adj*

birch *n* : abedul *m*

bird *n* : pájaro *m* (pequeño), ave *f* (grande)

birth *n* **1** : nacimiento *m*, parto *m* **2 give ∼ to** : dar a luz a — **birthday** *n* : cumpleaños *m* — **birthmark** *n* : mancha *f* de nacimiento — **birthplace** *n* : lugar *m* de nacimiento — **birthrate** *n* : índice *m* de natalidad

birth control *n* : control *m* de natalidad

biscuit *n* : bizcocho *m*

bisect *vt* : bisecar

bisexual *adj* : bisexual

bishop *n* : obispo *m*

bison *ns & pl* : bisonte *m*

bit[1] *n* : bocado *m* (de una brida)

bit[2] **1** : trozo *m*, pedazo *m* **2** : bit *m* (de información) **3 a ∼** : un poco

bitch *n* : perra *f* — **∼** *vi* COMPLAIN : quejarse, reclamar

bite *v* **bit; bitten; biting** *vt* **1** : morder **2** STING : picar — *vi* : morder — *n* **1** : picadura *f* (de un insecto), mordedura *f* (de un animal) **2** SNACK : bocado *m* — **biting** *adj* **1** PENETRATING : cortante, penetrante **2** CAUSTIC : mordaz

bitter *adj* **1** : amargo **2 it's ∼ cold** : hace un frío glacial **3 to the ∼ end** : hasta el final — **bitterness** *n* : amargura *f*

bizarre *adj* : extraño

black *adj* : negro — **∼** *n* **1** : negro *m* (color) **2** : negro *m*, **-gra** *f* (persona) — **black–and–blue** *adj* : amoratado — **blackberry** *n, pl* **-ries** : mora *f* — **blackbird** *n* : mirlo *m* — **blackboard** *n* : pizarra *f*, pizarrón *m Lat* — **blacken** *vt* : ennegrecer — **blackmail** *n* : chantaje *m* — **∼** *vt* : chantajear — **black market** *n* : mercado *m* negro — **blackout** *n* **1** : apagón *m* (de poder eléctrico) **2** FAINT : desmayo *m* — **blacksmith** *n* : herrero *m* — **blacktop** *n* : asfalto *m*

black box *n* : caja *f* negra

bladder *n* : vejiga *f*

blade *n* **1** : hoja *f* (de un cuchillo), cuchilla *f* (de un patín) **2** : pala *f* (de un remo, una hélice, etc.) **3 ∼ of grass** : brizna *f* (de hierba)

blame *vt* **blamed; blaming** : culpar, echar la culpa a — **∼** *n* : culpa *f* — **blameless** *adj* : inocente

bland *adj* : soso, insulso

blank *adj* **1** : en blanco (dícese de un papel), liso (dícese de una pared) **2** EMPTY : vacío — **∼** *n* : espacio *m* en blanco

blanket *n* **1** : manta *f*, cobija *f Lat* **2 ∼ of snow** : manto *m* de nieve — **∼** *vt* : cubrir

blare *vi* **blared; blaring** : resonar

blasphemy *n*, *pl* **-mies** : blasfemia *f*
blast *n* **1** GUST : ráfaga *f* **2** EXPLOSION : explosión *f* **3** : toque *m* (de trompeta, etc.) — ~ *vt* BLOW UP : volar — **blast-off** *n* : despegue *m*
blatant *adj* : descarado
blaze *n* **1** FIRE : fuego *m* **2** BRIGHTNESS : resplandor *m*, brillantez *f* **3** ~ **of anger** : arranque *m* de cólera — ~ *v* **blazed**; **blazing** *vi* : arder, brillar — *vt* ~ **a trail** : abrir un camino
blazer *n* : chaqueta *f* deportiva
bleach *vt* : blanquear, decolorar — ~ *n* : lejía *f*, blanqueador *m Lat*
bleachers *ns & pl* : gradas *fpl*
bleak *adj* **1** DESOLATE : desolado **2** GLOOMY : triste, sombrío
bleary–eyed *adj* : con los ojos nublados
bleat *vi* : balar — ~ *n* : balido *m*
bleed *v* **bled**; **bleeding** : sangrar
blemish *vt* : manchar, marcar — ~ *n* : mancha *f*, marca *f*
blend *vt* : mezclar, combinar — ~ *n* : mezcla *f*, combinación *f* — **blender** *n* : licuadora *f*
bless *vt* **blessed**; **blessing** : bendecir — **blessed** *or* **blest** *adj* : bendito — **blessing** *n* : bendición *f*
blew → **blow**
blind *adj* : ciego — ~ *vt* **1** : cegar, dejar ciego **2** DAZZLE : deslumbrar — ~ *n* **1** : persiana *f* (para una ventana) **2 the** ~ : los ciegos — **blindfold** *vt* : vendar los ojos — ~ *n* : venda *f* (para los ojos) — **blindly** *adv* : ciegamente — **blindness** *n* : ceguera *f*
blink *vi* **1** : parpadear **2** FLICKER : brillar intermitentemente — ~ *n* : parpadeo *m* — **blinker** *n* : intermitente *m*, direccional *f Lat*
bliss *n* : dicha *f*, felicidad *f* (absoluta) — **blissful** *adj* : feliz
blister *n* : ampolla *f* — ~ *vi* : ampollarse
blitz *n* : bombardeo *m* aéreo
blizzard *n* : ventisca *f* (de nieve)
bloated *adj* : hinchado
blob *n* **1** DROP : gota *f* **2** SPOT : mancha *f*
block *n* **1** : bloque *m* **2** OBSTRUCTION : obstrucción *f* **3** : manzana *f*, cuadra *f Lat* (de edificios) **4** *or* **building** ~ : cubo *m* de construcción — ~ *vt* : obstruir, bloquear — **blockade** *n* : bloqueo *m* — **blockage** *n* : obstrucción *f*
blockbuster *n* : gran éxito *m* (de taquilla)
blog *n* : blog *m*, bitácora *f*
blond *or* **blonde** *adj* : rubio — ~ *n* : rubio *m*, **-bia** *f*
blood *n* : sangre *f* — **bloodhound** *n* : sabueso *m* — **blood pressure** *n* : tensión *f* (arterial) — **bloodshed** *n* : derramamiento *m* de sangre — **bloodshot** *adj* : inyectado de sangre — **bloodstained** *adj* : manchado

de sangre — **bloodstream** *n* : sangre *f*, torrente *m* sanguíneo — **bloody** *adj* **bloodier**; **-est** : ensangrentado, sangriento
bloom *n* **1** : flor *f* **2 in full** ~ : en plena floración — ~ *vi* : florecer
blossom *n* : flor *f* — ~ *vi* : florecer
blot *n* **1** : borrón *m* (de tinta, etc.) **2** BLEMISH : mancha *f* — ~ *vt* **blotted**; **blotting** **1** : emborronar **2** DRY : secar
blotch *n* : mancha *f*, borrón *m* — **blotchy** *adj* **blotchier**; **-est** : lleno de manchas
blouse *n* : blusa *f*
blow *v* **blew**; **blown**; **blowing** *vi* **1** : soplar **2** SOUND : sonar **3** *or* ~ **out** : fundirse (dícese de un fusible eléctrico), reventarse (dícese de una llanta) — *vt* **1** : soplar **2** SOUND : tocar, sonar **3** BUNGLE : echar a perder — ~ *n* : golpe *m* — **blowout** *n* : reventón *m* — **blow up** *vi* : estallar, hacer explosión — *vt* **1** EXPLODE : volar **2** INFLATE : inflar
blubber *n* : esperma *f* de ballena
bludgeon *vt* : aporrear
blue *adj* **bluer**; **bluest** **1** : azul **2** MELANCHOLY : triste — ~ *n* : azul *m* — **blueberry** *n*, *pl* **-ries** : arándano *m* — **bluebird** *n* : azulejo *m* — **blue cheese** *n* : queso *m* azul — **blueprint** *n* PLAN : proyecto *m* — **blues** *npl* **1** SADNESS : tristeza *f* **2** : blues *m* (en música)
bluff *vi* : hacer un farol — ~ *n* : farol *m*
blunder *vi* : meter la pata *fam* — ~ *n* : metedura *f* de pata *fam*
blunt *adj* **1** DULL : desafilado **2** DIRECT : directo, franco
blur *n* : imágen *f* borrosa — ~ *vt* **blurred**; **blurring** : hacer borroso
blurb *n* : nota *f* publicitaria
blurt *vt or* ~ **out** : espetar
blush *n* : rubor *m* — ~ *vi* : ruborizarse
blustery *adj* : borrascoso, tempestuoso
boar *n* : cerdo *m* macho
board *n* **1** PLANK : tabla *f*, tablón *m* **2** COMMITTEE : junta *f*, consejo *m* **3** : tablero *m* (de juegos) **4 room and** ~ : comida y alojamiento — ~ *vt* **1** : subir a bordo de (una nave, un avión, etc.), subir a (un tren) **2** LODGE : hospedar **3** ~ **up** : cerrar con tablas — **boarder** *n* : huésped *mf*
boast *n* : jactancia *f* — ~ *vi* : alardear, jactarse — **boastful** *adj* : jactancioso
boat *n* : barco *m* (grande), barca *f* (pequeña)
boat person *n* : balsero *m*, **-ra** *f*
bob *vi* **bobbed**; **bobbing** *or* ~ **up and down** : subir y bajar
bobbin *n* : bobina *f*, carrete *m*
bobby pin *n* : horquilla *f*
body *n*, *pl* **bodies** **1** : cuerpo *m* **2** CORPSE : cadáver *m* **3** : carrocería (de un automóvil, etc.) **4** COLLECTION : conjunto *m*

5 ～ **of water** : masa *f* de agua — **bodily**
adj : corporal — **bodyguard** *n* : guardaespaldas *mf*

bodybuilding *n* : culturismo *m*

bog *n* : ciénaga *f* — ～ *vt* **bogged; bogging**
or ～ **down** : empantanarse

bogus *adj* : falso

boil *v* : hervir — **boiler** *n* : caldera *f*

bold *adj* 1 DARING : audaz 2 IMPUDENT
: descarado — **boldness** *n* : audacia *f*

Bolivian *adj* : boliviano *m*, **-na** *f*

bologna *n* : salchicha *f* ahumada

bolster *vt* **-stered; -stering** *or* ～ **up** : reforzar

bolt *n* 1 LOCK : cerrojo *m* 2 SCREW : tornillo *m* 3 ～ **of lightning** : relámpago *m*,
rayo *m* — ～ *vt* 1 FASTEN : atornillar 2
LOCK : echar el cerrojo a — *vi* FLEE : salir
corriendo

bomb *n* : bomba *f* — ～ *vt* : bombardear —
bombard *vt* : bombardear — **bombardment** *n* : bombardeo *m* — **bomber** *n* : bombardero *m*

bond *n* 1 TIE : vínculo *m*, lazo *m* 2 SURETY
: fianza *f* 3 : bono *m* (en finanzas) — ～ *vi*
STICK : adherirse

bondage *n* : esclavitud *f*

bone *n* : hueso *m* — ～ *vt* **boned; boning**
: deshuesar

bonfire *n* : hoguera *f*

bonus *n* 1 PAY : prima *f* 2 BENEFIT : beneficio *m* adicional

bony *adj* **bonier; -est** 1 : huesudo 2
: lleno de espinas (dícese de pescados)

boo *n*, *pl* **boos** : abucheo *m* — ～ *vt* : abuchear

book *n* 1 : libro *m* 2 NOTEBOOK : libreta *f*,
cuaderno *m* — ～ *vt* : reservar — **bookcase** *n* : estantería *f* — **bookkeeping** *n*
: teneduría *f* de libros, contabilidad *f* —
booklet *n* : folleto *m* — **bookseller** *n* : librero *m*, -ra *f* — **bookshelf** *n*, *pl* **-shelves**
: estante *m* — **bookstore** *n* : librería *f*

bookmark[1] *n* 1 : señalador *m* de libros, marcador *m* de libros 2 : marcador *m* (de Internet)

bookmark[2] *vt* : marcar (una página web)

boom *vi* 1 : tronar, resonar 2 PROSPER
: estar en auge, prosperar — ～ *n* 1 : bramido *m*, estruendo *m* 2 : auge *m*
(económico)

boon *n* : ayuda *f*, beneficio *m*

boost *vt* 1 LIFT : levantar 2 INCREASE : aumentar — ～ *n* 1 INCREASE : aumento *m*
2 ENCOURAGEMENT : estímulo *m*

boot *n* : bota *f*, botín *m* — ～ *vt* 1 : dar una
patada a 2 *or* ～ **up** : cargar (un ordenador)

booth *n*, *pl* **booths** : cabina *f* (de teléfono,
de votar), caseta *f* (de información)

bootleg[1] *adj* : pirata (**bootleg software**
: software pirata)

bootleg[2] *vt* : piratear (un video, etc.)

booty *n*, *pl* **-ties** : botín *m*

booze *n* : trago *m*, bebida *f* (alcohólica)

border *n* 1 EDGE : borde *m*, orilla *f* 2 TRIM
: ribete *m* 3 FRONTIER : frontera *f*

bore[1] *vt* **bored; boring** DRILL : taladrar

bore[2] *vt* TIRE : aburrir — ～ *n* : pesado *m*,
-da *fam f* (persona), lata *f fam* (cosa, situación) — **boredom** *n* : aburrimiento *m* —
boring *adj* : aburrido, pesado

born *adj* 1 : nacido 2 **be** ～ : nacer

borough *n* : distrito *m* municipal

borrow *vt* : pedir prestado, tomar prestado

Bosnian *adj* : bosnio *m*, **-nia** *f*

bosom *n* BREAST : pecho *m*, seno *m* — ～
adj ～ **friend** : amigo *m* íntimo

boss *n* : jefe *m*, **-fa** *f*; patrón *m*, **-trona** *f* —
～ *vt* SUPERVISE : dirigir — **bossy** *adj*

bossier; -est : autoritario

botany *n* : botánica *f* — **botanical** *adj* : botánico

botch *vt* : hacer una chapuza de, estropear

both *adj* : ambos, los dos, las dos — ～ *pron*
: ambos *m*, **-bas** *f*; los dos, las dos

bother *vt* 1 TROUBLE : preocupar 2 PESTER
: molestar, fastidiar — *vi* ～ **to** : molestarse
en — *n* : molestia *f*

bottle *n* 1 : botella *f*, frasco *m* 2 *or* baby
～ : biberón *m* — ～ *vt* **bottled; bottling**
: embotellar — **bottleneck** *n* : embotellamiento *m*

bottom *n* 1 : fondo *m* (de una caja, del mar,
etc.), pie *m* (de una escalera, una montaña,
etc.), final *m* (de una lista) 2 BUTTOCKS
: nalgas *fpl*, trasero *m* — ～ *adj* : más bajo,
inferior, de abajo — **bottomless** *adj* : sin
fondo

bough *n* : rama *f*

bought → **buy**

bouillon *n* : caldo *m*

boulder *n* : canto *m* rodado

boulevard *n* : bulevar *m*

bounce *v* **bounced; bouncing** *vt* : hacer rebotar — *vi* : rebotar — ～ *n* : rebote *m*

bound[1] *adj* **be** ～ **for** : ir rumbo a

bound[2] *adj* 1 OBLIGED : obligado 2 DETERMINED : decidido 3 **be** ～ **to** : tener
que

bound[3] *n* **out of** ～**s** : (en) zona prohibida
— **boundary** *n*, *pl* **-aries** : límite *m* —
boundless *adj* : sin límites

bouquet *n* : ramo *m*

bourgeois *adj* : burgués

bout *n* 1 : combate *m* (en deportes) 2
: ataque *m* (de una enfermedad) 3 : período
m (de actividad)

bow[1] *vi* : inclinarse — *vt* ～ **one's head**

: inclinar la cabeza — ～ *n* : reverencia *f*, inclinación *f*
bow² *n* **1** : arco *m* **2 tie a ～** : hacer un lazo
bow³ *n* : proa *f* (de un barco)
bowels *npl* **1** : intestinos *mpl* **2** DEPTHS : entrañas *fpl*
bowl¹ *n* : tazón *m*, cuenco *m*
bowl² *vi* : jugar a los bolos — **bowling** *n* : bolos *mpl*
box¹ *vi* FIGHT : boxear — **boxer** *n* : boxeador *m*, -dora *f* — **boxing** *n* : boxeo *m*
box² *n* **1** : caja *f*, cajón *m* **2** : palco *m* (en el teatro) — ～ *vt* : empaquetar — **box office** *n* : taquilla *f*, boletería *f Lat*
boy *n* : niño *m*, chico *m*
boycott *vt* : boicotear — ～ *n* : boicot *m*
boyfriend *n* : novio *m*
bra → **brassiere**
brace *n* **1** SUPPORT : abrazadera *f* **2 ～s** *npl* : aparatos *mpl* (para dientes) — ～ *vi* ～ **oneself for** : prepararse para
bracelet *n* : brazalete *m*
bracket *n* **1** SUPPORT : soporte *m* **2** : corchete *m* (marca de puntuación) **3** CATEGORY : categoría *f* — ～ *vt* **1** : poner entre corchetes **2** CATEGORIZE : catalogar
brag *vi* **bragged; bragging** : jactarse
braid *vt* : trenzar — ～ *n* : trenza *f*
braille *n* : braille *m*
brain *n* **1** : cerebro *m* **2 ～s** *npl* : inteligencia *f* — **brainstorm** *n* : idea *f* genial — **brainwash** *vt* : lavar el cerebro — **brainy** *adj* **brainier; -est** : inteligente, listo
brake *n* : freno *m* — ～ *v* **braked; braking** : frenar
bramble *n* : zarza *f*
bran *n* : salvado *m*
branch *n* **1** : rama *f* (de una planta) **2** DIVISION : ramal *m* (de un camino, etc.), sucursal *f* (de una empresa), agencia *f* (del gobierno) — ～ *vi or* ～ **off** : ramificarse, bifurcarse
brand *n* **1** : marca *f* (de ganado) **2** *or* ～ **name** : marca *f* de fábrica — ～ *vt* **1** : marcar (ganado) **2** LABEL : tachar, tildar
brandish *vt* : blandir
brand-new *adj* : flamante
brandy *n, pl* **-dies** : brandy *m*, coñac *m*
brass *n* **1** : latón *m* **2** : metales *mpl* (de una orquesta)
brassiere *n* : sostén *m*, brasier *m Lat*
brat *n* : mocoso *m*, -sa *f fam*
bravado *n, pl* **-does** *or* **-dos** : bravuconadas *fpl*
brave *adj* **braver; bravest** : valiente, valeroso — ～ *vt* **braved; braving** : afrontar, hacer frente a — ～ *n* : guerrero *m* indio —
bravery *n* : valor *m*, valentía *f*

brawl *n* : pelea *f*, reyerta *f*
brawn *n* : músculos *mpl* — **brawny** *adj* **brawnier; -est** : musculoso
bray *vi* : rebuznar
brazen *adj* : descarado
Brazilian *adj* : brasileño *m*, -ña *f*
breach *n* **1** VIOLATION : infracción *f*, violación *f* **2** GAP : brecha *f*
bread *n* **1** : pan *m* **2 ～ crumbs** : migajas *fpl*
breadth *n* : anchura *f*
break *v* **broke; broken; breaking** *vt* **1** : romper, quebrar **2** VIOLATE : infringir, violar **3** INTERRUPT : interrumpir **4** SURPASS : batir (un récord, etc.) **5 ～ a habit** : quitarse una costumbre **6 ～ the news** : dar la noticia — *vi* **1** : romperse, quebrarse **2 ～ away** : escapar **3 ～ down** : estropearse (dícese de una máquina), fallar (dícese de un sistema, etc.) **4 ～ into** : entrar en **5 ～ off** : interrumpirse **6 ～ out of** : escaparse de **7 ～ up** SEPARATE : separarse — ～ *n* **1** : ruptura *f*, fractura *f* **2** GAP : interrupción *f*, claro *m* (entre las nubes) **3 lucky ～** : golpe *m* de suerte **4 take a ～** : tomar(se) un descanso — **breakable** *adj* : quebradizo, frágil — **breakdown** *n* **1** : avería *f* (de máquinas), interrupción *f* (de comunicaciones), fracaso *m* (de negociaciones) **2** *or* **nervous ～** : crisis *f* nerviosa
breakfast *n* : desayuno *m*
breast *n* **1** : seno *m* (de una mujer) **2** CHEST : pecho *m* — **breast-feed** *vt* **-fed; -feeding** : amamantar
breath *n* : aliento *m*, respiración *f* — **breathe** *v* **breathed; breathing** : respirar — **breathless** *adj* : sin aliento, jadeante — **breathtaking** *adj* : impresionante
breed *v* **bred; breeding** *vt* **1** : criar (animales) **2** ENGENDER : engendrar, producir — *vi* : reproducirse — ～ *n* **1** : raza *f* **2** CLASS : clase *f*, tipo *m*
breeze *n* : brisa *f* — **breezy** *adj* **breezier; -est 1** WINDY : ventoso **2** NONCHALANT : despreocupado
brevity *n, pl* **-ties** : brevedad *f*
brew *vt* : hacer (cerveza, etc.), preparar (té) — *vi* **1** : fabricar cerveza **2** : amenazar (dícese de una tormenta) — **brewery** *n, pl* **-eries** : cervecería *f*
bribe *n* : soborno *m* — ～ *vt* **bribed; bribing** : sobornar — **bribery** *n, pl* **-eries** : soborno *m*
brick *n* : ladrillo *m* — **bricklayer** *n* : albañil *mf*
bride *n* : novia *f* — **bridal** *adj* : nupcial, de novia — **bridegroom** *n* : novio *m* — **bridesmaid** *n* : dama *f* de honor
bridge *n* **1** : puente *m* **2** : caballete *m* (de

la nariz) **3** : bridge *m* (juego de naipes) — ～ *vt* **bridged; bridging 1** : tender un puente sobre **2** ～ **the gap** : salvar las diferencias

bridle *n* : brida *f* — ～ *vt* **-dled; -dling** : embridar

brief *adj* : breve — ～ *n* **1** : resumen *m*, sumario *m* **2** ～**s** *npl* UNDERPANTS : calzoncillos *mpl* — ～ *vt* : dar órdenes a, instruir — **briefcase** *n* : portafolio *m*, maletín *m* — **briefly** *adv* : brevemente

bright *adj* **1** : brillante, claro **2** CHEERFUL : alegre, animado **3** INTELLIGENT : listo, inteligente — **brighten** *vi* **1** : hacerse más brillante **2** *or* ～ **up** : animarse, alegrarse — *vt* **1** ILLUMINATE : iluminar **2** ENLIVEN : alegrar, animar

brilliant *adj* : brillante — **brilliance** *n* **1** BRIGHTNESS : resplandor *m*, brillantez *f* **2** INTELLIGENCE : inteligencia *f*

brim *n* **1** : borde *m* (de una taza, etc.) **2** : ala *f* (de un sombrero) — ～ *vi* **brimmed; brimming** *or* ～ **over** : desbordarse, rebosar

brine *n* : salmuera *f*

bring *vt* **brought; bringing 1** : traer **2** ～ **about** : ocasionar **3** ～ **around** PERSUADE : convencer **4** ～ **back** : devolver **5** ～ **down** : derribar **6** ～ **on** CAUSE : provocar **7** ～ **out** : sacar **8** ～ **to an end** : terminar (con) **9** ～ **up** REAR : criar **10** ～ **up** MENTION : sacar

brink *n* : borde *m*

brisk *adj* **1** FAST : rápido **2** LIVELY : enérgico

bristle *n* : cerda *f* (de un animal), pelo *m* (de una planta) — ～ *vi* **-tled; -tling** : erizarse

British *adj* : británico

brittle *adj* **-tler; -tlest** : frágil, quebradizo

broach *vt* : abordar

broad *adj* **1** WIDE : ancho **2** GENERAL : general **3 in** ～ **daylight** : en pleno día

broadband[1] *adj* : de banda ancha

broadband[2] *n* : banda *f* ancha

broadcast *vt* **-cast; -casting** : emitir — ～ *n* : emisión *f*

broaden *vt* : ampliar, ensanchar — *vi* : ensancharse — **broadly** *adv* : en general — **broad–minded** *adj* : de miras amplias, tolerante

broccoli *n* : brócoli *m*, brécol *m*

brochure *n* : folleto *m*

broil *vt* : asar a la parrilla

broke → **break** — ～ *adj* : pelado *fam* — **broken** *adj* : roto, quebrado — **broken- hearted** *adj* : desconsolado, con el corazón destrozado

broker *n* : corredor *m*, -dora *f*

bronchitis *n* : bronquitis *f*

bronze *n* : bronce *m*

brooch *n* : broche *m*

brood *n* : nidada *f* (de pájaros), camada *f* (de mamíferos) — ～ *vi* **1** INCUBATE : empollar **2** ～ **about** : dar vueltas a, pensar demasiado en

brook *n* : arroyo *m*

broom *n* : escoba *f* — **broomstick** *n* : palo *m* de escoba

broth *n, pl* **broths** : caldo *m*

brothel *n* : burdel *m*

brother *n* : hermano *m* — **brotherhood** *n* : fraternidad *f* — **brother–in–law** *n, pl* **brothers–in–law:** cuñado *m* — **brotherly** *adj* : fraternal

brought → **bring**

brow *n* **1** EYEBROW : ceja *f* **2** FOREHEAD : frente *f* **3** : cima *f* (de una colina)

brown *adj* : marrón, castaño (dícese del pelo), moreno (dícese de la piel) — ～ *n* : marrón *m* — ～ *vt* : dorar (en cocinar)

browse *vi* **browsed; browsing** : mirar, echar un vistazo

browser *n* : navegador *m* (para la Internet)

bruise *vt* **bruised; bruising 1** : contusionar, magullar (a una persona) **2** : machucar (frutas) — ～ *n* : cardenal *m*, magulladura *f*

brunch *n* : brunch *m*

brunet *or* **brunette** *adj* : moreno — ～ *n* : moreno *m*, **-na** *f*

brunt *n* **bear the** ～ **of** : aguantar el mayor impacto de

brush *n* **1** : cepillo *m*, pincel *m* (de artista), brocha *f* (de pintor) **2** UNDERBRUSH : maleza *f* — ～ *vt* **1** : cepillar **2** GRAZE : rozar **3** ～ **aside** : rechazar **4** ～ **off** DISREGARD : hacer caso omiso de — *vi* ～ **up on** : repasar — **brush–off** *n* **give the** ～ **to** : dar calabazas a

brusque *adj* : brusco

brutal *adj* : brutal — **brutality** *n, pl* **-ties** : brutalidad *f*

brute *adj* : bruto — ～ *n* : bestia *f;* bruto *m*, **-ta** *f*

bubble *n* : burbuja *f* — ～ *vi* **-bled; -bling** : burbujear

buck *n, pl* **buck** *or* **bucks 1** : animal *m* macho, ciervo *m* (macho) **2** DOLLAR : dólar *m* — ～ *vi* **1** : corcovear (dícese de un caballo) **2** ～ **up** : animarse, levantar el ánimo — *vt* OPPOSE : oponerse a, ir en contra de

bucket *n* : cubo *m*

buckle *n* : hebilla *f* — ～ *v* **-led; -ling** *vt* **1** FASTEN : abrochar **2** BEND : combar, torcer — *vi* **1** : combarse, torcerse **2** : doblarse (dícese de las rodillas)

bud *n* **1** : brote *m* **2** *or* **flower** ～ : capullo *m* — ～ *vi* **budded; budding** : brotar, hacer brotes

Buddhism *n* : budismo *m* — **Buddhist** *adj* : budista — ～ *n* : budista *mf*

buddy *n, pl* **-dies** : compañero *m*, -ra *f*

budge *vi* **budged; budging** **1** MOVE : moverse **2** YIELD : ceder

budget *n* : presupuesto *m* — ～ *vi* : presupuestar — **budgetary** *adj* : presupuestario

buff *n* **1** : beige *m*, color *m* de ante **2** ENTHUSIAST : aficionado *m*, -da *f* — ～ *adj* : beige — ～ *vt* POLISH : pulir

buffalo *n, pl* **-lo** *or* **-loes** : búfalo *m*

buffet *n* **1** : bufé *m* (comida) **2** SIDEBOARD : aparador *m*

bug *n* **1** INSECT : bicho *m*, insecto *m* **2** FLAW : defecto *m* **3** GERM : microbio *m* **4** MICROPHONE : micrófono *m* (oculto) — ～ *vt* **bugged; bugging** **1** PESTER : fastidiar, molestar **2** : ocultar micrófonos en (una habitación, etc.)

buggy *n, pl* **-gies** **1** CARRIAGE : calesa *f* **2** *or* **baby** ～ : cochecito *m* (para niños)

bugle *n* : clarín *m*, corneta *f*

build *v* **built; building** *vt* **1** : construir **2** DEVELOP : desarrollar — *vi* **1** *or* ～ **up** INTENSIFY : aumentar, intensificar **2** *or* ～ **up** ACCUMULATE : acumularse — ～ *n* PHYSIQUE : físico *m*, complexión *f* — **builder** *n* : constructor *m*, -tora *f* — **building** *n* **1** STRUCTURE : edificio *m* **2** CONSTRUCTION : construcción *f* — **built–in** *adj* : empotrado

bulb *n* **1** : bulbo *m* (de una planta) **2** LIGHTBULB : bombilla *f*

bulge *vi* **bulged; bulging** : sobresalir — ～ *n* : bulto *m*, protuberancia *f*

bulk *n* **1** VOLUME : volumen *m*, bulto *m* **2** **in** ～ : en grandes cantidades — **bulky** *adj* **bulkier; -est** : voluminoso

bull *n* **1** : toro *m* **2** MALE : macho *m*

bulldog *n* : buldog *m*

bulldozer *n* : bulldozer *m*

bullet *n* : bala *f*

bulletin *n* : boletín *m* — **bulletin board** *n* : tablón *m* de anuncios

bulletproof *adj* : a prueba de balas

bullfight *n* : corrida *f* (de toros) — **bullfighter** *n* : torero *m*, -ra *f*; matador *m*

bullfighting *n* : lidia *f*, toreo *m*

bullion *n* : oro *m* en lingotes, plata *f* en lingotes

bull's–eye *n, pl* **bull's–eyes** : diana *f*

bully *n, pl* **-lies** : matón *m* — ～ *vt* **-lied; -lying** : intimidar

bum *n* : vagabundo *m*, -da *f*

bumblebee *n* : abejorro *m*

bump *n* **1** BULGE : bulto *m*, protuberancia *f*

2 IMPACT : golpe *m* **3** JOLT : sacudida *f* — ～ *vt* : chocar contra — *vi* ～ **into** MEET : encontrarse con — **bumper** *n* : parachoques *mpl* — ～ *adj* : extraordinario, récord — **bumpy** *adj* **bumpier; -est** **1** : desigual, lleno de baches (dícese de un camino) **2 a** ～ **flight** : un vuelo agitado

bun *n* : bollo *m*

bunch *n* : grupo *m* (de personas), racimo *m* (de frutas, etc.), ramo *m* (de flores), manojo *m* (de llaves) — ～ *vi or* ～ **up** : amontonarse, agruparse

bundle *n* **1** : lío *m*, bulto *m*, atado *m*, haz *m* (de palos) **2** PARCEL : paquete *m* **3** ～ **of nerves** : manojo *m* de nervios — ～ *vt* **-dled; -dling** *or* ～ **up** : liar, atar

bungalow *n* : casa *f* de un solo piso

bungle *vt* **-gled; -gling** : echar a perder

bunion *n* : juanete *m*

bunk *n or* **bunk bed** : litera *f*

bunny *n, pl* **-nies** : conejo *m*, -ja *f*

buoy *n* : boya *f* — ～ *vt or* ～ **up** HEARTEN : animar, levantar el ánimo a — **buoyant** *adj* **1** : boyante, flotante **2** LIGHTHEARTED : alegre, optimista

burden *n* : carga *f* — ～ *vt* ～ **s.o. with** : cargar a algn con — **burdensome** *adj* : oneroso

bureau *n* **1** : cómoda *f* (mueble) **2** : departamento *m* (del gobierno) **3** AGENCY : agencia *f* — **bureaucracy** *n, pl* **-cies** : burocracia *f* — **bureaucrat** *n* : burócrata *mf* — **bureaucratic** *adj* : burocrático

burglar *n* : ladrón *m*, -drona *f* — **burglarize** *vt* **-ized; -izing** : robar — **burglary** *n, pl* **-glaries** : robo *m*

burgundy *n, pl* **-dies** : borgoña *m*, vino *m* de Borgoña

burial *n* : entierro *m*

burly *adj* **-lier; -liest** : fornido

burn *v* **burned** *or* **burnt; burning** *vt* **1** : quemar **2** *or* ～ **down** : incendiar **3** *or* ～ **up** : consumir — *vi* **1** : arder (dícese de un fuego), quemarse (dícese de la comida, etc.) **2** : estar encendido (dícese de una luz) **3** ～ **out** : apagarse — ～ *n* : quemadura *f* — **burner** *n* : quemador *m*

burnish *vt* : pulir

burp *vi* : eructar — ～ *n* : eructo *m*

burrito *n, pl* **-tos** : burrito *m*

burro *n, pl* **-os** : burro *m*

burrow *n* : madriguera *f* — ～ *vi* **1** : cavar **2** ～ **into** : hurgar en

bursar *n* : tesorero *m*, -ra *f*

burst *v* **burst** *or* **bursted; bursting** *vi* : reventarse — *vt* : reventar — ～ *n* **1** EXPLOSION : estallido *m*, explosión *f* **2** OUTBURST : arranque *m*, arrebato *m* **3** ～ **of laughter** : carcajada *f*

bury *vt* **buried; burying 1** INTER : enterrar **2** HIDE : esconder

bus *n, pl* **buses** *or* **busses** : autobús *m*, bus *m* — ~ *v* **bused** *or* **bussed; busing** *or* **bussing** *vt* : transportar en autobús — *vi* : viajar en autobús

bush *n* SHRUB : arbusto *m*, mata *f*

bushel *n* : medida *f* de áridos igual a 35.24 litros

bushy *adj* **bushier; -est** : poblado, espeso

busily *adv* : afanosamente

business *n* **1** COMMERCE : negocios *mpl*, comercio *m* **2** COMPANY : empresa *f*, negocio *m* **3 it's none of your** ~ : no es asunto tuyo — **businessman** *n, pl* **-men** : empresario *m*, hombre *m* de negocios — **businesswoman** *n, pl* **-women** : empresaria *f*, mujer *f* de negocios

bust¹ *vt* BREAK : romper

bust² *n* **1** : busto *m* (en la escultura) **2** BREASTS : pecho *m*, senos *mpl*

bustle *vi* **-tled; -tling** *or* ~ **about** : ir y venir, ajetrearse — ~ *n or* **hustle and** ~ : bullicio *m*, ajetreo *m*

busy *adj* **busier; -est 1** : ocupado **2** BUSTLING : concurrido

busy signal *n* : señal *f* de comunicando

but *conj* **1** : pero **2 not one** ~ **two** : no uno sino dos — ~ *prep* : excepto, menos

butcher *n* : carnicero *m*, -ra *f* — ~ *vt* **1** : matar **2** BOTCH : hacer una carnicería de

butler *n* : mayordomo *m*

butt *vt* : embestir (con los cuernos), darle un cabezazo a — *vi* ~ **in** : interrumpir — ~ *n* **1** BUTTING : embestida *f* (de cuernos) **2** TARGET : blanco *m* **3** : extremo *m*, culata *f* (de un rifle), colilla *f* (de un cigarrillo)

butter *n* : mantequilla *f* — ~ *vt* : untar con mantequilla

buttercup *n* : ranúnculo *m*

butterfly *n, pl* **-flies** : mariposa *f*

buttocks *npl* : nalgas *fpl*

button *n* : botón *m* — ~ *vt* : abotonar — *vi or* ~ **up** : abotonarse — **buttonhole** *n* : ojal *m* — ~ *vt* **-holed; -holing** : acorralar

buy *vt* **bought; buying** : comprar — ~ *n* : compra *f* — **buyer** *n* : comprador *m*, -dora *f*

buzz *vi* : zumbar — ~ *n* : zumbido *m*

buzzard *n* : buitre *m*

buzzer *n* : timbre *m*

by *prep* **1** NEAR : cerca de **2** VIA : por **3** PAST : por, por delante de **4** DURING : de, durante **5** (*in expressions of time*) : para **6** (*indicating cause or agent*) : por, de, a — ~ *adv* **1** ~ **and** ~ : poco después **2** ~ **and large** : en general **3 go** ~ : pasar **4 stop** ~ : pasar por casa

bygone *adj* : pasado — ~ *n* **let** ~**s be** ~**s** : lo pasado, pasado está

bypass *n* : carretera *f* de circunvalación — ~ *vt* : evitar

by–product *n* : subproducto *m*

bystander *n* : espectador *m*, -dora *f*

byte *n* : byte *m*, octeto *m*

byword *n* **be a** ~ **for** : estar sinónimo de

C

c *n, pl* **c's** *or* **cs** : c, tercera letra del alfabeto inglés

cab *n* **1** : taxi *m* **2** : cabina *f* (de un camión, etc.)

cabbage *n* : col *f*, repollo *m*

cabin *n* **1** : cabaña *f* **2** : cabina *f* (de un avión, etc.), camarote *m* (de un barco)

cabinet *n* **1** CUPBOARD : armario *m* **2** : gabinete *m* (del gobierno) **3** *or* **medicine** ~ : botiquín *m*

cable *n* : cable *m* — **cable television** *n* : televisión *f* por cable

cackle *vi* **-led; -ling 1** CLUCK : cacarear **2** LAUGH : reírse a carcajadas

cactus *n, pl* **cacti** *or* **-tuses** : cactus *m*

cadence *n* : cadencia *f*, ritmo *m*

cadet *n* : cadete *mf*

café *n* : café *m*, cafetería *f* — **cafeteria** *n* : restaurante *m* autoservicio, cantina *f*

caffeine *n* : cafeína *f*

cage *n* : jaula *f* — ~ *vt* **caged; caging** : enjaular

cajole *vt* **-joled; -joling** : engatusar

cake *n* **1** : pastel *m*, torta *f* **2** : pastilla *f* (de jabón) **3 take the** ~ : ser el colmo — **caked** *adj* ~ **with** : cubierto de

calamity *n, pl* **-ties** : calamidad *f*

calcium *n* : calcio *m*

calculate *v* **-lated; -lating** : calcular — **calculating** *adj* : calculador — **calculation** *n* : cálculo *m* — **calculator** *n* : calculadora *f*

calendar *n* : calendario *m*

calf¹ *n, pl* **calves 1** : becerro *m*, -rra *f*; ternero *m*, -ra *f* (de vacunos) **2** : cría *f* (de otros mamíferos)

calf² *n, pl* **calves** : pantorrilla *f* (de la pierna)

caliber *or* calibre *n* : calibre *m*

call *vi* **1** : llamar **2** VISIT : pasar, hacer (una) visita **3** ~ **for** : requerir — *vt* **1** : llamar **2** ~ **off** : cancelar — ~ *n* **1** : llamada *f* **2** SHOUT : grito *m* **3** VISIT : visita *f* **4** DEMAND : petición *f* — **calling** *n* : vocación *f*

call center *n* : centro *m* de atención (telefónica), centro *m* de llamadas

callous *adj* : insensible, cruel

calm *n* : calma *f*, tranquilidad *f* — ~ *vt* : calmar — *vi or* ~ **down** : calmarse — ~ *adj* : tranquilo, en calma — **calmly** *adv* : con calma

calorie *n* : caloría *f*

came → **come**

camel *n* : camello *m*

camera *n* : cámara *f*

camouflage *n* : camuflaje *m* — ~ *vt* -flaged; -flaging : camuflar

camp *n* **1** : campamento *m* **2** FACTION : bando *m* — ~ *vi* : acampar, ir de camping

campaign *n* : campaña *f* — ~ *vi* : hacer (una) campaña

camping *n* : camping *m*

campus *n* : ciudad *f* universitaria

can¹ *v aux, past* **could**; *present s & pl* **can 1** (*expressing possibility or permission*) : poder **2** (*expressing knowledge or ability*) : saber **3 that cannot be!** : ¡no puede ser!

can² *n* : lata *f* — ~ *vt* **canned; canning** : enlatar

Canadian *adj* : canadiense

canal *n* : canal *m*

canary *n, pl* -naries : canario *m*

cancel *vt* -celed *or* -celled; -celing *or* -celling : cancelar — **cancellation** *n* : cancelación *f*

cancer *n* : cáncer *m* — **cancerous** *adj* : canceroso

candelabra *n, pl* -bra *or* -bras : candelabro *m*

candid *adj* : franco

candidate *n* : candidato *m*, -ta *f* — **candidacy** *n, pl* -cies : candidatura *f*

candle *n* : vela *f* — **candlestick** *n* : candelero *m*

candor *or Brit* candour *n* : franqueza *f*

candy *n, pl* -dies : dulce *m*, caramelo *m*

cane *n* **1** : bastón *m* (para andar), vara *f* (para castigar) **2** REED : caña *f*, mimbre *m* — ~ *vt* **caned; caning 1** : tapizar con mimbre **2** FLOG : azotar

canine *n or* ~ **tooth** : colmillo *m*, diente *m* canino — ~ *adj* : canino

canister *n* : lata *f*, bote *m* Spain

cannibal *n* : caníbal *mf*

cannon *n, pl* -nons *or* -non : cañón *m*

cannot (can not) → **can¹**

canny *adj* **cannier; -est** : astuto

canoe *n* : canoa *f*, piragua *f* — ~ *vt* -noed; -noeing : ir en canoa

canon *n* : canon *m* — **canonize** *vt* -ized; -izing : canonizar

can opener *n* : abrelatas *m*

canopy *n, pl* -pies : dosel *m*

can't (*contraction of* **can not**) → **can¹**

cantaloupe *n* : melón *m*, cantalupo *m*

cantankerous *adj* : irritable, irascible

canteen *n* **1** FLASK : cantimplora *f* **2** CAFETERIA : cantina *f*

canter *vi* : ir a medio galope — ~ *n* : medio galope *m*

canvas *n* **1** : lona *f* (tela) **2** : lienzo *m* (de pintar)

canvass *vt* **1** : solicitar votos de, hacer campaña entre **2** POLL : sondear — ~ *n* **1** : solicitación *f* (de votos) **2** POLL : sondeo *m*

canyon *n* : cañón *m*

cap *n* **1** : gorra *f*, gorro *m* **2** TOP : tapa *f*, tapón *m* (de botellas) **3** LIMIT : tope *m* — ~ *vt* **capped; capping 1** COVER : tapar, cubrir **2** OUTDO : superar

capable *adj* : capaz, competente — **capability** *n, pl* -ties : capacidad *f*

capacity *n, pl* -ties **1** : capacidad *f* **2** ROLE : calidad *f*

cape¹ *n* : cabo *m* (en geografía)

cape² *n* CLOAK : capa *f*

caper¹ *n* : alcaparra *f*

caper² *n* PRANK : broma *f*, travesura *f*

capital *adj* **1** : capital **2** : mayúsculo (dícese de las letras) — ~ *n* **1** *or* ~ **city** : capital *f* **2** WEALTH : capital *m* **3** *or* ~ **letter** : mayúscula *f* — **capitalism** *n* : capitalismo *m* — **capitalist** *or* **capitalistic** *adj* : capitalista — **capitalize** *vt* -ized; -izing **1** FINANCE : capitalizar **2** : escribir con mayúscula — *vi* ~ **on** : sacar partido de

capitol *n* : capitolio *m*

capitulate *vi* -lated; -lating : capitular

capsize *v* -sized; -sizing *vt* : hacer volcar — *vi* : zozobrar, volcar(se)

capsule *n* : cápsula *f*

captain *n* : capitán *m*, -tana *f*

caption *n* **1** : leyenda *f* (al pie de una ilustración) **2** SUBTITLE : subtítulo *m*

captivate *vt* -vated; -vating : cautivar, encantar

captive *adj* : cautivo — ~ *n* : cautivo *m*, -va *f* — **captivity** *n* : cautiverio *m*

capture *n* : captura *f*, apresamiento *m* — ~ *vt* -tured; -turing **1** SEIZE : capturar, apresar **2 ~ one's interest** : captar el interés de uno

car n **1** : automóvil m, coche m, carro m Lat **2** or **railroad ~** : vagón m

carafe n : garrafa f

caramel n : caramelo m, azúcar f quemada

carat n : quilate m

caravan n : caravana f

carbohydrate n : carbohidrato m, hidrato m de carbono

carbon n : carbono m — **carbon copy** n : copia f, duplicado m

carbon dioxide n : dióxido m de carbono

carbon footprint n : huella f de carbono

carbon monoxide n : monóxido m de carbono

carburetor n : carburador m

carcass n : cuerpo m (de un animal muerto)

card n **1** : tarjeta f **2** or **playing ~** : carta f, naipe m — **cardboard** n : cartón m

cardiac adj : cardíaco

cardigan n : cárdigan m

cardinal n : cardenal m — **~** adj : cardinal, fundamental

care n **1** : cuidado m **2** WORRY : preocupación **3 take ~ of** : cuidar (de) — **~** vi **cared; caring 1** : preocuparse, inquietarse **2 ~ for** TEND : cuidar (de), atender **3 ~ for** LIKE : querer **4 I don't ~** : no me importa

career n : carrera f — **~** vi : ir a toda velocidad

carefree adj : despreocupado

careful adj : cuidadoso — **carefully** adv : con cuidado, cuidadosamente — **careless** adj : descuidado — **carelessness** n : descuido m

caress n : caricia f — **~** vt : acariciar

cargo n, pl **-goes** or **-gos** : cargamento m, carga f

caricature n : caricatura f — **~** vt **-tured; -turing** : caricaturizar

caring adj : solícito, afectuoso

carnage n : matanza f, carnicería f

carnal adj : carnal

carnation n : clavel m

carnival n : carnaval m

carol n : villancico m

carp vi **~ at** : quejarse de

carpenter n : carpintero m, -ra f — **carpentry** n : carpintería f

carpet n : alfombra f

carriage n **1** : transporte m (de mercancías) **2** BEARING : porte m **3** or **baby ~** : cochecito m **4** or **horse–drawn ~** : carruaje m, coche m

carrier n **1** : transportista mf, empresa f de transportes **2** : portador m, -dora f (de una enfermedad)

carrot n : zanahoria f

carry v **-ried; -rying** vt **1** : llevar **2** TRANSPORT : transportar **3** STOCK : vender **4** ENTAIL : acarrear, implicar **5 ~ oneself** : portarse — vi : oírse (dícese de sonidos) — **carry away** vt **get carried away** : exaltarse, entusiasmarse — **carry on** vt CONDUCT : realizar — vi **1** : portarse inapropiadamente **2** CONTINUE : seguir, continuar — **carry out** vt **1** PERFORM : llevar a cabo, realizar **2** FULFILL : cumplir

cart n : carreta f, carro m — **~** vt or **~ around** : acarrear

cartilage n : cartílago m

carton n : caja f (de cartón)

cartoon n **1** : caricatura f **2** COMIC STRIP : historieta f **3** or **animated ~** : dibujos mpl animados

cartridge n : cartucho m

carve vt **carved; carving 1** : tallar, esculpir **2** : trinchar (carne)

case n **1** : caso m **2** BOX : caja f **3 in any ~** : en todo caso **4 in ~ of** : en caso de **5 just in ~** : por si acaso

cash register n : caja f registradora

cash n : efectivo m, dinero m en efectivo — **~** vt : convertir en efectivo, cobrar

cashew n : anacardo m

cashier n : cajero m, -ra f

cashmere n : cachemira f

casino n, pl **-nos** : casino m

cask n : barril m

casket n : ataúd m

casserole n **1** or **~ dish** : cazuela f **2** : guiso m (comida)

cassette n : cassette mf

cast iron n : hierro m fundido

cast vt **cast; casting 1** THROW : arrojar, lanzar **2** : depositar (un voto) **3** : repartir (papeles dramáticos) **4** MOLD : fundir — **~** n **1** : elenco m, reparto m (de actores) **2** or **plaster ~** : molde m de yeso, escayola f

castanets npl : castañuelas fpl

castaway n : náufrago m, -ga f

castle n **1** : castillo m **2** : torre f (en ajedrez)

castrate vt **-trated; -trating** : castrar

casual adj **1** CHANCE : casual, fortuito **2** INDIFFERENT : despreocupado **3** INFORMAL : informal — **casually** adv **1** : de manera despreocupada **2** INFORMALLY : informalmente

casualty n, pl **-ties 1** : accidente m **2** VICTIM : víctima f; herido m, -da f **3 casualties** npl : bajas fpl (militares)

cat n : gato m, -ta f

catalog or **catalogue** n : catálogo m — **~** vt **-loged** or **-logued; -loging** or **-loguing** : catalogar

catapult n : catapulta f

cataract *n* : catarata *f*

catastrophe *n* : catástrofe *f* — **catastrophic** *adj* : catastrófico

catch *v* **caught; catching** *vt* **1** CAPTURE, TRAP : capturar, atrapar **2** SURPRISE : sorprender **3** GRASP : agarrar, captar **4** SNAG : enganchar **5** : tomar (un tren, etc.) **6 ~ a cold** : resfriarse — *vi* **1** SNAG : engancharse **2 ~ fire** : prender fuego — **catching** *adj* : contagioso — **catchy** *adj* **catchier; -est** : pegadizo, pegajoso *Lat*

category *n, pl* **-ries** : categoría *f* — **categorical** *adj* : categórico

cater *vi* **1** : proveer comida **2 ~ to** : atender a — **caterer** *n* : proveedor *m*, -dora *f* de comida

caterpillar *n* : oruga *f*

catfish *n* : bagre *m*

cathedral *n* : catedral *f*

catholic *adj* **1** : universal **2 Catholic** : católico — **catholicism** *n* : catolicismo *m*

cattle *npl* : ganado *m* (vacuno)

caught → **catch**

cauldron *n* : caldera *f*

cauliflower *n* : coliflor *f*

cause *n* **1** : causa *f* **2** REASON : motivo *m* — **~** *vt* **caused; causing** : causar

caustic *adj* : cáustico

caution *n* **1** WARNING : advertencia *f* **2** CARE : precaución *f*, cautela *f* — **~** *vt* : advertir — **cautious** *adj* : cauteloso, precavido — **cautiously** *adv* : con precaución

cavalier *adj* : arrogante, desdeñoso

cavalry *n, pl* **-ries** : caballería *f*

cave *n* : cueva *f* — **~** *vi* **caved; caving** *or* **~ in** : hundirse

cavern *n* : caverna *f*

cavity *n, pl* **-ties** **1** : cavidad *f* **2** : caries *f* (dental)

cavort *vi* : brincar

CD *n* : CD *m*, disco *m* compacto

cease *v* **ceased; ceasing** *vt* : dejar de — *vi* : cesar — **cease-fire** *n* : alto *m* el fuego — **ceaseless** *adj* : incesante

cedar *n* : cedro *m*

ceiling *n* : techo *m*

celebrate *v* **-brated; -brating** *vt* : celebrar — *vi* : divertirse — **celebrated** *adj* : célebre — **celebration** *n* **1** : celebración *f* **2** FESTIVITY : fiesta *f* — **celebrity** *n, pl* **-ties** : celebridad *f*

celery *n, pl* **-eries** : apio *m*

cell *n* **1** : célula *f* **2** : celda *f* (en una cárcel, etc.)

cellar *n* **1** BASEMENT : sótano *m* **2** : bodega *f* (de vinos)

cello *n, pl* **-los** : violoncelo *m*

cell phone *n* : teléfono *m* celular

cellular *adj* : celular

cellulite *n* : celulitis *f*

cement *n* : cemento *m* — **~** *vt* : cementar

cemetery *n, pl* **-teries** : cementerio *m*

censor *vt* : censurar — **censorship** *n* : censura *f* — **censure** *n* : censura *f* — **~** *vt* **-sured; -suring** : censurar, criticar

census *n* : censo *m*

cent *n* : centavo *m*

centennial *n* : centenario *m*

center *or Brit* **centre** *n* : centro *m* — **~** *v* **centered** *or Brit* **centred; centering** *or Brit* **centring** *vt* : centrar — *vi* **~ on** : centrarse en

centigrade *adj* : centígrado

centimeter *n* : centímetro *m*

centipede *n* : ciempiés *m*

central *adj* **1** : central **2 a ~ location** : un lugar céntrico — **centralize** *vt* **-ized; -izing** : centralizar

centre → **center**

century *n, pl* **-ries** : siglo *m*

ceramics *npl* : cerámica *f*

cereal *n* : cereal *m*

ceremony *n, pl* **-nies** : ceremonia *f* — **ceremonial** *adj* : ceremonial

certain *adj* **1** : cierto **2 be ~ of** : estar seguro de **3 for ~** : seguro, con toda seguridad **4 make ~ of** : asegurarse de — **certainly** *adv* : desde luego, por supuesto — **certainty** *n, pl* **-ties** : certeza *f*, seguridad *f*

certify *vt* **-fied; -fying** : certificar — **certificate** *n* : certificado *m*, partida *f*, acta *f*

chafe *v* **chafed; chafing** *vi* : rozarse — *vt* : rozar

chain *n* **1** : cadena *f* **2 ~ of events** : serie *f* de acontecimientos — **~** *vt* : encadenar

chair *n* **1** : silla *f* **2** : cátedra *f* (en una universidad) — **~** *vt* : presidir — **chairman** *n, pl* **-men** : presidente *m* — **chairperson** *n* : presidente *m*, -ta *f*

chalk *n* : tiza *f*, gis *m Lat*

challenge *vt* **-lenged; -lenging** **1** DISPUTE : disputar, poner en duda **2** DARE : desafiar — **~** *n* : reto *m*, desafío *m* — **challenging** *adj* : estimulante

chamber *n* : cámara *f* — **chambermaid** *n* : camarera *f*

champagne *n* : champaña *m*, champán *m*

champion *n* : campeón *m*, -peona *f* — **~** *vt* : defender — **championship** *n* : campeonato *m*

chance *n* **1** LUCK : azar *m*, suerte *f* **2** OPPORTUNITY : oportunidad *f* **3** LIKELIHOOD : probabilidad *f* **4 by ~** : por casualidad **5 take a ~** : arriesgarse — **~** *vt* **chanced; chancing** RISK : arriesgar — **~** *adj* : fortuito

chandelier *n* : araña *f* (de luces)

change *v* **changed; changing** *vt* **1** : cambiar **2** SWITCH : cambiar de — *vi* **1** : cambiar **2** *or* ~ **clothes** : cambiarse (de ropa) — ~ *n* : cambio *m* — **changeable** *adj* : cambiable

channel *n* **1** : canal *m* **2** : cauce *m* (de un río) **3** MEANS : vía *f*, medio *m*

channel surfing *n* : zapping *m*

chant *v* : cantar — ~ *n* : canto *m*

chaos *n* : caos *m* — **chaotic** *adj* : caótico

chap¹ *vi* **chapped; chapping** : agrietarse

chap² *n* : tipo *m fam*

chapel *n* : capilla *f*

chaperon *or* chaperone *n* : acompañante *mf*

chaplain *n* : capellán *m*

chapter *n* : capítulo *m*

char *vt* **charred; charring** : carbonizar

character *n* **1** : carácter *m* **2** : personaje *m* (en una novela, etc.) — **characteristic** *adj* : característico — ~ *n* : característica *f* — **characterize** *vt* **-ized; -izing** : caracterizar

charcoal *n* : carbón *m*

charge *n* **1** : carga *f* (eléctrica) **2** COST : precio *m* **3** BURDEN : carga *f*, peso *m* **4** ACCUSATION : cargo *m*, acusación *f* **5 in** ~ **of** : encargado de **6 take** ~ **of** : hacerse cargo de — ~ *v* **charged; charging** *vt* **1** : cargar **2** ENTRUST : encargar **3** COMMAND : ordenar, mandar **4** ACCUSE : acusar — *vi* **1** : cargar **2** ~ **too much** : cobrar demasiado

charisma *n* : carisma *m* — **charismatic** *adj* : carismático

charity *n, pl* **-ties 1** : organización *f* benéfica **2** GOODWILL : caridad *f*

charlatan *n* : charlatán *m*, -tana *f*

charm *n* **1** : encanto *m* **2** SPELL : hechizo *m* — ~ *vt* : encantar, cautivar — **charming** *adj* : encantador

chart *n* **1** MAP : carta *f* **2** DIAGRAM : gráfico *m*, tabla *f* — ~ *vt* : trazar un mapa de

charter *n* : carta *f* — ~ *vt* : alquilar, fletar

chase *n* : persecución *f* — ~ *vt* **chased; chasing 1** PURSUE : perseguir **2** *or* ~ **away** : ahuyentar

chasm *n* : abismo *m*

chaste *adj* **chaster; -est** : casto — **chastity** *n* : castidad *f*

chat *vi* **chatted; chatting** : charlar — ~ *n* : charla *f* — **chatter** *vi* **1** : parlotear *fam* **2** : castañetear (dícese de los dientes) — ~ *n* : parloteo *m*, cháchara *f* — **chatterbox** *n* : parlanchín *m*, -china *f* — **chatty** *adj* **chattier; chattiest 1** : parlanchín **2** INFORMAL : familiar

chat room *n* : (sala *f* de) chat *m*

chauffeur *n* : chofer *mf*

chauvinist *or* **chauvinistic** *adj* : chauvinista, patriotero

cheap *adj* **1** INEXPENSIVE : barato **2** SHODDY : de baja calidad — ~ *adv* : barato

— **cheapen** *vt* : rebajar — **cheaply** *adv* : barato, a precio bajo

cheat *vt* : defraudar, estafar — *vi* **1** : hacer trampa(s) **2** ~ **on s.o.** : engañar a algn — ~ *or* **cheater** *n* : tramposo *m*, -sa *f*

check *n* **1** RESTRAINT : freno *m* **2** INSPECTION : inspección *f*, comprobación *f* **3** DRAFT : cheque *m* **4** BILL : cuenta *f* **5** : jaque *m* (en ajedrez) **6** : tela *f* a cuadros — ~ *vt* **1** RESTRAIN : frenar, contener **2** INSPECT : revisar **3** VERIFY : comprobar **4** : dar jaque (en ajedrez) **5** ~ **in** : enregistrarse (en un hotel) **6** ~ **out** : irse (de un hotel) **7** ~ **out** VERIFY : verificar, comprobar

checkers *n* : damas *fpl*

checkmate *n* : jaque *m* mate

checkpoint *n* : puesto *m* de control

checkup *n* : chequeo *m*, examen *m* médico

cheek *n* : mejilla *f*

cheer *n* **1** CHEERFULNESS : alegría *f* **2** APPLAUSE : aclamación *f* **3** ~**s!** : ¡salud! — ~ *vt* **1** GLADDEN : alegrar **2** APPLAUD, SHOUT : aclamar, aplaudir — **cheerful** *adj* : alegre

cheese *n* : queso *m*

cheetah *n* : guepardo *m*

chef *n* : chef *m*

chemical *adj* : químico — ~ *n* : sustancia *f* química — **chemist** *n* : químico *m*, -ca *f* — **chemistry** *n, pl* **-tries** : química *f*

chemical weapon *n* : arma *f* química

cheque *Brit* → **check**

cherish *vt* **1** : querer, apreciar **2** HARBOR : abrigar (un recuerdo, una esperanza, etc.)

cherry *n, pl* **-ries** : cereza *f*

chess *n* : ajedrez *m*

chest *n* **1** BOX : cofre *m* **2** : pecho *m* (del cuerpo) **3** *or* ~ **of drawers** : cómoda *f*

chestnut *n* : castaña *f*

chew *vt* : masticar, mascar — **chewing gum** *n* : chicle *m*

chic *adj* : elegante

chick *n* : polluelo *m*, -la *f* — **chicken** *n* : pollo *m* — **chicken pox** *n* : varicela *f*

chicory *n, pl* **-ries 1** : endivia *f* (para ensaladas) **2** : achicoria *f* (aditivo de café)

chief *adj* : principal — ~ *n* : jefe *m*, -fa *f* — **chiefly** *adv* : principalmente

child *n, pl* **children 1** : niño *m*, -ña *f* **2** OFFSPRING : hijo *m*, -ja *f* — **childbirth** *n* : parto *m* — **childhood** *n* : infancia *f*, niñez *f* — **childish** *adj* : infantil — **childlike** *adj* : infantil, inocente — **childproof** *adj* : a prueba de niños

Chilean *adj* : chileno

chili *or* **chile** *or* **chilli** *n, pl* **chilies** *or* **chiles** *or* **chillies 1** *or* ~ **pepper** : chile *m* **2** : chile *m* con carne

chill *n* **1** CHILLINESS : frío *m* **2 catch a** ~

: resfriarse **3 there's a ~ in the air** : hace fresco — ~ *adj* : frío — ~ *v* : enfriar —
chilly *adj* **chillier; -est** : fresco, frío
chime *vi* **chimed; chiming** : repicar, sonar — ~ *n* : carillón *m*
chimney *n, pl* **-neys** : chimenea *f*
chimpanzee *n* : chimpancé *m*
chin *n* : barbilla *f*
china *n* : porcelana *f*, loza *f*
Chinese *adj* : chino — ~ *n* : chino *m* (idioma)
chink *n* : grieta *f*
chip *n* **1** : astilla *f* (de madera o vidrio), lasca *f* (de piedra) **2** : ficha *f* (de póker, etc.) **3** NICK : desportilladura *f* **4** *or* **computer ~** : chip *m* **5** → **potato chips** — ~ *v* **chipped; chipping** *vt* : desportillar — *vi* **1** : desportillarse **2 ~ in** : contribuir
chipmunk *n* : ardilla *f* listada
chiropodist *n* : podólogo *m*, -ga *f*
chiropractor *n* : quiropráctico *m*, -ca *f*
chirp *vi* : piar, gorjear
chisel *n* : cincel *m* (para piedras, etc.), formón *m*, escoplo *m* (para madera) — ~ *vt* **-eled** *or* **-elled; -eling** *or* **-elling** : cincelar, tallar
chit *n* : nota *f*
chitchat *n* : cháchara *f fam*
chivalrous *adj* : caballeroso — **chivalry** *n, pl* **-ries** : caballerosidad *f*
chive *n* : cebollino *m*
chlorine *n* : cloro *m*
chock–full *adj* : repleto, atestado
chocolate *n* : chocolate *m*
choice *n* **1** : elección *f*, selección *f* **2** PREFERENCE : preferencia *f* — ~ *adj* **choicer; -est** : selecto
choir *n* : coro *m*
choke *v* **choked; choking** *vt* **1** : asfixiar, estrangular **2** BLOCK : atascar — *vi* : asfixiarse, atragantarse (con comida) — ~ *n* : estárter *m* (de un motor)
choose *v* **chose; chosen; choosing** *vt* **1** SELECT : escoger, elegir **2** DECIDE : decidir — *vi* : escoger — **choosy** *or* **choosey** *adj* **choosier; -est** : exigente
chop *vt* **chopped; chopping 1** : cortar, picar (carne, etc.) **2 ~ down** : talar — ~ *n* : chuleta *f* (de cerdo, etc.) — **choppy** *adj* **-pier; -est** : picado, agitado
chopsticks *npl* : palillos *mpl*
chord *n* : acorde *m* (en música)
chore *n* **1** : tarea *f* **2 household ~s** : faenas *fpl* domésticas
choreography *n, pl* **-phies** : coreografía *f*
chortle *vi* **-tled; -tling** : reírse (con satisfacción o júbilo)
chorus 1 : coro *m* (grupo de personas) **2** REFRAIN : estribillo *m*
chose, chosen → **choose**

christen *vt* : bautizar — **christening** *n* : bautizo *m*
Christian *n* : cristiano *m*, -na *f* — ~ *adj* : cristiano — **Christianity** *n* : cristianismo *m*
Christmas *n* : Navidad *f*
chrome *n* : cromo *m*
chronic *adj* : crónico
chronicle *n* : crónica *f*
chronology *n, pl* **-gies** : cronología *f* — **chronological** *adj* : cronológico
chrysanthemum *n* : crisantemo *m*
chubby *adj* **-bier; -est** : regordete *fam*, rechoncho *fam*
chuck *vt* : tirar, arrojar
chuckle *vi* **-led; -ling** : reírse (entre dientes) — ~ *n* : risa *f* ahogada
chum *n* : amigo *m*, -ga *f*; compinche *mf fam* — **chummy** *adj* **-mier; -est** : muy amigable
chunk *n* : trozo *m*, pedazo *m*
church *n* : iglesia *f*
churn *n* : mantequera *f* — ~ *vt* **1** : agitar **2 ~ out** : producir en grandes cantidades
chute *n* **1** : vertedor *m* **2** SLIDE : tobogán *m*
cider *n* : sidra *f*
cigar *n* : puro *m* — **cigarette** *n* : cigarrillo *m*, cigarro *m*
cinch *n* **it's a ~** : es pan comido
cinema *n* : cine *m*
cinnamon *n* : canela *f*
cipher *n* **1** ZERO : cero *m* **2** CODE : cifra *f*
circa *prep* : hacia
circle *n* : círculo *m* — ~ *v* **-cled; -cling** *vt* **1** : dar vueltas alrededor de **2** : trazar un círculo alrededor de (un número, etc.) — *vi* : dar vueltas
circuit *n* : circuito *m* — **circuitous** *adj* : tortuoso
circular *adj* : circular — ~ *n* LEAFLET : circular *f*
circulate *v* **-lated; -lating** *vt* : hacer circular — *vi* : circular — **circulation** *n* **1** : circulación *f* **2** : tirada *f* (de una publicación)
circumcise *vt* **-cised; -cising** : circuncidar — **circumcision** *n* : circuncisión *f*
circumference *n* : circunferencia *f*
circumspect *adj* : circunspecto, prudente
circumstance *n* **1** : circunstancia *f* **2 under no ~s** : bajo ningún concepto
circus *n* : circo *m*
cistern *n* : cisterna *f*
cite *vt* **cited; citing** : citar — **citation** *n* : citación *f*
citizen *n* : ciudadano *m*, -na *f* — **citizenship** *n* : ciudadanía *f*
citrus *n, pl* **-rus** *or* **-ruses** *or* **~ fruit** : cítrico *m*
city *n, pl* **cities** : ciudad *f*
civic *adj* : cívico — **civics** *ns & pl* : civismo *m*

203

clog

civil *adj* : civil — **civilian** *n* : civil *mf* — **civility** *n, pl* **-ties** : cortesía *f* — **civilization** *n* : civilización *f* — **civilize** *vt* **-lized; -lizing** : civilizar

clad *adj* ~ **in** : vestido de

claim *vt* **1** DEMAND : reclamar **2** MAINTAIN : afirmar, sostener **3** ~ **responsibility** : atribuirse la responsabilidad — ~ *n* **1** DEMAND : demanda *f*, reclamación *f* **2** ASSERTION : afirmación *f*

clam *n* : almeja *f*

clamber *vi* : trepar (con torpeza)

clammy *adj* **-mier; -est** : húmedo y algo frío

clamor *n* : clamor *m* — ~ *vi* : clamar

clamp *n* : abrazadera *f* — ~ *vt* : sujetar con abrazaderas — *vi* ~ **down on** : reprimir

clan *n* : clan *m*

clandestine *adj* : clandestino

clang *n* : ruido *m* metálico

clap *v* **clapped; clapping** *vt* **1** : aplaudir **2** ~ **one's hands** : dar palmadas — *vi* : aplaudir — ~ *n* : palmada *f*

clarify *vt* **-fied; -fying** : aclarar — **clarification** *n* : clarificación *f*

clarinet *n* : clarinete *m*

clarity *n* : claridad *f*

clash *vi* **1** : chocar, enfrentarse **2** CONFLICT : estar en conflicto — ~ *n* **1** CRASH : choque *m* **2** CONFLICT : conflicto *m*

clasp *n* : broche *m*, cierre *m* — ~ *vt* **1** : abrazar (a una persona), agarrar (una cosa) **2** FASTEN : abrochar

class *n* : clase *f*

classic *or* **classical** *adj* : clásico — **classic** *n* : clásico *m*

classify *vt* **-fied; -fying** : clasificar — **classification** *n* : clasificación *f* — **classified** *adj* RESTRICTED : secreto

classmate *n* : compañero *m*, -ra *f* de clase

classroom *n* : aula *f*, salón *m* de clase

clatter *vi* : hacer ruido — ~ *n* : estrépito *m*

clause *n* : cláusula *f*

claustrophobia *n* : claustrofobia *f*

claw *n* : garra *f*, uña *f* (de un gato), pinza *f* (de un crustáceo) — ~ *v* : arañar

clay *n* : arcilla *f*

clean *adj* **1** : limpio **2** UNADULTERATED : puro **3** SPOTLESS : impecable — ~ *vt* : limpiar — ~ *adv* : limpio — **cleaner** *n* **1** : limpiador *m*, -dora *f* **2** DRY CLEANER : tintorería *f* — **cleanliness** *n* : limpieza *f* — **cleanse** *vt* **cleansed; cleansing** : limpiar, purificar

clean sweep *n* : barrida *f* (en una competencia)

clear *adj* **1** : claro **2** TRANSPARENT : transparente **3** UNOBSTRUCTED : despejado, libre — ~ *vt* **1** : despejar (una superficie), desatascar (un tubo, etc.) **2** EXONERATE : absolver **3** : saltar por encima de (un ob-

stáculo) **4** ~ **the table** : levantar la mesa **5** ~ **up** RESOLVE : aclarar, resolver — *vi* **1** ~ **up** BRIGHTEN : despejarse (dícese del tiempo, etc.) **2** ~ **up** VANISH : desaparecer (dícese de una infección, etc.) — ~ *adv* **1** **make oneself** ~ : explicarse **2** **stand** ~ **!** : ¡aléjate! — **clearance** *n* **1** SPACE : espacio *m* (libre) **2** AUTHORIZATION : autorización *f* **3** ~ **sale** : liquidación *f* — **clearing** *n* : claro *m* — **clearly** *adv* **1** DISTINCTLY : claramente **2** OBVIOUSLY : obviamente

cleaver *n* : cuchillo *m* de carnicero

clef *n* : clave *f*

cleft *n* : hendidura *f*, grieta *f*

clement *adj* : clemente — **clemency** *n* : clemencia *f*

clench *vt* : apretar

clergy *n, pl* **-gies** : clero *m* — **clergyman** *n, pl* **-men** : clérigo *m* — **clerical** *adj* **1** : clerical **2** ~ **work** : trabajo *m* de oficina

clerk *n* **1** : oficinista *mf*; empleado *m*, -da *f* de oficina **2** SALESPERSON : dependiente *m*, -ta *f*

clever *adj* **1** SKILLFUL : ingenioso, hábil **2** SMART : listo, inteligente — **cleverly** *adv* : ingeniosamente — **cleverness** *n* **1** SKILL : ingenio *m* **2** INTELLIGENCE : inteligencia *f*

cliché *n* : cliché *m*

click *vt* : chasquear — *vi* **1** : chasquear **2** GET ALONG : llevarse bien — ~ *n* : chasquido *m*

client *n* : cliente *m*, -ta *f* — **clientele** *n* : clientela *f*

cliff *n* : acantilado *m*

climate *n* : clima *m*

climax *n* : clímax *m*, punto *m* culminante

climb *vt* : escalar, subir a, trepar a — *vi* **1** RISE : subir **2** *or* ~ **up** : subirse, treparse — ~ *n* : subida *f*

clinch *vt* : cerrar (un acuerdo, etc.)

cling *vi* **clung; clinging** : adherirse, pegarse

clinic *n* : clínica *f* — **clinical** *adj* : clínico

clink *vi* : tintinear

clip *vt* **clipped; clipping** **1** CUT : cortar, recortar **2** FASTEN : sujetar (con un clip) — ~ *n* **1** FASTENER : clip *m* **2** **at a good** ~ : a buen trote **3** → **paper clip** — **clippers** *npl* **1** : maquinilla *f* para cortar el pelo **2** *or* **nail** ~ : cortauñas *m*

cloak *n* : capa *f*

clock **1** : reloj *m* (de pared) **2** **around the** ~ : las veinticuatro horas — **clockwise** *adv & adj* : en el sentido de las agujas del reloj — **clockwork** *n* **1** : mecanismo *m* de relojería **2** **like** ~ : con precisión

clog *n* : zueco *m* — ~ *v* **clogged; clogging** *vt* : atascar, obstruir — *vi or* ~ **up** : atascarse

cloister *n* : claustro *m*

clone¹ *n* **1** : clon *m* (de un organismo) **2** COPY : copia *f*, reproducción *f*

clone² *vt* : clonar

close¹ *v* **closed; closing** *vt* : cerrar — *vi* **1** : cerrarse **2** TERMINATE : terminar **3** ~ **in** : acercarse — ~ *n* : final *m*

close² *adj* **closer; closest 1** NEAR : cercano, próximo **2** INTIMATE : íntimo **3** STRICT : estricto **4** STUFFY : sofocante **5 a** ~ **game** : un juego reñido — ~ *adv* : cerca, de cerca — **closely** *adv* : cerca, de cerca — **closeness** *n* **1** NEARNESS : cercanía *f* **2** INTIMACY : intimidad *f*

closet *n* : armario *m*, clóset *m Lat*

closure *n* : cierre *m*

clot *n* : coágulo *m* — ~ *v* **clotted; clotting** *vt* : coagular, cuajar — *vi* : coagularse

cloth *n*, *pl* **cloths 1** FABRIC : tela *f* **2** RAG : trapo *m*

clothe *vt* **clothed** *or* **clad; clothing** : vestir — **clothes** *npl* **1** : ropa *f* **2 put on one's** ~ : vestirse — **clothespin** *n* : pinza *f* (para la ropa) — **clothing** *n* : ropa *f*

cloud *n* : nube *f* — ~ *vt* : nublar — *vi or* ~ **over** : nublarse — **cloudy** *adj* **cloudier; -est** : nublado

clout *n* **1** BLOW : golpe *m*, tortazo *m fam* **2** INFLUENCE : influencia *f*

clove *n* **1** : clavo *m* **2** : diente *m* (de ajo)

clover *n* : trébol *m*

clown *n* : payaso *m*, **-sa** *f* — ~ *or* ~ **around** *vi* : payasear

cloying *adj* : empalagoso

club *n* **1** : garrote *m*, porra *f* **2** ASSOCIATION : club *m* **3** ~**s** *mpl* : tréboles *mpl* (en los naipes) — ~ *vt* **clubbed; clubbing** : aporrear

cluck *vi* : cloquear

clue *n* **1** : pista *f*, indicio *m* **2 I haven't got a** ~ : no tengo la menor idea

clump *n* : grupo *m* (de arbustos)

clumsy *adj* **-sier; -est** : torpe — **clumsiness** *n* : torpeza *f*

cluster *n* : grupo *m*, racimo *m* (de uvas, etc.) — ~ *vi* : agruparse

clutch *vt* : agarrar, asir — *vi* ~ **at** : tratar de agarrarse de — ~ *n* : embrague *m*, clutch *m Lat* (de un automóvil)

clutter *vt* : llenar desordenadamente — ~ *n* : desorden *m*, revoltijo *m*

coach *n* **1** CARRIAGE : carruaje *m*, carroza *f* **2** : vagón *m* de pasajeros (de un tren) **3** BUS : autobús *m* **4** : pasaje *m* aéreo de segunda clase **5** TRAINER : entrenador *m*, **-dora** *f* — *vt* : entrenar (un atleta), dar clases particulares a (un alumno)

coagulate *v* **-lated; -lating** *vt* : coagular — *vi* : coagularse

coal *n* : carbón *m*

coalition *n* : coalición *f*

coarse *adj* **coarser; -est 1** : tosco, basto **2** CRUDE, VULGAR : grosero, ordinario — **coarseness** *n* : aspereza *f*, tosquedad *f*

coast guard *n* : guardacostas *mpl*

coast *n* : costa *f* — ~ *vi* : ir en punto muerto (dícese del automóvil), deslizarse (dícese de una bicicleta) — **coastal** *adj* : costero

coaster *n* : posavasos *m*

coastline *n* : litoral *m*

coat *n* **1** : abrigo *m* **2** : pelaje *m* (de un animal) **3** : mano *f* (de pintura) — ~ *vt* : cubrir, revestir — **coating** *n* : capa *f* —

coat of arms *n* : escudo *m* de armas

coax *vt* : engatusar

cob → **corncob**

cobblestone *n* : adoquín *m*

cobweb *n* : telaraña *f*

cocaine *n* : cocaína *f*

cock *n* **1** ROOSTER : gallo *m* **2** FAUCET : grifo *m* **3** : martillo *m* (de un arma de fuego) — ~ *vt* **1** : amartillar (un arma de fuego) **2** ~ **one's head** : ladear la cabeza — **cockeyed** *adj* **1** ASKEW : ladeado **2** ABSURD : absurdo

cockpit *n* : cabina *f*

cockroach *n* : cucaracha *f*

cocktail *n* : coctel *m*, cóctel *m*

cocky *adj* **cockier; -est** : engreído, arrogante

cocoa *n* **1** : cacao *m* **2** : chocolate *m* (bebida)

coconut *n* : coco *m*

cocoon *n* : capullo *m*

cod *ns & pl* : bacalao *m*

coddle *vt* **-dled; -dling** : mimar

code *n* : código *m*

coeducational *adj* : mixto

coerce *vt* **-erced; -ercing** : coaccionar, forzar — **coercion** *n* : coacción *f*

coffee *n* : café *m* — **coffeepot** *n* : cafetera *f*

coffer *n* : cofre *m*

coffin *n* : ataúd *m*, féretro *m*

cog *n* : diente *m* (de una rueda)

cogent *adj* : convincente, persuasivo

cognac *n* : coñac *m*

cogwheel *n* : rueda *f* dentada

coherent *adj* : coherente

coil *vt* : enrollar — *vi* : enrollarse — ~ *n* **1** ROLL : rollo *m* **2** : tirabuzón *m* (de pelo), espiral *f* (de humo)

coin *n* : moneda *f* — ~ *vt* : acuñar

coincide *vi* **-cided; -ciding** : coincidir — **coincidence** *n* : coincidencia *f*, casualidad *f* — **coincidental** *adj* : casual, fortuito

coke *n* : coque *m* (combustible)

colander *n* : colador *m*

cold *adj* **1** : frío **2 be** ~ : tener frío **3 it's** ~ **today** : hace frío hoy — ~ *n* **1** : frío *m*

2 : resfriado *m* (en medicina) **3 catch a ~** : resfriarse

coleslaw *n* : ensalada *f* de col

colic *n* : cólico *m*

collaborate *vi* **-rated; -rating** : colaborar — **collaboration** *n* : colaboración *f* — **collaborator** *n* : colaborador *m*, -dora *f*

collapse *vi* **-lapsed; -lapsing 1** : derrumbarse, hundirse **2** : sufrir un colapso (físico o mental) — **~** *n* **1** FALL : derrumbamiento *m* **2** BREAKDOWN : colapso *m* — **collapsible** *adj* : plegable

collar *n* : cuello *m* (de camisa, etc.), collar *m* (para animales) — **collarbone** *n* : clavícula *f*

colleague *n* : colega *mf*

collect *vt* **1** GATHER : reunir **2** : coleccionar, juntar (timbres, etc.) **3** : recaudar (fondos, etc.) — *vi* **1** ACCUMULATE : acumularse, juntarse **2** CONGREGATE : congregarse, reunirse — **~** *adv* **call ~** : llamar a cobro revertido, llamar por cobrar *Lat* — **collection** *n* **1** : colección *f* **2** : colecta *f* (de contribuciones) — **collective** *adj* : colectivo — **collector** *n* **1** : coleccionista *mf* **2** : cobrador *m*, -dora *f* (de deudas)

college *n* **1** : instituto *m* (a nivel universitario) **2** : colegio *m* (electoral, etc.)

collide *vi* **-lided; -liding** : chocar, colisionar — **collision** *n* : choque *m*, colisión *f*

colloquial *adj* : coloquial, familiar

cologne *n* : colonia *f*

Colombian *adj* : colombiano

colon[1] *n, pl* **colons** *or* **cola** : colon *m* (en anatomía)

colon[2] *n, pl* **colons** : dos puntos *mpl* (signo de puntuación)

colonel *n* : coronel *m*

colony *n, pl* **-nies** : colonia *f* — **colonial** *adj* : colonial — **colonize** *vt* **-nized; -nizing** : colonizar

color *or Brit* **colour** *n* : color. *m* — **~** *vt* : colorear, pintar — *vi* BLUSH : sonrojarse — **color–blind** *or Brit* **colour-blind** *adj* : daltónico — **colored** *or Brit* **coloured** *adj* : de color — **colorful** *or Brit* **colourful** *adj* **1** : de vivos colores **2** PICTURESQUE : pintoresco — **colorless** *or Brit* **colourless** *adj* : incoloro

colossal *adj* : colosal

colt *n* : potro *m*

column *n* : columna *f* — **columnist** *n* : columnista *mf*

coma *n* : coma *m*

comb *n* **1** : peine *m* **2** : cresta *f* (de un gallo) — **~** *vt* : peinar

combat *n* : combate *m* — **~** *vt* **-bated** *or* **-batted; -bating** *or* **-batting** : combatir — **combatant** *n* : combatiente *mf*

combine *v* **-bined; -bining** *vt* : combinar —

vi : combinarse — **~** *n* HARVESTER : cosechadora *f* — **combination** *n* : combinación *f*

combustion *n* : combustión *f*

come *vi* **came; come; coming 1** : venir **2** ARRIVE : llegar **3 ~ about** : suceder **4 ~ back** : regresar, volver **5 ~ from** : venir de, provenir de **6 ~ in** : entrar **7 ~ out** : salir **8 ~ to** REVIVE : volver en sí **9 ~ on!** : ¡ándale! **10 ~ up** OCCUR : surgir **11 how ~?** : ¿por qué? — **comeback** *n* **1** RETURN : retorno *m* **2** RETORT : réplica *f*

comedy *n, pl* **-dies** : comedia *f* — **comedian** *n* : cómico *m*, -ca *f*

comet *n* : cometa *m*

comfort *vt* : consolar — **~** *n* **1** : comodidad *f* **2** SOLACE : consuelo *m* — **comfortable** *adj* : cómodo

comic *or* **comical** *adj* : cómico — **~** *n* **1** COMEDIAN : cómico *m*, -ca *f* **2** *or* **~ book** : revista *f* de historietas, cómic *m* — **comic strip** *n* : tira *f* cómica, historieta *f*

coming *adj* : próximo, que viene

comma *n* : coma *f*

command *vt* **1** ORDER : ordenar, mandar **2** : estar al mando de (un barco, etc.) **3 ~ respect** : inspirar (el) respeto — *vi* : dar órdenes — **~** *n* **1** ORDER : orden *f* **2** LEADERSHIP : mando *m* **3** MASTERY : maestría *f*, dominio *m* — **commander** *n* : comandante *mf* — **commandment** *n* : mandamiento *m*

commemorate *vt* **-rated; -rating** : conmemorar — **commemoration** *n* : conmemoración *f*

commence *v* **-menced; -mencing** : comenzar, empezar — **commencement** *n* **1** BEGINNING : comienzo *m* **2** GRADUATION : ceremonia *f* de graduación

commend *vt* **1** ENTRUST : encomendar **2** PRAISE : alabar — **commendable** *adj* : loable

comment *n* : comentario *m*, observación *f* — **~** *vi* : hacer comentarios — **commentary** *n, pl* **-taries** : comentario *m* — **commentator** *n* : comentarista *mf*

commerce *n* : comercio *m* — **commercial** *adj* : comercial — **~** *n* : anuncio *m*, aviso *m* *Lat* — **commercialize** *vt* **-ized; -izing** : comercializar

commiserate *vi* **-ated; -ating** : compadecerse

commission *n* : comisión *f* — **~** *vt* : encargar (una obra de arte) — **commissioner** *n* : comisario *m*, -ria *f*

commit *vt* **-mitted; -mitting 1** ENTRUST : confiar **2** : cometer (un crimen) **3** : internar (a algn en un hospital) **4 ~ oneself** : comprometerse **5 ~ to memory** : aprender de memoria — **commitment** n : compromiso m

committee n : comité m, comisión f

commodity n, pl **-ties** : artículo m de comercio, producto m

common adj **1** : común **2** ORDINARY : ordinario, común y corriente — ~ n in ~ : en común — **commonly** adv : comúnmente — **commonplace** adj : común, banal — **common sense** n : sentido m común

commotion n : alboroto m, jaleo m

commune[1] n : comuna f — **communal** adj : comunal

commune[2] vi **-muned; -muning** ~ **with** : comunicarse con

communicate v **-cated; -cating** vt : comunicar — vi : comunicarse — **communicable** adj : transmisible — **communication** n : comunicación f — **communicative** adj : comunicativo

communion n : comunión f

Communism n : comunismo m — **Communist** adj : comunista — ~ n : comunista mf

community n, pl **-ties** : comunidad f

commute v **-muted; -muting** vt : conmutar, reducir (una sentencia) — vi : viajar de la residencia al trabajo

compact adj : compacto — ~ n **1** or ~ **car** : auto m compacto **2** or **powder** ~ : polvera f — **compact disc** n : disco m compacto

companion n : compañero m, -ra f — **companionship** n : compañerismo m

company n, pl **-nies 1** : compañía f **2** GUESTS : visita f

compare v **-pared; -paring** vt : comparar — vi ~ **with** : poderse comparar con — **comparable** adj : comparable — **comparative** adj : comparativo, relativo — **comparison** n : comparación f

compartment n : compartimento m

compass n **1** : compás m **2 points of the** ~ : puntos mpl cardinales

compassion n : compasión f — **compassionate** adj : compasivo

compatible adj : compatible, afín — **compatibility** n : compatibilidad f

compel vt **-pelled; -pelling** : obligar — **compelling** adj : convincente

compensate v **-sated; -sating** vi ~ **for** : compensar — vt : indemnizar, compensar — **compensation** n : compensación f, indemnización f

compete vi **-peted; -peting** : competir — **competent** adj : competente — **competition** n **1** : competencia f **2** CONTEST : concurso m — **competitor** n : competidor m, -dora f

compile vt **-piled; -piling** : compilar, recopilar

complacency n : satisfacción f consigo mismo — **complacent** adj : satisfecho de sí mismo

complain vi : quejarse — **complaint** n **1** : queja f **2** AILMENT : enfermedad f

complement n : complemento m — ~ vt : complementar — **complementary** adj : complementario

complete adj **-pleter; -est 1** WHOLE : completo, entero **2** FINISHED : terminado **3** TOTAL : total — ~ vt **-pleted; -pleting** : completar — **completion** n : conclusión f

complex adj : complejo — ~ n : complejo m

complexion n : cutis m, tez f

complexity n, pl **-ties** : complejidad f

compliance n **1** : acatamiento m **2 in** ~ **with** : conforme a — **compliant** adj : sumiso

complicate vt **-cated; -cating** : complicar — **complicated** adj : complicado — **complication** n : complicación f

compliment n **1** : cumplido m **2** ~**s** npl : saludos mpl — ~ vt : felicitar — **complimentary** adj **1** FLATTERING : halagador, halagüeño **2** FREE : de cortesía, gratis

comply vi **-plied; -plying** ~ **with** : cumplir, obedecer

component n : componente m

compose vt **-posed; -posing 1** : componer **2** ~ **oneself** : serenarse — **composer** n : compositor m, -tora f — **composition** n **1** : composición f **2** ESSAY : ensayo m — **composure** n : calma f

compound[1] vt **1** COMPOSE : componer **2** : agravar (un problema, etc.) — ~ adj : compuesto — ~ n : compuesto m

compound[2] n ENCLOSURE : recinto m

comprehend vt : comprender — **comprehension** n : comprensión f — **comprehensive** adj **1** INCLUSIVE : inclusivo **2** BROAD : amplio

compress vt : comprimir — **compression** n : compresión f

comprise vt **-prised; -prising** : comprender

compromise n : acuerdo m, arreglo m — ~ v **-mised; -mising** vi : llegar a un acuerdo — vt : comprometer

compulsion n **1** COERCION : coacción f **2** URGE : impulso m — **compulsive** adj : compulsivo — **compulsory** adj : obligatorio

compute vt **-puted; -puting** : computar — **computer** n : computadora f, computador m, ordenador m Spain — **computerize** vt **-ized; -izing** : informatizar

computer programmer n : programador m, -dora f

computer programming n : programación f

computer science n : informática f

computing n : informática f

comrade n : camarada mf

con vt **conned; conning** : estafar — ~ n **1** SWINDLE : estafa f **2 the pros and ~s** : los pros y los contras

concave adj : cóncavo

conceal vt : ocultar

concede vt **-ceded; -ceding** : conceder, admitir

conceit n : vanidad f — **conceited** adj : engreído

conceive v **-ceived; -ceiving** vt : concebir — vi ~ **of** : concebir — **conceivable** adj : concebible

concentrate v **-trated; -trating** vt : concentrar — vi : concentrarse — **concentration** n : concentración f

concept n : concepto m — **conception** n : concepción f

concern vt **1** : concernir **2** ~ **oneself about** : preocuparse por — ~ n **1** AFFAIR : asunto m **2** WORRY : preocupación f **3** BUSINESS : negocio m — **concerned** adj **1** ANXIOUS : ansioso **2 as far as I'm** ~ : en cuanto a mí — **concerning** prep : con respecto a

concert n : concierto m — **concerted** adj : concertado

concession n : concesión f

concise adj : conciso

conclude v **-cluded; -cluding** : concluir — **conclusive** adj : concluyente

conclusion n **1** INFERENCE : conclusión f **2** END : fin m, final m

concoct vt **1** PREPARE : confeccionar **2** DEVISE : inventar, tramar — **concoction** n : mezcla f, brebaje m

concourse n : vestíbulo m, salón m

concrete adj : concreto — ~ n : hormigón m, concreto m Lat

concur vi **concurred; concurring** AGREE : estar de acuerdo

concussion n : conmoción f cerebral

condemn vt : condenar — **condemnation** n : condenación f

condense v **-densed; -densing** vt : condensar — vi : condensarse — **condensation** n : condensación f

condescending adj : condescendiente

condiment n : condimento m

condition n **1** : condición f **2 in good** ~ : en buen estado — **conditional** adj : condicional

condolences npl : pésame m

condom n : condón m

condominium n, pl **-ums** : condominio m Lat

condone vt **-doned; -doning** : aprobar

conducive adj : propicio, favorable

conduct n : conducta f — ~ vt **1** DIRECT, GUIDE : conducir, dirigir **2** CARRY OUT : llevar a cabo **3** ~ **oneself** : conducirse, comportarse — **conductor** n : revisor m, -sora f (en un tren); cobrador m, -dora f (en un autobús); director m, -tora f (de una orquesta)

cone n **1** : cono m **2** or **ice–cream** ~ : cucurucho m, barquillo m Lat

confection n : dulce m

confederation n : confederación f

confer v **-ferred; -ferring** vt : conferir, otorgar — vi ~ **with** : consultar — **conference** n : conferencia f

confess vt : confesar — vi **1** : confesarse **2** ~ **to** : confesar, admitir — **confession** n : confesión f

confetti n : confeti m

confide v **-fided; -fiding** : confiar — **confidence** n **1** TRUST : confianza f **2** SELF-ASSURANCE : confianza f en sí mismo **3** SECRET : confidencia f — **confident** adj **1** SURE : seguro **2** SELF-ASSURED : confiado, seguro de sí mismo — **confidential** adj : confidencial

confine vt **-fined; -fining 1** LIMIT : confinar, limitar **2** IMPRISON : encerrar — **confines** npl : confines mpl

confirm vt : confirmar — **confirmation** n : confirmación f — **confirmed** adj : inveterado

confiscate vt **-cated; -cating** : confiscar

conflict n : conflicto m — ~ vi : estar en conflicto, oponerse

conform vi **1** COMPLY : ajustarse **2** ~ **with** : corresponder a — **conformity** n, pl **-ties** : conformidad f

confound vt : confundir, desconcertar

confront vt : afrontar, encarar — **confrontation** n : confrontación f

confuse vt **-fused; -fusing** : confundir — **confusing** adj : confuso, desconcertante — **confusion** n : confusión f, desconcierto m

congeal vi : coagularse

congenial adj : agradable

congested adj : congestionado — **congestion** n : congestión f

congratulate vt **-lated; -lating** : felicitar — **congratulations** npl : felicitaciones fpl

congregate vi **-gated; -gating** : congregarse — **congregation** n : feligreses mpl (en religión)

congress n : congreso m — **congressional** adj : del congreso — **congressman** n, pl **-men** : congresista mf

conjecture

conjecture *n* : conjetura *f*, presunción *f* —
~ *v* **-tured; -turing** *vt* : conjeturar — *vi*
: hacer conjeturas
conjugal *adj* : conyugal
conjugate *vt* **-gated; -gating** : conjugar —
conjugation *n* : conjugación *f*
conjunction *n* **1** : conjunción *f* **2 in** ~
with : en combinación con
conjure *v* **-jured; -juring** *vi* : hacer juegos de
manos — ~ *vt or* ~ **up** : evocar
connect *vi* : conectarse — *vt* **1** JOIN : conectar, juntar **2** ASSOCIATE : asociar —
connection *n* **1** : conexión *f* **2** : enlace *m*
(con un tren, etc.) **3** ~**s** *npl* : relaciones
fpl (personas)
connoisseur *n* : conocedor *m*, -dora *f*
connote *vt* **-noted; -noting** : connotar, implicar
conquer *vt* : conquistar — **conqueror** *n*
: conquistador *m*, -dora *f* — **conquest** *n*
: conquista *f*
conscience *n* : conciencia *f* — **conscientious** *adj* : concienzudo
conscious *adj* **1** AWARE : consciente **2** IN-
TENTIONAL : intencional — **consciously**
adv : deliberadamente — **consciousness** *n*
1 AWARENESS : conciencia *f* **2 lose** ~
: perder el conocimiento
consecrate *vt* **-crated; -crating** : consagrar
— **consecration** *n* : consagración *f*
consecutive *adj* : consecutivo, sucesivo
consensus *n* : consenso *m*
consent *vi* : consentir — ~ *n* : consen-
timiento *m*
consequence *n* **1** : consecuencia *f* **2 of
no** ~ : sin importancia — **consequent** *adj*
: consiguiente — **consequently** *adv* : por
consiguiente
conserve *vt* **-served; -serving** : conservar,
preservar — **conservation** *n* : conservación
f — **conservative** *adj* **1** : conservador **2**
CAUTIOUS : moderado, prudente — ~ *n*
: conservador *m*, -dora *f* — **conservatory** *n*,
pl **-ries** : conservatorio *m*
consider *vt* **1** : considerar **2 all things
considered** : teniéndolo todo en cuenta —
considerable *adj* : considerable — **considerate** *adj* : considerado — **consideration** *n*
1 : consideración *f* **2 take into** ~ : tener
en cuenta — **considering** *prep* : teniendo
en cuenta
consign *vt* **1** : relegar **2** SEND : enviar —
consignment *n* : envío *m*
consist *vi* **1** ~ **in** : consistir en **2** ~ **of**
: constar de, componerse de — **consis-
tency** *n, pl* **-cies 1** TEXTURE : consistencia
f **2** COHERENCE : coherencia *f* **3** UNIFOR-
MITY : regularidad *f* — **consistent** *adj* **1**
UNCHANGING : constante, regular **2** ~ **with**
: consecuente con

console *vt* **-soled; -soling** : consolar —
consolation *n* **1** : consuelo *m* **2** ~ **prize**
: premio *m* de consolación
consolidate *vt* **-dated; -dating** : consolidar
— **consolidation** *n* : consolidación *f*
consonant *n* : consonante *f*
conspicuous *adj* **1** OBVIOUS : visible, evidente **2** STRIKING : llamativo — **conspicu-
ously** *adv* : de manera llama- tiva
conspire *vi* **-spired; -spiring** : conspirar —
conspiracy *n, pl* **-cies** : conspiración *f*
constant *adj* : constante — **constantly** *adv*
: constantemente
constellation *n* : constelación *f*
constipated *adj* : estreñido — **constipation**
n : estreñimiento *m*
constituent *n* **1** COMPONENT : componente
m **2** VOTER : elector *m*, -tora *f*; votante
mf
constitute *vt* **-tuted; -tuting** : constituir —
constitution *n* : constitución *f* — **constitutional** *adj* : constitucional
constraint *n* : restricción *f*, limitación *f*
construct *vt* : construir — **construction** *n*
: construcción *f* — **constructive** *adj* : constructivo
construe *vt* **-strued; -struing** : interpretar
consul *n* : cónsul *mf* — **consulate** *n* : consulado *m*
consult *v* : consultar — **consultant** *n*
: asesor *m*, -sora *f*; consultor *m*, -tora *f* —
consultation *n* : consulta *f*
consume *vt* **-sumed; -suming** : consumir
— **consumer** *n* : consumidor *m*, -dora *f* —
consumption *n* : consumo *m*
consumerism *n* : consumismo *m*
contact *n* : contacto *m* — ~ *vt* : ponerse en
contacto con — **contact lens** *n* : lente *mf*
(de contacto)
contagious *adj* : contagioso
contain *vt* **1** : contener **2** ~ **oneself**
: contenerse — **container** *n* : recipiente *m*,
envase *m*
contaminate *vt* **-nated; -nating** : contaminar — **contamination** *n* : contaminación
f
contemplate *v* **-plated; -plating** *vt* **1** : contemplar **2** CONSIDER : considerar, pensar en
— *vi* : reflexionar — **contemplation** *n*
: contemplación *f*
contemporary *adj* : contemporáneo — ~
n, pl **-raries** : contemporáneo *m*, -nea *f*
contempt *n* : desprecio *m* — **contemptible**
adj : despreciable — **contemptuous** *adj*
: desdeñoso
contend *vi* **1** COMPETE : contender, competir **2** ~ **with** : enfrentarse a — *vt* : sostener, afirmar — **contender** *n* : contendiente *mf*

content[1] *n* **1** : contenido *m* **2 table of ~s** : índice *m* de materias

content[2] *adj* : contento — **~** *vt* **~ oneself with** : contentarse con — **contented** *adj* : satisfecho, contento

contention *n* **1** DISPUTE : disputa *f* **2** OPINION : argumento *m*, opinión *f*

contentment *n* : satisfacción *f*

contest *vt* : disputar — **~** *n* **1** STRUGGLE : contienda *f* **2** COMPETITION : concurso *m*, competencia *f* — **contestant** *n* : concursante *mf*, contendiente *mf*

context *n* : contexto *m*

continent *n* : continente *m* — **continental** *adj* : continental

contingency *n, pl* **-cies** : contingencia *f*

continue *v* **-tinued; -tinuing** : continuar — **continual** *adj* : continuo, constante — **continuation** *n* : continuación *f* — **continuity** *n, pl* **-ties** : continuidad *f* — **continuous** *adj* : continuo

contort *vt* : retorcer — **contortion** *n* : contorsión *f*

contour *n* **1** : contorno *m* **2** *or* **~ line** : curva *f* de nivel

contraband *n* : contrabando *m*

contraception *n* : anticoncepción *f* — **contraceptive** *adj* : anticonceptivo — **~** *n* : anticonceptivo *m*

contract *n* : contrato *m* — **~** *vt* : contraer — *vi* : contraerse — **contraction** *n* : contracción *f* — **contractor** *n* : contratista *mf*

contradiction *n* : contradicción *f* — **contradict** *vt* : contradecir — **contradictory** *adj* : contradictorio

contraption *n* : artilugio *m*, artefacto *m*

contrary *n, pl* **-traries** **1** : contrario **2 on the ~** : al contrario — **~** *adj* **1** : contrario, opuesto **2 ~ to** : en contra de

contrast *v* : contrastar — **~** *n* : contraste *m*

contribute *v* **-uted; -uting** : contribuir — **contribution** *n* : contribución *f* — **contributor** *n* **1** : contribuyente *mf* **2** : colaborador *m*, -dora *f* (en periodismo)

contrite *adj* : arrepentido

contrive *vt* **-trived; -triving** **1** DEVISE : idear **2 ~ to do sth** : lograr hacer algo

control *vt* **-trolled; -trolling** : controlar — **~** *n* **1** : control *m* **2 ~s** *npl* : mandos *mpl*

controversy *n, pl* **-sies** : controversia *f* — **controversial** *adj* : polémico

convalescence *n* : convalecencia *f* — **convalescent** *adj* : convaleciente — **~** *n* : convaleciente *mf*

convene *v* **-vened; -vening** *vt* : convocar — *vi* : reunirse

convenience *n* : conveniencia *f*, comodidad *f* — **convenient** *adj* : conveniente

convent *n* : convento *m*

convention *n* : convención *f* — **conventional** *adj* : convencional

converge *vi* **-verged; -verging** : converger, convergir

converse[1] *vi* **-versed; -versing** : conversar — **conversation** *n* : conversación *f* — **conversational** *adj* : familiar

converse[2] *adj* : contrario, opuesto — **conversely** *adv* : a la inversa

conversion *n* : conversión *f* — **convert** *vt* : convertir — *vi* : convertirse — **convertible** *adj* : convertible — **~** *n* : descapotable *m*, convertible *m Lat*

convex *adj* : convexo

convey *vt* **1** TRANSPORT : llevar, transportar **2** TRANSMIT : comunicar

convict *vt* : declarar culpable a — **~** *n* : presidiario *m*, -ria *f* — **conviction** *n* **1** : condena *f* (de un acusado) **2** BELIEF : convicción *f*

convince *vt* **-vinced; -vincing** : convencer — **convincing** *adj* : convincente

convoke *vt* **-voked; -voking** : convocar

convoluted *adj* : complicado

convulsion *n* : convulsión *f* — **convulsive** *adj* : convulsivo

cook *n* : cocinero *m*, -ra *f* — **~** *vi* : cocinar, guisar — *vt* : preparar (comida) — **cookbook** *n* : libro *m* de cocina

cookie *or* **cooky** *n, pl* **-ies** : galleta *f* (dulce)

cooking *n* : cocina *f*

cool *adj* **1** : fresco **2** CALM : tranquilo **3** UNFRIENDLY : frío — **~** *vt* : enfriar — *vi* : enfriarse — **~** *n* **1** : fresco *m* **2** COMPOSURE : calma *f* — **cooler** *n* : nevera *f* portátil — **coolness** *n* : frescura *f*

coop *n* : gallinero *m* — **~** *vt or* **~ up** : encerrar

cooperate *vi* **-ated; -ating** : cooperar — **cooperation** *n* : cooperación *f* — **cooperative** *adj* : cooperativo

coordinate *vt* **-nated; -nating** *vt* : coordinar — **coordination** *n* : coordinación *f*

cop *n* **1** : poli *mf fam* **2 the ~s** : la poli *fam*

cope *vi* **coped; coping** **1** : arreglárselas **2 ~ with** : hacer frente a, poder con

copier *n* : fotocopiadora *f*

copious *adj* : copioso

copper *n* : cobre *m*

copy *n, pl* **copies** **1** : copia *f* **2** : ejemplar *m* (de un libro), número *m* (de una revista) — **~** *vt* **copied; copying** **1** DUPLICATE : hacer una copia de **2** IMITATE : copiar — **copyright** *n* : derechos *mpl* de autor

coral *n* : coral *m*

cord *n* **1** : cuerda *f* **2** *or* **electric ~** : cable *m* (eléctrico)
cordial *adj* : cordial
corduroy *n* : pana *f*
core *n* **1** : corazón *m* (de una fruta) **2** CENTER : núcleo *m*, centro *m*
cork *n* : corcho *m* — **corkscrew** *n* : sacacorchos *m*
corn *n* **1** : grano *m* **2** *or* **Indian ~** : maíz *m* **3** : callo *m* (del pie) — **corncob** *n* : mazorca *f*
corner *n* : ángulo *m*, rincón *m* (en una habitación), esquina *f* (de una intersección) — **~** *vt* **1** TRAP : acorralar **2** MONOPOLIZE : acaparar (un mercado) — **cornerstone** *n* : piedra *f* angular
cornmeal *n* : harina *f* de maíz — **cornstarch** *n* : maicena *f*
corny *adj* : cursi, sentimental
coronary *n, pl* **-naries** : trombosis *f* coronaria
coronation *n* : coronación *f*
corporal *n* : cabo *m*
corporation *n* : sociedad *f* anónima, compañía *f* — **corporate** *adj* : corporativo
corps *n, pl* **corps** : cuerpo *m*
corpse *n* : cadáver *m*
corpulent *adj* : obeso, gordo
corpuscle *n* : glóbulo *m*
corral *n* : corral *m* — **~** *vt* **-ralled; -ralling** : acorralar
correct *vt* : corregir — **~** *adj* : correcto — **correction** *n* : corrección *f*
correlation *n* : correlación *f*
correspond *vi* **1** WRITE : corresponderse **2 ~ to** : corresponder a — **correspondence** *n* : correspondencia *f*
corridor *n* : pasillo *m*
corroborate *vt* **-rated; -rating** : corroborar
corrode *v* **-roded; -roding** *vt* : corroer — *vi* : corroerse — **corrosion** *n* : corrosión *f* — **corrosive** *adj* : corrosivo
corrugated *adj* : ondulado
corrupt *vt* : corromper — **~** *adj* : corrupto, corrompido — **corruption** *n* : corrupción *f*
corset *n* : corsé *m*
cosmetic *n* : cosmético *m* — **~** *adj* : cosmético
cosmic *adj* : cósmico
cosmopolitan *adj* : cosmopolita
cosmos *n* : cosmos *m*
cost *n* : costo *m*, coste *m* — **~** *vi* **cost; costing 1** : costar **2 how much does it ~?** : ¿cuánto cuesta?, ¿cuánto vale?
Costa Rican *adj* : costarricense
costly *adj* : costoso
costume *n* **1** OUTFIT : traje *m* **2** DISGUISE : disfraz *m*
cot *n* : catre *m*

cottage *n* : casita *f* (de campo) — **cottage cheese** *n* : requesón *m*
cotton *n* : algodón *m*
couch *n* : sofá *m*
cough *vi* : toser — **~** *n* : tos *f*
could → **can¹**
council *n* **1** : concejo *m* **2** *or* **city ~** : ayuntamiento *m* — **councillor** *or* **councilor** *n* : concejal *m*, **-jala** *f*
counsel *n* **1** ADVICE : consejo *m* **2** LAWYER : abogado *m*, **-da** *f* — **~** *vt* **-seled** *or* **-selled; -seling** *or* **-selling** : aconsejar — **counselor** *or* **counsellor** *n* : consejero *m*, **-ra** *f*
count¹ *vt* : contar — *vi* **1** : contar **2 ~ on** : contar con **3 that doesn't ~** : eso no vale — **~** *n* **1** : recuento *m* **2 keep ~ of** : llevar la cuenta de
count² *n* : conde *m* (noble)
counter¹ *n* **1** : mostrador *m* (de un negocio) **2** TOKEN : ficha *f* (de un juego)
counter² *vt* : oponerse a — *vi* : contraatacar — **~** *adv* **~ to** : contrario a — **counteract** *vt* : contrarrestar — **counterattack** *n* : contraataque *m* — **counterbalance** *n* : contrapeso *m* — **counterclockwise** *adv* & *adj* : en sentido opuesto a las agujas del reloj — **counterfeit** *vt* : falsificar — **~** *adj* : falsificado — **~** *n* : falsificación *f* — **counterpart** *n* : homólogo *m* (de una persona), equivalente *m* (de una cosa) — **counterproductive** *adj* : contraproducente
countess *n* : condesa *f*
countless *adj* : incontable, innumerable
country *n, pl* **-tries 1** NATION : país *m* **2** COUNTRYSIDE : campo *m* — **~** *adj* : campestre, rural — **countryman** *n, pl* **-men** *or* **fellow ~** : compatriota *mf* — **countryside** *n* : campo *m*, campiña *f*
county *n, pl* **-ties** : condado *m*
coup *n, pl* **coups** *or* **~ d'etat** : golpe *m* (de estado)
couple *n* **1** : pareja *f* (de personas) **2 a ~ of** : un par de — **~** *vt* **-pled; -pling** : acoplar, unir
coupon *n* : cupón *m*
courage *n* : valor *m* — **courageous** *adj* : valiente
courier *n* : mensajero *m*, **-ra** *f*
course *n* **1** : curso *m* **2** : plato *m* (de una cena) **3** *or* **golf ~** : campo *m* de golf **4 in the ~ of** : en el transcurso de **5 of ~** : desde luego, por supuesto
court *n* **1** : corte *f* (de un rey, etc.) **2** : cancha *f*, pista *f* (en deportes) **3** TRIBUNAL : corte *f*, tribunal *m* — **~** *vt* : cortejar
courteous *adj* : cortés — **courtesy** *n, pl* **-sies** : cortesía *f*
courthouse *n* : palacio *m* de justicia,

juzgado *m* — **courtroom** *n* : sala *f* (de un tribunal)

courtship *n* : cortejo *m*, noviazgo *m*

courtyard *n* : patio *m*

cousin *n* : primo *m*, -ma *f*

cove *n* : ensenada *f*, cala *f*

covenant *n* : pacto *m*, convenio *m*

cover *vt* **1** : cubrir **2** *or* ~ **up** : encubrir, ocultar **3** TREAT : tratar — ~ *n* **1** : cubierta *f* **2** SHELTER : abrigo *m*, refugio *m* **3** LID : tapa *f* **4** : cubierta *f* (de un libro), portada *f* (de una revista) **5** ~s *npl* BED-CLOTHES : mantas *fpl*, cobijas *fpl Lat* **6** take ~ : ponerse a cubierto **7 under** ~ **of** : al amparo de — **coverage** *n* : cobertura *f* — **covert** *adj* : encubierto — **cover–up** *n* : encubrimiento *m*

covet *vt* : codiciar — **covetous** *adj* : codicioso

cow *n* : vaca *f* — ~ *vt* : intimidar, acobardar

coward *n* : cobarde *mf* — **cowardice** *n* : cobardía *f* — **cowardly** *adj* : cobarde

cowboy *n* : vaquero *m*

cower *vi* : encogerse (de miedo)

coy *adj* : tímido y coqueto

coyote *n*, *pl* **coyotes** *or* **coyote** : coyote *m*

cozy *adj* **-zier; -est** : acogedor

crab *n* : cangrejo *m*, jaiba *f Lat*

crack *vt* **1** SPLIT : rajar, partir **2** : cascar (nueces, huevos) **3** : chasquear (un látigo, etc.) **4** ~ **down on** : tomar medidas enérgicas contra — *vi* **1** SPLIT : rajarse, agrietarse **2** : chasquear (dícese de un látigo) **3** ~ **up** : sufrir una crisis nerviosa — ~ *n* **1** CRACKING : chasquido *m*, crujido *m* **2** CREVICE : raja *f*, grieta *f* **3 have a** ~ **at** : intentar

cracker *n* : galleta *f* (de soda, etc.)

crackle *vi* **-led; -ling** : crepitar, chisporrotear — ~ *n* : crujido *m*, chisporroteo *m*

cradle *n* : cuna *f* — ~ *vt* **-dled; -dling** : acunar

craft *n* **1** TRADE : oficio *m* **2** CUNNING : astucia *f* **3** → **craftsmanship 4** *pl usually* **craft** BOAT : embarcación *f* — **craftsman** *n*, *pl* **-men** : artesano *m*, -na *f* — **craftsmanship** *n* : artesanía *f*, destreza *f* — **crafty** *adj* **craftier; -est** : astuto, taimado

crag *n* : peñasco *m*

cram *v* **crammed; cramming** *vt* **1** STUFF : embutir **2** ~ **with** : atiborrar de — *vi* : estudiar a última hora

cramp *n* **1** : calambre *m*, espasmo *m* (de los músculos) **2** ~s *npl* : retorcijones *mpl*

cranberry *n*, *pl* **-berries** : arándano *m* (rojo y agrio)

crane *n* **1** : grulla *f* (ave) **2** : grúa *f* (máquina) — ~ *vt* **craned; craning** : estirar (el cuello)

crank *n* **1** : manivela *f* **2** ECCENTRIC : ex-

céntrico *m*, -ca *f* — **cranky** *adj* **crankier; -est** : malhumorado

crash *vi* **1** : caerse con estrépito **2** COLLIDE : estrellarse, chocar — *vt* : estrellar — ~ *n* **1** DIN : estrépito *m* **2** COLLISION : choque *m*

crass *adj* : burdo, grosero

crate *n* : cajón *m* (de madera)

crater *n* : cráter *m*

crave *vt* **craved; craving** : ansiar — **craving** *n* : ansia *f*

crawl *vi* : arrastrarse, gatear (dícese de un bebé) — ~ *n* **at a** ~ : a paso lento

crayon *n* : lápiz *m* de cera

craze *n* : moda *f* pasajera, manía *f*

crazy *adj* **-zier; -est** **1** : loco **2 go** ~ : volverse loco — **craziness** *n* : locura *f*

creak *vi* : chirriar, crujir — ~ *n* : chirrido *m*, crujido *m*

cream *n* : crema *f*, nata *f Spain* — **cream cheese** *n* : queso *m* crema — **creamy** *adj* **creamier; -est** : cremoso

crease *n* : pliegue *m*, raya *f* (del pantalón) — ~ *vt* **creased; creasing** : plegar, poner una raya en (el pantalón)

create *vt* **-ated; -ating** : crear — **creation** *n* : creación *f* — **creative** *adj* : creativo — **creator** *n* : creador *m*, -dora *f*

creature *n* : criatura *f*, animal *m*

credence *n* **lend** ~ **to** : dar crédito a

credentials *npl* : credenciales *fpl*

credible *adj* : creíble — **credibility** *n* : credibilidad *f*

credit *n* **1** : crédito *m* **2** RECOGNITION : reconocimiento *m* **3 be a** ~ **to** : ser el orgullo de — ~ *vt* **1** BELIEVE : creer **2** : abonar (en una cuenta) **3** ~ **s.o. with sth** : atribuir algo a algn — **credit card** *n* : tarjeta *f* de crédito

credulous *adj* : crédulo

creed *n* : credo *m*

creek *n* : arroyo *m*, riachuelo *m*

creep *vi* **crept; creeping** **1** CRAWL : arrastrarse **2** SLINK : ir a hurtadillas — ~ *n* **1** CRAWL : paso *m* lento **2 the** ~s : escalofríos *mpl* — **creeping** *adj* ~ **plant** : planta *f* trepadora

cremate *vt* **-mated; -mating** : incinerar

crescent *n* : media luna *f*

cress *n* : berro *m*

crest *n* : cresta *f* — **crestfallen** *adj* : alicaído

crevice *n* : grieta *f*

crew *n* **1** : tripulación *f* (de una nave) **2** TEAM : equipo *m*

crib *n* : cuna *f* (de un bebé)

cricket *n* **1** : grillo *m* (insecto) **2** : críquet *m* (juego)

crime *n* : crimen *m* — **criminal** *adj* : criminal — ~ *n* : criminal *mf*

crimp *vt* : rizar

crimson n : carmesí m
cringe vi **cringed; cringing** : encogerse
crinkle vt **-kled; -kling** : arrugar
cripple vt **-pled; -pling 1** DISABLE : lisiar, dejar inválido **2** INCAPACITATE : inutilizar, paralizar
crisis n, pl **crises** : crisis f
crisp adj **1** CRUNCHY : crujiente **2** : frío y vigoroso (dícese del aire) — **crispy** adj **crispier; -est** : crujiente
crisscross vt : entrecruzar
criterion n, pl **-ria** : criterio m
critic n : crítico m, -ca f — **critical** adj : crítico — **criticism** n : crítica f — **criticize** vt **-cized; -cizing** : criticar
croak vi : croar
crock n : vasija f de barro — **crockery** n : vajilla f, loza f
crocodile n : cocodrilo m
crony n, pl **-nies** : amigote m fam
crook n **1** STAFF : cayado m **2** THIEF : ratero m, -ra f; ladrón m, -drona f **3** BEND : pliegue m — **crooked** adj **1** BENT : torcido, chueco Lat **2** DISHONEST : deshonesto
crop n **1** WHIP : fusta f **2** HARVEST : cosecha f **3** : cultivo m (de maíz, tabaco, etc.) — ~ v **cropped; cropping** vt TRIM : recortar, cortar — vi ~ **up** : surgir
cross n **1** : cruz f **2** HYBRID : cruce m — ~ vt **1** : cruzar, atravesar **2** CROSSBREED : cruzar **3** or ~ **out** : tachar — ~ adj **1** : que atraviesa **2** ANGRY : enojado — **crossbreed** vt **-bred; -breeding** : cruzar — **cross–examine** vt : interrogar — **cross-eyed** adj : bizco — **cross fire** n : fuego m cruzado — **crossing** n **1** INTERSECTION : cruce m, paso m **2** VOYAGE : travesía f (del mar) — **cross–reference** n : referencia f — **crossroads** n : cruce m — **cross section** n **1** : corte m transversal **2** SAMPLE : muestra f representativa — **crosswalk** n : cruce m peatonal, paso m de peatones — **crossword puzzle** n : crucigrama m
crotch n : entrepierna f
crouch vi : agacharse
crouton n : crutón m
crow n : cuervo m — ~ vi **crowed** or Brit **crew; crowing** : cacarear
crowbar n : palanca f
crowd vi : amontonarse — vt : atestar, llenar — ~ n : multitud f, muchedumbre f
crown n **1** : corona f **2** : cima f (de una colina) — ~ vt : coronar
crucial adj : crucial
crucify vt **-fied; -fying** : crucificar — **crucifix** n : crucifijo m — **crucifixion** n : crucifixión f
crude adj **cruder; -est 1** RAW : crudo **2** VULGAR : grosero **3** ROUGH : tosco, rudo

cruel adj **-eler** or **-eller; -elest** or **-ellest** : cruel — **cruelty** n, pl **-ties** : crueldad f
cruet n : vinagrera f
cruise vi **cruised; cruising 1** : hacer un crucero **2** : ir a velocidad de crucero — ~ n : crucero m — **cruiser** n **1** WARSHIP : crucero m **2** : patrulla f (de policía)
crumb n : miga f, migaja f
crumble v **-bled; -bling** vt : desmenuzar — vi : desmenuzarse, desmoronarse
crumple vt **-pled; -pling** : arrugar
crunch vt : ronzar (con los dientes), hacer crujir (con los pies, etc.) — **crunchy** adj **crunchier; -est** : crujiente
crusade n : cruzada f
crush vt : aplastar, apachurrar Lat — ~ n **have a** ~ **on** : estar chiflado por
crust n : corteza f
crutch n : muleta f
crux n : quid m
cry vi **cried; crying 1** SHOUT : gritar **2** WEEP : llorar — ~ n, pl **cries** : grito m
crypt n : cripta f
crystal n : cristal m
cub n : cachorro m, -rra f
Cuban adj : cubano
cube n : cubo m — **cubic** adj : cúbico
cubicle n : cubículo m
cuckoo n : cuco m, cuclillo m
cucumber n : pepino m
cuddle v **-dled; -dling** vi : acurrucarse, abrazarse — vt : abrazar
cudgel n : porra f — ~ vt **-geled** or **-gelled; -geling** or **-gelling** : aporrear
cue¹ n SIGNAL : señal f
cue² n : taco m (de billar)
cuff¹ 1 : puño m (de una camisa) **2** ~**s** npl → **handcuffs**
cuff² vt : bofetear — ~ n SLAP : bofetada f
cuisine n : cocina f
culinary adj : culinario
cull vt : seleccionar, entresacar
culminate vi **-nated; -nating** : culminar — **culmination** n : culminación f
culprit n : culpable mf
cult n : culto m
cultivate vt **-vated; -vating** : cultivar — **cultivation** n : cultivo m
culture n **1** : cultura f **2** : cultivo m (en biología) — **cultural** adj : cultural — **cultured** adj : culto
cumbersome adj : torpe (y pesado), difícil de manejar
cumulative adj : acumulativo
cunning adj : astuto, taimado — ~ n : astucia f
cup n **1** : taza f **2** TROPHY : copa f
cupboard n : alacena f, armario m
curator n : conservador m, -dora f; director m, -tora f

curb *n* **1** RESTRAINT : freno *m* **2** : borde *m* de la acera — ~ *vt* : refrenar
curdle *v* **-dled; -dling** *vi* : cuajarse — *vt* : cuajar
cure *n* : cura *f,* remedio *m* — ~ *vt* **cured; curing** : curar
curfew *n* : toque *m* de queda
curious *adj* : curioso — **curio** *n, pl* **-rios** : curiosidad *f* — **curiosity** *n, pl* **-ties** : curiosidad *f*
curl *vt* **1** : rizar **2** COIL : enrollar, enroscar — *vi* **1** : rizarse **2** ~ **up** : acurrucarse — ~ *n* : rizo *m* — **curler** *n* : rulo *m* — **curly** *adj* **curlier; -est** : rizado
currant *n* **1** : grosella *f* (fruta) **2** RAISIN : pasa *f* de Corinto
currency *n, pl* **-cies** **1** MONEY : moneda *f* **2 gain** ~ : ganar aceptación
current *adj* **1** PRESENT : actual **2** PREVALENT : corriente — ~ *n* : corriente *f*
curriculum *n, pl* **-la** : plan *m* de estudios
curry *n, pl* **-ries** : curry *m*
curse *n* : maldición *f* — ~ *v* **cursed; cursing** : maldecir
cursor *n* : cursor *m*
cursory *adj* : superficial
curt *adj* : corto, seco
curtail *vt* : acortar
curtain *n* : cortina *f* (de una ventana), telón *m* (en un teatro)
curtsy *vi* **-sied** *or* **-seyed; -sying** *or* **-seying** : hacer una reverencia — ~ *n* : reverencia *f*
curve *v* **curved; curving** *vi* : hacer una curva — *vt* : encorvar — ~ *n* : curva *f*

cushion *n* : cojín *m* — ~ *vt* : amortiguar
custard *n* : natillas *fpl*
custody *n, pl* **-dies** **1** : custodia *f* **2 be in** ~ : estar detenido — **custodian** *n* : custodio *m,* **-dia** *f;* guardián, **-diana** *f*
custom *n* : costumbre *f* — **customary** *adj* : habitual, acostumbrado — **customer** *n* : cliente *m,* -ta *f* — **customs** *npl* : aduana *f*
cut *v* **cut; cutting** *vt* **1** : cortar **2** REDUCE : reducir, rebajar **3** ~ **oneself** : cortarse **4** ~ **up** : cortar en pedazos — *vi* **1** : cortar **2** ~ **in** : interrumpir — ~ *n* **1** : corte *m* **2** REDUCTION : rebaja *f,* reducción *f*
cute *adj* **cuter; -est** : mono *fam,* lindo
cutlery *n* : cubiertos *mpl*
cutlet *n* : chuleta *f*
cutting *adj* : cortante, mordaz
cyanide *n* : cianuro *m*
cyber- *pref* : ciber- *m*
cycle *n* **1** : ciclo *m* **2** BICYCLE : bicicleta *f* — ~ *vi* **-cled; -cling** : ir en bicicleta — **cyclic** *or* **cyclical** *adj* : cíclico — **cyclist** *n* : ciclista *mf*
cycling *n* : ciclismo *m*
cyclone *n* : ciclón *m*
cylinder *n* : cilindro *m* — **cylindrical** *adj* : cilíndrico
cymbal *n* : platillo *m,* címbalo *m*
cynic *n* : cínico *m,* -ca *f* — **cynical** *adj* : cínico — **cynicism** *n* : cinismo *m*
cypress *n* : ciprés *m*
cyst *n* : quiste *m*
czar *n* : zar *m*
Czech *adj* : checo — ~ *n* : checo *m* (idioma)

D

d *n, pl* **d's** *or* **ds** : d *f,* cuarta letra del alfabeto inglés
dab *n* : toque *m* — ~ *vt* **dabbed; dabbing** : dar toques ligeros a, aplicar suavemente
dabble *vi* **-bled; -bling** ~ **in** : interesarse superficialmente en — **dabbler** *n* : aficionado *m,* -da *f*
dad *n* : papá *m fam* — **daddy** *n, pl* **-dies** : papá *m fam*
daffodil *n* : narciso *m*
dagger *n* : daga *f,* puñal *m*
daily *adj* : diario — ~ *adv* : diariamente
dainty *adj* **-tier; -est** : delicado
dairy *n, pl* **-ies** **1** : lechería *f* (tienda) **2** *or* ~ **farm** : granja *f* lechera

daisy *n, pl* **-sies** : margarita *f*
dam *n* : presa *f* — ~ *vt* **dammed; damming** : represar
damage *n* **1** : daño *m,* perjuicio *m* **2** ~**s** *npl* : daños y perjuicios *mpl* — ~ *vt* **-aged; -aging** : dañar
damn *vt* **1** CONDEMN : condenar **2** CURSE : maldecir — ~ *n* **not give a** ~ : no importarse un comino *fam* — ~ *or* **damned** *adj* : maldito *fam*
damp *adj* : húmedo — **dampen** *vt* **1** MOISTEN : humedecer **2** DISCOURAGE : desalentar, desanimar — **dampness** *n* : humedad *f*

dance v **danced; dancing** : bailar — ~ n
: baile m — **dancer** n : bailarín m, -rina f
dandelion n : diente m de león
dandruff n : caspa f
dandy adj **-dier; -est** : de primera, excelente
danger n : peligro m — **dangerous** adj
: peligroso
dangle v **-gled; -gling** vi HANG : colgar,
pender — vt : hacer oscilar
Danish adj : danés — ~ n : danés m
(idioma)
dank adj : frío y húmedo
dare v **dared; daring** vt : desafiar — vi : osar
— ~ n : desafío m — **daredevil** n : persona
f temeraria — **daring** adj : atrevido, audaz
— ~ n : audacia f
dark adj **1** : oscuro **2** : moreno (dícese del
pelo o de la piel) **3** GLOOMY : sombrío **4**
get ~ : hacerse de noche — **darken** vt
: oscurecer — vi : oscurecerse — **darkness**
n : oscuridad f
darkroom n : cuarto m oscuro
darling n BELOVED : querido m, -da f — ~
adj : querido
darn vt : zurcir — ~ adj : maldito fam
dart n **1** : dardo m **2** ~s npl : juego m de
dardos — ~ vi : precipitarse
dash vt **1** SMASH : romper **2** HURL : lanzar
3 ~ **off** : hacer (algo) rápidamente — vi
: lanzarse, irse corriendo — ~ n **1** : guión
m largo (signo de puntuación) **2** PINCH : po-
quito m, pizca f **3** RACE : carrera f — **dashboard** n : tablero m de instrumentos —
dashing adj : gallardo, apuesto
data ns & pl : datos mpl — **database** n
: base f de datos
date[1] n : dátil m (fruta)
date[2] n **1** : fecha f **2** APPOINTMENT : cita f —
~ v **dated; dating** vt **1** : fechar (una carta,
etc.) **2** : salir con (algn) — vi ~ **from**
: datar de — **dated** adj : pasado de moda
daub vt : embadurnar
daughter n : hija f — **daughter–in–law** n, pl
daughters–in–law : nuera f
daunt vt : intimidar
dawdle vi **-dled; -dling** : entretenerse, perder
tiempo
dawn vi **1** : amanecer **2 it** ~**ed on him
that** : cayó en la cuenta de que — ~ n
: amanecer m
day n **1** : día m **2** or **working** ~ : jornada
f **3 the** ~ **before** : el día anterior **4 the**
~ **before yesterday** : anteayer **5 the** ~
after : el día siguiente **6 the** ~ **after tomorrow** : pasada mañana — **daybreak** n
: amanecer m — **daydream** n : ensueño m
— ~ vi : soñar despierto — **daylight** n
: luz f del día — **daytime** n : día m
daze vt **dazed; dazing** : aturdir — ~ n **in a**
~ : aturdido

dazzle vt **-zled; -zling** : deslumbrar
dead adj **1** LIFELESS : muerto **2** NUMB :
entumecido — ~ n **1 in the** ~ **of night**
: en plena noche **2 the** ~ : los muertos
— ~ adv ABSOLUTELY : absolutamente —
deaden vt **1** : atenuar (dolores) **2** MUFFLE
: amortiguar — **dead end** n : callejón m sin
salida — **deadline** n : fecha f límite —
deadlock n : punto m muerto — **deadly** adj
-lier; -est 1 : mortal, letal **2** ACCURATE
: certero, preciso
deaf adj : sordo — **deafen** vt : ensordecer
— **deafness** n : sordera f
deal n **1** TRANSACTION : trato m, transacción f **2** : reparto m (de naipes) **3 a good**
~ : mucho — ~ v **dealt; dealing** vt **1**
: dar **2** : repartir, dar (naipes) **3** ~ **a blow**
: asestar un golpe — vi **1** : dar, repartir (en
juegos de naipes) **2** ~ **in** : comerciar en
3 ~ **with** CONCERN : tratar de **4** ~ **with
s.o.** : tratar con algn — **dealer** n : comerciante mf — **dealings** npl : trato m, relaciones fpl
dean n : decano m, -na f
dear adj : querido — ~ n : querido m, -da f
— **dearly** adv **1** : mucho **2 pay** ~ : pagar
caro
death n : muerte f
debar vt : excluir
debate n : debate m, discusión f — ~ vt
-bated; -bating : debatir, discutir
debit vt : adeudar, cargar — ~ n : débito m,
debe m
debris n, pl **-bris** : escombros mpl
debt n : deuda f — **debtor** n : deudor m,
-dora f
debunk vt : desmentir
debut n : debut m — ~ vi : debutar
decade n : década f
decadence n : decadencia f — **decadent**
adj : decadente
decal n : calcomanía f
decanter n : licorera f
decapitate vt **-tated; -tating** : decapitar
decay vi **1** DECOMPOSE : descomponerse **2**
DETERIORATE : deteriorarse **3** : cariarse
(dícese de los dientes) — ~ n **1** : descomposición f **2** : deterioro m (de un edificio,
etc.) **3** : caries f (de los dientes)
deceased adj : difunto — ~ n **the** ~ : el
difunto, la difunta
deceive vt **-ceived; -ceiving** : engañar —
deceit n : engaño m — **deceitful** adj : engañoso
December n : diciembre m
decent adj **1** : decente **2** KIND : bueno,
amable — **decency** n, pl **-cies** : decencia f
deception n : engaño m — **deceptive** adj
: engañoso
decide v **-cided; -ciding** vt : decidir — vi

: decidirse — **decided** *adj* **1** UNQUESTION-ABLE : indudable **2** RESOLUTE : decidido — **decidedly** *adv* **1** DEFINITELY : decididamente **2** RESOLUTELY : con decisión

decimal *adj* : decimal — ~ *n* : número *m* decimal — **decimal point** *n* : coma *f* decimal

decipher *vt* : descifrar

decision *n* : decisión *f* — **decisive** *adj* **1** RESOLUTE : decidido **2** CONCLUSIVE : decisivo

deck *n* **1** : cubierta *f* (de un barco) **2** *or* ~ **of cards** : baraja *f* (de naipes) **3** TERRACE : entarimado *m*

declare *vt* **-clared; -claring** : declarar — **declaration** *n* : declaración *f*

decline *v* **-clined; -clining** *vt* REFUSE : declinar, rehusar — *vi* DECREASE : disminuir — ~ *n* **1** DETERIORATION : decadencia *f*, deterioro *m* **2** DECREASE : disminución *f*

decode *vt* **-coded; -coding** : descodificar

decompose *vt* **-posed; -posing** : descomponer — *vi* : descomponerse

decongestant *n* : descongestionante *m*

decorate *vt* **-rated; -rating** : decorar — **decor** *or* **décor** *n* : decoración *f* — **decoration** *n* : decoración *f* — **decorator** *n* : decorador *m*, -dora *f*

decoy *n* : señuelo *m*

decrease *v* **-creased; -creasing** : disminuir — ~ *n* : disminución *f*

decree *n* : decreto *m* — ~ *vt* **-creed; -creeing** : decretar

decrepit *adj* **1** FEEBLE : decrépito **2** DILAPIDATED : ruinoso

dedicate *vt* **-cated; -cating 1** : dedicar **2** ~ **oneself to** : consagrarse a — **dedication** *n* **1** DEVOTION : dedicación *f* **2** INSCRIPTION : dedicatoria *f*

deduce *vt* -duced; -ducing : deducir — **deduct** *vt* : deducir — **deduction** *n* : deducción *f*

deed *n* : acción *f*, hecho *m*

deem *vt* : considerar, juzgar

deep *adj* : hondo, profundo — ~ *adv* **1** DEEPLY : profundamente **2** ~ **down** : en el fondo **3 dig** ~ : cavar hondo — **deepen** *vt* : ahondar — *vi* : hacerse más profundo — **deeply** *adv* : hondo, profundamente

deer *ns* & *pl* : ciervo *m*

deface *vt* **-faced; -facing** : desfigurar

default *n* **by** ~ : en rebeldía — ~ *vi* **1** ~ **on** : no pagar (una deuda) **2** : no presentarse (en deportes)

defeat *vt* **1** BEAT : vencer, derrotar **2** FRUSTRATE : frustrar — ~ *n* : derrota *f*

defect *n* : defecto *m* — ~ *vi* : desertar — **defective** *adj* : defectuoso

defend *vt* : defender — **defendant** *n*

: acusado *m*, -da *f* — **defense** *or Brit* **defence** *n* : defensa *f* — **defenseless** *or Brit* **defenceless** *adj* : indefenso — **defensive** *adj* : defensivo — ~ *n* **on the** ~ : a la defensiva

defer *v* **-ferred; -ferring** *vt* : diferir, aplazar — *vi* ~ **to** : deferir a — **deference** *n* : deferencia *f* — **deferential** *adj* : deferente

defiance *n* **1** : desafío *m* **2 in** ~ **of** : a despecho de — **defiant** *adj* : desafiante

deficiency *n*, *pl* **-cies** : deficiencia *f* — **deficient** *adj* : deficiente

deficit *n* : déficit *m*

defile *vt* **-filed; -filing 1** DIRTY : ensuciar **2** DESECRATE : profanar

define *vt* **-fined; -fining** : definir — **definite** *adj* **1** : definido **2** CERTAIN : seguro, incuestionable — **definition** *n* : definición *f* — **definitive** *adj* : definitivo

deflate *v* **-flated; -flating** *vt* : desinflar (una llanta, etc.) — *vi* : desinflarse

deflect *vt* : desviar — *vi* : desviarse

deform *vt* : deformar — **deformity** *n*, *pl* **-ties** : deformidad *f*

defraud *vt* : defraudar

defrost *vt* : descongelar — *vi* : descongelarse

deft *adj* : hábil, diestro

defy *vt* **-fied; -fying 1** CHALLENGE : desafiar **2** RESIST : resistir

degenerate *vi* : degenerar — ~ *adj* : degenerado

degrade *vt* **-graded; -grading** : degradar — **degrading** *adj* : degradante

degree *n* **1** : grado *m* **2** *or* **academic** ~ : título *m*

dehydrate *vt* **-drated; -drating** : deshidratar

deign *vi* ~ **to** : dignarse (a)

deity *n*, *pl* **-ties** : deidad *f*

dejected *adj* : abatido — **dejection** *n* : abatimiento *m*

delay *n* : retraso *m* — ~ *vt* **1** POSTPONE : aplazar **2** HOLD UP : retrasar — *vi* : demorar

delectable *adj* : delicioso

delegate *n* : delegado *m*, -da *f* — ~ *v* **-gated; -gating** : delegar — **delegation** *n* : delegación *f*

delete *vt* **-leted; -leting** : borrar

deliberate *v* **-ated; -ating** *vt* : deliberar sobre — *vi* : deliberar — ~ *adj* : deliberado — **deliberately** *adv* INTENTIONALLY : a propósito — **deliberation** *n* : deliberación *f*

delicacy *n*, *pl* **-cies 1** : delicadeza *f* **2** FOOD : manjar *m*, exquisitez *f* — **delicate** *adj* : delicado

delicatessen *n* : charcutería *f*

delicious *adj* : delicioso

delight *n* : placer *m*, deleite *m* — ~ *vt* : deleitar, encantar — *vi* ~ **in** : deleitarse con — **delightful** *adj* : delicioso, encantador

delinquent *adj* : delincuente — ~ *n* : delincuente *mf*

delirious *adj* : delirante — **delirium** *n* : delirio *m*

deliver *vt* **1** DISTRIBUTE : entregar, repartir **2** FREE : liberar **3** : asistir en el parto de (un niño) **4** : pronunciar (un discurso, etc.) **5** DEAL : asestar (un golpe, etc.) — **delivery** *n, pl* **-eries** **1** DISTRIBUTION : entrega *f*, reparto *m* **2** LIBERATION : liberación *f* **3** CHILDBIRTH : parto *m*, alumbramiento *m*

delude *vt* **-luded; -luding** **1** : engañar **2** ~ **oneself** : engañarse

deluge *n* : diluvio *m*

delusion *n* : ilusión *f*

deluxe *adj* : de lujo

delve *vi* **delved; delving** **1** : escarbar **2** ~ **into** PROBE : investigar

demand *n* **1** REQUEST : petición *f* **2** CLAIM : reclamación *f*, exigencia *f* **3** → **supply** — ~ *vt* : exigir — **demanding** *adj* : exigente

demean *vt* ~ **oneself** : rebajarse

demeanor *n* : comportamiento *m*

demented *adj* : demente, loco

demise *n* : fallecimiento *m*

democracy *n, pl* **-cies** : democracia *f* — **democrat** *n* : demócrata *mf* — **democratic** *adj* : democrático

demolish *vt* : demoler — **demolition** *n* : demolición *f*

demon *n* : demonio *m*

demonstrate *v* **-strated; -strating** *vt* : demostrar — *vi* RALLY : manifestarse — **demonstration** *n* **1** : demostración *f* **2** RALLY : manifestación *f*

demoralize *vt* **-ized; -izing** : desmoralizar

demote *vt* **-moted; -moting** : bajar de categoría

demure *adj* : recatado

den *n* LAIR : guarida *f*

denial *n* **1** : negación *f*, rechazo *m* **2** REFUSAL : denegación *f*

denim *n* : tela *f* vaquera, mezclilla *f Lat*

denomination *n* **1** : confesión *f* (religiosa) **2** : valor *m* (de una moneda)

denounce *vt* **-nounced; -nouncing** : denunciar

dense *adj* **denser; -est** **1** THICK : denso **2** STUPID : estúpido — **density** *n, pl* **-ties** : densidad *f*

dent *vt* : abollar — ~ *n* : abolladura *f*

dental *adj* : dental — **dental floss** *n* : hilo *m* dental — **dentist** *n* : dentista *mf* — **dentures** *npl* : dentadura *f* postiza

deny *vt* **-nied; -nying** **1** : negar **2** REFUSE : denegar

deodorant *n* : desodorante *m*

depart *vi* **1** : salir **2** ~ **from** : apartarse de (la verdad, etc.)

department *n* : sección *f* (de una tienda, etc.), departamento *m* (de una empresa, etc.), ministerio *m* (del gobierno) — **department store** *n* : grandes almacenes *mpl*

departure *n* **1** : salida *f* **2** DEVIATION : desviación *f*

depend *vi* **1** ~ **on** : depender de **2** ~ **on s.o.** : contar con algn **3 that** ~**s** : eso depende — **dependable** *adj* : digno de confianza — **dependence** *n* : dependencia *f* — **dependent** *adj* : dependiente

depict *vt* **1** PORTRAY : representar **2** DESCRIBE : describir

deplete *vt* **-pleted; -pleting** : agotar, reducir

deplore *vt* **-plored; -ploring** : deplorar, lamentar — **deplorable** *adj* : lamentable

deploy *vt* : desplegar

deport *vt* : deportar, expulsar (de un país) — **deportation** *n* : deportación *f*

depose *vt* **-posed; -posing** : deponer

deposit *vt* **-ited; -iting** : depositar — ~ *n* **1** : depósito *m* **2** DOWN PAYMENT : entrega *f* inicial

depot *n* **1** WAREHOUSE : almacén *m*, depósito *m* **2** STATION : terminal *mf*

depreciate *vi* **-ated; -ating** : depreciarse — **depreciation** *n* : depreciación *f*

depress *vt* **1** : deprimir **2** PRESS : apretar — **depressed** *adj* : abatido, deprimido — **depressing** *adj* : deprimente — **depression** *n* : depresión *f*

deprive *vt* **-prived; -priving** : privar

depth *n, pl* **depths** **1** : profundidad *f* **2 in the** ~**s of night** : en lo más profundo de la noche

deputy *n, pl* **-ties** : suplente *mf*; sustituto *m*, -ta *f*

derail *vt* : hacer descarrilar

deranged *adj* : trastornado

derelict *adj* : abandonado

deride *vt* **-rided; -riding** : burlarse de — **derision** *n* : mofa *f*

derive *vi* **-rived; -riving** : derivar — **derivation** *n* : derivación *f*

derogatory *adj* : despectivo

descend *v* : descender, bajar — **descendant** *n* : descendiente *mf* — **descent** *n* **1** : descenso *m* **2** LINEAGE : descendencia *f*

describe *vt* **-scribed; -scribing** : describir — **description** *n* : descripción *f* — **descriptive** *adj* : descriptivo

desecrate *vt* **-crated; -crating** : profanar

desert *n* : desierto *m* — ~ *adj* ~ **island** : isla *f* desierta — ~ *vt* : abandonar — *vi* : desertar — **deserter** *n* : desertor *m*, -tora *f*

deserve *vt* **-served; -serving** : merecer

design *vt* **1** DEVISE : diseñar **2** PLAN

: proyectar — ~ *n* 1 : diseño *m* 2 PLAN : plan *m*, proyecto *m*

designate *vt* **-nated; -nating** : nombrar, designar

designer *n* : diseñador *m*, -dora *f*

desire *vt* **-sired; -siring** : desear — ~ *n* : deseo *m* — **desirable** *adj* : deseable

desk *n* : escritorio *m*, pupitre *m* (en la escuela)

desolate *adj* : desolado

despair *vi* : desesperar — ~ *n* : desesperación *f*

desperate *adj* : desesperado — **desperation** *n* : desesperación *f*

despise *vt* **-spised; -spising** : despreciar — **despicable** *adj* : despreciable

despite *prep* : a pesar de

despondent *adj* : desanimado

dessert *n* : postre *m*

destination *n* : destino *m* — **destined** *adj* 1 : destinado 2 ~ **for** : con destino a — **destiny** *n*, *pl* **-nies** : destino *m*

destitute *adj* : indigente

destroy *vt* : destruir — **destruction** *n* : destrucción *f* — **destructive** *adj* : destructivo

detach *vt* : separar — **detached** *adj* 1 : separado 2 IMPARTIAL : objetivo

detail *n* 1 : detalle *m* 2 **go into** ~ : entrar en detalles — ~ *vt* : detallar — **detailed** *adj* : detallado

detain *vt* 1 : detener (un prisionero) 2 DELAY : entretener

detect *vt* : detectar — **detection** *n* : detección *f*, descubrimiento *m* — **detective** *n* : detective *mf*

detention *n* : detención *m*

deter *vt* **-terred; -terring** : disuadir

detergent *n* : detergente *m*

deteriorate *vi* **-rated; -rating** : deteriorarse — **deterioration** *n* : deterioro *m*

determine *vt* **-mined; -mining** : determinar — **determined** *adj* RESOLUTE : decidido — **determination** *n* : determinación *f*

deterrent *n* : medida *f* disuasiva

detest *vt* : detestar — **detestable** *adj* : odioso

detonate *v* **-nated; -nating** *vt* : hacer detonar — *vi* EXPLODE : detonar, estallar — **detonation** *n* : detonación *f*

detour *n* 1 : desviación *f* 2 **make a** ~ : dar un rodeo — ~ *vi* : desviarse

detract *vi* ~ **from** : aminorar, restar importancia a

detrimental *adj* : perjudicial

devalue *vt* **-ued; -uing** : devaluar

devastate *vt* **-tated; -tating** : devastar — **devastating** *adj* : devastador — **devastation** *n* : devastación *f*

develop *vt* 1 : desarrollar 2 ~ **an illness** : contraer una enfermedad — *vi* 1 GROW : desarrollarse 2 HAPPEN : aparecer — **development** *n* : desarrollo *m*

deviate *v* **-ated; -ating** *vi* : desviarse — **deviation** *n* : desviación *f*

device *n* : dispositivo *m*, mecanismo *m*

devil *n* : diablo *m*, demonio *m* — **devilish** *adj* : diabólico

devious *adj* 1 CRAFTY : taimado 2 WINDING : tortuoso

devise *vt* **-vised; -vising** : idear, concebir

devoid *adj* ¶ **of** : desprovisto de

devote *vt* **-voted; -voting** : consagrar, dedicar — **devoted** *adj* : leal — **devotee** *n* : devoto *m*, -ta *f* — **devotion** *n* 1 : devoción *f*, dedicación *f* 2 : oración *f* (en religión)

devour *vt* : devorar

devout *adj* : devoto

dew *n* : rocío *m*

dexterity *n*, *pl* **-ties** : destreza *f*

diabetes *n* : diabetes *f* — **diabetic** *adj* : diabético — ~ *n* : diabético *m*, -ca *f*

diabolic *or* **diabolical** *adj* : diabólico

diagnosis *n*, *pl* **-noses** : diagnóstico *m* — **diagnose** *vt* **-nosed; -nosing** : diagnosticar — **diagnostic** *adj* : diagnóstico

diagonal *adj* : diagonal, en diagonal — ~ *n* : diagonal *f*

diagram *n* : diagrama *m*

dial *n* : esfera *f* (de un reloj), dial *m* (de un radio, etc.) — ~ *v* **dialed** *or* **dialled; dialing** *or* **dialling** : marcar

dialect *n* : dialecto *m*

dialogue *n* : diálogo *m*

diameter *n* : diámetro *m*

diamond *n* 1 : diamante *m* 2 : rombo *m* (forma) 3 *or* **baseball** ~ : cuadro *m*, diamante *m*

diaper *n* : pañal *m*

diaphragm *n* : diafragma *m*

diarrhea *n* : diarrea *f*

diary *n*, *pl* **-ries** : diario *m*

dice *ns & pl* : dados *mpl* (juego)

dictate *vt* **-tated; -tating** : dictar — **dictation** *n* : dictado *m* — **dictator** *n* : dictador *m*, -dora *f* — **dictatorship** *n* : dictadura *f*

dictionary *n*, *pl* **-naries** : diccionario *m*

did → do

die¹ *vi* **died; dying** 1 : morir 2 ~ **down** : amainar, disminuir 3 ~ **out** : extinguirse 4 **be dying for** : morirse por

die² *n* 1 *pl* **dice** : dado *m* (para jugar) 2 *pl* **dies** MOLD : molde *m*

diesel *n* : diesel *m*

diet *n* 1 FOOD : alimentación *f* 2 **go on a** ~ : ponerse a régimen — ~ *vi* : estar a régimen

differ *vi* **-ferred; -ferring** 1 : diferir, ser distinto 2 DISAGREE : no estar de acuerdo — **difference** *n* : diferencia *f* — **different** *adj*

: distinto, diferente — **differentiate** *v*
-ated; -ating *vt* : diferenciar — *vi* : distinguir — **differently** *adv* : de otra manera
difficult *adj* : difícil — **difficulty** *n, pl* **-ties**
: dificultad *f*
diffident *adj* : tímido, que falta confianza
dig *v* **dug; digging** *vt* **1** : cavar **2** ~ **up**
: desenterrar — *vi* : cavar — ~ *n* **1** GIBE
: pulla *f* **2** EXCAVATION : excavación *f*
digest *n* : resumen *m* — ~ *vt* **1** : digerir **2**
SUMMARIZE : resumir — **digestible** *adj* : digerible — **digestion** *n* : digestión *f* — **digestive** *adj* : digestivo
digit *n* **1** NUMERAL : dígito *m*, número *m* **2**
FINGER, TOE : dedo *m* — **digital** *adj* : digital
digitalize *vt* **-ized -izing** : digitalizar
dignity *n, pl* **-ties** : dignidad *f* — **dignified**
adj : digno, decoroso
digress *vi* : desviarse del tema, divagar —
digression *n* : digresión *f*
dike *n* : dique *m*
dilapidated *adj* : ruinoso
dilate *v* **-lated; -lating** *vt* : dilatar — *vi* : dilatarse
dilemma *n* : dilema *m*
diligence *n* : diligencia *f* — **diligent** *adj*
: diligente
dilute *vt* **-luted; -luting** : diluir
dim *v* **dimmed; dimming** *vt* : atenuar — *vi*
: irse atenuando — ~ *adj* **dimmer; dimmest** **1** DARK : oscuro **2** FAINT : débil,
tenue
dime *n* : moneda *f* de diez centavos
dimension *n* : dimensión *f*
diminish *v* : disminuir
diminutive *adj* : diminuto
dimple *n* : hoyuelo *m*
din *n* : estrépito *m*
dine *vi* **dined; dining** : cenar — **diner** *n* **1**
: comensal *mf* (persona) **2** : cafetería *f* (restaurante)
dingy *adj* **-gier; -est** : sucio, deslucido
dinner *n* : cena *f*, comida *f*
dinosaur *n* : dinosaurio *m*
dint *n* **by ¶ of** : a fuerza de
dip *v* **dipped; dipping** *vt* : mojar — *vi*
: bajar, descender — ~ *n* **1** DROP : descenso *m*, caída *f* **2** SWIM : chapuzón *m* **3**
SAUCE : salsa *f*
diploma *n, pl* **-mas** : diploma *m*
diplomacy *n* : diplomacia *f* — **diplomat** *n*
: diplomático *m*, -ca *f* — **diplomatic** *adj*
: diplomático
dire *adj* **direr; direst** **1** : grave, terrible **2**
EXTREME : extremo
direct *vt* **1** : dirigir **2** ORDER : mandar —
~ *adj* **1** STRAIGHT : directo **2** FRANK
: franco — ~ *adv* : directamente — **direct**

current *n* : corriente *f* continua — **direction**
n **1** : dirección *f* **2 ask** ~**s** : pedir indicaciones — **directly** *adv* **1** STRAIGHT : directamente **2** IMMEDIATELY : en seguida
— **director** *n* **1** : director *m*, -tora *f* **2**
board of ~**s** : directorio *m* — **directory** *n*,
pl **-ries** : guía *f* (telefónica)
dirt *n* **1** : suciedad *f* **2** SOIL : tierra *f* — **dirty**
adj **dirtier; -est** **1** : sucio **2** INDECENT
: obsceno, cochino *fam*
disability *n, pl* **-ties** : minusvalía *f*, invalidez
f — **disable** *vt* **-abled; -abling** : incapacitar
— **disabled** *adj* : minusválido
disadvantage *n* : desventaja *f*
disagree *vi* **1** : no estar de acuerdo (con
algn) **2** CONFLICT : no coincidir — **disagreeable** *adj* : desagradable — **disagreement** *n* **1** : desacuerdo *m* **2** ARGUMENT
: discusión *f*
disappear *vi* : desaparecer — **disappearance** *n* : desaparición *f*
disappoint *vt* : decepcionar, desilusionar —
disappointment *n* : decepción *f*, desilusión
f
disapprove *vi* **-proved; -proving** ~ **of** : desaprobar — **disapproval** *n* : desaprobación
f
disarm *vt* : desarmar — **disarmament** *n*
: desarme *m*
disarray *n* : desorden *m*
disaster *n* : desastre *m* — **disastrous** *adj*
: desastroso
disbelief *n* : incredulidad *f*
disc → **disk**
discard *vt* : desechar, deshacerse de
discern *vt* : percibir, discernir — **discernible** *adj* : perceptible
discharge *vt* **-charged; -charging** **1** UN-
LOAD : descargar **2** RELEASE : liberar,
poner en libertad **3** DISMISS : despedir **4**
CARRY OUT : cumplir con (una obligación)
— ~ *n* **1** : descarga *f* (de electricidad),
emisión *f* (de humo, etc.) **2** DISMISSAL : despido *m* **3** RELEASE : alta *f* (de un paciente),
puesta *f* en libertad (de un preso) **4** : supuración *f* (en medicina)
disciple *n* : discípulo *m*, -la *f*
discipline *n* **1** : disciplina *f* **2** PUNISHMENT
: castigo *m* — ~ *vt* **-plined; -plining** **1**
CONTROL : disciplinar **2** PUNISH : castigar
disclaim *vt* : negar
disclose *vt* **-closed; -closing** : revelar —
disclosure *n* : revelación *f*
discomfort *n* **1** : incomodidad *f* **2** PAIN
: malestar *m* **3** UNEASINESS : inquietud
f
disconcert *vt* : desconcertar
disconnect *vt* : desconectar
disconsolate *adj* : desconsolado
discontented *adj* : descontento

discontinue *vt* **-ued; -uing** : suspender, descontinuar

discount *n* : descuento *m*, rebaja *f* — ∼ *vt* **1** : descontar (precios) **2** DISREGARD : descartar

discourage *vt* **-aged; -aging** : desalentar, desanimar — **discouragement** *n* : desánimo *m*, desaliento *m*

discover *vt* : descubrir — **discovery** *n*, *pl* **-ries** : descubrimiento *m*

discredit *vt* : desacreditar — ∼ *n* : descrédito *m*

discreet *adj* : discreto

discrepancy *n*, *pl* **-cies** : discrepancia *f*

discretion *n* : discreción *f*

discriminate *vi* **-nated; -nating** **1** ∼ **against** : discriminar **2** ∼ **between** : distinguir entre — **discrimination** *n* **1** PREJUDICE : discriminación *f* **2** DISCERNMENT : discernimiento *m*

discuss *vt* : hablar de, discutir

discussion *n* : discusión *f*, debate *m*, conversación *f*

disdain *n* : desdén *m* — ∼ *vt* : desdeñar

disease *n* : enfermedad *f* — **diseased** *adj* : enfermo

disembark *vi* : desembarcar

disengage *vt* **-gaged; -gaging** **1** RELEASE : soltar **2** ∼ **the clutch** : desembragar

disentangle *vt* **-gled; -gling** : desenredar

disfavor *n* : desaprobación *f*

disfigure *vt* **-ured; -uring** : desfigurar

disgrace *vt* **-graced; -gracing** : deshonrar — ∼ *n* **1** DISHONOR : deshonra *f* **2** SHAME : vergüenza *f* — **disgraceful** *adj* : vergonzoso, deshonroso

disgruntled *adj* : descontento

disguise *vt* **-guised; -guising** : disfrazar — ∼ *n* : disfraz *m*

disgust *n* : asco *m*, repugnancia *f* — ∼ *vt* : asquear — **disgusting** *adj* : asqueroso

dish *n* **1** : plato *m* **2** *or* **serving** ∼ : fuente *f* **3** **wash the** ∼**es** : lavar los platos — ∼ *vt or* ∼ **up** : servir — **dishcloth** *n* : paño *m* de cocina (para secar), trapo *m* de fregar (para lavar)

dishearten *vt* : desanimar

disheveled *or* **dishevelled** *adj* : desaliñado, despeinado (dícese del pelo)

dishonest *adj* : deshonesto — **dishonesty** *n*, *pl* **-ties** : falta *f* de honrâdez

dishonor *n* : deshonra *f* — ∼ *vt* : deshonrar — **dishonorable** *adj* : deshonroso

dishwasher *n* : lavaplatos *m*, lavavajillas *m*

disillusion *vt* : desilusionar — **disillusionment** *n* : desilusión *f*

disinfect *vt* : desinfectar — **disinfectant** *n* : desinfectante *m*

disintegrate *vi* **-grated; -grating** : desintegrarse

disinterested *adj* : desinteresado

disk *or* **disc** *n* : disco *m*

dislike *n* : aversión *f*, antipatía *f* — ∼ *vt* **-liked; -liking** : tener aversión a **2 l** ∼ **dancing** : no me gusta bailar

dislocate *vt* **-cated; -cating** : dislocar

dislodge *vt* **-lodged; -lodging** : sacar, desalojar

disloyal *adj* : desleal — **disloyalty** *n*, *pl* **-ties** : deslealtad *f*

dismal *adj* : sombrío, deprimente

dismantle *vt* **-tled; -tling** : desmontar, desarmar

dismay *vt* : consternar — ∼ *n* : consternación *f*

dismiss *vt* **1** DISCHARGE : despedir, destituir **2** REJECT : descartar, rechazar — **dismissal** *n* **1** : despido *m* (de un empleado), destitución *f* (de un funcionario) **2** REJECTION : rechazo *m*

dismount *vi* : desmontar

disobey *v* : desobedecer — **disobedience** *n* : desobediencia *f* — **disobedient** *adj* : desobediente

disorder *n* **1** : desorden *m* **2** AILMENT : afección *f*, problema *m* — **disorderly** *adj* : desordenado

disorganize *vt* **-nized; -nizing** : desorganizar

disown *vt* : renegar de

dispassionate *adj* : desapasionado

dispatch *vt* : despachar, enviar

dispel *vt* **-pelled; -pelling** : disipar

dispensation *n* EXEMPTION : exención *m*, dispensa *f*

dispense *v* **-pensed; -pensing** *vt* : repartir, distribuir — *vi* ∼ **with** : prescindir de

disperse *v* **-persed; -persing** *vt* : dispersar — *vi* : dispersarse

displace *vt* **-placed; -placing** **1** : desplazar **2** REPLACE : reemplazar

display *vt* **1** EXHIBIT : exponer, exhibir **2** ∼ **anger** : manifestar la ira — ∼ *n* : muestra *f*, exposición *f*

displease *vt* **-pleased; -pleasing** : desagradar — **displeasure** *n* : desagrado *m*

dispose *v* **-posed; -posing** *vt* : disponer — *vi* ∼ **of** : deshacerse de — **disposable** *adj* : desechable — **disposal** *n* **1** REMOVAL : eliminación *f* **2 have at one's** ∼ : tener a su disposición — **disposition** *n* **1** ARRANGEMENT : disposición *f* **2** TEMPERAMENT : temperamento *m*, carácter *m*

disprove *vt* **-proved; -proving** : refutar

dispute *v* **-puted; -putting** *vt* QUESTION : cuestionar — *vi* ARGUE : discutir — ∼ *n* : disputa *f*, conflicto *m*

disqualification n : descalificación f — **disqualify** vt -**fied; -fying** : descalificar

disregard vt : ignorar, hacer caso omiso de — ∼ n : indiferencia f

disrepair n : mal estado m

disreputable adj : de mala fama

disrespect n : falta f de respeto — **disrespectful** adj : irrespetuoso

disrupt vt : trastornar, perturbar — **disruption** n : trastorno m

dissatisfaction n : descontento m — **dissatisfied** adj : descontento

dissect vt : disecar

disseminate vt -**nated; -nating** : diseminar, difundir

dissent vi : disentir — ∼ n : disentimiento m

dissertation THESIS : tesis f

disservice n do a ∼ to : no hacer justicia a

dissident n : disidente mf

dissimilar adj : distinto

dissipate vt -**pated; -pating 1** DISPEL : disipar **2** SQUANDER : desperdiciar

dissolve v -**solved; -solving** vt : disolver — vi : disolverse

dissuade vt -**suaded; -suading** : disuadir

distance n **1** : distancia f **2 in the** ∼ : a lo lejos — **distant** adj : distante

distaste n : desagrado m — **distasteful** adj : desagradable

distend vt : dilatar — vi : dilatarse

distill or Brit **distil** vt -**tilled; -tilling** : destilar

distinct adj **1** DIFFERENT : distinto **2** CLEAR : claro — **distinction** n : distinción f — **distinctive** adj : distintivo

distinguish vt : distinguir — **distinguished** adj : distinguido

distort vt : deformar, distorsionar — **distortion** n : deformación f

distract vt : distraer — **distraction** n : distracción f

distraught adj : muy afligido

distress n **1** : angustia f, aflicción f **2 in** ∼ : en peligro — ∼ vt : afligir — **distressing** adj : penoso

distribute vt -**uted; -uting** : distribuir, repartir — **distribution** n : distribución f — **distributor** n : distribuidor m, -dora f

district n **1** REGION : región f, zona f, barrio m (de una ciudad) **2** : distrito m (zona política)

distrust n : desconfianza f — ∼ vt : desconfiar de

disturb vt **1** BOTHER : molestar, perturbar **2** WORRY : inquietar — **disturbance** n **1** COMMOTION : alboroto m, disturbio m **2** INTERRUPTION : interrupción f

disuse n fall into ∼ : caer en desuso

ditch n : zanja f, cuneta f — ∼ vt DISCARD : deshacerse de, botar

ditto n, pl -**tos 1** : ídem m **2** ∼ **marks** : comillas fpl

dive vi **dived** or **dove; dived; diving 1** : zambullirse, tirarse al agua **2** DESCEND : bajar en picada (dícese de un avión, etc.) — ∼ n **1** : zambullida f, clavado m Lat **2** DESCENT : descenso m en picada — **diver** n : saltador m, -dora f

diverge vi -**verged; -verging** : divergir

diverse adj : diverso — **diversify** v -**fied; -fying** vt : diversificar — vi : diversificarse

diversion n **1** : desviación f **2** AMUSEMENT : diversión f, distracción f

diversity n, pl -**ties** : diversidad f

divert vt **1** : desviar **2** DISTRACT : distraer **3** AMUSE : divertir

divide v -**vided; -viding** vt : dividir — vi : dividirse

dividend n : dividendo m

divine adj -**viner; -est** : divino — **divinity** n, pl -**ties** : divinidad f

division n : división f

divorce n : divorcio m — ∼ v -**vorced; -vorcing** vt : divorciar — vi : divorciarse — **divorcée** n : divorciada f

divulge vt -**vulged; -vulging** : revelar, divulgar

dizzy adj **dizzier; -est 1** : mareado **2 a** ∼ **speed** : una velocidad vertiginosa — **dizziness** n : mareo m, vértigo m

DNA n : AND m

do v **did; done; doing; does** vt **1** : hacer **2** PREPARE : preparar — vi **1** BEHAVE : hacer **2** FARE : estar, ir, andar **3** SUFFICE : ser suficiente **4** ∼ **away with** : abolir, eliminar **5 how are you doing?** : ¿cómo estás? — v aux **1** (used in interrogative sentences) **do you know her?** : ¿la conoces? **2** (used in negative statements) **I don't know** : yo no sé **3** (used as a substitute verb to avoid repetition) **do you speak English? yes, I do** : ¿habla inglés? sí

dock n : muelle m — ∼ vt : descontar dinero de (un sueldo) — vi ANCHOR : fondear, atracar

doctor n **1** : doctor m, -tora f (en derecho, etc.) **2** PHYSICIAN : médico m, -ca; doctor m, -tora f — ∼ vt ALTER : alterar, falsificar

doctrine n : doctrina f

document n : documento m — ∼ vt : documentar — **documentary** n, pl -**ries** : documental m

dodge n : artimaña f, truco m — ∼ v **dodged; dodging** vt : esquivar, eludir — vi : echarse a un lado

doe n, pl **does** or **doe** : gama f, cierva f
does → **do**
dog n : perro m, -rra f — ~ vt **dogged; dogging** : perseguir — **dogged** adj : tenaz
dogma n : dogma m — **dogmatic** adj : dogmático
doily n, pl **-lies** : tapete m
doings npl : actividades fpl
doldrums npl **be in the** ~ : estar abatido
dole n : subsidio m de desempleo — ~ vt **doled; doling** or ~ **out** : repartir
doleful adj : triste, lúgubre
doll n : muñeco m, -ca f
dollar n : dólar m
dolphin n : delfín m
domain n 1 TERRITORY : dominio m 2 FIELD : campo m, esfera f
dome n : cúpula f
domestic adj 1 : doméstico 2 INTERNAL : nacional — ~ n SERVANT : empleado m doméstico, empleada f doméstica — **domesticate** vt **-cated; -cating** : domesticar
domination n : dominación f — **dominant** adj : dominante — **dominate** v **-nated; -nating** : dominar — **domineer** vi : dominar, tiranizar
dominos n : dominó m (juego)
donate vt **-nated; -nating** : donar, hacer un donativo de — **donation** n : donativo m
done → **do** — ~ adj 1 FINISHED : terminado, hecho 2 COOKED : cocido
donkey n, pl **-keys** : burro m
donor n : donante mf
don't (contraction of **do not**) → **do**
doodle v **-dled; -dling** : garabatear — ~ n : garabato m
doom n : perdición f, fatalidad f — ~ vt : condenar
door n 1 : puerta f 2 ENTRANCE : entrada f — **doorbell** n : timbre m — **doorknob** n : pomo m — **doorman** n, pl **-men** : portero m — **doormat** n : felpudo m — **doorstep** n : umbral m — **doorway** n : entrada f, portal m
dope n 1 DRUG : droga f 2 IDIOT : idiota mf — ~ vt **doped; doping** : drogar
dormant adj : inactivo, latente
dormitory n, pl **-ries** : dormitorio m
dose n : dosis f — **dosage** n : dosis f
dot n 1 : punto m 2 **on the** ~ : en punto
dot–com n : puntocom m
dote vi **doted; doting** ~ **on** : adorar
double adj : doble — ~ v **-bled; -bling** vt : doblar — vi : doblarse — ~ adv : (el) doble — ~ n : doble mf — **double bass** n : contrabajo m — **double–cross** vt : traicionar — **doubly** adv : doblemente
doubt vt 1 : dudar 2 DISTRUST : desconfiar de, dudar de — ~ n : duda f — **doubt-**

ful adj : dudoso — **doubtless** adv : sin duda
dough n : masa f — **doughnut** n : rosquilla f, dona f Lat
douse vt **doused; dousing** 1 DRENCH : empapar, mojar 2 EXTINGUISH : apagar
dove¹ → **dive**
dove² n : paloma f
dowdy adj **dowdier; -est** : poco elegante
down adv 1 DOWNWARD : hacia abajo 2 **come/go** ~ : bajar 3 ~ **here** : aquí abajo 4 **fall** ~ : caer 5 **lie** ~ : acostarse 6 **sit** ~ : sentarse — ~ prep 1 ALONG : a lo largo de 2 THROUGH : a través de 3 ~ **the hill** : cuesta abajo — ~ adj 1 DESCENDING : de bajada 2 DOWNCAST : abatido — ~ n : plumón m — **downcast** adj : triste, abatido — **downfall** n : ruina f — **downhearted** adj : desanimado — **downhill** adv & adj : cuesta abajo — **down payment** n : entrega f inicial — **downpour** n : chaparrón m — **downright** adv : absolutamente — ~ adj : absoluto, categórico — **downstairs** adv : abajo — ~ adj : de abajo — **downstream** adv : río abajo — **down-to–earth** adj : realista — **downtown** n : centro m (de la ciudad) — ~ adv : al centro, en el centro — ~ adj : del centro — **downward** or **downwards** adv & adj : hacia abajo
downloadable adj : descargable
dowry n, pl **-ries** : dote f
doze vi **dozed; dozing** : dormitar
dozen n, pl **dozens** or **dozen** : docena f
drab adj **drabber; drabbest** : monótono, apagado
draft n 1 : corriente f de aire 2 or **rough** ~ : borrador m 3 : conscripción f (militar) 4 or ~ **beer** : cerveza f de barril — ~ vt 1 SKETCH : hacer el borrador de 2 CONSCRIPT : reclutar — **drafty** adj **draftier; -est** : con corrientes de aire
drag v **dragged; dragging** vt 1 : arrastrar 2 DREDGE : dragar — vi : arrastrar(se) — ~ n 1 RESISTANCE : resistencia f (aerodinámica) 2 BORE : pesadez f, plomo m fam
dragon n : dragón m — **dragonfly** n, pl **-flies** : libélula f
drain vt 1 EMPTY : vaciar, drenar 2 EXHAUST : agotar — vi 1 : escurrir(se) (se dice de los platos) 2 or ~ **away** : desaparecer poco a poco — ~ n 1 : desagüe m 2 SEWER : alcantarilla f 3 DEPLETION : agotamiento m — **drainage** n : drenaje m — **drainpipe** n : tubo m de desagüe
drama n : drama m — **dramatic** adj : dramático — **dramatist** n : dramaturgo m, -ga f — **dramatize** vt **-tized; -tizing** : dramatizar

drank → **drink**
drape vt **draped; draping 1** COVER : cubrir (con tela) **2** HANG : drapear —**drapes** npl CURTAINS : cortinas fpl
drastic adj : drástico
draught → **draft**
draw v **drew** ; **drawn** ; **drawing** vt **1** PULL : tirar de **2** ATTRACT : atraer **3** SKETCH : dibujar, trazar **4** : sacar (una espada, etc.) **5** ~ **a conclusion** : llegar a una conclusión **6** ~ **up** DRAFT : redactar — vi **1** SKETCH : dibujar **2** ~ **near** : acercarse — ~ n **1** DRAWING : sorteo m **2** TIE : empate m **3** ATTRACTION : atracción f — **drawback** n : desventaja f — **drawer** n : gaveta f, cajón m (en un mueble) — **drawing** n **1** LOTTERY : sorteo m **2** SKETCH : dibujo m
drawl n : habla f lenta y con vocales prolongadas
dread vt : temer — ~ n : pavor m, temor m — **dreadful** adj : espantoso, terrible
dream n : sueño m — ~ v **dreamed** or **dreamt; dreaming** vi : soñar — vt **1** : soñar **2** ~ **up** : idear — **dreamer** n : soñador m, -dora f — **dreamy** adj **dreamier; -est** : soñador
dreary adj **-rier; -est** : sombrío, deprimente
dredge vt **dredged; dredging** : dragar — ~ n : draga f
dregs npl : heces fpl
drench vt : empapar
dress vt **1** : vestir **2** : preparar (pollo o pescado), aliñar (ensalada) — vi **1** : vestirse **2** ~ **up** : ponerse elegante — ~ n **1** CLOTHING : ropa f **2** : vestido m (de mujer) — **dresser** n : cómoda f con espejo — **dressing** n **1** : aliño m (de ensalada), relleno m (de pollo) **2** BANDAGE : vendaje m — **dressmaker** n : modista mf — **dressy** adj **dressier; -est** : elegante
drew → **draw**
dribble vi **-bled; -bling 1** DRIP : gotear **2** DROOL : babear **3** : driblar (en basquetbol) — ~ n **1** TRICKLE : goteo m, hilo m **2** DROOL : baba f
drier, driest → **dry**
drift n **1** MOVEMENT : movimiento m **2** HEAP : montón m (de arena, etc.), ventisquero m (de nieve) **3** MEANING : sentido m — ~ vi **1** : ir a la deriva **2** ACCUMULATE : amontonarse
drill n **1** : taladro m **2** : ejercicio m (en educación), simulacro m (de incendio, etc.) — ~ vt **1** : perforar, taladrar **2** TRAIN : instruir por repetición — vi ~ **for** : perforar en busca de
drink v **drank; drunk** or **drank; drinking** : beber — ~ n : bebida f
drip vi **dripped; dripping** : gotear — ~ n **1** DROP : gota f **2** DRIPPING : goteo m

drip–dry adj : de lavar y poner
drive v **drove; driven; driving** vt **1** : manejar **2** IMPEL : impulsar **3** ~ **crazy** : volver loco **4** ~ **s.o. to (do sth)** : llevar a algn a (hacer algo) — vi : manejar, conducir — ~ n **1** : paseo m (en coche) **2** CAMPAIGN : campaña f **3** VIGOR : energía f **4** NEED : instinto m
drivel n : tonterías fpl
driver n : conductor m, -tora f; chofer m
driveway n : camino m de entrada
drizzle n : llovizna f — ~ vi **-zled; -zling** : lloviznar
drone n **1** BEE : zángano m **2** HUM : zumbido m — ~ vi **droned; droning 1** BUZZ : zumbar **2** or ~ **on** : hablar con monotonía
drool vi : babear — ~ n : baba f
droop vi : inclinarse (dícese de la cabeza), encorvarse (dícese de los escombros), marchitarse (dícese de las flores)
drop n **1** : gota f (de líquido) **2** DECLINE, FALL : caída f — ~ v **dropped; dropping** vt **1** : dejar caer **2** LOWER : bajar **3** ABANDON : abandonar, dejar **4** ~ **off** LEAVE : dejar — vi **1** FALL : caer(se) **2** DECREASE : bajar, descender **3** ~ **by** or ~ **in** : pasar
drought n : sequía f
drove → **drive**
droves n **in** ~ : en manada
drown vt : ahogar — vi : ahogarse
drowsy adj **drowsier; -est** : somnoliento
drudgery n, pl **-eries** : trabajo m pesado
drug n **1** MEDICATION : medicamento m **2** NARCOTIC : droga f, estupefaciente m — ~ vt **drugged; drugging** : drogar — **drugstore** n : farmacia f
drum n **1** : tambor m **2** or **oil** ~ : bidón m (de petróleo) — ~ v **drummed; drumming** vt : tocar el tambor — vt : tamborilear con (los dedos, etc.) — **drumstick** n **1** : palillo m (de tambor) **2** : muslo m (de pollo)
drunk → **drink** — ~ adj : borracho — ~ or **drunkard** n : borracho m, -cha f — **drunken** adj : borracho, ebrio
dry adj **drier; driest** : seco — ~ v **dried; drying** vt : secar — vi : secarse — **dry-clean** vt : limpiar en seco — **dry cleaner** n : tintorería f (servicio) — **dry cleaning** n : limpieza f en seco — **dryer** n : secadora f — **dryness** n : sequedad f, aridez f
dual adj : doble
dub vt **dubbed; dubbing 1** CALL : apodar **2** : doblar (una película)
dubious adj **1** UNCERTAIN : dudoso **2** QUESTIONABLE : sospechoso
duchess n : duquesa f
duck n, pl **duck** or **ducks** : pato m, -ta f — ~ vt **1** LOWER : agachar, bajar **2** EVADE

: eludir, esquivar — *vi* : agacharse — **duck-ling** *n* : patito *m*, -ta *f*
duct *n* : conducto *m*
due *adj* **1** PAYABLE : pagadero **2** APPROPRI-ATE : debido, apropiado **3** EXPECTED : espe-rado **4** ~ **to** : debido a — ~ *n* **1 give s.o. their** ~ : hacer justicia a algn **2** ~**s** *npl* : cuota *f* — ~ *adv* ~ **east** : justo al este
duel *n* : duelo *m*
duet *n* : dúo *m*
dug → **dig**
duke *n* : duque *m*
dull *adj* **1** STUPID : torpe **2** BLUNT : desafi-lado **3** BORING : aburrido **4** LACKLUSTER : apagado — ~ *vt* : entorpecer (los senti-dos), aliviar (el dolor)
dumb *adj* **1** MUTE : mudo **2** STUPID : es-túpido
dumbfound *or* dumfound *vt* : dejar sin habla
dummy *n, pl* **-mies 1** SHAM : imitación *f* **2** MANNEQUIN : maniquí *m* **3** IDIOT : tonto *m*, -ta *f*
dump *vt* : descargar, verter — ~ *n* **1** : ver-tedero *m*, tiradero *m Lat* **2 down in the** ~**s** : triste, deprimido
dumpling *n* : bola *f* de masa hervida
dumpy *adj* **dumpier; -est** : regordete
dunce *n* : burro *m*, -rra *f fam*
dune *n* : duna *f*
dung *n* **1** : excrementos *mpl* **2** MANURE : estiércol *m*
dungarees *npl* JEANS : vaqueros *mpl*, jeans *mpl*
dungeon *n* : calabozo *m*
dunk *vt* : mojar

duo *n, pl* **duos** : dúo *m*
dupe *vt* **duped; duping** : engañar — ~ *n* : inocentón *m*, -tona *f*
duplex *n* : casa *f* de dos viviendas, dúplex *m*
duplicate *adj* : duplicado — ~ *vt* **-cated; -cating** : duplicar, hacer copias de — ~ *n* : duplicado *m*, copia *f*
durable *adj* : duradero
duration *n* : duración *f*
duress *n* : coacción *f*
during *prep* : durante
dusk *n* : anochecer *m*, crepúsculo *m*
dust *n* : polvo *m* — ~ *vt* **1** : quitar el polvo a **2** SPRINKLE : espolvorear — **dustpan** *n* : recogedor *m* — **dusty** *adj* **dustier; -est** : polvoriento
Dutch *adj* : holandés — ~ *n* **1** : holandés *m* (idioma) **2 the** ~ : los holandeses
duty *n, pl* **-ties 1** OBLIGATION : deber *m* **2** TAX : impuesto *m* **3 on** ~ : de servicio — **dutiful** *adj* : obediente
dwarf *n, pl* **dwarfs** *or* **dwarves** : enano *m*, -na *f* — ~ *vt* : hacer parecer pequeño
dwell *vi* **dwelled** *or* **dwelt; dwelling 1** RE-SIDE : morar, vivir **2** ~ **on** : pensar de-masiado en — **dweller** *n* : habitante *mf* — **dwelling** *n* : morada *f*, vivienda *f*
dwindle *vi* **-dled; -dling** : disminuir
dye *n* : tinte *m* — ~ *vt* **dyed; dyeing** : teñir
dying → **die**[1]
dynamic *adj* : dinámico
dynamite *n* : dinamita *f*
dynamo *n, pl* **-mos** : dínamo *m*
dynasty *n, pl* **-ties** : dinastía *f*
dysentery *n, pl* **-teries** : disentería *f*

E

e *n, pl* **e's** *or* **es** : e *f*, quinta letra del alfabeto inglés
e- *pref* : electrónico (**e-mail** : e-mail, correo electrónico)
each *adj* : cada — ~ *pron* **1** : cada uno *m*, cada una *f* **2** ~ **other** : el uno al otro **3 they hate** ~ **other** : se odian — ~ *adv* : cada uno, por persona
eager *adj* **1** ENTHUSIASTIC : entusiasta **2** IMPATIENT : impaciente — **eagerness** *n* : entusiasmo *m*, impaciencia *f*
eagle *n* : águila *f*
ear *n* **1** : oreja *f* **2** ~ **of corn** : mazorca *f*, choclo *m Lat* — **eardrum** *n* : tímpano *m*
earl *n* : conde *m*

earlobe *n* : lóbulo *m* de la oreja
early *adv* **earlier; -est 1** : temprano **2 as** ~ **as possible** : lo más pronto posible **3 ten minutes** ~ : diez minutos de adelanto — ~ *adj* **earlier; -est 1** FIRST : primero **2** ANCIENT : primitivo, antiguo **3 an** ~ **death** : una muerte prematura **4 be** ~ : llegar temprano **5 in the** ~ **spring** : a principios de la primavera
earmark *vt* : destinar
earn *vt* **1** : ganar **2** DESERVE : merecer
earnest *adj* : serio — ~ *n* **in** ~ : en serio
earnings *npl* **1** WAGES : ingresos *mpl* **2** PROFITS : ganancias *fpl*
earphone *n* : audífono *m*

earplug *n* : tapón *m* para el oído
earring *n* : pendiente *m*, arete *m Lat*
earshot *n* **within** ~ : al alcance del oído
earth *n* : tierra *f* — **earthenware** *n* : loza *f* — **earthly** *adj* : terrenal — **earthquake** *n* : terremoto *m* — **earthworm** *n* : lombriz *f* (de tierra) — **earthy** *adj* **earthier; -est** **1** : terroso **2** COARSE, CRUDE : grosero
ease *n* **1** FACILITY : facilidad *f* **2** COMFORT : comodidad *f* **3 feel at** ~ : sentir cómodo — ~ *v* **eased; easing** *vt* **1** ALLEVIATE : aliviar, calmar **2** FACILITATE : facilitar — *vi* **1** : calmarse **2** ~ **up** : disminuir
easel *n* : caballete *m*
easily *adv* **1** : fácilmente, con facilidad **2** UNQUESTIONABLY : con mucho, de lejos *Lat*
east *adv* : al este — ~ *adj* : este, del este — ~ *n* **1** : este *m* **2 the East** : el Oriente
Easter *n* : Pascua *f*
easterly *adv & adj* : del este
eastern *adj* **1** : del este **2 Eastern** : oriental, del este
easy *adj* **easier; -est** **1** : fácil **2** RELAXED : relajado — **easygoing** *adj* : tolerante, relajado
eat *v* **ate; eaten; eating** *vt* : comer — *vi* **1** : comer **2** ~ **into** CORRODE : corroer **3** ~ **into** DEPLETE : comerse — **eatable** *adj* : comestible
eaves *npl* : alero *m* — **eavesdrop** *vi* **-dropped; -dropping** : escuchar a escondidas
ebb *n* : reflujo *m* — ~ *vi* **1** : bajar (dícese de la marea) **2** DECLINE : decaer
ebony *n*, *pl* **-nies** : ébano *m*
e–book *n* : libro *m* electrónico, e-book *m*
eccentric *adj* : excéntrico — ~ *n* : excéntrico *m*, -ca *f* — **eccentricity** *n*, *pl* **-ties** : excentricidad *f*
echo *n*, *pl* **echoes** : eco *m* — ~ *v* **echoed; echoing** *vt* : repetir — *vi* : hacer eco, resonar
eclipse *n* : eclipse *m* — ~ *vt* **eclipsed; eclipsing** : eclipsar
ecology *n*, *pl* **-gies** : ecología *f* — **ecological** *adj* : ecológico
e–commerce *n* : comercio *m* electrónico
economy *n*, *pl* **-mies** : economía *f* — **economic** *or* **economical** *adj* : económico — **economics** *n* : economía *f* — **economist** *n* : economista *mf* — **economize** *v* **-mized; -mizing** : economizar
ecstasy *n*, *pl* **-sies** : éxtasis *m* — **ecstatic** *adj* : extático
Ecuadoran *or* **Ecuadorean** *or* **Ecuadorian** *adj* : ecuatoriano
edge *n* **1** BORDER : borde *m* **2** : filo *m* (de un cuchillo) **3** ADVANTAGE : ventaja *f* — ~ *v* **edged; edging** *vt* : bordear, ribetear — *vi* : avanzar poco a poco — **edgewise**

adv : de lado — **edgy** *adj* **edgier; -est** : nervioso
edible *adj* : comestible
edit *vt* **1** : editar, redactar, corregir **2** ~ **out** : suprimir, cortar — **edition** *n* : edición *f* — **editor** *n* : director *m*, -tora *f* (de un periódico); redactor *m*, -tora *f* (de un libro) — **editorial** *n* : editorial *m*
educate *vt* **-cated; -cating** **1** TEACH : educar, instruir **2** INFORM : informar — **education** *n* : educación *f* — **educational** *adj* **1** : educativo, instructivo **2** TEACHING : docente — **educator** *n* : educador *m*, -dora *f*
eel *n* : anguila *f*
eerie *adj* **-rier; -est** : extraño e inquietante, misterioso
effect *n* **1** : efecto *m* **2 go into** ~ : entrar en vigor — ~ *vt* : efectuar, llevar a cabo — **effective** *adj* **1** : eficaz **2** ACTUAL : efectivo, vigente — **effectiveness** *n* : eficacia *f*
effeminate *adj* : afeminado
effervescent *adj* : efervescente
efficient *adj* : eficiente — **efficiency** *n*, *pl* **-cies** : eficiencia *f*
effort *n* **1** : esfuerzo *m* **2 it's not worth the** ~ : no vale la pena — **effortless** *adj* : fácil, sin esfuerzo
egg *n* : huevo *m* — ~ *vt* ~ **on** : incitar
eggplant *n* : berenjena *f* — **eggshell** *n* : cascarón *m*
ego *n*, *pl* **egos** **1** SELF : ego *m*, yo *m* **2** SELF-ESTEEM : amor *m* propio — **egotism** *n* : egotismo *m* — **egotist** *n* : egotista *mf* — **egotistic** *or* **egotistical** *adj* : egotista
eiderdown *n* **1** DOWN : plumón *m* **2** COMFORTER : edredón *m*
eight *n* : ocho *m* — ~ *adj* : ocho — **eight hundred** *n* : ochocientos *m*
eighteen *n* : dieciocho *m* — ~ *adj* : dieciocho — **eighteenth** *adj* : decimoctavo — ~ *n* **1** : decimoctavo *m*, -va *f* (en una serie) **2** : dieciochoavo *m*, dieciochoava parte *f*
eighth *n* **1** : octavo *m*, -va *f* (en una serie) **2** : octavo *m*, octava parte *f* — ~ *adj* : octavo
eighty *n*, *pl* **eighties** : ochenta *m* — ~ *adj* : ochenta
either *adj* **1** : cualquiera (de los dos) **2** (*in negative constructions*) : ninguno (de los dos) **3** EACH : cada — ~ *pron* **1** : cualquiera *mf* (de los dos) **2** (*in negative constructions*) : ninguno *m*, -na *f* (de los dos) **3** *or* ~ **one** : algún *m*, alguna *f* — ~ *conj* **2** (*in negative constructions*) : ni
eject *vt* : expulsar, expeler
eke *vt* **eked; eking** *or* ~ **out** : ganar a duras penas
elaborate *adj* **1** DETAILED : detallado **2**

COMPLEX : complicado — ∼ v **-rated; -rat-ing** vt : elaborar — vi : entrar en detalles

elapse vi **elapsed; elapsing** : transcurrir

elastic adj : elástico — ∼ n 1 : elástico m 2 RUBBER BAND : goma f (elástica) — **elasticity** n, pl **-ties** : elasticidad f

elated adj : regocijado

elbow n : codo m

elder adj : mayor — ∼ n 1 : mayor mf 2 : anciano m, **-na** f (de un tribu, etc.) — **elderly** adj : mayor, anciano

elect vt : elegir — ∼ adj : electo — **election** n : elección f — **electoral** adj : electoral — **electorate** n : electorado m

electricity n, pl **-ties** : electricidad f — **electric** or **electrical** adj : eléctrico — **electrician** n : electricista mf — **electrify** vt **-fied; -fying** : electrificar — **electrocute** vt **-cuted; -cuting** : electrocutar

electron n : electrón m — **electronic** adj : electrónico — **electronic mail** n : correo m electrónico — **electronics** n : electrónica f

elegant adj : elegante — **elegance** n : elegancia f

element n 1 : elemento m 2 ∼s npl BASICS : elementos mpl, rudimentos mpl — **elementary** adj : elemental — **elementary school** n : escuela f primaria

elephant n : elefante m, **-ta** f

elevate vt **-vated; -vating** : elevar — **elevator** n : ascensor m

eleven n : once m — ∼ adj : once — **eleventh** adj : undécimo — ∼ n 1 : undécimo m, **-ma** f (en una serie) 2 : onceavo m, onceava parte f

elf n, pl **elves** : duende m

elicit vt : provocar

eligible adj : elegible

eliminate vt **-nated; -nating** : eliminar — **elimination** n : eliminación f

elite n : elite f

elk n : alce m (de Europa), uapití m (de América)

elliptical or **elliptic** adj : elíptico

elm n : olmo m

elongate vt **-gated; -gating** : alargar

elope vi **eloped; eloping** : fugarse — **elopement** n : fuga f

eloquence n : elocuencia f — **eloquent** adj : elocuente

else adv 1 **how** ∼ ? : ¿de qué otro modo? 2 **where** ∼ ? : ¿en qué otro sitio? 3 **or** ∼ : si no, de lo contrario — ∼ adj 1 **everyone** ∼ : todos los demás 2 **nobody** ∼ : ningún otro, nadie más 3 **nothing** ∼ : nada más 4 **what** ∼ ? : ¿qué más? — **elsewhere** adv : en otra parte

elude vt **eluded; eluding** : eludir, esquivar — **elusive** adj : esquivo

elves → **elf**

emaciated adj : escuálido, demacrado

E–mail → **electronic mail**

emanate vi **-nated; -nating** : emanar

emancipate vt **-pated; -pating** : emancipar — **emancipation** n : emancipación f

embalm vt : embalsamar

embankment n : terraplén m, dique m (de un río)

embargo n, pl **-goes** : embargo m

embark vt : embarcar — vi 1 : embarcarse 2 ∼ **upon** : emprender — **embarkation** n : embarque m, embarco m

embarrass vt : avergonzar — **embarrassing** adj : embarazoso — **embarrassment** n : vergüenza f

embassy n, pl **-sies** : embajada f

embed vt **-bedded; -bedding** : incrustar, enterrar

embellish vt : adornar, embellecer — **embellishment** n : adorno m

embers npl : ascuas fpl

embezzle vt **-zled; -zling** : desfalcar, malversar — **embezzlement** n : desfalco m, malversación f

emblem n : emblema m

embody vt **-bodied; -bodying** : encarnar, personificar

emboss vt : repujar, grabar en relieve

embrace v **-braced; -bracing** vt : abrazar — vi : abrazarse — ∼ n : abrazo m

embroider vt : bordar — **embroidery** n, pl **-deries** : bordado m

embryo n, pl **embryos** : embrión m

emerald n : esmeralda f

emerge vi **emerged; emerging** : salir, aparecer — **emergence** n : aparición f

emergency n, pl **-cies** 1 : emergencia f 2 ∼ **exit** : salida f de emergencia 3 ∼ **room** : sala f de urgencias, sala f de guardia

emery n, pl **-eries** 1 : esmeril m 2 ∼ **board** : lima f de uñas

emigrant n : emigrante mf — **emigrate** vi **-grated; -grating** : emigrar — **emigration** n : emigración f

eminence n : eminencia f — **eminent** adj : eminente

emission n : emisión f — **emit** vt **emitted; emitting** : emitir

emoticon n : emoticono m, emoticón m

emotion n : emoción f — **emotional** adj 1 : emocional 2 MOVING : emotivo

emperor n : emperador m

emphasis n, pl **-phases** : énfasis m — **emphasize** vt **-sized; -sizing** : subrayar, hacer hincapié en — **emphatic** adj : enérgico, categórico

empire n : imperio m

employ vt : emplear — **employee** n : empleado m, **-da** f — **employer** n : patrón m,

-trona *f;* empleador *m,* -dora *f* — **employment** *n* : trabajo *m,* empleo *m*
empower *vt* : autorizar
empress *n* : emperatriz *f*
empty *adj* **emptier; -est 1** : vacío **2** MEANINGLESS : vano — ~ *v* -**tied; -tying** *vt* : vaciar — *vi* : vaciarse — **emptiness** *n* : vacío *m*
emulate *vt* -**lated; -lating** : emular
enable *vt* -**abled; -abling** : hacer posible, permitir
enact *vt* **1** : promulgar (un ley o un decreto) **2** PERFORM : representar
enamel *n* : esmalte *m*
encampment *n* : campamento *m*
encase *vt* -**cased; -casing** : encerrar, revestir
enchant *vt* : encantar — **enchanting** *adj* : encantador — **enchantment** *n* : encanto *m*
enchilada *n* : enchilada *f*
encircle *vt* -**cled; -cling** : rodear
enclose *vt* -**closed; -closing 1** SURROUND : encerrar, cercar **2** INCLUDE : adjuntar (a una carta) — **enclosure** *n* **1** AREA : recinto *m* **2** : anexo *m* (con una carta)
encompass *vt* **1** ENCIRCLE : cercar **2** INCLUDE : abarcar
encore *n* **1** : bis *m*
encounter *vt* : encontrar — ~ *n* : encuentro *m*
encourage *vt* -**aged; -aging 1** : animar, alentar **2** FOSTER : promover, fomentar — **encouragement** *n* **1** : aliento *m* **2** PROMOTION : fomento *m*
encroach *vi* ~ **on** : invadir, usurpar, quitar (el tiempo)
encyclopedia *n* : enciclopedia *f*
end *n* **1** : fin **2** EXTREMITY : extremo *m,* punta *f* **3 come to an** ~ : llegar a su fin **4 in the** ~ : por fin — ~ *vt* : terminar, poner fin a — *vi* : terminar(se)
endanger *vt* : poner en peligro
endearing *adj* : simpático
endeavor *or Brit* **endeavour** *vt* ~ **to** : esforzarse por — ~ *n* : esfuerzo *m*
ending *n* : final *m,* desenlace *m*
endive *n* : endibia *f,* endivia *f*
endless *adj* **1** INTERMINABLE : interminable **2** INNUMERABLE : innumerable **3** ~ **possibilities** : posibilidades *fpl* infinitas
endorse *vt* -**dorsed; -dorsing 1** SIGN : endosar **2** APPROVE : aprobar — **endorsement** *n* APPROVAL : aprobación *f*
endow *vt* : dotar
endure *v* -**dured; -during** *vt* : soportar, aguantar — *vi* LAST : durar — **endurance** *n* : resistencia *f*
enemy *n, pl* -**mies** : enemigo *m,* -ga *f*
energy *n, pl* -**gies** : energía *f* — **energetic** *adj* : enérgico

enforce *vt* -**forced; -forcing 1** : hacer cumplir (un ley, etc.) **2** IMPOSE : imponer — **enforced** *adj* : forzoso — **enforcement** *n* : imposición *f* del cumplimiento
engage *v* -**gaged; -gaging** *vt* **1** : captar, atraer (la atención, etc.) **2** ~ **the clutch** : embragar — *vi* ~ **in** : dedicarse a, entrar en — **engagement** *n* **1** APPOINTMENT : cita *f,* hora *f* **2** BETROTHAL : compromiso *m* — **engaging** *adj* : atractivo
engine *n* **1** : motor *m* **2** LOCOMOTIVE : locomotora *f* — **engineer** *n* **1** : ingeniero *m,* -ra *f* **2** : maquinista *mf* (de locomotoras) — ~ *vt* **1** CONSTRUCT : construir **2** CONTRIVE : tramar — **engineering** *n* : ingeniería *f*
English *adj* : inglés — ~ *n* : inglés *m* (idioma) — **Englishman** *n* : inglés *m* — **Englishwoman** *n* : inglesa *f*
engrave *vt* -**graved; -graving** : grabar — **engraving** *n* : grabado *m*
engross *vt* : absorber
engulf *vt* : envolver
enhance *vt* -**hanced; -hancing** : aumentar, mejorar
enjoy *vt* **1** : disfrutar, gozar de **2** ~ **oneself** : divertirse — **enjoyable** *adj* : agradable — **enjoyment** *n* : placer *m*
enlarge *v* -**larged; -larging** *vt* : agrandar, ampliar — *vi* **1** : agrandarse **2** ~ **upon** : extenderse sobre — **enlargement** *n* : ampliación *f*
enlighten *vt* : aclarar, iluminar
enlist *vt* **1** ENROLL : alistar **2** OBTAIN : conseguir — *vi* : alistarse
enliven *vt* : animar
enmity *n, pl* -**ties** : enemistad *f*
enormous *adj* : enorme
enough *adj* : bastante, suficiente — ~ *adv* : bastante — ~ *pron* **1** : (lo) suficiente, (lo) bastante **2 it's not** ~ : no basta **3 I've had** ~ ! : ¡estoy harto!
enquire, enquiry → **inquire, inquiry**
enrage *vt* -**raged; -raging** : enfurecer
enrich *vt* : enriquecer
enroll *or* **enrol** *v* -**rolled; -rolling** *vt* : matricular, inscribir — *vi* : matricularse, inscribirse
ensemble *n* : conjunto *m*
ensign *n* **1** FLAG : enseña *f* **2** : alférez *mf* (de fragata)
enslave *vt* -**slaved; -slaving** : esclavizar
ensue *vi* -**sued; -suing** : seguir, resultar
ensure *vt* -**sured; -suring** : asegurar
entail *vt* : suponer, conllevar
entangle *vt* -**gled; -gling** : enredar — **entanglement** *n* : enredo *m*
enter *vt* **1** : entrar en **2** RECORD : inscribir — *vi* **1** : entrar **2** ~ **into** : firmar (un acuerdo), entablar (negociaciones, etc.)

enterprise *n* **1** : empresa *f* **2** INITIATIVE
: iniciativa *f* — **enterprising** *adj* : emprendedor
entertain *vt* **1** AMUSE : entretener, divertir
2 CONSIDER : considerar **3** ～ **guests** : recibir invitados — **entertainment** *n* : entretenimiento *m,* diversión *f*
enthrall *or* **enthral** *vt* **-thralled; -thralling**
: cautivar, embelesar
enthusiasm *n* : entusiasmo *m* — **enthusiast**
n : entusiasta *mf* — **enthusiastic** *adj* : entusiasta
entice *vt* **-ticed; -ticing** : atraer, tentar
entire *adj* : entero, completo — **entirely** *adv*
: completamente — **entirety** *n, pl* **-ties** : totalidad *f*
entitle *vt* **-tled; -tling 1** NAME : titular **2**
AUTHORIZE : dar derecho a — **entitlement**
n : derecho *m*
entity *n, pl* **-ties** : entidad *f*
entrails *npl* : entrañas *fpl,* vísceras *fpl*
entrance[1] *vt* **-tranced; -trancing** : encantar,
fascinar
entrance[2] *n* : entrada *f* — **entrant** *n* : participante *mf*
entreat *vt* : suplicar
entrée *or* **entree** *n* : plato *m* principal
entrepreneur *n* : empresario *m,* **-ria** *f*
entrust *vt* : confiar
entry *n, pl* **-tries 1** ENTRANCE : entrada *f* **2**
NOTATION : entrada *f,* anotación *f*
enumerate *vt* **-ated; -ating** : enumerar
enunciate *vt* **-ated; -ating 1** STATE : enunciar **2** PRONOUNCE : articular
envelop *vt* : envolver — **envelope** *n* : sobre
m
envious *adj* : envidioso — **enviously** *adv*
: con envidia
environment *n* : medio *m* ambiente — **environmental** *adj* : ambiental — **environmen-
talist** *n* : ecologista *mf*
envision *vt* : prever, imaginar
envoy *n* : enviado *m,* -da *f*
envy *n, pl* **envies** : envidia *f* — ～ *vt* **-vied;
-vying** : envidiar
enzyme *n* : enzima *f*
epic *adj* : épico — ～ *n* : epopeya *f*
epidemic *n* : epidemia *f* — ～ *adj* : epidémico
epilepsy *n, pl* **-sies** : epilepsia *f* — **epileptic**
adj : epiléptico — ～ *n* : epiléptico *m,* -ca *f*
episode *n* : episodio *m*
epitaph *n* : epitafio *m*
epitome *n* : personificación *f* — **epitomize**
vt **-mized; -mizing** : ser la personificación
de, personificar
epoch *n* : época *f*
equal *adj* **1** SAME : igual **2 be** ～ **to** : estar
a la altura de (una tarea, etc.) — ～ *n* : igual
mf — ～ *vt* **equaled** *or* **equalled; equaling**

or **equalling 1** : igualar **2** : ser igual a (en
matemáticas) — **equality** *n, pl* **-ties** : igualdad *f* — **equalize** *vt* **-ized; -izing** : igualar
— **equally** *adv* **1** : igualmente **2** ～ **important** : igual de importante
equate *vt* **equated; equating** ～ **with** : equiparar con — **equation** *n* : ecuación *f*
equator *n* : ecuador *m*
equilibrium *n, pl* **-riums** *or* **-ria** : equilibrio
m
equinox *n* : equinoccio *m*
equip *vt* **equipped; equipping** : equipar —
equipment *n* : equipo *m*
equity *n, pl* **-ties 1** FAIRNESS : equidad *f* **2**
equities *npl* STOCKS : acciones *fpl* ordinar-
ias
equivalent *adj* : equivalente — ～ *n* : equivalente *m*
era *n* : era *f,* época *f*
eradicate *vt* **-cated; -cating** : erradicar
erase *vt* **erased; erasing** : borrar — **eraser**
n : goma *f* de borrar, borrador *m*
erect *adj* : erguido — ～ *vt* : erigir, levantar
— **erection** *n* **1** BUILDING : construcción *f*
2 : erección *f* (en fisiología)
erode *vt* **eroded; eroding** : erosionar (el
suelo), corroer (metales) — **erosion** *n*
: erosión *f,* corrosión *f*
erotic *adj* : erótico
err *vi* : equivocarse, errar
errand *n* : mandado *m,* recado *m Spain*
erratic *adj* : errático, irregular
error *n* : error *m* — **erroneous** *adj* : erróneo
erupt *vi* **1** : hacer erupción (dícese de un
volcán) **2** : estallar (dícese de la cólera, la
violencia, etc.) — **eruption** *n* : erupción *f*
escalate *vi* **-lated; -lating** : intensificarse
escalator *n* : escalera *f* mecánica
escapade *n* : aventura *f*
escape *v* **-caped; -caping** *vt* : escapar a,
evitar — *vi* : escaparse, fugarse — ～ *n* **1**
: fuga *f* **2** ～ **from reality** : evasión *f* de la
realidad — **escapee** *n* : fugitivo *m,* **-va** *f*
escort *n* **1** GUARD : escolta *f* **2** COMPANION
: acompañante *mf* — ～ *vt* **1** : escoltar **2**
ACCOMPANY : acompañar
Eskimo *adj* : esquimal
especially *adv* : especialmente
espionage *n* : espionaje *m*
espresso *n, pl* **-sos** : café *m* exprés
essay *n* : ensayo *m* (literario), composición *f*
(académica)
essence *n* : esencia *f* — **essential** *adj*
: esencial — ～ *n* **1** : elemento *m* esencial
2 the ～ **s** : lo indispensable
establish *vt* : establecer — **establishment** *n*
: establecimiento *m*
estate *n* **1** POSSESSIONS : bienes *mpl* **2**
LAND, PROPERTY : finca *f*
esteem *n* : estima *f* — ～ *vt* : estimar

esthetic → aesthetic

estimate *vt* -mated; -mating : calcular, estimar — ~ *n* 1 : cálculo *m* (aproximado) 2 *or* ~ of costs : presupuesto *m* — estimation *n* 1 JUDGMENT : juicio *m* 2 ESTEEM : estima *f*

estuary *n, pl* -aries : estuario *m*, ría *f*

eternal *adj* : eterno — eternity *n, pl* -ties : eternidad *f*

ether *n* : éter *m*

ethical *adj* : ético — ethics *ns & pl* : ética *f*, moralidad *f*

ethnic *adj* : étnico

etiquette *n* : etiqueta *f*

Eucharist *n* : Eucaristía *f*

eulogy *n, pl* -gies : elogio *m*, panegírico *m*

euphemism *n* : eufemismo *m*

euphoria *n* : euforia *f*

euro *n, pl* -ros *or* -ro : euro *m*

European *adj* : europeo

evacuate *vt* -ated; -ating : evacuar — evacuation *n* : evacuación *f*

evade *vt* evaded; evading : evadir, eludir

evaluate *vt* -ated; -ating : evaluar

evaporate *vi* -rated; -rating : evaporarse

evasion *n* : evasión *f* — evasive *adj* : evasivo

eve *n* : víspera *f*

even *adj* 1 REGULAR, STEADY : regular, constante 2 LEVEL : plano, llano 3 SMOOTH : liso 4 EQUAL : igual 5 ~ number : número *m* par 6 get ~ with : desquitarse con — ~ *adv* 1 : hasta, incluso 2 ~ better : aún mejor, todavía mejor 3 ~ if : aunque 4 ~ so : aun así — ~ *vt* : igualar — *vi or* ~ out : nivelarse

evening *n* : tarde *f*, noche *f*

event *n* 1 : acontecimiento *m*, suceso *m* 2 : prueba *f* (en deportes) 3 in the ~ of : en caso de — eventful *adj* : lleno de incidentes

eventual *adj* : final — eventuality *n, pl* -ties : eventualidad *f* — eventually *adv* : al fin, finalmente

ever *adv* 1 ALWAYS : siempre 2 ~ since : desde entonces 3 hardly ~ : casi nunca 4 have you ~ done it? : ¿lo has hecho alguna vez?

evergreen *n* : planta *f* de hoja perenne

everlasting *adj* : eterno

every *adj* 1 EACH : cada 2 ~ month : todos los meses 3 ~ other day : cada dos días — everybody *pron* : todos *mpl*, -das *fpl;* todo el mundo — everyday *adj* : cotidiano, de todos los días — everyone → everybody — everything *pron* : todo — everywhere *adv* : en todas partes, por todas partes

evict *vt* : desahuciar, desalojar — eviction *n* : desahucio *m*

evidence *n* 1 PROOF : pruebas *fpl* 2 TESTIMONY : testimonio *m*, declaración *f* — evident *adj* : evidente — evidently *adv* 1 OBVIOUSLY : obviamente 2 APPARENTLY : evidentemente, al parecer

evil *adj* eviler *or* eviller; evilest *or* evillest : malvado, malo — ~ *n* : mal *m*, maldad *f*

evoke *vt* evoked; evoking : evocar

evolution *n* : evolución *f*, desarrollo *m* — evolve *vi* evolved; evolving : evolucionar, desarrollarse

exact *adj* : exacto, preciso — ~ *vt* : exigir — exacting *adj* : exigente — exactly *adv* : exactamente

exaggerate *v* -ated; -ating : exagerar — exaggeration *n* : exageración *f*

examine *vt* -ined; -ining 1 : examinar 2 INSPECT : revisar 3 QUESTION : interrogar — exam *n* : examen *m* — examination *n* : examen *m*

example *n* : ejemplo *m*

exasperate *vt* -ated; -ating : exasperar — exasperation *n* : exasperación *f*

excavate *vt* -vated; -vating : excavar — excavation *n* : excavación *f*

exceed *vt* : exceder, sobrepasar — exceedingly *adv* : extremadamente

excel *v* -celled; -celling *vi* : sobresalir — *vt* SURPASS : superar — excellence *n* : excelencia *f* — excellent *adj* : excelente

except *prep or* ~ for : excepto, menos, salvo — ~ *vt* : exceptuar — exception *n* : excepción *f* — exceptional *adj* : excepcional

excerpt *n* : extracto *m*

excess *n* : exceso *m* — ~ *adj* : excesivo, de sobra — excessive *adj* : excesivo

exchange *n* 1 : intercambio *m* 2 : cambio *m* (en finanzas) — ~ *vt* -changed; -changing : cambiar, intercambiar

excise *n* ~ tax : impuesto *m* interno, impuesto *m* sobre el consumo

excite *vt* -cited; -citing : excitar, emocionar — excited *adj* : excitado, entusiasmado — excitement *n* : entusiasmo *m*, emoción *f*

exclaim *v* : exclamar — exclamation *n* : exclamación *f* — exclamation point *n* : signo *m* de admiración

exclude *vt* -cluded; -cluding : excluir — excluding *prep* : excepto, con excepción de — exclusion *n* : exclusión *f* — exclusive *adj* : exclusivo

excrement *n* : excremento *m*

excruciating *adj* : insoportable, atroz

excursion *n* : excursión *f*

excuse *vt* -cused; -cusing 1 : perdonar 2 ~ me : perdóne, perdón — ~ *n* : excusa *f*

execute *vt* -cuted; -cuting : ejecutar — execution *n* : ejecución *f* — **executioner** *n* : verdugo *m*

executive *adj* : ejecutivo — ~ *n* **1** MANAGER : ejecutivo *m*, **-va** *f* **2** *or* ~ **branch** : poder *m* ejecutivo

exemplify *vt* **-fied; -fying** : ejemplificar — **exemplary** *adj* : ejemplar

exempt *adj* : exento — ~ *vt* : dispensar — **exemption** *n* : exención *f*

exercise *n* : ejercicio *m* — ~ *v* **-cised; -cising** *vt* USE : ejercer, hacer uso de — *vi* : hacer ejercicio

exert *vt* **1** : ejercer **2** ~ **oneself** : esforzarse — **exertion** *n* : esfuerzo *m*

exhale *v* **-haled; -haling** : exhalar

exhaust *vt* : agotar — ~ *n* **1** *or* ¶ **fumes** : gases *mpl* de escape **2** *or* ¶ **pipe** : tubo *m* de escape — **exhaustion** *n* : agotamiento *m* — **exhaustive** *adj* : exhaustivo

exhibit *vt* **1** DISPLAY : exponer **2** SHOW : mostrar — ~ *n* **1** : objeto *m* expuesto **2** EXHIBITION : exposición *f* — **exhibition** *n* : exposición *f*

exhilarate *vt* **-rated; -rating** : alegrar — **exhilaration** *n* : regocijo *m*

exile *n* **1** : exilio *m* **2** OUTCAST : exiliado *m*, **-da** *f* — ~ *vt* **exiled; exiling** : exiliar

exist *vi* : existir — **existence** *n* : existencia *f* — **existing** *adj* : existente

exit *n* : salida *f* — ~ *vi* : salir

exodus *n* : éxodo *m*

exonerate *vt* **-ated; -ating** : exonerar, disculpar

exorbitant *adj* : exorbitante, excesivo

exotic *adj* : exótico

expand *vt* **1** : ampliar, extender **2** : dilatar (metales, etc.) — *vi* **1** : ampliarse, extenderse **2** : dilatarse (dícese de metales, etc.) — **expanse** *n* : extensión *f* — **expansion** *n* : expansión *f*

expatriate *n* : expatriado *m*, **-da** *f* — ~ *adj* : expatriado

expect *vt* **1** : esperar **2** REQUIRE : contar con — *vi* **be expecting** : estar embarazada — **expectancy** *n*, *pl* **-cies** : esperanza *f* — **expectant** *adj* **1** : expectante **2** ~ **mother** : futura madre *f* — **expectation** *n* : esperanza *f*

expedient *adj* : conveniente — ~ *n* : expediente *m*, recurso *m*

expedition *n* : expedición *f*

expel *vt* **-pelled; -pelling** : expulsar (a una persona), expeler (humo, etc.)

expend *vt* : gastar — **expendable** *adj* : prescindible — **expenditure** *n* : gasto *m* — **expense** *n* **1** : gasto *m* **2** ~**s** *npl* : gastos *mpl*, expensas *fpl* **3 at the** ~ **of** : a expensas de — **expensive** *adj* : caro

experience *n* : experiencia *f* — ~ *vt*

-enced; -encing : experimentar — **experienced** *adj* : experimentado — **experiment** *n* : experimento *m* — ~ *vi* : experimentar — **experimental** *adj* : experimental

expert *adj* : experto — ~ *n* : experto *m*, **-ta** *f* — **expertise** *n* : pericia *f*, competencia *f*

expire *vi* **-pired; -piring** **1** : caducar, vencer **2** DIE : expirar, morir — **expiration** *n* : vencimiento *m*, caducidad *f*

explain *vt* : explicar — **explanation** *n* : explicación *f* — **explanatory** *adj* : explicativo

explicit *adj* : explícito

explode *v* **-ploded; -ploding** *vt* : hacer explotar — *vi* : explotar, estallar

exploit *n* : hazaña *f*, proeza *f* — ~ *vt* : explotar — **exploitation** *n* : explotación *f*

exploration *n* : exploración *f* — **explore** *vt* **-plored; -ploring** : explorar — **explorer** *n* : explorador *m*, **-dora** *f*

explosion *n* : explosión *f* — **explosive** *adj* : explosivo — ~ *n* : explosivo *m*

export *vt* : exportar — ~ *n* : exportación *f*

expose *vt* **-posed; -posing** **1** : exponer **2** REVEAL : descubrir, revelar — **exposed** *adj* : expuesto, al descubierto — **exposure** *n* : exposición *f*

express *adj* **1** SPECIFIC : expreso, específico **2** FAST : expreso, rápido — ~ *adv* : por correo urgente — ~ *n* *or* ~ **train** : expreso *m* — ~ *vt* : expresar — **expression** *n* : expresión *f* — **expressive** *adj* : expresivo — **expressly** *adv* : expresamente — **expressway** *n* : autopista *f*

expulsion *n* : expulsión *f*

exquisite *adj* : exquisito

extend *vt* **1** STRETCH : extender **2** LENGTHEN : prolongar **3** ENLARGE : ampliar **4** ~ **one's hand** : tender la mano — *vi* : extenderse — **extension** *n* **1** : extensión *f* **2** LENGTHENING : prolongación *f* **3** ANNEX : ampliación *f*, anexo *m* **4** ~ **cord** : alargador *m* — **extensive** *adj* : extenso — **extent** *n* **1** SIZE : extensión *f* **2** DEGREE : alcance *m*, grado *m* **3 to a certain** ~ : hasta cierto punto

extenuating *adj* ~ **circumstances** : circunstancias *fpl* atenuantes

exterior *adj* : exterior — ~ *n* : exterior *m*

exterminate *vt* **-nated; -nating** : exterminar — **extermination** *n* : exterminación *f*

external *adj* : externo — **externally** *adv* : exteriormente

extinct *adj* : extinto — **extinction** *n* : extinción *f*

extinguish *vt* : extinguir, apagar — **extinguisher** *n* : extintor *m*

extol *vt* **-tolled; -tolling** : ensalzar, alabar

extort *vt* : arrancar (algo a algn) por la fuerza — **extortion** *n* : extorsión *f*

extra *adj* : suplementario, de más — ~ *n* : extra *m* — ~ *adv* **1** : extra, más **2** ~ **special** : super especial

extract *vt* : extraer, sacar — ~ *n* : extracto *m* — **extraction** *n* : extracción *f*

extracurricular *adj* : extracurricular

extradite *vt* -**dited; -diting** : extraditar

extraordinary *adj* : extraordinario

extraterrestrial *adj* : extraterrestre — ~ *n* : extraterrestre *mf*

extravagant *adj* **1** WASTEFUL : despilfarrador, derrochador **2** EXAGGERATED : extravagante, exagerado — **extravagance** *n* **1** WASTEFULNESS : derroche *m*, despilfarro *m* **2** LUXURY : lujo *m* **3** EXAGGERATION : extravagancia *f*

extreme *adj* : extremo — ~ *n* : extremo *m*

— extremely *adv* : extremadamente — **extremity** *n*, *pl* -**ties** : extremidad *f*

extricate *vt* -**cated; -cating** : librar, (lograr) sacar

extrovert *n* : extrovertido *m*, -da *f* — **extroverted** *adj* : extrovertido

exuberant *adj* **1** JOYOUS : eufórico **2** LUSH : exuberante — **exuberance** *n* **1** JOYOUSNESS : euforia *f* **2** VIGOR : exuberancia *f*

exult *vi* : exultar

eye *n* **1** : ojo *m* **2** VISION : visión *f*, vista *f* **3** GLANCE : mirada *f* — ~ *vt* **eyed; eyeing** *or* **eying** : mirar — **eyeball** *n* : globo *m* ocular — **eyebrow** *n* : ceja *f* — **eyeglasses** *npl* : anteojos *mpl*, lentes *mpl* — **eyelash** *n* : pestaña *f* — **eyelid** *n* : párpado *m* — **eyesight** *n* : vista *f*, visión *f* — **eyesore** *n* : monstruosidad *f* — **eyewitness** *n* : testigo *mf* ocular

F

f *n*, *pl* **f's** *or* **fs** : f, sexta letra del alfabeto inglés

fable *n* : fábula *f*

fabric *n* : tela *f*, tejido *m*

fabulous *adj* : fabuloso

facade *n* : fachada *f*

face *n* **1** : cara *f*, rostro *m* (de una persona) **2** APPEARANCE : fisonomía *f*, aspecto *m* **3** : cara *f* (de una moneda), fachada *f* (de un edificio) **4** ~ **value** : valor *m* nominal **5** **in the** ~ **of** : en medio de, ante **6 lose** ~ : desprestigiarse **7 make** ~**s** : hacer muecas — ~ **faced; facing** *vt* **1** : estar frente a **2** CONFRONT : enfrentarse a **3** OVERLOOK : dar a — *vi* ~ **to the north** : mirar hacia el norte — **facedown** *adv* : boca abajo — **faceless** *adj* : anónimo — **face–lift** *n* : estiramiento *m* facial

facet *n* : faceta *f*

facetious *adj* : gracioso, burlón

face–to–face *adv* & *adj* : cara a cara

facial *adj* : de la cara, facial — ~ *n* : limpieza *f* de cutis

facility *n*, *pl* -**ties** **1** EASE : facilidad *f* **2** CENTER : centro *m* **3 facilities** *npl* : comodidades *fpl*, servicios *mpl*

facsimile *n* : facsímile *m*, facsímil *m*

fact *n* **1** : hecho *m* **2 in** ~ : en realidad, de hecho

faction *n* : facción *m*, bando *m*

factor *n* : factor *m*

factory *n*, *pl* -**ries** : fábrica *f*

factual *adj* : basado en hechos

faculty *n*, *pl* -**ties** : facultad *f*

fad *n* : moda *f* pasajera, manía *f*

fade *v* **faded; fading** *vi* **1** WITHER : marchitarse **2** DISCOLOR : desteñirse, decolorarse **3** DIM : apagarse **4** VANISH : desvanecerse — *vt* : desteñir

fail *vi* **1** : fracasar (dícese de una empresa, un matrimonio, etc.) **2** BREAK DOWN : fallar **3** ~ **in** : faltar a, no cumplir con **4** FLUNK : suspender *Spain*, ser reprobado *Lat* **5** ~ **to do sth** : no hacer algo — *vt* **1** DISAPPOINT : fallar **2** FLUNK : suspender *Spain*, reprobar *Lat* — ~ *n* **without** ~ : sin falta — **failing** *n* : defecto *m* — **failure** *n* **1** : fracaso *m* **2** BREAKDOWN : falla *f*

faint *adj* **1** WEAK : débil **2** INDISTINCT : tenue, indistinto **3 feel** ~ : estar mareado — ~ *vi* : desmayarse — ~ *n* : desmayo *m* — **fainthearted** *adj* : cobarde, pusilánime — **faintly** *adv* **1** WEAKLY : débilmente **2** SLIGHTLY : ligeramente, levemente

fair¹ *n* : feria *f*

fair² *adj* **1** BEAUTIFUL : bello, hermoso **2** : bueno (dícese del tiempo) **3** JUST : justo **4** : rubio (dícese del pelo), blanco (dícese de la tez) **5** ADEQUATE : adecuado — ~ *adv* **play** ~ : jugar limpio — **fairly** *adv* **1**

JUSTLY : justamente **2** QUITE : bastante —
fairness *n* : justicia *f*
fairy *n*, *pl* **fairies 1** : hada *f* **2** ~ **tale**
: cuento *m* de hadas
faith *n*, *pl* **faiths** : fe *f* — **faithful** *adj* : fiel
— **faithfully** *adv* : fielmente — **faithful-**
ness *n* : fidelidad *f*
fake *v* **faked; faking** *vt* **1** FALSIFY : falsificar, falsear **2** FEIGN : fingir — *vi* PRETEND
: fingir — ~ *adj* : falso — ~ *n* **1** IMITA-
TION : falsificación *f* **2** IMPOSTOR : impostor *m*, -tora *f*
falcon *n* : halcón *m*
fall *vi* **fell; fallen; falling 1** : caer, bajar
(dícese de los precios), descender (dícese de
la temperatura) **2** ~ **asleep** : dormirse **3**
~ **back** : retirarse **4** ~ **back on** : recurrir
a **5** ~ **down** : caerse **6** ~ **in love** : enamorarse **7** ~ **out** QUARREL : pelearse **8**
~ **through** : fracasar — ~ *n* **1** : caída *f*,
bajada *f* (de precios), descenso *m* (de temperatura) **2** AUTUMN : otoño *m* **3** ~**s** *npl*
WATERFALL : cascada *f*, catarata *f*
fallacy *n*, *pl* **-cies** : concepto *m* erróneo
fallible *adj* : falible
fallow *adj* **lie** ~ : estar en barbecho
false *adj* **falser; falsest 1** : falso **2** ~
alarm : falsa alarma *f* **3** ~ **teeth** : dentadura *f* postiza — **falsehood** *n* : mentira —
falseness *n* : falsedad *f* — **falsify** *vt* **-fied;**
fying : falsificar, falsear
falter *vi* **-tered; -tering 1** STUMBLE : tambalearse **2** WAVER : vacilar
fame *n* : fama *f*
familiar *adj* **1** : familiar **2 be** ~ **with**
: estar familiarizado con — **familiarity** *n*, *pl*
-ties : familiaridad *f* — **familiarize** *vt* **-ized;**
-izing ~ **oneself** : familiarizarse
family *n*, *pl* **-lies** : familia *f*
famine *n* : hambre *f*, hambruna *f*
famished *adj* : famélico
famous *adj* : famoso
fan 1 : ventilador *m*, abanico *m* **2** : aficionado *m*, -da *f* (a un pasatiempo); admirador *m*, -dora *f* (de una persona) — ~ *vt*
fanned; fanning : abanicar (a una persona),
avivar (un fuego)
fanatic *or* **fanatical** *adj* : fanático — ~ *n*
: fanático *m*, -ca *f* — **fanaticism** *n* : fanatismo *m*
fancy *vt* **-cied; -cying 1** IMAGINE : imaginarse **2** DESIRE : apetecerle (algo a uno)
— ~ *adj* **-cier; -est 1** ELABORATE : elaborado **2** LUXURIOUS : lujoso, elegante —
~ *n*, *pl* **-cies 1** WHIM : capricho *m* **2**
IMAGINATION : imaginación *f* **3 take a** ~
to : aficionarse a (una cosa), tomar cariño a
(una persona) — **fanciful** *adj* **1** CAPRI-
CIOUS : caprichoso **2** IMAGINATIVE : imaginativo

fanfare *n* : fanfarria *f*
fang *n* : colmillo *m* (de un animal), diente *m*
(de una serpiente)
fantasy *n*, *pl* **-sies** : fantasía *f* — **fantasize**
vi **-sized; -sizing** : fantasear — **fantastic**
adj : fantástico
FAQ *n*, *pl* **FAQs** : FAQ *m* (lista de preguntas)
far *adv* **farther** *or* **further; farthest** *or* **fur-**
thest 1 : lejos **2** MUCH : muy, mucho **3**
as ~ **as** : hasta (un lugar), con respecto a
(un tema) **4 by** ~ : con mucho **5** ~ **and**
wide : por todas partes **6** ~ **away** : a lo
lejos **7** ~ **from it!** : ¡todo lo contrario! **8**
so ~ : hasta ahora, todavía — ~ *adj* **far-**
ther *or* **further; farthest** *or* **furthest 1**
REMOTE : lejano **2** EXTREME : extremo —
faraway *adj* : remoto, lejano
farce *n* : farsa *f*
fare *vi* **fared; faring** : irle a uno — ~ *n* **1**
: precio *m* del pasaje **2** FOOD : comida *f*
farewell *n* : despedida *f* — ~ *adj* : de despedida
far–fetched *adj* : improbable, exagerado
farm *n* : granja *f*, hacienda *f* — ~ *vt* : cultivar (la tierra), criar (animales) — *vi* : ser
agricultor — **farmer** *n* : agricultor *m*, -tora *f*;
granjero *m*, -jera *f* — **farmhand** *n* : peón *m*
— **farmhouse** *n* : granja *f*, casa *f* de hacienda — **farming** *n* : agricultura *f*, cultivo *m*
(de plantas), crianza *f* (de animales) —
farmyard *n* : corral *m*
far–off *adj* : lejano
far–reaching *adj* : de gran alcance
farsighted *adj* **1** : hipermétrope **2** PRU-
DENT : previsor
farther *adv* **1** : más lejos **2** MORE : más —
adj : más lejano — **farthest** *adv* **1** : lo más
lejos **2** MOST : más — *adj* : más lejano
fascinate *vt* **-nated; -nating** : fascinar —
fascination *n* : fascinación *f*
fascism *n* : fascismo *m* — **fascist** *adj* : fascista — *n* : fascista *mf*
fashion *n* **1** MANNER : manera *f* **2** STYLE
: moda *f* **3 out of** ~ : pasada de moda —
fashionable *adj* : de moda
fast[1] *vi* : ayunar — ~ *n* : ayuno *m*
fast[2] *adj* **1** SWIFT : rápido **2** SECURE
: firme, seguro **3** : adelantado (dícese de un
reloj) **4** ~ **friends** : amigos *mpl* leales —
~ *adv* **1** SECURELY : firmemente **2**
SWIFTLY : rápidamente **3** ~ **asleep** : profundamente dormido
fasten *vt* : sujetar (papeles, etc.), abrochar
(una blusa, etc.), cerrar (una maleta, etc.)
— *vi* : abrocharse, cerrar — **fastener** *n*
: cierre *m*
fat *adj* **fatter; fattest 1** : gordo **2** THICK
: grueso — ~ *n* : grasa *f*
fatal *adj* **1** : mortal **2** FATEFUL : fatal,

fatídico — **fatality** *n, pl* **-ties** : víctima *f* mortal

fate *n* **1** : destino *m* **2** LOT : suerte *f* — **fateful** *adj* : fatídico

father *n* : padre *m* — ~ *vt* : engendrar — **fatherhood** *n* : paternidad *f* — **father–in–law** *n, pl* **fathers–in–law** : suegro *m* — **fatherly** *adj* : paternal

fathom *vt* : comprender

fatigue *n* : fatiga *f* — ~ *vt* **-tigued; -tiguing** : fatigar

fatten *vt* : engordar — **fattening** *adj* : que engorda

fatty *adj* **fattier; -est** : graso

faucet *n* : llave *f Lat*, grifo *m Spain*

fault *n* **1** FLAW : defecto *m* **2** RESPONSIBILITY : culpa *f* **3** : falla *f* (geológica) — *vt* : encontrar defectos a — **faultless** *adj* : impecable — **faulty** *adj* **faultier; -est** : defectuoso

fauna *n* : fauna *f*

favor *or Brit* **favour** *n* **1** : favor *m* **2 in ~ of** : a favor de — ~ *vt* **1** : favorecer **2** SUPPORT : estar a favor de **3** PREFER : preferir — **favorable** *or Brit* **favourable** *adj* : favorable — **favorite** *or Brit* **favourite** *n* : favorito *m*, -ta *f* — ~ *adj* : favorito — **favoritism** *or Brit* **favouritism** *n* : favoritismo *m*

fawn[1] *vi* ~ **over** : adular

fawn[2] *n* : cervato *m*

fax *n* : fax *m* — ~ *vt* : faxear, enviar por fax

fear *v* : temer — ~ *n* **1** : miedo *m*, temor *m* **2 for ~ of** : por temor a — **fearful** *adj* **1** FRIGHTENING : espantoso **2** AFRAID : temeroso

feasible *adj* : viable, factible

feast *n* **1** BANQUET : banquete *m*, festín *m* **2** FESTIVAL : fiesta *f* — ~ *vi* **1** : banquetear **2** ~ **upon** : darse un festín de

feat *n* : hazaña *f*

feather *n* : pluma *f*

feature *n* **1** : rasgo *m* (de la cara) **2** CHARACTERISTIC : característica *f* **3** : artículo *m* (en un periódico) **4** ~ **film** : largometraje *m* — *v* **-tured; -turing** *vt* **1** PRESENT : presentar **2** EMPHASIZE : destacar — *vi* : figurar

February *n* : febrero *m*

feces *npl* : excremento *mpl*

fed up *adj* : harto

federal *adj* : federal — **federation** *n* : federación *f*

fee *n* **1** : honorarios *mpl* **2 entrance ~** : entrada *f*

feeble *adj* **-bler; -blest** **1** : débil **2 a ~ excuse** : una pobre excusa

feed *v* **fed; feeding** *vt* **1** : dar de comer a, alimentar **2** SUPPLY : alimentar — *vi* : comer, alimentarse — ~ *n* : pienso *m*

feel *v* **felt; feeling** *vt* **1** : sentir (una sensación, etc.) **2** TOUCH : tocar, palpar **3** BELIEVE : creer — *vi* **1** : sentirse (bien, cansado, etc.) **2** SEEM : parecer **3** ~ **hot/thirsty** : tener calor/sed **4** ~ **like doing** : tener ganas de hacer — ~ *n* : tacto *m*, sensación *f*

feeling *n* **1** SENSATION : sensación *f*, sensibilidad *f* **2** EMOTION : sentimiento *m* **3** HUNCH, INTUITION : sensación *f* **4** OPINION : opinión *f* **5** ~**s** *npl* SENSIBILITIES : sentimientos *mpl* **to hurt/spare someone's feelings** : herir/no herir los sentimientos de alguien

feet → **foot**

feign *vt* : fingir

feline *adj* : felino — ~ *n* : felino *m*, **-na** *f*

fell[1] → **fall**

fell[2] *vt* : talar (un árbol)

fellow *n* **1** COMPANION : compañero *m*, -ra *f* **2** MEMBER : socio *m*, -cia *f* **3** MAN : tipo *m* — **fellowship** *n* **1** : compañerismo *m* **2** ASSOCIATION : fraternidad *f* **3** GRANT : beca *f*

felon *n* : criminal *mf* — **felony** *n, pl* **-nies** : delito *m* grave

felt[1] → **feel**

felt[2] *n* : fieltro *m*

female *adj* : femenino — ~ *n* **1** : hembra *f* (animal) **2** WOMAN : mujer *f*

feminine *adj* : femenino — **femininity** *n* : femineidad *f* — **feminism** *n* : feminismo *m* — **feminist** *adj* : feminista — ~ *n* : feminista *mf*

fence *n* : cerca *f*, valla *f*, cerco *m Lat* — ~ *v* **fenced; fencing** *vt or* ~ **in** : vallar, cercar — *vi* : hacer esgrima — **fencing** *n* : esgrima *m* (deporte)

fend *vt* ~ **off** : rechazar (un enemigo), eludir (una pregunta) — *vi* ~ **for oneself** : valerse por sí mismo

fender *n* : guardabarros *mpl*

fennel *n* : hinojo *m*

ferment *v* : fermentar — **fermentation** *n* : fermentación *f*

fern *n* : helecho *m*

ferocious *adj* : feroz — **ferocity** *n* : ferocidad *f*

ferret *n* : hurón *m* — ~ *vt* ~ **out** : descubrir

Ferris wheel *n* : noria *f*

ferry *vt* **-ried; -rying** : transportar — ~ *n, pl* **-ries** : ferry *m*

fertile *adj* : fértil — **fertility** *n* : fertilidad *f* — **fertilize** *vt* **-ized; -izing** : fecundar (un huevo), abonar (el suelo) — **fertilizer** *n* : fertilizante *m*, abono *m*

fervent *adj* : ferviente — **fervor** *or Brit* **fervour** *n* : fervor *m*
fester *vi* : enconarse
festival *n* **1** : fiesta *f* **2** film ~ : festival *m* de cine — **festive** *adj* : festivo — **festivity** *n, pl* **-ties** : festividad *f*
fetch *vt* **1** : ir a buscar **2** : venderse por (un precio)
fête *n* : fiesta *f*
fetid *adj* : fétido
fetish *n* : fetiche *m*
fetters *npl* : grillos *mpl* — **fetter** *vt* : encadenar
fetus *n* : feto *m*
feud *n* : enemistad *f* (entre familiares) — ~ *vi* : pelear
feudal *adj* : feudal — **feudalism** *n* : feudalismo *m*
fever *n* : fiebre *f* — **feverish** *adj* : febril
few *adj* **1** : pocos **2** a ~ **times** : varias veces — ~ *pron* **1** : pocos **2** a ~ : algunos, unos cuantos **3** quite a ~ : muchos — **fewer** *adj & pron* : menos
fiancé, fiancée *n* : prometido *m*, -da *f*; novio *m*, -via *f*
fiasco *n, pl* **-coes** : fiasco *m*
fib *n* : mentirilla *f* — ~ *vi* **fibbed; fibbing** : decir mentirillas
fiber *or* fibre *n* : fibra *f* — **fiberglass** *n* : fibra *f* de vidrio — **fibrous** *adj* : fibroso
fickle *adj* : inconstante
fiction *n* : ficción *f* — **fictional** *or* **fictitious** *adj* : ficticio
fiddle *n* : violín *m* — ~ *vi* **-dled; -dling 1** : tocar el violín **2** ~ **with** : juguetear con
fidelity *n, pl* **-ties** : fidelidad *f*
fidget *vi* **1** : estarse inquieto, moverse **2** ~ **with** : juguetear con — **fidgety** *adj* : inquieto, nervioso
field *n* : campo *m* — ~ *vt* : interceptar (una pelota), sortear (una pregunta) — **field glasses** *n* : binoculares *mpl*, gemelos *mpl* — **field trip** *n* : viaje *m* de estudio
fiend *n* **1** : demonio *m* **2** FANATIC : fanático *m*, -ca *f* — **fiendish** *adj* : diabólico
fierce *adj* **fiercer; -est 1** : feroz **2** INTENSE : fuerte (dícese del viento), acalorado (dícese de un debate) — **fierceness** *n* : ferocidad *f*
fiery *adj* **fierier; -est 1** BURNING : llameante **2** SPIRITED : ardiente, fogoso — **fieriness** *n* : pasión *f*, ardor *m*
fifteen *n* : quince *m* — ~ *adj* : quince — **fifteenth** *adj* : decimoquinto — ~ *n* **1** : decimoquinto *m*, -ta *f* (en una serie) **2** : quinceavo *m* (en matemáticas)
fifth *n* **1** : quinto *m*, -ta *f* (en una serie) **2** : quinto *m* (en matemáticas) — ~ *adj* : quinto

fiftieth *adj* : quincuagésimo — ~ *n* **1** : quincuagésimo *m*, -ma *f* (en una serie) **2** : cincuentavo *m* (en matemáticas)
fifty *n, pl* **-ties** : cincuenta *m* — ~ *adj* : cincuenta — **fifty–fifty** *adv* : a medias, mitad y mitad — ~ *adj* a ~ **chance** : un cincuenta por ciento de posibilidades
fig *n* : higo *m*
fight *v* **fought; fighting** *vi* **1** BATTLE : luchar **2** QUARREL : pelear **3** ~ **back** : defenderse — *vt* : luchar contra — ~ *n* **1** STRUGGLE : lucha *f* **2** QUARREL : pelea *f* — **fighter** *n* **1** : luchador *m*, -dora *f* **2** *or* ~ **plane** : avión *m* de caza
figment *n* ~ **of the imagination** : producto *m* de la imaginación
figurative *adj* : figurado
figure *n* **1** NUMBER : número *m*, cifra *f* **2** PERSON, SHAPE : figura *f* **3** ~ **of speech** : figura *f* retórica **4** watch one's ~ : cuidar la línea — ~ *v* **-ured; -uring** *vt* : calcular — *vi* **1** : figurar **2** that ~s! : ¡no me extraña! — **figurehead** *n* : testaferro *m* — **figure out** *vt* **1** UNDERSTAND : entender **2** RESOLVE : resolver
file[1] *n* : lima *f* (instrumento) — ~ *vt* **filed; filing** : limar
file[2] *vt* **filed; filing 1** : archivar (documentos) **2** ~ **charges** : presentar cargos — ~ *n* : archivo *m*
file[3] *n* LINE : fila *f* — ~ *vi* ~ **in/out** : entrar/salir en fila
fill *vt* **1** : llenar, rellenar **2** : cumplir con (un requisito) **3** : tapar (un agujero), empastar (un diente) — *vi* **1** ~ **in for** : reemplazar **2** *or* ~ **up** : llenarse — ~ *n* **1** eat one's ~ : comer lo suficiente **2** have one's ~ **of** : estar harto de
fillet *n* : filete *m*
filling *n* **1** : relleno *m* **2** : empaste *m* (de dientes) **3** ~ **station** → **service station**
filly *n, pl* **-lies** : potra *f*
film *n* : película *f* — ~ *vt* : filmar
filter *n* : filtro *m* — ~ *vt* : filtrar
filth *n* : mugre *f* — **filthy** *adj* **filthier; -est 1** : mugriento **2** OBSCENE : obsceno
fin *n* : aleta *f*
final *adj* **1** LAST : último **2** DEFINITIVE : definitivo **3** ULTIMATE : final — ~ *n* **1** : final *f* (en deportes) **2** ~**s** *npl* : exámenes *mpl* finales — **finalist** *n* : finalista *mf* — **finalize** *vt* **-ized; -izing** : finalizar — **finally** *adv* : finalmente
finance *n* **1** : finanzas *fpl* **2** ~**s** *npl* : recursos *mpl* financieros — ~ *vt* **-nanced; -nancing** : financiar — **financial** *adj* : financiero — **financially** *adv* : económicamente

find *vt* **found; finding 1** LOCATE : encontrar **2** REALIZE : darse cuenta de **3** ~ **guilty** : declarar culpable **4** *or* ~ **out** : descubrir — *vi* ~ **out** : enterarse — ~ *n* : hallazgo *m* — **finding** *n* **1** FIND : hallazgo *m* **2** ~**s** *npl* : conclusiones *fpl*

fine¹ *n* : multa *f* — ~ *vt* **fined; fining** : multar

fine² *adj* **finer; -est 1** DELICATE : fino **2** EXCELLENT : excelente **3** SUBTLE : sutil **4** : bueno (dícese del tiempo) **5** ~ **print** : letra *f* menuda **6 it's** ~ **with me** : me parece bien — ~ *adv* OK : bien — **fine arts** *npl* : bellas artes *fpl* — **finely** *adv* **1** EXCELLENTLY : excelentemente **2** PRECISELY : con precisión **3** MINUTELY : fino, menudo

finger *n* : dedo *m* — ~ *vt* : tocar, toquetear — **fingernail** *n* : uña *f* — **fingerprint** *n* : huella *f* digital — **fingertip** *n* : punta *f* del dedo

finicky *adj* : maniático, mañoso *Lat*

finish *v* : acabar, terminar — ~ *n* **1** END : fin *m*, final *m* **2** *or* ~ **line** : meta *f* **3** SURFACE : acabado *m*

finite *adj* : finito

fir *n* : abeto *m*

fire *n* **1** : fuego *m* **2** CONFLAGRATION : incendio *m* **3 catch** ~ : incendiarse (dícese de bosques, etc.), prenderse (dícese de fósforos, etc.) **4 on** ~ : en llamas **5 open** ~ **on** : abrir fuego sobre — ~ *vt* **fired; firing 1** DISMISS : despedir **2** SHOOT : disparar — *vi* : disparar — **fire alarm** *n* : alarma *f* contra incendios — **firearm** *n* : arma *f* de fuego — **firecracker** *n* : petardo *m* — **fire engine** *n* : carro *m* de bomberos *Lat*, coche *m* de bomberos *Spain* — **fire escape** *n* : escalera *f* de incendios — **fire extinguisher** *n* : extintor *m* (de incendios) — **firefighter** *n* : bombero *m*, -ra *f* — **firefly** *n*, *pl* **-flies** : luciérnaga *f* — **firehouse** → **fire station** — **fireman** *n*, *pl* **-men** → **firefighter** — **fireplace** *n* : hogar *m*, chimenea *f* — **fireproof** *adj* : ignífugo — **fireside** *n* : hogar *m* — **fire station** *n* : estación *f* de bomberos *Lat*, parque *m* de bomberos *Spain* — **firewood** *n* : leña *f* — **fireworks** *npl* : fuegos *mpl* artificiales

firm¹ *n* : empresa *f*

firm² *adj* : firme — **firmly** *adv* : firmemente — **firmness** *n* : firmeza *f*

first *adj* **1** : primero **2 at** ~ **sight** : a primera vista **3 for the** ~ **time** : por primera vez — ~ *adv* **1** : primero **2** ~ **and foremost** : ante todo **3** ~ **of all** : en primer lugar — ~ *n* **1** : primero *m*, -ra *f* **2 at** ~ : al principio — **first aid** *n* : primeros auxilios *mpl* — **first–class** *adv* : en primera — ~ *adj* : de primera *f* — **firsthand** *adv* : directamente — ~ *adj* : de primera mano

— **firstly** *adv* : en primer lugar — **first name** *n* : nombre *m* de pila — **first–rate** *adj* → **first–class**

fiscal *adj* : fiscal

fish *n*, *pl* **fish** *or* **fishes** : pez *m* (vivo), pescado *m* (para comer) — ~ *vi* **1** : pescar **2** ~ **for** SEEK : buscar **3 go** ~**ing** : ir de pesca — **fisherman** *n*, *pl* **-men** : pescador *m*, -dora *f* — **fishhook** *n* : anzuelo *m* — **fishing** *n* : pesca *f* — **fishing pole** *n* : caña *f* de pescar — **fish market** *n* : pescadería *f* — **fishy** *adj* **fishier; -est 1** : a pescado (dícese de sabores, etc.) **2** SUSPICIOUS : sospechoso

fist *n* : puño *m*

fit¹ *n* **1** : ataque *m* **2 he had a** ~ : le dio un ataque

fit² *adj* **fitter; fittest 1** SUITABLE : apropiado **2** HEALTHY : en forma **3 be** ~ **for** : ser apto para — ~ *v* **fitted; fitting** *vt* **1** : encajar en (un hueco, etc.) **2** *(relating to clothing)* : quedar bien a **3** SUIT : ser apropiado para **4** MATCH : coincidir con **5** *or* ~ **out** : equipar — *vi* **1** : caber (en una caja, etc.), encajar (en un hueco, etc.) **2** *or* ~ **in** BELONG : encajar **3 this dress doesn't** ~ : este vestido no me queda bien — ~ *n* **it's a good fit** : me queda bien — **fitful** *adj* : irregular — **fitness** *n* **1** HEALTH : salud *f* **2** SUITABILITY : idoneidad *f* — **fitting** *adj* : apropiado

five *n* : cinco *m* — ~ *adj* : cinco — **five hundred** *n* : quinientos *m* — ~ *adj* : quinientos

fix *vt* **1** ATTACH : fijar, sujetar **2** REPAIR : arreglar **3** PREPARE : preparar — ~ *n* PREDICAMENT : aprieto *m*, apuro *m* — **fixed** *adj* : fijo — **fixture** *n* : instalación *f*

fizz *vi* : burbujear — ~ *n* : efervescencia *f*

fizzle *vi* **-zled; -zling** *or* ~ **out** : quedar en nada

flabbergasted *adj* : estupefacto, pasmado

flabby *adj* **-bier; -est** : fofo

flaccid *adj* : fláccido

flag¹ *vi* WEAKEN : flaquear

flag² *n* : bandera *f* — ~ *vt* **flagged; flagging** *or* ~ **down** : hacer señales de parada a — **flagpole** *n* : asta *f*

flagrant *adj* : flagrante

flair *n* : don *m*, facilidad *f*

flake *n* : copo *m* (de nieve), escama *f* (de pintura, de la piel) — ~ *vi* **flaked; flaking** : pelarse

flamboyant *adj* : extravagante

flame *n* **1** : llama *f* **2 burst into** ~**s** : estallar en llamas **3 go up in** ~**s** : incendiarse

flamenco *n* : flamenco *m* (música o baile) — **flamenco** *adj*

flamingo *n*, *pl* **-gos** : flamenco *m*

flammable *adj* : inflamable
flank *n* : ijado *m* (de un animal), flanco *m* (militar) — ~ *vt* : flanquear
flannel *n* : franela *f*
flap *n* : solapa *f* (de un sobre, un libro, etc.), tapa *f* (de un recipiente) — ~ *v* **flapped; flapping** *vi* : agitarse — *vt* : batir, agitar
flapjack → **pancake**
flare *vi* **flared; flaring 1** ~ **up** BLAZE : llamear **2** ~ **up** EXPLODE, ERUPT : estallar, explotar — ~ *n* **1** BLAZE : llamarada *f* **2** SIGNAL : (luz *f* de) bengala *f*
flash *vi* **1** : brillar, destellar **2** ~ **past** : pasar como un rayo — *vt* **1** : dirigir (una luz) **2** SHOW : mostrar **3** ~ **a smile** : sonreír — ~ *n* **1** : destello *m* **2** ~ **of lightning** : relámpago *m* **3 in a** ~ : de repente — **flashlight** *n* : linterna *f* — **flashy** *adj* **flashier; -est** : ostentoso
flask *n* : frasco *m*
flat *adj* **flatter; flattest 1** LEVEL : plano, llano **2** DOWNRIGHT : categórico **3** FIXED : fijo **4** MONOTONOUS : monótono **5** : bemol (en la música) **6** ~ **tire** : neumático *m* desinflado — ~ *n* **1** : bemol *m* (en la música) **2** *Brit* APARTMENT : apartamento *m*, departamento *m Lat* **3** PUNCTURE : pinchazo *m* — *adv* **1** ~ **broke** : pelado **2 in one hour** ~ : en una hora justa — **flatly** *adv* : categóricamente — **flat–out** *adj* **1** : frenético **2** DOWNRIGHT : categórico — **flatten** *vt* **1** LEVEL : aplanar, allanar **2** KNOCK DOWN : arrasar
flatter *vt* **1** : halagar **2** BECOME : favorecer — **flatterer** *n* : adulador *m*, -dora *f* — **flattering** *adj* **1** : halagador **2** BECOMING : favorecedor — **flattery** *n*, *pl* **-ries** : halagos *mpl*
flaunt *vt* : hacer alarde de
flavor *or Brit* **flavour** *n* : gusto *m*, sabor *m* — ~ *vt* : sazonar — **flavorful** *or Brit* **flavourful** *adj* : sabroso — **flavoring** *or Brit* **flavouring** *n* : condimento *m*, sazón *f*
flaw *n* : defecto *m* — **flawless** *adj* : perfecto
flax *n* : lino *m*
flea *n* : pulga *f*
fleck *n* **1** PARTICLE : mota *f* **2** SPOT : pinta *f*
flee *v* **fled; fleeing** *vi* : huir — *vt* : huir de
fleece *n* : vellón *m* — ~ *vt* **fleeced; fleecing 1** SHEAR : esquilar **2** DEFRAUD : desplumar
fleet *n* : flota *f*
fleeting *adj* : fugaz
Flemish *adj* : flamenco
flesh *n* **1** : carne *f* **2** PULP : pulpa *f* **3 in the** ~ : en persona — **fleshy** *adj* **fleshier; -est 1** : gordo **2** PULPY : carnoso
flew → **fly**

flex *vt* : flexionar — **flexibility** *n*, *pl* **-ties** : flexibilidad *f* — **flexible** *adj* : flexible
flick *n* : golpecito *m* — ~ *vt* : dar un golpecito a — *vi* ~ **through** : hojear
flicker *vi* : parpadear — ~ *n* **1** : parpadeo *m* **2 a** ~ **of hope** : un rayo de esperanza
flier *n* **1** AVIATOR : aviador *m*, -dora *f* **2** *or* **flyer** LEAFLET : folleto *m*, volante *m Lat*
flight[1] *n* **1** : vuelo *m* **2** TRAJECTORY : trayectoria *f* **3** ~ **of stairs** : tramo *m*
flight[2] *n* ESCAPE : huida *f*
flimsy *adj* **flimsier; -est 1** LIGHT : ligero **2** SHAKY : poco sólido **3 a** ~ **excuse** : una excusa floja
flinch *vi* ~ **from** : encogerse ante
fling *vt* **flung; flinging 1** : arrojar **2** ~ **open** : abrir de un golpe — ~ *n* **1** AFFAIR : aventura *f* **2 have a** ~ **at** : intentar
flint *n* : pedernal *m*
flip *v* **flipped; flipping** *vt* **1** *or* ~ **over** : dar la vuelta a **2** ~ **a coin** : echarlo a cara o cruz — *vi* **1** *or* ~ **over** : volcarse **2** ~ **through** : hojear — ~ *n* SOMERSAULT : voltereta *f*
flippant *adj* : ligero, frívolo
flipper *n* : aleta *f*
flirt *vi* : coquetear — ~ *n* : coqueto *m*, -ta *f* — **flirtatious** *adj* : coqueto
flit *vi* **flitted; flitting** : revolotear
float *n* **1** : flotador *m* **2** : carroza *f* (en un desfile) — *vi* : flotar — *vt* : hacer flotar
flock *n* : rebaño *m* (de ovejas), bandada *f* (de pájaros) — ~ *vi* : congregarse
flog *vt* **flogged; flogging** : azotar
flood *n* **1** : inundación *f* **2** : torrente *m* (de palabras, de lágrimas, etc.) — ~ *vt* : inundar — **floodlight** *n* : foco *m*
floor *n* **1** : suelo *m*, piso *m Lat* **2** STORY : piso *m* **3 dance** ~ : pista *f* de baile **4** ground ~ : planta *f* baja — ~ *vt* **1** KNOCK DOWN : derribar **2** NONPLUS : desconcertar — **floorboard** *n* : tabla *f* del suelo
flop *vi* **flopped; flopping 1** FLAP : agitarse **2** COLLAPSE : dejarse caer **3** FAIL : fracasar — ~ *n* FAILURE : fracaso *m* — **floppy** *adj* **-pier; -est** : flojo, flexible — **floppy disk** *n* : diskette *m*, disquete *m*
flora *n* : flora *f* — **floral** *adj* : floral — **florid** *adj* **1** FLOWERY : florido **2** RUDDY : rojizo — **florist** *n* : florista *mf*
floss *n* → **dental floss**
flounder[1] *n*, *pl* **flounder** *or* **flounders** : platija *f*
flounder[2] *vi* **1** *or* ~ **about** : resbalarse, revolcarse **2** : titubear (en un discurso)
flour *n* : harina *f*
flourish *vi* : florecer — *vt* BRANDISH : blandir — ~ *n* : floritura *f* — **flourishing** *adj* : floreciente

flout vt : desacatar, burlarse de
flow vi : fluir, correr — ~ n 1 : flujo m, circulación f 2 : corriente f (de información, etc.)
flower n : flor f — ~ vi : florecer — **flowered** adj : floreado — **flowerpot** n : maceta f — **flowery** adj : florido
flown → **fly**
flu n : gripe f
fluctuate vi -ated; -ating : fluctuar — **fluctuation** n : fluctuación f
fluency n : fluidez f — **fluent** adj 1 : fluido 2 be ~ in : hablar con fluidez — **fluently** adv : con fluidez
fluff vt : pelusa f — **fluffy** adj fluffier; -est : de pelusa, velloso
fluid adj : fluido — ~ n : fluido m
flung → **fling**
flunk vt : reprobar Lat, suspender Spain — vi : ser reprobado Lat, suspender Spain
fluorescence n : fluorescencia f — **fluorescent** adj : fluorescente
flurry n, pl -ries 1 GUST : ráfaga f 2 or snow ~ : nevisca f 3 ~ of questions : aluvión m de preguntas
flush vi BLUSH : ruborizarse, sonrojarse — vt ~ the toilet : tirar de la cadena, jalarle a la cadena Lat — ~ n BLUSH : rubor m, sonrojo m — ~ adj ~ with : a nivel con, a ras de — ~ adv : al mismo nivel, a ras
fluster vt : poner nervioso
flute n : flauta f
flutter vi 1 FLIT : revolotear 2 WAVE : ondear 3 or ~ about : ir y venir — ~ n 1 : revoloteo m (de alas) 2 STIR : revuelo m
flux n be in a state of ~ : cambiar continuamente
fly¹ v flew; flown; flying vi 1 : volar 2 TRAVEL : ir en avión 3 WAVE : ondear 4 RUSH : correr 5 ~ by : pasar volando — vt 1 PILOT : pilotar 2 : hacer volar (una cometa), enarbolar (una bandera) — ~ n, pl flies : bragueta f (de un pantalón)
fly² n, pl flies : mosca f (insecto)
flyer → **flier**
flying saucer n : platillo m volador Lat, platillo m volante Spain
flyswatter n : matamoscas m
foal n : potro m, -tra f
foam n : espuma f — ~ vi : hacer espuma — **foamy** adj foamier; -est : espumoso
focus n, pl -ci 1 : foco m 2 be in ~ : estar enfocado 3 ~ of attention : centro m de atención — ~ v -cused or -cussed; -cusing or -cussing vt 1 : enfocar 2 : centrar (la atención, etc.) — vi ~ on : enfocar (con los ojos), concentrarse en (con la mente)
fodder n : forraje m
foe n : enemigo m, -ga f
fog n : niebla f — ~ v fogged; fogging vt

: empañar — vi or ~ up : empañarse — **foggy** adj foggier; -est : nebuloso — **foghorn** n : sirena f de niebla
foil¹ vt : frustrar
foil² n or aluminum ~ : papel m de aluminio
fold¹ n 1 : redil m (para ovejas) 2 return to the ~ : volver al redil
fold² vt 1 : doblar, plegar 2 ~ one's arms : cruzar los brazos — vi 1 or ~ up : doblarse, plegarse 2 FAIL : fracasar — ~ n : pliegue m — **folder** n : carpeta f
foliage n : follaje m
folk n, pl folk or folks 1 : gente f 2 ~s npl PARENTS : padres mpl — ~ adj 1 : popular 2 ~ dance : danza f folklórica — **folklore** n : folklore m
follow vt 1 : seguir 2 UNDERSTAND : entender 3 ~ up : seguir — vi 1 : seguir 2 UNDERSTAND : entender 3 ~ up on : seguir con — **follower** n : seguidor m, -dora f — **following** adj : siguiente — ~ n : seguidores mpl — ~ prep : después de
folly n, pl -lies : locura f
fond adj 1 : cariñoso 2 be ~ of sth : ser aficionado a algo 3 be ~ of s.o. : tener cariño a algn
fondle vt -dled; -dling : acariciar
fondness n 1 LOVE : cariño m 2 LIKING : afición f
food n : comida f, alimento m — **foodstuffs** npl : comestibles mpl
fool n 1 : idiota mf 2 JESTER : bufón m, -fona f — ~ vi 1 JOKE : bromear 2 ~ around : perder el tiempo — vt TRICK : engañar — **foolhardy** adj : temerario — **foolish** adj : tonto — **foolishness** n : tontería f — **foolproof** adj : infalible
foot n, pl feet : pie m — **footage** n : secuencias fpl (cinemáticas) — **football** n : fútbol m americano — **footbridge** n : pasarela f, puente m peatonal — **foothills** npl : estribaciones fpl — **foothold** n : punto m de apoyo — **footing** n 1 BALANCE : equilibrio m 2 on equal ~ : en igualdad — **footlights** npl : candilejas fpl — **footnote** n : nota f al pie de la página — **footpath** n : sendero m — **footprint** n : huella f — **footstep** n : paso m — **footstool** n : escabel m — **footwear** n : calzado m
for prep 1 (indicating purpose, etc.) : para 2 (indicating motivation, etc.) : por 3 (indicating duration) : durante 4 we walked ~ 3 miles : andamos 3 millas 5 AS FOR : con respecto a — ~ conj : puesto que, porque
forage n : forraje m — ~ vi -aged; -aging 1 : forrajear 2 ~ for : buscar
foray n : incursión f
forbid vt -bade or -bad; -bidden; -bidding

: prohibir — **forbidding** *adj* : intimidante, severo

force *n* **1** : fuerza *f* **2 by** ~ : por la fuerza **3 in** ~ : en vigor, en vigencia **4 armed** ~**s** : fuerzas *fpl* armadas — ~ *vt* **forced; forcing 1** : forzar **2** OBLIGATE : obligar — **forced** *adj* : forzado, forzoso — **forceful** *adj* : fuerte, energético

forceps *ns & pl* : fórceps *m*

forcibly *adv* : por la fuerza

ford *n* : vado *m* — ~ *vt* : vadear

fore *n* **come to the** ~ : empezar a destacarse

forearm *n* : antebrazo *m*

foreboding *n* : premonición *f*, presentimiento *m*

forecast *vt* **-cast; -casting** : predecir, pronosticar — ~ *n* : predicción *f*, pronóstico *m*

forefathers *n* : antepasados *mpl*

forefinger *n* : índice *m*, dedo *m* índice

forefront *n* **at/in the** ~ : a la vanguardia

forego → **forgo**

foregone *adj* ~ **conclusion** : resultado *m* inevitable

foreground *n* : primer plano *m*

forehead *n* : frente *f*

foreign *adj* **1** : extranjero **2** ~ **trade** : comercio *m* exterior — **foreigner** *n* : extranjero *m*, -ra *f*

foreman *n*, *pl* **-men** : capataz *mf*

foremost *adj* : principal — ~ *adv* **first and** ~ : ante todo

forensic *adj* : forense

forerunner *n* : precursor *m*, -sora *f*

foresee *vt* **-saw; -seen; -seeing** : prever — **foreseeable** *adj* : previsible

foreshadow *vt* : presagiar

foresight *n* : previsión *f*

forest *n* : bosque *m* — **forestry** *n* : silvicultura *f*

foretaste *n* : anticipo *m*

foretell *vt* **-told; -telling** : predecir

forethought *n* : reflexión *f* previa

forever *adv* **1** ETERNALLY : para siempre **2** CONTINUALLY : siempre, constantemente

forewarn *vt* : advertir, prevenir

foreword *n* : prólogo *m*

forfeit *n* **1** PENALTY : pena *f* **2** : prenda *f* (en un juego) — ~ *vt* : perder

forge *n* : forja *f* — ~ *v* **forged; forging** *vt* **1** : forjar (metal, etc.) **2** COUNTERFEIT : falsificar — *vi* ~ **ahead** : avanzar, seguir adelante — **forger** *n* : falsificador *m*, -dora *f* — **forgery** *n*, *pl* **-eries** : falsificación *f*

forget *v* **-got; -gotten** *or* **-got; -getting** *vt* : olvidar, olvidarse de — *vi* **1** : olvidarse **I forgot** : se me olvidó — **forgetful** *adj* : olvidadizo

forgive *vt* **-gave; -given; -giving** : perdonar — **forgiveness** *n* : perdón *m*

forgo *or* **forego** *vt* **-went; -gone; -going** : privarse de, renunciar a

fork *n* **1** : tenedor *m* **2** PITCHFORK : horca *f* **3** : bifurcación *f* (de un camino, etc.) — *vi* : ramificarse, bifurcarse — *vt* ~ **over** : desembolsar

forlorn *adj* : triste

form *n* **1** : forma *f* **2** DOCUMENT : formulario *m* **3** KIND : tipo *m* — ~ *vt* **1** : formar **2** ~ **a habit** : adquirir un hábito — *vi* : formarse

formal *adj* : formal — ~ *n* **1** BALL : baile *m* (formal) **2** *or* ~ **dress** : traje *m* de etiqueta — **formality** *n*, *pl* **-ties** : formalidad *f*

format *n* : formato *m* — ~ *vt* **-matted; -matting** : formatear

formation *n* **1** : formación *f* **2** SHAPE : forma *f*

former *adj* **1** PREVIOUS : antiguo, anterior **2** : primero (de dos) — **formerly** *adv* : anteriormente, antes

formidable *adj* : formidable

formula *n*, *pl* **-las** *or* **-lae 1** : fórmula *f* **2** *or* **baby** ~ : preparado *m* para biberón

forsake *vt* **-sook; -saken; -saking** : abandonar

fort *n* : fuerte *m*

forth *adv* **1 and so** ~ : etcétera **2 back and** ~ → **back 3 from this day** ~ : de hoy en adelante — **forthcoming** *adj* **1** COMING : próximo **2** OPEN : comunicativo — **forthright** *adj* : directo, franco

fortieth *adj* : cuadragésimo — ~ *n* **1** : cuadragésimo *m*, -ma *f* (en una serie) **2** : cuarentavo *m*, cuarentava parte *f*

fortify *vt* **-fied; -fying** : fortificar — **fortification** *n* : fortificación *f*

fortitude *n* : fortaleza *f*

fortnight *n* : quince días *mpl*, quincena *f*

fortress *n* : fortaleza *f*

fortunate *adj* : afortunado — **fortunately** *adv* : afortunadamente — **fortune** *n* : fortuna *f* — **fortune–teller** *n* : adivino *m*, -na *f*

forty *n*, *pl* **forties** : cuarenta *m* — ~ *adj* : cuarenta

forum *n*, *pl* **-rums** : foro *m*

forward *adj* **1** : hacia adelante (en dirección), delantero (en posición) **2** BRASH : descarado — ~ *adv* **1** : (hacia) adelante **2 from this day** ~ : de aquí en adelante — ~ *vt* : remitir, enviar — ~ *n* : delantero *m*, -ra *f* (en deportes) — **forwards** *adv* → **forward**

fossil *n* : fósil *m*

foster *adj* : adoptivo — ~ *vt* : promover, fomentar

fought → **fight**

foul *adj* **1** REPULSIVE : asqueroso **2** ~ **language** : palabrotas *fpl* **3** ~ **play** : actos *mpl* criminales **4** ~ **weather** : mal tiempo

m — $\sim$ n : falta f (en deportes) — $\sim$ vi : cometer faltas (en deportes) — vt : ensuciar

found[1] → **find**

found[2] vt : fundar, establecer — **foundation** n **1** : fundación f **2** BASIS : fundamento m **3** : cimientos mpl (de un edificio)

founder[1] n : fundador m, -dora f

founder[2] vi SINK : hundirse

fountain n : fuente f

four n : cuatro m — $\sim$ adj : cuatro — **fourfold** adj : cuadruple — **four hundred** adj : cuatrocientos — $\sim$ n : cuatrocientos m

fourteen n : catorce m — $\sim$ adj : catorce — **fourteenth** adj : decimocuarto — $\sim$ n **1** : decimocuarto m, -ta f (en una serie) **2** : catorceavo m, catorceava parte f

fourth n **1** : cuarto m, -ta f (en una serie) **2** : cuarto m, cuarta parte f — $\sim$ adj : cuarto

fowl n, pl **fowl** or **fowls** : ave f

fox n, pl **foxes** : zorro m, -ra f — $\sim$ vt TRICK : engañar — **foxy** adj **foxier; -est** SHREWD : astuto

foyer n : vestíbulo m

fraction n : fracción f

fracture n : fractura f — $\sim$ vt **-tured; -turing** : fracturar

fragile adj : frágil

fragment n : fragmento m

fragrant adj : fragante — **fragrance** n : fragancia f, aroma m

frail adj : débil, delicado

frame vt **framed; framing 1** ENCLOSE : enmarcar **2** COMPOSE, DRAFT : formular **3** INCRIMINATE : incriminar — $\sim$ n **1** : armazón mf (de un edificio, etc.) **2** : marco m (de un cuadro, una puerta, etc.) **3** or $\sim$**s** npl : montura f (para anteojos) **4** $\sim$ **of mind** : estado m de ánimo — **framework** n : armazón f

franc n : franco m

frank adj : franco — **frankly** adv : francamente — **frankness** n : franqueza f

frantic adj : frenético

fraternal adj : fraterno, fraternal — **fraternity** n, pl **-ties** : fraternidad f — **fraternize** vi **-nized; -nizing** : confraternizar

fraud n **1** DECEIT : fraude m **2** IMPOSTOR : impostor m, -tora f — **fraudulent** adj : fraudulento

fraught adj $\sim$ **with** : lleno de, cargado de

fray[1] n **1 join the** $\sim$: salir a la palestra **2 return to the** $\sim$: volver a la carga

fray[2] vt : crispar (los nervios) — vi : deshilacharse

freak n **1** ODDITY : fenómeno m **2** ENTHUSIAST : entusiasta mf — **freakish** adj : anormal

freckle n : peca f

free adj **freer; freest 1** : libre **2** or $\sim$ **of charge** : gratuito, gratis **3** LOOSE : suelto — $\sim$ vt **freed; freeing 1** : liberar, poner en libertad **2** RELEASE, UNFASTEN : soltar, desatar — $\sim$ adv or **for** $\sim$: gratis — **freedom** n : libertad f — **freelance** adj : por cuenta propia — **freely** adv **1** : libremente **2** LAVISHLY : con generosidad — **freeway** n : autopista f — **free will** n **1** : libre albedrío m **2 of one's own** $\sim$: por su propia voluntad

freeze v **froze; frozen; freezing** vi **1** : congelarse, helarse **2** STOP : quedarse inmóvil — vt : helar (agua, etc.), congelar (alimentos, precios, etc.) — **freeze–dry** vt **-dried; -drying** : liofilizar — **freezer** n : congelador m — **freezing** adj **1** CHILLY : helado **2 it's freezing!** : ¡hace un frío espantoso!

freight n **1** SHIPPING : porte m, flete m Lat **2** CARGO : carga f

French adj : francés — $\sim$ n **1** : francés m (idioma) **2 the** $\sim$ npl : los franceses — **Frenchman** n : francés m — **Frenchwoman** n : francesa f — **french fries** npl : papas fpl fritas

frenetic adj : frenético

frenzy n, pl **-zies** : frenesí m — **frenzied** adj : frenético

frequent vt : frecuentar — $\sim$ adj : frecuente — **frequency** n, pl **-cies** : frecuencia f — **frequently** adv : a menudo, frecuentemente

fresco n, pl **-coes** : fresco m

fresh adj **1** : fresco **2** IMPUDENT : descarado **3** CLEAN : limpio **4** NEW : nuevo **5** $\sim$ **water** : agua m dulce — **freshen** vt : refrescar — vi $\sim$ **up** : arreglarse — **freshly** adv : recién — **freshman** n, pl **-men** : estudiante mf de primer año — **freshness** n : frescura f

fret vi **fretted; fretting** : preocuparse — **fretful** adj : nervioso, irritable

friar n : fraile m

friction n : fricción f

Friday n : viernes m

friend n : amigo m, -ga f — **friendliness** n : simpatía f — **friendly** adj **-lier; -est** : simpático, amable — **friendship** n : amistad f

frigate n : fragata f

fright n : miedo m, susto m — **frighten** vt : asustar, espantar — **frightened** adj **1** : asustado, temeroso **2 be** $\sim$ **of** : tener miedo de — **frightening** adj : espantoso — **frightful** adj : espantoso, terrible

frigid adj : frío, glacial

frill n **1** RUFFLE : volante m **2** LUXURY : lujo m

fringe n **1** : fleco m **2** EDGE : periferia f, margen m **3** $\sim$ **benefits** : incentivos mpl, extras mpl

frisk vt SEARCH : cachear, registrar — **frisky** adj **friskier; -est** : retozón, juguetón

fritter *n* : buñuelo *m* — ~ *vt or* ~ **away** : malgastar (dinero), desperdiciar (tiempo)

frivolous *adj* : frívolo — **frivolity** *n*, *pl* **-ties** : frivolidad *f*

frizzy *adj* **frizzier; -est** : rizado, crespo

fro *adv* **to and** ~ → **to**

frock *n* : vestido *m*

frog *n* **1** : rana *f* **2 have a** ~ **in one's throat** : tener carraspera

frolic *vi* **-icked; -icking** : retozar

from *prep* **1** : de **2** (*indicating a starting point*) : desde **3** (*indicating a cause*) : de, por **4** ~ **now on** : a partir de ahora

front *n* **1** : parte *f* delantera **2** : delantera *f* (de un vestido, etc.), fachada *f* (de un edificio), frente *m* (military) **3 cold** ~ : frente *m* frío **4 in** ~ **of** : delante de, adelante de *Lat* — ~ *vi or* ~ **on** : dar a, estar orientado a — ~ *adj* **1** : delantero, de adelante **2 the** ~ **row** : la primera fila

frontier *n* : frontera *f*

frost *n* **1** : helada *f* **2** : escarcha *f* (en una superficie) — ~ *vt* ICE : bañar (pasteles) — **frostbite** *n* : congelación *f* — **frosting** *n* ICING : baño *m* — **frosty** *adj* **frostier; -est** **1** : cubierto de escarcha **2** CHILLY : helado, frío

froth *n*, *pl* **froths** : espuma *f* — **frothy** *adj* **frothier; -est** : espumoso

frown *vi* **1** : fruncir el ceño, fruncir el entrecejo **2** ~ **at** : mirar con ceño **3** ~ **upon** : desaprobar — ~ *n* : ceño *m* (fruncido)

froze, frozen → **freeze**

frugal *adj* : frugal

fruit *n* **1** : fruta *f* **2** PRODUCT, RESULT : fruto *m* — **fruitcake** *n* : pastel *m* de frutas — **fruitful** *adj* : fructífero — **fruition** *n* **come to** ~ : realizarse — **fruitless** *adj* : infructuoso — **fruity** *adj* **fruitier; -est** : (con sabor) a fruta

frustrate *vt* **-trated; -trating** : frustrar — **frustrating** *adj* : frustrante — **frustration** *n* : frustración *f*

fry *vt* **fried; frying** : freír — ~ *n*, *pl* **fries** **1 small** ~ : gente *f* de poca monta **2 fries** *npl* → **french fries** — **frying pan** *n* : sartén *mf*

fudge *n* : dulce *m* blando de chocolate y leche

fuel *n* : combustible *m* — ~ *vt* **-eled** *or* **-elled; -eling** *or* **-elling** **1** : alimentar (un horno), abastecer de combustible (un avión) **2** STIMULATE : estimular

fugitive *n* : fugitivo *m*, **-va** *f*

fulfill *or* **fulfil** *vt* **-filled; -filling** **1** : cumplir con (una obligación), desarrollar (potencial) **2** FILL, MEET : cumplir — **fulfillment** *n* **1** ACCOMPLISHMENT : cumplimiento *m* **2** SATISFACTION : satisfacción *f*

full *adj* **1** FILLED : lleno **2** COMPLETE : complete, detallado **3** : redondo (dícese de la cara), amplio (dícese de ropa) **4 at** ~ **speed** : a toda velocidad **5 in** ~ **bloom** : en plena flor — ~ *adv* **1** DIRECTLY : de lleno **2 know** ~ **well** : saber muy bien — ~ **n 1 pay in** ~ : pagar en su totalidad **2 to the** ~ : al máximo — **full–fledged** *adj* : hecho y derecho — **fully** *adv* **1** COMPLETELY : completamente **2** AT LEAST : al menos, por lo menos

fumble *vi* **-bled; -bling** **1** RUMMAGE : hurgar **2** ~ **with** : manejar con torpeza

fumble *vi* **-bled; -bling** **1** RUMMAGE : hurgar **2** ~ **with** : manejar con torpeza

fume *vi* **fumed; fuming** **1** SMOKE : echar humo, humear **2** RAGE : estar furioso — **fumes** *npl* : gases *mpl*

fume *vi* **fumed; fuming** **1** SMOKE : echar humo, humear **2** RAGE : estar furioso — **fumes** *npl* : gases *mpl*

fumigate *vt* **-gated; -gating** : fumigar

fumigate *vt* **-gated; -gating** : fumigar

fun *n* **1** AMUSEMENT : diversión *f* **2 have** ~ : divertirse **3 make** ~ **of** : reírse de, burlarse de — ~ *adj* : divertido

fun *n* **1** AMUSEMENT : diversión *f* **2 have** ~ : divertirse **3 make** ~ **of** : reírse de, burlarse de — ~ *adj* : divertido

function *n* **1** : función *f* **2** GATHERING : recepción *f*, reunión *f* social — ~ *vi* : funcionar — **functional** *adj* : funcional

function *n* **1** : función *f* **2** GATHERING : recepción *f*, reunión *f* social — ~ *vi* : funcionar — **functional** *adj* : funcional

fund *n* **1** : fondo *m* **2** ~ **s** *npl* RESOURCES : fondos *mpl* — ~ *vt* : financiar

fund *n* **1** : fondo *m* **2** ~ **s** *npl* RESOURCES : fondos *mpl* — ~ *vt* : financiar

fundamental *adj* : fundamental — **fundamentals** *npl* : fundamentos *mpl*

fundamental *adj* : fundamental — **fundamentals** *npl* : fundamentos *mpl*

funeral *adj* : funeral, fúnebre — ~ *n* : funeral *m*, funerales *mpl* — **funeral home** *or* **funeral parlor** *n* : funeraria *f*

funeral *adj* : funeral, fúnebre — ~ *n* : funeral *m*, funerales *mpl* — **funeral home** *or* **funeral parlor** *n* : funeraria *f*

fungus *n*, *pl* **fungi** : hongo *m*

fungus *n*, *pl* **fungi** : hongo *m*

funnel *n* **1** : embudo *m* **2** SMOKESTACK : chimenea *f*

funnel *n* **1** : embudo *m* **2** SMOKESTACK : chimenea *f*

funny *adj* **funnier; -est** **1** : divertido, gracioso **2** STRANGE.: extraño, raro — **funnies** *npl* : tiras *fpl* cómicas

funny *adj* **funnier; -est** **1** : divertido, gra-

cioso **2** STRANGE : extraño, raro — **fun-nies** *npl* : tiras *fpl* cómicas
fur *n* **1** : pelaje *m*, pelo *m* (de un animal) **2** *or* ~ **coat** : (prenda *f* de) piel *f* — ~ *adj* : de piel
fur *n* **1** : pelaje *m*, pelo *m* (de un animal) **2** *or* ~ **coat** : (prenda *f* de) piel *f* — ~ *adj* : de piel
furious *adj* : furioso
furious *adj* : furioso
furnace *n* : horno *m*
furnace *n* : horno *m*
furnish *vt* **1** SUPPLY : proveer **2** : amueblar (una casa, etc.) — **furnishings** *npl* : muebles *mpl*, mobiliario *m* — **furniture** *n* : muebles *mpl*, mobiliario *m*
furnish *vt* **1** SUPPLY : proveer **2** : amueblar (una casa, etc.) — **furnishings** *npl* : muebles *mpl*, mobiliario *m* — **furniture** *n* : muebles *mpl*, mobiliario *m*
furrow *n* : surco *m*
furrow *n* : surco *m*
furry *adj* **furrier; -est** : peludo (dícese de un animal), de peluche (dícese de un juguete, etc.)
furry *adj* **furrier; -est** : peludo (dícese de un animal), de peluche (dícese de un juguete, etc.)
further *adv* **1** FARTHER : más lejos **2** MOREOVER : además **3** MORE : más — ~ *vt* : promover, fomentar — ~ *adj* **1** FARTHER : más lejano **2** ADDITIONAL : adicional,

más **3** until ~ **notice** : hasta nuevo aviso — **furthermore** *adv* : además — **furthest** → **farthest**
further *adv* **1** FARTHER : más lejos **2** MOREOVER : además **3** MORE : más — ~ *vt* : promover, fomentar — ~ *adj* **1** FARTHER : más lejano **2** ADDITIONAL : adicional, más **3** until ~ **notice** : hasta nuevo aviso — **furthermore** *adv* : además — **furthest** → **farthest**
furtive *adj* : furtivo
fury *n*, *pl* **-ries** : furia *f*
fuse¹ *or* **fuze** *n* : mecha *f* (de una bomba, etc.)
fuse² *v* **fused; fusing** *vt* **1** MELT : fundir **2** UNITE : fusionar — *vi* : fundirse, fusionarse — ~ *n* **1** : fusible *m* **2** blow a ~ : fundir un fusible — **fusion** *n* : fusión *f*
fuss *n* **1** : jaleo *m*, alboroto *m* **2** make a ~ : armar un escándalo — ~ *vi* **1** WORRY : preocuparse **2** COMPLAIN : quejarse — **fussy** *adj* **fussier; -est** **1** IRRITABLE : irritable **2** ELABORATE : recargado **3** FINICKY : quisquilloso
futile *adj* : inútil, vano — **futility** *n*, *pl* **-ties** : inutilidad *f*
future *adj* : futuro — ~ *n* : futuro *m*
fuze → **fuse¹**
fuzz *n* : pelusa *f* — **fuzzy** *adj* **fuzzier; -est** **1** FURRY : con pelusa, peludo **2** BLURRY : borroso **3** VAGUE : confuso

G

g *n*, *pl* **g's** *or* **gs** : g *f*, séptima letra del alfabeto inglés
gab *vi* **gabbed; gabbing** : charlar, cotorrear *fam* — ~ *n* CHATTER : charla *f*
gable *n* : aguilón *m*
gadget *n* : artilugio *m*
gag *v* **gagged; gagging** *vt* : amordazar — *vi* CHOKE : atragantarse — ~ *n* **1** : mordaza *f* **2** JOKE : chiste *m*
gage → **gauge**
gaiety *n*, *pl* **-eties** : alegría *f* — **gaily** *adv* : alegremente
gain *n* **1** PROFIT : ganancia *f* **2** INCREASE : aumento *m* — ~ *vt* **1** OBTAIN : ganar, adquirir **2** ~ **weight** : aumentar de peso — *vi* **1** PROFIT : beneficiarse **2** : adelantar(se) (dícese de un reloj) — **gainful** *adj* : lucrativo
gait *n* : modo *m* de andar

gala *n* : fiesta *f*
galaxy *n*, *pl* **-axies** : galaxia *f*
gale *n* **1** : vendaval *f* **2** ~**s of laughter** : carcajadas *fpl*
gall *n* **have the** ~ **to** : tener el descaro de
gallant *adj* **1** BRAVE : valiente **2** CHIVALROUS : galante
gallbladder *n* : vesícula *f* biliar
gallery *n*, *pl* **-leries** : galería *f*
gallon *n* : galón *m*
gallop *vi* : galopar — ~ *n* : galope *m*
gallows *n*, *pl* **-lows** *or* **-lowses** : horca *f*
gallstone *n* : cálculo *m* biliar
galore *adj* : en abundancia
galoshes *npl* : galochas *fpl*, chanclos *mpl*
galvanize *vt* **-nized; -nizing** : galvanizar
gamble *v* **-bled; -bling** *vi* : jugar — *vt* : jugarse — ~ *n* **1** BET : apuesta *f* **2** RISK : riesga *f* — **gambler** *n* : jugador *m*, -dora *f*

game *n* **1** : juego *m* **2** MATCH : partido *m* **3** *or* ～ **animals** : caza *f* — ～ *adj* READY : listo, dispuesto

gamut *n* : gama *f*

gang *n* : banda *f*, pandilla *f* — ～ *vi* ～ **up on** : unirse contra

gangplank *n* : pasarela *f*

gangrene *n* : gangrena *f*

gangster *n* : gángster *mf*

gangway *n* → **gangplank**

gap *n* **1** OPENING : espacio *m* **2** INTERVAL : intervalo *m* **3** DISPARITY : brecha *f*, distancia *f* **4** DEFICIENCY : laguna *f*

gape *vi* **gaped; gaping 1** OPEN : estar abierto **2** STARE : mirar boquiabierto

garage *n* : garaje *m* — ～ *vt* **-raged; -raging** : dejar en un garaje

garb *n* : vestido *m*

garbage *n* : basura *f* — **garbage can** *n* : cubo *m* de la basura

garble *vt* **-bled; -bling** : tergiversar — **garbled** *adj* : confuso, incomprensible

garden *n* : jardín *m* — ～ *vi* : trabajar en el jardín — **gardener** *n* : jardinero *m*, -ra *f* — **gardening** *n* : jardinería *f*

gargle *vi* **-gled; -gling** : hacer gárgaras

garish *adj* : chillón

garland *n* : guirnalda *f*

garlic *n* : ajo *m*

garment *n* : prenda *f*

garnish *vt* : guarnecer — ～ *n* : adorno *m*, guarnición *f*

garret *n* : buhardilla *f*

garrison *n* : guarnición *f*

garrulous *adj* : charlatán, parlanchín

garter *n* : liga *f*

gas station *n* : gasolinera *f*

gas *n, pl* **gases 1** : gas *m* **2** GASOLINE : gasolina *f* — ～ *v* **gassed; gassing** *vt* : asfixiar con gas — *vi* ～ **up** : llenar el tanque con gasolina

gash *n* : tajo *m* — ～ *vt* : hacer un tajo en, cortar

gasket *n* : junta *f*

gasoline *n* : gasolina *f*

gasp *vi* **1** : dar un grito ahogado **2** PANT : jadear — ～ *n* : grito *m* ahogado

gastric *adj* : gástrico

gastronomy *n* : gastronomía *f*

gate *n* **1** DOOR : puerta *f* **2** BARRIER : barrera *f* — **gateway** *n* : puerta *f*

gather *vt* **1** ASSEMBLE : reunir **2** COLLECT : recoger **3** CONCLUDE : deducir **4** : fruncir (una tela) **5** ～ **speed** : acelerar — *vi* : reunirse (dícese de personas), acumularse (dícese de cosas) — **gathering** *n* : reunión *f*

gaudy *adj* **gaudier; -est** : chillón, llamativo

gauge *n* **1** INDICATOR : indicador *m* **2** CALIBER : calibre *m* — ～ *vt* **gauged;**

gauging 1 MEASURE : medir **2** ESTIMATE : calcular, evaluar

gaunt *adj* : demacrado, descarnado

gauze *n* : gasa *f*

gave → **give**

gawky *adj* **gawkier; -est** : desgarbado

gay *adj* **1** : alegre **2** HOMOSEXUAL : gay, homosexual

gaze *vi* **gazed; gazing** : mirar (fijamente) — ～ *n* : mirada *f*

gazelle *n* : gacela *f*

gazette *n* : gaceta *f*

gear *n* **1** EQUIPMENT : equipo *m* **2** POSSESSIONS : efectos *mpl* personales **3** : marcha *f* (de un vehículo) **4** *or* ～ **wheel** : rueda *f* dentada — ～ *vt* : orientar, adaptar — *vi* ～ **up** : prepararse — **gearshift** *n* : palanca *f* de cambio, palanca *f* de velocidades *Lat*

geese → **goose**

gelatin *n* : gelatina *f*

gem *n* : gema *f*, piedra *f* preciosa — **gemstone** *n* : piedra *f* preciosa

gender *n* **1** SEX : sexo *m* **2** : género *m* (en la gramática)

gene *n* : gen *m*, gene *m*

genealogy *n, pl* **-gies** : genealogía *f*

general *adj* : general — ～ *n* **1** : general *mf* (militar) **2 in** ～ : en general, por lo general — **generalize** *v* **-ized; -izing** : generalizar — **generally** *adv* : generalmente, en general — **general practitioner** *n* : médico *m*, -ca *f* de cabecera

generate *vt* **-ated; -ating** : generar — **generation** *n* : generación *f* — **generator** *n* : generador *m*

generous *adj* **1** : generoso **2** AMPLE : abundante — **generosity** *n, pl* **-ties** : generosidad *f*

genetic *adj* : genético — **genetics** *n* : genética *f*

genial *adj* : afable, simpático

genital *adj* : genital — **genitals** *npl* : genitales *mpl*

genius *n* : genio *m*

genocide *n* : genocidio *m*

genteel *adj* : refinado

gentle *adj* **-tler; -tlest 1** MILD : suave, dulce **2** LIGHT : ligero **3 a** ～ **hint** : una indirecta discreta — **gentleman** *n, pl* **-men 1** MAN : caballero *m*, señor *m* **2 a perfect** ～ : un perfecto caballero — **gentleness** *n* : delicadeza *f*, ternura *f*

genuine *adj* **1** AUTHENTIC : verdadero, auténtico **2** SINCERE : sincero

geography *n, pl* **-phies** : geografía *f* — **geographic** *or* **geographical** *adj* : geográfico

geology *n* : geología *f* — **geologic** *or* **geological** *adj* : geológico

geometry *n, pl* **-tries** : geometría *f* — **geometric** *or* **geometrical** *adj* : geométrico

geranium *n* : geranio *m*

geriatric *adj* : geriátrico — **geriatrics** *n* : geriatría *f*

germ *n* **1** : germen *m* **2** MICROBE : microbio *m*

German *adj* : alemán — ~ *n* : alemán *m* (idioma)

germinate *v* **-nated; -nating** *vi* : germinar — *vt* : hacer germinar

gestation *n* : gestación *f*

gesture *n* : gesto *m* — ~ *vi* **-tured; -turing** **1** : hacer gestos **2** ~ **to** : hacer señas a

get *v* **got; got** *or* **gotten; getting** *vt* **1** OBTAIN : conseguir, obtener **2** RECEIVE : recibir **3** EARN : ganar **4** FETCH : traer **5** CATCH : coger, agarrar *Lat* **6** UNDERSTAND : entender **7** PREPARE : preparar **8** ~ **one's hair cut** : cortarse el pelo **9** ~ **s.o. to do sth** : lograr que uno haga algo **10** **have got** : tener **11 have got to** : tener que — *vi* **1** BECOME : ponerse, hacerse **2** GO, MOVE : ir **3** PROGRESS : avanzar **4** ~ **ahead** : progresar **5** ~ **at** MEAN : querer decir **6** ~ **away** : escaparse **7** ~ **away with** : salir impune de **8** ~ **back at** : desquitarse con **9** ~ **by** : arreglárselas **10** ~ **home** : llegar a casa **11** ~ **out** : salir **12** ~ **over** : reponerse de, consolarse de **13** ~ **together** : reunirse **14** ~ **up** : levantarse — **getaway** *n* : fuga *f*, huida *f* — **get-together** *n* : reunión *f*

geyser *n* : géiser *m*

ghastly *adj* **-lier; -est** : horrible, espantoso

ghetto *n*, *pl* **-tos** *or* **-toes** : gueto *m*

ghost *n* : fantasma *f*, espectro *m* — **ghostly** *adv* : fantasmal

giant *n* : gigante *m*, -ta *f* — ~ *adj* : gigantesco

gibberish *n* : galimatías *m*, jerigonza *f*

gibe *vi* **gibed; gibing** ~ **at** : mofarse de — ~ *n* : pulla *f*, mofa *f*

giblets *npl* : menudillos *mpl*

giddy *adj* **-dier; -est** : mareado, vertiginoso — **giddiness** *n* : vértigo *m*

gift *n* **1** PRESENT : regalo *m* **2** TALENT : don *m* — **gifted** *adj* : talentoso, de talento

gigantic *adj* : gigantesco

giggle *vi* **-gled; -gling** : reírse tontamente — ~ *n* : risa *f* tonta

gild *vt* **gilded** *or* **gilt; gilding** : dorar

gill *n* : agalla *f*, branquia *f*

gilt *adj* : dorado

gimmick *n* : truco *m*, ardid *m*

gin *n* : ginebra *f*

ginger *n* : jengibre *m* — **ginger ale** *n* : refresco *m* de jengibre — **gingerbread** *n* : pan *m* de jengibre — **gingerly** *adv* : con cuidado, cautelosamente

giraffe *n* : jirafa *f*

girder *n* : viga *f*

girdle *n* CORSET : faja *f*

girl *n* **1** : niña *f*, muchacha *f*, chica *f* — **girlfriend** *n* : novia *f*, amiga *f*

girth *n* : circunferencia *f*

gist *n* **get the** ~ **of** : comprender lo esencial de

give *v* **gave; given; giving** *vt* **1** : dar **2** INDICATE : señalar **3** PRESENT : presentar **4** ~ **away** : regalar **5** ~ **back** : devolver **6** ~ **out** : repartir **7** ~ **up smoking** : dejar de fumar — *vi* **1** YIELD : ceder **2** COLLAPSE : romperse **3** ~ **out** : agotarse **4** ~ **up** : rendirse — ~ *n* : elasticidad *f* — **given** *adj* **1** SPECIFIED : determinado **2** INCLINED : dado, inclinado — **given name** *n* : nombre *m* de pila

glacier *n* : glaciar *m*

glad *adj* **gladder; gladdest** **1** : alegre, contento **2 be** ~ : alegrarse **3** ~ **to meet you!** : ¡mucho gusto! — **gladden** *vt* : alegrar — **gladly** *adv* : con mucho gusto — **gladness** *n* : alegría *f*, gozo *m*

glade *n* : claro *m*

glamor *or* **glamour** *n* : atractivo *m*, encanto *m* — **glamorous** *adj* : atractivo

glance *vi* **glanced; glancing** **1** ~ **at** : mirar, dar un vistazo a **2** ~ **off** : rebotar en — ~ *n* : mirada *f*, vistazo *m*

gland *n* : glándula *f*

glare *vi* **glared; glaring** **1** : brillar, relumbrar **2** ~ **at** : lanzar una mirada feroz a — ~ *n* **1** : luz *f* deslumbrante **2** STARE : mirada *f* feroz — **glaring** *adj* **1** BRIGHT : deslumbrante **2** FLAGRANT : flagrante

glass *n* **1** : vidrio *m*, cristal *m* **2 a** ~ **of milk** : un vaso de leche **3** ~**es** *npl* SPECTACLES : anteojos *mpl*, lentes *fpl* — ~ *adj* : de vidrio — **glassware** *n* : cristalería *f* — **glassy** *adj* **glassier; -est** **1** : vítreo **2** ~ **eyes** : ojos *mpl* vidriosos

glaze *vt* **glazed; glazing** **1** : poner vidrios a (una ventana, etc.) **2** : vidriar (cerámica) **3** ICE : glasear — ~ *n* **1** : vidriado *m*, barniz *m* (de cerámica) **2** ICING : glaseado *m*

gleam *n* **1** : destello *m* **2 a** ~ **of hope** : un rayo de esperanza — ~ *vi* : destellar, relucir

glee *n* : alegría *f* — **gleeful** *adj* : lleno de alegría

glib *adj* **glibber; glibbest** **1** : de mucha labia **2 a** ~ **reply** : una respuesta simplista — **glibly** *adv* : con mucha labia

glide *vi* **glided; gliding** : deslizarse (en una superficie), planear (en el aire) — **glider** *n* : planeador *m*

glimmer *vi* : brillar con luz trémula — ~ *n* : luz *f* trémula, luz *f* tenue

glimpse *vt* **glimpsed; glimpsing** : vislumbrar — ~ *n* : vislumbre

glint *vi* : destellar — ～ *n* : destello *m*
glisten *vi* : brillar
glitter *vi* : relucir, brillar
gloat *vi* ～ **over** : regodearse con
globalization *n* : globalización *f*
global warming *n* : calentamiento *m* global
globe *n* : globo *m* — **global** *adj* : global, mundial
gloom *n* **1** DARKNESS : oscuridad *f* **2** SADNESS : tristeza *f* — **gloomy** *adj* **gloomier; -est 1** DARK : sombrío, tenebroso **2** DISMAL : deprimente, lúgubre **3** PESSIMISTIC : pesimista
glory *n, pl* **-ries** : gloria *f* — **glorify** *vt* **-fied; -fying** : glorificar — **glorious** *adj* : glorioso, espléndido
gloss *n* : lustre *m*, brillo *m* — ～ *vt* ～ **over** : minimizar (la importancia de algo)
glossary *n, pl* **-ries** : glosario *m*
glossy *adj* **glossier; -est** : lustroso, brillante
glove *n* : guante *m*
glow *vi* **1** : brillar, resplandecer **2** ～ **with health** : rebosar de salud — ～ *n* : resplandor *m*, brillo *m*
glue *n* : pegamento *m*, cola *f* — ～ *vt* **glued; gluing** *or* **glueing** : pegar
glum *adj* **glummer; glummest** : sombrío, triste
glut *n* : superabundancia *f*, exceso *m*
glutton *n* : glotón *m*, **-tona** *f* — **gluttonous** *adj* : glotón — **gluttony** *n, pl* **-tonies** : glotonería *f*
gnarled *adj* : nudoso
gnash *vt* ～ **one's teeth** : hacer rechinar los dientes
gnat *n* : jején *m*
gnaw *vt* : roer
go *v* **went; gone; going; goes** *vi* **1** : ir **2** LEAVE : irse, salir **3** EXTEND : ir, extenderse **4** SELL : venderse **5** FUNCTION : funcionar, marchar **6** DISAPPEAR : desaparecer **7** ～ **back on one's word** : faltar a su palabra **8** ～ **crazy** : volverse loco **9** ～ **for** LIKE : gustar **10** ～ **off** EXPLODE : estallar **11** ～ **with** MATCH : armonizar con **12** ～ **without** : pasar sin — *v aux* **be going to** : ir a — ～ *n, pl* **goes 1 be on the** ～ : no parar **2 have a** ～ **at** : intentar
goad *vt* : aguijonear (un animal), incitar (a una persona)
goal *n* **1** AIM : meta *m*, objetivo *m* **2** : gol *m* (en deportes) — **goalkeeper** *or* **goalie** *n* : portero *m*, **-ra** *f*; arquero *m*, **-ra** *f*
goat *n* : cabra *f*
goatee *n* : barbita *f* de chivo
gobble *vt* **-bled; -bling** *or* ～ **up** : engullir
goblet *n* : copa *f*
goblin *n* : duende *m*
god *n* **1** : dios *m* **2 God** : Dios *m* — **goddess** *n* : diosa *f* — **godchild** *n, pl* **-children**

: ahijado *m*, **-da** *f* — **godfather** *n* : padrino *m* — **godmother** *n* : madrina *f* — **godparents** *npl* : padrinos *mpl* — **godsend** *n* : bendición *f* (del cielo)
goes → **go**
goggles *npl* : gafas *fpl* (protectoras), anteojos *mpl*
goings–on *npl* : sucesos *mpl*
gold *n* : oro *m* — **golden** *adj* **1** : (hecho) de oro **2** : dorado, de color oro — **goldfish** *n* : pez *m* de colores — **goldsmith** *n* : orfebre *mf*
golf *n* : golf *m* — ～ *vi* : jugar (al) golf — **golf ball** *n* : pelota *f* de golf — **golf course** *n* : campo *m* de golf — **golfer** *n* : golfista *mf*
gone *adj* **1** : ido, pasado **2** DEAD : muerto **3** LOST : desaparecido
good *adj* **better; best 1** : bueno **2** KIND : amable **3** ～ **afternoon (evening)** : buenas tardes **4 be** ～ **at** : tener facilidad para **5 feel** ～ : sentirse bien **6** ～ **for a cold** : beneficioso para los resfriados **7 have a** ～ **time** : divertirse **8** ～ **morning** : buenos días **9** ～ **night** : buenas noches — ～ *n* **1** : bien *m* **2** GOODNESS : bondad *f* **3** ～ **s** *npl* PROPERTY : bienes *mpl* **4** ～ **s** *npl* WARES : mercancías *fpl*, mercaderías *fpl* **5 for** ～ : para siempre — ～ *adv* : bien — **good–bye** *or* **good–by** *n* : adiós *m* — **Good Friday** *n* : Viernes *m* Santo — **good–looking** *adj* : bello, guapo — **goodness** *n* **1** : bondad *f* **2 thank** ～ **!** : ¡gracias a Dios!, ¡menos mal! — **goodwill** *n* : buena voluntad *f* — **goody** *n, pl* **goodies** : golosina *f*
gooey *adj* **gooier; gooiest** : pegajoso
goof *n* : pifia *f fam* — ～ *vi* **1** *or* ～ **up** : cometer un error **2** ～ **around** : hacer tonterías
goose *n, pl* **geese** : ganso *m*, **-sa** *f*; oca *f* — **goose bumps** *or* **goose pimples** *npl* : carne *f* de gallina
gopher *n* : taltuza *f*
gore[1] *n* BLOOD : sangre *f*
gore[2] *vt* **gored; goring** : cornear
gorge *n* RAVINE : cañon *m* — ～ *vt* **gorged; gorging** ～ **oneself** : hartarse
gorgeous *adj* : magnífico, espléndido
gorilla *n* : gorila *m*
gory *adj* **gorier; -est** : sangriento
gospel *n* **1** : evangelio *m* **2 the Gospel** : el Evangelio
gossip *n* **1** : chismoso *m*, **-sa** *f* (persona) **2** RUMOR : chisme *m* — ～ *vi* : chismear, contar chismes — **gossipy** *adj* : chismoso
got → **get**
Gothic *adj* : gótico
gotten → **get**
gourmet *n* : gastrónomo *m*, **-ma** *f*
gout *n* : gota *f*
govern *v* : gobernar — **governess** *n* : insti-

tutriz *f* — **government** *n* : gobierno *m* —
governor *n* : gobernador *m*, -dora *f*
gown *n* I : vestido *m* 2 : toga *f* (de magistrados, etc.)
grab *v* **grabbed; grabbing** *vt* : agarrar, arrebatar
grace *n* 1 : gracia *f* 2 **say** ~ : bendecir la
mesa — ~ *vt* **graced; gracing** 1 HONOR
: honrar 2 ADORN : adornar — **graceful** *adj*
: lleno de gracia, grácil — **gracious** *adj*
: cortés, gentil
grade *n* 1 QUALITY : calidad *f* 2 RANK
: grado *m*, rango *m* (militar) 3 YEAR : grado
m, año *m* (a la escuela) 4 MARK : nota *f* 5
SLOPE : cuesta *f* — ~ *vt* **graded; grading**
1 CLASSIFY : clasificar 2 MARK : calificar
(exámenes, etc.) — **grade school** → **elementary school**
gradual *adj* : gradual — **gradually** *adv*
: gradualmente, poco a poco
graduate *n* : licenciado *m*, -da *f* (de la universidad), bachiller *mf* (de la escuela secondaria) — ~ *v* **-ated; -ating** *vi* : graduarse, licenciarse — *vt* CALIBRATE
: graduar — **graduation** *n* : graduación *f*
graffiti *npl* : graffiti *mpl*
graft *n* : injerto *m* — ~ *vt* : injertar
grain *n* 1 : grano *m* 2 CEREALS : cereales
mpl 3 : veta *f*, vena *f* (de madera)
gram *n* : gramo *m*
grammar *n* : gramática *f* — **grammar
school** → **elementary school**
grand *adj* 1 : magnífico, espléndido 2
FABULOUS, GREAT : fabuloso, estupendo —
grandchild *n*, *pl* **-children** : nieto *m*, -ta *f*
— **granddaughter** *n* : nieta *f* — **grandeur** *n*
: grandiosidad *f* — **grandfather** *n* : abuelo
m — **grandiose** *adj* : grandioso — **grandmother** *n* : abuela *f* — **grandparents** *npl*
: abuelos *mpl* — **grandson** *n* : nieto *m* —
grandstand *n* : tribuna *f*
granite *n* : granito *m*
grant *vt* 1 : conceder 2 ADMIT : reconocer,
admitir 3 **take for granted** : dar (algo) por
sentado — ~ *n* 1 SUBSIDY : subvención *f*
2 SCHOLARSHIP : beca *f*
grape *n* : uva *f*
grapefruit *n* : toronja *f*, pomelo *m*
grapevine *n* 1 : vid *f*, parra *f* 2 **I heard it
through the** ~ : me lo dijo un pajarito *fam*
graph *n* : gráfica *f*, gráfico *m*
graphic¹ *adj* : gráfico
graphic² *n* 1 GRAPH, CHART: gráfica *f*, gráfico *m* 2 **graphics** *npl* : gráficos *mpl*, infografía *f*
grapple *vi* **-pled; -pling** ~ **with** : forcejear
con (una persona), luchar con (un problema)
grasp *vt* 1 : agarrar 2 UNDERSTAND : comprender, captar — ~ *n* 1 : agarre *m* 2 UN-
DERSTANDING : comprensión *f* 3 REACH
: alcance *m*
grass *n* 1 : hierba *f* (planta) 2 LAWN
: césped *m*, pasto *m* *Lat* — **grasshopper** *n*
: saltamontes *m* — **grassy** *adj* **grassier;
-est** : cubierto de hierba
grate¹ *v* **grated; -ing** *vt* 1 : rallar (en cocina) 2 ~ **one's teeth** : hacer rechinar los
dientes — *vi* RASP : chirriar
grate² *n* GRATING : reja *f*, rejilla *f*
grateful *adj* : agradecido — **gratefully** *adv*
: con agradecimiento — **gratefulness** *n*
: gratitud *f*, agradecimiento *m*
grater *n* : rallador *m*
gratify *vt* **-fied; -fying** 1 PLEASE : complacer 2 SATISFY : satisfacer
grating *n* : reja *f*, rejilla *f*
gratitude *n* : gratitud *f*
gratuitous *adj* : gratuito
grave¹ *n* : tumba *f*, sepultura *f*
grave² *adj* **graver; -est** : grave
gravel *n* : grava *f*, gravilla *f*
gravestone *n* : lápida *f* — **graveyard** *n* : cementerio *m*
gravity *n*, *pl* **-ties** : gravedad *f*
gravy *n*, *pl* **-vies** : salsa *f* (preparada con
jugo de carne)
gray *adj* 1 : gris 2 ~ **hair** : pelo *m* canoso
— ~ *n* : gris *m* — ~ *vi or* **turn** ~ : encanecer, ponerse gris
graze¹ *vi* **grazed; grazing** : pastar, pacer
graze² *vt* 1 TOUCH : rozar 2 SCRATCH : rasguñarse
grease *n* : grasa *f* — ~ *vt* **greased; greasing** : engrasar — **greasy** *adj* **greasier; -est**
1 : grasiento 2 OILY : graso, grasoso
great *adj* 1 : grande 2 FANTASTIC : estupendo, fabuloso — **great–grandchild** *n*, *pl*
-children : bisnieto *m*, -ta *f* — **great–
grandfather** *n* : bisabuelo *m* — **great–
grandmother** *n* : bisabuela *f* — **greatly** *adv*
1 MUCH : mucho 2 VERY : muy — **greatness** *n* : grandeza *f*
greed *n* 1 : codicia *f*, avaricia *f* 2 GLUT-
TONY : glotonería *f* — **greedily** *adv* : con
avaricia — **greedy** *adj* **greedier; -est** 1
: codicioso, avaro 2 GLUTTONOUS : glotón
Greek *adj* : griego — ~ *n* : griego *m* (idioma)
green *adj* 1 : verde 2 INEXPERIENCED
: novato — ~ *n* : verde *m* (color) 2
~**s** *npl* : verduras *fpl* — **greenery** *n*, *pl*
-eries : vegetación *f* — **greenhouse** *n* : invernadero *m*
greet *vt* 1 : saludar 2 WELCOME : recibir
— **greeting** *n* 1 : saludo *m* 2 ~**s** *npl*
REGARDS : saludos *mpl*, recuerdos *mpl*
gregarious *adj* : sociable
grenade *n* : granada *f*
grew → **grow**

grey → **gray**

greyhound *n* : galgo *m*

grid *n* **1** GRATING : rejilla *f* **2** NETWORK : red *f* **3** : cuadriculado *m* (de un mapa)

griddle *n* : plancha *f*

grief *n* : dolor *m*, pesar *m* — **grievance** *n* : queja *f* — **grieve** *v* **grieved; grieving** *vt* : entristecer — *vi* **for** : llorar (a), lamentar — **grievous** *adj* : grave, doloroso

grill *vt* **1** : asar a la parrilla **2** INTERROGATE : interrogar — **~** *n* : parrilla *f* (para cocinar) — **grille** *or* **grill** GRATING *n* : reja *f*, rejilla *f*

grim *adj* **grimmer; grimmest 1** STERN : severo **2** GLOOMY : sombrío

grimace *n* : mueca *f* — **~** *vi* **-maced; -macing** : hacer muecas

grime *n* : mugre *f*, suciedad *f* — **grimy** *adj* **grimier; -est** : mugriento, sucio

grin *vi* **grinned; grinning** : sonreír (abiertamente) — **~** *n* : sonrisa *f* (abierta)

grind *v* **ground; grinding** *vt* **1** : moler (el café, etc.) **2** SHARPEN : afilar **3 ~ one's teeth** : rechinar los dientes — *vi* : rechinar — **~** *n* **the daily ~** : la rutina diaria — **grinder** *n* : molinillo *m*

grip *vt* **gripped; gripping 1** : agarrar, asir **2** INTEREST : captar el interés de — **~** *n* **1** GRASP : agarre *m* **2** CONTROL : control *m*, dominio *m* **3** HANDLE : empuñadura *f* **4 come to ~s with** : llegar a entender de

gripe *vi* **griped; griping** : quejarse — **~** *n* : queja *f*

grisly *adj* **-lier; -est** : espeluznante, horrible

gristle *n* : cartílago *m*

grit *n* **1** : arena *f*, grava *f* **2** GUTS : agallas *fpl fam* **3 ~s** *npl* : sémola *f* de maíz — **~** *vt* **gritted; gritting ~ one's teeth** : acorazarse

groan *vi* : gemir — **~** *n* : gemido *m*

grocery *n*, *pl* **-ceries 1** *or* **~ store** : tienda *f* de comestibles, tienda *f* de abarrotes *Lat* **2 groceries** *npl* : comestibles *mpl*, abarrotes *mpl Lat* — **grocer** *n* : tendero *m*, -ra *f*

groggy *adj* **-gier; -est** : atontado, grogui *fam*

groin *n* : ingle *f*

groom *n* BRIDEGROOM : novio *m* — **~** *vt* **1** : almohazar (un animal) **2** PREPARE : preparar

groove *vi* : ranura *f*, surco *m*

grope *vi* **groped; groping 1** : andar a tientas **2 ~ for:** buscar a tientas

gross *adj* **1** SERIOUS : grave **2** OBESE : obeso **3** TOTAL : bruto **4** VULGAR : grosero, basto — **~** *n* **1** *or* **~ income** : ingresos *mpl* brutos **2** *pl* **~** : gruesa *f* (12 docenas) — **grossly** *adv* **1** EXTREMELY : enormemente **2** CRUDELY : groseramente

grotesque *adj* : grotesco

grouch *n* : gruñón *m*, -ñona *f fam* — **grouchy** *adj* **grouchier; -est** : gruñon *fam*

ground¹ → **grind**

ground² *n* **1** : suelo *m*, tierra *f* **2** *or* **~s** LAND : terreno *m* **3 ~s** REASON : razón *f*, motivos *mpl* **4 ~s** DREGS : pozo *m* (de café) — **~** *vt* **1** BASE : fundar, basar **2** : conectar a tierra (un aparato eléctrico) **3** : restringir (un avión o un piloto) a la tierra — **groundhog** *n* : marmota *f* (de América) — **groundless** *adj* : infundado — **groundwork** *n* : trabajo *m* preparatorio

group *n* : grupo *m* — **~** *vt* : agrupar — *vi or* **~ together** : agruparse

grove *n* : arboleda *f*

grovel *vi* **-eled** *or* **-elled; -eling** *or* **-elling** : arrastrarse, humillarse

grow *v* **grew; grown; growing** *vi* **1** : crecer **2** INCREASE : aumentar **3** BECOME : volverse, ponerse **4 ~ dark** : oscurecerse **5 ~ up** : hacerse mayor — *vt* **1** CULTIVATE : cultivar **2** : dejarse crecer (el pelo, etc.) — **grower** *n* : cultivador *m*, -dora *f*

growl *vi* : gruñir — **~** *n* : gruñido *m*

grown-up *adj* : mayor — **~** *n* : persona *f* mayor

growth *n* **1** : crecimiento *m* **2** INCREASE : aumento *m* **3** DEVELOPMENT : desarrollo *m* **4** TUMOR : tumor *m*

grub *n* **1** LARVA : larva *f* **2** FOOD : comida *f*

grubby *adj* **grubbier; -est** : mugriento, sucio

grudge *vt* **grudged; grudging** : dar de mala gana — **~** *n* **hold a ~** : guardar rencor

grueling *or* **gruelling** *adj* : extenuante, agotador

gruesome *adj* : horripilante

gruff *adj* **1** BRUSQUE : brusco **2** HOARSE : bronco

grumble *vi* **-bled; -bling** : refunfuñar, rezongar

grumpy *adj* **grumpier; -est** : malhumorado, gruñón *fam*

grunt *vi* : gruñir — **~** *n* : gruñido *m*

guarantee *n* : garantía *f* — **~** *vt* **-teed; -teeing** : garantizar

guard *n* **1** : guardia *f* **2** PRECAUTION : protección *f* — **~** *vt* : proteger, vigilar — *vi* **~ against** : protegerse contra — **guardian** *n* **1** : tutor *m*, -tora *f* (de niños) **2** PROTECTOR : guardián *m*, -diana *f*

guava *n* : guayaba *f*

guerrilla *or* **guerilla** *n* **1** : guerrillero *m*, -ra *f* **2 ~ warfare** : guerra *f* de guerrillas

guess *vt* **1** : adivinar **2** SUPPOSE : suponer, creer — *vi* **~ at** : adivinar — **~** *n* : conjetura *f*, suposición *f*

guest *n* **1** : invitado *m*, -da *f* **2** : huésped *mf* (a un hotel)

guide *n* : guía *mf* (persona), guía *f* (libro,

etc.) — ⁓ *vt* **guided; guiding** : guiar —
guidance *n* : orientación *f* — **guidebook** *n*
: guía *f* — **guideline** *n* : pauta *f*, directriz *f*
guild *n* : gremio *m*
guile *n* : astucia *f*
guilt *n* : culpa *f*, culpabilidad *f* — **guilty** *adj*
guiltier; -est : culpable
guinea pig *n* : conejillo *m* de Indias, cobaya
f
guise *n* : apariencia *f*
guitar *n* : guitarra *f*
gulf *n* **1** : golfo *m* **2** ABYSS : abismo *m*
gull *n* : gaviota *f*
gullet *n* **1** THROAT : garganta *f* **2** ESOPHA-
GUS : esófago *m*
gullible *adj* : crédulo
gully *n, pl* **-lies** : barranco *m*
gulp *vt or* ⁓ **down** : tragarse, engullir — *vi*
: tragar saliva — ⁓ *n* : trago *m*
gum¹ *n* : encía *f* (de la boca)
gum² *n* **1** : resina *f* (de plantas) **2** CHEWING
GUM : goma *f* de mascar, chicle *m*
gumption *n* : iniciativa *f*, agallas *fpl fam*
gun *n* **1** FIREARM : arma *f* de fuego **2** *or*
spray ⁓ : pistola *f* **3** → **cannon, pistol,**
revolver, rifle — ⁓ *vt* **gunned; gunning**
1 *or* ⁓ **down** : matar a tiros, asesinar **2** ⁓
the engine : acelerar (el motor) — **gun-**
boat *n* : cañonero *m* — **gunfire** *n* : disparos
mpl — **gunman** *n, pl* **-men** : pistolero *m*,
gatillero *m Lat* — **gunpowder** *n* : pólvora *f*
— **gunshot** *n* : disparo *m*, tiro *m*
gurgle *vi* **-gled; -gling** **1** : borbotar, gorgotear **2** : gorjear (dícese de un niño)
gush *vi* **1** SPOUT : salir a chorros **2** ⁓
with praise : deshacerse en elogios
gust *n* : ráfaga *f*
gusto *n, pl* **gustoes** : entusiasmo *m*
gusty *adj* **gustier; -est** : racheado, ventoso
gut *n* **1** : intestino *m* **2** ⁓s *npl* INNARDS
: tripas *fpl* **3** ⁓s *npl* COURAGE : agallas *fpl*
fam — ⁓ *vt* **gutted; gutting** **1** EVISCER-
ATE : destripar (un pollo, etc.), limpiar (un
pescado) **2** : destruir el interior de (un edificio)
gutter *n* : canaleta *f* (de un techo), cuneta *f*
(de una calle)
guy *n* : tipo *m fam*
guzzle *vt* **-zled; -zling** : chupar *fam*, tragar
gym *or* **gymnasium** *n, pl* **-siums** *or* **-sia**
: gimnasio *m* — **gymnast** *n* : gimnasta *mf*
— **gymnastics** *ns & pl* : gimnasia *f*
gynecology *n* : ginecología *f* — **gynecolo-**
gist *n* : ginecólogo *m*, -ga *f*
gyp *vt* **gypped; gypping** : estafar, timar
Gypsy *n, pl* **-sies** : gitano *m*, -na *f*
gyrate *vi* **-rated; -rating** : girar

H

h *n, pl* **h's** *or* **hs** : h *f*, octava letra del alfabeto
inglés
habit *n* **1** CUSTOM : hábito *m*, costumbre *f*
2 : hábito *m* (religioso)
habitat *n* : hábitat *m*
habitual *adj* **1** CUSTOMARY : habitual **2**
INVETERATE : empedernido
hack¹ *n* **1** : caballo *m* de alquiler **2** *or* ⁓
writer : escritorzuelo *m*, -la *f*
hack² *vt* : cortar — *vi or* ⁓ **into** : piratear
(un sistema informático)
hackneyed *adj* : manido, trillado
hacksaw *n* : sierra *f* para metales
had → **have**
haddock *ns & pl* : eglefino *m*
hadn't (*contraction of* **had not**) → **have**
hag *n* : bruja *f*
haggard *adj* : demacrado
haggle *vi* **-gled; -gling** : regatear
hail¹ *vt* **1** GREET : saludar **2** : llamar (un
taxi)
hail² *n* : granizo *m* (en meteorología) — ⁓
vi : granizar — **hailstone** *n* : piedra *f* de
granizo
hair *n* **1** : pelo *m*, cabello *m* **2** : vello *m* (en
las piernas, etc.) — **hairbrush** *n* : cepillo *m*
(para el pelo) — **haircut** *n* **1** : corte *m* de
pelo **2 get a** ⁓ : cortarse el pelo — **hairdo**
n, pl **-dos** : peinado *m* — **hairdresser** *n*
: peluquero *m*, -ra *f* — **hairless** *adj* : sin
pelo, calvo — **hairpin** *n* : horquilla *f* —
hair–raising *adj* : espeluznante — **hair-**
style → **hairdo** — **hair spray** *n* : laca *f* (para
el pelo) — **hairy** *adj* **hairier; -est** : peludo,
velludo
hale *adj* : saludable, robusto
half *n, pl* **halves** **1** : mitad *f* **2** *or* **halftime**
: tiempo *m* (en deportes) **3 in** ⁓ : por la
mitad — ⁓ *adj* **1** : medio **2** ⁓ **an hour**
: una media hora — ⁓ *adv* : medio — **half**
brother *n* : medio hermano *m*, hermanastro
m — **halfhearted** *adj* : sin ánimo, poco en-

tusiasta — **half sister** n : media hermana f, hermanastra f — **halfway** adv : a medio camino — ~ adj : medio

halibut ns & pl : halibut m

hall n **1** HALLWAY : corredor m, pasillo m **2** AUDITORIUM : sala f **3** LOBBY : vestíbulo m **4** DORMITORY : residencia f universitaria

hallmark n : sello m (distintivo)

Halloween n : víspera f de Todos los Santos

hallucination n : alucinación f

hallway n **1** ENTRANCE : entrada f **2** CORRIDOR : corredor m, pasillo m

halo n, pl **-los** or **-loes** : aureola f, halo m

halt n **1 call a ~ to** : poner fin a **2 come to a ~** : pararse — ~ vi : pararse — vt : parar

halve vt **halved; halving 1** DIVIDE : partir por la mitad **2** REDUCE : reducir a la mitad — **halves** → **half**

ham n : jamón m

hamburger or **hamburg** n **1** : carne f molida **2** or ~ **patty** : hamburguesa f

hammer n : martillo m — ~ v : martillar, martillear

hammock n : hamaca f

hamper[1] vt : obstaculizar, dificultar

hamper[2] n : cesto m, canasta f (para ropa sucia)

hamster n : hámster m

hand n **1** : mano f **2** : manecilla f, aguja f (de un reloj, etc.) **3** HANDWRITING : letra f, escritura f **4** WORKER : obrero m, -ra f **5 by ~** : a mano **6 lend a ~** : echar una mano **7 on ~** : a mano, disponible **8 on the other ~** : por otro lado — ~ vt **1** : pasar, dar **2 ~ out** : distribuir **3 ~ over** : entregar — **handbag** n : cartera f Lat, bolso m Spain — **handbook** n : manual m — **handcuffs** npl : esposas fpl — **handful** n : puñado m — **handgun** n : pistola f, revólver m

handicap n **1** : minusvalía f (física) **2** : hándicap m (en deportes) — ~ vt **-capped; -capping 1** : asignar un handicap a (en deportes) **2** HAMPER : obstaculizar — **handicapped** adj : minusválido

handicrafts npl : artesanía(s) f(pl)

handiwork n : trabajo m (manual)

handkerchief n, pl **-chiefs** : pañuelo m

handle n : asa m (de una taza, etc.), mango m (de un utensilio), pomo m (de una puerta), tirador m (de un cajón) — ~ vt **-dled; -dling 1** TOUCH : tocar **2** MANAGE : tratar, manejar — **handlebars** npl : manillar m, manubrio m Lat

handmade adj : hecho a mano

handout n **1** ALMS : dádiva f, limosna f **2** LEAFLET : folleto m

handrail n : pasamanos m

handshake n : apretón m de manos

handsome adj **-somer; -est 1** ATTRACTIVE : apuesto, guapo **2** GENEROUS : generoso **3** SIZABLE : considerable

handwriting n : letra f, escritura f — **handwritten** adj : escrito a mano

handy adj **handier; -est 1** NEARBY : a mano **2** USEFUL : práctico, útil **3** DEFT : habilidoso — **handyman** n, pl **-men** : hombre m habilidoso

hang v **hung; hanging** vt **1** : colgar **2** (past tense often **hanged**) EXECUTE : ahorcar **3 ~ one's head** : bajar la cabeza — vi **1** : colgar, pender **2** : caer (dícese de la ropa, etc.) **3 ~ up on s.o.** : colgar a algn — ~ n **1** DRAPE : caída f **2 get the ~ of** : agarrar la onda de

hangar n : hangar m

hanger n : percha f, gancho m (para ropa) Lat

hangover n : resaca f

hanker vi ~ **for** : tener ansias de — **hankering** n : ansia f, anhelo m

haphazard adj : casual, fortuito

happen vi **1** : pasar, suceder, ocurrir **2 ~ to do sth** : hacer algo por casualidad **3 it so happens that...** : da la casualidad de que... — **happening** n : suceso m, acontecimiento m

happy adj **-pier; -est 1** : feliz **2 be ~** : alegrarse **3 be ~ with** : estar contento con **4 be ~ to do sth** : hacer algo con mucho gusto — **happily** adv : alegremente — **happiness** n : felicidad f — **happy–go–lucky** adj : despreocupado

harass vt : acosar — **harassment** n : acoso m

harbor or Brit **harbour** n : puerto m — vt **1** SHELTER : albergar **2 ~ a grudge against** : guardar rencor a

hard adj **1** : duro **2** DIFFICULT : difícil **3 be a ~ worker** : ser muy trabajador **4 ~ liquor** : bebidas fpl fuertes **5 ~ water** : agua f dura — ~ adv **1** FORCEFULLY : fuerte **2 work ~** : trabajar duro **3 take sth ~** : tomarse algo muy mal — **harden** vt : endurecer — **hardheaded** adj : testarudo, terco — **hard–hearted** adj : duro de corazón — **hardly** adv **1** : apenas **2 ~ ever** : casi nunca — **hardness** n **1** : dureza f **2** DIFFICULTY : dificultad f — **hardship** n : dificultad f — **hardware** n **1** : ferretería f **2** : hardware m (en informática) — **hardworking** adj : trabajador

hardy adj **-dier; -est** : fuerte (dícese de personas), resistente (dícese de las plantas)

hare n, pl **hare** or **hares** : liebre f

harm n : daño m — ~ vt : hacer daño a (una persona), dañar (una cosa), perjudicar (la reputación de algn, etc.) — **harmful** adj : perjudicial — **harmless** adj : inofensivo

harmonica *n* : armónica *f*
harmony *n, pl* **-nies** : armonía *f* — **harmonious** *adj* : armonioso — **harmonize** *v* **-nized; -nizing** : armonizar
harness *n* : arnés *m* — ~ *vt* **1** : enjaezar **2** UTILIZE : utilizar
harp *n* : arpa *m* — ~ *vi* ~ **on** : insistir sobre
harpoon *n* : arpón *m*
harpsichord *n* : clavicémbalo *m*
harsh *adj* **1** ROUGH : áspero **2** SEVERE : duro, severo **3** : fuerte (dícese de una luz), discordante (dícese de sonidos) — **harshness** *n* : severidad *f*
harvest *n* : cosecha *f* — ~ *v* : cosechar
has → **have**
hash *vt* **1** CHOP : picar **2** ~ **over** DISCUSS : discutir — ~ *n* : picadillo *m* (comida)
hasn't (*contraction of* **has not**) → **has**
hassle *n* : problemas *mpl*, lío *m* — ~ *vt* **-sled; -sling** : fastidiar
haste *n* **1** : prisa *f*, apuro *m Lat* **2 make ~** : darse prisa, apurarse *Lat* — **hasten** *vt* : acelerar — *vi* : apresurarse, apurarse *Lat* — **hasty** *adj* **hastier; -est** : precipitado
hat *n* : sombrero *m*
hatch *n* : escotilla *f* — ~ *vt* **1** : empollar (huevos) **2** CONCOCT : tramar — *vi* : salir del cascarón
hatchet *n* : hacha *f*
hate *n* : odio *m* — ~ *vt* **hated; hating** : odiar, aborrecer — **hateful** *adj* : odioso, aborrecible — **hatred** *n* : odio *m*
haughty *adj* **-tier; -est** : altanero, altivo
haul *vt* : arrastrar, jalar *Lat* — ~ *n* **1** CATCH : redada *f* (de peces) **2** LOOT : botín *m* **3 a long ~** : un trayecto largo
haunch *n* : cadera *f* (de una persona), anca *f* (de un animal)
haunt *vt* **1** : frecuentar, rondar **2** TROUBLE : inquietar — ~ *n* : sitio *m* predilecto — **haunted** *adj* : embrujado
have *v* **had; having; has** *vt* **1** : tener **2** CONSUME : comer, tomar **3** ALLOW : permitir **4** : dar (una fiesta, etc.), convocar (una reunión) **5 ~ one's hair cut** : cortarse el pelo **6 ~ sth done** : mandar hacer algo — ~ *aux* **1** : haber **2 ~ just done sth** : acabar de hacer algo **4 you've finished, haven't you?** : has terminado, ¿no?
haven *n* : refugio *m*
havoc *n* : estragos *mpl*
hawk¹ *n* : halcón *m*
hawk² *vt* : pregonar (mercancías)
hay *n* : heno *m* — **hay fever** *n* : fiebre *f* del heno — **haystack** *n* : almiar *m* — **haywire** *adj* **go ~** : estropearse
hazard *n* : peligro *m*, riesgo *m* — ~ *vt* : arriesgar, aventurar — **hazardous** *adj* : arriesgado, peligroso

haze *n* : bruma *f*, neblina *f*
hazel *n* : color *m* avellana — **hazelnut** *n* : avellana *f*
hazy *adj* **hazier; -est** : nebuloso
he'd (*contraction of* **he had** *or* **he would**) → **have, would**
he'll (*contraction of* **he shall** *or* **he will**) → **shall, will**
he's (*contraction of* **he is** *or* **he has**) → **be, have**
he *pron* : él
head *n* **1** : cabeza *f* **2** END, TOP : cabeza *f* (de un clavo, etc.), cabecera *f* (de una mesa) **3** LEADER : jefe *m*, **-fa** *f* **4 be out of one's ~** : estar loco **5 come to a ~** : llegar a un punto crítico **6 ~s or tails** : cara o cruz **7 per ~** : por cabeza — ~ *adj* MAIN : principal — ~ *vt* : encabezar — *vi* : dirigirse — **headache** *n* : dolor *m* de cabeza — **headband** *n* : cinta *f* del pelo — **headdress** *n* : tocado *m* — **headfirst** *adv* : de cabeza — **heading** *n* : encabezamiento *m*, título *m* — **headland** *n* : cabo *m* — **headlight** *n* : faro *m* — **headline** : titular *m* — **headlong** *adv* **1** HEADFIRST : de cabeza **2** HASTILY : precipitadamente — **headmaster** *n* : director *m* — **headmistress** *n* : directora *f* — **head-on** *adv & adj* : de frente — **headphones** *npl* : auriculares *mpl*, audífonos *mpl Lat* — **headquarters** *ns & pl* : oficina *f* central (de una compañía), cuartel *m* general (de los militares) — **head start** *n* : ventaja *f* — **headstrong** *adj* : testarudo, obstinado — **headwaiter** *n* : jefe *m*, **-fa** *f* de comedor — **headway** *n* **1** : progreso *m* **2 make ~** : avanzar — **heady** *adj* **headier; -est** : embriagador
heal *vt* : curar — *vi* : cicatrizar
health *n* : salud *f* — **healthy** *adj* **healthier; -est** : sano, saludable
heap *n* : montón *m* — ~ *vt* : amontonar
hear *v* **heard; hearing** *vt* : oír — *vi* **1** : oír **2 ~ about** : enterarse de **3 ~ from** : tener noticias de — **hearing** *n* **1** : oído *m* **2** : vista *f* (en un tribunal) — **hearing aid** *n* : audífono *m* — **hearsay** *n* : rumores *mpl*
hearse *n* : coche *m* fúnebre
heart *n* **1** : corazón *m* **2 at ~** : en el fondo **3 by ~** : de memoria **4 lose ~** : descorazonarse **5 take ~** : animarse — **heartache** *n* : pena *f*, dolor *m* — **heart attack** *n* : infarto *m*, ataque *m* al corazón — **heartbeat** *n* : latido *m* (del corazón) — **heartbreak** *n* : congoja *f*, angustia *f* — **heartbroken** *adj* : desconsolado — **heartburn** *n* : acidez *f* estomacal
hearth *n* : hogar *m*
heartily *adv* : de buena gana
heartless *adj* : de mal corazón, cruel

hearty *adj* **heartier; -est 1** : cordial, caluroso **2** : abundante (dícese de una comida)
heat *vt* : calentar — *vi or* ~ **up** : calentarse — ~ *n* **1** : calor *m* **2** HEATING : calefacción *f* — **heated** *adj* : acalorado — **heater** *n* : calentador *m*
heath *n* : brezal *m*
heathen *adj* : pagano — ~ *n, pl* **-thens** *or* **-then** : pagano *m*, **-na** *f*
heather *n* : brezo *m*
heave *v* **heaved** *or* **hove; heaving** *vt* **1** LIFT : levantar (con esfuerzo) **2** HURL : lanzar, tirar **3** ~ **a sigh** : suspirar — ~ *vi or* ~ **up** : levantarse
heaven *n* : cielo *m* — **heavenly** *adj* **1** : celestial **2** ~ **body** : cuerpo *m* celeste
heavy *adj* **heavier; -est 1** : pesado **2** INTENSE : fuerte **3** ~ **sigh** : suspiro *m* profundo **4** ~ **traffic** : tráfico *m* denso — **heavily** *adv* **1** : pesadamente **2** EXCESSIVELY : mucho — **heaviness** *n* : peso *m*, pesadez *f* — **heavyweight** *n* : peso *m* pesado
Hebrew *adj* : hebreo — ~ *n* : hebreo *m* (idioma)
heckle *vt* **-led; -ling** : interrumpir (a un orador) con preguntas molestas
hectic *adj* : agitado, ajetreado
hedge *n* : seto *m* vivo — ~ *v* **hedged; hedging** *vt* ~ **one's bets** : cubrirse — *vi* : contestar con evasivas — **hedgehog** *n* : erizo *m*
heed *vt* : prestar atención a, hacer caso de — ~ *n* **take** ~ : tener cuidado — **heedless** *adj* **be** ~ **of** : hacer caso omiso de
heel *n* : talón *m* (del pie), tacón *m* (de un zapato)
hefty *adj* **heftier; -est** : robusto y pesado
heifer *n* : novilla *f*
height *n* **1** : estatura *f* (de una persona), altura *f* (de un objeto) **2** PEAK : cumbre *f* **3** **the** ~ **of folly** : el colmo de la locura **4** **what is your** ~ ? : ¿cuánto mides? — **heighten** *vt* : aumentar, intensificar
heir *n* : heredero *m*, **-ra** *f* — **heiress** *n* : heredera *f* — **heirloom** *n* : reliquia *f* de familia
held → **hold**
helicopter *n* : helicóptero *m*
hell *n* : infierno *m* — **hellish** *adj* : infernal
hello *interj* : ¡hola!
helm *n* : timón *m*
helmet *n* : casco *m*
help *vt* **1** : ayudar **2** ~ **oneself** : servirse **3 I can't** ~ **it** : no lo puedo remediar — ~ *n* **1** : ayuda *f* **2** STAFF : personal *m* — **help!** : ¡socorro!, ¡auxilio! — **helper** *n* : ayudante *mf* — **helpful** *adj* **1** OBLIGING : servicial, amable **2** USEFUL : útil — **helping** *n* : porción *f* — **helpless** *adj* **1** POWERLESS : incapaz **2** DEFENSELESS : indefenso

hem *n* : dobladillo *m* — ~ *vt* **hemmed; hemming** ~ **in** : encerrar
hemisphere *n* : hemisferio *m*
hemorrhage *n* : hemorragia *f*
hemorrhoids *npl* : hemorroides *fpl*, almorranas *fpl*
hemp *n* : cáñamo *m*
hen *n* : gallina *f*
hence *adv* **1** : de aquí, de ahí **2** THEREFORE : por lo tanto **3 ten years** ~ : de aquí a 10 años — **henceforth** *adv* : de ahora en adelante
henpeck *vt* : dominar (al marido)
hepatitis *n, pl* **-titides** : hepatitis *f*
her *adj* : su, sus — ~ *pron* **1** (*used as direct object*) : la **2** (*used as indirect object*) : le, se **3** (*used as object of a preposition*) : ella
herald *vt* : anunciar
herb *n* : hierba *f*
herd *n* : manada *f* — ~ *vt* : conducir (en manada) — *vi or* ~ **together** : reunir
here *adv* **1** : aquí, acá **2** ~ **you are!** : ¡toma! — **hereabouts** *or* **hereabout** *adv* : por aquí (cerca) — **hereafter** *adv* : en el futuro — **hereby** *adv* : por este medio
hereditary *adj* : hereditario — **heredity** *n* : herencia *f*
heresy *n, pl* **-sies** : herejía *f*
herewith *adv* : adjunto
heritage *n* **1** : herencia *f* **2** : patrimonio *m* (nacional)
hermit *n* : ermitaño *m*, **-ña** *f*
hernia *n, pl* **-nias** *or* **-niae** : hernia *f*
hero *n, pl* **-roes** : héroe *m* — **heroic** *adj* : heroico — **heroine** *n* : heroína *f* — **heroism** *n* : heroísmo *m*
heron *n* : garza *f*
herring *n, pl* **-ring** *or* **-rings** : arenque *m*
hers *pron* **1** : (el) suyo, (la) suya, (los) suyos, (las) suyas **2 some friends of** ~ : unos amigos suyos, unos amigos de ella — **herself** *pron* **1** (*used reflexively*) : se **2** (*used emphatically*) : ella misma
hesitant *adj* : titubeante, vacilante — **hesitate** *vi* **-tated; -tating** : vacilar, titubear — **hesitation** *n* : vacilación *f*, titubeo *m*
heterosexual *adj* : heterosexual — ~ *n* : heterosexual *mf*
hexagon *n* : hexágono *m*
hey *interj* : ¡eh!, ¡oye!
heyday *n* : auge *m*, apogeo *m*
hi *interj* : ¡hola!
hibernate *vi* **-nated; -nating** : hibernar
hiccup *n* **have the** ~**s** : tener hipo — ~ *vi* **-cuped; -cuping** : tener hipo
hide[1] *n* : piel *f*, cuero *m*
hide[2] *v* **hid; hidden** *or* **hid; hiding** *vt* **1** : esconder **2** : ocultar (motivos, etc.) — *vi*

: esconderse — **hide–and–seek** n : escondite m, escondidas fpl Lat

hideous adj : horrible, espantoso

hideout n : escondite m, guarida f

hierarchy n, pl **-chies** : jerarquía f — **hierarchical** adj : jerárquico

high adj **1** : alto **2** INTOXICATED : borracho, drogado **3 a ~ voice** : una voz aguda **4 it's two feet ~** : tiene dos pies de alto **5 ~ winds** : fuertes vientos mpl — ~ adv : alto — ~ n : récord m, máximo m — **higher** adj **1** : superior **2 ~ education** : enseñanza f superior — **highlight** n : punto m culminante — **highly** adv **1** VERY : muy, sumamente **2 think ~ of** : tener en mucho a — **Highness** n **His/Her ~** : Su Alteza f — **high school** n : escuela f superior, escuela f secundaria — **high–strung** adj : nervioso, excitable — **highway** n : carretera f

hijack vt : secuestrar — **hijacker** n : secuestrador m, -dora f — **hijacking** n : secuestro m

hike v **hiked; hiking** vi : ir de caminata — vt or ~ **up** RAISE : subir — ~ n : caminata f, excursión f — **hiker** n : excursionista mf

hilarious adj : muy divertido — **hilarity** n : hilaridad f

hill n **1** : colina f, cerro m **2** SLOPE : cuesta f — **hillside** n : ladera f, cuesta f — **hilly** adj **hillier; -est** : accidentado

hilt n : puño m

him pron **1** (used as direct object) : lo **2** (used as indirect object) : le, se **3** (used as object of a preposition) : él — **himself** pron **1** (used reflexively) : se **2** (used emphatically) : él mismo

hind adj : trasero, posterior

hinder vt : dificultar, estorbar — **hindrance** n : obstáculo m

hindsight n **in ~** : en retrospectiva

Hindu adj : hindú

hinge n : bisagra f, gozne m — ~ vi **hinged; hinging ~ on** : depender de

hint n **1** : indirecta f **2** TIP : consejo m **3** TRACE : asomo m, toque m — ~ vt : dar a entender — vi ~ **at** : insinuar

hip n : cadera f

hippopotamus n, pl **-muses** or **-mi** : hipopótamo m

hire n **1** : alquiler m **2 for ~** : se alquila — ~ vt **hired; hiring 1** EMPLOY : contratar, emplear **2** RENT : alquilar

his adj : su, sus, de él — ~ pron **1** : (el) suyo, (la) suya, (los) suyos, (las) suyas **2 some friends of ~** : unos amigos suyos, unos amigos de él

Hispanic adj : hispano, hispánico

hiss vi : silbar — n : silbido m

history n, pl **-ries 1** : historia f **2** BACK-

GROUND : historial m — **historian** n : historiador m, -dora f — **historic** or **historical** adj : histórico

hit v **hit; hitting** vt **1** : golpear, pegar **2** : dar (con un proyectil) **3** AFFECT : afectar **4** REACH : alcanzar **5 the car ~ a tree** : el coche chocó contra un árbol — vi : pegar — ~ n **1** : golpe m **2** SUCCESS : éxito m

hitch vt **1** ATTACH : enganchar **2** or ~ **up** RAISE : subirse **3 ~ a ride** : hacer autostop — ~ n PROBLEM : problema m — **hitch-hike** vi **-hiked; -hiking** : hacer autostop — **hitchhiker** n : autostopista mf

hitherto adv : hasta ahora

HIV n : VIH m, virus m del sida

hive n : colmena f

hives ns & pl : urticaria f

hoard n : tesoro m (de dinero), reserva f (de provisiones) — ~ vt : acumular

hoarse adj **hoarser; -est** : ronco

hoax n : engaño m

hobble vi **-bled; -bling** : cojear

hobby n, pl **-bies** : pasatiempo m

hobo n, pl **-boes** : vagabundo m, -da f

hockey n : hockey m

hoe n : azada f — ~ vt **hoed; hoeing** : azadonar

hog n : cerdo m — ~ vt **hogged; hogging** MONOPOLIZE : acaparar

hoist vt **1** : izar (una vela, etc.) **2** LIFT : levantar — ~ n : grúa f

hold[1] n : bodega f (en un barco o un avión)

hold[2] v **held; holding** vt **1** GRIP : agarrar **2** POSSESS : tener **3** SUPPORT : sostener **4** : celebrar (una reunión, etc.), mantener (una conversación) **5** CONTAIN : contener **6** CONSIDER : considerar **7** or ~ **back** : detener **8 ~ hands** : agarrarse de la mano **9 ~ up** ROB : atracar **10 ~ up** DELAY : retrasar — vi **1** LAST : durar, continuar **2** APPLY : ser válido — ~ n **1** GRIP : agarre m **2 get ~ of** : conseguir **3 get ~ of oneself** : controlarse — **holder** n : tenedor m, -dora f — **holdup** n **1** ROBBERY : atraco m **2** DELAY : retraso m, demora f

hole n : agujero m, hoyo m

holiday n **1** : día m feriado, fiesta f **2** Brit VACATION : vacaciones fpl

holiness n : santidad f

holler vi : gritar — ~ n : grito m

hollow adj **1** : hueco **2** VALLEY : hondonada f — ~ adj **-lower; -est 1** : hueco **2** FALSE : vacío, falso — ~ vt or ~ **out** : ahuecar

holly n, pl **-lies** : acebo m

holocaust n : holocausto m

holster n : pistolera f

holy adj **-lier; -est** : santo, sagrado

homage n : homenaje m

home n **1** : casa f **2** FAMILY : hogar m **3**

INSTITUTION : residencia *f*, asilo *m* **4 at ~ and abroad** : dentro y fuera del país — ~ *adv* **go** — : ir a casa — **homeland** *n* : patria *f* — **homeless** *adj* : sin hogar — **homely** *adj* **-lier; -est 1** DOMESTIC : casero **2** UGLY : feo — **homemade** *adj* : casero, hecho en casa — **homemaker** *n* : ama *f* de casa — **home run** *n* : jonrón *m* — **homesick** *adj* **be ~** : echar de menos a la familia — **homeward** *adj* : de vuelta, de regreso — **homework** *n* : tarea *f*, deberes *mpl* — **homey** *adj* **homier; -est** : hogareño, acogedor

homicide *n* : homicidio *m*

homogeneous *adj* : homogéneo

homosexual *adj* : homosexual — ~ *n* : homosexual *mf* — **homosexuality** *n* : homosexualidad *f*

honest *adj* **1** : honrado **2** FRANK : sincero — **honestly** *adv* : sinceramente — **honesty** *n*, *pl* **-ties** : honradez *f*

honey *n*, *pl* **-eys** : miel *f* — **honeycomb** *n* : panal *m* — **honeymoon** *n* : luna *f* de miel

honk *vi* : tocar la bocina — ~ *n* : bocinazo *m*

honor *or Brit* **honour** *n* : honor *m* — ~ *vt* **1** : honrar **2** : aceptar (un cheque, etc.), cumplir con (una promesa) — **honorable** *or Brit* **honourable** *adj* : honorable, honroso — **honorary** *adj* : honorario

hood *n* **1** : capucha *f* (de un abrigo, etc.) **2** : capó *m* (de un automóvil)

hoodlum *n* : matón *m*

hoodwink *vt* : engañar

hoof *n*, *pl* **hooves** *or* **hoofs** : pezuña *f* (de una vaca, etc.), casco *m* (de un caballo)

hook *n* **1** : gancho *m* **2** *or* **~ and eye** : corchete *m* **3** → **fishhook** **4 off the ~** : descolgado — ~ *vt* : enganchar — *vi* : engancharse

hoop *n* : aro *m*

hooray → **hurrah**

hoot *vi* **1** : ulular (dícese de un búho) **2 ~ with laughter** : reírse a carcajadas — ~ *n* **1** : ululato *m* (de un búho) **2 I don't give a ~** : me importa un comino

hop[1] *vi* **hopped; hopping** : saltar a la pata coja — ~ *n* : salto *m* a la pata coja

hop[2] *n* **~s** : lúpulo *m* (planta)

hope *v* **hoped; hoping** *vi* : esperar — *vt* : esperar que — ~ *n* : esperanza *f* — **hopeful** *adj* : esperanzado — **hopefully** *adv* **1** : con esperanza **2 ~ it will help** : se espera que ayude — **hopeless** *adj* : desesperado — **hopelessly** *adv* : desesperadamente

horde *n* : horda *f*

horizon *n* : horizonte *m* — **horizontal** *adj* : horizontal

hormone *n* : hormona *f*

horn *n* **1** : cuerno *m* (de un animal) **2** : trompa *f* (instrumento musical) **3** : bocina *f*, claxon *m* (de un vehículo)

hornet *n* : avispón *m*

horoscope *n* : horóscopo *m*

horror *n* : horror *m* — **horrendous** *adj* : horrendo — **horrible** *adj* : horrible — **horrid** *adj* : horroroso, horrible — **horrify** *vt* **-fied; -fying** : horrorizar

hors d'oeuvre *n*, *pl* **hors d'oeuvres** : entremés *m*

horse *n* : caballo *m* — **horseback** *n* **on ~** : a caballo — **horsefly** *n*, *pl* **-flies** : tábano *m* — **horseman** *n*, *pl* **-men** : jinete *m* — **horseplay** *n* : payasadas *fpl* — **horsepower** *n* : caballo *m* de fuerza — **horseradish** *n* : rábano *m* picante — **horseshoe** *n* : herradura *f* — **horsewoman** *n*, *pl* **-women** : jinete *f*

horticulture *n* : horticultura *f*

hose *n* **1** *pl* **hoses** : manguera *f*, manga *f* **2** **hose** *pl* STOCKINGS : medias *fpl* — ~ *vt* **hosed; hosing** : regar (con manguera) — **hosiery** *n* : calcetería *f*

hospice *n* : hospicio *m*

hospital *n* : hospital *m* — **hospitable** *adj* : hospitalario — **hospitality** *n*, *pl* **-ties** : hospitalidad *f* — **hospitalize** *vt* **-ized; -izing** : hospitalizar

host[1] *n* **a ~ of** : toda una serie de

host[2] *n* **1** : anfitrión *m*, **-triona** *f* **2** : presentador *m*, **-dora** *f* (de televisión, etc.) — ~ *vt* : presentar (un programa de televisión, etc.)

host[3] *n* EUCHARIST : hostia *f*, Eucaristía *f*

hostage *n* : rehén *m*

hostel *n or* **youth ~** : albergue *m* juvenil

hostess *n* : anfitriona *f*

hostile *adj* : hostil — **hostility** *n*, *pl* **-ties** : hostilidad *f*

hot dog *n* : perro *m* caliente

hot *adj* **hotter; hottest 1** : caliente, caluroso (dícese del tiempo), cálido (dícese del clima) **2** SPICY : picante **3 feel ~** : tener calor **4 have a ~ temper** : tener mal genio **5 ~ news** : noticias *fpl* de última hora **6 it's ~ today** : hace calor

hotel *n* : hotel *m*

hotheaded *adj* : exaltado

hound *n* : perro *m* (de caza) — ~ *vt* : acosar, perseguir

hour *n* : hora *f* — **hourglass** *n* : reloj *m* de arena — **hourly** *adv* & *adj* : cada hora, por hora

house *n*, *pl* **houses 1** : casa *f* **2** : cámara *f* (del gobierno) **3 publishing ~** : editorial *f* — ~ *vt* **housed; housing** : albergar — **houseboat** *n* : casa *f* flotante — **housefly** *n*, *pl* **-flies** : mosca *f* común — **household**

adj **1** : doméstico **2** ~ **name** : nombre *m* muy conocido — ~ *n* : casa *f* — **housekeeper** *n* : ama *f* de llaves — **housekeeping** *n* : gobierno *m* de la casa — **housewarming** *n* : fiesta *f* de estreno de una casa — **housewife** *n, pl* **-wives** : ama *f* de casa — **housework** *n* : faenas *fpl* domésticas — **housing** *n* **1** : viviendas *fpl* **2** CASE : caja *f* protectora

hove → **heave**

hovel *n* : casucha *f*, tugurio *m*

hover *vi* **1** : cernerse **2** ~ **about** : rondar

hovercraft *n* : aerodeslizador *m*

how *adv* **1** : cómo **2** (*used in exclamations*) : qué **3** ~ **are you?** : ¿cómo está Ud.? **4** ~ **come** : por qué **5** ~ **much** : cuánto **6** ~ **do you do?** : mucho gusto **7** ~ **old are you?** : ¿cuántos años tienes? — ~ *conj* : como

however *conj* **1** : de cualquier manera que **2** ~ **you like** : como quieras — ~ *adv* **1** NEVERTHELESS : sin embargo, no obstante **2** ~ **difficult it is** : por díficil que sea **3** ~ **hard I try** : por más que me esfuerce

howl *vi* : aullar — ~ *n* : aullido *m*

hub *n* **1** CENTER : centro *m* **2** : cubo *m* (de una rueda)

hubbub *n* : alboroto *m*, jaleo *m*

hubcap *n* : tapacubos *m*

huddle *vi* **-dled; -dling** *or* ~ **together** : apiñarse

hue *n* : color *m*, tono *m*

huff *n* **be in a** ~ : estar enojado

hug *vt* **hugged; hugging** : abrazar — ~ *n* : abrazo *m*

huge *adj* **huger; hugest** : inmenso, enorme

hull *n* : casco *m* (de un barco, etc.)

hum *v* **hummed; humming** *vi* **1** : tararear **2** BUZZ : zumbar — *vt* : tararear (una melodía) — ~ *n* : zumbido *m*

human *adj* : humano — ~ *n* : (ser *m*) humano *m* — **humane** *adj* : humano, humanitario — **humanitarian** *adj* : humanitario — **humanity** *n, pl* **-ties** : humanidad *f*

humble *vt* **-bled; -bling** **1** : humillar **2** ~ **oneself** : humillarse — ~ *adj* **-bler; -blest** : humilde

humdrum *adj* : monótono, rutinario

humid *adj* : húmedo — **humidity** *n, pl* **-ties** : humedad *f*

humiliate *vt* **-ated; -ating** : humillar — **humiliating** *adj* : humillante — **humiliation** *n* : humillación *f* — **humility** *n* : humildad *f*

humor *or Brit* **humour** *n* : humor *m* — ~ *vt* : seguir la corriente a, complacer — **humorous** *adj* : humorístico, cómico

hump *n* : joroba *f*

hunch *vi or* ~ **over** : encorvarse — ~ *n* : presentimiento *m*

hundred *adj* : cien, ciento — ~ *n, pl* **-dreds** *or* **-dred** : ciento *m* — **hundredth** *adj* : centésimo — ~ *n* **1** : centésimo *m*, -ma *f* (en una serie) **2** : centésimo *m* (en matemáticas)

hung → **hang**

Hungarian *adj* : húngaro — ~ *n* : húngaro *m* (idioma)

hunger *n* : hambre *m* — ~ *vi* **1** : tener hambre **2** ~ **for** : ansiar, anhelar — **hungry** *adj* **-grier; -est** **1** : hambriento **2 be** ~ : tener hambre

hunk *n* : pedazo *m* (grande)

hunt *vt* **1** : cazar **2** ~ **for** : buscar — ~ *n* **1** : caza *f*, cacería *f* **2** SEARCH : búsqueda *f*, busca *f* — **hunter** *n* : cazador *m*, -dora *f* — **hunting** *n* **1** : caza *f* **2 go** ~ : ir de caza

hurdle *n* **1** : valla *f* (en deportes) **2** OBSTACLE : obstáculo *m*

hurl *vt* : lanzar, arrojar

hurrah *interj* : ¡hurra!

hurricane *n* : huracán *m*

hurry *n* : prisa *f*, apuro *f Lat* — *v* **-ried; -rying** *vi* : darse prisa, apurarse *Lat* — *vt* : apurar, dar prisa a — **hurried** *adj* : apresurado — **hurriedly** *adv* : apresuradamente, de prisa

hurt *v* **hurt; hurting** *vt* **1** INJURE : hacer daño a, lastimar **2** OFFEND : ofender, herir — *vi* **1** : doler **2 my foot** ~ **s** : me duele el pie — ~ *n* **1** INJURY : herida *f* **2** DISTRESS : dolor *m*, pena *f* — **hurtful** *adj* : hiriente, doloroso

hurtle *vi* **-tled; -tling** : lanzarse, precipitarse

husband *n* : esposo *m*, marido *m*

hush *vt* : hacer callar, acallar — ~ *n* : silencio *m*

husk *n* : cáscara *f*

husky[1] *adj* **-kier; -est** HOARSE : ronco

husky[2] *n, pl* **-kies** : perro *m*, -rra *f* esquimal

husky[3] *adj* BURLY : fornido

hustle *v* **-tled; -tling** *vt* : dar prisa a, apurar *Lat* — *vi* : darse prisa, apurarse *Lat* — ~ *n* ~ **and bustle** : ajetreo *m*, bullicio *m*

hut *n* : cabaña *f*

hutch *n or* **rabbit** ~ : conejera *f*

hyacinth *n* : jacinto *m*

hybrid *n* : híbrido *m* — ~ *adj* : híbrido

hydrant *n or* **fire** ~ : boca *f* de incendios

hydraulic *adj* : hidráulico

hydroelectric *adj* : hidroeléctrico

hydrogen *n* : hidrógeno *m*

hyena *n* : hiena *f*

hygiene *n* : higiene *f* — **hygienic** *adj* : higiénico

hymn *n* : himno *m*

hyperactive *adj* : hiperactivo

hyperlink *n* : hiperenlace *m*

hypermarket *n* : hipermercado *m*

hyphen *n* : guión *m*

hypnosis *n*, *pl* **-noses** : hipnosis *f* — **hypnotic** *adj* : hipnótico — **hypnotism** *n* : hipnotismo *m* — **hypnotize** *vt* **-tized; -tizing** : hipnotizar

hypochondriac *n* : hipocondríaco *m*, -ca *f*

hypocrisy *n*, *pl* **-sies** : hipocresía *f* — **hypocrite** *n* : hipócrita *mf* — **hypocritical** *adj* : hipócrita

hypothesis *n*, *pl* **-eses** : hipótesis *f* — **hypothetical** *adj* : hipotético

hysteria *n* : histeria *f*, histerismo *m* — **hysterical** *adj* : histérico

I

i *n*, *pl* **i's** *or* **is** : i *f*, novena letra del alfabeto inglés

I *pron* : yo

ice *n* : hielo *m* — ~ *v* **iced; icing** *vt* **1** FREEZE : congelar **2** CHILL : enfriar **3** : bañar (pasteles, etc.) — ~ *vi or* ~ **up** : helarse, congelarse — **iceberg** *n* : iceberg *m* — **icebox** → **refrigerator** — **ice–cold** *adj* : helado — **ice cream** *n* : helado *m* — **ice cube** *n* : cubito *m* de hielo — **ice–skate** *vi* **-skated; -skating** : patinar — **ice skate** *n* : patín *m* de cuchilla — **icicle** *n* : carámbano *m* — **icing** *n* : baño *m*

icon *n* : icono *m*

icy *adj* **icier; -est 1** : cubierto de hielo (dícese de pavimento, etc.) **2** FREEZING : helado

I'd (*contraction of* **I should** *or* **I would**) → **should, would**

idea *n* : idea *f*

ideal *adj* : ideal — ~ *n* : ideal *m* — **idealist** *n* : idealista *mf* — **idealistic** *adj* : idealista — **idealize** *vt* **-ized; -izing** : idealizar

identity *n*, *pl* **-ties** : identidad *f* — **identical** *adj* : idéntico — **identify** *v* **-fied; -fying** *vt* : identificar — *vi* ~ **with** : identificarse con — **identification** *n* **1** : identificación *f* **2** ~ **card** : carnet *m*, carné *m*

ideology *n*, *pl* **-gies** : ideología *f* — **ideological** *adj* : ideológico

idiocy *n*, *pl* **-cies** : idiotez *f*

idiom *n* EXPRESSION : modismo *m* — **idiomatic** *adj* : idiomático

idiosyncrasy *n*, *pl* **-sies** : idiosincrasia *f*

idiot *n* : idiota *mf* — **idiotic** *adj* : idiota

idle *adj* **idler; idlest 1** LAZY : haragán, holgazán **2** INACTIVE : parado (dícese de una máquina) **3** UNEMPLOYED : desocupado **4** VAIN : frívolo, vano **5 out of** ~ **curiosity** : por pura curiosidad — ~ *v* **idled; idling** *vi* : andar al ralentí (dícese de un motor) — *vt* ~ **away the hours** : pasar el rato — **idleness** *n* : ociosidad *f*

idol *n* : ídolo *m* — **idolize** *vt* **-ized; -izing** : idolatrar

idyllic *adj* : idílico

if *conj* **1** : si **2** THOUGH : aunque, si bien **3** ~ **so** : si es así

igloo *n*, *pl* **-loos** : iglú *m*

ignite *v* **-nited; -niting** *vt* : encender — *vi* : encenderse — **ignition** *n* **1** : ignición *f* **2** *or* ~ **switch** : encendido *m*

ignore *vt* **-nored; -noring** : ignorar, no hacer caso de — **ignorance** *n* : ignorancia *f* — **ignorant** *adj* **1** : ignorante **2 be** ~ **of** : desconocer, ignorar

ilk *n* : tipo *m*, clase *f*

ill *adj* **worse; worst 1** SICK : enfermo **2** BAD : malo — *adv* **worse; worst** : mal — **ill–advised** *adj* : imprudente — **ill at ease** *adj* : incómodo

I'll (*contraction of* **I shall** *or* **I will**) → **shall, will**

illegal *adj* : ilegal

illegible *adj* : ilegible

illegitimate *adj* : ilegítimo — **illegitimacy** *n* : ilegitimidad *f*

illicit *adj* : ilícito

illiterate *adj* : analfabeto — **illiteracy** *n*, *pl* **-cies** : analfabetismo *m*

ill–mannered *adj* : descortés, maleducado

ill–natured *adj* : de mal genio

illness *n* : enfermedad *f*

illogical *adj* : ilógico

ill–treat *vt* : maltratar

illuminate *vt* **-nated; -nating** : iluminar — **illumination** *n* : iluminación *f*

illusion *n* : ilusión *f* — **illusory** *adj* : ilusorio

illustrate *v* **-trated; -trating** : ilustrar — **illustration** *n* **1** : ilustración *f* **2** EXAMPLE : ejemplo *m* — **illustrative** *adj* : ilustrativo

illustrious *adj* : ilustre, glorioso

ill will *n* : animadversión *f*, mala voluntad *f*

I'm (*contraction of* **I am**) → **be**

image *n* : imagen *f* — **imaginary** *adj* : imaginario — **imagination** *n* : imaginación *f* —

imaginative *adj* : imaginativo — **imagine** *vt* **-ined; -ining** : imaginar(se)
imbalance *n* : desequilibrio *m*
imbecile *n* : imbécil *mf*
imbue *vt* **-bued; -buing** : imbuir
imitation *n* : imitación *f* — ~ *adj* : de imitación, artificial — **imitate** *vt* **-tated; -tating** : imitar, remedar — **imitator** *n* : imitador *m*, -dora *f*
immaculate *adj* : inmaculado
immaterial *adj* : irrelevante, sin importancia
immature *adj* : inmaduro — **immaturity** *n*, *pl* **-ties** : inmadurez *f*
immediate *adj* : inmediato — **immediately** *adv* : inmediatamente
immense *adj* : inmenso — **immensity** *n*, *pl* **-ties** : inmensidad *f*
immerse *vt* **-mersed; -mersing** : sumergir — **immersion** *n* : inmersión *f*
immigrate *vi* **-grated; -grating** : inmigrar — **immigrant** *n* : inmigrante *mf* — **immigration** *n* : inmigración *f*
imminent *adj* : inminente — **imminence** *n* : inminencia *f*
immobile *adj* : inmóvil — **immobilize** *vt* **-lized; -lizing** : inmovilizar
immoral *adj* : inmoral — **immorality** *n*, *pl* **-ties** : inmoralidad *f*
immortal *adj* : inmortal — ~ *n* : inmortal *mf* — **immortality** *n* : inmortalidad *f*
immune *adj* : inmune — **immunity** *n*, *pl* **-ties** : inmunidad *f* — **immunization** *n* : inmunización *f* — **immunize** *vt* **-nized; -nizing** : inmunizar
imp *n* RASCAL : diablillo *m*
impact *n* : impacto *m*
impair *vt* : dañar, perjudicar
impart *vt* : impartir (información), conferir (una calidad, etc.)
impartial *adj* : imparcial — **impartiality** *n*, *pl* **-ties** : imparcialidad *f*
impassable *adj* : intransitable
impasse *n* : impasse *m*
impassioned *adj* : apasionado
impassive *adj* : impasible
impatience *n* : impaciencia *f* — **impatient** *adj* : impaciente — **impatiently** *adv* : con impaciencia
impeccable *adj* : impecable
impede *vt* **-peded; -peding** : dificultar — **impediment** *n* : impedimento *m*, obstáculo *m*
impel *vt* **-pelled; -pelling** : impeler
impending *adj* : inminente
impenetrable *adj* : impenetrable
imperative *adj* **1** COMMANDING : imperativo **2** NECESSARY : imprescindible — ~ *n* : imperativo *m*
imperceptible *adj* : imperceptible
imperfection *n* : imperfección *f* — **imper-**

fect *adj* : imperfecto — ~ *n or* ~ **tense** : imperfecto *m*
imperial *adj* : imperial — **imperialism** *n* : imperialismo *m* — **imperious** *adj* : imperioso
impersonal *adj* : impersonal
impersonate *vt* **-ated; -ating** : hacerse pasar por, imitar — **impersonation** *n* : imitación *f* — **impersonator** *n* : imitador *m*, -dora *f*
impertinent *adj* : impertinente — **impertinence** *n* : impertinencia *f*
impervious *adj* ~ **to** : impermeable a
impetuous *adj* : impetuoso, impulsivo
impetus *n* : ímpetu *m*, impulso *m*
impinge *vi* **-pinged; -pinging** ~ **on** : afectara, incidir en
impish *adj* : pícaro, travieso
implant *vt* : implantar
implausible *adj* : inverosímil
implement *n* : instrumento *m*, implemento *m* *Lat* — ~ *vt* : poner en práctica
implicate *vt* **-cated; -cating** : implicar — **implication** *n* **1** INVOLVEMENT : implicación *f* **2** CONSEQUENCE : consecuencia *f* **3** by ~ : de forma indirecta
implicit *adj* **1** : implícito **2** UNQUESTIONING : absoluto, incondicional
implore *vt* **-plored; -ploring** : implorar, suplicar
imply *vt* **-plied; -plying** **1** HINT : insinuar **2** ENTAIL : implicar
impolite *adj* : descortés, maleducado
import *vt* : importar (mercancías) — **important** *adj* : importante — **importance** *n* : importancia *f* — **importation** *n* : importación *f* — **importer** *n* : importador *m*, -dora *f*
impose *v* **-posed; -posing** *vt* : imponer — *vi* ~ **on** : importunar, molestar — **imposing** *adj* : imponente — **imposition** *n* **1** ENFORCEMENT : imposición *f* **2** be an ~ on : molestar
impossible *adj* : imposible — **impossibility** *n*, *pl* **-ties** : imposibilidad *f*
impostor *or* imposter *n* : impostor *m*, -tora *f*
impotent *adj* : impotente — **impotence** *n* : impotencia *f*
impound *vt* : incautar, embargar
impoverished *adj* : empobrecido
impracticable *adj* : impracticable
impractical *adj* : poco práctico
imprecise *adj* : impreciso — **imprecision** *n* : imprecisión *f*
impregnable *adj* : impenetrable
impregnate *vt* **-nated; -nating** **1** : impregnar **2** FERTILIZE : fecundar
impress *vt* **1** : causar una buena impresión a **2** AFFECT : impresionar **3** ~ sth on s.o. : recalcar algo a algn — *vi* : impresionar — **impression** *n* : impresión *f* — **impression-**

able *adj* : impresionable — **impressive** *adj* : impresionante

imprint *vt* : imprimir — ~ *n* MARK : impresión *f*, huella *f*

imprison *vt* : encarcelar — **imprisonment** *n* : encarcelamiento *m*

improbable *adj* : improbable — **improbability** *n*, *pl* **-ties** : improbabilidad *f*

impromptu *adj* : improvisado

improper *adj* **1** UNSEEMLY : indecoroso **2** INCORRECT : impropio — **impropriety** *n*, *pl* **-eties** : inconveniencia *f*

improve *v* **-proved; -proving** : mejorar — **improvement** *n* : mejora *f*

improvise *v* **-vised; -vising** : improvisar — **improvisation** *n* : improvisación *f*

impudent *adj* : insolente — **impudence** *n* : insolencia *f*

impulse *n* **1** : impulso *m* **2** on ~ : sin reflexionar — **impulsive** *adj* : impulsivo — **impulsiveness** *n* : impulsividad *f*

impunity *n* **1** : impunidad *f* **2** with ~ : impunemente

impure *adj* : impuro — **impurity** *n*, *pl* **-ties** : impureza *f*

in *prep* **1** : en **2** DURING : por, en *Lat* **3** WITHIN : dentro de **4** dressed ~ red : vestido de rojo **5** ~ the rain : bajo la lluvia **6** ~ the sun : al sol **7** ~ this way : de esta manera **8** the best ~ the world : el mejor del mundo **9** written ~ ink/ French : escrito con tinta/en francés — *adv* **1** INSIDE : dentro, adentro **2** be ~ : estar (en casa) **3** be ~ on : participar en **4** come in! : ¡entre!, ¡pase! **5** he's ~ for a shock : se va a llevar un shock — ~ *adj* : de moda

inability *n*, *pl* **-ties** : incapacidad *f*

inaccessible *adj* : inaccesible

inaccurate *n* : inexacto

inactive *n* : inactivo — **inactivity** *n*, *pl* **-ties** : inactividad *f*

inadequate *adj* : insuficiente

inadvertently *adv* : sin querer

inadvisable *adj* : desaconsejable

inane *adj* **inaner; -est** : estúpido, tonto

inanimate *adj* : inanimado

inapplicable *adj* : inaplicable

inappropriate *adj* : impropio, inoportuno

inarticulate *adj* : incapaz de expresarse

inasmuch as *conj* : ya que, puesto que

inattentive *adj* : poco atento

inaudible *adj* : inaudible

inaugural *adj* **1** : inaugural **2** ~ address : discurso *m* de investidura — **inaugurate** *vt* **-rated; -rating** **1** : investir (a un presidente, etc.) **2** BEGIN : inaugurar — **inauguration** *n* : investidura *f* (de una persona), inauguración *f* (de un edificio, etc.)

inborn *adj* : innato

inbred *adj* INNATE : innato

incalculable *adj* : incalculable

incapable *adj* : incapaz — **incapacitate** *vt* **-tated; -tating** : incapacitar — **incapacity** *n*, *pl* **-ties** : incapacidad *f*

incarcerate *vt* **-ated; -ating** : encarcelar

incarnate *adj* : encarnado — **incarnation** *n* : encarnación *f*

incendiary *adj* : incendiario

incense[1] *n* : incienso *m*

incense[2] *vt* **-censed; -censing** : indignar, enfurecer

incentive *n* : incentivo *m*

inception *n* : comienzo *m*, principio *m*

incessant *adj* : incesante

incest *n* : incesto *m* — **incestuous** *adj* : incestuoso

inch *n* : pulgada *f* — ~ *v* : avanzar poco a poco

incident *n* : incidente *m* — **incidence** *n* : índice *m* (de crímenes, etc.) — **incidental** *adj* **1** MINOR : incidental **2** CHANCE : casual — **incidentally** *adv* : a propósito

incinerate *vt* **-ated; -ating** : incinerar — **incinerator** *n* : incinerador *m*

incision *n* : incisión *f*

incite *vt* **-cited; -citing** : incitar, instigar

incline *v* **-clined; -clining** *vt* **1** BEND : inclinar **2** be ~ed to : inclinarse a, tender a — ~ *vi* : inclinarse — ~ *n* : pendiente *f* — **inclination** *n* **1** : inclinación *f* **2** DESIRE : deseo *m*, ganas *fpl*

include *vt* **-cluded; -cluding** : incluir — **inclusion** *n* : inclusión *f* — **inclusive** *adj* : inclusivo

incognito *adv* & *adj* : de incógnito

incoherent *adj* : incoherente — **incoherence** *n* : incoherencia *f*

income *n* : ingresos *mpl* — **income tax** *n* : impuesto *m* sobre la renta

incomparable *adj* : incomparable

incompatible *adj* : incompatible

incompetent *adj* : incompetente — **incompetence** *n* : incompetencia *f*

incomplete *adj* : incompleto

incomprehensible *adj* : incomprensible

inconceivable *adj* : inconcebible

inconclusive *adj* : no concluyente

incongruous *adj* : incongruente

inconsiderate *adj* : desconsiderado

inconsistent *adj* **1** : inconsecuente **2** be ~ with : no concordar con — **inconsistency** *n*, *pl* **-cies** : inconsecuencia *f*

inconspicuous *adj* : que no llama la atención

inconvenient *adj* : incómodo, inconveniente — **inconvenience** *n* **1** BOTHER : incomodidad *f*, molestia *f* **2** DRAWBACK : inconveniente *m* — ~ *vt* **-nienced; -niencing** *vt* : importunar, molestar

incorporate *vt* **-rated; -rating** : incorporar
incorrect *adj* : incorrecto
increase *n* : aumento *m* — ∿ *v* **-creased; -creasing** : aumentar — **increasingly** *adv* : cada vez más
incredible *adj* : increíble
incredulous *adj* : incrédulo
incriminate *vt* **-nated; -nating** : incriminar
incubator *n* : incubadora *f*
incumbent *n* : titular *mf*
incur *vt* **incurred; incurring** : provocar (al enojo, etc.), incurrir en (gastos)
incurable *adj* : incurable
indebted *adj* **1** : endeudado **2 be ∿ to s.o.** : estar en deuda con algn
indecent *adj* : indecente — **indecency** *n, pl* **-cies** : indecencia *f*
indecisive *adj* : indeciso
indeed *adv* **1** TRULY : verdaderamente, sin duda **2** IN FACT : en efecto **3 ∿?** : ¿de veras?
indefinite *adj* **1** : indefinido **2** VAGUE : impreciso — **indefinitely** *adv* : indefinidamente
indelible *adj* : indeleble
indent *vt* : sangrar (un párrafo) — **indentation** *n* DENT, NOTCH : mella *f*
independent *adj* : independiente — **independence** *n* : independencia *f*
indescribable *adj* : indescriptible
indestructible *adj* : indestructible
index *n, pl* **-dexes** *or* **-dices** : índice *m* — ∿ *vt* : incluir en un índice — **index finger** *n* : dedo *m* índice
Indian *adj* : indio *m*, **-dia** *f*
indication *n* : indicio *m*, señal *f* — **indicate** *vt* **-cated; -cating** : indicar — **indicative** *adj* : indicativo — **indicator** *n* : indicador *m*
indict *vt* : acusar (de un crimen) — **indictment** *n* : acusación *f*
indifferent *adj* **1** : indiferente **2** MEDIOCRE : mediocre — **indifference** *n* : indiferencia *f*
indigenous *adj* : indígena
indigestion *n* : indigestión *f* — **indigestible** *adj* : indigesto
indignation *n* : indignación *f* — **indignant** *adj* : indignado — **indignity** *n, pl* **-ties** : indignidad *f*
indigo *n, pl* **-gos** *or* **-goes** : añil *m*
indirect *adj* : indirecto
indiscreet *adj* : indiscreto — **indiscretion** *n* : indiscreción *f*
indiscriminate *adj* : indiscriminado
indispensable *adj* : indispensable, imprescindible
indisputable *adj* : indiscutible
indistinct *adj* : indistinto
individual *adj* **1** : individual **2** PARTICULAR : particular — ∿ *n* : individuo *m* —

individuality *n, pl* **-ties** : individualidad *f* — **individually** *adv* : individualmente
indoctrinate *vt* **-nated; -nating** : adoctrinar — **indoctrination** *n* : adoctrinamiento *m*
indoor *adj* **1** : (de) interior **2 ∿ plant** : planta *f* de interior **3 ∿ pool** : piscina *f* cubierta **4 ∿ sports** : deportes *mpl* bajo techo — **indoors** *adv* : adentro, dentro
induce *vt* **-duced; -ducing** **1** : inducir **2** CAUSE : provocar — **inducement** *n* : incentivo *m*
indulge *v* **-dulged; -dulging** *vt* **1** GRATIFY : satisfacer **2** PAMPER : consentir — *vi* **∿ in** : permitirse — **indulgence** *n* **1** : indulgencia *f* **2** SATISFYING : satisfacción *f* — **indulgent** *adj* : indulgente
industry *n, pl* **-tries** **1** : industria *f* **2** DILIGENCE : diligencia *f* — **industrial** *adj* : industrial — **industrialize** *vt* **-ized; -izing** : industrializar — **industrious** *adj* : diligente, trabajador
inebriated *adj* : ebrio, embriagado
inedible *adj* : no comestible
ineffective *adj* **1** : ineficaz **2** INCOMPETENT : incompetente — **ineffectual** *adj* : inútil, ineficaz
inefficient *adj* **1** : ineficiente **2** INCOMPETENT : incompetente — **inefficiency** *n, pl* **-cies** : ineficiencia *f*
ineligible *adj* : ineligible
inept *adj* **1** : inepto **2 ∿ at** : incapaz para
inequality *n, pl* **-ties** : desigualdad *f*
inert *adj* : inerte — **inertia** *n* : inercia *f*
inescapable *adj* : ineludible
inevitable *adj* : inevitable — **inevitably** *adv* : inevitablemente
inexcusable *adj* : inexcusable
inexpensive *adj* : barato, económico
inexperienced *adj* : inexperto
inexplicable *adj* : inexplicable
infallible *adj* : infalible
infamous *adj* : infame
infancy *n, pl* **-cies** : infancia *f* — **infant** *n* : bebé *m;* niño *m*, **-ña** *f* — **infantile** *adj* : infantil
infantry *n, pl* **-tries** : infantería *f*
infatuated *adj* **be ∿ with** : estar encaprichado con — **infatuation** *n* : encaprichamiento *m*
infect *vt* : infectar — **infection** *n* : infección *f* — **infectious** *adj* : contagioso
infer *vt* **inferred; inferring** : deducir, inferir — **inference** *n* : deducción *f*
inferior *adj* : inferior — ∿ *n* : inferior *mf* — **inferiority** *n, pl* **-ties** : inferioridad *f*
infernal *adj* : infernal — **inferno** *n, pl* **-nos** : infierno *m*
infertile *adj* : estéril — **infertility** *n* : esterilidad *f*
infest *vt* : infestar

infidelity *n*, *pl* **-ties** : infidelidad *f*
infiltrate *v* **-trated; -trating** *vt* : infiltrar — *vi* : infiltrarse
infinite *adj* : infinito
infinitive *n* : infinitivo *m*
infinity *n*, *pl* **-ties** **1** : infinito *m* **2 an** ～ **of** : una infinidad de
infirm *adj* : enfermizo, endeble — **infirmary** *n*, *pl* **-ries** : enfermería *f* — **infirmity** *n*, *pl* **-ties** **1** FRAILTY : endeblez *f* **2** AILMENT : enfermedad *f*
inflame *vt* **-flamed; -flaming** : inflamar — **inflammable** *adj* : inflamable — **inflammation** *n* : inflamación *f* — **inflammatory** *adj* : inflamatorio
inflate *vt* **-flated; -flating** : inflar — **inflation** *n* : inflación *f* — **inflationary** *adj* : inflacionario, inflacionista
inflexible *adj* : inflexible
inflict *vt* : infligir
influence *n* **1** : influencia *f* **2 under the** ～ : embriagado — ～ *vt* **-enced; -encing** : influir en, influenciar — **influential** *adj* : influyente
influenza *n* : gripe *f*, influenza *f*
influx *n* : afluencia *f*
inform *vt* **1** : informar **2 keep me** ～**ed** : manténme al corriente — *vi* ～ **on** : delatar, denunciar
informal *adj* **1** : informal **2** : familiar (dícese del lenguaje) — **informality** *n*, *pl* **-ties** : falta *f* de ceremonia — **informally** *adv* : de manera informal
information *n* : información *f* — **informative** *adj* : informativo — **informer** *n* : informante *mf*
information technology *n* : informática *f*
infrared *adj* : infrarrojo
infrastructure *n* : infraestructura *f*
infrequent *adj* : infrequente — **infrequently** *adv* : raramente
infringe *v* **-fringed; -fringing** *vt* : infringir — *vi* ～ **on** : violar — **infringement** *n* : violación *f*
infuriate *vt* **-ated; -ating** : enfurecer, poner furioso — **infuriating** *adj* : exasperante
infuse *vt* **-fused; -fusing** : infundir — **infusion** *n* : infusión *f*
ingenious *adj* : ingenioso — **ingenuity** *n*, *pl* **-ities** : ingenio
ingenuous *adj* : ingenuo
ingest *vt* : ingerir
ingot *n* : lingote *m*
ingrained *adj* : arraigado
ingratiate *vt* **-ated; -ating** ～ **oneself with** : congraciarse con
ingratitude *n* : ingratitud *f*
ingredient *n* : ingrediente *m*
ingrown *adj* ～ **nail** : uña *f* encarnada

inhabit *vt* : habitar — **inhabitant** *n* : habitante *mf*
inhale *v* **-haled; -haling** *vt* : inhalar, aspirar — *vi* : inspirar
inherent *adj* : inherente — **inherently** *adv* : intrínsecamente
inherit *vt* : heredar — **inheritance** *n* : herencia *f*
inhibit *vt* IMPEDE : inhibir — **inhibition** *n* : inhibición *f*
inhuman *adj* : inhumano — **inhumane** *adj* : inhumano — **inhumanity** *n*, *pl* **-ties** : inhumanidad *f*
initial *adj* : inicial — *n* : inicial *f* — *vt* **-tialed** *or* **-tialled; -tialing** *or* **-tialling** : poner las iniciales a
initiate *vt* **-ated; -ating** **1** BEGIN : iniciar **2** ～ **s.o. into sth** : iniciar a algn en algo — **initiation** *n* : iniciación *f* — **initiative** *n* : iniciativa *f*
inject *vt* : inyectar — **injection** *n* : inyección *f*
injure *vt* **-jured; -juring** **1** : herir **2** ～ **oneself** : hacerse daño — **injurious** *adj* : perjudicial — **injury** *n*, *pl* **-ries** **1** : herida *f* **2** HARM : perjuicio *m*
injustice *n* : injusticia *f*
ink *n* : tinta *f* — **inkwell** *n* : tintero *m*
inland *adj* : interior — ～ *adv* : hacia el interior, tierra adentro
in–laws *npl* : suegros *mpl*
inlet *n* : ensenada *f*, cala *f*
inmate *n* **1** PATIENT : paciente *mf* **2** PRISONER : preso *m*, **-sa** *f*
inn *n* : posada *f*, hostería *f*
innards *npl* : entrañas *fpl*, tripas *fpl fam*
innate *adj* : innato
inner *adj* : interior, interno — **innermost** *adj* : más íntimo, más profundo
inning *n* : entrada *f*
innocent *adj* : inocente — ～ *n* : inocente *mf* — **innocence** *n* : inocencia *f*
innocuous *adj* : inocuo
innovate *vi* **-vated; -vating** : innovar — **innovation** *n* : innovación *f* — **innovative** *adj* : innovador — **innovator** *n* : innovador *m*, **-dora** *f*
innuendo *n*, *pl* **-dos** *or* **-does** : insinuación *f*, indirecta *f*
innumerable *adj* : innumerable
inoculate *vt* **-lated; -lating** : inocular — **inoculation** *n* : inoculación *f*
inoffensive *adj* : inofensivo
inpatient *n* : paciente *mf* hospitalizado
input *n* **1** : contribución *f* **2** : entrada *f* (de datos) — ～ *vt* **-putted** *or* **-put; -putting** : entrar (datos, etc.)
inquire *v* **-quired; -quiring** *vt* : preguntar — *vi* **1** ～ **about** : informarse sobre **2** ～ **into** : investigar — **inquiry** *n*, *pl* **-ries** **1**

QUESTION : pregunta *f* **2** INVESTIGATION : investigación *f* — **inquisition** *n* : inquisición *f* — **inquisitive** *adj* : curioso

insane *adj* : loco — **insanity** *n, pl* **-ties** : locura *f*

insatiable *adj* : insaciable

inscribe *vt* **-scribed; -scribing** : inscribir — **inscription** *n* : inscripción *f*

inscrutable *adj* : inescrutable

insect *n* : insecto *m* — **insecticide** *n* : insecticida *m*

insecure *adj* : inseguro, poco seguro — **insecurity** *n, pl* **-ties** : inseguridad *f*

insensitive *adj* : insensible — **insensitivity** *n, pl* **-ties** : insensibilidad *f*

inseparable *adj* : inseparable

insert *vt* : insertar (texto), introducir (una moneda, etc.)

inside *n* **1** : interior *m* **2** ~ **out** : al revés — *adv* : dentro, adentro — ~ *adj* : interior — ~ *prep* **1** *or* ~ **of** : dentro de **2** ~ **an hour** : en menos de una hora

insidious *adj* : insidioso

insight *n* : perspicacia *f*

insignia *or* **insigne** *n, pl* **-nia** *or* **-nias** : insignia *f*, enseña *f*

insignificant *adj* : insignificante

insincere *adj* : insincero

insinuate *vt* **-ated; -ating** : insinuar — **insinuation** *n* : insinuación *f*

insipid *adj* : insípido

insist *v* : insistir — **insistent** *adj* : insistente

insofar as *conj* : en la medida en que

insole *n* : plantilla *f*

insolent *adj* : insolente — **insolence** *n* : insolencia *f*

insolvent *adj* : insolvente

insomnia *n* : insomnio *m*

inspect *vt* : inspeccionar, revisar — **inspection** *n* : inspección *f* — **inspector** *n* : inspector *m*, -tora *f*

inspire *vt* **-spired; -spiring** : inspirar — **inspiration** *n* : inspiración *f* — **inspirational** *adj* : inspirador

instability *n, pl* **-ties** : inestabilidad *f*

install *vt* **-stalled; -stalling** : instalar — **installation** *n* : instalación *f* — **installment** *n* **1** PAYMENT : plazo *m*, cuota *f* **2** : entrega *f* (de una publicación o telenovela)

instance *n* **1** : ejemplo *m* **2 for** ~ : por ejemplo **3 in this** ~ : en este caso

instant *n* : instante *m* — ~ *adj* **1** IMMEDIATE : inmediato **2** ~ **coffee** : café *m* instantáneo — **instantaneous** *adj* : instantáneo — **instantly** *adv* : al instante, instantáneamente

instead *adv* **1** : en cambio **2 I went** ~ : fui en su lugar — **instead of** *prep* : en vez de, en lugar de

instep *n* : empeine *m*

instigate *vt* **-gated; -gating** : instigar a — **instigation** *n* : instigación *f* — **instigator** *n* : instigador *m*, -dora *f*

instill *or Brit* **instil** *vt* **-stilled; -stilling** : inculcar, infundir

instinct *n* : instinto *m* — **instinctive** *or* **instinctual** *adj* : instintivo

institute *vt* **-tuted; -tuting** **1** : instituir **2** INITIATE : iniciar — ~ *n* : instituto *m* — **institution** *n* : institución *f*

instruct *vt* **1** : instruir **2** COMMAND : mandar — **instruction** *n* : instrucción *f* — **instructor** *n* : instructor *m*, -tora *f*

instrument *n* : instrumento *m* — **instrumental** *adj* **1** : instrumental **2 be** ~ **in** : jugar un papel fundamental en

insubordinate *adj* : insubordinado — **insubordination** *n* : insubordinación *f*

insufferable *adj* : insoportable

insufficient *adj* : insuficiente

insular *adj* **1** : insular **2** NARROW-MINDED : estrecho de miras

insulate *vt* **-lated; -lating** : aislar — **insulation** *n* : aislamiento *m*

insulin *n* : insulina *f*

insult *vt* : insultar — ~ *n* : insulto *m* — **insulting** *adj* : insultante, ofensivo

insure *vt* **-sured; -suring** : asegurar — **insurance** *n* : seguro *m*

insurmountable *adj* : insuperable

intact *adj* : intacto

intake *n* : consumo *m* (de alimentos), entrada *f* (de aire, etc.)

intangible *adj* : intangible

integral *adj* : integral

integrate *v* **-grated; -grating** *vt* : integrar — *vi* : integrarse

integrity *n* : integridad *f*

intellect *n* : intelecto *m* — **intellectual** *adj* : intelectual — ~ *n* : intelectual *mf* — **intelligence** *n* : inteligencia *f* — **intelligent** *adj* : inteligente — **intelligible** *adj* : inteligible

intend *vt* **1 be** ~**ed for** : ser para **2** ~ **to do** : pensar hacer, tener la intención de hacer — **intended** *adj* : intencionado, deliberado

intense *adj* : intenso — **intensely** *adv* : sumamente, profundamente — **intensify** *v* **-fied; -fying** *vt* : intensificar — *vi* : intensificarse — **intensity** *n, pl* **-ties** : intensidad *f* — **intensive** *adj* : intensivo

intent *n* : intención *f* — ~ *adj* **1** : atento, concentrado **2** ~ **on doing** : resuelto a hacer — **intention** *n* : intención *f* — **intentional** *adj* : intencional, deliberado — **intently** *adv* : atentamente, fijamente

interact *vi* **1** : interactuar **2** ~ **with** : relacionarse con — **interaction** *n* : interacción *f* — **interactive** *adj* : interactivo

intercede *vi* **-ceded; -ceding** : interceder
intercept *vt* : interceptar
interchange *vt* **-changed; -changing** : intercambiar — ~ *n* **1** : intercambio *m* **2** JUNCTION : enlace *m* — **interchangeable** *adj* : intercambiable
intercom *n* : interfono *m*, interfón *m Mex*
intercourse *n* : relaciones *fpl* (sexuales)
interest *n* : interés *m* — ~ *vt* : interesar — **interested** *adj* : interesado — **interesting** *adj* : interesante
interface *n* : interfaz *mf* (de una computadora)
interfere *vi* **-fered; -fering** **1** ~ **in** : entrometerse en, interferir en **2** ~ **with** DISRUPT : afectar (una actividad, etc.) — **interference** *n* **1** : interferencia *f* **2** : intromisión *f* (en el radio, etc.)
interim *n* I : interín *m* **2 in the** ~ : mientras tanto — ~ *adj* : interino, provisional
interior *adj* : interior — ~ *n* : interior *m*
interjection *n* : interjección *f*
interlock *vt* : engranar
interloper *n* : intruso *m*, **-sa** *f*
interlude *n* **1** : intervalo *m* **2** : interludio *m* (en música, etc.)
intermediate *adj* : intermedio — **intermediary** *n*, *pl* **-aries** : intermediario *m*, **-ria** *f*
interminable *adj* : interminable
intermission *n* : intervalo *m*, intermedio *m*
intermittent *adj* : intermitente
intern[1] *vt* : confinar
intern[2] *vi* : hacer las prácticas — ~ *n* : interno *m*, **-na** *f*
internal *adj* : interno
international *adj* : internacional
interpret *vt* : interpretar — **interpretation** *n* : interpretación *f* — **interpreter** *n* : intérprete *mf*
interrogate *vt* **-gated; -gating** : interrogar — **interrogation** *n* QUESTIONING : interrogatorio *m* — **interrogative** *adj* : interrogativo
interrupt *v* : interrumpir — **interruption** *n* : interrupción *f*
intersect *vt* : cruzar (dícese de calles), cortar (dícese de líneas) — *vi* : cruzarse, cortarse — **intersection** *n* : cruce *m*, intersección *f*
intersperse *vt* **-spersed; -spersing** : intercalar
interstate *n or* ~ **highway** : carretera *f* interestatal
intertwine *vi* **-twined; -twining** : entrelazarse
interval *n* : intervalo *m*
intervene *vi* **-vened; -vening** **1** : intervenir **2** ELAPSE : transcurrir, pasar — **intervention** *n* : intervención *f*
interview *n* : entrevista *f* — ~ *vt* : entrevis-

tar — **interviewer** *n* : entrevistador *m*, -dora *f*
intestine *n* : intestino *m* — **intestinal** *adj* : intestinal
intimate[1] *vt* **-mated; -mating** : insinuar, dar a entender
intimate[2] *adj* : íntimo — **intimacy** *n*, *pl* **-cies** : intimidad *f*
intimidate *vt* **-dated; -dating** : intimidar — **intimidation** *n* : intimidación *f*
into *prep* **1** : en, a **2 bump** ~ : darse contra **3** (*used in mathematics*) **3** ~ **12** : 12 dividido por 3
intolerable *adj* : intolerable — **intolerance** *n* : intolerancia *f* — **intolerant** *adj* : intolerante
intoxicate *vt* **-cated; -cating** : embriagar — **intoxicated** *adj* **1** : embriagado **2** ~ **with** : ebrio de
intransitive *adj* : intransitivo
intravenous *adj* : intravenoso
intrepid *adj* : intrépido
intricate *adj* : complicado, intrincado — **intricacy** *n*, *pl* **-cies** : complejidad *f*
intrigue *n* : intriga *f* — ~ *v* **-trigued; -triguing** : intrigar — **intriguing** *adj* : intrigante
intrinsic *adj* : intrínseco
introduce *vt* **-duced; -ducing** **1** : introducir **2** : presentar (a una persona) — **introduction** *n* **1** : introducción *f* **2** : presentación *f* (de una persona) — **introductory** *adj* : introductorio
introvert *n* : introvertido *m*, -da *f* — **introverted** *adj* : introvertido
intrude *vi* **-truded; -truding** **1** : entrometerse **2** ~ **on s.o.** : molestar a algn — **intruder** *n* : intruso *m*, **-sa** *f* — **intrusion** *n* : intrusión *f* — **intrusive** *adj* : intruso
intuition *n* : intuición *f* — **intuitive** *adj* : intuitivo
inundate *vt* **-dated; -dating** : inundar
invade *vt* **-vaded; -vading** : invadir
invalid[1] *adj* : inválido
invalid[2] *n* : inválido *m*, -da *f*
invaluable *adj* : inestimable, invalorable *Lat*
invariable *adj* : invariable
invasion *n* : invasión *f*
invent *vt* : inventar — **invention** *n* : invención *f* — **inventive** *adj* : inventivo — **inventor** *n* : inventor *m*, -tora *f*
inventory *n*, *pl* **-ries** : inventario *m*
invert *vt* : invertir
invertebrate *adj* : invertebrado — ~ *n* : invertebrado *m*
invest *vt* : invertir
investigate *v* **-gated; -gating** : investigar — **investigation** *n* : investigación *f* — **investigator** *n* : investigador *m*, -dora *f*
investment *n* : inversión *f* — **investor** *n* : inversor *m*, -sora *f*

inveterate *adj* : inveterado
invigorating *adj* : vigorizante
invincible *adj* : invencible
invisible *adj* : invisible
invitation *n* : invitación *f* — **invite** *vt* **-vited;**
   -viting 1 : invitar **2** SEEK : buscar (problemas, etc.) — **inviting** *adj* : atrayente
invoice *n* : factura *f*
invoke *vt* **-voked; -voking** : invocar
involuntary *adj* : involuntario
involve *vt* **-volved; -volving 1** CONCERN
   : concernir, afectar **2** ENTAIL : suponer —
   involved *adj* **1** COMPLEX : complicado **2**
   CONCERNED : afectado — **involvement** *n*
   : participación *f*
invulnerable *adj* : invulnerable
inward *adj* INNER : interior, interno — **~** *or*
   inwards *adv* : hacia adentro, hacia el interior
iodine *n* : yodo *m*, tintura *f* de yodo
ion *n* : ion *m*
iota *n* : pizca *f*, ápice *m*
IOU *n* : pagaré *m*, vale *m*
Iranian *adj* : iraní
Iraqi *adj* : iraquí
ire *n* : ira *f* — **irate** *adj* : furioso
iris *n, pl* **irises** *or* **irides 1** : iris *m* (del ojo)
   2 : lirio *m* (planta)
Irish *adj* : irlandés
irksome *adj* : irritante, fastidioso
iron *n* **1** : hierro *m*, fierro *m Lat* (metal) **2**
   : plancha *f* (para la ropa) — **~** *v* : planchar
ironic *or* **ironical** *adj* : irónico
ironing board *n* : tabla *f* (de planchar)
irony *n, pl* **-nies** : ironía *f*
irrational *adj* : irracional
irreconcilable *adj* : irreconciliable
irrefutable *adj* : irrefutable
irregular *adj* : irregular — **irregularity** *n, pl*
   -ties : irregularidad *f*
irrelevant *adj* : irrelevante
irreparable *adj* : irreparable
irreplaceable *adj* : irreemplazable
irresistible *adj* : irresistible
irresolute *adj* : irresoluto
irrespective of *prep* : sin tener en cuenta
irresponsible *adj* : irresponsable — **irresponsibility** *n, pl* **-ties** : irresponsabilidad *f*
irreverent *adj* : irreverente
irreversible *adj* : irreversible, irrevocable

irrigate *vt* **-gated; -gating** : irrigar, regar —
   irrigation *n* : irrigación *f*, riego *m*
irritate *vt* **-tated; -tating** : irritar — **irritable**
   adj : irritable — **irritably** *adv* : con irritación — **irritating** *adj* : irritante — **irritation** *n* : irritación *f*
is → **be**
Islam *n* : el Islam — **Islamic** *adj* : islámico
island *n* : isla *f* — **isle** *n* : isla *f*
isolate *vt* **-lated; -lating** : aislar — **isolation**
   n : aislamiento *m*
Israeli *adj* : israelí
issue *n* **1** MATTER : asunto *m*, cuestión *f* **2**
   : número *m* (de una revista, etc.) **3 make**
   an ~ of : insistir demasiado sobre **4 take**
   ~ with : disentir de — **~** *v* **-sued; -suing**
   vi **~ from** : surgir de — *vt* **1** : emitir
   (sellos, etc.), distribuir (provisiones, etc.)
   2 PUBLISH : publicar
isthmus *n* : istmo *m*
it'd (*contraction of* **it had** *or* **it would**) →
   have, would
it'll (*contraction of* **it shall** *or* **it will**) → **shall,**
   will
it's (*contraction of* **it is** *or* **it has**) → **be,**
   have
it *pron* **1** (*as subject*) : él, ella **2** (*as indirect
   object*) : le, se **3** (*as direct object*) : lo, la
   4 (*as object of a preposition*) : él, ella **5 it's**
   raining : está lloviendo **6 it's 8 o'clock**
   : son las ocho **7 it's hot out** : hace calor **8**
   ~ is necessary : es necesario **9 who is**
   ~? : ¿quién es? **10 it's me** : soy yo
Italian *adj* : italiano — **~** *n* : italiano *m*
   (idioma)
italics *n* : cursiva *f*
itch *vi* **1** : picar **2 be ~ing to** : morirse
   por — **~** *n* : picazón *f* — **itchy** *adj* **itchier;**
   -est : que pica
item *n* **1** : artículo *m* **2** : punto *m* (en una
   agenda) **3 ~ of clothing** : prenda *f* de
   vestir **4 news ~** : noticia *f* — **itemize** *vt*
   -ized; -izing : detallar, enumerar
itinerant *adj* : ambulante
itinerary *n, pl* **-aries** : itinerario *m*
its *adj* : su, sus
itself *pron* **1** (*used reflexively*) : se **2** (*used
   for emphasis*) : (él) mismo, (ella) misma, sí
   (mismo) **3 by ~** : solo
I've (*contraction of* **I have**) → **have**
ivory *n, pl* **-ries** : marfil *m*
ivy *n, pl* **ivies** : hiedra *f*

J

j *n*, *pl* **j's** *or* **js** : j *f*, décima letra del alfabeto inglés

jab *vt* **jabbed; jabbing** **1** PIERCE : pinchar **2** POKE : golpear (con la punta de algo) — ~ *n* **1** PRICK : pinchazo *m* **2** POKE : golpe *m* abrupto

jabber *vi* : farfullar

jack–o'–lantern *n* : linterna *f* hecha de una calabaza

jack *n* **1** : gato *m* (mecanismo) **2** : sota *f* (de naipes) — ~ *vt or* ~ **up** **1** : levantar (con un gato) **2** INCREASE : subir

jackal *n* : chacal *m*

jackass *n* : asno *m*, burro *m*

jacket *n* **1** : chaqueta *f* **2** : sobrecubierta *f* (de un libro), carátula *f* (de un disco)

jackhammer *n* : martillo *m* neumático

jackknife *n* : navaja *f* — ~ *vi* **-knifed; -knifing** : plegarse (dícese de un camión)

jackpot *n* : premio *m* gordo

jaded *adj* **1** TIRED : agotado **2** BORED : hastiado

jagged *adj* : dentado

jail *n* : cárcel *f* — ~ *vt* : encarcelar — **jailer** *or* **jailor** *n* : carcelero *m*, -ra *f*

jalapeño *n* : jalapeño *m Lat*

jam¹ *v* **jammed; jamming** *vt* **1** CRAM : apiñar, embutir **2** BLOCK : atascar, atorar — *vi* : atascarse, atrancarse — ~ *n* **1** *or* **traffic** ~ : embotellamiento *m* (de tráfico) **2** FIX : lío *m*, aprieto *m*

jam² *n* PRESERVES : mermelada *f*

jangle *v* **-gled; -gling** *vi* : hacer un ruido metálico — *vt* : hacer sonar — ~ *n* : ruido *m* metálico

janitor *n* : portero *m*, -ra *f*; conserje *mf*

January *n* : enero *m*

Japanese *adj* : japonés — ~ *n* : japonés *m* (idioma)

jar¹ *v* **jarred; jarring** *vi* **1** GRATE : chirriar **2** CLASH : desentonar **3** ~ **on** IRRITATE : crispar, enervar (a algn) — *vt* JOLT : sacudir — ~ *n* : sacudida *f*

jar² *n* : tarro *m*

jargon *n* : jerga *f*

jaundice *n* : ictericia *f*

jaunt *n* : excursión *f*

jaunty *adj* **-tier; -est** : garboso, desenvuelto

jaw *n* : mandíbula *f* (de una persona), quijada *f* (de un animal) — **jawbone** *n* : mandíbula *f*, quijada *f*

jay *n* : arrendajo *m*

jazz *n* : jazz *m* — ~ *vt or* ~ **up** : animar, alegrar — **jazzy** *adj* **jazzier; -est** FLASHY : llamativo

jealous *adj* : celoso — **jealousy** *n* : celos *mpl*, envidia *f*

jeans *npl* : jeans *mpl*, vaqueros *mpl*

jeer *vt* **1** BOO : abuchear **2** MOCK : mofarse de — *vi* ~ **at** : mofarse de — ~ *n* : mofa *f*

jell *vi* : cuajar

jelly *n*, *pl* **-lies** : jalea *f* — **jellyfish** *n* : medusa *f*

jeopardy *n* : peligro *m*, riesgo *m* — **jeopardize** *vt* **-dized; -dizing** : arriesgar, poner en peligro

jerk *n* **1** JOLT : sacudida *f* brusca **2** FOOL : idiota *mf* — ~ *vt* : sacudir — *vi* JOLT : dar sacudidas

jersey *n*, *pl* **-seys** : jersey *m*

jest *n* : broma *f* — ~ *vi* : bromear — **jester** *n* : bufón *m*

Jesus *n* : Jesús *m*

jet *n* **1** STREAM : chorro *m* **2** *or* ~ **airplane** : avión *m* a reacción, reactor *m* — **jet–propelled** *adj* : a reacción

jettison *vt* **1** : echar al mar **2** DISCARD : deshacerse de

jetty *n*, *pl* **-ties** : desembarcadero *m*, muelle *m*

jewel *n* **1** : joya *f* **2** GEM : piedra *f* preciosa — **jeweler** *or* **jeweller** *n* : joyero *m*, -ra *f* — **jewelry** *n* : joyas *fpl*, alhajas *fpl*

Jewish *adj* : judío

jibe *vi* **jibed; jibing** AGREE : concordar

jiffy *n*, *pl* **-fies** : santiamén *m*, segundo *m*

jig *n* : giga *f*

jiggle *vt* **-gled; -gling** : sacudir, zarandear — ~ *n* : sacudida *f*

jigsaw *n* **1** : sierra *f* de vaivén **2** *or* ~ **puzzle** : rompecabezas *m*

jilt *vt* : dejar plantado

jingle *v* **-gled; -gling** *vi* : tintinear — *vt* : hacer sonar — ~ *n* TINKLE : tintineo *m*

jinx *n* CURSE : maldición *f*

jitters *npl* **have the** ~ : estar nervioso — **jittery** *adj* : nervioso

job *n* **1** EMPLOYMENT : empleo *m*, trabajo *m* **2** TASK : trabajo *m*

jockey *n*, *pl* **-eys** : jockey *mf*

jog *v* **jogged; jogging** *vt* ~ **s.o.'s memory** : refrescar la memoria a algn — *vi* : hacer footing — **jogging** *n* : footing *m*

join *vt* **1** UNITE : unir, juntar **2** MEET : reunirse con **3** : hacerse socio de (una organización, etc.) — *vi* **1** *or* ~ **together** : unirse **2** : hacerse socio (de una organización, etc.)

joint n **1** : articulación f (en anatomía) **2** JUNCTURE : juntura f, unión f — ~ adj : conjunto — **jointly** adv : conjuntamente

joke n : chiste m, broma f — ~ vi **joked; joking** : bromear — **joker** n **1** : bromista mf **2** : comodín m (en los naipes)

jolly adj **-lier; -est** : alegre, jovial

jolt vt : sacudir — ~ n **1** : sacudida f brusca **2** SHOCK : golpe m (emocional)

jostle v **-tled; -tling** vt : empujar, dar empujones — vi : empujarse

jot vt **jotted; jotting** or ~ **down** : anotar, apuntar

journal n **1** DIARY : diario m **2** PERIODICAL : revista f — **journalism** n : periodismo m — **journalist** n : periodista mf

journey n, pl **-neys** : viaje m — ~ vi **-neyed; -neying** : viajar

jovial adj : jovial

joy n : alegría f — **joyful** adj : alegre, feliz — **joyous** adj : jubiloso, alegre

jubilant adj : jubiloso — **jubilee** n : aniversario m especial

Judaism n : judaísmo m

judge vt **judged; judging** : juzgar — ~ n : juez mf — **judgment** or **judgement** n **1** RULING : fallo m, sentencia f **2** VIEW : juicio m

judicial adj : judicial — **judicious** adj : juicioso

jug n : jarra f

juggle vi **-gled; -gling** : hacer juegos malabares — **juggler** n : malabarista mf

jugular vein n : vena f yugular

juice n : jugo m — **juicy** adj **juicier; -est** : jugoso

jukebox n : máquina f de discos

July n : julio m

jumble vt **-bled; -bling** : mezclar — ~ n : revoltijo m

jumbo adj : gigante

jump vi **1** LEAP : saltar **2** START : sobresaltarse **3** RISE : subir de un golpe **4** ~ **at** : no dejar escapar (una oportunidad, etc.) — vt : saltar — ~ n **1** LEAP : salto m **2** INCREASE : aumento m — **jumper** n **1** : saltador m, -dora f (en deportes) **2** : jumper m (vestido) — **jumpy** adj **jumpier; -est** : nervioso

junction n **1** JOINING : unión f **2** : cruce m (de calles), empalme m (de un ferrocarril) — **juncture** n : coyuntura f

June n : junio m

jungle n : selva f

junior adj **1** YOUNGER : más joven **2** SUBORDINATE : subalterno — ~ n **1** : persona f de menor edad **2** SUBORDINATE : subalterno m, -na f **3** : estudiante mf de penúltimo año

junk n : trastos mpl (viejos) — ~ vt : echar a la basura

junta n : junta f (militar)

jurisdiction n : jurisdicción f

jury n, pl **-ries** : jurado m — **juror** n : jurado mf

just adj : justo — ~ adv **1** BARELY : apenas **2** EXACTLY : exactamente **3** ONLY : sólo, solamente **4** ~ **now** : ahora mismo **5 she has** ~ **left** : acaba de salir **6 we were** ~ **leaving** : justo íbamos a salir

justice n **1** : justicia f **2** JUDGE : juez mf

justify vt **-fied; -fying** : justificar — **justification** n : justificación f

jut vi **jutted; jutting** or ~ **out** : sobresalir

juvenile adj **1** YOUNG : juvenil **2** CHILDISH : infantil — ~ n : menor mf

juxtapose vt **-posed; -posing** : yuxtaponer

K

k n, pl **k's** or **ks** : k f, undécima letra del alfabeto inglés

kaleidoscope n : calidoscopio m

kangaroo n, pl **-roos** : canguro m

karat n : quilate m

karate n : karate m

keel n : quilla f — ~ vi or ~ **over** : volcarse (dícese de un barco), desplomarse (dícese de una persona)

keen adj **1** SHARP : afilado **2** PENETRAT- ING : cortante, penetrante **3** ENTHUSIASTIC : entusiasta **4** ~ **eyesight** : visión f aguda

keep v **kept; keeping** vt **1** : guardar **2** : cumplir (una promesa), acudir a (una cita) **3** DETAIN : hacer quedar, detener **4** PREVENT : impedir **5** ~ **up** : mantener — vi **1** REMAIN : mantenerse **2** LAST : conservarse **3** or ~ **on** CONTINUE : no dejar — ~ n **1 earn one's** ~ : ganarse el pan **2 for** ~**s** : para siempre — **keeper** n : guarda mf — **keeping** n **1** CARE : cuidado m **2 in**

~ **with** : de acuerdo con — **keepsake** *n* : recuerdo *m*

keg *n* : barril *m*

kennel *n* : caseta *f* para perros, perrera *f*

kept → **keep**

kerchief *n* : pañuelo *m*

kernel *n* **1** : almendra *f* **2** CORE : meollo *m*

kerosene *or* **kerosine** *n* : queroseno *m*

ketchup *n* : salsa *f* de tomate

kettle *n* : hervidor *m*, tetera *f* (para hervir)

key *n* **1** : llave *f* **2** : tecla *f* (de un piano o una máquina) — ~ *vt* **be keyed up** : estar nervioso — ~ *adj* : clave — **keyboard** *n* : teclado *m* — **keyhole** *n* : ojo *m* (de la cerradura) — **keynote** *n* : tónica *f* — **key ring** *n* : llavero *m*

keypad *n* : teclado *m* numérico

khaki *adj* : caqui

kick *vt* **1** : dar una patada a **2** ~ **out** : echar a patadas — *vi* **1** : dar patadas (dícese de una persona), cocear (dícese de un animal) **2** RECOIL : dar un culatazo — ~ *n* **1** : patada *f*, coz *f* (de un animal) **2** RECOIL : culatazo *m* **3** PLEASURE, THRILL : placer *m*

kid *n* **1** GOAT : chivo *m*, -va *f*; cabrito *m* **2** CHILD : niño *m*, -ña *f* — ~ *v* **kidded; kidding** *vi or* ~ **around** : bromear — *vt* TEASE : tomar el pelo a — **kidnap** *vt* **-napped** *or* **-naped; -napping** *or* **-naping** : secuestrar, raptar

kidney bean *n* : frijol *m*

kidney *n*, *pl* **-neys** : riñón *m*

kill *vt* **1** : matar **2** DESTROY : acabar con **3** ~ **time** : matar el tiempo — ~ *n* **1** KILLING : matanza *f* **2** PREY : presa *f* — **killer** *n* : asesino *m*, -na *f* — **killing** *n* **1** : matanza *f* **2** MURDER : asesinato *m*

kiln *n* : horno *m*

kilo *n*, *pl* **-los** : kilo *m* — **kilogram** *n* : kilogramo *m* — **kilometer** *n* : kilómetro *m* — **kilowatt** *n* : kilovatio *m*

kin *n* : parientes *mpl*

kind *n* : tipo *m*, clase *f* — ~ *adj* : amable

kindergarten *n* : jardín *m* infantil, jardín *m* de niños *Lat*

kindhearted *adj* : de buen corazón

kindle *vt* **-dled; -dling 1** : encender (un fuego) **2** AROUSE : despertar

kindly *adj* **-lier; -est** : bondadoso, amable — ~ *adv* **1** : amablemente **2 take** ~ **to** : aceptar de buena gana **3 we** ~ **ask you not smoke** : les rogamos que no fumen — **kindness** *n* : bondad *f* — **kind of** *adv* SOMEWHAT : un tanto, algo

kindred *adj* **1** : emparentado **2** ~ **spirit** : alma *f* gemela

king *n* : rey *m* — **kingdom** *n* : reino *m*

kink *n* **1** TWIST : vuelta *f*, curva *f* **2** FLAW : problema *m*

kinship *n* : parentesco *m*

kiss *vt* : besar — *vi* : besarse — ~ *n* : beso *m*

kit *n* **1** : juego *m*, kit *m* **2 first–aid** ~ : botiquín *m* **3 tool** ~ : caja *f* de herramientas

kitchen *n* : cocina *f*

kite *n* : cometa *f*, papalote *m* *Lat*

kitten *n* : gatito *m*, -ta *f* — **kitty** *n*, *pl* **-ties** FUND : fondo *m* común

knack *n* : maña *f*, facilidad *f*

knapsack *n* : mochila *f*

knead *vt* **1** : amasar, sobar **2** MASSAGE : masajear

knee *n* : rodilla *f* — **kneecap** *n* : rótula *f*

kneel *vi* **knelt** *or* **kneeled; kneeling** : arrodillarse

knew → **know**

knickknack *n* : chuchería *f*

knife *n*, *pl* **knives** : cuchillo *m* — ~ *vt* **knifed; knifing** : acuchillar

knight *n* **1** : caballero *m* **2** : caballo *m* (en ajedrez) — **knighthood** *n* : título *m* de Sir

knit *v* **knit** *or* **knitted; knitting** *v* : tejer — ~ *n* : prenda *f* tejida

knob *n* : tirador *m*, botón *m*, perilla *f* *Lat*

knock *vt* **1** : golpear **2** CRITICIZE : criticar **3** ~ **down** : derribar, echar al suelo — *vi* **1** : dar un golpe, llamar (a la puerta) **2** COLLIDE : darse, chocar — ~ *n* : golpe *m*, llamada *f* (a la puerta)

knot *n* : nudo *m* — ~ *vt* **knotted; knotting** : anudar — **knotty** *adj* **-tier; -est 1** : nudoso **2** : enredado (dícese de un problema)

know *v* **knew; known; knowing** *vt* **1** : saber **2** : conocer (a una persona, un lugar) **3** ~ **how to** : saber — *vi* : saber — **knowing** *adj* : cómplice — **knowingly** *adv* **1** : de manera cómplice **2** DELIBERATELY : a sabiendas — **know–it–all** *n* : sabelotodo *mf fam* — **knowledge** *n* **1** : conocimiento *m* **2** LEARNING : conocimientos *mpl*, saber *m* — **knowledgeable** *adj* : informado, entendido

knuckle *n* : nudillo *m*

Koran *n* **the Koran** : el Corán *m*

Korean *adj* : coreano *m*, -na *f* — ~ *n* : coreano *m* (idioma)

kosher *adj* : aprobado por la ley judía

L

l *n*, *pl* **l's** *or* **ls** : l *f*, duodécima letra del alfabeto inglés

lab → **laboratory**

label *n* **1** TAG : etiqueta *f* **2** BRAND : marca *f* — ~ *vt* **-beled** *or* **-belled; -beling** *or* **-belling** : etiquetar

labor *n* **1** : trabajo *m* **2** WORKERS : mano *f* de obra **3 in** ~ : de parto — ~ *vi* **1** : trabajar **2** STRUGGLE : avanzar penosamente — *vt* BELABOR : insistir en (un punto)

laboratory *n*, *pl* **-ries** : laboratorio *m*

laborer *n* : trabajador *m*, -dora *f*

laborious *adj* : laborioso

lace *n* **1** : encaje *m* **2** SHOELACE : cordón *m* (de zapatos), agujeta *f Lat* — ~ *vt* **laced; lacing 1** TIE : atar **2 be laced with** : echar licor a (una bebida, etc.)

lacerate *vt* **-ated; -ating** : lacerar

lack *vt* : carecer de, no tener — *vi* **be lacking** : faltar — ~ *n* : falta *f*, carencia *f*

lackadaisical *adj* : apático, indolente

lackluster *adj* : sin brillo, apagado

laconic *adj* : lacónico

lacquer *n* : laca *f*

lacrosse *n* : lacrosse *f*

lacy *adj* **lacier; -est** : como de encaje

lad *n* : muchacho *m*, niño *m*

ladder *n* : escalera *f*

laden *adj* : cargado

ladle *n* : cucharón *m* — ~ *vt* **-dled; -dling** : servir con cucharón

lady *n*, *pl* **-dies** : señora *f*, dama *f* — **ladybug** *n* : mariquita *f* — **ladylike** *adj* : elegante, como señora

lag *n* **1** DELAY : retraso *m* **2** INTERVAL : intervalo *m* — ~ *vi* **lagged; lagging** : quedarse atrás, rezagarse

lager *n* : cerveza *f* rubia

lagoon *n* : laguna *f*

laid *pp* → **lay¹**

lain *pp* → **lie¹**

lair *n* : guarida *f*

lake *n* : lago *m*

lamb *n* : cordero *m*

lame *adj* **lamer; lamest 1** : cojo, renco **2 a** ~ **excuse** : una excusa poco convincente

lament *vt* **1** MOURN : llorar **2** DEPLORE : lamentar — ~ *n* : lamento *m* — **lamentable** *adj* : lamentable

laminate *vt* **-nated; -nating** : laminar

lamp *n* : lámpara *f* — **lamppost** *n* : farol *m* — **lampshade** *n* : pantalla *f*

lance *n* : lanza *f* — ~ *vt* **lanced; lancing** : abrir con lanceta (en medecina)

land *n* **1** : tierra *f* **2** COUNTRY : país *m* **3** *or* **plot of** ~ : terreno *m* — ~ *vt* **1** : desembarcar (pasajeros de un barco), hacer aterrizar (un avión) **2** CATCH : sacar (un pez) del agua **3** SECURE : conseguir (empleo, etc.) — *vi* **1** : aterrizar (dícese de un avión) **2** FALL : caer — **landing** *n* **1** : aterrizaje *m* (de aviones) **2** : desembarco *m* (de barcos) **3** : descanso *m* (de una escalera) — **landlady** *n*, *pl* **-dies** : casera *f* — **landlord** *n* : casero *m* — **landmark** *n* **1** : punto *m* de referencia **2** MONUMENT : monumento *m* histórico — **landowner** *n* : hacendado *m*, -da *f*; terrateniente *mf* — **landscape** *n* : paisaje *m* — ~ *vt* **-scaped; -scaping** : ajardinar — **landslide** *n* **1** : desprendimiento *m* de tierras **2** *or* ~ **victory** : victoria *f* arrolladora

lane *n* **1** : carril *m* (de una carretera) **2** PATH, ROAD : camino *m*

language *n* **1** : idioma *m*, lengua *f* **2** SPEECH : lenguaje *m*

languid *adj* : lánguido — **languish** *vi* : languidecer

lanky *adj* **lankier; -est** : delgado, larguirucho *fam*

lantern *n* : linterna *f*

lap *n* **1** : regazo *m* (de una persona) **2** : vuelta *f* (en deportes) — ~ *v* **lapped; lapping** *vt or* ~ **up** : beber a lengüetadas — *vi* ~ **against** : lamer

lapel *n* : solapa *f*

lapse *n* **1** : lapsus *m*, falla *f* (de memoria, etc.) **2** INTERVAL : lapso *m*, intervalo *m* — ~ *vi* **lapsed; lapsing 1** EXPIRE : caducar **2** ELAPSE : transcurrir, pasar **3** ~ **into** : caer en

laptop *adj* : portátil

larceny *n*, *pl* **-nies** : robo *m*

lard *n* : manteca *f* de cerdo

large *adj* **larger; largest 1** : grande **2 at** ~ : en libertad **3 by and** ~ : por lo general — **largely** *adv* : en gran parte

lark *n* **1** : alondra *f* (pájaro) **2 for a** ~ : por divertirse

larva *n*, *pl* **-vae** : larva *f*

larynx *n*, *pl* **-rynges** *or* **-ynxes** : laringe *f* — **laryngitis** *n* : laringitis *f*

lasagna *n* : lasaña *f*

laser *n* : láser *m*

lash *vt* **1** WHIP : azotar **2** BIND : amarrar — *vi* ~ **out at** : arremeter contra — ~ *n* **1** BLOW : latigazo *m* (con un látigo) **2** EYELASH : pestaña *f*

lass *or* **lassie** *n* : muchacha *f*, chica *f*

lasso *n*, *pl* **-sos** *or* **-soes** : lazo *m*

last *vi* : durar — ~ *n* **1** : último *m*, -ma *f* **2**
at ~ : por fin, finalmente — ~ *adv* **1**
: por última vez, en último lugar **2 arrive**
~ : llegar el último — ~ *adj* **1** : último
2 ~ **year** : el año pasado — **lastly** *adv* : por
último, finalmente
latch *n* : picaporte *m*, pestillo *m*
late *adj* **later; latest 1** : tarde **2** : avanzado
(dícese de la hora) **3** DECEASED : difunto
4 RECENT : reciente — ~ *adv* **later; latest**
: tarde — **lately** *adv* : recientemente, últimamente — **lateness** *n* **1** : retraso *m* **2**
: lo avanzado (de la hora)
latent *adj* : latente
lateral *adj* : lateral
latest *n* **at the** ~ : a más tardar
lathe *n* : torno *m*
lather *n* : espuma *f* — ~ *vt* : enjabonar — *vi*
: hacer espuma
Latin–American *adj* : latinoamericano
latitude *n* : latitud *f*
latter *adj* **1** : último **2** SECOND : segundo
— ~ *pron* **the** ~ : éste, ésta, éstos *pl*, éstas
pl
lattice *n* : enrejado *m*
laugh *vi* : reír(se) — ~ *n* : risa *f* — **laughable** *adj* : risible, ridículo — **laughter** *n*
: risa *f*, risas *fpl*
launch *vt* : lanzar — ~ *n* : lanzamiento *m*
launder *vt* **1** : lavar y planchar (ropa) **2**
: blanquear, lavar (dinero) — **laundry** *n, pl*
-dries 1 : ropa *f* sucia **2** : lavandería *f*
(servicio) **3 do the** ~ : lavar la ropa
lava *n* : lava *f*
lavatory *n, pl* **-ries** BATHROOM : baño *m*, cuarto *m* de baño
lavender *n* : lavanda *f*
lavish *adj* **1** EXTRAVAGANT : pródigo **2**
ABUNDANT : abundante **3** LUXURIOUS : lujoso — ~ *vt* : prodigar
law *n* **1** : ley *f* **2** : derecho *m* (profesión,
etc.) **3 practice** ~ : ejercer la abogacía
— **lawful** *adj* : legal, legítimo
lawn *n* : césped *m* — **lawn mower** *n* : corta-
dora *f* de césped
lawsuit *n* : pleito *m*
lawyer *n* : abogado *m*, -da *f*
lax *adj* : poco estricto, relajado
laxative *n* : laxante *m*
lay[1] *vt* **laid; laying 1** PLACE, PUT : poner,
colocar **2** ~ **eggs** : poner huevos **3** ~
off : despedir (un empleado) **4** ~ **out**
PRESENT : presentar, exponer **5** ~ **out** DE-
SIGN : diseñar (el trazado de)
lay[2] *pp* → **lie**[1]
lay[3] *adj* **1** SECULAR : laico **2** NONPROFES-
SIONAL : lego, profano
layer *n* : capa *f*
layman *n, pl* **-men** : lego *m*, laico *m* (en religión)

layout *n* ARRANGEMENT : disposición *f*
lazy *adj* **-zier; -est** : perezoso — **laziness** *n*
: pereza *f*
lead[1] *vt* **led; leading 1** GUIDE : conducir **2**
DIRECT : dirigir **3** HEAD : encabezar, ir al
frente de — *vi* : llevar, conducir (a algo) —
~ *n* **1** : delantera *f* **2 follow s.o.'s** ~
: seguir el ejemplo de algn
lead[2] *n* **1** : plomo *m* (metal) **2** GRAPHITE
: mina *f* — **leaden** *adj* **1** : de plomo **2**
HEAVY : pesado
leader *n* : jefe *m*, -fa *f* — **leadership** *n*
: mando *m*, dirección *f*
leaf *n, pl* **leaves 1** : hoja *f* **2 turn over a
new** ~ : hacer borrón y cuenta nueva — ~
vi ~ **through** : hojear (un libro, etc.) —
leaflet *n* : folleto *m*
league *n* **1** : liga *f* **2 be in** ~ **with** : estar
confabulado con
leak *vt* **1** : dejar escapar (un líquido o un
gas) **2** : filtrar (información) — *vi* **1**
: gotear, escaparse (dícese de un líquido o
un gas) **2** : filtrarse (dícese de información)
— ~ *n* **1** : agujero *m* (de un cubo, etc.),
gotera *f* (de un techo) **2** : fuga *f*, escape *m*
(de un líquido o un gas) **3** : filtración *f* (de
información) — **leaky** *adj* **leakier; -est**
: que hace agua
lean[1] *v* **leaned** *or Brit* **leant; leaning** *vi* **1**
BEND : inclinarse **2** ~ **against** : apoyarse
contra — *vt* : apoyar
lean[2] *adj* **1** THIN : delgado **2** : sin grasa
(dícese de la carne)
leaning *n* : inclinación *f*
leanness *n* : delgadez *f* (de una persona), lo
magro (de la carne)
leap *vi* **leapt** *or* **leaped; leaping** : saltar,
brincar — ~ *n* : salto *m*, brinco *m* — **leap
year** *n* : año *m* bisiesto
learn *v* **learned; learning** : aprender —
learned *adj* : sabio, erudito — **learner** *n*
: principiante *mf*, estudiante *mf* — **learning**
n : erudición *f*, saber *m*
lease *n* : contrato *m* de arrendamiento — ~
vt **leased; leasing** : arrendar
leash *n* : correa *f*
least *adj* **1** : menor **2** SLIGHTEST : más
minimo — ~ *n* **1 at** ~ : por lo menos **2
the** ~ : lo menos **3 to say the** ~ : por no
decir más — ~ *adv* : menos
leather *n* : cuero *m*
leave *v* **left; leaving** *vt* **1** : dejar **2**
: salir(se) de (un lugar) **3** ~ **out** : omitir
— *vi* DEPART : irse — ~ *n* **1** *or* ~ **of absence** : permiso *m*, licencia *f* **2 take one's**
~ : despedirse
leaves → **leaf**
lecture *n* **1** TALK : conferencia *f* **2** REPRI-
MAND : sermón *m*, reprimenda *f* — ~ *v*

-tured; -turing *vt* : sermonear — *vi* : dar clase, dar una conferencia
led *pp* → **lead¹**
ledge *n* : antepecho *m* (de una ventana), saliente *m* (de una montaña)
leech *n* : sanguijuela *f*
leek *n* : puerro *m*
leer *vi* : lanzar una mirada lascivia — ~ *n* : mirada *f* lasciva
leery *adj* : receloso
leeway *n* : libertad *f* de acción, margen *m*
left¹ → **leave**
left² *adj* : izquierdo — ~ *adv* : a la izquierda — ~ *n* : izquierda *f* — **left–handed** *adj* : zurdo
leftovers *npl* : restos *mpl*, sobras *fpl*
leg *n* **1** : pierna *f* (de una persona, de ropa), pata *f* (de un animal, de muebles) **2** : etapa *f* (de un viaje)
legacy *n, pl* **-cies** : legado *m*
legal *adj* **1** LAWFUL : legítimo, legal **2** JUDICIAL : legal, jurídico — **legality** *n, pl* **-ties** : legalidad *f* — **legalize** *vt* **-ized; -izing** : legalizar
legend *n* : leyenda *f* — **legendary** *adj* : lengendario
legible *adj* : legible
legion *n* : legión *f*
legislate *vi* **-lated; -lating** : legislar — **legislation** *n* : legislación *f* — **legislative** *adj* : legislativo, legislador — **legislature** *n* : asamblea *f* legislativa
legitimate *adj* : legítimo — **legitimacy** *n* : legitimidad *f*
leisure *n* **1** : ocio *m*, tiempo *m* libre **2 at your** ~ : cuando te venga bien — **leisurely** *adj & adv* : lento, sin prisas
lemon *n* : limón *m* — **lemonade** *n* : limonada *f*
lend *vt* **lent; lending** : prestar
length *n* **1** : largo *m* **2** DURATION : duración *f* **3 at** ~ FINALLY : por fin **4 at** ~ : EXTENSIVELY : extensamente **5 go to any** ~**s** : hacer todo lo posible — **lengthen** *vt* **1** : alargar **2** PROLONG : prolongar — *vi* : alargarse — **lengthways** *or* **lengthwise** *adv* : a lo largo — **lengthy** *adj* **lengthier; -est** : largo
lenient *adj* : indulgente — **leniency** *n, pl* **-cies** : indulgencia *f*
lens *n* **1** : cristalino *m* (del ojo) **2** : lente *mf* (de un instrumento) **3** → **contact lens**
Lent *n* : Cuaresma *f*
lentil *n* : lenteja *f*
leopard *n* : leopardo *m*
leotard *n* : leotardo *m*, malla *f*
lesbian *n* : lesbiana *f*
less *adv* (*comparative of* **little**) : menos — ~ *adj* (*comparative of* **little**) : menos — ~

pron : menos — ~ *prep* MINUS : menos —
lessen *v* : disminuir — **lesser** *adj* : menor
lesson *n* **1** CLASS : clase *f*, curso *m* **2 learn one's** ~ : aprender la lección
lest *conj* ~ **we forget** : para que no olvidemos
let's (*contraction of* **let us**) → **let**
let *vt* **let; letting 1** ALLOW : dejar, permitir **2** RENT : alquilar **3** ~**'s go!** : ¡vamos!, ¡vámonos! **4** ~ **down** DISAPPOINT : fallar **5** ~ **in** : dejar entrar **6** ~ **off** FORGIVE : perdonar **7** ~ **up** ABATE : amainar, disminuir
letdown *n* : chasco *m*, decepción *f*
lethal *adj* : letal
lethargic *adj* : letárgico
letter *n* **1** : carta *f* **2** : letra *f* (del alfabeto)
lettuce *n* : lechuga *f*
letup *n* : pausa *f*, descanso *m*
leukemia *n* : leucemia *f*
level *n* **1** : nivel *m* **2 be on the** ~ : ser honrado — ~ *vt* **-eled** *or* **-elled; -eling** *or* **-elling 1** : nivelar **2** AIM : apuntar **3** RAZE : arrasar — ~ *adj* **1** FLAT : llano, plano **2** : nivel (de altura) — **levelheaded** *adj* : sensato, equilibrado
lever *n* : palanca *f* — **leverage** *n* **1** : apalancamiento *m* (en física) **2** INFLUENCE : influencia *f*
levity *n* : ligereza *f*
levy *n, pl* **levies** : impuesto *m* — ~ *vt* **levied; levying** : imponer, exigir (un impuesto)
lewd *adj* : lascivo
lexicon *n, pl* **-ica** *or* **-icons** : léxico *m*, lexicón *m*
liable *adj* **1** : responsable **2** LIKELY : probable **3** SUSCEPTIBLE : propenso — **liability** *n, pl* **-ties 1** RESPONSIBILITY : responsabilidad *f* **2** DRAWBACK : desventaja *f* **3 liabilities** *npl* DEBTS : deudas *fpl*, pasivo *m*
liaison *n* **1** : enlace *m* **2** AFFAIR : amorío *m*
liar *n* : mentiroso *m*, **-sa** *f*
libel *n* : libelo *m*, difamación *f* — ~ *vt* **-beled** *or* **-belled; -beling** *or* **-belling** : difamar
liberal *adj* : liberal — ~ *n* : liberal *mf*
liberate *vt* **-ated; -ating** : liberar — **liberation** *n* : liberación *f*
liberty *n, pl* **-ties** : libertad *f*
library *n, pl* **-braries** : biblioteca *f* — **librarian** *n* : bibliotecario *m*, **-ria** *f*
lice → **louse**
license *or* **licence** *n* **1** PERMIT : licencia *f* **2** FREEDOM : libertad *f* **3** AUTHORIZATION : permiso *m* — ~ *vt* **licensed; licensing** : autorizar
lick *vt* **1** : lamer **2** DEFEAT : dar una paliza a *fam* — ~ *n* : lamida *f*
licorice *n* : regaliz *m*
lid *n* **1** : tapa *f* **2** EYELID : párpado *m*

lie¹ *vi* **lay; lain; lying 1** *or* ~ **down** : acostarse, echarse **2** BE : estar, encontrarse

lie² *vi* lied; lying : mentir — ~ *n* : mentira *f*

lieutenant *n* : teniente *mf*

life *n, pl* **lives** : vida *f* — **lifeboat** *n* : bote *m* salvavidas — **lifeguard** *n* : socorrista *mf* — **lifeless** *adj* : sin vida — **lifelike** *adj* : natural, realista — **lifelong** *adj* : de toda la vida — **life preserver** *n* : salvavidas *m* — **lifestyle** *n* : estilo *m* de vida — **lifetime** *n* : vida *f*

lift *vt* **1** RAISE : levantar **2** STEAL : robar — *vi* **1** CLEAR UP : despejarse **2** *or* ~ **off** : despegar (dícese de un avión, etc.) — ~ *n* **1** LIFTING : levantamiento *m* **2 give s.o. a** ~ : llevar en coche a algn — **liftoff** *n* : despegue *m*

light¹ *n* **1** : luz *f* **2** LAMP : lámpara *f* **3** HEADLIGHT : faro *m* **4 do you have a** ~**?** : ¿tienes fuego? — ~ *adj* **1** BRIGHT : bien iluminado **2** : claro (dícese de los colores), rubio (dícese del pelo) — ~ *v* **lit** *or* **lighted; lighting** *vt* **1** : encender (un fuego) **2** ILLUMINATE : iluminar — *vi or* ~ **up** : iluminarse — **lightbulb** *n* : bombilla *f*, bombillo *m* *Lat* — **lighten** *vt* BRIGHTEN : iluminar — **lighter** *n* : encendedor *m* — **lighthouse** *n* : faro *m* — **lighting** *n* : alumbrado *m* — **lightning** *n* : relámpago *m*, rayo *m* — **lightyear** *n* : año *m* luz

light² *adj* : ligero — **lighten** *vt* : aligerar — **lightly** *adv* **1** : suavemente **2 let off** ~ : tratar con indulgencia — **lightness** *n* : ligereza *f* — **lightweight** *adj* : ligero

like¹ *v* **liked; liking** *vt* **1** : gustarle (a uno) **2** WANT : querer — *vi* **if you** ~ : si quieres — **likes** *npl* : preferencias *fpl*, gustos *mpl* — **likable** *or* **likeable** *adj* : simpático

like² *adj* SIMILAR : parecido — ~ *prep* : como — ~ *conj* **1** AS : como **2** AS IF : como si — **likelihood** *n* : probabilidad *f* — **likely** *adj* **-lier; -est** : probable — **liken** *vt* : comparar — **likeness** *n* : semejanza *f*, parecido *m* — **likewise** *adv* **1** : lo mismo **2** ALSO : también

liking *n* : afición *f* (por una cosa), simpatía *f* (por una persona)

lilac *n* : lila *f*

lily *n, pl* **lilies** : lirio *m*, azucena *f* — **lily of the valley** *n* : lirio *m* de los valles

lima bean *n* : frijol *m* de media luna

limb *n* **1** : miembro *m* (en anatomía) **2** : rama *f* (de un árbol)

limber *vi or* ~ **up** : calentarse, hacer ejercicios preliminares — ~ *adj* : ágil

limbo *n, pl* **-bos** : limbo *m*

lime *n* : lima *f*, limón *m* verde *Lat*

limelight *n* **be in the** ~ : estar en el candelero

limerick *n* : poema *m* jocoso de cinco versos

limestone *n* : (piedra *f*) caliza *f*

limit *n* : límite *m* — ~ *vt* : limitar, restringir — **limitation** *n* : limitación *f*, restricción *f* — **limited** *adj* : limitado

limousine *n* : limusina *f*

limp¹ *vi* : cojear — ~ *n* : cojera *f*

limp² *adj* : flojo, fláccido

line *n* **1** : línea *f* **2** ROPE : cuerda *f* **3** ROW : fila *f* **4** QUEUE : cola *f* **5** WRINKLE : arruga *f* **6 drop a** ~ : mándar unas líneas — ~ *v* **lined; lining** *vt* **1** : forrar (un vestido, etc.), cubrir (las paredes, etc.) **2** MARK : rayar, trazar líneas en **3** BORDER : bordear — *vi or* ~ **up** : ponerse in fila, hacer cola

lineage *n* : linaje *m*

linear *adj* : lineal

linen *n* : lino *m*

liner *n* **1** LINING : forro *m* **2** SHIP : buque *m*, transatlántico *m*

lineup *n* **1** *or* **police** ~ : fila *f* de sospechosos **2** : alineación *f* (en deportes)

linger *vi* **1** : quedarse, entretenerse **2** PERSIST : persistir

lingerie *n* : ropa *f* íntima femenina, lencería *f*

lingo *n, pl* **-goes** JARGON : jerga *f*

linguistics *n* : lingüística *f* — **linguist** *n* : lingüista *mf* — **linguistic** *adj* : lingüístico

lining *n* : forro *m*

link *n* **1** : eslabón *m* (de una cadena) **2** BOND : lazo *m* **3** CONNECTION : conexión *f* — ~ *vt* : enlazar, conectar — *vi* ~ **up** : unirse, conectar

linoleum *n* : linóleo *m*

lint *n* : pelusa *f*

lion *n* : león *m* — **lioness** *n* : leona *f*

lip *n* **1** : labio *m* **2** EDGE : borde *m* — **lipstick** *n* : lápiz *m* de labios

lip-read *vi* : leer los labios

liqueur *n* : licor *m*

liquid *adj* : líquido — ~ *n* : líquido *m* — **liquidate** *vt* **-dated; -dating** : liquidar — **liquidation** *n* : liquidación *f*

liquor *n* : bebidas *fpl* alcohólicas

lisp *vi* : cecear — ~ *n* : ceceo *m*

list¹ *n* : lista *f* — ~ *vt* **1** ENUMERATE : hacer una lista de, enumerar **2** INCLUDE : incluir (en una lista)

list² *vi* : escorar (dícese de un barco)

listen *vi* **1** : escuchar **2 ~ to** HEED : hacer caso de **3 ~ to reason** : atender a razones — **listener** *n* : oyente *mf*

listless *adj* : apático

lit *pp* → **light**

litany *n, pl* **-nies** : letanía *f*

liter *n* : litro *m*

literacy *n* : alfabetismo *m*

literal *adj* : literal — **literally** *adv* : literalmente, al pie de la letra

literate adj : alfabetizado
literature n : literatura f — **literary** adj : literario
lithe adj : ágil y grácil
litigation n : litigio m
litre → **liter**
litter n **1** RUBBISH : basura f **2** : camada f (de animales) **3** or **kitty ~** : arena f higiénica — **~** vt : tirar basura en, ensuciar — vi : tirar basura
little adj **littler** or **less** or **lesser**; **littlest** or **least 1** SMALL : pequeño **2 a ~** SOME : un poco de **3 he speaks ~ English** : habla poco inglés — **~** adv **less; least** : poco — **~** pron **1** : poco m, -ca f **2 ~ by ~** : poco a poco
liturgy n, pl **-gies** : liturgia f — **liturgical** adj : litúrgico
live vi **lived; living 1** : vivir **2** RESIDE : residir **3 ~ on** : vivir de — vt : vivir, llevar (una vida) — **~** adj **1** : vivo **2** : con corriente (dícese de cables eléctricos) **3** : en vivo, en directo (dícese de programas de televisión, etc.) — **livelihood** n : sustento m, medio m de vida — **lively** adj **-lier; -est** : animado, alegre — **liven** vt or **~ up** : animar — vi : animarse
liver n : hígado m
livestock n : ganado m
livid adj **1** : lívido **2** ENRAGED : furioso
living adj : vivo — **~** n **make a ~** : ganarse la vida — **living room** n : living m, sala f (de estar)
lizard n : lagarto m
llama n : llama f
load n **1** CARGO : carga f **2** BURDEN : carga f, peso m **3 ~s of** : un montón de — **~** vt : cargar
loaf¹ n, pl **loaves** : pan m, barra f (de pan)
loaf² vi : holgazanear — **loafer** n **1** : holgazán m, -zana f **2** : mocasín m (zapato)
loan n : préstamo m — **~** vt : prestar
loathe vt **loathed; loathing** : odiar — **loathsome** adj : odioso
lobby n, pl **-bies 1** : vestíbulo m **2** or **political ~** : grupo m de presión, lobby m — **~** v **-bied; -bying** vt : ejercer presión sobre
lobe n : lóbulo m
lobster n : langosta f
local adj : local — **~** n **the ~s** : los vecinos del lugar — **locale** n : escenario m — **locality** n, pl **-ties** : localidad f
locate vt **-cated; -cating 1** SITUATE : situar, ubicar **2** FIND : localizar — **location** n : situación f, lugar m
lock¹ n : mechón m (de pelo)

lock² n **1** : cerradura f (de una puerta, etc.) **2** : esclusa f (de un canal) — **~** vt **1** : cerrar (con llave) **2** or **~ up** CONFINE : encerrar — vi **1** : cerrarse con llave **2** : bloquearse (dícese de una rueda, etc.) —
locker n : armario m — **locket** n : medallón m — **locksmith** n : cerrajero m, -ra f
locomotive n : locomotora f
locust n : langosta f, chapulín m Lat
lodge v **lodged; lodging** vt **1** HOUSE : hospedar, alojar **2** FILE : presentar — vi **1** : hospedarse, alojarse — **~** n : pabellón m — **lodger** n : huésped m, -peda f — **lodging** n **1** : alojamiento m **2 ~s** npl : habitaciones fpl
loft n **1** : desván m (en una casa) **2** HAYLOFT : pajar m — **lofty** adj **loftier; -est 1** : noble, elevado **2** HAUGHTY : altanero
log n **1** : tronco m, leño m **2** RECORD : diario m — **~** vi **logged; logging 1** : talar (árboles) **2** RECORD : registrar, anotar **3 ~ on** : entrar (en el sistema) **4 ~ off** : salir (del sistema) — **logger** n : leñador m, -dora f
logic n : lógica f — **logical** adj : lógico —
logistics ns & pl : logística f
logo n, pl **logos** : logotipo m
loin n : lomo m
loiter vi : vagar, holgazanear
lollipop or **lollypop** n : pirulí m, chupete m Lat
lone adj : solitario — **loneliness** n : soledad f — **lonely** adj **-lier; -est** : solitario, solo — **loner** n : solitario m, -ria f — **lonesome** adj : solo, solitario
long¹ adj **longer; longest** : largo — **~** adv **1** : mucho tiempo **2 all day ~** : todo el día **3 as ~ as** : mientras **4 no ~er** : ya no **5 so ~!** : ¡hasta luego!, ¡adiós! — **~** n **1 before ~** : dentro de poco **2 the ~ and the short** : lo esencial
long² vi **~ for** : anhelar, desear
longevity n : longevidad f
longing n : ansia f, anhelo m
longitude n : longitud f
look vi **1** : mirar **2** SEEM : parecer **3 ~ after** : cuidar (de) **4 ~ for** EXPECT : esperar **5 ~ for** SEEK : buscar **6 ~ into** : investigar **7 ~ out** : tener cuidado **8 ~ over** EXAMINE : revisar **9 ~ up to** : respetar — vt : mirar — **~** n **1** : mirada f **2** APPEARANCE : aspecto m, aire m — **lookout** n **1** : puesto m de observación **2** WATCHMAN : vigía mf **3 be on the ~ for** : estar al acecho de
loom¹ n : telar m
loom² vi **1** APPEAR : aparecer, surgir **2** APPROACH : ser inminente
loop n : lazada f, lazo m — **~** vt : hacer

lazadas con — **loophole** n : escapatoria f

loose adj **looser; -est** **1** MOVABLE : flojo, suelto **2** SLACK : flojo **3** ROOMY : holgado **4** APPROXIMATE : libre, aproximado **5** FREE : suelto **6** IMMORAL : relajado — **loosely** adv **1** : sin apretar **2** ROUGHLY : aproximadamente — **loosen** vt : aflojar

loot n : botín m — ～ vt : saquear, robar — **looter** n : saqueador m, -dora f — **looting** n : saqueo m

lop vt **lopped; lopping** : cortar, podar

lopsided adj : torcido, chueco Lat

lord n **1** : señor m, noble m **2 the Lord** : el Señor

lore n : saber m popular, tradición f

lose v **lost; losing** vt **1** : perder **2** ～ **one's way** : perderse **3** ～ **time** : atrasarse (dícese de un reloj) — vi : perder — **loser** n : perdedor m, -dora f — **lost** adj **1** : perdido **2 get** ～ : perderse

loss n **1** : pérdida f **2** DEFEAT : derrota f **3 be at a** ～ **for words** : no encontrar palabras

lot n **1** FATE : suerte f **2** PLOT : solar m **3 a** ～ **of** or ～**s of** : mucho, un montón de

lotion n : loción f

lottery n, pl **-teries** : lotería f

loud adj **1** : alto, fuerte **2** NOISY : ruidoso **3** FLASHY : llamativo — ～ adv **1** : fuerte **2 out** ～ : en voz alta — **loudly** adv : en voz alta — **loudspeaker** n : altavoz m

lounge vi **lounged; lounging** **1** : repantigarse **2** or ～ **about** : holgazanear — ～ n : salón m

louse n, pl **lice** : piojo m — **lousy** adj **lousier; -est** **1** : piojoso **2** BAD : pésimo, muy malo

love n **1** : amor m **2 fall in** ～ : enamorarse — v **loved; loving** : querer, amar — **lovable** adj : adorable, amoroso Lat — **lovely** adj **-lier; -est** : lindo, precioso — **lover** n : amante mf — **loving** adj : cariñoso

low adj **lower; -est** **1** : bajo **2** SCARCE : escaso **3** DEPRESSED : deprimido — ～ adv **1** : bajo **2 turn the lights down** ～ : bajar las luces — ～ n **1** : punto m bajo **2** or ～ **gear** : primera velocidad f — **lower** adj : inferior, más bajo — ～ vt : bajar — **lowly** adj **-lier; -est** : humilde

loyal adj : leal, fiel — **loyalty** n, pl **-ties** : lealtad f

lozenge n : pastilla f

lubricate vt **-cated; -cating** : lubricar — **lubricant** n : lubricante m — **lubrication** n : lubricación f

lucid adj : lúcido — **lucidity** n : lucidez f

luck n **1** : suerte f **2 good** ～**!**: ¡buena suerte! — **luckily** adv : afortunadamente — **lucky** adj **luckier; -est** **1** : afortunado **2** ～ **charm** : amuleto m (de la suerte)

lucrative adj : lucrativo

ludicrous adj : ridículo, absurdo

lug vt **lugged; lugging** : arrastrar

luggage n : equipaje m

lukewarm adj : tibio

lull vt **1** CALM : calmar **2** ～ **to sleep** : adormecer — ～ n : período m de calma, pausa f

lullaby n, pl **-bies** : canción f de cuna, nana f

lumber n : madera f — **lumberjack** n : leñador m, -dora f

luminous adj : luminoso

lump n **1** CHUNK, PIECE : pedazo m, trozo m **2** SWELLING : bulto m **3** : grumo m (en un líquido) — ～ vt or ～ **together** : juntar, agrupar — **lumpy** adj **lumpier; -est** : grumoso (dícese de una salsa), lleno de bultos (dícese de un colchón)

lunacy n, pl **-cies** : locura f

lunar adj : lunar

lunatic n : loco m, -ca f

lunch n : almuerzo m, comida f — ～ vi : almorzar, comer — **luncheon** n : comida f, almuerzo m

lung n : pulmón m

lunge vi **lunged; lunging** **1** : lanzarse **2** ～ **at** : arremeter contre

lurch[1] vi **1** STAGGER : tambalearse **2** : dar bandazos (dícese de un vehículo)

lurch[2] n **leave in a** ～ : dejar en la estacada

lure n **1** BAIT : señuelo m **2** ATTRACTION : atractivo m — ～ vt **lured; luring** : atraer

lurid adj **1** GRUESOME : espeluznante **2** SENSATIONAL : sensacionalista **3** GAUDY : chillón

lurk vi : estar al acecho

luscious adj : delicioso, exquisito

lush adj : exuberante, suntuoso

lust n **1** : lujuria f **2** CRAVING : ansia f, anhelo m — ～ vi **after** : desear (a una persona), codiciar (riquezas, etc.)

luster or **lustre** n : lustre m

lusty adj **lustier; -est** : fuerte, vigoroso

luxurious adj : lujoso — **luxury** n, pl **-ries** : lujo m

lye n : lejía f

lying → **lie**

lynch vt : linchar

lynx n : lince m

lyric or **lyrical** adj : lírico — **lyrics** npl : letra f (de una canción)

M

m *n, pl* **m's** *or* **ms** : m *f,* decimotercera letra del alfabeto inglés

ma'am → **madam**

macabre *adj* : macabro

macaroni *n* : macarrones *mpl*

mace *n* **1** : maza *f* (arma o símbolo) **2** : macis *f* (especia)

machete *n* : machete *m*

machine *n* : máquina *f* — **machinery** *n, pl* **-eries 1** : maquinaria *f* **2** WORKS : mecanismo *m* — **machine gun** *n* : ametralladora *f*

mad *adj* **madder; maddest 1** INSANE : loco **2** FOOLISH : insensato **3** ANGRY : furioso

madam *n, pl* **mesdames** : señora *f*

madden *vt* : enfurecer

made → **make**

madly *adv* : como un loco, locamente — **madman** *n, pl* **-men** : loco *m* — **madness** *n* : locura *f*

Mafia *n* : Mafia *f*

magazine *n* **1** PERIODICAL : revista *f* **2** : recámara *f* (de un arma de fuego)

maggot *n* : gusano *m*

magic *n* : magia *f* — ~ *or* **magical** *adj* : mágico — **magician** *n* : mago *m,* -ga *f*

magistrate *n* : magistrado *m,* -da *f*

magnanimous *adj* : magnánimo

magnate *n* : magnate *mf*

magnet *n* : imán *m* — **magnetic** *adj* : magnético — **magnetism** *n* : magnetismo *m* — **magnetize** *vt* **-tized; -tizing** : magnetizar

magnificent *adj* : magnífico — **magnificence** *n* : magnificencia *f*

magnify *vt* **-fied; -fying 1** ENLARGE : ampliar **2** EXAGGERATE : exagerar — **magnifying glass** *n* : lupa *f*

magnitude *n* : magnitud *f*

magnolia *n* : magnolia *f*

mahogany *n, pl* **-nies** : caoba *f*

maid *n* : sirvienta *f,* criada *f,* muchacha *f* — **maiden** *adj* FIRST : inaugural — **maiden name** *n* : nombre *m* de soltera

mail *n* **1** : correo *m* **2** LETTERS : correspondencia *f* — ~ *vt* : enviar por correo — **mailbox** *n* : buzón *m* — **mailman** *n, pl* **-men** : cartero *m*

maim *vt* : mutilar

main *n* : tubería *f* principal (de agua o gas), cable *m* principal (de un circuito) — ~ *adj* : principal — **mainframe** *n* : computadora *f* central — **mainland** *n* : continente *m* — **mainly** *adv* : principalmente — **mainstay** *n* : sostén *m* (principal) — **mainstream** *n*

: corriente *f* principal — ~ *adj* : dominante, convencional

maintain *vt* : mantener — **maintenance** *n* : mantenimiento *m*

maize *n* : maíz *m*

majestic *adj* : majestuoso — **majesty** *n, pl* **-ties** : majestad *f*

major *adj* **1** : muy importante, principal **2** : mayor (en música) — ~ *n* **1** : mayor *mf,* comandante *mf* (en las fuerzas armadas) **2** : especialidad *f* (universitaria) — ~ *vi* **-jored; -joring** : especializarse — **majority** *n, pl* **-ties** : mayoría *f*

make *v* **made; making** *vt* **1** : hacer **2** MANUFACTURE : fabricar **3** CONSTITUTE : constituir **4** PREPARE : preparar **5** RENDER : poner **6** COMPEL : obligar **7** ~ **a decision** : tomar una decisión **8** ~ **a living** : ganar la vida — *vi* **1** ~ **do** : arreglárselas **2** ~ **for** : dirigirse a **3** ~ **good** SUCCEED : tener éxito — ~ *n* BRAND : marca *f* — **make–believe** *n* : fantasía *f* — ~ *adj* : imaginario — **make out** *vt* **1** : hacer (un cheque, etc.) **2** DISCERN : distinguir **3** UNDERSTAND : comprender — *vi* **how did you** ~? : ¿qué tal te fue? — **maker** *n* MANUFACTURER : fabricante *mf* — **makeshift** *adj* : improvisado — **makeup** *n* **1** COMPOSITION : composición *f* **2** COSMETICS : maquillaje *m* — **make up** *vt* **1** PREPARE : preparar **2** INVENT : inventar **3** CONSTITUTE : formar — *vi* RECONCILE : hacer las paces

maladjusted *adj* : inadaptado

malaria *n* : malaria *f,* paludismo *m*

male *n* : macho *m* (de animales o plantas), varón *m* (de personas) — ~ *adj* **1** : macho **2** MASCULINE : masculino

malevolent *adj* : malévolo

malfunction *vi* : funcionar mal — ~ *n* : mal funcionamiento *m*

malice *n* : mala intención *f,* rencor *m* — **malicious** *adj* : malicioso

malign *adj* : maligno — ~ *vt* : calumniar

malignant *adj* : maligno

mall *n or* **shopping** ~ : centro *m* comercial

malleable *adj* : maleable

mallet *n* : mazo *m*

malnutrition *n* : desnutrición *f*

malpractice *n* : mala práctica *f,* negligencia *f*

malt *n* : malta *f*

mama *or* **mamma** *n* : mamá *f*

mammal *n* : mamífero *m*

mammogram *n* : mamografía *f*

mammoth *adj* : gigantesco

man *n, pl* **men** : hombre *m* — ~ *vt* **manned;**
manning : tripular (un barco o avión), encargarse de (un servicio)
manage *v* **-aged; -aging** *vt* **1** HANDLE
: manejar **2** DIRECT : administrar, dirigir
— *vi* COPE : arreglárselas — **manageable**
adj : manejable — **management** *n* : dirección *f* — **manager** *n* : director *m*, -tora *f;*
gerente *mf* — **managerial** *adj* : directivo
mandarin *n or* ~ **orange** : mandarina *f*
mandate *n* : mandato *m* — **mandatory** *adj*
: obligatorio
mane *n* : crin *f* (de un caballo), melena *f* (de
un león)
maneuver *n* : maniobra *f* — ~ *v* **-vered;**
-vering : maniobrar
mangle *vt* **-gled; -gling** : destrozar
mango *n, pl* **-goes** : mango *m*
mangy *adj* **mangier; -est** : sarnoso
manhandle *vi* **-dled; -dling** : maltratar
manhole *n* : boca *f* de alcantarilla
manhood *n* **1** : madurez *f* (de un hombre)
2 VIRILITY : virilidad *f*
mania *n* : manía *f* — **maniac** *n* : maníaco *m,*
-ca *f*
manicure *n* : manicura *f* — ~ *vt* **-cured;**
-curing : hacer la manicura a
manifest *adj* : manifiesto, patente — ~ *vt*
: manifestar — **manifesto** *n, pl* **-tos** *or*
-toes : manifiesto *m*
manipulate *vt* **-lated; -lating** : manipular —
manipulation *n* : manipulación *f*
mankind *n* : género *m* humano, humanidad *f*
manly *adj* **-lier; -est** : viril — **manliness** *n*
: virilidad *f*
man–made *adj* : artificial
mannequin *n* : maniquí *m*
manner *n* **1** : manera *f* **2** KIND : clase *f* **3**
~**s** *npl* ETIQUETTE : modales *mpl*, edu-
cación *f* — **mannerism** *n* : peculiaridad *f*
(de una persona)
manoeuvre *Brit* → **maneuver**
manor *n* : casa *f* solariega
manpower *n* : mano *f* de obra
mansion *n* : mansión *f*
manslaughter *n* : homicidio *m* sin premeditación
mantel *or* **mantelpiece** *n* : repisa *f* de la
chimenea
manual *adj* : manual — ~ *n* : manual *m*
manufacture *n* : fabricación *f* — ~ *vt*
-tured; -turing : fabricar — **manufacturer**
n : fabricante *mf*
manure *n* : estiércol *m*
manuscript *n* : manuscrito *m*
many *adj* **more; most** **1** : muchos **2 as** ~
: tantos **3 how** ~ : cuántos **4 too** ~
: demasiados — ~ *pron* : muchos *pl,* **-chas**
pl
map *n* : mapa *m* — ~ *vt* **mapped; mapping**

1 : trazar el mapa de **2** *or* ~ **out** : planear,
proyectar
maple *n* : arce *m*
mar *vt* **marred; marring** : estropear
maraca *n* : maraca *f*
marathon *n* : maratón *m*
marble *n* **1** : mármol *m* **2** ~**s** *npl* : canicas *fpl* (para jugar)
march *n* : marcha *f* — ~ *vi* : marchar, desfilar
March *n* : marzo *m*
mare *n* : yegua *f*
margarine *n* : margarina *f*
margin *n* : margen *m* — **marginal** *adj* : marginal
marigold *n* : caléndula *f*
marijuana *n* : marihuana *f*
marinate *vt* **-nated; -nating** : marinar
marine *adj* : marino — ~ *n* : soldado *m* de
marina
marionette *n* : marioneta *f*
marital *adj* **1** : matrimonial **2** ~ **status**
: estado *m* civil
maritime *adj* : marítimo
mark *n* **1** : marca *f* **2** STAIN : mancha *f* **3**
IMPRINT : huella *f* **4** TARGET : blanco *m* **5**
GRADE : nota *f* — ~ *vt* **1** : marcar **2** STAIN
: manchar **3** POINT OUT : señalar **4** : calificar (un examen, etc.) **5** COMMEMORATE
: conmemorar **6** CARACTERIZE : caracterizar **7** ~ **off** : delimitar — **marked** *adj*
: marcado, notable — **markedly** *adv* : notablemente — **marker** *n* : marcador *m*
market *n* : mercado *m* — ~ *vt* : vender, comercializar — **marketable** *adj* : vendible
— **marketplace** *n* : mercado *m*
marksman *n, pl* **-men** : tirador *m* — **marks-**
manship *n* : puntería *f*
marmalade *n* : mermelada *f*
maroon[1] *vt* : abandonar, aislar
maroon[2] *n* : rojo *m* oscuro
marquee *n* CANOPY : marquesina *f*
marriage *n* **1** : matrimonio *m* **2** WEDDING
: casamiento *m*, boda *f* — **married** *adj* **1**
: casado **2 get** ~ : casarse
marrow *n* : médula *f*, tuétano *m*
marry *v* **-ried; -rying** *vt* **1** : casar **2** WED
: casarse con — *vi* : casarse
Mars *n* : Marte *m*
marsh *n* **1** : pantano *m* **2** *or* **salt** ~ : marisma *f*
marshal *n* : mariscal *m* (en el ejército); jefe
m, **-fa** *f* (de policía, de bomberos, etc.) — ~
vt **-shaled** *or* **-shalled; -shaling** *or* **-shal-**
ling : poner en orden (los pensamientos,
etc.), reunir (las tropas)
marshmallow *n* : malvavisco *m*
marshy *adj* **marshier; -est** : pantanoso
mart *n* : mercado *m*
martial *adj* : marcial

martyr *n* : mártir *mf* — ~ *vt* : martirizar
marvel *n* : maravilla *f* — ~ *vi* **-veled** *or* **-velled; -veling** *or* **-velling** : maravillarse — **marvelous** *or* **marvellous** *adj* : maravilloso
mascara *n* : rímel *m*
mascot *n* : mascota *f*
masculine *adj* : masculino — **masculinity** *n* : masculinidad *f*
mash *vt* **1** CRUSH : aplastar, majar **2** PUREE : hacer puré de — **mashed potatoes** *npl* : puré *m* de patatas, puré *m* de papas *Lat*
mask *n* : máscara *f* — ~ *vt* : enmascarar
masochism *n* : masoquismo *m* — **masochist** *n* : masoquista *mf* — **masochistic** *adj* : masoquista
mason *n* : albañil *mf* — **masonry** *n, pl* **-ries** : albañilería *f*
masquerade *n* : mascarada *f* — ~ *vi* **-aded; -ading** ~ **as** : disfrazarse de, hacerse pasar por
Mass *n* : misa *f*
mass *n* **1** : masa *f* **2** MULTITUDE : cantidad *f* **3 the** ~**es** : las masas
massacre *n* : masacre *f* — ~ *vt* **-cred; -cring** : masacrar
massage *n* : masaje *m* — ~ *vt* **-saged; -saging** : dar masaje a, masajear — **masseur** *n* : masajista *m* — **masseuse** *n* : masajista *f*
massive *adj* **1** BULKY, SOLID : macizo **2** HUGE : enorme, masivo
mast *n* : mástil *m*
master *n* **1** : amo *m*, señor *m* (de la casa) **2** EXPERT : maestro *m*, -tra *f* **3** ~**'s degree** : maestría *f* — ~ *vt* : dominar — **masterful** *adj* : magistral — **masterpiece** *n* : obra *f* maestra — **mastery** *n* : maestría *f*
masturbate *v* **-bated; -bating** *vi* : masturbarse — **masturbation** *n* : masturbación *f*
mat *n* **1** DOORMAT : felpudo *m* **2** RUG : estera *f*
matador *n* : matador *m*
match *n* **1** EQUAL : igual *mf* **2** : fósforo *m*, cerilla *f* (para encender) **3** GAME : partido *m*, combate *m* (en boxeo) **4 be a good** ~ : hacer buena pareja — ~ *vt* **1** *or* ~ **up** : emparejar **2** EQUAL : igualar **3** : combinar con, hacer juego con (ropa, colores, etc.) — *vi* : concordar, coincidir
mate *n* **1** COMPANION : compañero *m*, -ra *f*; amigo *m*, -ga *f* **2** : macho *m*, hembra *f* (de animales) — ~ *vi* **mated; mating** : aparearse
maté *n* : yerba *f*, mate *m*
material *adj* **1** : material **2** IMPORTANT : importante — ~ *n* **1** : material *m* **2** CLOTH : tela *f*, tejido *m* — **materialistic** *adj* : materialista — **materialize** *vi* **-ized; -izing** : aparecer

maternal *adj* : maternal — **maternity** *n, pl* **-ties** : maternidad *f* — ~ *adj* **1** : de maternidad **2** ~ **clothes** : ropa *f* de futura mamá
math → **mathematics**
mathematics *ns* & *pl* : matemáticas *fpl* — **mathematical** *adj* : matemático — **mathematician** *n* : matemático *m*, -ca *f*
matinee *or* **matinée** *n* : matiné(e) *f*, fonción *f* de tarde
matrimony *n* : matrimonio *m* — **matrimonial** *adj* : matrimonial
matrix *n, pl* **-trices** *or* **-trixes** : matriz *f*
matte *adj* : mate
matter *n* **1** SUBSTANCE : materia *f* **2** QUESTION : asunto *m*, cuestión *f* **3 as a** ~ **of fact** : en efecto, en realidad **4 for that** ~ : de hecho **5 to make** ~**s worse** : para colmo de males **6 what's the** ~**?** : ¿qué pasa? — ~ *vi* : importar
mattress *n* : colchón *m*
mature *adj* **-turer; -est** : maduro — ~ *vi* **-tured; -turing** : madurar — **maturity** *n* : madurez *f*
maul *vt* : maltratar, aporrear
mauve *n* : malva *m*
maxim *n* : máxima *f*
maximum *n, pl* **-ma** *or* **-mums** : máximo *m* — ~ *adj* : máximo — **maximize** *vt* **-mized; -mizing** : llevar al máximo
May *n* : mayo *m*
may *v aux, past* **might;** *present s* & *pl* **may 1** : poder **2 come what** ~ : pase lo que pase **3 it** ~ **happen** : puede pasar **4** ~ **the best man win** : que gane el mejor
maybe *adv* : quizás, tal vez
mayhem *n* : alboroto *m*
mayonnaise *n* : mayonesa *f*
mayor *n* : alcalde *m*, **-desa** *f*
maze *n* : laberinto *m*
me *pron* **1** : me **2 for** ~ : para mí **3 give it to** ~**!** : ¡dámelo! **4 it's** ~ : soy yo **5 with** ~ : conmigo
meadow *n* : prado *m*, pradera *f*
meager *or* **meagre** *adj* : escaso
meal *n* **1** : comida *f* **2** : harina *f* (de maíz, etc.) — **mealtime** *n* : hora *f* de comer
mean[1] *vt* **meant; meaning 1** SIGNIFY : querer decir **2** INTEND : querer, tener la intención de **3 be meant for** : estar destinado a **4 he didn't** ~ **it** : no lo dijo en serio
mean[2] *adj* **1** UNKIND : malo **2** STINGY : mezquino, tacaño **3** HUMBLE : humilde
mean[3] *adj* AVERAGE : medio — ~ *n* : promedio *m*
meander *vi* **-dered; -dering 1** WIND : serpentear **2** WANDER : vagar
meaning *n* : significado *m*, sentido *m* — **meaningful** *adj* : significativo — **meaningless** *adj* : sin sentido

meanness *n* **1** UNKINDNESS : maldad *f* **2** STINGINESS : mezquinidad *f*

means *n* **1** : medio *m* **2 by all ~** : por supuesto **3 by ~ of** : por medio de **4 by no ¶** : de ninguna manera

meantime *n* **1** : interín *m* **2 in the ~** : mientras tanto — **~** *adv* → **meanwhile**

meanwhile *adv* : mientras tanto — **~** *n* → **meantime**

measles *npl* : sarampión *m*

measly *adj* **-slier; -est** : miserable, misero

measure *n* : medida *f* — **~** *v* **-sured; -suring** : medir — **measurable** *adj* : mensurable — **measurement** *n* : medida *f* — **measure up ~ to** : estar a la altura de

meat *n* : carne *f* — **meatball** *n* : albóndiga *f* — **meaty** *adj* **meatier; -est 1** : carnoso **2** SUBSTANTIAL : sustancioso

mechanic *n* : mecánico *m*, -ca *f* — **mechanical** *adj* : mecánico — **mechanics** *ns & pl* **1** : mecánica *f* **2** WORKINGS : mecanismo *m* — **mechanism** *n* : mecanismo *m* — **mechanize** *vt* **-nized; -nizing** : mecanizar

medal *n* : medalla *f* — **medallion** *n* : medallón *m*

meddle *vi* **-dled; -dling** : entrometerse

media *or* **mass ~** *npl* : medios *mpl* de comunicación

median *adj* : medio

mediate *vi* **-ated; -ating** : mediar — **mediation** *n* : mediación *f* — **mediator** *n* : mediador *m*, -dora *f*

medical *adj* : médico — **medicated** *adj* : medicinal — **medication** *n* : medicamento *m* — **medicinal** *adj* : medicinal — **medicine** **1** : medicina *f* **2** MEDICATION : medicina *f*, medicamento *m*

medieval *or* **mediaeval** *adj* : medieval

mediocre *adj* : mediocre — **mediocrity** *n, pl* **-ties** : mediocridad *f*

meditate *vi* **-tated; -tating** : meditar — **meditation** *n* : meditación *f*

medium *n, pl* **-diums** *or* **-dia 1** MEANS : medio *m* **2** MEAN : punto *m* medio, término *m* medio **3** → **media** — **~** *adj* : mediano

medley *n, pl* **-leys 1** : mezcla *f* **2** : popurrí *m* (de canciones)

meek *adj* : dócil

meet *v* **met; meeting** *vt* **1** ENCOUNTER : encontrarse con **2** SATISFY : satisfacer **3 pleased to ~ you** : encantado de conocerlo — *vi* **1** : encontrarse **2** ASSEMBLE : reunirse **3** BE INTRODUCED : conocerse — **~** *n* : encuentro *m* — **meeting** *n* : reunión *f*

megabyte *n* : megabyte *m*

megaphone *n* : megáfono *m*

melancholy *n, pl* **-cholies** : melancolía *f* — **~** *adj* : melancólico, triste

mellow *adj* **1** : suave, dulce **2** CALM : apacible **3** : maduro (dícese de frutas), añejo (dícese de vinos) — **~** *vt* : suavizar, endulzar — *vi* : suavizarse

melody *n, pl* **-dies** : melodía *f*

melon *n* : melón *m*

melt *vi* : derretirse, fundirse — *vt* : derretir

member *n* : miembro *m* — **membership** **1** : calidad *f* de miembro **2** MEMBERS : miembros *mpl*

membrane *n* : membrana *f*

memory *n, pl* **-ries 1** : memoria *f* **2** RECOLLECTION : recuerdo *m* — **memento** *n, pl* **-tos** *or* **-toes** : recuerdo *m* — **memo** *n, pl* **memos** *or* **memorandum** *n, pl* **-dums** *or* **-da** : memorándum *m* — **memoirs** *npl* : memorias *fpl* — **memorable** *adj* : memorable — **memorial** *adj* : conmemorativo — **~** *n* : monumento *m* (conmemorativo) — **memorize** *vt* **-rized; -rizing** : aprender de memoria

men → **man**

menace *n* : amenaza *f* — **~** *vt* **-aced; -acing** : amenazar — **menacing** *adj* : amenazador

mend *vt* **1** : reparar, arreglar **2** DARN : zurcir — *vi* HEAL : curarse

menial *adj* : servil, bajo

meningitis *n, pl* **-gitides** : meningitis *f*

menopause *n* : menopausia *f*

menstruate *vi* **-ated; -ating** : menstruar — **menstruation** *n* : menstruación *f*

mental *adj* : mental — **mentality** *n, pl* **-ties** : mentalidad *f*

mention *n* : mención *f* — **mention** *vt* **1** : mencionar **2 don't ~ it!** : ¡de nada!, ¡no hay de qué!

menu *n* : menú *m*

meow *n* : maullido *m*, miau *m* — **~** *vi* : maullar

mercenary *n, pl* **-naries** : mercenario *m*, -ria *f* — **~** *adj* : mercenario

merchant *n* : comerciante *mf* — **merchandise** *n* : mercancía *f*, mercadería *f*

merciful *adj* : misericordioso, compasivo — **merciless** *adj* : despiadado

Mercury *n* : Mercurio *m*

mercury *n, pl* **-ries** : mercurio *m*

mercy *n, pl* **-cies 1** : misericordia *f*, compasión *f* **2 at the ~ of** : a merced de

mere *adj, superlative* **merest** : mero, simple — **merely** *adv* : simplemente

merge *v* **merged; merging** *vi* : unirse, fusionarse (dícese de las compañías), confluir (dícese de los ríos, las calles, etc.) — *vt* : unir, fusionar, combinar — **merger** *n* : unión *f*, fusión *f*

merit *n* : mérito *m* — **~** *vt* : merecer

mermaid *n* : sirena *f*

merry *adj* **-rier; -est** : alegre — **merry–go–round** *n* : tiovivo *m*

mesa *n* : mesa *f*

mesh *n* : malla *f*

mesmerize *vt* **-ized; -izing** : hipnotizar

mess *n* **1** : desorden *m* **2** MUDDLE : lío *m* **3** : rancho *m* (militar) — ~ *vt* **1** *or* ~ **up** SOIL : ensuciar **2** ~ **up** DISARRANGE : desordenar **3** ~ **up** BUNGLE : echar a perder — *vi* **1** ~ **around** PUTTER : entretenerse **2** ~ **with** PROVOKE : meterse con

message *n* : mensaje *m* — **messenger** *n* : mensajero *m*, -ra *f*

messy *adj* **messier; -est** : desordenado, sucio

met → **meet**

metabolism *n* : metabolismo *m*

metal *n* : metal *m* — **metallic** *adj* : metálico

metamorphosis *n, pl* **-phoses** : metamorfosis *f*

metaphor *n* : metáfora *f*

meteor *n* : meteoro *m* — **meteorological** *adj* : meteorológico — **meteorologist** *n* : meteorólogo *m*, -ga *f* — **meteorology** *n* : meteorología *f*

meter *or Brit* **metre** *n* **1** : metro *m* **2** : contador *m* (de electricidad, etc.)

method *n* : método *m* — **methodical** *adj* : metódico

meticulous *adj* : meticuloso

metric *or* **metrical** *adj* : métrico

metropolis *n* : metrópoli *f* — **metropolitan** *adj* : metropolitano

Mexican *adj* : mexicano

mice → **mouse**

microbe *n* : microbio *m*

microfilm *n* : microfilm *m*

microphone *n* : micrófono *m*

microscope *n* : microscopio *m* — **microscopic** *adj* : microscópico

microwave *n or* ~ **oven** : microondas *m*

mid *adj* **1** ~ **morning** : a media mañana **2 in** ~**-August** : a mediados de agosto **3 she is in her mid thirties** : tiene alrededor de 35 años — **midair** *n* **in** ~ : en el aire — **midday** *n* : mediodía *m*

middle *adj* : de en medio, del medio — ~ *n* **1** : medio *m*, centro *m* **2 in the** ~ **of** : en medio de (un espacio), a mitad de (una actividad) **3 in the** ~ **of the month** : a mediados del mes — **middle–aged** *adj* : de mediana edad — **Middle Ages** *npl* : Edad *f* Media — **middle class** *n* : clase *f* media — **middleman** *n, pl* **-men** : intermediario *m*, -ria *f*

midget *n* : enano *m*, -na *f*

midnight *n* : medianoche *f*

midriff *n* : diafragma *m*

midst *n* **1 in the** ~ **of** : en medio de **2 in our** ~ : entre nosotros

midsummer *n* : pleno verano *m*

midway *adv* : a mitad de camino, a medio camino

midwife *n, pl* **-wives** : comadrona *f*

midwinter *n* : pleno invierno *m*

miff *vt* : ofender

might[1] (*used to express permission or possibility or as a polite alternative to* **may**) → **may**

might[2] *n* : fuerza *f*, poder *m* — **mighty** *adj* **mightier; -est 1** : fuerte, poderoso **2** GREAT : enorme — ~ *adv* : muy

migraine *n* : jaqueca *f*, migraña *f*

migrate *vi* **-grated; -grating** : emigrar — **migrant** *n* : trabajador *m*, -dora *f* ambulante

mild *adj* **1** GENTLE : suave **2** LIGHT : leve **3** *a* ~ **climate** : una clima templada

mildew *n* : moho *m*

mildly *adv* : ligeramente, suavemente — **mildness** *n* : apacibilidad *f* (de personas), suavedad *f* (de sabores, etc.)

mile *n* : milla *f* — **mileage** *n* : distancia *f* recorrida (en millas), kilometraje *m* — **milestone** *n* : hito *m*

military *adj* : militar — ~ *n* **the** ~ : las fuerzas armadas — **militant** *adj* : militante — ~ *n* : militante *mf* — **militia** *n* : milicia *f*

milk *n* : leche *f* — ~ *vt* **1** : ordeñar (una vaca, etc.) **2** EXPLOIT : explotar — **milky** *adj* **milkier; -est** : lechoso — **Milky Way** *n* **the** ~ : la Vía Láctea

mill *n* **1** : molino *m* **2** FACTORY : fábrica *f* **3** GRINDER : molinillo *m* — ~ *vt* : moler — *vi or* ~ **about** : arremolinarse

millennium *n, pl* **-nia** *or* **-niums** : milenio *m*

miller *n* : molinero *m*, -ra *f*

milligram *n* : miligramo *m* — **millimeter** *or Brit* **millimetre** *n* : milímetro *m*

million *n, pl* **millions** *or* **million 1** : millón *m* **2 a** ~ **people** : un millón de personas — ~ *adj* **a** ~ : un millón de — **millionaire** *n* : millonario *m*, -ria *f* — **millionth** *adj* : millonésimo

mime *n* **1** : mimo *mf* **2** PANTOMIME : pantomima *f* — ~ *v* **mimed; miming** *vt* : imitar — *vi* : hacer la mímica — **mimic** *vt* **-icked; -icking** : imitar, remedar — ~ *n* : imitador *m*, -dora *f* — **mimicry** *n, pl* **-ries** : imitación *f*

mince *v* **minced; mincing** *vt* **1** : picar, moler **2 not to** ~ **one's words** : no tener pelos en la lengua

mind *n* **1** : mente *f* **2** INTELLECT : capacidad *f* intelectual **3** OPINION : opinión *f* **4** REASON : razón *f* **5 have a** ~ **to** : tener intención de — ~ *vt* **1** TEND : cuidar **2** OBEY : obedecer **3** WATCH : tener cuidado con   **4 I don't ~ the heat** : no me molesta el calor — *vi* **1** OBEY : obedecer   **2 I don't ~** : no me importa, me es igual — **mindful** *adj* : atento — **mindless** *adj* **1** SENSELESS : estúpido, sin sentido   **2** DULL : aburrido

mine[1] *pron* **1** : (el) mío, (la) mía, (los) míos, (las) mías   **2 a friend of ~** : un amigo mío

mine[2] *n* : mina *f* — **~** *vt* **mined; mining   1** : extraer (oro, etc.)   **2** : minar (con artefactos explosivos) — **minefield** *n* : campo *m* de minas — **miner** *n* : minero *m*, -ra *f*

mineral *n* : mineral *m*

mingle *v* **-gled; -gling** *vt* : mezclar — *vi* **1** : mezclarse   **2** : circular (a una fiesta, etc.)

miniature *n* : miniatura *f* — **~** *adj* : en miniatura

minimal *adj* : mínimo — **minimize** *vt* **-mized; -mizing** : minimizar — **minimum** *adj* : mínimo — **~** *n, pl* **-ma** *or* **-mums** : mínimo *m*

mining *n* : minería *f*

minister *n* **1** : pastor *m*, -tora *f* (de una iglesia)   **2** : ministro *m*, **-tra** *f* (en política) — **~** *vi* **~ to** : cuidar (de), atender a — **ministerial** *adj* : ministerial — **ministry** *n, pl* **-tries** : ministerio *m*

minivan *n* : minivan *f*

mink *n, pl* **mink** *or* **minks** : visón *m*

minnow *n, pl* **-nows** : pececillo *m* de agua dulce

minor *adj* **1** : menor   **2** INSIGNIFICANT : sin importancia — **~** *n* **1** : menor *mf* (de edad)   **2** : asignatura *f* secundaria (de estudios) — **minority** *n, pl* **-ties** : minoría *f*

mint[1] *n* **1** : menta *f* (planta)   **2** : pastilla *f* de menta (dulce)

mint[2] *n* **1 the U.S. Mint** : la casa de la moneda de los EE.UU.   **2 be worth a ~** : valer un dineral — **~** *vt* : acuñar — **~** *adj* **in ~ condition** : como nuevo

minus *prep* **1** : menos   **2** WITHOUT : sin — **~** *n or* **~ sign** : signo *m* de menos

minuscule *adj* : minúsculo

minute[1] *n* **1** : minuto *m*   **2** MOMENT : momento *m*   **3 ~s** *npl* : actas *fpl* (de una reunión)

minute[2] *adj* **-nuter; -est** **1** TINY : diminuto, minúsculo   **2** DETAILED : minucioso

miracle *n* : milagro *m* — **miraculous** *adj* : milagroso

mirage *n* : espejismo *m*

mire *n* : lodo *m*, fango *m*

mirror *n* : espejo *m* — **~** *vt* : reflejar

mirth *n* : alegría *f*, risas *fpl*

misapprehension *n* : malentendido *m*

misbehave *vi* **-haved; -having** : portarse mal — **misbehavior** *n* : mala conducta *f*

miscalculate *v* **-lated; -lating** : calcular mal

miscarriage *n* **1** : aborto *m*   **2 ~ of justice** : error *m* judicial

miscellaneous *adj* : diverso, vario

mischief *n* : travesuras *fpl* — **mischievous** *adj* : travieso

misconception *n* : concepto *m* erróneo

misconduct *n* : mala conducta *f*

misdeed *n* : fechoría *f*

misdemeanor *n* : delito *m* menor

miser *n* : avaro *m*, -ra *f*; tacaño *m*, -ña *f*

miserable *adj* **1** UNHAPPY : triste   **2** WRETCHED : miserable   **3 ~ weather** : tiempo *m* malo

miserly *adj* : mezquino

misery *n, pl* **-eries   1** : sufrimiento *m*   **2** WRETCHEDNESS : miseria *f*

misfire *vi* **-fired; -firing** : fallar

misfit *n* : inadaptado *m*, -da *f*

misfortune *n* : desgracia *f*

misgiving *n* : duda *f*

misguided *adj* : descaminado, equivocado

mishap *n* : contratiempo *m*

misinform *vt* : informar mal

misinterpret *vt* : interpretar mal

misjudge *vt* **-judged; -judging** : juzgar mal

mislay *vt* **-laid; -laying** : extraviar, perder

mislead *vt* **-led; -leading** : engañar — **misleading** *adj* : engañoso

misnomer *n* : nombre *m* inapropiado

misplace *vt* **-placed; -placing** : extraviar, perder

misprint *n* : errata *f*, error *m* de imprenta

Miss *n* : señorita *f*

miss *vt* **1** : errar, faltar   **2** OVERLOOK : pasar por alto   **3** : perder (una oportunidad, un vuelo, etc.)   **4** AVOID : evitar   **5** OMIT : saltarse   **6 I ~ you** : te echo de menos — **~** *n* **1** : fallo *m* (de un tiro, etc.)   **2** FAILURE : fracaso *m*

missile *n* **1** : misil *m*   **2** PROJECTILE : proyectil *m*

missing *adj* : perdido, desaparecido

mission *n* : misión *f* — **missionary** *n, pl* **-aries** : misionero *m*, -ra *f*

misspell *vt* : escribir mal

mist *n* : neblina *f*, bruma *f*

mistake *vt* **mistook; mistaken; -taking   1** MISINTERPRET : entender mal   **2** CONFUSE : confundir — **~** *n* **1** : error *m*   **2 make a ~** : equivocarse — **mistaken** *adj* : equivocado

mister *n* : señor *m*

mistletoe *n* : muérdago *m*

mistreat *vt* : maltratar

mistress *n* **1** : dueña *f*, señora *f* (de una casa)   **2** LOVER : amante *f*

mistrust *n* : desconfianza *f* — **~** *vt* : desconfiar de

misty *adj* **mistier; -est** : neblinoso, nebuloso

misunderstand *vt* **-stood; -standing** : entender mal — **misunderstanding** *n* : malentendido *m*

misuse vt **-used; -using 1** : emplear mal **2** MISTREAT : maltratar — ～ n : mal empleo m, abuso m

mitigate vt **-gated; -gating** : mitigar

mitt n : manopla f, guante m (de béisbol) — **mitten** n : manopla f, mitón m

mix vt **1** : mezclar **2** ～ **up** : confundir — vi : mezclarse — ～ n : mezcla f — **mixture** n : mezcla f — **mix-up** n : confusión f, lío m fam

moan n : gemido m — ～ vi : gemir

mob n : muchedumbre f — ～ vt **mobbed; mobbing** : acosar

mobile adj : móvil — ～ n : móvil m — **mobile home** n : caravana f — **mobility** n : movilidad f — **mobilize** vt **-lized; -lizing** : movilizar

moccasin n : mocasín m

mock vt : burlarse de, mofarse de — ～ adj : falso — **mockery** n, pl **-eries** : burla f — **mock-up** n : maqueta f

mode n **1** : modo m **2** FASHION : moda f

model n **1** : modelo m **2** MOCK-UP : maqueta f **3** : modelo mf (persona) — ～ v **-eled** or **-elled; -eling** or **-elling** vt **1** SHAPE : modelar **2** WEAR : lucir — vi : trabajar de modelo — ～ adj : modelo

modem n : módem m

moderate adj : moderado — ～ n : moderado m, -da f — ～ v **-ated; -ating** vt : moderar — vi : moderarse — **moderation** n : moderación f — **moderator** n : moderador m, -dora f

modern adj : moderno — **modernize** vt **-ized; -izing** : modernizar

modest adj : modesto — **modesty** n : modestia f

modify vt **-fied; -fying** : modificar

moist adj : húmedo — **moisten** vt : humedecer — **moisture** n : humedad f — **moisturizer** n : crema f hidratante

molar n : muela f

molasses n : melaza f

mold¹ n FORM : molde m — ～ vt : moldear, formar

mold² n FUNGUS : moho m — **moldy** adj **moldier; -est** : mohoso

mole¹ n : lunar m (en la piel)

mole² n : topo m (animal)

molecule n : molécula f

molest vt **1** HARASS : importunar **2** : abusar (sexualmente)

molten adj : fundido

mom n : mamá f

moment n : momento m — **momentarily** adv **1** : momentáneamente **2** SOON : dentro de poco, pronto — **momentary** adj : momentáneo

momentous adj : muy importante

momentum n, pl **-ta** or **-tums 1** : momento m (en física) **2** IMPETUS : ímpetu m

monarch n : monarca mf — **monarchy** n, pl **-chies** : monarquía f

monastery n, pl **-teries** : monasterio m

Monday n : lunes m

money n, pl **-eys** or **-ies** : dinero m — **monetary** adj : monetario — **money order** n : giro m postal

mongrel n : perro m mestizo

monitor n : monitor m (de una computadora, etc.) — ～ vt : controlar

monk n : monje m

monkey n, pl **-keys** : mono m, -na f — **monkey wrench** n : llave f inglesa

monogram n : monograma m

monologue n : monólogo m

monopoly n, pl **-lies** : monopolio m — **monopolize** vt **-lized; -lizing** : monopolizar

monotonous adj : monótono — **monotony** n : monotonía f

monster n : monstruo m — **monstrosity** n, pl **-ties** : monstruosidad f — **monstrous** adj **1** : monstruoso **2** HUGE : gigantesco

month n : mes m — **monthly** adv : mensualmente — ～ adj : mensual

monument n : monumento m — **monumental** adj : monumental

moo vi : mugir — ～ n : mugido m

mood n : humor m — **moody** adj **moodier; -est 1** GLOOMY : melancólico, deprimido **2** IRRITABLE : malhumorado **3** TEMPERAMENTAL : de humor variable

moon n : luna f — **moonlight** n : luz f de la luna

moor¹ n : brezal m, páramo m

moor² vt : amarrar — **mooring** n DOCK : atracadero m

moose ns & pl : alce m

moot adj : discutible

mop n **1** : trapeador m Lat, fregona f Spain **2** or ～ **of hair** : pelambrera f — ～ vt **mopped; mopping** : trapear Lat, pasar la fregona a Spain

mope vi **moped; moping** : andar deprimido

moped n : ciclomotor m

moral adj : moral — ～ n **1** : moraleja f (de un cuento, etc.) **2** ～**s** npl : moral f, moralidad f — **morale** n : moral f — **morality** n, pl **-ties** : moralidad f

morbid adj : morboso

more adj : más — ～ adv **1** : más **2** ～ **and** ～ : cada vez más **3** ～ **or less** : más o menos **4** once ～ : una vez más — ～ n : más m — ～ pron : más — **moreover** adv : además

morgue n : depósito m de cadáveres

morning n **1** : mañana f **2** good ～! : ¡buenos días! **3** in the ～ : por la mañana

moron n : estúpido m, -da f; imbécil mf

morose *adj* : malhumorado

morphine *n* : morfina *f*

morsel *n* **1** BITE : bocado *m* **2** FRAGMENT : pedazo *m*

mortal *adj* : mortal — ~ *n* : mortal *mf* — mortality *n* : mortalidad *f*

mortar *n* : mortero *m*

mortgage *n* : hipoteca *f* — ~ *vt* -gaged; -gaging : hipotecar

mortify *vt* -fied; -fying **1** : mortificar **2** HUMILIATE : avergonzar

mosaic *n* : mosaico *m*

Moslem → Muslim

mosque *n* : mezquita *f*

mosquito *n, pl* -toes : mosquito *m*, zancudo *m Lat*

moss *n* : musgo *m*

most *adj* **1** : la mayoría de, la mayor parte de **2** (the) ~ : más — ~ *adv* : más — ~ *n* : más *m*, máximo *m* — ~ *pron* : la mayoría, la mayor parte — mostly *adv* **1** MAINLY : en su mayor parte, principalmente **2** USUALLY : normalmente

motel *n* : motel *m*

moth *n* : palomilla *f*, polilla *f*

mother *n* : madre *f* — ~ *vt* **1** : cuidar de **2** SPOIL : mimar — motherhood *n* : maternidad *f* — mother–in–law *n, pl* mothers–in–law : suegra *f* — motherly *adj* : maternal — mother–of–pearl *n* : nácar *m*

motif *n* : motivo *m*

motion *n* **1** : movimiento *m* **2** PROPOSAL : moción *f* **3** set in ~ : poner en marcha — ~ *vi* ~ to s.o. : hacer una señal a algn — motionless *adj* : inmóvil — motion picture *n* : película *f*

motive *n* : motivo *m* — motivate *vt* -vated; -vating : motivar — motivation *n* : motivación *f*

motor *n* : motor *m* — motorbike *n* : motocicleta *f* (pequeña), moto *f* — motorboat *n* : lancha *f* motora — motorcycle *n* : motocicleta *f* — motorcyclist *n* : motociclista *mf* — motorist *n* : automovilista *mf*, motorista *mf Lat*

motto *n, pl* -toes : lema *m*

mould → mold

mound *n* **1** PILE : montón *m* **2** HILL : montículo *m*

mount¹ *n* **1** HORSE : montura *f* **2** SUPPORT : soporte *m* — ~ *vt* : montar (un caballo, etc.), subir (una escalera) — *vi* INCREASE : aumentar

mount² *n* HILL : monte *m* — mountain *n* : montaña *f* — mountainous *adj* : montañoso

mourn *vt* : llorar (por) — *vi* : lamentarse — mourner *n* : doliente *mf* — mournful *adj* : triste — mourning *n* : luto *m*

mouse *n, pl* mice : ratón *m* — mousetrap *n* : ratonera *f*

moustache → mustache

mouth *n* : boca *f* (de una persona o un animal), desembocadura *f* (de un río) — mouthful *n* : bocado *m* — mouthpiece *n* : boquilla *f* (de un instrumento musical)

move *v* moved; moving *vi* **1** GO : ir **2** RELOCATE : mudarse **3** STIR : moverse **4** ACT : tomar medidas — *vt* **1** : mover **2** AFFECT : conmover **3** TRANSPORT : transportar, trasladar **4** PROPOSE : proponer — ~ *n* **1** MOVEMENT : movimiento *m* **2** RELOCATION : mudanza *f* **3** STEP : medida *f* — movable *or* moveable *adj* : movible, móvil — movement *n* : movimiento *m*

movie *n* **1** : película *f* **2** ~s *npl* : cine *m*

mow *vt* mowed; mowed *or* mown ; mowing : cortar (la hierba) — mower → lawn mower

MP3 *n* : MP3 *m*

Mr. *n, pl* Messrs. : señor *m*

Mrs. *n, pl* Mesdames : señora *f*

Ms. *n* : señora *f*, señorita *f*

much *adj* more; most : mucho — ~ *adv* more; most **1** : mucho **2** as ~ as : tanto como **3** how ~? : ¿cuánto? **4** too ~ : demasiado — ~ *pron* : mucho, -cha

muck *n* **1** DIRT : mugre *f*, suciedad *f* **2** MANURE : estiércol *m*

mucus *n* : mucosidad *f*

mud *n* : barro *m*, lodo *m*

muddle *v* -dled; -dling *vt* **1** CONFUSE : confundir **2** JUMBLE : desordenar — *vi* ~ through : arreglárselas — ~ *n* : confusión *f*, lío *m fam*

muddy *adj* -dier; -est : fangoso, lleno de barro

muffin *n* : mollete *m*

muffle *vt* -fled; -fling : amortiguar (un sonido) — muffler *n* **1** SCARF : bufanda *f* **2** : silenciador *m*, mofle *m Lat* (de un automóvil)

mug *n* CUP : tazón *m* — ~ *vt* : asaltar, atracar — mugger *n* : atracador *m*, -dora *f*

muggy *adj* -gier; -est : bochornoso

mule *n* : mula *f*

mull *vt or* ~ over : reflexionar sobre

multicolored *adj* : multicolor

multimedia *adj* : multimedia

multinational *adj* : multinacional

multiple *adj* : múltiple — ~ *n* : múltiplo *m* — multiplication *n* : multiplicación *f* — multiply *v* -plied; -plying *vt* : multiplicar — *vi* : multiplicarse

multitude *n* : multitud *f*

mum *adj* keep ~ : guardar silencio

mumble *v* -bled; -bling *vt* : mascullar — *vi* : hablar entre dientes

mummy *n, pl* -mies : momia *f*

mumps *ns & pl* : paperas *fpl*
munch *v* : mascar, masticar
mundane *adj* : rutinario, ordinario
municipal *adj* : municipal — **municipality** *n, pl* **-ties** : municipio *m*
munitions *npl* : municiónes *fpl*
mural *n* : mural *m*
murder *n* : asesinato *m*, homicidio *m* — **~** *vt* : asesinar, matar — *vi* : matar — **murderer** *n* : asesino *m*, **-na** *f*; homicida *mf* — **murderous** *adj* : asesino, homicida
murky *adj* **-kier; -est** : turbio, oscuro
murmur *n* : murmullo *m* — **murmur** *v* : murmurar
muscle *n* : músculo *m* — **~** *vi* **-cled; -cling** *or* **~ in** : meterse por la fuerza en — **muscular** *adj* **1** : muscular **2** STRONG : musculoso
muse[1] *n* : musa *f*
muse[2] *vi* **mused; musing** : meditar
museum *n* : museo *m*
mushroom *n* **1** : hongo *m*, seta *f* **2** : champiñón *m* (en la cocina) — **~** *vi* GROW : crecer rápidamente, multiplicarse
mushy *adj* **mushier; -est 1** SOFT : blando **2** MAWKISH : sensiblero
music *n* : música *f* — **musical** *adj* : musical — **~** *n* : comedia *f* musical — **musician** *n* : músico *m*, **-ca** *f*
Muslim *adj* : musulmán — **~** *n* : musulmán *m*, **-mana** *f*
muslin *n* : muselina *f*
mussel *n* : mejillón *m*
must *v aux* **1** : deber, tener que **2 you ~ come** : tienes que venir **3 you ~ be tired** : debes (de) estar cansado — **~** *n* : necesidad *f*
mustache *n* : bigote *m*, bigotes *mpl*
mustang *n* : mustang *m*
mustard *n* : mostaza *f*
muster *vt* **1** : reunir **2** *or* **~ up** : armarse de, cobrar (valor, fuerzas, etc.)
musty *adj* **mustier; -est** : que huele a cerrado
mute *adj* **muter; mutest** : mudo — **~** *n* : mudo *m*, **-da** *f*
mutilate *vt* **-lated; -lating** : mutilar
mutiny *n, pl* **-nies** : motín *m* — **~** *vi* **-nied; -nying** : amotinarse
mutter *vi* : murmurar
mutton *n* : carne *f* de carnero
mutual *adj* **1** : mutuo **2** COMMON : común — **mutually** *adv* : mutuamente
muzzle *n* **1** SNOUT : hocico *m* **2** : bozal *m* (para un perro, etc.) **3** : boca *f* (de un arma de fuego) — **~** *vt* **-zled; -zling** : poner un bozal a (un animal)
my *adj* : mi
myopia *n* : miopía *f* — **myopic** *adj* : miope
myself *pron* **1** (*reflexive*) : me **2** (*emphatic*) : yo mismo **3 by ~** : solo
mystery *n, pl* **-teries** : misterio *m* — **mysterious** *adj* : misterioso
mystic *adj or* **mystical** : místico
mystify *vt* **-fied; -fying** : dejar perplejo, confundir
mystique *n* : aura *f* de misterio
myth *n* : mito *m* — **mythical** *adj* : mítico

N

n *n, pl* **n's** *or* **ns** : n *f*, decimocuarta letra del alfabeto inglés
nab *vt* **nabbed; nabbing 1** ARREST : pescar *fam* **2** GRAB : agarrar
nag *v* **nagged; nagging** *vi* COMPLAIN : quejarse — *vt* **1** ANNOY : fastidiar, dar la lata a **2** SCOLD : regañar — **nagging** *adj* : persistente
nail *n* **1** : clavo *m* **2** : uña *f* (de un dedo) — **~** *vt or* **~ down** : clavar — **nail file** *n* : lima *f* de uñas
naïve *or* naïve *adj* **-iver; -est** : ingenuo — **naïveté** *n* : ingenuidad *f*
naked *adj* **1** : desnudo **2 the ~ truth** : la pura verdad **3 to the ~ eye** : a simple vista
name *n* **1** : nombre *m* **2** REPUTATION : fama *f* **3 what is your ~?** : ¿cómo se llama? **4 → first name, surname** — **~** *vt* **named; naming 1** : poner nombre a **2** APPOINT : nombrar **3 ~ a price** : fijar un precio — **nameless** *adj* : anónimo — **namely** *adv* : a saber — **namesake** *n* : tocayo *m*, **-ya** *f*
nap[1] *vi* **napped; napping** : echarse una siesta — **~** *n* : siesta *f*
nap[2] *n* : pelo *m* (de una tela)
nape *n or* **~ of the neck** : nuca *f*
napkin *n* **1** : servilleta *f* **2 → sanitary napkin**
narcotic *n* : narcótico *m*, estupefaciente *m*

narrate *vt* **-rated; -rating** : narrar — **narration** *n* : narración *f* — **narrative** *n* : narración *f* — **narrator** *n* : narrador *m*, -dora *f*
narrow *adj* **1** : estrecho, angosto **2** RESTRICTED : limitado — ～ *vi* : estrecharse — *vt* **1** : estrechar **2** *or* ～ **down** : limitar — **narrowly** *adv* : por poco — **narrow-minded** *adj* : de miras estrechas
nasal *adj* : nasal
nasty *adj* **-tier; -est 1** MEAN : malo, cruel **2** UNPLEASANT : desagradable **3** REPUGNANT : asqueroso — **nastiness** *n* : maldad *f*
nation *n* : nación *f* — **national** *adj* : nacional — **nationalism** *n* : nacionalismo *m* — **nationality** *n*, *pl* **-ties** : nacionalidad *f* — **nationalize** *vt* **-ized; -izing** : nacionalizar — **nationwide** *adj* : por todo el país
native *adj* **1** : natal (dícese de un país, etc.) **2** INNATE : innato **3** ～ **language** : lengua *f* materna — ～ *n* **1** : nativo *m*, -va *f* **2 be a** ～ **of** : ser natural de — **Native American** : indio *m* americano, india *f* americana — **nativity** *n*, *pl* **-ties the Nativity** : la Navidad
nature *n* **1** : naturaleza *f* **2** KIND : índole *f*, clase *f* **3** DISPOSITION : carácter *m*, natural *m* — **natural** *adj* : natural — **naturalize** *vt* **-ized; -izing** : naturalizar — **naturally** *adv* : naturalmente
naught *n* **1** NOTHING : nada *f* **2** ZERO : cero *m*
naughty *adj* **-tier; -est 1** : travieso, pícaro **2** RISQUÉ : picante
nausea *n* : náuseas *fpl* — **nauseating** *adj* : nauseabundo — **nauseous** *adj* **1 feel** ～ : sentir náuseas **2** SICKENING : nauseabundo
nautical *adj* : náutico
naval *adj* : naval
nave *n* : nave *f* (de una iglesia)
navel *n* : ombligo *m*
navigate *v* **-gated; -gating** *vi* : navegar — *vt* **1** : gobernar (un barco), pilotar (un avión) **2** : navegar por (un río, etc.) — **navigable** *adj* : navegable — **navigation** *n* : navegación *f* — **navigator** *n* : navegante *mf*
navy *n*, *pl* **-vies 1** : marina *f* de guerra **2** *or* ～ **blue** : azul *m* marino
near *adv* : cerca — ～ *prep* : cerca de — ～ *adj* : cercano, próximo — ～ *vt* : acercarse a — **nearby** *adv* : cerca — ～ *adj* : cercano — **nearly** *adv* : casi — **nearsighted** *adj* : miope, corto de vista
neat *adj* **1** TIDY : muy arreglado **2** CLEVER : hábil, ingenioso — **neatly** *adv* **1** : ordenadamente **2** CLEVERLY : hábilmente — **neatness** *n* : pulcritud *f*, orden *m*
nebulous *adj* : nebuloso
necessary *adj* : necesario — **necessarily** *adv* : necesariamente — **necessitate** *vt*

-tated; -tating : exigir, requerir — **necessity** *n*, *pl* **-ties 1** : necesidad *f* **2 necessities** *npl* : cosas *fpl* indispensables
neck *n* **1** : cuello *m* (de una persona o una botella), pescuezo *m* (de un animal) **2** COLLAR : cuello *m* — **necklace** *n* : collar *m* — **necktie** *n* : corbata *f*
nectar *n* : néctar *m*
nectarine *n* : nectarina *f*
need *n* **1** : necesidad *f* **2 if** ～ **be** : si hace falta — ～ *vt* **1** : necesitar, exigir **2** ～ **to** : tener que — *v aux* : tener que
needle *n* : aguja *f* — ～ *vt* **-dled; -dling** : pinchar
needless *adj* **1** : innecesario **2** ～ **to say** : de más está decir
needlework *n* : bordado *m*
needn't (*contraction of* **need not**) → **need**
needy **needier; -est** *adj* : necesitado
negative *adj* : negativo — ～ *n* **1** : negación *f* (en gramática) **2** : negativo *m* (en fotografía)
neglect *vt* : descuidar — ～ *n* : descuido *m*, abandono *m*
negligee *n* : negligé *m*
negligence *n* : negligencia *f*, descuido *m* — **negligent** *adj* : negligente, descuidado
negligible *adj* : insignificante
negotiate *v* **-ated; -ating** : negociar — **negotiable** *adj* : negociable — **negotiation** *n* : negociación *f* — **negotiator** *n* : negociador *m*, -dora *f*
Negro *n*, *pl* **-groes** *sometimes considered offensive* : negro *m*, -gra *f*
neigh *vi* : relinchar — ～ *n* : relincho *m*
neighbor *or Brit* **neighbour** *n* : vecino *m*, -na *f* — **neighborhood** *or Brit* **neighbourhood** *n* **1** : barrio *m*, vecindario *m* **2 in the** ～ **of** : alrededor de — **neighborly** *or Brit* **neighbourly** *adv* : amable
neither *conj* **1** ～...**nor** : ni...ni **2** ～ **am/do I** : yo tampoco — ～ *pron* : ninguno, -na — ～ *adj* : ninguno (de los dos)
neon *n* : neón *m*
nephew *n* : sobrino *m*
Neptune *n* : Neptuno *m*
nerve *n* **1** : nervio *m* **2** COURAGE : coraje *m* **3** GALL : descaro *m* **4** ～**s** *npl* JITTERS : nervios *mpl* — **nervous** *adj* : nervioso — **nervousness** *n* : nerviosismo *m* — **nervy** *adj* **nervier; -est** : descarado
nest *n* : nido *m* — ～ *vi* : anidar
nestle *vi* **-tled; -tling** : acurrucarse
net[1] *n* : red *f* — ～ *vt* **netted; netting** : pescar, atrapar (con una red)
net[2] *adj* : neto — ～ *vt* netted; netting YIELD : producir neto
nettle *n* : ortiga *f*
network *n* : red *f*
neurology *n* : neurología *f*

neurosis *n, pl* **-roses** : neurosis *f* — **neurotic** *adj* : neurótico
neuter *adj* : neutro — ~ *vt* : castrar
neutral *n* : punto *m* muerto (de un automóvil) — ~ *adj* **1** : neutral **2** : neutro (en electrotecnia o química) — **neutrality** *n* : neutralidad *f* — **neutralize** *vt* **-ized; -izing** : neutralizar
neutron *n* : neutrón *m*
never *adv* **1** : nunca, jamás **2** NOT : no **3** ~ **again** : nunca más **4** ~ **mind** : no importa — **nevermore** *adv* : nunca jamás — **nevertheless** *adv* : sin embargo, no obstante
New Year's Day *n* : día *m* del Año Nuevo
new *adj* : nuevo — **newborn** *adj* : recién nacido — **newcomer** *n* : recién llegado *m*, -da *f* — **newly** *adv* : recién, recientemente — **newlywed** *n* : recién casado *m*, -da *f* — **news** *n* : noticias *fpl* — **newscast** *n* : noticiario *m*, noticiero *m Lat* — **newscaster** *n* : presentador *m*, -dora *f* (de un noticiario) — **newsletter** *n* : boletín *m* informativo — **newspaper** *n* : periódico *m*, diario *m* — **newsstand** *n* : puesto *m* de periódicos
newt *n* : tritón *m*
next *adj* **1** : próximo **2** FOLLOWING : siguiente — ~ *adv* **1** : la próxima vez **2** AFTERWARD : después, luego **3** NOW : ahora — **next–door** *adj* : de al lado — **next to** *adv* ALMOST : casi — ~ *prep* BESIDE : al lado de
nib *n* : plumilla *f*
nibble *vt* **-bled; -bling** : mordisquear
Nicaraguan *adj* : nicaragüense
nice *adj* **nicer; nicest 1** PLEASANT : agradable, bueno **2** KIND : amable — **nicely** *adv* **1** WELL : bien **2** KINDLY : amablemente — **niceness** *n* : amabilidad *f* — **niceties** *npl* : detalles *mpl*, sutilezas *fpl*
niche *n* **1** : nicho *m* **2** find one's ~ : hacerse su hueco
nick *n* **1** : corte *m* pequeño, muesca *f* **2 in the** ~ **of time** : justo a tiempo — ~ *vt* : hacer una muesca en
nickel *n* **1** : níquel *m* (metal) **2** : moneda *f* de cinco centavos
nickname *n* : apodo *m*, sobrenombre *m* — ~ *vt* **-named; -naming** : apodar
nicotine *n* : nicotina *f*
niece *n* : sobrina *f*
niggling *adj* **1** PETTY : insignificante **2** PERSISTENT : constante
night *n* **1** : noche *f* **2 at** ~ : de noche **3 last** ~ : anoche **4 tomorrow** ~ : mañana por la noche — **nightclub** *n* : club *m* nocturno — **nightfall** *n* : anochecer *m* — **nightgown** *n* : camisón *m* (de noche) — **nightly** *adj* : de todas las noches — ~ *adv* : cada

noche — **nightmare** *n* : pesadilla *f* — **nighttime** *n* : noche *f*
nil *n* NOTHING : nada *f*
nimble *adj* **-bler; -blest** : ágil
nine *adj* : nueve — ~ *n* : nueve *m* — **nine hundred** *adj* : novecientos — ~ *n* : novecientos *m* — **nineteen** *adj* : diecinueve — ~ *n* : diecinueve *m* — **nineteenth** *adj* : decimonoveno, decimonono — ~ *n* **1** : decimonoveno *m*, -na *f;* decimonono *m*, -na *f* (en una serie) **2** : diecinueveavo *m* (en matemáticas) — **ninetieth** *adj* : nonagésimo — ~ *n* **1** : nonagésimo *m*, -ma *f* (en una serie) **2** : noventavo *m* (en matemáticas) — **ninety** *adj* : noventa — ~ *n, pl* **-ties** : noventa *m* — **ninth** *adj* : noveno — ~ *n* **1** : noveno *m*, -na *f* (en una serie) **2** : noveno *m* (en matemáticas)
nip *vt* **nipped; nipping 1** PINCH : pellizcar **2** BITE : mordisquear **3** ~ **in the bud** : cortar de raíz — ~ *n* **1** PINCH : pellizco *m* **2** NIBBLE : mordisco *m*
nipple *n* **1** : pezón *m* (de una mujer) **2** : tetilla *f* (de un hombre o un biberón)
nitrogen *n* : nitrógen *m*
nitwit *n* : idiota *mf*
no one *pron* : nadie
no *adv* : no — ~ *adj* **1** : ninguno **2 I have** ~ **money** : no tengo dinero **3 it's** ~ **trouble** : no es ningún problema **4** ~ **smoking** : prohibido fumar — ~ *n, pl* **noes** *or* **nos** : no *m*
noble *adj* **-bler; -blest** : noble — ~ *n* : noble *mf* — **nobility** *n* : nobleza *f*
nobody *pron* : nadie
nocturnal *adj* : nocturno
nod *v* **nodded; nodding** *vi* **1** *or* ~ **yes** : asentir con la cabeza **2** ~ **off** : dormirse — *vt* ~ **one's head** : asentir con la cabeza — ~ *n* : señal *m* con la cabeza
noes → **no**
noise *n* : ruido *m* — **noisily** *adv* : ruidosamente — **noisy** *adj* **noisier; -est** : ruidoso
nomad *n* : nómada *mf* — **nomadic** *adj* : nómada
nominal *adj* : nominal
nominate *vt* **-nated; -nating 1** : proponer, postular *Lat* **2** APPOINT : nombrar — **nomination** *n* **1** : propuesta *f*, postulación *f Lat* **2** APPOINTMENT : nombramiento *m*
nonalcoholic *adj* : no alcohólico
nonchalant *adj* : despreocupado
noncommissioned officer *n* : suboficial *mf*
noncommittal *adj* : evasivo
nondescript *adj* : anodino, soso
none *pron* **1** : ninguno, ninguna **2 there are** ~ **left** : no hay más — ~ *adv* **1 be** ~ **the worse** : no sufrir daño alguno **2** ~ **too happy** : nada contento **3** ~ **too soon** : a buena hora

nonentity *n, pl* **-ties** : persona *f* insignificante

nonetheless *adv* : sin embargo, no obstante

nonexistent *adj* : inexistente

nonfat *adj* : sin grasa

nonfiction *n* : no ficción *f*

nonprofit *adj* : sin fines lucrativos

nonsense *n* : tonterías *fpl*, disparates *mpl* — **nonsensical** *adj* : absurdo

nonsmoker *n* : no fumador *m*, -dora *f*

nonstop *adj* : directo — ~ *adv* : sin parar

noodle *n* : fideo *m*

nook *n* : rincón *m*

noon *n* : mediodía *m*

noose *n* **1** : dogal *m*, soga *f* **2** LASSO : lazo *m*

nor *conj* **1 neither...**~ : ni...ni **2** ~ **I** : yo tampoco

norm *n* **1** : norma *f* **2 the** ~ : lo normal — **normal** *adj* : normal — **normality** *n* : normalidad *f* — **normally** *adv* : normalmente

north *adv* : al norte — ~ *adj* : norte, del norte — ~ *n* **1** : norte *m* **2 the North** : el Norte — **North American** *adj* : norteamericano — **northeast** *adv* : hacia el nordeste — ~ *adj* : nordeste, del nordeste — ~ *n* : nordeste *m*, noreste *m* — **northeastern** *adj* : nordeste, del nordeste — **northerly** *adj* : del norte — **northern** *adj* : del norte, norteño — **northwest** *adv* : hacia el noroeste — ~ *adj* : noroeste, del noroeste — ~ *n* : noroeste *m* — **northwestern** *adj* : noroeste, del noroeste

Norwegian *adj* : noruego

nose *n* **1** : nariz *f* (de una persona), hocico *m* (de un animal) **2 blow one's** ~ : sonarse las narices — ~ *vi* **nosed; nosing** *or* ~ **around** : meter las narices — **nosebleed** *n* : hemorragia *f* nasal — **nosedive** *n* : descenso *m* en picada

nostalgia *n* : nostalgia *f* — **nostalgic** *adj* : nostálgico

nostril *n* : ventana *f* de la nariz

nosy *or* **nosey** *adj* **nosier; -est** : entrometido

not *adv* **1** : no **2 he's** ~ **tired** : no esta cansado **3 I hope** ~ : espero que no **4** ~ **... anything** : no...nada

notable *adj* : notable — ~ *n* : personaje *m* — **notably** *adv* : notablemente

notary public *n, pl* **notaries public** *or* **notary publics** : notario *m*, -ria *f*

notation *n* : anotación *f*

notch *n* : muesca *f*, corte *m* — ~ *vt* : hacer un corte en

note *vt* **noted; noting 1** NOTICE : observar, notar **2** RECORD : anotar — ~ *n* **1** : nota *f* **2 of** ~ : destacado **3 take** ~ **of** : prestar atención a **4 take** ~**s** : apuntar — **notebook** *n* : libreta *f*, cuaderno *m* — **noted** *adj*

: renombrado, célebre — **noteworthy** *adj* : notable

nothing *pron* **1** : nada **2 be** ~ **but** : no ser más que **3 for** ~ FREE : gratis — ~ *n* **1** ZERO : zero *m* **2** TRIFLE : nimiedad *f*

notice *n* **1** SIGN : letrero *m*, aviso *m* **2 at a moment's** ~ : sin previo aviso **3 be given one's** ~ : ser despedido **4 take** ~ **of** : prestar atención a — ~ *vt* **-ticed; -ticing** : notar — **noticeable** *adj* : perceptible, evidente

notify *vt* **-fied; -fying** : notificar, avisar — **notification** *n* : notificación *f*, aviso *m*

notion *n* **1** : noción *f*, idea *f* **2** ~**s** *npl* : artículos *mpl* de mercería

notorious *adj* : de mala fama — **notoriety** *n* : mala fama *f*, notoriedad *f*

notwithstanding *prep* : a pesar de, no obstante — ~ *adv* : sin embargo — ~ *conj* : a pesar de que

nougat *n* : turrón *m*

nought → **naught**

noun *n* : nombre *m*, sustantivo *m*

nourish *vt* : nutrir — **nourishing** *adj* : nutritivo — **nourishment** *n* : alimento *m*

novel *adj* : original, novedoso — ~ *n* : novela *f* — **novelist** *n* : novelista *mf* — **novelty** *n, pl* **-ties** : novedad *f*

November *n* : noviembre *m*

novice *n* : novato *m*, -ta *f*; principiante *mf*

now *adv* **1** : ahora **2** THEN : entonces **3 from** ~ **on** : de ahora en adelante **4** ~ **and then** : de vez en cuando **5 right** ~ : ahora mismo — ~ *conj or* ~ **that** : ahora que, ya que — ~ *n* **1 a year from** ~ : dentro de un año **2 by** ~ : ya **3 until** ~ : hasta ahora — **nowadays** *adv* : hoy en día

nowhere *adv* **1** (*indicating location*) : por ninguna parte, por ningún lado **2** (*indicating motion*) : a ninguna parte, a ningún lado **3 I'm** ~ **near finished** : aún me falta mucho para terminar **4 it's** ~ **near here** : queda bastante lejos de aquí — ~ *n* : ninguna parte *f*

nozzle *n* : boca *f* (de una manguera, etc.)

nuance *n* : matiz *m*

nucleus *n, pl* **-clei** : núcleo *m* — **nuclear** *adj* : nuclear

nude *adj* **nuder; nudest** : desnudo — ~ *n* : desnudo *m*

nudge *vt* **nudged; nudging** : dar un codazo a — ~ *n* : toque *m* (con el codo)

nudity *n* : desnudez *f*

nugget *n* : pepita *f* (de oro, etc.)

nuisance *n* **1** ANNOYANCE : fastidio *m*, molestia *f* **2** PEST : pesado *m*, -da *f fam*

nuke[1] *n* : arma *m* nuclear

nuke[2] *vt* **nuked nuking 1** : atacar con armas nucleares **2** : cocinar en el microondas

null *adj* ~ **and void** : nulo y sin efecto

numb *adj* **1** : entumecido, dormido **2** ~ **with fear** : paralizado de miedo — ~ *vt* : entumecer, adormecer

number *n* **1** : número *m* **2 a** ~ **of** : varios — ~ *vt* **1** : numerar **2** INCLUDE : contar, incluir **3** TOTAL : ascender a

numeral *n* : número *m* — **numeric** *or* **numerical** *adj* : numérico — **numerous** *adj* : numeroso

nun *n* : monja *f*

nuptial *adj* : nupcial

nurse *n* **1** : enfermero *m*, -ra *f* **2** → **nursemaid** — ~ *vt* **nursed; nursing 1** : cuidar (de), atender **2** SUCKLE : amamantar — **nursemaid** *n* : niñera *f* — **nursery** *n, pl* **-eries 1** : cuarto *m* de los niños **2** *or* **day** ~ : guardería *f* **3** : vivero *m* (de plantas) — **nursing home** *n* : asilo *m* de ancianos

nurture *vt* **-tured; -turing 1** NOURISH : nu-trir **2** EDUCATE : criar, educar **3** FOSTER : alimentar

nut *n* **1** : nuez *f* **2** LUNATIC : loco *m*, -ca *f* **3** ENTHUSIAST : fanático *m*, -ca *f* **4** ~ **s and bolts** : tuercas y tornillos — **nutcracker** *n* : cascanueces *m*

nutmeg *n* : nuez *f* moscada

nutrient *n* : nutriente *m*

nutrition *n* : nutrición *f* — **nutritional** *adj* : nutritivo — **nutritious** *adj* : nutritivo

nuts *adj* : loco

nutshell *n* **1** : cáscara *f* de nuez **2 in a** ~ : en pocas palabras

nutty *adj* **-tier; -tiest** : loco

nuzzle *v* **-zled; -zling** *vi* : acurrucarse — *vt* : acariciar con el hocico

nylon *n* **1** : nilón *m* **2** ~ **s** *npl* : medias *fpl* de nilón

nymph *n* : ninfa *f*

O

o'clock *adv* **1 at 6** ~ : a las seis **2 it's one** ~ : es la una **3 it's ten** ~ : son las diez

o *n, pl* **o's** *or* **os 1** : o *f*, decimoquinta letra del alfabeto inglés **2** ZERO : cero *m*

O → **oh**

oaf *n* : zoquete *m*

oak *n, pl* **oaks** *or* **oak** : roble *m*

oar *n* : remo *m*

oasis *n, pl* **oases** : oasis *m*

oath *n, pl* **oaths 1** : juramento *m* **2** SWEAR-WORD : palabrota *f*

oats *npl* : avena *f* — **oatmeal** *n* : harina *f* de avena

obedient *adj* : obediente — **obedience** *n* : obediencia *f*

obese *adj* : obeso — **obesity** *n* : obesidad *f*

obey *v* **obeyed; obeying** : obedecer

obituary *n, pl* **-aries** : obituario *m*

object *n* **1** : objeto *m* **2** AIM : objetivo *m* **3** : complemento *m* (en gramática) — ~ *vt* : objetar — *vi* ~ **to** : oponerse a — **objection** *n* : objeción *f* — **objectionable** *adj* : desagradable — **objective** *adj* : objetivo — ~ *n* : objetivo *m*

oblige *vt* **obliged; obliging 1** : obligar **2 be much** ~ **d** : estar muy agradecido **3** ~ **s.o.** : hacer un favor a algn — **obligation** *n* : obligación *f* — **obligatory** *adj* : obligatorio — **obliging** *adj* : atento, servicial

oblique *adj* **1** SLANTING : oblicuo **2** INDI-RECT : indirecto

obliterate *vt* **-ated; -ating 1** ERASE : borrar **2** DESTROY : arrasar

oblivion *n* : olvido *m* — **oblivious** *adj* : inconsciente

oblong *adj* : oblongo — ~ *n* : rectángulo *m*

obnoxious *adj* : odioso

oboe *n* : oboe *m*

obscene *adj* : obsceno — **obscenity** *n, pl* **-ties** : obscenidad *f*

obscurity *n, pl* **-ties** : oscuridad *f* — **obscure** *adj* : oscuro — ~ *vt* **-scured; -scuring 1** DARKEN : oscurecer **2** HIDE : ocultar

observe *v* **-served; -serving** *vt* : observar — *vi* WATCH : mirar — **observance** *n* **1** : observancia *f* **2 religious** ~ **s** : prácticas *fpl* religiosas — **observant** *adj* : observador — **observation** *n* : observación *f* — **observatory** *n, pl* **-ries** : observatorio *m*

obsess *vt* : obsesionar — **obsession** *n* : obsesión *f* — **obsessive** *adj* : obsesivo

obsolete *adj* : obsoleto, desusado

obstacle *n* : obstáculo *m*

obstetrics *n* : obstetricia *f*

obstinate *adj* : obstinado

obstruct *vt* **1** BLOCK : obstruir **2** HINDER : obstaculizar — **obstruction** *n* : obstrucción *f*

obtain *vt* : obtener, conseguir — **obtainable** *adj* : asequible

obtrusive *adj* : entrometido (dícese de las

personas), demasiado prominente (dícese de las cosas)
obtuse *adj* : obtuso
obvious *adj* : obvio, evidente — **obviously** *adv* **1** CLEARLY : obviamente **2** OF COURSE : claro, por supuesto

occasion *n* **1** : ocasión *f* **2 on ~** : de vez en cuando — **~** *vt* : ocasionar — **occasional** *adj* : poco frecuente, ocasional — **occasionally** *adv* : de vez en cuando
occult *adj* : oculto
occupy *vt* -**pied; -pying 1** : ocupar **2 ~ oneself** : entretenerse — **occupancy** *n, pl* -**cies** : ocupación *f* — **occupant** *n* : ocupante *mf* — **occupation** *n* : ocupación *f* — **occupational** *adj* : profesional
occur *vi* **occurred; occurring 1** : ocurrir **2** APPEAR : encontrarse **3 ~ to s.o.** : ocurrirse a algn — **occurrence** *n* **1** EVENT : acontecimiento *m*, suceso *m* **2** INCIDENCE : incidencia *f*
ocean *n* : océano *m*
ocher *or* ochre *n* : ocre *m*
octagon *n* : octágono *m* — **octagonal** *adj* : octagonal
octave *n* : octava *f*
October *n* : octubre *m*
octopus *n, pl* -**puses** *or* -**pi** : pulpo *m*
oculist *n* : oculista *mf*
odd *adj* **1** STRANGE : extraño, raro **2** : sin pareja (dícese de un calcetín, etc.) **3 forty ~ years** : cuarenta y tantos años **4 ~ jobs** : algunos trabajos *mpl* **5 ~ number** : número *m* impar — **oddity** *n, pl* -**ties** : rareza *f* — **oddly** *adv* : de manera extraña — **odds** *npl* **1** CHANCES : probabilidades *fpl* **2 at ~** : en desacuerdo **3 five to one ~** : cinco contra uno (en apuestas) — **odds and ends** *npl* : cosas *fpl* sueltas
ode *n* : oda *f*
odious *adj* : odioso
odor *or Brit* odour *n* : olor *m* — **odorless** *or Brit* **odourless** *adj* : inodoro
of *prep* **1** : de **2 five minutes ~ ten** : las diez menos cinco **3 the eighth ~ April** : el ocho de abril
off *adv* **1 be ~** LEAVE : irse **2 cut ~** : cortar **3 day ~** : día *m* de descanso **4 fall ~** : caerse **5 doze ~** : dormirse **6 far ~** : lejos **7 ~ and on** : de vez en cuando **8 shut ~** : apagar **9 ten miles ~** : a diez millas de aquí — **~** *prep* **1** : de **2 be ~ duty** : estar libre **3 ~ center** : descentrado — **~** *adj* **1** CANCELED : cancelado **2** OUT : apagado **3 an ~ chance** : una posibilidad remota
offend *vt* : ofender — **offender** *n* : delincuente *mf* — **offense** *or* **offence** *n* **1** AFFRONT : afrenta *f* **2** ASSAULT : ataque *m* **3** : ofensiva *f* (en deportes) **4** CRIME : delito

m **5 take ~** : ofenderse — **offensive** *adj* : ofensivo — **~** *n* : ofensiva *f*
offer *vt* : ofrecer — **~** *n* : oferta *f* — **offering** *n* : ofrenda *f*
offhand *adv* : de improviso, en este momento — **~** *adj* : improvisado
office *n* **1** : oficina *f* **2** POSITION : cargo *m* **3 run for ~** : presentarse como candidato — **officer** *n* **1** : oficial *mf* **2** *or* **police ~** : agente *mf* (de policía) — **official** *n* : funcionario *m*, -ria *f* — **~** *adj* : oficial
offing *n* **in the ~** : en perspectiva
offset *vt* -**set; -setting** : compensar
offshore *adv* : a una distancia de la costa
offspring *ns & pl* : prole *f*, progenie *f*
often *adv* **1** : muchas veces, a menudo, con frecuencia **2 every so ~** : de vez en cuando
ogle *vt* **ogled; ogling** : comerse con los ojos
ogre *n* : ogro *m*
oh *interj* **1** : ¡oh!, ¡ah! **2 ~ no!** : ¡ay no! **3 ~ really?** : ¿de veras?
oil *n* **1** : aceite *m* **2** PETROLEUM : petróleo *m* **3** *or* **~ painting** : óleo *m* — **~** *vt* : lubricar — **oilskin** *n* : hule *m* — **oily** *adj* **oilier; -est** : aceitoso, grasiento
ointment *n* : ungüento *m*, pomada *f*
OK *or* **okay** *adv* **1** : muy bien **2 ~!** : ¡de acuerdo!, ¡bueno! — **~** *adj* **1** ALL RIGHT : bien **2 it's ~ with me** : por mí no hay problema — **~** *n* : visto *m* bueno — **~** *vt* **OK'd** *or* **okayed; OK'ing** *or* **okaying** : dar el visto bueno a
okra *n* : quingombó *m*
old *adj* **1** : viejo **2** FORMER : antiguo **3 any ~** : cualquier **4 be ten years ~** : tener diez años (de edad) **5 ~ age** : vejez *f* **6 ~ man** : anciano *m* **7 ~ woman** : anciana *f* — **~ in the ~** : los viejos, los ancianos — **old-fashioned** *adj* : anticuado
olive *n* **1** : aceituna *f* (fruta) **2** *or* **~ green** : verde *m* oliva
Olympic *adj* : olímpico — **Olympics** *npl* **the ~** : las Olimpiadas, las Olimpíadas
omelet *or* **omelette** *n* : omelette *mf Lat*, tortilla *f* francesa *Spain*
omen *n* : agüero *m* — **ominous** *adj* : ominoso, de mal agüero
omit *vt* **omitted; omitting** : omitir — **omission** *n* : omisión *f*
omnipotent *adj* : omnipotente
on *prep* **1** : en **2** ABOUT : sobre **3 ~ foot** : a pie **4 ~ Monday** : el lunes **5 ~ the right** : a la derecha **6 ~ vacation** : de vacaciones **7 talk ~ the phone** : hablar por teléfono — **~** *adv* **1 and so ~** : etcétera **2 from that moment ~** : a partir de ese momento **3 keep ~** : seguir **4 later ~** : más tarde **5 ~ and ~** : sin parar **6 put ~** : ponerse (ropa), poner (música,

etc.) **7 turn ~** : encender (una luz, etc.), abrir (una llave) — **~** *adj* **1** : encendido (dícese de luces, etc.), abierto (dícese de llaves) **2 be ~ to** : estar enterado de
once *adv* **1** : una vez **2** FORMERLY : antes — **~** *n* **1 at ~** TOGETHER : al mismo tiempo **2 at ~** IMMEDIATELY : inmediatamente — **~** *conj* : una vez que
oncoming *adj* : que viene
one *adj* **1** : un, uno **2** ONLY : único **3** *or* **~ and the same** : el mismo — **~** *n* **1** : uno *m* (número) **2 ~ by ~** : uno a uno — **~** *pron* **1** : uno, una **2 ~ another** : el uno al otro **3 ~ never knows** : nunca se sabe **4 that ~** : aquél, aquella **5 which ~?** : ¿cuál? — **oneself** *pron* **1** (*used reflexively*) : se **2** (*used after prepositions*) : sí mismo, sí misma **3** (*used emphatically*) : uno mismo, una misma **4 by ~** : solo — **one–sided** *adj* **1** UNEQUAL : desigual **2** BIASED : parcial — **one–way** *adj* **1** : de sentido único (dícese de una calle) **2 ~ ticket** : boleto *m* de ida
ongoing *adj* : en curso, corriente
onion *n* : cebolla *f*
only *adj* : único — **~** *adv* **1** : sólo, solamente **2 if ~** : ojalá, por lo menos — **~** *conj* BUT : pero
onset *n* : comienzo *m*, llegada *f*
onslaught *n* : ataque *m*, arremetida *f*
onto *prep* : sobre
onus *n* : responsabilidad *f*
onward *adv* & *adj* : hacia adelante
onyx *n* : ónix *m*
ooze *v* **oozed; oozing** : rezumar
opal *n* : ópalo *m*
opaque *adj* : opaco
open *adj* **1** : abierto **2** AVAILABLE : vacante, libre **3 an ~ question** : una cuestión pendiente — **~** *vt* : abrir — *vi* **1** : abrirse **2** BEGIN : comenzar — **~** *n* **in the ~** **1** OUTDOORS : al aire libre **2** KNOWN : sacado a la luz — **open–air** *adj* : al aire libre — **opener** *n* **1** : abridor *m* **2** *or* **bottle ~** : abrebotellas *m* **3** *or* **can ~** : abrelatas *m* — **opening** *n* **1** : abertura *f* **2** BEGINNING : comienzo *m*, apertura *f* **3** OPPORTUNITY : oportunidad *f* — **openly** *adv* : abiertamente
opera *n* : ópera *f*
operate *v* **-ated; -ating** *vi* **1** FUNCTION : funcionar **2 ~ on s.o.** : operar a algn — *vt* **1** : hacer funcionar (una máquina) **2** MANAGE : dirigir, manejar — **operation** *n* **1** : operación *f* **2** FUNCTIONING : funcionamiento *m* — **operational** *adj* : operacional — **operative** *adj* : en vigor — **operator** *n* **1** : operador *m*, -dora *f* **2** *or* **machine ~** : operario *m*, -ria *f*

opinion *n* : opinión *f* — **opinionated** *adj* : dogmático
opium *n* : opio *m*
opossum *n* : zarigüeya *f*, oposum *m*
opponent *n* : adversario *m*, -ria *f*; contrincante *mf* (en deportes)
opportunity *n, pl* **-ties** : oportunidad *f* — **opportune** *adj* : oportuno — **opportunist** *n* : oportunista *mf*
oppose *vt* **-posed; -posing** : oponerse a — **opposed** *adj* **~ to** : en contra de
opposite *adj* **1** FACING : de enfrente **2** CONTRARY : opuesto — **~** *n* **the ~** : lo contrario, lo opuesto — **~** *adv* : enfrente — **~** *prep* : enfrente de, frente a — **opposition** *n* **1** : oposición *f* **2 in ~ to** : en contra de
oppress *vt* : oprimir — **oppression** *n* : opresión *f* — **oppressive** *adj* **1** : opresivo **2** STIFLING : agobiante — **oppressor** *n* : opresor *m*, -sora *f*
opt *vi* **~ for** : optar por
optic *or* **optical** *adj* : óptico — **optician** *n* : óptico *m*, -ca *f*
optimism *n* : optimismo *m* — **optimist** *n* : optimista *mf* — **optimistic** *adj* : optimista
optimum *n, pl* **-ma** : lo óptimo, lo ideal
option *n* **1** : opción *f* **2 have no ~** : no tener más remedio — **optional** *adj* : facultativo, opcional
opulence *n* : opulencia *f* — **opulent** *adj* : opulento
or *conj* **1** (*indicating an alternative*) : o (u *before* o- *or* ho-) **2** (*following a negative*) : ni **3 ~ else** : si no
oracle *n* : oráculo *m*
oral *adj* : oral
orange *n* **1** : naranja *f* (fruta) **2** : naranja *m* (color)
orator *n* : orador *m*, -dora *f*
orbit *n* : órbita *f* — **~** *vt* : girar alrededor de — *vi* : orbitar
orchard *n* : huerto *m*
orchestra *n* : orquesta *f*
orchid *n* : orquídea *f*
ordain *vt* **1** : ordenar (un sacerdote, etc.) **2** DECREE : decretar
ordeal *n* : prueba *f* dura
order *vt* **1** : ordenar **2** : pedir (mercancías, etc.) — *vi* : hacer un pedido — **~** *n* **1** ARRANGEMENT : orden *m* **2** COMMAND : orden *f* **3** REQUEST : pedido *m* **4** : orden *f* (religiosa) **5 in ~ that** : para que **6 in ~ to** : para **7 out of ~** : averiado, descompuesto *Lat* — **orderly** *adj* : ordenado — **~** *n, pl* **-lies** **1** : ordenanza *m* (en el ejército) **2** : camillero *m* (en un hospital)
ordinary *adj* **1** : normal, corriente **2** MEDIOCRE : ordinario — **ordinarily** *adv* : generalmente

ore *n* : mena *f*
oregano *n* : orégano *m*
organ *n* : órgano *m* — **organic** *adj* : orgánico — **organism** *n* : organismo *m* — **organist** *n* : organista *mf* — **organize** *vt* **-nized; -nizing** : organizar — **organization** *n* : organización *f* — **organizer** *n* : organizador *m*, -dora *f*
orgasm *n* : orgasmo *m*
orgy *n, pl* **-gies** : orgía *f*
Orient *n* the **~** : el Oriente — **orient** *vt* : orientar — **oriental** *adj* : del Oriente, oriental — **orientation** *n* : orientación *f*
orifice *n* : orificio *m*
origin *n* : origen *m* — **original** *n* : original *m* — **~** *adj* : original — **originality** *n* : originalidad *f* — **originally** *adv* : originariamente — **originate** *v* **-nated; -nating** *vt* : originar — *vi* **1** : originarse **2 ~ from** : provenir de — **originator** *n* : creador *m*, -dora *f*
ornament *n* : adorno *m* — **~** *vt* : adornar — **ornamental** *adj* : ornamental, de adorno — **ornate** *adj* : elaborado, adornado
ornithology *n, pl* **-gies** : ornitología *f*
orphan *n* : huérfano *m*, -na *f* — **~** *vt* : dejar huérfano — **orphanage** *n* : orfelinato *m*, orfanato *m*
orthodox *adj* : ortodoxo — **orthodoxy** *n, pl* **-doxies** : ortodoxia *f*
orthopedic *adj* : ortopédico
oscillation *n* : oscilación *f* — **oscillate** *vi* **-lated; -lating** : oscilar
ostensible *adj* : aparente, ostensible
ostentation *n* : ostentación *f* — **ostentatious** *adj* : ostentoso
osteopath *n* : osteópata *f*
ostracism *n* : ostracismo *m* — **ostracize** *vt* **-cized; -cizing** : aislar
ostrich *n* : avestruz *m*
other *adj* **1** : otro **2 every ~ day** : cada dos días **3 on the ~ hand** : por otra parte, por otro lado — **~** *pron* **1** : otro, otra **2 the ~s** : los otros, las otras, los demás, las demás — **other than** *prep* : aparte de, fuera de — **otherwise** *adv* **1** : eso aparte, por lo demás **2** DIFFERENTLY : de otro modo **3** OR ELSE : si no
otter *n* : nutria *f*
ought *v aux* **1** : deber **2 you ~ to have done it** : deberías haberlo hecho
ounce *n* : onza *f*
our *adj* : nuestro — **ours** *pron* **1** : (el) nuestro, (la) nuestra, (los) nuestros, (las) nuestras **2 a friend of ~** : un amigo nuestro — **ourselves** *pron* **1** (*used reflexively*) : nos **2** (*used after prepositions*) : nosotros, nosotras **3** (*used for emphasis*) : nosotros mismos, nosotras mismas
oust *vt* : desbancar

out of *prep* **1** FROM : de **2** THROUGH : por **3** WITHOUT : sin **4 ~ curiosity** : por curiosidad **5 ~ control** : fuera de control **6 one ~ four** : uno de cada cuatro — **out-of-date** *adj* : anticuado — **out-of-door** *or* **out-of-doors** *adj* → **outdoor**
out *adv* **1** OUTSIDE : fuera, afuera **2 cry ~** : gritar **3 eat ~** : comer afuera **4 go ~** : salir **5 look ~** : mirar para afuera **6 run ~ of** : agotar **7 turn ~** : apagar (una luz) **8 take ~** REMOVE : sacar — **~** *prep* → **out of** — **~** *adj* **1** ABSENT : ausente **2** UNFASHIONABLE : fuera de moda **3** EXTINGUISHED : apagado **4 the sun is ~** : hace sol
outboard motor *n* : motor *m* fuera de borde
outbreak *n* : brote *m* (de una enfermedad), comienzo *m* (de guerra)
outburst *n* : arranque *m*, arrebato *m*
outcast *n* : paria *mf*
outcome *n* : resultado *m*
outcry *n, pl* **-cries** : protesta *f*
outdated *adj* : anticuado
outdo *vt* **-did; -done; -doing; -does** : superar
outdoor *adj* : al aire libre — **outdoors** *adv* : al aire libre
outer *adj* : exterior — **outer space** *n* : espacio *m* exterior
outfit *n* **1** EQUIPMENT : equipo *m* **2** CLOTHES : conjunto *m* — **~** *vt* **-fitted; -fitting** EQUIP : equipar
outgoing *adj* **1** SOCIABLE : extrovertido **2 ~ mail** : correo *m* (para enviar) **3 ~ president** : presidente *m*, -ta *f* saliente
outgrow *vt* **-grew; -grown; -growing** : crecer más que
outing *n* : excursión *f*
outlandish *adj* : estrafalario
outlast *vt* : durar más que
outlaw *n* : forajido *m*, -da *f* — **~** *vt* : declarar ilegal
outlay *n* : desembolso *m*
outlet *n* **1** EXIT : salida *f* **2** RELEASE : desahogo *m* **3** *or* **electrical ~** : toma *f* de corriente **4** *or* **retail ~** : tienda *f* al por menor
outline *n* **1** CONTOUR : contorno *m* **2** SKETCH : bosquejo *m*, boceto *m* **3** SUMMARY : esquema *m* — **~** *vt* **-lined; -lining** **1** SKETCH : bosquejar **2** EXPLAIN : delinear, esbozar
outlive *vt* **-lived; -living** : sobrevivir a
outlook *n* **1** PROSPECTS : perspectivas *fpl* **2** VIEWPOINT : punto *m* de vista
outlying *adj* : alejado, distante
outmoded *adj* : pasado de moda, anticuado
outnumber *vt* : superar en número a
outpatient *n* : paciente *m* externo
outpost *n* : puesto *m* avanzado

output *n* **1** : producción *f*, rendimiento *m* **2** : salida *f* (informática) — ~ *vt* **-putted** *or* **-put; -putting** : producir

outrage *n* **1** : atrocidad *f*, escándalo *m* **2** ANGER : ira *f*, indignación *f* — ~ *vt* **-raged; -raging** : ultrajar — **outrageous** *adj* : escandaloso

outright *adv* **1** COMPLETELY : por completo **2** INSTANTLY : en el acto — ~ *adj* : completo, absoluto

outset *n* : comienzo *m*, principio *m*

outside *n* **1** : exterior *m* **2 from the** ~ : desde fuera, desde afuera — ~ *adj* **1** : exterior, externo **2 an** ~ **chance** : una posibilidad remota — ~ *adv* : fuera, afuera — ~ *prep or* ~ **of** : fuera de — **outsider** *n* : forastero *m*, -ra *f*

outskirts *npl* : afueras *fpl*, alrededores *mpl*

outspoken *adj* : franco, directo

outstanding *adj* **1** UNPAID : pendiente **2** EXCELLENT : excepcional

outstretched *adj* : extendido

outstrip *vt* **-stripped** *or* **-stript; -stripping** : aventajar

outward *adj* **1** : hacia afuera **2** EXTERNAL : externo, external — ~ *or* **outwards** *adv* : hacia afuera — **outwardly** *adv* apparently : aparentemente

outweigh *vt* : pesar más que

outwit *vt* **-witted; -witting** : ser más listo que

oval *n* : óvalo *m* — ~ *adj* : ovalado

ovary *n*, *pl* **-ries** : ovario *m*

ovation *n* : ovación *f*

oven *n* : horno *m*

over *adv* **1** ABOVE : por encima **2** AGAIN : otra vez, de nuevo **3** MORE : más **4 all** ~ : por todas partes **5 ask** ~ : invitar **6 cross** ~ : cruzar **7 fall** ~ : caerse **8** ~ **and** ~ : una y otra vez **9** ~ **here** : aquí **10** ~ **there** : allí — ~ *prep* **1** ABOVE, UPON : encima de, sobre **2** ACROSS : por encima de, sobre **3** DURING : en, durante **4 fight** ~ : pelearse por **5** ~ **$5** : más de $5 **6** ~ **the phone** : por teléfono — ~ *adj* : terminado, acabado

overall *adv* GENERALLY : en general — *adj* : total, en conjunto — **overalls** *npl* : overol *m* Lat

overbearing *adj* : dominante, imperioso

overboard *adv* **fall** ~ : caer al agua

overburden *vt* : sobrecargar

overcast *adj* : nublado

overcharge *vt* **-charged; -charging** : cobrar demasiado

overcoat *n* : abrigo *m*

overcome *v* **-came; -come; -coming** *vt* **1** CONQUER : vencer **2** OVERWHELM : agobiar — *vi* : vencer

overcook *vt* : cocer demasiado

overcrowded *adj* : abarrotado de gente

overdo *vt* **-did; -done; -doing; -does 1** : hacer demasiado **2** EXAGGERATE : exagerar **3** → **overcook**

overdose *n* : sobredosis *f*

overdraw *vt* **-drew; -drawn; -drawing** : girar en descubierto — **overdraft** *n* : sobregiro *m*, descubierto *m*

overdue *adj* : fuera de plazo (dícese de pagos, libros, etc.)

overeat *vi* **-ate; -eaten; -eating** : comer demasiado

overestimate *vt* **-mated; -mating** : sobreestimar

overflow *vt* : desbordar — *vi* : desbordarse — ~ *n* : desbordamiento *m* (de un río)

overgrown *adj* : cubierto (de malas hierbas, etc.)

overhand *adv* : por encima de la cabeza

overhang *v* **-hung; -hanging** : sobresalir

overhaul *vt* : revisar (un motor, etc.)

overhead *adv* : por encima — ~ *adj* : de arriba — ~ *n* : gastos *mpl* generales

overhear *vt* **-heard; -hearing** : oír por casualidad

overheat *vt* : calentar demasiado — *vi* : recalentarse

overjoyed *adj* : encantado

overland *adv* & *adj* : por tierra

overlap *v* **-lapped; -lapping** *vt* : traslapar — *vi* : traslaparse

overload *vt* : sobrecargar

overlook *vt* **1** : dar a (un jardín, el mar, etc.) **2** MISS : pasar por alto

overly *adv* : demasiado

overnight *adv* **1** : por la noche **2** SUDDENLY : de la noche a la mañana — ~ *adj* **1** : de noche **2** SUDDEN : repentino

overpass *n* : paso *m* elevado

overpopulated *adj* : superpoblado

overpower *vt* **1** SUBDUE : dominar **2** OVERWHELM : agobiar, abrumar

overrated *adj* : sobreestimado

override *vt* **-rode; -ridden; -riding 1** : predominar sobre **2** : anular (una decisión, etc.)

overrule *vt* **-ruled; -ruling** : anular (una decisión), rechazar (una protesta)

overrun *vt* **-ran; -running 1** INVADE : invadir **2** EXCEED : exceder

overseas *adv* : en el extranjero — ~ *adj* : extranjero, exterior

oversee *vt* **-saw; -seen; -seeing** : supervisar

overshadow *vt* : eclipsar

oversight *n* : descuido *m*

oversleep *vi* **-slept; -sleeping** : quedarse dormido

overstep *vt* **-stepped; -stepping** : sobrepasar

overt *adj* : manifiesto

overtake *vt* **-took; -taken; -taking 1** PASS : adelantar **2** SURPASS : superar

overthrow *vt* **-threw; -thrown; -throwing** : derrocar

overtime *n* **1** : horas *fpl* extras (de trabajo) **2** : prórroga *f* (en deportes)

overtone *n* SUGGESTION : tinte *m*, insinuación *f*

overture *n* : obertura *f* (en música)

overturn *vt* **1** : dar la vuelta a **2** NULLIFY : anular — *vi* : volcar

overweight *adj* : demasiado gordo

overwhelm *vt* **1** : abrumar, agobiar **2** : aplastar (a un enemigo) — **overwhelming** *adj* : abrumador, apabullante

overwork *vt* : hacer trabajar demasiado — *vi* : trabajar demasiado

overwrought *adj* : alterado, sobreexitado

owe *vt* **owed; owing** : deber — **owing to** *prep* : debido a

owl *n* : búho *m*

own *adj* : propio — ~ *vt* : poseer, tener — *vi* ~ **up** : confesar — ~ *pron* **1** my (**your, his/her/their, our**) ~ : el mío, la mía; el tuyo, la tuya; el suyo, la suya; el nuestro, la nuestra **2 be on one's** ~ : estar solo **3 to each his** ~ : cada uno a lo suyo — **owner** *n* : propietario *m*, **-ria** *f* — **ownership** *n* : propiedad *f*

ox *n*, *pl* **oxen** : buey *m*

oxygen *n* : oxígeno *m*

oyster *n* : ostra *f*

ozone *n* : ozono *m*

P

p *n*, *pl* **p's** *or* **ps** : p *f*, decimosexta letra del alfabeto inglés

pace *n* **1** STEP : paso *m* **2** RATE : ritmo *m* **3 keep** ~ **with** : andar al mismo paso que — ~ *vi* **paced; pacing** *or* ~ **up and down** : caminar de arriba para abajo

pacify *vt* **-fied; -fying** : apaciguar — **pacifier** *n* : chupete *m* — **pacifist** *n* : pacifista *mf*

pack *n* **1** BUNDLE : fardo *m* **2** BACKPACK : mochila *f* **3** PACKAGE : paquete *m* **4** : baraja *f* (de naipes) **5** : manada *f* (de lobos, etc.), jauría *f* (de perros) — ~ *vt* **1** PACKAGE : empaquetar **2** FILL : llenar **3** : hacer (una maleta) — *vi* : hacer las maletas — **package** *vt* **-aged; -aging** : empaquetar — ~ *n* : paquete *m* — **packet** *n* : paquete *m*

pact *n* : pacto *m*, acuerdo *m*

pad *n* **1** CUSHION : almohadilla *f* **2** TABLET : bloc *m* (de papel) **3** *or* **ink** ~ : tampón *m* **4 launching** ~ : plataforma *f* (de lanzamiento) — ~ *vt* **padded; padding** : rellenar — **padding** *n* **1** : relleno *m* **2** : paja *f* (en un discurso, etc.)

paddle *n* **1** : canalete *m* (de una canoa) **2** : pala *f*, paleta *f* (en deportes) — ~ *vt* **-dled; -dling** : hacer avanzar (una canoa) con canalete

padlock *n* : candado *m* — ~ *vt* : cerrar con candado

paella *n* : paella *f*

pagan *n* : pagano *m*, **-na** *f* — ~ *adj* : pagano

page[1] *vt* **paged; paging** : llamar por altavoz

page[2] *n* : página *f* (de un libro, etc.)

pageant *n* : espectáculo *m* — **pageantry** *n* : pompa *f*, boato *m*

paid → **pay**

pail *n* : cubo *m* Spain, cubeta *f* Lat

pain *n* **1** : dolor *m* **2** : pena *f* (mental) **3** ~**s** *npl* EFFORT : esfuerzos *mpl* — ~ *vt* : doler — **painful** *adj* : doloroso — **painkiller** *n* : analgésico *m* — **painless** *adj* : indoloro, sin dolor — **painstaking** *adj* : meticuloso, esmerado

paint *v* : pintar — ~ *n* : pintura *f* — **paintbrush** *n* : pincel *m* (de un artista), brocha *f* (para pintar casas, etc.) — **painter** *n* : pintor *m*, **-tora** *f* — **painting** *n* : pintura *f*

pair *n* **1** : par *m* **2** COUPLE : pareja *f* — ~ *vt* : emparejar

pajamas *npl* : pijama *m*, piyama *mf* Lat

Pakistani *adj* : paquistaní

pal *n* : amigo *m*, **-ga** *f*

palace *n* : palacio *m*

palate *n* : paladar *m* — **palatable** *adj* : sabroso

pale *adj* **paler; palest 1** PALLID : pálido **2** : claro (dícese de los colores, etc.) — ~ *vi* **paled; paling** : palidecer — **paleness** *n* : palidez *f*

Palestinian *adj* : palestino

palette *n* : paleta *f*

pallbearer *n* : portador *m*, **-dora** *f* del féretro

pallid *adj* : pálido — **pallor** *n* : palidez *f*

palm[1] *n* : palma *f* (de la mano)

palm[2] *or* ~ **tree** : palmera *f* — **Palm** Sunday *n* : Domingo *m* de Ramos

palpitate *vi* **-tated; -tating** : palpitar — **palpitation** *n* : palpitación *f*
paltry *adj* **-trier; -est** : mísero, mezquino
pamper *vt* : mimar
pamphlet *n* : panfleto *m*, folleto *m*
pan *n* **1** SAUCEPAN : cacerola *f* **2** FRYING PAN : sartén *mf* — *vt* **panned; panning** CRITICIZE : poner por los suelos
pancake *n* : crepe *mf*, panqueque *m Lat*
panda *n* : panda *mf*
pandemonium *n* : pandemonio *m*
pander *vi* **~ to** : complacer a
pane *n* : cristal *m*, vidrio *m*
panel *n* **1** : panel *m* **2** GROUP : jurado *m* **3** *or* **instrument ~** : tablero *m* (de instrumentos) — **~** *vt* **-eled** *or* **-elled; -eling** *or* **-elling** : adornar con paneles — **paneling** *n* : paneles *mpl*
pang *n* : punzada *f*
panic *n* : pánico *m* — **~** *v* **-icked; -icking** *vt* : llenar del pánico — *vi* : ser presa del pánico — **panicky** *adj* : presa de pánico
panorama *n* : panorama *m* — **panoramic** *adj* : panorámico
pansy *n, pl* **-sies** : pensamiento *m*
pant *vi* : jadear, resoplar
panther *n* : pantera *f*
panties *npl* : bragas *fpl Spain*, calzones *mpl Lat*
pantomime *n* : pantomima *f*
pantry *n, pl* **-tries** : despensa *f*
pants *npl* TROUSERS : pantalón *m*, pantalones *mpl*
papa *n* : papá *m fam*
papal *adj* : papal
papaya *n* : papaya *f*
paper *n* **1** : papel *m* **2** DOCUMENT : documento *m* **3** NEWSPAPER : periódico *m* — **~** *vt* WALLPAPER : empapelar — **~** *adj* : de papel — **paperback** *n* : libro *m* en rústica — **paper clip** *n* : clip *m*, sujetapapeles *m* — **paperweight** *n* : pisapapeles *m* — **paperwork** *n* : papeleo *m*
paprika *n* : pimentón *m*
par *n* **1** : par *m* (en golf) **2 below ~** : debajo de la par **3 on a ~ with** : al nivel de
parable *n* : parábola *f*
parachute *n* : paracaídas *m* — **~** *vi* **-chuted; -chuting** : lanzarse en paracaídas
parade *n* **1** : desfile *m* **2** DISPLAY : alarde *m* — **~** *v* **-raded; -rading** *vi* MARCH : desfilar — *vt* DISPLAY : hacer alarde de
paradise *n* : paraíso *m*
paradox *n* : paradoja *f* — **paradoxical** *adj* : paradójico
paraffin *n* : parafina *f*
paragraph *n* : párrafo *m*
Paraguayan *adj* : paraguayo
parakeet *n* : periquito *m*
parallel *adj* : paralelo — **~** *n* **1** : paralelo

m (en geografía) **2** SIMILARITY : paralelismo *m*, semejanza *f* — **~** *vt* : ser paralelo a
paralysis *n, pl* **-yses** : parálisis *f* — **paralyze** *or Brit* **paralise** *vt* **-lyzed** *or Brit* **-lised; -lyzing** *or Brit* **-lising** : paralizar
parameter *n* : parámetro *m*
paramount *adj* **of ~ importance** : de suma importancia
paranoia *n* : paranoia *f* — **paranoid** *adj* : paranoico
paraphernalia *ns & pl* : parafernalia *f*
paraphrase *n* : paráfrasis *f* — **~** *vt* **-phrased; -phrasing** : parafrasear
paraplegic *n* : parapléjico *m*, -ca *f*
parasite *n* : parásito *m*
paratrooper *n* : paracaidista *mf* (militar)
parcel *n* : paquete *m*
parch *vt* : resecar
parchment *n* : pergamino *m*
pardon *n* **1** : perdón *m* **2** REPRIEVE : indulto *m* **3 I beg your ~** : perdone Ud., disculpe Ud. *Lat* — **~** *vt* **1** : perdonar **2** REPRIEVE : indultar (a un delincuente)
parent *n* **1** : madre *f*, padre *m* **2 ~s** *npl* : padres *mpl* — **parental** *adj* : de los padres
parenthesis *n, pl* **-theses** : paréntesis *m*
parish *n* **1** : parroquia *f* — **parishioner** *n* : feligrés *m*, -gresa *f*
parity *n, pl* **-ties** : igualdad *f*
park *n* : parque *m* — **~** *v* : estacionar, parquear *Lat*
parka *n* : parka *f*
parking *n* : estacionamiento *m*
parliament *n* : parlamento *m* — **parliamentary** *adj* : parlamentario
parlor *or Brit* **parlour** *n* : salón *m*
parochial *adj* **1** : parroquial **2** PROVINCIAL : de miras estrechas
parody *n, pl* **-dies** : parodia *f* — **~** *vt* **-died; -dying** : parodiar
parole *n* : libertad *f* condicional
parrot *n* : loro *m*, papagayo *m*
parry *vt* **-ried; -rying 1** : parar (un golpe) **2** EVADE : eludir (una pregunta, etc.)
parsley *n* : perejil *m*
parsnip *n* : chirivía *f*
parson *n* : clérigo *m*
part *n* **1** : parte *f* **2** PIECE : pieza *f* **3** ROLE : papel *m* **4** : raya *f* (del pelo) — **~** *vi* **1** *or* **~ company** : separarse **2 ~ with** : dehacerse de — *vt* SEPARATE : separar
partake *vi* **-took; -taken; -taking ~ in** : participar en
partial *adj* **1** : parcial **2 be ~ to** : ser aficionado a
participate *vi* **-pated; -pating** : participar — **participant** *n* : participante *mf*
participle *n* : participio *m*
particle *n* : partícula *f*

particular *adj* **1** : particular **2** FUSSY : exigente — ~ *n* **1 in** ~ : en particular, en especial **2** ~**s** *npl* DETAILS : detalles *mpl* — **particularly** *adv* : especialmente
partisan *n* : partidario *m*, **-ria** *f*
partition *n* **1** DISTRIBUTION : partición *f* **2** DIVIDER : tabique *m* — ~ *vt* : dividir
partly *adv* : en parte
partner *n* **1** : pareja *f* (en un juego, etc.) **2** *or* **business** ~ : socio *m*, **-cia** *f* — **partnership** *n* : asociación *f*
party *n*, *pl* **-ties 1** : partido *m* (político) **2** GATHERING : fiesta *f* **3** GROUP : grupo *m*
pass *vi* **1** : pasar **2** CEASE : pasarse : aprobar (en un examen) **4** *or* ~ **away** DIE : morir **5** ~ **for** : pasar por **6** ~ **out** FAINT : desmayarse — *vt* **1** : pasar **2** *or* ~ **in front of** : pasar por **3** OVERTAKE : adelantar **4** : aprobar (un examen, una ley, etc.) **5** ~ **down** : transmitir — ~ *n* **1** PERMIT : pase *m*, permiso *m* **2** : pase *m* (en deportes) **3** *or* **mountain** ~ : paso *m* de montaña — **passable** *adj* **1** ADEQUATE : adecuado **2** : transitable (dícese de un camino, etc.) — **passage** *n* **1** : paso *m* **2** CORRIDOR : pasillo *m* (dentro de un edificio), pasaje *m* (entre edificios) **3** VOYAGE : travesía *f* (por el mar) — **passageway** *n* : pasillo *m*, corredor *m*
passenger *n* : pasajero *m*, **-ra** *f*
passerby *n*, *pl* **passersby** : transeúnte *mf*
passion *n* : pasión *f* — **passionate** *adj* : apasionado
passive *adj* : pasivo
Passover *n* : Pascua *f* (en el judaísmo)
passport *n* : pasaporte *m*
password *n* : contraseña *f*
past *adj* **1** : pasado **2** FORMER : anterior **3 the** ~ **few months** : los últimos meses — ~ *prep* **1** IN FRONT OF : por delante de **2** BEYOND : más allá de **3 half** ~ **two** : las dos y media — ~ *n* : pasado *m* — ~ *adv* : por delante
pasta *n* : pasta *f*
paste *n* **1** : pasta *f* **2** GLUE : engrudo *m* — ~ *vt* **pasted; pasting** : pegar
pastel *n* : pastel *m* — ~ *adj* : pastel
pasteurize *vt* **-ized; -izing** : pasteurizar
pastime *n* : pasatiempo *m*
pastor *n* : pastor *m*, **-tora** *f*
pastry *n*, *pl* **-ries** : pasteles *mpl*
pasture *n* : pasto *m*
pasty *adj* **pastier; -est 1** DOUGHY : pastoso **2** PALLID : pálido
pat *n* **1** : palmadita *f* **2 a** ~ **of butter** : una porción de mantequilla — ~ *vt* **patted; patting** : dar palmaditas a — ~ *adv* **have down** ~ : saberse de memoria — ~ *adj* GLIB : fácil
patch *n* **1** : parche *m*, remiendo *m* (para la ropa) **2** SPOT : mancha *f*, trozo *m* **3** PLOT : parcela *f* (de tierra) — ~ *vt* **1** MEND : remendar **2** ~ **up** : arreglar — **patchy** *adj* **patchier; -est 1** : desigual **2** INCOMPLETE : parcial, incompleto
patent *adj* **1** *or* **patented** : patentado **2** OBVIOUS : patente, evidente — ~ *n* : patente *f* — ~ *vt* : patentar
paternal *adj* **1** FATHERLY : paternal **2** ~ **grandmother** : abuela *f* paterna — **paternity** *n* : paternidad *f*
path *n* **1** TRACK, TRAIL : camino *m*, sendero *m* **2** COURSE : trayectoria *f*
pathetic *adj* : patético
pathology *n*, *pl* **-gies** : patología *f*
pathway *n* : camino *m*, sendero *m*
patience *n* : paciencia *f* — **patient** *adj* : paciente — ~ *n* : paciente *mf* — **patiently** *adv* : con paciencia
patio *n*, *pl* **-tios** : patio *m*
patriot *n* : patriota *mf* — **patriotic** *adj* : patriótico
patrol *n* : patrulla *f* — ~ *v* **-trolled; -trolling** : patrullar
patron *n* **1** SPONSOR : patrocinador *m*, **-dora** *f* **2** CUSTOMER : cliente *m*, **-ta** *f* — **patronage** *n* **1** SPONSORSHIP : patrocinio *m* **2** CLIENTELE : clientela *f* — **patronize** *vt* **-ized; -izing 1** : ser cliente de (una tienda, etc.) **2** : tratar (a algn) con condescencia
patter *n* : tamborileo *m* (de la lluvia), correteo *m* (de los pies)
pattern *n* **1** MODEL : modelo *m* **2** DESIGN : diseño *m* **3** STANDARD : pauta *f*, modo *m* **4** : patrón *m* (en costura) — ~ *vt* : basar (en un modelo)
paunch *n* : panza *f*
pause *n* : pausa *f* — ~ *vi* **paused; pausing** : hacer una pausa
pave *vt* **paved; paving** : pavimentar — **pavement** *n* : pavimento *m*
pavilion *n* : pabellón *m*
paw *n* **1** : pata *f* **2** : garra *f* (de un gato) — ~ *vt* : tocar con la pata
pawn[1] *n* : peón *m* (en ajedrez)
pawn[2] *vt* : empeñar — **pawnbroker** *n* : prestamista *mf* — **pawnshop** *n* : casa *f* de empeños
pay *v* **paid; paying** *vt* **1** : pagar **2** ~ **attention** : prestar atención **3** ~ **back** : devolver **4** ~ **one's respects** : presentar uno sus respetos **5** ~ **a visit** : hacer una visita — *vi* **1** : pagar **2 crime doesn't** ~ : no hay crimen sin castigo — ~ *n* : paga *f* — **payable** *adj* : pagadero — **paycheck** *n* : cheque *m* del sueldo — **payment** *n* **1** : pago *m* **2** INSTALLMENT : plazo *m*, cuota *f Lat* — **payroll** *n* : nómina *f*

PC *n, pl* **PCs** *or* **PC's** : PC *mf,* computadora *f* personal

pea *n* : guisante *m,* arveja *f Lat*

peace *n* : paz *f* — **peaceful** *adj* **1** : pacífico **2** CALM : tranquilo

peach *n* : melocotón *m,* durazno *m Lat*

peacock *n* : pavo *m* real

peak *n* **1** SUMMIT : cumbre *f,* cima *f,* pico *m* (de una montaña) **2** APEX : nivel *m* máximo — ～ *adj* : máximo — ～ *vi* : alcanzar su nivel máximo

peal *n* **1** : repique *m* **2** ～s of laughter : carcajadas *fpl*

peanut *n* : cacajuete *m,* maní *m Lat*

pear *n* : pera *f*

pearl *n* : perla *f*

peasant *n* : campesino *m,* -na *f*

peat *n* : turba *f*

pebble *n* : guijarro *m*

pecan *n* : pacana *f,* nuez *f Lat*

peck *vt* : picar, picotear — ～ *n* **1** : picotazo *m* (de un pájaro) **2** KISS : besito

peculiar *adj* **1** DISTINCTIVE : peculiar, característico **2** STRANGE : extraño, raro — **peculiarity** *n, pl* -ties **1** : peculiaridad *f* **2** ODDITY : rareza *f*

pedal *n* : pedal *m* — ～ *vi* -aled *or* -alled; -aling *or* -alling : pedalear

pedantic *adj* : pedante

peddle *vt* -dled; -dling : vender en las calles — **peddler** *n* : vendedor *m,* -dora *f* ambulante

pedestal *n* : pedestal *m*

pedestrian *n* : peatón *m,* -tona *f* — ～ *adj* ～ **crossing** : paso *m* de peatones

pediatrics *ns & pl* : pediatría *f* — **pediatrician** *n* : pediatra *mf*

pedigree *n* : pedigrí *m* (de un animal), linaje *m* (de una persona)

pee¹ *vi* URINATE : hacer pipí *fam*

pee² *n* : pipí *m fam* **to take a pee** : hacer pipí

peek *vi* : mirar a hurtadillas — ～ *n* : miradita *f* (furtiva)

peel *vt* : pelar (fruta, etc.) — *vi* : pelarse (dícese de la piel), desconcharse (dícese de la pintura) — ～ *n* : piel *f,* cáscara *f*

peep¹ *vi* CHEEP : piar — ～ *n* : pío *m* (de un pajarito)

peep² *vi* **1** PEEK : mirar a hurtadillas **2** *or* ～ **out** : asomar — ～ *n* GLANCE : mirada *f* (furtiva)

peer¹ *n* : par *mf*

peer² *vi* : mirar (con atención)

peeve *vt* : irritar — **peevish** *adj* : malhumorado

peg *n* **1** : clavija *f* **2** HOOK : gancho *m*

pelican *n* : pelícano *m*

pellet *n* **1** : bolita *f* **2** SHOT : perdigón *m*

pelt¹ *n* : piel *f* (de un animal)

pelt² *vt* : lanzar (algo a algn)

pelvis *n, pl* -vises *or* -ves : pelvis *f* — **pelvic** *adj* : pélvico

pen name *n* : seudónimo *m*

pen¹ *vt* **penned; penning** ENCLOSE : encerrar — ～ *n* : corral *m,* redil *m*

pen² *n* **1** *or* **ballpoint** ～ : bolígrafo *m* **2** *or* **fountain** ～ : pluma *f*

penal *adj* : penal — **penalize** *vt* -ized; -izing : penalizar — **penalty** *n, pl* -ties **1** : pena *f,* castigo *m* **2** : penalty *m* (en deportes)

penance *n* : penitencia *f*

pencil *n* : lápiz *m* — **pencil sharpener** *n* : sacapuntas *m*

pendant *n* : colgante *m*

pending *adj* : pendiente — ～ *prep* : en espera de

penetrate *v* -trated; -trating : penetrar — **penetrating** *adj* : penetrante — **penetration** *n* : penetración *f*

penguin *n* : pingüino *m*

penicillin *n* : penicilina *f*

peninsula *n* : península *f*

penis *n, pl* -nes *or* -nises : pene *m*

penitentiary *n, pl* -ries : penitenciaría *f*

pennant *n* : banderín *m*

penny *n, pl* -nies *or* **pence** : centavo *m* (de los Estados Unidos), penique *m* (del Reino Unido) — **penniless** *adj* : sin un centavo

pension *n* : pensión *f,* jubilación *f*

pensive *adj* : pensativo

pentagon *n* : pentágono *m*

penthouse *n* : ático *m*

pent–up *adj* : reprimado

people *ns & pl* **1** people *npl* : gente *f,* personas *fpl* **2** *pl* ～s : pueblo *m*

pep *n* : energía *f,* vigor *m* — ～ *vt or* ～ **up** : animar

pepper *n* **1** : pimienta *f* (condimento) **2** : pimiento *m* (fruta) — **peppermint** *n* : menta *f*

per *prep* **1** : por **2** ACCORDING TO : según **3** ～ **day** : al día **4** **miles** ～ **hour** : millas *fpl* por hora

perceive *vt* -ceived; -ceiving : percibir

percent *adv* : por ciento — **percentage** *n* : porcentaje *m*

perception *n* : percepción *f* — **perceptive** *adj* : perspicaz

perch¹ *n* : percha *f* (para los pájaros) — ～ *vi* : posarse

perch² *n* : perca *f* (pez)

percolate *vt* -lated; -lating : filtrarse — **percolator** *n* : cafetera *f* de filtro

percussion *n* : percusión *f*

perennial *adj* : perenne — ～ *n* : planta *f* perenne

perfect *adj* : perfecto — ～ *vt* : perfeccionar — **perfection** *n* : perfección *f* — **perfectionist** *n* : perfeccionista *mf*

perforate *vt* -rated; -rating : perforar

perform *vt* **1** CARRY OUT : realizar, hacer **2** : representar (una obra teatral), interpretar (una obra musical) — *vi* **1** FUNCTION : funcionar **2** ACT : actuar — **performance** *n* **1** : realización *f* **2** INTERPRETATION : interpretación *f* **3** PRESENTATION : representación *f* — **performer** *n* : actor *m*, **-triz** *f*; intérprete *mf* (de música)

perfume *n* : perfume *m*

perhaps *adv* : tal vez, quizá, quizás

peril *n* : peligro *m* — **perilous** *adj* : peligroso

perimeter *n* : perímetro *m*

period *n* **1** : período *m* (de tiempo) **2** : punto *m* (en puntuación) **3** ERA : época *f* — **periodic** *adj* : periódico — **periodical** *n* : revista *f*

peripheral *adj* : periférico

perish *vi* : perecer — **perishable** *adj* : perecedero — **perishables** *npl* : productos *mpl* perecederos

perjury *n* : perjurio *m*

perk *vi* ~ **up** : animarse, reanimarse — ~ *n* : extra *m* — **perky** *adj* **perkier; -est** : alegre

permanence *n* : permanencia *f* — **permanent** *adj* : permanente — ~ *n* : permanente *f*

permeate *v* **-ated; -ating** : penetrar

permission *n* : permiso *m* — **permissible** *adj* : permisible — **permissive** *adj* : permisivo — **permit** *vt* **-mitted; -mitting** : permitir — ~ *n* : permiso *m*

peroxide *n* : peróxido *m*

perpendicular *adj* : perpendicular

perpetrate *vt* **-trated; -trating** : cometer — **perpetrator** *n* : autor *m*, **-tora** *f* (de un delito)

perpetual *adj* : perpetuo

perplex *vt* : dejar perplejo — **perplexing** *adj* : desconcertante — **perplexity** *n*, *pl* **-ties** : perplejidad *f*

persecute *vt* **-cuted; -cuting** : perseguir — **persecution** *n* : persecución *f*

persevere *vi* **-vered; -vering** : perseverar — **perseverance** *n* : perseverancia *f*

persist *vi* : persistir — **persistence** *n* : persistencia *f* — **persistent** *adj* : persistente

person *n* : persona *f* — **personal** *adj* : personal — **personality** *n*, *pl* **-ties** : personalidad *f* — **personally** *adv* : personalmente, en persona — **personnel** *n* : personal *m*

perspective *n* : perspectiva *f*

perspiration *n* : transpiración *f* — **perspire** *vi* **-spired; -spiring** : transpirar

persuade *vt* **-suaded; -suading** : persuadir — **persuasion** *n* : persuasión *f*

pertain *vi* ~ **to** : estar relacionado con — **pertinent** *adj* : pertinente

perturb *vt* : perturbar

Peruvian *adj* : peruano

pervade *vt* **-vaded; -vading** : penetrar — **pervasive** *adj* : penetrante

perverse *adj* **1** CORRUPT : perverso **2** STUBBORN : obstinado — **pervert** *n* : pervertido *m*, **-da** *f*

peso *n*, *pl* **-sos** : peso *m*

pessimism *n* : pesimismo *m* — **pessimist** *n* : pesimista *mf* — **pessimistic** *adj* : pesimista

pest *n* **1** : insecto *m* nocivo, animal *m* nocivo **2** : peste *f fam* (persona)

pester *vt* **-tered; -tering** : molestar

pesticide *n* : pesticida *m*

pet *n* **1** : animal *m* doméstico **2** FAVORITE : favorito *m*, **-ta** *f* — ~ *vt* **petted; petting** : acariciar

petal *n* : pétalo *m*

petite *adj* : chiquita

petition *n* : petición *f* — ~ *vt* : dirigir una petición a

petrify *vt* **-fied; -fying** : petrificar

petroleum *n* : petróleo *m*

petticoat *n* : enagua *f*, fondo *m Lat*

petty *adj* **-tier; -est** **1** UNIMPORTANT : insignificante, nimio **2** MEAN : mezquino — **pettiness** *n* : mezquindad *f*

petulant *adj* : irritable, de mal genio

pew *n* : banco *m* (de iglesia)

pewter *n* : peltre *m*

phallic *adj* : fálico

phantom *n* : fantasma *m*

pharmacy *n*, *pl* **-cies** : farmacia *f* — **pharmacist** *n* : farmacéutico *m*, **-ca** *f*

phase *n* : fase *f* — ~ *vt* **phased; phasing** **1** ~ **in** : introducir progresivamente **2** ~ **out** : retirar progresivamente

phenomenon *n*, *pl* **-na** *or* **-nons** : fenómeno *m* — **phenomenal** *adj* : fenomenal

philanthropy *n*, *pl* **-pies** : filantropía *f* — **philanthropist** *n* : filántropo *m*, **-pa** *f*

philosophy *n*, *pl* **-phies** : filosofía *f* — **philosopher** *n* : filósofo *m*, **-fa** *f*

phlegm *n* : flema *f*

phobia *n* : fobia *f*

phone → telephone

phonetic *adj* : fonético

phony *or* **phoney** *adj* **-nier; -est** : falso — ~ *n*, *pl* **-nies** : farsante *mf*

phosphorus *n* : fósforo *m*

photo *n*, *pl* **-tos** : foto *f* — **photocopier** *n* : fotocopiadora *f* — **photocopy** *n*, *pl* **-copies** : fotocopia *f* — ~ *vt* **-copied; -copying** : fotocopiar — **photograph** *n* : fotografía *f*, foto *f* — ~ *vt* : fotografiar — **photographer** *n* : fotógrafo *m*, **-fa** *f* — **photographic** *adj* : fotográfico — **photography** *n* : fotografía *f*

phrase *n* : frase *f* — ~ *vt* **phrased; phrasing** : expresar

physical *adj* : físico — ~ *n* : reconocimiento *m* médico

physician *n* : médico *m*, -ca *f*

physics *ns & pl* : física *f* — **physicist** *n* : físico *m*, -ca *f*

physiology *n* : fisiología *f*

physique *n* : físico *m*

piano *n*, *pl* **-anos** : piano *m* — **pianist** *n* : pianista *mf*

pick *vt* **1** CHOOSE : escoger **2** GATHER : recoger **3** REMOVE : quitar (poco a poco) **4** ~ **a fight** : buscar camorra — *vi* **1** ~ **and choose** : ser exigente **2** ~ **on** : meterse con — ~ *n* **1** CHOICE : selección *f* **2** *or* **pickax** : pico *m* **3 the** ~ **of** : lo mejor de

picket *n* **1** STAKE : estaca *f* **2** *or* ~ **line** : piquete *m* — ~ *v* : piquetear

pickle *n* **1** : pepinillo *m* (encurtido) **2** JAM : lío *m fam*, apuro *m* — ~ *vt* **-led; -ling** : encurtir

pickpocket *n* : carterista *mf*

pickup *n* **1** IMPROVEMENT : mejora *f* **2** *or* ~ **truck** : camioneta *f* — **pick up** *vt* **1** LIFT : levantar **2** TIDY : arreglar, ordenar — *vi* IMPROVE : mejorar

picnic *n* : picnic *m* — ~ *vi* **-nicked; -nicking** : ir de picnic

picture *n* **1** PAINTING : cuadro *m* **2** DRAWING : dibujo *m* **3** PHOTO : fotografía *f* **4** IMAGE : imagen *f* **5** MOVIE : película *f* — ~ *vt* **-tured; -turing 1** DEPICT : representar **2** IMAGINE : imaginarse — **picturesque** *adj* : pintoresco

pie *n* : pastel *m* (con fruta o carne), empanada *f* (con carne)

piece *n* **1** : pieza *f* **2** FRAGMENT : trozo *m*, pedazo *m* **3 a** ~ **of advice** : un consejo — ~ *vt* **pieced; piecing** *or* ~ **together** : juntar, componer — **piecemeal** *adv* : poco a poco — ~ *adj* : poco sistemático

pier *n* : muelle *m*

pierce *vt* **pierced; piercing** : perforar — **piercing** *adj* : penetrante

piety *n*, *pl* **-eties** : piedad *f*

pig *n* : cerdo *m*, -da *f*; puerco *m*, -ca *f*

pigeon *n* : paloma *f* — **pigeonhole** *n* : casilla *f*

piggyback *adv & adj* : a cuestas

pigment *n* : pigmento *m*

pigpen *n* : pocilga *f*

pigtail *n* : coleta *f*, trenza *f*

pile¹ *n* HEAP : montón *m*, pila *f* — ~ *v* **piled; piling** *vt* : amontonar, apilar — *vi* ~ **up** : amontonarse, acumularse

pile² *n* NAP : pelo *m* (de telas)

pilfer *vt* : robar, hurtar

pilgrim *n* : peregrino *m*, -na *f* — **pilgrimage** *n* : peregrinación *f*

pill *n* : pastilla *f*, píldora *f*

pillage *n* : saqueo *m* — ~ *vt* **-laged; -laging** : saquear

pillar *n* : pilar *m*, columna *f*

pillow *n* : almohada *f* — **pillowcase** *n* : funda *f* (de almohada)

pilot *n* : piloto *mf* — ~ *vt* : pilotar, pilotear — **pilot light** *n* : piloto *m*

pimp *n* : proxeneta *m*

pimple *n* : grano *m*

pin *n* **1** : alfiler *m* **2** BROOCH : broche *m* **3** *or* **bowling** ~ : bolo *m* — ~ *vt* **pinned; pinning 1** FASTEN : prender, sujetar (con alfileres) **2** *or* ~ **down** : inmovilizar

pincers *npl* : tenazas *fpl*

pinch *vt* **1** : pellizcar **2** STEAL : robar — *vi* : apretar — ~ *n* **1** : pellizco *m* **2** BIT : pizca *f* **3 in a** ~ : en caso necesario

pine¹ *n* : pino *m* (árbol)

pine² *vi* **pined; pining 1** LANGUISH : languidecer **2** ~ **for** : suspirar por

pineapple *n* : piña *f*, ananás *m*

pink *n* : rosa *m*, rosado *m* — ~ *adj* : rosa, rosado

pinnacle *n* : pináculo *m*

pinpoint *vt* : localizar, precisar

pint *n* : pinta *f*

pioneer *n* : pionero *m*, -ra *f*

pious *adj* : piadoso

pipe *n* **1** : tubo *m*, caño *m* **2** : pipa *f* (para fumar) — **pipeline** *n* **1** : conducto *m*, oleoducto *m* (para petróleo)

piquant *adj* : picante

pique *n* : resentimiento *m*

pirate *n* : pirata *mf*

pistachio *n*, *pl* **-chios** : pistacho *m*

pistol *n* : pistola *f*

piston *n* : pistón *m*

pit *n* **1** HOLE : hoyo *m*, fosa *f* **2** MINE : mina *f* **3** : hueso *m* (de una fruta) **4** ~ **of the stomach** : boca *f* del estómago — ~ *vt* **pitted; pitting 1** : marcar de hoyos **2** : deshuesar (una fruta) **3** ~ **against** : enfrentar a

pitch *vt* **1** : armar (una tienda) **2** THROW : lanzar — *vi* **1** *or* ~ **forward** : caerse **2** LURCH : cabecear (dícese de un barco o un avión) — ~ *n* **1** DEGREE, LEVEL : grado *m*, punto *m* **2** TONE : tono *m* **3** THROW : lanzamiento *m* **4** *or* **sales** ~ : presentación *f* (de un vendedor)

pitcher *n* **1** JUG : jarro *m* **2** : lanzador *m*, -dora *f* (en béisbol, etc.)

pitchfork *n* : horquilla *f*, horca *f*

pitfall *n* : riesgo *m*, dificultad *f*

pith *n* **1** : médula *f* (de un hueso, etc.) **2** CORE : meollo *m* — **pithy** *adj* **pithier; -est** : conciso y sustancioso

pity *n*, *pl* **pities 1** COMPASSION : compasión *f* **2 what a** ~! : ¡qué lástima! — ~ *vt* **pitied; pitying** : compadecerse de — **pitiful** *adj* : lastimoso — **pitiless** *adj* : despiadado

pivot *n* : pivote *m* — ~ *vi* **1** : girar sobre un eje **2** ~ **on** : depender de

pizza *n* : pizza *f*

placard *n* POSTER : cartel *m*, póster *m*

placate *vt* **-cated; -cating** : apaciguar

place *n* **1** : sitio *m*, lugar *m* **2** SEAT : asiento *m* **3** POSITION : puesto *m* **4** ROLE : papel *m* **5 take** ~ : tener lugar **6 take the** ~ **of** : sustituir a — ~ *vt* **placed; placing 1** PUT, SET : poner, colocar **2** IDENTIFY : identificar, recordar **3** ~ **an order** : hacer un pedido — **placement** *n* : colocación *f*

placid *adj* : plácido, tranquilo

plagiarism *n* : plagio *m* — **plagiarize** *vt* **-rized; -rizing** : plagiar

plague *n* **1** : plaga *f* (de insectos, etc.) **2** : peste *f* (en medicina)

plaid *n* : tela *f* escocesa — ~ *adj* : escocés

plain *adj* **1** SIMPLE : sencillo **2** CLEAR : claro, evidente **3** CANDID : franco **4** HOMELY : poco atractivo **5 in** ~ **sight** : a la vista (de todos) — ~ *n* : llanura *f*, planicie *f* — **plainly** *adv* **1** CLEARLY : claramente **2** FRANKLY : francamente **3** SIMPLY : sencillamente

plaintiff *n* : demandante *mf*

plan *n* **1** : plan *m*, proyecto *m* **2** DIAGRAM : plano *m* — ~ *v* **planned; planning** *vt* **1** : planear, proyectar **2** INTEND : tener planeado — *vi* : hacer planes

plane[1] *n* **1** LEVEL : plano *m*, nivel *m* **2** AIRPLANE : avión *m*

plane[2] *n or* **carpenter's** ~ : cepillo *m*

planet *n* : planeta *f*

plank *n* : tabla *f*

planning *n* : planificación *f*

plant *vt* : plantar (flores, árboles), sembrar (semillas) — ~ *n* **1** : planta *f* **2** FACTORY : fábrica *f*

plantain *n* : plátano *m* (grande)

plantation *n* : plantación *f*

plaque *n* : placa *f*

plaster *n* : yeso *m* — ~ *vt* **1** : enyesar **2** COVER : cubrir — **plaster cast** *n* : escayola *f*

plastic *adj* **1** : de plástico **2** FLEXIBLE : plástico, flexible **3** ~ **surgery** : cirugía *f* plástica — ~ *n* : plástico *m*

plate *n* **1** SHEET : placa *f* **2** DISH : plato *m* **3** ILLUSTRATION : lámina *f* — ~ *vt* **plated; plating** : chapar (en metal)

plateau *n*, *pl* **-teaus** *or* **-teaux** : meseta *f*

platform *n* **1** : plataforma *f* **2** : andén *m* (de una estación de ferrocarril) **3** *or* **political** ~ : programa *m* electoral

platinum *n* : platino *m*

platitude *n* : lugar *m* común

platoon *n* : sección *f* (en el ejército)

platter *n* : fuente *f*

plausible *adj* : creíble, verosímil

play *n* **1** : juego *m* **2** DRAMA : obra *f* de teatro — ~ *vi* **1** : jugar **2** ~ **in a band** : tocar en un grupo — *vt* **1** : jugar (deportes, etc.), jugar a (juegos) **2** : tocar (música o un instrumento) **3** ~ **the role of** : representar el papel de — **player** *n* **1** : jugador *m*, -dora *f* **2** ACTOR : actor *m*, actriz *f* **3** MUSICIAN : músico *m*, -ca *f* — **playful** *adj* : juguetón — **playground** *n* : patio *m* de recreo — **playing card** *n* : naipe *m*, carta *f* — **playmate** *n* : compañero *m*, -ra *f* de juego — **play–off** *n* : desempate *m* — **playpen** *n* : corral *m* (para niños) — **plaything** *n* : juguete *m* — **playwright** *n* : dramaturgo *m*, -ga *f*

plea *n* **1** : acto *m* de declararse (en derecho) **2** APPEAL : ruego *m*, súplica *f* — **plead** *v* **pleaded** *or* **pled; pleading** *vi* **1** ~ **for** : suplicar **2** ~ **guilty** : declararse culpable **3** ~ **not guilty** : negar la acusación — *vt* **1** : alegar, pretextar **2** ~ **a case** : defender un caso

pleasant *adj* : agradable, grato — **please** *v* **pleased; pleasing** *vt* **1** GRATIFY : complacer **2** SATISFY : satisfacer — *vi* **1** : agradar **2 do as you** ~ : haz lo que quieras — ~ *adv* : por favor — **pleased** *adj* : contento — **pleasing** *adj* : agradable — **pleasure** *n* : placer *m*, gusto *m*

pleat *vt* : plisar — ~ *n* : pliegue *m*

pledge *n* **1** SECURITY : prenda *f* **2** PROMISE : promesa *f* — ~ *vt* **pledged; pledging 1** PAWN : empeñar **2** PROMISE : prometer

plenty *n* **1** : abundancia *f* **2** ~ **of time** : tiempo *m* de sobra — **plentiful** *adj* : abundante

pliable *adj* : flexible

pliers *npl* : alicates *mpl*

plight *n* : situación *f* difícil

plod *vi* **plodded; plodding 1** : caminar con paso pesado **2** DRUDGE : trabajar laboriosamente

plot *n* **1** LOT : parcela *f* **2** : argumento *m* (de una novela, etc.) **3** CONSPIRACY : complot *m*, intriga *f* — ~ *v* **plotted; plotting** *vt* : tramar (un plan), trazar (una gráfica, etc.) — *vi* CONSPIRE : conspirar

plow *or* **plough** *n* **1** : arado *m* **2** → **snowplow** — ~ *v* : arar

ploy *n* : estratagema *f*

pluck *vt* **1** : arrancar **2** : desplumar (un pollo, etc.) **3** : recoger (flores) **4** ~ **one's eyebrows** : depilarse las cejas

plug *n* **1** STOPPER : tapón *m* **2** : enchufe *m* (eléctrico) — ~ *vt* **plugged; plugging 1** BLOCK : tapar **2** ADVERTISE : dar publicidad a **3** ~ **in** : enchufar

plum *n* : ciruela *f*

plumb *adj* : a plomo, vertical — **plumber** *n* : fontanero *m*, -ra *f*; plomero *m*, -ra *f Lat* — **plumbing** *n* **1** : fontanería *f*, plomería *f Lat* **2** PIPES : cañerías *fpl*

plume *n* : pluma *f*

plummet *vi* : caer en picado

plump *adj* : rechoncho *fam*

plunder *vi* : saquear, robar — ~ *n* : botín *m*

plunge *v* **plunged; plunging** *vt* **1** IMMERSE : sumergir **2** THRUST : hundir — *vi* **1** : zambullirse (en el agua) **2** DESCEND : descender en picada — ~ *n* **1** DIVE : zambullida *f* **2** DROP : descenso *m* abrupto

plural *adj* : plural — ~ *n* : plural *m*

plus *adj* : positivo — ~ *n* **1** *or* ~ **sign** : signo *m* (de) más **2** ADVANTAGE : ventaja *f* — ~ *prep* : más — ~ *conj* : y, además

plush *n* : felpa *f* — ~ *adj* **1** : de felpa **2** LUXURIOUS : lujoso

plutonium *n* : plutonio *m*

ply *vt* **plied; plying 1** : ejercer (un oficio) **2** ~ **with questions** : acosar con preguntas

plywood *n* : contrachapado *m*

pneumatic *adj* : neumático

pneumonia *n* : pulmonía *f*

poach[1] *vt* : cocer a fuego lento

poach[2] *vt or* ~ **game** : cazar ilegalmente — **poacher** *n* : cazador *m* furtivo, cazadora *f* furtiva

pocket *n* : bolsillo *m* — ~ *vt* : meterse en el bolsillo — **pocketbook** *n* : cartera *f*, bolsa *f Lat* — **pocketknife** *n, pl* **-knives** : navaja *f*

pod *n* : vaina *f*

podcast *n* : podcast *m*

poem *n* : poema *m* — **poet** *n* : poeta *mf* — **poetic** *or* **poetical** *adj* : poético — **poetry** *n* : poesía *f*

poignant *adj* : conmovedor

point *n* **1** : punto *m* **2** PURPOSE : sentido *m* **3** TIP : punta *f* **4** FEATURE : cualidad *f* **5 be beside the** ~ : no venir al caso **6 there's no** ~ ... : no sirve de nada... — ~ *vt* **1** AIM : apuntar **2** *or* ~ **out** : señalar, indicar — *vi* ~ **at** : señalar (con el dedo) — **point-blank** *adv* : a quemarropa — **pointer** *n* **1** NEEDLE : aguja *f* **2** : perro *m* de muestra **3** TIP : consejo *m* — **pointless** *adj* : inútil — **point of view** *n* : perspectiva *f*, punto *m* de vista

poise *n* **1** : elegancia *f* **2** COMPOSURE : aplomo *m*

poison *n* : veneno *m* — ~ *vt* : envenenar — **poisonous** *adj* : venenoso (dícese de una culebra, etc.), tóxico (dícese de una sustancia)

poke *vt* **poked; poking 1** JAB : golpear (con la punta de algo), dar **2** THRUST : introducir, asomar — ~ *n* : golpe *m* abrupto (con la punta de algo)

poker[1] *n* : atizador *m* (para el fuego)

poker[2] *n* : póquer *m* (juego de naipes)

polar *adj* : polar — **polar bear** *n* : oso *m* blanco — **polarize** *vt* **-ized; -izing** : polarizar

pole[1] *n* : palo *m*, poste *m*

pole[2] *n* : polo *m* (en geografía)

police *vt* **-liced; -licing** : mantener el orden en — ~ *ns & pl* **the** ~ : la policía — **policeman** *n, pl* **-men** : policía *m* — **police officer** *n* : policía *mf*, agente *mf* de policía — **policewoman** *n, pl* **-women** : (mujer *f*) policía *f*

policy *n, pl* **-cies 1** : política *f* **2** *or* **insurance** ~ : póliza *f* de seguros

polio *or* **poliomyelitis** *n* : polio *f*, poliomielitis *f*

Polish *adj* : polaco — ~ *n* : polaco *m* (idioma)

polish *vt* **1** : pulir **2** : limpiar (zapatos), encerar (un suelo) — ~ *n* **1** LUSTER : brillo *m*, lustre *m* **2** : betún *m* (para zapatos), cera *f* (para suelos y muebles), esmalte *m* (para las uñas)

polite *adj* **-liter; -est** : cortés — **politeness** *n* : cortesía *f*

political *adj* : político — **politician** *n* : político *m*, -ca *f* — **politics** *ns & pl* : política *f*

polka *n* : polka *f* — **polka dot** *n* : lunar *m*

poll *n* **1** : encuesta *f*, sondeo *m* **2 the** ~**s** : las urnas — ~ *vt* **1** : obtener (votos) **2** CANVASS : encuestar, sondear

pollen *n* : polen *m*

pollute *vt* **-luted; -luting** : contaminar — **pollution** *n* : contaminación *f*

polyester *n* : poliéster *m*

polygon *n* : polígono *m*

pomegranate *n* : granada *f*

pomp *n* : pompa *f* — **pompous** *adj* : pomposo

pond *n* : charca *f* (natural), estanque *m* (artificial)

ponder *vt* : considerar — *vi* ~ **over** : reflexionar sobre

pony *n, pl* **-nies** : poni *m* — **ponytail** *n* : cola *f* de caballo

poodle *n* : caniche *m*

pool *n* **1** PUDDLE : charco *m* **2** : fondo *m* común (de recursos) **3** BILLIARDS : billar *m* **4** *or* **swimming** ~ : piscina *f* — ~ *vt* : hacer un fondo común de

poor *adj* **1** : pobre **2** INFERIOR : malo **3 the ~** : los pobres — **poorly** *adv* : mal
pop¹ *v* **popped; popping** *vt* **1** : hacer reventar **2 ~ sth into** : meter algo en — *vi* **1** BURST : reventarse, estallar **2 ~ in** : entrar (un momento) **3 ~ out** : saltar (dícese de los ojos) **4 ~ up** APPEAR : aparecer — **~** *n* **1** : ruido *m* seco **2 → soda pop**
pop² *n or* **~ music** : música *f* popular
popcorn *n* : palomitas *fpl*
pope *n* : papa *m*
poplar *n* : álamo *m*
poppy *n*, *pl* **-pies** : amapola *f*
popular *adj* : popular — **popularity** *n* : popularidad *f* — **popularize** *vt* **-ized; -izing** : popularizar
populate *vt* **-lated; -lating** : poblar — **population** *n* : población *f*
porcelain *n* : porcelana *f*
porch *n* : porche *m*
porcupine *n* : puerco *m* espín
pore¹ *vi* **pored; poring ~ over** : estudiar esmeradamente
pore² *n* : poro *m*
pork *n* : carne *f* de cerdo
pornography *n* : pornografía *f* — **pornographic** *adj* : pornográfico
porous *adj* : poroso
porpoise *n* : marsopa *f*
porridge *n* : avena *f* (cocida), gachas *fpl* (de avena)
port¹ *n* HARBOR : puerto *m*
port² *n or* **~ side** : babor *m*
port³ *n* : oporto *m* (vino)
portable *adj* : portátil
portent *n* : presagio *m*
porter *n* : maletero *m*, mozo *m* (de estación)
portfolio *n*, *pl* **-lios** : cartera *f*
porthole *n* : portilla *f*
portion *n* : porción *f*
portrait *n* : retrato *m*
portray *vt* **1** : representar, retratar **2** : interpretar (un personaje)
Portuguese *adj* : portugués — **~** *n* : portugués *m* (idioma)
pose *v* **posed; posing** *vt* : plantear (una pregunta, etc.), representar (una amenaza) — *vi* **1** : posar **2 ~ as** : hacerse pasar por — **~** *n* : pose *f*
posh *adj* : elegante, de lujo
position *n* **1** : posición *f* **2** JOB : puesto *m* — **~** *vt* : colocar, situar
positive *adj* **1** : positivo **2** CERTAIN : seguro
possess *vt* : poseer — **possession** *n* **1** : posesión *f* **2 ~s** *npl* BELONGINGS : bienes *mpl* — **possessive** *adj* : posesivo
possible *adj* : posible — **possibility** *n*, *pl* **-ties** : posibilidad *f* — **possibly** *adv* : posiblemente

post¹ *n* POLE : poste *m*, palo *m*
post² *n* POSITION : puesto *m*
post³ *n* MAIL : cartas *fpl* — **~** *vt* **1** : echar al correo **2 keep ~ed** : tener al corriente — **postage** *n* : franqueo *m* — **postal** *adj* : postal — **postcard** *n* : tarjeta *f* postal
poster *n* : cartel *m*
posterity *n* : posteridad *f*
posthumous *adj* : póstumo
postman → mailman — **post office** *n* : oficina *f* de correos
postpone *vt* **-poned; -poning** : aplazar — **postponement** *n* : aplazamiento *m*
postscript *n* : posdata *f*
posture *n* : postura *f*
postwar *adj* : de (la) posguerra
pot *n* **1** : olla *f* (de cocina) **2** FLOWERPOT : maceta *f* **3 ~s and pans** : cacharros *mpl*
potassium *n* : potasio *m*
potato *n*, *pl* **-toes** : patata *f*, papa *f Lat*
potent *adj* **1** POWERFUL : poderoso **2** EFFECTIVE : eficaz
potential *adj* : potencial — **~** *n* : potencial *m*
pothole *n* : bache *m*
potion *n* : poción *f*
pottery *n*, *pl* **-teries** : cerámica *f*
pouch *n* **1** BAG : bolsa *f* pequeña **2** : bolsa *f* (de un animal)
poultry *n* : aves *fpl* de corral
pounce *vi* **pounced; pouncing** : abalanzarse
pound¹ *n* : libra *f* (unidad de dinero o de peso)
pound² *n or* **dog ~** : perrera *f*
pound³ *vt* **1** CRUSH : machacar **2** HIT : golpear — *vi* : palpitar (dícese del corazón)
pour *vt* : verter — *vi* **1** FLOW : fluir, salir **2 it's ~ing** : está lloviendo a cántaros
pout *vi* : hacer pucheros — **~** *n* : puchero *m*
poverty *n* : pobreza *f*
powder *vt* **1** : empolvar **2** CRUSH : pulverizar — **~** *n* **1** : polvo *m* **2 or face ~** : polvos *mpl* — **powdery** *adj* : polvoriento
power *n* **1** CONTROL : poder *m* **2** ABILITY : capacidad *f* **3** STRENGTH : fuerza *f* **4** : potencia *f* (política) **5** ENERGY : energía *f* **6** ELECTRICITY : electricidad *f* — **~** *vt* : impulsar — **powerful** *adj* : poderoso — **powerless** *adj* : impotente
practical *adj* : práctico — **practically** *adv* : casi, prácticamente
practice *or* **practise** *v* **-ticed** *or* **-tised; -ticing** *or* **-tising** *vt* **1** : practicar **2** : ejercer (una profesión) — *vi* : practicar — **practice** *n* **1** : práctica *f* **2** CUSTOM : costumbre *f* **3** : ejercicio *m* (de una profesión) **4 be out of ~** : no estar en forma — **practitioner** *n* **1** : profesional *mf* **2 general ~** : médico *m*, -ca *f* de medicina general
pragmatic *adj* : pragmático

prairie *n* : pradera *f*

praise *vt* **praised; praising** : elogiar, alabar — ~ *n* : elogio *m*, alabanza *f* — **praiseworthy** *adj* : loable

prance *vi* **pranced; prancing** : hacer cabriolas

prank *n* : travesura *f*

prawn *n* : gamba *f*

pray *vi* **1** : rezar **2** ~ **for** : rogar — **prayer** *n* : oración *f*

preach *v* : predicar — **preacher** *n* MINISTER : pastor *m*, -tora *f*

precarious *adj* : precario

precaution *n* : precaución *f*

precede *vt* **-ceded; -ceding** : preceder a — **precedence** *n* : precedencia *f* — **precedent** *n* : precedente *m*

precinct *n* **1** DISTRICT : distrito *m* **2** ~s *npl* : recinto *m*

precious *adj* : precioso

precipice *n* : precipicio *m*

precipitate *vt* **-tated; -tating** : precipitar — **precipitation** *n* **1** HASTE : precipitación *f* **2** : precipitaciones *fpl* (en meteorología)

precise *adj* : preciso — **precisely** *adv* : precisamente — **precision** *n* : precisión *f*

preclude *vt* **-cluded; -cluding 1** PREVENT : impedir **2** EXCLUDE : excluir

precocious *adj* : precoz

preconceived *adj* : preconcebido

predator *n* : depredador *m*

predecessor *n* : antecesor *m*, -sora *f*; predecesor *m*, -sora *f*

predicament *n* : apuro *m*

predict *vt* : pronosticar, predecir — **predictable** *adj* : previsible — **prediction** *n* : pronóstico *m*, predicción *f*

predispose *vt* **-posed; -posing** : predisponer

predominant *adj* : predominante

preeminent *adj* : preeminente

preempt *vt* : adelantarse a (un ataque, etc.)

preen *vt* **1** : arreglarse (las plumas) **2** ~ **oneself** : acicalarse

prefabricated *adj* : prefabricado

preface *n* : prefacio *m*, prólogo *m*

prefer *vt* **-ferred; -ferring** : preferir — **preferable** *adj* : preferible — **preference** *n* : preferencia *f* — **preferential** *adj* : preferente

prefix *n* : prefijo *m*

pregnancy *n*, *pl* **-cies** : embarazo *m* — **pregnant** *adj* : embarazada

prehistoric *or* **prehistorical** *adj* : prehistórico

prejudice *n* **1** BIAS : prejuicio *m* **2** HARM : perjuicio *m* — ~ *vt* **-diced; -dicing 1** BIAS : predisponer **2** HARM : perjudicar — **prejudiced** *adj* : parcial

preliminary *adj* : preliminar

prelude *n* : preludio *m*

premarital *adj* : prematrimonial

premature *adj* : prematuro

premeditated *adj* : premeditado

premier *adj* : principal — ~ *n* PRIME MINISTER : primer ministro *m*, primera ministra *f*

premiere *n* : estreno *m*

premise *n* **1** : premisa *f* (de un argumento) **2** ~s *npl* : recinto *m*, local *m*

premium *n* **1** : premio *m* **2** *or* **insurance** ~ : prima *f* (de seguro)

preoccupied *adj* : preocupado

prepare *v* **-pared; -paring** *vt* : preparar — *vi* : prepararse — **preparation** *n* **1** : preparación *f* **2** ~s *npl* ARRANGEMENTS : preparativos *mpl* — **preparatory** *adj* : preparatorio

prepay *vt* **-paid; -paying** : pagar por adelantado

preposition *n* : preposición *f*

preposterous *adj* : absurdo, ridículo

prerequisite *n* : requisito *m* previo

prerogative *n* : prerrogativa *f*

prescribe *vt* **-scribed; -scribing 1** : prescribir **2** : recetar (en medicina) — **prescription** *n* : receta *f*

presence *n* : presencia *f*

present[1] *adj* **1** CURRENT : actual **2 be** ~ **at** : estar presente en — ~ *n* **1** : presente *m* **2 at** ~ : actualmente

present[2] *n* GIFT : regalo *m* — ~ *vt* **1** INTRODUCE : presentar **2** GIVE : entregar — **presentation** *n* **1** : presentación *f* **2** *or* ~ **ceremony** : ceremonia *f* de entrega

presently *adv* **1** SOON : dentro de poco **2** NOW : actualmente

preserve *vt* **-served; -serving 1** : conservar **2** MAINTAIN : mantener — ~ *n* **1** JAM : confitura *f* **2** *or* **game** ~ : coto *m* de caza — **preservation** *n* : preservación *f*, conservación *f* — **preservative** *n* : conservante *m*

president *n* : presidente *m*, -ta *f* — **presidency** *n*, *pl* **-cies** : presidencia *f* — **presidential** *adj* : presidencial

press *n* : prensa *f* — ~ *vt* **1** : apretar **2** IRON : planchar — *vi* **1** : apretar **2** URGE : presionar — **pressing** *adj* : urgente — **pressure** *n* : presión *f* — ~ *vt* **-sured; -suring** : presionar, apremiar

prestige *n* : prestigio *m* — **prestigious** *adj* : prestigioso

presume *vt* **-sumed; -suming** : presumir — **presumably** *adv* : es de suponer, supuestamente — **presumption** *n* : presunción *f* — **presumptuous** *adj* : presuntuoso

pretend *vt* **1** CLAIM : pretender **2** FEIGN : fingir — *vi* **1** : fingir — **pretense** *or* **pretence** *n* **1** CLAIM : pretensión *f* **2 under false** ~s : con pretextos falsos — **pretentious** *adj* : pretencioso

preterit *nm* : pretérito *m*

pretext *n* : pretexto *m*
pretty *adj* **-tier; -est** : lindo, bonito — ~ *adv* FAIRLY : bastante
pretzel *n* : galleta *f* salada
prevail *vi* **1** TRIUMPH : prevalecer **2** PREDOMINATE : predominar **3** ~ **upon** : persuadir — **prevalent** *adj* : extendido
prevent *vt* : impedir — **prevention** *n* : prevención *f* — **preventive** *adj* : preventivo
preview *n* : preestreno *m*
previous *adj* : previo, anterior — **previously** *adv* : anteriormente
prey *n, pl* **preys** : presa *f* — **prey on** *vt* **1** : alimentarse de **2** ~ **on one's mind** : atormentar a algn
price *n* : precio *m* — ~ *vt* **priced; pricing** : poner un precio a — **priceless** *adj* : inestimable
prick *n* : pinchazo *m* — ~ *vt* **1** : pinchar **2** ~ **up one's ears** : levantar las orejas — **prickly** *adj* : espinoso
pride *n* : orgullo *m* — ~ *vt* **prided; priding** ~ **oneself on** : enorgullecerse de
priest *n* : sacerdote *m* — **priesthood** *n* : sacerdocio *m*
prim *adj* **primmer; primmest** : remilgado
primary *adj* **1** FIRST : primario **2** PRINCIPAL : principal — **primarily** *adv* : principalmente
prime[1] *vt* **primed; priming** **1** : cebar (un arma de fuego, etc.) **2** PREPARE : preparar
prime[2] *n* **the** ~ **of one's life** : la flor de la vida — ~ *adj* **1** MAIN : principal, primero **2** EXCELLENT : excelente — **prime minister** *n* : primer ministro *m*, primera ministra *f*
primer[1] *n* : base *f* (de pintura)
primer[2] *n* READER : cartilla *f*
primitive *adj* : primitivo
primrose *n* : primavera *f*
prince *n* : príncipe *m* — **princess** *n* : princesa *f*
principal *adj* : principal — ~ *n* : director *m*, -tora *f* (de un colegio)
principle *n* : principio *m*
print *n* **1** MARK : huella *f* **2** LETTERING : letra *f* **3** ENGRAVING : grabado *m* **4** : estampado *m* (de tela) **5** : copia *f* (en fotografía) **6 out of** ~ : agotado — ~ *vt* : imprimir (libros, etc.) — *vi* : escribir con letra de molde — **printer** *n* **1** : impresor *m*, -sora *f* (persona) **2** : impresora *f* (máquina) — **printing** *n* **1** : impresión *f* **2** : imprenta *f* (profesión) **3** LETTERING : letras *fpl* de molde
prior *adj* **1** : previo **2** ~ **to** : antes de — **priority** *n, pl* **-ties** : prioridad *f*
prison *n* : prisión *f*, cárcel *f* — **prisoner** *n* **1** : preso *m*, -sa *f* **2** ~ **of war** : prisionero *m*, -ra *f* de guerra
privacy *n, pl* **-cies** : intimidad *f* — **private** *adj* **1** : privado **2** SECRET : secreto — ~ *n*

: soldado *m* raso — **privately** *adv* : en privado
privilege *n* : privilegio *m* — **privileged** *adj* : privilegiado
prize *n* : premio *m* — ~ *adj* : premiado — ~ *vt* **prized; prizing** : valorar, apreciar — **prizefighter** *n* : boxeador *m*, -dora *f* profesional — **prizewinning** *adj* : premiado
pro *n* **1** → **professional 2 the** ~**s and cons** : los pros y los contras
probability *n, pl* **-ties** : probabilidad *f* — **probable** *adj* : probable — **probably** *adv* : probablemente
probation *n* **1** : período *m* de prueba (de un empleado, etc.) **2** : libertad *f* condicional (de un preso)
probe *n* **1** : sonda *f* (en medicina, etc.) **2** INVESTIGATION : investigación *f* — ~ *vt* **probed; probing** **1** : sondar **2** INVESTIGATE : investigar
problem *n* : problema *m*
procedure *n* : procedimiento *m*
proceed *vi* **1** ACT : proceder **2** CONTINUE : continuar **3** ADVANCE : avanzar — **proceedings** *npl* **1** EVENTS : actos *mpl* **2** : proceso *m* (en derecho) — **proceeds** *npl* : ganancias *fpl*
process *n, pl* **-cesses** **1** : proceso *m* **2 in the** ~ **of** : en vías de — ~ *vt* : procesar — **procession** *n* : desfile *m*
proclaim *vt* : proclamar — **proclamation** *n* : proclamación *f*
procrastinate *vi* **-nated; -nating** : demorar, aplazar
procure *vt* **-cured; -curing** : obtener
prod *vt* **prodded; prodding** : pinchar, aguijonear
prodigal *adj* : pródigo
prodigy *n, pl* **-gies** : prodigio *m*
produce *vt* **-duced; -ducing** **1** : producir **2** CAUSE : causar **3** SHOW : presentar, mostrar **4** : poner en escena (una obra de teatro) — ~ *n* : productos *mpl* agrícolas — **producer** *n* : productor *m*, -tora *f* — **product** *n* : producto *m* — **productive** *adj* : productivo
profane *adj* **1** : profano **2** IRREVERENT : blasfemo — **profanity** *n, pl* **-ties** : blasfemia *f*
profess *vt* : profesar — **profession** *n* : profesión *f* — **professional** *adj* : profesional — ~ *n* : profesional *mf* — **professor** *n* : profesor *m*, -sora *f*
proficiency *n* : competencia *f* — **proficient** *adj* : competente
profile *n* **1** : perfil *m* **2 keep a low** ~ : no llamar la atención
profit *n* : beneficio *m*, ganancia *f* — ~ *vi* : sacar provecho (de), beneficiarse (de) — **profitable** *adj* : provechoso

profound *adj* : profundo

profuse *adj* : profuso — **profusion** *n* : profusión *f*

prognosis *n, pl* **-noses** : pronóstico *m*

program *n* : programa *m* — ~ *vt* **-grammed** *or* **-gramed; -gramming** *or* **-graming** : programar

progress *n* 1 : progreso *m* 2 ADVANCE : avance *m* — ~ *vi* : progresar, avanzar — **progressive** *adj* 1 : progresista (dícese de la política, etc.) 2 INCREASING : progresiva

prohibit *vt* : prohibir — **prohibition** *n* : prohibición *f*

project *n* : proyecto *m* — ~ *vt* : proyectar — *vi* PROTRUDE : sobresalir — **projectile** *n* : proyectil *m* — **projection** *n* 1 : proyección *f* 2 PROTRUSION : saliente *m* — **projector** *n* : proyector *m*

proliferate *vi* **-ated; -ating** : proliferar — **proliferation** *n* : proliferación *f* — **prolific** *adj* : prolífico

prologue *n* : prólogo *m*

prolong *vt* : prolongar

prom *n* : baile *m* formal (en un colegio)

prominent *adj* : prominente — **prominence** *n* 1 : prominencia *f* 2 IMPORTANCE : eminencia *f*

promiscuous *adj* : promiscuo

promise *n* : promesa *f* — ~ *v* **-ised; -ising** : prometer — **promising** *adj* : prometedor

promote *vt* **-moted; -moting** 1 : ascender (a un alumno o un empleado) 2 FURTHER : promover, fomentar 3 ADVERTISE : promocionar — **promoter** *n* : promotor *m*, -tora *f*; empresario *m*, **-ria** *f* (en deportes) — **promotion** *n* 1 : ascenso *m* (de un alumno o un empleado) 2 ADVERTISING : publicidad *f*, propaganda *f*

prompt *vt* 1 INCITE : provocar (una cosa), inducir (a una persona) 2 : apuntar (a un actor, etc.) — ~ *adj* 1 : rápido 2 PUNCTUAL : puntual

prone *adj* 1 : boca abajo, decúbito prono 2 **be** ~ **to** : ser propenso a

prong *n* : punta *f*, diente *m*

pronoun *n* : pronombre *m*

pronounce *vt* **-nounced; -nouncing** : pronunciar — **pronouncement** *n* : declaración *f* — **pronunciation** *n* : pronunciación *f*

proof *n* : prueba *f* — ~ *adj* ~ **against** : a prueba de — **proofread** *vt* **-read; -reading** : corregir

prop *n* 1 SUPPORT : puntal *m*, apoyo *m* 2 : accesorio *m* (en teatro) — ~ *vt* **propped; propping** 1 ~ **against** : apoyar contra 2 ~ **up** SUPPORT : apoyar

propaganda *n* : propaganda *f*

propagate *v* **-gated; -gating** *vt* : propagar — *vi* : propagarse

propel *vt* **-pelled; -pelling** : propulsar — **propeller** *n* : hélice *f*

propensity *n, pl* **-ties** : propensión *f*

proper *adj* 1 SUITABLE : apropiado 2 REAL : verdadero 3 CORRECT : correcto 4 GENTEEL : cortés 5 ~ **name** : nombre *m* propio — **properly** *adv* : correctamente

property *n, pl* **-ties** 1 : propiedad *f* 2 BUILDING : inmueble *m* 3 LAND, LOT : parcela *f*

prophet *n* : profeta *m*, profetisa *f* — **prophecy** *n, pl* **-cies** : profecía *f* — **prophesy** *v* **-sied; -sying** *vt* : profetizar — *vi* : hacer profecías — **prophetic** *adj* : profético

proportion *n* 1 : proporción *f* 2 SHARE : parte *f* — **proportional** *adj* : proporcional — **proportionate** *adj* : proporcional

proposal *n* : propuesta *f*

propose *v* **-posed; -posing** *vt* 1 SUGGEST : proponer 2 ~ **to do sth** : pensar hacer algo — *vi* : proponer matrimonio — **proposition** *n* : proposición *f*

proprietor *n* : propietario *m*, **-ria** *f*

propriety *n, pl* **-eties** : decencia *f*, decoro *m*

propulsion *n* : propulsión *f*

prose *n* : prosa *f*

prosecute *vt* **-cuted; -cuting** : procesar — **prosecution** *n* 1 : procesamiento *m* 2 **the** ~ : la acusación — **prosecutor** *n* : acusador *m*, -dora *f*

prospect *n* 1 : perspectiva *f* 2 POSSIBILITY : posibilidad *f* — **prospective** *adj* : futuro, posible

prospector *n* : prospector *m*, -tora *f*; explorador *m*, -dora *f*

prosper *vi* : prosperar — **prosperity** *n* : prosperidad *f* — **prosperous** *adj* : próspero

prostitute *n* : prostituta *f* — **prostitution** *n* : prostitución *f*

prostrate *adj* : postrado

protagonist *n* : protagonista *mf*

protect *vt* : proteger — **protection** *n* : protección *f* — **protective** *adj* : protector — **protector** *n* : protector *m*, -tora *f*

protégé *n* : protegido *m*, -da *f*

protein *n* : proteína *f*

protest *n* : protesta *f* — ~ *vt* : protestar — *vi* ~ **against** : protestar contra — **Protestant** *n* : protestante *mf* — **protester** *or* **protestor** *n* : manifestante *mf*

protocol *n* : protocolo *m*

prototype *n* : prototipo *m*

protract *vt* : prolongar

protrude *vi* **-truded; -truding** : sobresalir

proud *adj* : orgulloso

prove *v* **proved; proved** *or* **proven; proving** *vt* : probar — *vi* : resultar

proverb *n* : proverbio *m*, refrán *m* — **proverbial** *adj* : proverbial

provide *v* **-vided; -viding** *vt* : proveer — *vi* ~ **for** SUPPORT : mantener — **provided** *or* ~ **that** *conj* : con tal (de) que, siempre que — **providence** *n* : providencia *f*

province *n* **1** : provincia *f* **2** SPHERE : campo *m*, competencia *f* — **provincial** *adj* : provinciano

provision *n* **1** : provisión *f*, suministro *m* **2** STIPULATION : condición *f* **3** ~**s** *npl* : víveres *mpl* — **provisional** *adj* : provisional — **proviso** *n*, *pl* **-sos** *or* **-soes** : condición *f*

provoke *vt* **-voked; -voking** : provocar — **provocation** *n* : provocación *f* — **provocative** *adj* : provocador, provocativo

prow *n* : proa *f*

prowess *n* **1** BRAVERY : valor *m* **2** SKILL : habilidad *f*

prowl *vi* : merodear, rondar — *vt* : merodear por — **prowler** *n* : merodeador *m*, -dora *f*

proximity *n* : proximidad *f* — **proxy** *n*, *pl* **proxies by** ~ : por poder

prude *n* : mojigato *m*, -ta *f*

prudence *n* : prudencia *f* — **prudent** *adj* : prudente

prune¹ *n* : ciruela *f* pasa

prune² *vt* **pruned; pruning** : podar (arbustos, etc.)

pry *v* **pried; prying** *vi* ~ **into** : entrometerse en — *vt or* ~ **open** : abrir (a la fuerza)

psalm *n* : salmo *m*

pseudonym *n* : seudónimo *m*

psychiatry *n* : psiquiatría *f* — **psychiatric** *adj* : psiquiátrico — **psychiatrist** *n* : psiquiatra *mf*

psychic *adj* : psíquico

psychoanalysis *n*, *pl* **-yses** : psicoanálisis *m* — **psychoanalyst** *n* : psicoanalista *mf* — **psychoanalyze** *vt* **-lyzed; -lyzing** : psicoanalizar

psychology *n*, *pl* **-gies** : psicología *f* — **psychological** *adj* : psicológico — **psychologist** *n* : psicólogo *m*, -ga *f*

psychopath *n* : psicópata *mf*

psychotherapy *n*, *pl* **-pies** : psicoterapia *f*

psychotic *adj* : psicótico

puberty *n* : pubertad *f*

pubic *adj* : púbico

public *adj* : público — ~ *n* : público *m* — **publication** *n* : publicación *f* — **publicity** *n* : publicidad *f* — **publicize** *vt* **-cized; -cizing** : publicitar, divulgar

publish *vt* : publicar — **publisher** *n* **1** : editor *m*, -tora *f* (persona) **2** : casa *f* editorial (negocio)

pucker *vt* : fruncir, arrugar — *vi* : arrugarse

pudding *n* : budín *m*, pudín *m*

puddle *n* : charco *m*

pudgy *adj* **pudgier; -est** : rechoncho *fam*

Puerto Rican *adj* : puertorriqueño

puff *vi* **1** BLOW : soplar **2** PANT : resoplar **3** ~ **up** SWELL : hincharse — *vt* ~ **out** : hinchar — ~ *n* **1** : bocanada *f* (de humo) **2** : chupada *f* (a un cigarrillo) **3** *or* **cream** ~ : pastelito *m* de crema **4** *or* **powder** ~ : borla *f* — **puffy** *adj* **puffier; -est** : hinchado

pull *vt* **1** : tirar de **2** EXTRACT : sacar **3** TEAR : desgarrarse (un músculo, etc.) **4** ~ **off** REMOVE : quitar **5** ~ **oneself together** : calmarse **6** ~ **up** : levantar, subir — *vi* **1** : tirar **2** ~ **through** RECOVER : reponerse **3** ~ **together** COOPERATE : reunir **4** ~ **up** STOP : parar — ~ *n* **1** : tirón *m* **2** INFLUENCE : influencia *f* — **pulley** *n*, *pl* **-leys** : polea *f* — **pullover** *n* : suéter *m*

pulp *n* **1** : pulpa *f* (de frutas, etc.) **2** *or* **wood** ~ : pasta *f* de papel

pulpit *n* : púlpito *m*

pulsate *vi* **-sated; -sating** : palpitar — **pulse** *n* : pulso *m*

pulverize *vt* **-ized; -izing** : pulverizar

pummel *vt* **-meled; -meling** : aporrear

pump¹ *n* : bomba *f* — ~ *vt* **1** : bombear **2** ~ **up** : inflar

pump² *n* SHOE : zapato *m* de tacón

pumpernickel *n* : pan *m* negro de centeno

pumpkin *n* : calabaza *f*, zapallo *m Lat*

pun *n* : juego *m* de palabras — ~ *vi* **punned; punning** : hacer juegos de palabras

punch¹ *vt* **1** : dar un puñetazo a **2** PERFORATE : perforar (papeles, etc.), picar (un boleto) — ~ *n* **1** : golpe *m*, puñetazo *m* **2** *or* **paper** ~ : perforadora *f*

punch² *n* : ponche *m* (bebida)

punctual *adj* : puntual — **punctuality** *n* : puntualidad *f*

punctuate *vt* **-ated; -ating** : puntuar — **punctuation** *n* : puntuación *f*

puncture *n* : pinchazo *m*, ponchadura *f Lat* — ~ *vt* **-tured; -turing** : pinchar, ponchar *Lat*

pungent *adj* : acre

punish *vt* : castigar — **punishment** *n* : castigo *m* — **punitive** *adj* : punitivo

puny *adj* **-nier; -est** : enclenque

pup *n* : cachorro *m*, -rra *f* (de un perro); cría *f* (de otros animales)

pupil¹ *n* : alumno *m*, -na *f* (de colegio)

pupil² *n* : pupila *f* (del ojo)

puppet *n* : títere *m*

puppy *n*, *pl* **-pies** : cachorro *m*, -rra *f*

purchase *vt* **-chased; -chasing** : comprar — ~ *n* : compra *f*

pure *adj* **purer; purest** : puro

puree *n* : puré *m*

purely *adv* : puramente

purgatory *n*, *pl* **-ries** : purgatorio *m* — **purge** *vt* **purged; purging** : purgar — ~ *n* : purga *f*

purify *vt* **-fied; -fying** : purificar — **purification** *n* : purificación *f*
puritanical *adj* : puritano
purity *n* : pureza *f*
purple *n* : morado *m*
purport *vt* ~ **to be** : pretender ser
purpose *n* **1** : propósito *m* **2** RESOLUTION : determinación *f* **3 on** ~ : a propósito — **purposeful** *adj* : resuelto — **purposely** *adv* : a propósito
purr *n* : ronroneo *m* — ~ *vi* : ronronear
purse *n* **1** *or* **change** ~ : monedero *m* **2** HANDBAG : cartera *f*, bolso *m* *Spain*, bolsa *f* *Lat* — ~ *vt* **pursed; pursing** : fruncir
pursue *vt* **-sued; -suing 1** CHASE : perseguir **2** SEEK : buscar — **pursuer** *n* : perseguidor *m*, -dora *f* — **pursuit** *n* **1** CHASE : persecución *f* **2** SEARCH : búsqueda *f* **3** OCCUPATION : actividad *f*
pus *n* : pus *m*
push *vt* **1** SHOVE : empujar **2** PRESS : apretar **3** URGE : presionar **4** ~ **around** BULLY : mangonear — *vi* **1** : empujar **2** ~ **for** : presionar para — ~ *n* **1** SHOVE : empujón *m* **2** DRIVE : dinamismo *m* **3**

EFFORT : esfuerzo *m* — **pushy** *adj* **pushier; -est** : mandón, prepotente
pussy *n*, *pl* **pussies** : gatito *m*, -ta *f*; minino *m*, -na *f*
put *v* **put; putting** *vt* **1** : poner **2** INSERT : meter **3** EXPRESS : decir **4** ~ **one's mind to sth** : proponerse hacer algo — *vi* ~ **up with** : aguantar — **put away** *vt* **1** STORE : guardar **2** *or* ~ **aside** : dejar a un lado — **put down** *vt* **1** SUPPRESS : aplastar, sofocar **2** ATTRIBUTE : atribuir — **put off** *vt* DEFER : aplazar, posponer — **put on** *vt* **1** ASSUME : adoptar **2** PRESENT : presentar (una obra de teatro, etc.) **3** WEAR : ponerse — **put out** *vt* INCONVENIENCE : incomodar — **put up** *vt* **1** BUILD : construir **2** LODGE : alojar **3** PROVIDE : poner (dinero)
putrefy *vi* **-fied; -fying** : pudrirse
putty *n*, *pl* **-ties** : masilla *f*
puzzle *v* **-zled; -zling** *vt* : confundir, dejar perplejo — *vi* ~ **over** : tratar de descifrar — ~ *n* **1** : rompecabezas *m* **2** MYSTERY : enigma *m*
pylon *n* : pilón *m*
pyramid *n* : pirámide *f*
python *n* : pitón *f*

Q

q *n*, *pl* **q's** *or* **qs** : q *f*, decimoséptima letra del alfabeto inglés
quack[1] *vi* : graznar (dícese del pato) — ~ *n* : graznido *m*
quack[2] *n* CHARLATAN : charlatán *m*, -tana *f*
quadruple *v* **-pled; -pling** *vt* : cuadruplicar — *vi* : cuadruplicarse
quagmire *n* : atolladero *m*
quail *n*, *pl* **quail** *or* **quails** : codorniz *f*
quaint *adj* **1** ODD : curioso **2** PICTURESQUE : pintoresco
quake *vi* **quaked; quaking** : temblar — ~ *n* → **earthquake**
qualify *v* **-fied; -fying** *vt* **1** LIMIT : matizar **2** : calificar (en gramática) **3** EQUIP : habilitar — *vi* **1** : titularse (de abogado, etc.) **2** : clasificarse (en deportes) — **qualification** *n* I REQUIREMENT : requisito *m* **2** ~**s** *npl* ABILITY : capacidad *f* **3 without** ~ : sin reservas — **qualified** *adj* : capacitado
quality *n*, *pl* **-ties 1** : calidad *f* **2** PROPERTY : cualidad *f*
qualm *n* **1** DOUBT : duda *f* **2 have no** ~**s about** : no tener ningún escrúpulo en

quandary *n*, *pl* **-ries** : dilema *m*
quantify *vt* **-fied -fying** : cuantificar
quantity *n*, *pl* **-ties** : cantidad *f*
quarantine *n* : cuarentena *f* — ~ *vt* **-tined; -tining** : poner en cuarentena
quarrel *n* : pelea *f*, riña *f* — ~ *vi* **-reled** *or* **-relled; -reling** *or* **-relling** : pelearse, reñir — **quarrelsome** *adj* : pendenciero
quarry[1] *n*, *pl* **quarries** PREY : presa *f*
quarry[2] *n*, *pl* **quarries** EXCAVATION : cantera *f*
quart *n* : cuarto *m* de galón
quarter *n* **1** : cuarto *m* (en matemáticas) **2** : moneda *f* de 25 centavos **3** DISTRICT : barrio *m* **4** ~ **after three** : las tres y cuarto **5** ~**s** *npl* LODGING : alojamiento *m* — ~ *vt* **1** : dividir en cuatro partes **2** : acuartelar (tropas) — **quarterly** *adv* : cada tres meses — ~ *adj* : trimestral — ~ *n*, *pl* **-lies** : publicación *f* trimestral
quartet *n* : cuarteto *m*
quartz *n* : cuarzo *m*
quash *vt* **1** ANNUL : anular **2** SUPPRESS : aplastar, sofocar

quaver *vi* : temblar

quay *n* : muelle *m*

queasy *adj* **-sier; -est** : mareado

queen *n* : reina *f*

queer *adj* ODD : extraño

quell *vt* SUPPRESS : sofocar, aplastar

quench *vt* **1** EXTINGUISH : apagar **2** ~ **one's thirst** : quitar la sed

query *n*, *pl* **-ries** : pregunta *f* — ~ *vt* **-ried; -rying** **1** ASK : preguntar **2** QUESTION : cuestionar

quest *n* : búsqueda *f*

question *n* **1** QUERY : pregunta *f* **2** ISSUE : cuestión *f* **3 be out of the** ~ : ser indiscutible **4 call into** ~ : poner en duda **5 without** ~ : sin duda — ~ *vt* **1** ASK : preguntar **2** DOUBT : cuestionar **3** INTERROGATE : interrogar — *vi* : preguntar — **questionable** *adj* : discutible — **question mark** *n* : signo *m* de interrogación — **questionnaire** *n* : cuestionario *m*

queue *n* : cola *f* — ~ *vi* **queued; queuing** *or* **queueing** : hacer cola

quibble *vi* **-bled; -bling** : discutir, quejarse por nimiedades

quick *adj* **1** : rápido **2** CLEVER : agudo — ~ *n* **to the** ~ : en lo vivo — ~ *adv* : rápidamente — **quicken** *vt* : acelerar — **quickly** *adv* : rápidamente — **quicksand** *n* : arena *f* movediza — **quick–tempered** *adj* : irascible — **quick–witted** *adj* : agudo

quiet *n* **1** : silencio *m* **2** CALM : tranquilidad *f* — ~ *adj* **1** : silencioso **2** CALM : tranquilo **3** RESERVED : callado **4** : discreto (dícese de colores, etc.) — ~ *vt* **1** SILENCE : hacer callar **2** CALM : calmar — *vi or* ~ **down** : calmarse — **quietly** *adv* **1** : silenciosamente **2** CALMLY : tranquilamente

quilt *n* : edredón *m*

quintet *n* : quinteto *m*

quip *n* : ocurrencia *f*, salida *f* — ~ *vt* **quipped; quipping** : decir bromeando

quirk *n* : peculiaridad *f*

quit *v* **quit; quitting** *vt* **1** LEAVE : dejar, abandonar **2** ~ **doing** : dejar de hacer — *vi* **1** STOP : parar **2** RESIGN : dimitir, renunciar

quite *adv* **1** COMPLETELY : completamente **2** RATHER : bastante

quits *adj* **call it** ~ : quedar en paz

quiver *vi* : temblar

quiz *n*, *pl* **quizzes** TEST : prueba *f* — ~ *vt* **quizzed; quizzing** : interrogar

quota *n* : cuota *f*, cupo *m*

quotation *n* **1** : cita *f* **2** ESTIMATE : presupuesto *m* — **quotation marks** *npl* : comillas *fpl* — **quote** *vt* **quoted; quoting** **1** CITE : citar **2** : cotizar (en finanzas) — ~ *n* **1** → **quotation** **2** ~**s** *npl* → **quotation marks**

quotient *n* : cociente *m*

R

r *n*, *pl* **r's** *or* **rs** : r *f*, decimoctava letra del alfabeto inglés

rabbi *n* : rabino *m*, **-na** *f*

rabbit *n*, *pl* **-bit** *or* **-bits** : conejo *m*, **-ja** *f*

rabble *n* : chusma *f*, populacho *m*

rabies *ns & pl* : rabia *f* — **rabid** *adj* **1** : rabioso **2** FANATIC : fanático

raccoon *n*, *pl* **-coon** *or* **-coons** : mapache *m*

race[1] *n* **1** : raza *f* **2 human** ~ : género *m* humano

race[2] *n* : carrera *f* (competitiva) — ~ *vi* **raced; racing** **1** : correr (en una carrera) **2** RUSH : ir corriendo — **racehorse** *n* : caballo *m* de carreras — **racetrack** *n* : pista *f* (de carreras)

racial *adj* : racial — **racism** *n* : racismo *m* — **racist** *n* : racista *mf*

rack *n* **1** SHELF : estante *m* **2 luggage** ~ : portaequipajes *m* — ~ *vt* **1** ~**ed with** : atormentado por **2** ~ **one's brains** : devanarse los sesos

racket[1] *n* : raqueta *f* (en deportes)

racket[2] *n* **1** DIN : alboroto *m*, bulla *f* **2** SWINDLE : estafa *f*

racy *adj* **racier; -est** : subido de tono, picante

radar *n* : radar *m*

radiant *adj* : radiante — **radiance** *n* : resplandor *m* — **radiate** *v* **-ated; -ating** *vt* : irradiar — *vi* **1** : irradiar **2** *or* ~ **out** : extenderse (desde un centro) — **radiation** *n* : radiación *f* — **radiator** *n* : radiador *m*

radical *adj* : radical — ~ *n* : radical *mf*

radii → **radius**

radio *n*, *pl* **-dios** : radio *mf* (aparato), radio *f* (medio) — ~ *vt* : transmitir por radio —

radioactive *adj* : radioactivo, radiactivo

radish *n* : rábano *m*

radius *n, pl* **radii** : radio *m*
raffle *vt* **-fled; -fling** : rifar — ~ *n* : rifa *f*
raft *n* : balsa *f*
rafter *n* : cabrio *m*
rag *n* **1** : trapo *m* **2** ~**s** *npl* TATTERS : harapos *mpl*, andrajos *mpl*
rage *n* **1** : cólera *f*, rabia *f* **2 be all the** ~ : hacer furor — ~ *vi* **raged; raging 1** : estar furioso **2** : bramar (dícese del viento, etc.)
ragged *adj* **1** UNEVEN : irregular **2** TATTERED : andrajoso, harapiento
raid *n* **1** : invasión *f* (militar) **2** : asalto *m* (por delincuentes), redada *f* (por la policía) — ~ *vt* **1** INVADE : invadir **2** ROB : asaltar **3** : hacer una redada en (dícese de la policía) — **raider** *n* ATTACKER : asaltante *mf*
rail¹ *vi* ~ **at s.o.** : recriminar a algn
rail² *n* **1** BAR : barra *f* **2** HANDRAIL : pasamanos *m* **3** TRACK : riel *m* **4 by** ~ : por ferrocarril — **railing** *n* **1** : baranda *f* (de un balcón), pasamanos *m* (de una escalera) **2** RAILS : reja *f* — **railroad** *n* : ferrocarril *m* — **railway** → **railroad**
rain *n* : lluvia *f* — ~ *vi* : llover — **rainbow** *n* : arco *m* iris — **raincoat** *n* : impermeable *m* — **rainfall** *n* : precipitación *f* — **rainy** *adj* **rainier; -est** : lluvioso
rain forest *n* : bosque *m* tropical
raise *vt* **raised; raising 1** : levantar **2** COLLECT : recaudar **3** REAR : criar **4** GROW : cultivar **5** INCREASE : aumentar **6** : sacar (objeciones, etc.) — ~ *n* : aumento *m*
raisin *n* : pasa *f*
rake *n* : rastrillo *m* — ~ *vt* **raked; raking** : rastrillar
rally *v* **-lied; -lying** *vi* **1** : unirse, reunirse **2** RECOVER : recuperarse — *vt* : conseguir (apoyo), unir a (la gente) — ~ *n, pl* **-lies** : reunión *f*, mitin *m*
RAM *n* : RAM *f*
ram *n* : carnero *m* (animal) — ~ *vt* **rammed; ramming 1** CRAM : meter con fuerza **2** *or* ~ **into** : chocar contra
ramble *vi* **-bled; -bling 1** WANDER : pasear **2** *or* ~ **on** : divagar — ~ *n* : paseo *m*, excursión *f*
ramp *n* : rampa *f*
rampage *vi* **-paged; -paging** : andar arrasando todo — ~ *n* : frenesí *m* (de violencia)
rampant *adj* : desenfrenado
rampart *n* : muralla *f*
ramshackle *adj* : destartalado
ran → **run**
ranch *n* : hacienda *f* — **rancher** *n* : hacendado *m*, -da *f*
rancid *adj* : rancio
rancor *n* : rencor *m*
random *adj* **1** : aleatorio **2 at** ~ : al azar

rang → **ring**
range *n* **1** GRASSLAND : pradera *f* **2** STOVE : cocina *f* **3** VARIETY : gama *f* **4** SCOPE : amplitud *f* **5** *or* **mountain** ~ : cordillera *f* — ~ *vi* **ranged; ranging 1** EXTEND : extenderse **2** ~ **from...to...** : variar entre...y... — **ranger** *n or* **forest** ~ : guardabosque *mf*
rank¹ *adj* **1** SMELLY : fétido **2** OUTRIGHT : completo
rank² *n* **1** ROW : fila *f* **2** : rango *m* (militar) **3** ~**s** *npl* : soldados *mpl* rasos **4 the** ~ **and file** : las bases — ~ *vt* RATE : clasificar — *vi* : clasificarse
rankle *vi* **-kled; -kling** : causar rencor, doler
ransack *vt* **1** SEARCH : registrar **2** LOOT : saquear
ransom *n* : rescate *m* — ~ *vt* : rescatar
rant *vi or* ~ **and rave** : despotricar
rap¹ *n* KNOCK : golpecito *m* — ~ *v* **rapped; rapping** : golpear
rap² *n or* ~ **music** : rap *m*
rapacious *adj* : rapaz
rape *vt* **raped; raping** : violar — ~ *n* : violación *f*
rapid *adj* : rápido — **rapids** *npl* : rápidos *mpl*
rapist *n* : violador *m*, -dora *f*
rapport *n* **have a good** ~ : entenderse bien
rapt *adj* : absorto, embelesado
rapture *n* : éxtasis *m*
rare *adj* **rarer; rarest 1** FINE : excepcional **2** UNCOMMON : raro **3** : poco cocido (dícese de la carne) — **rarely** *adv* : raramente — **rarity** *n, pl* **-ties** : rareza *f*
rascal *n* : pillo *m*, -lla *f*; pícaro *m*, -ra *f*
rash¹ *adj* : imprudente, precipitado
rash² *n* : sarpullido *m*, erupción *f*
rasp *vt* SCRAPE : raspar — ~ *n* : escofina *f*
raspberry *n, pl* **-ries** : frambuesa *f*
rat *n* : rata *f*
rate *n* **1** PACE : velocidad *f*, ritmo *m* **2** : tipo *m*, tasa *m* (de interés, etc.) **3** PRICE : tarifa *f* **4 at any** ~ : de todos modos **5 birth** ~ : índice *m* de natalidad — ~ *vt* **rated; rating 1** REGARD : considerar **2** DESERVE : merecer
rather *adv* **1** FAIRLY : bastante **2 I'd** ~... : prefiero... **3** *or* ~ : o mejor dicho
ratify *vt* **-fied; -fying** : ratificar — **ratification** *n* : ratificación *f*
rating *n* **1** : clasificación *f* **2** ~**s** *npl* : índice *m* de audiencia
ratio *n, pl* **-tios** : proporción *f*
ration *n* **1** : ración *f* **2** ~**s** *npl* PROVISIONS : víveres *mpl* — ~ *vt* **rationed; rationing** : racionar
rational *adj* : racional — **rationale** *n* : lógica *f*, razones *fpl* — **rationalize** *vt* **-ized; -izing** : racionalizar

rattle *v* **-tled; -tling** *vi* : traquetear — *vt* **1** SHAKE : agitar **2** UPSET : desconcertar **3** ~ **off** : decir de corrido — ~ *n* **1** : traqueteo *m* **2** *or* **baby's** ~ : sonajero *m* —
rattlesnake *n* : serpiente *f* de cascabel
raucous *adj* **1** HOARSE : ronco **2** BOISTEROUS : bullicioso
ravage *vt* **-aged; -aging** : estragar, asolar — **ravages** *npl* : estragos *mpl*
rave *vi* **raved; raving 1** : delirar **2** ~ **about** : hablar con entusiasmo sobre
raven *n* : cuervo *m*
ravenous *adj* **1** HUNGRY : hambriento **2** VORACIOUS : voraz
ravine *n* : barranco *m*
ravishing *adj* : encantador
raw *adj* **rawer; rawest 1** UNCOOKED : crudo **2** INEXPERIENCED : inexperto **3** CHAFED : en carne viva **4** : frío y húmedo (dícese del tiempo) **5** ~ **deal** : trato *m* injusto **6** ~ **materials** : materias *fpl* primas
ray *n* : rayo *m*
rayon *n* : rayón *m*
raze *vt* **razed; razing** : arrasar
razor *n* : maquinilla *f* de afeitar — **razor blade** *n* : hoja *f* de afeitar
reach *vt* **1** : alcanzar **2** *or* ~ **out** : extender **3** : llegar a (un acuerdo, un límite, etc.) **4** CONTACT : contactar — *vi* **1** : extenderse **2** ~ **for** : tratar de agarrar — ~ *n* **1** : alcance *m* **2 within** ~ : al alcance
react *vi* : reaccionar — **reaction** *n* : reacción *f* — **reactionary** *adj* : reaccionario — ~ *n, pl* **-ries** : reaccionario *m*, **-ria** *f* — **reactor** *n* : reactor *m*
read *v* **read; reading** *vt* **1** : leer **2** INTERPRET : interpretar **3** SAY : decir **4** INDICATE : marcar — *vi* **1** : leer **2 it** ~**s as follows** : dice lo siguiente — **readable** *adj* : legible — **reader** *n* : lector *m*, **-tora** *f*
readily *adv* **1** WILLINGLY : de buena gana **2** EASILY : fácilmente
reading *n* : lectura *f*
readjust *vt* : reajustar — *vi* : volverse a adaptar
ready *adj* **readier; -est 1** : listo, preparado **2** WILLING : dispuesto **3** AVAILABLE : disponible **4 get** ~ : prepararse — ~ *vt* **readied; readying** : preparar
real *adj* **1** : verdadero, real **2** GENUINE : auténtico — ~ *adv* VERY : muy — **real estate** *n* : propiedad *f* inmobiliaria, bienes *mpl* raices — **realism** *n* : realismo *m* — **realist** *n* : realista *mf* — **realistic** *adj* : realista — **reality** *n, pl* **-ties** : realidad *f*
realize *vt* **-ized; -izing 1** : darse cuenta de **2** ACHIEVE : realizar — **realization** *n* **1** : comprensión *f* **2** FULFILLMENT : realización *f*
really *adv* : verdaderamente

realm *n* **1** KINGDOM : reino *m* **2** SPHERE : esfera *f*
ream *n* : resma *f* (de papel)
reap *v* : cosechar
reappear *vi* : reaparecer
rear¹ *vt* **1** RAISE : levantar **2** : criar (niños, etc.) — *vi or* ~ **up** : encabritarse
rear² *n* **1** BACK : parte *f* de atrás **2** BUTTOCKS : trasero *m fam* — ~ *adj* : trasero, posterior
rearrange *vt* **-ranged; -ranging** : reorganizar, cambiar
reason *n* : razón *f* — ~ *vt* THINK : pensar — *vi* : razonar — **reasonable** *adj* : razonable — **reasoning** *n* : razonamiento *m*
reassure *vt* **-sured; -suring** : tranquilizar — **reassurance** *n* : (palabras *fpl* de) consuelo *m*
rebate *n* : reembolso *m*
rebel *n* : rebelde *mf* — ~ *vi* **-belled; -belling** : rebelarse — **rebellion** *n* : rebelión *f* — **rebellious** *adj* : rebelde
rebirth *n* : renacimiento *m*
rebound *vi* : rebotar — ~ *n* : rebote *m*
rebuff *vt* : rechazar — ~ *n* : desaire *m*
rebuild *vt* **-built; -building** : reconstruir
rebuke *vt* **-buked; -buking** : reprender — ~ *n* : reprimenda *f*
rebut *vt* **-butted; -butting** : rebatir — **rebuttal** *n* : refutación *f*
recall *vt* **1** : llamar (al servicio, etc.) **2** REMEMBER : recordar **3** REVOKE : revocar — ~ *n* **1** : retirada *f* **2** MEMORY : memoria *f*
recant *vi* : retractarse
recapitulate *v* **-lated; -lating** : recapitular
recapture *vt* **-tured; -turing 1** : recobrar **2** RELIVE : revivir
recede *vi* **-ceded; -ceding** : retirarse
receipt *n* **1** : recibo *m* **2** ~**s** *npl* : ingresos *mpl*
receive *vt* **-ceived; -ceiving** : recibir — **receiver** *n* **1** : receptor *m* (de radio, etc.) **2** *or* **telephone** ~ : auricular *m*
recent *adj* : reciente — **recently** *adv* : recientemente
receptacle *n* : receptáculo *m*, recipiente *m*
reception *n* : recepción *f* — **receptionist** *n* : recepcionista *mf* — **receptive** *adj* : receptivo
recess *n* **1** ALCOVE : hueco *m* **2** : recreo *m* (escolar) **3** ADJOURNMENT : suspensión *f* de actividades *Spain*, receso *m Lat* — **recession** *n* : recesión *f*
recharge *vt* **-charged; -charging** : recargar — **rechargeable** *adj* : recargable
recipe *n* : receta *f*
recipient *n* : recipiente *mf*
reciprocal *adj* : recíproco
recite *vt* **-cited; -citing 1** : recitar (un

poema, etc.) **2** LIST : enumerar — **recital** n
: recital m
reckless adj : imprudente — **recklessness**
n : imprudencia f
reckon vt **1** COMPUTE : calcular **2** CON-
SIDER : considerar — **reckoning** n : cálcu-
los mpl
reclaim vt **1** : reclamar **2** RECOVER : recuperar
recline vi -**clined; -clining** : reclinarse —
reclining adj : reclinable (dícese de un
asiento, etc.)
recluse n : solitario m, -**ria** f
recognition n : reconocimiento m — **recognizable** adj : reconocible — **recognize** vt
-**nized; -nizing** : reconocer
recoil vi : retroceder — ∼ n : culatazo m (de
un arma de fuego)
recollect v : recordar — **recollection** n : recuerdo m
recommend vt : recomendar — **recommendation** n : recomendación f
reconcile v -**ciled; -ciling** vt **1** : reconciliar
(personas), conciliar (datos, etc.) **2** ∼
oneself to : resignarse a — vi MAKE UP
: reconciliarse — **reconciliation** n : reconciliación f
reconnaissance n : reconocimiento m (militar)
reconsider vt : reconsiderar
reconstruct vt : reconstruir
record vt **1** WRITE DOWN : anotar, apuntar
2 REGISTER : registrar **3** : grabar (música,
etc.) — ∼ n **1** DOCUMENT : documento m
2 REGISTER : registro m **3** HISTORY : historial m **4** : disco m (de música, etc.) **5**
criminal ∼ : antecedentes mpl penales **6**
world ∼ : récord m mundial — **recorder** n
1 : flauta f dulce **2** or **tape** ∼ : grabadora
f — **recording** n : disco m — **record player**
n : tocadiscos m
recount¹ vt NARRATE : narrar, relatar
recount² vt : volver a contar (votos, etc.) ∼
— n : recuento m
recourse n **1** : recurso m **2 have** ∼ **to**
: recurrir a
recover vt : recobrar — vi RECUPERATE : recuperarse — **recovery** n, pl -**eries** : recuperación f
recreation n : recreo m — **recreational** adj
: de recreo
recruit vt : reclutar — ∼ n : recluta mf —
recruitment n : reclutamiento m
rectangle n : rectángulo m — **rectangular**
adj : rectangular
rectify vt -**fied; -fying** : rectificar
rector n **1** : parroco m (clérigo) **2** : rector
m, -**tora** f (de una universidad) — **rectory** n,
pl -**ries** : rectoría f
rectum n, pl -**tums** or -**ta** : recto m

recuperate v -**ated; -ating** vt : recuperar —
vi : recuperarse — **recuperation** n : recuperación f
recur vi -**curred; -curring** : repetirse — **re-
currence** n : repetición f — **recurrent** adj
: que se repite
recycle vt -**cled; -cling** : reciclar
red adj : rojo — ∼ n : rojo m — **redden** vt
: enrojecer — vi : enrojecerse — **reddish**
adj : rojizo
redecorate vt -**rated; -rating** : pintar de
nuevo
redeem vt **1** SAVE : salvar, rescatar **2** : desempeñar (de un monte de piedad) **3** : canjear (cupones, etc.) — **redemption** n : redención f
red–handed adv or adj : con las manos en la
masa
redhead n : pelirrojo m, -**ja** f
red–hot adj : al rojo vivo
redness n : rojez f
redo vt -**did; -done; -doing** : hacer de nuevo
redouble vt -**bled; -bling** : redoblar
red tape n : papeleo m
reduce v -**duced; -ducing** vt : reducir — vi
SLIM : adelgazar — **reduction** n : reducción
f
redundant adj : redundante
reed n **1** : caña f **2** : lengüeta f (de un instrumento)
reef n : arrecife m
reek vi : apestar
reel n : carrete m (de hilo, etc.) — ∼ vt **1**
∼ **in** : enrollar (un sedal), sacar (un pez)
del agua **2** ∼ **off** : enumerar — vi **1** SPIN
: dar vueltas **2** STAGGER : tambalearse
reestablish vt : restablecer
refer v -**ferred; -ferring** vt **1** DIRECT : enviar, mandar **2** SUBMIT : remitir — vi ∼ **to**
1 MENTION : referirse a **2** CONSULT : consultar
referee n : árbitro m, -**tra** f — ∼ v -**eed;
-eeing** : arbitrar
reference n **1** : referencia f **2** CONSULTA-
TION : consulta f **3** or ∼ **book** : libro m de
consulta **4 in** ∼ **to** : con referencia a
refill vt : rellenar — ∼ n : recambio m
refine vt -**fined; -fining** : refinar — **refined**
adj : refinado — **refinement** n : refinamiento m — **refinery** n, pl -**eries** : refinería
f
reflect vt : reflejar — vi **1** : reflejarse **2** ∼
badly on : desacreditar **3** ∼ **upon** : reflexionar sobre — **reflection** n **1** : reflexión f **2** IMAGE : reflejo m — **reflector** n
: reflector m
reflex n : reflejo m
reflexive adj : reflexivo
reform vt : reformar — vi : reformarse — ∼

n : reforma *f* — **reformer** *n* : reformador *m*, -dora *f*

refrain¹ *vi* ～ **from** : abstenerse de

refrain² *n* : estribillo *m* (en música)

refresh *vt* : refrescar — **refreshments** *npl* : refrigerio *m*

refrigerate *vt* -ated; -ating : refrigerar — **refrigeration** *n* : refrigeración *f* — **refrigerator** *n* : nevera *f*, refrigerador *m* *Lat*, frigorífico *m* *Spain*

refuel *v* -eled *or* -elled; -eling *or* -elling *vt* : llenar de carburante — *vi* : repostar

refuge *n* : refugio *m* — **refugee** *n* : refugiado *m*, -da *f*

refund *vt* : reembolsar — ～ *n* : reembolso *m*

refurbish *vt* : renovar, restaurar

refuse¹ *v* -fused; -fusing *vt* **1** : rehusar, rechazar **2** ～ **to do sth** : negarse a hacer algo — *vi* : negarse — **refusal** *n* : negativa *f*

refuse² *n* : residuos *mpl*, desperdicios *mpl*

refute *vt* -futed; -futing : refutar

regain *vt* : recuperar, recobrar

regal *adj* : regio, majestuoso — **regalia** *n* : ropaje *m*, insignias *fpl*

regard *n* **1** : consideración *f* **2** ESTEEM : estima *f* **3 in this** ～ : en este sentido **4** ～**s** *npl* : saludos *mpl* **5 with** ～ **to** : respecto a — ～ *vt* **1** : mirar (con recelo, etc.) **2** HEED : tener en cuenta **3** ESTEEM : estimar **4 as** ～**s** : en lo que se refiere a **5** ～ **as** : considerar — **regarding** *prep* : respecto a — **regardless** *adv* : a pesar de todo — **regardless of** *prep* **1** : sin tener en cuenta **2** IN SPITE OF : a pesar de

regent *n* : regente *mf*

reggae *n* : reggae *m*

regime *n* : régimen *m* — **regimen** *n* : régimen *m*

regiment *n* : regimiento *m*

region *n* : región *f* — **regional** *adj* : regional

register *n* : registro *m* — ～ *vt* **1** : registrar (a personas), matricular (vehículos) **2** SHOW : marcar, manifestar **3** : certificar (correo) — *vi* ENROLL : inscribirse, matricularse — **registrar** *n* : registrador *m*, -dora *f* oficial — **registration** *n* **1** : inscripción *f*, matriculación *f* **2** *or* ～ **number** : número *m* de matrícula — **registry** *n*, *pl* -tries : registro *m*

regret *vt* -gretted; -gretting : lamentar — ～ *n* **1** REMORSE : arrepentimiento *m* **2** SORROW : pesar *m* — **regrettable** *adj* : lamentable

regular *adj* **1** : regular **2** CUSTOMARY : habitual — ～ *n* : cliente *mf* habitual — **regularity** *n*, *pl* -ties : regularidad *f* — **regularly** *adv* : regularmente — **regulate** *vt* -lated;

-lating : regular — **regulation** *n* **1** CONTROL : regulación *f* **2** RULE : regla *f*

rehabilitate *vt* -tated; -tating : rehabilitar — **rehabilitation** *n* : rehabilitación *f*

rehearse *v* -hearsed; -hearsing : ensayar — **rehearsal** *n* : ensayo *m*

reign *n* : reinado *m* — ～ *vi* : reinar

reimburse *vt* -bursed; -bursing : reembolsar — **reimbursement** *n* : reembolso *m*

rein *n* : rienda *f*

reincarnation *n* : reencarnación *f*

reindeer *n* : reno *m*

reinforce *vt* -forced; -forcing : reforzar — **reinforcement** *n* : refuerzo *m*

reinstate *vt* -stated; -stating **1** : restablecer **2** : restituir (a algn en su cargo)

reiterate *vt* -ated; -ating : reiterar

reject *vt* : rechazar — **rejection** *n* : rechazo *m*

rejoice *vi* -joiced; -joicing : regocijarse

rejuvenate *vt* -nated; -nating : rejuvenecer

rekindle *vt* -dled; -dling : reavivar

relapse *n* : recaída *f* — ～ *vi* -lapsed; -lapsing : recaer

relate *v* -lated; -lating *vt* **1** TELL : relatar **2** ASSOCIATE : relacionar — *vi* ～ **to 1** CONCERN : estar relacionado con **2** UNDERSTAND : identificarse con **3** : relacionarse con (socialmente) — **related** *adj* ～ **to** : emparentado con — **relation** *n* **1** CONNECTION : relación *f* **2** RELATIVE : pariente *mf* **3 in** ～ **to** : en relación con **4** ～**s** *npl* : relaciones *fpl* — **relationship** *n* **1** : relación *f* **2** KINSHIP : parentesco *m* — **relative** *n* : pariente *mf* — ～ *adj* : relativo — **relatively** *adv* : relativamente

relax *vt* : relajar — *vi* : relajarse — **relaxation** *n* **1** : relajación *f* **2** RECREATION : esparcimiento *m*

relay *n* **1** : relevo *m* **2** *or* ～ **race** : carrera *f* de relevos — ～ *vt* -layed; -laying : transmitir

release *vt* -leased; -leasing **1** FREE : liberar, poner en libertad **2** : soltar (un freno, etc.) **3** EMIT : despedir **4** : sacar (un libro, etc.), estrenar (una película) — ～ *n* **1** : liberación *f* **2** : estreno *m* (de una película), publicación *f* (de un libro) **3** : fuga *f* (de gases)

relegate *vt* -gated; -gating : relegar

relent *vi* : ceder — **relentless** *adj* : implacable

relevant *adj* : pertinente — **relevance** *n* : pertinencia *f*

reliable *adj* : fiable (dícese de personas), fidedigno (dícese de información, etc.) — **reliability** *n*, *pl* -ties : fiabilidad *f* (de una cosa), responsabilidad *f* (de una persona) — **reliance** *n* **1** : dependencia *f* **2** TRUST : confianza *f* — **reliant** *adj* : dependiente

relic *n* : reliquia *f*
relief *n* **1** : alivio *m* **2** AID : ayuda *f* **3** : relieve *m* (en la escultura) **4** REPLACEMENT : relevo *m* — **relieve** *vt* -**lieved; -lieving 1** : aliviar **2** REPLACE : relevar (a algn) **3** ~ **s.o. of** : liberar a algn de
religion *n* : religión *f* — **religious** *adj* : religioso
relinquish *vt* : renunciar a, abandonar
relish *n* **1** : salsa *f* (condimento) **2 with** ~ : con gusto — ~ *vt* : saborear
relocate *vt* -**cated; -cating** : trasladar — *vi* : trasladarse — **relocation** *n* : traslado *m*
reluctance *n* : reticencia *f*, desgana *f* — **reluctant** *adj* : reacio, reticente — **reluctantly** *adv* : a regañadientes
rely *vi* -**lied; -lying** ~ **on 1** DEPEND ON : depender de **2** TRUST : confiar (en)
remain *vi* **1** : quedar **2** STAY : quedarse **3** CONTINUE : seguir, continuar — **remainder** *n* : resto *m* — **remains** *npl* : restos *mpl*
remark *n* : comentario *m*, observación *f* — ~ *vt* : observar — *vi* ~ **on** : observar — **remarkable** *adj* : extraordinario, notable
remedy *n, pl* -**dies** : remedio *m* — ~ *vt* -**died; -dying** : remediar — **remedial** *adj* : correctivo
remember *vt* **1** : acordarse de, recordar **2** ~ **to** : acordarse de — *vi* : acordarse, recordar — **remembrance** *n* : recuerdo *m*
remind *vt* : recordar — **reminder** *n* : recordatorio *m*
reminiscence *n* : recuerdo *m*, reminiscencia *f* — **reminisce** *vi* -**nisced; -niscing** : rememorar los viejos tiempos — **reminiscent** *adj* **be** ~ **of** : recordar
remiss *adj* : negligente, remiso
remit *vt* -**mitted; -mitting 1** PARDON : perdonar **2** : enviar (dinero) — **remission** *n* : remisión *f*
remnant *n* **1** : resto *m* **2** TRACE : vestigio *m*
remorse *n* : remordimiento *m* — **remorseful** *adj* : arrepentido
remote *adj* -**moter; -est 1** : remoto **2** ALOOF : distante **3** ~ **from** : apartado de, alejado de — **remote control** *n* : control *m* remoto — **remotely** *adv* SLIGHTLY : remotamente
remove *vt* -**moved; -moving 1** : quitar (una tapa, etc.), quitarse (ropa) **2** EXTRACT : sacar **3** DISMISS : destituir **4** ELIMINATE : eliminar — **removable** *adj* : separable, de quita y pon — **removal** *n* **1** : eliminación *f* **2** EXTRACTION : extracción *f*
remunerate *vt* -**ated; -ating** : remunerar
render *vt* **1** : rendir (homenaje), prestar (ayuda) **2** MAKE : hacer **3** TRANSLATE : traducir
rendezvous *ns & pl* : cita *f*
rendition *n* : interpretación *f*

renegade *n* : renegado *m*, -da *f*
renew *vt* **1** : renovar **2** RESUME : reanudar — **renewal** *n* : renovación *f*
renounce *vt* -**nounced; -nouncing** : renunciar a
renovate *vt* -**vated; -vating** : renovar — **renovation** *n* : renovación *f*
renown *n* : renombre *m* — **renowned** *adj* : célebre, renombrado
rent *n* **1** : alquiler *m*, arrendamiento *m*, renta *f* **2 for** ~ : se alquila — ~ *vt* : alquilar — **rental** *n* : alquiler *m* — ~ *adj* : de alquiler — **renter** *n* : arrendatario *m*, -ria *f*
renunciation *n* : renuncia *f*
reopen *vt* : volver a abrir
reorganize *vt* -**nized; -nizing** : reorganizar — **reorganization** *n* : reorganización *f*
repair *vt* : reparar, arreglar — ~ *n* **1** : reparación *f*, arreglo *m* **2 in bad** ~ : en mal estado
repay *vt* -**paid; -paying 1** : devolver (dinero), pagar (una deuda) **2** : corresponder a (un favor, etc.)
repeal *vt* : abrogar, revocar — ~ *n* : abrogación *f*, revocación *f*
repeat *vt* : repetir — ~ *n* : repetición *f* — **repeatedly** *adv* : repetidas veces
repel *vt* -**pelled; -pelling** : repeler — **repellent** *n* : repelente *m*
repent *vi* : arrepentirse — **repentance** *n* : arrepentimiento *m*
repercussion *n* : repercusión *f*
repertoire *n* : repertorio *m*
repetition *n* : repetición *f* — **repetitious** *adj* : repetitivo — **repetitive** *adj* : repetitivo
replace *vt* -**placed; -placing 1** : reponer **2** SUBSTITUTE : reemplazar, sustituir **3** EXCHANGE : cambiar — **replacement** *n* **1** : sustitución *f* **2** : sustituto *m*, -ta *f* (persona) **3** *or* ~ **part** : repuesto *m*
replenish *vt* **1** : reponer **2** REFILL : rellenar
replete *adj* ~ **with** : repleto de
replica *n* : réplica *f*
reply *vi* -**plied; -plying** : contestar, responder — ~ *n, pl* -**plies** : respuesta *f*
report *n* **1** : informe *m* **2** RUMOR : rumor *m* **3** *or* **news** ~ : reportaje *m* **4 weather** ~ : boletín *m* meteorológico — ~ *vt* **1** RELATE : anunciar **2** ~ **a crime** : denunciar un delito **3** *or* ~ **on** : informar sobre — *vi* **1** : informar **2** ~ **for duty** : presentarse — **report card** *n* : boletín *m* de calificaciones — **reportedly** *adv* : según se dice — **reporter** *n* : periodista *mf*; reportero *m*, -ra *f*
repose *vi* -**posed; -posing** : reposar — ~ *n* : reposo *m*
reprehensible *adj* : reprensible
represent *vt* **1** : representar **2** PORTRAY : presentar — **representation** *n* : represen-

tación *f* — **representative** *adj* : representativo — ~ *n* : representante *mf*

repress *vt* : reprimir — **repression** *n* : represión *f*

reprieve *n* : indulto *m*

reprimand *n* : reprimenda *f* — ~ *vt* : reprender

reprint *vt* : reimprimir — ~ *n* : reedición *f*

reprisal *n* : represalia *f*

reproach *n* **1** : reproche *m* **2 beyond** ~ : irreprochable — ~ *vt* : reprochar — **reproachful** *adj* : de reproche

reproduce *v* **-duced; -ducing** *vt* : reproducir — *vi* : reproducirse — **reproduction** *n* : reproducción *f* — **reproductive** *adj* : reproductor

reproof *n* : reprobación *f*

reptile *n* : reptil *m*

republic *n* : república *f* — **republican** *n* : republicano *m*, **-na** *f* — ~ *adj* : republicano

repudiate *vt* **-ated; -ating** : repudiar

repugnant *adj* : repugnante, asqueroso — **repugnance** *n* : repugnancia *f*

repulse *vt* **-pulsed; -pulsing** : repeler, rechazar — **repulsive** *adj* : repulsivo

reputation *n* : reputación *f* — **reputable** *adj* : de confianza, acreditado — **reputed** *adj* : supuesto

request *n* : petición *f* — ~ *vt* : pedir

requiem *n* : réquiem *m*

require *vt* **-quired; -quiring** **1** CALL FOR : requerir **2** NEED : necesitar — **requirement** *n* **1** NEED : necesidad *f* **2** DEMAND : requisito *m* — **requisite** *adj* : necesario

resale *n* : reventa *f*

rescind *vt* : rescindir (un contrato), revocar (una ley, etc.)

rescue *vt* **-cued; -cuing** : rescatar, salvar — ~ *n* : rescate *m* — **rescuer** *n* : salvador *m*, -dora *f*

research *n* : investigación *f* — ~ *vt* : investigar — **researcher** *n* : investigador *m*, -dora *f*

resemble *vt* **-sembled; -sembling** : parecerse a — **resemblance** *n* : parecido *m*

resent *vt* : resentirse de, ofenderse por — **resentful** *adj* : resentido — **resentment** *n* : resentimiento *m*

reserve *vt* **-served; -serving** : reservar — ~ *n* **1** : reserva *f* **2** ~**s** *npl* : reservas *fpl* (militares) — **reservation** *n* : reserva *f* — **reserved** *adj* : reservado — **reservoir** *n* : embalse *m*

reset *vt* **-set; -setting** : volver a poner (un reloj, etc.)

residence *n* : residencia *f* — **reside** *vi* **-sided; -siding** : residir — **resident** *adj* : residente — ~ *n* : residente *mf* — **residential** *adj* : residencial

residue *n* : residuo *m*

resign *vt* **1** QUIT : dimitir **2** ~ **oneself to** : resignarse a — **resignation** *n* **1** : dimisión *f* **2** ACCEPTANCE : resignación *f*

resilient *adj* **1** : resistente (dícese de personas) **2** ELASTIC : elástico — **resilience** *n* **1** : resistencia *f* **2** ELASTICITY : elasticidad *f*

resin *n* : resina *f*

resist *vt* : resistir — *vi* : resistirse — **resistance** *n* : resistencia *f* — **resistant** *adj* : resistente

resolve *vt* **-solved; -solving** : resolver — ~ *n* : resolución *f* — **resolution** *n* **1** : resolución *f* **2** DECISION, INTENTION : propósito *m* — **resolute** *adj* : resuelto

resonance *n* : resonancia *f* — **resonant** *adj* : resonante

resort *n* **1** RECOURSE : recurso *m* **2** *or* **tourist** ~ : centro *m* turístico — ~ *vi* ~ **to** : recurrir a

resounding *adj* **1** RESONANT : resonante **2** ABSOLUTE : rotundo

resource *n* : recurso *m* — **resourceful** *adj* : ingenioso

respect *n* **1** ESTEEM : respeto *m* **2 in some** ~**s** : en algún sentido **3 pay one's** ~**s** : presentar uno sus respetos **4 with** ~ **to** : (con) respecto a — ~ *vt* : respetar — **respectable** *adj* : respetable — **respectful** *adj* : respetuoso — **respective** *adj* : respectivo — **respectively** *adv* : respectivamente

respiration *n* : respiración *f* — **respiratory** *adj* : respiratorio

respite *n* : respiro *m*

response *n* : respuesta *f* — **respond** *vi* : responder — **responsibility** *n*, *pl* **-ties** : responsabilidad *f* — **responsible** *adj* : responsable — **responsive** *adj* : sensible, receptivo

rest[1] *n* **1** : descanso *m* **2** SUPPORT : apoyo *m* **3** : silencio *m* (en música) — ~ *vi* **1** : descansar **2** LEAN : apoyarse **3** ~ **on** DEPEND ON : depender de — *vt* **1** RELAX : descansar **2** LEAN : apoyar

rest[2] *n* REMAINDER : resto *m*

restaurant *n* : restaurante *m*

restful *adj* : tranquilo, apacible

restitution *n* : restitución *f*

restless *adj* : inquieto, agitado

restore *vt* **-stored; -storing** **1** RETURN : devolver **2** REESTABLISH : restablecer **3** REPAIR : restaurar — **restoration** *n* **1** : restablecimiento *m* **2** REPAIR : restauración *f*

restrain *vt* **1** : contener **2** ~ **oneself** : contenerse — **restrained** *adj* : comedido, moderado — **restraint** *n* **1** : restricción *f* **2** SELF-CONTROL : moderación *f*, control *m* de sí mismo

restriction *n* : restricción *f* — **restrict** *vt*

: restringir — **restricted** *adj* : restringido
— **restrictive** *adj* : restrictivo

result *vi* : resultar — **~** *n* **1** : resultado *m*
2 as a ~ of : como consecuencia de

résumé *or* resume *or* resumé *n* : currículum
m (vitae)

resume *v* **-sumed; -suming** *vt* : reanudar —
vi : reanudarse

resumption *n* : reanudación *f*

resurgence *n* : resurgimiento *m*

resurrection *n* : resurrección *f* — **resurrect**
vt : resucitar

resuscitate *vt* **-tated; -tating** : resucitar

retail *vt* : vender al por menor — **~** *n* : venta
f al por menor — **~** *adj* : detallista, minorista — **~** *adv* : al detalle, al por menor
— **retailer** *n* : detallista *mf*, minorista *mf*

retain *vt* : retener

retaliate *vi* **-ated; -ating** : tomar represalias
— **retaliation** *n* : represalias *fpl*

retard *vt* : retardar, retrasar — **retarded** *adj*
: retrasado

retention *n* : retención *f*

reticence *n* : reticencia *f* — **reticent** *adj*
: reticente

retina *n*, *pl* **-nas** *or* **-nae** : retina *f*

retinue *n* : séquito *m*

retire *vi* **-tired; -tiring 1** WITHDRAW : retirarse **2** : jubilarse, retirarse (de un trabajo)
3 : acostarse (en la cama) — **retirement** *n*
: jubilación *f* — **retiring** *adj* SHY : retraído

retort *vt* : replicar — **~** *n* : réplica *f*

retrace *vt* **-traced; -tracing ~ one's steps**
: volver sobre sus pasos

retract *vt* **1** WITHDRAW : retirar **2** : retraer
(garras, etc.) — *vi* : retractarse

retrain *vt* : reciclar

retreat *n* **1** : retirada *f* **2** REFUGE : refugio
m — **~** *vi* : retirarse

retribution *n* : castigo *m*

retrieve *vt* **-trieved; -trieving 1** : cobrar,
recuperar **2** RESCUE : salvar — **retrieval** *n*
: recuperación *f* — **retriever** *n* : perro *m*
cobrador

retroactive *adj* : retroactivo

retrospect *n* **in ~** : mirando hacia atrás —
retrospective *adj* : retrospectivo

return *vi* **1** : volver, regresar **2** REAPPEAR
: reaparecer — *vt* **1** : devolver **2** YIELD
: producir — **~** *n* **1** : regreso *m*, vuelta *f*
2 : devolución *f* (de algo prestado) **3** YIELD
: rendimiento *m* **4 in ~ for** : a cambio de **5**
or **tax ~** : declaración *f* de impuestos —
~ *adj* : de vuelta

reunite *vt* **-nited; -niting** : reunir — **reunion**
n : reunión *f*

revamp *vt* : renovar

reveal *vt* **1** : revelar **2** SHOW : dejar ver

revel *vi* **-eled** *or* **-elled; -eling** *or* **-elling ~**
in : deleitarse en

revelation *n* : revelación *f*

revelry *n*, *pl* **-ries** : jolgorio *m*, regocijos *mpl*

revenge *vt* **-venged; -venging** : vengar —
~ *n* **1** : venganza *f* **2 take ~ on** : vengarse de

revenue *n* : ingresos *mpl*

reverberate *vi* **-ated; -ating** : retumbar, resonar

reverence *n* : reverencia *f*, veneración *f* —
revere *vt* **-vered; -vering** : venerar — **reverend** *adj* : reverendo — **reverent** *adj*
: reverente

reverie *n*, *pl* **-eries** : ensueño *m*

reverse *adj* : inverso, contrario — **~** *v*
-versed; -versing *vt* **1** : invertir **2** : cambiar (una política), revocar (una decisión)
3 : dar marcha atrás a (un automóvil) — *vi*
: invertirse — **~** *n* **1** BACK : dorso *m*, revés
m **2** *or* **~ gear** : marcha *f* atrás **3 the ~**
: lo contrario — **reversible** *adj* : reversible
— **reversal** *n* **1** : inversión *f* **2** CHANGE
: cambio *m* total **3** SETBACK : revés *m* —

revert *vi* : revertir

review *n* **1** : revisión *f* **2** OVERVIEW : resumen *m* **3** CRITIQUE : reseña *f*, crítica *f* **4**
: repaso *m* (para un examen) — **~** *vt* **1**
EXAMINE : examinar **2** : repasar (una lección) **3** CRITIQUE : reseñar — **reviewer** *n*
: crítico *m*, -ca *f*

revile *vt* **-viled; -viling** : injuriar

revise *vt* **-vised; -vising 1** : modificar (una
política, etc.) **2** : revisar, corregir (una publicación) — **revision** *n* : corrección *f*, modificación *f*

revive *v* **-vived; -viving** *vt* **1** : reanimar,
reactivar **2** : resucitar (a una persona) **3**
RESTORE : restablecer — *vi* **1** : reanimarse,
reactivarse **2** COME TO : volver en sí — **revival** *n* : reanimación *f*, reactivación *f*

revoke *vt* **-voked; -voking** : revocar

revolt *vi* : rebelarse, sublevarse — *vt* : dar
asco a — **~** *n* : revuelta *f*, sublevación *f* —
revolting *adj* : asqueroso

revolution *n* : revolución *f* — **revolutionary**
adj : revolucionario — **~** *n*, *pl* **-aries** : revolucionario *m*, **-ria** *f* — **revolutionize** *vt*
-ized; -izing : revolucionar

revolve *v* **-volved; -volving** *vt* : hacer girar
— *vi* : girar

revolver *n* : revólver *m*

revue *n* : revista *f* (teatral)

revulsion *n* : repugnancia *f*

reward *vt* : recompensar — **~** *n* : recompensa *f*

rewrite *vt* **-wrote; -written; -writing** : volver
a escribir

rhetoric *n* : retórica *f* — **rhetorical** *adj*
: retórico

rheumatism *n* : reumatismo *m* — **rheu-
matic** *adj* : reumático

rhino *n, pl* **-no** *or* **-nos** → **rhinoceros** — **rhinoceros** *n, pl* **-noceroses** *or* **-noceros** *or* **-noceri** : rinoceronte *m*

rhubarb *n* : ruibarbo *m*

rhyme *n* **1** : rima *f* **2** VERSE : verso *m* (en rima) — *vi* **rhymed; rhyming** : rimar

rhythm *n* : ritmo *m* — **rhythmic** *or* **rhythmical** *adj* : rítmico

rib *n* : costilla *f* — ~ *vt* TEASE : tomar el pelo a

ribbon *n* : cinta *f*

rice *n* : arroz *m*

rich *adj* **1** : rico **2** ~ **foods** : comidas *fpl* pesadas — **riches** *npl* : riquezas *fpl* — **richness** *n* : riqueza *f*

rickety *adj* : desvencijado, destartalado

ricochet *n* : rebote *m* — ~ *vi* **-cheted** *or* **-chetted; -cheting** *or* **-chetting** : rebotar

rid *vt* **rid; ridding 1** : librar **2 get ~ of** : deshacerse de — **riddance** *n* **good ~!** : ¡adiós y buen viaje!

riddle[1] *n* : acertijo *m*, adivinanza *f*

riddle[2] *vt* **-dled; -dling 1** : acribillar **2 riddled with** : lleno de

ride *v* **rode; ridden; riding** *vt* **1** : montar (a caballo, en bicicleta), ir (en autobús, etc.) **2** TRAVERSE : recorrer — *vi* **1** *or* ~ **horseback** : montar a caballo **2** : ir (en auto, etc.) — ~ *n* **1** : paseo *m*, vuelta *f* **2** : aparato *m* (en un parque de diversiones) — **rider** *n* **1** : jinete *mf* (a caballo) **2** CYCLIST : ciclista *mf*, motociclista *mf*

ridge *n* : cadena *f* (de montañas)

ridiculous *adj* : ridículo — **ridicule** *n* : burlas *fpl* — ~ *vt* **-culed; -culing** : ridiculizar

rife *adj* **1** : extendido **2 be ~ with** : estar plagado de

rifle[1] *vi* **-fled; -fling ~ through** : revolver

rifle[2] *n* : rifle *m*, fusil *m*

rift *n* **1** : grieta *f* **2** : ruptura *f* (entre personas)

rig[1] *vt* : amañar (una elección)

rig[2] *vt* **rigged; rigging 1** : aparejar (un barco) **2** EQUIP : equipar **3** *or* ~ **out** DRESS : vestir **4** *or* ~ **up** CONSTRUCT : construir — ~ *n* **1** : aparejo *m* (de un barco) **2** *or* **oil** ~ : plataforma *f* petrolífera — **rigging** *n* : aparejo *m*

right *adj* **1** JUST : bueno, justo **2** CORRECT : correcto **3** APPROPRIATE : apropiado, adecuado **4** STRAIGHT : recto **5 be ~** : tener razón **6** → **right–hand** — ~ *n* **1** GOOD : bien *m* **2** ENTITLEMENT : derecho *m* **3 on the ~** : a la derecha **4** *or* ~ **side** : derecha *f* — ~ *adv* **1** WELL : bien **2** PRECISELY : justo **3** DIRECTLY : derecho **4** IMMEDIATELY : inmediatamente **5** COMPLETELY : completamente **6** *or* **to the ~** : a la derecha — ~ *vt* **1** STRAIGHTEN : enderezar **2 ~ a wrong** : reparar un

daño — **right angle** *n* : ángulo *m* recto — **righteous** *adj* : recto, honrado — **rightful** *adj* : legítimo — **right–hand** *adj* : derecho — **right–handed** *adj* : diestro — **rightly** *adv* **1** : justamente **2** CORRECTLY : correctamente — **right–wing** *adj* : derechista

rigid *adj* : rígido

rigor *or Brit* **rigour** *n* : rigor *m* — **rigorous** *adj* : riguroso

rim *n* **1** EDGE : borde *m* **2** : llanta *f* (de una rueda) **3** : montura *f* (de anteojos)

rind *n* : corteza *f*

ring[1] *v* **rang; rung; ringing** *vi* **1** : sonar (dícese de un timbre, etc.) **2** RESOUND : resonar — *vt* : tocar (un timbre, etc.) — ~ *n* **1** : toque *m* (de un timbre, etc.) **2** CALL : llamada *f* (por teléfono)

ring[2] *n* **1** : anillo *m*, sortija *f* **2** BAND, HOOP : aro *m* **3** CIRCLE : círculo *m* **4** *or* **boxing** ~ : cuadrilátero *m* **5** NETWORK : red *f* — ~ *vt* : cercar, rodear — **ringleader** *n* : cabecilla *mf*

ringlet *n* : rizo *m*, bucle *m*

rink *n* : pista *f* (de patinaje)

rinse *vt* **rinsed; rinsing** : enjuagar — ~ *n* : enjuague *m*

riot *n* : disturbio *m* — ~ *vi* : causar disturbios — **rioter** *n* : alborotador *m*, -dora *f*

rip–off *n* : timo *m fam*

rip *v* **ripped; ripping** *vt* **1** : rasgar, desgarrar **2** ~ **off** : arrancar — *vi* : rasgarse — ~ *n* : rasgón *m*, desgarrón *m*

ripe *adj* **riper; ripest 1** : maduro **2** ~ **for** : listo por — **ripen** *v* : madurar — **ripeness** *n* : madurez *f*

ripple *v* **-pled; -pling** *vi* : rizarse (dícese de agua) — *vt* : rizar — ~ *n* : onda *f*, rizo *m*

rise *vi* **rose; risen; rising 1** GET UP : levantarse **2** : salir (dícese del sol, etc.) **3** ASCEND : subir **4** INCREASE : aumentar **5** ~ **up** REBEL : sublevarse — ~ *n* **1** ASCENT : subida *f* **2** INCREASE : aumento *m* **3** SLOPE : cuesta *f* — **riser** *n* **1 early ~** : madrugador *m*, -dora *f* **2 late ~** : dormilón *m*, -lona *f*

risk *n* : riesgo *m* — ~ *vt* : arriesgar — **risky** *adj* **riskier; -est** : arriesgado, riesgoso *Lat*

rite *n* : rito *m* — **ritual** *adj* : ritual — ~ *n* : ritual *m*

rival *n* : rival *mf* — ~ *adj* : rival — ~ *vt* **-valed** *or* **-valled; -valing** *or* **-valling** : rivalizar con — **rivalry** *n, pl* **-ries** : rivalidad *f*

river *n* : río *m*

rivet *n* : remache *m* — ~ *vt* **1** : remachar **2** FIX : fijar (los ojos, etc.) **3 be ~ed by** : estar fascinado con

roach → **cockroach**

road *n* **1** : carretera *f* **2** STREET : calle *f* **3** PATH : camino *m* — **roadblock** *n* : control *m*

— **roadside** *n* : borde *m* de la carretera — **roadway** *n* : carretera *f*

roam *vi* : vagar — *vt* : vagar por

roar *vi* 1 : rugir 2 ~ **with laughter** : reírse a carcajadas — *vt* : decir a gritos — ~ *n* : rugido *m* (de un animal), estruendo *m* (de un avión, etc.)

roast *vt* : asar (carne, etc.), tostar (café, etc.) — *vi* : asarse — ~ *n* : asado *m* — ~ *adj* : asado — **roast beef** *n* : rosbif *m*

rob *v* **robbed; robbing** *vt* 1 : robar 2 ~ **of** : privar de — *vi* : robar — **robber** *n* : ladrón *m*, **-drona** *f* — **robbery** *n*, *pl* **-beries** : robo *m*

robe *n* 1 : toga *f* (de un magistrado, etc.) 2 → **bathrobe**

robin *n* : petirrojo *m*

robot *n* : robot *m*

robust *adj* : robusto

rock[1] *vt* 1 : acunar (a un niño), mecer (una cuna) 2 SHAKE : sacudir — *vi* : mecerse — ~ *n or* ~ **music** : música *f* rock

rock[2] *n* 1 : roca *f* (sustancia) 2 BOULDER : peña *f*, peñasco *m* 3 STONE : piedra *f*

rocket *n* : cohete *m*

rocking chair *n* : mecedora *f*

rocky *adj* **rockier; -est** 1 : rocoso 2 SHAKY : tambaleante

rod *n* 1 : varilla *f* 2 *or* **fishing** ~ : caña *f* de pescar

rode → **ride**

rodent *n* : roedor *m*

rodeo *n*, *pl* **-deos** : rodeo *m*

roe *n* : hueva *f*

rogue *n* : pícaro *m*, **-ra** *f*

role *n* : papel *m*

roll *n* 1 : rollo *m* (de película, etc.) 2 LIST : lista *f* 3 : redoble *m* (de un tambor) 4 SWAYING : balanceo *m* 5 BUN : pancito *m Lat*, panecillo *m Spain* — ~ *vt* 1 : hacer rodar 2 *or* ~ **out** : estirar (masa) 3 ~ **up** : enrollar (papel, etc.), arremangar (una manga) — *vi* 1 : rodar 2 SWAY : balancearse 3 ~ **around** : revolcarse 4 ~ **over** : darse la vuelta — **roller** *n* 1 : rodillo *m* 2 CURLER : rulo *m* — **roller coaster** *n* : montaña *f* rusa — **roller-skate** *vi* **-skated; -skating** : patinar (sobre ruedas) — **roller skate** *n* : patín *m* (de ruedas)

Roman *adj* : romano — **Roman Catholic** *adj* : católico

romance *n* 1 : novela *f* romántica 2 AFFAIR : romance *m*

Romanian *adj* : rumano — ~ *n* : rumano *m* (idioma)

romantic *adj* : romántico

romp *n* : retozo *m* — ~ *vi* : retozar

roof *n*, *pl* **roofs** 1 : tejado *m*, techo *m* 2 ~ **of the mouth** : paladar *m* — **roofing** *n* : techumbre *f* — **rooftop** *n* : tejado *m*, techo *m*

rook[1] *n* : grajo *m* (ave)

rook[2] *n* : torre *f* (en ajedrez)

rookie *n* : novato *m*, **-ta** *f*

room *n* 1 : cuarto *m*, habitación *f* 2 BEDROOM : dormitorio *m* 3 SPACE : espacio *m* 4 OPPORTUNITY : posibilidad *f* — **roommate** *n* : compañero *m*, **-ra** *f* de cuarto — **roomy** *adj* **roomier; -est** : espacioso

roost *n* : percha *f* — ~ *vi* : posarse — **rooster** *n* : gallo *m*

root[1] *n* : raíz *f* — ~ *vt* ~ **out** : extirpar

root[2] *vi* ~ **around in** : hurgar en

root[3] *vi* ~ **for** SUPPORT : alentar

rope *n* : cuerda *f* — ~ *vt* **roped; roping** 1 : atar (con cuerda) 2 ~ **off** : acordonar

rosary *n*, *pl* **-ries** : rosario *m*

rose[1] → **rise**

rose[2] *n* : rosa *f* (flor), rosa *m* (color) — ~ *adj* : rosa — **rosebush** *n* : rosal *m*

rosemary *n*, *pl* **-maries** : romero *m*

Rosh Hashanah *n* : el Año Nuevo judío

roster *n* : lista *f*

rostrum *n*, *pl* **-tra** *or* **-trums** : tribuna *f*

rosy *adj* **rosier; -est** 1 : sonrosado 2 PROMISING : halagüeno

rot *v* **rotted; rotting** *vi* : pudrirse — *vt* : pudrir — ~ *n* : putrefacción *f*

rotary *adj* : rotativo — ~ *n* : rotonda *f*, glorieta *f Spain*

rotate *v* **-tated; -tating** *vi* : girar — *vt* 1 : girar 2 ALTERNATE : alternar — **rotation** *n* : rotación *f*

rote *n* **by** ~ : de memoria

rotor *n* : rotor *m*

rotten *adj* 1 : podrido 2 BAD : malo

rouge *n* : colorete *m*

rough *adj* 1 COARSE : áspero 2 RUGGED : accidentado 3 CHOPPY : agitado 4 DIFFICULT : duro 5 FORCEFUL : brusco 6 APPROXIMATE : aproximado 7 UNREFINED : tosco 8 ~ **draft** : borrador *m* — ~ *vt* 1 → **roughen** 2 ~ **up** BEAT : dar una paliza a — **roughage** *n* : fibra *f* — **roughen** *vt* : poner áspero — *vi* : ponerse áspero — **roughly** *adv* 1 : bruscamente 2 ABOUT : aproximadamente — **roughness** *n* COARSENESS : aspereza *f*

roulette *n* : ruleta *f*

round *adj* : redondo — ~ *adv* → **around** — ~ *n* 1 : círculo *m* 2 : ronda *f* (de bebidas, negociaciones, etc.) 3 : asalto *m* (en boxeo), vuelta *f* (en juegos) 4 ~ **of applause** : aplauso *m* 5 ~**s** *npl* : visitas *fpl* (de un médico), rondas *fpl* (de un policía, etc.) — ~ *vt* 1 TURN : doblar 2 ~ **off** : redondear 3 ~ **off** *or* ~ **out** COMPLETE : rematar 4 ~ **up** GATHER : reunir (personas), rodear (ganado) — ~ *prep* → **around**

— **roundabout** *adj* : indirecto — **round–trip** *n* : viaje *m* de ida y vuelta — **roundup** *n* : rodeo *m* (de animales), redada *f* (de delincuentes, etc.)

rouse *vt* **roused; rousing 1** AWAKEN : despertar **2** EXCITE : excitar

rout *n* : derrota *f* aplastante — ~ *vt* : derrotar

route *n* **1** : ruta *f* **2** *or* **delivery** ~ : recorrido *m*

routine *n* : rutina *f* — ~ *adj* : rutinario

rove *v* **roved; roving** *vi* : errar, vagar — *vt* : errar por

row¹ *vt* **1** : llevar a remo **2** ~ **a boat** : remar — *vi* : remar

row² *n* **1** : fila *f* (de gente o asientos), hilera *f* (de casas, etc.) **2 in a** ~ SUCCESSIVELY : seguido

row³ *n* **1** RACKET : bulla *f* **2** QUARREL : pelea *f*

rowboat *n* : bote *m* de remos

rowdy *adj* **-dier; -est** : escandaloso, alborotador — ~ *n*, *pl* **-dies** : alborotador *m*, -dora *f*

royal *adj* : real — **royalty** *n*, *pl* **-ties 1** : realeza *f* **2 royalties** *npl* : derechos *mpl* de autor

rub *v* **rubbed; rubbing** *vt* **1** : frotar **2** CHAFE : rozar **3** ~ **in** : aplicar frotando — *vi* **1** ~ **against** : rozar **2** ~ **off** : salir (al frotar) — ~ *n* : frotamiento *m*

rubber *n* **1** : goma *f*, caucho *m* **2** ~**s** *npl* : chanclos *mpl* — **rubber band** *n* : goma *f* (elástica) — **rubber stamp** *n* : sello *m* (de goma) — **rubbery** *adj* : gomoso

rubbish *n* **1** : basura *f* **2** NONSENSE : tonterías *fpl*

rubble *n* : escombros *mpl*

ruby *n*, *pl* **-bies** : rubí *m*

rudder *n* : timón *m*

ruddy *adj* **-dier; -est** : rubicundo

rude *adj* **ruder; rudest 1** IMPOLITE : grosero, mal educado **2** ABRUPT : brusco — **rudely** *adv* : groseramente — **rudeness** *n* : mala educación *f*

rudiment *n* : rudimento *m* — **rudimentary** *adj* : rudimentario

rue *vt* **rued; ruing** : lamentar — **rueful** *adj* : triste, arrepentido

ruffle *vt* **-fled; -fling 1** : despeinar (pelo), erizar (plumas) **2** VEX : alterar, contrariar — ~ *n* : volante *m* (de un vestido, etc.)

rug *n* : alfombra *f*, tapete *m*

rugged *adj* **1** : escabroso (dícese del terreno), escarpado (dícese de montañas) **2** HARSH : duro **3** STURDY : fuerte

ruin *n* : ruina *f* — ~ *vt* : arruinar

rule *n* **1** : regla *f* **2** CONTROL : dominio *m* **3 as a** ~ : por lo general — ~ *v* **ruled; ruling** *vt* **1** GOVERN : gobernar **2** : fallar

(dícese de un juez) **3** ~ **out** : descartar — *vi* : gobernar, reinar — **ruler** *n* **1** : gobernante *mf*; soberano *m*, -na *f* **2** : regla *f* (para medir) — **ruling** *n* VERDICT : fallo *m*

rum *n* : ron *m*

Rumanian → **Romanian**

rumble *vi* **-bled; -bling 1** : retumbar **2** : hacer ruidos (dícese del estómago) — ~ *n* : retumbo *m*, estruendo *m*

rummage *vi* **-maged; -maging** : hurgar

rumor *n* : rumor *m* — ~ *vt* **be** ~**ed** : rumorearse

rump *n* **1** : grupa *f* (de un animal) **2** ~ **steak** : filete *m* de cadera

rumpus *n* : lío *m*, jaleo *m fam*

run *v* **ran; run; running** *vi* **1** : correr **2** FUNCTION : funcionar **3** LAST : durar **4** : desteñir (dícese de colores) **5** EXTEND : correr, extenderse **6** : presentarse (como candidato) **7** ~ **away** : huir **8** ~ **into** ENCOUNTER : tropezar con **9** ~ **into** HIT : chocar contra **10** ~ **late** : ir retrasado **11** ~ **out of** : quedarse sin **12** ~ **over** : atropellar — *vt* **1** : correr **2** OPERATE : hacer funcionar **3** : hacer correr (agua) **4** MANAGE : dirigir **5** ~ **a fever** : tener fiebre — ~ *n* **1** : carrera *f* **2** TRIP : viaje *m*, paseo *m* (en coche) **3** SERIES : serie *f* **4 in the long** ~ : a la larga **5 in the short** ~ : a corto plazo — **runaway** *n* : fugitivo *m*, -va *f* — ~ *adj* : fugitivo — **rundown** *n* : resumen *m* — **run–down** *adj* **1** : destartalado **2** EXHAUSTED : agotado

rung¹ → **ring¹**

rung² *n* : peldaño *m* (de una escalera, etc.)

runner *n* **1** : corredor *m*, -dora *f* **2** : patín *m* (de un trineo), riel *m* (de un cajón, etc.) — **runner–up** *n*, *pl* **runners–up** : subcampeón *m*, -peona *f* — **running** *adj* **1** FLOWING : corriente **2** CONTINUOUS : continuo **3** CONSECUTIVE : seguido

runt *n* : animal *m* más pequeño (de una camada)

runway *n* : pista *f* de aterrizaje

rupture *n* : ruptura *f* — ~ *v* **-tured; -turing** *vt* : romper — *vi* : reventar

rural *adj* : rural

ruse *n* : ardid *m*

rush¹ *n* : junco *m* (planta)

rush² *vi* : ir de prisa — *vt* **1** : apresurar, apurar **2** ATTACK : asaltar **3** : llevar rápidamente (al hospital, etc.) — ~ *n* **1** : prisa *f*, apuro *m* **2** : ráfaga *f* (de aire), torrente *m* (de agua) — ~ *adj* : urgente — **rush hour** *n* : hora *f* punta

russet *n* : color *m* rojizo

Russian *adj* : ruso — ~ *n* : ruso *m* (idioma)

rust *n* : herrumbre *f*, óxido *m* — ~ *vi* : oxidarse — *vt* : oxidar

rustic *adj* : rústico

rustle *v* **-tled; -tling** *vt* **1** : hacer susurrar **2** : robar (ganado) — *vi* : susurrar — **~** *n* : susurro *m*

rusty *adj* **rustier; -est** : oxidado

rut *n* **1** : surco *m* **2 be in a ~** : ser esclavo de la rutina

ruthless *adj* : despiadado, cruel

rye *n* : centeno *m*

S

s *n, pl* **s's** *or* **ss** : s *f*, decimonovena letra del alfabeto inglés

Sabbath *n* **1** : sábado *m* (día santo judío) **2** : domingo *m* (día santo cristiano)

sabotage *n* : sabotaje *m* — **~** *vt* **-taged; -taging** : sabotear

saccharin *n* : sacarina *f*

sack *n* : saco *m* — **~** *vt* **1** FIRE : despedir **2** PLUNDER : saquear

sacrament *n* : sacramento *m*

sacred *adj* : sagrado

sacrifice *n* : sacrificio *m* — **~** *vt* **-ficed; -ficing** : sacrificar

sacrilege *n* : sacrilegio *m* — **sacrilegious** *adj* : sacrílego

sad *adj* **sadder; saddest** : triste — **sadden** *vt* : entristecer

saddle *n* : silla *f* (de montar) — **~** *vt* **-dled; -dling 1** : ensillar (un caballo, etc.) **2 ~ s.o. with sth** : cargar a algn con algo

sadistic *adj* : sádico

sadness *n* : tristeza *f*

safari *n* : safari *m*

safe *adj* **safer; safest 1** : seguro **2** UN-HARMED : ileso **3** CAREFUL : prudente **4 ~ and sound** : sano y salvo — **~** *n* : caja *f* fuerte — **safeguard** *n* : salvaguarda *f* — **~** *vt* : salvaguardar — **safely** *adv* **1** : sin peligro **2 arrive ~** : llegar sin novedad — **safety** *n, pl* **-ties** : seguridad *f* — **safety belt** *n* : cinturón *m* de seguridad — **safety pin** *n* : imperdible *m*

saffron *n* : azafrán *m*

sag *vi* **sagged; sagging 1** : combarse **2** GIVE : aflojarse **3** FLAG : flaquear

saga *n* : saga *f*

sage[1] *n* : salvia *f* (planta)

sage[2] *adj* **sager; -est** : sabio — **~** *n* : sabio *m*, -bia *f*

said → **say**

sail *n* **1** : vela *f* (de un barco) **2 go for a ~** : salir a navegar **3 set ~** : zarpar — **~** *vi* : navegar — *vt* : gobernar (un barco), navegar (el mar) — **sailboat** *n* : velero *m* — **sailor** *n* : marinero *m*

saint *n* : santo *m*, -ta *f* — **saintly** *adj* **saint-lier; -est** : santo

sake *n* **1 for goodness' ~!** : ¡por Dios! **2 for the ~ of** : por (el bien de)

salad *n* : ensalada *f*

salamander *n* : salamandra *f*

salami *n* : salami *m*

salary *n, pl* **-ries** : sueldo *m*

sale *n* **1** : venta *f* **2 for ~** : se vende **3 on ~** : de rebaja — **salesman** *n, pl* **-men** : vendedor *m*, dependiente *m* — **saleswoman** *n, pl* **-women** : vendedora *f*, dependienta *f*

salient *adj* : saliente

saliva *n* : saliva *f*

sallow *adj* : amarillento, cetrino

salmon *ns & pl* : salmón *m*

salon *n* → **beauty salon**

saloon *n* : bar *m*

salsa *n* : salsa *f* mexicana, salsa *f* picante

salt *n* : sal *f* — **~** *vt* : salar — **saltwater** *adj* : de agua salada — **salty** *adj* **saltier; -est** : salado

salute *v* **-luted; -luting** *vt* : saludar — *vi* : hacer un saludo — **~** *n* : saludo *m*

salvage *n* : salvamento *m* — **~** *vt* **-vaged; -vaging** : salvar

salvation *n* : salvación *f*

salve *n* : ungüento *m*

same *adj* **1** : mismo **2 be the ~ (as)** : ser igual (que) **3 the ~ thing (as)** : la misma cosa (que) — **~** *pron* **1 all the ~** : igual **2 the ~** : lo mismo — **~** *adv* **the ~** : igual

sample *n* : muestra *f* — **~** *vt* **-pled; -pling** : probar

sanatorium *n, pl* **-riums** *or* **-ria** : sanatorio *m*

sanctify *vt* **-fied; -fying** : santificar

sanction *n* : sanción *f* — **~** *vt* : sancionar

sanctity *n, pl* **-ties** : santidad *f*

sanctuary *n, pl* **-aries** : santuario *m*

sand *n* : arena *f* — **~** *vt* : lijar (madera)

sandal *n* : sandalia *f*

sandpaper *n* : papel *m* de lija — **~** *vt* : lijar

sandwich *n* : sandwich *m*, bocadillo *m Spain* — ~ *vt* ~ **between** : meter entre

sandy *adj* **sandier; -est** : arenoso

sane *adj* **saner; sanest 1** : cuerdo **2** SENSIBLE : sensato

sang → **sing**

sanitarium *n, pl* **-iums** *or* **-ia** → **sanatorium**

sanitary *adj* **1** : sanitario **2** HYGIENIC : higiénico — **sanitary napkin** *n* : compresa *f* (higiénica) — **sanitation** *n* : sanidad *f*

sanity *n* : cordura *f*

sank → **sink**

Santa Claus *n* : Papá *m* Noel

sap¹ *n* **1** : savia *f* (de una planta) **2** SUCKER : inocentón *m*, **-tona** *f*

sap² *vt* **sapped; sapping** : minar (la fuerza, etc.)

sapphire *n* : zafiro *m*

sarcasm *n* : sarcasmo *m* — **sarcastic** *adj* : sarcástico

sardine *n* : sardina *f*

sash *n* : faja *f* (de un vestido), fajín *m* (de un uniforme)

sat → **sit**

satanic *adj* : satánico

satchel *n* : cartera *f*

satellite *n* : satélite *m*

satin *n* : raso *m*

satire *n* : sátira *f* — **satiric** *or* **satirical** *adj* : satírico

satisfaction *n* : satisfacción *f* — **satisfactory** *adj* : satisfactorio — **satisfy** *v* **-fied; -fying** *vt* **1** : satisfacer **2** CONVINCE : convencer — **satisfying** *adj* : satisfactorio

saturate *vt* **-rated; -rating 1** : saturar **2** DRENCH : empapar — **saturation** *n* : saturación *f*

Saturday *n* : sábado *m*

Saturn *n* : Saturno *m*

sauce *n* : salsa *f* — **saucepan** *n* : cacerola *f* — **saucer** *n* : platillo *m* — **saucy** *adj* **saucier; -est** IMPUDENT : descarado

sauna *n* : sauna *mf*

saunter *vi* : pasear

sausage *n* : salchicha *f*

sauté *vt* **-téed** *or* **-téd; -téing** : saltear, sofreír

savage *adj* : salvaje, feroz — ~ *n* : salvaje *mf* — **savagery** *n, pl* **-ries** : ferocidad *f*

save *vt* **saved; saving 1** RESCUE : salvar **2** RESERVE : guardar **3** : ahorrar (dinero, tiempo, etc.) — ~ *prep* EXCEPT : salvo

savior *n* : salvador *m*, **-dora** *f*

savor *vt* : saborear — **savory** *adj* : sabroso

saw¹ → **see**

saw² *n* : sierra *f* — ~ *vt* **sawed; sawed** *or* **sawn; sawing** : serrar — **sawdust** *n* : serrín *m*, aserrín *m*

saxophone *n* : saxofón *m*

say *v* **said; saying; says** *vt* **1** : decir **2** INDICATE : marcar (dícese de relojes, etc.) — *vi* **1** : decir **2 that is to** ~ : es decir — ~ *n, pl* **says 1 have no** ~ : no tener ni voz ni voto **2 have one's** ~ : dar su opinión — **saying** *n* : refrán *m*

scab *n* **1** : costra *f* (en una herida) **2** STRIKEBREAKER : esquirol *mf*

scaffold *n* : andamio *m* (en construcción)

scald *vt* : escaldar

scale¹ *n* : balanza *f* (para pesar)

scale² *n* : escama *f* (de un pez, etc.) — ~ *vt* **scaled; scaling** : escamar

scale³ *vt* **scaled; scaling 1** CLIMB : escalar **2 down** : reducir — ~ *n* : escala *f* (musical, salarial, etc.)

scallion *n* : cebolleta *f*

scallop *n* : vieira *f*

scalp *n* : cuero *m* cabelludo

scam *n* : estafa *f*, timo *m fam*

scamper *vi* ~ **away** : irse corriendo

scan *vt* **scanned; scanning 1** : escandir (versos) **2** EXAMINE : escudriñar **3** SKIM : echar un vistazo a **4** : escanear (en informática)

scandal *n* **1** : escándalo *m* **2** GOSSIP : habladurías *fpl* — **scandalous** *adj* : escandaloso

Scandinavian *adj* : escandinavo

scant *adj* : escaso

scapegoat *n* : chivo *m* expiatorio

scar *n* : cicatriz *f* — ~ *v* **scarred; scarring** *vt* : dejar una cicatriz en — *vi* : cicatrizar

scarce *adj* **scarcer; -est** : escaso — **scarcely** *adv* : apenas — **scarcity** *n, pl* **-ties** : escasez *f*

scare *vt* **scared; scaring 1** : asustar **2 be ~d of** : tener miedo a — ~ *n* **1** FRIGHT : susto *m* **2** ALARM : pánico *m* — **scarecrow** *n* : espantapájaros *m*, espantajo *m*

scarf *n, pl* **scarves** *or* **scarfs 1** : bufanda *f* **2** KERCHIEF : pañuelo *m*

scarlet *adj* : escarlata — **scarlet fever** *n* : escarlatina *f*

scary *adj* **scarier; -est** : que da miedo

scathing *adj* : mordaz

scatter *vt* **1** STREW : esparcir **2** DISPERSE : dispersar — *vi* : dispersarse

scavenger *n* : carroñero *m*, **-ra** *f* (animal)

scenario *n, pl* **-ios 1** : guión *m* (cinemático) **2 the worst-case** ~ : el peor de los casos

scene *n* **1** : escena *f* **2 behind the** ~**s** : entre bastidores **3 make a** ~ : armar un escándalo **2** LANDSCAPE : paisaje *m* — **scenery** *n, pl* **-eries 1** : decorado *m* **2** LANDSCAPE : paisaje *m* — **scenic** *adj* : pintoresco

scent *n* **1** : aroma *m* **2** PERFUME : perfume *m* **3** TRAIL : rastro *m* — **scented** *adj* : perfumado

sceptic → **skeptic**

schedule *n* **1** : programa *m* **2** TIMETABLE
: horario *m* **3 behind** ~ : atrasado, con retraso **4 on** ~ : según lo previsto — ~ *vt*
-uled; -uling : planear, programar
scheme *n* **1** PLAN : plan *m* **2** PLOT : intriga
f **3** DESIGN : esquema *f* — ~ *vi* **schemed;**
scheming : intrigar
schism *n* : cisma *m*
schizophrenia *n* : esquizofrenia *f* — **schizophrenic** *adj* : esquizofrénico
scholar *n* : erudito *m*, -ta *f* — **scholarly** *adj*
: erudito — **scholarship** *n* **1** : erudición *f*
2 GRANT : beca *f*
school¹ *n* : banco *m* (de peces)
school² *n* **1** : escuela *f* **2** COLLEGE : universidad *f* **3** DEPARTMENT : facultad *f* —
~ *vt* : instruir — **schoolboy** *n* : colegial *m*
— **schoolgirl** *n* : colegiala *f* — **school-**
teacher *n* → **teacher**
science *n* : ciencia *f* — **scientific** *adj*
: científico — **scientist** *n* : científico *m*, -ca
f
scissors *npl* : tijeras *fpl*
scoff *vi* ~ **at** : burlarse de, mofarse de
scold *vt* : regañar
scoop *n* **1** : pala *f* **2** : noticia *f* exclusiva
(en periodismo) — ~ *vt* **1** : sacar (con
pala) **2** ~ **out** : ahuecar **3** ~ **up** : recoger
scoot *vi* : ir rápidamente — **scooter** *n* **1**
: patinete *m* **2** *or* **motor** ~ : escúter *m*
scope *n* **1** RANGE : alcance *m* **2** OPPORTUNITY : posibilidades *fpl*
scorch *vt* : chamuscar
score *n*, *pl* **scores** **1** : tanteo *m* (en deportes) **2** RATING : puntuación *f* **3** : partitura *f* (musical) **4** *or pl* **score** TWENTY
: veintena *f* **5 keep** ~ : llevar la cuenta **6**
on that ~ : en ese sentido — ~ *v* **scored;**
scoring *vt* **1** : marcar, anotarse *Lat* (un
tanto) **2** : sacar (una nota) — *vi* : marcar
(en deportes)
scorn *n* : desdén *m* — ~ *vt* : desdeñar —
scornful *adj* : desdeñoso
scorpion *n* : alacrán *m*, escorpión *m*
Scot *n* : escocés *m*, -cesa *f* — **Scotch** *adj* →
Scottish — ~ *n or* ~ **whiskey** : whisky
m escocés — **Scottish** *adj* : escocés
scoundrel *n* : sinvergüenza *mf*
scour *vt* **1** SCRUB : fregar **2** SEARCH : registrar
scourge *n* : azote *m*
scout *n* : explorador *m*, -dora *f*
scowl *vi* : fruncir el ceño — ~ *n* : ceño *m*
fruncido
scram *vi* **scrammed; scramming** : largarse
scramble *v* **-bled; -bling** *vi* **1** CLAMBER
: trepar **2** ~ **for** : pelearse por — *vt* : mez-

clar — ~ *n* : rebatiña *f*, pelea *f* — **scram-**
bled eggs *npl* : huevos *mpl* revueltos
scrap¹ *n* **1** PIECE : pedazo *m* **2** *or* ~ **metal**
: chatarra *f* **3** ~ **s** *npl* : sobras — ~ *vt*
scrapped; scrapping : desechar
scrap² *n* FIGHT : pelea *f*
scrapbook *n* : álbum *m* de recortes
scrape *v* **scraped; scraping** *vt* **1** : rascar
2 : rasparse (la rodilla, etc.) **3** *or* ~ **off**
: raspar **4** ~ **together** : reunir — *vi* **1**
RUB : rozar **2** ~ **by** : arreglárselas — ~ *n*
1 : rasguño *m* **2** PREDICAMENT : apuro *m*
scratch *vt* **1** CLAW : arañar **2** MARK : rayar
3 : rascarse (la cabeza, etc.) **4** ~ **out**
: tachar — ~ *n* **1** : arañazo *m* **2** MARK
: rayón *m* **3 start from** ~ : empezar desde
cero
scrawl *v* : garabatear — ~ *n* : garabato *m*
scrawny *adj* **scrawnier; -est** : escuálido
scream *vi* : gritar, chillar — ~ *n* : grito *m*,
chillido *m*
screech *n* **1** : chillido *m* (de personas) **2**
: chirrido *m* (de frenos, etc.) — ~ *vi* **1**
: chillar **2** : chirriar (dícese de los frenos,
etc.)
screen *n* **1** : pantalla *f* **2** PARTITION
: mampara *f* **3** *or* **window** ~ : mosquitero
m — ~ *vt* **1** SHIELD : proteger **2** HIDE
: ocultar **3** : seleccionar (candidatos, etc.)
screw *n* : tornillo *m* — ~ *vt* **1** : atornillar
2 ~ **up** RUIN : fastidiar — **screwdriver** *n*
: destornillador *m*
scribble *v* **-bled; -bling** : garabatear — ~ *n*
: garabato *m*
script *n* **1** HANDWRITING : escritura *f* **2**
: guión *m* (de cine, etc.) — **scripture** *n* **1**
: escritos *mpl* sagrados **2 the Scriptures**
npl : las Escrituras *fpl*
scroll *n* : rollo *m* (de pergamino, etc.)
scrounge *v* **scrounged; scrounging** *vt*
: gorrear *fam* — *vi* ~ **around for sth**
: andar buscando algo
scrub¹ *n* UNDERBRUSH : maleza *f*
scrub² *vt* **scrubbed; scrubbing** SCOUR : fregar
— ~ *n* : fregado *m*
scruff *n* **by the** ~ **of the neck** : por el pescuezo
scruple *n* : escrúpulo *m* — **scrupulous** *adj*
: escrupuloso
scrutiny *n*, *pl* **-nies** : análisis *m* cuidadoso
— **scrutinize** *vt* **-nized; -nizing** : escudriñar
scuff *vt* : raspar, rayar
scuffle *n* : refriega *f*
sculpture *n* : escultura *f* — **sculpt** *v* : esculpir — **sculptor** *n* : escultor *m*, -tora *f*
scum *n* **1** FROTH : espuma *f* **2** : escoria *f*
(dícese de personas)
scurry *vi* **-ried; -rying** : corretear
scuttle¹ *n* : cubo *m* (para carbón)

scuttle² vt **-tled; -tling** : hundir (un barco)
scuttle³ vi SCAMPER : corretear
sea n **1** : mar mf **2 at ~** : en el mar — **~**
adj : del mar — **seafarer** n : marinero m —
seafood n : mariscos mpl — **seagull** n
: gaviota f
seal¹ n : foca f (animal)
seal² n **1** STAMP : sello m **2** CLOSURE
: cierre m (hermético) — **~** vt : sellar
seam n **1** : costura f **2** VEIN : veta f
seaman n, pl **-men** : marinero m
seamy adj **seamier; -est** : sórdido
seaplane n : hidroavión m
seaport n : puerto m marítimo
search vt : registrar — vi **for** : buscar —
~ n **1** : registro m **2** HUNT : búsqueda f
— **searchlight** n : reflector m
search engine n : buscador m
seashell n : concha f (marina) — **seashore**
n : orilla f del mar — **seasick** adj **1** : mareado **2 be ~** : marearse — **seasickness**
n : mareo m
season n **1** : estación f (del año) **2** : temporada f (en deportes, etc.) — **~** vt **1** FLA-
VOR : sazonar **2** : secar (madera) — **seasonal** adj : estacional — **seasoned** adj
EXPERIENCED : veterano — **seasoning** n
: condimento m
seat n **1** : asiento m **2** : fondillos mpl (de
un pantalón) **3** BUTTOCKS : trasero m **4**
CENTER : sede f — vt **1 be ~ed** : sentarse **2 the bus ~s 30** : el autobús tiene
cabida para 30 — **seat belt** n : cinturón m
de seguridad
seaweed n : alga f marina
secede vi **-ceded; -ceding** : separarse (de
una nación, etc.)
secluded adj : aislado — **seclusion** n : aislamiento m
second adj : segundo — **~** or **secondly**
adv : en segundo lugar — **~** n **1** : segundo
m, -da f **2** MOMENT : segundo m **3 have**
~s : repetir (en una comida) — **~** vt : secundar — **secondary** adj : secundario —
secondhand adj : de segunda mano —
second–rate adj : mediocre
secret adj : secreto — **~** n : secreto m —
secrecy n, pl **-cies** : secreto m
secretary n, pl **-taries 1** : secretario m, -ria
f **2** : ministro m, -tra f (del gobierno)
secretion n : secreción f — **secrete** vt
-creted; -creting : secretar
secretive adj : reservado — **secretly** adv
: en secreto
sect n : secta f
section n : sección f, parte f
sector n : sector m
secular adj : secular
security n, pl **-ties 1** : seguridad f **2** GUAR-
ANTEE : garantía f **3 securities** npl : va-

lores mpl — **secure** adj **-curer; -est** : seguro — **~** vt **-cured; -curing 1** FASTEN
: asegurar **2** GET : conseguir
sedan n : sedán m
sedate adj : sosegado
sedative adj : sedante — **~** n : sedante m
sedentary adj : sedentario
sediment n : sedimento m
seduce vt **-duced; -ducing** : seducir — **seduction** n : seducción f — **seductive** adj
: seductor
see v **saw; seen; seeing** vt **1** : ver **2** UN-
DERSTAND : entender **3** ESCORT : acompa-
ñar **4 ~ s.o. off** : despedirse de algn **5**
~ sth through : llevar algo a cabo **6 ~**
you later! : ¡hasta luego! — vi **1** : ver **2**
UNDERSTAND : entender **3 let's ~** : vamos
a ver **4 ~ to** : ocuparse de
seed n, pl **seed** or **seeds 1** : semilla f **2**
SOURCE : germen m — **seedy** adj **seedier;**
-est SQUALID : sórdido
seek v **sought; seeking** vt **1** or **~ out**
: buscar **2** REQUEST : pedir **3 ~ to** : tratar
de — vi SEARCH : buscar
seem vi : parecer
seep vi : filtrarse
seesaw n : balancín m
seethe vi **seethed; seething** : rabiar, estar
furioso
segment n : segmento m
segregate vt **-gated; -gating** : segregar —
segregation n : segregación f
seize v **seized; seizing** vt **1** GRASP : agarrar **2** CAPTURE : tomar **3** : aprovechar
(una oportunidad) — vi or **~ up** : agarro-
tarse — **seizure** n **1** CAPTURE : toma f **2**
: ataque m (en medicina)
seldom adv : pocas veces, raramente
select adj : selecto — **~** vt : seleccionar —
selection n : selección f — **selective** adj
: selectivo
self n, pl **selves 1** : ser m **2 her better ~**
: su lado bueno — **self–addressed** adj
: con la dirección del remitente — **self–as-
sured** adj : seguro de sí mismo — **self–
centered** adj : egocéntrico — **self–confidence** : confianza f en sí mismo — **self–
confident** adj : seguro de sí mismo — **self–
conscious** adj : cohibido — **self–control** n
: dominio m de sí mismo — **self–defense** n
: defensa f propia — **self–employed** adj
: que trabaja por cuenta propia — **self–esteem** n : amor m propio — **self–evident** adj
: evidente — **self–help** n : autoayuda f —
self– important adj : presumido — **self–interest** n : interés m personal — **selfish** adj
: egoísta — **selfishness** n : egoísmo m —
selfless adj : desinteresado — **self–pity** n,
pl **-ties** : autocompasión f — **self–portrait** n
: autorretrato m — **self– respect** n : amor m

propio — **self-righteous** *adj* : santurrón —
self-service *adj* : de autoservicio — **self-sufficient** *adj* : autosuficiente — **self-taught** *adj* : autodidacta
sell *v* **sold; selling** *vt* : vender — *vi* : venderse — **seller** *n* : vendedor *m*, -dora *f*
selves → **self**
semantics *ns & pl* : semántica *f*
semblance *n* : apariencia *f*
semester *n* : semestre *m*
semicolon *n* : punto y coma *m*
semifinal *n* : semifinal *f*
seminary *n, pl* **-naries** : seminario *m* — **seminar** *n* : seminario *m*
senate *n* : senado *m* — **senator** *n* : senador *m*, -dora *f*
send *vt* **sent; sending** **1** : mandar, enviar **2** ~ **away for** : pedir **3** ~ **back** : devolver (mercancías, etc.) **4** ~ **for** : mandar a buscar — **sender** *n* : remitente *mf*
senile *adj* : senil — **senility** *n* : senilidad *f*
senior *n* **1** SUPERIOR : superior *m* **2** : estudiante *mf* de último año (en educación) **3** *or* ~ **citizen** : persona *f* mayor **4 be s.o.'s** ~ : ser mayor que algn — ~ *adj* **1** : superior (en rango) **2** ELDER : mayor — **seniority** *n* : antigüedad *f*
sensation *n* : sensación *f* — **sensational** *adj* : sensacional
sense *n* **1** : sentido *m* **2** FEELING : sensación *f* **3** COMMON SENSE : sentido *m* común **4 make** ~ : tener sentido — ~ *vt* **sensed; sensing** : sentir — **senseless** *adj* **1** : sin sentido **2** UNCONSCIOUS : inconsciente — **sensible** *adj* : sensato, práctico — **sensibility** *n, pl* **-ties** : sensibilidad *f* — **sensitive** *adj* **1** : sensible **2** TOUCHY : susceptible — **sensitivity** *n, pl* **-ties** : sensibilidad *f* — **sensual** *adj* : sensual — **sensuous** *adj* : sensual
sent → **send**
sentence *n* **1** : frase *f* **2** JUDGMENT : sentencia *f* — ~ *vt* **-tenced; -tencing** : sentenciar
sentiment *n* **1** : sentimiento *m* **2** BELIEF : opinión *f* — **sentimental** *adj* : sentimental — **sentimentality** *n, pl* **-ties** : sentimentalismo *m*
sentry *n, pl* **-tries** : centinela *m*
separation *n* : separación *f* — **separate** *v* **-rated; -rating** *vt* **1** : separar **2** DISTINGUISH : distinguir — *vi* : separarse — ~ *adj* **1** : separado **2** DETACHED : aparte **3** DISTINCT : distinto — **separately** *adv* : por separado
September *n* : septiembre *m*, setiembre *m*
sequel *n* **1** : continuación *f* **2** CONSEQUENCE : secuela *f*
sequence *n* **1** ORDER : orden *m* **2** : secuencia *f* (de números o escenas)

Serb *or* **Serbian** *adj* : serbio
serene *adj* : sereno — **serenity** *n* : serenidad *f*
sergeant *n* : sargento *mf*
serial *adj* : seriado — ~ *n* : serial *m* — **series** *n, pl* **series** : serie *f*
serious *adj* : serio — **seriously** *adv* **1** : seriamente **2** GRAVELY : gravemente **3 take** ~ : tomar en serio
sermon *n* : sermón *m*
serpent *n* : serpiente *f*
servant *n* : criado *m*, -da *f*
serve *v* **served; serving** *vi* **1** : servir **2** : sacar (en deportes) **3** ~ **as** : servir de — *vt* **1** : servir **2** ~ **time** : cumplir una condena — **server** *n* **1** WAITER : camarero *m*, -ra *f* **2** : servidor *m* (en informática)
service *n* **1** : servicio *m* **2** CEREMONY : oficio *m* **3** MAINTENANCE : revisión *f* **4 armed** ~**s** : fuerzas *fpl* armadas — ~ *vt* **-viced; -vicing** : revisar (un vehículo, etc.) — **serviceman** *n, pl* **-men** : militar *m* — **service station** *n* : estación *f* de servicio — **serving** *n* : porción *f*, ración *f*
session *n* : sesión *f*
set *n* **1** : juego *m* (de platos, etc.) **2** : set *m* (en tenis, etc.) **3** *or* **stage** ~ : decorado *m* **4 television** ~ : aparato *m* de televisión — ~ *v* **set; setting** *vt* **1** *or* ~ **down** : poner **2** : poner en hora (un reloj) **3** FIX : fijar (una fecha, etc.) **4** ~ **fire to** : prender fuego a **5** ~ **free** : poner en libertad **6** ~ **off** : hacer sonar (una alarma), hacer estallar (una bomba) **7** ~ **out to (do sth)** : proponerse (hacer algo) **8** ~ **up** ASSEMBLE : montar, armar **9** ~ **up** ESTABLISH : establecer — *vi* **1** : cuajarse (dícese de la gelatina, etc.), fraguar (dícese del cemento) **2** : ponerse (dícese del sol, etc.) **3** ~ **in** BEGIN : empezar **4** ~ **off** *or* ~ **out** : salir (de viaje) — ~ *adj* **1** FIXED : fijo **2** READY : listo, preparado — **setback** *n* : revés *m* — **setting** *n* **1** : posición *f* (de un control) **2** MOUNTING : engaste *m* (de joyas) **3** SCENE : escenario *m*
settle *v* **settled; settling** *vi* **1** : asentarse (dícese de polvo, colonos, etc.) **2** ~ **down** RELAX : calmarse **3** ~ **for** : conformarse con **4** ~ **in** : instalarse — *vt* **1** DECIDE : fijar, decidir **2** RESOLVE : resolver **3** PAY : pagar **4** CALM : calmar **5** COLONIZE : colonizar — **settlement** *n* **1** PAYMENT : pago *m* **2** COLONY : colonia *f*, poblado *m* **3** AGREEMENT : acuerdo *m* — **settler** *n* : colono *m*, -na *f*
seven *adj* : siete — ~ *n* : siete *m* — **seven hundred** *adj* : setecientos — ~ *n* : setecientos *m* — **seventeen** *adj* : diecisiete — ~ *n* : diecisiete *m* — **seventeenth** *adj* : decimoséptimo — ~ *n* **1** : decimosép-

timo *m*, -ma *f* (en una serie) **2** : diecisieteavo *m* (en matemáticas) — **seventh** *adj*
: séptimo — ∼ *n* **1** : séptimo *m*, -ma *f* (en
una serie) **2** : séptimo *m* (en matemáticas)
— **seventieth** *adj* : septuagésimo — ∼ *n*
1 : septuagésimo *m*, -ma *f* (en una serie) **2**
: setentavo *m* (en matemáticas) — **seventy**
adj : setenta — ∼ *n*, *pl* **-ties** : setenta *m*
sever *vt* **-ered; -ering** : cortar, romper
several *adj* : varios — ∼ *pron* : varios, varias
severance *n* : ruptura *f*
severe *adj* **severer; -est 1** : severo **2** SERI-
OUS : grave — **severely** *adv* **1** : severa-
mente **2** SERIOUSLY : gravemente — **severity** *n* **1** : severidad *f* **2** SERIOUSNESS
: gravedad *f*
sew *v* **sewed; sewn** *or* **sewed; sewing**
: coser
sewer *n* : cloaca *f* — **sewage** *n* : aguas *fpl*
negras
sewing *n* : costura *f*
sex *n* **1** : sexo *m* **2** INTERCOURSE : relaciones *fpl* sexuales — **sexism** *n* : sexismo *m*
— **sexist** *adj* : sexista — **sexual** *adj* : sexual — **sexuality** *n* : sexualidad *f* — **sexy** *adj*
sexier; -est : sexy
shabby *adj* **shabbier; -est 1** WORN
: gastado **2** UNFAIR : malo, injusto
shack *n* : choza *f*
shackle *n* : grillete *m*
shade *n* **1** : sombra *f* **2** : tono *m* (de un
color) **3** NUANCE : matiz *m* **4** *or* **lampshade** : pantalla *f* **5** *or* **window** ∼ : persiana *f* — ∼ *vt* **shaded; shading** : proteger
de la luz — **shadow** *n* : sombra *f* — **shad-
owy** *adj* INDISTINCT : vago — **shady** *adj*
shadier; -est 1 : sombreado **2** DISREPU-
TABLE : sospechoso
shaft *n* **1** : asta *f* (de una flecha, etc.) **2**
HANDLE : mango *m* **3** AXLE : eje *m* **4**
: rayo *m* (de luz) **5** *or* **mine** ∼ : pozo *m*
shaggy *adj* **shaggier; -est** : peludo
shake *v* **shook; shaken; shaking** *vt* **1** : sacudir **2** MIX : agitar **3** ∼ **hands with s.o.**
: dar la mano a algn **4** ∼ **one's head**
: negar con la cabeza **5** ∼ **up** UPSET
: afectar — *vi* : temblar — ∼ *n* **1** : sacudida
f **2** → **handshake** — **shaker** *n* **1** **salt** ∼
: salero *m* **2** **pepper** ∼ : pimentero *m* —
shaky *adj* **shakier; -est 1** : tembloroso **2**
UNSTABLE : poco firme
shall *v* *aux*, *past* **should**; *pres sing & pl*
shall 1 (*expressing volition or futurity*) →
will 2 (*expressing possibility or obligation*) → **should 3** ∼ **we go?** : ¿nos
vamos?
shallow *adj* **1** : poco profundo **2** SUPERFI-
CIAL : superficial

sham *n* : farsa *f* — ∼ *v* **shammed; sham-
ming** : fingir
shambles *ns & pl* : caos *m*, desorden *m*
shame *n* **1** : vergüenza *f* **2 what a** ∼!
: ¡qué lástima! — ∼ *vt* **shamed; shaming**
: avergonzar — **shameful** *adj* : vergonzoso
— **shameless** *adj* : desvergonzado
shampoo *vt* : lavar (el pelo) — ∼ *n*, *pl*
-poos : champú *m*
shamrock *n* : trébol *m*
shan't (*contraction of* **shall not**) → **shall**
shape *v* **shaped; shaping** *vt* **1** : formar **2**
DETERMINE : determinar **3 be** ∼**d like**
: tener forma de — *vi or* ∼ **up** : tomar
forma — ∼ *n* **1** : forma *f* **2 get in** ∼
: ponerse en forma — **shapeless** *adj* : informe
share *n* **1** : porción *f* **2** : acción *f* (en una
compañía) — ∼ *v* **shared; sharing** *vt* **1**
: compartir **2** DIVIDE : dividir — *vi* : compartir — **shareholder** *n* : accionista *mf*
shark *n* : tiburón *m*
sharp *adj* **1** : afilado **2** POINTY : puntiagudo **3** ACUTE : agudo **4** HARSH : duro,
severo **5** CLEAR : nítido **6** : sostenido (en
música) **7 a** ∼ **curve** : una curva cerrada
— ∼ *adv* **at two o'clock** ∼ : a las dos en
punto — ∼ *n* : sostenido (en música) —
sharpen *vt* : afilar (un cuchillo, etc.), sacar
punta a (un lápiz) — **sharpener** *n* **1** *or*
knife ∼ : afilador *m* **2** *or* **pencil** ∼
: sacapuntas *m* — **sharply** *adv* : bruscamente
shatter *vt* **1** : hacer añicos **2** DEVASTATE
: destrozar — *vi* : hacerse añicos
shave *v* **shaved; shaved** *or* **shaven; shav-
ing** *vt* **1** : afeitar **2** SLICE : cortar — *vi*
: afeitarse — ∼ *n* : afeitada *f* — **shaver** *n*
: máquina *f* de afeitar
shawl *n* : chal *m*
she'd (*contraction of* **she had** *or* **she
would**) → **have, would**
she'll (*contraction of* **she shall** *or* **she will**)
→ **shall, will**
she's (*contraction of* **she is** *or* **she has**) →
be, have
she *pron* : ella
sheaf *n*, *pl* **sheaves 1** : gavilla *f* **2** : fajo *m*
(de papeles)
shear *vt* **sheared; sheared** *or* **shorn;
shearing** : esquilar — **shears** *npl* : tijeras
fpl (grandes)
sheath *n*, *pl* **sheaths** : funda *f*, vaina *f*
shed[1] *v* **shed; shedding** *vt* **1** : derramar
(lágrimas, etc.) **2** : mudar (de piel, etc.),
quitarse (ropa) **3** ∼ **light on** : aclarar
shed[2] *n* : cobertizo *m*
sheen *n* : brillo *m*, lustre *m*
sheep *n*, *pl* **sheep** : oveja *f* — **sheepish** *adj*
: avergonzado

sheer *adj* **1** THIN : transparente **2** PURE : puro **3** STEEP : escarpado

sheet *n* **1** : sábana *f* (de la cama) **2** : hoja *f* (de papel) **3** : capa *f* (de hielo, etc.) **4** PLATE : placa *f*, lámina *f*

shelf *n, pl* **shelves** : estante *m*

shell *n* **1** : concha *f* **2** : caparazón *m* (de un crustáceo, etc.) **3** : cáscara *f* (de un huevo, etc.) **4** : armazón *mf* (de un edificio, etc.) **5** POD : vaina *f* **6** MISSILE : proyectil *m* — ~ *vt* **1** : pelar (nueces, etc.) **2** BOMBARD : bombardear

shellfish *n* : marisco *m*

shelter *n* **1** : refugio *m* **2 take** ~ : refugiarse — ~ *vt* **1** PROTECT : proteger **2** HARBOR : albergar

shelve *vt* **shelved; shelving** DEFER : dar carpetazo a

shepherd *n* : pastor *m* — ~ *vt* GUIDE : conducir, guiar

sherbet *n* : sorbete *m*

sheriff *n* : sheriff *mf*

sherry *n, pl* **-ries** : jerez *m*

shield *n* : escudo *m* — ~ *vt* : proteger

shier, shiest → **shy**

shift *vt* **1** MOVE : mover **2** SWITCH : transferir — *vi* **1** : cambiar **2** MOVE : moverse **3** *or* ~ **gears** : cambiar de velocidad — ~ *n* **1** CHANGE : cambio *m* **2** : turno *m* (de trabajo) — **shiftless** *adj* : holgazán — **shifty** *adj* **shiftier; -est** : sospechoso

shimmer *vi* : brillar, relucir

shin *n* : espinilla *f*

shine *v* **shone** *or* **shined; shining** *vi* : brillar — *vt* **1** : alumbrar (una luz) **2** POLISH : sacar brillo a — ~ *n* : brillo *m*

shingle *n* : teja *f* plana y delgada (en construcción) — ~ *vt* **-gled; -gling** : techar —

shingles *npl* : herpes *m*

shiny *adj* **shinier; -est** : brillante

ship *n* **1** : barco *m*, buque *m* **2** → **spaceship** — ~ *vt* **shipped; shipping** : transportar, enviar (por barco) — **shipbuilding** *n* : construcción *f* naval — **shipment** *n* : envío *m* — **shipping** *n* **1** : transporte *m* **2** SHIPS : barcos *mpl* — **shipshape** *adj* : ordenado — **shipwreck** *n* : naufragio *m* — ~ *vt* **be** ~**ed** : naufragar — **shipyard** *n* : astillero *m*

shirk *vt* : esquivar

shirt *n* : camisa *f*

shiver *vi* : temblar (del frío, etc.) — ~ *n* : escalofrío *m*

shoal *n* : banco *m*

shock *n* **1** IMPACT : choque *m* **2** SURPRISE, UPSET : golpe *m* emocional **3** : shock *m* (en medicina) **4** *or* **electric** ~ : descarga *f* (eléctrica) — ~ *vt* : escandalizar — **shock absorber** *n* : amortiguador *m* — **shocking** *adj* : escandaloso

shoddy *adj* **shoddier; -est** : de mala calidad

shoe *n* : zapato *m* — ~ *vt* **shod; shoeing** : herrar (un caballo) — **shoelace** *n* : cordón *m* (de zapato) — **shoemaker** *n* : zapatero *m*, -ra *f*

shone → **shine**

shook → **shake**

shoot *v* **shot; shooting** *vt* **1** : disparar **2** : echar (una mirada) **3** PHOTOGRAPH : fotografiar **4** FILM : rodar — *vi* **1** : disparar **2** ~ **by** : pasar como una bala — ~ *n* : brote *m*, retoño *m* (de una planta) — **shooting star** *n* : estrella *f* fugaz

shop *n* **1** : tienda *f* **2** WORKSHOP : taller *m* — ~ *vi* **shopped; shopping** **1** : hacer compras **2 go shopping** : ir de compras — **shopkeeper** *n* : tendero *m*, -ra *f* — **shoplift** *vi* : hurtar mercancía (en tiendas) — **shoplifter** *n* : ladrón *m*, **-drona** *f* (que roba en tiendas) — **shopper** *n* : comprador *m*, -dora *f*

shore *n* : orilla *f*

shorn → **shear**

short *adj* **1** : corto **2** : bajo (de estatura) **3** CURT : brusco **4 a** ~ **time ago** : hace poco **5 be** ~ **of** : estar corto de — ~ *adv* **1 stop** ~ : parar en seco **2 fall** ~ : quedarse corto — **shortage** *n* : escasez *f*, carencia *f* — **shortcake** *n* : tarta *f* de fruta — **shortcoming** *n* : defecto *m* — **shortcut** *n* : atajo *m* — **shorten** *vt* : acortar — **shorthand** *n* : taquigrafía *f* — **short–lived** *adj* : efímero — **shortly** *adv* : dentro de poco — **shortness** *n* **1** : lo corto (de una cosa), baja estatura *f* (de una persona) **2** ~ **of breath** : falta *f* de aliento — **shorts** *npl* : shorts *mpl*, pantalones *mpl* cortos — **shortsighted** → **nearsighted**

shot *n* **1** : disparo *m*, tiro *m* **2** : tiro *m* (en deportes) **3** ATTEMPT : intento *m* **4** PHOTOGRAPH : foto *f* **5** INJECTION : inyección *f* **6** : trago *m* (de licor) — **shotgun** *n* : escopeta *f*

should *past of* **shall** **1 if she** ~ **call** : si llama **2 I** ~ **have gone** : debería haber ido **3 they** ~ **arrive soon** : deben llegar pronto **4 what** ~ **we do?** : ¿qué hacemos?

shoulder *n* **1** : hombro *m* **2** : arcén *m* (de una carretera) — ~ *vt* : cargar con (la responsabilidad, etc.) — **shoulder blade** *n* : omóplato *m*

shouldn't (*contraction of* **should not**) → **should**

shout *v* : gritar — ~ *n* : grito *m*

shove *v* **shoved; shoving** : empujar — ~ *n* : empujón *m*

shovel *n* : pala *f* — ~ *vt* **-veled** *or* **-velled; -veling** *or* **-velling** **1** : mover (tierra, etc.) con una pala **2** DIG : cavar (con una pala)

show *v* **showed; shown** *or* **showed; showing** *vt* **1** : mostrar **2** TEACH : enseñar **3** PROVE : demostrar **4** ESCORT : acompañar **5** : proyectar (una película), dar (un programa de televisión) **6** ~ **off** : hacer alarde de — *vi* **1** : notarse, verse **2** ~ **off** : lucirse **3** ~ **up** ARRIVE : aparecer — ~ *n* **1** : demostración *f* **2** EXHIBITION : exposición *f* **3** : espectáculo *m* (teatral), programa *m* (de televisión, etc.) — **showdown** *n* : confrontación *f*

shower *n* **1** : ducha *f* **2** : chaparrón *m* (en meteorología) **3** PARTY : fiesta *f* — ~ *vt* **1** SPRAY : regar **2** ~ **s.o. with** : colmar a algn de — *vi* **1** : ducharse **2** RAIN : llover

showy *adj* **showier; -est** : llamativo, ostentoso

shrank → **shrink**

shrapnel *ns & pl* : metralla *f*

shred *n* **1** : tira *f* (de tela, etc.) **2** IOTA : pizca *f* — ~ *vt* **shredded; shredding 1** : hacer tiras **2** GRATE : rallar

shrewd *adj* : astuto

shriek *vi* : chillar — ~ *n* : chillido *m*, alarido *m*

shrill *adj* : agudo, estridente

shrimp *n* : camarón *m*

shrine *n* **1** TOMB : sepulcro *m* **2** SANCTUARY : santuario *m*

shrink *v* **shrank; shrunk** *or* **shrunken; shrinking** *vt* : encoger — *vi* **1** : encogerse (dícese de ropa), reducirse (dícese de números, etc.) **2** *or* ~ **back** : retroceder

shrivel *vi* **-veled** *or* **-velled; -veling** *or* **-velling** *or* ~ **up** : arrugarse, marchitarse

shroud *n* **1** : sudario *m*, mortaja *f* **2** VEIL : velo *m* — ~ *vt* : envolver

shrub *n* : arbusto *m*, mata *f*

shrug *vi* **shrugged; shrugging** : encogerse de hombros

shrunk → **shrink**

shudder *vi* : estremecerse — ~ *n* : estremecimiento *m*

shuffle *v* **-fled; -fling** *vt* : barajar (naipes), revolver (papeles, etc.) — *vi* : caminar arrastrando los pies

shun *vi* **shunned; shunning** : evitar, esquivar

shut *v* **shut; shutting** *vt* **1** CLOSE : cerrar **2** ~ **off** → **turn off 3** ~ **up** CONFINE : encerrar — *vi* **1** *or* ~ **down** : cerrarse **2** ~ **up!** : ¡cállate! — **shutter** *n* **1** *or* **window** ~ : contraventana *f* **2** : obturador *m* (de una cámara)

shuttle *n* **1** : lanzadera *f* (para tejer) **2** *or* ~ **bus** : autobús *m* (de corto recorrido) **3** → **space shuttle** — ~ *v* **-tled; -tling** *vt* : transportar — *vi* : ir y venir

shy *adj* **shier** *or* **shyer; shiest** *or* **shyest**

: tímido — ~ *vi* **shied; shying** *or* ~ **away** : retroceder — **shyness** *n* : timidez *f*

sibling *n* : hermano *m*, hermana *f*

sick *adj* **1** : enfermo **2** **be** ~ VOMIT : vomitar **3** **be** ~ **of** : estar harto de **4** **feel** ~ : tener náuseas — **sicken** *vt* DISGUST : dar asco a — **sickening** *adj* : nauseabundo

sickle *n* : hoz *f*

sickly *adj* **sicklier; -est 1** UNHEALTHY : enfermizo **2** → **sickening** — **sickness** *n* : enfermedad *f*

side *n* **1** : lado *m* **2** : costado *m* (de una persona), ijada *f* (de un animal) **3** : parte *f* (en una disputa, etc.) **4** ~ **by** ~ : uno al lado de otro **5** **take** ~**s** : tomar partido — ~ *vi* ~ **with** : ponerse de parte de — **sideboard** *n* : aparador *m* — **sideburns** *npl* : patillas *fpl* — **side effect** *n* : efecto *m* secundario — **sideline** *n* : línea *f* de banda (en deportes) — **sidestep** *vt* **-stepped; -stepping** : eludir, esquivar — **sidetrack** *vt* **get** ~**ed** : distraerse — **sidewalk** *n* : acera *f* — **sideways** *adj & adv* : de lado — **siding** *n* : revestimiento *m* exterior

siege *n* : sitio *m*

sieve *n* : tamiz *m*, cedazo *m*

sift *vt* **1** : cerner, tamizar **2** *or* ~ **through** : pasar por el tamiz

sigh *vi* : suspirar — ~ *n* : suspiro *m*

sight *n* **1** : vista *f* **2** SPECTACLE : espectáculo *m* **3** : lugar *m* de interés (turístico) **4** **catch** ~ **of** : avistar — ~ *vt* : avistar — **sightseer** *n* : turista *mf*

sign **language** *n* : lenguaje *m* gestual — **signpost** *n* : poste *m* indicador

sign *n* **1** : signo *m* **2** NOTICE : letrero *m* **3** GESTURE : seña *f*, señal *f* — ~ *vt* : firmar (un cheque, etc.) — *vi* **1** : firmar **2** ~ **up** ENROLL : inscribirse

signal *n* : señal *f* — ~ *v* **-naled** *or* **-nalled; -naling** *or* **-nalling** *vt* **1** : hacer señas a **2** INDICATE : señalar — *vi* **1** : hacer señas **2** : señalizar (en un vehículo)

signature *n* : firma *f*

significance *n* **1** : significado *m* **2** IMPORTANCE : importancia *f* — **significant** *adj* : importante — **signify** *vt* **-fied; -fying** : significar

silence *n* : silencio *m* — ~ *vt* **-lenced; -lencing** : silenciar — **silent** *adj* **1** : silencioso **2** MUM : callado **3** : mudo (dícese de películas y letras)

silhouette *n* : silueta *f* — ~ *vt* **-etted; -etting** **be** ~**d against** : perfilarse contra

silicon *n* : silicio *m*

silk *n* : seda *f* — **silky** *adj* **silkier; -est** : sedoso

sill *n* : alféizar *m* (de una ventana), umbral *m* (de una puerta)

silly *adj* **sillier; -est** : tonto, estúpido

silt *n* : cieno *m*

silver *n* **1** : plata *f* **2** → **silverware** — ～ *adj* : de plata — **silverware** *n* : plata *f* — **silvery** *adj* : plateado

similar *adj* : similar, parecido — **similarity** *n*, *pl* **-ties** : semejanza *f*, parecido *m*

simmer *v* : hervir a fuego lento

simple *adj* **simpler; -plest 1** : simple **2** EASY : sencillo — **simplicity** *n* : simplicidad *f*, sencillez *f* — **simplify** *vt* **-fied; -fying** : simplificar — **simply** *adv* **1** : sencillamente **2** ABSOLUTELY : realmente

simulate *vt* **-lated; -lating** : simular

simultaneous *adj* : simultáneo

sin *n* : pecado *m* — ～ *vi* **sinned; sinning** : pecar

since *adv* **1** *or* ～ **then** : desde entonces **2 long** ～ : hace mucho — ～ *conj* **1** : desde que **2** BECAUSE : ya que, como **3 it's been years** ～... : hace años que... — ～ *prep* : desde

sincere *adj* **-cerer; -est** : sincero — **sincerely** *adv* : sinceramente — **sincerity** *n* : sinceridad *f*

sinful *adj* : pecador (dícese de las personas), pecaminoso (dícese de las acciones)

sing *v* **sang** *or* **sung; sung; singing** : cantar

singe *vt* **singed; singeing** : chamuscar

singer *n* : cantante *mf*

single *adj* **1** : solo, único **2** UNMARRIED : soltero **3 every** ～ **day** : cada día, todos los días — ～ *n* **1** : soltero *m*, -ra *f* **2** *or* ～ **room** : habitación *f* individual — ～ *vt* **-gled; -gling** ～ **out 1** SELECT : escoger **2** DISTINGUISH : señalar — **single–handed** *adj* : sin ayuda, solo

singular *adj* : singular — ～ *n* : singular *m*

sinister *adj* : siniestro

sink *v* **sank** *or* **sunk; sunk; sinking** *vi* **1** : hundirse (en un líquido) **2** DROP : bajar, caer — *vt* **1** : hundir **2** ～ **sth into** : clavar algo en — ～ *n* **1** *or* **kitchen** ～ : fregadero *m* **2** *or* **bathroom** ～ : lavabo *m*, lavamanos *m*

sinner *n* : pecador *m*, -dora *f*

sip *v* **sipped; sipping** *vt* : sorber — *vi* : beber a sorbos — ～ *n* : sorbo *m*

siphon *n* : sifón *m* — ～ *vt* : sacar con sifón

sir *n* **1** (*in titles*) : sir *m* **2** (*as a form of address*) : señor *m* **3 Dear Sir** : Estimado señor

siren *n* : sirena *f*

sirloin *n* : solomillo *m*

sissy *n*, *pl* **-sies** : mariquita *mf fam*

sister *n* : hermana *f* — **sister–in–law** *n*, *pl* **sisters–in–law** : cuñada *f*

sit *v* **sat; sitting** *vi* **1** *or* ～ **down** : sentarse **2** LIE : estar (ubicado) **3** MEET : estar en

sesión **4** *or* ～ **up** : incorporarse — *vt* : sentar

site *n* **1** : sitio *m*, lugar *m* **2** LOT : solar *m*

sitter → **baby–sitter**

sitting room → **living room**

situated *adj* : ubicado, situado — **situation** *n* : situación *f*

six *adj* : seis — ～ *n* : seis *m* — **six hundred** *adj* : seiscientos — ～ *n* : seiscientos *m* — **sixteen** *adj* : dieciséis — ～ *n* : dieciséis *m* — **sixteenth** *adj* : decimosexto — ～ *n* **1** : decimosexto *m*, -ta *f* (en una serie) **2** : dieciseisavo *m*, dieciseisava parte *f* — **sixth** *adj* : sexto — ～ *n* **1** : sexto *m*, -ta *f* (en una serie) **2** : sexto *m* (en matemáticas) — **sixtieth** *adj* : sexagésimo — ～ *n* **1** : sexagésimo *m*, -ma *f* (en una serie) **2** : sesentavo *m* (en matemáticas) — **sixty** *adj* : sesenta — ～ *n*, *pl* **-ties** : sesenta *m*

size *n* **1** : tamaño *m*, talla *f* (de ropa), número *m* (de zapatos) **2** EXTENT : magnitud *f* — ～ *vt* **sized; sizing** ～ **up** : evaluar — **sizable** *or* **sizeable** *adj* : considerable

sizzle *vi* **-zled; -zling** : chisporrotear

skate¹ *n* : raya *f* (pez)

skate² *n* : patín *m* — ～ *vi* **skated; skating** : patinar — **skateboard** *n* : monopatín *m* — **skater** *n* : patinador *m*, -dora *f*

skeleton *n* : esqueleto *m*

skeptic *n* : escéptico *m*, -ca *f* — **skeptical** *adj* : escéptico — **skepticism** *n* : escepticismo *m*

sketch *n* **1** : esbozo *m*, bosquejo *m* **2** SKIT : sketch *m* — ～ *vt* : bosquejar — *vi* : hacer bosquejos — **sketchy** *adj* **sketchier; -est** : incompleto

skewer *n* : brocheta *f*, broqueta *f*

ski *n*, *pl* **skis** : esquí *m* — ～ *vi* **skied; skiing** : esquiar

skid *n* : derrape *m*, patinazo *m* — ～ *vi* **skidded; skidding** : derrapar, patinar

skier *n* : esquiador *m*, -dora *f*

skill *n* **1** : habilidad *f*, destreza *f* **2** TECHNIQUE : técnica *f* — **skilled** *adj* : hábil

skillet *n* : sartén *mf*

skillful *adj* : hábil, diestro

skim *vt* **skimmed; skimming 1** : espumar (sopa, etc.), descremar (leche) **2** : pasar rozando (una superficie) **3** *or* ～ **through** : echar un vistazo a — ～ *adj* : descremado

skimp *vi* ～ **on** : escatimar — **skimpy** *adj* **skimpier; -est 1** : exiguo, escaso **2** : brevísimo (dícese de ropa)

skin *n* : piel *f* — ～ *vt* **skinned; skinning** : despellejar — **skin diving** *n* : buceo *m*, submarinismo *m* — **skinny** *adj* **skinnier; -est** : flaco

skip *v* **skipped; skipping** *vi* : ir brincando — *vt* OMIT : saltarse — ～ *n* : brinco *m*, salto *m*

skipper *n* : capitán *m*, **-tana** *f*
skirmish *n* : escaramuza *f*
skirt *n* : falda *f* — ∼ *vt* **1** BORDER : bordear **2** EVADE : eludir
skull *n* : cráneo *m* (de una persona viva), calavera *f* (de un esqueleto)
skunk *n* : mofeta *f*, zorrillo *m Lat*
sky *n, pl* **skies** : cielo *m* — **skylight** *n* : claraboya *f*, tragaluz *m* — **skyline** *n* : horizonte *m* — **skyscraper** *n* : rascacielos *m*
slab *n* : bloque *m* (de piedra, etc.)
slack *adj* **1** LOOSE : flojo **2** CARELESS : descuidado — ∼ *n* **1 take up the** ∼ : tensar (una cuerda, etc.) **2** ∼**s** *npl* : pantalones *mpl* — **slacken** *vt* : aflojar — *vi* : aflojarse
slain → **slay**
slam *n* : golpe *m*, portazo *m* (de una puerta) — ∼ *v* **slammed; slamming** *vt* **1** *or* ∼ **down** : tirar, plantar **2** *or* ∼ **shut** : cerrar de golpe **3** ∼ **the door** : dar un portazo — *vi* **1** : cerrarse de golpe **2** ∼ **into** : chocar contra
slam dunk *n* : clavada *f*
slander *vt* : calumniar, difamar — ∼ *n* : calumnia *f*, difamación *f*
slang *n* : argot *m*
slant *n* : inclinación *f* — ∼ *vi* : inclinarse
slap *vt* **slapped; slapping** **1** : dar una bofetada a **2** ∼ **s.o. on the back** : dar una palmada en la espalda a algn — ∼ *n* : bofetada *f*, cachetada *f Lat*
slash *vt* **1** : hacer un tajo en **2** : rebajar (precios) drásticamente — ∼ *n* : tajo *m*
slat *n* : tablilla *f*
slate *n* : pizarra *f*
slaughter *n* : matanza *f* — ∼ *vt* **1** : matar (animales) **2** MASSACRE : masacrar — **slaughterhouse** *n* : matadero *m*
slave *n* : esclavo *m*, **-va** *f* — ∼ *vi* **slaved; slaving** : trabajar como un burro — **slavery** *n* : esclavitud *f*
Slavic *adj* : eslavo
slay *vt* **slew; slain; slaying** : asesinar
sleazy *adj* **sleazier; -est** : sórdido
sled *n* : trineo *m*
sledgehammer *n* : almádena *f*
sleek *adj* : liso y brillante
sleep *n* **1** : sueño *m* **2 go to** ∼ : dormirse — ∼ *vi* **slept; sleeping** : dormir — **sleeper** *n* **be a light** ∼ : tener el sueño ligero — **sleepless** *adj* **have a** ∼ **night** : pasar la noche en blanco — **sleepwalker** *n* : sonámbulo *m*, **-la** *f* — **sleepy** *adj* **sleepier; -est** **1** : somnoliento, soñoliento **2 be** ∼ : tener sueño
sleet *n* : aguanieve *f* — ∼ *vi* : caer aguanieve
sleeve *n* : manga *f* — **sleeveless** *adj* : sin mangas

sleigh *n* : trineo *m*
slender *adj* : delgado
slew → **slay**
slice *vt* **sliced; slicing** : cortar — ∼ *n* : trozo *m*, rebanada *f* (de pan, etc.), tajada *f* (de carne)
slick *adj* SLIPPERY : resbaladizo, resbaloso *Lat*
slide *v* **slid; sliding** *vi* : deslizarse — *vt* : deslizar — ∼ *n* **1** : deslizamiento *m* **2** : tobogán *m* (para niños) **3** : diapositiva *f* (fotográfica) **4** DECLINE : descenso *m*
slier, sliest → **sly**
slight *adj* **1** : ligero, leve **2** SLENDER : delgado — ∼ *vt* : desairar — **slightly** *adv* : ligeramente, un poco
slim *adj* **slimmer; slimmest** **1** : delgado **2 a** ∼ **chance** : escasas posibilidades *fpl* — ∼ *v* **slimmed; slimming** : adelgazar
slime *n* **1** : baba *f* (de un caracol, etc.) **2** MUD : limo *m* — **slimy** *adj* **slimier; -est** : viscoso
sling *vt* **slung; slinging** **1** THROW : lanzar **2** HANG : colgar — ∼ *n* **1** : honda *f* **2** : cabestrillo *m* (en medicina) — **slingshot** *n* : tirachinas *m*
slink *vi* **slunk; slinking** : andar furtivamente
slip[1] *v* **slipped; slipping** *vi* **1** SLIDE : resbalarse **2 let sth** ∼ : dejar escapar algo **3** ∼ **away** : escabullirse **4** ∼ **up** : equivocarse — *vt* **1** : deslizar **2** ∼ **into** : ponerse (una prenda) **3 it slipped my mind** : se me olvidó — ∼ *n* **1** MISTAKE : error *m*, desliz *m* **2** ∼ **of the tongue** : lapsus *m* **3** PETTICOAT : enagua *f*
slip[2] *n* — ∼ **of paper** : papelito *m*
slipper *n* : zapatilla *f*, pantufla *f*
slippery *adj* **slipperier; -est** : resbaladizo, resbaloso *Lat*
slit *n* **1** OPENING : rendija *f* **2** CUT : corte *m*, raja *f* — ∼ *vt* **slit; slitting** : cortar
slither *vi* : deslizarse
sliver *n* : astilla *f*
slogan *n* : eslogan *m*
slop *v* **slopped; slopping** *vt* : derramar — *vi* : derramarse
slope *vi* **sloped; sloping** : inclinarse — ∼ *n* : pendiente *f*, declive *m*
sloppy *adj* **sloppier; -est** **1** CARELESS : descuidado **2** UNKEMPT : desaliñado
slot *n* : ranura *f*
sloth *n* : pereza *f*
slouch *vi* : andar con los hombros caídos (en una silla)
slovenly *adj* : desaliñado
slow *adj* **1** : lento **2 be** ∼ : estar atrasado (dícese de un reloj) — ∼ *adv* → **slowly** — ∼ *vt* : retrasar, retardar — *vi or* ∼ **down** : ir más despacio — **slowly** *adv* : lentamente, despacio — **slowness** *n* : lentitud *f*

sludge *n* SEWAGE : aguas *fpl* negras

slug¹ *n* **1** : babosa *f* (molusco) **2** BULLET : bala *f* **3** TOKEN : ficha *f*

slug² *vt* slugged; slugging : pegar un porrazo a

sluggish *adj* : lento

slum *n* : barrio *m* bajo

slumber *vi* : dormir — ~ *n* : sueño *m*

slump *vi* **1** DROP : bajar **2** COLLAPSE : dejarse caer **3** → **slouch** — ~ *n* : bajón *m*

slung → **sling**

slunk → **slink**

slur¹ *n* ASPERSION : calumnia *f*, difamación *f*

slur² *vt* slurred; slurring : arrastrar (las palabras)

slurp *v* : beber haciendo ruido — ~ *n* : sorbo *m* (ruidoso)

slush *n* : nieve *f* medio derretida

sly *adj* slier; sliest **1** : astuto, taimado **2** on the ~ : a escondidas

smack¹ *vi* ~ of : oler a

smack² *vt* **1** : pegar una bofetada a **2** KISS : besar **3** ~ one's lips : relamerse — ~ *n* : **1** SLAP : bofetada *f* **2** KISS : beso *m* — ~ *adv* : justo, exactamente

small *adj* : pequeño, chico — **smallpox** *n* : viruela *f*

smart *adj* **1** : listo, inteligente **2** STYLISH : elegante — ~ *vi* STING : escocer — **smartly** *adv* : elegantemente

smash *n* **1** BLOW : golpe *m* **2** COLLISION : choque *m* **3** BANG, CRASH : estrépito *m* — ~ *vt* **1** BREAK : romper **2** DESTROY : aplastar — *vi* **1** SHATTER : hacerse pedazos **2** ~ into : estrellarse contra

smattering *n* : nociones *fpl*

smear *n* : mancha *f* — ~ *vt* **1** : embadurnar (de pinta, etc.), untar (de aceite, etc.) **2** SMUDGE : manchar

smell *v* smelled *or* smelt; smelling : oler — ~ *n* **1** : (sentido *m* del) olfato *m* **2** ODOR : olor *m* — **smelly** *adj* smellier; -est : maloliente

smelt *vt* : fundir

smile *vi* smiled; smiling : sonreír — ~ *n* : sonrisa *f*

smirk *vi* : sonreír con suficiencia — ~ *n* : sonrisa *f* satisfecha

smith → **blacksmith**

smitten *adj* be ~ with : estar enamorado de

smock *n* : blusón *m*, bata *f*

smog *n* : smog *m*

smoke *n* : humo *m* — ~ *v* smoked; smoking *vi* **1** : humear (dícese de fuegos, etc.) **2** : fumar (dícese de personas) — *vt* **1** : ahumar (carne, etc.) **2** : fumar (cigarrillos) — **smoker** *n* : fumador *m*, -dora *f* — **smokestack** *n* : chimenea *f* — **smoky** *adj* smokier; -est **1** : lleno de humo **2** : a humo (dícese de sabores, etc.)

smolder *vi* : arder (sin llama)

smooth *adj* **1** : liso (dícese de superficies), suave (dícese de movimientos), tranquilo (dícese del mar) **2** : sin grumos (dícese de salsas, etc.) — ~ *vt* : alisar — **smoothly** *adv* : suavemente — **smoothness** *n* : suavidad *f*

smother *vt* : asfixiar (a algn), sofocar (llamas, etc.)

smudge *v* smudged; smudging *vt* : emborronar — *vi* : correrse — ~ *n* : mancha *f*, borrón *m*

smug *adj* smugger; smuggest : suficiente

smuggle *vt* -gled; -gling : pasar de contrabando — **smuggler** *n* : contrabandista *mf*

snack *n* : refrigerio *m*, tentempié *m fam*

snag *n* : problema *m* — ~ *v* snagged; snagging *vt* : enganchar — *vi* : engancharse

snail *n* : caracol *m*

snake *n* : culebra *f*, serpiente *f*

snap *v* snapped; snapping *vi* **1** BREAK : romperse **2** : intentar morder (dícese de un perro, etc.) **3** ~ at : contestar bruscamente a — *vt* **1** BREAK : romper **2** ~ one's fingers : chasquear los dedos **3** ~ open/shut : abrir/cerrar de golpe — ~ *n* **1** : chasquido *m* **2** FASTENER : broche *m* (de presión) **3** be a ~ : ser facilísimo — **snappy** *adj* snappier; -est **1** FAST : rápido **2** STYLISH : elegante — **snapshot** *n* : instantánea *f*

snare *n* : trampa *f* — ~ *vt* snared; snaring : atrapar

snarl¹ *vi* TANGLE : enmarañar, enredar — ~ *n* : enredo *m*, maraña *f*

snarl² *vi* GROWL : gruñir — *n* : gruñido *m*

snatch *vt* : arrebatar

sneak *vi* : ir a hurtadillas — *vt* : hacer furtivamente — ~ *n* : soplón *m*, -plona *f fam* — **sneakers** *npl* : tenis *mpl*, zapatillas *fpl* — **sneaky** *adj* sneakier; -est : solapado

sneer *vi* : sonreír con desprecio — ~ *n* : sonrisa *f* de desprecio

sneeze *vi* sneezed; sneezing : estornudar — ~ *n* : estornudo *m*

snide *adj* : sarcástico

sniff *vi* : oler — *vt* **1** : oler **2** → **sniffle** — ~ *n* : aspiración *f* por la nariz — **sniffle** *vi* -fled; -fling : sorberse la nariz — **sniffles** *npl* have the ~ : estar resfriado

snip *n* : tijeretada *f* — ~ *vt* snipped; snipping : cortar (con tijeras)

snivel *vi* -veled *or* -velled; -veling *or* -velling : lloriquear

snob *n* : esnob *mf* — **snobbish** *adj* : esnob

snoop *vi* : husmear — ~ *n* : fisgón *m*, -gona *f*

snooze *vi* snoozed; snoozing : dormitar — ~ *n* : siestecita *f*, siestita *f*

snore *vi* **snored; snoring** : roncar — ~ *n* : ronquido *m*

snort *vi* : bufar — ~ *n* : bufido *m*

snout *n* : hocico *m*, morro *m*

snow *n* : nieve *f* — ~ *vi* : nevar — **snowfall** *n* : nevada *f* — **snowflake** *n* : copo *m* de nieve — **snowman** *n* : muñeco *m* de nieve — **snowplow** *n* : quitanieves *m* — **snowshoe** *n* : raqueta *f* (para nieve) — **snowstorm** *n* : tormenta *f* de nieve — **snowy** *adj* snowier; -est **1 a** ~ **day** : un día nevoso **2** ~ **mountains** : montañas *fpl* nevadas

snub *vt* **snubbed; snubbing** : desairar — ~ *n* : desaire *m*

snuff *vt or* ~ **out** : apagar

snug *adj* **snugger; snuggest 1** : cómodo **2** TIGHT : ajustado — **snuggle** *vi* -gled; -gling : acurrucarse

so *adv* **1** LIKEWISE : también **2** THUS : así **3** THEREFORE : por lo tanto **4** *or* ~ **much** : tanto **5** *or* ~ **very** : tan **6 and** ~ **on** : etcétera **7 I think** ~ : creo que sí **8 I told you** ~ : te lo dije — ~ *conj* **1** THEREFORE : así que **2** *or* ~ **that** : para que **3** ~ **what?** : ¿y qué? — ~ *adj* TRUE : cierto — ~ *pron or* ~ : más o menos

soak *vi* : estar en remojo — *vt* **1** : poner en remojo **2** ~ **up** : absorber — ~ *n* : remojo *m*

soap *n* : jabón *m* — ~ *vt or* ~ **up** : enjabonar — **soapy soapier; -est** *adj* : jabonoso

soap opera *n* : culebrón *m*, telenovela *f*

soar *vi* **1** : planear **2** SKYROCKET : dispararse

sob *vi* **sobbed; sobbing** : sollozar — ~ *n* : sollozo *m*

sober *adj* **1** : sobrio **2** SERIOUS : serio — **sobriety** *n* **1** : sobriedad *f* **2** SERIOUSNESS : seriedad *f*

so—called *adj* : supuesto, presunto

soccer *n* : futbol *m*, fútbol *m*

social *adj* : social — ~ *n* : reunión *f* social — **sociable** *adj* : sociable — **socialism** *n* : socialismo *m* — **socialist** *n* : socialista *mf* — ~ *adj* : socialista — **socialize** *v* -ized; -izing *vt* : socializar — *vi* ~ **with** : alternar con — **society** *n*, *pl* -eties : sociedad *f* — **sociology** *n* : sociología *f*

sock¹ *n*, *pl* **socks** *or* **sox** : calcetín *m*

sock² *vt* : pegar, golpear — ~ *n* PUNCH : puñetazo *m*

socket *n* **1** *or* **electric** ~ : enchufe *m*, toma *f* de corriente **2** *or* **eye** ~ : órbita *f*, cuenca *f* **3** : glena *f* (de una articulación)

soda *n* **1** *or* ~ **pop** : refresco *m*, gaseosa *f* **2** *or* ~ **water** : soda *f*

sodium *n* : sodio *m*

sofa *n* : sofá *m*

soft *adj* **1** : blando **2** SMOOTH : suave —

softball *n* : softbol *m* — **soft drink** *n* : refresco *m* — **soften** *vt* **1** : ablandar **2** EASE, SMOOTH : suavizar — *vi* **1** : ablandarse **2** EASE : suavizarse — **softly** *adv* : suavemente — **software** *n* : software *m*

soggy *adj* **soggier; -est** : empapado

soil *vt* : ensuciar — ~ *n* DIRT : tierra *f*

solace *n* : consuelo *m*

solar *adj* : solar

sold → **sell**

solder *n* : soldadura *f* — ~ *vt* : soldar

soldier *n* : soldado *mf*

sole¹ *n* : lenguado *m* (pez)

sole² *n* : planta *f* (del pie), suela *f* (de un zapato)

sole³ *adj* : único — **solely** *adv* : únicamente, sólo

solemn *adj* : solemne — **solemnity** *n*, *pl* -ties : solemnidad *f*

solicit *vt* : solicitar

solid *adj* **1** : sólido **2** UNBROKEN : continuo **3** ~ **gold** : oro *m* macizo **4 two** ~ **hours** : dos horas seguidas — ~ *n* : sólido *m* — **solidarity** *n* : solidaridad *f* — **solidify** *v* -fied; -fying *vt* : solidificar — *vi* : solidificarse — **solidity** *n*, *pl* -ties : solidez *f*

solitary *adj* : solitario — **solitude** *n* : soledad *f*

solo *n*, *pl* **solos** : solo *m* — **soloist** *n* : solista *mf*

solution *n* : solución *f* — **soluble** *adj* : soluble — **solve** *vt* **solved; solving** : resolver — **solvent** *n* : solvente *m*

somber *adj* : sombrío

some *adj* **1** (*of unspecified identity*) : un **2** (*of an unspecified amount*) : algo de, un poco de **3** (*of an unspecified number*) : unos **4** CERTAIN : algunos **5 that was** ~ **game!** : ¡fue un partidazo! — ~ *pron* **1** SEVERAL : algunos, unos **2** PART : un poco, algo — ~ *adv* ~ **twenty people** : unas veinte personas — **somebody** *pron* : alguien — **someday** *adv* : algún día — **somehow** *adv* **1** : de algún modo **2** ~ **or other** : de alguna manera u otra — **someone** *pron* : alguien

somersault *n* : voltereta *f*, salto *m* mortal

something *pron* **1** : algo **2** ~ **else** : otra cosa — **sometime** *adv* **1** : algún día, en algún momento **2** ~ **next month** : (durante) el mes que viene — **sometimes** *adv* : a veces — **somewhat** *adv* : algo — **somewhere** *adv* **1** : en alguna parte, en algún lado **2** ~ **around** : alrededor de **3** ~ **else** → **elsewhere**

son–in–law *n*, *pl* **sons–in– law** : yerno *m*

son *n* : hijo *m*

song *n* : canción *f*

sonnet *n* : soneto *m*

soon *adv* **1** : pronto **2** SHORTLY : dentro de

poco **3 as ~ as** : en cuanto **4 as ~ as
possible** : lo más pronto posible **5 ~
after** : poco después **6 ~er or later** : tarde
o temprano **7 the ~er the better** : cuanto
antes mejor

soot *n* : hollín *m*

soothe *vt* **soothed; soothing 1** CALM
: calmar **2** RELIEVE : aliviar

sop *vt* **sopped; sopping ~ up** : absorber

sophistication *n* : sofisticación *f* — **sophisticated** *adj* : sofisticado

sophomore *n* : estudiante *mf* de segundo
año

soprano *n, pl* **-nos** : soprano *mf*

sorcerer *n* : hechicero *m*, brujo *m* — **sorcery** *n* : hechicería *f*, brujería *f*

sordid *adj* : sórdido

sore *adj* **sorer; sorest 1** : dolorido **2**
ANGRY : enfadado **3 ~ throat** : dolor *m* de
garganta **4 I have a ~ throat** : me duele la
garganta — **~** *n* : llaga *f* — **sorely** *adv*
: muchísimo — **soreness** *n* : dolor *m*

sorrow *n* : pesar *m*, pena *f* — **sorry** *adj* **sorrier; -est 1** PITIFUL : lamentable **2 feel
~ for** : compadecer **3 I'm ~** : lo siento

sort *n* **1** : tipo *m*, clase *f* **2 a ~ of** : una
especie de — **~** *vt* : clasificar — **sort of**
adv **1** SOMEWHAT : algo **2** MORE OR LESS
: más o menos

SOS *n* : SOS *m*

so–so *adj & adv* : así así *fam*

soufflé *n* : suflé *m*

sought → seek

soul *n* : alma *f*

sound¹ *adj* **1** HEALTHY : sano **2** FIRM : sólido **3** SENSIBLE : lógico **4 a ~ sleep** : un
sueño profundo **5 safe and ~** : sano y
salvo

sound² *n* : sonido *m* — *vt* : hacer sonar, tocar
(una trompeta, etc.) — *vi* **1** : sonar **2** SEEM
: parecer

sound³ *n* CHANNEL : brazo *m* de mar — **~**
vt **1** : sondar (en navegación) **2** *or* **~ out**
: sondear

soundly *adv* **1** SOLIDLY : sólidamente **2**
DEEPLY : profundamente

soundproof *adj* : insonorizado

soup *n* : sopa *f*

sour *adj* **1** : agrio **2 ~ milk** : leche *f* cortada — **~** *vt* : agriar

source *n* : fuente *f*, origen *m*

south *adv* : al sur — **~** *adj* : (del) sur — **~**
n : sur *m* — **South African** *adj* : sudafricano — **South American** *adj* : sudamericano — **southeast** *adv* : hacia el sureste —
~ *adj* : (del) sureste — **~** *n* : sureste *m*,
sudeste *m* — **southeastern** *adj* → **southeast** — **southerly** *adv & adj* : del sur —
southern *adj* : del sur, meridional —
southwest *adv* : hacia el suroeste — **~** *adj*

: (del) suroeste — **~** *n* : suroeste *m*, sudoeste *m* — **southwestern** *adj* → **southwest**

souvenir *n* : recuerdo *m*

sovereign *n* : soberano *m*, **-na** *f* — **~** *adj*
: soberano — **sovereignty** *n, pl* **-ties** : soberanía *f*

Soviet *adj* : soviético

sow¹ *n* : cerda *f*

sow² *vt* **sowed; sown** *or* **sowed; sowing**
: sembrar

sox → sock

soybean *n* : soya *f*, soja *f*

spa *n* : balneario *m*

space *n* **1** : espacio *m* **2** ROOM, SPOT : sitio
m, lugar *m* — **~** *vt* **spaced; spacing** : espaciar — **spaceship** *n* : nave *f* espacial —
space shuttle *n* : transbordador *m* espacial
— **spacious** *adj* : espacioso, amplio

spade¹ *n* SHOVEL : pala *f*

spade² *n* : pica *f* (naipe)

spaghetti *n* : espaguetis *mpl*

span *n* **1** PERIOD : espacio *m* **2** : luz *f*
(entre dos soportes) — **~** *vt* **spanned;
spanning 1** : abarcar (un período) **2**
CROSS : extenderse sobre

Spaniard *n* : español *m*, **-ñola** *f*

spaniel *n* : spaniel *m*

Spanish *adj* : español — **~** *n* : español *m*
(idioma)

spank *vt* : dar palmadas a (en las nalgas)

spar *vi* **sparred; sparring** : entrenarse (en
boxeo)

spare *vt* **spared; sparing 1** PARDON : perdonar **2** SAVE : ahorrar **3 can you ~ a
dollar?** : ¿me das un dólar? **4 I can't ~
the time** : no tengo tiempo **5 ~ no expense** : no reparar en gastos **6 to ~** : de
sobra — **~** *adj* **1** : de repuesto **2** EXCESS
: de más **3** LEAN : delgado — **~** *n or* **~
part** : repuesto *m* — **spare time** *n* : tiempo
m libre — **sparing** *adj* : parco, económico

spark *n* : chispa *f* — *vi* : chispear, echar
chispas — *vt* : despertar (interés), provocar
(crítica) — **sparkle** *vi* **-kled; -kling** : destellar, centellear — **~** *n* : destello *m*, centelleo
m — **spark plug** *n* : bujía *f*

sparrow *n* : gorrión *m*

sparse *adj* **sparser; -est** : escaso

spasm *n* : espasmo *m*

spat¹ → spit

spat² *n* QUARREL : disputa *f*, pelea *f*

spatter *vt* : salpicar

spawn *vi* : desovar — *vt* : engendrar, producir — **~** *n* : hueva *f*

speak *v* **spoke; spoken; speaking** *vi* **1**
: hablar **2 ~ out against** : denunciar **3
~ up** : hablar más alto **4 ~ up for** : defender — *vt* **1** : decir **2** : hablar (un
idioma) — **speaker** *n* **1** ORATOR : orador

m, -dora *f* **2** : hablante *mf* (de un idioma) **3** LOUDSPEAKER : altavoz *m*

spear *n* : lanza *f* — **spearhead** *n* : punta *f* de lanza — ∼ *vt* : encabezar — **spearmint** *n* : menta *f* verde

special *adj* : especial — **specialist** *n* : especialista *mf* — **specialization** *n* : especialización *f* — **specialize** *vi* **-ized; -izing** : especializarse — **specially** *adv* : especialmente — **specialty** *n*, *pl* **-ties** : especialidad *f*

special effects *npl* : efectos *mpl* especiales

species *ns & pl* : especie *f*

specify *vt* **-fied; -fying** : especificar — **specific** *adj* : específico — **specifically** *adv* **1** : específicamente **2** EXPLICITLY : expresamente — **specification** *n* : especificación *f*

specimen *n* : espécimen *m*

speck *n* **1** SPOT : mancha *f* **2** BIT : mota *f* — **speckled** *adj* : moteado

spectacle *n* **1** : espectáculo *m* **2** ∼s *npl* GLASSES : gafas *fpl*, lentes *fpl*, anteojos *mpl* — **spectacular** *adj* : espectacular — **spectator** *n* : espectador *m*, -dora *f*

specter *or* **spectre** *n* : espectro *m*

spectrum *n*, *pl* **-tra** *or* **-trums** **1** : espectro *m* **2** RANGE : gama *f*

speculation *n* : especulación *f*

speech *n* **1** : habla *f* **2** ADDRESS : discurso *m* — **speechless** *adj* : mudo

speed *n* **1** : rapidez *f* **2** VELOCITY : velocidad *f* — *v* **sped** *or* **speeded; speeding** *vi* **1** : conducir a exceso de velocidad **2** ∼ **off** : irse a toda velocidad **3** ∼ **up** : acelerarse — *vt or* ∼ **up** : acelerar — **speed limit** *n* : velocidad *f* máxima — **speedometer** *n* : velocímetro *m* — **speedy** *adj* **speedier, -est** : rápido

spell[1] *vt* **1** : escribir (las letras de) **2** *or* ∼ **out** : deletrear **3** MEAN : significar

spell[2] *n* ENCHANTMENT : hechizo *m*

spell[3] *n* : período *m* (de tiempo)

spellbound *adj* : embelesado

spelling *n* : ortografía *f*

spend *vt* **spent; spending** **1** : gastar (dinero) **2** : pasar (las vacaciones, etc.) **3** ∼ **time on** : dedicar tiempo a

sperm *n*, *pl* **sperm** *or* **sperms** : esperma *mf*

spew *vt* : vomitar, arrojar (lava, etc.)

sphere *n* : esfera *f* — **spherical** *adj* : esférico

spice *n* : especia *f* — ∼ *vt* **spiced; spicing** : condimentar, sazonar — **spicy** *adj* **spicier; -est** : picante

spider *n* : araña *f*

spigot *n* : grifo *m Spain*, llave *f Lat*

spike *n* **1** : clavo *m* (grande) **2** POINT : punta *f* — **spiky** *adj* : puntiagudo

spill *vt* : derramar — *vi* : derramarse

spin *v* **spun; spinning** *vi* : girar — *vt* **1**

: hilar (lana, etc.) **2** TWIRL : hacer girar — ∼ *n* **1** : vuelta *f*, giro *m* **2 go for a** ∼ : dar una vuelta (en auto)

spinach *n* : espinacas *fpl*

spinal cord *n* : médula *f* espinal

spindle *n* : huso *m* (para hilar) — **spindly** *adj* : larguirucho *fam*

spine *n* **1** : columna *f* vertebral **2** QUILL : púa *f* **3** THORN : espina *f* **4** : lomo *m* (de un libro)

spinster *n* : soltera *f*

spiral *adj* : de espiral, en espiral — ∼ *n* : espiral *f* — ∼ *vi* **-raled** *or* **-ralled; -raling** *or* **-ralling** : ir en espiral

spire *n* : aguja *f*

spirit *n* **1** : espíritu *m* **2 in good** ∼s : animado **3** ∼s *npl* : licores *mpl* — **spirited** *adj* : animado — **spiritual** *adj* : espiritual — **spirituality** *n*, *pl* **-ties** : espiritualidad *f*

spit[1] *n* ROTISSERIE : asador *m*

spit[2] *v* **spit** *or* **spat; spitting** : escupir — *n* SALIVA : saliva *f*

spite *n* **1** : rencor *m* **2 in** ∼ **of** : a pesar de — ∼ *vt* **spited; spiting** : fastidiar — **spiteful** *adj* : rencoroso

spittle *n* : saliva *f*

splash *vt* : salpicar — *vi* **1** : salpicar **2** *or* ∼ **about** : chapotear — ∼ *n* **1** : salpicadura *f* **2** : mancha *f* (de color, etc.)

splatter → **spatter**

spleen *n* : bazo *m* (órgano)

splendor *n* : esplendor *m* — **splendid** *adj* : espléndido

splint *n* : tablilla *f*

splinter *n* : astilla *f* — *vi* : astillarse

split *v* **split; splitting** *vt* **1** : partir **2** BURST : reventar **3** *or* ∼ **up** : dividir — *vi* **1** : partirse, rajarse **2** *or* ∼ **up** : dividirse — ∼ *n* **1** CRACK : rajadura *f* **2** *or* ∼ **seam** : descosido *m* **3** DIVISION : división *f*

splurge *vi* **splurged; splurging** : derrochar dinero

spoil *vt* **spoiled** *or* **spoilt; spoiling** **1** RUIN : estropear **2** PAMPER : consentir, mimar — **spoils** *npl* : botín *m*

spoke[1] → **speak**

spoke[2] *n* : rayo *m* (de una rueda)

spoken → **speak**

spokesman *n*, *pl* **-men** : portavoz *mf* — **spokeswoman** *n*, *pl* **-women** : portavoz *f*

sponge *n* : esponja *f* — ∼ *vt* **sponged; sponging** : limpiar con una esponja — **spongy** *adj* **spongier; -est** : esponjoso

sponsor *n* : patrocinador *m*, -dora *f* — ∼ *vt* : patrocinar — **sponsorship** *n* : patrocinio *m*

spontaneity *n* : espontaneidad *f* — **spontaneous** *adj* : espontáneo

spooky *adj* **spookier; -est** : espeluznante

spool *n* : carrete *m*

spoon *n* : cuchara *f* — **spoonful** *n* : cucharada *f*

sporadic *adj* : esporádico

spore *n* : espora *f*

sport *n* **1** : deporte *m* **2 be a good ~** : tener espíritu deportivo — **sportsman** *n*, *pl* **-men** : deportista *m* — **sportswoman** *n*, *pl* **-women** : deportista *f* — **sporty** *adj* **sportier; -est** : deportivo

sports center *n* : centro *m* deportivo

spot *n* **1** : mancha *f* **2** DOT : punto *m* **3** PLACE : lugar *m*, sitio *m* **4 in a tight ~** : en apuros **5 on the ~** INSTANTLY : en ese mismo momento — **~** *vt* **spotted; spotting 1** STAIN : manchar **2** DETECT, NOTICE : ver, descubrir — **spotless** *adj* : impecable — **spotlight** *n* **1** : foco *m*, reflector *m* **2 be in the ~** : ser el centro de atención — **spotty** *adj* **spottier; -est** : irregular

spouse *n* : cónyuge *mf*

spout *vi* : salir a chorros — **~** *n* **1** : pico *m* (de una jarra, etc.) **2** STREAM : chorro *m*

sprain *n* : esguince *m* — **~** *vt* : sufrir un esguince en

sprawl *vi* **1** : repantigarse (en un sillón, etc.) **2** EXTEND : extenderse — **~** *n* : extensión *f*

spray[1] *n* BOUQUET : ramillete *m*

spray[2] *n* **1** MIST : rocío *m* **2** *or* **aerosol ~** : spray *m* **3** *or* **~ bottle** : atomizador *m* — **~** *vt* : rociar (una superficie), pulverizar (un líquido)

spread *v* **spread; spreading** *vt* **1** : propagar (enfermedades), difundir (noticias, etc.) **2** *or* **~ out** : extender **3** : untar (con mantequilla, etc.) — *vi* **1** : propagarse, difundirse **2** *or* **~ out** : extenderse — **~** *n* **1** : propagación *f*, difusión *f* **2** PASTE : pasta *f* (para untar) — **spreadsheet** *n* : hoja *f* de cálculo

spree *n* **go on a ~** : ir de juerga *fam*

sprig *n* : ramito *m*

sprightly *adj* **sprightlier; -est** : vivo

spring *v* **sprang** *or* **sprung; sprung; springing** *vi* **1** : saltar **2 ~ from** : surgir de **3 ~ up** : surgir — *vt* **1** ACTIVATE : accionar **2 ~ a leak** : hacer agua **3 ~ sth on s.o.** : sorprender a algn con algo — **~** *n* **1** : manantial *m* (de aguas) **2** : primavera *f* (estación) **3** LEAP : salto *m* **4** RESILIENCE : elasticidad *f* **5** : resorte *m* (mecanismo) **6** *or* **bedspring** : muelle *m* — **springboard** *n* : trampolín *m* — **springtime** *n* : primavera *f* — **springy** *adj* **springier; -est** : mullido

sprinkle *vt* **-kled; -kling 1** : salpicar, rociar **2** DUST : espolvorear — **~** *n* : llovizna *f* — **sprinkler** *n* : aspersor *m*

sprint *vi* **1** : correr **2** : esprintar (en deportes) — **~** *n* : esprint *m* (en deportes)

sprout *vi* : brotar — **~** *n* : brote *m*

spruce[1] *vt* **spruced; sprucing ~ up** : arreglar

spruce[2] *n* : picea *f* (árbol)

spry *adj* **sprier** *or* **spryer; spriest** *or* **spryest** : ágil, activo

spun → spin

spur *n* **1** : espuela *f* **2** STIMULUS : acicate *m* **3 on the ~ of the moment** : sin pensarlo — **~** *vt* **spurred; spurring** *or* **~ on 1** : espolear (un caballo) **2** MOTIVATE : motivar

spurn *vt* : desdeñar, rechazar

spurt[1] *vi* : salir a chorros — **~** *n* : chorro *m*

spurt[2] *n* **1** : arranque *m* (de energía, etc.) **2 work in ~s** : trabajar por rachas

spy *v* **spied; spying** *vt* : ver, divisar — *vi* **~ on s.o.** : espiar a algn — **~** *n* : espía *mf*

squabble *n* : riña *f*, pelea *f* — **~** *vi* **-bled; -bling** : reñir, pelearse

squad *n* : pelotón *m* (militar), brigada *f* (de policías)

squadron *n* : escuadrón *m* (de soldados), escuadra *f* (de aviones o naves)

squalid *adj* : miserable

squall *n* : turbión *m*

squalor *n* : miseria *f*

squander *vt* : derrochar (dinero, etc.), desperdiciar (oportunidades, etc.)

square *n* **1** : cuadrado *m* **2** : plaza *f* (de una ciudad) — **~** *adj* **squarer; -est 1** : cuadrado **2** HONEST : justo **3** EVEN : en paz **4 a ~ meal** : una comida decente — **~** *vt* **squared; squaring 1** : elevar al cuadrado (un número) **2** : saldar (una cuenta) — **square root** *n* : raíz *f* cuadrada

squash[1] *vt* **1** : aplastar **2** : acallar (protestas, etc.) — **~** *n* : squash *m* (deporte)

squash[2] *n*, *pl* **squashes** *or* **squash** : calabaza *f* (vegetal)

squat *vi* **squatted; squatting 1** *or* **~ down** : ponerse en cuclillas **2** : ocupar un lugar sin derecho — **~** *adj* **squatter; squattest** : achaparrado

squawk *n* : graznido *m* — **~** *vi* : graznar

squeak *vi* **1** : chillar **2** CREAK : chirriar — **~** *n* **1** : chillido *m* **2** CREAK : chirrido *m* — **squeaky** *adj* **squeakier; -est** : chirriante

squeal *vi* **1** : chillar (dícese de personas, etc.), chirriar (dícese de frenos, etc.) **2** PROTEST : quejarse — **~** *n* : chillido *m* (de una persona), chirrido *m* (de frenos, etc.)

squeamish *adj* : impresionable, delicado

squeeze *vt* **squeezed; squeezing 1** : apretar **2** : exprimir (frutas, etc.) **3** : extraer (jugo, etc.) — **~** *n* : apretón *m*

squid *n*, *pl* **squid** *or* **squids** : calamar *m*

squint *vi* : entrecerrar los ojos — **~** *n* : estrabismo *m*

squirm *vi* : retorcerse

squirrel *n* : ardilla *f*

squirt *vt* : lanzar un chorro de — *vi* : salir a chorros — ~ *n* : chorrito *m*

stab *n* **1** : puñalada *f* **2** ~ **of pain** : pinchazo *m* **3 take a** ~ **at** : intentar — ~ *vt* **stabbed; stabbing 1** KNIFE : apuñalar **2** STICK : clavar

stable 1 : establo *m* (para ganado) **2** *or* **horse** ~ : caballeriza *f* — ~ *adj* **-bler; -blest** : estable — **stability** *n*, *pl* **-ties** : estabilidad *f* — **stabilize** *vt* **-lized; -lizing** : estabilizar

stack *n* : montón *m*, pila *f* — ~ *vt* : amontonar, apilar

stadium *n*, *pl* **-dia** *or* **-diums** : estadio *m*

staff *n*, *pl* **staffs** *or* **staves 1** : bastón *m* **2** *pl* **staffs** PERSONNEL : personal *m* **3** *pl* **staffs** : pentagrama *m* (en música) — ~ *vt* : proveer de personal

stag *n*, *pl* **stags** *or* **stag** : ciervo *m*, venado *m* — ~ *adj* : sólo para hombres — ~ *adv* **go** ~ : ir solo

stage *n* **1** : escenario *m* (de un teatro) **2** PHASE : etapa *f* **3 the** ~ : el teatro — ~ *vt* **staged; staging 1 the** : poner en escena **2** ARRANGE : montar — **stagecoach** *n* : diligencia *f*

stagger *vi* : tambalearse — *vt* **1** : escalonar (turnos, etc.) **2 be** ~**ed by** : quedarse estupefacto por — ~ *n* : tambaleo *m* — **staggering** *adj* : asombroso

stagnant *adj* : estancado — **stagnate** *vi* **-nated; -nating** : estancarse

stain *vt* **1** : manchar **2** : teñir (madera) — ~ *n* **1** : mancha *f* **2** DYE : tinte *m*, tintura *f* — **stainless steel** *n* : acero *m* inoxidable

stair *n* **1** STEP : escalón *m*, peldaño *m* **2** ~**s** *npl* : escalera(s) *f(pl)* — **staircase** *n* : escalera(s) *f(pl)* — **stairway** *n* : escalera(s) *f(pl)*

stake *n* **1** POST : estaca *f* **2** BET : apuesta *f* **3** INTEREST : intereses *mpl* **4 be at** ~ : estar en juego — ~ *vt* **staked; staking 1** : estacar **2** BET : jugarse **3** ~ **a claim to** : reclamar

stale *adj* **staler; stalest 1** : duro (dícese del pan) **2** OLD : viejo **3** STUFFY : viciado

stalk[1] *n* : tallo *m* (de una planta)

stalk[2] *vt* : acechar — *vi* *or* ~ **off** : irse con altivez

stall[1] *n* **1** : compartimiento *m* (de un establo) **2** STAND : puesto *m* — ~ *vt* : parar (un motor) — *vi* : pararse

stall[2] *vt* DELAY : entretener — *vi* : andar con rodeos

stallion *n* : caballo *m* semental

stalwart *adj* **1** STRONG : fornido **2** ~ **supporter** : partidario *m* leal

stamina *n* : resistencia *f*

stammer *vi* : tartamudear — ~ *n* : tartamudeo *m*

stamp 1 SEAL : sello *m* **2** DIE : cuño *m* **3** *or* **postage** ~ : sello *m*, estampilla *f* *Lat*, timbre *m* *Lat* — ~ *vt* **1** : franquear (una carta) **2** IMPRINT : sellar **3** MINT : acuñar **4** ~ **one's foot** : dar una patada (en el suelo)

stampede *n* : estampida *f* — ~ *vi* **-peded; -peding** : salir en estampida

stance *n* : postura *f*

stand *v* **stood; standing** *vi* **1** : estar de pie, estar parado *Lat* **2** BE : estar **3** CONTINUE : seguir vigente **4** LIE, REST : reposar **5** ~ **aside** *or* ~ **back** : apartarse **6** ~ **out** : sobresalir **7** *or* ~ **up** : ponerse de pie, pararse *Lat* — *vt* **1** PLACE : poner, colocar **2** ENDURE : soportar **3** ~ **a chance** : tener una posibilidad — **stand by** *vt* **1** : mantener (una promesa, etc.) **2** SUPPORT : apoyar — **stand for** *vt* **1** MEAN : significar **2** PERMIT : permitir — **stand up** *vi* **1** ~ **for** : defender **2** ~ **up to** : resistir a — ~ *n* **1** RESISTANCE : resistencia *f* **2** STALL : puesto *m* **3** BASE : base *f* **4** POSITION : posición *f* **5** ~**s** *npl* : tribuna *f*

standard *n* **1** : norma *f* **2** BANNER : estandarte *m* **3** CRITERION : criterio *m* **4** ~ **of living** : nivel *m* de vida — ~ *adj* : estándar — **standardize** *vt* **-ized; -izing** : estandarizar

standing *n* **1** RANK : posición *f* **2** DURATION : duración *f*

standpoint *n* : punto *m* de vista

standstill *n* **1 be at a** ~ : estar paralizado **2 come to a** ~ : pararse

stank → **stink**

stanza *n* : estrofa *f*

staple[1] *n* : producto *m* principal — ~ *adj* : principal, básico

staple[2] *n* : grapa *f* (para papeles) — ~ *vt* **-pled; -pling** : grapar, engrapar *Lat* — **stapler** *n* : grapadora *f*, engrapadora *f* *Lat*

star *n* : estrella *f* — ~ *v* **starred; starring** *vt* FEATURE : estar protagonizado por — *vi* ~ **in** : protagonizar

starboard *n* : estribor *m*

starch *vt* : almidonar — ~ *n* **1** : almidón *m* **2** : fécula *f* (comida)

stardom *n* : estrellato *m*

stare *vi* **stared; staring** : mirar fijamente — ~ *n* : mirada *f* fija

starfish *n* : estrella *f* de mar

stark *adj* **1** PLAIN : austero **2** HARSH : severo, duro **3** SHARP : marcado — ~ *adv* **1** : completamente **2** ~ **naked** : en cueros (vivos)

starlight *n* : luz *f* de las estrellas

starling *n* : estornino *m*

starry *adj* **starrier; -est** : estrellado

start *vi* **1** : empezar, comenzar **2** SET OUT
: salir **3** JUMP : sobresaltarse **4** *or* ~ **up**
: arrancar — *vt* **1** : empezar, comenzar **2**
CAUSE : provocar **3** *or* ~ **up** ESTABLISH
: montar **4** *or* ~ **up** : arrancar (un motor,
etc.) — ~ *n* **1** : principio *m* **2 get an
early** ~ : salir temprano **3 give s.o. a** ~
: asustar a algn — **starter** *n* : motor *m* de
arranque (de un vehículo)
startle *vt* **-tled; -tling** : asustar
starve *v* **starved; starving** *vi* : morirse de
hambre — *vt* : privar de comida — **starvation** *n* : inanición *f*, hambre *f*
stash *vt* : esconder
state *n* **1** : estado *m* **2 the States** : los
Estados Unidos — ~ *vt* **stated; stating 1**
SAY : decir **2** REPORT : exponer — **stately**
adj **statelier; -est** : majestuoso — **statement** *n* **1** : declaración *f* **2** *or* **bank** ~
: estado *m* de cuenta — **statesman** *n*, *pl*
-men : estadista *mf*
static *adj* : estático — ~ *n* : estática *f*
station wagon *n* : camioneta *f* (familiar)
station *n* **1** : estación *f* (de trenes, etc.) **2**
RANK : condición *f* (social) **3** : canal *m* (de
televisión), emisora *f* (de radio) **4** → **fire
station, police station** — *vt* : apostar, estacionar — **stationary** *adj* : estacionario
stationery *n* : papel *m* y sobres *mpl* (para
cartas)
statistic *n* : estadística *f* — **statistical** *adj*
: estadístico
statue *n* : estatua *f*
stature *n* : estatura *f*, talla *f*
status *n* **1** : situación *f* **2** *or* **social** ~
: estatus *m* **3 marital** ~ : estado *m* civil
statute *n* : estatuto *m*
staunch *adj* : leal
stave *vt* **staved** *or* **stove; staving 1** ~ **in**
: romper **2** ~ **off** : evitar
staves → **staff**
stay[1] *vi* **1** REMAIN : quedarse, permanecer
2 LODGE : alojarse **3** ~ **awake** : mantenerse despierto **4** ~ **in** : quedarse en casa
— *vt* : suspender (una ejecución, etc.) — ~
n **1** : estancia *f*, estadía *f* *Lat* **2** SUSPEN-
SION : suspensión *f*
stay[2] *n* SUPPORT : soporte *m*
stead *n* **1 in s.o.'s** ~ : en lugar de algn **2**
stand s.o. in good ~ : ser muy útil a algn
— **steadfast** *adj* **1** FIRM : firme **2** LOYAL
: leal, fiel — **steadily** *adv* **1** : progresivamente **2** INCESSANTLY : sin parar **3**
FIXEDLY : fijamente — **steady** *adj* **steadier;
-est 1** FIRM, SURE : firme, seguro **2** FIXED
: fijo **3** DEPENDABLE : responsable **4** CON-
STANT : constante — ~ *vt* **steadied;
steadying 1** : mantener firme **2** : calmar
(los nervios)
steak *n* : bistec *m*, filete *m*

steal *v* **stole; stolen; stealing** *vt* : robar —
vi **1** : robar **2** ~ **away** : escabullirse
stealth *n* : sigilo *m* — **stealthy** *adj* **stealth-
ier; -est** : furtivo, sigiloso
steam *n* **1** : vapor *m* **2 let off** ~ : desahogarse — ~ *vi* : echar vapor — *vt* **1**
: cocer al vapor **2** ~ **up** : empañar —
steam engine *n* : motor *m* de vapor —
steamship *n* : (barco *m* de) vapor *m* —
steamy *adj* **steamier; -est 1** : lleno de
vapor **2** PASSIONATE : tórrido
steel *n* : acero *m* — ~ *vt* ~ **oneself** : armarse de valor — ~ *adj* : de acero
steep[1] *adj* **1** : empinado **2** CONSIDERABLE
: considerable **3** : muy alto (dícese de precios)
steep[2] *vt* : dejar (té, etc.) en infusión
steeple *n* : aguja *f*, campanario *m*
steer[1] *n* : buey *m*
steer[2] *vt* : dirigir (un auto, etc.), pilotear (un
barco) — **steering wheel** *n* : volante *m*
stem[1] *n* : tallo *m* (de una planta), pie *m* (de
una copa) — ~ *vi* ~ **from** : provenir de
stem[2] *vt* **stemmed; stemming** : contener, detener
stench *n* : hedor *m*, mal olor *m*
stencil *n* : plantilla *f* (para marcar)
step *n* **1** : paso *m* **2** RUNG, STAIR : escalón
m **3** ~ **by** ~ : paso por paso **4 take** ~**s**
: tomar medidas **5 watch your** ~ : mira
por dónde caminas — ~ *vi* **stepped; step-
ping 1** : dar un paso **2** ~ **back** : reto-
ceder **3** ~ **down** RESIGN : retirarse **4** ~
in : intervenir **5** ~ **out** : salir (por un momento) **6** ~ **this way** : pase por aquí —
step up *vt* INCREASE : aumentar
stepbrother *n* : hermanastro *m* — **stepdaughter** *n* : hijastra *f* — **stepfather** *n* : padrastro *m*
stepladder *n* : escalera *f* de tijera
stepmother *n* : madrastra *f* — **stepsister** *n*
: hermanastra *f* — **stepson** *n* : hijastro *m*
stereo *n*, *pl* **stereos** : estéreo *m* — ~ *adj*
: estéreo
stereotype *vt* **-typed; -typing** : estereotipar
— ~ *n* : estereotipo *m*
sterile *adj* : estéril — **sterility** *n* : esterilidad
f — **sterilization** *n* : esterilización *f* — **sterilize** *vt* **-ized; -izing** : esterilizar
sterling *adj* : excelente — **sterling silver** *n*
: plata *f* de ley
stern[1] *adj* : severo, adusto
stern[2] *n* : popa *f*
stethoscope *n* : estetoscopio *m*
stew *n* : estofado *m*, guiso *m* — ~ *vt* : estofar, guisar — *vi* **1** : cocer **2** FRET : preocuparse
steward *n* **1** : administrador *m*, -dora *f* **2**
: auxiliar *m* de vuelo (en un avión) **3** : camarero *m* (en un barco) — **stewardess** *n* **1**

: auxiliar *f* de vuelo, azafata *f* (en un avión) **2** : camarera *f* (en un barco)

stick¹ *n* **1** : palo *m* **2** TWIG : ramita *f* (suelta) **3** WALKING STICK : bastón *m*

stick² *v* **stuck; sticking** *vt* **1** : pegar **2** STAB : clavar **3** PUT : poner **4** ~ **out** : sacar (la lengua, etc.) — *vi* **1** : pegarse JAM : atascarse **3** ~ **around** : quedarse **4** ~ **out** PROTRUDE : sobresalir **5** ~ **out** SHOW : asomar **6** ~ **up** : sobresalir **7** ~ **up for** : defender — **sticker** *n* : etiqueta *f* adhesiva — **stickler** *n* **be a** ~ **for** : insistir mucho en — **sticky** *adj* **stickier; -est** : pegajoso

stiff *adj* **1** RIGID : rígido, tieso **2** STILTED : forzado **3** STRONG : fuerte **4** DIFFICULT : difícil **5** : entumecido (dícese de múscu-los) — **stiffen** *vt* : fortalecer, hacer más duro — *vi* **1** HARDEN : endurecerse **2** : en-tumecerse (dícese de músculos) — **stiff-ness** *n* : rigidez *f*

stifle *vt* **-fled; -fling** : sofocar

stigmatize *vt* **-tized; -tizing** : estigmatizar

still *adj* **1** : inmóvil **2** SILENT : callado — ~ *adv* **1** : todavía, aún **2** NEVERTHELESS : de todos modos, aún así **3 sit** ~**!** : ¡qué-date quieto! — ~ *n* : quietud *f*, calma *f* — **stillborn** *adj* : nacido muerto — **stillness** *n* : calma *f*, silencio *m*

stilt *n* : zanco *m* — **stilted** *adj* : forzado

stimulate *vt* **-lated; -lating** : estimular — **stimulant** *n* : estimulante *m* — **stimulation** *n* : estimulación *f* — **stimulus** *n, pl* **-li** : estímulo *m*

sting *v* **stung; stinging** : picar — ~ *n* : pic-adura *f* — **stinger** *n* : aguijón *m*

stingy *adj* **stingier; -est** : tacaño — **stingi-ness** *n* : tacañería *f*

stink *vi* **stank** *or* **stunk; stunk; stinking** : apestar, oler mal — ~ *n* : hedor *m*, peste *f fam*

stint *vi* ~ **on** : escatimar — ~ *n* : período *m*

stipulate *vt* **-lated; -lating** : estipular

stir *v* **stirred; stirring** *vt* **1** : remover, re-volver **2** MOVE : mover **3** INCITE : incitar **4** *or* ~ **up** : despertar (memorias, etc.), provocar (ira, etc.) — *vi* : moverse, agitarse — ~ *n* COMMOTION : revuelo *m*

stirrup *n* : estribo *m*

stitch *n* **1** : puntada *f* **2** PAIN : punzada *f* (en el costado) — ~ *v* : coser

stock **market** *n* : bolsa *f* — **stockpile** *n* : reservas *fpl* — ~ *vt* **-piled; -piling** : alma-cenar — **stocky** *adj* **stockier; -est** : ro-busto, fornido

stock *n* **1** INVENTORY : existencias *fpl* **2** SECURITIES : acciones *fpl* **3** ANCESTRY : linaje *m*, estirpe *f* **4** BROTH : caldo *m* **5 out of** ~ : agotado **6 take** ~ **of** : evaluar

— ~ *vt* : surtir, abastecer — *vi* ~ **up on** : abastecerse de — **stockbroker** *n* : corre-dor *m*, -dora *f* de bolsa

stocking *n* : media *f*

stodgy *adj* **stodgier; -est** **1** DULL : pesado **2** OLD-FASHIONED : anticuado

stoic *n* : estoico *m*, -ca *f* — ~ *or* **stoical** *adj* : estoico — **stoicism** *n* : estoicismo *m*

stoke *vt* **stoked; stoking** : echar carbón o leña a

stole¹ → **steal**

stole² *n* : estola *f*

stolen → **steal**

stomach *n* : estómago *m* — ~ *vt* : aguantar, soportar — **stomachache** *n* : dolor *m* de estómago

stone *n* **1** : piedra *f* **2** : hueso *m* (de una fruta) — ~ *vt* **stoned; stoning** : apedrear — **stony** *adj* **stonier; -est** **1** : pedregoso **2 a** ~ **silence** : un silencio sepulcral

stood → **stand**

stool *n* : taburete *m*

stoop *vi* **1** : agacharse **2** ~ **to** : rebajarse a — ~ *n* **have a** ~ : ser encorvado

stop *v* **stopped; stopping** *vt* **1** PLUG : tapar **2** PREVENT : impedir **3** HALT : parar, de-tener **4** CEASE : dejar de — *vi* **1** : deten-erse, parar **2** CEASE : cesar, dejar **3** ~ **by** : visitar — ~ *n* **1** : parada *f*, alto *m* **2 come to a** ~ : pararse, detenerse **3 put a** ~ **to** : poner fin a — **stopgap** *n* : arreglo *m* provisorio — **stoplight** *n* : semáforo *m* — **stoppage** *n or* **work** ~ : paro *m* — **stop-per** *n* : tapón *m*

store *vt* **stored; storing** : guardar (comida, etc.), almacenar (datos, mercancías, etc.) — ~ *n* **1** SUPPLY : reserva *f* **2** SHOP : tienda *f* — **storage** *n* : almacenamiento *m* — **storehouse** *n* : almacén *m* — **storekeeper** *n* : tendero *m*, -ra *f* — **storeroom** *n* : alma-cén *m*

stork *n* : cigüeña *f*

storm *n* : tormenta *f*, tempestad *f* — ~ *vi* **1** RAGE : ponerse furioso **2** ~ **in/out** : en-trar/salir furioso — *vt* ATTACK : asaltar — **stormy** *adj* **stormier; -est** : tormentoso

story¹ *n, pl* **stories** **1** TALE : cuento *m* **2** ACCOUNT : historia *f* **3** RUMOR : rumor *m*

story² *n* FLOOR : piso *m*, planta *f*

stout *adj* **1** BRAVE : valiente **2** RESOLUTE : tenaz **3** STURDY : fuerte **4** FAT : corpu-lento

stove¹ *n* **1** : estufa *f* (para calentar) **2** RANGE : cocina *f*

stove² → **stave**

stow *vt* **1** : guardar **2** LOAD : cargar — *vi* ~ **away** : viajar de polizón — **stowaway** *n* : polizón *m*

straddle *vt* **-dled; -dling** : sentarse a hor-cajadas sobre

straggle *vi* **-gled; -gling** : rezagarse, quedarse atrás — **straggler** *n* : rezagado *m*, -da *f*

straight *adj* **1** : recto, derecho **2** : lacio (dícese del pelo) **3** HONEST : franco **4** TIDY : arreglado — ~ *adv* **1** DIRECTLY : derecho **2** EXACTLY : justo **3** CLEARLY : con claridad **4** FRANKLY : con franqueza — **straightaway** *adv* : inmediatamente — **straighten** *vt* **1** : enderezar **2** ~ **up** : arreglar — **straightforward** *adj* **1** FRANK : franco **2** CLEAR : claro, sencillo

strain[1] *n* **1** LINEAGE : linaje *m* **2** STREAK : veta *f* **3** VARIETY : variedad *f* **4** ~**s** *npl* : acordes *mpl* (de música)

strain[2] *vt* **1** : forzar (la vista o la voz) **2** FILTER : colar **3** : tensar (relaciones, etc.) **4** ~ **a muscle** : sufrir un esguince **5** ~ **oneself** : hacerse daño — *vi* : esforzarse (por) — ~ *n* **1** STRESS : tensión *f* **2** SPRAIN : esguince *m* — **strainer** *n* : colador *m*

strait *n* **1** : estrecho *m* **2 in dire** ~**s** : en grandes apuros

strand[1] *vt* **be** ~**ed** : quedar(se) varado

strand[2] *n* **1** : hebra *f* **2 a** ~ **of hair** : un pelo

strange *adj* **stranger; -est 1** : extraño, raro **2** UNFAMILIAR : desconocido — **strangely** *adv* : de manera extraña — **strangeness** *n* **1** : rareza *f* **2** UNFAMILIARITY : lo desconocido — **stranger** *n* : desconocido *m*, -da *f*

strangle *vt* **-gled; -gling** : estrangular

strap *n* **1** : correa *f* **2** *or* **shoulder** ~ : tirante *m* — ~ *vt* **strapped; strapping** : sujetar con una correa — **strapless** *n* : sin tirantes — **strapping** *adj* : robusto, fornido

strategy *n, pl* **-gies** : estrategia *f* — **strategic** *adj* : estratégico

straw *n* **1** : paja *f* **2** *or* **drinking** ~ : pajita *f* **3 the last** ~ : el colmo

strawberry *n, pl* **-ries** : fresa *f*

stray *n* : animal *m* perdido — ~ *vi* **1** : perderse, extraviarse **2** : apartarse (de un grupo, etc.) **3** DEVIATE : desviarse — ~ *adj* : perdido

streak *n* **1** : raya *f* **2** VEIN : veta *f* **3** ~ **of luck** : racha *f* de suerte — *vi* ~ **by** : pasar como una flecha

stream *n* **1** : arroyo *m*, riachuelo *m* **2** FLOW : chorro *m*, corriente *f* — ~ *vi* : correr — **streamer** *n* **1** PENNANT : banderín *m* **2** : serpentina *f* (de papel) — **streamlined** *adj* **1** : aerodinámico **2** EFFICIENT : eficiente

street *n* : calle *f* — **streetcar** *n* : tranvía *m* — **streetlight** *n* : farol *m*

strength *n* **1** : fuerza *f* **2** FORTITUDE : fortaleza *f* **3** TOUGHNESS : resistencia *f*, solidez *f* **4** INTENSITY : intensidad *f* **5** ~**s**

and weaknesses : virtudes y defectos — **strengthen** *vt* **1** : fortalecer **2** REINFORCE : reforzar **3** INTENSIFY : intensificar

strenuous *adj* **1** : enérgico **2** ARDUOUS : duro, riguroso

stress *n* **1** : tensión *f* **2** EMPHASIS : énfasis *m* **3** : acento *m* (en lingüística) — ~ *vt* **1** EMPHASIZE : enfatizar **2** *or* ~ **out** : estresar — **stressful** *adj* : estresante

stretch *vt* **1** : estirar (músculos, elástico, etc.) **2** EXTEND : extender **3** ~ **the truth** : forzar la verdad — *vi* **1** : estirarse **2** EXTEND : extenderse — ~ *n* **1** : extensión *f* **2** ELASTICITY : elasticidad *f* **3** EXPANSE : tramo *m* **4** : período *m* (de tiempo) — **stretcher** *n* : camilla *f*

strew *vt* **strewed; strewed** *or* **strewn; strewing** : esparcir (semillas, etc.), desparramar (papeles, etc.)

stricken *adj* ~ **with** : aquejado de (una enfermedad), afligido por (tristeza, etc.)

strict *adj* : estricto — **strictly** *adv* ~ **speaking** : en rigor

stride *vi* **strode; stridden; striding** : ir dando zancadas — ~ *n* **1** : zancada *f* **2 make great** ~**s** : hacer grandes progresos

strident *adj* : estridente

strife *n* : conflictos *mpl*

strike *v* **struck; struck; striking** *vt* **1** HIT : golpear **2** *or* ~ **against** : chocar contra **3** *or* ~ **out** DELETE : tachar **4** : dar (la hora) **5** IMPRESS : impresionar **6** : descubrir (oro o petróleo) **7 it** ~**s me as...** : me parece... **8** ~ **up** START : entablar — *vi* **1** : golpear **2** ATTACK : atacar **3** : declararse en huelga **4** : sobrevenir (dícese de una enfermedad, etc.) — ~ *n* **1** BLOW : golpe *m* **2** : huelga *f*, paro *m Lat* (de trabajadores) **3** ATTACK : ataque *m* — **strikebreaker** *n* : esquirol *mf* — **striker** *n* : huelguista *mf* — **striking** *adj* : notable, llamativo

string *n* **1** : cordel *m* **2** : sarta *f* (de perlas, insultos, etc.), serie *f* (de eventos, etc.) **3** ~**s** *npl* : cuerdas *fpl* (en música) — ~ *vt* **strung; stringing 1** : ensartar **2** *or* ~ **up** : colgar — **string bean** *n* : habichuela *f* verde

stringent *adj* : estricto, severo

strip[1] *v* **stripped; stripping** *vt* **1** REMOVE : quitar **2** UNDRESS : desnudar **3** ~ **s.o. of sth** : despojar a algn de algo — *vi* UNDRESS : desnudarse

strip[2] *n* : tira *f*

stripe *n* : raya *f*, lista *f* — **striped** *adj* : a rayas, rayado

strive *vi* **strove; striven** *or* **strived; striving 1** ~ **for** : luchar por **2** ~ **to** : esforzarse por

strode → **stride**

stroke *vt* **stroked; stroking** : acariciar —

~ *n* **1** : golpe *m* **2** : derrame *m* cerebral (en medicina)
stroll *vi* : pasearse — ~ *n* : paseo *m* — **stroller** *n* : cochecito *m* (para niños)
strong *adj* : fuerte — **stronghold** *n* : bastión *m* — **strongly** *adv* **1** DEEPLY : profundamente **2** WHOLEHEARTEDLY : totalmente **3** VIGOROUSLY : enérgicamente
strove → **strive**
struck → **strike**
structure *n* : estructura *f* — **structural** *adj* : estructural
struggle *vi* -gled; -gling **1** : forcejear **2** STRIVE : luchar — ~ *n* : lucha *f*
strum *vt* strummed; strumming : rasguear
strung → **string**
strut *vi* strutted; strutting : pavonearse — ~ *n* : puntal *m* (en construcción)
stub *n* : colilla *f* (de un cigarrillo), cabo *m* (de un lápiz, etc.), talón *m* (de un cheque) — ~ *vt* stubbed; stubbing ~ one's toe : darse en el dedo
stubble *n* : barba *f* de varios días
stubborn *adj* **1** : terco, obstinado **2** PERSISTENT : tenaz
stucco *n, pl* stuccos *or* stuccoes : estuco *m*
stuck → **stick** — **stuck–up** *adj* : engreído, creído *fam*
stud¹ *n* : semental *m* (animal)
stud² *n* **1** NAIL, TACK : tachuela *f*, tachón *m* **2** *or* ~ earring : arete *m* Lat, pendiente *m* Spain **3** : montante *m* (en construcción)
student *n* : estudiante *mf*; alumno *m*, -na *f* (de un colegio) — **studio** *n, pl* studios : estudio *m* — **study** *n, pl* studies : estudio *m* — ~ *v* studied; studying : estudiar — **studious** *adj* : estudioso
stuff *n* **1** : cosas *fpl* **2** MATTER, SUBSTANCE : cosa *f* **3** know one's ~ : ser experto — ~ *vt* **1** FILL : rellenar **2** CRAM : meter — **stuffing** *n* : relleno *m* — **stuffy** *adj* stuffier; -est **1** STODGY : pesado, aburrido **2** : tapado (dícese de la nariz) **3** ~ rooms : salas *fpl* mal ventiladas
stumble *vi* -bled; -bling **1** : tropezar **2** ~ across *or* upon : tropezar con
stump *n* **1** : muñón *m* (de una pierna, etc.) **2** *or* tree ~ : tocón *m* — ~ *vt* : dejar perplejo
stun *vt* stunned; stunning **1** : aturdir (con un golpe) **2** ASTONISH : dejar atónito
stung → **sting**
stunk → **stink**
stunning *adj* **1** : increíble, sensacional **2** STRIKING : imponente
stunt¹ *vt* : atrofiar
stunt² *n* : proeza *f* (acrobática)
stupendous *adj* : estupendo

stupid *adj* **1** : estúpido **2** SILLY : tonto, bobo — **stupidity** *n* : tontería *f*, estupidez *f*
sturdy *adj* sturdier; -est **1** : fuerte, resistente **2** ROBUST : robusto
stutter *vi* : tartamudear — ~ *n* : tartamudeo *m*
sty *n* **1** *pl* sties PIGPEN : pocilga *f* **2** *pl* sties *or* styes : orzuelo *m* (en el ojo)
style *n* **1** : estilo *m* **2** FASHION : moda *f* **3** be in ~ : estar de moda — ~ *vt* styled; styling : peinar (pelo), diseñar (vestidos, etc.) — **stylish** *adj* : elegante, chic — **stylist** *n* : estilista *mf*
suave *adj* : refinado y afable
sub¹ *vi* subbed; subbing → substitute — ~ *n* → substitute
sub² *n* → submarine
subconscious *adj* : subconsciente — ~ *n* : subconsciente *m*
subdivide *vt* -vided; -viding : subdividir — **subdivision** *n* : subdivisión *f*
subdue *vt* -dued; -duing **1** CONQUER : sojuzgar **2** CONTROL : dominar **3** SOFTEN : atenuar — **subdued** *adj* : apagado
subject *n* **1** : sujeto *m* **2** : súbdito *m*, -ta *f* (de un gobierno) **3** TOPIC : tema *m* — ~ *adj* : sometido **2** ~ to : sujeto a — ~ *vt* ~ to : someter a — **subjective** *adj* : subjetivo
subjunctive *n* : subjuntivo *m* — **subjunctive** *adj* : subjuntivo
sublime *adj* : sublime
submarine *adj* : submarino — ~ *n* : submarino *m*
submerge *v* -merged; -merging *vt* : sumergir — *vi* : sumergirse
submit *v* -mitted; -mitting *vi* **1** YIELD : rendirse **2** ~ to : someterse a — *vt* : presentar — **submission** *n* **1** : sumisión *f* **2** PRESENTATION : presentación *f* — **submissive** *adj* : sumiso
subordinate *adj* : subordinado — ~ *n* : subordinado *m*, -da *f* — ~ *vt* -nated; -nating : subordinar
subpoena *n* : citación *f*
subscribe *vi* -scribed; -scribing ~ to : suscribirse a (una revista, etc.), suscribir (una opinión, etc.) — **subscriber** *n* : suscriptor *m*, -tora *f* (de una revista, etc.); abonado *m*, -da *f* (de un servicio) — **subscription** *n* : suscripción *f*
subsequent *adj* **1** : subsiguiente **2** ~ to : posterior a — **subsequently** *adv* : posteriormente
subservient *adj* : servil
subside *vi* -sided; -siding **1** SINK : hundirse **2** : amainar (dícese de tormentas, pasiones, etc.), remitir (dícese de fiebres, etc.)
subsidiary *adj* : secundario — ~ *n, pl* -ries : filial *f*

subsidy *n, pl* **-dies** : subvención *f* — **subsidize** *vt* **-dized; -dizing** : subvencionar

subsistence *n* : subsistencia *f* — **subsist** *vi* : subsistir

substance *n* : sustancia *f*

substandard *adj* : inferior

substantial *adj* **1** CONSIDERABLE : considerable **2** STURDY : sólido **3** : sustancioso (dícese de una comida, etc.) — **substantially** *adv* : considerablemente

substitute *n* : sustituto *m*, -ta *f* (de una persona); sucedáneo *m* (de una cosa) — ~ *vt* **-tuted; -tuting** : sustituir — **substitution** *n* : sustitución *f*

subterranean *adj* : subterráneo

subtitle *n* : subtítulo *m*

subtle *adj* **-tler; -tlest** : sutil — **subtlety** *n, pl* **-ties** : sutileza *f*

subtraction *n* : resta *f* — **subtract** *vt* : restar

suburb *n* **1** : barrio *m* residencial, suburbio *m* **2 the ~s** : las afueras — **suburban** *adj* : de las afueras (de una ciudad)

subversion *n* : subversión *f* — **subversive** *adj* : subversivo

subway *n* : metro *m*

succeed *vt* : suceder a — *vi* : tener éxito (dícese de personas), dar resultado (dícese de planes, etc.) — **success** *n* : éxito *m* — **successful** *adj* : de éxito, exitoso *Lat* — **successfully** *adv* : con éxito

succession *n* **1** : sucesión *f* **2 in ~** : sucesivamente, seguidos — **successive** *adj* : sucesivo — **successor** *n* : sucesor *m*, -sora *f*

succinct *adj* : sucinto

succulent *adj* : suculento

succumb *vi* : sucumbir

such *adj* **1** : tal **2 ~ as** : como **3 ~ a pity!** : ¡qué lástima! — *pron* **1** : tal **2 and ~** : y cosas por el estilo **3 as ~** : como tal — ~ *adv* **1** VERY : muy **2 ~ a nice man!** : ¡qué hombre tan simpático! **3 ~ that** : de tal manera que

suck *vt* **1** *or* **~ on** : chupar **2** *or* **~ up** : sorber (bebidas), aspirar (con una máquina) — **sucker** *n* **1** SHOOT : chupón *m* **2** FOOL : imbécil *mf* — **suckle** *vt* **-led; -ling** : amamantar — **suction** *n* : succión *f*

sudden *adj* **1** : repentino **2 all of a ~** : de repente — **suddenly** *adv* : de repente

suds *npl* : espuma *f* (de jabón)

sue *vt* **sued; suing** : demandar (por)

suede *n* : ante *m*, gamuza *f*

suet *n* : sebo *m*

suffer *vi* : sufrir — *vt* **1** : sufrir **2** BEAR : tolerar — **suffering** *n* : sufrimiento *m*

suffice *vi* **-ficed; -ficing** : bastar — **sufficient** *adj* : suficiente — **sufficiently** *adv* : (lo) suficientemente

suffix *n* : sufijo *m*

suffocate *v* **-cated; -cating** *vt* : asfixiar — *vi* : asfixiarse — **suffocation** *n* : asfixia *f*

suffrage *n* : sufragio *m*

sugar *n* : azúcar *mf* — **sugarcane** *n* : caña *f* de azúcar — **sugary** *adj* : azucarado

suggestion *n* **1** : sugerencia *f* **2** TRACE : indicio *m* — **suggest** *vt* **1** : sugerir **2** INDICATE : indicar

suicide *n* **1** : suicidio *m* (acto) **2** : suicida *mf* (persona) — **suicidal** *adj* : suicida

suit *n* **1** LAWSUIT : pleito *m* **2** : traje *m* (ropa) **3** : palo *m* (de naipes) — ~ *vt* **1** ADAPT : adaptar **2** BEFIT : ser apropiado para **3 ~ s.o.** : convenir a algn (dícese de fechas, etc.), quedar bien a algn (dícese de ropa) — **suitable** *adj* : apropiado — **suitcase** *n* : maleta *f*, valija *f Lat*

suite *n* **1** : suite *f* (de habitaciones) **2** : juego *m* (de muebles)

suitor *n* : pretendiente *m*

sulfur *n* : azufre *m*

sulk *vi* : enfurruñarse *fam* — **sulky** *adj* **sulkier; -est** : malhumorado

sullen *adj* : hosco

sultry *adj* **sultrier; -est 1** : bochornoso **2** SENSUAL : sensual

sum *n* : suma *f* — ~ *vt* **summed; summing ~ up** : resumir — **summarize** *v* **-rized; -rizing** : resumir — **summary** *n, pl* **-ries** : resumen *m*

summer *n* : verano *m*

summit *n* : cumbre *f*

summon *vt* **1** : llamar (a algn), convocar (una reunión) **2** : citar (en derecho) — **summons** *n, pl* **summonses** SUBPOENA : citación *f*

sumptuous *adj* : suntuoso

sun *n* : sol *m* — **sunbathe** *vi* **-bathed; -bathing** : tomar el sol — **sunbeam** *n* : rayo *m* de sol — **sunburn** *n* : quemadura *f* de sol

Sunday *n* : domingo *m*

sundry *adj* : varios, diversos

sunflower *n* : girasol *m*

sung → sing

sunglasses *npl* : gafas *fpl* de sol, lentes *mpl* de sol

sunk → sink — **sunken** *adj* : hundido

sunlight *n* : (luz *f* del) sol *m* — **sunny** *adj* **-nier; -est** : soleado — **sunrise** *n* : salida *f* del sol — **sunset** *n* : puesta *f* del sol — **sunshine** *n* : sol *m*, luz *f* del sol — **suntan** *n* : bronceado *m*

super *adj* : súper *fam*

superb *adj* : magnífico, espléndido

superficial *adj* : superficial

superfluous *adj* : superfluo

superimpose *vt* **-posed; -posing** : sobreponer

superintendent *n* **1** : superintendente *mf*

(de policía) **2** *or* **building ~** : portero *m*, -ra *f* **3** *or* **school ~** : director *m*, -tora *f* (de un colegio)

superior *adj* : superior — **~** *n* : superior *m* — **superiority** *n, pl* **-ties** : superioridad *f*

superlative *adj* **1** : superlativo (en gramática) **2** EXCELLENT : excepcional — **~** *n* : superlativo *m*

supermarket *n* : supermercado *m*

supernatural *adj* : sobrenatural

superpower *n* : superpotencia *f*

supersede *vt* **-seded; -seding** : reemplazar, suplantar

supersonic *adj* : supersónico

superstition *n* : superstición *f* — **superstitious** *adj* : supersticioso

supervisor *n* : supervisor *m*, -sora *f* — **supervise** *vt* **-vised; -vising** : supervisar — **supervision** *n* : supervisión *f* — **supervisory** *adj* : de supervisor

supper *n* : cena *f*, comida *f*

supplant *vt* : suplantar

supple *adj* **-pler; -plest** : flexible

supplement *n* : suplemento *m* — **~** *vt* : complementar — **supplementary** *adj* : suplementario

supply *vt* **-plied; -plying** **1** : suministrar **2** **~ with** : proveer de — **~** *n, pl* **-plies** **1** : suministro *m*, provisión *f* **2 ~ and demand** : oferta y demanda **3 supplies** *npl* PROVISIONS : provisiones *fpl*, víveres *mpl* — **supplier** *n* : proveedor *m*, -dora *f*

support *vt* **1** BACK : apoyar **2** : mantener (una familia, etc.), **3** PROP UP : sostener — **~** *n* **1** : apoyo *m* (moral), ayuda *f* (económica) **2** PROP : soporte *m* — **supporter** *n* : partidario *m*, -ria *f*

suppose *vt* **-posed; -posing** **1** : suponer **2 be ~d to (do sth)** : tener que (hacer algo) — **supposedly** *adv* : supuestamente

suppress *vt* **1** : reprimir **2** : suprimir (noticias, etc.) — **suppression** *n* **1** : represión *f* **2** : supresión *f* (de información)

supreme *adj* : supremo — **supremacy** *n, pl* **-cies** : supremacía *f*

sure *adj* **surer; -est** **1** : seguro **2 make ~ that** : asegurarse de que — **~** *adv* **1** OF COURSE : por supuesto, claro **2 it ~ is hot!** : ¡qué calor! — **surely** *adv* : seguramente

surface *n* : superficie *f* — **~** *v* **-faced; -facing** *vi* : salir a la superficie — *vt* : revestir

surfeit *n* : exceso *m*

surfer *n* **1** : surfista *mf* **2** : internauta *mf*

surfing *n* : surf *m*, surfing *m*

surfing *n* : surf *m*, surfing *m*

surge *vi* **surged; surging** **1** SWELL : hincharse (dícese del mar) **2** SWARM : moverse en tropel — **~** *n* **1** : oleaje *m*

(del mar), oleada *f* (de gente) **2** INCREASE : aumento *m* (súbito)

surgeon *n* : cirujano *m*, -na *f* — **surgery** *n, pl* **-geries** : cirugía *f* — **surgical** *adj* : quirúrgico

surly *adj* **surlier; -est** : hosco, arisco

surmount *vt* : superar

surname *n* : apellido *m*

surpass *vt* : superar

surplus *n* : excedente *m*

surprise *n* **1** : sorpresa *f* **2 take by ~** : sorprender — **~** *vt* **-prised; -prising** : sorprender — **surprising** *adj* : sorprendente

surrender *vt* : entregar, rendir — *vi* : rendirse — **~** *n* : rendición *m* (de una ciudad, etc.), entrega *f* (de posesiones)

surrogate *n* : sustituto *m*

surround *vt* : rodear — **surroundings** *npl* : ambiente *m*

surveillance *n* : vigilancia *f*

survey *vt* **-veyed; -veying** **1** : medir (un solar) **2** INSPECT : inspeccionar **3** POLL : sondear — **~** *n, pl* **-veys** **1** INSPECTION : inspección *f* **2** : medición *f* (de un solar) **3** POLL : encuesta *f*, sondeo *m* — **surveyor** *n* : agrimensor *m*, -sora *f*

survive *v* **-vived; -viving** *vi* : sobrevivir — *vt* : sobrevivir a — **survival** *n* : supervivencia *f* — **survivor** *n* : superviviente *mf*

susceptible *adj* **~ to** : propenso a — **susceptibility** *n, pl* **-ties** : propensión *f* (a enfermedades, etc.)

suspect *adj* : sospechoso — **~** *n* : sospechoso *m*, **-sa** *f* — **~** *vt* : sospechar (algo), sospechar de (algn)

suspend *vt* : suspender — **suspense** *n* **1** : incertidumbre *m* **2** : suspenso *m* *Lat*, suspense *m* *Spain* (en el cine, etc.) — **suspension** *n* : suspensión *f*

suspicion *n* : sospecha *f* — **suspicious** *adj* **1** QUESTIONABLE : sospechoso **2** DISTRUSTFUL : suspicaz

sustain *vt* **1** : sostener **2** SUFFER : sufrir

swagger *vi* : pavonearse

swallow[1] *v* : tragar — **~** *n* : trago *m*

swallow[2] *n* : golondrina *f* (pájaro)

swam → swim

swamp *n* : pantano *m*, ciénaga *f* — **~** *vt* : inundar — **swampy** *adj* **swampier; -est** : pantanoso, cenagoso

swan *n* : cisne *f*

swap *vt* **swapped; swapping** **1** : intercambiar **2 ~ sth for sth** : cambiar algo por algo **3 ~ sth with s.o.** : cambiar algo a algn — **~** *n* : cambio *m*

swarm *n* : enjambre *m* — **~** *vi* : enjambrar

swat *vt* **swatted; swatting** : aplastar (un insecto)

sway *n* **1** : balanceo *m* **2** INFLUENCE : influjo *m* — ~ *vi* : balancearse — *vt* : influir en

swear *v* **swore; sworn; swearing** *vi* **1** : jurar **2** CURSE : decir palabrotas — *vt* : jurar — **swearword** *n* : palabrota *f*

sweat *vi* **sweat** *or* **sweated; sweating** : sudar — ~ *n* : sudor *m* — **sweater** *n* : suéter *m* — **sweatshirt** *n* : sudadera *f* — **sweaty** *adj* **sweatier; -est** : sudado

Swedish *adj* : sueco — ~ *n* : sueco *m* (idioma)

sweep *v* **swept; sweeping** *vt* **1** : barrer **2** ~ **aside** : apartar **3** ~ **through** : extenderse por — *vi* : barrer — ~ *n* **1** : barrido *m* **2** : movimiento *m* circular (de la mano, etc.) **3** SCOPE : alcance — **sweeping** *adj* **1** WIDE : amplio **2** EXTENSIVE : extenso — **sweepstakes** *ns & pl* : lotería *f*

sweet *adj* **1** : dulce **2** PLEASANT : agradable — ~ *n* : dulce *m* — **sweeten** *vt* : endulzar — **sweetener** *n* : endulzante *m* — **sweetheart** *n* **1** : novio *m*, -via *f* **2** (*used as a form of address*) : cariño *m* — **sweetness** *n* : dulzura *f* — **sweet potato** *n* : batata *f*, boniato *m*

swell *vi* **swelled; swelled** *or* **swollen; swelling 1** *or* ~ **up** : hincharse **2** INCREASE : aumentar, crecer — ~ *n* : oleaje *m* (del mar) — **swelling** *n* : hinchazón *f*

sweltering *adj* : sofocante

swept → **sweep**

swerve *vi* **swerved; swerving** : virar bruscamente

swift *adj* : rápido — **swiftly** *adv* : rápidamente

swig *n* : trago *m* — ~ *vi* **swigged; swigging** : beber a tragos

swim *vi* **swam; swum; swimming 1** : nadar **2** REEL : dar vueltas — ~ *n* **1** : baño *m* **2 go for a** ~ : ir a nadar — **swimmer** *n* : nadador *m*, -dora *f*

swindle *vt* **-dled; -dling** : estafar, timar — ~ *n* : estafa *f*, timo *m fam*

swine *ns & pl* : cerdo *m*, -da *f*

swing *v* **swung; swinging** *vt* **1** : balancear, hacer oscilar **2** MANAGE : arreglar — *vi* **1** : balancearse, oscilar **2** SWIVEL : girar — ~ *n* **1** : vaivén *m*, balanceo *m* **2** SHIFT : cambio *m* **3** : columpio *m* (para niños) **4 in full** ~ : en pleno proceso

swipe *v* **swiped; swiping** *vt* STEAL : birlar *fam*, robar — *vi* ~ **at** : intentar pegar

swirl *vi* : arremolinarse — ~ *n* **1** EDDY : remolino *m* **2** SPIRAL : espiral *f*

swish *vt* : agitar (haciendo un sonido) — *vi* **1** RUSTLE : hacer frufrú **2** ~ **by** : pasar silbando

Swiss *adj* : suizo

switch *n* **1** WHIP : vara *f* **2** CHANGE : cambio *m* **3** : interruptor *m*, llave *f* (de la luz, etc.) — ~ *vt* **1** CHANGE : cambiar de **2** EXCHANGE : intercambiar **3** ~ **on** : encender, prender *Lat* **4** ~ **off** : apagar — *vi* **1** : sacudir (la cola, etc.) **2** CHANGE : cambiar **3** SWAP : intercambiarse — **switchboard** *n* : centralita *f*, conmutador *m Lat*

swivel *vi* **-veled** *or* **-velled; -veling** *or* **-velling** : girar (sobre un pivote)

swollen → **swell**

swoon *vi* : desvanecerse

swoop *vi* ~ **down on** : abatirse sobre — ~ *n* : descenso *m* en picada

sword *n* : espada *f*

swordfish *n* : pez *m* espada

swore, sworn → **swear**

swum → **swim**

swung → **swing**

syllable *n* : sílaba *f*

syllabus *n, pl* **-bi** *or* **-buses** : programa *m* (de estudios)

symbol *n* : símbolo *m* — **symbolic** *adj* : simbólico — **symbolism** *n* : simbolismo *m* — **symbolize** *vt* **-ized; -izing** : simbolizar

symmetry *n, pl* **-tries** : simetría *f* — **symmetrical** *adj* : simétrico

sympathy *n, pl* **-thies 1** COMPASSION : compasión *f* **2** UNDERSTANDING : comprensión *f* **3** CONDOLENCES : pésame *m* **4 sympathies** *npl* LOYALTY : simpatías *fpl* — **sympathize** *vi* **-thized; -thizing 1** ~ **with** PITY : compadecerse de **2** ~ **with** UNDERSTAND : comprender — **sympathetic** *adj* **1** COMPASSIONATE : compasivo **2** UNDERSTANDING : comprensivo

symphony *n, pl* **-nies** : sinfonía *f*

symposium *n, pl* **-sia** *or* **-siums** : simposio *m*

symptom *n* : síntoma *m* — **symptomatic** *adj* : sintomático

synagogue *n* : sinagoga *f*

synchronize *vt* **-nized; -nizing** : sincronizar

syndrome *n* : síndrome *m*

synonym *n* : sinónimo *m* — **synonymous** *adj* : sinónimo

synopsis *n, pl* **-opses** : sinopsis *f*

syntax *n* : sintaxis *f*

synthesis *n, pl* **-theses** : síntesis *f* — **synthesize** *vt* **-sized; -sizing** : sintetizar — **synthetic** *adj* : sintético

syphilis *n* : sífilis *f*

Syrian *adj* : sirio

syringe *n* : jeringa *f*, jeringuilla *f*

syrup *n* : jarabe *m*

system *n* **1** : sistema *m* **2** BODY : organismo *m* **3 digestive** ~ : aparato *m* digestivo — **systematic** *adj* : sistemático

T

t *n, pl* **t's** *or* **ts** : t *f*, vigésima letra del alfabeto inglés

tab *n* **1** TAG : etiqueta *f* **2** FLAP : lengüeta *f* **3** ACCOUNT : cuenta *f* **4 keep ~s on** : vigilar

table *n* **1** : mesa *f* **2** LIST : tabla *f* **3 ~ of contents** : índice *m* de materias — **tablecloth** *n* : mantel *m* — **tablespoon** *n* **1** : cuchara *f* grande **2** : cucharada *f* (cantidad)

tablet *n* **1** PAD : bloc *m* **2** PILL : pastilla *f* **3** *or* **stone ~** : lápida *f*

tabloid *n* : tabloide *m*

taboo *adj* : tabú — **~** *n* : tabú *m*

tacit *adj* : tácito

taciturn *adj* : taciturno

tack *vt* **1** : fijar con tachuelas **2 ~ on** ADD : añadir — **~** *n* **1** : tachuela *f* **2 change ~** : cambiar de rumbo

tackle *n* **1** GEAR : aparejo *m* **2** : placaje *m*, tacle *m Lat* (acción) — **~** *vt* **-led; -ling** **1** : placar, taclear *Lat* **2** CONFRONT : abordar

tacky *adj* **tackier; -est 1** : pegajoso **2** GAUDY : de mal gusto

tact *n* : tacto *m* — **tactful** *adj* : diplomático, discreto

tactical *adj* : táctico — **tactic** *n* : táctica *f* — **tactics** *ns & pl* : táctica *f*

tactless *adj* : indiscreto

tadpole *n* : renacuajo *m*

tag[1] *n* LABEL : etiqueta *f* — **~** *v* **tagged; tagging** *vt* : etiquetar — *vi* **~ along with s.o.** : acompañar a algn

tag[2] *vt* : tocar (en varios juegos)

tail *n* **1** : cola *f* **2 ~s** *npl* : cruz *f* (de una moneda) — **~** *vt* FOLLOW : seguir

tailor *n* : sastre *m*, -tra *f* — **~** *vt* **1** : confeccionar (ropa) **2** ADAPT : adaptar

taint *vt* : contaminar

take *v* **took; taken; taking** *vt* **1** : tomar **2** BRING : llevar **3** REMOVE : sacar **4** BEAR : soportar, aguantar **5** ACCEPT : aceptar **6 I ~ it that...** : supongo que... **7 ~ a bath** : bañarse **8 ~ a walk** : dar un paseo **9 ~ back** : retirar (palabras, etc.) **10 ~ in** ALTER : achicar **11 ~ in** GRASP : entender **12 ~ in** TRICK : engañar **13 ~ off** REMOVE : quitar, quitarse (ropa) **14 ~ on** : asumir (una responsabilidad, etc.) **15 ~ out** : sacar **16 ~ over** : tomar el poder de **17 ~ place** : tener lugar **18 ~ up** SHORTEN : acortar **19 ~ up** OCCUPY : ocupar — *vi* **1** : prender (dícese de una vacuna, etc.) **2 ~ off** : despegar (dícese de

aviones, etc.) **3 ~ over** : asumir el mando — **~** *n* **1** PROCEEDS : ingresos *mpl* **2** : toma *f* (en el cine) — **takeoff** *n* : despegue *m* (de un avión, etc.) — **takeover** *n* : toma *f* (de poder, etc.), adquisición *f* (de una empresa)

talcum powder *n* : polvos *mpl* de talco

tale *n* : cuento *m*

talent *n* : talento *m* — **talented** *adj* : talentoso

talk *vi* **1** : hablar **2 ~ about** : hablar de **3 ~ to/with** : hablar con — *vt* **1** SPEAK : hablar **2 ~ over** : hablar de, discutir — **~** *n* **1** CHAT : conversación *f* **2** SPEECH : charla *f* — **talkative** *adj* : hablador

tall *adj* **1** : alto **2 how ~ are you?** : ¿cuánto mides?

tally *n, pl* **-lies** : cuenta *f* — **~** *v* **-lied; -lying** *vt* RECKON : calcular — *vi* MATCH : concordar, cuadrar

talon *n* : garra *f*

tambourine *n* : pandereta *f*

tame *adj* **tamer; -est 1** : domesticado **2** DOCILE : manso **3** DULL : insípido, soso — **~** *vt* **tamed; taming** : domar

tamper *vi* **~ with** : forzar (una cerradura), amañar (documentos, etc.)

tampon *n* : tampón *m*

tan *v* **tanned; tanning** *vt* : curtir (cuero) — *vi* : broncearse — **~** *n* **1** SUNTAN : bronceado *m* **2** : (color *m*) café *m* con leche

tang *n* : sabor *m* fuerte

tangent *n* : tangente *f*

tangerine *n* : mandarina *f*

tangible *adj* : tangible

tangle *v* **-gled; -gling** *vt* : enredar — *vi* : enredarse — **~** *n* : enredo *m*

tango *n, pl* **-gos** : tango *m*

tank *n* **1** : tanque *m*, depósito *m* **2** : tanque *m* (militar) — **tanker** *n* **1** : buque *m* tanque **2** *or* **~ truck** : camión *m* cisterna

tantalizing *adj* : tentador

tantrum *n* **throw a ~** : hacer un berrinche

tap[1] *n* FAUCET : llave *f*, grifo *m Spain* — **~** *vt* **tapped; tapping 1** : sacar (un líquido, etc.), sangrar (un árbol) **2** : intervenir (un teléfono)

tap[2] *vt* **tapped; tapping** STRIKE : tocar, dar un golpecito en — **~** *n* : golpecito *m*, toque *m*

tape *n* : cinta *f* — **~** *vt* **taped; taping 1** : pegar con cinta **2** RECORD : grabar — **tape measure** *n* : cinta *f* métrica

taper *n* : vela *f* (larga) — **~** *vi* **1** NARROW : estrecharse **2** *or* **~ off** : disminuir

tapestry *n, pl* **-tries** : tapiz *m*

tar *n* : alquitrán *m* — ~ *vt* **tarred; tarring** : alquitranar

tarantula *n* : tarántula *f*

target *n* **1** : blanco *m* **2** GOAL : objetivo *m*

tariff *n* : tarifa *f*, arancel *m*

tarnish *vt* **1** : deslustrar **2** : empañar (una reputación, etc.) — *vi* : deslustrarse

tart¹ *adj* SOUR : ácido, agrio

tart² *n* : pastel *m*

tartan *n* : tartán *m*

task *n* : tarea *f*

tassel *n* : borla *f*

taste *v* **tasted; tasting** *vt* TRY : probar — *vi* **1** : saber **2** ~ **like** : saber a — ~ *n* **1** FLAVOR : gusto *m*, sabor *m* **2** **have a** ~ **of** : probar **3** **in good/bad** ~ : de buen/mal gusto — **tasteful** *adj* : de buen gusto — **tasteless** *adj* **1** : sin sabor **2** COARSE : de mal gusto — **tasty** *adj* **tastier; -est** : sabroso

tatters *npl* : harapos *mpl* — **tattered** *adj* : harapiento

tattle *vi* **-tled; -tling** ~ **on s.o.** : acusar a algn

tattoo *vt* : tatuar — ~ *n* : tatuaje *m*

taught → **teach**

taunt *n* : pulla *f*, burla *f* — ~ *vt* : mofarse de, burlarse de

taut *adj* : tirante, tenso

tavern *n* : taberna *f*

tax *vt* **1** : gravar **2** STRAIN : poner a prueba — ~ *n* **1** : impuesto *m* **2** BURDEN : carga *f* — **taxable** *adj* : imponible — **taxation** *n* : impuestos *mpl* — **tax– exempt** *adj* : libre de impuestos

taxi *n*, *pl* **taxis** : taxi *m* — ~ *vi* **taxied; taxiing** *or* **taxying; taxis** *or* **taxies** : rodar por la pista (dícese de un avión)

taxpayer *n* : contribuyente *mf*

tea *n* : té *m*

teach *v* **taught; teaching** *vt* : enseñar, dar clases de (una asignatura) — *vi* : dar clases — **teacher** *n* : profesor *m*, -sora *f*; maestro *m*, -tra *f* (de niños pequeños) — **teaching** *n* : enseñanza *f*

teacup *n* : taza *f* de té

team *n* : equipo *m* — ~ *vi or* ~ **up** : asociarse — **teammate** *n* : compañero *m*, -ra *f* de equipo — **teamwork** *n* : trabajo *m* de equipo

teapot *n* : tetera *f*

tear¹ *v* **tore; torn; tearing** *vt* **1** : romper, rasgar **2** ~ **apart** : destrozar **3** ~ **down** : derribar **4** ~ **off** *or* ~ **out** : arrancar **5** ~ **up** : romper (papel, etc.) — *vi* **1** : romperse, rasgarse **2** RUSH : ir a toda velocidad — ~ *n* : desgarro *m*, rasgón *m*

tear² *n* : lágrima *f* — **tearful** *adj* : lloroso

tease *vt* **teased; teasing** **1** : tomar el pelo a, burlarse de **2** ANNOY : fastidiar

teaspoon *n* **1** : cucharita *f* **2** : cucharadita *f* (cantidad)

technical *adj* : técnico — **technicality** *n*, *pl* **-ties** : detalle *m* técnico — **technically** *adv* : técnicamente — **technician** *n* : técnico *m*, -ca *f*

technique *n* : técnica *f*

technological *adj* : tecnológico — **technology** *n*, *pl* **-gies** : tecnología *f*

teddy bear *n* : oso *m* de peluche

tedious *adj* : tedioso, aburrido — **tedium** *n* : tedio *m*

tee *n* : tee *m* (en deportes)

teem *vi* **1** POUR : llover a cántaros **2** **be** ~**ing with** : estar repleto de

teenage *or* **teenaged** *adj* : adolescente — **teenager** *n* : adolescente *mf* — **teens** *npl* : adolescencia *f*

teepee → **tepee**

teeter *vi* : tambalearse

teeth → **tooth** — **teethe** *vi* **teethed; teething** : echar los dientes

telecommunication *n* : telecomunicación *f*

telegram *n* : telegrama *m*

telegraph *n* : telégrafo *m* — ~ *v* : telegrafiar

telephone *n* : teléfono *m* — ~ *v* **-phoned; -phoning** : llamar por teléfono

telescope *n* : telescopio *m*

televise *vt* **-vised; -vising** : televisar — **television** *n* : televisión *f*

tell *v* **told; telling** *vt* **1** : decir **2** RELATE : contar **3** DISTINGUISH : distinguir **4** ~ **s.o. off** : regañar a algn — *vi* **1** : decir **2** KNOW : saber **3** SHOW : tener efecto **4** ~ **on s.o.** : acusar a algn — **teller** *n or* **bank** ~ : cajero *m*, -ra *f*

temp *n* : empleado *m*, -da *f* temporal

temper *vt* MODERATE : temperar — ~ *n* **1** MOOD : humor *m* **2** **have a bad** ~ : tener mal genio **3** **lose one's** ~ : perder los estribos — **temperament** *n* : temperamento *m* — **temperamental** *adj* : temperamental — **temperate** *adj* **1** : moderado **2** ~ **zone** : zona *f* templada

temperature *n* **1** : temperatura *f* **2** **have a** ~ : tener fiebre

tempest *n* : tempestad *f*

temple *n* **1** : templo *m* **2** : sien *f* (en anatomía)

tempo *n*, *pl* **-pi** *or* **-pos** **1** : tempo *m* **2** PACE : ritmo *m*

temporarily *adv* : temporalmente — **temporary** *adj* : temporal

tempt *vt* : tentar — **temptation** *n* : tentación *f*

ten *adj* : diez — ~ *n* : diez *m*

tenacity *n* : tenacidad *f* — **tenacious** *adj* : tenaz

tenant *n* : inquilino *m*, **-na** *f*; arrendatario *m*, **-ria** *f*

tend[1] *vt* MIND : cuidar

tend[2] *vi* ~ **to** : tender a — **tendency** *n*, *pl* **-cies** : tendencia *f*

tender[1] *adj* **1** : tierno **2** PAINFUL : dolorido

tender[2] *vt* : presentar — ~ *n* **1** : oferta *f* **2** **legal** ~ : moneda *f* de curso legal

tenderloin *n* : lomo *f* (de cerdo o vaca)

tenderness *n* : ternura *f*

tendon *n* : tendón *m*

tenet *n* : principio *m*

tennis *n* : tenis *m*

tenor *n* : tenor *m*

tense[1] *n* : tiempo *m* (de un verbo)

tense[2] *v* tensed; tensing *vt* : tensar — *vi* : tensarse — ~ *adj* tenser; tensest : tenso — **tension** *n* : tensión *f*

tent *n* : tienda *f* de campaña

tentacle *n* : tentáculo *m*

tentative *adj* **1** HESITANT : vacilante **2** PROVISIONAL : provisional

tenth *adj* : décimo — ~ *n* **1** : décimo *m*, **-ma** *f* (en una serie) **2** : décimo *m* (en matemáticas)

tenuous *adj* : tenue, endeble

tepid *adj* : tibio

term *n* **1** WORD : término *m* **2** PERIOD : período *m* **3** **be on good** ~**s** : tener buenas relaciones **4** **in** ~**s of** : con respecto a — ~ *vt* : calificar de

terminal *adj* : terminal — ~ *n* **1** : terminal *m* **2** *or* **bus** ~ : terminal *f*

terminate *v* **-nated; -nating** *vi* : terminar(se) — *vt* : poner fin a — **termination** *n* : terminación *f*

termite *n* : termita *f*

terrace *n* : terraza *f*

terrain *n* : terreno *m*

terrestrial *adj* : terrestre

terrible *adj* : espantoso, terrible — **terribly** *adv* : terriblemente

terrier *n* : terrier *mf*

terrific *adj* **1** HUGE : tremendo **2** EXCELLENT : estupendo

terrify *vt* **-fied; -fying** : aterrar, aterrorizar — **terrifying** *adj* : aterrador

territory *n*, *pl* **-ries** : territorio *m* — **territorial** *adj* : territorial

terror *n* : terror *m* — **terrorism** *n* : terrorismo *m* — **terrorist** *n* : terrorista *mf* — **terrorize** *vt* **-ized; -izing** : aterrorizar

terse *adj* **terser; tersest** : seco, lacónico

test tube *n* : probeta *f*, tubo *m* de ensayo

test *n* **1** TRIAL : prueba *f* **2** EXAM : examen *m*, prueba *f* **3** : análisis *m* (en medicina) — ~ *vt* **1** TRY : probar **2** QUIZ : examinar **3** : analizar (la sangre, etc.), examinar (los ojos, etc.)

testament *n* **1** WILL : testamento *m* **2** **the**

Old/New Testament : el Antiguo/Nuevo Testamento

testicle *n* : testículo *m*

testify *v* **-fied; -fying** : testificar

testimony *n*, *pl* **-nies** : testimonio *m*

tetanus *n* : tétano *m*

tether *vt* : atar

text *n* : texto *m* — **textbook** *n* : libro *m* de texto

textile *n* : textil *m*

text message *n* : mensaje *m* de texto, SMS *m*

texture *n* : textura *f*

than *conj & prep* : que, de (con cantidades)

thank *vt* **1** : agradecer, dar (las) gracias a **2** ~ **you!** : ¡gracias! — **thankful** *adj* : agradecido — **thankfully** *adv* **1** : con agradecimiento **2** FORTUNATELY : gracias a Dios — **thanks** *npl* **1** : agradecimiento *m* **2** ~! : ¡gracias!

Thanksgiving *n* : día *m* de Acción de Gracias

that *pron, pl* **those** **1** : ése, ésa, eso **2** (*more distant*) : aquél, aquélla, aquello **3** **is** ~ **you?** : ¿eres tú? **4** **like** ~ : así **5** ~ **is...** : es decir... **6** **those who...** : los que... — ~ *conj* : que — ~ *adj, pl* **those** **1** : ese, esa **2** (*more distant*) : aquel, aquella **3** ~ **one** : ése, ésa — ~ *adv* : tan

thatched *adj* : con techo de paja

thaw *vt* : descongelar (alimentos), derretir (hielo) — *vi* **1** : descongelarse **2** MELT : derretirse — ~ *n* : deshielo *m*

the *art* **1** : el, la, los, las **2** PER : por — ~ *adv* **1** ~ **sooner** ~ **better** : cuanto más pronto, mejor **2** **I like this one** ~ **best** : éste es el que más me gusta

theater *or* theatre *n* : teatro *m* — **theatrical** *adj* : teatral

theft *n* : robo *m*, hurto *m*

their *adj* : su, sus, de ellos, de ellas — **theirs** *pron* **1** : (el) suyo, (la) suya, (los) suyos, (las) suyas **2** **some friends of** ~ : unos amigos suyos, unos amigos de ellos

them *pron* **1** (*used as direct object*) : los, las **2** (*used as indirect object*) : les, se **3** (*used as object of a preposition*) : ellos, ellas

theme *n* **1** : tema *m* **2** ESSAY : trabajo *m* (escrito)

themselves *pron* **1** (*used reflexively*) : se **2** (*used emphatically*) : ellos mismos, ellas mismas **3** (*used after a preposition*) : sí (mismos), sí (mismas)

then *adv* **1** : entonces **2** NEXT : luego, después **3** BESIDES : además — ~ *adj* : entonces

thence *adv* : de ahí (en adelante)

theology *n*, *pl* **-gies** : teología *f* — **theological** *adj* : teológico

theorem

theorem *n* : teorema *m* — **theoretical** *adj* : teórico — **theory** *n, pl* **-ries** : teoría *f*

therapeutic *adj* : terapéutico — **therapist** *n* : terapeuta *mf* — **therapy** *n, pl* **-pies** : terapia *f*

there *adv* **1** *or* **over** ~ : allí, allá **2** *or* **right** ~ : ahí **3 in** ~ : ahí (dentro) **4** ~, **it's done!** : ¡listo! **5 up/down** ~ : ahí arriba / abajo **6 who's** ~? : ¿quién es? — ~ *pron* **1** ~ **is/are** : hay **2** ~ **are three of us** : somos tres — **thereabouts** *or* **thereabout** *adv* **or** ~ : por ahí — **thereafter** *adv* : después — **thereby** *adv* : así — **therefore** *adv* : por lo tanto

thermal *adj* : térmico

thermometer *n* : termómetro *m*

thermos *n* : termo *m*

thermostat *n* : termostato *m*

thesaurus *n, pl* **-sauri** *or* **-sauruses** : diccionario *m* de sinónimos

these → **this**

thesis *n, pl* **theses** : tesis *f*

they *pron* **1** : ellos, ellas **2 where are** ~? : ¿dónde están? **3 as** ~ **say** : como dicen — **they'd** (*contraction of* **they had** *or* **they would**) → **have, would** — **they'll** (*contraction of* **they shall** *or* **they will**) → **shall, will** — **they're** (*contraction of* **they are**) → **be** — **they've** (*contraction of* **they have**) → **have**

thick *adj* **1** : grueso **2** DENSE : espeso **3 a** ~ **accent** : un acento marcado **4 it's two inches** ~ : tiene dos pulgadas de grosor — ~ *n* **in the** ~ **of** : en medio de — **thicken** *vt* : espesar — *vi* : espesarse — **thicket** *n* : matorral *m* — **thickness** *n* : grosor *m*, espesor *m*

thief *n, pl* **thieves** : ladrón *m*, -drona *f*

thigh *n* : muslo *m*

thimble *n* : dedal *m*

thin *adj* **thinner; -est 1** : delgado **2** : ralo (dícese del pelo) **3** WATERY : claro, aguado **4** FINE : fino — ~ *v* **thinned; thinning** *vt* DILUTE : diluir — *vi* : ralear (dícese del pelo)

thing *n* **1** : cosa *f* **2 for one** ~ : en primer lugar **3 how are** ~s? : ¿qué tal? **4 it's a good** ~ **that...** : menos mal que... **5 the important** ~ **is...** : lo importante es...

think *v* **thought; thinking** *vt* **1** : pensar **2** BELIEVE : creer **3** ~ **up** : idear — *vi* **1** : pensar **2** ~ **about** *or* ~ **of** CONSIDER : pensar en **3** ~ **of** REMEMBER : acordarse de **4 what do you** ~ **of it?** : ¿qué te parece? — **thinker** *n* : pensador *m*, -dora *f*

third *adj* : tercero — ~ *or* **thirdly** *adv* : en tercer lugar — ~ *n* **1** : tercero *m*, -ra *f* (en una serie) **2** : tercero *m* (en matemáticas) — **Third World** *n* : Tercer Mundo *m*

thirst *n* : sed *f* — **thirsty** *adj* **thirstier; -est 1** : sediento **2 be** ~ : tener sed

thirteen *adj* : trece — ~ *n* : trece *m* — **thirteenth** *adj* : décimo tercero — ~ *n* **1** : decimotercero *m*, -ra *f* (en una serie) **2** : treceavo *m* (en matemáticas)

thirty *adj* : treinta — ~ *n, pl* **thirties** : treinta *m* — **thirtieth** *adj* : trigésimo — ~ *n* **1** : trigésimo *m*, -ma *f* (en una serie) **2** : treintavo *m* (en matemáticas)

this *pron, pl* **these 1** : éste, ésta, esto **2 like** ~ : así — ~ *adj, pl* **these 1** : este, esta **2** ~ **one** : éste, ésta **3** ~ **way** : por aquí — ~ *adv* ~ **big** : así de grande

thistle *n* : cardo *m*

thong *n* **1** : correa *f* **2** SANDAL : chancla *f*

thorn *n* : espina *f* — **thorny** *adj* : espinoso

thorough *adj* **1** : meticuloso **2** COMPLETE : completo — **thoroughly** *adv* **1** : a fondo **2** COMPLETELY : completamente — **thoroughbred** *adj* : de pura sangre — **thoroughfare** *n* : vía *f* pública

those → **that**

though *conj* : aunque — ~ *adv* **1** : sin embargo **2 as** ~ : como si

thought → **think** — ~ *n* **1** : pensamiento *m* **2** IDEA : idea *f* — **thoughtful** *adj* **1** : pensativo **2** KIND : amable — **thoughtless** *adj* **1** CARELESS : descuidado **2** RUDE : desconsiderado

thousand *adj* : mil — ~ *n, pl* **-sands** *or* **-sand** : mil *m* — **thousandth** *adj* : milésimo — ~ *n* **1** : milésimo *m*, -ma *f* (en una serie) **2** : milésimo *m* (en matemáticas)

thrash *vt* : dar una paliza a — *vi or* ~ **around** : agitarse, revolcarse

thread *n* **1** : hilo *m* **2** : rosca *f* (de un tornillo) — ~ *vt* : enhilar (una aguja), ensartar (cuentas) — **threadbare** *adj* : raído

threat *n* : amenaza *f* — **threaten** *v* : amenazar — **threatening** *adj* : amenazador

three *adj* : tres — ~ *n* : tres *m* — **three hundred** *adj* : trescientos — ~ *n* : trescientos *m*

threshold *n* : umbral *m*

threw → **throw**

thrift *n* : frugalidad *f* — **thrifty** *adj* **thriftier; -est** : económico, frugal

thrill *vt* : emocionar — ~ *n* : emoción *f* — **thriller** *n* : película *f* de suspense *Spain*, película *f* de suspenso *Lat* — **thrilling** *adj* : emocionante

thrive *vi* **throve** *or* **thrived; thriven 1** FLOURISH : florecer **2** PROSPER : prosperar

throat *n* : garganta *f*

throb *vi* **throbbed; throbbing 1** PULSATE : palpitar **2** VIBRATE : vibrar **3** ~ **with pain** : tener un dolor punzante

throes *npl* **1** PANGS : agonía *f* **2 in the** ~ **of** : en medio de

throne *n* : trono *m*

throng *n* : muchedumbre *f*, multitud *f*

throttle *vt* **-tled; -tling** : estrangular — ~ *n* : válvula *f* reguladora

through *prep* **1** : por, a través de **2** BE-TWEEN : entre **3** BECAUSE OF : a causa de **4** DURING : durante **5** → **throughout 6 Monday** ~ **Friday** : de lunes a viernes — ~ *adv* **1** : de un lado a otro (en el espacio), de principio a fin (en el tiempo) **2** COMPLETELY : completamente — ~ *adj* **1 be** ~ : haber terminado **2** ~ **traffic** : tráfico *m* de paso — **throughout** *prep* : por todo (un lugar), a lo largo de (un período de tiempo)

throw *v* **threw; thrown; throwing** *vt* **1** : tirar, lanzar **2** : proyectar (una sombra) **3** CONFUSE : desconcertar **4** ~ **a party** : dar una fiesta **5** ~ **away** *or* ~ **out** : tirar, botar *Lat* — *vi* ~ **up** VOMIT : vomitar — ~ *n* : tiro *m*, lanzamiento *m*

thrush *n* : tordo *m*, zorzal *m*

thrust *vt* **thrust; thrusting 1** : empujar (bruscamente) **2** PLUNGE : clavar **3** ~ **upon** : imponer a — ~ *n* **1** : empujón *m* **2** : estocada *f* (en esgrima)

thud *n* : ruido *m* sordo

thug *n* : matón *m*

thumb *n* : (dedo *m*) pulgar *m* — ~ *vt or* ~ **through** : hojear — **thumbnail** *n* : uña *f* del pulgar — **thumbtack** *n* : tachuela *f*, chinche *f Lat*

thump *vt* : golpear — *vi* : latir con fuerza (dícese del corazón) — ~ *n* : ruido *m* sordo

thunder *n* : truenos *mpl* — ~ *vi* : tronar — *vt* SHOUT : bramar — **thunderbolt** *n* : rayo *m* — **thunderous** *adj* : atronador — **thunderstorm** *n* : tormenta *f* eléctrica

Thursday *n* : jueves *m*

thus *adv* **1** : así **2** THEREFORE : por lo tanto

thwart *vt* : frustrar

thyme *n* : tomillo *m*

thyroid *n* : tiroides *mf*

tiara *n* : diadema *f*

tic *n* : tic *m* (nervioso)

tick¹ *n* : garrapata *f* (insecto)

tick² *n* **1** : tictac *m* (sonido) **2** CHECK : marca *f* — ~ *vi* : hacer tictac — *vt* **1** *or* ~ **off** CHECK : marcar **2** ~ **off** ANNOY : fastidiar

ticket *n* **1** : pasaje *m* (de avión), billete *m* *Spain* (de tren, avión, etc.), boleto *m Lat* (de tren o autobús) **2** : entrada *f* (al teatro, etc.) **3** FINE : multa *f*

tickle *v* **-led; -ling** *vt* **1** : hacer cosquillas a **2** AMUSE : divertir — *vi* : picar — ~ *n* : cosquilleo *m* — **ticklish** *adj* **1** : cosquilloso **2** TRICKY : delicado

tidal wave *n* : maremoto *m*

tidbit *n* MORSEL : golosina *f*

tide *n* : marea *f* — ~ *vt* **tided; tiding** ~ **over** : ayudar a superar un apuro

tidy *adj* **-dier; -est** : ordenado, arreglado — ~ *vt* **-died; -dying** *or* ~ **up** : ordenar, arreglar

tie *n* **1** : atadura *f*, cordón *m* **2** BOND : lazo *m* **3** : empate *m* (en deportes) **4** NECKTIE : corbata *f* — ~ *v* **tied; tying** *or* **tieing** *vt* **1** : atar, amarrar *Lat* **2** ~ **a knot** : hacer un nudo — *vi* : empatar (en deportes)

tier *n* : nivel *m*, piso (de un pastel), grada *f* (de un estadio)

tiger *n* : tigre *m*

tight *adj* **1** : apretado **2** SNUG : ajustado, ceñido **3** TAUT : tirante **4** STINGY : agarrado **5** SCARCE : escaso **6 a** ~ **seal** : un cierre hermético **7 a** ~ **spot** : un aprieto — ~ *adv* **closed** : bien cerrado — **tighten** *vt* **1** : apretar **2** TENSE : tensar **3** : hacer más estricto (reglas, etc.) — **tightly** *adv* : bien, fuerte — **tightrope** *n* : cuerda *f* floja — **tights** *npl* : leotardo *m*, mallas *fpl*

tile *n* **1** : azulejo *m*, baldosa *f* (de piso) **2** *or* **roofing** ~ : teja *f* — ~ *vt* **tiled; tiling 1** : revestir de azulejos, embaldosar (un piso) **2** : tejar (un techo)

till¹ *prep & conj* → **until**

till² *vt* : cultivar

till³ *n* : caja *f* (registradora)

tilt *n* **1** : inclinación *f* **2 at full** ~ : a toda velocidad — ~ *vt* : inclinar — *vi* : inclinarse

timber *n* **1** : madera *f* (para construcción) **2** BEAM : viga *f*

timbre *n* : timbre *m*

time *n* **1** : tiempo *m* **2** AGE : época *f* **3** : compás *m* (en música) **4 at** ~ **s** : a veces **5 at this** ~ : en este momento **6 for the** ~ **being** : por el momento **7 from** ~ **to** ~ : de vez en cuando **8 have a good** ~ : pasarlo bien **9 many** ~ **s** : muchas veces **10 on** ~ : a tiempo **11** ~ **after** ~ : una y otra vez **12 what** ~ **is it?** : ¿qué hora es? — ~ *vt* **timed; timing** : tomar el tiempo a (algn), cronometrar (una carrera, etc.) — **timeless** *adj* : eterno — **timely** *adj* **-lier; -est** : oportuno — **timer** *n* : temporizador *m*, avisador *m* (de cocina) — **times** *prep* **3** ~ **4 is 12** : 3 por 4 son 12 — **timetable** *n* : horario *m*

timid *adj* : tímido

tin *n* **1** : estaño *m* **2** CAN : lata *f*, bote *m Spain* — **tinfoil** *n* : papel *m* (de) aluminio

tinge *vt* **tinged; tingeing** *or* **tinging** : matizar — ~ *n* **1** TINT : matiz *m* **2** TOUCH : dejo *m*

tingle *vi* **-gled; -gling** : sentir (un) hormigueo — ~ *n* : hormigueo *m*

tinker *vi* ~ **with** : intentar arreglar (con pequeños ajustes)

tinkle *vi* **-kled; -kling** : tintinear — **~** *n* : tintineo *m*

tint *n* : tinte *m* — **~** *vt* : teñir

tiny *adj* **-nier; -est** : diminuto, minúsculo

tip–top *adj* : excelente

tip¹ *v* **tipped; tipping** *vt* **1** TILT : inclinar **2** *or* **~ over** : volcar — *vi* : inclinarse

tip² *n* END : punta *f*

tip³ *n* ADVICE : consejo *m* — **~** *vt* **~ off** : avisar

tip⁴ *vt* : dar una propina a — **~** *n* GRATUITY : propina *f*

tipsy *adj* **-sier; -est** : achispado

tiptoe *n* **on ~** : de puntillas — **~** *vi* **-toed; -toeing** : caminar de puntillas

tire¹ *n* : neumático *m*, llanta *f Lat*

tire² *v* **tired; tiring** *vt* : cansar — *vi* : cansarse — **tired** *adj* **1 ~ of** : cansado de, harto de **2 ~ out** : agotado — **tireless** *adj* : incansable — **tiresome** *adj* : pesado

tissue *n* **1** : pañuelo *m* de papel **2** : tejido *m* (en biología)

title *n* : título *m* — **~** *vt* **-tled; -tling** : titular

to *prep* **1** : a **2** TOWARD : hacia **3** IN ORDER TO : para **4** UP TO : hasta **5 a quarter ~ seven** : las siete menos cuarto **6 be nice ~ them** : trátalos bien **7 ten ~ the box** : diez por caja **8 the mate ~ this shoe** : el compañero de este zapato **9 two ~ four years old** : entre dos y cuatro años de edad **10 want ~ do** : querer hacer — **~** *adv* **1 come ~** : volver en sí **2 ~ and fro** : de un lado a otro

toad *n* : sapo *m*

toast *vt* **1** : tostar (pan, etc.) **2** : brindar por (una persona) — **~** *n* **1** : pan *m* tostado, tostadas *fpl* **2** DRINK : brindis *m* — **toaster** *n* : tostador *m*

tobacco *n*, *pl* **-cos** : tabaco *m*

toboggan *n* : tobogán *m*

today *adv* : hoy — **~** *n* : hoy *m*

toddler *n* : niño *m* pequeño, niña *f* pequeña (que comienza a caminar)

toe *n* : dedo *m* (del pie) — **toenail** *n* : uña *f* (del pie)

together *adv* **1** : juntos **2 ~ with** : junto con

toil *n* : trabajo *m* duro — **~** *vi* : trabajar duro

toilet *n* **1** BATHROOM : baño *m*, servicio *m* **2** : inodoro *m* (instalación) — **toilet paper** *n* : papel *m* higiénico — **toiletries** *npl* : artículos *mpl* de tocador

token *n* **1** SIGN : muestra *f* **2** MEMENTO : recuerdo *m* **3** : ficha *f* (para un tren, etc.)

told → **tell**

tolerable *adj* : tolerable — **tolerance** *n* : tolerancia *f* — **tolerant** *adj* : tolerante — **tolerate** *vt* **-ated; -ating** : tolerar

toll¹ *n* **1** : peaje *m* **2 death ~** : número *m* de muertos **3 take a ~ on** : afectar

toll² *vi* RING : tocar, doblar — **~** *n* : tañido *m*

tomato *n*, *pl* **-toes** : tomate *m*

tomb *n* : tumba *f*, sepulcro *m* — **tombstone** *n* : lápida *f*

tome *n* : tomo *m*

tomorrow *adv* : mañana — **~** *n* : mañana *m*

ton *n* : tonelada *f*

tone *n* : tono *m* — **~** *vt* **toned; toning** *or* **~ down** : atenuar

tongs *npl* : tenazas *fpl*

tongue *n* : lengua *f*

tonic *n* **1** : tónico *m* **2** *or* **~ water** : tónica *f*

tonight *adv* : esta noche — **~** *n* : esta noche *f*

tonsil *n* : amígdala *f*

too *adv* **1** ALSO : también **2** EXCESSIVELY : demasiado

took → **take**

tool *n* : herramienta *f* — **toolbox** *n* : caja *f* de herramientas

toolbar *n* : barra *f* de herramientas

toot *vt* : sonar (un claxon, etc.) — **~** *n* **1** WHISTLE : pitido *m* **2** HONK : bocinazo *m*

tooth *n*, *pl* **teeth** : diente *m* — **toothache** *n* : dolor *m* de muelas — **toothbrush** *n* : cepillo *m* de dientes — **toothpaste** *n* : pasta *f* de dientes, pasta *f* dentífrica

top¹ *n* **1** : parte *f* superior **2** SUMMIT : cima *f*, cumbre *f* **3** COVER : tapa *f*, cubierta *f* **4 on ~ of** : encima de — **~** *vt* **topped; topping 1** COVER : rematar (un edificio, etc.), bañar (un pastel, etc.) **2** SURPASS : superar **3 ~ off** : llenar — **~** *adj* **1** : de arriba, superior **2** BEST : mejor **3 a ~ executive** : un alto ejecutivo

top² *n* : trompo *m* (juguete)

topic *n* : tema *m* — **topical** *adj* : de interés actual

topmost *adj* : más alto

topple *v* **-pled; -pling** *vi* : caerse — *vt* **1** OVERTURN : volcar **2** OVERTHROW : derrocar

torch *n* : antorcha *f*

tore → **tear¹**

torment *n* : tormento *m* — **~** *vt* : atormentar

torn → **tear¹**

tornado *n*, *pl* **-does** *or* **-dos** : tornado *m*

torpedo *n*, *pl* **-does** : torpedo *m* — **~** *vt* : torpedear

torrent *n* : torrente *m*

torrid *adj* : tórrido

torso *n*, *pl* **-sos** *or* **-si** : torso *m*

tortilla *n* : tortilla *f*

tortoise *n* : tortuga *f* (terrestre) — **tortoiseshell** *n* : carey *m*, concha *f*

tortuous *adj* : tortuoso

torture *n* : tortura *f* — **~** *vt* **-tured; -turing** : torturar

toss *vt* **1** : tirar, lanzar **2** : mezclar (una ensalada) — *vi* ~ **and turn** : dar vueltas — ~ *n* : lanzamiento *m*

tot *n* : pequeño *m*, -ña *f*

total *adj* : total — ~ *n* : total *m* — ~ *vt* -taled *or* -talled; -taling *or* -talling **1** : ascender a **2** *or* ~ **up** : totalizar, sumar

totalitarian *adj* : totalitario

tote *vt* toted; toting : llevar

totter *vi* : tambalearse

touch *vt* **1** : tocar **2** MOVE : conmover **3** AFFECT : afectar **4** ~ **up** : retocar — *vi* : tocarse — ~ *n* **1** : tacto *m* (sentido) **2** HINT : toque *m* **3** BIT : pizca *f* **4 keep in** ~ : mantenerse en contacto **5 lose one's** ~ : perder la habilidad — **touchdown** *n* : touchdown *m* — **touchy** *adj* **touchier; -est 1** : delicado **2 be** ~ **about** : picarse a la mención de

tough *adj* **1** : duro **2** STRONG : fuerte **3** STRICT : severo **4** DIFFICULT : difícil — **toughen** *vt or* ~ **up** : endurecer — *vi* : endurecerse — **toughness** *n* : dureza *f*

tour *n* **1** : viaje *m* (por un país, etc.), visita *f* (a un museo, etc.) **2** : gira *f* (de un equipo, etc.) — ~ *vi* **1** TRAVEL : viajar **2** : hacer una gira (dícese de equipos, etc.) — *vt* : viajar por, recorrer — **tourist** *n* : turista *mf*

tournament *n* : torneo *m*

tousle *vt* -sled; -sling : despeinar

tout *vt* : promocionar

tow truck *n* : grúa *f*

tow *vt* : remolcar — ~ *n* : remolque *m*

toward *or* **towards** *prep* : hacia

towel *n* : toalla *f*

tower *n* : torre *f* — ~ *vi* ~ **over** : descollar sobre — **towering** *adj* : altísimo

town *n* **1** VILLAGE : pueblo *m* **2** CITY : ciudad *f* — **township** *n* : municipio *m*

toxic *adj* : tóxico

toy *n* : juguete *m* — ~ *vi* ~ **with** : juguetear con

trace *n* **1** SIGN : rastro *m*, señal *f* **2** HINT : dejo *m* — ~ *vt* traced; tracing **1** : calcar (un dibujo, etc.) **2** DRAW : trazar **3** FIND : localizar

track *n* **1** : pista *f* **2** PATH : sendero *m* **3** *or* **railroad** ~ : vía *f* (férrea) **4 keep** ~ **of** : llevar la cuénta de — ~ *vt* TRAIL : seguir la pista de

tract¹ *n* **1** EXPANSE : extensión *f* **2** : tracto *m* (en anatomía)

tract² *n* PAMPHLET : folleto *m*

traction *n* : tracción *f*

tractor *n* **1** : tractor *m* **2** *or* ~ **-trailer** : camión *m* (con remolque)

trade *n* **1** PROFESSION : oficio *m* **2** COMMERCE : comercio *m* **3** INDUSTRY : industria *f* **4** EXCHANGE : cambio *m* — ~ *v* traded; trading *vi* : comerciar — *vt* ~ **sth**

with s.o. : cambiar algo a algn — **trademark** *n* : marca *f* registrada

tradition *n* : tradición *f* — **traditional** *adj* : tradicional

traffic *n* : tráfico *m* — ~ *vi* trafficked; trafficking — **in** : traficar con — **traffic light** *n* : semáforo *m*

tragedy *n, pl* -dies : tragedia *f* — **tragic** *adj* : trágico

trail *vi* **1** DRAG : arrastrar **2** LAG : rezagarse **3** ~ **off** : apagarse — *vt* **1** DRAG : arrastrar **2** PURSUE : seguir la pista de — ~ *n* **1** : rastro *m*, huellas *fpl* **2** PATH : sendero *m* — **trailer** *n* **1** : remolque *m* **2** : caravana *f* (vivienda)

train *n* **1** : tren *m* **2** : cola *f* (de un vestido) **3** SERIES : serie *f* **4** ~ **of thought** : hilo *m* (de las ideas) — ~ *vt* **1** : adiestrar, entrenar (atletas, etc.) **2** AIM : apuntar — *vi* : prepararse, entrenarse (en deportes, etc.) — **trainer** *n* : entrenador *m*, -dora *f*

trait *n* : rasgo *m*

traitor *n* : traidor *m*, -dora *f*

tramp *vi* : caminar (pesadamente) — ~ *n* VAGRANT : vagabundo *m*, -da *f*

trample *vt* -pled; -pling : pisotear

trampoline *n* : trampolín *m*

trance *n* : trance *m*

tranquillity *or* **tranquility** *n* : tranquilidad *f* — **tranquil** *adj* : tranquilo — **tranquilize** *vt* -ized; -izing : tranquilizar — **tranquilizer** *n* : tranquilizante *m*

transaction *n* : transacción *f*

transatlantic *adj* : transatlántico

transcend *vt* **1** : ir más allá de **2** OVERCOME : superar

transcribe *vt* -scribed; -scribing : transcribir — **transcript** *n* : transcripción *f*

transfer *v* -ferred; -ferring *vt* **1** : transferir (fondos, etc.) **2** : trasladar (a un empleado, etc.) — *vi* **1** : cambiarse (de escuelas, etc.) **2** : hacer transbordo (entre trenes, etc.) — ~ *n* **1** : transferencia *f* (de fondos, etc.), traslado *m* (de una persona) **2** : boleto *m* (para hacer transbordo) **3** DECAL : calcomanía *f*

transform *vt* : transformar — **transformation** *n* : transformación *f*

transfusion *n* : transfúsión *f*

transgression *n* : transgresión *f* — **transgress** *vt* : transgredir

transient *adj* : pasajero

transit *n* **1** : tránsito *m* **2** TRANSPORTATION : transporte *m* — **transition** *n* : transición *f* — **transitive** *adj* : transitivo — **transitory** *adj* : transitorio

translate *vt* -lated; -lating : traducir — **translation** *n* : traducción *f* — **translator** *n* : traductor *m*, -tora *f*

translucent *adj* : translúcido

transmit *vt* **-mitted; -mitting** : transmitir — **transmission** *n* : transmisión *f* — **transmitter** *n* : transmisor *m*

transparent *adj* : transparente — **transparency** *n, pl* **-cies** : transparencia *f*

transpire *vi* **-spired; -spiring** **1** TURN OUT : resultar **2** HAPPEN : suceder

transplant *vt* : trasplantar — ~ *n* : trasplante *m*

transport *vt* : transportar — ~ *n* : transporte *m* — **transportation** *n* : transporte *m*

transpose *vt* **-posed; -posing** **1** : trasponer **2** : transportar (en música)

trap *n* : trampa *f* — ~ *vt* **trapped; trapping** : atrapar — **trapdoor** *n* : trampilla *f*

trapeze *n* : trapecio *m*

trappings *npl* : adornos *mpl*, atavíos *mpl*

trash *n* : basura *f*

trauma *n* : trauma *m* — **traumatic** *adj* : traumático

travel *vi* **-eled** *or* **-elled; -eling** *or* **-elling** **1** : viajar **2** MOVE : desplazarse — ~ *n* : viajes *mpl* — **traveler** *or* **traveller** *n* : viajero *m*, -ra *f*

traverse *vt* **-versed; -versing** : atravesar

travesty *n, pl* **-ties** : parodia *f*

trawl *vi* : pescar (con red de arrastre) — **trawler** *n* : barco *m* de pesca

tray *n* : bandeja *f*

treachery *n, pl* **-eries** : traición *f* — **treacherous** *adj* **1** : traidor **2** DANGEROUS : peligroso

tread *v* **trod; trodden** *or* **trod; treading** *vt* **1** *or* ~ **on** : pisar **2** ~ **water** : flotar — *vi* **1** STEP : pisar **2** WALK : caminar — ~ *n* **1** STEP : paso *m* **2** : banda *f* de rodadura (de un neumático) — **treadmill** *n* : rueda *f* de andar

treason *n* : traición *f* (a la patria)

treasure *n* : tesoro *m* — ~ *vt* **-sured; -suring** : apreciar — **treasurer** *n* : tesorero *m*, -ra *f* — **treasury** *n, pl* **-suries** : erario *m*, tesoro *m*

treat *vt* **1** : tratar **2** CONSIDER : considerar **3** ~ **s.o. to (dinner, etc.)** : invitar a algn (a cenar, etc.) — ~ *n* **1** : gusto *m*, placer *m* **2 it's my** ~ : invito yo

treatise *n* : tratado *m*

treatment *n* : tratamiento *m*

treaty *n, pl* **-ties** : tratado *m*

treble *adj* **1** TRIPLE : triple **2** : de tiple (en música) — ~ *vt* **-bled; -bling** : triplicar — **treble clef** : clave *f* de sol

tree *n* : árbol *m*

trek *vi* **trekked; trekking** : viajar (con dificultad) — ~ *n* : viaje *m* difícil

trellis *n* : enrejado *m*

tremble *vi* **-bled; -bling** : temblar

tremendous *adj* : tremendo

tremor *n* : temblor *m*

trench *n* **1** : zanja *f* **2** : trinchera *f* (militar)

trend *n* **1** : tendencia *f* **2** FASHION : moda *f* — **trendy** *adj* **trendier; -est** : de moda

trepidation *n* : inquietud *f*

trespass *vi* : entrar ilegalmente (en propiedad ajena)

trial *n* **1** : juicio *m*, proceso *m* **2** TEST : prueba *f* **3** ORDEAL : dura prueba *f* — ~ *adj* : de prueba

triangle *n* : triángulo *m* — **triangular** *adj* : triangular

tribe *n* : tribu *f* — **tribal** *adj* : tribal

tribulation *n* : tribulación *f*

tribunal *n* : tribunal *m*

tribute *n* : tributo *m* — **tributary** *n, pl* **-taries** : afluente *m*

trick *n* **1** : trampa *f* **2** PRANK : broma *f* **3** KNACK, FEAT : truco *m* **4** : baza *f* (en naipes) — ~ *vt* : engañar — **trickery** *n* : engaño *m*

trickle *vi* **-led; -ling** : gotear — ~ *n* : goteo *m*

tricky *adj* **trickier; -est** **1** SLY : astuto, taimado **2** DIFFICULT : difícil

tricycle *n* : triciclo *m*

trifle *n* **1** TRIVIALITY : nimiedad *f* **2 a** ~ : un poco — ~ *vi* **-fled; -fling** ~ **with** : jugar con — **trifling** *adj* : insignificante

trigger *n* : gatillo *m* — ~ *vt* : causar, provocar

trill *n* : trino *m* — ~ *vi* : trinar

trillion *n* : billón *m*

trilogy *n, pl* **-gies** : trilogía *f*

trim *vt* **trimmed; trimming** **1** : recortar **2** ADORN : adornar — ~ *adj* **trimmer; trimmest** **1** SLIM : esbelto **2** NEAT : arreglado — ~ *n* **1** : recorte *m* **2** DECORATION : adornos *mpl* **3 in** ~ : en buena forma — **trimming** *npl* **1** : adornos *mpl* **2** GARNISH : guarnición *f*

Trinity *n* : Trinidad *f*

trinket *n* : chuchería *f*

trio *n, pl* **trios** : trío *m*

trip *v* **tripped; tripping** *vi* **1** : caminar (a paso ligero) **2** STUMBLE : tropezar **3** ~ **up** : equivocarse — *vt* **1** ACTIVATE : activar **2** ~ **s.o.** : hacer una zancadilla a algn **3** ~ **s.o. up** : hacer equivocar a algn — ~ *n* **1** : viaje *m* **2** STUMBLE : traspié *m*

tripe *n* **1** : mondongo *m*, callos *mpl* **2** NONSENSE : tonterías *fpl*

triple *vt* **-pled; -pling** : triplicar — ~ *n* : triple *m* — ~ *adj* : triple — **triplet** *n* : trillizo *m*, -za *f* — **triplicate** *n* : triplicado *m*

tripod *n* : trípode *m*

trite *adj* **triter; tritest** : trillado

triumph *n* : triunfo *m* — ~ *vi* : triunfar — **triumphal** *adj* : triunfal — **triumphant** *adj* : triunfante

trivial *adj* : trivial — **trivia** *ns & pl* : trivialidades *fpl* — **triviality** *n, pl* **-ties** : trivialidad *f*

trod, trodden → **tread**
trolley *n, pl* **-leys** : tranvía *m*
trombone *n* : trombón *m*
troop *n* **1** : escuadrón *m* (de caballería), compañía *f* (de soldados) **2 ~s** *npl* : tropas *fpl* — **~** *vi* **in/out** : entrar/salir en tropel — **trooper** *n* **1** : soldado *m* **2** *or* **state ~** : policía *mf* estatal
trophy *n, pl* **-phies** : trofeo *m*
tropic *n* **1** : trópico *m* **2 the ~s** : el trópico — *or* **tropical** *adj* : tropical
trot *n* : trote *m* — **~** *vi* **trotted; trotting** : trotar
trouble *v* **-bled; -bling** *vt* **1** WORRY : preocupar **2** BOTHER : molestar — *vi* : molestarse — **~** *n* **1** PROBLEMS : problemas *mpl* **2** EFFORT : molestia *f* **3 be in ~** : estar en apuros **4 get in ~** : meterse en problemas **5 I had ~ doing it** : me costó hacerlo — **troublemaker** *n* : alborotador *m*, -dora *f* — **troublesome** *adj* : problemático
trough *n, pl* **troughs 1** : depresión *f* **2** *or* **feeding ~** : comedero *m* **3** *or* **drinking ~** : bebedero *m*
troupe *n* : compañía *f* (de teatro)
trousers *npl* : pantalón *m*, pantalones *mpl*
trout *n, pl* **trout** : trucha *f*
trowel *n* : paleta *f* (de albañil), desplantador *m* (de jardinero)
truant *n* : alumno *m*, -na *f* que falta a clase
truce *n* : tregua *f*
truck *vt* : transportar en camión — **~** *n* **1** : camión *m* **2** CART : carro *m* — **trucker** *n* : camionero *m*, -ra *f*
trudge *vi* **trudged; trudging** : caminar a paso pesado
true *adj* **truer; truest 1** : verdadero **2** LOYAL : fiel **3** GENUINE : auténtico **4 be ~** : ser cierto, ser verdad
truffle *n* : trufa *f*
truly *adv* : verdaderamente
trump *n* : triunfo *m* (en naipes)
trumpet *n* : trompeta *f*
trunk *n* **1** STEM, TORSO : tronco *m* **2** : trompa *f* (de un elefante) **3** : baúl *m* (equipaje) **4** : maletero *m* (de un auto) **5 ~s** *npl* : traje *m* de baño (de hombre)
truss *n* **1** FRAMEWORK : armazón *m* **2** : braguero *m* (en medicina)
trust *n* **1** CONFIDENCE : confianza *f* **2** HOPE : esperanza *f* **3** CREDIT : crédito *m* **4** : trust *m* (en finanzas) **5 in ~** : en fideicomiso — **~** *vi* **1** : confiar **2** HOPE : esperar — *vt* **1** : confiar en, fiarse de (en frases negativas) **2 ~ s.o. with sth** : confiar algo a algn — **trustee** *n* : fideicomisario *m*, -ria *f* — **trustworthy** *adj* : digno de confianza
truth *n, pl* **truths** : verdad *f* — **truthful** *adj* : sincero, veraz
try *v* **tried; trying** *vt* **1** ATTEMPT : tratar (de), intentar **2** : juzgar (un caso, etc.) **3** TEST : poner a prueba **4** *or* **~ out** : probar **5 ~ on** : probarse (ropa) — *vi* : hacer un esfuerzo — **~** *n, pl* **tries** : intento *m* — **trying** *adj* **1** ANNOYING : irritante, pesado **2** DIFFICULT : duro — **tryout** *n* : prueba *f*
tsar → **czar**
T-shirt *n* : camiseta *f*
tub *n* **1** : cuba *f*, tina *f* **2** CONTAINER : envase *m* **3** BATHTUB : bañera *f*
tuba *n* : tuba *f*
tube *n* **1** : tubo *m* **2** *or* **inner ~** : cámara *f* **3 the ~** : la tele
tuberculosis *n, pl* **-loses** : tuberculosis *f*
tubing *n* : tubería *f* — **tubular** *adj* : tubular
tuck *vt* **1** : meter **2 ~ away** : guardar **3 ~ in** : meter por dentro (una blusa, etc.) **4 ~ s.o. in** : arropar a algn — **~** *n* : jareta *f*
Tuesday *n* : martes *m*
tuft *n* : mechón *m* (de pelo), penacho *m* (de plumas)
tug *vt* **tugged; tugging** *or* **~ at** : tirar de, jalar de — **~** *n* **1** : tirón *m*, jalón *m* — **tugboat** *n* : remolcador *m* — **tug-of-war** *n, pl* **tugs-of-war** : tira y afloja *m*
tuition *n* **1** : enseñanza *f* **2** *or* **~ fees** : matrícula *f*
tulip *n* : tulipán *m*
tumble *vi* **-bled; -bling** : caerse — **~** *n* : caída *f* — **tumbler** *n* : vaso *m* (sin pie)
tummy *n, pl* **-mies** : barriga *f*, panza *f*
tumor *n* : tumor *m*
tumult *n* : tumulto *m* — **tumultuous** *adj* : tumultuoso
tuna *n, pl* **-na** *or* **-nas** : atún *m*
tune *n* **1** MELODY : melodía *f* **2** SONG : tonada *f* **3 in ~** : afinado **4 out of ~** : desafinado — **~** *v* **tuned; tuning** *vt* : afinar — *vi* : sintonizar — **tuner** *n* **1** : afinador *m*, -dora *f* (de pianos, etc.) **2** : sintonizador *m* (de un receptor)
tunic *n* : túnica *f*
tunnel *n* : túnel *m* — **~** *vi* **-neled** *or* **-nelled; -neling** *or* **-nelling** : hacer un túnel
turban *n* : turbante *m*
turbine *n* : turbina *f*
turbulent *adj* : turbulento — **turbulence** *n* : turbulencia *f*
turf *n* **1** GRASS : césped *m* **2** SOD : tepe *m*
turgid *adj* : ampuloso (dícese de prosa, etc.)
turkey *n, pl* **-keys** : pavo *m*
turmoil *n* : confusión *f*
turn *vt* **1** : hacer girar (una rueda, etc.), volver (la cabeza, una página, etc.) **2** : dar la vuelta a (una esquina) **3** SPRAIN : torcer **4 ~ down** REFUSE : rechazar **5 ~ down** LOWER : bajar **6 ~ in** : entregar **7 ~ off** : cerrar (una llave), apagar (la luz, etc.) **8 ~ on** : abrir (una llave), encender, prender *Lat* (la luz, etc.) **9 ~ out** EXPEL : echar

10 ~ out PRODUCE : producir **11 ~ out →
turn off 12** *or* **~ over** FLIP : dar la vuelta a,
voltear *Lat* **13 ~ over** TRANSFER : entregar **14 ~ s.o.'s stomach** : revolver el
estómago a algn **15 ~ sth into sth** : convertir algo en algo **16 ~ up** RAISE : subir
— *vi* **1** ROTATE : girar, dar vueltas **2** BE-
COME : ponerse **3** SOUR : agriarse **4** RE-
SORT : recurrir **5** *or* **~ around** : darse la
vuelta, volverse **6 ~ into** : convertirse en
7 ~ left : doblar a la izquierda **8 ~ out**
COME : acudir **9 ~ out** RESULT : resultar
10 ~ up APPEAR : aparecer — **~** *n* **1**
: vuelta *f* **2** CHANGE : cambio *m* **3** CURVE
: curva *f* **4 do a good ~** : hacer un favor
5 whose ~ is it? : ¿a quién le toca?
turnip *n* : nabo *m*
turnout *n* : concurrencia *f* — **turnover** *n* **1**
: tartaleta *f* (postre) **2** : volumen *m* (de ven-
tas) **3** : movimiento *f* (de personal) —
turnpike *n* : carretera *f* de peaje — **turnta-
ble** *n* : plato *m* giratorio
turpentine *n* : trementina *f*
turquoise *n* : turquesa *f*
turret *n* **1** : torrecilla *f* **2** : torreta *f* (de un
tanque, etc.)
turtle *n* : tortuga *f* (marina) — **turtleneck** *n*
: cuello *m* de tortuga
tusk *n* : colmillo *m*
tussle *n* : pelea *f* — **~** *vi* **-sled; -sling**
: pelearse
tutor *n* : profesor *m*, -sora *f* particular — **~**
vt : dar clases particulares a
tuxedo *n, pl* **-dos** *or* **-does** : esmoquin *m*,
smoking *m*
TV → television
twang *n* **1** : tañido *m* **2** : acento *m* nasal
(de la voz)
tweak *vt* : pellizcar — **~** *n* : pellizco *m*
tweed *n* : tweed *m*
tweet *n* : gorjeo *m*, pío *m* — **~** *vi* : piar
tweezers *npl* : pinzas *fpl*
twelve *adj* : doce — **~** *n* : doce *m* — **twelfth**
adj : duodécimo — **~** *n* **1** : duodécimo *m*,
-ma *f* (en una serie) **2** : doceavo *m* (en
matemáticas)

twenty *adj* : veinte — **~** *n, pl* **-ties** : veinte
m — **twentieth** *adj* : vigésimo — **~** *n* **1**
: vigésimo *m*, -ma *f* (en una serie) **2** : veinteavo *m* (en matemáticas)
twice *adv* **1** : dos veces **2 ~ as much/
many as** : el doble de (algo), el doble que
(algn)
twig *n* : ramita *f*
twilight *n* : crepúsculo *m*
twin *n* : gemelo *m*, -la *f*; mellizo *m*, -za *f* —
~ *adj* : gemelo, mellizo
twine *n* : cordel *m*, bramante *m Spain*
twinge *n* : punzada *f*
twinkle *vi* **-kled; -kling 1** : centellear **2**
: brillar (dícese de los ojos) — **~** *n* : centelleo *m*, brillo *m* (de los ojos)
twirl *vt* : girar, dar vueltas a — *vi* : girar, dar
vueltas — **~** *n* : giro *m*, vuelta *f*
twist *vt* **1** : retorcer **2** TURN : girar **3**
SPRAIN : torcerse **4** : tergiversar (palabras)
— *vi* **1** : retorcerse **2** COIL : enrollarse **3**
: serpentear (entre montañas, etc.) — **~** *n*
1 BEND : vuelta *f* **2** TURN : giro *m* **3 ~ of
lemon** : rodajita *f* de limón — **twister →
tornado**
twitch *vi* : moverse (espasmódicamente) —
~ *n* **nervous ~** : tic *m* nervioso
two *adj* : dos — **~** *n, pl* **twos** : dos *m* —
twofold *adj* : doble — **~** *adv* : al doble —
two hundred *adj* : doscientos — **~** *n*
: doscientos *m*
tycoon *n* : magnate *mf*
tying → tie
type *n* : tipo *m* — **~** *v* **typed; typing** : escribir a máquina — **typewritten** *adj* : escrito a
máquina — **typewriter** *n* : máquina *f* de escribir
typhoon *n* : tifón *m*
typical *adj* : típico, característico — **typify** *vt*
-fied; -fying : tipificar
typist *n* : mecanógrafo *m*, -fa *f*
typography *n* : tipografía *f*
tyranny *n, pl* **-nies** : tiranía *f* — **tyrant** *n*
: tirano *m*, -na *f*
tzar → czar

U

u *n, pl* **u's** *or* **us** : u *f*, vigésima primera letra
del alfabeto inglés
udder *n* : ubre *f*
UFO (*unidentified flying object*) *n, pl* **UFO's**
or **UFOs** : ovni *m*, OVNI *m*

ugly *adj* **uglier; -est** : feo — **ugliness** *n*
: fealdad *f*
ulcer *n* : úlcera *f*
ulterior *adj* **~ motive** : segunda intención *f*
ultimate *adj* **1** FINAL : final, último **2** UT-

MOST : máximo **3** FUNDAMENTAL : fundamental — **ultimately** *adv* **1** FINALLY : por último, finalmente **2** EVENTUALLY : a la larga

ultimatum *n, pl* **-tums** *or* **-ta** : ultimátum *m*

ultrasonic *adj* : ultrasónico

ultraviolet *adj* : ultravioleta

umbilical cord *n* : cordón *m* umbilical

umbrella *n* : paraguas *m*

umpire *n* : árbitro *m*, **-tra** *f* — ~ *vt* **-pired; -piring** : arbitrar

umpteenth *adj* : enésimo

unable *adj* **1** : incapaz **2 be ~ to** : no poder

unabridged *adj* : íntegro

unacceptable *adj* : inaceptable

unaccountable *adj* : inexplicable

unaccustomed *adj* **be ~ to** : no estar acostumbrado a

unadulterated *adj* : puro

unaffected *adj* **1** : no afectado **2** NATURAL : sin afectación, natural

unafraid *adj* : sin miedo

unaided *adj* : sin ayuda

unanimous *adj* : unánime

unannounced *adj* : sin dar aviso

unarmed *adj* : desarmado

unassuming *adj* : modesto, sin pretensiones

unattached *adj* **1** : suelto **2** UNMARRIED : soltero

unattractive *adj* : poco atractivo

unauthorized *adj* : no autorizado

unavailable *adj* : no disponible

unavoidable *adj* : inevitable

unaware *adj* **1** : inconsciente **2 be ~ of** : ignorar — **unawares** *adv* **catch s.o. ~** : agarrar a algn desprevenido

unbalanced *adj* : desequilibrado

unbearable *adj* : inaguantable, insoportable

unbelievable *adj* : increíble

unbending *adj* : inflexible

unbiased *adj* : imparcial

unborn *adj* : aún no nacido

unbreakable *adj* : irrompible

unbridled *adj* : desenfrenado

unbroken *adj* **1** INTACT : intacto **2** CONTINUOUS : continuo

unbutton *vt* : desabrochar, desabotonar

uncalled-for *adj* : inapropiado, innecesario

uncanny *adj* **-nier; -est** : extraño, misterioso

unceasing *adj* : incesante

unceremonious *adj* **1** INFORMAL : poco ceremonioso **2** ABRUPT : brusco

uncertain *adj* **1** : incierto **2 in no ~ terms** : de forma vehemente — **uncertainty** *n, pl* **-ties** : incertidumbre *f*

unchanged *adj* : igual, sin alterar — **unchanging** *adj* : inmutable

uncivilized *adj* : incivilizado

uncle *n* : tío *m*

unclear *adj* : poco claro

uncomfortable *adj* **1** : incómodo **2** DISCONCERTING : inquietante, desagradable

uncommon *adj* : raro

uncompromising *adj* : intransigente

unconcerned *adj* : indiferente

unconditional *adj* : incondicional

unconscious *adj* : inconsciente

unconstitutional *adj* : inconstitucional

uncontrollable *adj* : incontrolable

unconventional *adj* : poco convencional

uncouth *adj* : grosero

uncover *vt* **1** : destapar **2** REVEAL : descubrir

undecided *adj* : indeciso

undeniable *adj* : innegable

under way *adv* **get ~** : ponerse en marcha

under *adv* **1** : debajo **2** LESS : menos **3** *or* **~ anesthetic** : bajo los efectos de la anestesia — **~** *prep* **1** BELOW, BENEATH : debajo de, abajo de **2 ~ 20 minutes** : menos de 20 minutos **3 ~ the circumstances** : dadas las circunstancias

underage *adj* : menor de edad

underclothes → **underwear**

undercover *adj* : secreto

undercurrent *n* : tendencia *f* oculta

underdeveloped *adj* : subdesarrollado

underestimate *vt* **-mated; -mating** : subestimar

underfoot *adv* : bajo los pies

undergo *vt* **-went; -gone; -going** : sufrir, experimentar

undergraduate *n* : estudiante *m* universitario, estudiante *f* universitaria

underground *adv* **1** : bajo tierra **2 go ~** : pasar a la clandestinidad — **~** *adj* **1** : subterráneo **2** SECRET : secreto, clandestino — **~** *n* : movimiento *m* clandestino

undergrowth *n* : maleza *f*

underhanded *adj* SLY : solapado

underline *vt* **-lined; -lining** : subrayar

underlying *adj* : subyacente

undermine *vt* **-mined; -mining** : socavar, minar

underneath *adv* : debajo, abajo — **~** *prep* : debajo de, abajo de *Lat*

underpants *npl* : calzoncillos *mpl,* calzones *mpl Lat*

underpass *n* : paso *m* inferior

underprivileged *adj* : desfavorecido

underrate *vt* **-rated; -rating** : subestimar

undershirt *n* : camiseta *f*

understand *v* **-stood** ; **-standing** : comprender, entender — **understandable** *adj* : comprensible — **understanding** *adj* : comprensivo, compasivo — **~** *n* **1** : comprensión *f* **2** AGREEMENT : acuerdo *m*

understatement *n* **that's an ~** : decir sólo eso es quedarse corto

understand

understudy n, pl **-dies** : sobresaliente mf (en el teatro)
undertake vt **-took; -taken; -taking** : emprender (una tarea), encargarse de (una responsabilidad) — **undertaker** n : director m, -tora f de una funeraria — **undertaking** n : empresa f, tarea f
undertone n **1** : voz f baja **2** SUGGESTION : matiz m
undertow n : resaca f
underwater adj : submarino — ～ adv : debajo (del agua)
underwear n : ropa f interior
underwent → undergo
underworld n the ～ CRIMINALS : la hampa, los bajos fondos
underwriter n : asegurador m, -dora f
undesirable adj : indeseable
undeveloped adj : sin desarrollar
undignified adj : indecoroso
undisputed adj : indiscutible
undo vt **-did; -done; -doing 1** UNFASTEN : deshacer, desatar **2** : reparar (daños, etc.)
undoubtedly adv : indudablemente
undress vt : desnudar — vi : desnudarse
undue adj : indebido, excesivo
undulate vi **-lated; -lating** : ondular
unduly adv : excesivamente
undying adj : eterno
unearth vt : desenterrar
unearthly adj **-lier; -est** : sobrenatural, de otro mundo
uneasy adj **-easier; -est 1** AWKWARD : incómodo **2** WORRIED : inquieto **3** RESTLESS : agitado — **uneasily** adv : inquietamente — **uneasiness** n : inquietud f
uneducated adj : inculto
unemployed adj : desempleado — **unemployment** n : desempleo m
unerring adj : infalible
unethical adj : poco ético
uneven adj **1** : desigual **2** : impar (dícese de un número)
unexpected adj : inesperado
unfailing adj I CONSTANT : constante **2** INEXHAUSTIBLE : inagotable
unfair adj : injusto — **unfairly** adv : injustamente — **unfairness** n : injusticia f
unfaithful adj : infiel — **unfaithfulness** n : infidelidad f
unfamiliar adj **1** : desconocido **2** be ～ **with** : desconocer
unfasten vt **1** : desabrochar (ropa, etc.) **2** UNDO : desatar (una cuerda, etc.)
unfavorable adj : desfavorable
unfeeling adj : insensible
unfinished adj : sin terminar
unfit adj **1** UNSUITABLE : impropio **2** UNSUITED : no apto, incapaz
unfold vt **1** : desplegar, desdoblar **2** RE-

VEAL : revelar (un plan, etc.) — vi **1** : extenderse, desplegarse **2** DEVELOP : desarrollarse
unforeseen adj : imprevisto
unforgettable adj : inolvidable
unforgivable adj : imperdonable
unfortunate adj **1** UNLUCKY : desgraciado, desafortunado **2** INAPPROPRIATE : inoportuno — **unfortunately** adv : desgraciadamente
unfounded adj : infundado
unfriendly adj **-lier; -est** : poco amistoso
unfurl vt : desplegar
unfurnished adj : desamueblado
ungainly adj : desgarbado
ungodly adj **1** : impío **2** an ～ **hour** : una hora intempestiva
ungrateful adj : desagradecido
unhappy adj **-pier; -est 1** SAD : infeliz, triste **2** UNFORTUNATE : desafortunado — **unhappily** adv **1** SADLY : tristemente **2** UNFORTUNATELY : desgraciadamente — **unhappiness** n : tristeza f
unharmed adj : salvo, ileso
unhealthy adj **-thier; -est 1** : malsano **2** SICKLY : enfermizo
unheard—of adj : sin precedente, insólito
unhook vt : desenganchar
unhurt adj : ileso
unicorn n : unicornio m
unification n : unificación f
uniform adj : uniforme — ～ n : uniforme m — **uniformity** n, pl **-ties** : uniformidad f
unify vt **-fied; -fying** : unificar
unilateral adj : unilateral
unimaginable adj : inconcebible
unimportant adj : insignificante
uninhabited adj : deshabitado, despoblado
uninjured adj : ileso
unintentional adj : involuntario
union n **1** : unión f **2** or **labor** ～ : sindicato m, gremio m Lat
unique adj : único — **uniquely** adv EXCEPTIONALLY : excepcionalmente
unison n in ～ : al unísono
unit n **1** : unidad f **2** : módulo m (de un mobiliario)
unite v **united; uniting** vt : unir — vi : unirse — **unity** n, pl **-ties 1** : unidad f **2** HARMONY : acuerdo m
universe n : universo m — **universal** adj : universal
university n, pl **-ties** : universidad f
unjust adj : injusto — **unjustified** adj : injustificado
unkempt adj **1** : descuidado, desaseado **2** : despeinado (dícese del pelo)
unkind adj : poco amable, cruel — **unkindness** n : falta f de amabilidad, crueldad f
unknown adj : desconocido

unlawful *adj* : ilegal

unless *conj* : a menos que, a no ser que

unlike *adj* : diferente — ~ *prep* : a diferencia de — **unlikelihood** *n* : improbabilidad *f* — **unlikely** *adj* **-lier; -est** : improbable

unlimited *adj* : ilimitado

unload *v* : descargar

unlock *vt* : abrir (con llave)

unlucky *adj* **-luckier; -est 1** UNFORTUNATE : desgraciado **2** : de mala suerte (dícese de un número, etc.)

unmarried *adj* : soltero

unmask *vt* : desenmascarar

unmistakable *adj* : inconfundible

unnatural *adj* **1** : anormal **2** AFFECTED : afectado, forzado

unnecessary *adj* : innecesario — **unnecessarily** *adv* : innecesariamente

unnerving *adj* : desconcertante

unnoticed *adj* : inadvertido

unobtainable *adj* : inasequible

unobtrusive *adj* : discreto

unofficial *adj* : no oficial

unorthodox *adj* : poco ortodoxo

unpack *vt* **1** : desempaquetar, desempacar *Lat* (un paquete, etc.) **2** : deshacer (una maleta) — *vi* : deshacer las maletas

unparalleled *adj* : sin igual

unpleasant *adj* : desagradable

unplug *vt* **-plugged; -plugging** : desconectar, desenchufar

unpopular *adj* : poco popular

unprecedented *adj* : sin precedente

unpredictable *adj* : imprevisible

unprepared *adj* **1** : no preparado **2** UNREADY : deprevenido

unqualified *adj* **1** : no calificado, sin título **2** COMPLETE : absoluto

unquestionable *adj* : indiscutible — **unquestioning** *adj* : incondicional

unravel *v* **-eled** *or* **-elled; -eling** *or* **-elling** *vt* : desenmarañar — *vi* : deshacerse

unreal *adj* : irreal — **unrealistic** *adj* : poco realista

unreasonable *adj* **1** : irrazonable **2** EXCESSIVE : excesivo

unrecognizable *adj* : irreconocible

unrelated *adj* : no relacionado

unrelenting *adj* : implacable

unreliable *adj* : que no es de fiar

unrepentant *adj* : impenitente

unrest *n* **1** : inquietud *f*, malestar *m* **2** *or* **political** ~ : disturbios *mpl*

unripe *adj* : verde, no maduro

unrivaled *or* **unrivalled** *adj* : incomparable, sin par

unroll *vt* : desenrollar — *vi* : desenrollarse

unruly *adj* : indisciplinado

unsafe *adj* : inseguro

unsaid *adj* : sin decir

unsanitary *adj* : antihigiénico

unsatisfactory *adj* : insatisfactorio

unscathed *adj* : ileso

unscrew *vt* : destornillar

unscrupulous *adj* : sin escrúpulos

unseemly *adj* **-lier; -est** : indecoroso

unseen *adj* **1** : no visto **2** UNNOTICED : inadvertido

unselfish *adj* : desinteresado

unsettle *vt* **-tled; -tling** DISTURB : perturbar — **unsettled** *adj* **1** CHANGEABLE : inestable **2** DISTURBED : agitado, inquieto **3** : variable (dícese del tiempo)

unsightly *adj* : feo

unskilled *adj* : no calificado — **unskillful** *adj* : torpe, poco hábil

unsociable *adj* : poco sociable

unsound *adj* **1** : defectuoso, erróneo **2 of** ~ **mind** : demente

unspeakable *adj* **1** : indecible **2** TERRIBLE : atroz

unstable *adj* : inestable

unsteady *adj* **1** : inestable **2** SHAKY : tembloroso

unsuccessful *adj* **1** : fracasado **2 be** ~ : no tener éxito

unsuitable *adj* **1** : inadecuado **2** INCONVENIENT : inconveniente

unsure *adj* : inseguro

unsuspecting *adj* : confiado

unsympathetic *adj* : indiferente

unthinkable *adj* : inconcebible

untidy *adj* : desordenado (dícese de una sala, etc.), desaliñado (dícese de una persona)

untie *vt* **-tied; -tying** *or* **-tieing** : desatar

until *prep* : hasta — ~ *conj* : hasta que

untimely *adj* **1** PREMATURE : prematuro **2** INOPPORTUNE : inoportuno

untold *adj* : incalculable

untoward *adj* **1** ADVERSE : adverso **2** IMPROPER : indecoroso

untroubled *adj* **1** : tranquilo **2 be** ~ **by** : no estar afectado por

untrue *adj* : falso

unused *adj* **1** NEW : nuevo **2 be** ~ **to** : no estar acustumbrado a

unusual *adj* : poco común, insólito — **unusually** *adv* : excepcionalmente

unveil *vt* : descubrir, revelar

unwanted *adj* : superfluo (dícese de un objeto), no deseado (dícese de un niño, etc.)

unwarranted *adj* : injustificado

unwelcome *adj* : inoportuno, molesto

unwell *adj* **be** ~ : sentirse mal

unwieldy *adj* : difícil de manejar

unwilling *adj* : poco dispuesto — **unwillingly** *adv* : de mala gana

unwind *v* **-wound; -winding** *vt* : desenrollar — *vi* **1** : desenrollarse **2** RELAX : relajarse

unwise *adj* : imprudente

unworthy *adj* be ~ of : no ser digno de

unwrap *vt* -wrapped; -wrapping : desenvolver

up–to–date *adj* **1** : corriente, al día **2** MODERN : moderno

up *adv* **1** ABOVE : arriba **2** UPWARDS : hacia arriba **3 ten miles farther** ~ : diez millas más adelante **4** ~ **here/there** : aquí/allí arriba **5** ~ **north** : en el norte **6** ~ **until** : hasta — ~ *adj* **1** AWAKE : levantado **2** FINISHED : terminado **3 be** ~ **against** : enfrentarse con **4 be** ~ **on** : estar al corriente de **5 it's** ~ **to you** : depende de tí **6 prices are** ~ : los precios han aumentado **7 the sun is** ~ : ha salido el sol **8 what's** ~? : ¿qué pasa? — ~ *prep* **1 go** ~ **the river** : ir río arriba **2 go** ~ **the stairs** : subir la escalera **3** ~ **the coast** : a lo largo de la costa — ~ *v* upped; upping; ups *vt* : aumentar — *vi* **she** ~ **and left** : agarró y se fue

upbringing *n* : educación *f*

upcoming *adj* : próximo

update *vt* -dated; -dating : poner al día, actualizar — ~ *n* : puesta *f* al día

upgrade *vt* -graded; -grading : elevar la categoría de (un puesto, etc.), mejorar (una facilidad, etc.)

upheaval *n* : trastorno *m*

uphill *adv* : cuesta arriba — ~ *adj* **1** : en subida **2 be an** ~ **battle** : ser muy difícil

uphold *vt* -held; -holding : sostener, apoyar

upholstery *n, pl* -steries : tapicería *f*

upkeep *n* : mantenimiento *m*

upon *prep* **1** : en, sobre **2** ~ **leaving** : al salir

upper class *n* : clase *f* alta

upper hand *n* : ventaja *f*, dominio *m*

upper *adj* : superior — ~ *n* : parte *f* superior (del calzado, etc.)

uppercase *adj* : mayúsculo

uppermost *adj* : más alto

upright *adj* **1** VERTICAL : vertical **2** ERECT : derecho **3** JUST : recto, honesto — ~ *n* : montante *m*, poste *m*

uprising *n* : insurrección *f*, revuelta *f*

uproar *n* COMMOTION : alboroto *m*

uproot *vt* : desarraigar

upset *vt* -set; -setting **1** OVERTURN : volcar **2** DISTRESS : alterar, inquietar **3** DISRUPT : trastornar — ~ *adj* **1** DISTRESSED : alterado **2 have an** ~ **stomach** : estar mal del estómago — ~ *n* : trastorno *m*

upshot *n* : resultado *m* final

upside down *adv* **1** : al revés **2 turn** ~ : volver — **upside– down** *adj* : al revés

upstairs *adv* : arriba — ~ *adj* : de arriba — ~ *ns & pl* : piso *m* de arriba

upstart *n* : advenedizo *m*, -za *f*

upstream *adv* : río arriba

upswing *n* **be on the** ~ : estar mejorándose

uptown *adv* : hacia la parte alta de la ciudad, hacia el distrito residencial

upturn *n* : mejora *f*, auge *m* (económico)

upward *or* **upwards** *adv* : hacia arriba — **upward** *adj* : ascendente, hacia arriba

uranium *n* : uranio *m*

urban *adj* : urbano

urbane *adj* : urbano, cortés

urge *vt* **urged; urging 1** PRESS : instar, exhortar **2** ~ **on** : animar — ~ *n* : impulso *m*, ganas *fpl* — **urgency** *n, pl* -cies : urgencia *f* — **urgent** *adj* **1** : urgente **2 be** ~ : urgir

urine *n* : orina *f* — **urinate** *vi* -nated; -nating : orinar

urn *n* : urna *f*

Uruguayan *adj* : uruguayo

us *pron* **1** (*as direct or indirect object*) : nos **2** (*as object of a preposition*) : nosotros, nosotras **3 both of** ~ : nosotros dos **4 it's** ~! : ¡somos nosotros!

usage *n* : uso *m*

use *v* **used; using 1** : usar **2** CONSUME : consumir, tomar (drogas, etc.) **3** ~ **up** : agotar, consumir — *vi* **1 she** ~d **to dance** : acostumbraba bailar **2 winters** ~d **to be colder** : los inviernos solían ser más fríos — ~ *n* **1** : uso *m* **2 have no** ~ **for** : no necesitar **3 have the** ~ **of** : poder usar, tener acceso a **4 it's no** ~! : ¡es inútil! — **used** *adj* **1** SECONDHAND : usado **2 be** ~ **to** : estar acostumbrado a — **useful** *adj* : útil, práctico — **usefulness** *n* : utilidad *f* — **useless** *adj* : inútil — **user** *n* : usuario *m*, -ria *f*

usher *vt* **1** : acompañar, conducir **2** ~ **in** : hacer entrar — ~ *n* : acomodador *m*, -dora *f*

usual *adj* **1** : habitual, usual **2 as** ~ : como de costumbre — **usually** *adv* : usualmente

usurp *vt* : usurpar

utensil *n* : utensilio *m*

uterus *n, pl* **uteri** : útero *m*, matriz *f*

utility *n, pl* -ties **1** : utilidad *f* **2** *or* **public** ~ : empresa *f* de servicio público

utilize *vt* -lized; -lizing : utilizar

utmost *adj* **1** FARTHEST : extremo **2 of the** ~ **importance** : de suma importancia — ~ *n* **do one's** ~ : hacer todo lo posible

utopia *n* : utopía *f* — **utopian** *adj* : utópico

utter¹ *adj* : absoluto, completo

utter² *vt* : decir, pronunciar (palabras) — **utterance** *n* : declaración *f*, expresión *f*

utterly *adv* : completamente, totalmente

V

v *n, pl* **v's** *or* **vs** : v *f*, vigésima segunda letra del alfabeto inglés
vacant *adj* **1** AVAILABLE : libre **2** UNOCCUPIED : desocupado **3** : vacante (dícese de un puesto) **4** : ausente (dícese de una mirada) — **vacancy** *n, pl* **-cies 1** : (puesto *m*) vacante *f* **2** : habitación *f* libre (en un hotel, etc.)
vacate *vt* **-cated; -cating** : desalojar, desocupar
vacation *n* : vacaciones *fpl*
vaccination *n* : vacunación *f* — **vaccinate** *vt* **-nated; -nating** : vacunar — **vaccine** *n* : vacuna *f*
vacuum *n, pl* **vacuums** *or* **vacua** : vacío *m* — ~ *vt* : pasar la aspiradora por — **vacuum cleaner** *n* : aspiradora *f*
vagina *n, pl* **-nae** *or* **-nas** : vagina *f*
vagrant *n* : vagabundo *m*, -da *f*
vague *adj* **vaguer; -est** : vago, indistinto
vain *adj* **1** CONCEITED : vanidoso **2 in** ~ : en vano
valentine *n* : tarjeta *f* del día de San Valentín
valiant *adj* : valiente, valeroso
valid *adj* : válido — **validate** *vt* **-dated; -dating** : validar — **validity** *n* : validez *f*
valley *n, pl* **-leys** : valle *m*
valor *n* : valor *m*, valentía *f*
value *n* : valor *m* — ~ *vt* **-ued; -uing** : valorar — **valuable** *adj* : valioso — **valuables** *npl* : objetos *mpl* de valor
valve *n* : válvula *f*
vampire *n* : vampiro *m*
van *n* : furgoneta *f*, camioneta *f*
vandal *n* : vándalo *m* — **vandalism** *n* : vandalismo *m* — **vandalize** *vt* : destrozar, destruir
vane *n or* **weather** ~ : veleta *f*
vanguard *n* : vanguardia *f*
vanilla *n* : vainilla *f*
vanish *vi* : desaparecer
vanity *n, pl* **-ties 1** : vanidad *f* **2** *or* ~ **table** : tocador *m*
vantage point *n* : posición *f* ventajosa
vapor *n* : vapor *m*
variable *adj* : variable — ~ *n* : variable *f* — **variance** *n* **at** ~ **with** : en desacuerdo con — **variant** *n* : variante *f* — **variation** *n* : variación *f* — **varied** *adj* : variado — **variegated** *adj* : abigarrado, multicolor — **variety** *n, pl* **-ties 1** : variedad *f* **2** ASSORTMENT : surtido *m* **3** SORT : clase *f* — **various** *adj* : varios, diversos
varnish *n* : barniz *f* — ~ *vt* : barnizar
vary *v* **varied; varying** : variar

vase *n* **1** : jarrón *m* **2** *or* **flower** ~ : florero *m*
vast *adj* : vasto, enorme — **vastness** *n* : inmensidad *f*
vat *n* : cuba *f*
vault[1] *vi* LEAP : saltar — ~ *n* : salto *m*
vault[2] *n* **1** DOME : bóveda *f* **2** *or* **bank** ~ : cámara *f* acorazada, bóveda *f* de seguridad *Lat* **3** CRYPT : cripta *f*
VCR (*videocassette recorder*) *n* : video *m*
veal *n* : (carne *f* de) ternera *f*
veer *vi* : virar
vegetable *adj* : vegetal — ~ *n* **1** : vegetal *m* (planta) **2** ~**s** *npl* : verduras *fpl* — **vegetarian** *n* : vegetariano *mf* — **vegetation** *n* : vegetación *f*
vehemence *n* : vehemencia *f* — **vehement** *adj* : vehemente
vehicle *n* : vehículo *m*
veil *n* : velo *m* — ~ *vt* **1** : cubrir con un velo **2** CONCEAL : velar
vein *n* **1** : vena *f* **2** : veta *f* (de un mineral, etc.)
velocity *n, pl* **-ties** : velocidad *f*
velvet *n* : terciopelo *m* — **velvety** *adj* : aterciopelado
vending machine *vt* : máquina *f* expendedora
vendor *n* : vendedor *m*, -dora *f*
veneer *n* **1** : chapa *f* **2** FACADE : apariencia *f*
venerable *adj* : venerable — **venerate** *vt* **-ated; -ating** : venerar — **veneration** *n* : veneración *f*
venereal *adj* : venéreo
venetian blind *n* : persiana *f* veneciana
Venezuelan *adj* : venezolano
vengeance *n* **1** : venganza *f* **2 take** ~ **on** : vengarse de — **vengeful** *adj* : vengativo
venison *n* : (carne *f* de) venado *m*
venom *n* : veneno *m* — **venomous** *adj* : venenoso
vent *vt* : desahogar — ~ *n* **1** *or* **air** ~ : rejilla *f* de ventilación **2** OUTLET : desahogo *m* — **ventilate** *vt* **-lated; -lating** : ventilar — **ventilation** *n* : ventilación *f* — **ventilator** *n* : ventilador *m*
ventriloquist *n* : ventrílocuo *m*, -cua *f*
venture *v* **-tured; -turing** *vt* **1** RISK : arriesgar **2** : aventurar (una opinión, etc.) — *vi* : atreverse — ~ *n or* **business** ~ : empresa *f*
venue *n* : lugar *m*
Venus *n* : Venus *m*
veranda *or* **verandah** *n* : veranda *f*

verb *n* : verbo *m* — **verbal** *adj* : verbal — **verbatim** *adv* : palabra por palabra — ∼ *adj* : literal — **verbose** *adj* : verboso

verdict *n* **1** : veredicto *m* **2** OPINION : opinión *f*

verge *n* **1** : borde *m* **2 on the** ∼ **of** : a punto de (hacer algo), al borde de (algo) — ∼ *vi* **verged; verging** ∼ **on** : rayar en

verify *vt* **-fied; -fying** : verificar — **verification** *n* : verificación *f*

vermin *ns & pl* : alimañas *fpl*

vermouth *n* : vermut *m*

versatile *adj* : versátil — **versatility** *n* : versatilidad *f*

verse *n* **1** LINE : verso *m* **2** POETRY : poesía *f* **3** : versículo *m* (en la Biblia) — **versed** *adj* **be well** ∼ **in** : ser muy versado en

version *n* : versión *f*

versus *prep* : versus

vertebra *n*, *pl* **-brae** *or* **-bras** : vértebra *f*

vertical *adj* : vertical — ∼ *n* : vertical *f*

vertigo *n*, *pl* **-goes** *or* **-gos** : vértigo *m*

verve *n* : brío *m*

very *adv* **1** : muy **2 at the** ∼ **least** : por lo menos **3 the** ∼ **same thing** : la misma cosa **4** ∼ **much** : mucho **5** ∼ **well** : muy bien — ∼ *adj* **verier; -est 1** PRECISE, SAME : mismo **2** MERE : solo, mero **3 the** ∼ **thing** : justo lo que hacía falta

vessel *n* **1** CONTAINER : recipiente *m* **2** SHIP : nave *f*, buque *m* **3** *or* **blood** ∼ : vaso *m* sanguíneo

vest *n* **1** : chaleco *m* **2** *Brit* UNDERSHIRT : camiseta *f*

vestibule *n* : vestíbulo *m*

vestige *n* : vestigio *m*

vet *n* **1** → **veterinarian 2** → **veteran**

veteran *n* : veterano *m*, **-na** *f*

veterinarian *n* : veterinario *m*, **-ria** *f* — **veterinary** *adj* : veterinario

veto *n*, *pl* **-toes** : veto *m* — ∼ *vt* : vetar

vex *vt* ANNOY : irritar

via *prep* : por, vía

viable *adj* : viable

viaduct *n* : viaducto *m*

vial *n* : frasco *m*

vibrant *adj* : vibrante — **vibrate** *vi* **-brated; -brating** : vibrar — **vibration** *n* : vibración *f*

vicar *n* : vicario *m*, **-ria** *f*

vicarious *adj* : indirecto

vice president *n* : vicepresidente *m*, **-ta** *f*

vice versa *adv* : viceversa

vice *n* : vicio *m*

vicinity *n*, *pl* **-ties 1** : inmediaciones *fpl* **2 in the** ∼ **of** ABOUT : alrededor de

vicious *adj* **1** SAVAGE : feroz **2** MALICIOUS : malicioso

victim *n* : víctima *f*

victor *n* : vencedor *m*, **-dora** *f*

victory *n*, *pl* **-ries** : victoria *f* — **victorious** *adj* : victorioso

video *n* : video *m*, vídeo *m Spain* — ∼ *adj* : de video — **videocassette** *n* : videocasete *m* — **videotape** *n* : videocinta *f* — ∼ *vt* **-taped; -taping** : videograbar

video game *n* : videojuego *m*, juego *m* de video

vie *vi* **vied; vying** : competir

Vietnamese *adj* : vietnamita

view *n* **1** : vista *f* **2** OPINION : opinión *f* **3 come into** ∼ : aparecer **4 in** ∼ **of** : en vista de (que) — ∼ *vt* **1** : ver **2** CONSIDER : considerar — **viewer** *n* *or* **television** ∼ : televidente *mf* — **viewpoint** *n* : punto *m* de vista

vigil *n* : vela *f* — **vigilance** *n* : vigilancia *f* — **vigilant** *adj* : vigilante

vigor *or Brit* **vigour** *n* : vigor *m* — **vigorous** *adj* **1** : enérgico **2** ROBUST : vigoroso

Viking *n* : vikingo *m*, **-ga** *f*

vile *adj* **viler; vilest 1** : vil **2** REVOLTING : asqueroso **3** TERRIBLE : horrible

villa *n* : casa *f* de campo

village *n* : pueblo *m* (grande), aldea *f* (pequeña) — **villager** *n* : vecino *m*, **-na** *f* (de un pueblo); aldeano *m*, **-na** *f* (de una aldea)

villain *n* : villano *m*, **-na** *f*

vindicate *vt* **-cated; -cating 1** : vindicar **2** JUSTIFY : justificar

vindictive *adj* : vengativo

vine *n* **1** : enredadera *f* **2** GRAPEVINE : vid *f*

vinegar *n* : vinagre *m*

vineyard *n* : viña *f*, viñedo *m*

vintage *n* **1** : cosecha *f* (de vino) **2** ERA : época *f* — ∼ *adj* **1** : añejo (dícese de un vino) **2** CLASSIC : de época

vinyl *n* : vinilo *m*

viola *n* : viola *f*

violate *vt* **-lated; -lating** : violar — **violation** *n* : violación *f*

violence *n* : violencia *f* — **violent** *adj* : violento

violet *n* : violeta *f* (flor), violeta *m* (color)

violin *n* : violín *m* — **violinist** *n* : violinista *mf* — **violoncello** → **cello**

VIP *n*, *pl* **VIPs** : VIP *mf*

viper *n* : víbora *f*

virgin *n* : virgen *mf* — ∼ *adj* **1** : virgen (dícese de la lana, etc.) **2** CHASTE : virginal — **virginity** *n* : virginidad *f*

virile *adj* : viril — **virility** *n* : virilidad *f*

virtual *adj* : virtual — **virtually** *adv* : prácticamente

virtue *n* **1** : virtud *f* **2 by** ∼ **of** : en virtud de

virtuoso *n*, *pl* **-sos** *or* **-si** : virtuoso *m*, **-sa** *f*

virtuous *adj* : virtuoso

virulent *adj* : virulento

virus *n* : virus *m*

visa *n* : visado *m*, visa *f Lat*
vis-à-vis *prep* : con respecto a
viscous *adj* : viscoso
vise *n* : torno *m* de banco
visible *adj* **1** : visible **2** NOTICEABLE : evidente — **visibility** *n, pl* **-ties** : visibilidad *f*
vision *n* **1** : visión *f* **2 have ~s of** : imaginarse — **visionary** *adj* : visionario — ~ *n, pl* **-ries** : visionario *m*, **-ria** *f*
visit *vt* : visitar — *vi* **1** : hacer una visita **2 be ~ing** : estar de visita — ~ *n* : visita *f* — **visitor** *n* **1** : visitante *mf* **2** GUEST : visita *f*
visor *n* : visera *f*
vista *n* : vista *f*
visual *adj* : visual — **visualize** *vt* **-ized; -izing** : visualizar
vital *adj* **1** : vital **2** CRUCIAL : esencial — **vitality** *n, pl* **-ties** : vitalidad *f*, energía *f*
vitamin *n* : vitamina *f*
vivacious *adj* : vivaz, animado
vivid *adj* : vivo (dícese de colores), vívido (dícese de sueños, etc.)
vocabulary *n, pl* **-laries** : vocabulario *m*
vocal *adj* **1** : vocal **2** OUTSPOKEN : vociferante — **vocal cords** *npl* : cuerdas *fpl* vocales — **vocalist** *n* : cantante *mf*, vocalista *mf*
vocation *n* : vocación *f* — **vocational** *adj* : profesional
vociferous *adj* : vociferante, ruidoso
vodka *n* : vodka *m*
vogue *n* **1** : moda *f*, boga *f* **2 be in ~** : estar de moda, estar en boga
voice *n* : voz *f* — ~ *vt* **voiced; voicing** : expresar

void *adj* **1** INVALID : nulo **2 ~ of** : falto de — ~ *n* : vacío *m* — ~ *vt* : anular
volatile *adj* : volátil — **volatility** *n* : volatilidad *f*
volcano *n, pl* **-noes** *or* **-nos** : volcán *m* — **volcanic** *adj* : volcánico
volition *n* **of one's own ~** : por voluntad propia
volley *n, pl* **-leys** **1** : descarga *f* (de tiros) **2** : torrente *m* (de insultos, etc.) **3** : volea *f* (en deportes) — **volleyball** *n* : voleibol *m*
volt *n* : voltio *m* — **voltage** *n* : voltaje *m*
voluble *adj* : locuaz
volume *n* : volumen *m* — **voluminous** *adj* : voluminoso
voluntary *adj* : voluntario — **volunteer** *n* : voluntario *m*, **-ria** *f* — ~ *vt* : ofrecer — *vi* **~ to** : ofrecerse a
voluptuous *adj* : voluptuoso
vomit *n* : vómito *m* — ~ *v* : vomitar
voracious *adj* : voraz
vote *n* **1** : voto *m* **2** SUFFRAGE : derecho *m* al voto — ~ *vi* **voted; voting** : votar — **voter** *n* : votante *mf* — **voting** *n* : votación *f*
vouch *vi* **~ for** : responder de (algo), responder por (algn) — **voucher** *n* : vale *m*
vow *n* : voto *m* — ~ *vt* : jurar
vowel *n* : vocal *m*
voyage *n* : viaje *m*
vulgar *adj* **1** COMMON : ordinario **2** CRUDE : grosero, vulgar — **vulgarity** *n, pl* **-ties** : vulgaridad *f*
vulnerable *adj* : vulnerable — **vulnerability** *n, pl* **-ties** : vulnerabilidad *f*
vulture *n* : buitre *m*
vying → **vie**

W

w *n, pl* **w's** *or* **ws** : w *f*, vigésima tercera letra del alfabeto inglés
wad *n* : taco *m* (de papel, etc.), fajo *m* (de billetes)
waddle *vi* **-dled; -dling** : andar como un pato
wade *v* **waded; wading** *vi* : caminar por el agua — *vt or* **~ across** : vadear
wafer *n* : barquillo *m*
waffle *n* : gofre *m Spain*, wafle *m Lat*
waft *vt* : llevar por el aire — *vi* : flotar
wag *v* **wagged; wagging** *vt* : menear — *vi* : menearse
wage *n or* **wages** *npl* : salario *m* — ~ *vt* **waged; waging** **~ war** : hacer la guerra
wager *n* : apuesta *f* — ~ *v* : apostar

wagon *n* **1** CART : carrito *m* **2** → **station wagon**
waif *n* : niño *m* abandonado
wail *vi* : lamentarse — ~ *n* : lamento *m*
waist *n* : cintura *f* — **waistline** *n* : cintura *f*
wait *vi* : esperar — *vt* **1** AWAIT : esperar **2 ~ tables** : servir a la mesa — ~ *n* **1** : espera *f* **2 lie in ~** : estar al acecho — **waiter** *n* : camarero *m*, mozo *m Lat* — **waiting room** *n* : sala *f* de espera — **waitress** *n* : camarera *f*, moza *f Lat*
waive *vt* **waived; waiving** : renunciar a — **waiver** *n* : renuncia *f*
wake[1] *v* **woke; woken** *or* **waked; waking** *vi*

or ~ **up** : despertarse — *vt* : despertar —
~ *n* : velatorio *m* (de un difunto)
wake² *n* **1** : estela *f* (de un barco) **2 in the**
~ **of** : tras, como consecuencia de
waken *vt* : despertar — *vi* : despertarse
walk *vi* **1** : caminar, andar **2** STROLL : pasear **3 too far to** ~ : demasiado lejos para
ir a pie — *vt* **1** : caminar por **2** : sacar a
pasear (a un perro) — ~ *n* **1** : paseo *m* **2**
PATH : camino *m* **3** GAIT : andar *m* —
walker *n* **1** : paseante *mf* **2** HIKER : excursionista *mf* — **walking stick** *n* : bastón *m*
— **walkout** *n* STRIKE : huelga *f* — **walk out**
vi **1** STRIKE : declararse en huelga **2**
LEAVE : salir, irse **3** ~ **on** : abandonar
wall *n* : muro *m* (exterior), pared *f* (interior),
muralla *f* (de una ciudad)
wallet *n* : billetera *f*, cartera *f*
wallflower *n* **be a** ~ : comer pavo
wallop *vt* : pegar fuerte — ~ *n* : golpe *m*
fuerte
wallow *vi* : revolcarse
wallpaper *n* : papel *m* pintado — ~ *vt* : empapelar
walnut *n* : nuez *f*
walrus *n*, *pl* **-rus** *or* **-ruses** : morsa *f*
waltz *n* : vals *m* — ~ *vi* : valsar
wan *adj* **wanner; -est** : pálido
wand *n* : varita *f* (mágica)
wander *vi* **1** : vagar, pasear **2** STRAY : divagar — *vt* : pasear por — **wanderer** *n*
: vagabundo *m*, -da *f* — **wanderlust** *n* : pasión *f* por viajar
wane *vi* **waned; waning** : menguar — ~ *n*
be on the ~ : estar disminuyendo
want *vt* **1** DESIRE : querer **2** NEED : necesitar **3** LACK : carecer de — ~ *n* **1** NEED
: necesidad *f* **2** LACK : falta *f* **3** DESIRE
: deseo *m* — **wanting** *adj* **be** ~ : carecer
wanton *adj* **1** LEWD : lascivo **2** ~ **cruelty**
: crueldad *f* despiadada
war *n* : guerra *f*
ward *n* **1** : sala *f* (de un hospital, etc.) **2**
: distrito *m* electoral **3** : pupilo *m*, **-la** *f* (de
un tutor, etc.) — ~ *vt* ~ **off** : protegerse
contra — **warden** *n* **1** : guardián *m*, -diana
f **2** *or* **game** ~ : guardabosque *mf* **3** *or*
prison ~ : alcaide *m*
wardrobe *n* **1** CLOSET : armario *m* **2**
CLOTHES : vestuario *m*
warehouse *n* : almacén *m*, bodega *f* *Lat* —
wares *npl* : mercancías *fpl*
warfare *n* : guerra *f*
warily *adv* : cautelosamente
warlike *adj* : belicoso
warm *adj* **1** : caliente **2** LUKEWARM : tibio
3 CARING : cariñoso **4 I feel** ~ : tengo
calor **5** ~ **clothes** : ropa *f* de abrigo — ~
vt or ~ **up** : calentar — *vi* **1** *or* ~ **up**

: calentarse **2** ~ **to** : tomar simpatía a
(algn), entusiasmarse con (algo) — **warm-
blooded** *adj* : de sangre caliente — **warm-
hearted** *adj* : cariñoso — **warmly** *adv* **1**
: calurosamente **2 dress** ~ : abrigarse —
warmth *n* **1** : calor *m* **2** AFFECTION
: cariño *m*, afecto *m*
warn *vt* : advertir, avisar— **warning** *n* : advertencia *f*, aviso *m*
warp *vt* **1** : alabear (madera, etc.) **2** DISTORT : deformar — *vi* : alabearse
warrant *n* **1** : autorización *f* **2 arrest** ~
: orden *f* judicial — ~ *vt* : justificar — **warranty** *n*, *pl* **-ties** : garantía *f*
warrior *n* : guerrero *m*, -ra *f*
warship *n* : buque *m* de guerra
wart *n* : verruga *f*
wartime *n* : tiempo *m* de guerra
wary *adj* **warier; -est** : cauteloso
was → **be**
wash *vt* **1** : lavar(se) **2** CARRY : arrastrar
3 ~ **away** : llevarse **4** ~ **over** : bañar —
vi : lavarse — ~ *n* **1** : lavado *m* **2** LAUNDRY : ropa *f* sucia — **washable** *adj* : lavable
— **washcloth** *n* : toallita *f* (para lavarse) —
washed–out *adj* **1** : desvaído (dícese de
colores) **2** EXHAUSTED : agotado —
washer *n* **1** → **washing machine 2**
: arandela *f* (de una llave, etc.) — **washing
machine** *n* : máquina *f* de lavar, lavadora *f*
— **washroom** *n* : servicios *mpl* (públicos),
baño *m*
wasn't (*contraction of* **was not**) → **be**
wasp *n* : avispa *f*
waste *v* **wasted; wasting** *vt* **1** : desperdiciar, derrochar, malgastar **2** ~ **time**
: perder tiempo — *vi or* ~ **away** : consumirse — ~ *adj* : de desecho — ~ *n* **1** : derroche *m*, desperdicio *m* **2** RUBBISH
: desechos *mpl* **3 a** ~ **of time** : una pérdida de tiempo — **wastebasket** *n* : papelera *f* — **wasteful** *adj* : derrochador —
wasteland *n* : yermo *m*
watch *vi* **1** : mirar **2** *or* **keep** ~ : velar **3**
~ **out!** : ¡ten cuidado!, ¡ojo! — *vt* **1**: mirar
2 *or* ~ **over** : vigilar, cuidar **3** ~ **what
you do** : ten cuidado con lo que haces — ~
n **1** reloj *m* **2** SURVEILLANCE : vigilancia *f*
3 LOOKOUT : guardia *mf* — **watchdog** *n*
: perro *m* guardián — **watchful** *adj* : vigilante — **watchman** *n*, *pl* **-men** : vigilante
m, guarda *m* — **watchword** *n* : santo *m* y
seña
water *n* : agua *f* — ~ *vt* **1** : regar (el jardín,
etc.) **2** ~ **down** DILUTE : diluir, aguar —
vi **1** : lagrimear (dícese de los ojos) **2 my
mouth is** ~**ing** : se me hace agua la boca
— **watercolor** *n* : acuarela *f* — **watercress**
n : berro *m* — **waterfall** *n* : cascada *f*, salto
m de agua — **water lily** *n* : nenúfar *m* — **wa-**

terlogged *adj* : lleno de agua, empapado — **watermelon** *n* : sandía *f* — **waterpower** *n* : energía *f* hidráulica — **waterproof** *adj* : impermeable — **watershed** *n* 1 : cuenca *f* (de un río) 2 : momento *m* crítico — **waterskiing** *n* : esquí *m* acuático — **watertight** *adj* : hermético — **waterway** *n* : vía *f* navegable — **waterworks** *npl* : central *f* de abastecimiento de agua — **watery** *adj* 1 : acuoso 2 DILUTED : aguado, diluido 3 WASHED-OUT : desvaído (dícese de colores)

watt *n* : vatio *m* — **wattage** *n* : vataje *m*

wave *v* **waved; waving** *vi* 1 : saludar con la mano 2 : flotar (dícese de una bandera) — *vt* 1 SHAKE : agitar 2 CURL : ondular 3 SIGNAL : hacer señas a (con la mano) — ~ *n* 1 : ola *f* (de agua) 2 CURL : onda *f* 3 : onda *f* (en física) 4 : señal *f* (con la mano) 5 SURGE : oleada *f* — **wavelength** *n* : longitud *f* de onda

waver *vi* : vacilar

wax¹ *vi* : crecer (dícese de la luna)

wax² *n* : cera *f* (para pisos, etc.) — ~ *vt* : encerar — **waxy** *adj* **waxier; -est** : ceroso

way *n* 1 : camino *m* 2 MEANS : manera *f*, modo *m* 3 **by the** ~ : a propósito, por cierto 4 **by** ~ **of** : vía, pasando por 5 **come a long** ~ : hacer grandes progresos 6 **get in the** ~ : meterse en el camino 7 **get one's own** ~ : salirse uno con la suya 8 **mend one's** ~**s** : dejar las malas costumbres 9 **out of the** ~ REMOTE : remoto, recóndito 10 **which** ~ **did he go?** : ¿por dónde fue?

we *pron* : nosotros, nosotras

weak *adj* 1 : débil 2 DILUTED : aguado 3 **a** ~ **excuse** : una excusa poco convincente — **weaken** *vt* : debilitar — *vi* : debilitarse — **weakling** *n* : debilucho *m*, -cha *f* — **weakly** *adv* : débilmente — ~ *adj* **weaklier; -est** : enfermizo — **weakness** *n* 1 : debilidad *f* 2 FLAW : flaqueza *f*, punto *m* débil

wealth *n* : riqueza *f* — **wealthy** *adj* **wealthier; -est** : rico

wean *vt* : destetar

weapon *n* : arma *f*

wear *v* **wore; worn; wearing** *vt* 1 : llevar (ropa, etc.), calzar (zapatos) 2 *or* ~ **away** : desgastar 3 ~ **oneself out** : agotarse 4 ~ **out** : gastar — *vi* 1 LAST : durar 2 ~ **off** : desaparecer 3 ~ **out** : gastarse — ~ *n* 1 USE : uso *m* 2 CLOTHING : ropa *f* 3 **be the worse for** ~ : estar deteriorado — **wear and tear** *n* : desgaste *m*

weary *adj* **-rier; -est** : cansado — ~ *v* **-ried; -rying** *vt* : cansar — *vi* : cansarse — **weariness** *n* : cansancio *m* — **wearisome** *adj* : cansado

weasel *n* : comadreja *f*

weather *n* : tiempo *m* — ~ *vt* 1 WEAR : erosionar, desgastar 2 ENDURE, OVERCOME : superar — **weather–beaten** *adj* : curtido — **weatherman** *n, pl* **-men** : meteorólogo *m*, -ga *f* — **weather vane** *n* : valeta *f*

weave *v* **wove** *or* **weaved; woven** *or* **weaved; weaving** *vt* 1 : tejer (tela) 2 INTERLACE : entretejer 3 ~ **one's way** : abrirse camino — *vi* : tejer — ~ *n* : tejido *m* — **weaver** *n* : tejedor *m*, -dora *f*

web *n* 1 : telaraña *f* (de araña) 2 : membrana *f* interdigital (de aves) 3 NETWORK : red *f*

web browser *n* : navegador *m*

webcam *n* : webcam *f*

webmaster *n* : webmaster *mf*

Web page *n* : página *f* web

wed *v* **wedded; wedding** *vt* : casarse con — *vi* : casarse

we'd (*contraction of* **we had, we should,** *or* **we would**) → **have, should, would**

wedding *n* : boda *f*, casamiento *m*

wedge *n* 1 : cuña *f* 2 PIECE : porción *f*, trozo *m* — ~ *vt* **wedged; wedging** 1 : apretar (con una cuña) 2 CRAM : meter

Wednesday *n* : miércoles *m*

wee *adj* 1 : pequeñito 2 **in the** ~ **hours** : a las altas horas

weed *n* : mala hierba *f* — ~ *vt* 1 : desherbar 2 ~ **out** : eliminar

week *n* : semana *f* — **weekday** *n* : día *m* laborable — **weekend** *n* : fin *m* de semana — **weekly** *adv* : semanalmente — ~ *adj* : semanal — ~ *n, pl* **-lies** : semanario *m*

weep *v* **wept; weeping** : llorar — **weeping willow** *n* : sauce *m* llorón — **weepy** *adj* **weepier; -est** : lloroso

weigh *vt* 1 : pesar 2 CONSIDER : sopesar 3 ~ **down** : sobrecargar (con una carga), abrumar (con preocupaciones, etc.) — *vi* : pesar

weight *n* 1 : peso *m* 2 **gain** ~ : engordar 3 **lose** ~ : adelgazar — **weighty** *adj* **weightier; -est** 1 HEAVY : pesado 2 IMPORTANT : importante, de peso

weird *adj* 1 : misterioso 2 STRANGE : extraño

welcome *vt* **-comed; -coming** : dar la bienvenida a, recibir — ~ *adj* 1 : bienvenido 2 **you're** ~ : de nada — ~ *n* : bienvenida *f*, acojida *f*

weld *v* : soldar

welfare *n* 1 WELL-BEING : bienestar *m* 2 AID : asistencia *f* social

well¹ *adv* **better; best** 1 : bien 2 CONSIDERABLY : bastante 3 **as** ~ : también 4 **as** ~ **as** : además de — ~ *adj* : bien — ~ *interj* 1 (*used to introduce a remark*)

: bueno **2** (*used to express surprise*)
: ¡vaya!

well² *n* : pozo *m* — ∼ *vi or* ∼ up : brotar,
manar

we'll (*contraction of* **we shall** *or* **we will**) →
shall, will

well–being *n* : bienestar *m* — **well–bred** *adj*
: fino, bien educado — **well–done** *adj* **1**
: bien hecho **2** : bien cocido (dícese de la
carne, etc.) — **well–known** *adj* : famoso,
bien conocido — **well–meaning** *adj* : bienintencionado — **well–off** *adj* : acomodado
— **well–rounded** *adj* : completo — **well-
to– do** *adj* : próspero, adinerado

Welsh *adj* : galés — ∼ *n* **1** : galés *m*
(idioma) **2 the** ∼ : los galeses

went → **go**

wept → **weep**

were → **be**

we're (*contraction of* **we are**) → **be**

weren't (*contraction of* **were not**) → **be**

west *adv* : al oeste — ∼ *adj* : oeste, del
oeste — ∼ *n* **1** : oeste *m* **2 the West** : el
Oeste, el Occidente — **westerly** *adv & adj*
: del oeste — **western** *adj* **1** : del oeste **2**
Western : occidental — **Westerner** *n* : habitante *mf* del oeste — **westward** *adv & adj*
: hacia el oeste

wet *adj* **wetter; wettest 1** : mojado **2**
RAINY : lluvioso **3** ∼ **paint** : pintura *f*
fresca — ∼ *vt* **wet** *or* **wetted; wetting**
: mojar, humedecer

we've (*contraction of* **we have**) → **have**

whack *vt* : golpear fuertemente — ∼ *n*
: golpe *m* fuerte

whale *n, pl* **whales** *or* **whale** : ballena *f*

wharf *n, pl* **wharves** : muelle *m*, embarcadero *m*

what *adj* **1** (*used in questions and exclamations*) : qué **2** WHATEVER : cualquier — ∼
pron **1** (*used in questions*) : qué **2** (*used in
indirect statements*) : lo que, que **3** ∼
does it cost? : ¿cuánto cuesta? **4** ∼ **for?**
: ¿por qué? **5** ∼ **if** : y si — **whatever** *adj*
1 : cualquier **2 there's no chance** ∼ : no
hay ninguna posibilidad **3 nothing** ∼
: nada en absoluto — ∼ *pron* **1** ANYTHING
: lo que **2** (*used in questions*) : qué **3** ∼
it may be : sea lo que sea — **whatsoever**
adj & pron → **whatever**

wheat *n* : trigo *m*

wheedle *vt* -**dled; -dling** : engatusar

wheel *n* **1** : rueda *f* **2** *or* **steering** ∼ : volante *m* (de automóviles, etc.), timón *m* (de
barcos) — ∼ *vt* : empujar (algo sobre ruedas) — *vi or* ∼ **around** : darse la vuelta
— **wheelbarrow** *n* : carretilla *f* — **wheelchair** *n* : silla *f* de ruedas

wheeze *vi* **wheezed; wheezing** : resollar —
∼ *n* : resuello *m*

when *adv* : cuándo — ∼ *conj* **1** : cuando
2 the days ∼ **I clean the house** : los días
(en) que limpio la casa — ∼ *pron* : cuándo
— **whenever** *adv* : cuando sea — ∼ *conj*
1 : cada vez que **2** ∼ **you like** : cuando
quieras

where *adv* **1** : dónde **2** ∼ **are you going?**
: ¿adónde vas? — ∼ *conj & pron* : donde
— **whereabouts** *adv* : (por) dónde — ∼ *ns*
& pl : paradero *m* — **wherever** *adv* **1** : en
cualquier parte **2** WHERE : dónde, adónde
— ∼ *conj* : dondequiera que

whet *vt* **whetted; whetting 1** : afilar **2** ∼
the appetite : estimular el apetito

whether *conj* **1** : si **2 we doubt** ∼ **he'll**
show up : dudamos que aparezca **3** ∼
you like it or not : tanto si quieras como si
no

which *adj* **1** : qué, cuál **2 in** ∼ **case** : en
cuyo caso — ∼ *pron* **1** (*used in questions*)
: cuál **2** (*used in relative clauses*) : que, el
(la) cual — **whichever** *adj* : cualquier — ∼
pron : el (la) que, cualquiera que

whiff *n* **1** PUFF : soplo *m* **2** SMELL : olor-
cillo *m*

while *n* **1** : rato *m* **2 be worth one's** ∼
: valer la pena **3 in a** ∼ : dentro de poco
— ∼ *conj* **1** : mientras **2** WHEREAS
: mientras que **3** ALTHOUGH : aunque —
∼ *vt* **whiled; whiling** ∼ **away the time**
: matar el tiempo

whim *n* : capricho *m*, antojo *m*

whimper *vi* : lloriquear— ∼ *n* : quejido *m*

whimsical *adj* : caprichoso, fantasioso

whine *vi* **whined; whining 1** : gimotear **2**
COMPLAIN : quejarse — ∼ *n* : quejido *m*,
gemido *m*

whip *v* **whipped; whipping** *vt* **1** : azotar **2**
BEAT : batir (huevos, crema, etc.) **3** ∼ **up**
AROUSE : avivar, despertar — *vi* FLAP : agi-
tarse — ∼ *n* : látigo *m*

whir *vi* **whirred; whirring** : zumbar — ∼ *n*
: zumbido *m*

whirl *vi* **1** : dar vueltas, girar **2** *or* ∼
about : arremolinarse — ∼ *n* **1** : giro *m*
2 SWIRL : torbellino *m* — **whirlpool** *n* : remolino *m* — **whirlwind** *n* : torbellino *m*

whisk *vt* **1** : batir **2** ∼ **away** : llevarse —
∼ *n or* **egg** ∼ : batidor *m* — **whisk broom**
n : escobilla *f*

whisker *n* **1** : pelo *m* (de la barba) **2** ∼**s**
npl : bigotes *mpl* (de animales)

whiskey *or* **whisky** *n, pl* -**keys** *or* -**kies**
: whisky *m*

whisper *vi* : cuchichear, susurrar — *vt* : susurrar — ∼ *n* : susurro *m*

whistle *v* -**tled; -tling** *vi* **1** : silbar, chiflar
Lat **2** : pitar (dícese de un tren, etc.) — *vt*
: silbar — ∼ *n* **1** : silbido *m*, chiflido *m*
(sonido) **2** : silbato *m*, pito *m* (instrumento)

white *adj* **whiter; -est** : blanco — ~ *n* **1**
: blanco *m* (color) **2** : clara *f* (de huevos) **3**
or ~ **person** : blanco *m*, -ca *f* — **white-
collar** *adj* **1** : de oficina **2** ~ **worker**
: oficinista *mf* — **whiten** *vt* : blanquear —
whiteness *n* : blancura *f* — **whitewash** *vt*
1 : enjalbegar **2** CONCEAL : encubrir (un
escándalo, etc.) — ~ *n* **1** : jalbegue *m*,
lechada *f* **2** COVER-UP : encubrimiento *m*
whittle *vt* **-tled; -tling** **1** : tallar (madera) **2**
or ~ **down** : reducir
whiz *or* **whizz** *vi* **whizzed; whizzing** **1**
BUZZ : zumbar **2** ~ **by** : pasar muy rápido
— ~ *or* **whizz** *n, pl* **whizzes** : zumbido *m*
— **whiz kid** *n* : joven *m* prometedor
who *pron* **1** (*used in direct and indirect
questions*) : quién **2** (*used in relative
clauses*) : que, quien — **whodunit** *n* : novela *f*
policíaca — **whoever** *pron* **1** : quienquiera
que, quien **2** (*used in questions*) : quién
whole *adj* **1** : entero **2** INTACT : intacto **3 a**
~ **lot** : muchísimo — ~ *n* **1** : todo *m* **2**
as a ~ : en conjunto **3 on the** ~ : en
general — **wholehearted** *adj* : sincero —
wholesale *n* : venta *f* al por mayor — ~
adj **1** : al por mayor **2** ~ **slaughter**
: matanza *f* sistemática — ~ *adv* : al por
mayor — **wholesaler** *n* : mayorista *mf* —
wholesome *adj* : sano — **whole wheat** *adj*
: de trigo integral — **wholly** *adv* : completamente
whom *pron* **1** (*used in direct questions*) : a
quién **2** (*used in indirect questions*) : de
quién, con quién, en quién **3** (*used in relative clauses*) : que, a quien
whooping cough *n* : tos *f* ferina
whore *n* : puta *f*
whose *adj* **1** (*used in questions*) : de quién
2 (*used in relative clauses*) : cuyo — ~
pron : de quién
why *adv* : por qué — ~ *n, pl* **whys** : porqué
m — ~ *conj* : por qué — ~ *interj* (*used to
express surprise*) : ¡vaya!, ¡mira!
wick *n* : mecha *f*
wicked *adj* **1** : malo, malvado **2** MISCHIE-
VOUS : travieso **3** TERRIBLE : terrible, horrible — **wickedness** *n* : maldad *f*
wicker *n* : mimbre *m* — ~ *adj* : de mimbre
wide *adj* **wider; widest** **1** : ancho **2** VAST
: amplio, extenso **3** *or* ~ **of the mark**
: desviado — ~ *adv* **1** ~ **apart** : muy
separados **2 far and** ~ : por todas partes
3 ~ **open** : abierto de par en par — **wide-
awake** *adj* : (completamente) despierto —
widely *adv* : extensivamente — **widespread** *adj* : extendido
widow *n* : viuda *f* — ~ *vt* : dejar viuda —
widower *n* : viudo *m*
width *n* : ancho *m*, anchura *f*
wield *vt* **1** : usar, manejar **2** EXERT : ejercer

wiener → **frankfurter**
wife *n, pl* **wives** : esposa *f*, mujer *f*
wig *n* : peluca *f*
wiggle *v* **-gled; -gling** *vt* : menear, contonear
— *vi* : menearse — ~ *n* : meneo *m*
wigwam *n* : wigwam *m*
wild *adj* **1** : salvaje **2** DESOLATE : agreste
3 UNRULY : desenfrenado **4** RANDOM : al
azar **5** FRANTIC : frenético **6** OUTRA-
GEOUS : extravagante — ~ *adv* **1** → **wildly**
2 run ~ : volver al estado silvestre (dícese
de las plantas), desmandarse (dícese de los
niños) — **wildcat** *n* : gato *m* montés — **wil-
derness** *n* : yermo *m*, desierto *m* — **wildfire** *n* **1** : fuego *m* descontrolado **2 spread
like** ~ : propagarse como un reguero de
pólvora — **wildflower** *n* : flor *f* silvestre —
wildlife *n* : fauna *f* — **wildly** *adv* **1** FRANTI-
CALLY : frenéticamente **2** EXTREMELY : locamente
will[1] *v past* **would**; *pres sing & pl* **will** *vi*
WISH : querer — *v aux* **1 tomorrow we** ~
go shopping : mañana iremos de compras
2 he ~ **get angry over nothing** : se pone
furioso por cualquier cosa **3 I** ~ **go despite them** : iré a pesar de ellos **4 I won't
do it** : no lo haré **5 that** ~ **be the mailman** : eso ha de ser el cartero **6 the couch**
~ **hold three people** : en el sofá cabrán
tres personas **7 accidents** ~ **happen**
: los accidentes ocurrirán **8 you** ~ **do as
I say** : harás lo que digo
will[2] *n* **1** : voluntad *f* **2** TESTAMENT : testamento *m* **3 free** ~ : libre albedrío *m* —
willful *or* **wilful** *adj* **1** OBSTINATE : terco **2**
INTENTIONAL : intencionado — **willing** *adj*
1 : complaciente **2 be** ~ **to** : estar dispuesto a — **willingly** *adv* : con gusto — **willingness** *n* : buena voluntad *f*
willow *n* : sauce *m*
willpower *n* : fuerza *f* de voluntad
wilt *vi* : marchitarse
wily *adj* **wilier; -est** : artero, astuto
win *v* **won; winning** *vi* : ganar — *vt* **1**
: ganar, conseguir **2** ~ **over** : ganarse a
— ~ *n* : triunfo *m*, victoria *f*
wince *vi* **winced; wincing** : hacer una
mueca de dolor — ~ *n* : mueca *f* de dolor
winch *n* : torno *m*
wind instrument *n* : instrumento *m* de viento
wind up *vt* : terminar, concluir — *vi* : terminar, acabar — **windup** *n* : conclusión *f*
wind[1] *n* **1** : viento *m* **2** BREATH : aliento *m*
3 FLATULENCE : flatulencia *f* **4 get** ~ **of**
: enterarse de
wind[2] *v* **wound; winding** *vi* : serpentear —
vt **1** COIL : enrollar **2** ~ **a clock** : dar
cuerda a un reloj
windfall *n* : beneficio *m* imprevisto
winding *adj* : tortuoso

windmill *n* : molino *m* de viento

window *n* : ventana *f* (de un edificio o una computadora), ventanilla *f* (de un vehículo), vitrina *f* (de una tienda) — **windowpane** *n* : vidrio *m* — **windowsill** *n* : repisa *f* de la ventana

window–shop *vi* -shopped; -shopping : mirar las vitrinas

windpipe *n* : tráquea *f*

windshield *n* **1** : parabrisas *m* **2 ~ wiper** : limpiaparabrisas *m*

windsurfing *n* : windsurf *m*

windy *adj* **windier; -est 1** : ventoso **2 it's ~** : hace viento

wine *n* : vino *m* — **wine cellar** *n* : bodega *f*

wing *n* **1** : ala *f* **2 under s.o.'s ~** : bajo el cargo de algn — **winged** *adj* : alado

wink *vi* : guiñar — **~** *n* **1** : guiño *m* **2 not sleep a ~** : no pegar el ojo

winner *n* : ganador *m*, -dora *f* — **winning** *adj* **1** : ganador **2** CHARMING : encantador — **winnings** *npl* : ganancias *fpl*

winter *n* : invierno *m* — **~** *adj* : invernal, de invierno — **wintergreen** *n* : gaulteria *f* — **wintertime** *n* : invierno *m* — **wintry** *adj* **wintrier; -est** : invernal, de invierno

wipe *vt* **wiped; wiping 1** : limpiar **2 ~ away** : enjugar (lágrimas), borrar (una memoria) **3 ~ out** : aniquilar, destruir — **~** *n* : pasada *f* (con un trapo, etc.)

wire *n* **1** : alambre *m* **2** : cable *m* (eléctrico o telefónico) **3** TELEGRAM : telegrama *m* — **~** *vt* **-wired; wiring 1** : instalar el cableado en (una casa, etc.) **2** BIND : atar con alambre **3** TELEGRAPH : enviar un telegrama a — **wireless** *adj* : inalámbrico — **wiring** *n* : cableado *m* — **wiry** *adj* **wirier; -est 1** : hirsuto, tieso (dícese del pelo) **2** : esbelto y musculoso (dícese del cuerpo)

wisdom *n* : sabiduría *f* — **wisdom tooth** *n* : muela *f* de juicio

wise *adj* **wiser; wisest 1** : sabio **2** SENSIBLE : prudente — **wisecrack** *n* : broma *f*, chiste *m* — **wisely** *adv* : sabiamente

wish *vt* **1** : desear **2 ~ s.o. well** : desear lo mejor a algn — *vi* **1** : pedir (como deseo) **2 as you ~** : como quieras — **~** *n* **1** : deseo *m* **2 best ~es** : muchos recuerdos — **wishbone** *n* : espoleta *f* — **wishful** *adj* **1** : deseoso **2 ~ thinking** : ilusiones *fpl*

wishy–washy *adj* : insípido, soso

wisp *n* **1** : mechón *m* (de pelo) **2** : voluta *f* (de humo)

wistful *adj* : melancólico

wit *n* **1** CLEVERNESS : ingenio *m* **2** HUMOR : agudeza *f* **3 at one's ~'s end** : desesperado **4 scared out of one's ~s** : muerto de miedo

witch *n* : bruja *f* — **witchcraft** *n* : brujería *f*, hechicería *f*

with *prep* **1** : con **2 I'm going ~ you** : voy contigo **3 it varies ~ the season** : varía según la estación **4 the girl ~ red hair** : la muchacha de pelo rojo **5 ~ all his work, the business failed** : a pesar de su trabajo, el negocio fracasó

withdraw *v* **-drew; -drawn; -drawing** *vt* : retirar — *vi* : apartarse — **withdrawal** *n* **1** : retirada *f* **2** : abandono (de drogas, etc.) — **withdrawn** *adj* : introvertido

wither *vi* : marchitarse

withhold *vt* **-held; -holding** : retener (fondos), negar (permiso, etc.)

within *adv* : dentro — **~** *prep* **1** : dentro de **2** (*in expressions of distance*) : a menos de **3** (*in expressions of time*) : dentro de, en menos de **4 ~ reach** : al alcance de la mano

without *adv* **do ~** : pasar sin algo — **~** *prep* : sin

withstand *vt* **-stood; -standing 1** BEAR : aguantar **2** RESIST : resistir

witness *n* **1** : testigo *mf* **2** EVIDENCE : testimonio *m* **3 bear ~** : atestiguar — **~** *vt* **1** SEE : ser testigo de **2** : atestiguar (una firma, etc.)

witticism *n* : agudeza *f*, ocurrencia *f*

witty *adj* **-tier; -est** : ingenioso, ocurrente

wives → wife

wizard *n* **1** : mago *m*, brujo *m* **2 a math ~** : un genio de matemáticas

wizened *adj* : arrugado

wobble *vi* **-bled; -bling 1** : tambalearse **2** : temblar (dícese de la voz, etc.) — **wobbly** *adj* : cojo

woe *n* **1** : aflicción *f* **2 ~s** *npl* TROUBLES : penas *fpl* — **woeful** *adj* : triste

woke, woken → wake

wolf *n*, *pl* **wolves** : lobo *m*, -ba *f* — **~** *vt or* **~ down** : engullir

woman *n*, *pl* **women** : mujer *f* — **womanly** *adj* : femenino

womb *n* : útero *m*, matriz *f*

won → win

wonder *n* **1** MARVEL : maravilla *f* **2** AMAZEMENT : asombro *m* — **~** *v* : preguntarse — **wonderful** *adj* : maravilloso, estupendo

won't (*contraction of* **will not**) **→ will**

woo *vt* **1** COURT : cortejar **2** : buscar el apoyo de (clientes, votantes, etc.)

wood *n* **1** : madera *f* (materia) **2** FIREWOOD : leña *f* **3** *or* **~s** *npl* FOREST : bosque *m* — **~** *adj* : de madera — **woodchuck** *n* : marmota *f* de América — **wooded** *adj* : arbolado, boscoso — **wooden** *adj* : de madera — **woodpecker** *n* : pájaro *m* carpintero — **woodshed** *n* : leñera *f* — **woodwind** *n* : instrumento *m* de viento de madera — **woodwork** *n* : carpintería *f*

wool *n* : lana *f* — **woolen** *or* **woollen** *adj* : de lana — ~ *n* **1** : lana *f* (tela) **2** ~**s** *npl* : prendas *fpl* de lana — **woolly** *adj* **-lier; -est** : lanudo

word *n* **1** : palabra *f* **2** NEWS : noticias *fpl* **3** ~**s** *npl* : letra *f* (de una canción, etc.) **4 have** ~**s with** : reñir con **5 just say the** ~ : no tienes que decirlo **6 keep one's** ~ : cumplir su palabra — ~ *vt* : expresar — **word processing** *n* : procesamiento *m* de textos — **word processor** *n* : procesador *m* de textos — **wordy** *adj* **wordier; -est** : prolijo

wore → **wear**

work *n* **1** LABOR : trabajo *m* **2** EMPLOY-MENT : trabajo *m*, empleo *m* **3** : obra *f* (de arte, etc.) **4** ~**s** *npl* FACTORY : fábrica *f* **5** ~**s** *npl* MECHANISM : mecanismo *m* — ~ *v* **worked** *or* **wrought; working** *vt* **1** : hacer trabajar (a una persona) **2** : manejar, operar (una máquina, etc.) — *vi* **1** : trabajar **2** FUNCTION : funcionar **3** : surtir efecto (dícese de una droga), resultar (dícese de una idea, etc.) — **worked up** *adj* : nervioso — **worker** *n* : trabajador *m*, -dora *f*; obrero *m*, -ra *f* — **working** *adj* **1** : que trabaja (dícese de personas), de trabajo (dícese de la ropa, etc.) **2 be in** ~ **order** : funcionar bien — **working class** *n* : clase *f* obrera — **workingman** *n, pl* **-men** : obrero *m* — **workman** *n, pl* **-men** **1** : obrero *m* **2** ARTISAN : artesano *m* — **workmanship** *n* : artesanía *f*, destreza *f* — **workout** *n* : ejercicios *mpl* (físicos) — **work out** *vt* **1** DE-VELOP : elaborar **2** SOLVE : resolver — *vi* **1** TURN OUT : resultar **2** SUCCEED : lograr, salir bien **3** EXERCISE : hacer ejercicio — **workshop** *n* : taller *m* — **work up** *vt* **1** EXCITE : ponerse como loco **2** GENERATE : desarrollar

world *n* : mundo *m* **2 think the** ~ **of s.o.** : tener a algn en alta estima — ~ *adj* : mundial, del mundo — **worldly** *adj* : mundano — **worldwide** *adv* : en todo el mundo — ~ *adj* : global, mundial

worm *n* **1** : gusano *m*, lombriz *f* **2** ~**s** *npl* : lombrices *fpl* (parásitos)

worn → **wear** — **worn-out** *adj* **1** USED : gastado **2** TIRED : agotado

worry *v* **-ried; -rying** *vt* : preocupar, inquietar — *vi* : preocuparse, inquietarse — ~ *n, pl* **-ries** : preocupación *f* — **worried** *adj* : preocupado — **worrisome** *adj* : inquietante

worse *adv* (*comparative of* **bad** *or of* **ill**) : peor — ~ *adj* (*comparative of* **bad** *or of* **ill**) **1** : peor **2 from bad to** ~ : de mal en peor **3 get** ~ : empeorar — ~ *n* **1 the** ~ : el (la) peor, lo peor **2 take a turn for the** ~ : ponerse peor — **worsen** *v* : empeorar

worship *v* **-shiped** *or* **-shipped; -shiping** *or* **-shipping** *vt* : adorar — *vi* : practicar una religión — ~ *n* : adoración *f*, culto *m* — **worshiper** *or* **worshipper** *n* : adorador *m*, -dora *f*

worst *adv* (*superlative of* **ill** *or of* **bad** *or* **badly**) : peor — ~ *adj* (*superlative of* **bad** *or of* **ill**) : peor — ~ *n* **the** ~ : lo peor, el (la) peor

worth *n* **1** : valor *m* (monetario) **2** MERIT : mérito *m*, valía *f* **3 ten dollars'** ~ **of gas** : diez dólares de gasolina — ~ *prep* **1 it's** ~ **$ 10** : vale $ 10 **2 it's** ~ **doing** : vale la pena hacerlo — **worthless** *adj* **1** : sin valor **2** USELESS : inútil — **worthwhile** *adj* : que vale la pena — **worthy** *adj* **-thier; -est** : digno

would *past of* **will** **1 he** ~ **often take his children to the park** : solía llevar a sus hijos al parque **2 I** ~ **go if I had the money** : iría yo si tuviera el dinero **3 I** ~ **rather go alone** : preferiría ir sola **4 she** ~ **have won if she hadn't tripped** : habría ganado si no hubiera tropezado **5** ~ **you kindly help me with this?** : ¿tendría la bondad de ayudarme con esto? — **would-be** *adj* **a** ~ **poet** : un aspirante a poeta — **wouldn't** (*contraction of* **would not**) → **would**

wound¹ *n* : herida *f* — ~ *vt* : herir

wound² → **wind**

wove, woven → **weave**

wrangle *vi* **-gled; -gling** : reñir — ~ *n* : riña *f*, disputa *f*

wrap *vt* **wrapped; wrapping** **1** : envolver **2** ~ **up** FINISH : dar fin a — ~ *n* **1** : prenda *f* que envuelve (como un chal) **2** WRAPPER : envoltura *f* — **wrapper** *n* : envoltura *f*, envoltorio *m* — **wrapping** *n* : envoltura *f*, envoltorio *m*

wrath *n* : ira *f*, cólera *f* — **wrathful** *adj* : iracundo

wreath *n, pl* **wreaths** : corona *f* (de flores, etc.)

wreck *n* **1** WRECKAGE : restos *mpl* **2** RUIN : ruina *f*, desastre *m* **3 be a nervous** ~ : tener los nervios destrozados — ~ *vt* : destrozar (un automóvil), naufragar (un barco) — **wreckage** *n* : restos *mpl* (de un buque naufragado, etc.), ruinas *fpl* (de un edificio)

wren *n* : chochín *m*

wrench *vt* **1** PULL : arrancar (de un tirón) **2** SPRAIN, TWIST : torcerse — ~ *n* **1** TUG : tirón *m*, jalón *m* **2** SPRAIN : torcedura *f* **3** *or* **monkey** ~ : llave *f* inglesa

wrestle *vi* **-tled; -tling** : luchar — **wrestler** *n* : luchador *m*, -dora *f* — **wrestling** *n* : lucha *f*

wretch *n* : desgraciado *m*, -da *f* — **wretched** *adj* **1** : miserable **2** ~ **weather** : tiempo *m* espantoso

wriggle *vi* **-gled; -gling** : retorcerse, menearse

wring *vt* **wrung; wringing 1** *or* ~ **out** : escurrir (el lavado, etc.) **2** TWIST : retorcer **3** EXTRACT : arrancar (información, etc.)

wrinkle *n* : arruga *f* — ~ *v* **-kled; -kling** *vt* : arrugar — *vi* : arrugarse

wrist *n* : muñeca *f* — **wristwatch** *n* : reloj *m* de pulsera

writ *n* : orden *f* (judicial)

write *v* **wrote; written; writing** : escribir —

write down *vt* : apuntar, anotar — **write off** *vt* CANCEL : cancelar — **writer** *n* : escritor *m*, -tora *f*

writhe *vi* **writhed; writhing** : retorcerse

writing *n* : escritura *f*

wrong *n* **1** INJUSTICE : injusticia *f*, mal *m* **2** : agravio *m* (en derecho) **3 be in the** ~ : haber hecho mal — ~ *adj* **wronger; wrongest 1** : malo **2** UNSUITABLE : inadecuado, inapropiado **3** INCORRECT : incorrecto, equivocado **4 be** ~ : no tener razón — ~ *adv* : mal, incorrectamente — ~ *vt* **wronged; wronging** : ofender, ser injusto con — **wrongful** *adj* **1** UNJUST : injusto **2** UNLAWFUL : ilegal — **wrongly** *adv* **1** UNJUSTLY : injustamente **2** INCORRECTLY : mal

wrote → **write**

wrought iron *n* : hierro *m* forjado

wrung → **wring**

wry *adj* **wrier; wriest** : irónico, sardónico (dícese del humor)

XYZ

x *n, pl* **x's** *or* **xs** : x *f*, vigésima cuarta letra del alfabeto inglés

X ray *n* **1** : rayo *m* X **2** *or* ~ **photograph** : radiografía *f* — **x–ray** *vt* : radiografiar

xenophobia *n* : xenofobia *f*

Xmas *n* : Navidad *f*

xylophone *n* : xilófono *m*

y *n, pl* **y's** *or* **ys** : y *f*, vigésima quinta letra del alfabeto inglés

yacht *n* : yate *m*

yam *n* **1** : ñame *m* **2** SWEET POTATO : batata *f*, boniato *m*

yank *vt* : tirar de, jalar *Lat* — ~ *n* : tirón *m*, jalón *m Lat*

Yankee *n* : yanqui *mf*

yap *vi* **yapped; yapping** : ladrar — ~ *n* : ladrido *m*

yard *n* **1** : yarda *f* (medida) **2** COURTYARD : patio *m* **3** : jardín *m* (de una casa) — **yardstick** *n* **1** : vara *f* (de medir) **2** CRITERION : criterio *m*

yarn *n* **1** : hilado *m* **2** TALE : historia *f*, cuento *m*

yawn *vi* : bostezar — ~ *n* : bostezo *m*

year *n* **1** : año *m* **2 she's ten** ~**s old** : tiene diez años **3 I haven't seen them in** ~**s** : hace siglos que no los veo — **yearbook** *n* : anuario *m* — **yearling** *n* : animal *m* menor de dos años — **yearly** *adv* **1** : anualmente **2 three times** ~ : tres veces al año — ~ *adj* : anual

yearn *vi* : anhelar — **yearning** *n* : anhelo *m*, ansia *f*

yeast *n* : levadura *f*

yell *vi* : gritar, chillar — *vt* : gritar — ~ *n* : grito *m*, chillido *m*

yellow *adj* : amarillo — ~ *n* : amarillo *m* — **yellowish** *adj* : amarillento

yelp *n* : gañido *m* — ~ *vi* : dar un gañido

yes *adv* **1** : sí **2 say** ~ : decir que sí — ~ *n* : sí *m*

yesterday *adv* : ayer — ~ *n* **1** : ayer *m* **2 the day before** ~ : anteayer

yet *adv* **1** : aún, todavía **2 has he come** ~? : ¿ya ha venido? **3 not** ~ : todavía no **4** ~ **more problems** : más problemas aún **5** NEVERTHELESS : sin embargo — ~ *conj* : pero

yield *vt* **1** PRODUCE : producir **2** ~ **the right of way** : ceder el paso — *vi* : ceder — ~ *n* : rendimiento *m*, rédito *m* (en finanzas)

yoga *n* : yoga *m*

yogurt *n* : yogur *m*, yogurt *m*

yoke *n* : yugo *m*

yolk *n* : yema *f* (de un huevo)

you're (*contraction of* **you are**) → **be**

you've (*contraction of* **you have**) → **have**

you *pron* **1** (*used as subject—familiar*) : tú; vos (*in some Latin American countries*); ustedes *pl;* vosotros, vosotras *pl Spain* **2** (*used as subject—formal*) : usted, ustedes *pl* **3** (*used as indirect object—familiar*) : te, les *pl* (se *before* lo, la, los, las), os *pl Spain* **4** (*used as indirect object—formal*) : lo (*Spain sometimes* le), la; los (*Spain sometimes* les), las *pl* **5** (*used after a preposition—familiar*) : ti; vos (*in some Latin American countries*); ustedes *pl;* vosotros, vosotras *pl Spain* **6** (*used after a preposition—formal*) : usted, ustedes *pl* **7** *with* ~ (*familiar*) : contigo; con ustedes *pl;* con vosotros, con vosotras *pl Spain* **8** *with* ~ (*formal*) : con usted, con ustedes *pl* **9** ~ **never know** : nunca se sabe — **you'd** (*contraction of* **you had** *or* **you would**) → **have**, **would** — **you'll** (*contraction of* **you shall** *or* **you will**) → **shall, will**

young *adj* **younger; youngest 1** : joven **2** **my** ~**er brother** : mi hermano menor **3** **she is the** ~**est** : es la más pequeña **4** **the** ~ : los jóvenes — ~ *npl* : jóvenes *mfpl* (de los humanos), crías *fpl* (de los animales) — **youngster** *n* : chico *m*, -ca *f;* joven *mf*

your *adj* **1** (*familiar singular*) : tu **2** (*familiar plural*) : su, vuestro *Spain* **3** (*formal*) : su **4** **on** ~ **left** : a la izquierda

yours *pron* **1** (*belonging to one person—familiar*) : (el) tuyo, (la) tuya, (los) tuyos, (las) tuyas **2** (*belonging to more than one person—familiar*) : (el) suyo, (la) suya, (los) suyos, (las) suyas; (el) vuestro, (la) vuestra, (los) vuestros, (las) vuestras *Spain* **3** (*formal*) : (el) suyo, (la) suya, (los) suyos, (las) suyas

yourself *pron, pl* **yourselves 1** (*used reflexively—familiar*) : te, se *pl,* os *pl Spain* **2** (*used reflexively—formal*) : se **3** (*used for emphasis*) : tú mismo, tú misma; usted mismo, usted misma; ustedes mismos, ustedes mismas *pl;* vosotros mismos, vosotras mismas *pl Spain*

youth *n, pl* **youths 1** : juventud *f* **2** BOY : joven *m* **3** **today's** ~ : los jóvenes de hoy — **youthful** *adj* **1** : juvenil, de juventud **2** YOUNG : joven

yowl *vi* : aullar — ~ *n* : aullido *m*

yucca *n* : yuca *f*

Yugoslavian *adj* : yugoslavo

yule *n* CHRISTMAS : Navidad *f* — **yuletide** *n* : Navidades *fpl*

z *n, pl* **z's** *or* **zs** : z *f,* vigésima sexta letra del alfabeto inglés

zany *adj* **-nier; -est** : alocado, disparatado

zeal *n* : fervor *m*, celo *m* — **zealous** *adj* : entusiasta

zebra *n* : cebra *f*

zenith *n* **1** : cenit *m* (en astronomía) **2** PEAK : apogeo *m*

zero *n, pl* **-ros** : cero *m*

zest *n* **1** : gusto *m* **2** FLAVOR : sazón *f*

zigzag *n* : zigzag *m* — ~ *vi* **-zagged; -zagging** : zigzaguear

zinc *n* : cinc *m*, zinc *m*

zip *v* **zipped; zipping** *vt or* ~ **up** : cerrar la cremallera de, cerrar el cierre de *Lat* — *vi* SPEED : pasarse volando — **zip code** *n* : código *m* postal — **zipper** *n* : cremallera *f,* cierre *m Lat*

zodiac *n* : zodíaco *m*

zone *n* : zona *f*

zoo *n, pl* **zoos** : zoológico *m,* zoo *m* — **zoology** *n* : zoología *f*

zoom *vi* : zumbar, ir volando — ~ *n* **1** : zumbido *m* **2** *or* ~ **lens** : zoom *m*

zucchini *n, pl* **-ni** *or* **-nis** : calabacín *m*, calabacita *f Lat*

Common Spanish Abbreviations

abr.	abril	Apr.	April
A.C., a.C.	antes de Cristo	BC	before Christ
a. de J.C.	antes de Jesucristo	BC	before Christ
admon., admón.	administración	—	administration
a/f	a favor	—	in favor
ago.	agosto	Aug.	August
Apdo.	apartado (de correos)	—	P.O. box
aprox.	aproximadamente	approx.	approximately
Aptdo.	apartado (de correos)	—	P.O. box
Arq.	arquitecto	arch.	architect
A.T.	Antiguo Testamento	O.T.	Old Testament
atte.	atentamente	—	sincerely
atto., atta.	atento, atenta	—	kind, courteous
av., avda.	avenida	ave.	avenue
a/v.	a vista	—	on receipt
BID	Banco Interamericano de Desarrollo	IDB	Interamerican Development Bank
Bo	banco	—	bank
BM	Banco Mundial	—	World Bank
c/, C/	calle	st.	street
C	centígrado, Celsius	C	centigrade, Celsius
C.	compañía	Co.	company
CA	corriente alterna	AC	alternating current
cap.	capítulo	ch., chap.	chapter
c/c	cuenta corriente	—	current account, checking account
c.c.	centímetros cúbicos	cu. cm	cubic centimeters
CC	corriente continua	DC	direct current
c/d	con descuento	—	with discount
Cd.	ciudad	—	city
CE	Comunidad Europea	EC	European Community
CEE	Comunidad Económica Europea	EEC	European Economic Community
cf.	confróntese	cf.	compare
cg.	centígramo	cg	centigram
CGT	Confederación General de Trabajadores o del Trabajo	—	confederation of workers, workers' union
CI	coeficiente intelectual o de inteligencia	IQ	intelligence quotient
Cía.	compañía	Co.	company
cm.	centímetro	cm	centimeter
Cnel.	coronel	Col.	colonel
col.	columna	col.	column
Col. Mex	colonia	—	residential area
Com.	comandante	Cmdr.	commander
comp.	compárese	comp.	compare
Cor.	coronel	Col.	colonel
C.P.	código postal	—	zip code
CSF, c.s.f.	coste, seguro y flete	c.i.f.	cost, insurance, and freight
cta.	cuenta	ac., acct.	account
cte.	corriente	cur.	current

SPANISH ABBREVIATION AND EXPANSION		ENGLISH EQUIVALENT	
c/u	cada uno, cada una	ea.	each
CV	caballo de vapor	hp	horsepower
D.	Don	—	—
Da., D.ª	Doña	—	—
d.C.	después de Cristo	AD	anno Domini (in the year of our Lord)
dcha.	derecha	—	right
d. de J.C.	después de Jesucristo	AD	anno Domini (in the year of our lord)
dep.	departamento	dept.	department
DF, D.F.	Distrito Federal	—	Federal District
dic.	diciembre	Dec.	December
dir.	director, directora	dir.	director
dir.	dirección	—	address
Dña.	Doña	—	—
do.	domingo	Sun.	Sunday
dpto.	departamento	dept.	department
Dr.	doctor	Dr.	doctor
Dra.	doctora	Dr.	doctor
dto.	descuento	—	discount
E, E.	Este, este	E	East, east
Ed.	editorial	—	publishing house
Ed., ed.	edición	ed.	edition
edif.	edificio	bldg.	building
edo.	estado	st.	state
EEUU, EE.UU.	Estados Unidos	US, U.S.	United States
ej.	por ejemplo	e.g.	for example
E.M.	esclerosis multiple	MS	multiple sclerosis
ene.	enero	Jan.	January
etc.	etcétera	etc.	et cetera
ext.	extensión	ext.	extension
F	Fahrenheit	F	Fahrenheit
f.a.b.	franco a bordo	f.o.b.	free on board
FC	ferrocarril	RR	railroad
feb.	febrero	Feb.	February
FF AA, FF.AA.	Fuerzas Armadas	—	armed forces
FMI	Fondo Monetario Internacional	IMF	International Monetary Fund
g.	gramo	g., gm, gr.	gram
G.P.	giro postal	M.O.	money order
gr.	gramo	g., gm, gr.	gram
Gral.	general	Gen.	general
h.	hora	hr.	hour
Hnos.	hermanos	Bros.	brothers
I + D, I & D, I y D	investigación y desarrollo	R & D	research and development
i.e.	esto es, es decir	i.e.	that is
incl.	inclusive	incl.	inclusive, inclusively
Ing.	ingeniero, ingeniera	eng.	engineer
IPC	indice de precios al consumo	CPI	consumer price index
IVA	impuesto al valor agregado	VAT	value-added tax
izq.	izquierda	l.	left
juev.	jueves	Thurs.	Thursday
jul.	julio	Jul.	July

SPANISH ABBREVIATION AND EXPANSION		ENGLISH EQUIVALENT	
jun.	junio	Jun.	June
kg.	kilogramo	kg	kilogram
km.	kilómetro	km	kilometer
km/h	kilómetros por hora	kph	kilometers per hour
kv, kV	kilovatio	kw, kW	kilowatt
l.	litro	l, lit.	liter
Lic.	licenciado, licenciada	—	—
Ltda.	limitada	Ltd.	limited
lun.	lunes	Mon.	Monday
m	masculino	m	masculine
m	metro	m	meter
m	minuto	m	minute
mar.	marzo	Mar.	March
mart.	martes	Tues.	Tuesday
mg.	miligramo	mg	milligram
miérc.	miércoles	Wed.	Wednesday
min	minuto	min.	minute
mm.	milímetro	mm	millimeter
M-N, m/n	moneda nacional	—	national currency
Mons.	monseñor	Msgr.	monsignor
Mtra.	maestra	—	teacher
Mtro.	maestro	—	teacher
N, N.	Norte, norte	N, no.	North, north
n/o	nuestro	—	our
n.º	número	no.	number
N. de (la) R.	nota de (la) redacción	—	editor's note
NE	nordeste	NE	northeast
NN.UU.	Naciones Unidas	UN	United Nations
NO	noroeste	NW	northwest
nov.	noviembre	Nov.	November
N.T.	Nuevo Testamento	N.T.	New Testament
ntra., ntro.	nuestra, nuestro	—	our
NU	Naciones Unidas	UN	United Nations
núm.	número	num.	number
O, O.	Oeste, oeste	W	West, west
oct.	octubre	Oct.	October
OEA, O.E.A.	Organización de Estados Americanos	OAS	Organization of American States
OMS	Organización Mundial de la Salud	WHO	World Health Organization
ONG	organización no gubernamental	NGO	non-governmental organization
ONU	Organización de las Naciones Unidas	UN	United Nations
OTAN	Organización del Tratado del Atlántico Norte	NATO	North Atlantic Treaty Organization
p.	página	p.	page
P, P.	padre	Fr.	father
pág.	página	pg.	page
pat.	patente	pat.	patent
PCL	pantalla de cristal líquido	LCD	liquid crystal display
P.D.	post data	P.S.	postscript
p. ej.	por ejemplo	e.g.	for example
PNB	Producto Nacional Bruto	GNP	gross national product
pº	paseo	Ave.	avenue
p.p.	porte pagado	ppd.	postpaid

SPANISH ABBREVIATION AND EXPANSION		ENGLISH EQUIVALENT	
PP, p.p.	por poder, por poderes	p.p.	by proxy
prom.	promedio	av., avg.	average
ptas., pts.	pesetas	—	—
q.e.p.d.	que en paz descanse	R.I.P.	may he/she rest in peace
R, R/	remite	—	sender
RAE	Real Academia Española	—	—
ref., ref.^a	referencia	ref.	reference
rep.	república	rep.	republic
r.p.m.	revoluciones por minuto	rpm.	revolutions per minute
rte.	remite, remitente	—	sender
s.	siglo	c., cent.	century
s/	su, sus	—	his, her, your, their
S, S.	Sur, sur	S, so.	South, south
S.	san, santo	St.	saint
S.A.	sociedad anónima	Inc.	incorporated (company)
sáb.	sábado	Sat.	Saturday
s/c	su cuenta	—	your account
SE	sudeste, sureste	SE	southeast
seg.	segundo, segundos	sec.	second, seconds
sep., sept.	septiembre	Sept.	September
s.e.u.o.	salvo error u omisión	—	errors and omissions excepted
Sgto.	sargento	Sgt.	sergeant
S.L.	sociedad limitada	Ltd.	limited (corporation)
S.M.	Su Majestad	HM	His Majesty, Her Majesty
s/n	sin número	—	no (street) number
s.n.m.	sobre el nivel de mar	a.s.l.	above sea level
SO	sudoeste/suroeste	SW	southwest
S.R.C.	se ruega contestación	R.S.V.P.	please reply
ss.	siguientes	—	the following ones
SS, S.S.	Su Santidad	H.H.	His Holiness
Sta.	santa	St.	Saint
Sto.	santo	St.	saint
t, t.	tonelada	t., tn	ton
TAE	tasa anual efectiva	APR	annual percentage rate
tb.	también	—	also
tel., Tel.	teléfono	tel.	telephone
Tm.	tonelada métrica	MT	metric ton
Tn.	tonelada	t., tn	ton
trad.	traducido	tr., trans., transl.	translated
UE	Unión Europea	EU	European Union
Univ.	universidad	Univ., U.	university
UPC	unidad procesadora central	CPU	central processing unit
Urb.	urbanización	—	residential area
v	versus	v., vs.	versus
v	verso	v., ver., vs.	verse
v.	véase	vid.	see
Vda.	viuda	—	widow
v.g., v.gr.	verbigracia	e.g.	for example
vier., viern.	viernes	Fri.	Friday
V.M.	Vuestra Majestad	—	Your Majesty
V^OB^O, V.^OB.^O	visto bueno	—	OK, approved
vol, vol.	volumen	vol.	volume
vra., vro.	vuestra, vuestro	—	your

Spanish Numbers

Cardinal Numbers

1	uno	28	veintiocho
2	dos	29	veintinueve
3	tres	30	treinta
4	cuatro	31	treinta y uno
5	cinco	40	cuarenta
6	seis	50	cincuenta
7	siete	60	sesenta
8	ocho	70	setenta
9	nueve	80	ochenta
10	diez	90	noventa
11	once	100	cien
12	doce	101	ciento uno
13	trece	200	doscientos
14	catorce	300	trescientos
15	quince	400	cuatrocientos
16	dieciséis	500	quinientos
17	diecisiete	600	seiscientos
18	dieciocho	700	setecientos
19	diecinueve	800	ochocientos
20	veinte	900	novecientos
21	veintiuno	1,000	mil
22	veintidós	1,001	mil uno
23	veintitrés	2,000	dos mil
24	veinticuatro	100,000	cien mil
25	veinticinco	1,000,000	un millón
26	veintiséis	1,000,000,000	mil millones
27	veintisiete	1,000,000,000,000	un billón

Ordinal Numbers

1st	primero, -ra	17th	decimoséptimo, -ma
2nd	segundo, -da	18th	decimoctavo, -va
3rd	tercero, -ra	19th	decimonoveno, -na; *or*
4th	cuarto, -ta		decimonono, -na
5th	quinto, -ta	20th	vigésimo, -ma
6th	sexto, -ta	21st	vigésimoprimero,
7th	séptimo, -ta		vigésimaprimera
8th	octavo, -ta	30th	trigésimo, -ma
9th	noveno, -na	40th	cuadragésimo, -ma
10th	décimo, -ma	50th	quincuagésimo, -ma
11th	undécimo, -ca	60th	sexagésimo, -ma
12th	duodécimo, -ma	70th	septuagésimo, -ma
13th	decimotercero, -ra	80th	octogésimo, -ma
14th	decimocuarto, -ta	90th	nonagésimo, -ma
15th	decimoquinto, -ta	100th	centésimo, -ma
16th	decimosexto, -ta	1,000th	milésimo, -ma

English Numbers

Cardinal Numbers

1	one	20	twenty
2	two	21	twenty-one
3	three	30	thirty
4	four	40	forty
5	five	50	fifty
6	six	60	sixty
7	seven	70	seventy
8	eight	80	eighty
9	nine	90	ninety
10	ten	100	one hundred
11	eleven	101	one hundred and one
12	twelve	200	two hundred
13	thirteen	1,000	one thousand
14	fourteen	1,001	one thousand and one
15	fifteen	2,000	two thousand
16	sixteen	100,000	one hundred thousand
17	seventeen	1,000,000	one million
18	eighteen	1,000,000,000	one billion
19	nineteen	1,000,000,000,000	one trillion

Ordinal Numbers

1st	first	16th	sixteenth
2nd	second	17th	seventeenth
3rd	third	18th	eighteenth
4th	fourth	19th	nineteenth
5th	fifth	20th	twentieth
6th	sixth	21st	twenty-first
7th	seventh	30th	thirtieth
8th	eighth	40th	fortieth
9th	ninth	50th	fiftieth
10th	tenth	60th	sixtieth
11th	eleventh	70th	seventieth
12th	twelfth	80th	eightieth
13th	thirteenth	90th	ninetieth
14th	fourteenth	100th	hundredth
15th	fifteenth	1,000th	thousandth